9th Edition

Accounting Principles

Volume 2: Chapters 13–26

Jerry J. Weygandt PhD, CPA
University of Wisconsin
Madison, Wisconsin

Paul D. Kimmel PhD, CPA
University of Wisconsin—Milwaukee
Milwaukee, Wisconsin

Donald E. Kieso PhD, CPA
Northern Illinois University
DeKalb, Illinois

John Wiley & Sons, Inc.

WILEY

Dedicated to
Amaya, Christina, Max, Quinn, Venden, Evan, and Nolan, and their grandmother Enid; Morgan, Cole, and Erin, and their grandmother Donna; Croix, Marais, and Kale, and their mother Merlynn

Publisher George Hoffman
Associate Publisher Christopher DeJohn
Senior Editor Brian Kamins
Senior Marketing Manager Julia Flohr
Assistant Marketing Manager Carly DeCardia
Executive Marketing Manager Amy Scholz
Senior Production Editor Valerie A. Vargas
Senior Media Editor Allie K. Morris
Development Editor Ann Torbert
Production Management Services Ingrao Associates
Creative Director Harry Nolan
Senior Designer Madelyn Lesure
Project Editor Ed Brislin
Senior Photo Editor Elle Wagner
Editorial Assistant Kathryn Fraser
Marketing Assistant Alana Filipovich
Cover Photo OJO Images/SuperStock

This book was set in Times Ten Roman 10.5/12 by Aptara®, Inc. and printed and bound by RRD-JC. The cover was printed by RRD-JC.

This book is printed on acid free paper. ∞

Copyright © 2009 John Wiley & Sons, Inc. All rights reserved. No part of this publication may be reproduced, stored in a retrieval system or transmitted in any form or by any means, electronic, mechanical, photocopying, recording, scanning or otherwise, except as permitted under Sections 107 or 108 of the 1976 United States Copyright Act, without either the prior written permission of the Publisher, or authorization through payment of the appropriate per-copy fee to the Copyright Clearance Center, Inc. 222 Rosewood Drive, Danvers, MA 01923, website www.copyright.com. Requests to the Publisher for permission should be addressed to the Permissions Department, John Wiley & Sons, Inc., 111 River Street, Hoboken, NJ 07030-5774, (201)748-6011, fax (201)748-6008, website http://www.wiley.com/go/permissions.

To order books or for customer service please, call 1-800-CALL WILEY (225-5945).

ISBN-13 978-0470-31757-0

Printed in the United States of America

10 9 8 7 6 5 4 3 2 1

Achieve Positive Learning Outcomes

WILEY PLUS
www.wileyplus.com

WileyPLUS combines robust course management tools with interactive teaching and learning resources all in one easy-to-use system. It has helped over half a million students and instructors achieve positive learning outcomes in their courses.

WileyPLUS contains everything you and your students need— and nothing more, including:

- The entire textbook online—with dynamic links from homework to relevant sections. Students can use the online text and save up to half the cost of buying a new printed book.
- Automated assigning & grading of homework & quizzes.
- An interactive variety of ways to teach and learn the material.
- Instant feedback and help for students... available 24/7.

"*WileyPLUS* helped me become more prepared. There were more resources available using *WileyPLUS* than just using a regular [printed] textbook, which helped out significantly. Very helpful...and very easy to use."

– Student Victoria Cazorla,
Dutchess County Community College

See and try WileyPLUS *in action!*
Details and Demo:
www.wileyplus.com

Why WileyPLUS for Accounting?

"It was easier to do my homework problems online and receive quick responses. WileyPLUS helped me understand what I was doing wrong and confirmed what I was doing right."

– Student Brenda Cintron, Accounting Major at UMUC

WileyPLUS helps today's students succeed in the classroom and become globally competitive with step-by-step instruction, instant feedback, and support material to reinforce accounting concepts. Instructors can easily monitor progress by student or by class, and spend more time teaching and less time grading homework.

- **WileyPLUS links students directly from homework problems to specific sections of their online text to read about specific topics.**

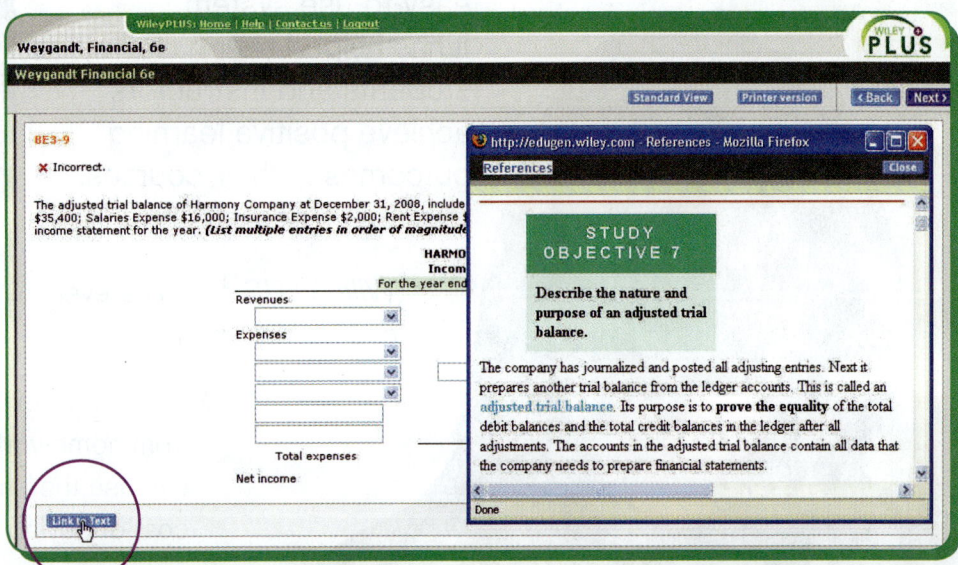

- **Students can also link to contextual help such as interactive tutorials, chapter reviews, and demonstration problems; simulations; and video for visual review or help when they need it most.**

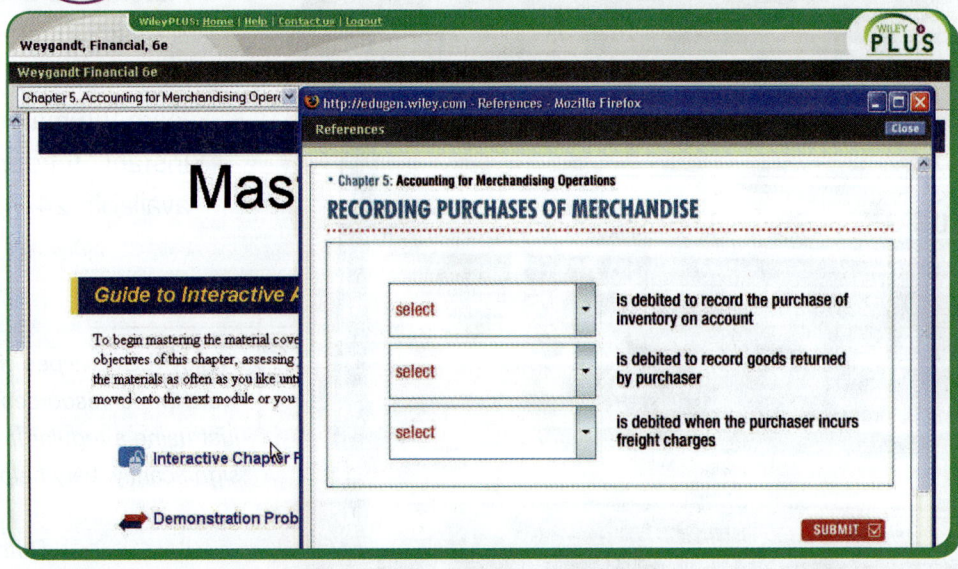

"I really liked the demonstrations and examples with the pictures and interactive quizzes...very helpful. WileyPLUS gave me motivation and confidence..."
– Student Victoria Sniezek, Anne Arundel Community College

See and try WileyPLUS in action!
Details and Demo: www.wileyplus.com

WileyPLUS combines robust course management tools with the complete online text and all of the interactive teaching and learning resources you and your students need in one easy to use system.

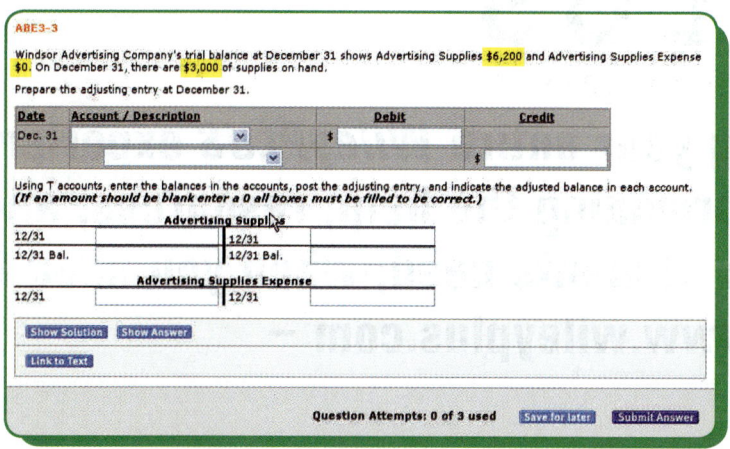

⊕ *Algorithmically generated, end-of-chapter exercises and problems allow a number of students to take the same assignment with differing variables.*

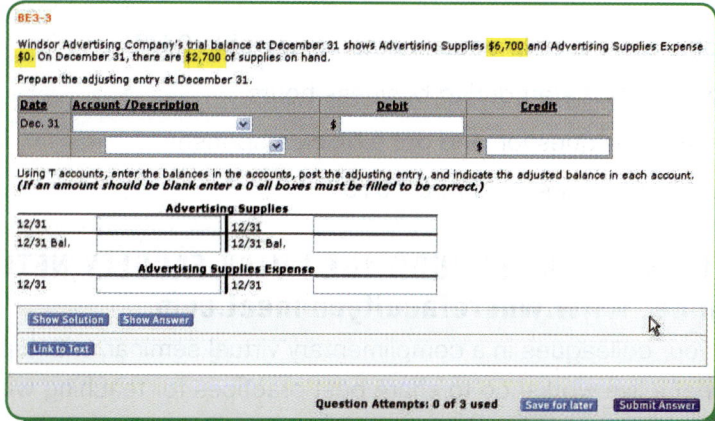

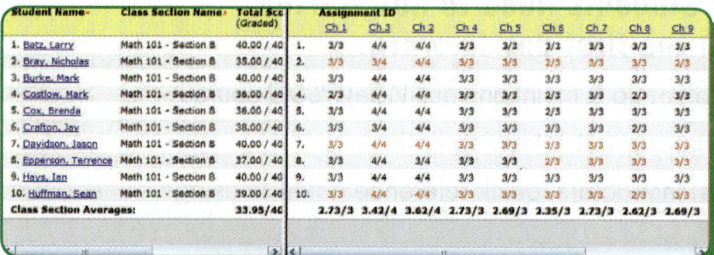

⊕ *Assessment and Homework Management tools help instructors monitor students' progress individually—or by class.*

"I received an A in accounting because *WileyPLUS* helped me understand the material by practicing."
– Student Crista Dixon, University of Nevada, Reno

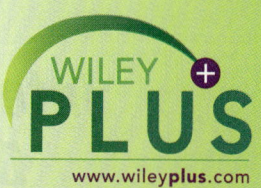

www.wileyplus.com

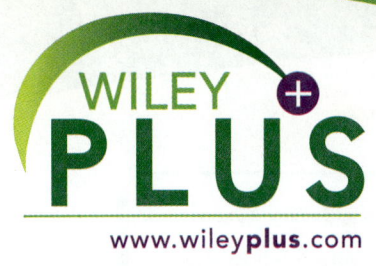

www.wileyplus.com

Wiley is committed to making your entire *WileyPLUS* experience productive & enjoyable by providing the help, resources, and personal support you & your students need, when you need it. It's all here: www.wileyplus.com –

TECHNICAL SUPPORT:

- A fully searchable knowledge base of FAQs and help documentation, available 24/7
- Live chat with a trained member of our support staff during business hours
- A form to fill out and submit online to ask any question and get a quick response
- **Instructor-only** phone line during business hours: 1.877.586.0192

FACULTY-LED TRAINING THROUGH THE WILEY FACULTY NETWORK:
Register online: www.wherefacultyconnect.com
Connect with your colleagues in a complimentary virtual seminar, with a personal mentor in your field, or at a live workshop to share best practices for teaching with technology.

1ST DAY OF CLASS...AND BEYOND!
Resources You & Your Students Need to Get Started & Use *WileyPLUS* from the first day forward.

- 2-Minute Tutorials on how to set up & maintain your *WileyPLUS* course
- User guides, links to technical support & training options
- ***WileyPLUS for Dummies***: Instructors' quick reference guide to using *WileyPLUS*
- Student tutorials & instruction on how to register, buy, and use *WileyPLUS*

YOUR *WileyPLUS* ACCOUNT MANAGER:
Your personal *WileyPLUS* connection for any assistance you need!

SET UP YOUR *WileyPLUS* COURSE IN MINUTES!
Selected *WileyPLUS* courses with QuickStart contain pre-loaded assignments & presentations created by subject matter experts who are also experienced *WileyPLUS* users.

Interested? See and try WileyPLUS *in action!*
Details and Demo: www.wileyplus.com

Dear Student,

Why This Course?
Remember your biology course in high school? Did you have one of those "invisible man" models (or maybe something more high-tech than that) that gave you the opportunity to look "inside" the human body? This accounting course offers something similar: To understand a business, you have to understand the financial insides of a business organization. An accounting course will help you understand the essential financial components of businesses. Whether you are looking at a large multinational company like Microsoft or Starbucks or a single-owner software consulting business or coffee shop, knowing the fundamentals of accounting will help you understand what is happening. As an employee, a manager, an investor, a business owner, or a manager of your own personal finances—any of which roles you will have at some point in your life—you will be much the wiser for having taken this course.

Why This Book?
Hundreds of thousands of students have used this textbook. Your instructor has chosen it for you because of its trusted reputation. The authors have worked hard to keep the book fresh, timely, and accurate.

The book contains features to help you learn best, whatever your learning style. To understand what your learning style is, spend about ten minutes to take the online learning style quiz discussed at the top of page ix and then look at pages ix, x, and xi for how you can apply an understanding of your learning style to this course. Then, when you know more about your own learning style, browse through the Student Owner's Manual online at the book's companion website (www.wiley.com/college/sc/weyprin). It shows you the main features you will find in this textbook and explains their purpose.

How to Succeed?
We've asked many students and many instructors whether there is a secret for success in this course. The nearly unanimous answer turns out to be not much of a secret: "Do the homework." This is one course where doing is learning, and the more time you spend on the homework assignments—using the various tools that this book provides—the more likely you are to learn the essential concepts, techniques, and methods of accounting. Besides the textbook itself, the companion website offers various support resources.

Good luck in this course. We hope you enjoy the experience and that you put to good use throughout a lifetime of success the lessons you learn about accounting and about business! We are sure you will not be disappointed.

Jerry J. Weygandt
Paul D. Kimmel
Donald E. Kieso

ABOUT THE AUTHORS

Jerry J. Weygandt, PhD, CPA, is Arthur Andersen Alumni Professor of Accounting at the University of Wisconsin—Madison. He holds a Ph.D. in accounting from the University of Illinois. Articles by Professor Weygandt have appeared in the *Accounting Review, Journal of Accounting Research, Accounting Horizons, Journal of Accountancy*, and other academic and professional journals. These articles have examined such financial reporting issues as accounting for price-level adjustments, pensions, convertible securities, stock option contracts, and interim reports. Professor Weygandt is author of other accounting and financial reporting books and is a member of the American Accounting Association, the American Institute of Certified Public Accountants, and the Wisconsin Society of Certified Public Accountants. He has seved on numerous committees of the American Accounting Association and as a member of the editorial board of the *Accounting Review;* he also has served as President and Secretary-Treasurer of the American Accounting Association. In addition, he has been actively involved with the American Institute of Certified Public Accountants and has been a member of the Accounting Standards Executive Committee (AcSEC) of that organization. He has served on the FASB task force that examined the reporting issues related to accounting for income taxes and served as a trustee of the Financial Accounting Foundation. Professor Weygandt has received the Chancellor's Award for Excellence in Teaching and the Beta Gamma Sigma Dean's Teaching Award. He is on the board of directors of M & I Bank of Southern Wisconsin. He is the recipient of the Wisconsin Institute of CPA's Outstanding Educator's Award and the Lifetime Achievement Award. In 2001 he received the American Accounting Association's Outstanding Accounting Educator Award.

Paul D. Kimmel, PhD, CPA, received his bachelor's degree from the University of Minnesota and his doctorate in accounting from the University of Wisconsin. He is an Associate Professor at the University of Wisconsin—Milwaukee, and has public accounting experience with Deloitte & Touche (Minneapolis). He was the recipient of the UWM School of Business Advisory Council Teaching Award, the Reggie Taite Excellence in Teaching Award. and a three-time winner of the Outstanding Teaching Assistant Award at the University of Wisconsin. He is also a recipient of the Elijah Watts Sells Award for Honorary Distinction for his results on the CPA exam. He is a member of the American Accounting Association and the Institute of Management Accountants and has published articles in *Accounting Review, Accounting Horizons, Advances in Management Accounting, Managerial Finance, Issues in Accounting Education, Journal of Accounting Education*, as well as other journals. His research interests include accounting for financial instruments and innovation in accounting education. He has published papers and given numerous talks on incorporating critical thinking into accounting education, and helped prepare a catalog of critical thinking resources for the Federated Schools of Accountancy.

Donald E. Kieso, PhD, CPA, received his bachelor's degree from Aurora University and his doctorate in accounting from the University of Illinois. He has served as chairman of the Department of Accountancy and is currently the KPMG Emeritus Professor of Accountancy at Northern Illinois University. He has public accounting experience with Price Waterhouse & Co. (San Francisco and Chicago) and Arthur Andersen & Co. (Chicago) and research experience with the Research Division of the American Institute of Certified Public Accountants (New York). He has done postdoctorate work as a Visiting Scholar at the University of California at Berkeley and is a recipient of NIU's Teaching Excellence Award and four Golden Apple Teaching Awards. Professor Kieso is the author of other accounting and business books and is a member of the American Accounting Association, the American Institute of Certified Public Accountants, and the Illinois CPA Society. He has served as a member of the Board of Directors of the Illinois CPA Society, the AACSB's Accounting Accreditation Committees, the State of Illinois Comptroller's Commission, as Secretary-Treasurer of the Federation of Schools of Accountancy, and as Secretary-Treasurer of the American Accounting Association. Professor Kieso is currently serving on the Board of Trustees and Executive Committee of Aurora University, as a member of the Board of Directors of Kishwaukee Community Hospital, and as Treasurer and Director of Valley West Community Hospital. From 1989 to 1993 he served as a charter member of the national Accounting Education Change Commission. He is the recipient of the Outstanding Accounting Educator Award from the Illinois CPA Society, the FSA's Joseph A. Silvoso Award of Merit, the NIU Foundation's Humanitarian Award for Service to Higher Education, a Distinguished Service Award from the Illinois CPA Society, and in 2003 an honorary doctorate from Aurora University.

WHAT ARE LEARNING STYLES?

Have you ever repeated something to yourself over and over to help remember it? Or does your best friend ask you to draw a map to someplace where the two of you are planning to meet, rather than just *tell* her the directions? If so, then you already have an intuitive sense that people learn in different ways.

Researchers in learning theory have developed various categories of learning styles. Some people, for example, learn best by reading or writing. Others learn best by using various senses—seeing, hearing, feeling, tasting, or even smelling.

When you understand how you learn best, you can make use of learning strategies that will optimize the time you spend studying. To find out what your particular learning style is, go to WileyPLUS and take the learning styles quiz you find there. The quiz will help you determine your primary learning style:

Visual learner	Auditory learner	Haptic learner	Olfactory learner
Print learner	Interactive learner	Kinesthetic learner	

Then, consult the information below and on the following pages for study tips for each learning style. This information will help you better understand your learning style and how to apply it to the study of accounting.

✓ Study Tips for Visual Learners

If you are a **Visual Learner,** you prefer to work with images and diagrams. It is important that you *see* information.

Visual Learning:
- Draw charts/diagrams during lecture.
- Examine textbook figures and graphs.
- Look at images and videos on WileyPLUS and other websites.
- Pay close attention to charts, drawings, and handouts your instructors use.
- Underline; use different colors.
- Use symbols, flow charts, graphs, different arrangements on the page, white spaces.

Visual Reinforcement:
- Make flashcards by drawing tables/charts on one side and definition or description on the other side.
- Use art-based worksheets. Cover labels on images in text and then rewrite the labels.
- Use colored pencils/markers and colored paper to organize information into types.
- Convert your lecture notes into "page pictures." To do this:
  - Use the visual learning strategies outlined above.
  - Reconstruct images in different ways.
  - Redraw pages from memory.
  - Replace words with symbols and initials.
  - Draw diagrams where appropriate.
  - Practice turning your visuals back into words.

If visual learning is your weakness: If you are **not** a Visual Learner but want to improve your visual learning, try re-keying tables/charts from the textbook.

✓ Study Tips for Print Learners

If you are a **Print Learner,** reading will be important but writing will be much more important.

Print Learning:
- Write text lecture notes during lecture.
- Read relevant topics in textbook, especially textbook tables.
- Look at text descriptions in animations and websites.
- Use lists and headings.
- Use dictionaries, glossaries, and definitions.
- Read handouts, textbooks, and supplementary library readings.
- Use lecture notes.

Print Reinforcement:
- Rewrite your notes from class and copy classroom handouts in your own handwriting.
- Make your own flashcards.
- Write out essays summarizing lecture notes or textbook topics.
- Develop mnemonics.
- Identify word relationships.
- Create tables with information extracted from textbook or lecture notes.
- Use text-based worksheets or crossword puzzles.
- Write out words again and again.
- Reread notes silently.
- Rewrite ideas and principles into other words.
- Turn charts, diagrams, and other illustrations into statements.
- Practice writing exam answers.
- Practice with multiple-choice questions.
- Write paragraphs, especially beginnings and endings.
- Write your lists in outline form.
- Arrange your words into hierarchies and points.

If print learning is your weakness: If you are **not** a Print Learner but want to improve your print learning, try covering labels of figures from the textbook and writing in the labels.

✓ Study Tips for Auditory Learners

If you are an **Auditory Learner,** you prefer listening as a way to learn information. Hearing will be very important, and sound helps you focus.

Auditory Learning:
- Make audio recordings during lecture.
- Do not skip class. Hearing the lecture is essential to understanding.

- Play audio files provided by instructor and textbook.
- Listen to narration of animations.
- Attend lectures and tutorials.
- Discuss topics with students and instructors.
- Explain new ideas to other people.
- Leave spaces in your lecture notes for later recall.
- Describe overheads, pictures, and visuals to somebody who was not in class.

Auditory Reinforcement:

- Record yourself reading the notes and listen to the recording.
- Write out transcripts of the audio files.
- Summarize information that you have read, speaking out loud.
- Use a recorder to create self-tests.
- Compose "songs" about information.
- Play music during studying to help focus.
- Expand your notes by talking with others and with information from your textbook.
- Read summarized notes out loud.
- Explain your notes to another auditory learner.
- Talk with the instructor.
- Spend time in quiet places recalling the ideas.
- Say your answers out loud.

If auditory learning is your weakness: If you are **not** an Auditory Learner but want to improve your auditory learning, try writing out the scripts from pre-recorded lectures.

✓ Study Tips for Interactive Learners

If you are an **Interactive Learner,** you will want to share your information. A study group will be important.

Interactive Learning:

- Ask a lot of questions during lecture or laboratory meetings.
- Contact other students, via email or discussion forums, and ask them to explain what they learned.

Interactive Reinforcement:

- "Teach" the content to a group of other students.
- Talking to an empty room may seem odd, but it will be effective for you.
- Discuss information with others, making sure that you both ask and answer questions.
- Work in small group discussions, making a verbal and written summary of what others say.

If interactive learning is your weakness: If you are **not** an Interactive Learner but want to improve your interactive learning, try asking your study partner questions and then repeating them to the instructor.

✓ Study Tips for Haptic Learners

If you are a **Haptic Learner,** you prefer to work with your hands. It is important to physically manipulate material.

Haptic Learning:

- Take blank paper to lecture to draw charts/tables/diagrams.
- Using the textbook, run your fingers along the figures and graphs to get a "feel" for shapes and relationships.

Haptic Reinforcement:

- Trace words and pictures on flash cards.
- Perform electronic exercises that involve drag-and-drop activities.
- Alternate between speaking and writing information.
- Observe someone performing a task that you would like to learn.
- Make sure you have freedom of movement while studying.

If haptic learning is your weakness: If you are **not** a Haptic Learner but want to improve your haptic learning, try spending more time in class working with formulas, financial statements, and tables while speaking or writing down information.

✓ Study Tips for Kinesthetic Learners

If you are a **Kinesthetic Learner,** it will be important that you involve your body during studying.

Kinesthetic Learning:

- Ask permission to get up and move during lecture.
- Participate in role playing activities, in the classroom.
- Use all your senses.
- Use hands-on approaches.
- Go to labs, take field trips.
- Use trial-and-error methods.
- Listen to real-life examples.
- Pay attention to applications.

Kinesthetic Reinforcement:

- Make flash cards, place them on the floor and move around them as you study.
- Move while you are "teaching" the material to others.
- Put examples in your summaries.
- Use case studies and applications to help with principles and abstract concepts.
- Talk about your notes with another Kinesthetic person.
- Use pictures and photographs that illustrate an idea.
- Write practice answers.
- Role-play the exam situation.

If kinesthetic learning is your weakness: If you are **not** a Kinesthetic Learner but want to improve your kinesthetic learning, try moving flash cards to reconstruct balance sheets, income statements, cash flow statements, etc.

✓ Study Tips for Olfactory Learners

If you are an **Olfactory Learner,** you will prefer to use the sense of smell (sometimes taste) and to reinforce learning. This is a rare learning modality.

Olfactory Learning:

- During lecture, use different scented markers to identify different types of information.

Olfactory Reinforcement:

- Rewrite notes with scented markers.
- If possible, go back to the computer lab to do your studying.
- Burn aromatic candles while studying.
- Try to associate the material that you're studying with a pleasant smell or taste.

If olfactory learning is your weakness: If you are **not** an Olfactory Learner, but want to improve your olfactory learning, try surrounding yourself with pleasant scents during study sessions.

WileyPLUS and Textbook Resources for Various Learning Styles

RESOURCES	Visual	Print	Auditory	Interactive	Haptic	Kinesthetic	Olfactory*
Content of textbook		✓					
The Navigator/Feature Story/Preview	✓	✓					
Study Objectives		✓					
Infographics/Illustrations	✓	✓					
Accounting Equation Analyses	✓	✓	✓	✓	✓	✓	
Do It! Exercises/Comprehensive Do It! Problem/Action Plan	✓	✓		✓	✓	✓	
Graph in *All About You*	✓	✓					
Summary of Study Objectives		✓					
Glossary/Self-study questions		✓		✓	✓	✓	
Questions/Exercises/Problems	✓	✓		✓			
Alternate versions of exercises & Problems (B exercises; Problem sets B&C)	✓	✓		✓			
Financial Reporting/Comparative Analysis Problems	✓	✓		✓	✓	✓	
Writing activities—Exercises and Problems marked with a pencil icon	✓	✓		✓	✓	✓	
Exploring the Web activity	✓	✓	✓	✓	✓	✓	
Communication Activity		✓		✓	✓	✓	
AAY Activity		✓		✓	✓	✓	
Practice quizzes		✓		✓	✓	✓	
Flash cards	✓	✓		✓	✓	✓	
Audio Reviews/Video Clips/Clicker Content			✓	✓	✓	✓	
Flash Tutorial Reviews (Comprehensive Do It/Accounting Cycle/Annual Report)	✓	✓	✓	✓	✓	✓	
Crossword Puzzles	✓	✓	✓	✓	✓	✓	
Excel Templates/Excel Working Papers	✓	✓		✓	✓	✓	
Checklist of Key Figures	✓	✓					
Peachtree/Quickbooks/GLS	✓	✓		✓	✓	✓	
Self-study/Self-test web quizzes	✓	✓		✓	✓	✓	

* To improve your learning using your olfactory modality, look at the resources recommended for your other most preferred learning styles. Then, pair olfactory study techniques with other resources, to enhance your learning. For example, you can burn aromatic candles while working on Flash tutorial reviews or Excel templates in WileyPLUS, or you can use scented markers to create flashcards.

ACKNOWLEDGMENTS

From the first edition of this textbook and through the years since, we have benefited greatly from feedback provided by numerous instructors and students of accounting principles courses throughout the country. We offer our thanks to those many people for their criticism, constructive suggestions, and innovative ideas. We are indebted to the following people for their contributions to the most recent editions of the book.

Reviewers and Focus Group Participants for the Ninth Edition

John Ahmad, *Northern Virginia Community College—Annandale;* Colin Battle, *Broward Community College;* Beverly Beatty, *Anne Arundel Community College;* Jaswinder Bhangal, *Chabot College;* Leroy Bugger, *Edison Community College;* Ann Cardozo, *Broward Community College;* Kimberly Charland, *Kansas State University;* Lisa Cole, *Johnson County Community College.*

Tony Dellarte, *Luzerne Community College;* Pam Donahue, *Northern Essex Community College;* Dora Estes, *Volunteer State Community College;* Mary Falkey, *Prince Georges Community College;* Lori Grady, *Bucks County Community College;* Joyce Griffin, *Kansas City Community College;* Lester Hall, *Danville Community College;* Becky Hancock, *El Paso Community College;* Audrey Hunter, *Broward Community College.*

Naomi Karolinski, *Monroe Community College;* Kenneth Koerber, *Bucks County Community College;* Sandra Lang, *McKendree College;* Cathy Xanthaky Larsen, *Middlesex Community College;* David Laurel, *South Texas Community College;* Suneel Maheshwari, *Marshall University;* Lori Major, *Luzerne County Community College;* Jim Martin, *University of Montevallo.*

Yvonne Phang, *Borough of Manhattan Community College;* Mike Prockton, *Finger Lakes Community College;* Richard Sarkisian, *Camden Community College;* Beth Secrest, *Walsh University;* Lois Slutsky, *Broward Community College;* Shafi Ullah, *Broward Community College;* Patricia Walczack, *Lansing Community College;* Kenton Walker, *University of Wyoming;* Patricia Wall, *Middle Tennessee State University.*

Reviewers and Focus Group Participants for Recent Editions

Sylvia Allen, *Los Angeles Valley College;* Matt Anderson, *Michigan State University;* Alan Applebaum, *Broward Community College;* Juanita Ardovany, *Los Angeles Valley College;* Yvonne Baker, *Cincinnati State Tech Community College;* Peter Battelle, *University of Vermont;* Jim Benedum, *Milwaukee Area Technical College;* Bernard Bieg, *Bucks County College;* Michael Blackett, *National American University;* Barry Bomboy, *J. Sargeant Reynolds Community College;* Kent D. Bowen, *Butler County Community College;* David Boyd, *Arkansas State University;* Greg Brookins, *Santa Monica College;* Kurt H. Buerger, *Angelo State University;* Leon Button, *Scottsdale Community College.*

Steve Carlson, *University of North Dakota;* Fatma Cebenoyan, *Hunter College;* Trudy Chiaravelli, *Lansing Community College;* Shifei Chung, *Rowan University;* Siu Chung, *Los Angeles Valley College;* Kenneth Couvillion, *San Joaquin Delta College;* Alan B. Czyzewski, *Indiana State University;* Thomas Davies, *University of South Dakota;* Peggy DeJong, *Kirkwood Community College;* John Delaney, *Augustana College;* Kevin Dooley, *Kapi'olani Community College;* Edmond Douville, *Indiana University Northwest;* Pamela Druger, *Augustana College;* Russell Dunn, *Broward Community College;* John Eagan, *Erie Community College;* Richard Ellison, *Middlesex Community College.*

Raymond Gardner, *Ocean County College;* Richard Ghio, *San Joaquin Delta College;* Amy Haas, *Kingsborough Community College, CUNY;* Jeannie Harrington, *Middle Tennessee State University;* Bonnie Harrison, *College of Southern Maryland;* William Harvey, *Henry Ford Community College;* Michelle Heard, *Metropolitan Community College;* Ruth Henderson, *Union Community College;* Ed Hess, *Butler County Community College;* Kathy Hill, *Leeward Community College;* Patty Holmes, *Des Moines Area Community College;* Zach Holmes, *Oakland Community College;* Paul Holt, *Texas A&M-Kingsville;* Audrey Hunter, *Broward Community College;* Verne Ingram, *Red Rocks Community College.*

Joanne Johnson, *Caldwell Community College;* Anil Khatri, *Bowie State University;* Shirley Kleiner, *Johnson County Community College;* Jo Koehn, *Central Missouri State University;* Ken Koerber, *Bucks County Community College;* Adriana Kulakowski, *Mynderse Academy;* Robert Laycock, *Montgomery College;* Natasha Librizzi, *Madison Area Technical College;* William P. Lovell, *Cayuga Community College;*. Melanie Mackey, *Ocean County College;* Jerry Martens, *Community College of Aurora;* Maureen McBeth, *College of DuPage;* Francis McCloskey, *Community College of Philadelphia;* Chris McNamara, *Finger Lakes Community College;* Edwin Mah, *University of Maryland, University College;* Thomas Marsh, *Northern Virginia Community College—Annandale;* Shea Mears, *Des Moines Area Community College;* Pam Meyer, *University of Louisiana—Lafayette;* Cathy Montesarchio, *Broward Community College.*

Robin Nelson, *Community College of Southern Nevada;* Joseph M. Nicassio, *Westmoreland County Community College;* Michael O'Neill, *Seattle Central Community College;* Mike Palma, *Gwinnett Tech;* George Palz, *Erie Community College;* Michael Papke, *Kellogg Community College;* Ruth Parks, *Kellogg Community College;* Al Partington, *Los Angeles Pierce College;* Jennifer Patty, *Des Moines Area Community College;* Jan Pitera, *Broome Community College;* Laura M. Prosser, *Black Hills State University;* Bill Rencher, *Seminole Community College;* Jenny Resnick, Santa Monica College; Renee Rigoni, *Monroe Community College;* Kathie Rogers, *SUNY Suffolk;* Al Ruggiero, *SUNY Suffolk;* Jill Russell, *Camden County College.*

Roger Sands, *Milwaukee Area Technical College;* Marcia Sandvold, *Des Moines Area Community College;* Kent Schneider, *East Tennessee State University;* Karen Searle, Paul J. Shinal, *Cayuga Community College;* Kevin Sinclair,

Lehigh University; Alice Sineath, *Forsyth Tech Community College;* Leon Singleton, *Santa Monica College;* Michael S. Skaff, *College of the Sequoias;* Jeff Slater, *North Shore Community College;* Lois Slutsky, *Broward Community College;* Dan Small, *J. Sargeant Reynolds Community College;* Lee Smart, *Southwest Tennessee Community College;* James Smith, *Ivy Tech State College;* Carol Springer, *Georgia State University;* Jeff Spoelman, *Grand Rapids Community College;* Norman Sunderman, *Angelo State University.*

Donald Terpstra, *Jefferson; Community College;* Lynda Thompson, *Massasoit Community College;* Sue Van Boven, *Paradise Valley Community College;* Christian Widmer, *Tidewater Community College;* Wanda Wong, *Chabot College;* Pat Walczak, *Lansing Community College;* Carol N. Welsh, *Rowan University;* Idalene Williams, *Metropolitan Community College;* Gloria Worthy, *Southwest Tennessee Community College.*

Thanks also to "perpetual reviewers" Robert Benjamin, *Taylor University;* Charles Malone, Tammy Wend, and Carol Wysocki, all of *Columbia Basin College;* and William Gregg of *Montgomery College.* We appreciate their continuing interest in the book and their regular contributions of ideas to improve it.

Special Thanks

Our thanks also go to the following for their work on the Ninth Edition: Melanie Yon, for preparing end-of-chapter content for WileyPLUS; Sheila Viel, *University of Wisconsin-Milwaukee,* for production of interactive chapter reviews and demonstration problems; Richard Campbell, *Rio Grande College,* for WileyPLUS Accounting Tutors and video material; Naomi Karolinski, *Monroe Community College,* for General Ledger Software review; Sally Nelson, for General Ledger Software review; Chris Tomas, for General Ledger Software review.

Thanks, too, to the following for their authorship of supplements: Linda Batiste, *Baton Rouge Community College,* Test Bank; Mel Coe, *DeVry Institute of Technology, Atlanta,* Peachtree Workbook; Joan Cook, *Milwaukee Area Technical College,* Heritage Home Furniture Practice Set; Larry Falcetto, *Emporia State University,* Test Bank, Instructor's Manual, Campus Cycle Practice Set; Mark Gleason, *Metropolitan State University*, Algorithmic Computerized Test Bank; Larry Falcetto, *Emporia State University,* Test Bank, Lori Grady, *Bucks County Community College,* Web Quizzes; Coby Harmon, *University of California, Santa Barbara*, PowerPoint presentations; Marilyn Hunt, M.A., C.P.A., Problem-Solving Survival Guide; Douglas W. Kieso, *Aurora University,* Study Guide; Jill Misuraca, *Central Connecticut State University,* Web Quizzes; Yvonne Phang, *Borough of Manhattan Community College*, WileyPLUS Web Quizzes. Rex A. Schildhouse, *San Diego Community College—Miramar,* Peachtree Workbook, Excel Workbook and Templates, and QuickBooks Tutorials; Dick Wasson, *Southwestern College,* Excel Working Papers, Working Papers, and Test Bank.

We also thank those who have ensured the accuracy of our supplements: LuAnn Bean, *Florida Institute of Technology;* Jack Borke, *University of Wisconsin—Platteville;* Robert Derstine, *Villanova University;* Terry Elliott, *Morehead State University*; James Emig, *Villanova University;* Larry Falcetto, *Emporia State University;* Anthony Falgiani, *Western Illinois University;* Jennifer Laudermilch, *PricewaterhouseCoopers;* Kevin McNelis, *New Mexico State University;* Richard Merryman, *Jefferson Community College, State University of New York;* Barbara Muller, *Arizona State University;* Yvonne Phang, *Borough of Manhattan Community College;* John Plouffe, *California State University—Los Angeles;* Renee Rigoni, *Monroe Community College;* Rex Schildhouse, *San Diego Community College–Miramar;* Alice Sineath, *Forsyth Tech Community College;* Teresa Speck, *St. Mary's University;* Lynn Stallworth, *Appalachian State University;* Sheila Viel, *University of Wisconsin—Milwaukee;* Dick Wasson, *Southwestern College;* Bernie Weinrich, *Lindenwood University.*

In addition, special recognition goes to Karen Huffman, *Palomar College,* for her assessment of the text's pedagogy and her suggestions on how to increase its helpfulness to students; to Gary R., Morrison, *Wayne State University,* for his review of the instructional design; and to Nancy Galli, *Palomar College,* for her work on learning styles. Finally, special thanks to Wayne Higley, *Buena Vista University*, for his technical proofing.

Our thanks to the publishing "pros" who contribute to our efforts to publish high-quality products that benefit both teachers and students: Ann Torbert, development editor; Ed Brislin, project editor; Brian Kamins, associate editor; Allie Morris, media editor; Katie Fraser, editorial assistant; Valerie Vargas, senior production editor; Maddy Lesure, textbook designer; Dorothy Sinclair, managing editor; Pam Kennedy, director of production and manufacturing; Ann Berlin, VP of higher education production and manufacturing; Elle Wagner, photo cditor; Sandra Rigby, illustration editor; Suzanne Ingrao of Ingrao Associates, project manager; Karyn Morrison, permissions editor; Jane Shifflet of Aptara Inc., product manager at Aptara Inc.; and Amanda Grant, project manager at Elm Street Publishing Services. They provided innumerable services that helped this project take shape.

We also appreciate the exemplary support and professional commitment given us by Chris DeJohn, associate publisher, and the enthusiasm and ideas that Julia Flohr, senior marketing manager, brings to the project.

Finally, our thanks for the support provided by the management of John Wiley & Sons, Inc.—Joe Heider, Vice President of Product and e-Business Development; Bonnie Lieberman, Senior Vice President of the College Division; and Will Pesce, President and Chief Executive Officer of John Wiley & Sons, Inc..

We thank PepsiCo, Inc. for permitting us the use of their 2007 annual reports for our specimen financial statements and accompanying notes.

We will appreciate suggestions and comments from users—instructors and students alike. You can send your thought to us via email at

AccountingAuthors@yahoo.com

Jerry J. Weygandt, *Madison, Wisconsin*
Paul D. Kimmel, *Milwaukee, Wisconsin*
Donald E. Kieso, *DeKalb, Illinois*

BRIEF CONTENTS

1 Accounting in Action 2
2 The Recording Process 48
3 Adjusting the Accounts 94
4 Completing the Accounting Cycle 144
5 Accounting for Merchandising Operations 198
6 Inventories 248
7 Accounting Information Systems 300
8 Fraud, Internal Control, and Cash 344
9 Accounting for Receivables 396
10 Plant Assets, Natural Resources, and Intangible Assets 436
11 Current Liabilities and Payroll Accounting 484
12 Accounting for Partnerships 526
13 Corporations: Organization and Capital Stock Transactions 568
14 Corporations: Dividends, Retained Earnings, and Income Reporting 606
15 Long-Term Liabilities 642
16 Investments 694
17 Statement of Cash Flows 730
18 Financial Statement Analysis 790
19 Managerial Accounting 842
20 Job Order Costing 886
21 Process Costing 928
22 Cost-Volume-Profit 974
23 Budgetary Planning 1016
24 Budgetary Control and Responsibility Accounting 1060
25 Standard Costs and Balanced Scorecard 1108
26 Incremental Analysis and Capital Budgeting 1154

APPENDICES

A Specimen Financial Statements: PepsiCo, Inc. A1
B Specimen Financial Statements: The Coca-Cola Company, Inc. B1
C Present-Value Concepts C1
D Using Financial Calculators D1
E Standards of Ethical Conduct for Management Accountants E1

CONTENTS

1 Accounting in Action   2

Feature Story: KNOWING THE NUMBERS   2
What Is Accounting?   4
   Three Activities   4
   Who Uses Accounting Data   6
The Building Blocks of Accounting   7
   Ethics in Financial Reporting   7
   Generally Accepted Accounting Principles   8
   Assumptions   9
The Basic Accounting Equation   11
   Assets   12
   Liabilities   12
   Owner's Equity   12
Using the Basic Accounting Equation   14
   Transaction Analysis   14
   Summary of Transactions   19
Financial Statements   20
   Income Statement   22
   Owner's Equity Statement   22
   Balance Sheet   22
   Statement of Cash Flows   23
All About You: ETHICS: MANAGING PERSONAL FINANCIAL REPORTING   25
APPENDIX: Accounting Career Opportunities   29
   Public Accounting   29
   Private Accounting   29
   Opportunities in Government   30
   Forensic Accounting   30
   "Show Me the Money"   30

2 The Recording Process   48

Feature Story: ACCIDENTS HAPPEN   48
The Account   50
   Debits and Credits   51
   Summary of Debit/Credit Rules   54
Steps in the Recording Process   55
   The Journal   55
   The Ledger   58
The Recording Process Illustrated   61
   Summary Illustration of Journalizing and Posting   67
The Trial Balance   68
   Limitations of a Trial Balance   69
   Locating Errors   70
   Use of Dollar Signs   70
All About You: YOUR PERSONAL ANNUAL REPORT   72

3 Adjusting the Accounts   94

Feature Story: WHAT WAS YOUR PROFIT?   94
Timing Issues   96
   Fiscal and Calendar Years   96
   Accrual- vs. Cash-Basis Accounting   97
   Recognizing Revenues and Expenses   97
The Basics of Adjusting Entries   99
   Types of Adjusting Entries   99
   Adjusting Entries for Deferrals   100
   Adjusting Entries for Accruals   107
   Summary of Journalizing and Posting   112
The Adjusted Trial Balance and Financial Statements   114
   Preparing the Adjusted Trial Balance   114
   Preparing Financial Statements   115
APPENDIX: Alternative Treatment of Prepaid Expenses and Unearned Revenues   119
   Prepaid Expenses   120
   Unearned Revenues   121
   Summary of Additional Adjustment Relationships   122

4 Completing the Accounting Cycle   144

Feature Story: EVERYONE LIKES TO WIN   144
Using a Worksheet   146
   Steps in Preparing a Worksheet   146
   Preparing Financial Statements from a Worksheet   150
   Preparing Adjusting Entries from a Worksheet   150
Closing the Books   152
   Preparing Closing Entries   153
   Posting Closing Entries   155
   Preparing a Post-Closing Trial Balance   157
Summary of the Accounting Cycle   159
   Reversing Entries—An Optional Step   160
   Correcting Entries—An Avoidable Step   160
The Classified Balance Sheet   162
   Current Assets   164
   Long-Term Investments   164
   Property, Plant, and Equipment   165
   Intangible Assets   165
   Current Liabilities   166
   Long-Term Liabilities   167
   Owner's Equity   167
All About You: YOUR PERSONAL BALANCE SHEET   169
APPENDIX: Reversing Entries   173
   Reversing Entries Example   173

5 Accounting for Merchandising Operations   198

Feature Story: WHO DOESN'T SHOP AT WAL-MART?   198

xvi Contents

Merchandising Operations 200
- Operating Cycles 201
- Flow of Costs 201

Recording Purchases of Merchandise 203
- Freight Costs 205
- Purchase Returns and Allowances 206
- Purchase Discounts 206
- Summary of Purchasing Transactions 207

Recording Sales of Merchandise 208
- Sales Returns and Allowances 209
- Sales Discounts 210

Completing the Accounting Cycle 211
- Adjusting Entries 211
- Closing Entries 212
- Summary of Merchandising Entries 212

Forms of Financial Statements 214
- Multiple-Step Income Statement 214
- Single-Step Income Statement 217
- Classified Balance Sheet 217

APPENDIX 5A: Periodic Inventory System 221
- Determining Cost of Goods Sold Under a Periodic System 221
- Recording Merchandise Transactions 222
- Recording Purchases of Merchandise 222
- Recording Sales of Merchandise 223

APPENDIX 5B: Worksheet for a Merchandising Company 225
- Using a Worksheet 225

6 Inventories 248

Feature Story: WHERE IS THAT SPARE BULLDOZER BLADE? 248

Classifying Inventory 250

Determining Inventory Quantities 251
- Taking a Physical Inventory 251
- Determining Ownership of Goods 252

Inventory Costing 254
- Specific Identification 254
- Cost Flow Assumptions 255
- Financial Statement and Tax Effects of Cost Flow Methods 260
- Using Inventory Cost Flow Methods Consistently 262
- Lower-of-Cost-or-Market 262

Inventory Errors 263
- Income Statement Effects 263
- Balance Sheet Effects 265

Statement Presentation and Analysis 265
- Presentation 265
- Analysis 266

All About You: EMPLOYEE THEFT—AN INSIDE JOB 268

APPENDIX 6A: Inventory Cost Flow Methods in Perpetual Inventory Systems 271
- First-In, First-Out (FIFO) 271
- Last-In, First-Out (LIFO) 272
- Average-Cost 272

APPENDIX 6B: Estimating Inventories 274
- Gross Profit Method 275
- Retail Inventory Method 276

7 Accounting Information Systems 300

Feature Story: QUICKBOOKS® HELPS THIS RETAILER SELL GUITARS 300

Basic Concepts of Accounting Information Systems 302
- Computerized Accounting Systems 302
- Manual Accounting Systems 305

Subsidiary Ledgers 305
- Subsidiary Ledger Example 306
- Advantages of Subsidiary Ledgers 307

Special Journals 308
- Sales Journal 309
- Cash Receipts Journal 311
- Purchases Journal 315
- Cash Payments Journal 317
- Effects of Special Journals on the General Journal 320

8 Fraud, Internal Control, and Cash 344

Feature Story: MINDING THE MONEY IN MOOSE JAW 344

Fraud and Internal Control 346
- Fraud 346
- The Sarbanes-Oxley Act 348
- Internal Control 348
- Principles of Internal Control Activities 349
- Limitations of Internal Control 356

Cash Controls 357
- Cash Receipts Controls 357
- Cash Disbursements Controls 360

Control Features: Use of a Bank 364
- Making Bank Deposits 365
- Writing Checks 365
- Bank Statements 365
- Reconciling the Bank Account 367
- Electronic Funds Transfer (EFT) System 371

Reporting Cash 372

All About You: PROTECTING YOURSELF FROM IDENTITY THEFT 373

9 Accounting for Receivables 396

Feature Story: A DOSE OF CAREFUL MANAGEMENT KEEPS RECEIVABLES HEALTHY 396

Types of Receivables 398

Accounts Receivable 398
- Recognizing Accounts Receivable 399
- Valuing Accounts Receivable 400
- Disposing of Accounts Receivable 406

Notes Receivable 409
  Determining the Maturity Date 410
  Computing Interest 411
  Recognizing Notes Receivable 411
  Valuing Notes Receivable 411
  Disposing of Notes Receivable 412
Statement Presentation and Analysis 414
  Presentation 414
  Analysis 414
All About You: SHOULD YOU BE CARRYING PLASTIC? 416

10 Plant Assets, Natural Resources, and Intangible Assets 436

Feature Story: HOW MUCH FOR A RIDE TO THE BEACH? 436
SECTION 1 **Plant Assets** 438
Determining the Cost of Plant Assets 439
  Land 439
  Land Improvements 439
  Buildings 440
  Equipment 440
Depreciation 442
  Factors in Computing Depreciation 443
  Depreciation Methods 444
  Depreciation and Income Taxes 448
  Revising Periodic Depreciation 448
Expenditures During Useful Life 449
Plant Assets Disposals 450
  Retirement of Plant Assets 450
  Sale of Plant Assets 451
SECTION 2 **Natural Resources** 453
SECTION 3 **Intangible Assets** 454
Accounting for Intangible Assets 454
  Patents 455
  Copyrights 455
  Trademarks and Trade Names 455
  Franchises and Licenses 456
  Goodwill 456
Research and Development Costs 457
Statement Presentation and Analysis 458
  Presentation 458
  Analysis 459
All About You: BUYING A WRECK OF YOUR OWN 460
APPENDIX: **Exchange of Plant Assets** 464
  Loss Treatment 464
  Gain Treatment 464

11 Current Liabilities and Payroll Accounting 484

Feature Story: FINANCING HIS DREAMS 484
Accounting for Current Liabilities 486
  Notes Payable 486
  Sales Taxes Payable 487
  Unearned Revenues 488
  Current Maturities of Long-Term Debt 489
  Statement Presentation and Analysis 490
Contingent Liabilities 491
  Recording a Contingent Liability 492
  Disclosure of Contingent Liabilities 493
Payroll Accounting 494
  Determining the Payroll 495
  Recording the Payroll 498
  Employer Payroll Taxes 501
  Filing and Remitting Payroll Taxes 503
  Internal Control for Payroll 504
All About You: YOUR BOSS WANTS TO KNOW IF YOU JOGGED TODAY 506
APPENDIX: **Additional Fringe Benefits** 509
Paid Absences 509
  Post-Retirement Benefits 510
  Post-Retirement Healthcare and Life Insurance Benefits 510

12 Accounting for Partnerships 526

Feature Story: FROM TRIALS TO TOP TEN 526
Partnership Form of Organization 528
  Characteristics of Partnerships 528
  Organizations with Partnership Characteristics 529
  Advantages and Disadvantages of Partnerships 530
  The Partnership Agreement 532
Basic Partnership Accounting 533
  Forming a Partnership 533
  Dividing Net Income or Net Loss 534
  Partnership Financial Statements 537
Liquidation of a Partnership 538
  No Capital Deficiency 539
  Capital Deficiency 542
APPENDIX: **Admission and Withdrawal of Partners** 546
  Admission of a Partner 546
  Withdrawal of a Partner 550

13 Corporations: Organization and Capital Stock Transactions 568

Feature Story: "HAVE YOU DRIVEN A FORD LATELY?" 568
The Corporate Form of Organization 570
  Characteristics of a Corporation 571
  Forming a Corporation 573
  Ownership Rights of Stockholders 574
  Stock Issue Considerations 575
  Corporate Capital 577
Accounting for Issues of Common Stock 579
  Issuing Par Value Common Stock for Cash 579
  Issuing No-Par Common Stock for Cash 580
  Issuing Common Stock for Services or Noncash Assets 580

xviii Contents

Accounting for Treasury Stock 582
   Purchase of Treasury Stock 582
   Disposal of Treasury Stock 584
Preferred Stock 586
   Dividend Preferences 586
   Liquidation Preference 587
Statement Presentation 587

14 Corporations: Dividends, Retained Earnings, and Income Reporting 606

Feature Story: OWNING A PIECE OF THE ACTION 606
Dividends 608
   Cash Dividends 608
   Stock Dividends 612
   Stock Splits 614
Retained Earnings 616
   Retained Earnings Restrictions 617
   Prior Period Adjustments 618
   Retained Earnings Statement 619
Statement Presentation and Analysis 620
   Stockholders' Equity Presentation 620
   Stockholders' Equity Analysis 621
   Income Statement Presentation 621
   Income Statement Analysis 622
All About You: CORPORATIONS HAVE GOVERNANCE STRUCTURES—DO YOU? 624

15 Long-Term Liabilities 642

Feature Story: THANKS GOODNESS FOR BANKRUPTCY 642
Bond Basics 644
   Types of Bonds 645
   Issuing Procedures 646
   Bond Trading 646
   Determining the Market Value of Bonds 648
Accounting for Bond Issues 649
   Issuing Bonds at Face Value 649
   Discount or Premium on Bonds 649
   Issuing Bonds at a Discount 650
   Issuing Bonds at a Premium 651
Accounting for Bond Retirements 653
   Redeeming Bonds at Maturity 653
   Redeeming Bonds before Maturity 653
   Converting Bonds into Common Stock 653
Accounting for Other Long-Term Liabilities 654
   Long-Term Notes Payable 654
   Lease Liabilities 656
Statement Presentation and Analysis 658
   Presentation 658
   Analysis 659
APPENDIX 15A: Present Value Concepts Related to Bond Pricing 663
   Present Value of Face Value 664
   Present Value of Interest Payments (Annuities) 665

   Time Periods and Discounting 667
   Computing the Present Value of a Bond 667
APPENDIX 15B: Effective-Interest Method of Bond Amortization 669
   Amortizing Bond Discount 669
   Amortizing Bond Premium 671
APPENDIX 15C: Straight-Line Amortization 673
   Amortizing Bond Discount 673
   Amortizing Bond Premium 674

16 Investments 694

Feature Story: "IS THERE ANYTHING ELSE WE CAN BUY?" 694
Why Corporations Invest 696
Accounting for Debt Investments 698
   Recording Acquisition of Bonds 698
   Recording Bond Interest 698
   Recording Sale of Bonds 698
Accounting for Stock Investments 699
   Holdings of Less than 20% 700
   Holdings Between 20% and 50% 701
   Holdings of More than 50% 702
Valuing and Reporting Investments 704
   Categories of Securities 705
   Balance Sheet Presentation 708
   Presentation of Realized and Unrealized Gain or Loss 709
   Classified Balance Sheet 710

17 Statement of Cash Flows 730

Feature Story: GOT CASH? 730
The Statement of Cash Flows: Usefulness and Format 731
   Usefulness of the Statement of Cash Flows 731
   Classification of Cash Flows 733
   Significant Noncash Activities 734
   Format of the Statement of Cash Flows 735
   Preparing the Statement of Cash Flows 736
   Indirect and Direct Methods 737
Preparing the Statement of Cash Flows—Indirect Method 738
   Step 1: Operating Activities 739
   Step 2: Investing and Financing Activities 744
   Step 3: Net Change in Cash 745
Using Cash Flows to Evaluate a Company 748
   Free Cash Flow 748
APPENDIX 17A: Using a Work Sheet to Prepare the Statement of Cash Flows—Indirect Method 752
   Preparing the Worksheet 753
APPENDIX 17B: Statement of Cash Flows—Direct Method 758
   Step 1: Operating Activities 759
   Step 2: Investing and Financing Activities 763
   Step 3: Net Change in Cash 764

18 Financial Statement Analysis 790

Feature Story: IT PAYS TO BE PATIENT 790
Basics of Financial Statement Analysis 792
    Need for Comparative Analysis 792
    Tools of Analysis 793
Horizontal Analysis 793
    Balance Sheet 794
    Income Statement 795
    Retained Earnings Statement 796
Vertical Analysis 797
    Balance Sheet 797
    Income Statement 797
Ratio Analysis 799
    Liquidity Ratios 800
    Profitability Ratios 803
    Solvency Ratios 807
    Summary of Ratios 809
Earning Power and Irregular Items 811
    Discontinued Operations 811
    Extraordinary Items 812
    Changes in Accounting Principle 814
    Comprehensive Income 814
Quality of Earnings 815
    Alternative Accounting Methods 816
    Pro Forma Income 816
    Improper Recognition 816

19 Managerial Accounting 842

Feature Story: WHAT A DIFFERENCE A DAY MAKES 842
Managerial Accounting Basics 844
    Comparing Managerial and Financial Accounting 845
    Management Functions 846
    Business Ethics 847
Managerial Cost Concepts 849
    Manufacturing Costs 849
    Product versus Period Costs 851
Manufacturing Costs in Financial Statements 852
    Income Statement 852
    Balance Sheet 855
    Cost Concepts—A Review 856
Managerial Accounting Today 858
    Service-Industry Trends 585
    Managerial Accounting Practices 858

20 Job Order Costing 886

Feature Story: ". . . AND WE'D LIKE IT IN RED" 886
Cost Accounting Systems 888
    Job Order Cost System 888
    Process Cost System 889
Job Order Cost Flow 890
    Accumulating Manufacturing Costs 891
    Assigning Manufacturing Costs to Work in Process 893

    Assigning Costs to Finished Goods 900
    Assigning Costs to Cost of Goods Sold 901
    Summary of Job Order Cost Flows 901
Reporting Job Cost Data 903
Under- or Overapplied Manufacturing Overhead 904
All About You: MINDING YOUR OWN BUSINESS 906

21 Process Costing 928

Feature Story: BEN & JERRY'S TRACKS ITS MIX-UPS 928
The Nature of Process Cost Systems 930
    Uses of Process Cost Systems 930
    Similarities and Differences between Job Order Cost and Process Cost Systems 931
    Process Cost Flow 933
    Assignment of Manufacturing Costs—Journal Entries 933
Equivalent Units 936
    Weighted-Average Method 937
    Refinements on the Weighted-Average Method 937
    Production Cost Report 939
Comprehensive Example of Process Costing 940
    Compute the Physical Unit Flow (Step 1) 941
    Compute Equivalent Units of Production (Step 2) 941
    Compute Unit Production Costs (Step 3) 942
    Prepare a Cost Reconciliation Schedule (Step 4) 943
    Preparing the Production Cost Report 943
    Costing Systems—Final Comments 945
Contemporary Developments 946
    Just-in-Time Processing 946
    Activity-Based Costing 948
APPENDIX: Example of Traditional Costing versus Activity-Based Costing 953
    Production and Cost Data 953
    Unit Costs Under Traditional Costing 953
    Unit Costs Under ABC 953
    Comparing Unit Costs 954
    Benefits and Limitations of Activity-Based Costing 955

22 Cost-Volume-Profit 974

Feature Story: GROWING BY LEAPS AND LEOTARDS 974
Cost Behavior Analysis 976
    Variable Costs 977
    Fixed Costs 977
    Relevant Range 978
    Mixed Costs 980
    Importance of Identifying Variable and Fixed Costs 982
Cost-Volume-Profit Analysis 983
    Basic Components 983
    CVP Income Statement 984
    Break-even Analysis 986

xx Contents

    Target Net Income 989
    Margin of Safety 991
    CVP and Changes in the Business Environment 992
    CVP Income Statement Revisited 993
All About You: A HYBRID DILEMMA 995
APPENDIX: Variable Costing 998
    Effects of Variable Costing on Income 999
    Rationale for Variable Costing 1001

23 Budgetary Planning 1016

Feature Story: THE NEXT AMAZON.COM? NOT QUITE 1016
Budgeting Basics 1018
    Budgeting and Accounting 1018
    The Benefits of Budgeting 1019
    Essentials of Effective Budgeting 1019
    Length of the Budget Period 1019
    The Budgeting Process 1020
    Budgeting and Human Behavior 1020
    Budgeting and Long-Range Planning 1021
    The Master Budget 1022
Preparing the Operating Budgets 1023
    Sales Budget 1023
    Production Budget 1024
    Direct Materials Budget 1025
    Direct Labor Budget 1027
    Manufacturing Overhead Budget 1028
    Selling and Administrative Expense Budget 1029
    Budgeted Income Statement 1029
Preparing the Financial Budgets 1031
    Cash Budget 1031
    Budgeted Balance Sheet 1034
Budgeting in Non-Manufacturing Companies 1036
    Merchandisers 1036
    Service Enterprises 1037
    Not-for-Profit Organizations 1037
All About You: AVOIDING PERSONAL FINANCIAL DISASTER 1038

24 Budgetary Control and Responsibility Accounting 1060

Feature Story: TRYING TO AVOID AN ELECTRIC SHOCK 1060
The Concept of Budgetary Control 1062
Static Budget Reports 1063
    Examples 1064
    Uses and Limitations 1065
Flexible Budgets 1065
    Why Flexible Budgets? 1065
    Developing the Flexible Budget 1067
    Flexible Budget—A Case Study 1068
    Flexible Budget Reports 1070
    Management by Exception 1071

The Concept of Responsibility Accounting 1072
    Controllable versus Non-controllable Revenues and Costs 1074
    Responsibility Reporting System 1074
Types of Responsibility Centers 1077
    Responsibility Accounting for Cost Centers 1078
    Responsibility Accounting for Profit Centers 1078
    Responsibility Accounting for Investment Centers 1080
    Principles of Performance Evaluation 1083

25 Standard Costs and Balanced Scorecard 1108

Feature Story: HIGHLIGHTING PERFORMANCE EFFICIENCY 1108
The Need for Standards 1110
    Distinguishing between Standards and Budgets 1111
    Why Standard Costs? 1111
Setting Standard Costs—A Difficult Task 1112
    Ideal versus Normal Standards 1112
    A Case Study 1112
Analyzing and Reporting Variances from Standards 1116
    Direct Materials Variances 1116
    Direct Labor Variances 1119
    Manufacturing Overhead Variances 1121
    Reporting Variances 1122
    Statement Presentation of Variances 1123
Balanced Scorecard 1124
APPENDIX 25A: Standard Cost Accounting System 1130
    Journal Entries 1130
    Ledger Accounts 1132
APPENDIX 25B: A Closer Look at Overhead Variances 1133
    Overhead Controllable Variance 1133
    Overhead Volume Variance 1134

26 Incremental Analysis and Capital Budgeting 1154

Feature Story: SOUP IS GOOD FOOD 1154
SECTION 1 Incremental Analysis 1156
Management's Decision-Making Process 1156
    The Incremental Analysis Approach 1157
    How Incremental Analysis Works 1157
Types of Incremental Analysis 1158
    Accept an Order at a Special Price 1158
    Make or Buy 1159
    Sell or Process Further 1162
    Retain or Replace Equipment 1163
    Eliminate an Unprofitable Segment 1164
    Allocate Limited Resources 1165
SECTION 2 Capital Budgeting 1166
Evaluation Process 1167
Annual Rate of Return 1167
Cash Payback 1168

Contents **xxi**

Discounted Cash Flow 1170
   Net Present Value Method 1171
   Internal Rate of Return Method 1173
   Comparing Discounted Cash Flow Methods 1174
All About You: WHAT IS A DEGREE WORTH? 1176

APPENDIX A Specimen Financial Statements: PepsiCo, Inc. A1

APPENDIX B Specimen Financial Statements: The Coca-Cola Company B1

APPENDIX C Time Value of Money C1
Nature of Interest C1
   Simple Interest C1
   Compound Interest C2
Present Value Variables C3
Present Value of a Single Amount C3
Present Value of an Annuity C5
Time Periods and Discounting C7
Computing the Present Value of a Long-Term Note or Bond C7

APPENDIX D Using Financial Calculators D1
Present Value of a Single Sum D1
   Plus and Minus D2
   Compounding Periods D2
   Rounding D2
Present Value of an Annuity D2
Useful Applications of the Financial Calculator D3
   Auto Loan D3
   Mortgage Loan Amount D3

APPENDIX E Standards of Ethical Conduct for Management Accountants E1
IMA Statement of Ethical Professional Practice E1
   Principles E1
   Standards E1
   Resolution of Ethical Conflict E2

Photo Credits PC1
Company Index I1
Subject Index I3

all about YOU — quick guide

The *"All About You"* feature promotes financial literacy. These full-page boxes will get students thinking and talking about how accounting impacts their personal lives. Students are more likely to understand the accounting concept being made within the textbook when accounting material is linked to a familiar topic. Each *All About You* box presents a high-interest issue related to the chapter topic, offers facts about it, poses a situation for students to think about, and offers brief opposing answers as a starting place for further discussion. As a feedback mechanism, the authors' comments and opinions about the situation appear at the end of the chapter.

In addition, an *"All About You" Activity*, located in the *Broadening Your Perspective* section near the end of the assignment material, offers further opportunity to explore aspects of the topic in a homework assignment.

CHAPTER 1 Accounting in Action
Ethics: Managing Personal Financial Reporting (p. 25)
Compares filing for financial aid to corporate financial reporting. Presents facts about student debt loads. Asks whether students should present a negative financial picture to increase the chance of receiving financial aid.

CHAPTER 2 The Recording Process
Your Personal Annual Report (p. 72)
Likens a student's résumé to a company's annual report. Asks students to consider whether firing Radio Shack's CEO for résumé falsehoods was warranted.

CHAPTER 4 Completing the Accounting Cycle
Your Personal Balance Sheet (p. 169)
Walks students through identification of personal assets and personal liabilities. Presents facts about Americans' wealth and attitudes toward saving versus spending. Asks if college is a good time to prepare a personal balance sheet.

CHAPTER 6 Inventories
Employee Theft—An Inside Job (p. 268)
Discusses the problem of inventory theft and how companies keep it in check. Asks students' opinions on the use of video cameras to reduce theft.

CHAPTER 8 Internal Control and Cash
Protecting Yourself from Identity Theft (p. 373)
Likens corporate internal controls to individuals' efforts to protect themselves from identity thieves. Presents facts about how thieves use stolen data. Asks students about the safety of storing personal financial data on computers.

CHAPTER 9 Accounting for Receivables
Should You Be Carrying Plastic? (p. 416)
Discusses the need for individuals to evaluate their credit positions as thoughtfully as companies do. Presents facts about college-student debt and Americans' use of credit cards. Asks whether students should cut up their credit cards.

CHAPTER 10 Plant Assets, Natural Resources, and Intangible Assets
Buying a Wreck of Your Own (p. 460)
Presents information about costs of new versus used cars. Asks whether students could improve their economic well-being by buying a used car.

CHAPTER 11 Current Liabilities and Payroll Accounting
Your Boss Wants to Know If You Jogged Today (p. 506)
Discusses ways to contain costs of health-care spending. Asks students to consider whose responsibility it is to maintain healthy lifestyles to control health-care costs.

CHAPTER 14 Corporations: Dividends, Retained Earnings, and Income Reporting
Corporations Have Governance Structures— Do You? (p. 624)
Discusses codes of ethics in business and at college. Presents facts about abuse of workplace codes of ethics and responses of stockholders. Asks students for opinions on whether schools' codes of ethics serve a useful purpose.

CHAPTER 20 Job Order Cost Accounting
Minding Your Own Business (p. 906)
Focuses on how small business owners calculate product costs. Presents facts about sole proprietorships and franchises. Poses a start-up business idea and asks students to evaluate the cost of labor input.

CHAPTER 22 Cost-Volume-Profit
A Hybrid Dilemma (p. 995)
Explores the cost tradeoffs of hybrid vehicles. Asks students to evaluate the pros and cons of buying a hybrid vehicle.

CHAPTER 23 Budgetary Planning
Avoiding Personal Financial Disaster (p. 1038)
Explores personal budgets for college students. Asks students to look at a budgeting calculator and consider whether student loans should be considered a source of income.

CHAPTER 26 Incremental Analysis and Capital Budgeting
What Is a Degree Worth? (p. 1176)
Presents facts about cost of college, and benefits of college education. Asks students to consider the value of a college education.

th Edition

Accounting Principles

Volume 2: Chapters 13–26

Chapter 13

Corporations: Organization and Capital Stock Transactions

STUDY OBJECTIVES

After studying this chapter, you should be able to:

1. Identify the major characteristics of a corporation.
2. Differentiate between paid-in capital and retained earnings.
3. Record the issuance of common stock.
4. Explain the accounting for treasury stock.
5. Differentiate preferred stock from common stock.
6. Prepare a stockholders' equity section.

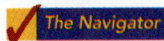

✓ The Navigator

Scan **Study Objectives**	■
Read **Feature Story**	■
Read **Preview**	■
Read text and answer **DO IT!** p. 577 ■ p. 579 ■ p. 581 ■ p. 585 ■ p. 589 ■	
Work **Comprehensive** **DO IT!** p. 589	■
Review **Summary of Study Objectives**	■
Answer **Self-Study Questions**	■
Complete **Assignments**	■

Feature Story

"HAVE YOU DRIVEN A FORD LATELY?"

A company that has produced such renowned successes as the Model T and the Mustang, and such a dismal failure as the Edsel, would have some interesting tales to tell. Henry Ford was a defiant visionary from the day he formed Ford Motor Company (www.ford.com) in 1903. His goal from day one was to design a car he could mass-produce and sell at a price that was affordable to the masses. In short order he accomplished this goal. By 1920,

60% of all vehicles on U.S. roads were Fords.

Henry Ford was intolerant of anything that stood between him and success. In the early years Ford had issued shares to the public in order to finance the company's exponential growth. In 1916 he decided not to pay a dividend in order to increase the funds available to expand the company.

The shareholders sued. Henry Ford's reaction was swift and direct: If the shareholders didn't see things his way, he would get rid of them. In 1919 the Ford family purchased 100 percent of the outstanding shares of Ford, eliminating any outside "interference." It was over 35 years before the company again issued shares to the public.

Ford Motor Company has continued to evolve and grow over the years into one of the largest international corporations. Today there are nearly a billion shares of publicly traded Ford stock outstanding. But some aspects of the company have changed very little: The chairman and chief executive of the company is a member of the Ford family. Also, the Ford family still retains a significant stake in Ford Motor Company. In a move Henry Ford might have supported, top management recently decided to centralize decision making—that is, to have more key decisions made by top management, rather than by division managers. And, reminiscent of Henry Ford's most famous car, the company is attempting to make a "global car"—a mass-produced car that can be sold around the world with only minor changes.

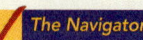

Inside Chapter 13...

- **How to Read Stock Quotes** (p. 576)
- **Why Did Reebok Buy Its Own Stock?** (p. 584)

Preview of Chapter 13

Corporations like Ford Motor Company have substantial resources. In fact, the corporation is the dominant form of business organization in the United States in terms of number of employees and dollar volume of sales and earnings. All of the 500 largest companies in the United States are corporations. In this chapter we will explain the essential features of a corporation and the accounting for a corporation's capital stock transactions. In Chapter 14 we will look at other issues related to accounting for corporations.

The content and organization of Chapter 13 are as follows.

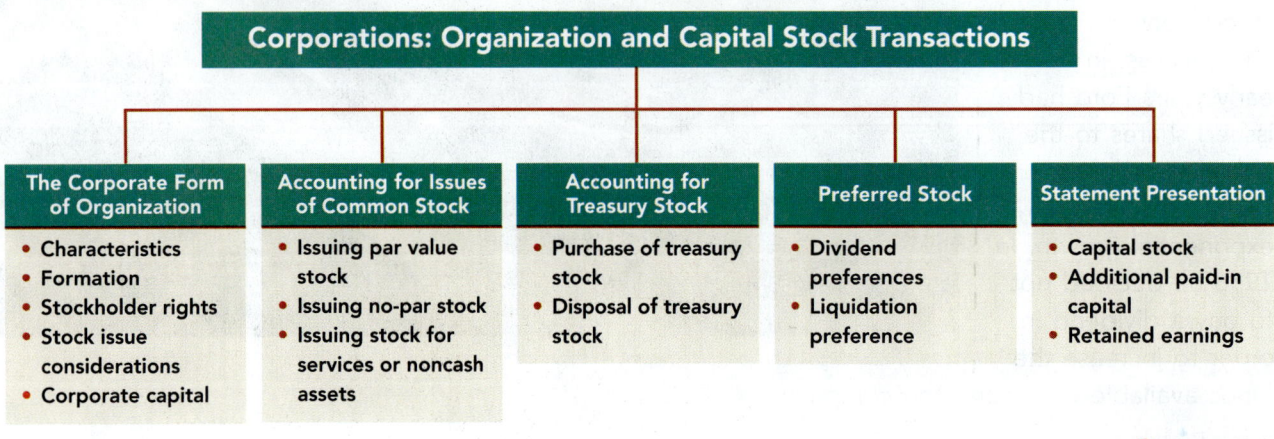

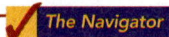

THE CORPORATE FORM OF ORGANIZATION

In 1819, Chief Justice John Marshall defined a corporation as "an artificial being, invisible, intangible, and existing only in contemplation of law." This definition is the foundation for the prevailing legal interpretation that a **corporation** is an **entity separate and distinct from its owners**.

A corporation is created by law, and its continued existence depends upon the statutes of the state in which it is incorporated. As a legal entity, a corporation has most of the rights and privileges of a person. The major exceptions relate to privileges that only a living person can exercise, such as the right to vote or to hold public office. A corporation is subject to the same duties and responsibilities as a person. For example, it must abide by the laws, and it must pay taxes.

Two common ways to classify corporations are by purpose and by ownership. A corporation may be organized for the purpose of making a **profit**, or it may be **not-for-profit**. For-profit corporations include such well-known companies as McDonald's, Ford Motor Company, PepsiCo, and Google. Not-for-profit corporations are organized for charitable, medical, or educational purposes. Examples are the Salvation Army, the American Cancer Society, and the Bill & Melinda Gates Foundation.

Classification by **ownership** distinguishes between publicly held and privately held corporations. A **publicly held corporation** may have thousands of stockholders. Its stock is regularly traded on a national securities exchange such as the New York Stock Exchange. Most of the largest U.S. corporations are publicly held. Examples of publicly held corporations are Intel, IBM, Caterpillar Inc., and General Electric.

In contrast, a **privately held corporation** usually has only a few stockholders, and does not offer its stock for sale to the general public. Privately held companies are generally much smaller than publicly held companies, although some notable

ALTERNATIVE TERMINOLOGY

Privately held corporations are also referred to as *closely held corporations.*

exceptions exist. Cargill Inc., a private corporation that trades in grain and other commodities, is one of the largest companies in the United States.

Characteristics of a Corporation

A number of characteristics distinguish corporations from proprietorships and partnerships. We explain the most important of these characteristics below.

STUDY OBJECTIVE 1
Identify the major characteristics of a corporation.

SEPARATE LEGAL EXISTENCE

As an entity separate and distinct from its owners, the corporation acts under its own name rather than in the name of its stockholders. Ford Motor Company may buy, own, and sell property. It may borrow money, and may enter into legally binding contracts in its own name. It may also sue or be sued, and it pays its own taxes.

Remember that in a partnership the acts of the owners (partners) bind the partnership. In contrast, the acts of its owners (stockholders) do not bind the corporation unless such owners are **agents** of the corporation. For example, if you owned shares of Ford Motor Company stock, you would not have the right to purchase automobile parts for the company unless you were appointed as an agent of the company, such as a purchasing manager.

LIMITED LIABILITY OF STOCKHOLDERS

Since a corporation is a separate legal entity, creditors have recourse only to corporate assets to satisfy their claims. The liability of stockholders is normally limited to their investment in the corporation. Creditors have no legal claim on the personal assets of the owners unless fraud has occurred. Even in the event of bankruptcy, stockholders' losses are generally limited to their capital investment in the corporation.

TRANSFERABLE OWNERSHIP RIGHTS

Shares of capital stock give ownership in a corporation. These shares are transferable units. Stockholders may dispose of part or all of their interest in a corporation simply by selling their stock. Remember that the transfer of an ownership interest in a partnership requires the consent of each owner. In contrast, the transfer of stock is entirely at the discretion of the stockholder. It does not require the approval of either the corporation or other stockholders.

The transfer of ownership rights between stockholders normally has no effect on the daily operating activities of the corporation. Nor does it affect the corporation's assets, liabilities, and total ownership equity. The transfer of these ownership rights is a transaction between individual owners. After it first issues the capital stock, the company does not participate in such transfers.

ABILITY TO ACQUIRE CAPITAL

It is relatively easy for a corporation to obtain capital through the issuance of stock. Investors buy stock in a corporation to earn money over time as the share price grows, and because a stockholder has limited liability and shares of stock are readily transferable. Also, individuals can become stockholders by investing relatively small amounts of money. In sum, the ability of a successful corporation to obtain capital is virtually unlimited.

CONTINUOUS LIFE

The life of a corporation is stated in its charter. The life may be perpetual, or it may be limited to a specific number of years. If it is limited, the company can extend the life through renewal of the charter. Since a corporation is a separate legal entity, its

Continuous life

continuance as a going concern is not affected by the withdrawal, death, or incapacity of a stockholder, employee, or officer. As a result, a successful enterprise can have a continuous and perpetual life.

CORPORATION MANAGEMENT

As in **Ford Motor Company**, stockholders legally own the corporation. But they manage the corporation indirectly through a board of directors they elect. The board, in turn, formulates the operating policies for the company. The board also selects officers, such as a president and one or more vice presidents, to execute policy and to perform daily management functions.

Illustration 13-1 presents a typical organization chart showing the delegation of responsibility. The chief executive officer (CEO) has overall responsibility for managing the business. As the organization chart shows, the CEO delegates responsibility to other officers.

Illustration 13-1
Corporation organization chart

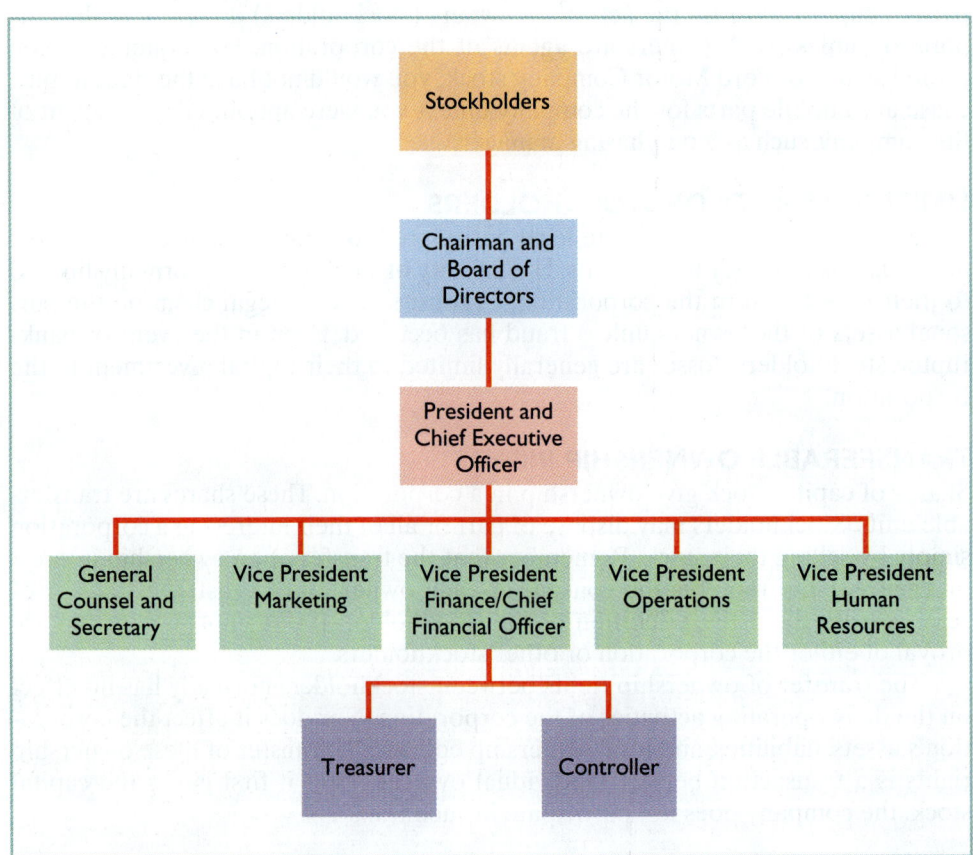

The chief accounting officer is the **controller**. The controller's responsibilities include (1) maintaining the accounting records, (2) maintaining an adequate system of internal control, and (3) preparing financial statements, tax returns, and internal reports. The **treasurer** has custody of the corporation's funds and is responsible for maintaining the company's cash position.

The organizational structure of a corporation enables a company to hire professional managers to run the business. On the other hand, the separation of ownership and management prevents owners from having an active role in managing the company, which some owners like to have.

> **ETHICS NOTE**
> Managers who are not owners are often compensated based on the performance of the firm. They thus may be tempted to exaggerate firm performance by inflating income figures.

GOVERNMENT REGULATIONS

A corporation is subject to numerous state and federal regulations. State laws usually prescribe the requirements for issuing stock, the distributions of earnings permitted to stockholders, and the effects of retiring stock. Federal securities laws govern the sale of capital stock to the general public. Also, most publicly held corporations are required to make extensive disclosure of their financial affairs to the Securities and Exchange Commission (SEC) through quarterly and annual reports. In addition, when a corporation lists its stock on organized securities exchanges, it must comply with the reporting requirements of these exchanges. Government regulations are designed to protect the owners of the corporation.

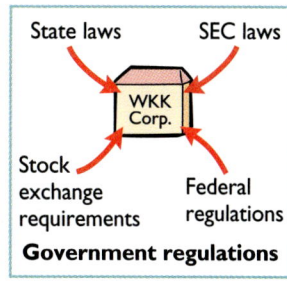

Government regulations

ADDITIONAL TAXES

Neither proprietorships nor partnerships pay income taxes separate from the owner's share of earnings. Sole proprietors and partners report earnings on their personal income tax returns and pay taxes on this amount. Corporations, on the other hand, must pay federal and state income taxes **as a separate legal entity**. These taxes are substantial.

In addition, stockholders must pay taxes on cash dividends (pro rata distributions of net income). Thus, many argue that the government taxes corporate income **twice (double taxation)**—once at the corporate level, and again at the individual level.

In summary, we can identify the following advantages and disadvantages of a corporation compared to a proprietorship and a partnership.

Additional taxes

Advantages	Disadvantages
Separate legal existence	Corporation management—separation of ownership and management
Limited liability of stockholders	
Transferable ownership rights	Government regulations
Ability to acquire capital	Additional taxes
Continuous life	
Corporation management—professional managers	

Illustration 13-2
Advantages and disadvantages of a corporation

Forming a Corporation

The initial step in forming a corporation is to file an application with the Secretary of State in the state in which incorporation is desired. The application contains such information as: (1) the name and purpose of the proposed corporation; (2) amounts, kinds, and number of shares of capital stock to be authorized; (3) the names of the incorporators; and (4) the shares of stock to which each has subscribed.

After the state approves the application, it grants a **charter**. The charter may be an approved copy of the application form, or it may be a separate document containing the same basic data. The issuance of the charter creates the corporation. Upon receipt of the charter, the corporation develops its by-laws. The **by-laws** establish the internal rules and procedures for conducting the affairs of the corporation. They also indicate the powers of the stockholders, directors, and officers of the enterprise.[1]

Regardless of the number of states in which a corporation has operating divisions, it is incorporated in only one state. It is to the company's advantage to incorporate in a state whose laws are favorable to the corporate form of business

ALTERNATIVE TERMINOLOGY

The charter is often referred to as the *articles of incorporation*.

---

[1]Following approval by two-thirds of the stockholders, the by-laws become binding upon all stockholders, directors, and officers. Legally, a corporation is regulated first by the laws of the state, second by its charter, and third by its by-laws. Corporations must take care to ensure that the provisions of the by-laws are not in conflict with either state laws or the charter.

574 Chapter 13 Corporations: Organization and Capital Stock Transactions

organization. General Motors, for example, is incorporated in Delaware, whereas Qualcomm is a New Jersey corporation. Many corporations choose to incorporate in states with rules favorable to existing management. For example, Gulf Oil at one time changed its state of incorporation to Delaware to thwart possible unfriendly takeovers. There, state law allows boards of directors to approve certain defensive tactics against takeovers without a vote by shareholders.

Corporations engaged in interstate commerce must also obtain a license from each state in which they do business. The license subjects the corporation's operating activities to the corporation laws of the state.

Costs incurred in the formation of a corporation are called **organization costs**. These costs include legal and state fees, and promotional expenditures involved in the organization of the business. **Corporations expense organization costs as incurred.** To determine the amount and timing of future benefits is so difficult that it is standard procedure to take a conservative approach of expensing these costs immediately.

Ownership Rights of Stockholders

When chartered, the corporation may begin selling ownership rights in the form of shares of stock. When a corporation has only one class of stock, it is **common stock**. Each share of common stock gives the stockholder the ownership rights pictured in Illustration 13-3. A corporation's articles of incorporation or its by-laws state the ownership rights of a share of stock.

Illustration 13-3
Ownership rights of stockholders

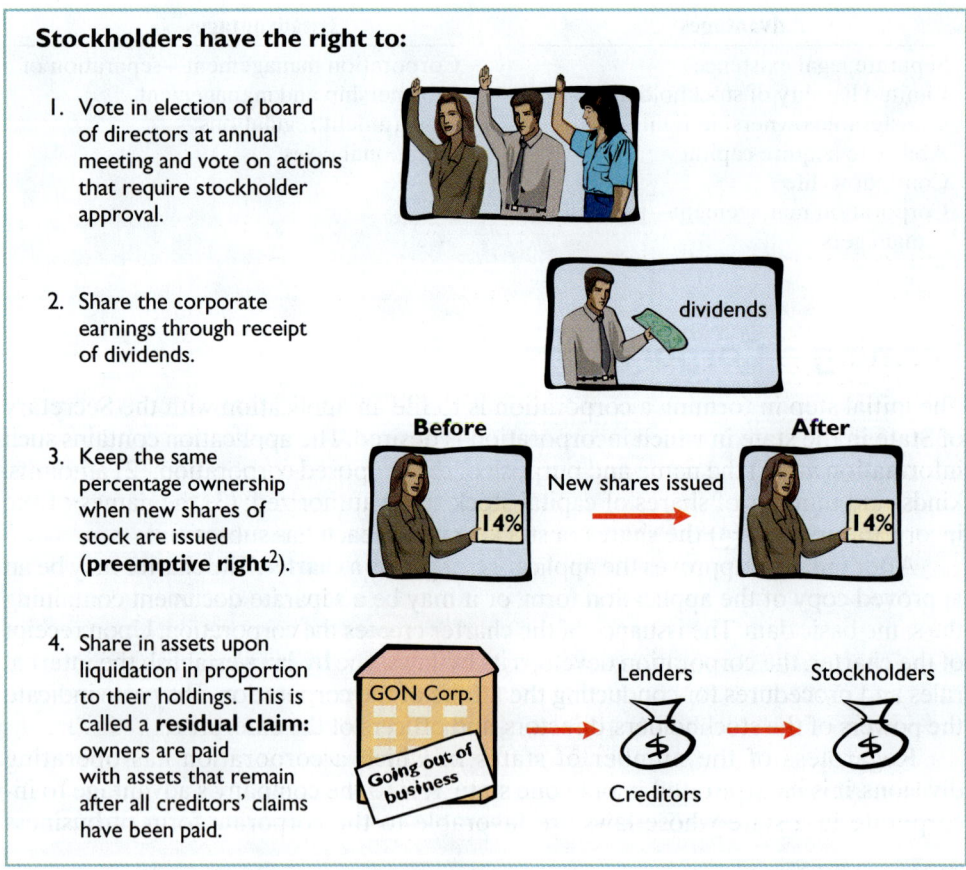

Stockholders have the right to:

1. Vote in election of board of directors at annual meeting and vote on actions that require stockholder approval.

2. Share the corporate earnings through receipt of dividends.

3. Keep the same percentage ownership when new shares of stock are issued (**preemptive right**[2]).

4. Share in assets upon liquidation in proportion to their holdings. This is called a **residual claim:** owners are paid with assets that remain after all creditors' claims have been paid.

---

[2] A number of companies have eliminated the preemptive right, because they believe it makes an unnecessary and cumbersome demand on management. For example, by stockholder approval, IBM has dropped its preemptive right for stockholders.

Proof of stock ownership is evidenced by a form known as a **stock certificate**. As Illustration 13-4 shows, the face of the certificate shows the name of the corporation, the stockholder's name, the class and special features of the stock, the number of shares owned, and the signatures of authorized corporate officials. Prenumbered certificates facilitate accountability. They may be issued for any quantity of shares.

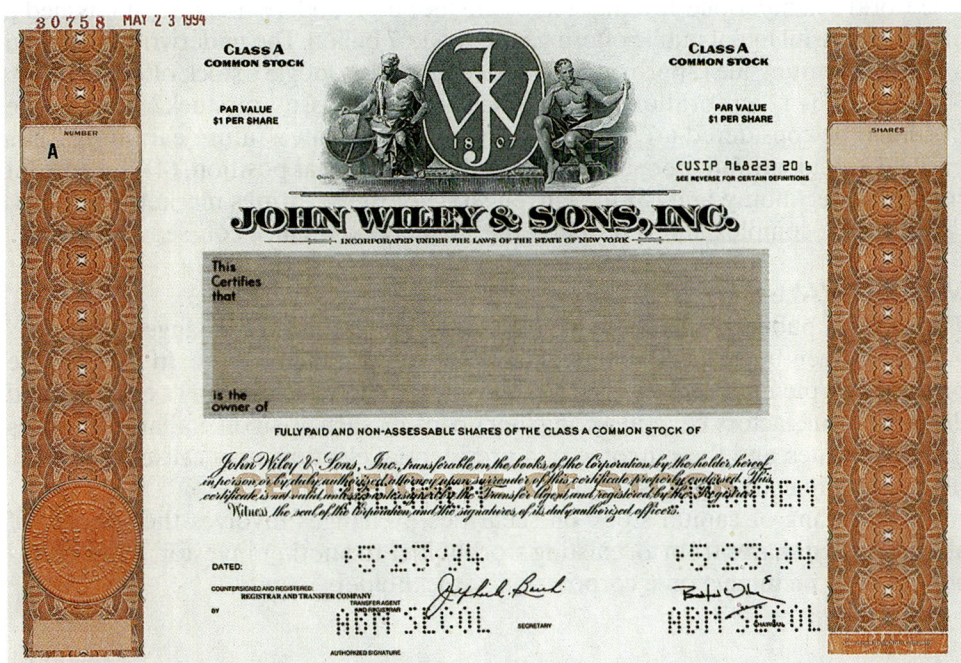

Illustration 13-4
A stock certificate

Stock Issue Considerations

In considering the issuance of stock, a corporation must resolve a number of basic questions: How many shares should it authorize for sale? How should it issue the stock? At what price should it issue the shares? What value should the corporation assign to the stock? These questions are addressed in the following sections.

AUTHORIZED STOCK
The charter indicates the amount of stock that a corporation is **authorized** to sell. The total amount of authorized stock at the time of incorporation normally anticipates both initial and subsequent capital needs. As a result, the number of shares authorized generally exceeds the number initially sold. If it sells all authorized stock, a corporation must obtain consent of the state to amend its charter before it can issue additional shares.

The authorization of capital stock does not result in a formal accounting entry. This event has no immediate effect on either corporate assets or stockholders' equity. However, the number of authorized shares is often reported in the stockholders' equity section. It is then simple to determine the number of unissued shares that the corporation can issue without amending the charter: subtract the total shares issued from the total authorized. For example, if Advanced Micro was authorized to sell 100,000 shares of common stock and issued 80,000 shares, 20,000 shares would remain unissued.

ISSUANCE OF STOCK
A corporation can issue common stock **directly** to investors. Or it can issue the stock **indirectly** through an investment banking firm that specializes in bringing securities to market. Direct issue is typical in closely held companies. Indirect issue is customary for a publicly held corporation.

Indirect Issuance

In an indirect issue, the investment banking firm may agree to **underwrite** the entire stock issue. In this arrangement, the investment banker buys the stock from the corporation at a stipulated price and resells the shares to investors. The corporation thus avoids any risk of being unable to sell the shares. Also, it obtains immediate use of the cash received from the underwriter. The investment banking firm, in turn, assumes the risk of reselling the shares, in return for an underwriting fee.[3] For example, Google (the world's number-one Internet search engine) used underwriters when it issued a highly successful initial public offering, raising $1.67 billion. The underwriters charged a 3% underwriting fee (approximately $50 million) on Google's stock offering.

How does a corporation set the price for a new issue of stock? Among the factors to be considered are: (1) the company's anticipated future earnings, (2) its expected dividend rate per share, (3) its current financial position, (4) the current state of the economy, and (5) the current state of the securities market. The calculation can be complex and is properly the subject of a finance course.

MARKET VALUE OF STOCK

The stock of publicly held companies is traded on organized exchanges. The interaction between buyers and sellers determines the prices per share. In general, the prices set by the marketplace tend to follow the trend of a company's earnings and dividends. But, factors beyond a company's control, such as an oil embargo, changes in interest rates, and the outcome of a presidential election, may cause day-to-day fluctuations in market prices.

The trading of capital stock on securities exchanges involves the transfer of **already issued shares** from an existing stockholder to another investor. These transactions have **no impact** on a corporation's stockholders' equity.

INVESTOR INSIGHT

How to Read Stock Quotes

The volume of trading on national and international exchanges is heavy. Daily trading on the New York Stock Exchange (NYSE) alone often exceeds one billion shares. For each listed stock, the *Wall Street Journal* and other financial media report the total volume of stock traded for a given day, the high and low price for the day, the closing market price, and the net change for the day. A recent stock quote for PepsiCo, listed on the NYSE under the ticker symbol PEP, is shown below.

Stock	Volume	High	Low	Close	Net Change
PepsiCo	4,305,600	60.30	59.32	60.02	+0.41

These numbers indicate that PepsiCo's trading volume was 4,305,600 shares. The high, low, and closing prices for that date were $60.30, $59.32, and $60.02, respectively. The net change for the day was an increase of $0.41 per share.

? For stocks traded on organized stock exchanges, how are the dollar prices per share established? What factors might influence the price of shares in the marketplace?

---

[3] Alternatively, the investment banking firm may agree only to enter into a **best-efforts** contract with the corporation. In such cases, the banker agrees to sell as many shares as possible at a specified price. The corporation bears the risk of unsold stock. Under a best-efforts arrangement, the banking firm is paid a fee or commission for its services.

PAR AND NO-PAR VALUE STOCKS

Par value stock is capital stock to which the charter has assigned a value per share. Years ago, par value determined the **legal capital** per share that a company must retain in the business for the protection of corporate creditors; that amount was not available for withdrawal by stockholders. Thus, in the past, most states required the corporation to sell its shares at par or above.

However, par value was often immaterial relative to the value of the company's stock—even at the time of issue. Thus, its usefulness as a protective device to creditors was questionable. For example, Reebok's par value is $0.01 per share, yet a new issue in 2006 would have sold at a **market value** in the $33 per share range. Thus, par has no relationship with market value; in the vast majority of cases, it is an immaterial amount. As a consequence, today many states do not require a par value. Instead, they use other means to determine legal capital to protect creditors.

No-par value stock is capital stock to which the charter has not assigned a value. No-par value stock is quite common today. For example, Nike, Procter & Gamble, and North American Van Lines all have no-par stock. In many states the board of directors assigns a **stated value** to no-par shares.

DO IT!

CORPORATE ORGANIZATION

Indicate whether each of the following statements is true or false.

_____ 1. Similar to partners in a partnership, stockholders of a corporation have unlimited liability.

_____ 2. It is relatively easy for a corporation to obtain capital through the issuance of stock.

_____ 3. The separation of ownership and management is an advantage of the corporate form of business.

_____ 4. The journal entry to record the authorization of capital stock includes a credit to the appropriate capital stock account.

_____ 5. Most states require a par value per share for capital stock.

action plan

✔ Review the characteristics of a corporation and understand which are advantages and which are disadvantages.

✔ Understand that corporations raise capital through the issuance of stock, which can be par or no-par.

Solution

1. False. The liability of stockholders is normally limited to their investment in the corporation.
2. True.
3. False. The separation of ownership and management is a disadvantage of the corporate form of business.
4. False. The authorization of capital stock does not result in a formal accounting entry.
5. False. Many states do not require a par value.

Related exercise material: **BE13-1, E13-1, E13-2,** and **DO IT! 13-1.**

Corporate Capital

Owners' equity is identified by various names: **stockholders' equity, shareholders' equity,** or **corporate capital**. The stockholders' equity section of a corporation's balance sheet consists of two parts: (1) paid-in (contributed) capital and (2) retained earnings (earned capital).

STUDY OBJECTIVE 2

Differentiate between paid-in capital and retained earnings.

578 Chapter 13 Corporations: Organization and Capital Stock Transactions

The distinction between **paid-in capital** and **retained earnings** is important from both a legal and a financial point of view. Legally, corporations can make distributions of earnings (declare dividends) out of retained earnings in all states. However, in many states they cannot declare dividends out of paid-in capital. Management, stockholders, and others often look to retained earnings for the continued existence and growth of the corporation.

PAID-IN CAPITAL

Paid-in capital is the total amount of cash and other assets paid in to the corporation by stockholders in exchange for capital stock. As noted earlier, when a corporation has only one class of stock, it is **common stock**.

RETAINED EARNINGS

Retained earnings is net income that a corporation retains for future use. Net income is recorded in Retained Earnings by a closing entry that debits Income Summary and credits Retained Earnings. For example, assuming that net income for Delta Robotics in its first year of operations is $130,000, the closing entry is:

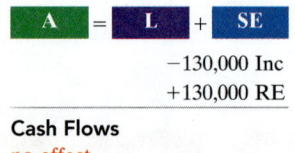
−130,000 Inc
+130,000 RE

Cash Flows
no effect

Income Summary	130,000	
Retained Earnings		130,000
(To close Income Summary and transfer net income to retained earnings)		

If Delta Robotics has a balance of $800,000 in common stock at the end of its first year, its stockholders' equity section is as follows.

Illustration 13-5
Stockholders' equity section

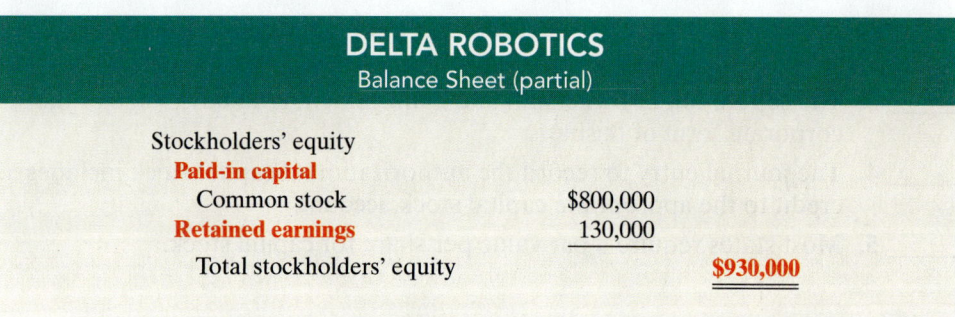

DELTA ROBOTICS
Balance Sheet (partial)

Stockholders' equity	
Paid-in capital	
Common stock	$800,000
Retained earnings	130,000
Total stockholders' equity	**$930,000**

The following illustration compares the owners' equity (stockholders' equity) accounts reported on a balance sheet for a proprietorship, a partnership, and a corporation.

Illustration 13-6
Comparison of owners' equity accounts

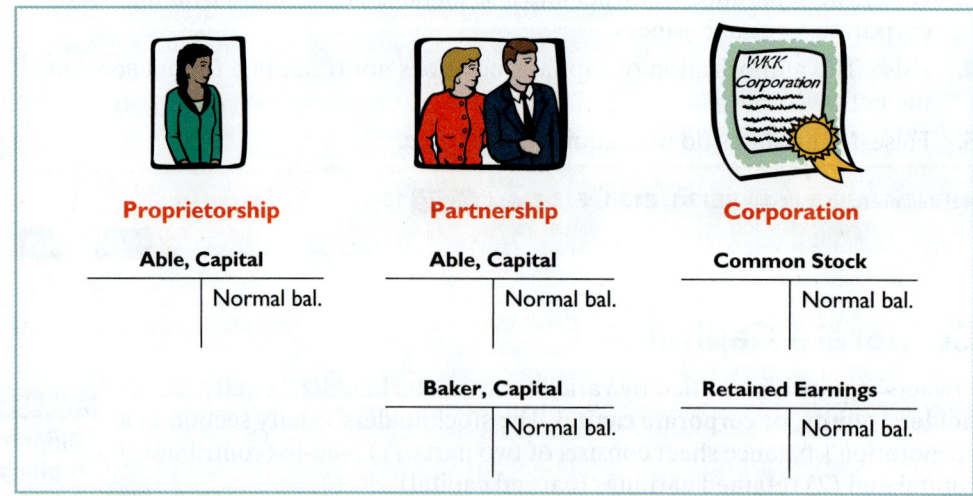

DO IT!

At the end of its first year of operation, Doral Corporation has $750,000 of common stock and net income of $122,000. Prepare (a) the closing entry for net income and (b) the stockholders' equity section at year-end.

CORPORATE CAPITAL

action plan

✔ Record net income in Retained Earnings by a closing entry in which Income Summary is debited and Retained Earnings is credited.

✔ In the stockholders' equity section, show (1) paid-in capital and (2) retained earnings.

Solution

(a) Income Summary   122,000
      Retained Earnings   122,000
      (To close Income Summary and transfer net income to retained earnings)

(b) Stockholders' equity
      Paid-in capital
        Common stock $750,000
      Retained earnings   122,000
        Total stockholders' equity $872,000

Related exercise material: **BE13-2** and **DO IT!** **13-2**.

ACCOUNTING FOR ISSUES OF COMMON STOCK

Let's now look at how to account for issues of common stock. The primary objectives in accounting for the issuance of common stock are: (1) to identify the specific sources of paid-in capital, and (2) to maintain the distinction between paid-in capital and retained earnings. **The issuance of common stock affects only paid-in capital accounts.**

STUDY OBJECTIVE 3
Record the issuance of common stock.

Issuing Par Value Common Stock for Cash

As discussed earlier, par value does not indicate a stock's market value. Therefore, the cash proceeds from issuing par value stock may be equal to, greater than, or less than par value. When the company records issuance of common stock for cash, it credits to Common Stock the par value of the shares. It records in a separate paid-in capital account the portion of the proceeds that is above or below par value.

To illustrate, assume that Hydro-Slide, Inc. issues 1,000 shares of $1 par value common stock at par for cash. The entry to record this transaction is:

Cash   1,000
    Common Stock   1,000
    (To record issuance of 1,000 shares of $1 par common stock at par)

If Hydro-Slide issues an additional 1,000 shares of the $1 par value common stock for cash at $5 per share, the entry is:

Cash   5,000
    Common Stock   1,000
    Paid-in Capital in Excess of Par Value   4,000
    (To record issuance of 1,000 shares of $1 par common stock)

The total paid-in capital from these two transactions is $6,000, and the legal capital is $2,000. Assuming Hydro-Slide, Inc. has retained earnings of $27,000, Illustration 13-7 (page 580) shows the company's stockholders' equity section.

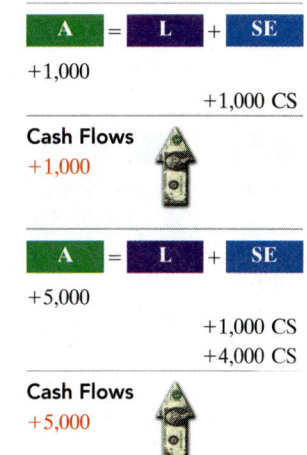

Illustration 13-7
Stockholders' equity—paid-in capital in excess of par value

HYDRO-SLIDE, INC.
Balance Sheet (partial)

Stockholders' equity		
Paid-in capital		
Common stock		$ 2,000
Paid-in capital in excess of par value		**4,000**
Total paid-in capital		6,000
Retained earnings		27,000
Total stockholders' equity		$33,000

> **ALTERNATIVE TERMINOLOGY**
>
> Paid-in Capital in Excess of Par is also called *Premium on Stock*.

When a corporation issues stock for less than par value, it debits the account Paid-in Capital in Excess of Par Value, if a credit balance exists in this account. If a credit balance does not exist, then the corporation debits to Retained Earnings the amount less than par. This situation occurs only rarely: Most states do not permit the sale of common stock below par value, because stockholders may be held personally liable for the difference between the price paid upon original sale and par value.

Issuing No-Par Common Stock for Cash

When no-par common stock has a stated value, the entries are similar to those illustrated for par value stock. The corporation credits the stated value to Common Stock. Also, when the selling price of no-par stock exceeds stated value, the corporation credits the excess to Paid-in Capital in Excess of Stated Value.

For example, assume that instead of $1 par value stock, Hydro-Slide, Inc. has $5 stated value no-par stock and the company issues 5,000 shares at $8 per share for cash. The entry is:

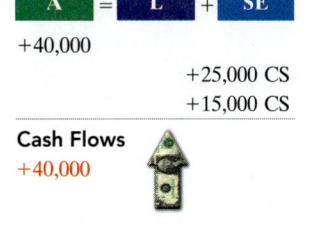

Cash	40,000	
Common Stock		25,000
Paid-in Capital in Excess of Stated Value		15,000
(To record issue of 5,000 shares of $5 stated value no-par stock)		

Hydro-Slide, Inc. reports Paid-in Capital in Excess of Stated Value as part of paid-in capital in the stockholders' equity section.

What happens when no-par stock does not have a stated value? In that case, the corporation credits the entire proceeds to Common Stock. Thus, if Hydro-Slide does not assign a stated value to its no-par stock, it would record the issuance of the 5,000 shares at $8 per share for cash as follows.

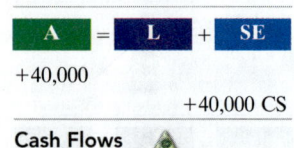

Cash	40,000	
Common Stock		40,000
(To record issue of 5,000 shares of no-par stock)		

Issuing Common Stock for Services or Noncash Assets

Corporations also may issue stock for services (compensation to attorneys or consultants) or for noncash assets (land, buildings, and equipment). In such cases, what cost should be recognized in the exchange transaction? To comply with the **cost**

principle, in a noncash transaction **cost is the cash equivalent price**. Thus, **cost is either the fair market value of the consideration given up, or the fair market value of the consideration received**, whichever is more clearly determinable.

To illustrate, assume that attorneys have helped Jordan Company incorporate. They have billed the company $5,000 for their services. They agree to accept 4,000 shares of $1 par value common stock in payment of their bill. At the time of the exchange, there is no established market price for the stock. In this case, the market value of the consideration received, $5,000, is more clearly evident. Accordingly, Jordan Company makes the following entry:

Organization Expense	5,000	
Common Stock		4,000
Paid-in Capital in Excess of Par Value		1,000
(To record issuance of 4,000 shares of $1 par value stock to attorneys)		

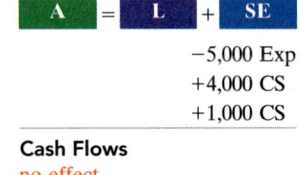

As explained on page 574, organization costs are expensed as incurred.

In contrast, assume that Athletic Research Inc. is an existing publicly held corporation. Its $5 par value stock is actively traded at $8 per share. The company issues 10,000 shares of stock to acquire land recently advertised for sale at $90,000. The most clearly evident value in this noncash transaction is the market price of the consideration given, $80,000. The company records the transaction as follows.

Land	80,000	
Common Stock		50,000
Paid-in Capital in Excess of Par Value		30,000
(To record issuance of 10,000 shares of $5 par value stock for land)		

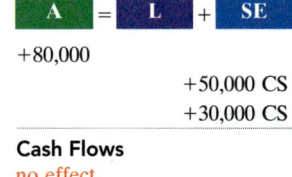

As illustrated in these examples, **the par value of the stock is never a factor in determining the cost of the assets received**. This is also true of the stated value of no-par stock.

DO IT!

ISSUANCE OF STOCK

Cayman Corporation begins operations on March 1 by issuing 100,000 shares of $10 par value common stock for cash at $12 per share. On March 15 it issues 5,000 shares of common stock to attorneys in settlement of their bill of $50,000 for organization costs. Journalize the issuance of the shares, assuming the stock is not publicly traded.

action plan

✔ In issuing shares for cash, credit Common Stock for par value per share.

✔ Credit any additional proceeds in excess of par value to a separate paid-in capital account.

✔ When stock is issued for services, use the cash equivalent price.

Solution

Mar. 1	Cash	1,200,000	
	Common Stock		1,000,000
	Paid-in Capital in Excess of Par Value		200,000
	(To record issuance of 100,000 shares at $12 per share)		

582 Chapter 13 Corporations: Organization and Capital Stock Transactions

action plan (cont'd)

✓ For the cash equivalent price use either the fair market value of what is given up or the fair market value of what is received, whichever is more clearly determinable.

Mar. 15	Organization Expense		50,000	
	Common Stock			50,000
	(To record issuance of 5,000 shares for attorneys' fees)			

Related exercise material: **BE13-3, BE13-4, BE13-5, E13-3, E13-4, E13-6,** and **DO IT! 13-3.**

ACCOUNTING FOR TREASURY STOCK

STUDY OBJECTIVE 4
Explain the accounting for treasury stock.

Treasury stock is a corporation's own stock that it has issued and subsequently reacquired from shareholders, but not retired. A corporation may acquire treasury stock for various reasons:

1. To reissue the shares to officers and employees under bonus and stock compensation plans.
2. To signal to the stock market that management believes the stock is underpriced, in the hope of enhancing its market value.
3. To have additional shares available for use in the acquisition of other companies.
4. To reduce the number of shares outstanding and thereby increase earnings per share.
5. To rid the company of disgruntled investors, perhaps to avoid a takeover, as illustrated in the Ford Motor Company Feature Story.

HELPFUL HINT
Treasury shares do not have dividend rights or voting rights.

Many corporations have treasury stock. One survey of 600 U.S. companies found that approximately two-thirds have treasury stock.[4] Buybacks are becoming more popular. For example, **Exxon Mobil Corp.**, **Microsoft Corp.**, and **Time Warner Inc.** purchased a combined $14.37 billion of their shares in the first quarter of a recent year.

Purchase of Treasury Stock

Companies generally account for treasury stock by **the cost method**. This method uses the cost of the shares purchased to value the treasury stock. Under the cost method, the company debits **Treasury Stock** for the **price paid to reacquire the shares**.

When the company disposes of the shares, it credits to Treasury Stock **the same amount** it paid to reacquire the shares. To illustrate, assume that on January 1, 2010, the stockholders' equity section of Mead, Inc. has 100,000 shares of $5 par value common stock outstanding (all issued at par value) and Retained Earnings of $200,000. The stockholders' equity section before purchase of treasury stock is as follows.

---
[4]*Accounting Trends & Techniques 2007* (New York: American Institute of Certified Public Accountants).

Illustration 13-8
Stockholders' equity with no treasury stock

MEAD, INC.
Balance Sheet (partial)

Stockholders' equity	
Paid-in capital	
Common stock, $5 par value, 100,000 shares issued and outstanding	$500,000
Retained earnings	200,000
Total stockholders' equity	$700,000

On February 1, 2010, Mead acquires 4,000 shares of its stock at $8 per share. The entry is:

Feb. 1	Treasury Stock	32,000	
	Cash		32,000
	(To record purchase of 4,000 shares of treasury stock at $8 per share)		

A = L + SE

−32,000 TS
−32,000

Cash Flows
−32,000

Note that Mead debits Treasury Stock for the cost of the shares purchased. Is the original paid-in capital account, Common Stock, affected? No, because the number of issued shares does not change. In the stockholders' equity section of the balance sheet, Mead deducts treasury stock from total paid-in capital and retained earnings. Treasury Stock is a **contra stockholders' equity account**. Thus, the acquisition of treasury stock reduces stockholders' equity.

The stockholders' equity section of Mead, Inc. after purchase of treasury stock is as follows.

Illustration 13-9
Stockholders' equity with treasury stock

MEAD, INC.
Balance Sheet (partial)

Stockholders' equity	
Paid-in capital	
Common stock, $5 par value, 100,000 shares issued and 96,000 shares outstanding	$500,000
Retained earnings	200,000
Total paid-in capital and retained earnings	700,000
Less: Treasury stock (4,000 shares)	**32,000**
Total stockholders' equity	$668,000

In the balance sheet, Mead discloses both the number of shares issued (100,000) and the number in the treasury (4,000). The difference between these two amounts is the number of shares of stock outstanding (96,000). The term **outstanding stock** means the number of shares of issued stock that are being held by stockholders.

Some maintain that companies should report treasury stock as an asset because it can be sold for cash. Under this reasoning, companies should also show unissued stock as an asset, clearly an erroneous conclusion. Rather than being an asset, treasury stock reduces stockholder claims on corporate assets. This effect is correctly shown by reporting treasury stock as a deduction from total paid-in capital and retained earnings.

ETHICS NOTE
The purchase of treasury stock reduces the cushion for creditors and preferred stockholders. A restriction for the cost of treasury stock purchased is often required. The restriction is usually applied to retained earnings.

ACCOUNTING ACROSS THE ORGANIZATION

Why Did Reebok Buy Its Own Stock?

In a bold (and some would say risky) move, Reebok at one time bought back nearly a *third* of its shares. This repurchase of shares dramatically reduced Reebok's available cash. In fact, the company borrowed significant funds to accomplish the repurchase. In a press release, management stated that it was repurchasing the shares because it believed its stock was severely underpriced. The repurchase of so many shares was meant to signal management's belief in good future earnings.

Skeptics, however, suggested that Reebok's management was repurchasing shares to make it less likely that another company would acquire Reebok (in which case Reebok's top managers would likely lose their jobs). By depleting its cash, Reebok became a less likely acquisition target. Acquiring companies like to purchase companies with large cash balances so they can pay off debt used in the acquisition.

 What signal might a large stock repurchase send to investors regarding management's belief about the company's growth opportunities?

Disposal of Treasury Stock

Treasury stock is usually sold or retired. The accounting for its sale differs when treasury stock is sold above cost than when it is sold below cost.

SALE OF TREASURY STOCK ABOVE COST

If the selling price of the treasury shares is equal to their cost, the company records the sale of the shares by a debit to Cash and a credit to Treasury Stock. When the selling price of the shares is greater than their cost, the company credits the difference to Paid-in Capital from Treasury Stock.

To illustrate, assume that on July 1, Mead sells for $10 per share the 1,000 shares of its treasury stock, previously acquired at $8 per share. The entry is as follows.

> **HELPFUL HINT**
> Treasury stock transactions are classified as capital stock transactions. As in the case when stock is issued, the income statement is not involved.

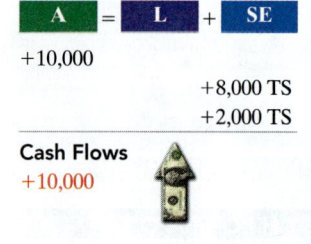

July 1	Cash	10,000	
	Treasury Stock		8,000
	Paid-in Capital from Treasury Stock		2,000
	(To record sale of 1,000 shares of treasury		
	stock above cost)		

Mead does not record a $2,000 gain on sale of treasury stock for two reasons: (1) Gains on sales occur when **assets** are sold, and treasury stock is not an asset. (2) A corporation does not realize a gain or suffer a loss from stock transactions with its own stockholders. Thus, companies should not include in net income any paid-in capital arising from the sale of treasury stock. Instead, they report Paid-in Capital from Treasury Stock separately on the balance sheet, as a part of paid-in capital.

SALE OF TREASURY STOCK BELOW COST

When a company sells treasury stock below its cost, it usually debits to Paid-in Capital from Treasury Stock the excess of cost over selling price. Thus, if Mead, Inc.

sells an additional 800 shares of treasury stock on October 1 at $7 per share, it makes the following entry.

Oct. 1	Cash		5,600	
	Paid-in Capital from Treasury Stock		800	
	Treasury Stock			6,400
	(To record sale of 800 shares of treasury			
	stock below cost)			

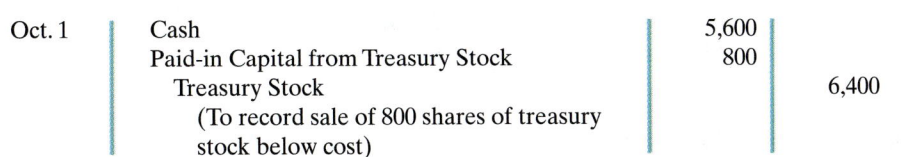

A = L + SE
+5,600
      −800 TS
      +6,400 TS

Cash Flows
+5,600

Observe the following from the two sales entries: (1) Mead credits Treasury Stock at cost in each entry. (2) Mead uses Paid-in Capital from Treasury Stock for the difference between cost and the resale price of the shares. (3) The original paid-in capital account, Common Stock, is not affected. **The sale of treasury stock increases both total assets and total stockholders' equity.**

After posting the foregoing entries, the treasury stock accounts will show the following balances on October 1.

Treasury Stock				Paid-in Capital from Treasury Stock			
Feb. 1	32,000	July 1	8,000	Oct. 1	800	July 1	2,000
		Oct. 1	6,400				
						Oct. 1 Bal.	1,200
Oct. 1 Bal.	17,600						

Illustration 13-10
Treasury stock accounts

When a company fully depletes the credit balance in Paid-in Capital from Treasury Stock, it debits to Retained Earnings any additional excess of cost over selling price. To illustrate, assume that Mead, Inc. sells its remaining 2,200 shares at $7 per share on December 1. The excess of cost over selling price is $2,200 [2,200 × ($8 − $7)]. In this case, Mead debits $1,200 of the excess to Paid-in Capital from Treasury Stock. It debits the remainder to Retained Earnings. The entry is:

Dec. 1	Cash		15,400	
	Paid-in Capital from Treasury Stock		1,200	
	Retained Earnings		1,000	
	Treasury Stock			17,600
	(To record sale of 2,200 shares of treasury			
	stock at $7 per share)			

A = L + SE
+15,400
      −1,200 TS
      −1,000 RE
      +17,600 TS

Cash Flows
+15,400

DO IT!

Santa Anita Inc. purchases 3,000 shares of its $50 par value common stock for $180,000 cash on July 1. It will hold the shares in the treasury until resold. On November 1, the corporation sells 1,000 shares of treasury stock for cash at $70 per share. Journalize the treasury stock transactions.

TREASURY STOCK

action plan

✔ Record the purchase of treasury stock at cost.
✔ When treasury stock is sold above its cost, credit the excess of the selling price over cost to Paid-in Capital from Treasury Stock.

Solution

July 1	Treasury Stock		180,000	
	Cash			180,000
	(To record the purchase of 3,000 shares at			
	$60 per share)			

586 Chapter 13 Corporations: Organization and Capital Stock Transactions

action plan (cont'd)

✔ When treasury stock is sold below its cost, debit the excess of cost over selling price to Paid-in Capital from Treasury Stock.

Nov. 1	Cash		70,000	
	Treasury Stock			60,000
	Paid-in Capital from Treasury Stock			10,000
	(To record the sale of 1,000 shares at $70 per share)			

Related exercise material: **BE13-6, E13-5, E13-7, E13-8,** and **DO IT! 13-4.**

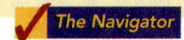

PREFERRED STOCK

STUDY OBJECTIVE 5
Differentiate preferred stock from common stock.

To appeal to more investors, a corporation may issue an additional class of stock, called preferred stock. **Preferred stock** has provisions that give it some preference or priority over common stock. Typically, preferred stockholders have a priority as to (1) distributions of earnings (dividends) and (2) assets in the event of liquidation. However, they generally do not have voting rights.

Like common stock, corporations may issue preferred stock for cash or for noncash assets. The entries for these transactions are similar to the entries for common stock. When a corporation has more than one class of stock, each paid-in capital account title should identify the stock to which it relates. A company might have the following accounts: Preferred Stock, Common Stock, Paid-in Capital in Excess of Par Value—Preferred Stock, and Paid-in Capital in Excess of Par Value—Common Stock. For example, if Stine Corporation issues 10,000 shares of $10 par value preferred stock for $12 cash per share, the entry to record the issuance is:

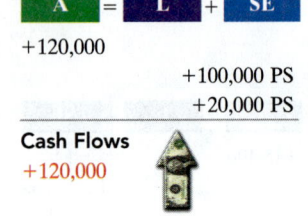

	Cash		120,000	
	Preferred Stock			100,000
	Paid-in Capital in Excess of Par Value–Preferred Stock			20,000
	(To record the issuance of 10,000 shares of $10 par value preferred stock)			

Preferred stock may have either a par value or no-par value. In the stockholders' equity section of the balance sheet, companies list preferred stock first because of its dividend and liquidation preferences over common stock.

We discuss various features associated with the issuance of preferred stock on the following pages.

Dividend Preferences

As noted earlier, **preferred stockholders have the right to receive dividends before common stockholders**. For example, if the dividend rate on preferred stock is $5 per share, common shareholders will not receive any dividends in the current year until preferred stockholders have received $5 per share. The first claim to dividends does not, however, guarantee the payment of dividends. Dividends depend on many factors, such as adequate retained earnings and availability of cash. If a company does not pay dividends to preferred stockholders, it cannot of course pay dividends to common stockholders.

The per share dividend amount is stated as a percentage of the preferred stock's par value or as a specified amount. For example, at one time **Crane Company** specified a 3¾% dividend on its $100 par value preferred ($100 × 3¾% = $3.75 per share). **PepsiCo** has a $5.46 series of no-par preferred stock.

CUMULATIVE DIVIDEND

Preferred stock often contains a **cumulative dividend** feature. This means that preferred stockholders must be paid both current-year dividends and any unpaid prior-year dividends before common stockholders receive dividends. When preferred stock is cumulative, preferred dividends not declared in a given period are called **dividends in arrears**.

To illustrate, assume that Scientific Leasing has 5,000 shares of 7%, $100 par value, cumulative preferred stock outstanding. The annual dividend is $35,000 (5,000 × $7 per share), but dividends are two years in arrears. In this case, preferred stockholders are entitled to receive the following dividends in the current year.

Dividends in arrears ($35,000 × 2)	$ 70,000
Current-year dividends	35,000
Total preferred dividends	**$105,000**

Illustration 13-11
Computation of total dividends to preferred stock

The company cannot pay dividends to common stockholders until it pays the entire preferred dividend. In other words, companies cannot pay dividends to common stockholders while any preferred stock is in arrears.

Are dividends in arrears considered a liability? **No—no payment obligation exists until the board of directors declares a dividend.** However, companies should disclose in the notes to the financial statements the amount of dividends in arrears. Doing so enables investors to assess the potential impact of this commitment on the corporation's financial position.

Companies that are unable to meet their dividend obligations are not looked upon favorably by the investment community. As a financial officer noted in discussing one company's failure to pay its cumulative preferred dividend for a period of time, "Not meeting your obligations on something like that is a major black mark on your record." The accounting entries for preferred stock dividends are explained in Chapter 14.

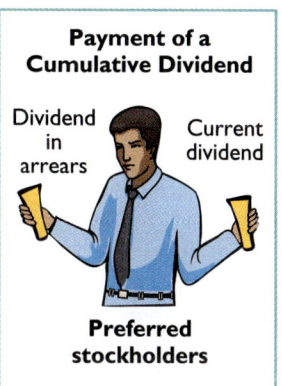

Payment of a Cumulative Dividend

Liquidation Preference

Most preferred stocks also have a preference on corporate assets if the corporation fails. This feature provides security for the preferred stockholder. The preference to assets may be for the par value of the shares or for a specified liquidating value. For example, EarthLink's preferred stock entitles its holders to receive $20.83 per share, plus accrued and unpaid dividends. The liquidation preference establishes the respective claims of creditors and preferred stockholders.

STATEMENT PRESENTATION

Companies report paid-in capital and retained earnings in the stockholders' equity section of the balance sheet. They identify the specific sources of paid-in capital, using the following classifications.

STUDY OBJECTIVE 6
Prepare a stockholders' equity section.

1. **Capital stock.** This category consists of preferred and common stock. Preferred stock appears before common stock because of its preferential rights. Companies report par value, shares authorized, shares issued, and shares outstanding for each class of stock.

2. **Additional paid-in capital.** This category includes the excess of amounts paid in over par or stated value and paid-in capital from treasury stock.

ALTERNATIVE TERMINOLOGY
Paid-in capital is sometimes called *contributed capital*.

The stockholders' equity section of Connally Inc. in Illustration 13-12 (page 588) includes most of the accounts discussed in this chapter. The disclosures pertaining to

Connally's common stock indicate that: the company issued 400,000 shares; 100,000 shares are unissued (500,000 authorized less 400,000 issued); and 390,000 shares are outstanding (400,000 issued less 10,000 shares in treasury).

Illustration 13-12
Stockholders' equity section

CONNALLY INC.
Balance Sheet (partial)

Stockholders' equity		
Paid-in capital		
Capital stock		
9% preferred stock, $100 par value cumulative, 10,000 shares authorized, 6,000 shares issued and outstanding		$ 600,000
Common stock, no par, $5 stated value, 500,000 shares authorized, 400,000 shares issued, and 390,000 outstanding		2,000,000
Total capital stock		2,600,000
Additional paid-in capital		
In excess of par value—preferred stock	$ 30,000	
In excess of stated value—common stock	860,000	
From treasury stock	140,000	
Total additional paid-in capital		1,030,000
Total paid-in capital		3,630,000
Retained earnings		1,058,000
Total paid-in capital and retained earnings		4,688,000
Less: Treasury stock—common (10,000 shares) (at cost)		(80,000)
Total stockholders' equity		$4,608,000

Published annual reports often combine and report as a single amount the individual sources of additional paid-in capital, as shown in Illustration 13-13. In addition, authorized shares are sometimes not reported.

Illustration 13-13
Published stockholders' equity section

KELLOGG COMPANY
Balance Sheet (partial)
($ in millions)

Stockholders' equity	
Common stock, $0.25 par value, 1,000,000,000 shares authorized	
Issued: 418,669,193 shares	$ 105
Capital in excess of par value	388
Retained earnings	4,217
Treasury stock, at cost	
28,618,052 shares	(1,357)
Accumulated other comprehensive income (loss)	(827)
Total stockholders' equity	$2,526

In practice, companies sometimes use the term "Capital surplus" in place of "Additional paid-in capital," and "Earned surplus" in place of "Retained earnings." The use of the term "surplus" suggests that the company has available an excess amount of funds. Such is not necessarily the case. Therefore, **the term "surplus" should not be employed in accounting**. Unfortunately, a number of financial statements still do use it.

DO IT!

STOCKHOLDERS' EQUITY SECTION

Jennifer Corporation has issued 300,000 shares of $3 par value common stock. It authorized 600,000 shares. The paid-in capital in excess of par value on the common stock is $380,000. The corporation has reacquired 15,000 shares at a cost of $50,000 and is currently holding those shares. Treasury stock was reissued in prior years for $72,000 more than its cost.

The corporation also has 4,000 shares issued and outstanding of 8%, $100 par-value preferred stock. It authorized 10,000 shares. The paid-in capital in excess of par value on the preferred stock is $25,000. Retained earnings is $610,000.

Prepare the stockholders' equity section of the balance sheet.

action plan

✔ Present capital stock first; list preferred stock before common stock.

✔ Present additional paid-in capital after capital stock.

✔ Report retained earnings after capital stock and additional paid-in capital.

✔ Deduct treasury stock from total paid-in capital and retained earnings.

Solution

JENNIFER CORPORATION
Balance Sheet (partial)

Stockholders' equity		
Paid-in capital		
Capital stock		
8% preferred stock, $100 par value, 10,000 shares authorized, 4,000 shares issued and outstanding		$ 400,000
Common stock, $3 par value, 600,000 shares authorized, 300,000 shares issued, and 285,000 shares outstanding		900,000
Total capital stock		1,300,000
Additional paid-in capital		
In excess of par value—preferred stock	$ 25,000	
In excess of par value—common stock	380,000	
From treasury stock	72,000	
Total additional paid-in capital		477,000
Total paid-in capital		1,777,000
Retained earnings		610,000
Total paid-in capital and retained earnings		2,387,000
Less: Treasury stock—common (15,000 shares) (at cost)		(50,000)
Total stockholders' equity		$2,337,000

Related exercise material: **BE13-8, E13-9, E13-12, E13-13, E13-14, E13-15,** and **DO IT! 13-5.**

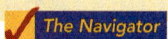

Comprehensive DO IT!

The Rolman Corporation is authorized to issue 1,000,000 shares of $5 par value common stock. In its first year, the company has the following stock transactions.

Jan. 10   Issued 400,000 shares of stock at $8 per share.
July 1   Issued 100,000 shares of stock for land. The land had an asking price of $900,000. The stock is currently selling on a national exchange at $8.25 per share.
Sept. 1   Purchased 10,000 shares of common stock for the treasury at $9 per share.
Dec. 1   Sold 4,000 shares of the treasury stock at $10 per share.

Instructions

(a) Journalize the transactions.
(b) Prepare the stockholders' equity section assuming the company had retained earnings of $200,000 at December 31.

Chapter 13 Corporations: Organization and Capital Stock Transactions

action plan

✔ When common stock has a par value, credit Common Stock for par value.

✔ Use fair market value in a noncash transaction.

✔ Debit and credit the Treasury Stock account at cost.

✔ Record differences between the cost and selling price of treasury stock in stockholders' equity accounts, not as gains or losses.

Solution to Comprehensive DO IT!

(a)

Date	Account	Debit	Credit
Jan. 10	Cash	3,200,000	
	Common Stock		2,000,000
	Paid-in Capital in Excess of Par Value		1,200,000
	(To record issuance of 400,000 shares of $5 par value stock)		
July 1	Land	825,000	
	Common Stock		500,000
	Paid-in Capital in Excess of Par Value		325,000
	(To record issuance of 100,000 shares of $5 par value stock for land)		
Sept. 1	Treasury Stock	90,000	
	Cash		90,000
	(To record purchase of 10,000 shares of treasury stock at cost)		
Dec. 1	Cash	40,000	
	Treasury Stock		36,000
	Paid-in Capital from Treasury Stock		4,000
	(To record sale of 4,000 shares of treasury stock above cost)		

(b)

ROLMAN CORPORATION
Balance Sheet (partial)

Stockholders' equity		
Paid-in capital		
Capital stock		
Common stock, $5 par value, 1,000,000 shares authorized, 500,000 shares issued, 494,000 shares outstanding		$2,500,000
Additional paid-in capital		
In excess of par value	$1,525,000	
From treasury stock	4,000	
Total additional paid-in capital		1,529,000
Total paid-in capital		4,029,000
Retained earnings		200,000
Total paid-in capital and retained earnings		4,229,000
Less: Treasury stock (6,000 shares)		(54,000)
Total stockholders' equity		$4,175,000

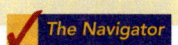

SUMMARY OF STUDY OBJECTIVES

1 Identify the major characteristics of a corporation. The major characteristics of a corporation are separate legal existence, limited liability of stockholders, transferable ownership rights, ability to acquire capital, continuous life, corporation management, government regulations, and additional taxes.

2 Differentiate between paid-in capital and retained earnings. Paid-in capital is the total amount paid in on capital stock. It is often called contributed capital. Retained earnings is net income retained in a corporation. It is often called earned capital.

3 Record the issuance of common stock. When companies record the issuance of common stock for cash, they credit the par value of the shares to Common Stock. They record in a separate paid-in capital account the portion of the proceeds that is above or below par value. When no-par common stock has a stated value, the entries are similar to those for par value stock. When no-par stock does not have a stated value, companies credit the entire proceeds to Common Stock.

4 Explain the accounting for treasury stock. The cost method is generally used in accounting for treasury stock. Under this approach, companies debit Treasury Stock at the price paid to reacquire the shares. They credit the same amount to Treasury Stock when they sell the shares. The difference between the sales price and cost is recorded in stockholders' equity accounts, not in income statement accounts.

5 Differentiate preferred stock from common stock. Preferred stock has contractual provisions that give it priority over common stock in certain areas. Typically, preferred stockholders have a preference (1) to dividends and (2) to assets in liquidation. They usually do not have voting rights.

6 Prepare a stockholders' equity section. In the stockholders' equity section, companies report paid-in capital and retained earnings and identify specific sources of paid-in capital. Within paid-in capital, two classifications are shown: capital stock and additional paid-in capital. If a corporation has treasury stock, it deducts the cost of treasury stock from total paid-in capital and retained earnings to obtain total stockholders' equity.

GLOSSARY

Authorized stock The amount of stock that a corporation is authorized to sell as indicated in its charter. (p. 575).

By-laws The internal rules and procedures for conducting the affairs of a corporation. (p. 573).

Charter A document that creates a corporation. (p. 573).

Corporation A business organized as a legal entity separate and distinct from its owners under state corporation law. (p. 570).

Cumulative dividend A feature of preferred stock entitling the stockholder to receive current and unpaid prior-year dividends before common stockholders receive dividends. (p. 587).

No-par value stock Capital stock that has not been assigned a value in the corporate charter. (p. 577).

Organization costs Costs incurred in the formation of a corporation. (p. 574).

Outstanding stock Capital stock that has been issued and is being held by stockholders. (p. 583).

Paid-in capital Total amount of cash and other assets paid in to the corporation by stockholders in exchange for capital stock. (p. 578).

Par value stock Capital stock that has been assigned a value per share in the corporate charter. (p. 577).

Preferred stock Capital stock that has some preferences over common stock. (p. 586).

Privately held corporation A corporation that has only a few stockholders and whose stock is not available for sale to the general public. (p. 570).

Publicly held corporation A corporation that may have thousands of stockholders and whose stock is regularly traded on a national securities exchange. (p. 570).

Retained earnings Net income that is retained in the corporation for future use. (p. 578).

Stated value The amount per share assigned by the board of directors to no-par stock. (p. 577).

Treasury stock A corporation's own stock that has been issued and subsequently reacquired from shareholders by the corporation but not retired. (p. 582).

SELF-STUDY QUESTIONS

Answers are at the end of the chapter.

(SO 1) **1.** Which of the following is *not* a major advantage of a corporation?
 a. Separate legal existence.
 b. Continuous life.
 c. Government regulations.
 d. Transferable ownership rights.

(SO 1) **2.** A major disadvantage of a corporation is:
 a. limited liability of stockholders.
 b. additional taxes.
 c. transferable ownership rights.
 d. none of the above.

3. Costs incurred in the formation of a corporation: (SO 2)
 a. do not include legal fees.
 b. are expensed as incurred.
 c. are recorded as an asset.
 d. provide future benefits whose amounts and timing are easily determined.

4. Which of the following statements is *false*? (SO 1)
 a. Ownership of common stock gives the owner a voting right.
 b. The stockholders' equity section begins with paid-in capital.
 c. The authorization of capital stock does not result in a formal accounting entry.

592 Chapter 13 Corporations: Organization and Capital Stock Transactions

   d. Legal capital per share applies to par value stock but not to no-par value stock.

(SO 2) **5.** Total stockholders' equity (in the absence of treasury stock) equals:
   a. Paid-in capital + Additional paid-in capital + Retained earnings.
   b. Paid-in capital + Capital stock + Retained earnings.
   c. Capital stock + Additional paid-in capital − Retained earnings.
   d. Paid in capital + Retained earnings.

(SO 2) **6.** The account Retained Earnings is:
   a. a subdivision of paid-in capital.
   b. net income retained in the corporation.
   c. reported as an expense in the income statement.
   d. closed to capital stock.

(SO 3) **7.** A-Team Corporation issued 1,000 shares of $5 par value stock for land. The stock is actively traded at $9 per share. The land was advertised for sale at $10,500. The land should be recorded at:
   a. $4,000.
   b. $5,000.
   c. $9,000.
   d. $10,500.

(SO 3) **8.** ABC Corporation issues 1,000 shares of $10 par value common stock at $12 per share. In recording the transaction, credits are made to:
   a. Common Stock $10,000 and Paid-in Capital in Excess of Stated Value $2,000.
   b. Common Stock $12,000.
   c. Common Stock $10,000 and Paid-in Capital in Excess of Par Value $2,000.
   d. Common Stock $10,000 and Retained Earnings $2,000.

(SO 4) **9.** Treasury stock may be repurchased:
   a. to reissue the shares to officers and employees under bonus and stock compensation plans.
   b. to signal to the stock market that management believes the stock is underpriced.
   c. to have additional shares available for use in the acquisition of other companies.
   d. more than one of the above.

(SO 4) **10.** XYZ, Inc. sells 100 shares of $5 par value treasury stock at $13 per share. If the cost of acquiring the shares was $10 per share, the entry for the sale should include credits to:

   a. Treasury Stock $1,000 and Paid-in Capital from Treasury Stock $300.
   b. Treasury Stock $500 and Paid-in Capital from Treasury Stock $800.
   c. Treasury Stock $1,000 and Retained Earnings $300.
   d. Treasury Stock $500 and Paid-in Capital in Excess of Par Value $800.

11. In the stockholders' equity section, the cost of treasury (SO 4) stock is deducted from:
   a. total paid-in capital and retained earnings.
   b. retained earnings.
   c. total stockholders' equity.
   d. common stock in paid-in capital.

12. Preferred stock may have priority over common stock (SO 5) *except* in:
   a. dividends.
   b. assets in the event of liquidation.
   c. cumulative dividend features.
   d. voting.

13. Which of the following is *not* reported under additional (SO 6) paid-in capital?
   a. Paid-in capital in excess of par value.
   b. Common stock.
   c. Paid-in capital in excess of stated value.
   d. Paid-in capital from treasury stock.

14. M-Bot Corporation has 10,000 shares of 8%, $100 (SO 5) par value, cumulative preferred stock outstanding at December 31, 2010. No dividends were declared in 2008 or 2009. If M-Bot wants to pay $375,000 of dividends in 2010, common stockholders will receive:
   a. $0.
   b. $295,000.
   c. $215,000.
   d. $135,000.

15. In the stockholders' equity section of the balance sheet, (SO 6) common stock:
   a. is listed before preferred stock.
   b. is added to total capital stock.
   c. is part of paid-in capital.
   d. is part of additional paid-in capital.

Go to the book's companion website, **www.wiley.com/college/weygandt**, for Additional Self-Study questions.

QUESTIONS

1. Eric Fink, a student, asks your help in understanding the following characteristics of a corporation: (a) separate legal existence, (b) limited liability of stockholders, and (c) transferable ownership rights. Explain these characteristics to Eric.

2. (a) Your friend Vicky Biel cannot understand how the characteristic of corporation management is both an advantage and a disadvantage. Clarify this problem for Vicky.

(b) Identify and explain two other disadvantages of a corporation.

3. (a) The following terms pertain to the forming of a corporation: (1) charter, (2) by-laws, and (3) organization costs. Explain the terms.

(b) Linda Merando believes a corporation must be incorporated in the state in which its headquarters office is located. Is Linda correct? Explain.

4. What are the basic ownership rights of common stockholders in the absence of restrictive provisions?

5. (a) What are the two principal components of stockholders' equity?
   (b) What is paid-in capital? Give three examples.

6. How do the financial statements for a corporation differ from the statements for a proprietorship?

7. The corporate charter of Hawes Corporation allows the issuance of a maximum of 100,000 shares of common stock. During its first two years of operations, Hawes sold 70,000 shares to shareholders and reacquired 7,000 of these shares. After these transactions, how many shares are authorized, issued, and outstanding?

8. Which is the better investment—common stock with a par value of $5 per share, or common stock with a par value of $20 per share? Why?

9. What factors help determine the market value of stock?

10. What effect does the issuance of stock at a price above par value have on the issuer's net income? Explain.

11. Why is common stock usually not issued at a price that is less than par value?

12. Land appraised at $80,000 is purchased by issuing 1,000 shares of $20 par value common stock. The market price of the shares at the time of the exchange, based on active trading in the securities market, is $95 per share. Should the land be recorded at $20,000, $80,000, or $95,000? Explain.

13. For what reasons might a company like IBM repurchase some of its stock (treasury stock)?

14. Kwun, Inc. purchases 1,000 shares of its own previously issued $5 par common stock for $12,000. Assuming the shares are held in the treasury, what effect does this transaction have on (a) net income, (b) total assets, (c) total paid-in capital, and (d) total stockholders' equity?

15. The treasury stock purchased in question 14 is resold by Kwun, Inc. for $18,000. What effect does this transaction have on (a) net income, (b) total assets, (c) total paid-in capital, and (d) total stockholders' equity?

16. (a) What are the principal differences between common stock and preferred stock?
    (b) Preferred stock may be cumulative. Discuss this feature.
    (c) How are dividends in arrears presented in the financial statements?

17. Ruiz Inc.'s common stock has a par value of $1 and a current market value of $15. Explain why these amounts are different.

18. Indicate how each of the following accounts should be classified in the stockholders' equity section.
    (a) Common stock
    (b) Paid-in capital in excess of par value
    (c) Retained earnings
    (d) Treasury stock
    (e) Paid-in capital from treasury stock
    (f) Paid-in capital in excess of stated value
    (g) Preferred stock

19.  How many shares of treasury stock did PepsiCo have at December 29, 2007, and at December 30, 2006?

BRIEF EXERCISES

BE13-1 Ken Fritz is studying for his accounting midterm examination. Identify for Ken the advantages and disadvantages of the corporate form of business organization.

List the advantages and disadvantages of a corporation.
(SO 1)

BE13-2 At December 31, Kunkel Corporation reports net income of $450,000. Prepare the entry to close net income.

Prepare closing entries for a corporation. (SO 2)

BE13-3 On May 10, Mazili Corporation issues 2,000 shares of $10 par value common stock for cash at $18 per share. Journalize the issuance of the stock.

Prepare entries for issuance of par value common stock.
(SO 3)

BE13-4 On June 1, Mendoza Inc. issues 3,000 shares of no-par common stock at a cash price of $6 per share. Journalize the issuance of the shares assuming the stock has a stated value of $1 per share.

Prepare entries for issuance of no-par value common stock.
(SO 3)

BE13-5 Kane Inc.'s $10 par value common stock is actively traded at a market value of $15 per share. Kane issues 5,000 shares to purchase land advertised for sale at $85,000. Journalize the issuance of the stock in acquiring the land.

Prepare entries for issuance of stock in a noncash transaction.
(SO 3)

BE13-6 On July 1, Goetz Corporation purchases 500 shares of its $5 par value common stock for the treasury at a cash price of $8 per share. On September 1, it sells 300 shares of the treasury stock for cash at $11 per share. Journalize the two treasury stock transactions.

Prepare entries for treasury stock transactions.
(SO 4)

BE13-7 Acker Inc. issues 5,000 shares of $100 par value preferred stock for cash at $130 per share. Journalize the issuance of the preferred stock.

Prepare entries for issuance of preferred stock.
(SO 5)

594 Chapter 13 Corporations: Organization and Capital Stock Transactions

Prepare stockholders' equity section.

(SO 6)

BE13-8 Ermler Corporation has the following accounts at December 31: Common Stock, $10 par, 5,000 shares issued, $50,000; Paid-in Capital in Excess of Par Value $20,000; Retained Earnings $45,000; and Treasury Stock—Common, 500 shares, $11,000. Prepare the stockholders' equity section of the balance sheet.

DO IT! REVIEW

Analyze statements about corporate organization.

(SO 1)

DO IT! 13-1 Indicate whether each of the following statements is true or false.

_____ 1. The corporation is an entity separate and distinct from its owners.
_____ 2. The liability of stockholders is normally limited to their investment in the corporation.
_____ 3. The relative lack of government regulation is an advantage of the corporate form of business.
_____ 4. There is no journal entry to record the authorization of capital stock.
_____ 5. No-par value stock is quite rare today.

Close net income and prepare stockholders' equity section.

(SO 2)

DO IT! 13-2 At the end of its first year of operation, Dade Corporation has $1,000,000 of common stock and net income of $216,000. Prepare (a) the closing entry for net income and (b) the stockholders' equity section at year-end.

Journalize issuance of stock.

(SO 3)

DO IT! 13-3 Caribbean Corporation began operations on April 1 by issuing 60,000 shares of $5 par value common stock for cash at $13 per share. On April 19, it issued 2,000 shares of common stock to attorneys in settlement of their bill of $27,500 for organization costs. Journalize both issuances, assuming the stock is not publicly traded.

Journalize treasury stock transactions.

(SO 4)

DO IT! 13-4 Chiapas Corporation purchased 2,000 shares of its $10 par value common stock for $120,000 on August 1. It will hold these shares in the treasury until resold. On December 1, the corporation sold 1,200 shares of treasury stock for cash at $72 per share. Journalize the treasury stock transactions.

Prepare stockholders' equity section.

(SO 6)

DO IT! 13-5 Connolly Corporation has issued 100,000 shares of $5 par value common stock. It authorized 500,000 shares. The paid-in capital in excess of par value on the common stock is $240,000. The corporation has reacquired 7,000 shares at a cost of $46,000 and is currently holding those shares. Treasury stock was reissued in prior years for $47,000 more than its cost.

The corporation also has 2,000 shares issued and outstanding of 7%, $100 par-value preferred stock. It authorized 10,000 shares. The paid-in capital in excess of par value on the preferred stock is $23,000.

Retained earnings is $372,000.

Prepare the stockholders' equity section of the balance sheet.

EXERCISES

Identify characteristics of a corporation.

(SO 1)

E13-1 Jeff Lynne has prepared the following list of statements about corporations.

1. A corporation is an entity separate and distinct from its owners.
2. As a legal entity, a corporation has most of the rights and privileges of a person.
3. Most of the largest U.S. corporations are privately held corporations.
4. Corporations may buy, own, and sell property; borrow money; enter into legally binding contracts; and sue and be sued.
5. The net income of a corporation is not taxed as a separate entity.
6. Creditors have a legal claim on the personal assets of the owners of a corporation if the corporation does not pay its debts.
7. The transfer of stock from one owner to another requires the approval of either the corporation or other stockholders.
8. The board of directors of a corporation legally owns the corporation.
9. The chief accounting officer of a corporation is the controller.
10. Corporations are subject to less state and federal regulations than partnerships or proprietorships.

Instructions
Identify each statement as true or false. If false, indicate how to correct the statement.

E13-2 Jeff Lynne (see E13-1) has studied the information you gave him in that exercise and has come to you with more statements about corporations.

1. Corporation management is both an advantage and a disadvantage of a corporation compared to a proprietorship or a partnership.
2. Limited liability of stockholders, government regulations, and additional taxes are the major disadvantages of a corporation.
3. When a corporation is formed, organization costs are recorded as an asset.
4. Each share of common stock gives the stockholder the ownership rights to vote at stockholder meetings, share in corporate earnings, keep the same percentage ownership when new shares of stock are issued, and share in assets upon liquidation.
5. The number of issued shares is always greater than or equal to the number of authorized shares.
6. A journal entry is required for the authorization of capital stock.
7. Publicly held corporations usually issue stock directly to investors.
8. The trading of capital stock on a securities exchange involves the transfer of already issued shares from an existing stockholder to another investor.
9. The market value of common stock is usually the same as its par value.
10. Retained earnings is the total amount of cash and other assets paid in to the corporation by stockholders in exchange for capital stock.

Identify characteristics of a corporation.
(SO 1, 2)

Instructions
Identify each statement as true or false. If false, indicate how to correct the statement.

E13-3 During its first year of operations, Harlan Corporation had the following transactions pertaining to its common stock.

Jan. 10 Issued 70,000 shares for cash at $5 per share.
July 1 Issued 40,000 shares for cash at $7 per share.

Journalize issuance of common stock.
(SO 3)

Instructions
(a) Journalize the transactions, assuming that the common stock has a par value of $5 per share.
(b) Journalize the transactions, assuming that the common stock is no-par with a stated value of $1 per share.

E13-4 Grossman Corporation issued 1,000 shares of stock.

Instructions
Prepare the entry for the issuance under the following assumptions.

(a) The stock had a par value of $5 per share and was issued for a total of $52,000.
(b) The stock had a stated value of $5 per share and was issued for a total of $52,000.
(c) The stock had no par or stated value and was issued for a total of $52,000.
(d) The stock had a par value of $5 per share and was issued to attorneys for services during incorporation valued at $52,000.
(e) The stock had a par value of $5 per share and was issued for land worth $52,000.

Journalize issuance of common stock.
(SO 3)

E13-5 Leone Co. had the following transactions during the current period.

Mar. 2 Issued 5,000 shares of $5 par value common stock to attorneys in payment of a bill for $30,000 for services provided in helping the company to incorporate.
June 12 Issued 60,000 shares of $5 par value common stock for cash of $375,000.
July 11 Issued 1,000 shares of $100 par value preferred stock for cash at $110 per share.
Nov. 28 Purchased 2,000 shares of treasury stock for $80,000.

Journalize issuance of common and preferred stock and purchase of treasury stock.
(SO 3, 4, 5)

Instructions
Journalize the transactions.

E13-6 As an auditor for the CPA firm of Bunge and Dodd, you encounter the following situations in auditing different clients.

1. Desi Corporation is a closely held corporation whose stock is not publicly traded. On December 5, the corporation acquired land by issuing 5,000 shares of its $20 par value common stock. The owners' asking price for the land was $120,000, and the fair market value of the land was $115,000.

Journalize noncash common stock transactions.
(SO 3)

2. Lucille Corporation is a publicly held corporation whose common stock is traded on the securities markets. On June 1, it acquired land by issuing 20,000 shares of its $10 par value stock. At the time of the exchange, the land was advertised for sale at $250,000. The stock was selling at $12 per share.

Instructions

Prepare the journal entries for each of the situations above.

Journalize treasury stock transactions.

(SO 4)

E13-7 On January 1, 2010, the stockholders' equity section of Nunez Corporation shows: Common stock ($5 par value) $1,500,000; paid-in capital in excess of par value $1,000,000; and retained earnings $1,200,000. During the year, the following treasury stock transactions occurred.

Mar. 1 Purchased 50,000 shares for cash at $15 per share.
July 1 Sold 10,000 treasury shares for cash at $17 per share.
Sept. 1 Sold 8,000 treasury shares for cash at $14 per share.

Instructions

(a) Journalize the treasury stock transactions.
(b) Restate the entry for September 1, assuming the treasury shares were sold at $12 per share.

Journalize treasury stock transactions.

(SO 4)

E13-8 Mad City Corporation purchased from its stockholders 5,000 shares of its own previously issued stock for $250,000. It later resold 2,000 shares for $54 per share, then 2,000 more shares for $49 per share, and finally 1,000 shares for $40 per share.

Instructions

Prepare journal entries for the purchase of the treasury stock and the three sales of treasury stock.

Journalize preferred stock transactions and indicate statement presentation.

(SO 5, 6)

E13-9 Polzin Corporation is authorized to issue both preferred and common stock. The par value of the preferred is $50. During the first year of operations, the company had the following events and transactions pertaining to its preferred stock.

Feb. 1 Issued 20,000 shares for cash at $53 per share.
July 1 Issued 12,000 shares for cash at $57 per share.

Instructions

(a) Journalize the transactions.
(b) Post to the stockholders' equity accounts.
(c) Indicate the financial statement presentation of the related accounts.

Differentiate between preferred and common stock.

(SO 5)

E13-10 AI Corporation issued 100,000 shares of $20 par value, cumulative, 8% preferred stock on January 1, 2009, for $2,100,000. In December 2011, AI declared its first dividend of $500,000.

Instructions

(a) Prepare AI's journal entry to record the issuance of the preferred stock.
(b) If the preferred stock is *not* cumulative, how much of the $500,000 would be paid to **common** stockholders?
(c) If the preferred stock is cumulative, how much of the $500,000 would be paid to **common** stockholders?

Prepare correct entries for capital stock transactions.

(SO 3, 4, 5)

E13-11 Roemer Corporation recently hired a new accountant with extensive experience in accounting for partnerships. Because of the pressure of the new job, the accountant was unable to review his textbooks on the topic of corporation accounting. During the first month, the accountant made the following entries for the corporation's capital stock.

May 2	Cash		130,000	
	Capital Stock			130,000
	(Issued 10,000 shares of $10 par value common stock at $13 per share)			
10	Cash		600,000	
	Capital Stock			600,000
	(Issued 10,000 shares of $50 par value preferred stock at $60 per share)			

15	Capital Stock	15,000	
	Cash		15,000
	(Purchased 1,000 shares of common stock for the treasury at $15 per share)		
31	Cash	8,000	
	Capital Stock		5,000
	Gain on Sale of Stock		3,000
	(Sold 500 shares of treasury stock at $16 per share)		

Instructions

On the basis of the explanation for each entry, prepare the entry that should have been made for the capital stock transactions.

E13-12 The following stockholders' equity accounts, arranged alphabetically, are in the ledger of Freeze Corporation at December 31, 2010.

Prepare a stockholders' equity section.

(SO 6)

Common Stock ($5 stated value)	$1,700,000
Paid-in Capital in Excess of Par Value—Preferred Stock	280,000
Paid-in Capital in Excess of Stated Value—Common Stock	900,000
Preferred Stock (8%, $100 par, noncumulative)	500,000
Retained Earnings	1,134,000
Treasury Stock—Common (10,000 shares)	120,000

Instructions

Prepare the stockholders' equity section of the balance sheet at December 31, 2010.

E13-13 The stockholders' equity section of Jarvis Corporation at December 31 is as follows.

Answer questions about stockholders' equity section.

(SO 3, 4, 5, 6)

JARVIS CORPORATION
Balance Sheet (partial)

Paid-in capital		
Preferred stock, cumulative, 10,000 shares authorized, 6,000 shares issued and outstanding		$ 300,000
Common stock, no par, 750,000 shares authorized, 600,000 shares issued		1,200,000
Total paid-in capital		1,500,000
Retained earnings		1,858,000
Total paid-in capital and retained earnings		3,358,000
Less: Treasury stock (10,000 common shares)		(64,000)
Total stockholders' equity		$3,294,000

Instructions

From a review of the stockholders' equity section, as chief accountant, write a memo to the president of the company answering the following questions.

(a) How many shares of common stock are outstanding?
(b) Assuming there is a stated value, what is the stated value of the common stock?
(c) What is the par value of the preferred stock?
(d) If the annual dividend on preferred stock is $30,000, what is the dividend rate on preferred stock?
(e) If dividends of $60,000 were in arrears on preferred stock, what would be the balance in Retained Earnings?

E13-14 In a recent year, the stockholders' equity section of Aluminum Company of America (Alcoa) showed the following (in alphabetical order): additional paid-in capital $6,101, common stock $925, preferred stock $55, retained earnings $7,428, and treasury stock 2,828. All dollar data are in millions.

Prepare a stockholders' equity section.

(SO 6)

The preferred stock has 557,740 shares authorized, with a par value of $100 and an annual $3.75 per share cumulative dividend preference. At December 31, 557,649 shares of preferred are issued and 546,024 shares are outstanding. There are 1.8 billion shares of $1 par value common stock authorized, of which 924.6 million are issued and 844.8 million are outstanding at December 31.

Instructions
Prepare the stockholders' equity section, including disclosure of all relevant data.

Classify stockholders' equity accounts.
(SO 6)

E13-15 The ledger of Mathis Corporation contains the following accounts: Common Stock, Preferred Stock, Treasury Stock—Common, Paid-in Capital in Excess of Par Value—Preferred Stock, Paid-in Capital in Excess of Stated Value—Common Stock, Paid-in Capital from Treasury Stock, and Retained Earnings.

Instructions
Classify each account using the following table headings.

	Paid-in Capital			
Account	Capital Stock	Additional	Retained Earnings	Other

EXERCISES: SET B

Visit the book's companion website at **www.wiley.com/college/weygandt**, and choose the Student Companion site, to access Exercise Set B.

PROBLEMS: SET A

Journalize stock transactions, post, and prepare paid-in capital section.
(SO 3, 5, 6)

P13-1A Franco Corporation was organized on January 1, 2010. It is authorized to issue 10,000 shares of 8%, $100 par value preferred stock, and 500,000 shares of no-par common stock with a stated value of $2 per share. The following stock transactions were completed during the first year.

Jan. 10 Issued 80,000 shares of common stock for cash at $4 per share.
Mar. 1 Issued 5,000 shares of preferred stock for cash at $105 per share.
Apr. 1 Issued 24,000 shares of common stock for land. The asking price of the land was $90,000. The fair market value of the land was $85,000.
May 1 Issued 80,000 shares of common stock for cash at $4.50 per share.
Aug. 1 Issued 10,000 shares of common stock to attorneys in payment of their bill of $30,000 for services provided in helping the company organize.
Sept. 1 Issued 10,000 shares of common stock for cash at $5 per share.
Nov. 1 Issued 1,000 shares of preferred stock for cash at $109 per share.

Instructions
(a) Journalize the transactions.
(b) Post to the stockholders' equity accounts. (Use J5 as the posting reference.)
(c) Prepare the paid-in capital section of stockholders' equity at December 31, 2010.

(c) Total paid-in capital $1,479,000

Journalize and post treasury stock transactions, and prepare stockholders' equity section.
(SO 4, 6)

P13-2A Jacobsen Corporation had the following stockholders' equity accounts on January 1, 2010: Common Stock ($5 par) $500,000, Paid-in Capital in Excess of Par Value $200,000, and Retained Earnings $100,000. In 2010, the company had the following treasury stock transactions.

Mar. 1 Purchased 5,000 shares at $9 per share.
June 1 Sold 1,000 shares at $12 per share.
Sept. 1 Sold 2,000 shares at $10 per share.
Dec. 1 Sold 1,000 shares at $6 per share.

Jacobsen Corporation uses the cost method of accounting for treasury stock. In 2010, the company reported net income of $30,000.

Instructions
(a) Journalize the treasury stock transactions, and prepare the closing entry at December 31, 2010, for net income.
(b) Open accounts for (1) Paid-in Capital from Treasury Stock, (2) Treasury Stock, and (3) Retained Earnings. Post to these accounts using J10 as the posting reference.
(c) Prepare the stockholders' equity section for Jacobsen Corporation at December 31, 2010.

(b) Treasury Stock $9,000
(c) Total stockholders' equity $823,000

P13-3A The stockholders' equity accounts of Neer Corporation on January 1, 2010, were as follows.

Preferred Stock (8%, $50 par, cumulative, 10,000 shares authorized)	$ 400,000
Common Stock ($1 stated value, 2,000,000 shares authorized)	1,000,000
Paid-in Capital in Excess of Par Value—Preferred Stock	100,000
Paid-in Capital in Excess of Stated Value—Common Stock	1,450,000
Retained Earnings	1,816,000
Treasury Stock—Common (10,000 shares)	50,000

Journalize and post transactions, prepare stockholders' equity section.
(SO 2, 3, 4, 5, 6)

During 2010, the corporation had the following transactions and events pertaining to its stockholders' equity.

Feb. 1 Issued 25,000 shares of common stock for $120,000.
Apr. 14 Sold 6,000 shares of treasury stock—common for $33,000.
Sept. 3 Issued 5,000 shares of common stock for a patent valued at $35,000.
Nov. 10 Purchased 1,000 shares of common stock for the treasury at a cost of $6,000.
Dec. 31 Determined that net income for the year was $452,000.

No dividends were declared during the year.

Instructions
(a) Journalize the transactions and the closing entry for net income.
(b) Enter the beginning balances in the accounts, and post the journal entries to the stockholders' equity accounts. (Use J5 for the posting reference.)
(c) Prepare a stockholders' equity section at December 31, 2010, including the disclosure of the preferred dividends in arrears.

(c) Total stockholders' equity $5,350,000

P13-4A Vargas Corporation is authorized to issue 20,000 shares of $50 par value, 10% preferred stock and 125,000 shares of $3 par value common stock. On January 1, 2010, the ledger contained the following stockholders' equity balances.

Preferred Stock (10,000 shares)	$500,000
Paid-in Capital in Excess of Par Value—Preferred	75,000
Common Stock (70,000 shares)	210,000
Paid-in Capital in Excess of Par Value—Common	700,000
Retained Earnings	300,000

Journalize and post stock transactions, and prepare stockholders' equity section.
(SO 2, 3, 5, 6)

During 2010, the following transactions occurred.

Feb. 1 Issued 2,000 shares of preferred stock for land having a fair market value of $125,000.
Mar. 1 Issued 1,000 shares of preferred stock for cash at $65 per share.
July 1 Issued 16,000 shares of common stock for cash at $7 per share.
Sept. 1 Issued 400 shares of preferred stock for a patent. The asking price of the patent was $30,000. Market values were preferred stock $70 and patent indeterminable.
Dec. 1 Issued 8,000 shares of common stock for cash at $7.50 per share.
Dec. 31 Net income for the year was $260,000. No dividends were declared.

Instructions
(a) Journalize the transactions and the closing entry for net income.
(b) Enter the beginning balances in the accounts, and post the journal entries to the stockholders' equity accounts. (Use J2 for the posting reference.)
(c) Prepare a stockholders' equity section at December 31, 2010.

(c) Total stockholders' equity $2,435,000

P13-5A The following stockholders' equity accounts arranged alphabetically are in the ledger of Tyner Corporation at December 31, 2010.

Common Stock ($5 stated value)	$2,000,000
Paid-in Capital from Treasury Stock	10,000
Paid-in Capital in Excess of Stated Value—Common Stock	1,600,000
Paid-in Capital in Excess of Par Value—Preferred Stock	679,000
Preferred Stock (8%, $50 par, noncumulative)	800,000
Retained Earnings	1,748,000
Treasury Stock—Common (10,000 shares)	130,000

Prepare stockholders' equity section.
(SO 6)

Instructions
Prepare a stockholders' equity section at December 31, 2010.

Total stockholders' equity $6,707,000

Prepare entries for stock transactions and prepare stockholders' equity section.

(SO 3, 4, 5, 6)

P13-6A Palmaro Corporation has been authorized to issue 20,000 shares of $100 par value, 10%, noncumulative preferred stock and 1,000,000 shares of no-par common stock. The corporation assigned a $2.50 stated value to the common stock. At December 31, 2010, the ledger contained the following balances pertaining to stockholders' equity.

Preferred Stock	$120,000
Paid-in Capital in Excess of Par Value—Preferred	20,000
Common Stock	1,000,000
Paid-in Capital in Excess of Stated Value—Common	1,800,000
Treasury Stock—Common (1,000 shares)	13,000
Paid-in Capital from Treasury Stock	500
Retained Earnings	82,000

The preferred stock was issued for land having a fair market value of $140,000. All common stock issued was for cash. In November, 1,500 shares of common stock were purchased for the treasury at a per share cost of $13. In December, 500 shares of treasury stock were sold for $14 per share. No dividends were declared in 2010.

Instructions
(a) Prepare the journal entries for the:
  (1) Issuance of preferred stock for land.
  (2) Issuance of common stock for cash.
  (3) Purchase of common treasury stock for cash.
  (4) Sale of treasury stock for cash.
(b) Prepare the stockholders' equity section at December 31, 2010.

(b) Total stockholders' equity $3,009,500

PROBLEMS: SET B

Journalize stock transactions, post, and prepare paid-in capital section.

(SO 3, 5, 6)

P13-1B Donelson Corporation was organized on January 1, 2010. It is authorized to issue 20,000 shares of 6%, $40 par value preferred stock, and 500,000 shares of no-par common stock with a stated value of $2 per share. The following stock transactions were completed during the first year.

Jan. 10 Issued 100,000 shares of common stock for cash at $3 per share.
Mar. 1 Issued 10,000 shares of preferred stock for cash at $55 per share.
Apr. 1 Issued 25,000 shares of common stock for land. The asking price of the land was $90,000. The company's estimate of fair market value of the land was $75,000.
May 1 Issued 75,000 shares of common stock for cash at $4 per share.
Aug. 1 Issued 10,000 shares of common stock to attorneys in payment of their bill for $50,000 for services provided in helping the company organize.
Sept. 1 Issued 5,000 shares of common stock for cash at $6 per share.
Nov. 1 Issued 2,000 shares of preferred stock for cash at $60 per share.

Instructions
(a) Journalize the transactions.
(b) Post to the stockholders' equity accounts. (Use J1 as the posting reference.)
(c) Prepare the paid-in capital section of stockholders' equity at December 31, 2010.

(c) Total paid-in capital $1,425,000

Journalize and post treasury stock transactions, and prepare stockholders' equity section.

(SO 4, 6)

P13-2B Gentry Corporation had the following stockholders' equity accounts on January 1, 2010: Common Stock ($1 par) $400,000, Paid-in Capital in Excess of Par Value $500,000, and Retained Earnings $100,000. In 2010, the company had the following treasury stock transactions.

Mar. 1 Purchased 5,000 shares at $7 per share.
June 1 Sold 1,000 shares at $10 per share.
Sept. 1 Sold 2,000 shares at $9 per share.
Dec. 1 Sold 1,000 shares at $5 per share.

Gentry Corporation uses the cost method of accounting for treasury stock. In 2010, the company reported net income of $80,000.

Instructions
(a) Journalize the treasury stock transactions, and prepare the closing entry at December 31, 2010, for net income.

(b) Open accounts for (1) Paid-in Capital from Treasury Stock, (2) Treasury Stock, and (3) Retained Earnings. Post to these accounts using J12 as the posting reference.
(c) Prepare the stockholders' equity section for Gentry Corporation at December 31, 2010.

(b) Treasury Stock $7,000
(c) Total stockholders' equity $1,078,000

P13-3B The stockholders' equity accounts of Miles Corporation on January 1, 2010, were as follows.

Preferred Stock (10%, $100 par, noncumulative, 5,000 shares authorized)	$ 300,000
Common Stock ($5 stated value, 300,000 shares authorized)	1,000,000
Paid-in Capital in Excess of Par Value—Preferred Stock	20,000
Paid-in Capital in Excess of Stated Value—Common Stock	425,000
Retained Earnings	488,000
Treasury Stock—Common (5,000 shares)	40,000

Journalize and post transactions, prepare stockholders' equity section.

(SO 2, 3, 4, 5, 6)

During 2010, the corporation had the following transactions and events pertaining to its stockholders' equity.

Feb. 1 Issued 3,000 shares of common stock for $25,500.
Mar. 20 Purchased 1,500 additional shares of common treasury stock at $8 per share.
June 14 Sold 4,000 shares of treasury stock—common for $36,000.
Sept. 3 Issued 2,000 shares of common stock for a patent valued at $19,000.
Dec. 31 Determined that net income for the year was $350,000.

Instructions
(a) Journalize the transactions and the closing entry for net income.
(b) Enter the beginning balances in the accounts and post the journal entries to the stockholders' equity accounts. (Use J1 as the posting reference.)
(c) Prepare a stockholders' equity section at December 31, 2010.

(c) Total stockholders' equity $2,611,500

P13-4B Molina Corporation is authorized to issue 10,000 shares of $40 par value, 10% preferred stock and 200,000 shares of $5 par value common stock. On January 1, 2010, the ledger contained the following stockholders' equity balances.

Preferred Stock (5,000 shares)	$200,000
Paid-in Capital in Excess of Par Value—Preferred	60,000
Common Stock (70,000 shares)	350,000
Paid-in Capital in Excess of Par Value—Common	700,000
Retained Earnings	300,000

Journalize and post stock transactions, and prepare stockholders' equity section.

(SO 2, 3, 5, 6)

During 2010, the following transactions occurred.

Feb. 1 Issued 1,000 shares of preferred stock for land having a fair market value of $65,000.
Mar. 1 Issued 2,000 shares of preferred stock for cash at $60 per share.
July 1 Issued 20,000 shares of common stock for cash at $5.80 per share.
Sept. 1 Issued 800 shares of preferred stock for a patent. The asking price of the patent was $60,000. Market values were preferred stock $65 and patent, indeterminable.
Dec. 1 Issued 10,000 shares of common stock for cash at $6 per share.
Dec. 31 Net income for the year was $210,000. No dividends were declared.

Instructions
(a) Journalize the transactions and the closing entry for net income.
(b) Enter the beginning balances in the accounts, and post the journal entries to the stockholders' equity accounts. (Use J2 as the posting reference.)
(c) Prepare a stockholders' equity section at December 31, 2010.

(c) Total stockholders' equity $2,233,000

P13-5B The following stockholders' equity accounts arranged alphabetically are in the ledger of Jenkins Corporation at December 31, 2010.

Common Stock ($10 stated value)	$1,200,000
Paid-in Capital from Treasury Stock	6,000
Paid-in Capital in Excess of Stated Value—Common Stock	690,000
Paid-in Capital in Excess of Par Value—Preferred Stock	288,400
Preferred Stock (8%, $100 par, noncumulative)	300,000
Retained Earnings	826,000
Treasury Stock—Common (8,000 shares)	88,000

Prepare stockholders' equity section.

(SO 6)

602 Chapter 13 Corporations: Organization and Capital Stock Transactions

Total stockholders' equity $3,222,400

Instructions
Prepare a stockholders' equity section at December 31, 2010.

Prepare entries for stock transactions and prepare stockholders' equity section.
(SO 3, 4, 5, 6)

P13-6B Steven Corporation has been authorized to issue 40,000 shares of $100 par value, 8%, noncumulative preferred stock and 2,000,000 shares of no-par common stock. The corporation assigned a $5 stated value to the common stock. At December 31, 2010, the ledger contained the following balances pertaining to stockholders' equity.

Preferred Stock	$ 240,000
Paid-in Capital in Excess of Par Value—Preferred	56,000
Common Stock	2,000,000
Paid-in Capital in Excess of Stated Value—Common	4,400,000
Treasury Stock—Common (1,000 shares)	22,000
Paid-in Capital from Treasury Stock	3,000
Retained Earnings	560,000

The preferred stock was issued for land having a fair market value of $296,000. All common stock issued was for cash. In November, 1,500 shares of common stock were purchased for the treasury at a per share cost of $22. In December, 500 shares of treasury stock were sold for $28 per share. No dividends were declared in 2010.

Instructions
(a) Prepare the journal entries for the:
  (1) Issuance of preferred stock for land.
  (2) Issuance of common stock for cash.
  (3) Purchase of common treasury stock for cash.
  (4) Sale of treasury stock for cash.

(b) Total stockholders' equity $7,237,000

(b) Prepare the stockholders' equity section at December 31, 2010.

PROBLEMS: SET C

Visit the book's companion website at **www.wiley.com/college/weygandt**, and choose the Student Companion site, to access Problem Set C.

CONTINUING COOKIE CHRONICLE

(Note: This is a continuation of the Cookie Chronicle from Chapters 1 through 12.)

CCC13 Natalie's friend, Curtis Lesperance, decides to meet with Natalie after hearing that her discussions about a possible business partnership with her friend Katy Peterson have failed. Because Natalie has been so successful with Cookie Creations and Curtis has been just as successful with his coffee shop, they both conclude that they could benefit from each other's business expertise. Curtis and Natalie next evaluate the different types of business organization, and because of the advantage of limited personal liability, decide to form a corporation. Natalie and Curtis are very excited about this new business venture. They come to you with information about their businesses and with a number of questions.

Go to the book's companion website,
www.wiley.com/college/weygandt,
to see the completion of this problem.

BROADENING YOUR PERSPECTIVE

FINANCIAL REPORTING AND ANALYSIS

Financial Reporting Problem: PepsiCo

BYP13-1 The stockholders' equity section for PepsiCo, Inc. is shown in Appendix A. You will also find data relative to this problem on other pages of the appendix.

Instructions

(a) What is the par or stated value per share of PepsiCo's common stock?
(b) What percentage of PepsiCo's authorized common stock was issued at December 29, 2007?
(c) How many shares of common stock were outstanding at December 29, 2007, and at December 30, 2006?
(d) What was the high and low market price per share in the fourth quarter of fiscal 2007, as reported under Selected Financial Data?

Comparative Analysis Problem: PepsiCo vs. Coca-Cola

BYP13-2 PepsiCo, Inc.'s financial statements are presented in Appendix A. Financial statements of The Coca-Cola Company are presented in Appendix B.

Instructions

(a) What is the par or stated value of Coca-Cola's and PepsiCo's common of capital, stock?
(b) What percentage of authorized shares was issued by Coca-Cola at December 31, 2007, and by PepsiCo at December 29, 2007?
(c) How many shares are held as treasury stock by Coca-Cola at December 31, 2007, and by PepsiCo at December 29, 2007?
(d) How many Coca-Cola common shares are outstanding at December 31, 2007? How many PepsiCo shares of capital stock are outstanding at December 29, 2007?

Exploring the Web

BYP13-3 SEC filings of publicly traded companies are available to view online.

Address: http://biz.yahoo.com/i, or go to **www.wiley.com/college/weygandt**

Steps
1. Pick a company and type in the company's name.
2. Choose **Quote**.

Instructions
Answer the following questions.

(a) What company did you select?
(b) What is its stock symbol?
(c) What was the stock's trading range today?
(d) What was the stock's trading range for the year?

CRITICAL THINKING

Decision Making Across the Organization

BYP13-4 The stockholders' meeting for Strauder Corporation has been in progress for some time. The chief financial officer for Strauder is presently reviewing the company's financial statements and is explaining the items that comprise the stockholders' equity section of the

balance sheet for the current year. The stockholders' equity section of Strauder Corporation at December 31, 2010, is as follows.

STRAUDER CORPORATION
Balance Sheet (partial)
December 31, 2010

Paid-in capital		
Capital stock		
Preferred stock, authorized 1,000,000 shares cumulative, $100 par value, $8 per share, 6,000 shares issued and outstanding		$ 600,000
Common stock, authorized 5,000,000 shares, $1 par value, 3,000,000 shares issued, and 2,700,000 outstanding		3,000,000
Total capital stock		3,600,000
Additional paid-in capital		
In excess of par value—preferred stock	$ 50,000	
In excess of par value—common stock	25,000,000	
Total additional paid-in capital		25,050,000
Total paid-in capital		28,650,000
Retained earnings		900,000
Total paid-in capital and retained earnings		29,550,000
Less: Common treasury stock (300,000 shares)		9,300,000
Total stockholders' equity		$20,250,000

At the meeting, stockholders have raised a number of questions regarding the stockholders' equity section.

Instructions

With the class divided into groups, answer the following questions as if you were the chief financial officer for Strauder Corporation.

(a) "What does the cumulative provision related to the preferred stock mean?"

(b) "I thought the common stock was presently selling at $29.75, but the company has the stock stated at $1 per share. How can that be?"

(c) "Why is the company buying back its common stock? Furthermore, the treasury stock has a debit balance because it is subtracted from stockholders' equity. Why is treasury stock not reported as an asset if it has a debit balance?"

Communication Activity

BYP13-5 Sid Hosey, your uncle, is an inventor who has decided to incorporate. Uncle Sid knows that you are an accounting major at U.N.O. In a recent letter to you, he ends with the question, "I'm filling out a state incorporation application. Can you tell me the difference in the following terms: (1) authorized stock, (2) issued stock, (3) outstanding stock, (4) preferred stock?"

Instructions

In a brief note, differentiate for Uncle Sid among the four different stock terms. Write the letter to be friendly, yet professional.

Ethics Case

BYP13-6 The R&D division of Marco Chemical Corp. has just developed a chemical for sterilizing the vicious Brazilian "killer bees" which are invading Mexico and the southern states of the United States. The president of Marco is anxious to get the chemical on the market to boost Marco's profits. He believes his job is in jeopardy because of decreasing sales and profits. Marco has an opportunity to sell this chemical in Central American countries, where the laws are much more relaxed than in the United States.

The director of Marco's R&D division strongly recommends further testing in the laboratory for side-effects of this chemical on other insects, birds, animals, plants, and even humans.

He cautions the president, "We could be sued from all sides if the chemical has tragic side-effects that we didn't even test for in the labs." The president answers, "We can't wait an additional year for your lab tests. We can avoid losses from such lawsuits by establishing a separate wholly owned corporation to shield Marco Corp. from such lawsuits. We can't lose any more than our investment in the new corporation, and we'll invest just the patent covering this chemical. We'll reap the benefits if the chemical works and is safe, and avoid the losses from lawsuits if it's a disaster." The following week Marco creates a new wholly owned corporation called Brecht Inc., sells the chemical patent to it for $10, and watches the spraying begin.

Instructions
(a) Who are the stakeholders in this situation?
(b) Are the president's motives and actions ethical?
(c) Can Marco shield itself against losses of Brecht Inc.?

"All About You" Activity

BYP13-7 A high percentage of Americans own stock in corporations. As a shareholder in a corporation, you will receive an annual report. One of the goals of this course is for you to learn how to navigate your way around an annual report.

Instructions
Use the annual report provided in Appendix A to answer the following questions.

(a) What CPA firm performed the audit of PepsiCo's financial statements?
(b) What was the amount of PepsiCo's earnings per share in 2007?
(c) What was net revenue in 2007?
(d) How many shares of treasury stock did the company have at the end of 2007?
(e) How much cash did PepsiCo spend on capital expenditures in 2007?
(f) Over what life does the company depreciate its buildings?
(g) What was the total amount of dividends paid in 2007?

Answers to Insight and Accounting Across the Organization Questions

p. 576 How to Read Stock Quotes
Q: For stocks traded on organized stock exchanges, how are the dollar prices per share established?
A: The dollar prices per share are established by the interaction between buyers and sellers of the shares.
Q: What factors might influence the price of shares in the marketplace?
A: The price of shares is influenced by a company's earnings and dividends as well as by factors beyond a company's control, such as changes in interest rates, labor strikes, scarcity of supplies or resources, and politics. The number of willing buyers and sellers (demand and supply) also plays a part in the price of shares.

p. 584 Why Did Reebok Buy Its Own Stock?
Q: What signal might a large stock repurchase send to investors regarding management's belief about the company's growth opportunities?
A: When a company has many growth opportunities it will normally conserve its cash in order to be better able to fund expansion. A large use of cash to buy back stock (and essentially shrink the company) would suggest that management was not optimistic about its growth opportunities.

Answers to Self-Study Questions
1. c   2. b   3. b   4. d   5. d   6. b   7. c   8. c   9. d   10. a   11. a   12. d   13. b
14. d   15. c

Remember to go back to the Navigator box on the chapter-opening page and check off your completed work.

Chapter 14

Corporations: Dividends, Retained Earnings, and Income Reporting

STUDY OBJECTIVES

After studying this chapter, you should be able to:

1 Prepare the entries for cash dividends and stock dividends.
2 Identify the items reported in a retained earnings statement.
3 Prepare and analyze a comprehensive stockholders' equity section.
4 Describe the form and content of corporation income statements.
5 Compute earnings per share.

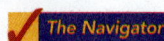

✓ The Navigator

Scan **Study Objectives**	■
Read **Feature Story**	■
Read **Preview**	■
Read text and answer **DO IT!** p. 612 ■ p. 615 ■ p. 619 ■ p. 623 ■	
Work **Comprehensive** **DO IT!** p. 625	■
Review **Summary of Study Objectives**	■
Answer **Self-Study Questions**	■
Complete **Assignments**	■

Feature Story

OWNING A PIECE OF THE ACTION

Van Meter Industrial, Inc., an electrical-parts distributor in Cedar Rapids, Iowa, is 100% employee-owned. For many years the company has issued bonuses in the form of shares of company stock to all of its employees. These bonus distributions typically have a value equal to several weeks of pay. Top management always thought that this was a great program. Therefore, it came as quite a surprise a few years ago when an employee stood up at a company-wide meeting and said that he did not see any real value in receiving the company's shares. Instead, he wanted "a few hundred extra bucks for beer and cigarettes."

As it turned out, many of the company's 340 employees felt this way. Rather than end the stock bonus program, however, the company decided to educate its employees on the value of share ownership. The employees now are taught how to determine the worth of their shares, the rights that come with share ownership, and what they can do to help increase the value of those shares.

As part of the education program, management developed a slogan, "Work ten, get five free." The idea is that after working 10 years, an employee's shares would be worth the equivalent of about five years' worth of salary. For example, a person earning a $30,000 salary would earn $300,000 in wages over a 10-year period. During that same 10-year period it was likely that the value of the employee's shares would accumulate to about $150,000 (five years' worth of salary). This demonstrates in more concrete terms why employees should be excited about share ownership.

A 12-member employee committee has the responsibility of educating new employees about the program. The committee also runs training programs so that employees understand how their cost-saving actions improve the company's results—and its stock price. It appears that the company's education program to encourage employees to act like owners is working. Profitability has increased rapidly, and employee turnover has fallen from 18% to 8%. Given Van Meter's success, many of the 10,000 other employee-owned companies in the United States might want to investigate whether their employees understand the benefits of share ownership.

Source: Adapted from Simona Covel, "How to Get Workers to Think and Act Like Owners," *Wall Street Journal Online*, February 15, 2008.

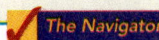

Inside Chapter 14...

- **Why Companies Are Increasing Their Dividends** (p. 611)
- **Would You Pay $133,900 for One Share of Stock?** (p. 615)
- ***All About You:* Corporations Have Governance Structures— Do You?** (p. 624)

Preview of Chapter 14

As indicated in the Feature Story, a profitable corporation like Van Meter Industrial, Inc. can provide real benefits to employees through its stock bonus plan. And as employees learn more about the role of dividends, retained earnings, and earnings per share, they develop an understanding and appreciation for what the company is providing to them.

The content and organization of Chapter 14 are as follows.

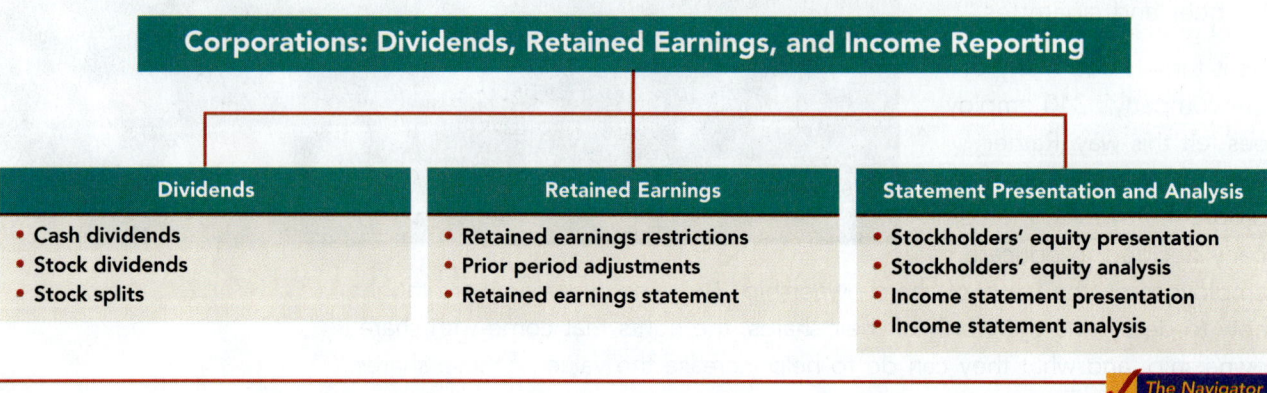

DIVIDENDS

STUDY OBJECTIVE 1
Prepare the entries for cash dividends and stock dividends.

A **dividend** is a corporation's distribution of cash or stock to its stockholders on a pro rata (proportional) basis. Investors are very interested in a company's dividend policies and practices. Dividends can take four forms: cash, property, scrip (a promissory note to pay cash), or stock. Cash dividends predominate in practice. Also, companies declare stock dividends with some frequency. These two forms of dividends will be the focus of discussion in this chapter.

Dividends may be expressed in two ways: (1) as a percentage of the par or stated value of the stock, or (2) as a dollar amount per share. The financial press generally reports **dividends as a dollar amount per share**. For example, Boeing Company's dividend rate is $1.60 a share, Hershey Foods Corp.'s is $1.19, and McDonald's is $1.50.

Cash Dividends

A **cash dividend** is a pro rata distribution of cash to stockholders. For a corporation to pay a cash dividend, it must have:

1. **Retained earnings.** The legality of a cash dividend depends on the laws of the state in which the company is incorporated. Payment of cash dividends from retained earnings is legal in all states. In general, cash dividend distributions from only the balance in common stock (legal capital) are illegal.

    A dividend declared out of paid-in capital is termed a **liquidating dividend**. Such a dividend reduces or "liquidates" the amount originally paid in by stockholders. Statutes vary considerably with respect to cash dividends based on paid-in capital in excess of par or stated value. Many states permit such dividends.

2. **Adequate cash.** The legality of a dividend and the ability to pay a dividend are two different things. For example, Nike, with retained earnings of over

$4.8 billion, could legally declare a dividend of at least $4.8 billion. But Nike's cash balance is only $1.8 billion.

Before declaring a cash dividend, a company's board of directors must carefully consider both current and future demands on the company's cash resources. In some cases, current liabilities may make a cash dividend inappropriate. In other cases, a major plant expansion program may warrant only a relatively small dividend.

3. **A declaration of dividends.** A company does not pay dividends unless its board of directors decides to do so, at which point the board "declares" the dividend. The board of directors has full authority to determine the amount of income to distribute in the form of a dividend and the amount to retain in the business. Dividends do not accrue like interest on a note payable, and they are not a liability until declared.

The amount and timing of a dividend are important issues. The payment of a large cash dividend could lead to liquidity problems for the company. On the other hand, a small dividend or a missed dividend may cause unhappiness among stockholders. Many stockholders expect to receive a reasonable cash payment from the company on a periodic basis. Many companies declare and pay cash dividends quarterly.

ENTRIES FOR CASH DIVIDENDS

Three dates are important in connection with dividends: (1) the declaration date, (2) the record date, and (3) the payment date. Normally, there are two to four weeks between each date. Companies make accounting entries on two of the dates—the declaration date and the payment date.

On the **declaration date**, the board of directors formally declares (authorizes) the cash dividend and announces it to stockholders. Declaration of a cash dividend **commits the corporation to a legal obligation**. The obligation is binding and cannot be rescinded. The company makes an entry to recognize the decrease in retained earnings and the increase in the liability Dividends Payable.

To illustrate, assume that on December 1, 2010, the directors of Media General declare a 50¢ per share cash dividend on 100,000 shares of $10 par value common stock. The dividend is $50,000 (100,000 × 50¢) The entry to record the declaration is:

Declaration Date

Dec. 1	Retained Earnings	50,000	
	Dividends Payable		50,000
	(To record declaration of cash dividend)		

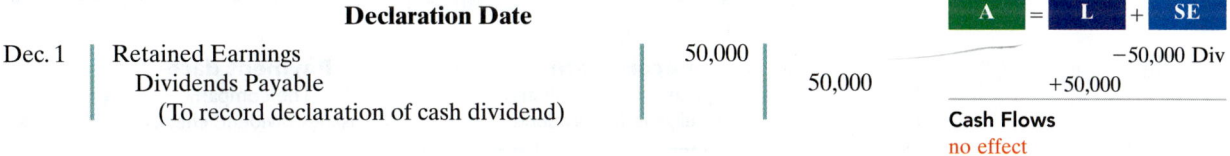

Dividends Payable is a current liability: it will normally be paid within the next several months.

Instead of debiting Retained Earnings, the company may debit the account Dividends. This account provides additional information in the ledger. Also, a company may have separate dividend accounts for each class of stock. When using a dividend account, the company transfers the balance of that account to Retained Earnings at the end of the year by a closing entry. Whichever account is used for the dividend declaration, the effect is the same: Retained earnings decreases, and a current liability increases. *For homework problems, you should use the Retained Earnings account for recording dividend declarations.*

At the **record date**, the company determines ownership of the outstanding shares for dividend purposes. The records maintained by the corporation supply this information. In the interval between the declaration date and the record date, the corporation updates its stock ownership records. For Media General, the

610 Chapter 14 Corporations: Dividends, Retained Earnings, and Income Reporting

HELPFUL HINT
The purpose of the record date is to identify the persons or entities that will receive the dividend, not to determine the amount of the dividend liability.

record date is December 22. No entry is required on this date because the corporation's liability recognized on the declaration date is unchanged.

Record Date

Dec. 22 | No entry necessary

On the **payment date**, the company mails dividend checks to the stockholders and records the payment of the dividend. Assuming that the payment date is January 20 for Media General, the entry on that date is:

Payment Date

Jan. 20	Dividends Payable	50,000	
	Cash		50,000
	(To record payment of cash dividend)		

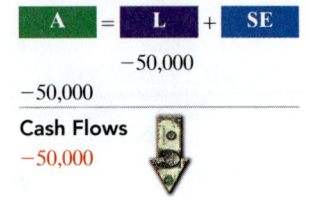

Note that payment of the dividend reduces both current assets and current liabilities. It has no effect on stockholders' equity. The **cumulative effect** of the **declaration and payment** of a cash dividend is to **decrease both stockholders' equity and total assets**. Illustration 14-1 summarizes the three important dates associated with dividends for Media General.

Illustration 14-1
Key dividend dates

ALLOCATING CASH DIVIDENDS BETWEEN PREFERRED AND COMMON STOCK

As explained in Chapter 13, preferred stock has priority over common stock in regard to dividends. Holders of cumulative preferred stock must be paid any unpaid prior-year dividends and its current year's dividend before common stockholders receive dividends.

To illustrate, assume that at December 31, 2010, IBR Inc. has 1,000 shares of 8%, $100 par value cumulative preferred stock. It also has 50,000 shares of $10 par value common stock outstanding. The dividend per share for preferred stock is $8 ($100 par value × 8%). The required annual dividend for preferred stock is therefore $8,000 (1,000 × $8). At December 31, 2010, the directors declare a $6,000 cash dividend. In this case, the entire dividend amount goes to preferred stockholders because of their dividend preference. The entry to record the declaration of the dividend is:

Dec. 31	Retained Earnings	6,000	
	Dividends Payable		6,000
	(To record $6 per share cash dividend to preferred stockholders)		

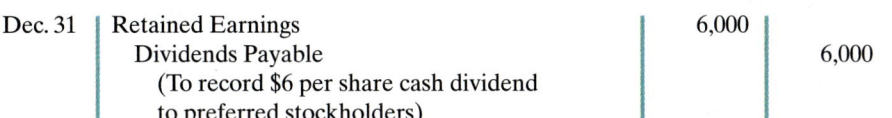

A = L + SE
−6,000 Div
+6,000

Cash Flows
no effect

Because of the cumulative feature, dividends of $2 per share are in arrears on preferred stock for 2010. The company must pay these dividends to preferred stockholders before it can pay any future dividends to common stockholders. IBR should disclose dividends in arrears in the financial statements.

At December 31, 2011, IBR declares a $50,000 cash dividend. The allocation of the dividend to the two classes of stock is as follows.

Total dividend			$50,000
Allocated to preferred stock			
Dividends in arrears, 2010 (1,000 × $2)	$2,000		
2011 dividend (1,000 × $8)	8,000	10,000	
Remainder allocated to common stock			$40,000

Illustration 14-2
Allocating dividends to preferred and common stock

The entry to record the declaration of the dividend is:

Dec. 31	Retained Earnings	50,000	
	Dividends Payable		50,000
	(To record declaration of cash dividends of $10,000 to preferred stock and $40,000 to common stock)		

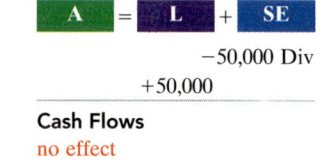

A = L + SE
−50,000 Div
+50,000

Cash Flows
no effect

What if IBR's preferred stock were not cumulative? In that case preferred stockholders would have received only $8,000 in dividends in 2011. Common stockholders would have received $42,000.

ACCOUNTING ACROSS THE ORGANIZATION

Why Companies Are Increasing Their Dividends

The decision whether to pay a dividend, and how much to pay, is a very important management decision. In recent years, many companies have substantially increased their dividends, and total dividends paid by U.S. companies hit record levels.

One explanation for the increase is that Congress lowered, from 39% to 15%, the tax rate paid by investors on dividends received, making dividends more attractive to investors. Another driving force for the dividend increases was that companies were sitting on record amounts of cash. Because they did not see a lot of profitable investment opportunities, companies decided to return the cash to shareholders.

Bigger dividends are still possible in the future. Large companies paid out 32% of their earnings as dividends in 2007—well below the historical average payout of 54% of earnings.

Source: Alan Levinsohn, "Divine Dividends," *Strategic Finance*, May 2005, pp. 59–60.

 What factors must management consider in deciding how large a dividend to pay?

DO IT!

DIVIDENDS ON PREFERRED AND COMMON STOCK

MasterMind Corporation has 2,000 shares of 6%, $100 par value preferred stock outstanding at December 31, 2010. At December 31, 2010, the company declared a $60,000 cash dividend. Determine the dividend paid to preferred stockholders and common stockholders under each of the following scenarios.

1. The preferred stock is noncumulative, and the company has not missed any dividends in previous years.
2. The preferred stock is noncumulative, and the company did not pay a dividend in each of the two previous years.
3. The preferred stock is cumulative, and the company did not pay a dividend in each of the two previous years.

action plan

✔ Determine dividends on preferred shares by multiplying the dividend rate times the par value of the stock times the number of preferred shares.

✔ Understand the cumulative feature: If preferred stock is cumulative, then any missed dividends (dividends in arrears) and the current year's dividend must be paid to preferred stockholders before dividends are paid to common stockholders.

Solution

1. The company has not missed past dividends and the preferred stock is noncumulative; thus, the preferred stockholders are paid only this year's dividend. The dividend paid to preferred stockholders would be $12,000 (2,000 × .06 × $100). The dividend paid to common stockholders would be $48,000 ($60,000 − $12,000).
2. The preferred stock is noncumulative; thus, past unpaid dividends do not have to be paid. The dividend paid to preferred stockholders would be $12,000 (2,000 × .06 × $100). The dividend paid to common stockholders would be $48,000 ($60,000 − $12,000).
3. The preferred stock is cumulative; thus, dividends that have been missed (dividends in arrears) must be paid. The dividend paid to preferred stockholders would be $36,000 (3 × 2,000 × .06 × $100). The dividend paid to common stockholders would be $24,000 ($60,000 − $36,000).

Related exercise material: **E14-2, E14-17,** and **DO IT! 14-1.**

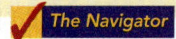

Stock Dividends

A **stock dividend** is a pro rata distribution to stockholders of the corporation's own stock. Whereas a company pays cash in a cash dividend, a company issues shares of stock in a stock dividend. **A stock dividend results in a decrease in retained earnings and an increase in paid-in capital.** Unlike a cash dividend, a stock dividend does not decrease total stockholders' equity or total assets.

To illustrate, assume that you have a 2% ownership interest in Cetus Inc.; you own 20 of its 1,000 shares of common stock. If Cetus declares a 10% stock dividend, it would issue 100 shares (1,000 × 10%) of stock. You would receive two shares (2% × 100). Would your ownership interest change? No, it would remain at 2% (22 ÷ 1,100). **You now own more shares of stock, but your ownership interest has not changed.** Illustration 14-3 (next page) shows the effect of a stock dividend for stockholders.

The company has disbursed no cash, and has assumed no liabilities. What are the purposes and benefits of a stock dividend? Corporations issue stock dividends generally for one or more of the following reasons.

1. To satisfy stockholders' dividend expectations without spending cash.
2. To increase the marketability of the corporation's stock. When the number of shares outstanding increases, the market price per share decreases. Decreasing

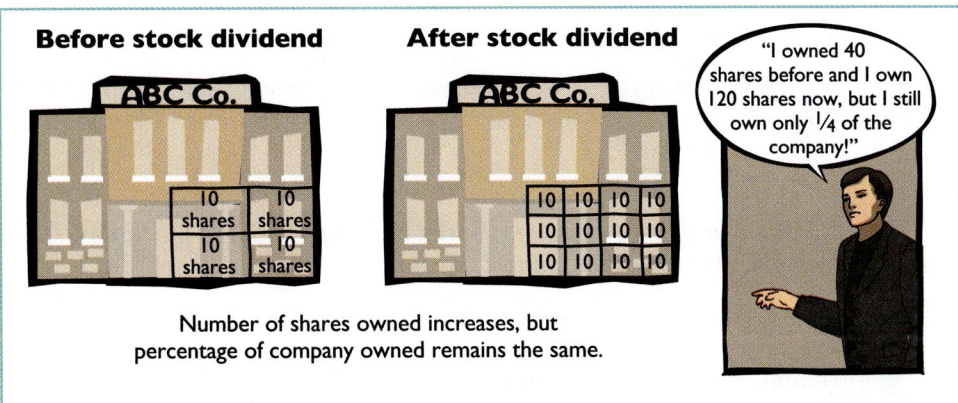

Illustration 14-3
Effect of stock dividend for stockholders

the market price of the stock makes it easier for smaller investors to purchase the shares.

3. To emphasize that a portion of stockholders' equity has been permanently reinvested in the business (and is unavailable for cash dividends).

When the dividend is declared, the board of directors determines the size of the stock dividend and the value assigned to each dividend. Generally, if the company issues a **small stock dividend** (less than 20–25% of the corporation's issued stock), the value assigned to the dividend is the fair market value per share. This treatment is based on the assumption that a small stock dividend will have little effect on the market price of the outstanding shares. Many stockholders consider small stock dividends to be distributions of earnings equal to the fair market value of the shares distributed. If a company issues a **large stock dividend** (greater than 20–25%), the value assigned to the dividend is the par or stated value. Small stock dividends predominate in practice. Thus, we will illustrate only entries for small stock dividends.

ENTRIES FOR STOCK DIVIDENDS

To illustrate the accounting for small stock dividends, assume that Medland Corporation has a balance of $300,000 in retained earnings. It declares a 10% stock dividend on its 50,000 shares of $10 par value common stock. The current fair market value of its stock is $15 per share. The number of shares to be issued is 5,000 (10% × 50,000). Therefore the total amount to be debited to Retained Earnings is $75,000 (5,000 × $15). The entry to record the declaration of the stock dividend is as follows.

Retained Earnings	75,000	
Common Stock Dividends Distributable		50,000
Paid-in Capital in Excess of Par Value		25,000
(To record declaration of 10% stock dividend)		

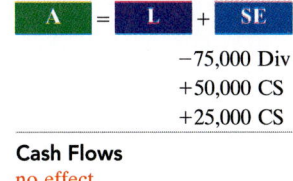

−75,000 Div
+50,000 CS
+25,000 CS

Cash Flows
no effect

Medland debits Retained Earnings for the fair market value of the stock issued ($15 × 5,000). It credits Common Stock Dividends Distributable for the par value of the dividend shares ($10 × 5,000), and credits Paid-in Capital in Excess of Par Value for the excess over par ($5 × 5,000).

Common Stock Dividends Distributable is a **stockholders' equity account**. It is not a liability because assets will not be used to pay the dividend. If the company prepares a balance sheet before it issues the dividend shares, it reports the distributable account under Paid-in capital as shown in Illustration 14-4 (next page).

Illustration 14-4
Statement presentation of common stock dividends distributable

Paid-in capital		
Common stock	$500,000	
Common stock dividends distributable	**50,000**	$550,000

When Medland issues the dividend shares, it debits Common Stock Dividends Distributable, and credits Common Stock, as follows.

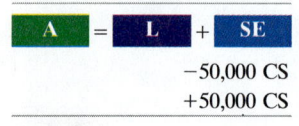

−50,000 CS
+50,000 CS

Cash Flows
no effect

Common Stock Dividends Distributable	50,000	
Common Stock		50,000
(To record issuance of 5,000 shares in a stock dividend)		

EFFECTS OF STOCK DIVIDENDS

How do stock dividends affect stockholders' equity? They **change the composition of stockholders' equity**, because they transfer to paid-in capital a portion of retained earnings. However, **total stockholders' equity remains the same**. Stock dividends also have no effect on the par or stated value per share. But the number of shares outstanding increases. Illustration 14-5 shows these effects for Medland Corporation.

Illustration 14-5
Stock dividend effects

	Before Dividend	After Dividend
Stockholders' equity		
Paid-in capital		
Common stock, $10 par	$500,000	$550,000
Paid-in capital in excess of par value	—	25,000
Total paid-in capital	500,000	575,000
Retained earnings	300,000	225,000
Total stockholders' equity	**$800,000**	**$800,000**
Outstanding shares	**50,000**	**55,000**
Par value per share	**$10.00**	**$10.00**

In this example, total paid-in capital increases by $75,000, and retained earnings decreases by the same amount. Note also that total stockholders' equity remains unchanged at $800,000.

Stock Splits

A **stock split**, like a stock dividend, involves issuance of additional shares to stockholders according to their percentage ownership. **A stock split results in a reduction in the par or stated value per share.** The purpose of a stock split is to increase the marketability of the stock by lowering its market value per share.

The effect of a split on market value is generally *inversely proportional* to the size of the split. For example, after a recent 2-for-1 stock split, the market value of Nike's stock fell from $111 to approximately $55. The lower market value stimulated market activity, and within one year the stock was trading above $100 again.

In a stock split, the number of shares increases in the same proportion that par or stated value per share decreases. For example, in a 2-for-1 split, one share of $10 par value stock is exchanged for two shares of $5 par value stock. **A stock split does**

HELPFUL HINT
A stock split changes the par value per share but does not affect any balances in stockholders' equity.

not have any effect on total paid-in capital, retained earnings, or total stockholders' equity. But the number of shares outstanding increases, and par value per share decreases. Illustration 14-6 shows these effects for Medland Corporation, assuming that it splits its 50,000 shares of common stock on a 2-for-1 basis.

	Before Stock Split	After Stock Split
Stockholders' equity		
Paid-in capital		
Common stock	$500,000	$500,000
Paid-in capital in excess of par value	–0–	–0–
Total paid-in capital	500,000	500,000
Retained earnings	300,000	300,000
Total stockholders' equity	**$800,000**	**$800,000**
Outstanding shares	**50,000**	**100,000**
Par value per share	**$10.00**	**$5.00**

Illustration 14-6
Stock split effects

A stock split does not affect the balances in any stockholders' equity accounts. Therefore **it is not necessary to journalize a stock split**.

Illustration 14-7 summarizes the significant differences between stock splits and stock dividends.

Item	Stock Split	Stock Dividend
Total paid-in capital	No change	Increase
Total retained earnings	No change	Decrease
Total par value (common stock)	No change	Increase
Par value per share	Decrease	No change

Illustration 14-7
Differences between the effects of stock splits and stock dividends

INVESTOR INSIGHT

Would You Pay $133,900 for One Share of Stock?

A handful of U.S. companies have no intention of keeping their stock trading in a range accessible to mere mortals. These companies never split their stock, no matter how high their stock price gets. The king is investment company Berkshire Hathaway's Class A stock, which sells for a pricey $133,900—per share! The company's Class B stock is a relative bargain at roughly $4,452 per share. And who is the CEO of Berkshire Hathaway? Warren Buffett, one of the richest individuals in the world.

 How does the effect on share price following a stock split compare to the effect on share price of treasury shares acquired?

DO IT!

Sing CD Company has had five years of record earnings. Due to this success, the market price of its 500,000 shares of $2 par value common stock has tripled from $15 per share to $45. During this period, paid-in capital remained the same at $2,000,000. Retained earnings increased from $1,500,000 to $10,000,000. CEO

STOCK DIVIDENDS AND STOCK SPLITS

action plan

✔ Calculate the stock dividend's effect on retained earnings by multiplying the number of new shares times the market price of the stock (or par value for a large stock dividend).

✔ Recall that a stock dividend increases the number of shares without affecting total stockholders' equity.

✔ Recall that a stock split only increases the number of shares outstanding and decreases the par value per share.

Joan Elbert is considering either (1) a 10% stock dividend or (2) a 2-for-1 stock split. She asks you to show the before-and-after effects of each option on (a) retained earnings and (b) total stockholders' equity.

Solution

(a) (1) The stock dividend amount is $2,250,000 [(500,000 × 10%) × $45]. The new balance in retained earnings is $7,750,000 ($10,000,000 − $2,250,000).
(2) The retained earnings balance after the stock split would be the same as it was before the split: $10,000,000.

(b) (1) Stock dividends change the composition of stockholders' equity because they transfer to paid-in capital a portion of retained earnings. However, total stockholders' equity remains the same.
(2) In a stock split, the number of shares increases in the same proportion that par or stated value per share decreases. A stock split therefore does not have any effect on total paid-in capital, retained earnings, or total stockholders' equity.

Related exercise material: BE14-3, E14-4, E14-5, E14-6, E14-7, and DO IT! 14-2.

RETAINED EARNINGS

STUDY OBJECTIVE 2
Identify the items reported in a retained earnings statement.

As you learned in Chapter 13, **retained earnings** is net income that a company retains for use in the business. The balance in retained earnings is part of the stockholders' claim on the total assets of the corporation. It does not, though, represent a claim on any specific asset. Nor can the amount of retained earnings be associated with the balance of any asset account. For example, a $100,000 balance in retained earnings does not mean that there should be $100,000 in cash. The reason is that the company may have used the cash resulting from the excess of revenues over expenses to purchase buildings, equipment, and other assets.

To demonstrate that retained earnings and cash may be quite different, Illustration 14-8 shows recent amounts of retained earnings and cash in selected companies.

Illustration 14-8
Retained earnings and cash balances

Company	Retained Earnings (in millions)	Cash
Disney Co.	$24,207	$3,670
Intel Corp.	28,984	6,598
Kellogg Co.	4,217	1,026
Amazon.com	(1,837)	1,022

HELPFUL HINT
Remember that Retained Earnings is a stockholders' equity account, whose normal balance is a credit.

Remember from Chapter 13 that when a company has net income, it closes net income to retained earnings. The closing entry is a debit to Income Summary and a credit to Retained Earnings.

When a company has a **net loss** (expenses exceed revenues), it also closes this amount to retained earnings. The closing entry in this case is a debit to Retained

Earnings and a credit to Income Summary. This is done even if it results in a debit balance in Retained Earnings. **Companies do not debit net losses to paid-in capital accounts.** To do so would destroy the distinction between paid-in and earned capital. A debit balance in Retained Earnings is identified as a **deficit**. It is reported as a deduction in the stockholders' equity section, as shown below.

Illustration 14-9
Stockholders' equity with deficit

Balance Sheet (partial)

Stockholders' equity	
Paid-in capital	
Common stock	$800,000
Retained earnings (deficit)	(50,000)
Total stockholders' equity	$750,000

Retained Earnings Restrictions

The balance in retained earnings is generally available for dividend declarations. Some companies state this fact. For example, Lockheed Martin Corporation states the following in the notes to its financial statements.

LOCKHEED MARTIN CORPORATION
Notes to the Financial Statements

At December 31, retained earnings were unrestricted and available for dividend payments.

Illustration 14-10
Disclosure of unrestricted retained earnings

In some cases, there may be **retained earnings restrictions**. These make a portion of the retained earnings balance currently unavailable for dividends. Restrictions result from one or more of the following causes.

1. **Legal restrictions.** Many states require a corporation to restrict retained earnings for the cost of treasury stock purchased. The restriction keeps intact the corporation's legal capital that is being temporarily held as treasury stock. When the company sells the treasury stock, the restriction is lifted.
2. **Contractual restrictions.** Long-term debt contracts may restrict retained earnings as a condition for the loan. The restriction limits the use of corporate assets for payment of dividends. Thus, it increases the likelihood that the corporation will be able to meet required loan payments.
3. **Voluntary restrictions.** The board of directors may voluntarily create retained earnings restrictions for specific purposes. For example, the board may authorize a restriction for future plant expansion. By reducing the amount of retained earnings available for dividends, the company makes more cash available for the planned expansion.

Companies generally disclose **retained earnings restrictions** in the notes to the financial statements. For example, Tektronix Inc., a manufacturer of electronic measurement devices, had total retained earnings of $774 million, but the unrestricted portion was only $223.8 million.

Illustration 14-11
Disclosure of restriction

TEKTRONIX INC.
Notes to the Financial Statements

Certain of the Company's debt agreements require compliance with debt covenants. Management believes that the Company is in compliance with such requirements. The Company had unrestricted retained earnings of $223.8 million after meeting those requirements.

Prior Period Adjustments

Suppose that a corporation has closed its books and issued financial statements. The corporation then discovers that it made a material error in reporting net income of a prior year. How should the company record this situation in the accounts and report it in the financial statements?

The correction of an error in previously issued financial statements is known as a **prior period adjustment**. The company makes the correction directly to Retained Earnings, because the effect of the error is now in this account. The net income for the prior period has been recorded in retained earnings through the journalizing and posting of closing entries.

To illustrate, assume that General Microwave discovers in 2010 that it understated depreciation expense in 2009 by $300,000 due to computational errors. These errors overstated both net income for 2009 and the current balance in retained earnings. The entry for the prior period adjustment, ignoring all tax effects, is as follows.

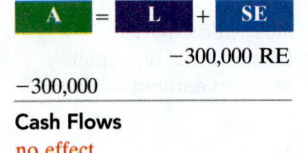

−300,000
Cash Flows
no effect

Retained Earnings	300,000	
Accumulated Depreciation		300,000
(To adjust for understatement of depreciation in a prior period)		

A debit to an income statement account in 2010 is incorrect because the error pertains to a prior year.

Companies report prior period adjustments in the retained earnings statement.[1] They add (or deduct, as the case may be) these adjustments from the beginning retained earnings balance. This results in an adjusted beginning balance. For example, assuming a beginning balance of $800,000 in retained earnings, General Microwave reports the prior period adjustment as follows.

Illustration 14-12
Statement presentation of prior period adjustments

GENERAL MICROWAVE
Retained Earnings Statement (partial)

Balance, January 1, as reported	$ 800,000
Correction for overstatement of net income in prior period (depreciation error)	(300,000)
Balance, January 1, as adjusted	$ 500,000

Again, reporting the correction in the current year's income statement would be incorrect because it applies to a prior year's income statement.

---

[1] A complete retained earnings statement is shown in Illustration 14-14 on the next page.

Retained Earnings Statement

The **retained earnings statement** shows the changes in retained earnings during the year. The company prepares the statement from the Retained Earnings account. Illustration 14-13 shows (in account form) transactions that affect retained earnings.

Illustration 14-13
Debits and credits to retained earnings

Retained Earnings	
1. Net loss	1. Net income
2. Prior period adjustments for overstatement of net income	2. Prior period adjustments for understatement of net income
3. Cash dividends and stock dividends	
4. Some disposals of treasury stock	

As indicated, net income increases retained earnings, and a net loss decreases retained earnings. Prior period adjustments may either increase or decrease retained earnings. Both cash dividends and stock dividends decrease retained earnings. The circumstances under which treasury stock transactions decrease retained earnings are explained in Chapter 13, page 585.

A complete retained earnings statement for Graber Inc., based on assumed data, is as follows.

Illustration 14-14
Retained earnings statement

GRABER INC.
Retained Earnings Statement
For the Year Ended December 31, 2010

Balance, January 1, as reported		$1,050,000
Correction for understatement of net income in prior period (inventory error)		50,000
Balance, January 1, as adjusted		1,100,000
Add: Net income		360,000
		1,460,000
Less: Cash dividends	$100,000	
Stock dividends	200,000	300,000
Balance, December 31		$1,160,000

DO IT!

RETAINED EARNINGS STATEMENT

Vega Corporation has retained earnings of $5,130,000 on January 1, 2010. During the year, Vega earned $2,000,000 of net income. It declared and paid a $250,000 cash dividend. In 2010, Vega recorded an adjustment of $180,000 due to the understatement (from a mathematical error) of 2009 depreciation expense. Prepare a retained earnings statement for 2010.

620 Chapter 14 Corporations: Dividends, Retained Earnings, and Income Reporting

action plan

✔ Recall that a retained earnings statement begins with retained earnings, as reported at the end of the previous year.

✔ Add or subtract any prior period adjustments to arrive at the adjusted beginning figure.

✔ Add net income and subtract dividends declared to arrive at the ending balance in retained earnings.

Solution

VEGA CORPORATION
Retained Earnings Statement
For the Year Ended December 31, 2010

Balance, January 1, as reported	$5,130,000
Correction for overstatement of net income in prior period (depreciation error)	(180,000)
Balance, January 1, as adjusted	4,950,000
Add: Net income	2,000,000
	6,950,000
Less: Cash dividends	250,000
Balance, December 31	$6,700,000

Related exercise material: **BE14-4, BE14-5, E14-8, E14-9,** and **DO IT! 14-3**.

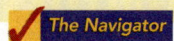

STATEMENT PRESENTATION AND ANALYSIS

Stockholders' Equity Presentation

STUDY OBJECTIVE 3
Prepare and analyze a comprehensive stockholders' equity section.

Illustration 14-15 presents the stockholders' equity section of Graber Inc.'s balance sheet. Note the following: (1) "Common stock dividends distributable" is shown under "Capital stock," in "Paid-in capital." (2) A note (Note R) discloses a retained earnings restriction.

Illustration 14-15
Comprehensive stockholders' equity section

GRABER INC.
Balance Sheet (partial)

Stockholders' equity		
Paid-in capital		
Capital stock		
9% Preferred stock, $100 par value, cumulative, callable at $120, 10,000 shares authorized, 6,000 shares issued and outstanding		$ 600,000
Common stock, no par, $5 stated value, 500,000 shares authorized, 400,000 shares issued and 390,000 outstanding	$2,000,000	
Common stock dividends distributable	50,000	2,050,000
Total capital stock		2,650,000
Additional paid-in capital		
In excess of par value—preferred stock	30,000	
In excess of stated value—common stock	1,050,000	
Total additional paid-in capital		1,080,000
Total paid-in capital		3,730,000
Retained earnings **(see Note R)**		1,160,000
Total paid-in capital and retained earnings		4,890,000
Less: Treasury stock—common (10,000 shares)		80,000
Total stockholders' equity		$4,810,000

Note R: Retained earnings is restricted for the cost of treasury stock, $80,000.

Instead of presenting a detailed stockholders' equity section in the balance sheet and a retained earnings statement, many companies prepare a **stockholders' equity statement**. This statement shows the changes (1) in each stockholders' equity account and (2) in total that occurred during the year. An example of a stockholders' equity statement appears in PepsiCo's financial statements in Appendix A (page A7).

Stockholders' Equity Analysis

Investors and analysts can measure profitability from the viewpoint of the common stockholder by the **return on common stockholders' equity**. This ratio shows how many dollars of net income the company earned for each dollar invested by the common stockholders. It is computed by dividing **net income available to common stockholders** (which is net income minus preferred stock dividends) by average common stockholders' equity.

To illustrate, Walt Disney Company's beginning-of-the-year and end-of-the-year common stockholders' equity were $31,820 and $30,753 million respectively. Its net income was $4,687 million, and no preferred stock was outstanding. The return on common stockholders' equity ratio is computed as follows.

Net Income Available to Common Stockholders	÷	Average Common Stockholders' Equity	=	Return on Common Stockholders' Equity
($4,687 − $0)	÷	($31,820 + $30,753) / 2	=	15.0%

Illustration 14-16
Return on common stockholders' equity ratio and computation

As shown above, if a company has preferred stock, we would deduct the amount of **preferred dividends** from the company's net income to compute income available to common stockholders. Also, the par value of preferred stock is deducted from total average stockholders' equity to arrive at the amount of common stockholders' equity.

Income Statement Presentation

Income statements for **corporations are the same as the statements for proprietorships or partnerships except for one thing: the reporting of income taxes**. For income tax purposes, corporations are a separate legal entity. As a result, corporations report **income tax expense** in a separate section of the corporation income statement, before net income. The condensed income statement for Leads Inc. in Illustration 14-17 shows a typical presentation.

STUDY OBJECTIVE 4
Describe the form and content of corporation income statements.

LEADS INC.
Income Statement
For the Year Ended December 31, 2010

Sales	$800,000
Cost of goods sold	600,000
Gross profit	200,000
Operating expenses	50,000
Income from operations	150,000
Other revenues and gains	10,000
Other expenses and losses	(4,000)
Income before income taxes	**156,000**
Income tax expense	**46,800**
Net income	$109,200

Illustration 14-17
Income statement with income taxes

622 Chapter 14 Corporations: Dividends, Retained Earnings, and Income Reporting

Note that the corporation reports income before income taxes as one line item and income tax expense as another.

Companies record income tax expense and the related liability for income taxes payable as part of the adjusting process. Using the data for Leads Inc., in Illustration 14-17, the adjusting entry for income tax expense at December 31, 2010, is:

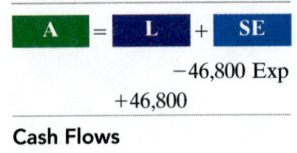

−46,800 Exp
+46,800

Cash Flows
no effect

Income Tax Expense	46,800	
Income Taxes Payable		46,800
(To record income taxes for 2010)		

The income statement of PepsiCo, in Appendix A presents another illustration of income taxes.

Income Statement Analysis

STUDY OBJECTIVE 5
Compute earnings per share.

The financial press frequently reports earnings data. Stockholders and potential investors widely use these data in evaluating the profitability of a company. A convenient measure of earnings is **earnings per share (EPS)**, which indicates the net income earned by each share of outstanding **common stock**.

EPS AND PREFERRED DIVIDENDS

The existence of preferred dividends slightly complicates the calculation of EPS. When a corporation has both preferred and common stock, we must subtract the current year's preferred dividend from net income, to arrive at **income available to common stockholders**. Illustration 14-18 shows the formula for computing EPS.

Illustration 14-18
Formula for earnings per share

Net Income minus Preferred Dividends	÷	Weighted-Average of Common Shares Outstanding	=	Earnings per Share

ETHICS NOTE
In order to meet market expectations for EPS, some managers engage in elaborate treasury stock transactions. These transactions can be very costly for the remaining shareholders.

To illustrate, assume that Rally Inc. reports net income of $211,000 on its 102,500 weighted-average common shares.[2] During the year it also declares a $6,000 dividend on its preferred stock. Therefore, the amount Rally has available for common stock dividends is $205,000 ($211,000 − $6,000). Earnings per share is $2 ($205,000 ÷ 102,500). If the preferred stock is cumulative, Rally deducts the dividend for the current year, whether or not it is declared. Remember that companies report **earnings per share only for common stock**.

Investors often attempt to link earnings per share to the market price per share of a company's stock.[3] Because of the importance of earnings per share, most companies must report it on the face of the income statement. Generally companies

---

[2]The calculation of the weighted average of common shares outstanding is discussed in advanced accounting courses.

[3]The ratio of the market price per share to the earnings per share is called the *price/earnings (P/E) ratio*. The financial media report this ratio for common stocks listed on major stock exchanges.

simply report this amount below net income on the statement. For Rally Inc. the presentation is as follows.

RALLY INC.
Income Statement (partial)

Net income	$211,000
Earnings per share	**$2.00**

Illustration 14-19
Basic earnings per share disclosure

DO IT!

STOCKHOLDERS' EQUITY AND EPS

On January 1, 2010, Sienna Corporation purchased 2,000 shares of treasury stock. Other information regarding Siena Corporation is provided below.

	2009	2010
Net income	$110,000	$110,000
Dividends on preferred stock	$10,000	$10,000
Dividends on common stock	$2,000	$1,600
Weighted average number of shares outstanding	10,000	8,000*
Common stockholders' equity, beginning of year	$500,000	$400,000*
Common stockholders' equity, end of year	$500,000	$400,000

*Adjusted for purchase of treasury stock.

Compute (a) return on common stockholders' equity for each year and (b) earnings per share for each year, and (c) discuss the changes in each.

action plan

✔ Determine return on common stockholders' equity by dividing net income available to common stockholders by the average common stockholders' equity.

✔ Determine earnings per share by dividing net income available to common stockholders by the weighted-average number of common shares outstanding.

Solution

(a)

2009: Return on common stockholders' equity $= \dfrac{(\$110{,}000 - \$10{,}000)}{(\$500{,}000 + \$500{,}000)/2} = 20\%$

2010: $\dfrac{(\$110{,}000 - \$10{,}000)}{(\$400{,}000 + \$400{,}000)/2} = 25\%$

(b)

2009: Earnings per share $= \dfrac{(\$110{,}000 - \$10{,}000)}{10{,}000} = \$10$

2010: $\dfrac{(\$110{,}000 - \$10{,}000)}{8{,}000} = \$12.50$

(c) Between 2009 and 2010, return on common stockholders' equity improved from 20% to 25%. Earnings per share increased from $10 to $12.50. While this would appear to be good news for the company's common stockholders, these increases should be carefully evaluated. It is important to note that net income did not change during this period. The increase in both ratios was due to the purchase of treasury shares, which reduced the denominator of each ratio. As the company repurchases its own shares, it becomes more reliant on debt and thus increases its risk.

Related exercise material: BE14-6, BE14-7, BE14-9, BE14-10, E14-12, E14-13, E14-14, E14-15, E14-16, E14-17, and DO IT! 14-4.

 Be sure to read **ALL ABOUT YOU: Corporations Have Governance Structures—Do You?** on page 624 for information on how topics in this chapter apply to your personal life.

all about YOU

Corporations Have Governance Structures—Do You?

As discussed previously in this text, the scandals and bankruptcies at Enron, WorldCom, and other companies brought many changes to the way America does business. One of the primary lessons has been that companies need to take corporate governance and management oversight more seriously. As part of this effort, many companies have developed a code of ethics. The purpose of a code of ethics is to clearly specify standards of conduct to deter wrongdoing and promote honest and ethical conduct. It also is intended to be an expression by top management of its "tone at the top"—that is, to indicate that top management takes ethics seriously. Many other organizations, including university student groups, also have formulated ethics codes.

Some Facts

* Under Sarbanes-Oxley, a company must disclose in its annual report whether it has a code of ethics. It must also disclose any changes to or waivers of the code of ethics.

* Enron had a code of ethics. In a number of instances, Enron's board of directors knowingly waived requirements of the code so that the CFO could set up and run special purpose entities. Ultimately these waivers contributed to Enron's downfall.

* In some instances U.S. federal prosecutors have pressured companies to not pay the legal-defense bills of employees accused of wrong-doing, thus making it harder for the employees to defend themselves.

* In a recent survey of 1,436 workers, 34% said that they have seen unethical activities at their workplace, but only 47% said they are likely to report these activities. Many cited fear of retaliation by their bosses as the reason for not reporting.

About the Numbers

Stockholders often lose money as a result of unethical behavior by management. When they do, they often file lawsuits against the company in an effort to recoup these losses. The graph below shows just how expensive these class-action lawsuits can be for companies.

Top Class-Action Securities Settlements

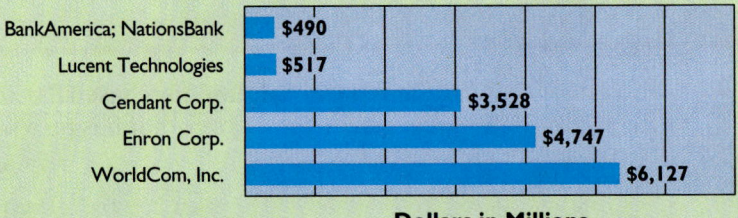

Company	Settlement
BankAmerica; NationsBank	$490
Lucent Technologies	$517
Cendant Corp.	$3,528
Enron Corp.	$4,747
WorldCom, Inc.	$6,127

Dollars in Millions

Source: Elaine Buckberg, Todd Foster, and Ronald I. Miller, "Recent Trends in Shareholder Class Action Litigation: Are WorldCom and Enron the New Standard?" NERA Economic Consulting, www.nera.com (accessed June 26, 2006).

What Do You Think

Many universities have become concerned about student cheating. In particular, the prevalence of digital documents on the Internet has made it very easy to plagiarize. Many schools now have student ethics codes. Do you think that these ethics codes serve a useful purpose?

YES: Anything that will reduce unethical behavior is a good thing. An ethics code establishes what is and is not acceptable behavior, which helps universities maintain ethical standards for academic work and weed out those students who try to get ahead by non-ethical means.

NO: The existence of an ethics code won't affect student behavior. If students have a propensity to cheat, a document that tells them what is and is not good behavior is not going to be a deterrent. Students already know what cheating is, and that it is wrong.

Sources: "Whistleblowing Workers: Becoming an Endangered Species?" *HR Focus*, June 2006, p. 9; Lauren Etter, "The Enron Trial Finally Begins," *Wall Street Journal*, February 4, 2006, p. A7.

The authors' comments on this situation appear on page 640.

Comprehensive DO IT!

On January 1, 2010, Hayslett Corporation had the following stockholders' equity accounts.

Common Stock ($10 par value, 260,000 shares issued and outstanding)	$2,600,000
Paid-in Capital in Excess of Par Value	1,500,000
Retained Earnings	3,200,000

During the year, the following transactions occurred.

April	1	Declared a $1.50 cash dividend per share to stockholders of record on April 15, payable May 1.
May	1	Paid the dividend declared in April.
June	1	Announced a 2-for-1 stock split. Prior to the split, the market price per share was $24.
Aug.	1	Declared a 10% stock dividend to stockholders of record on August 15, distributable August 31. On August 1, the market price of the stock was $10 per share.
	31	Issued the shares for the stock dividend.
Dec.	1	Declared a $1.50 per share dividend to stockholders of record on December 15, payable January 5, 2009.
	31	Determined that net income for the year was $600,000.

Instructions
(a) Journalize the transactions and the closing entry for net income.
(b) Prepare a stockholders' equity section at December 31.

action plan
✔ Award dividends to outstanding shares only.
✔ Adjust the par value and number of shares for stock splits, but make no journal entry.
✔ Use market value of stock to determine the value of a small stock dividend.
✔ Close Income Summary to Retained Earnings.

Solution to Comprehensive DO IT!

(a)

Apr. 1		Retained Earnings (260,000 × $1.50)	390,000	
		Dividends Payable		390,000
May 1		Dividends Payable	390,000	
		Cash		390,000
June 1		Memo—two-for-one stock split increases number of shares to 520,000 (260,000 × 2) and reduces par value to $5 per share.		
Aug. 1		Retained Earnings (52,000* × $10)	520,000	
		Common Stock Dividends Distributable (52,000 × $5)		260,000
		Paid-in Capital in Excess of Par Value (52,000 × $5)		260,000
		*520,000 × .10		
	31	Common Stock Dividends Distributable	260,000	
		Common Stock		260,000
Dec. 1		Retained Earnings (572,000** × $1.50)	858,000	
		Dividends Payable		858,000
		**(260,000 × 2) + 52,000		
	31	Income Summary	600,000	
		Retained Earnings		600,000

(b)

HAYSLETT CORPORATION

Stockholders' equity	
Paid-in capital	
Capital stock	
Common stock, $5 par value, 572,000 shares issued and outstanding	$2,860,000
Additional paid-in capital in excess of par value	1,760,000
Total paid-in capital	4,620,000
Retained earnings	2,032,000
Total stockholders' equity	$6,652,000

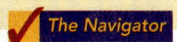

SUMMARY OF STUDY OBJECTIVES

1. **Prepare the entries for cash dividends and stock dividends.** Companies make entries for both cash and stock dividends at the declaration date and at the payment date. At the *declaration date* the entries are: cash dividend—debit Retained Earnings, and credit Dividends Payable; small stock dividend—debit Retained Earnings, credit Paid-in Capital in Excess of Par (or Stated) Value, and credit Common Stock Dividends Distributable. At the *payment date,* the entries for cash and stock dividends are: cash dividend—debit Dividends Payable and credit Cash; small stock dividend—debit Common Stock Dividends Distributable and credit Common Stock.

2. **Identify the items reported in a retained earnings statement.** Companies report each of the individual debits and credits to retained earnings in the retained earnings statement. Additions consist of net income and prior period adjustments to correct understatements of prior years' net income. Deductions consist of net loss, adjustments to correct overstatements of prior years' net income, cash and stock dividends, and some disposals of treasury stock.

3. **Prepare and analyze a comprehensive stockholders' equity section.** A comprehensive stockholders' equity section includes all stockholders' equity accounts. It consists of two sections: paid-in capital and retained earnings. It should also include notes to the financial statements that explain any restrictions on retained earnings and any dividends in arrears. One measure of profitability is the return on common stockholders' equity. It is calculated by dividing net income minus preferred stock dividends by average common stockholders' equity.

4. **Describe the form and content of corporation income statements.** The form and content of corporation income statements are similar to the statements of proprietorships and partnerships with one exception: Corporations must report income taxes or income tax expense in a separate section before net income in the income statement.

5. **Compute earnings per share.** Companies compute earnings per share by dividing net income by the weighted-average number of common shares outstanding during the period. When preferred stock dividends exist, they must be deducted from net income in order to calculate EPS.

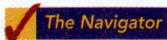

GLOSSARY

Cash dividend A pro rata distribution of cash to stockholders. (p. 608).

Declaration date The date the board of directors formally declares a dividend and announces it to stockholders. (p. 609).

Deficit A debit balance in retained earnings. (p. 617).

Dividend A corporation's distribution of cash or stock to its stockholders on a pro rata (proportional) basis. (p. 608).

Earnings per share The net income earned by each share of outstanding common stock. (p 622).

Liquidating dividend A dividend declared out of paid-in capital. (p. 608).

Payment date The date dividend checks are mailed to stockholders. (p. 610).

Prior period adjustment The correction of an error in previously issued financial statements. (p. 618).

Record date The date when ownership of outstanding shares is determined for dividend purposes. (p. 609).

Retained earnings Net income that is retained in the business. (p. 616).

Retained earnings restrictions Circumstances that make a portion of retained earnings currently unavailable for dividends. (p. 617).

Retained earnings statement A financial statement that shows the changes in retained earnings during the year. (p. 619).

Return on common stockholders' equity A measure of profitability that shows how many dollars of net income were earned for each dollar invested by the owners; computed as net income minus preferred dividends divided by average common stockholders' equity. (p. 621).

Stock dividend A pro rata distribution to stockholders of the corporation's own stock. (p. 612).

Stockholders' equity statement A statement that shows the changes in each stockholders' equity account and in total stockholders' equity during the year. (p. 621).

Stock split The issuance of additional shares of stock to stockholders according to their percentage ownership; is accompanied by a reduction in the par or stated value per share. (p. 614).

SELF-STUDY QUESTIONS

Answers are at the end of the chapter.

(SO 1) **1.** Entries for cash dividends are required on the:
   a. declaration date and the payment date.
   b. record date and the payment date.
   c. declaration date, record date, and payment date.
   d. declaration date and the record date.

(SO 1) **2.** Which of the following statements about small stock dividends is true?
   a. A debit to Retained Earnings for the par value of the shares issued should be made.
   b. A small stock dividend decreases total stockholders' equity.
   c. Market value per share should be assigned to the dividend shares.
   d. A small stock dividend ordinarily will have no effect on book value per share of stock.

(SO 1) **3.** Which of the following statements about a 3-for-1 stock split is true?
   a. It will triple the market value of the stock.
   b. It will triple the amount of total stockholders' equity.
   c. It will have no effect on total stockholders' equity.
   d. It requires the company to distribute cash.

(SO 1) **4.** Encore Inc. declared an $80,000 cash dividend. It currently has 3,000 shares of 7%, $100 par value cumulative preferred stock outstanding. It is one year in arrears on its preferred stock. How much cash will Encore distribute to the common stockholders?
   a. $38,000.
   b. $42,000.
   c. $59,000.
   d. None.

(SO 1) **5.** Raptor Inc. has retained earnings of $500,000 and total stockholders' equity of $2,000,000. It has 100,000 shares of $8 par value common stock outstanding, which is currently selling for $30 per share. If Raptor declares a 10% stock dividend on its common stock:
   a. net income will decrease by $80,000.
   b. retained earnings will decrease by $80,000 and total stockholders' equity will increase by $80,000.
   c. retained earnings will decrease by $300,000 and total stockholders' equity will increase by $300,000.
   d. retained earnings will decrease by $300,000 and total paid-in capital will increase by $300,000.

(SO 2) **6.** Which of the following can cause a restriction in retained earnings?
   a. State laws regarding treasury stock.
   b. Long-term debt contract terms.
   c. Authorizations by the board of directors in light of planned expansion of corporate facilities.
   d. All of the above.

(SO 2) **7.** All *but one* of the following is reported in a retained earnings statement. The exception is:
   a. cash and stock dividends.
   b. net income and net loss.
   c. sales revenue.
   d. prior period adjustments.

(SO 2) **8.** A prior period adjustment is:
   a. reported in the income statement as a nontypical item.
   b. a correction of an error that is made directly to retained earnings.
   c. reported directly in the stockholders' equity section.
   d. reported in the retained earnings statement as an adjustment of the ending balance of retained earnings.

(SO 3) **9.** In the stockholders' equity section, Common Stock Dividends Distributable is reported as a(n):
   a. deduction from total paid-in capital and retained earnings.
   b. addition to additional paid-in capital.
   c. deduction from retained earnings.
   d. addition to capital stock.

(SO 3) **10.** Katie Inc. reported net income of $186,000 during 2010 and paid dividends of $26,000 on common stock. It also has 10,000 shares of 6%, $100 par value, noncumulative preferred stock outstanding. Common stockholders' equity was $1,200,000 on January 1, 2010, and $1,600,000 on December 31, 2010. The company's return on common stockholders' equity for 2010 is:
   a. 10.0%.
   b. 9.0%.
   c. 7.1%.
   d. 13.3%.

(SO 4) 11. Corporation income statements may be the same as the income statements for unincorporated companies *except* for:
  a. gross profit.
  b. income tax expense.
  c. operating income.
  d. net sales.

(SO 4) 12. During 2010 Talon Inc. had sales revenue $376,000, gross profit $176,000, operating expenses $66,000, cash dividends $30,000, other expenses and losses $20,000. Its corporate tax rate is 30%. What was Talon's income tax expense for the year?
  a. $18,000.
  b. $52,800.
  c. $112,800.
  d. $27,000.

(SO 3) 13. The return on common stockholders' equity is defined as:
  a. Net income divided by total assets.
  b. Cash dividends divided by average common stockholders' equity.
  c. Income available to common stockholders divided by average common stockholders' equity.
  d. None of these is correct.

(SO 5) 14. If everything else is held constant, earnings per share is increased by:
  a. the payment of a cash dividend to common shareholders.
  b. the payment of a cash dividend to preferred shareholders.
  c. the issuance of new shares of common stock.
  d. the purchase of treasury stock.

(SO 5) 15. The income statement for Nadeen, Inc. shows income before income taxes $700,000, income tax expense $210,000, and net income $490,000. If Nadeen has 100,000 shares of common stock outstanding throughout the year, earnings per share is:
  a. $7.00.
  b. $4.90.
  c. $2.10.
  d. No correct answer is given.

Go to the book's companion website,
www.wiley.com/college/weygandt,
for Additional Self-Study questions.

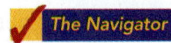

QUESTIONS

1. (a) What is a dividend? (b) "Dividends must be paid in cash." Do you agree? Explain.
2. Sue DeVine maintains that adequate cash is the only requirement for the declaration of a cash dividend. Is Sue correct? Explain.
3. (a) Three dates are important in connection with cash dividends. Identify these dates, and explain their significance to the corporation and its stockholders.
   (b) Identify the accounting entries that are made for a cash dividend and the date of each entry.
4. Conger Inc. declares a $45,000 cash dividend on December 31, 2010. The required annual dividend on preferred stock is $10,000. Determine the allocation of the dividend to preferred and common stockholders assuming the preferred stock is cumulative and dividends are 1 year in arrears.
5. Contrast the effects of a cash dividend and a stock dividend on a corporation's balance sheet.
6. Todd Huebner asks, "Since stock dividends don't change anything, why declare them?" What is your answer to Todd?
7. Meenen Corporation has 30,000 shares of $10 par value common stock outstanding when it announces a 2-for-1 stock split. Before the split, the stock had a market price of $120 per share. After the split, how many shares of stock will be outstanding? What will be the approximate market price per share?
8. The board of directors is considering either a stock split or a stock dividend. They understand that total stockholders' equity will remain the same under either action. However, they are not sure of the different effects of the two types of actions on other aspects of stockholders' equity. Explain the differences to the directors.
9. What is a prior period adjustment, and how is it reported in the financial statements?
10. KSU Corporation has a retained earnings balance of $210,000 on January 1. During the year, a prior period adjustment of $50,000 is recorded because of the understatement of depreciation in the prior period. Show the retained earnings statement presentation of these data.
11. What is the purpose of a retained earnings restriction? Identify the possible causes of retained earnings restrictions.
12. How are retained earnings restrictions generally reported in the financial statements?
13. Identify the events that result in debits and credits to retained earnings.
14. Juan Ortega believes that both the beginning and ending balances in retained earnings are shown in the stockholders' equity section. Is Juan correct? Discuss.
15. Gene Remington, who owns many investments in common stock, says, "I don't care what a company's net income is. The stock price tells me everything I need to know!" How do you respond to Gene?
16. What is the unique feature of a corporation income statement? Illustrate this feature, using assumed data.
17. Why must preferred stock dividends be subtracted from net income in computing earnings per share?
18. **PEPSICO** What were the amounts of the dividends PepsiCo declared per share of common stock in the years 2003 to 2007? Is the trend in dividends consistent with the company's net income trend during the period?

BRIEF EXERCISES

BE14-1 Eidman Corporation has 80,000 shares of common stock outstanding. It declares a $1 per share cash dividend on November 1 to stockholders of record on December 1. The dividend is paid on December 31. Prepare the entries on the appropriate dates to record the declaration and payment of the cash dividend.

Prepare entries for a cash dividend.
(SO 1)

BE14-2 Tidwell Corporation has 50,000 shares of $10 par value common stock outstanding. It declares a 10% stock dividend on December 1 when the market value per share is $16. The dividend shares are issued on December 31. Prepare the entries for the declaration and payment of the stock dividend.

Prepare entries for a stock dividend.
(SO 1)

BE14-3 The stockholders' equity section of O'Vear Corporation consists of common stock ($10 par) $2,000,000 and retained earnings $500,000. A 10% stock dividend (20,000 shares) is declared when the market value per share is $14. Show the before and after effects of the dividend on the following.

(a) The components of stockholders' equity.
(b) Shares outstanding.
(c) Par value per share.

Show before and after effects of a stock dividend.
(SO 1)

BE14-4 For the year ending December 31, 2010, Kerns Inc. reports net income $140,000 and dividends $85,000. Prepare the retained earnings statement for the year assuming the balance in retained earnings on January 1, 2010, was $220,000.

Prepare a retained earnings statement.
(SO 2)

BE14-5 The balance in retained earnings on January 1, 2010, for Persinger Inc, was $800,000. During the year, the corporation paid cash dividends of $90,000 and distributed a stock dividend of $8,000. In addition, the company determined that it had understated its depreciation expense in prior years by $50,000. Net income for 2010 was $120,000. Prepare the retained earnings statement for 2010.

Prepare a retained earnings statement.
(SO 2)

BE14-6 SUPERVALU, one of the largest grocery retailers in the United States, is headquartered in Minneapolis. The following financial information (in millions) was taken from the company's 2007 annual report. Net sales $37,406; net income $452; beginning stockholders' equity $2,619; ending stockholders' equity $5,306. Compute the return on common stockholders' equity ratio.

Calculate the return on common stockholders' equity.
(SO 3)

BE14-7 Fuentes Corporation reported net income of $152,000, declared dividends on common stock of $50,000, and had an ending balance in retained earnings of $360,000. Stockholders' equity was $700,000 at the beginning of the year and $820,000 at the end of the year. Compute the return on common stockholders' equity.

Compute return on common stockholders' equity.
(SO 3)

BE14-8 The following information is available for Dixen Corporation for the year ended December 31, 2010: Cost of goods sold $205,000; Sales $450,000; Other revenues and gains $50,000; Operating expenses $75,000. Assuming a corporate tax rate of 30%, prepare an income statement for the company.

Prepare a corporate income statement.
(SO 4)

BE14-9 Quayle Corporation reports net income of $380,000 and a weighted average of 200,000 shares of common stock outstanding for the year. Compute the earnings per share of common stock.

Compute earnings per share.
(SO 5)

BE14-10 Income and common stock data for Quayle Corporation are presented in BE14-9. Assume also that Quayle has cumulative preferred stock dividends for the current year of $20,000 that were declared and paid. Compute the earnings per share of common stock.

Compute earnings per share with cumulative preferred stock.
(SO 5)

DO IT! REVIEW

DO IT! 14-1 Mensa Corporation has 3,000 shares of 7%, $100 par value preferred stock outstanding at December 31, 2010. At December 31, 2010, the company declared a $105,000 cash dividend. Determine the dividend paid to preferred stockholders and common stockholders under each of the following scenarios.

Determine dividends paid to preferred and common stockholders.
(SO 1)

1. The preferred stock is noncumulative, and the company has not missed any dividends in previous years.

Chapter 14 Corporations: Dividends, Retained Earnings, and Income Reporting

2. The preferred stock is noncumulative, and the company did not pay a dividend in each of the two previous years.
3. The preferred stock is cumulative, and the company did not pay a dividend in each of the two previous years.

Determine effects of stock dividend and stock split.
(SO 1)

DO IT! 14-2 Riff CD Company has had 4 years of retained earnings. Due to this success, the market price of its 400,000 shares of $3 par value common stock has increased from $12 per share to $51. During this period, paid-in capital remained the same at $2,400,000. Retained earnings increased from $1,800,000 to $12,000,000. CEO Josh Borke is considering either (1) a 15% stock dividend or (2) a 2-for-1 stock split. He asks you to show the before-and-after effects of each option on (a) retained earnings and (b) total stockholders' equity.

Prepare a retained earnings statement.
(SO 2)

DO IT! 14-3 Alpha Centuri Corporation has retained earnings of $3,100,000 on January 1, 2010. During the year, Alpha Centuri earned $1,200,000 of net income. It declared and paid a $150,000 cash dividend. In 2010, Alpha Centuri recorded an adjustment of $110,000 due to the overstatement (from mathematical error) of 2009 depreciation expense. Prepare a retained earnings statement for 2010.

Compute return on stockholders' equity and EPS and discuss changes in each.
(SO 3, 5)

DO IT! 14-4 On January 1, 2010, Tuscany Corporation purchased 1,000 shares of treasury stock. Other information regarding Tuscany Corporation is provided below.

	2009	2010
Net income	$200,000	$210,000
Dividends on preferred stock	$30,000	$30,000
Dividends on common stock	$20,000	$25,000
Weighted average number of common shares outstanding	10,000	9,000
Common stockholders' equity beginning of year	$600,000	$750,000
Common stockholders' equity end of year	$750,000	$830,000

Compute (a) return on common stockholders' equity for each year and (b) earnings per share for each year, and (c) discuss the changes in each.

EXERCISES

Journalize cash dividends; indicate statement presentation.
(SO 1)

E14-1 On January 1, Molini Corporation had 95,000 shares of no-par common stock issued and outstanding. The stock has a stated value of $5 per share. During the year, the following occurred.

Apr. 1 Issued 25,000 additional shares of common stock for $17 per share.
June 15 Declared a cash dividend of $1 per share to stockholders of record on June 30.
July 10 Paid the $1 cash dividend.
Dec. 1 Issued 2,000 additional shares of common stock for $19 per share.
     15 Declared a cash dividend on outstanding shares of $1.20 per share to stockholders of record on December 31.

Instructions
(a) Prepare the entries, if any, on each of the three dividend dates.
(b) How are dividends and dividends payable reported in the financial statements prepared at December 31?

Allocate cash dividends to preferred and common stock.
(SO 1)

E14-2 Perez Corporation was organized on January 1, 2009. During its first year, the corporation issued 2,000 shares of $50 par value preferred stock and 100,000 shares of $10 par value common stock. At December 31, the company declared the following cash dividends: 2009, $6,000, 2010, $12,000, and 2011, $28,000.

Instructions
(a) Show the allocation of dividends to each class of stock, assuming the preferred stock dividend is 7% and not cumulative.
(b) Show the allocation of dividends to each class of stock, assuming the preferred stock dividend is 8% and cumulative.
(c) Journalize the declaration of the cash dividend at December 31, 2011, under part (b).

Journalize stock dividends.
(SO 1)

E14-3 On January 1, 2010, Deweese Corporation had $1,000,000 of common stock outstanding that was issued at par. It also had retained earnings of $750,000. The company issued 40,000 shares of common stock at par on July 1 and earned net income of $400,000 for the year.

Instructions

Journalize the declaration of a 15% stock dividend on December 10, 2010, for the following independent assumptions.

1. Par value is $10, and market value is $18.
2. Par value is $5, and market value is $20.

E14-4 On October 31, the stockholders' equity section of Huth Company consists of common stock $300,000 and retained earnings $900,000. Huth is considering the following two courses of action: (1) declaring a 5% stock dividend on the 30,000, $10 par value shares outstanding, or (2) effecting a 2-for-1 stock split that will reduce par value to $5 per share. The current market price is $14 per share.

Compare effects of a stock dividend and a stock split.
(SO 1)

Instructions

Prepare a tabular summary of the effects of the alternative actions on the components of stockholders' equity, outstanding shares, and par value per share. Use the following column headings: Before Action, After Stock Dividend, and After Stock Split.

E14-5 On October 1, Kosko Corporation's stockholders' equity is as follows.

Indicate account balances after a stock dividend.
(SO 1, 3)

Common stock, $5 par value	$400,000
Paid-in capital in excess of par value	25,000
Retained earnings	155,000
Total stockholders' equity	$580,000

On October 1, Kosko declares and distributes a 10% stock dividend when the market value of the stock is $15 per share.

Instructions

(a) Compute the par value per share (1) before the stock dividend and (2) after the stock dividend.
(b) Indicate the balances in the three stockholders' equity accounts after the stock dividend shares have been distributed.

E14-6 During 2010, Jester Corporation had the following transactions and events.

1. Declared a cash dividend.
2. Issued par value common stock for cash at par value.
3. Completed a 2-for-1 stock split in which $10 par value stock was changed to $5 par value stock.
4. Declared a small stock dividend when the market value was higher than par value.
5. Made a prior period adjustment for overstatement of net income.
6. Issued the shares of common stock required by the stock dividend declaration in item no. 4 above.
7. Paid the cash dividend in item no. 1 above.
8. Issued par value common stock for cash above par value.

Indicate the effects on stockholders' equity components.
(SO 1, 2, 3)

Instructions

Indicate the effect(s) of each of the foregoing items on the subdivisions of stockholders' equity. Present your answer in tabular form with the following columns. Use (I) for increase, (D) for decrease, and (NE) for no effect. Item no. 1 is given as an example.

	Paid-in Capital		
Item	Capital Stock	Additional	Retained Earnings
1	NE	NE	D

E14-7 Before preparing financial statements for the current year, the chief accountant for Reynolds Company discovered the following errors in the accounts.

Prepare correcting entries for dividends and a stock split.
(SO 1)

1. The declaration and payment of $50,000 cash dividend was recorded as a debit to Interest Expense $50,000 and a credit to Cash $50,000.
2. A 10% stock dividend (1,000 shares) was declared on the $10 par value stock when the market value per share was $18. The only entry made was: Retained Earnings (Dr.) $10,000 and Dividend Payable (Cr.) $10,000. The shares have not been issued.

3. A 4-for-1 stock split involving the issue of 400,000 shares of $5 par value common stock for 100,000 shares of $20 par value common stock was recorded as a debit to Retained Earnings $2,000,000 and a credit to Common Stock $2,000,000.

Instructions
Prepare the correcting entries at December 31.

E14-8 On January 1, 2010, Felter Corporation had retained earnings of $550,000. During the year, Felter had the following selected transactions.

1. Declared cash dividends $120,000.
2. Corrected overstatement of 2009 net income because of depreciation error $40,000.
3. Earned net income $350,000.
4. Declared stock dividends $60,000.

Instructions
Prepare a retained earnings statement for the year.

E14-9 Sasha Company reported retained earnings at December 31, 2009, of $310,000. Sasha had 200,000 shares of common stock outstanding throughout 2010.
   The following transactions occurred during 2010.

1. An error was discovered: in 2008, depreciation expense was recorded at $70,000, but the correct amount was $50,000.
2. A cash dividend of $0.50 per share was declared and paid.
3. A 5% stock dividend was declared and distributed when the market price per share was $15 per share.
4. Net income was $285,000.

Instructions
Prepare a retained earnings statement for 2010.

E14-10 Kelly Groucutt Company reported the following balances at December 31, 2009: common stock $400,000; paid-in capital in excess of par value $100,000; retained earnings $250,000. During 2010, the following transactions affected stockholder's equity.

1. Issued preferred stock with a par value of $125,000 for $200,000.
2. Purchased treasury stock (common) for $40,000.
3. Earned net income of $140,000.
4. Declared and paid cash dividends of $56,000.

Instructions
Prepare the stockholders' equity section of Kelly Groucutt Company's December 31, 2010, balance sheet.

E14-11 The following accounts appear in the ledger of Ortiz Inc. after the books are closed at December 31.

Common Stock, no par, $1 stated value, 400,000 shares authorized; 300,000 shares issued	$ 300,000
Common Stock Dividends Distributable	30,000
Paid-in Capital in Excess of Stated Value—Common Stock	1,200,000
Preferred Stock, $5 par value, 8%, 40,000 shares authorized; 30,000 shares issued	150,000
Retained Earnings	800,000
Treasury Stock (10,000 common shares)	74,000
Paid-in Capital in Excess of Par Value—Preferred Stock	344,000

Instructions
Prepare the stockholders' equity section at December 31, assuming retained earnings is restricted for plant expansion in the amount of $100,000.

E14-12 The following information is available for Patel Corporation for the year ended December 31, 2010: Sales $800,000; Other revenues and gains $92,000; Operating expenses $110,000; Cost of goods sold $465,000; Other expenses and losses $32,000; Preferred stock dividends $30,000. The company's tax rate was 20%, and it had 50,000 shares outstanding during the entire year.

Instructions

(a) Prepare a corporate income statement.
(b) Calculate earnings per share.

E14-13 In 2010, Mike Singletary Corporation had net sales of $600,000 and cost of goods sold of $360,000. Operating expenses were $153,000, and interest expense was $7,500. The corporation's tax rate is 30%. The corporation declared preferred dividends of $15,000 in 2010, and its average common stockholders' equity during the year was $200,000.

Prepare an income statement and compute return on equity.
(SO 3, 4)

Instructions

(a) Prepare an income statement for Mike Singletary Corporation.
(b) Compute Mike Singletary Corporation's return on common stockholders' equity for 2010.

E14-14 McCoy Corporation has outstanding at December 31, 2010, 50,000 shares of $20 par value, cumulative, 8% preferred stock and 200,000 shares of $5 par value common stock. All shares were outstanding the entire year. During 2010, McCoy earned total revenues of $2,000,000 and incurred total expenses (except income taxes) of $1,200,000. McCoy's income tax rate is 30%.

Compute EPS.
(SO 4, 5)

Instructions
Compute McCoy's 2010 earnings per share.

E14-15 The following financial information is available for Cheney Corporation.

Calculate ratios to evaluate earnings performance.
(SO 3, 5)

	2010	2009
Average common stockholders' equity	$1,200,000	$900,000
Dividends paid to common stockholders	50,000	30,000
Dividends paid to preferred stockholders	20,000	20,000
Net income	290,000	200,000
Market price of common stock	20	15

The weighted average number of shares of common stock outstanding was 80,000 for 2009 and 100,000 for 2010.

Instructions
Calculate earnings per share and return on common stockholders' equity for 2010 and 2009.

E14-16 This financial information is available for Hoyle Corporation.

Calculate ratios to evaluate earnings performance.
(SO 3, 5)

	2010	2009
Average common stockholders' equity	$1,800,000	$1,900,000
Dividends paid to common stockholders	90,000	70,000
Dividends paid to preferred stockholders	20,000	20,000
Net income	290,000	248,000
Market price of common stock	20	25

The weighted-average number of shares of common stock outstanding was 180,000 for 2009 and 150,000 for 2010.

Instructions
Calculate earnings per share and return on common stockholders' equity for 2010 and 2009.

E14-17 At December 31, 2010, Cali Corporation has 2,000 shares of $100 par value, 8%, preferred stock outstanding and 100,000 shares of $10 par value common stock issued. Cali's net income for the year is $241,000.

Compute earnings per share under different assumptions.
(SO 5)

Instructions
Compute the earnings per share of common stock under the following independent situations. (Round to two decimals.)

(a) The dividend to preferred stockholders was declared. There has been no change in the number of shares of common stock outstanding during the year.
(b) The dividend to preferred stockholders was not declared. The preferred stock is cumulative. Cali held 10,000 shares of common treasury stock throughout the year.

634 Chapter 14 Corporations: Dividends, Retained Earnings, and Income Reporting

EXERCISES: SET B

Visit the book's companion website at **www.wiley.com/college/weygandt**, and choose the Student Companion site, to access Exercise Set B.

PROBLEMS: SET A

Prepare dividend entries and stockholders' equity section.

(SO 1, 3)

P14-1A On January 1, 2010, Carolinas Corporation had the following stockholders' equity accounts.

Common Stock ($20 par value, 60,000 shares issued and outstanding)	$1,200,000
Paid-in Capital in Excess of Par Value	200,000
Retained Earnings	600,000

During the year, the following transactions occurred.

- Feb. 1 Declared a $1 cash dividend per share to stockholders of record on February 15, payable March 1.
- Mar. 1 Paid the dividend declared in February.
- Apr. 1 Announced a 2-for-1 stock split. Prior to the split, the market price per share was $36.
- July 1 Declared a 10% stock dividend to stockholders of record on July 15, distributable July 31. On July 1, the market price of the stock was $13 per share.
- 31 Issued the shares for the stock dividend.
- Dec. 1 Declared a $0.50 per share dividend to stockholders of record on December 15, payable January 5, 2011.
- 31 Determined that net income for the year was $350,000.

Instructions

(a) Journalize the transactions and the closing entry for net income.
(b) Enter the beginning balances, and post the entries to the stockholders' equity accounts. (*Note*: Open additional stockholders' equity accounts as needed.)
(c) Prepare a stockholders' equity section at December 31.

(c) Total stockholders' equity $2,224,000

Journalize and post transactions; prepare retained earnings statement and stockholders' equity section.

(SO 1, 2, 3)

P14-2A The stockholders' equity accounts of Hashmi Company at January 1, 2010, are as follows.

Preferred Stock, 6%, $50 par	$600,000
Common Stock, $5 par	800,000
Paid-in Capital in Excess of Par Value—Preferred Stock	200,000
Paid-in Capital in Excess of Par Value—Common Stock	300,000
Retained Earnings	800,000

There were no dividends in arrears on preferred stock. During 2010, the company had the following transactions and events.

- July 1 Declared a $0.50 cash dividend on common stock.
- Aug. 1 Discovered $25,000 understatement of 2009 depreciation. Ignore income taxes.
- Sept. 1 Paid the cash dividend declared on July 1.
- Dec. 1 Declared a 10% stock dividend on common stock when the market value of the stock was $18 per share.
- 15 Declared a 6% cash dividend on preferred stock payable January 15, 2011.
- 31 Determined that net income for the year was $355,000.
- 31 Recognized a $200,000 restriction of retained earnings for plant expansion.

Instructions

(a) Journalize the transactions, events, and closing entry.
(b) Enter the beginning balances in the accounts, and post to the stockholders' equity accounts. (*Note*: Open additional stockholders' equity accounts as needed.)
(c) Prepare a retained earnings statement for the year.
(d) Prepare a stockholders' equity section at December 31, 2010.

(c) Ending balance $726,000
(d) Total stockholders' equity $2,914,000

P14-3A The post-closing trial balance of Dold Corporation at December 31, 2010, contains the following stockholders' equity accounts.

Preferred Stock (15,000 shares issued)	$ 750,000
Common Stock (250,000 shares issued)	2,500,000
Paid-in Capital in Excess of Par Value—Preferred	250,000
Paid-in Capital in Excess of Par Value—Common	400,000
Common Stock Dividends Distributable	250,000
Retained Earnings	1,042,000

Prepare retained earnings statement and stockholders' equity section, and compute earnings per share.

(SO 1, 2, 3, 5)

A review of the accounting records reveals the following.

1. No errors have been made in recording 2010 transactions or in preparing the closing entry for net income.
2. Preferred stock is $50 par, 6%, and cumulative; 15,000 shares have been outstanding since January 1, 2009.
3. Authorized stock is 20,000 shares of preferred, 500,000 shares of common with a $10 par value.
4. The January 1 balance in Retained Earnings was $1,170,000.
5. On July 1, 20,000 shares of common stock were issued for cash at $16 per share.
6. On September 1, the company discovered an understatement error of $90,000 in computing depreciation in 2009. The net of tax effect of $63,000 was properly debited directly to Retained Earnings.
7. A cash dividend of $250,000 was declared and properly allocated to preferred and common stock on October 1. No dividends were paid to preferred stockholders in 2009.
8. On December 31, a 10% common stock dividend was declared out of retained earnings on common stock when the market price per share was $16.
9. Net income for the year was $585,000.
10. On December 31, 2010, the directors authorized disclosure of a $200,000 restriction of retained earnings for plant expansion. (Use Note X.)

Instructions
(a) Reproduce the Retained Earnings account for 2010.
(b) Prepare a retained earnings statement for 2010.
(c) Prepare a stockholders' equity section at December 31, 2010.
(d) Compute the allocation of the cash dividend to preferred and common stock.
(e) Compute the earnings per share of common stock using 240,000 as the weighted average shares outstanding for the year.

(c) Total stockholders' equity, $5,192,000

P14-4A On January 1, 2010, Pattini Corporation had the following stockholders' equity accounts.

Common Stock (no par value, 90,000 shares issued and outstanding)	$1,400,000
Retained Earnings	500,000

Prepare the stockholders' equity section, reflecting dividends and stock split.

(SO 1, 2, 3)

During the year, the following transactions occurred.

Feb. 1 Declared a $1 cash dividend per share to stockholders of record on February 15, payable March 1.
Mar. 1 Paid the dividend declared in February.
Apr. 1 Announced a 4-for-1 stock split. Prior to the split, the market price per share was $36.
July 1 Declared a 5% stock dividend to stockholders of record on July 15, distributable July 31. On July 1, the market price of the stock was $13 per share.
    31 Issued the shares for the stock dividend.
Dec. 1 Declared a $0.50 per share dividend to stockholders of record on December 15, payable January 5, 2011.
    31 Determined that net income for the year was $350,000.

Instructions
Prepare the stockholders' equity section of the balance sheet at: (a) March 31, (b) June 30, (c) September 30, and (d) December 31, 2010.

(d) Total stockholders' equity $1,971,000

P14-5A On January 1, 2010, Yadier Inc. had the following stockholders' equity account balances.

Common Stock, no-par value (500,000 shares issued)	$1,500,000
Common Stock Dividends Distributable	200,000
Retained Earnings	600,000

Prepare the stockholders' equity section, reflecting various events.

(SO 1, 3)

636 Chapter 14 Corporations: Dividends, Retained Earnings, and Income Reporting

During 2010, the following transactions and events occurred.

1. Issued 50,000 shares of common stock as a result of a 10% stock dividend declared on December 15, 2009.
2. Issued 30,000 shares of common stock for cash at $6 per share.
3. Corrected an error that had understated the net income for 2008 by $70,000.
4. Declared and paid a cash dividend of $80,000.
5. Earned net income of $300,000.

Total stockholders' equity $2,770,000

Instructions

Prepare the stockholders' equity section of the balance sheet at December 31, 2010.

PROBLEMS: SET B

Prepare dividend entries and stockholders' equity section.

(SO 1, 3)

P14-1B On January 1, 2010, Weiser Corporation had the following stockholders' equity accounts.

Common Stock ($5 par value, 200,000 shares issued and outstanding)	$1,000,000
Paid-in Capital in Excess of Par Value	200,000
Retained Earnings	840,000

During the year, the following transactions occurred.

Jan. 15 Declared a $1 cash dividend per share to stockholders of record on January 31, payable February 15.
Feb. 15 Paid the dividend declared in January.
Apr. 15 Declared a 10% stock dividend to stockholders of record on April 30, distributable May 15. On April 15, the market price of the stock was $15 per share.
May 15 Issued the shares for the stock dividend.
July 1 Announced a 2-for-1 stock split. The market price per share prior to the announcement was $17. (The new par value is $2.50.)
Dec. 1 Declared a $0.50 per share cash dividend to stockholders of record on December 15, payable January 10, 2011.
31 Determined that net income for the year was $250,000.

Instructions

(a) Journalize the transactions and the closing entry for net income.
(b) Enter the beginning balances, and post the entries to the stockholders' equity accounts. (*Note*: Open additional stockholders' equity accounts as needed.)
(c) Prepare a stockholders' equity section at December 31.

(c) Total stockholders' equity $1,870,000

Journalize and post transactions; prepare retained earnings statement and stockholders' equity section.

(SO 1, 2, 3)

P14-2B The stockholders' equity accounts of Holmes Inc., at January 1, 2010, are as follows.

Preferred Stock, $100 par, 7%	$600,000
Common Stock, $10 par	900,000
Paid-in Capital in Excess of Par Value—Preferred Stock	100,000
Paid-in Capital in Excess of Par Value—Common Stock	200,000
Retained Earnings	500,000

There were no dividends in arrears on preferred stock. During 2010, the company had the following transactions and events.

July 1 Declared a $0.50 cash dividend on common stock.
Aug. 1 Discovered a $72,000 overstatement of 2009 depreciation. Ignore income taxes.
Sept. 1 Paid the cash dividend declared on July 1.
Dec. 1 Declared a 10% stock dividend on common stock when the market value of the stock was $16 per share.
15 Declared a 7% cash dividend on preferred stock payable January 31, 2011.
31 Determined that net income for the year was $350,000.

Instructions

(a) Journalize the transactions and the closing entry for net income.
(b) Enter the beginning balances in the accounts and post to the stockholders' equity accounts. (*Note*: Open additional stockholders' equity accounts as needed.)

(c) Prepare a retained earnings statement for the year.
(d) Prepare a stockholders' equity section at December 31, 2010.

(c) Ending balance $691,000
(d) Total stockholders' equity $2,635,000

P14-3B The ledger of Yakima Corporation at December 31, 2010, after the books have been closed, contains the following stockholders' equity accounts.

Prepare retained earnings statement and stockholders' equity section, and compute earnings per share.
(SO 1, 2, 3, 5)

Preferred Stock (10,000 shares issued)	$1,000,000
Common Stock (400,000 shares issued)	2,000,000
Paid-in Capital in Excess of Par Value—Preferred	200,000
Paid-in Capital in Excess of Stated Value—Common	1,180,000
Common Stock Dividends Distributable	200,000
Retained Earnings	2,560,000

A review of the accounting records reveals the following.

1. No errors have been made in recording 2010 transactions or in preparing the closing entry for net income.
2. Preferred stock is 6%, $100 par value, noncumulative, and callable at $125. Since January 1, 2009, 10,000 shares have been outstanding; 20,000 shares are authorized.
3. Common stock is no-par with a stated value of $5 per share; 600,000 shares are authorized.
4. The January 1 balance in Retained Earnings was $2,450,000.
5. On October 1, 100,000 shares of common stock were sold for cash at $8 per share.
6. A cash dividend of $500,000 was declared and properly allocated to preferred and common stock on November 1. No dividends were paid to preferred stockholders in 2009.
7. On December 31, a 10% common stock dividend was declared out of retained earnings on common stock when the market price per share was $9.
8. Net income for the year was $970,000.
9. On December 31, 2010, the directors authorized disclosure of a $100,000 restriction of retained earnings for plant expansion. (Use Note A.)

Instructions
(a) Reproduce the Retained Earnings account (T-account) for 2010.
(b) Prepare a retained earnings statement for 2010.
(c) Prepare a stockholders' equity section at December 31, 2010.
(d) Compute the allocation of the cash dividend to preferred and common stock.
(e) Compute the earnings per share of common stock using 325,000 as the weighted average shares outstanding for the year.

(c) Total stockholders' equity: $7,140,000

P14-4B On January 1, 2010, Carne Corporation had the following stockholders' equity accounts.

Prepare the stockholders' equity section, reflecting dividends and stock split.
(SO 1, 2, 3)

Common Stock (no-par value, 100,000 shares issued and outstanding)	$2,800,000
Retained Earnings	1,000,000

During the year, the following transactions occurred.

Feb. 1 Declared a $1 cash dividend per share to stockholders of record on February 15, payable March 1.
Mar. 1 Paid the dividend declared in February.
Apr. 1 Announced a 4-for-1 stock split. Prior to the split, the market price per share was $36.
July 1 Declared a 5% stock dividend to stockholders of record on July 15, distributable July 31. On July 1, the market price of the stock was $13 per share.
   31   Issued the shares for the stock dividend.
Dec. 1 Declared a $0.50 per share dividend to stockholders of record on December 15, payable January 5, 2011.
   31   Determined that net income for the year was $700,000.

Instructions
Prepare the stockholders' equity section of the balance sheet at: (a) March 31, (b) June 30, (c) September 30, and (d) December 31, 2010.

(d) Total, stockholders' equity $4,190,000

P14-5B On January 1, 2010, Garcia Inc. had the following shareholders' equity balances.

Prepare the stockholders' equity section, reflecting various events.
(SO 1, 3)

Common Stock, no-par value (1,000,000 shares issued)	$3,000,000
Common Stock Dividends Distributable	400,000
Retained Earnings	1,200,000

Chapter 14 Corporations: Dividends, Retained Earnings, and Income Reporting

During 2010, the following transactions and events occurred.

1. Issued 100,000 shares of common stock as a result of a 10% stock dividend declared on December 15, 2009.
2. Issued 60,000 shares of common stock for cash at $5 per share.
3. Corrected an error that had understated the net income for 2008 by $140,000.
4. Declared and paid a cash dividend of $300,000.
5. Earned net income of $600,000.

Total stockholders' equity $5,340,000

Instructions

Prepare the stockholders' equity section of the balance sheet at December 31, 2010.

PROBLEMS: SET C

Visit the book's companion website at **www.wiley.com/college/weygandt**, and choose the Student Companion site, to access Problem Set C.

CONTINUING COOKIE CHRONICLE

(*Note:* This is a continuation of the Cookie Chronicle from Chapters 1 through 13.)

CCC14 After establishing their company's fiscal year end to be October 31, Natalie and Curtis began operating Cookie & Coffee Creations Inc. on November 1, 2010. On that date, they issued both preferred and common stock. After the first year of operations, Natalie and Curtis want to prepare financial information for the year.

Go to the book's companion website,
www.wiley.com/college/weygandt,
to see the completion of this problem.

BROADENING YOUR PERSPECTIVE

FINANCIAL REPORTING AND ANALYSIS

Financial Reporting Problem: PepsiCo, Inc.

BYP14-1 The financial statements of *PepsiCo, Inc.* are presented in Appendix A.

Instructions

Refer to PepsiCo's financial statements and answer the following questions.

(a) What amount did PepsiCo declare in dividends on common stock in the year ended December 29, 2007?
(b) How does this amount compare with dividends declared on common stock in the year ended December 30, 2006?

Comparative Analysis Problem: PepsiCo, Inc. vs. The Coca-Cola Company

BYP14-2 PepsiCo's financial statements are presented in Appendix A. Financial statements of *The Coca-Cola Company* are presented in Appendix B.

Instructions

(a) Compute earnings per share and return on common stockholders' equity for both companies for the year ending December 31, 2007. Assume PepsiCo's weighted average shares were 1,625 million and Coca-Cola's weighted average shares were 2,313 million. Can these measures be used to compare the profitability of the two companies? Why or why not?

(b) What was the total amount of dividends paid by each company in 2007?

Exploring the Web

BYP14-3 Use the stockholders' equity section of an annual report and identify the major components.

Address: www.reportgallery.com, or go to **www.wiley.com/college/weygandt**

Steps
1. From Report Gallery Homepage, choose **Search by Alphabet**, and choose a letter.
2. Select a particular company.
3. Choose Annual Report.
4. Follow instructions below.

Instructions
Answer the following questions.

(a) What is the company's name?
(b) What classes of capital stock has the company issued?
(c) For each class of stock:
  (1) How many shares are authorized, issued, and/or outstanding?
  (2) What is the par value?
(d) What are the company's retained earnings?
(e) Has the company acquired treasury stock? How many shares?

CRITICAL THINKING

Decision Making Across the Organization

BYP14-4 The stockholders' equity accounts of Fernandez, Inc., at January 1, 2010, are as follows.

Preferred Stock, no par, 4,000 shares issued	$400,000
Common Stock, no par, 140,000 shares issued	700,000
Retained Earnings	500,000

During 2010, the company had the following transactions and events.

July 1   Declared a $0.50 cash dividend on common stock.
Aug. 1   Discovered a $72,000 overstatement of 2009 depreciation expense. (Ignore income taxes.)
Sept. 1   Paid the cash dividend declared on July 1.
Dec. 1   Declared a 10% stock dividend on common stock when the market value of the stock was $12 per share.
    15   Declared a $9 per share cash dividend on preferred stock, payable January 31, 2011.
    31   Determined that net income for the year was $320,000.

Instructions
With the class divided into groups, answer the following questions.

(a) Prepare a retained earnings statement for the year. There are no preferred dividends in arrears.
(b) Discuss why the overstatement of 2009 depreciation expense is not treated as an adjustment of the current year's income.
(c) Discuss the reasons why a company might decide to issue a stock dividend rather than a cash dividend.

Communication Activity

BYP14-5 In the past year, Cormier Corporation declared a 10% stock dividend, and Fegan, Inc. announced a 2-for-1 stock split. Your parents own 100 shares of each company's $50 par value common stock. During a recent phone call, your parents ask you, as an accounting student, to explain the differences between the two events.

Instructions
Write a letter to your parents that explains the effects of the two events to them as stockholders and the effects of each event on the financial statements of each corporation.

Ethics Case

BYP14-6 Garcia Corporation has paid 60 consecutive quarterly cash dividends (15 years). The last 6 months, however, have been a cash drain on the company, as profit margins have been greatly narrowed by increasing competition. With a cash balance sufficient to meet only day-to-day operating needs, the president, Tom Henson, has decided that a stock dividend instead of a cash dividend should be declared. He tells Garcia's financial vice president, Andrea Lane, to issue a press release stating that the company is extending its consecutive dividend record with the issuance of a 5% stock dividend. "Write the press release convincing the stockholders that the stock dividend is just as good as a cash dividend," he orders. "Just watch our stock rise when we announce the stock dividend; it must be a good thing if that happens."

Instructions
(a) Who are the stakeholders in this situation?
(b) Is there anything unethical about Henson's intentions or actions?
(c) What is the effect of a stock dividend on a corporation's stockholders' equity accounts? Which would you rather receive as a stockholder—a cash dividend or a stock dividend? Why?

"All About You" Activity

BYP14-7 In the **All About You** feature in this chapter (p. 624), you learned that in response to the Sarbanes-Oxley Act, many companies have implemented formal ethics codes. Many other organizations also have ethics codes.

Instructions
Obtain the ethics code from an organization that you belong to (e.g., student organization, business school, employer, or a volunteer organization). Evaluate the ethics code based on how clearly it identifies proper and improper behavior. Discuss its strengths, and how it might be improved.

Answers to Insight and Accounting Across the Organization Questions

p. 611 Why Companies Are Increasing Their Dividends
Q: What factors must management consider in deciding how large a dividend to pay?
A: *Management must consider the size of the company's retained earnings balance, the amount of available cash, the company's expected near-term cash needs, the company's growth opportunities, and what level of dividend the company will be able to sustain based upon its expected future earnings.*

p. 615 Would You Pay $133,900 for One Share of Stock?
Q: How does the effect on share price following a stock split compare to the effect on share price of treasury shares acquired?
A: *A stock split and the acquisition of treasury shares have the opposite effects on share price: A stock split* decreases *the share price, whereas the acquisition of treasury shares* increases *the share price.*

Authors' Comments on *All About You:* Corporations Have Governance Structures—Do You? (p. 624)

Before we address the usefulness of a student code of ethics, let's first ask whether a corporate code of ethics will ensure that employees no longer commit fraud. The answer is, "Clearly not." Does that mean a code of ethics is a waste of time? No. A code of ethics is a useful statement by the leaders of an organization about what kind of behavior is expected of the members of that organization. It provides a concrete reference point by which wrongdoing can be identified and evaluated.

Now, suppose that you were taking an exam and that you observed a number of people cheating. It would be very frustrating if you thought that your instructor, the school administrators, and other students didn't care that people were cheating. Ultimately this would encourage even more people to cheat. But if the school has defined unethical behavior, stated that it won't be tolerated, and created the necessary mechanisms for detecting and punishing unethical behavior, then it has begun the first steps in creating a more ethical environment. For an example of an ethics code for university students, see the ethics section of the Student Resources at **www.bus.wisc.edu/accounting**.

Answers to Self-Study Questions
1. a **2.** c **3.** c **4.** a **5.** d **6.** d **7.** c **8.** b **9.** d **10.** b **11.** b **12.** d **13.** c **14.** d **15.** b

Chapter 15

Long-Term Liabilities

STUDY OBJECTIVES

After studying this chapter, you should be able to:

1. Explain why bonds are issued.
2. Prepare the entries for the issuance of bonds and interest expense.
3. Describe the entries when bonds are redeemed or converted.
4. Describe the accounting for long-term notes payable.
5. Contrast the accounting for operating and capital leases.
6. Identify the methods for the presentation and analysis of long-term liabilities.

✓ The Navigator

- Scan **Study Objectives**
- Read **Feature Story**
- Read **Preview**
- Read text and answer **DO IT!**
  p. 648   p. 652   p. 654   p. 656
  p. 659
- Work **Comprehensive** **DO IT!** p. 660
- Review **Summary of Study Objectives**
- Answer **Self-Study Questions**
- Complete **Assignments**

✓ The Navigator

Feature Story

THANK GOODNESS FOR BANKRUPTCY

One piece of baggage America's first settlers carried with them from England was the belief that not repaying one's debts was a moral failure. As in England, the colonists' penalty for such wickedness was often prison.

The theory behind jailing debtors was that the threat of incarceration might persuade them to reveal hidden assets. Or their families might take pity and pay their ransom. But if the debtor was truly penniless, he could be sentenced to what amounted to life in prison. Unlike murderers, rapists, and thieves, the debtors were also responsible for paying their own upkeep, thus putting them even further into debt. . . .

The colonies gradually developed more forgiving laws on debt, recognizing that owing money could be the result of bad luck rather than evidence of fraud or indolence. "Crops fail, prices fall, ships sink, warehouses burn, owners die, partners steal, pirates pillage, wars ravage, and people simply make mistakes," wrote Bruce Mann in his 2002 book *Republic of Debtors.* "Failure was the down side of entrepreneurial risk. This made failure the potential common fate of all merchants." . . .

Colonial lawmakers began taking a more charitable view toward debtors, but they were likelier to excuse a rich defaulter than a poor one. . . . Indeed, when some large speculative financial schemes collapsed after the Revolutionary War, many wealthy men were suddenly bankrupt. One of them, Robert Morris, who had signed the Declaration of Independence and provided critical financing for the war, lost his fortune speculating on land. Sentenced to debtors' prison in Philadelphia, Morris rented the best room in the jail and outfitted it with a settee, writing desks, a bed, a trunk of clothes and other comforts of home.

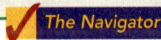

However lavishly they could outfit their prison cells, though, rich and poor faced the same dim future. There was no way an insolvent could get a fresh start—the "holy grail of debt relief," as Mr. Mann put it. In prison or out, debtors were expected to repay every penny they owed their creditors, even if it took them the rest of their lives. . . .

Congress passed a bankruptcy law in 1800 but then repealed it three years later. Not until 1831 did New York abolish prison for most debtors; Pennsylvania kept its debtors' prisons open until 1842. . . .

Source: Excerpted from Cynthia Crossen, "Early Debtors Faced Jail at Own Expense Until All Was Repaid," *Wall Street Journal,* January 30, 2006, p. B1. By permission.

✓ The Navigator

Inside Chapter 15...

- **Search for Your Best Rate** (p. 656)
- **"Covenant-Lite" Debt** (p. 660)

Preview of Chapter 15

As you can see from the Feature Story, having liabilities can be dangerous in difficult economic times. In this chapter we will explain the accounting for the major types of long-term liabilities reported on the balance sheet. **Long-term liabilities** are obligations that are expected to be paid after one year. These liabilities may be bonds, long-term notes, or lease obligations.

The content and organization of Chapter 15 are as follows.

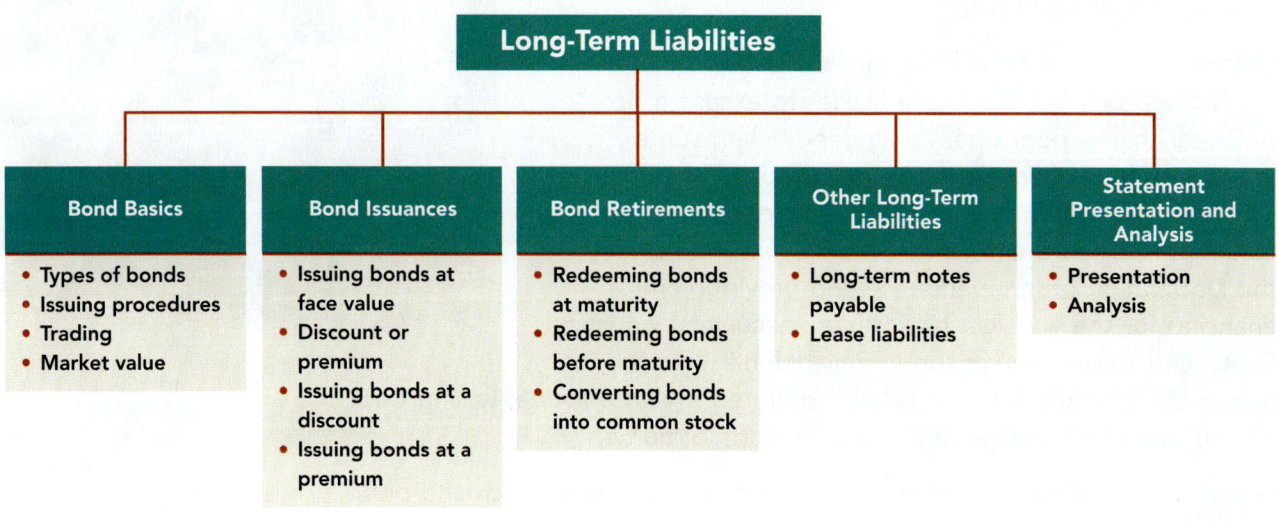

BOND BASICS

STUDY OBJECTIVE 1
Explain why bonds are issued.

Bonds are a form of interest-bearing notes payable. To obtain **large amounts of long-term capital**, corporate management usually must decide whether to issue common stock (equity financing) or bonds. Bonds offer three advantages over common stock, as shown in Illustration 15-1.

Illustration 15-1
Advantages of bond financing over common stock

Bond Financing	Advantages
	1. **Stockholder control is not affected.** Bondholders do not have voting rights, so current owners (stockholders) retain full control of the company.
	2. **Tax savings result.** Bond interest is deductible for tax purposes; dividends on stock are not.
	3. **Earnings per share may be higher.** Although bond interest expense reduces net income, earnings per share on common stock often is higher under bond financing because no additional shares of common stock are issued.

As the illustration shows, one reason to issue bonds is that they do not affect stockholder control. Because bondholders do not have voting rights, owners can raise capital with bonds and still maintain corporate control. In addition, bonds are attractive to corporations because the cost of bond interest is tax-deductible. As a result of this tax treatment, which stock dividends do not offer, bonds may result in lower cost of capital than equity financing.

To illustrate the third advantage, on earnings per share, assume that Microsystems, Inc. is considering two plans for financing the construction of a new $5 million plant. Plan A involves issuance of 200,000 shares of common stock at the current market price of $25 per share. Plan B involves issuance of $5 million, 8% bonds at face value. Income before interest and taxes on the new plant will be $1.5 million. Income taxes are expected to be 30%. Microsystems currently has 100,000 shares of common stock outstanding. Illustration 15-2 shows the alternative effects on earnings per share.

	Plan A Issue Stock	Plan B Issue Bonds
Income before interest and taxes	$1,500,000	$1,500,000
Interest (8% × $5,000,000)	—	400,000
Income before income taxes	1,500,000	1,100,000
Income tax expense (30%)	450,000	330,000
Net income	$1,050,000	$ 770,000
Outstanding shares	300,000	100,000
Earnings per share	**$3.50**	**$7.70**

Illustration 15-2
Effects on earnings per share—stocks vs. bonds

Note that net income is $280,000 less ($1,050,000 − $770,000) with long-term debt financing (bonds). However, earnings per share is higher because there are 200,000 fewer shares of common stock outstanding.

One disadvantage in using bonds is that the company must **pay interest** on a periodic basis. In addition, the company must also **repay the principal** at the due date. A company with fluctuating earnings and a relatively weak cash position may have great difficulty making interest payments when earnings are low.

A corporation may also obtain long-term financing from notes payable and leasing. However, notes payable and leasing are seldom sufficient to furnish the amount of funds needed for plant expansion and major projects like new buildings.

Bonds are sold in relatively small denominations (usually $1,000 multiples). As a result of their size, and the variety of their features, bonds attract many investors.

HELPFUL HINT
Besides corporations, governmental agencies and universities also issue bonds to raise capital.

Types of Bonds

Bonds may have many different features. In the following sections, we describe the types of bonds commonly issued.

SECURED AND UNSECURED BONDS

Secured bonds have specific assets of the issuer pledged as collateral for the bonds. A bond secured by real estate, for example, is called a mortgage bond. A bond secured by specific assets set aside to retire the bonds is called a sinking fund bond.

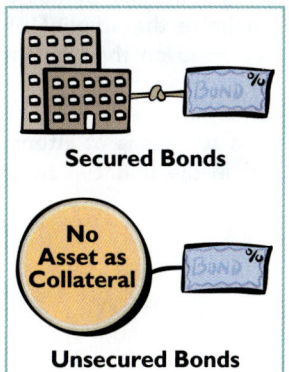

Unsecured bonds, also called **debenture bonds**, are issued against the general credit of the borrower. Companies with good credit ratings use these bonds extensively. For example, in a recent annual report, DuPont reported over $2 billion of debenture bonds outstanding.

TERM AND SERIAL BONDS
Bonds that mature—are due for payment—at a single specified future date are **term bonds**. In contrast, bonds that mature in installments are **serial bonds**.

REGISTERED AND BEARER BONDS
Bonds issued in the name of the owner are **registered bonds**. Interest payments on registered bonds are made by check to bondholders of record. Bonds not registered are **bearer** (or **coupon**) **bonds**. Holders of bearer bonds must send in coupons to receive interest payments. Most bonds issued today are registered bonds.

CONVERTIBLE AND CALLABLE BONDS
Bonds that can be converted into common stock at the bondholder's option are **convertible bonds**. The conversion feature generally is attractive to bond buyers. Bonds that the issuing company can retire at a stated dollar amount prior to maturity are **callable bonds**. A call feature is included in nearly all corporate bond issues.

Convertible Bonds

Callable Bonds

Issuing Procedures
State laws grant corporations the power to issue bonds. Both the board of directors and stockholders usually must approve bond issues. **In authorizing the bond issue, the board of directors must stipulate the number of bonds to be authorized, total face value, and contractual interest rate.** The total bond authorization often exceeds the number of bonds the company originally issues. This gives the corporation the flexibility to issue more bonds, if needed, to meet future cash requirements.

The **face value** is the amount of principal the issuing company must pay at the maturity date. The **contractual interest rate**, often referred to as the **stated rate**, is the rate used to determine the amount of cash interest the borrower pays and the investor receives. Usually the contractual rate is stated as an annual rate. Interest is generally paid semiannually.

The terms of the bond issue are set forth in a legal document called a **bond indenture**. The indenture shows the terms and summarizes the rights of the bondholders and their trustees, and the obligations of the issuing company. The **trustee** (usually a financial institution) keeps records of each bondholder, maintains custody of unissued bonds, and holds conditional title to pledged property.

In addition, the issuing company arranges for the printing of **bond certificates**. The indenture and the certificate are separate documents. As shown in Illustration 15-3, a bond certificate provides the following information: name of the issuer, face value, contractual interest rate, and maturity date. An investment company that specializes in selling securities generally sells the bonds for the issuing company.

> **ETHICS NOTE**
> Some companies try to minimize the amount of debt reported on their balance sheet by not reporting certain types of commitments as liabilities. This subject is of intense interest in the financial community.

Bond Trading
Bondholders have the opportunity to convert their holdings into cash at any time by selling the bonds at the current market price on national securities exchanges. **Bond prices are quoted as a percentage of the face value of the bond, which is usually $1,000.** A $1,000 bond with a quoted price of 97 means that the selling price of

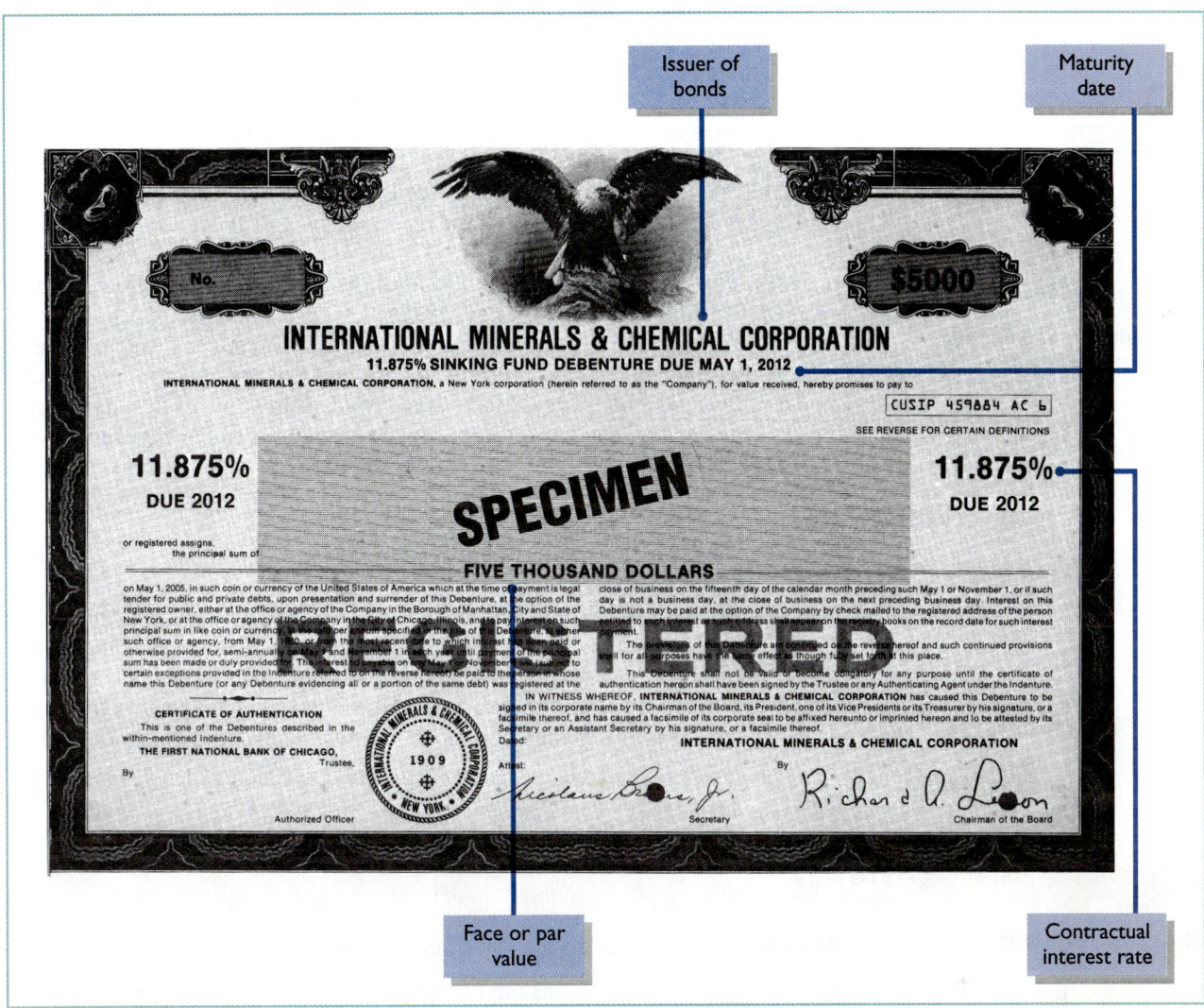

Illustration 15-3
Bond certificate

the bond is 97% of face value, or $970. Newspapers and the financial press publish bond prices and trading activity daily as illustrated by the following.

Bonds	Maturity	Close	Yield
Wal-Mart Stores 4.125	Feb. 2011	101.880	3.898

Illustration 15-4
Market information for bonds

This bond listing indicates that Wal-Mart has outstanding 4.125%, $1,000 bonds that mature in 2011. They currently yield a 3.898% return. At the close of trading, the price was 101.880% of face value, or $1,018.80.

A corporation makes journal entries **when it issues or buys back bonds**, when it records interest, or when bondholders convert bonds into common stock. For example, DuPont **does not journalize** transactions between its bondholders and other investors. If Tom Smith sells his DuPont bonds to Faith Jones, DuPont does not journalize the transaction. (DuPont or its trustee does, however, keep records of the names of bondholders in the case of registered bonds.)

HELPFUL HINT
(1) What is the price of a $1,000 bond trading at 95¼?
(2) What is the price of a $1,000 bond trading at 101⅞?
Answers: (1) $952.50.
(2) $1,018.75.

Determining the Market Value of Bonds

If you were an investor wanting to purchase a bond, how would you determine how much to pay? To be more specific, assume that Coronet, Inc. issues a **zero-interest bond** (pays no interest) with a face value of $1,000,000 due in 20 years. For this bond, the only cash you receive is a million dollars at the end of 20 years. Would you pay a million dollars for this bond? We hope not! A million dollars received 20 years from now is not the same as a million dollars received today.

The reason you should not pay a million dollars for Coronet's bond relates to what is called the **time value of money**. If you had a million dollars today, you would invest it. From that investment, you would earn interest such that at the end of 20 years, you would have much more than a million dollars. If someone is going to pay you a million dollars 20 years from now, you would want to find its equivalent today. In other words, you would want to determine how much you must invest today at current interest rates to have a million dollars in 20 years. The amount that must be invested today at a given rate of interest over a specified time is called **present value**.

The present value of a bond is the value at which it should sell in the marketplace. Market value therefore is a function of the three factors that determine present value: (1) the dollar amounts to be received, (2) the length of time until the amounts are received, and (3) the market rate of interest. The **market interest rate** is the rate investors demand for loaning funds. Appendix 15A discusses the process of finding the present value for bonds. Appendix C near the end of the book also provides additional material for time value of money computations.

Same dollars at different times are not equal.

DO IT!

BOND TERMINOLOGY

State whether each of the following statements is true or false.

_____ 1. Mortgage bonds and sinking fund bonds are both examples of secured bonds.

_____ 2. Unsecured bonds are also known as debenture bonds.

_____ 3. The stated rate is the rate investors demand for loaning funds.

_____ 4. The face value is the amount of principal the issuing company must pay at the maturity date.

_____ 5. The bond issuer must make journal entries to record transfers of its bonds among investors.

action plan

✔ Review the types of bonds and the basic terms associated with bonds.

Solution

1. True.
2. True.
3. False. The stated rate is the contractual interest rate used to determine the amount of cash interest the borrower pays.
4. True.
5. False. The bond issuer makes journal entries only when it issues or buys back bonds, when it records interest, and when bonds are converted.

Related exercise material: **BE15-1, E15-1, E15-2,** and **DO IT! 15-1.**

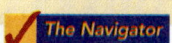

ACCOUNTING FOR BOND ISSUES

Bonds may be issued at face value, below face value (at a discount), or above face value (at a premium).

STUDY OBJECTIVE 2
Prepare the entries for the issuance of bonds and interest expense.

Issuing Bonds at Face Value

To illustrate the accounting for bonds, assume that on January 1, 2010, Candlestick Corporation issues $100,000, five-year, 10% bonds at 100 (100% of face value). The entry to record the sale is:

Jan. 1	Cash	100,000	
	Bonds Payable		100,000
	(To record sale of bonds at face value)		

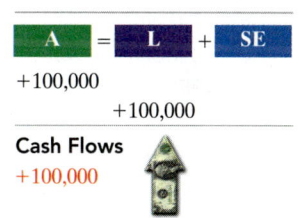

Candlestick reports bonds payable in the long-term liabilities section of the balance sheet because the maturity date is more than one year away.

Over the term (life) of the bonds, companies make entries to record bond interest. Interest on bonds payable is computed in the same manner as interest on notes payable, as explained in Chapter 11 (page 487). Assume that interest is payable semiannually on January 1 and July 1 on the bonds described above. In that case, Candlestick must pay interest of $5,000 ($100,000 × 10% × 6/12) on July 1, 2010. The entry for the payment, assuming no previous accrual of interest, is:

July 1	Bond Interest Expense	5,000	
	Cash		5,000
	(To record payment of bond interest)		

At December 31, Candlestick recognizes the $5,000 of interest expense incurred since July 1 with the following adjusting entry:

Dec. 31	Bond Interest Expense	5,000	
	Bond Interest Payable		5,000
	(To accrue bond interest)		

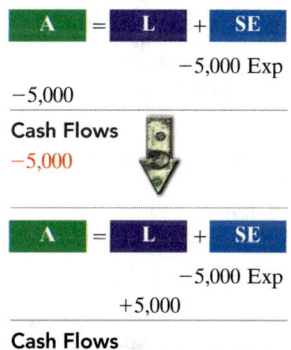

Companies classify bond interest payable as a current liability, because it is scheduled for payment within the next year. When Candlestick pays the interest on January 1, 2011, it debits (decreases) Bond Interest Payable and credits (decreases) Cash for $5,000.

Discount or Premium on Bonds

In the Candlestick illustrations above, we assumed that the contractual (stated) interest rate paid on the bonds and the market (effective) interest rate were the same. Recall that the **contractual interest rate** is the rate applied to the face (par) value to arrive at the interest paid in a year. The **market interest rate** is the rate investors demand for loaning funds to the corporation. When the contractual interest rate and the market interest rate are the same, bonds sell **at face value (par value)**.

However, market interest rates change daily. The type of bond issued, the state of the economy, current industry conditions, and the company's performance all affect market interest rates. Contractual and market interest rates often differ. As a result, bonds often sell below or above face value.

To illustrate, suppose that a company issues 10% bonds at a time when other bonds of similar risk are paying 12%. Investors will not be interested in buying the 10% bonds, so their value will fall below their face value. In this case, we say the 10% bonds are **selling at a discount**. As a result of the decline in the bonds' selling price, the actual interest rate incurred by the company increases to the level of the current market interest rate.

Conversely, if the market rate of interest is **lower than** the contractual interest rate, investors will have to pay more than face value for the bonds. That is, if the market rate of interest is 8% but the contractual interest rate on the bonds is 10%, the issuer will require more funds from the investor. In these cases, **bonds sell at a premium**. Illustration 15-5 shows these relationships graphically.

Illustration 15-5
Interest rates and bond prices

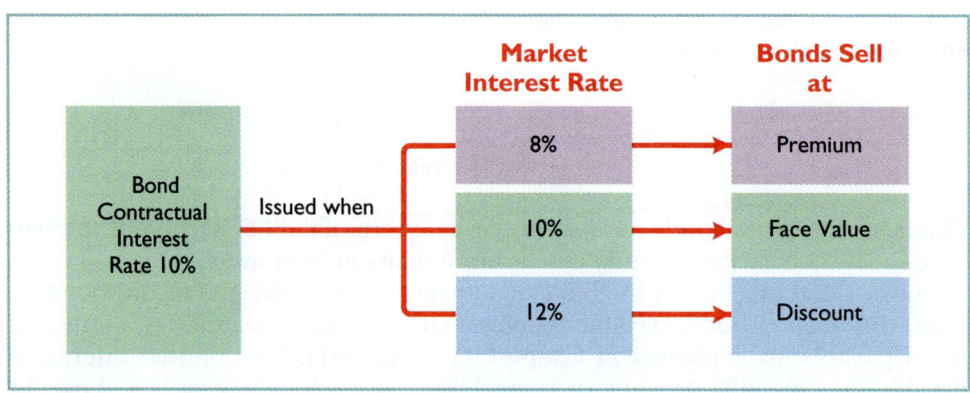

Issuing bonds at an amount different from face value is quite common. By the time a company prints the bond certificates and markets the bonds, it will be a coincidence if the market rate and the contractual rate are the same. Thus, the sale of bonds at a discount does not mean that the issuer's financial strength is suspect. Nor does the sale of bonds at a premium indicate exceptional financial strength.

Issuing Bonds at a Discount

To illustrate issuance of bonds at a discount, assume that on January 1, 2010, Candlestick, Inc. sells $100,000, five-year, 10% bonds for $92,639 (92.639% of face value). Interest is payable on July 1 and January 1. The entry to record the issuance is:

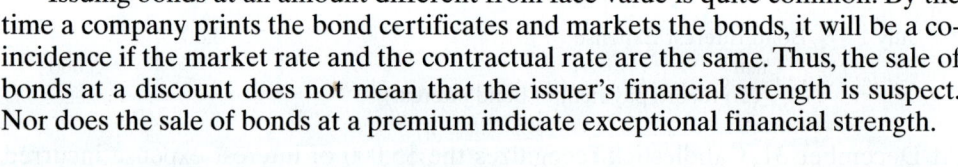

Although Discount on Bonds Payable has a debit balance, **it is not an asset**. Rather, it is a **contra account**. This account is **deducted from bonds payable** on the balance sheet, as shown in Illustration 15-6.

Illustration 15-6
Statement presentation of discount on bonds payable

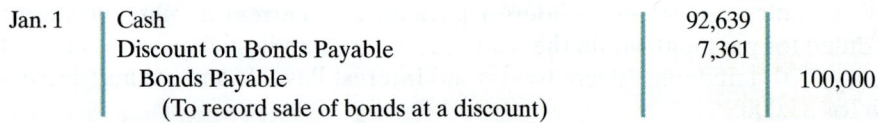

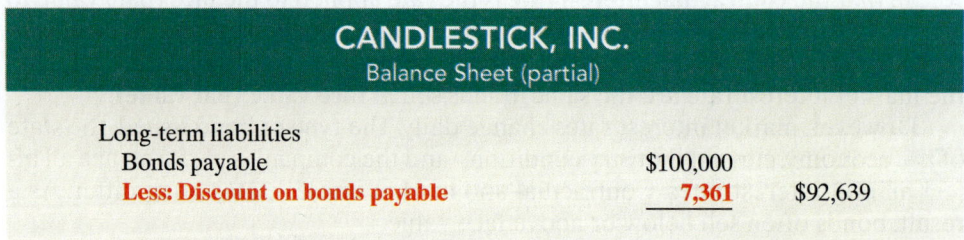

The $92,639 represents the **carrying (or book) value** of the bonds. On the date of issue this amount equals the market price of the bonds.

The issuance of bonds below face value—at a discount—causes the total cost of borrowing to differ from the bond interest paid. That is, the issuing corporation must pay not only the contractual interest rate over the term of the bonds, but also the face value (rather than the issuance price) at maturity. Therefore, the difference between the issuance price and face value of the bonds—the discount—is an **additional cost of borrowing**. The company records this additional cost as **bond interest expense** over the life of the bonds. Appendixes 15B and 15C show the procedures for recording this additional cost.

The total cost of borrowing $92,639 for Candlestick, Inc. is $57,361, computed as follows.

> **HELPFUL HINT**
> Carrying value (book value) of bonds issued at a discount is determined by subtracting the balance of the discount account from the balance of the Bonds Payable account.

Bonds Issued at a Discount

Semiannual interest payments ($100,000 × 10% × ½ = $5,000; $5,000 × 10)	$50,000
Add: Bond discount ($100,000 − $92,639)	7,361
Total cost of borrowing	**$57,361**

Illustration 15-7
Total cost of borrowing—bonds issued at a discount

Alternatively, we can compute the total cost of borrowing as follows.

Bonds Issued at a Discount

Principal at maturity	$100,000
Semiannual interest payments ($5,000 × 10)	50,000
Cash to be paid to bondholders	150,000
Cash received from bondholders	92,639
Total cost of borrowing	**$ 57,361**

Illustration 15-8
Alternative computation of total cost of borrowing—bonds issued at a discount

Issuing Bonds at a Premium

To illustrate the issuance of bonds at a premium, we now assume the Candlestick, Inc. bonds described above sell for $108,111 (108.111% of face value) rather than for $92,639. The entry to record the sale is:

Jan. 1	Cash	108,111	
	Bonds Payable		100,000
	Premium on Bonds Payable		8,111
	(To record sale of bonds at a premium)		

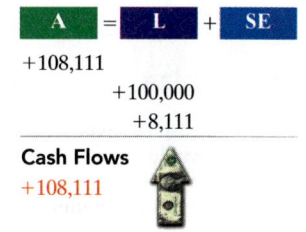

Candlestick adds the premium on bonds payable **to the bonds payable amount** on the balance sheet, as shown in Illustration 15-9.

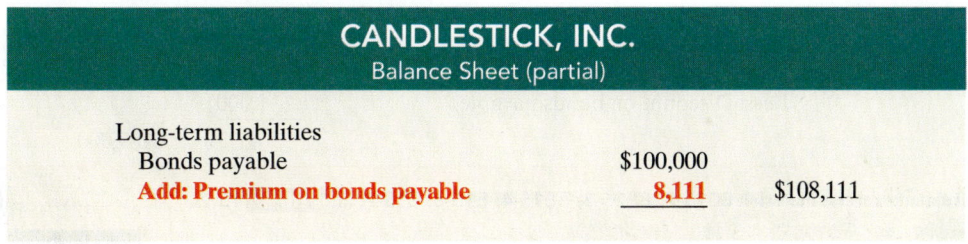

Illustration 15-9
Statement presentation of bond premium

652 Chapter 15 Long-Term Liabilities

HELPFUL HINT
Premium on Bonds Payable

Decrease Debit	Increase Credit ↓ Normal Balance

The sale of bonds above face value causes the total cost of borrowing to be **less than the bond interest paid**. The bond premium is considered to be **a reduction in the cost of borrowing**. The company credits the bond premium to Bond Interest Expense over the life of the bonds. Appendixes 15B and 15C show the procedures for recording this reduction in the cost of borrowing. The total cost of borrowing $108,111 for Candlestick, Inc. is computed as follows.

Illustration 15-10
Total cost of borrowing—bonds issued at a premium

Bonds Issued at a Premium	
Semiannual interest payments ($100,000 × 10% × ½ = $5,000; $5,000 × 10)	$50,000
Less: Bond premium ($108,111 − $100,000)	8,111
Total cost of borrowing	**$41,889**

Alternatively, we can compute the cost of borrowing as follows.

Illustration 15-11
Alternative computation of total cost of borrowing—bonds issued at a premium

Bonds Issued at a Premium	
Principal at maturity	$100,000
Semiannual interest payments ($5,000 × 10)	50,000
Cash to be paid to bondholders	150,000
Cash received from bondholders	108,111
Total cost of borrowing	**$ 41,889**

DO IT!

BOND ISSUANCE

Giant Corporation issues $200,000 of bonds for $189,000. (a) Prepare the journal entry to record the issuance of the bonds, and (b) show how the bonds would be reported on the balance sheet at the date of issuance.

action plan

✔ Record cash received, bonds payable at face value, and the difference as a discount or premium.

✔ Report discount as a deduction from bonds payable and premium as an addition to bonds payable.

Solution

(a)
Cash	189,000	
Discount on Bonds Payable	11,000	
Bonds Payable		200,000
(To record sale of bonds at a discount)		

(b)
Long-term liabilities
Bonds payable	$200,000	
Less: Discount on bonds payable	(11,000)	
		$189,000

Related exercise material: **BE15-2, BE15-3, BE15-4, E15-6, E15-7,** and **DO IT! 15-2.**

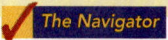

ACCOUNTING FOR BOND RETIREMENTS

An issuing corporation retires bonds either when it redeems the bonds or when bondholders convert them into common stock. We explain the entries for these transactions in the following sections.

STUDY OBJECTIVE 3
Describe the entries when bonds are redeemed or converted.

Redeeming Bonds at Maturity

Regardless of the issue price of bonds, the book value of the bonds at maturity will equal their face value. Assuming that the company pays and records separately the interest for the last interest period, Candlestick records the redemption of its bonds at maturity as follows:

Bonds Payable	100,000	
Cash		100,000
(To record redemption of bonds at maturity)		

A = L + SE
       −100,000
−100,000

Cash Flows
−100,000

Redeeming Bonds before Maturity

Bonds also may be redeemed before maturity. A company may decide to retire bonds before maturity to reduce interest cost and to remove debt from its balance sheet. A company should retire debt early only if it has sufficient cash resources.

When a company retires bonds before maturity, it is necessary to: (1) eliminate the carrying value of the bonds at the redemption date; (2) record the cash paid; and (3) recognize the gain or loss on redemption. The carrying value of the bonds is the face value of the bonds less any remaining bond discount or plus any remaining bond premium at the redemption date.

To illustrate, assume that Candlestick, Inc. has sold its bonds at a premium. At the end of the eighth period, Candlestick retires these bonds at 103 after paying the semiannual interest. Assume also that the carrying value of the bonds at the redemption date is $101,623. Candlestick makes the following entry to record the redemption at the end of the eighth interest period (January 1, 2014):

HELPFUL HINT
Question: A bond is redeemed prior to its maturity date. Its carrying value exceeds its redemption price. Will the retirement result in a gain or a loss on redemption?
Answer: Gain.

Jan. 1	Bonds Payable	100,000	
	Premium on Bonds Payable	1,623	
	Loss on Bond Redemption	1,377	
	Cash		103,000
	(To record redemption of bonds at 103)		

A = L + SE
      −100,000
      −1,623
                −1,377 Exp
−103,000

Cash Flows
−103,000

Note that the loss of $1,377 is the difference between the cash paid of $103,000 and the carrying value of the bonds of $101,623.

Converting Bonds into Common Stock

Convertible bonds have features that are attractive both to bondholders and to the issuer. The conversion often gives bondholders an opportunity to benefit if the market price of the common stock increases substantially. Until conversion, though, the bondholder receives interest on the bond. For the issuer of convertible bonds, the bonds sell at a higher price and pay a lower rate of interest than comparable debt securities without the conversion option. Many corporations, such as USAir, USX Corp., and DaimlerChrysler Corporation, have convertible bonds outstanding.

654 Chapter 15 Long-Term Liabilities

When the issuing company records a conversion, the company ignores the current market prices of the bonds and stock. Instead, the company transfers the **carrying value** of the bonds to paid-in capital accounts. **No gain or loss is recognized.**

To illustrate, assume that on July 1 Saunders Associates converts $100,000 bonds sold at face value into 2,000 shares of $10 par value common stock. Both the bonds and the common stock have a market value of $130,000. Saunders makes the following entry to record the conversion:

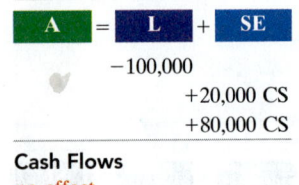

Cash Flows
no effect

July 1	Bonds Payable	100,000	
	Common Stock		20,000
	Paid-in Capital in Excess of Par Value		80,000
	(To record bond conversion)		

Note that the company does not consider the current market price of the bonds and stock ($130,000) in making the entry. This method of recording the bond conversion is often referred to as the **carrying (or book) value method**.

DO IT!

BOND REDEMPTION

action plan

✔ Determine and eliminate the carrying value of the bonds.
✔ Record the cash paid.
✔ Compute and record the gain or loss (the difference between the first two items).

R & B Inc. issued $500,000, 10-year bonds at a premium. Prior to maturity, when the carrying value of the bonds is $508,000, the company retires the bonds at 102. Prepare the entry to record the redemption of the bonds.

Solution

There is a loss on redemption: The cash paid, $510,000 ($500,000 × 102%), is greater than the carrying value of $508,000. The entry is:

Bonds Payable	500,000	
Premium on Bonds Payable	8,000	
Loss on Bond Redemption	2,000	
Cash		510,000
(To record redemption of bonds at 102)		

Related exercise material: **BE15-5, E15-5, E15-6, E15-8, E15-9**, and **DO IT! 15-3**.

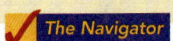

ACCOUNTING FOR OTHER LONG-TERM LIABILITIES

Other common types of long-term obligations are notes payable and lease liabilities. The accounting for these liabilities is explained in the following sections.

Long-Term Notes Payable

STUDY OBJECTIVE 4
Describe the accounting for long-term notes payable.

The use of notes payable in long-term debt financing is quite common. **Long-term notes payable** are similar to short-term interest-bearing notes payable except that the term of the notes exceeds one year.

A long-term note may be secured by a **mortgage** that pledges title to specific assets as security for a loan. Individuals widely use **mortgage notes payable** to purchase homes, and many small and some large companies use them to acquire plant assets. At one time, approximately 18% of McDonald's long-term debt related to mortgage notes on land, buildings, and improvements.

Mortgage loan terms may stipulate either a **fixed** or an **adjustable** interest rate. The interest rate on a fixed-rate mortgage remains the same over the life of the mortgage. The interest rate on an adjustable-rate mortgage is adjusted periodically to reflect changes in the market rate of interest. Typically, the terms require the borrower to make installment payments over the term of the loan. Each payment consists of (1) interest on the unpaid balance of the loan and (2) a reduction of loan principal. While the total amount of the payment remains constant, the interest decreases each period, while the portion applied to the loan principal increases.

Companies initially record mortgage notes payable at face value. They subsequently make entries for each installment payment. To illustrate, assume that Porter Technology Inc. issues a $500,000, 12%, 20-year mortgage note on December 31, 2010, to obtain needed financing for a new research laboratory. The terms provide for semiannual installment payments of $33,231 (not including real estate taxes and insurance). The installment payment schedule for the first two years is as follows.

Illustration 15-12
Mortgage installment payment schedule

Semiannual Interest Period	(A) Cash Payment	(B) Interest Expense (D) × 6%	(C) Reduction of Principal (A) − (B)	(D) Principal Balance (D) − (C)
12/31/10				$500,000
06/30/11	$33,231	$30,000	$3,231	496,769
12/31/11	33,231	29,806	3,425	493,344
06/30/12	33,231	29,601	3,630	489,714
12/31/12	33,231	29,383	3,848	485,866

Porter records the mortgage loan and first installment payment as follows.

Dec. 31	Cash	500,000	
	Mortgage Notes Payable		500,000
	(To record mortgage loan)		

June 30	Interest Expense	30,000	
	Mortgage Notes Payable	3,231	
	Cash		33,231
	(To record semiannual payment on mortgage)		

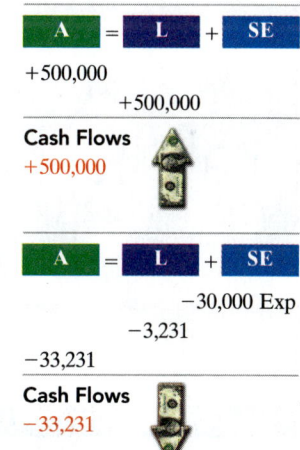

In the balance sheet, the company reports the reduction in principal for the next year as a current liability, and it classifies the remaining unpaid principal balance as a long-term liability. At December 31, 2011, the total liability is $493,344. Of that amount, $7,478 ($3,630 + $3,848) is current, and $485,866 ($493,344 − $7,478) is long-term.

656 Chapter 15 Long-Term Liabilities

DO IT!

LONG-TERM NOTE

action plan

✔ Record the issuance of the note as a cash receipt and a liability.

✔ Each installment payment consists of interest and payment of principal.

Cole Research issues a $250,000, 8%, 20-year mortgage note to obtain needed financing for a new lab. The terms call for semiannual payments of $12,631 each. Prepare the entries to record the mortgage loan and the first installment payment.

Solution

Cash	250,000	
Mortgage Notes Payable		250,000
(To record mortgage loan)		
Interest Expense	10,000*	
Mortgage Notes Payable	2,361	
Cash		12,361
(To record semiannual payment on mortgage)		

*Interest expense = $250,000 × 8% × 6/12.

Related exercise material: **BE15-6, E15-10, E15-11**, and **DO IT! 15-4**.

ACCOUNTING ACROSS THE ORGANIZATION

Search for Your Best Rate

Companies spend a great deal of time shopping for the best loan terms. You should do the same. Suppose that you have a used car that you are planning to trade in on the purchase of a new car. Experts suggest that you view this deal as three separate transactions: (1) the purchase of a new car, (2) the trade in or sale of an old car, and (3) shopping for an interest rate.

Studies suggest that too many people neglect transaction number 3. One survey found that 63% of people planned on shopping for the best car-loan interest rate online the next time they bought a car. But a separate study found that only 15% of people who bought a car actually shopped around for the best online rate. Too many people simply take the interest rate offered at the car dealership. Many lenders will pre-approve you for a loan up to a specific dollar amount, and many will then give you a blank check (negotiable for up to that amount) that you can take to the car dealer.

Source: Ron Lieber, "How to Haggle the Best Car Loan," *Wall Street Journal*, March 25, 2006, p. B1.

 What should you do if the dealer "trash-talks" your lender, or refuses to sell you the car for the agreed-upon price unless you get your car loan through the dealer?

Lease Liabilities

STUDY OBJECTIVE 5
Contrast the accounting for operating and capital leases.

A lease is a contractual arrangement between a lessor (owner of the property) and a lessee (renter of the property). It grants the right to use specific property for a period of time in return for cash payments. Leasing is big business. U.S. companies leased an estimated $125 billion of capital equipment in a recent year. This represents approximately one-third of equipment financed that year. The two most common types of leases are operating leases and capital leases.

OPERATING LEASES

The renting of an apartment and the rental of a car at an airport are examples of **operating leases. In an operating lease the intent is temporary use of the property by the lessee, while the lessor continues to own the property.**

In an operating lease, the lessee records the lease (or rental) payments as an expense. The lessor records the payments as revenue. For example, assume that a sales representative for Western Inc. leases a car from Hertz Car Rental at the Los Angeles airport and that Hertz charges a total of $275. Western, the lessee, records the rental as follows:

Car Rental Expense	275	
Cash		275
(To record payment of lease rental charge)		

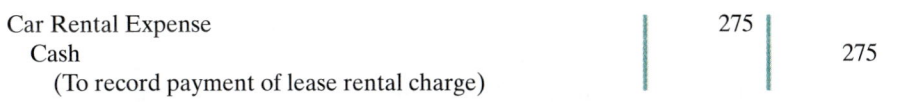

The lessee may incur other costs during the lease period. For example, in the case above, Western will generally incur costs for gas. Western would report these costs as an expense.

CAPITAL LEASES

In most lease contracts, the lessee makes a periodic payment and records that payment in the income statement as rent expense. In some cases, however, the lease contract transfers to the lessee substantially all the benefits and risks of ownership. Such a lease is in effect a purchase of the property. This type of lease is a **capital lease**. Its name comes from the fact that the company capitalizes the present value of the cash payments for the lease and records that amount as an asset. Illustration 15-13 indicates the major difference between operating and capital leases.

Illustration 15-13
Types of leases

HELPFUL HINT
A capital lease situation is one that, although legally a rental case, is *in substance* an installment purchase by the lessee. Accounting standards require that substance over form be used in such a situation.

If **any one** of the following conditions exists, the lessee must record a lease **as an asset**—that is, as a capital lease:

1. **The lease transfers ownership of the property to the lessee.** *Rationale:* If during the lease term the lessee receives ownership of the asset, the lessee should report the leased item as an asset on its books.

2. **The lease contains a bargain purchase option.** *Rationale:* If during the term of the lease the lessee can purchase the asset at a price substantially below its fair market value, the lessee will exercise this option. Thus, the lessee should report the leased item as an asset on its books.

3. **The lease term is equal to 75% or more of the economic life of the leased property.** *Rationale:* If the lease term is for much of the asset's useful life, the lessee should report the leased item as an asset on its books.

4. **The present value of the lease payments equals or exceeds 90% of the fair market value of the leased property.** *Rationale:* If the present value of the lease payments is equal to or almost equal to the fair market value of the asset, the lessee has essentially purchased the asset. As a result, the lessee should report the leased item as an asset on its books.

To illustrate, assume that Gonzalez Company decides to lease new equipment. The lease period is four years; the economic life of the leased equipment is estimated to be five years. The present value of the lease payments is $190,000, which is equal to the fair market value of the equipment. There is no transfer of ownership during the lease term, nor is there any bargain purchase option.

In this example, Gonzalez has essentially purchased the equipment. Conditions 3 and 4 have been met. First, the lease term is 75% or more of the economic life of the asset. Second, the present value of cash payments is equal to the equipment's fair market value. Gonzalez records the transaction as follows.

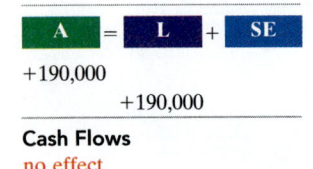

Cash Flows
no effect

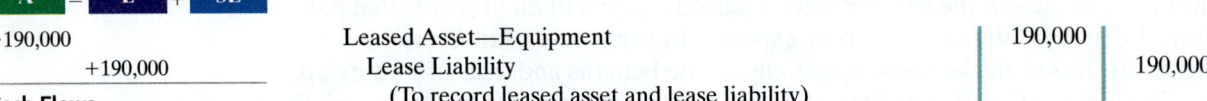

Leased Asset—Equipment	190,000	
Lease Liability		190,000
(To record leased asset and lease liability)		

The lessee reports a leased asset on the balance sheet under plant assets. It reports the lease liability on the balance sheet as a liability. **The portion of the lease liability expected to be paid in the next year is a current liability. The remainder is classified as a long-term liability.**

Most lessees do not like to report leases on their balance sheets. Why? Because the lease liability increases the company's total liabilities. This, in turn, may make it more difficult for the company to obtain needed funds from lenders. As a result, companies attempt to keep leased assets and lease liabilities off the balance sheet by structuring leases so as not to meet any of the four conditions discussed earlier. The practice of keeping liabilities off the balance sheet is referred to as **off–balance-sheet financing**.

ETHICS NOTE

Accounting standard setters are attempting to rewrite rules on lease accounting because of concerns that abuse of the current standards is reducing the usefulness of financial statements.

STATEMENT PRESENTATION AND ANALYSIS

Presentation

STUDY OBJECTIVE 6
Identify the methods for the presentation and analysis of long-term liabilities.

Companies report long-term liabilities in a separate section of the balance sheet immediately following current liabilities, as shown in Illustration 15-14. Alternatively, companies may present summary data in the balance sheet, with detailed data (interest rates, maturity dates, conversion privileges, and assets pledged as collateral) shown in a supporting schedule.

Illustration 15-14
Balance sheet presentation of long-term liabilities

LAX CORPORATION
Balance Sheet (partial)

Long-term liabilities		
Bonds payable 10% due in 2017	$1,000,000	
Less: Discount on bonds payable	80,000	$ 920,000
Mortgage notes payable, 11%, due in 2023 and secured by plant assets		500,000
Lease liability		440,000
Total long-term liabilities		$1,860,000

Companies report the current maturities of long-term debt under current liabilities if they are to be paid from current assets.

Analysis

Long-term creditors and stockholders are interested in a company's long-run solvency. Of particular interest is the company's ability to pay interest as it comes due and to repay the face value of the debt at maturity. Here we look at two ratios that provide information about debt-paying ability and long-run solvency.

The **debt to total assets ratio** measures the percentage of the total assets provided by creditors. As shown in the formula in Illustration 15-15, it is computed by dividing total debt (both current and long-term liabilities) by total assets. The higher the percentage of debt to total assets, the greater the risk that the company may be unable to meet its maturing obligations.

The **times interest earned ratio** indicates the company's ability to meet interest payments as they come due. It is computed by dividing income before income taxes and interest expense by interest expense.

To illustrate these ratios, we will use data from **Kellogg Company**'s recent annual report. The company had total liabilities of $8,871 million, total assets of $11,397 million, interest expense of $319 million, income taxes of $444 million, and net income of $1,103 million. Kellogg's debt to total assets ratio and times interest earned ratio are shown below.

Total Debt	÷	Total Assets	=	Debt to Total Assets
$8,871	÷	$11,397	=	77.8%
Income before Income Taxes and Interest Expense	÷	Interest Expense	=	Times Interest Earned
$1,103 + $444 + $319	÷	$319	=	5.85 times

Illustration 15-15
Debt to total assets and times interest earned ratios, with computations

Kellogg has a relatively high debt to total assets percentage of 78.4%. Its interest coverage of 5.75 times is considered safe.

DO IT!

LEASE LIABILITY; ANALYSIS OF LONG-TERM LIABILITIES

FX Corporation leases new equipment on December 31, 2010. The lease transfers ownership to FX at the end of the lease. The present value of the lease payments is $240,000. After recording this lease, FX has assets of $2,000,000, liabilities of $1,200,000, and stockholders' equity of $800,000. (a) Prepare the entry to record the lease, and (b) compute and discuss the debt to total assets ratio at year-end.

action plan

✔ Record the present value of the lease payments as an asset and a liability.

✔ Use the formula for the debt to total assets ratio (total debt divided by total assets).

Solution

(a)

Leased Asset—Equipment	240,000	
Lease Liability		240,000
(To record leased asset and lease liability)		

(b) The debt to total assets ratio = $1,200,000 ÷ $2,000,000 = 60%. This means that 60% of the total assets were provided by creditors. The higher the percentage of debt to total assets, the greater the risk that the company may be unable to meet its maturing obligations.

Related exercise material: **BE15-7, E15-12, E15-14,** and **DO IT! 15-5.**

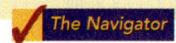

INVESTOR INSIGHT

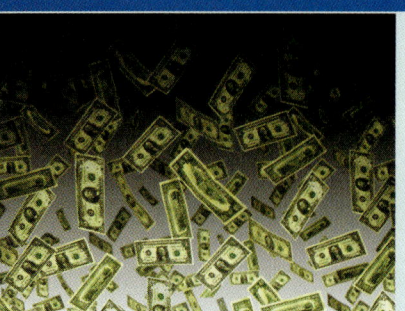

"Covenant-Lite" Debt

In many corporate loans and bond issuances the lending agreement specifies debt covenants. These covenants typically are specific financial measures, such as minimum levels of retained earnings, cash flows, times interest earned ratios, or other measures that a company must maintain during the life of the loan. If the company violates a covenant it is considered to have violated the loan agreement; the creditors can demand immediate repayment, or they can renegotiate the loan's terms. Covenants protect lenders because they enable lenders to step in and try to get their money back before the borrower gets too deep into trouble.

During the 1990s most traditional loans specified between three to six covenants or "triggers." In more recent years, when lots of cash was available, lenders began reducing or completely eliminating covenants from loan agreements in order to be more competitive with other lenders. In a slower economy these lenders will be more likely to lose big money when companies default.

Source: Cynthia Koons, "Risky Business: Growth of 'Covenant-Lite' Debt," *Wall Street Journal,* June 18, 2007, p. C2.

 How can financial ratios such as those covered in this chapter provide protection for creditors?

Comprehensive DO IT!

Snyder Software Inc. has successfully developed a new spreadsheet program. To produce and market the program, the company needed $2 million of additional financing. On January 1, 2011, Snyder borrowed money as follows.

1. Snyder issued $500,000, 11%, 10-year convertible bonds. The bonds sold at face value and pay semiannual interest on January 1 and July 1. Each $1,000 bond is convertible into 30 shares of Snyder's $20 par value common stock.
2. Snyder issued $1 million, 10%, 10-year bonds at face value. Interest is payable semiannually on January 1 and July 1.
3. Snyder also issued a $500,000, 12%, 15-year mortgage note payable. The terms provide for semiannual installment payments of $36,324 on June 30 and December 31.

Instructions

1. For the convertible bonds, prepare journal entries for:
   (a) The issuance of the bonds on January 1, 2011.
   (b) Interest expense on July 1 and December 31, 2011.
   (c) The payment of interest on January 1, 2012.
   (d) The conversion of all bonds into common stock on January 1, 2012, when the market value of the common stock was $67 per share.
2. For the 10-year, 10% bonds:
   (a) Journalize the issuance of the bonds on January 1, 2011.
   (b) Prepare the journal entries for interest expense in 2011. Assume no accrual of interest on July 1.
   (c) Prepare the entry for the redemption of the bonds at 101 on January 1, 2014, after paying the interest due on this date.

3. For the mortgage note payable:
   (a) Prepare the entry for the issuance of the note on January 1, 2011.
   (b) Prepare a payment schedule for the first four installment payments.
   (c) Indicate the current and noncurrent amounts for the mortgage note payable at December 31, 2011.

Solution to Comprehensive DO IT!

1. (a) 2011
Jan. 1 Cash   500,000
          Bonds Payable   500,000
          (To record issue of 11%, 10-year convertible bonds at face value)

(b) 2011
July 1 Bond Interest Expense   27,500
          Cash ($500,000 × 0.055)   27,500
          (To record payment of semiannual interest)

Dec. 31 Bond Interest Expense   27,500
          Bond Interest Payable   27,500
          (To record accrual of semiannual bond interest)

(c) 2012
Jan. 1 Bond Interest Payable   27,500
          Cash   27,500
          (To record payment of accrued interest)

(d) Jan. 1 Bonds Payable   500,000
          Common Stock   300,000*
          Paid-in Capital in Excess of Par Value   200,000
          (To record conversion of bonds into common stock)
          *($500,000 ÷ $1,000 = 500 bonds;
          500 × 30 = 15,000 shares;
          15,000 × $20 = $300,000)

2. (a) 2011
Jan. 1 Cash   1,000,000
          Bonds Payable   1,000,000
          (To record issuance of bonds)

(b) 2011
July 1 Bond Interest Expense   50,000
          Cash   50,000
          (To record payment of semiannual interest)

Dec. 31 Bond Interest Expense   50,000
          Bond Interest Payable   50,000
          (To record accrual of semiannual interest)

action plan
- Compute interest semiannually (six months).
- Record the accrual and payment of interest on appropriate dates.
- Record the conversion of the bonds into common stock by removing the book (carrying) value of the bonds from the liability account.

action plan
- Record the issuance of the bonds.
- Compute interest expense for each period.
- Compute the loss on bond redemption as the excess of the cash paid over the carrying value of the redeemed bonds.

662 Chapter 15 Long-Term Liabilities

(c) 2014
Jan. 1 Bonds Payable   1,000,000
        Loss on Bond Redemption   10,000*
            Cash   1,010,000
        (To record redemption of bonds at 101)
        *($1,010,000 − $1,000,000)

action plan

✔ Compute periodic interest expense on a mortgage note, recognizing that as the principal amount decreases, so does the interest expense.

✔ Record mortgage payments, recognizing that each payment consists of (1) interest on the unpaid loan balance and (2) a reduction of the loan principal.

3. (a) 2011
Jan. 1 Cash   500,000
            Mortgage Notes Payable   500,000
        (To record issuance of mortgage note payable)

(b)

Semiannual Interest Period	Cash Payment	Interest Expense	Reduction of Principal	Principal Balance
Issue date				$500,000
1	$36,324	$30,000	$6,324	493,676
2	36,324	29,621	6,703	486,973
3	36,324	29,218	7,106	479,867
4	36,324	28,792	7,532	472,335

(c) Current liability $14,638 ($7,106 + $7,532)
    Long-term liability $472,335

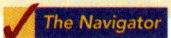

SUMMARY OF STUDY OBJECTIVES

1 Explain why bonds are issued. Companies may sell bonds to investors to raise long-term capital. Bonds offer the following advantages over common stock: (a) stockholder control is not affected, (b) tax savings result, (c) earnings per share of common stock may be higher.

2 Prepare the entries for the issuance of bonds and interest expense. When companies issue bonds, they debit Cash for the cash proceeds, and credit Bonds Payable for the face value of the bonds. The account Premium on Bonds Payable shows a bond premium; Discount on Bonds Payable shows a bond discount.

3 Describe the entries when bonds are redeemed or converted. When bondholders redeem bonds at maturity, the issuing company credits Cash and debits Bonds Payable for the face value of the bonds. When bonds are redeemed before maturity, the issuing company (a) eliminates the carrying value of the bonds at the redemption date, (b) records the cash paid, and (c) recognizes the gain or loss on redemption. When bonds are converted to common stock, the issuing company transfers the carrying (or book) value of the bonds to appropriate paid-in capital accounts; no gain or loss is recognized.

4 Describe the accounting for long-term notes payable. Each payment consists of (1) interest on the unpaid balance of the loan and (2) a reduction of loan principal. The interest decreases each period, while the portion applied to the loan principal increases.

5 Contrast the accounting for operating and capital leases. For an operating lease, the lessee (renter) records lease (rental) payments as an expense. For a capital lease, the lessee records the asset and related obligation at the present value of the future lease payments.

6 Identify the methods for the presentation and analysis of long-term liabilities. Companies should report the nature and amount of each long-term debt in the balance sheet or in the notes accompanying the financial statements. Stockholders and long-term creditors are interested in a company's long-run solvency. Debt to total assets and times interest earned are two ratios that provide information about debt-paying ability and long-run solvency.

GLOSSARY

Bearer (coupon) bonds Bonds not registered in the name of the owner. (p. 646).

Bond certificate A legal document that indicates the name of the issuer, the face value of the bonds, the contractual interest rate and maturity date of the bonds. (p. 646).

Bond indenture A legal document that sets forth the terms of the bond issue. (p. 646).

Bonds A form of interest-bearing notes payable issued by corporations, universities, and governmental entities. (p. 644).

Callable bonds Bonds that are subject to retirement at a stated dollar amount prior to maturity at the option of the issuer. (p. 646).

Capital lease A contractual arrangement that transfers substantially all the benefits and risks of ownership to the lessee so that the lease is in effect a purchase of the property. (p. 657).

Contractual interest rate Rate used to determine the amount of cash interest the borrower pays and the investor receives. (p. 646).

Convertible bonds Bonds that permit bondholders to convert them into common stock at the bondholders' option. (p. 646).

Debenture bonds Bonds issued against the general credit of the borrower. Also called unsecured bonds. (p. 646).

Debt to total assets ratio A solvency measure that indicates the percentage of total assets provided by creditors; computed as total debt divided by total assets. (p. 659).

Discount (on a bond) The difference between the face value of a bond and its selling price, when the bond is sold for less than its face value. (p. 649).

Face value (par value) Amount of principal the issuer must pay at the maturity date of the bond. (p. 646).

Long-term liabilities Obligations expected to be paid after one year. (p. 644).

Market interest rate The rate investors demand for loaning funds to the corporation. (p. 648).

Mortgage bond A bond secured by real estate. (p. 645).

Mortgage notes payable A long-term note secured by a mortgage that pledges title to specific assets as security for a loan. (p. 655).

Operating lease A contractual arrangement giving the lessee temporary use of the property, with continued ownership of the property by the lessor. (p. 657).

Premium (on a bond) The difference between the selling price and the face value of a bond, when the bond is sold for more than its face value. (p. 650).

Registered bonds Bonds issued in the name of the owner. (p. 646).

Secured bonds Bonds that have specific assets of the issuer pledged as collateral. (p. 645).

Serial bonds Bonds that mature in installments. (p. 646).

Sinking fund bonds Bonds secured by specific assets set aside to retire them. (p. 645).

Term bonds Bonds that mature at a single specified future date. (p. 646).

Times interest earned ratio A solvency measure that indicates a company's ability to meet interest payments; computed by dividing income before income taxes and interest expense by interest expense. (p. 659).

Unsecured bonds Bonds issued against the general credit of the borrower. Also called debenture bonds. (p. 646).

APPENDIX 15A Present Value Concepts Related to Bond Pricing

Congratulations! You have a winning lottery ticket and the state has provided you with three possible options for payment. They are:

1. Receive $10,000,000 in three years.
2. Receive $7,000,000 immediately.
3. Receive $3,500,000 at the end of each year for three years.

Which of these options would you select? The answer is not easy to determine at a glance. To make a dollar-maximizing choice, you must perform present value computations. A present value computation is based on the concept of time value of money. Time value of money concepts are useful for the lottery situation and for pricing other amounts to be received in the future. This appendix discusses how to use present value concepts to price bonds. It also will tell you how to determine what option you should take as a lottery winner.

Present Value of Face Value

STUDY OBJECTIVE 7
Compute the market price of a bond.

To illustrate present value concepts, assume that you are willing to invest a sum of money that will yield $1,000 at the end of one year. In other words, what amount would you need to invest today to have $1,000 one year from now? If you want to earn 10%, the investment (or present value) is $909.09 ($1,000 ÷ 1.10). Illustration 15A-1 shows the computation.

Illustration 15A-1
Present value computation—$1,000 discounted at 10% for one year

Present value	×	(1 + Interest rate)	=	Future amount
Present value	×	(1 + 10%)	=	$1,000
Present value			=	$1,000 ÷ 1.10
Present value			=	**$909.09**

The future amount ($1,000), the interest rate (10%), and the number of periods (1) are known. We can depict the variables in this situation as shown in the time diagram in Illustration 15A-2.

Illustration 15A-2
Finding present value if discounted for one period

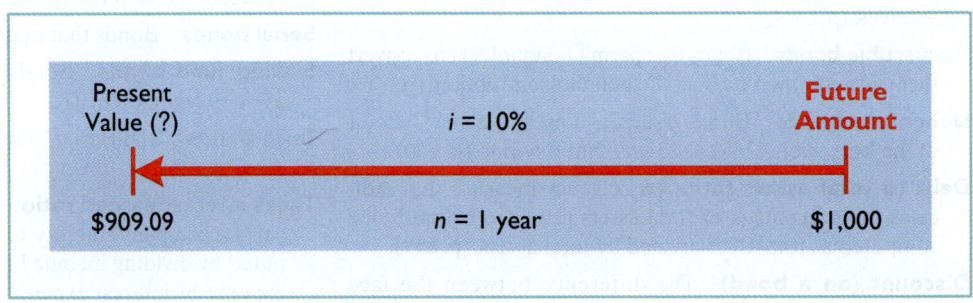

If you are to receive the single future amount of $1,000 **in two years**, discounted at 10%, its present value is $826.45 [($1,000 ÷ 1.10) ÷ 1.10], depicted as follows.

Illustration 15A-3
Finding present value if discounted for two periods

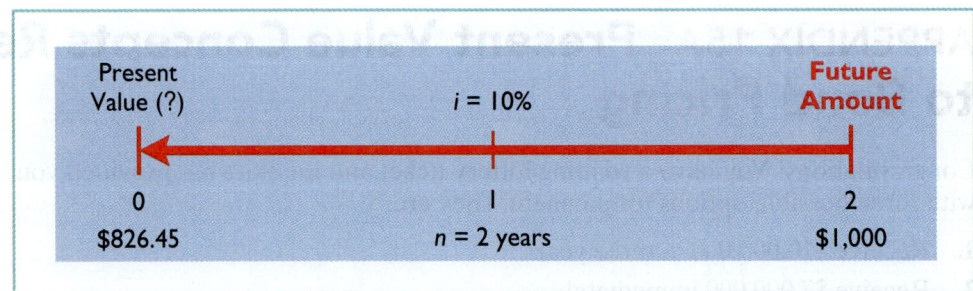

We also can determine the present value of 1 through tables that show the present value of 1 for n periods. In Table 15A-1 (page 665), n is the number of discounting periods involved. The percentages are the periodic interest rates, and the 5-digit decimal numbers in the respective columns are the factors for the present value of 1.

When using Table 15A-1, we multiply the future amount by the present value factor specified at the intersection of the number of periods and the interest rate. For example, the present value factor for 1 period at an interest rate of 10% is .90909, which equals the $909.09 ($1,000 × .90909) computed in Illustration 15A-1.

TABLE 15A-1
Present Value of 1

(n) Periods	4%	5%	6%	8%	9%	10%	11%	12%	15%
1	.96154	.95238	.94340	.92593	.91743	.90909	.90090	.89286	.86957
2	.92456	.90703	.89000	.85734	.84168	.82645	.81162	.79719	.75614
3	.88900	.86384	.83962	.79383	.77218	.75132	.73119	.71178	.65752
4	.85480	.82270	.79209	.73503	.70843	.68301	.65873	.63552	.57175
5	.82193	.78353	.74726	.68058	.64993	.62092	.59345	.56743	.49718
6	.79031	.74622	.70496	.63017	.59627	.56447	.53464	.50663	.43233
7	.75992	.71068	.66506	.58349	.54703	.51316	.48166	.45235	.37594
8	.73069	.67684	.62741	.54027	.50187	.46651	.43393	.40388	.32690
9	.70259	.64461	.59190	.50025	.46043	.42410	.39092	.36061	.28426
10	.67556	.61391	.55839	.46319	.42241	.38554	.35218	.32197	.24719

For two periods at an interest rate of 10%, the present value factor is .82645, which equals the $826.45 ($1,000 × .82645) computed previously.

Let's now go back to our lottery example. Given the present value concepts just learned, we can determine whether receiving $10,000,000 in three years is better than receiving $7,000,000 today, assuming the appropriate discount rate is 9%. The computation is as follows.

$10,000,000 × PV of 1 due in 3 years at 9% =	
$10,000,000 × .77218 (Table 15A-1)	$7,721,800
Amount to be received from state immediately	7,000,000
Difference	$ 721,800

Illustration 15A-4
Present value of $10,000,000 to be received in three years

What this computation shows you is that you would be $721,800 better off receiving the $10,000,000 at the end of three years rather than taking $7,000,000 immediately.

Present Value of Interest Payments (Annuities)

In addition to receiving the face value of a bond at maturity, an investor also receives periodic interest payments over the life of the bonds. These periodic payments are called **annuities**.

In order to compute the present value of an annuity, we need to know: (1) the interest rate, (2) the number of interest periods, and (3) the amount of the periodic receipts or payments. To illustrate the computation of the present value of an annuity, assume that you will receive $1,000 cash annually for three years and the interest rate is 10%. The time diagram in Illustration 15A-5 depicts this situation.

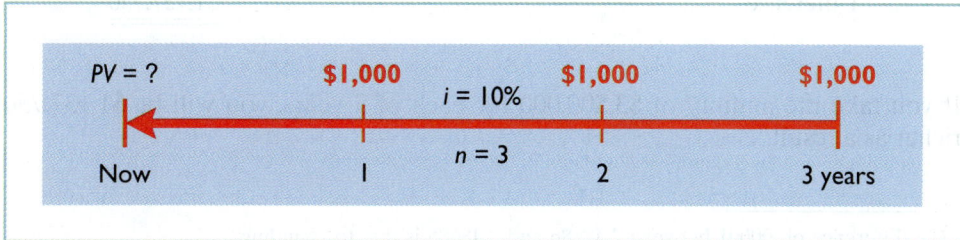

Illustration 15A-5
Time diagram for a three-year annuity

Chapter 15 Long-Term Liabilities

The present value in this situation may be computed as follows.

Illustration 15A-6
Present value of a series of future amounts computation

Future Amount	×	Present Value of 1 Factor at 10%	=	Present Value
$1,000 (1 year away)		.90909		$ 909.09
1,000 (2 years away)		.82645		826.45
1,000 (3 years away)		.75132		751.32
		2.48686		**$2,486.86**

We also can use annuity tables to value annuities. As illustrated in Table 15A-2 below, these tables show the present value of 1 to be received periodically for a given number of periods.

TABLE 15A-2
Present Value of an Annuity of 1

(n) Periods	4%	5%	6%	8%	9%	10%	11%	12%	15%
1	.96154	.95238	.94340	.92593	.91743	.90909	.90090	.89286	.86957
2	1.88609	1.85941	1.83339	1.78326	1.75911	1.73554	1.71252	1.69005	1.62571
3	2.77509	2.72325	2.67301	2.57710	2.53130	2.48685	2.44371	2.40183	2.28323
4	3.62990	3.54595	3.46511	3.31213	3.23972	3.16986	3.10245	3.03735	2.85498
5	4.45182	4.32948	4.21236	3.99271	3.88965	3.79079	3.69590	3.60478	3.35216
6	5.24214	5.07569	4.91732	4.62288	4.48592	4.35526	4.23054	4.11141	3.78448
7	6.00205	5.78637	5.58238	5.20637	5.03295	4.86842	4.71220	4.56376	4.16042
8	6.73274	6.46321	6.20979	5.74664	5.53482	5.33493	5.14612	4.96764	4.48732
9	7.43533	7.10782	6.80169	6.24689	5.99525	5.75902	5.53705	5.32825	4.77158
10	8.11090	7.72173	7.36009	6.71008	6.41766	6.14457	5.88923	5.65022	5.01877

From Table 15A-2 you can see that the present value factor of an annuity of 1 for three periods at 10% is 2.48685.[1] This present value factor is the total of the three individual present value factors as shown in Illustration 15A-6. Applying this amount to the annual cash flow of $1,000 produces a present value of $2,486.85.

Let's now go back to our lottery example. We determined that you would get more money if you wait and take the $10,000,000 in three years rather than take $7,000,000 immediately. But there is still another option—to receive $3,500,000 at the end of **each year** for three years (an annuity). The computation to evaluate this option (again assuming a 9% discount rate) is as follows.

Illustration 15A-7
Present value of lottery payments to be received over three years

$3,500,000 × PV of 1 due yearly for 3 years at 9% =	
$3,500,000 × 2.53130 (Table 15A-2)	$8,859,550
Present value of $10,000,000 to be received in 3 years	7,721,800
Difference	$1,137,750

If you take the annuity of $3,500,000 for each of 3 years, you will be $1,137,750 richer as a result.

---

[1] The difference of .00001 between 2.48686 and 2.48685 is due to rounding.

Time Periods and Discounting

We have used an **annual** interest rate to determine present value. Present value computations may also be done over shorter periods of time, such as monthly, quarterly, or semiannually. When the time frame is less than one year, it is necessary to convert the annual interest rate to the shorter time frame.

Assume, for example, that the investor in Illustration 15A-6 received $500 **semiannually** for three years instead of $1,000 annually. In this case, the number of periods becomes 6 (3 × 2), the interest rate is 5% (10% ÷ 2), the present value factor from Table 15A-2 is 5.07569, and the present value of the future cash flows is $2,537.85 (5.07569 × $500). This amount is slightly higher than the $2,486.86 computed in Illustration 15A-6 because interest is computed twice during the same year. That is, interest is earned on the first half year's interest.

Computing the Present Value of a Bond

The present value (or market price) of a bond is a function of three variables: (1) the payment amounts, (2) the length of time until the amounts are paid, and (3) the interest (discount) rate.

The first variable (dollars to be paid) is made up of two elements: (1) a series of interest payments (an annuity), and (2) the principal amount (a single sum). To compute the present value of the bond, we must discount both the interest payments and the principal amount.

When the investor's interest (discount) rate is equal to the bond's contractual interest rate, the present value of the bonds will equal the face value of the bonds. To illustrate, assume a bond issue of 10%, five-year bonds with a face value of $100,000 with interest payable **semiannually** on January 1 and July 1. If the discount rate is the same as the contractual rate, the bonds will sell **at face value**. In this case, the investor will receive: (1) $100,000 at maturity and (2) a series of ten $5,000 interest payments [$100,000 × (10% ÷ 2)] over the term of the bonds. The length of time is expressed in terms of interest periods (in this case, 10) and the discount rate per interest period (5%). The time diagram in Illustration 15A-8 depicts the variables involved in this discounting situation.

Illustration 15A-8
Time diagram for the present value of a 10%, five-year bond paying interest semiannually

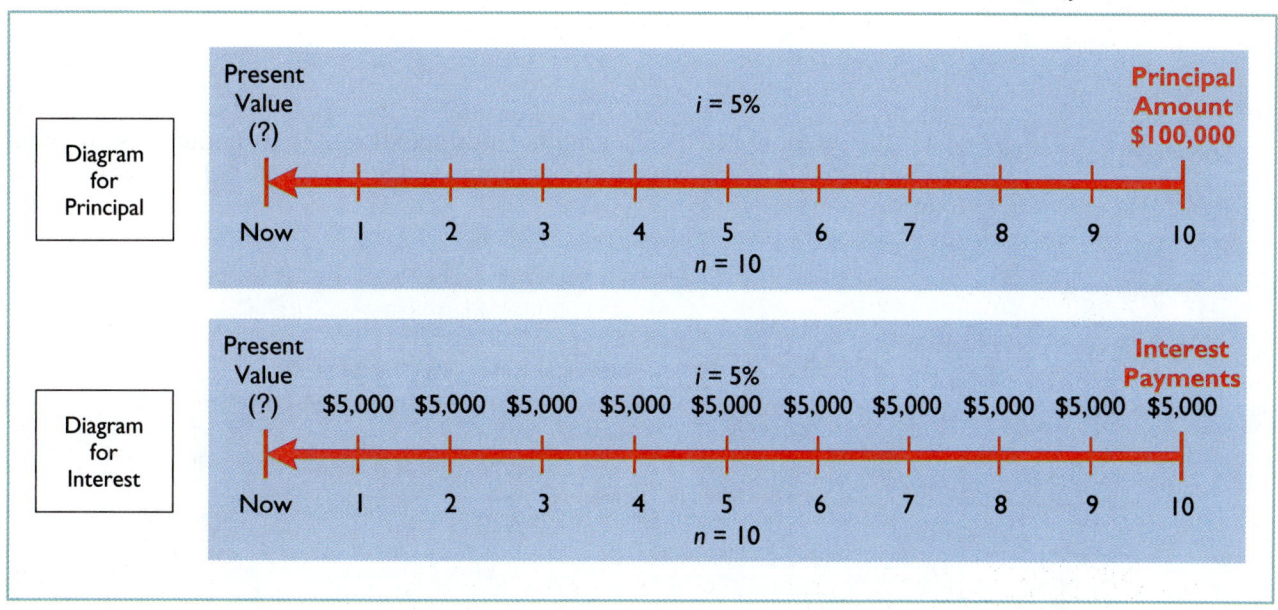

The computation of the present value of Candlestick's bonds, assuming they were issued at face value (page 649), is shown below.

Illustration 15A-9
Present value of principal and interest (face value)

10% Contractual Rate—10% Discount Rate	
Present value of principal to be received at maturity	
$100,000 × PV of 1 due in 10 periods at 5%	
$100,000 × .61391 (Table 15A-1)	$ 61,391
Present value of interest to be received periodically over the term of the bonds	
$5,000 × PV of 1 due periodically for 10 periods at 5%	
$5,000 × 7.72173 (Table 15A-2)	38,609*
Present value of bonds	**$100,000**

*(Rounded).

Now assume that the investor's required rate of return is 12%, not 10%. The future amounts are again $100,000 and $5,000, respectively. But now we must use a discount rate of 6% (12% ÷ 2). The present value of Candlestick's bonds issued at a discount (page 650) is $92,639 as computed below.

Illustration 15A-10
Present value of principal and interest (discount)

10% Contractual Rate—12% Discount Rate	
Present value of principal to be received at maturity	
$100,000 × .55839 (Table 15A-1)	$55,839
Present value of interest to be received periodically over the term of the bonds	
$5,000 × 7.36009 (Table 15A-2)	36,800
Present value of bonds	**$92,639**

If the discount rate is 8% and the contractual rate is 10%, the present value of Candlestick's bonds issued at a premium (page 651) is $108,111, computed as follows.

Illustration 15A-11
Present value of principal and interest (premium)

10% Contractual Rate—8% Discount Rate	
Present value of principal to be received at maturity	
$100,000 × .67556 (Table 15A-1)	$ 67,556
Present value of interest to be received periodically over the term of the bonds	
$5,000 × 8.11090 (Table 15A-2)	40,555
Present value of bonds	**$108,111**

SUMMARY OF STUDY OBJECTIVE FOR APPENDIX 15A

7 Compute the market price of a bond. Time value of money concepts are useful for pricing bonds. The present value (or market price) of a bond is a function of three variables: (1) the payment amounts, (2) the length of time until the amounts are paid, and (3) the interest rate.

APPENDIX 15B Effective-Interest Method of Bond Amortization

Under the **effective-interest method**, the amortization of bond discount or bond premium results in periodic interest expense equal to a **constant percentage** of the carrying value of the bonds. The effective-interest method results in varying amounts of amortization and interest expense per period but **a constant percentage rate**.

> **STUDY OBJECTIVE 8**
> Apply the effective-interest method of amortizing bond discount and bond premium.

The following steps are required under the effective-interest method.

1. Compute the **bond interest expense**. To do so, multiply the carrying value of the bonds at the beginning of the interest period by the effective-interest rate.
2. Compute the **bond interest paid** (or accrued). To do so, multiply the face value of the bonds by the contractual interest rate.
3. Compute the **amortization amount**. To do so, determine the difference between the amounts computed in steps (1) and (2).

Illustration 15B-1 depicts these steps.

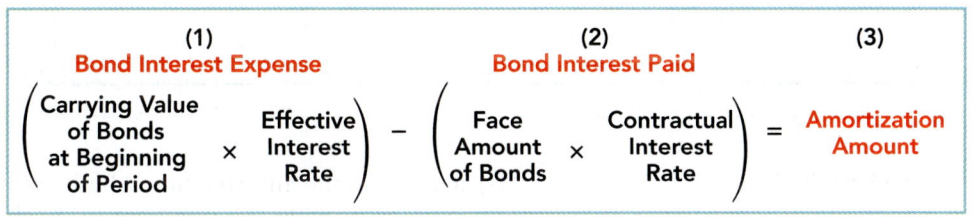

Illustration 15B-1
Computation of amortization—effective-interest method

When the difference between the straight-line method of amortization (Appendix 15C) and the effective-interest method is material, GAAP requires the use of the effective-interest method.

Amortizing Bond Discount

To illustrate the effective-interest method of bond discount amortization, assume that Candlestick, Inc. issues $100,000 of 10%, five-year bonds on January 1, 2010, with interest payable each July 1 and January 1 (pages 650–651). The bonds sell for $92,639 (92.639% of face value). This sales price results in bond discount of $7,361 ($100,000 − $92,639) and an effective-interest rate of 12%. A bond discount amortization schedule, as shown in Illustration 15B-2 (page 670), facilitates the recording of interest expense and the discount amortization. Note that interest expense as a percentage of carrying value remains constant at 6%.

CANDLESTICK, INC.
Bond Discount Amortization
Effective-Interest Method—Semiannual Interest Payments
10% Bonds Issued at 12%

Semiannual Interest Periods	(A) Interest to Be Paid (5% × $100,000)	(B) Interest Expense to Be Recorded (6% × Preceding Bond Carrying Value)		(C) Discount Amortization (B) − (A)	(D) Unamortized Discount (D) − (C)	(E) Bond Carrying Value ($100,000 − D)
Issue date					$7,361	$92,639
1	$ 5,000	$ 5,558	(6% × $92,639)	$ 558	6,803	93,197
2	5,000	5,592	(6% × $93,197)	592	6,211	93,789
3	5,000	5,627	(6% × $93,789)	627	5,584	94,416
4	5,000	5,665	(6% × $94,416)	665	4,919	95,081
5	5,000	5,705	(6% × $95,081)	705	4,214	95,786
6	5,000	5,747	(6% × $95,786)	747	3,467	96,533
7	5,000	5,792	(6% × $96,533)	792	2,675	97,325
8	5,000	5,840	(6% × $97,325)	840	1,835	98,165
9	5,000	5,890	(6% × $98,165)	890	945	99,055
10	5,000	5,945*	(6% × $99,055)	945	−0−	100,000
	$50,000	$57,361		$7,361		

Column **(A)** remains constant because the face value of the bonds ($100,000) is multiplied by the semiannual contractual interest rate (5%) each period.
Column **(B)** is computed as the preceding bond carrying value times the semiannual effective-interest rate (6%).
Column **(C)** indicates the discount amortization each period.
Column **(D)** decreases each period until it reaches zero at maturity.
Column **(E)** increases each period until it equals face value at maturity.

*$2 difference due to rounding.

Illustration 15B-2
Bond discount amortization schedule

We have highlighted columns (A), (B), and (C) in the amortization schedule to emphasize their importance. These three columns provide the numbers for each period's journal entries. They are the primary reason for preparing the schedule.

For the first interest period, the computations of bond interest expense and the bond discount amortization are:

Illustration 15B-3
Computation of bond discount amortization

Bond interest expense ($92,639 × 6%)	$5,558
Contractual interest ($100,000 × 5%)	5,000
Bond discount amortization	**$ 558**

Candlestick records the payment of interest and amortization of bond discount on July 1, 2010, as follows.

July 1	Bond Interest Expense	5,558	
	Discount on Bonds Payable		558
	Cash		5,000
	(To record payment of bond interest and amortization of bond discount)		

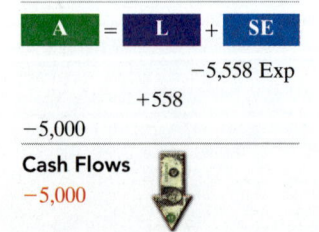

A = L + SE
       −5,558 Exp
   +558
−5,000

Cash Flows
−5,000

For the second interest period, bond interest expense will be $5,592 ($93,197 × 6%), and the discount amortization will be $592. At December 31, Candlestick makes the following adjusting entry.

Dec. 31	Bond Interest Expense	5,592	
	Discount on Bonds Payable		592
	Bond Interest Payable		5,000
	(To record accrued interest and amortization of bond discount)		

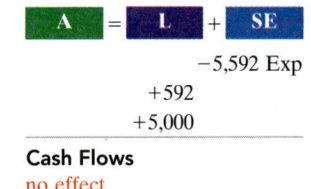

Cash Flows
no effect

Total bond interest expense for 2010 is $11,150 ($5,558 + $5,592). On January 1, Candlestick records payment of the interest by a debit to Bond Interest Payable and a credit to Cash.

Amortizing Bond Premium

The amortization of bond premium by the effective-interest method is similar to the procedures described for bond discount. For example, assume that Candlestick, Inc. issues $100,000, 10%, five-year bonds on January 1, 2010, with interest payable on July 1 and January 1 (pages 651–652). In this case, the bonds sell for $108,111. This sales price results in bond premium of $8,111 and an effective-interest rate of 8%. Illustration 15B-4 shows the bond premium amortization schedule.

HELPFUL HINT
When a bond sells for $108,111, it is quoted as 108.111% of face value. Note that $108,111 can be proven as shown in Appendix 15A.

Illustration 15B-4
Bond premium amortization schedule

CANDLESTICK, INC.
Bond Premium Amortization
Effective-Interest Method—Semiannual Interest Payments
10% Bonds Issued at 8%

Semiannual Interest Periods	(A) Interest to Be Paid (5% × $100,000)	(B) Interest Expense to Be Recorded (4% × Preceding Bond Carrying Value)	(C) Premium Amortization (A) − (B)	(D) Unamortized Premium (D) − (C)	(E) Bond Carrying Value ($100,000 + D)
Issue date				$8,111	$108,111
1	$ 5,000	$ 4,324 (4% × $108,111)	$ 676	7,435	107,435
2	5,000	4,297 (4% × $107,435)	703	6,732	106,732
3	5,000	4,269 (4% × $106,732)	731	6,001	106,001
4	5,000	4,240 (4% × $106,001)	760	5,241	105,241
5	5,000	4,210 (4% × $105,241)	790	4,451	104,451
6	5,000	4,178 (4% × $104,451)	822	3,629	103,629
7	5,000	4,145 (4% × $103,629)	855	2,774	102,774
8	5,000	4,111 (4% × $102,774)	889	1,885	101,885
9	5,000	4,075 (4% × $101,885)	925	960	100,960
10	5,000	4,040* (4% × $100,960)	960	–0–	100,000
	$50,000	$41,889	$8,111		

Column (A) remains constant because the face value of the bonds ($100,000) is multiplied by the semiannual contractual interest rate (5%) each period.
Column (B) is computed as the carrying value of the bonds times the semiannual effective-interest rate (4%).
Column (C) indicates the premium amortization each period.
Column (D) decreases each period until it reaches zero at maturity.
Column (E) decreases each period until it equals face value at maturity.

*$2 difference due to rounding.

672 Chapter 15 Long-Term Liabilities

For the first interest period, the computations of bond interest expense and the bond premium amortization are:

Illustration 15B-5 Computation of bond premium amortization

Bond interest expense ($108,111 × 4%)	$4,324
Contractual interest ($100,000 × 5%)	5,000
Bond premium amortization	**$ 676**

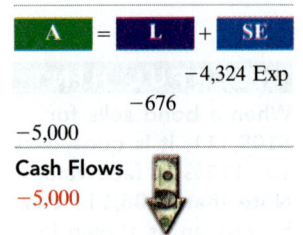

Candlestick records payments on the first interest date as follows.

July 1	Bond Interest Expense	4,324	
	Premium on Bonds Payable	676	
	Cash		5,000
	(To record payment of bond interest and amortization of bond premium)		

For the second interest period, interest expense will be $4,297, and the premium amortization will be $703. Total bond interest expense for 2010 is $8,621 ($4,324 + $4,297).

Comprehensive DO IT! for Appendix 15B

Gardner Corporation issues $1,750,000, 10-year, 12% bonds on January 1, 2010, at $1,968,090, to yield 10%. The bonds pay semiannual interest July 1 and January 1. Gardner uses the effective-interest method of amortization.

action plan

✔ Compute interest expense by multiplying bond carrying value at the beginning of the period by the effective-interest rate.

✔ Compute credit to cash (or bond interest payable) by multiplying the face value of the bonds by the contractual interest rate.

✔ Compute bond premium or discount amortization, which is the difference between interest expense and cash paid.

✔ Interest expense decreases when the effective-interest method is used for bonds issued at a premium. The reason is that a constant percentage is applied to a decreasing book value to compute interest expense.

Instructions

(a) Prepare the journal entry to record the issuance of the bonds.
(b) Prepare the journal entry to record the payment of interest on July 1, 2010.

Solution to Comprehensive DO IT! for Appendix 15B

(a) 2010

Jan. 1	Cash	1,968,090	
	Bonds Payable		1,750,000
	Premium on Bonds Payable		218,090
	(To record issuance of bonds at a premium)		

(b) 2010

July 1	Bond Interest Expense	98,405*	
	Premium on Bonds Payable	6,595**	
	Cash		105,000
	(To record payment of semiannual interest and amortization of bond premium)		
	*($1,968,090 × 5%)		
	**($105,000 − $98,405)		

SUMMARY OF STUDY OBJECTIVE FOR APPENDIX 15B

8 Apply the effective-interest method of amortizing bond discount and bond premium. The effective-interest method results in varying amounts of amortization and interest expense per period but a *constant percentage rate* of interest. When the difference between the straight-line and effective-interest method is material, GAAP requires the use of the effective-interest method.

GLOSSARY FOR APPENDIX 15B

Effective-interest method of amortization A method of amortizing bond discount or bond premium that results in periodic interest expense equal to a constant percentage of the carrying value of the bonds. (p. 669).

APPENDIX 15C Straight-Line Amortization

Amortizing Bond Discount

To follow the matching principle, companies should allocate bond discount systematically to each period in which the bonds are outstanding. The **straight-line method of amortization** allocates the **same amount to interest expense** in each interest period. The amount is determined using the formula in Illustration 15C-1.

> **STUDY OBJECTIVE 9**
> Apply the straight-line method of amortizing bond discount and bond premium.

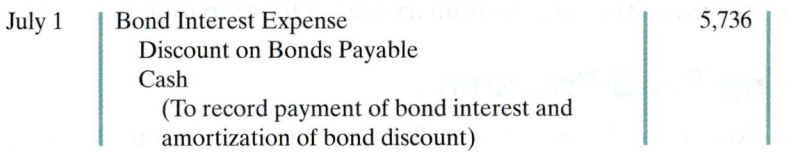

Illustration 15C-1
Formula for straight-line method of bond discount amortization

In the Candlestick, Inc. example (pages 650–651), the company sold $100,000, five-year, 10% bonds on January 1, 2010, for $92,639. This price resulted in a $7,361 bond discount ($100,000 − $92,639). Interest is payable on July 1 and January 1. The bond discount amortization for each interest period is $736 ($7,361 ÷ 10). Candlestick records the payment of bond interest and the amortization of bond discount on the first interest date (July 1, 2010) as follows.

July 1	Bond Interest Expense	5,736	
	Discount on Bonds Payable		736
	Cash		5,000
	(To record payment of bond interest and amortization of bond discount)		

A	=	L	+	SE
				−5,736 Exp
		+736		
−5,000				

Cash Flows
−5,000

At December 31, Candlestick makes the following adjusting entry.

Dec. 31	Bond Interest Expense	5,736	
	Discount on Bonds Payable		736
	Bond Interest Payable		5,000
	(To record accrued bond interest and amortization of bond discount)		

A	=	L	+	SE
				−5,736 Exp
		+736		
		+5,000		

Cash Flows
no effect

Over the term of the bonds, the balance in Discount on Bonds Payable will decrease annually by the **same amount** until it has a zero balance at the maturity date of the bonds. Thus, the carrying value of the bonds at maturity will be equal to the face value.

It is useful to prepare a bond discount amortization schedule as shown in Illustration 15C-2 (page 674). The schedule shows interest expense, discount amortization, and the carrying value of the bond for each interest period. As indicated, the interest expense recorded **each period** for the Candlestick bond is $5,736. Also note that the carrying value of the bond increases $736 each period until it reaches its face value $100,000 at the end of period 10.

Illustration 15C-2
Bond discount amortization schedule

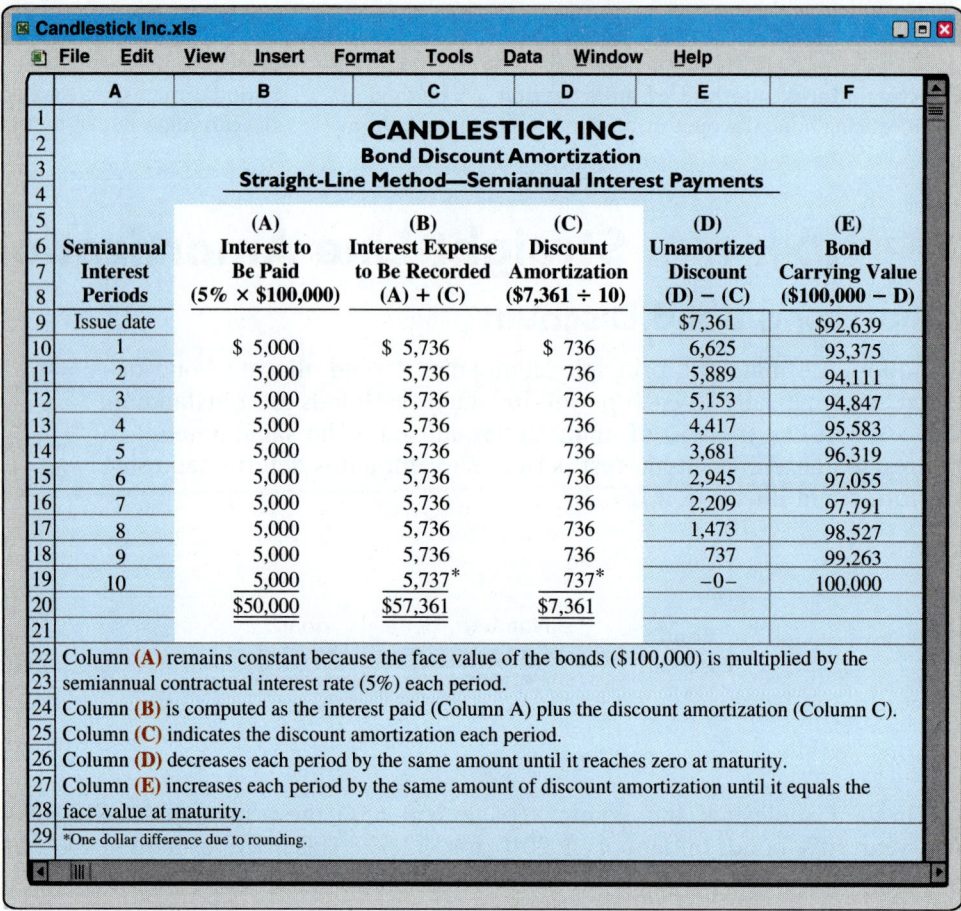

CANDLESTICK, INC.
Bond Discount Amortization
Straight-Line Method—Semiannual Interest Payments

Semiannual Interest Periods	(A) Interest to Be Paid (5% × $100,000)	(B) Interest Expense to Be Recorded (A) + (C)	(C) Discount Amortization ($7,361 ÷ 10)	(D) Unamortized Discount (D) − (C)	(E) Bond Carrying Value ($100,000 − D)
Issue date				$7,361	$92,639
1	$ 5,000	$ 5,736	$ 736	6,625	93,375
2	5,000	5,736	736	5,889	94,111
3	5,000	5,736	736	5,153	94,847
4	5,000	5,736	736	4,417	95,583
5	5,000	5,736	736	3,681	96,319
6	5,000	5,736	736	2,945	97,055
7	5,000	5,736	736	2,209	97,791
8	5,000	5,736	736	1,473	98,527
9	5,000	5,736	736	737	99,263
10	5,000	5,737*	737*	−0−	100,000
	$50,000	$57,361	$7,361		

Column **(A)** remains constant because the face value of the bonds ($100,000) is multiplied by the semiannual contractual interest rate (5%) each period.
Column **(B)** is computed as the interest paid (Column A) plus the discount amortization (Column C).
Column **(C)** indicates the discount amortization each period.
Column **(D)** decreases each period by the same amount until it reaches zero at maturity.
Column **(E)** increases each period by the same amount of discount amortization until it equals the face value at maturity.
*One dollar difference due to rounding.

We have highlighted columns (A), (B), and (C) in the amortization schedule to emphasize their importance. These three columns provide the numbers for each period's journal entries. They are the primary reason for preparing the schedule.

Amortizing Bond Premium

The amortization of bond premium parallels that of bond discount. Illustration 15C-3 presents the formula for determining bond premium amortization under the straight-line method.

Illustration 15C-3
Formula for straight-line method of bond premium amortization

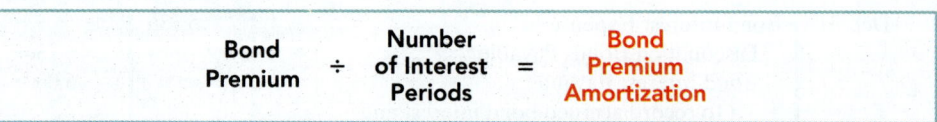

Bond Premium ÷ Number of Interest Periods = Bond Premium Amortization

Continuing our example, assume that Candlestick sells the bonds for $108,111, rather than $92,639 (pages 651–652). This sale price results in a bond premium of $8,111 ($108,111 − $100,000). The bond premium amortization for each interest period is $811 ($8,111 ÷ 10). Candlestick records the first payment of interest on July 1 as follows.

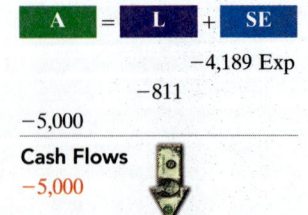

July 1	Bond Interest Expense	4,189	
	Premium on Bonds Payable	811	
	Cash		5,000
	(To record payment of bond interest and amortization of bond premium)		

At December 31, the company makes the following adjusting entry.

Dec. 31	Bond Interest Expense	4,189	
	Premium on Bonds Payable	811	
	Bond Interest Payable		5,000
	(To record accrued bond interest and amortization of bond premium)		

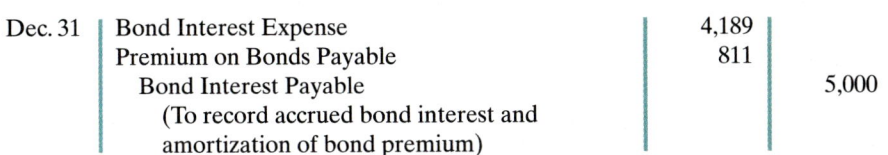

A = L + SE
−4,189 Exp
−811
+5,000

Cash Flows
no effect

Over the term of the bonds, the balance in Premium on Bonds Payable will decrease annually **by the same amount** until it has a zero balance at maturity.

It is useful to prepare a bond premium amortization schedule as shown in Illustration 15C-4. It shows interest expense, premium amortization, and the carrying value of the bond. The interest expense recorded each period for the Candlestick bond is $4,189. Also note that the carrying value of the bond decreases $811 each period until it reaches its face value $100,000 at the end of period 10.

Illustration 15C-4
Bond premium amortization schedule

CANDLESTICK, INC.
Bond Premium Amortization
Straight-Line Method—Semiannual Interest Payments

Semiannual Interest Periods	(A) Interest to Be Paid (5% × $100,000)	(B) Interest Expense to Be Recorded (A) − (C)	(C) Premium Amortization ($8,111 ÷ 10)	(D) Unamortized Premium (D) − (C)	(E) Bond Carrying Value ($100,000 + D)
Issue date				$8,111	$108,111
1	$ 5,000	$ 4,189	$ 811	7,300	107,300
2	5,000	4,189	811	6,489	106,489
3	5,000	4,189	811	5,678	105,678
4	5,000	4,189	811	4,867	104,867
5	5,000	4,189	811	4,056	104,056
6	5,000	4,189	811	3,245	103,245
7	5,000	4,189	811	2,434	102,434
8	5,000	4,189	811	1,623	101,623
9	5,000	4,189	811	812	100,812
10	5,000	4,188*	812*	–0–	100,000
	$50,000	$41,889	$8,111		

Column **(A)** remains constant because the face value of the bonds ($100,000) is multiplied by the semiannual contractual interest rate (5%) each period.
Column **(B)** is computed as the interest paid (Column A) less the premium amortization (Column C).
Column **(C)** indicates the premium amortization each period.
Column **(D)** decreases each period by the same amount until it reaches zero at maturity.
Column **(E)** decreases each period by the amount of premium amortization until it equals the face value at maturity.

*One dollar difference due to rounding.

Comprehensive DO IT! for Appendix 15C

Glenda Corporation issues $1,968,090, 10-year, 12% bonds on January 1, 2010, for $1,820,000 to yield 10%. The bonds pay semiannual interest July 1 and January 1. Glenda uses the straight-line method of amortization.

Instructions

(a) Prepare the journal entry to record the issuance of the bonds.
(b) Prepare the journal entry to record the payment of interest on July 1, 2010.

676 Chapter 15 Long-Term Liabilities

action plan

✔ Compute credit to cash (or bond interest payable) by multiplying the face value of the bonds by the contractual interest rate.

✔ Compute bond premium or discount amortization by dividing bond premium or discount by the total number of periods.

✔ Understand that interest expense decreases when bonds are issued at a premium. The reason is that the amortization of premium reduces the total cost of borrowing.

Solution to Comprehensive DO IT! for Appendix 15C

(a) 2010
Jan. 1 Cash   1,968,090
          Bonds Payable   1,750,000
          Premium on Bonds Payable   218,090

(b) 2010
July 1 Bond Interest Expense   94,095.50**
          Premium on Bonds Payable   10,904.50*
          Cash   105,000
*$218,090 ÷ 20
**$105,000 − $10,904.50

SUMMARY OF STUDY OBJECTIVE FOR APPENDIX 15C

9 Apply the straight-line method of amortizing bond discount and bond premium. The straight-line method of amortization results in a *constant amount* of amortization and interest expense per period.

GLOSSARY FOR APPENDIX 15C

Straight-line method of amortization. A method of amortizing bond discount or bond premium that results in allocating the same amount to interest expense in each interest period. (p. 673)

*Note: All asterisked Questions, Exercises, and Problems relate to material in the appendices to the chapter.

SELF-STUDY QUESTIONS

Answers are at the end of the chapter.

(SO 1) **1.** The term used for bonds that are unsecured is:
  a. callable bonds.
  b. indenture bonds.
  c. debenture bonds.
  d. bearer bonds.

(SO 1) **2.** The market interest rate:
  a. is the contractual interest rate used to determine the amount of cash interest paid by the borrower.
  b. is listed in the bond indenture.
  c. is the rate investors demand for loaning funds.
  d. More than one of the above is true.

(SO 2) **3.** Karson Inc. issues 10-year bonds with a maturity value of $200,000. If the bonds are issued at a premium, this indicates that:
  a. the contractual interest rate exceeds the market interest rate.
  b. the market interest rate exceeds the contractual interest rate.
  c. the contractual interest rate and the market interest rate are the same.
  d. no relationship exists between the two rates.

4. Four-Nine Corporation issued bonds that pay interest (SO 2) every July 1 and January 1. The entry to accrue bond interest at December 31 includes a:
  a. debit to Interest Payable.
  b. credit to Cash.
  c. credit to Interest Expense.
  d. credit to Interest Payable.

5. Gester Corporation retires its $100,000 face value bonds (SO 3) at 105 on January 1, following the payment of semiannual interest. The carrying value of the bonds at the redemption date is $103,745. The entry to record the redemption will include a:
  a. credit of $3,745 to Loss on Bond Redemption.
  b. debit of $3,745 to Premium on Bonds Payable.
  c. credit of $1,255 to Gain on Bond Redemption.
  d. debit of $5,000 to Premium on Bonds Payable.

(SO 3) **6.** Colson Inc. converts $600,000 of bonds sold at face value into 10,000 shares of common stock, par value $1. Both the bonds and the stock have a market value of $760,000. What amount should be credited to Paid-in Capital in Excess of Par as a result of the conversion?
   a. $10,000.
   b. $160,000.
   c. $600,000.
   d. $590,000.

(SO 4) **7.** Howard Corporation issued a 20-year mortgage note payable on January 1, 2010. At December 31, 2010, the unpaid principal balance will be reported as:
   a. a current liability.
   b. a long-term liability.
   c. part current and part long-term liability.
   d. interest payable.

(SO 4) **8.** Andrews Inc. issues a $497,000, 10% 3-year mortgage note on January 1. The note will be paid in three annual installments of $200,000, each payable at the end of the year. What is the amount of interest expense that should be recognized by Andrews Inc. in the second year?
   a. $16,567.
   b. $49,700.
   c. $34,670.
   d. $346,700.

(SO 5) **9.** Lease A does not contain a bargain purchase option, but the lease term is equal to 90 percent of the estimated economic life of the leased property. Lease B does not transfer ownership of the property to the lessee by the end of the lease term, but the lease term is equal to 75 percent of the estimated economic life of the leased property. How should the lessee classify these leases?

	Lease A	Lease B
a.	Operating lease	Capital lease
b.	Operating lease	Operating lease
c.	Capital lease	Operating lease
d.	Capital lease	Capital lease

(SO 6) **10.** For 2010, Corn Flake Corporation reported net income of $300,000. Interest expense was $40,000 and income taxes were $100,000. The times interest earned ratio was:
   a. 3 times.
   b. 4.4 times.
   c. 7.5 times.
   d. 11 times.

*11. The market price of a bond is dependent on: (SO 7)
   a. the payment amounts.
   b. the length of time until the amounts are paid.
   c. the interest rate.
   d. All of the above.

*12. On January 1, Besalius Inc. issued $1,000,000, 9% bonds (SO 8) for $939,000. The market rate of interest for these bonds is 10%. Interest is payable annually on December 31. Besalius uses the effective-interest method of amortizing bond discount. At the end of the first year, Besalius should report unamortized bond discount of:
   a. $54,900.   c. $51,610.
   b. $57,100.   d. $51,000.

*13. On January 1, Dias Corporation issued $1,000,000, 10%, (SO 8) 5-year bonds with interest payable on July 1 and January 1. The bonds sold for $1,081,105. The market rate of interest for these bonds was 8%. On the first interest date, using the effective-interest method, the debit entry to Bond Interest Expense is for:
   a. $50,000.   c. $43,244.
   b. $54,055.   d. $100,811.

*14. On January 1, Hurley Corporation issues $500,000, 5-year, (SO 9) 12% bonds at 96 with interest payable on July 1 and January 1. The entry on July 1 to record payment of bond interest and the amortization of bond discount using the straight-line method will include a:
   a. debit to Interest Expense $30,000.
   b. debit to Interest Expense $60,000.
   c. credit to Discount on Bonds Payable $4,000.
   d. credit to Discount on Bonds Payable $2,000.

*15. For the bonds issued in question 9, above, what is the carry- (SO 9) ing value of the bonds at the end of the third interest period?
   a. $486,000.   c. $472,000.
   b. $488,000.   d. $464,000.

Go to the book's companion website,
www.wiley.com/college/weygandt,
for Additional Self-Study questions.

QUESTIONS

1. (a) What are long-term liabilities? Give three examples. (b) What is a bond?

2. (a) As a source of long-term financing, what are the major advantages of bonds over common stock? (b) What are the major disadvantages in using bonds for long-term financing?

3. Contrast the following types of bonds: (a) secured and unsecured, (b) term and serial, (c) registered and bearer, and (d) convertible and callable.

4. The following terms are important in issuing bonds: (a) face value, (b) contractual interest rate, (c) bond indenture, and (d) bond certificate. Explain each of these terms.

5. Describe the two major obligations incurred by a company when bonds are issued.

6. Assume that Koslowski Inc. sold bonds with a face value of $100,000 for $104,000. Was the market interest rate equal to, less than, or greater than the bonds' contractual interest rate? Explain.

7. If a 7%, 10-year, $800,000 bond is issued at face value and interest is paid semiannually, what is the amount of the interest payment at the end of the first semiannual period?

8. If the Bonds Payable account has a balance of $900,000 and the Discount on Bonds Payable account has a balance of $40,000, what is the carrying value of the bonds?

9. Which accounts are debited and which are credited if a bond issue originally sold at a premium is redeemed before maturity at 97 immediately following the payment of interest?

10. Henricks Corporation is considering issuing a convertible bond. What is a convertible bond? Discuss the advantages of a convertible bond from the standpoint of (a) the bondholders and (b) the issuing corporation.

11. Tim Brown, a friend of yours, has recently purchased a home for $125,000, paying $25,000 down and the remainder financed by a 10.5%, 20-year mortgage, payable at $998.38 per month. At the end of the first month, Tim receives a statement from the bank indicating that only $123.38 of principal was paid during the month. At this rate, he calculates that it will take over 67 years to pay off the mortgage. Is he right? Discuss.

12. (a) What is a lease agreement? (b) What are the two most common types of leases? (c) Distinguish between the two types of leases.

13. Clooney Company rents a warehouse on a month-to-month basis for the storage of its excess inventory. The company periodically must rent space when its production greatly exceeds actual sales. What is the nature of this type of lease agreement, and what accounting treatment should be used?

14. Rondelli Company entered into an agreement to lease 12 computers from Estes Electronics Inc. The present value of the lease payments is $186,300. Assuming that this is a capital lease, what entry would Rondelli Company make on the date of the lease agreement?

15. In general, what are the requirements for the financial statement presentation of long-term liabilities?

*16. Laura Hiatt is discussing the advantages of the effective-interest method of bond amortization with her accounting staff. What do you think Laura is saying?

*17. Markham Corporation issues $500,000 of 9%, 5-year bonds on January 1, 2010, at 104. If Markham uses the effective-interest method in amortizing the premium, will the annual interest expense increase or decrease over the life of the bonds? Explain.

*18. Tina Cruz and Dale Commons are discussing how the market price of a bond is determined. Tina believes that the market price of a bond is solely a function of the amount of the principal payment at the end of the term of a bond. Is she right? Discuss.

*19. Explain the straight-line method of amortizing discount and premium on bonds payable.

*20. DeWeese Corporation issues $400,000 of 8%, 5-year bonds on January 1, 2010, at 105. Assuming that the straight-line method is used to amortize the premium, what is the total amount of interest expense for 2010?

21.  Did PepsiCo redeem any of its debt during the fiscal year ended December 29, 2007? (*Hint:* Examine PepsiCo's statement of cash flows.)

BRIEF EXERCISES

Compare bond versus stock financing.
(SO 1)

BE15-1 Mareska Inc. is considering two alternatives to finance its construction of a new $2 million plant.

(a) Issuance of 200,000 shares of common stock at the market price of $10 per share.
(b) Issuance of $2 million, 8% bonds at face value.

Complete the following table, and indicate which alternative is preferable.

	Issue Stock	Issue Bond
Income before interest and taxes	$700,000	$700,000
Interest expense from bonds		
Income before income taxes	$	$
Income tax expense (30%)		
Net income	$	$
Outstanding shares		500,000
Earnings per share		

Prepare entries for bonds issued at face value.
(SO 2)

BE15-2 Pruitt Corporation issued 3,000, 8%, 5-year, $1,000 bonds dated January 1, 2010, at 100.

(a) Prepare the journal entry to record the sale of these bonds on January 1, 2010.
(b) Prepare the journal entry to record the first interest payment on July 1, 2010 (interest payable semiannually), assuming no previous accrual of interest.
(c) Prepare the adjusting journal entry on December 31, 2010, to record interest expense.

Prepare entries for bonds sold at a discount and a premium.
(SO 2)

BE15-3 Ratzlaff Company issues $2 million, 10-year, 8% bonds at 97, with interest payable on July 1 and January 1.

(a) Prepare the journal entry to record the sale of these bonds on January 1, 2010.
(b) Assuming instead that the above bonds sold for 104, prepare the journal entry to record the sale of these bonds on January 1, 2010.

BE15-4 Halloway Company has issued three different bonds during 2010. Interest is payable semiannually on each of these bonds.

1. On January 1, 2010, 1,000, 8%, 5-year, $1,000 bonds dated January 1, 2010, were issued at face value.
2. On July 1, $800,000, 9%, 5-year bonds dated July 1, 2010, were issued at 102.
3. On September 1, $200,000, 7%, 5-year bonds dated September 1, 2010, were issued at 98.

Prepare the journal entry to record each bond transaction at the date of issuance.

Prepare entries for bonds issued.
(SO 2)

BE15-5 The balance sheet for Lemay Company reports the following information on July 1, 2010.

> Long-term liabilities
> Bonds payable $1,000,000
> Less: Discount on bonds payable 60,000 $940,000

Lemay decides to redeem these bonds at 101 after paying semiannual interest. Prepare the journal entry to record the redemption on July 1, 2010.

Prepare entry for redemption of bonds.
(SO 3)

BE15-6 Pickeril Inc. issues a $600,000, 10%, 10-year mortgage note on December 31, 2010, to obtain financing for a new building. The terms provide for semiannual installment payments of $48,145. Prepare the entry to record the mortgage loan on December 31, 2010, and the first installment payment.

Prepare entries for long-term notes payable.
(SO 4)

BE15-7 Prepare the journal entries that the lessee should make to record the following transactions.

1. The lessee makes a lease payment of $80,000 to the lessor in an operating lease transaction.
2. Veatch Company leases a new building from Joel Construction, Inc. The present value of the lease payments is $700,000. The lease qualifies as a capital lease.

Contrast accounting for operating and capital lease.
(SO 5)

BE15-8 Presented below are long-term liability items for Molini Company at December 31, 2010. Prepare the long-term liabilities section of the balance sheet for Molini Company.

> Bonds payable, due 2012 $500,000
> Lease liability 70,000
> Notes payable, due 2015 80,000
> Discount on bonds payable 45,000

Prepare statement presentation of long-term liabilities.
(SO 6)

***BE15-9** (a) What is the present value of $10,000 due 8 periods from now, discounted at 10%?
(b) What is the present value of $20,000 to be received at the end of each of 6 periods, discounted at 8%?

Determine present value.
(SO 7)

***BE15-10** Presented below is the partial bond discount amortization schedule for Morales Corp. Morales uses the effective-interest method of amortization.

Semiannual Interest Periods	Interest to Be Paid	Interest Expense to Be Recorded	Discount Amortization	Unamortized Discount	Bond Carrying Value
Issue date				$62,311	$937,689
1	$45,000	$46,884	$1,884	60,427	939,573
2	45,000	46,979	1,979	58,448	941,552

Use effective-interest method of bond amortization.
(SO 8)

Instructions
(a) Prepare the journal entry to record the payment of interest and the discount amortization at the end of period 1.
(b) Explain why interest expense is greater than interest paid.
(c) Explain why interest expense will increase each period.

***BE15-11** Deane Company issues $5 million, 10-year, 9% bonds at 96, with interest payable on July 1 and January 1. The straight-line method is used to amortize bond discount.

(a) Prepare the journal entry to record the sale of these bonds on January 1, 2010.
(b) Prepare the journal entry to record interest expense and bond discount amortization on July 1, 2010, assuming no previous accrual of interest.

Prepare entries for bonds issued at a discount.
(SO 9)

***BE15-12** Coates Inc. issues $3 million, 5-year, 10% bonds at 102, with interest payable on July 1 and January 1. The straight-line method is used to amortize bond premium.

(a) Prepare the journal entry to record the sale of these bonds on January 1, 2010.
(b) Prepare the journal entry to record interest expense and bond premium amortization on July 1, 2010, assuming no previous accrual of interest.

Prepare entries for bonds issued at a premium.
(SO 9)

680 Chapter 15 Long-Term Liabilities

DO IT! REVIEW

Evaluate statements about bonds.

(SO 1)

DO IT! 15-1 State whether each of the following statements is true or false.
_____ 1. Mortgage bonds and sinking fund bonds are both examples of debenture bonds.
_____ 2. Convertible bonds are also known as callable bonds.
_____ 3. The market rate is the rate investors demand for loaning funds.
_____ 4. Semiannual interest on bonds is equal to the face value times the stated rate times 6/12.
_____ 5. The present value of a bond is the value at which it should sell in the market.

Prepare journal entry for bond issuance and show balance sheet presentation.

(SO 2)

DO IT! 15-2 Goliath Corporation issues $300,000 of bonds for $312,000. (a) Prepare the journal entry to record the issuance of the bonds, and (b) show how the bonds would be reported on the balance sheet at the date of issuance.

Prepare entry for bond redemption.

(SO 3)

DO IT! 15-3 Hucklebuckers Corporation issued $400,000 of 10-year bonds at a discount. Prior to maturity, when the carrying value of the bonds was $390,000, the company retired the bonds at 99. Prepare the entry to record the redemption of the bonds.

Prepare entries for mortgage note and installment payment on note.

(SO 4)

DO IT! 15-4 Nitro-Sort Corporation issues a $350,000, 6%, 15-year mortgage note to obtain needed financing for a new lab. The terms call for semiannual payments of $17,857 each. Prepare the entries to record the mortgage loan and the first installment payment.

Prepare entry for lease, and compute debt to total assets ratio.

(SO 5)

DO IT! 15-5 James Morrison Corporation leases new equipment on December 31, 2010. The lease transfers ownership of the equipment to James Morrison at the end of the lease. The present value of the lease payments is $192,000. After recording this lease, James Morrison has assets of $1,800,000, liabilities of $1,100,000, and stockholders' equity of $700,000. (a) Prepare the entry to record the lease, and (b) compute and discuss the debt to total assets ratio at year-end.

EXERCISES

Evaluate statements about bonds.

(SO 1)

E15-1 Jim Thome has prepared the following list of statements about bonds.
1. Bonds are a form of interest-bearing notes payable.
2. When seeking long-term financing, an advantage of issuing bonds over issuing common stock is that stockholder control is not affected.
3. When seeking long-term financing, an advantage of issuing common stock over issuing bonds is that tax savings result.
4. Secured bonds have specific assets of the issuer pledged as collateral for the bonds.
5. Secured bonds are also known as debenture bonds.
6. Bonds that mature in installments are called term bonds.
7. A conversion feature may be added to bonds to make them more attractive to bond buyers.
8. The rate used to determine the amount of cash interest the borrower pays is called the stated rate.
9. Bond prices are usually quoted as a percentage of the face value of the bond.
10. The present value of a bond is the value at which it should sell in the marketplace.

Instructions
Identify each statement as true or false. If false, indicate how to correct the statement.

Compare two alternatives of financing—issuance of common stock vs. issuance of bonds.

(SO 1)

E15-2 Northeast Airlines is considering two alternatives for the financing of a purchase of a fleet of airplanes. These two alternatives are:
1. Issue 60,000 shares of common stock at $45 per share. (Cash dividends have not been paid nor is the payment of any contemplated).
2. Issue 10%, 10-year bonds at face value for $2,700,000.

It is estimated that the company will earn $800,000 before interest and taxes as a result of this purchase. The company has an estimated tax rate of 30% and has 90,000 shares of common stock outstanding prior to the new financing.

Instructions
Determine the effect on net income and earnings per share for these two methods of financing.

E15-3 On January 1, Neuer Company issued $500,000, 10%, 10-year bonds at face value. Interest is payable semiannually on July 1 and January 1.

Prepare entries for issuance of bonds, and payment and accrual of bond interest.

(SO 2)

Instructions
Present journal entries to record the following.

(a) The issuance of the bonds.
(b) The payment of interest on July 1, assuming that interest was not accrued on June 30.
(c) The accrual of interest on December 31.

E15-4 On January 1, Flory Company issued $300,000, 8%, 5-year bonds at face value. Interest is payable semiannually on July 1 and January 1.

Prepare entries for bonds issued at face value.

(SO 2)

Instructions
Prepare journal entries to record the following events.

(a) The issuance of the bonds.
(b) The payment of interest on July 1, assuming no previous accrual of interest.
(c) The accrual of interest on December 31.

E15-5 Jaurez Company issued $400,000 of 9%, 10-year bonds on January 1, 2010, at face value. Interest is payable semiannually on July 1 and January 1.

Prepare entries for bonds issued at face value.

(SO 2, 3)

Instructions
Prepare the journal entries to record the following events.

(a) The issuance of the bonds.
(b) The payment of interest on July 1, assuming no previous accrual of interest.
(c) The accrual of interest on December 31.
(d) The redemption of bonds at maturity, assuming interest for the last interest period has been paid and recorded.

E15-6 Nocioni Company issued $1,000,000 of bonds on January 1, 2010.

Prepare entries for issuance, retirement, and conversion of bonds.

(SO 2, 3)

Instructions
(a) Prepare the journal entry to record the issuance of the bonds if they are issued at (1) 100, (2) 98, and (3) 103.
(b) Prepare the journal entry to record the retirement of the bonds at maturity, assuming the bonds were issued at 100.
(c) Prepare the journal entry to record the retirement of the bonds before maturity at 98. Assume the balance in Premium on Bonds Payable is $9,000.
(d) Prepare the journal entry to record the conversion of the bonds into 30,000 shares of $10 par value common stock. Assume the bonds were issued at par.

E15-7 Deng Company issued $500,000 of 5-year, 8% bonds at 97 on January 1, 2010. The bonds pay interest twice a year.

Prepare entries to record issuance of bonds at discount and premium.

(SO 2)

Instructions
(a) (1) Prepare the journal entry to record the issuance of the bonds.
    (2) Compute the total cost of borrowing for these bonds.
(b) Repeat the requirements from part (a), assuming the bonds were issued at 105.

E15-8 The following section is taken from Budke Corp.'s balance sheet at December 31, 2009.

Prepare entries for bond interest and redemption.

(SO 2, 3)

Current liabilities
   Bond interest payable $ 72,000
Long-term liabilities
   Bonds payable, 9%, due January 1, 2014   1,600,000

Interest is payable semiannually on January 1 and July 1. The bonds are callable on any interest date.

Instructions
(a) Journalize the payment of the bond interest on January 1, 2010.
(b) Assume that on January 1, 2010, after paying interest, Budke calls bonds having a face value of $600,000. The call price is 104. Record the redemption of the bonds.
(c) Prepare the entry to record the payment of interest on July 1, 2010, assuming no previous accrual of interest on the remaining bonds.

Chapter 15 Long-Term Liabilities

Prepare entries for redemption of bonds and conversion of bonds into common stock.
(SO 3)

E15-9 Presented below are three independent situations.

1. Sigel Corporation retired $130,000 face value, 12% bonds on June 30, 2010, at 102. The carrying value of the bonds at the redemption date was $117,500. The bonds pay semiannual interest, and the interest payment due on June 30, 2010, has been made and recorded.
2. Diaz Inc. retired $150,000 face value, 12.5% bonds on June 30, 2010, at 98. The carrying value of the bonds at the redemption date was $151,000. The bonds pay semiannual interest, and the interest payment due on June 30, 2010, has been made and recorded.
3. Haas Company has $80,000, 8%, 12-year convertible bonds outstanding. These bonds were sold at face value and pay semiannual interest on June 30 and December 31 of each year. The bonds are convertible into 30 shares of Haas $5 par value common stock for each $1,000 worth of bonds. On December 31, 2010, after the bond interest has been paid, $20,000 face value bonds were converted. The market value of Haas common stock was $44 per share on December 31, 2010.

Instructions
For each independent situation above, prepare the appropriate journal entry for the redemption or conversion of the bonds.

Prepare entries to record mortgage note and installment payments.
(SO 4)

E15-10 Leoni Co. receives $240,000 when it issues a $240,000, 10%, mortgage note payable to finance the construction of a building at December 31, 2010. The terms provide for semiannual installment payments of $20,000 on June 30 and December 31.

Instructions
Prepare the journal entries to record the mortgage loan and the first two installment payments.

Prepare entries to record mortgage note and installment payments.
(SO 4)

E15-11 TPo1 Company borrowed $300,000 on January 1, 2010, by issuing a $300,000, 8% mortgage note payable. The terms call for semiannual installment payments of $20,000 on June 30 and December 31.

Instructions
(a) Prepare the journal entries to record the mortgage loan and the first two installment payments.
(b) Indicate the amount of mortgage note payable to be reported as a current liability and as a long-term liability at December 31, 2010.

Prepare entries for operating lease and capital lease.
(SO 5)

E15-12 Presented below are two independent situations.

1. Speedy Car Rental leased a car to Mayfield Company for one year. Terms of the operating lease agreement call for monthly payments of $500.
2. On January 1, 2010, Olsen Inc. entered into an agreement to lease 20 computers from Gage Electronics. The terms of the lease agreement require three annual rental payments of $30,000 (including 10% interest) beginning December 31, 2010. The present value of the three rental payments is $74,606. Olsen considers this a capital lease.

Instructions
(a) Prepare the appropriate journal entry to be made by Mayfield Company for the first lease payment.
(b) Prepare the journal entry to record the lease agreement on the books of Olsen Inc. on January 1, 2010.

Prepare long-term liabilities section.
(SO 6)

E15-13 The adjusted trial balance for Gilligan Corporation at the end of the current year contained the following accounts.

Bond Interest Payable	$ 9,000
Lease Liability	89,500
Bonds Payable, due 2015	180,000
Premium on Bonds Payable	32,000

Instructions
Prepare the long-term liabilities section of the balance sheet.

E15-14 Seven Corporation reports the following amounts in their 2010 financial statements:

	At December 31, 2010	For the Year 2010
Total assets	$1,000,000	
Total liabilities	620,000	
Total stockholders' equity	?	
Interest expense		$ 7,000
Income tax expense		100,000
Net income		150,000

Compute debt to total assets and times interest earned ratios.
(SO 6)

Instructions
(a) Compute the December 31, 2010, balance in stockholders' equity.
(b) Compute the debt to total assets ratio at December 31, 2010.
(c) Compute times interest earned for 2010.

*E15-15 Banzai Corporation is issuing $200,000 of 8%, 5-year bonds when potential bond investors want a return of 10%. Interest is payable semiannually.

Compute market price of bonds.
(SO 7)

Instructions
Compute the market price (present value) of the bonds.

*E15-16 Hrabik Corporation issued $600,000, 9%, 10-year bonds on January 1, 2010, for $562,613. This price resulted in an effective-interest rate of 10% on the bonds. Interest is payable semiannually on July 1 and January 1. Hrabik uses the effective-interest method to amortize bond premium or discount.

Prepare entries for issuance of bonds, payment of interest, and amortization of discount using effective-interest method
(SO 8)

Instructions
Prepare the journal entries to record the following. (Round to the nearest dollar.)
(a) The issuance of the bonds.
(b) The payment of interest and the discount amortization on July 1, 2010, assuming that interest was not accrued on June 30.
(c) The accrual of interest and the discount amortization on December 31, 2010.

*E15-17 Siburo Company issued $300,000, 11%, 10-year bonds on January 1, 2010, for $318,694. This price resulted in an effective-interest rate of 10% on the bonds. Interest is payable semiannually on July 1 and January 1. Siburo uses the effective-interest method to amortize bond premium or discount.

Prepare entries for issuance of bonds, payment of interest, and amortization of premium using effective-interest method.
(SO 8)

Instructions
Prepare the journal entries to record the following. (Round to the nearest dollar).
(a) The issuance of the bonds.
(b) The payment of interest and the premium amortization on July 1, 2010, assuming that interest was not accrued on June 30.
(c) The accrual of interest and the premium amortization on December 31, 2010.

*E15-18 Patino Company issued $400,000, 9%, 20-year bonds on January 1, 2010, at 103. Interest is payable semiannually on July 1 and January 1. Patino uses straight-line amortization for bond premium or discount.

Prepare entries to record issuance of bonds, payment of interest, amortization of premium, and redemption at maturity.
(SO 3, 9)

Instructions
Prepare the journal entries to record the following.
(a) The issuance of the bonds.
(b) The payment of interest and the premium amortization on July 1, 2010, assuming that interest was not accrued on June 30.
(c) The accrual of interest and the premium amortization on December 31, 2010.
(d) The redemption of the bonds at maturity, assuming interest for the last interest period has been paid and recorded.

*E15-19 Joseph Company issued $800,000, 11%, 10-year bonds on December 31, 2009, for $730,000. Interest is payable semiannually on June 30 and December 31. Joseph Company uses the straight-line method to amortize bond premium or discount.

Prepare entries to record issuance of bonds, payment of interest, amortization of discount, and redemption at maturity.
(SO 3, 9)

684 Chapter 15 Long-Term Liabilities

Instructions

Prepare the journal entries to record the following.

(a) The issuance of the bonds.
(b) The payment of interest and the discount amortization on June 30, 2010.
(c) The payment of interest and the discount amortization on December 31, 2010.
(d) The redemption of the bonds at maturity, assuming interest for the last interest period has been paid and recorded.

EXERCISES: SET B

Visit the book's companion website at **www.wiley.com/college/weygandt**, and choose the Student Companion site, to access Exercise Set B.

PROBLEMS: SET A

Prepare entries to record issuance of bonds, interest accrual, and bond redemption.

(SO 2, 3, 6)

P15-1A On May 1, 2010, Newby Corp. issued $600,000, 9%, 5-year bonds at face value. The bonds were dated May 1, 2010, and pay interest semiannually on May 1 and November 1. Financial statements are prepared annually on December 31.

Instructions

(a) Prepare the journal entry to record the issuance of the bonds.
(b) Prepare the adjusting entry to record the accrual of interest on December 31, 2010.
(c) Show the balance sheet presentation on December 31, 2010.

(d) Int. exp. $18,000

(d) Prepare the journal entry to record payment of interest on May 1, 2011, assuming no accrual of interest from January 1, 2011, to May 1, 2011.
(e) Prepare the journal entry to record payment of interest on November 1, 2011.

(f) Loss $12,000

(f) Assume that on November 1, 2011, Newby calls the bonds at 102. Record the redemption of the bonds.

Prepare entries to record issuance of bonds, interest accrual, and bond redemption.

(SO 2, 3, 6)

P15-2A Kusmaul Electric sold $500,000, 10%, 10-year bonds on January 1, 2010. The bonds were dated January 1 and paid interest on January 1 and July 1. The bonds were sold at 104.

Instructions

(a) Prepare the journal entry to record the issuance of the bonds on January 1, 2010.
(b) At December 31, 2010, the balance in the Premium on Bonds Payable account is $18,000. Show the balance sheet presentation of accrued interest and the bond liability at December 31, 2010.

(c) Loss $9,000

(c) On January 1, 2012, when the carrying value of the bonds was $516,000, the company redeemed the bonds at 105. Record the redemption of the bonds assuming that interest for the period has already been paid.

Prepare installment payments schedule and journal entries for a mortgage note payable.

(SO 4)

P15-3A Fordyce Electronics issues a $400,000, 8%, 10-year mortgage note on December 31, 2009. The proceeds from the note are to be used in financing a new research laboratory. The terms of the note provide for semiannual installment payments, exclusive of real estate taxes and insurance, of $29,433. Payments are due June 30 and December 31.

Instructions

(a) Prepare an installment payments schedule for the first 2 years.
(b) Prepare the entries for (1) the loan and (2) the first two installment payments.
(c) Show how the total mortgage liability should be reported on the balance sheet at December 31, 2010.

(b) June 30 Mortgage Notes Payable $13,433
(c) Current liability—2010: $29,639

Analyze three different lease situations and prepare journal entries.

(SO 5)

P15-4A Presented on the next page are three different lease transactions that occurred for Kear Inc. in 2010. Assume that all lease contracts start on January 1, 2010. In no case does Kear receive title to the properties leased during or at the end of the lease term.

	Lessor		
	Jansen Delivery	**Flood Co.**	**Louis Auto**
Type of property	Computer	Delivery equipment	Automobile
Yearly rental	$ 6,000	$ 4,200	$ 3,700
Lease term	6 years	4 years	2 years
Estimated economic life	7 years	7 years	5 years
Fair market value of lease asset	$33,000	$19,000	$11,000
Present value of the lease rental payments	$31,000	$13,000	$ 6,400
Bargain purchase option	None	None	None

Instructions

(a) Which of the leases above are operating leases and which are capital leases? Explain.
(b) How should the lease transaction for Flood Co. be recorded in 2010?
(c) How should the lease transaction for Jansen Delivery be recorded on January 1, 2010?

*P15-5A On July 1, 2010, Atwater Corporation issued $2,000,000 face value, 10%, 10-year bonds at $2,271,813. This price resulted in an effective-interest rate of 8% on the bonds. Atwater uses the effective-interest method to amortize bond premium or discount. The bonds pay semiannual interest July 1 and January 1.

Prepare entries to record issuance of bonds, payment of interest, and amortization of bond premium using effective-interest method.

(SO 2, 8)

Instructions
(Round all computations to the nearest dollar.)
(a) Prepare the journal entry to record the issuance of the bonds on July 1, 2010.
(b) Prepare an amortization table through December 31, 2011 (3 interest periods) for this bond issue.
(c) Prepare the journal entry to record the accrual of interest and the amortization of the premium on December 31, 2010.
(d) Prepare the journal entry to record the payment of interest and the amortization of the premium on July 1, 2011, assuming no accrual of interest on June 30.
(e) Prepare the journal entry to record the accrual of interest and the amortization of the premium on December 31, 2011.

(c) Amortization $9,127

(d) Amortization $9,493

(e) Amortization $9,872

*P15-6A On July 1, 2010, Rossillon Company issued $4,000,000 face value, 8%, 10-year bonds at $3,501,514. This price resulted in an effective-interest rate of 10% on the bonds. Rossillon uses the effective-interest method to amortize bond premium or discount. The bonds pay semiannual interest July 1 and January 1.

Prepare entries to record issuance of bonds, payment of interest, and amortization of discount using effective-interest method. In addition, answer questions.

(SO 2, 8)

Instructions
(Round all computations to the nearest dollar.)
(a) Prepare the journal entries to record the following transactions.
   (1) The issuance of the bonds on July 1, 2010.
   (2) The accrual of interest and the amortization of the discount on December 31, 2010.
   (3) The payment of interest and the amortization of the discount on July 1, 2011, assuming no accrual of interest on June 30.
   (4) The accrual of interest and the amortization of the discount on December 31, 2011.
(b) Show the proper balance sheet presentation for the liability for bonds payable on the December 31, 2011, balance sheet.
(c) Provide the answers to the following questions in letter form.
   (1) What amount of interest expense is reported for 2011?
   (2) Would the bond interest expense reported in 2011 be the same as, greater than, or less than the amount that would be reported if the straight-line method of amortization were used?
   (3) Determine the total cost of borrowing over the life of the bond.
   (4) Would the total bond interest expense be greater than, the same as, or less than the total interest expense that would be reported if the straight-line method of amortization were used?

(a) (3) Amortization $15,830

(a) (4) Amortization $16,621

(b) Bond carrying value $3,549,041

*P15-7A Soprano Electric sold $3,000,000, 10%, 10-year bonds on January 1, 2010. The bonds were dated January 1 and pay interest July 1 and January 1. Soprano Electric uses the straight-line method to amortize bond premium or discount. The bonds were sold at 104. Assume no interest is accrued on June 30.

Prepare entries to record issuance of bonds, interest accrual, and straight-line amortization for 2 years.

(SO 6, 9)

Chapter 15 Long-Term Liabilities

(b) Amortization $6,000
(d) Premium on bonds payable $96,000

Prepare entries to record issuance of bonds, interest, and straight-line amortization of bond premium and discount.

(SO 6, 9)

(a) Amortization $5,000
(b) Amortization $2,500
(c) Premium on bonds payable $95,000
   Discount on bonds payable $47,500

Prepare entries to record interest payments, straight-line premium amortization, and redemption of bonds.

(SO 2, 3, 9)

Instructions

(a) Prepare the journal entry to record the issuance of the bonds on January 1, 2010.
(b) Prepare a bond premium amortization schedule for the first 4 interest periods.
(c) Prepare the journal entries for interest and the amortization of the premium in 2010 and 2011.
(d) Show the balance sheet presentation of the bond liability at December 31, 2011.

*P15-8A Elkins Company sold $2,500,000, 8%, 10-year bonds on July 1, 2010. The bonds were dated July 1, 2010, and pay interest July 1 and January 1. Elkins Company uses the straight-line method to amortize bond premium or discount. Assume no interest is accrued on June 30.

Instructions

(a) Prepare all the necessary journal entries to record the issuance of the bonds and bond interest expense for 2010, assuming that the bonds sold at 104.
(b) Prepare journal entries as in part (a) assuming that the bonds sold at 98.
(c) Show balance sheet presentation for each bond issue at December 31, 2010.

*P15-9A The following is taken from the Pinkston Company balance sheet.

PINKSTON COMPANY
Balance Sheet (partial)
December 31, 2010

Current liabilities		
Bond interest payable (for 6 months from July 1 to December 31)		$ 105,000
Long-term liabilities		
Bonds payable, 7% due January 1, 2021	$3,000,000	
Add: Premium on bonds payable	200,000	$3,200,000

Interest is payable semiannually on January 1 and July 1. The bonds are callable on any semiannual interest date. Pinkston uses straight-line amortization for any bond premium or discount. From December 31, 2010, the bonds will be outstanding for an additional 10 years (120 months).

Instructions

(a) Journalize the payment of bond interest on January 1, 2011.

(b) Amortization $10,000

(b) Prepare the entry to amortize bond premium and to pay the interest due on July 1, 2011, assuming no accrual of interest on June 30.

(c) Gain $64,000

(c) Assume that on July 1, 2011, after paying interest, Pinkston Company calls bonds having a face value of $1,200,000. The call price is 101. Record the redemption of the bonds.

(d) Amortization $6,000

(d) Prepare the adjusting entry at December 31, 2011, to amortize bond premium and to accrue interest on the remaining bonds.

PROBLEMS: SET B

Prepare entries to record issuance of bonds, interest accrual, and bond redemption.

(SO 2, 3, 6)

P15-1B On June 1, 2010, Mordica Corp. issued $2,000,000, 9%, 5-year bonds at face value. The bonds were dated June 1, 2010, and pay interest semiannually on June 1 and December 1. Financial statements are prepared annually on December 31.

Instructions

(a) Prepare the journal entry to record the issuance of the bonds.
(b) Prepare the adjusting entry to record the accrual of interest on December 31, 2010.
(c) Show the balance sheet presentation on December 31, 2010.

(d) Int. exp. $75,000

(d) Prepare the journal entry to record payment of interest on June 1, 2011, assuming no accrual of interest from January 1, 2011, to June 1, 2011.
(e) Prepare the journal entry to record payment of interest on December 1, 2011.

(f) Loss $40,000

(f) Assume that on December 1, 2011, Mordica calls the bonds at 102. Record the redemption of the bonds.

Prepare entries to record issuance of bonds, interest accrual, and bond redemption.

(SO 2, 3, 6)

P15-2B Mueller Co. sold $800,000, 9%, 10-year bonds on January 1, 2010. The bonds were dated January 1, and interest is paid on January 1 and July 1. The bonds were sold at 105.

Instructions

(a) Prepare the journal entry to record the issuance of the bonds on January 1, 2010.
(b) At December 31, 2010, the balance in the Premium on Bonds Payable account is $36,000. Show the balance sheet presentation of accrued interest and the bond liability at December 31, 2010.
(c) On January 1, 2012, when the carrying value of the bonds was $832,000, the company redeemed the bonds at 105. Record the redemption of the bonds assuming that interest for the period has already been paid.

(c) Loss $8,000

P15-3B Colt Electronics issues an $600,000, 8%, 10-year mortgage note on December 31, 2010, to help finance a plant expansion program. The terms provide for semiannual installment payments, not including real estate taxes and insurance, of $44,149. Payments are due June 30 and December 31.

Prepare installment payments schedule and journal entries for a mortgage note payable.
(SO 4)

Instructions

(a) Prepare an installment payments schedule for the first 2 years.
(b) Prepare the entries for (1) the mortgage loan and (2) the first two installment payments.
(c) Show how the total mortgage liability should be reported on the balance sheet at December 31, 2011.

(b) June 30 Mortgage Notes Payable $20,149
(c) Current liability—2011: $44,458

P15-4B Presented below are three different lease transactions in which Ortiz Enterprises engaged in 2010. Assume that all lease transactions start on January 1, 2010. In no case does Ortiz receive title to the properties leased during or at the end of the lease term.

Analyze three different lease situations and prepare journal entries.
(SO 5)

	Lessor		
	Renner Co.	**Flynn Co.**	**Miley Inc.**
Type of property	Bulldozer	Truck	Furniture
Bargain purchase option	None	None	None
Lease term	4 years	6 years	3 years
Estimated economic life	8 years	7 years	5 years
Yearly rental	$13,000	$20,000	$ 3,000
Fair market value of leased asset	$80,000	$96,000	$20,500
Present value of the lease rental payments	$48,000	$82,000	$ 9,000

Instructions

(a) Identify the leases above as operating or capital leases. Explain.
(b) How should the lease transaction for Flynn Co. be recorded on January 1, 2010?
(c) How should the lease transaction for Miley Inc. be recorded in 2010?

*P15-5B On July 1, 2010, Wheeler Satellites issued $4,500,000 face value, 9%, 10-year bonds at $4,219,600. This price resulted in an effective-interest rate of 10% on the bonds. Wheeler uses the effective-interest method to amortize bond premium or discount. The bonds pay semiannual interest July 1 and January 1.

Prepare entries to record issuance of bonds, payment of interest, and amortization of bond discount using effective-interest method.
(SO 2, 8)

Instructions
(Round all computations to the nearest dollar.)

(a) Prepare the journal entry to record the issuance of the bonds on July 1, 2010.
(b) Prepare an amortization table through December 31, 2011 (3 interest periods) for this bond issue.
(c) Prepare the journal entry to record the accrual of interest and the amortization of the discount on December 31, 2010.
(d) Prepare the journal entry to record the payment of interest and the amortization of the discount on July 1, 2011, assuming that interest was not accrued on June 30.
(e) Prepare the journal entry to record the accrual of interest and the amortization of the discount on December 31, 2011.

(c) Amortization $8,480
(d) Amortization $8,904
(e) Amortization $9,349

*P15-6B On July 1, 2010, Remington Chemical Company issued $4,000,000 face value, 10%, 10-year bonds at $4,543,627. This price resulted in an 8% effective-interest rate on the bonds. Remington uses the effective-interest method to amortize bond premium or discount. The bonds pay semiannual interest on each July 1 and January 1.

Prepare entries to record issuance of bonds, payment of interest, and amortization of premium using effective-interest method. In addition, answer questions.
(SO 2, 8)

688 Chapter 15 Long-Term Liabilities

Instructions

(Round all computations to the nearest dollar.)

(a) Prepare the journal entries to record the following transactions.
  (1) The issuance of the bonds on July 1, 2010.
  (2) The accrual of interest and the amortization of the premium on December 31, 2010.
  (3) The payment of interest and the amortization of the premium on July 1, 2011, assuming no accrual of interest on June 30.
  (4) The accrual of interest and the amortization of the premium on December 31, 2011.

(b) Show the proper balance sheet presentation for the liability for bonds payable on the December 31, 2011, balance sheet.

(c) Provide the answers to the following questions in letter form.
  (1) What amount of interest expense is reported for 2011?
  (2) Would the bond interest expense reported in 2011 be the same as, greater than, or less than the amount that would be reported if the straight-line method of amortization were used?
  (3) Determine the total cost of borrowing over the life of the bond.
  (4) Would the total bond interest expense be greater than, the same as, or less than the total interest expense if the straight-line method of amortization were used?

Sidebar notes:
- (a) (2) Amortization $18,255
- (a) (3) Amortization $18,985
- (a) (4) Amortization $19,745
- (b) Bond carrying value $4,486,642

Prepare entries to record issuance of bonds, interest accrual, and straight-line amortization for 2 years.

(SO 6, 9)

*P15-7B Suppan Company sold $6,000,000, 9%, 20-year bonds on January 1, 2010. The bonds were dated January 1, 2010, and pay interest on January 1 and July 1. Suppan Company uses the straight-line method to amortize bond premium or discount. The bonds were sold at 96. Assume no interest is accrued on June 30.

Instructions

(a) Prepare the journal entry to record the issuance of the bonds on January 1, 2010.
(b) Prepare a bond discount amortization schedule for the first 4 interest periods.
(c) Prepare the journal entries for interest and the amortization of the discount in 2010 and 2011.
(d) Show the balance sheet presentation of the bond liability at December 31, 2011.

Sidebar notes:
- (b) Amortization $6,000
- (d) Discount on bonds payable $216,000

Prepare entries to record issuance of bonds, interest, and straight-line amortization of bond premium and discount.

(SO 6, 9)

*P15-8B Jinkens Corporation sold $4,000,000, 8%, 10-year bonds on January 1, 2010. The bonds were dated January 1, 2010, and pay interest on July 1 and January 1. Jinkens Corporation uses the straight-line method to amortize bond premium or discount. Assume no interest is accrued on June 30.

Instructions

(a) Prepare all the necessary journal entries to record the issuance of the bonds and bond interest expense for 2010, assuming that the bonds sold at 103.
(b) Prepare journal entries as in part (a) assuming that the bonds sold at 96.
(c) Show balance sheet presentation for each bond issue at December 31, 2010.

Sidebar notes:
- (a) Amortization $6,000
- (b) Amortization $8,000
- (c) Premium on bonds payable $108,000
  Discount on bonds payable $144,000

Prepare entries to record interest payments, straight-line discount amortization, and redemption of bonds.

(SO 2, 3, 9)

*P15-9B The following is taken from the Nilson Corp. balance sheet.

NILSON CORPORATION
Balance Sheet (partial)
December 31, 2010

Current liabilities		
Bond interest payable (for 6 months from July 1 to December 31)		$ 108,000
Long-term liabilities		
Bonds payable, 9%, due January 1, 2021	$2,400,000	
Less: Discount on bonds payable	90,000	2,310,000

Interest is payable semiannually on January 1 and July 1. The bonds are callable on any semi-annual interest date. Nilson uses straight-line amortization for any bond premium or discount. From December 31, 2010, the bonds will be outstanding for an additional 10 years (120 months).

Instructions

(Round all computations to the nearest dollar.)

(a) Journalize the payment of bond interest on January 1, 2011.
(b) Prepare the entry to amortize bond discount and to pay the interest due on July 1, 2011, assuming that interest was not accrued on June 30.

Sidebar note:
- (b) Amortization $4,500

(c) Assume that on July 1, 2011, after paying interest, Nilson Corp. calls bonds having a face value of $800,000. The call price is 102. Record the redemption of the bonds. **(c) Loss $44,500**

(d) Prepare the adjusting entry at December 31, 2011, to amortize bond discount and to accrue interest on the remaining bonds. **(d) Amortization $3,000**

PROBLEMS: SET C

Visit the book's companion website at **www.wiley.com/college/weygandt**, and choose the Student Companion site, to access Problem Set C.

COMPREHENSIVE PROBLEM: CHAPTERS 13–15

Nordham Corporation's trial balance at December 31, 2010, is presented below. All 2010 transactions have been recorded except for the items described below and on the next page.

	Debit	Credit
Cash	$ 23,000	
Accounts Receivable	51,000	
Merchandise Inventory	22,700	
Land	65,000	
Building	95,000	
Equipment	40,000	
Allowance for Doubtful Accounts		$ 450
Accumulated Depreciation—Building		30,000
Accumulated Depreciation—Equipment		14,400
Accounts Payable		19,300
Bond Interest Payable		–0–
Dividends Payable		–0–
Unearned Rent Revenue		8,000
Bonds Payable (10%)		50,000
Common Stock ($10 par)		30,000
Paid-in Capital in Excess of Par—Common Stock		6,000
Preferred Stock ($20 par)		–0–
Paid-in Capital in Excess of Par—Preferred Stock		–0–
Retained Earnings		75,050
Treasury Stock	–0–	
Dividends	–0–	
Sales		570,000
Rent Revenue		–0–
Bad Debts Expense	–0–	
Bond Interest Expense	2,500	
Cost of Goods Sold	400,000	
Depreciation Expense—Buildings	–0–	
Depreciation Expense—Equipment	–0–	
Other Operating Expenses	39,000	
Salaries Expense	65,000	
Total	$803,200	$803,200

Unrecorded transactions

1. On January 1, 2010, Nordham issued 1,000 shares of $20 par, 6% preferred stock for $22,000.
2. On January 1, 2010, Nordham also issued 1,000 shares of common stock for $23,000.
3. Nordham reacquired 300 shares of its common stock on July 1, 2010, for $49 per share.
4. On December 31, 2010, Nordham declared the annual preferred stock dividend and a $1.50 per share dividend on the outstanding common stock, all payable on January 15, 2011.
5. Nordham estimates that uncollectible accounts receivable at year-end is $5,100.
6. The building is being depreciated using the straight-line method over 30 years. The salvage value is $5,000.
7. The equipment is being depreciated using the straight-line method over 10 years. The salvage value is $4,000.

690 Chapter 15 Long-Term Liabilities

8. The unearned rent was collected on October 1, 2010. It was receipt of 4 months' rent in advance (October 1, 2010 through January 31, 2011).
9. The 10% bonds payable pay interest every January 1 and July 1. The interest for the 6 months ended December 31, 2010, has not been paid or recorded.

Instructions
(Ignore income taxes.)

(a) Prepare journal entries for the transactions listed above.
(b) Prepare an updated December 31, 2010, trial balance, reflecting the unrecorded transactions.
(c) Prepare a multiple-step income statement for the year ending December 31, 2010.
(d) Prepare a statement of retained earnings for the year ending December 31, 2010.
(e) Prepare a classified balance sheet as of December 31, 2010.

(b) Total $868,700

(e) Total assets $270,900

CONTINUING COOKIE CHRONICLE

(*Note:* This is a continuation of the Cookie Chronicle from Chapters 1 through 14.)

CCC15 Natalie and Curtis have been experiencing great demand for their cookies and muffins. As a result, they are now thinking about buying a commercial oven. They know which oven they want and how much it will cost. They have some cash set aside for the purchase and will need to borrow the rest. They met with a bank manager to discuss their options.

Go to the book's companion website, www.wiley.com/college/weygandt, to see the completion of this problem.

BROADENING YOUR PERSPECTIVE

FINANCIAL REPORTING AND ANALYSIS

Financial Reporting Problem: PepsiCo, Inc.

BYP15-1 Refer to the financial statements of PepsiCo, Inc. and the Notes to Consolidated Financial Statements in Appendix A.

Instructions
(a) What was PepsiCo's total long-term debt at December 29, 2007? What was the increase/decrease in total long-term debt from the prior year? What does Note 9 to the financial statements indicate about the composition of PepsiCo's long-term debt obligation?
(b) What type of leases, operating or capital, does PepsiCo report? (See Note 9.) Are these leases reported on PepsiCo's financial statements?
(c) What are the total long-term contractual commitments that PepsiCo reports as of December 29, 2007? (See Note 9.)

Comparative Analysis Problem: PepsiCo, Inc. vs. The Coca-Cola Company

BYP15-2 PepsiCo's financial statements are presented in Appendix A. Financial statements of The Coca-Cola Company are presented in Appendix B.

Instructions

(a) Based on the information contained in these financial statements, compute the following 2007 ratios for each company.
  (1) Debt to total assets.
  (2) Times interest earned.
(b) What conclusions concerning the companies' long-run solvency can be drawn from these ratios?
(c) Which company has reported the greater amount of future long-term commitments for the 5 succeeding years?

Exploring the Web

BYP15-3 Bond or debt securities pay a stated rate of interest. This rate of interest is dependent on the risk associated with the investment. Moody's Investment Service provides ratings for companies that issue debt securities.

Address: www.moodys.com, or go to **www.wiley.com/college/weygandt**

Steps: From Moody's homepage, choose **About Moody's**.

Instructions

(a) What year did Moody's introduce the first bond rating? (See **Moody's History**.)
(b) What is the total amount of debt securities that Moody's analysts "track"? (See **An Introduction**.)
(c) What characteristics must debt ratings have in order to be useful to the capital markets? (See **Understand Risk: The Truth About Credit Ratings**.)

CRITICAL THINKING

Decision Making Across the Organization

*BYP15-4 On January 1, 2008, Carlin Corporation issued $2,400,000 of 5-year, 8% bonds at 95; the bonds pay interest semiannually on July 1 and January 1. By January 1, 2010, the market rate of interest for bonds of risk similar to those of Carlin Corporation had risen. As a result the market value of these bonds was $2,000,000 on January 1, 2010—below their carrying value. Andrea Carlin, president of the company, suggests repurchasing all of these bonds in the open market at the $2,000,000 price. To do so the company will have to issue $2,000,000 (face value) of new 10-year, 11% bonds at par. The president asks you, as controller, "What is the feasibility of my proposed repurchase plan?"

Instructions

With the class divided into groups, answer the following.

(a) What is the carrying value of the outstanding Carlin Corporation 5-year bonds on January 1, 2010? (Assume straight-line amortization.)
(b) Prepare the journal entry to retire the 5-year bonds on January 1, 2010. Prepare the journal entry to issue the new 10-year bonds.
(c) Prepare a short memo to the president in response to her request for advice. List the economic factors that you believe should be considered for her repurchase proposal.

Communication Activity

BYP15-5 Joe Penner, president of Penner Corporation, is considering the issuance of bonds to finance an expansion of his business. He has asked you to (1) discuss the advantages of bonds over common stock financing, (2) indicate the types of bonds he might issue, and (3) explain the issuing procedures used in bond transactions.

Instructions

Write a memo to the president, answering his request.

Ethics Case

BYP15-6 Sam Farr is the president, founder, and majority owner of Galena Medical Corporation, an emerging medical technology products company. Galena is in dire need of additional capital to keep operating and to bring several promising products to final development, testing, and production. Sam, as owner of 51% of the outstanding stock, manages the company's operations. He places heavy emphasis on research and development and on long-term growth. The other principal stockholder is Jill Hutton who, as a nonemployee investor, owns 40% of the stock. Jill would like to deemphasize the R&D functions and emphasize the marketing function, to maximize short-run sales and profits from existing products. She believes this strategy would raise the market price of Galena's stock.

All of Sam's personal capital and borrowing power is tied up in his 51% stock ownership. He knows that any offering of additional shares of stock will dilute his controlling interest because he won't be able to participate in such an issuance. But, Jill has money and would likely buy enough shares to gain control of Galena. She then would dictate the company's future direction, even if it meant replacing Sam as president and CEO.

The company already has considerable debt. Raising additional debt will be costly, will adversely affect Galena's credit rating, and will increase the company's reported losses due to the growth in interest expense. Jill and the other minority stockholders express opposition to the assumption of additional debt, fearing the company will be pushed to the brink of bankruptcy. Wanting to maintain his control and to preserve the direction of "his" company, Sam is doing everything to avoid a stock issuance. He is contemplating a large issuance of bonds, even if it means the bonds are issued with a high effective-interest rate.

Instructions
(a) Who are the stakeholders in this situation?
(b) What are the ethical issues in this case?
(c) What would you do if you were Sam?

"All About You" Activity

BYP15-7 Numerous articles have been written that identify early warning signs that you might be getting into trouble with your personal debt load. You can find many good articles on this topic on the Web.

Instructions
Find an article that identifies early warning signs of personal debt trouble. Write up a summary of the article and bring your summary and the article to class to share.

Answers to Insight and Accounting Across the Organization Questions

p. 656 Search for Your Best Rate
Q: What should you do if the dealer "trash-talks" your lender, or refuses to sell you the car for the agreed-upon price unless you get your car loan through the dealer?
A: *Experts suggest that if the dealer "trash-talks" your lender or refuses to sell you the car at the agreed-upon price unless you get your financing through the dealer, get up and leave, and buy your car somewhere else.*

p. 660 "Covenant-Lite" Debt
Q: How can financial ratios such as those covered in this chapter provide protection for creditors?
A: *Financial ratios such as the current ratio, debt to total assets ratio, and the times interest earned ratio provide indications of a company's liquidity and solvency. By specifying minimum levels of liquidity and solvency, as measured by these ratios, a creditor creates triggers that enable it to step in before a company's financial situation becomes too dire.*

Answers to Self-Study Questions
1. c **2.** c **3.** a **4.** d **5.** b **6.** d **7.** c **8.** c **9.** d **10.** d *****11.** d *****12.** b *****13.** c *****14.** d *****15.** a

Remember to go back to the Navigator box on the chapter-opening page and check off your completed work.

Chapter 16

Investments

STUDY OBJECTIVES

After studying this chapter, you should be able to:

1. Discuss why corporations invest in debt and stock securities.
2. Explain the accounting for debt investments.
3. Explain the accounting for stock investments.
4. Describe the use of consolidated financial statements.
5. Indicate how debt and stock investments are reported in financial statements.
6. Distinguish between short-term and long-term investments.

✓ The Navigator

- Scan **Study Objectives**
- Read **Feature Story**
- Read **Preview**
- Read text and answer **DO IT!** p. 699   p. 704   p. 707   p. 710
- Work **Comprehensive** **DO IT!** p. 712
- Review **Summary of Study Objectives**
- Answer **Self-Study Questions**
- Complete **Assignments**

Feature Story

"IS THERE ANYTHING ELSE WE CAN BUY?"

In a rapidly changing world you must change rapidly or suffer the consequences. In business, change requires investment.

A case in point is found in the entertainment industry. Technology is bringing about innovations so quickly that it is nearly impossible to guess which technologies will last and which will soon fade away. For example, will both satellite TV and cable TV survive, or will just one succeed, or will both be replaced by something else? Or consider the publishing industry. Will paper newspapers and magazines be replaced by online news via the World Wide Web? If you are a publisher, you have to make your best guess about what the future holds and invest accordingly.

Time Warner, Inc. (*www.timewarner.com*) lives at the center of this arena. It is not an environment for the timid, and Time Warner's philosophy is anything but timid. It might be characterized as, "If we can't beat you, we will buy you." Its mantra is "invest, invest, invest." A list of Time Warner's holdings gives an idea of its reach. Magazines: *People, Time, Life, Sports Illustrated, Fortune.* Book publishers: Time-Life Books, Book-of-the-Month Club, Little, Brown & Co, Sunset Books. Television and movies: Warner Bros. ("ER," "Without a Trace," the WB Network), HBO, and movies like *Harry Potter and the Goblet of Fire, and Batman Begins.* Broadcasting: TNT, CNN news, and Turner's library of thousands of classic movies. Internet: America Online, and AOL Anywhere. Time Warner owns more information and entertainment copyrights and brands than any other company in the world.

The merger of America Online (AOL) with Time Warner, one of the biggest mergers ever, was originally perceived by many as the gateway to the future. In actuality, it was a financial disaster. It is largely responsible for much of the decline in Time Warner's stock price, from a high of $95.80 to a recent level of $14.07. Ted Turner, who was at one time Time Warner's largest shareholder, lost billions of dollars on the deal and eventually sold most of his shares.

Inside Chapter 16...

- **How Procter & Gamble Accounts for Gillette** (p. 703)
- **And the Correct Way to Report Investments Is...?** (p. 706)

Preview of Chapter 16

Time Warner's management believes in aggressive growth through investing in the stock of existing companies. Besides purchasing stock, companies also purchase other securities such as bonds issued by corporations or by governments. Companies can make investments for a short or long period of time, as a passive investment, or with the intent to control another company. As you will see in this chapter, the way in which a company accounts for its investments is determined by a number of factors.

The content and organization of Chapter 16 are as follows.

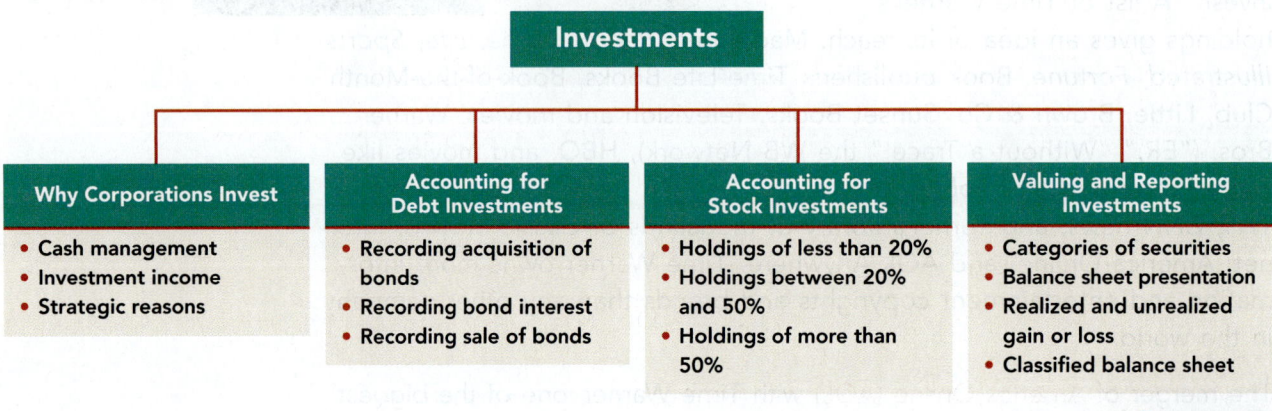

WHY CORPORATIONS INVEST

STUDY OBJECTIVE 1
Discuss why corporations invest in debt and stock securities.

Corporations purchase investments in debt or stock securities generally for one of three reasons. First, a corporation may **have excess cash** that it does not need for the immediate purchase of operating assets. For example, many companies experience seasonal fluctuations in sales. A Cape Cod marina has more sales in the spring and summer than in the fall and winter. At the end of an operating cycle, the marina may have cash on hand that is temporarily idle until the start of another operating cycle. It may invest the excess funds to earn a greater return than it would get by just holding the funds in the bank. Illustration 16-1 depicts the role that such temporary investments play in the operating cycle.

Illustration 16-1
Temporary investments and the operating cycle

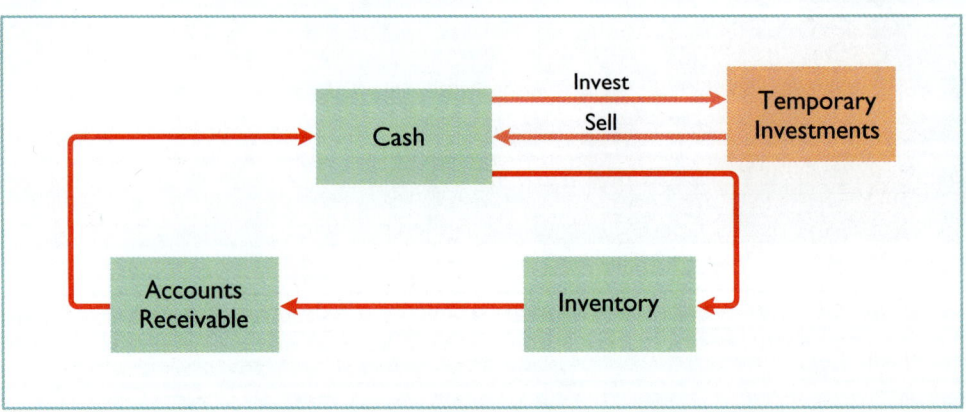

696

Excess cash may also result from economic cycles. For example, when the economy is booming, General Electric generates considerable excess cash. It uses some of this cash to purchase new plant and equipment and pays out some of the cash in dividends. But it may also invest excess cash in liquid assets in anticipation of a future downturn in the economy. It can then liquidate these investments during a recession, when sales slow and cash is scarce.

When investing excess cash for short periods of time, corporations invest in low-risk, highly liquid securities—most often short-term government securities. It is generally not wise to invest short-term excess cash in shares of common stock because stock investments can experience rapid price changes. If you did invest your short-term excess cash in stock and the price of the stock declined significantly just before you needed cash again, you would be forced to sell your stock investment at a loss.

A second reason some companies purchase investments is to generate **earnings from investment income**. For example, banks make most of their earnings by lending money, but they also generate earnings by investing in debt. Conversely, mutual stock funds invest primarily in equity securities in order to benefit from stock-price appreciation and dividend revenue.

Third, companies also invest for **strategic reasons**. A company can exercise some influence over a customer or supplier by purchasing a significant, but not controlling, interest in that company. Or, a company may purchase a noncontrolling interest in another company in a related industry in which it wishes to establish a presence. For example, Time Warner initially purchased an interest of less than 20% in Turner Broadcasting to have a stake in Turner's expanding business opportunities. At a later date Time Warner acquired the remaining 80%. Subsequently, Time Warner merged with AOL and became AOL Time Warner, Inc. Now, it is again just Time Warner, Inc., having dropped the "AOL" from its name in late 2003.

A corporation may also choose to purchase a controlling interest in another company. For example, as the *Accounting Across the Organization* box on page 703 shows, Procter & Gamble purchased Gillette. Such purchases might be done to enter a new industry without incurring the tremendous costs and risks associated with starting from scratch. Or a company might purchase another company in its same industry.

In summary, businesses invest in other companies for the reasons shown in Illustration 16-2.

Illustration 16-2
Why corporations invest

Reason	Typical Investment
To house excess cash until needed	Low-risk, high-liquidity, short-term securities such as government-issued securities
To generate earnings (I need 1,000 Treasury bills by tonight)	Debt securities (banks and other financial institutions); and stock securities (mutual funds and pension funds)
To meet strategic goals	Stocks of companies in a related industry or in an unrelated industry that the company wishes to enter

ACCOUNTING FOR DEBT INVESTMENTS

STUDY OBJECTIVE 2
Explain the accounting for debt investments.

Debt investments are investments in government and corporation bonds. In accounting for debt investments, companies make entries to record (1) the acquisition, (2) the interest revenue, and (3) the sale.

Recording Acquisition of Bonds

At acquisition, the cost principle applies. Cost includes all expenditures necessary to acquire these investments, such as the price paid plus brokerage fees (commissions), if any.

Assume, for example, that Kuhl Corporation acquires 50 Doan Inc. 8%, 10-year, $1,000 bonds on January 1, 2010, for $54,000, including brokerage fees of $1,000. The entry to record the investment is:

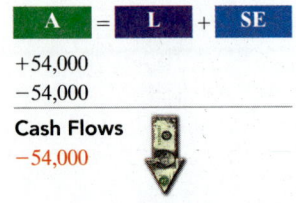

Jan. 1	Debt Investments	54,000	
	Cash		54,000
	(To record purchase of 50 Doan Inc. bonds)		

Recording Bond Interest

The Doan, Inc. bonds pay interest of $2,000 semiannually on July 1 and January 1 ($50,000 × 8% × ½). The entry for the receipt of interest on July 1 is:

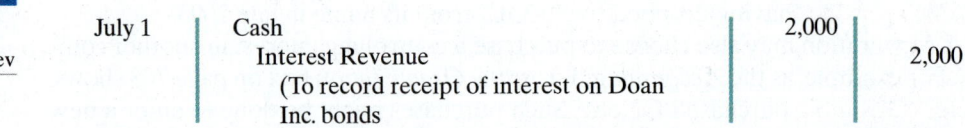

July 1	Cash	2,000	
	Interest Revenue		2,000
	(To record receipt of interest on Doan Inc. bonds		

If Kuhl Corporation's fiscal year ends on December 31, it accrues the interest of $2,000 earned since July 1. The adjusting entry is:

Dec. 31	Interest Receivable	2,000	
	Interest Revenue		2,000
	(To accrue interest on Doan Inc. bonds)		

Kuhl reports Interest Receivable as a current asset in the balance sheet. It reports Interest Revenue under "Other revenues and gains" in the income statement.

Kuhl reports receipt of the interest on January 1 as follows.

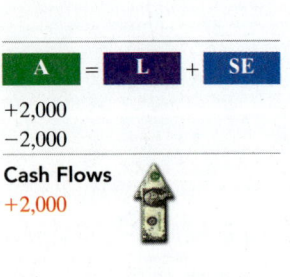
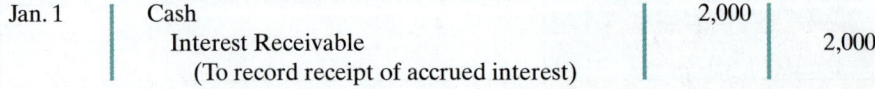

Jan. 1	Cash	2,000	
	Interest Receivable		2,000
	(To record receipt of accrued interest)		

A credit to Interest Revenue at this time is incorrect because the company earned and accrued interest revenue in the *preceding* accounting period.

Recording Sale of Bonds

When Kuhl sells the bonds, it credits the investment account for the cost of the bonds. Kuhl records as a gain or loss any difference between the net proceeds from the sale (sales price less brokerage fees) and the cost of the bonds.

Assume, for example, that Kuhl Corporation receives net proceeds of $58,000 on the sale of the Doan Inc. bonds on January 1, 2011, after receiving the interest due. Since the securities cost $54,000, the company realizes a gain of $4,000. It records the sale as:

Jan. 1	Cash	58,000	
	Debt Investments		54,000
	Gain on Sale of Debt Investments		4,000
	(To record sale of Doan Inc. bonds)		

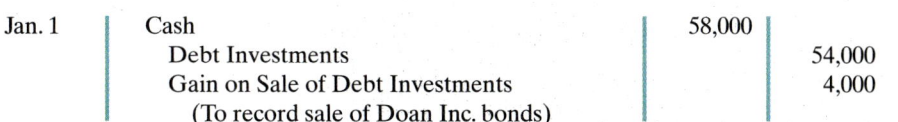

Kuhl reports the gain on sale of debt investments under "Other revenues and gains" in the income statement and reports losses under "Other expenses and losses."

DO IT!

Waldo Corporation had the following transactions pertaining to debt investments.

Jan. 1 Purchased 30, $1,000 Hillary Co. 10% bonds for $30,000, plus brokerage fees of $900. Interest is payable semiannually on July 1 and January 1.
July 1 Received semiannual interest on Hillary Co. bonds.
July 1 Sold 15 Hillary Co. bonds for $15,000, less $400 brokerage fees.

(a) Journalize the transactions, and (b) prepare the adjusting entry for the accrual of interest on December 31.

DEBT INVESTMENTS

Solution

(a)
Jan. 1	Debt Investments	30,900	
	Cash		30,900
	(To record purchase of 30 Hillary Co. bonds)		

July 1	Cash	1,500	
	Interest Revenue ($30,000 × .10 × 6/12)		1,500
	(To record receipt of interest on Hillary Co. bonds)		

July 1	Cash	14,600	
	Loss on Sale of Debt Investments	850	
	Debt Investments ($30,900 × 15/30)		15,450
	(To record sale of 15 Hillary Co. bonds)		

(b)
Dec. 31	Interest Receivable	750	
	Interest Revenue ($15,000 × .10 × 6/12)		750
	(To accrue interest on Hillary Co. bonds)		

action plan

✔ Record bond investments at cost.
✔ Record interest when received and/or accrued.
✔ When bonds are sold, credit the investment account for the cost of the bonds.
✔ Record any difference between the cost and the net proceeds as a gain or loss.

Related exercise material: **BE16-1, E16-2, E16-3,** and **DO IT! 16-1.**

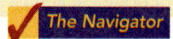

ACCOUNTING FOR STOCK INVESTMENTS

Stock investments are investments in the capital stock of other corporations. When a company holds stock (and/or debt) of several different corporations, the group of securities is identified as an **investment portfolio**.

The accounting for investments in common stock depends on the extent of the investor's influence over the operating and financial affairs of the issuing corporation (the **investee**). Illustration 16-3 (page 700) shows the general guidelines.

STUDY OBJECTIVE 3
Explain the accounting for stock investments.

Illustration 16-3
Accounting guidelines for stock investments

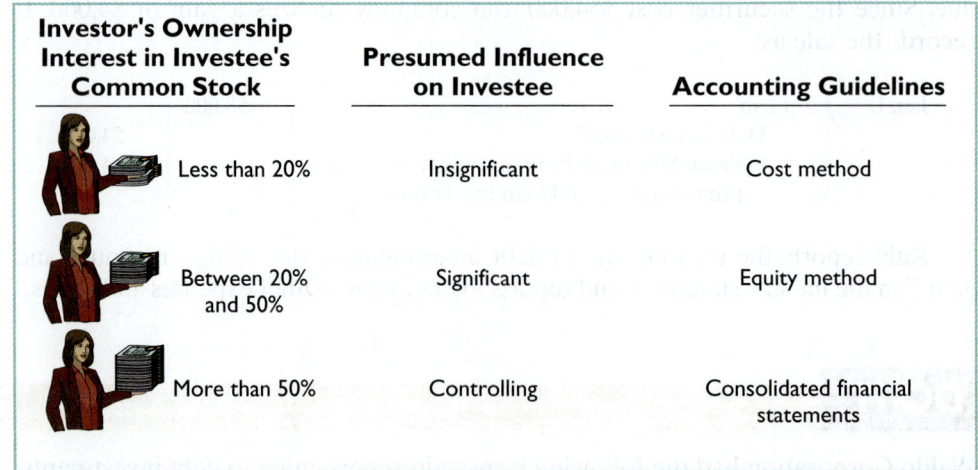

Companies are required to use judgment instead of blindly following the guidelines.[1] On the following pages we will explain the application of each guideline.

Holdings of Less than 20%

HELPFUL HINT
The entries for investments in common stock also apply to investments in preferred stock.

In accounting for stock investments of less than 20%, companies use the cost method. Under the **cost method**, companies record the investment at cost, and recognize revenue only when cash dividends are received.

RECORDING ACQUISITION OF STOCK INVESTMENTS

At acquisition, the cost principle applies. Cost includes all expenditures necessary to acquire these investments, such as the price paid plus any brokerage fees (commissions).

Assume, for example, that on July 1, 2010, Sanchez Corporation acquires 1,000 shares (10% ownership) of Beal Corporation common stock. Sanchez pays $40 per share plus brokerage fees of $500. The entry for the purchase is:

July 1	Stock Investments		40,500	
	Cash			40,500
	(To record purchase of 1,000 shares of Beal Corporation common stock)			

A = L + SE
+40,500
−40,500

Cash Flows
−40,500

RECORDING DIVIDENDS

During the time Sanchez owns the stock, it makes entries for any cash dividends received. If Sanchez receives a $2 per share dividend on December 31, the entry is:

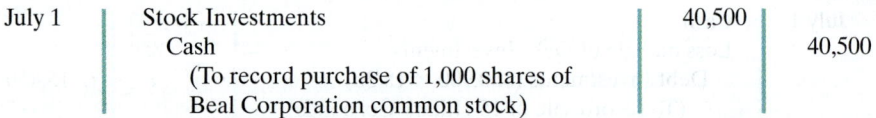

Dec. 31	Cash (1,000 × $2)		2,000	
	Dividend Revenue			2,000
	(To record receipt of a cash dividend)			

A = L + SE
+2,000
    +2,000 Rev

Cash Flows
+2,000

Sanchez reports Dividend Revenue under "Other revenues and gains" in the income statement. Unlike interest on notes and bonds, dividends do not accrue. Therefore, companies do not make adjusting entries to accrue dividends.

---

[1] Among the questions that are considered in determining an investor's influence are these: (1) Does the investor have representation on the investee's board? (2) Does the investor participate in the investee's policy-making process? (3) Are there material transactions between the investor and investee? (4) Is the common stock held by other stockholders concentrated or dispersed?

RECORDING SALE OF STOCK

When a company sells a stock investment, it recognizes as a gain or a loss the difference between the net proceeds from the sale (sales price less brokerage fees) and the cost of the stock.

Assume that Sanchez Corporation receives net proceeds of $39,500 on the sale of its Beal stock on February 10, 2011. Because the stock cost $40,500, Sanchez incurred a loss of $1,000. The entry to record the sale is:

Feb. 10	Cash	39,500	
	Loss on Sale of Stock Investments	1,000	
	Stock Investments		40,500
	(To record sale of Beal common stock)		

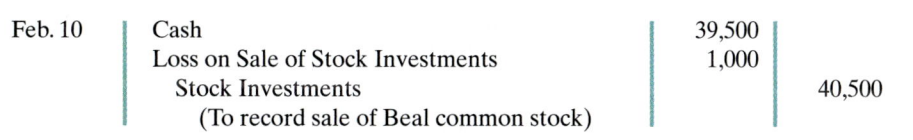

Sanchez reports the loss under "Other expenses and losses" in the income statement. It would show a gain on sale under "Other revenues and gains."

Holdings Between 20% and 50%

When an investor company owns only a small portion of the shares of stock of another company, the investor cannot exercise control over the investee. But, when an investor owns between 20% and 50% of the common stock of a corporation, it is presumed that the investor has significant influence over the financial and operating activities of the investee. The investor probably has a representative on the investee's board of directors, and through that representative, may exercise some control over the investee. The investee company in some sense becomes part of the investor company.

For example, even prior to purchasing all of Turner Broadcasting, Time Warner owned 20% of Turner. Because it exercised significant control over major decisions made by Turner, Time Warner used an approach called the equity method. Under the equity method, **the investor records its share of the net income of the investee in the year when it is earned**. An alternative might be to delay recognizing the investor's share of net income until the investee declares a cash dividend. But that approach would ignore the fact that the investor and investee are, in some sense, one company, making the investor better off by the investee's earned income.

Under the equity method, the investor company initially records the investment in common stock at cost. After that, it **annually adjusts** the investment account to show the investor's equity in the investee. Each year, the investor does the following: (1) It increases (debits) the investment account and increases (credits) revenue for its share of the investee's net income.[2] (2) The investor also decreases (credits) the investment account for the amount of dividends received. The investment account is reduced for dividends received, because payment of a dividend decreases the net assets of the investee.

> **HELPFUL HINT**
> Under the equity method, the investor recognizes revenue on the accrual basis—i.e., when it is earned by the investee.

RECORDING ACQUISITION OF STOCK INVESTMENTS

Assume that Milar Corporation acquires 30% of the common stock of Beck Company for $120,000 on January 1, 2010. Milar records this transaction as:

Jan. 1	Stock Investments	120,000	
	Cash		120,000
	(To record purchase of Beck common stock)		

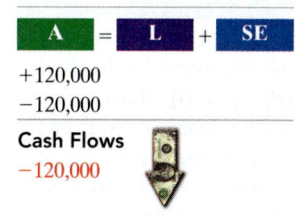

---

[2] Or, the investor increases (debits) a loss account and decreases (credits) the investment account for its share of the investee's net loss.

RECORDING REVENUE AND DIVIDENDS

For 2010, Beck reports net income of $100,000. It declares and pays a $40,000 cash dividend. Milar records (1) its share of Beck's income, $30,000 (30% × $100,000) and (2) the reduction in the investment account for the dividends received, $12,000 ($40,000 × 30%). The entries are:

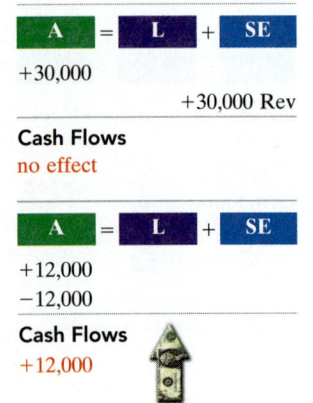

		(1)		
Dec. 31	Stock Investments		30,000	
	Revenue from Investment in Beck Company			30,000
	(To record 30% equity in Beck's 2010 net income)			

		(2)		
Dec. 31	Cash		12,000	
	Stock Investments			12,000
	(To record dividends received)			

After Milar posts the transactions for the year, its investment and revenue accounts will show the following.

Illustration 16-4
Investment and revenue accounts after posting

Stock Investments				Revenue from Investment in Beck Company	
Jan. 1	120,000	Dec. 31	12,000		
Dec. 31	30,000			Dec. 31	30,000
Dec. 31 Bal.	138,000				

During the year, the net increase in the investment account was $18,000. As indicated above, the investment account increased by $30,000 due to Milar's share of Beck's income, and it decreased by $12,000 due to dividends received from Beck. In addition, Milar reports $30,000 of revenue from its investment, which is 30% of Beck's net income of $100,000.

Note that the difference between reported revenue under the cost method and reported revenue under the equity method can be significant. For example, Milar would report only $12,000 of dividend revenue (30% × $40,000) if it used the cost method.

Holdings of More than 50%

STUDY OBJECTIVE 4
Describe the use of consolidated financial statements.

A company that owns more than 50% of the common stock of another entity is known as the **parent company**. The entity whose stock the parent company owns is called the **subsidiary (affiliated) company**. Because of its stock ownership, the parent company has a **controlling interest** in the subsidiary.

When a company owns more than 50% of the common stock of another company, it usually prepares **consolidated financial statements**. These statements present the total assets and liabilities controlled by the parent company. They also present the total revenues and expenses of the subsidiary companies. Companies prepare consolidated statements **in addition to** the financial statements for the parent and individual subsidiary companies.

As noted earlier, when Time Warner had a 20% investment in Turner, it reported this investment in a single line item—Other Investments. After the merger, Time Warner instead consolidated Turner's results with its own. Under this

HELPFUL HINT
If parent (A) has three wholly owned subsidiaries (B, C, & D), there are four separate legal entities. From the viewpoint of the shareholders of the parent company, there is only one economic entity.

approach, Time Warner included Turner's individual assets and liabilities with its own: its plant and equipment were added to Time Warner's plant and equipment, its receivables were added to Time Warner's receivables, and so on.

ACCOUNTING ACROSS THE ORGANIZATION

How Procter & Gamble Accounts for Gillette

Recently, Procter & Gamble Company acquired Gillette Company for $53.4 billion. The common stockholders of Procter & Gamble elect the board of directors of the company, who, in turn, select the officers and managers of the company. Procter & Gamble's board of directors controls the property owned by the corporation, which includes the common stock of Gillette. Thus, they are in a position to elect the board of directors of Gillette and, in effect, control its operations. These relationships are graphically illustrated here.

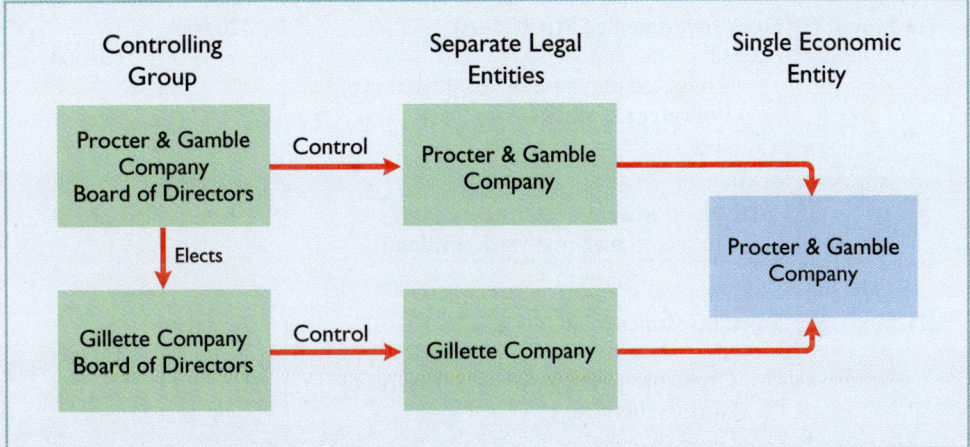

? Where on Procter & Gamble's balance sheet will you find its investment in Gillette Company?

Consolidated statements are useful to the stockholders, board of directors, and managers of the parent company. These statements indicate the magnitude and scope of operations of the companies under common control. For example, regulators and the courts undoubtedly used the consolidated statements of AT&T to determine whether a breakup of AT&T was in the public interest. Listed below are three companies that prepare consolidated statements and some of the companies they have owned. One, Disney, is Time Warner's arch rival.

Toys "R" Us, Inc.	Cendant	The Disney Company
Kids "R" Us	Howard Johnson	Capital Cities/ABC, Inc.
Babies "R" Us	Ramada Inn	Disneyland, Disney World
Imaginarium	Century 21	Mighty Ducks
Toysrus.com	Coldwell Banker	Anaheim Angels
	Avis	ESPN

Illustration 16-5
Examples of consolidated companies and their subsidiaries

DO IT!

STOCK INVESTMENTS

Presented below are two independent situations.

1. Rho Jean Inc. acquired 5% of the 400,000 shares of common stock of Stillwater Corp. at a total cost of $6 per share on May 18, 2010. On August 30, Stillwater declared and paid a $75,000 dividend. On December 31, Stillwater reported net income of $244,000 for the year.

2. Debbie, Inc. obtained significant influence over North Sails by buying 40% of North Sails' 60,000 outstanding shares of common stock at a cost of $12 per share on January 1, 2010. On April 15, North Sails declared and paid a cash dividend of $45,000. On December 31, North Sails reported net income of $120,000 for the year.

Prepare all necessary journal entries for 2010 for (1) Rho Jean Inc. and (2) Debbie, Inc.

action plan

✔ Presume that the investor has relatively little influence over the investee when an investor owns less than 20% of the common stock of another corporation. In this case, net income earned by the investee is not considered a proper basis for recognizing income from the investment by the investor.

✔ Presume significant influence for investments of 20%–50%. Therefore, record the investor's share of the net income of the investee.

Solution

(1)	May 18	Stock Investments (20,000 × $6)	120,000	
		Cash		120,000
		(To record purchase of 20,000 shares of Stillwater Co. stock)		
	Aug. 30	Cash	3,750	
		Dividend Revenue ($75,000 × 5%)		3,750
		(To record receipt of cash dividend)		
(2)	Jan. 1	Stock Investments (60,000 × 40% × $12)	288,000	
		Cash		288,000
		(To record purchase of 24,000 shares of North Sails' stock)		
	Apr. 15	Cash	18,000	
		Stock Investments ($45,000 × 40%)		18,000
		(To record receipt of cash dividend)		
	Dec. 31	Stock Investments ($120,000 × 40%)	48,000	
		Revenue from Investment in North Sails		48,000
		(To record 40% equity in North Sails' net income)		

Related exercise material: **BE16-2, BE16-3, E16-4, E16-5, E16-6, E16-7, E16-8,** and **DO IT! 16-2**.

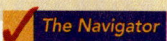

VALUING AND REPORTING INVESTMENTS

STUDY OBJECTIVE 5
Indicate how debt and stock investments are reported in financial statements.

The value of debt and stock investments may fluctuate greatly during the time they are held. For example, in one 12-month period, the stock price of **Dell Computer Corp.** hit a high of $30.77 and a low of $18.87. In light of such price fluctuations, how should companies value investments at the balance sheet date? Valuation could be at cost, at fair value (market value), or at the lower-of-cost-or-market value.

Many people argue that fair value offers the best approach because it represents the expected cash realizable value of securities. **Fair value** is the amount for which a security could be sold in a normal market. Others counter that, unless a security is going to be sold soon, the fair value is not relevant because the price of the security will likely change again.

Categories of Securities

For purposes of valuation and reporting at a financial statement date, companies classify debt and stock investments into three categories:

1. **Trading securities** are bought and held primarily for sale in the near term to generate income on short-term price differences.
2. **Available-for-sale securities** are held with the intent of selling them sometime in the future.
3. **Held-to-maturity securities** are debt securities that the investor has the intent and ability to hold to maturity.[3]

Illustration 16-6 shows the valuation guidelines for these securities. **These guidelines apply to all debt securities and all stock investments in which the holdings are less than 20%.**

> **INTERNATIONAL NOTE**
> A recent U.S. accounting standard gives companies the "option" of applying fair value accounting, rather than historical cost, to certain types of assets and liabilities. This makes U.S. accounting more similar to international standards.

Illustration 16-6
Valuation guidelines

TRADING SECURITIES

Companies hold trading securities with the intention of selling them in a short period (generally less than a month). *Trading* means frequent buying and selling. Companies report trading securities at fair value, and report changes from cost as part of net income. The changes are reported as **unrealized gains or losses** because the securities have not been sold. The unrealized gain or loss is the difference between the **total cost** of trading securities and their **total fair value**. Companies classify trading securities as current assets.

Illustration 16-7 shows the cost and fair values for investments Pace Corporation classified as trading securities on December 31, 2010. Pace has an unrealized gain of $7,000 because total fair value of $147,000 is $7,000 greater than total cost of $140,000.

> **HELPFUL HINT**
> The fact that trading securities are short-term investments increases the likelihood that they will be sold at fair value (the company may not be able to time their sale) and the likelihood that there will be realized gains or losses.

Illustration 16-7
Valuation of trading securities

Trading Securities, December 31, 2010			
Investments	Cost	Fair Value	Unrealized Gain (Loss)
Yorkville Company bonds	$ 50,000	$ 48,000	$ (2,000)
Kodak Company stock	90,000	99,000	9,000
Total	$140,000	$147,000	**$ 7,000**

---

[3]This category is provided for completeness. The accounting and valuation issues related to held-to-maturity securities are discussed in more advanced accounting courses.

706 Chapter 16 Investments

Pace records fair value and unrealized gain or loss through an adjusting entry at the time it prepares financial statements. In this entry, the company uses a valuation allowance account, Market Adjustment—Trading, to record the difference between the total cost and the total fair value of the securities. The adjusting entry for Pace Corporation is:

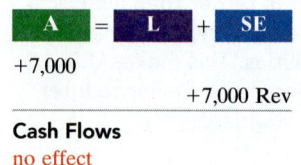

Cash Flows
no effect

Dec. 31	Market Adjustment—Trading	7,000	
	Unrealized Gain—Income		7,000
	(To record unrealized gain on trading securities)		

Use of a Market Adjustment—Trading account enables Pace to maintain a record of the investment cost. It needs actual cost to determine the gain or loss realized when it sells the securities. Pace adds the Market Adjustment—Trading balance to the cost of the investments to arrive at a fair value for the trading securities. **The fair value of the securities is the amount Pace reports on its balance sheet.** It reports the unrealized gain in the income statement in the "Other revenues and gains" section. The term "Income" in the account title indicates that the gain affects net income.

If the total cost of the trading securities is greater than total fair value, an unrealized loss has occurred. In such a case, the adjusting entry is a debit to Unrealized Loss—Income and a credit to Market Adjustment—Trading. Companies report the unrealized loss under "Other expenses and losses" in the income statement.

The market adjustment account is carried forward into future accounting periods. The company does not make any entry to the account until the end of each reporting period. At that time, the company adjusts the balance in the account to the difference between cost and fair value. For trading securities, it closes the Unrealized Gain (Loss)—Income account at the end of the reporting period.

ACCOUNTING ACROSS THE ORGANIZATION

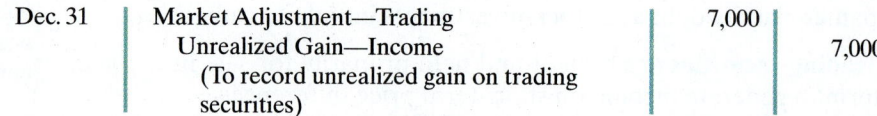

And the Correct Way to Report Investments Is...?

The accompanying graph presents an estimate of the percentage of companies on the major exchanges that have investments in the equity of other entities.

As the graph indicates, many companies have equity investments of some type. These investments can be substantial. For example, the total amount of equity-method investments appearing on company balance sheets is approximately $403 billion, and the amount shown in the income statements in any one year for all companies is approximately $38 billion.

Source: "Report and Recommendations Pursuant to Section 401(c) of the Sarbanes-Oxley Act of 2002 on Arrangements with Off-Balance Sheet Implications, Special Purpose Entities, and Transparency of Filings by Issuers," United States Securities and Exchange Commission—Office of Chief Accountant, Office of Economic Analyses, Division of Corporation Finance (June 2005), pp. 36–39.

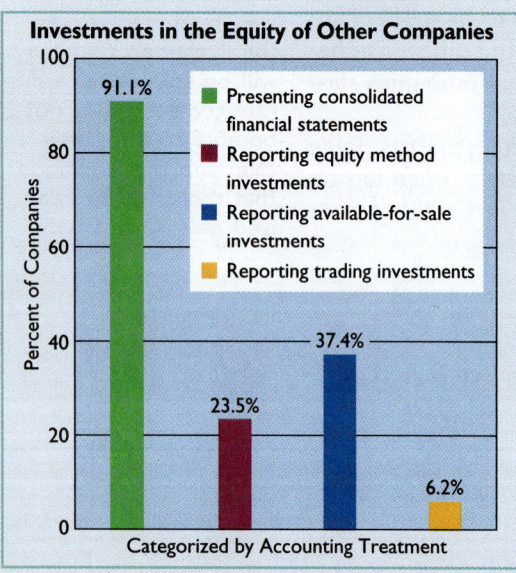

 Why might the use of the equity method not lead to full disclosure in the financial statements?

AVAILABLE-FOR-SALE SECURITIES

As indicated earlier, companies hold available-for-sale securities with the intent of selling these investments sometime in the future. If the intent is to sell the securities within the next year or operating cycle, the investor classifies the securities as current assets in the balance sheet. Otherwise, it classifies them as long-term assets in the investments section of the balance sheet.

Companies report available-for-sale securities at fair value. The procedure for determining fair value and the unrealized gain or loss for these securities is the same as for trading securities. To illustrate, assume that Ingrao Corporation has two securities that it classifies as available-for-sale. Illustration 16-8 provides information on their valuation. There is an unrealized loss of $9,537 because total cost of $293,537 is $9,537 more than total fair value of $284,000.

> **ETHICS NOTE**
> Some managers seem to hold their available-for-sale securities that have experienced losses, while selling those that have gains, thus increasing income. Do you think this is ethical?

Illustration 16-8
Valuation of available-for-sale securities

Available-for-Sale Securities, December 31, 2010

Investments	Cost	Fair Value	Unrealized Gain (Loss)
Campbell Soup Corporation 8% bonds	$ 93,537	$103,600	$10,063
Hershey Corporation stock	200,000	180,400	(19,600)
Total	$293,537	$284,000	**$(9,537)**

Both the adjusting entry and the reporting of the unrealized gain or loss for Ingrao's available-for-sale securities differ from those illustrated for trading securities. The differences result because Ingrao does not expect to sell these securities in the near term. Thus, prior to actual sale it is more likely that changes in fair value may change either unrealized gains or losses. Therefore, Ingrao does not report an unrealized gain or loss in the income statement. Instead, it reports it as a **separate component of stockholders' equity**.

In the adjusting entry, Ingrao identifies the market adjustment account with available-for-sale securities, and it identifies the unrealized gain or loss account with stockholders' equity. Ingrao records the unrealized loss of $9,537 as follows:

Dec. 31	Unrealized Gain or Loss—Equity	9,537	
	Market Adjustment—Available-for-Sale		9,537
	(To record unrealized loss on available-for-sale securities)		

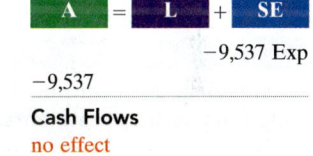

A = L + SE
−9,537 Exp
−9,537
Cash Flows
no effect

If total fair value exceeds total cost, Ingrao debits Market Adjustment—Available for Sale and credits Unrealized Gain or Loss—Equity.

For available-for-sale securities, the company carries forward the Unrealized Gain or Loss—Equity account to future periods. At each future balance sheet date, Ingrao adjusts the market adjustment account to show the difference between cost and fair value at that time.

> **ETHICS NOTE**
> Recently the SEC accused investment bank **Morgan Stanley** of overstating the value of certain bond investments by $75 million. The SEC stated that, in applying market value accounting, Morgan Stanly used its own more-optimistic assumptions rather than relying on external pricing sources.

DO IT!

TRADING AND AVAILABLE-FOR-SALE SECURITIES

Some of Powderhorn Corporation's investment securities are classified as trading securities and some are classified as available-for-sale. The cost and market value of each category at December 31, 2010, are shown on page 708.

	Cost	Fair Value	Unrealized Gain (Loss)
Trading securities	$93,600	$94,900	$1,300
Available-for-sale securities	$48,800	$51,400	$2,600

At December 31, 2009, the Market Adjustment—Trading account had a debit balance of $9,200, and the Market Adjustment—Available-for-Sale account had a credit balance of $5,750. Prepare the required journal entries for each group of securities for December 31, 2010.

action plan

✔ Mark trading securities to fair value and report the adjustment in current-period income.

✔ Mark available-for-sale securities to fair value and report the adjustment as a separate component of stockholders' equity.

Solution

Trading securities:

Unrealized Loss—Income	7,900*	
Market Adjustment—Trading		7,900
(To record unrealized loss on trading securities)		
*$9,200 − $1,300		

Available-for-sale securities:

Market Adjustment—Available-for-Sale	8,350**	
Unrealized Gain or Loss—Equity		8,350
(To record unrealized gain on available-for-sale securities)		
**$5,750 + $2,600		

Related exercise material: **BE16-4, BE16-5, BE16-6, BE16-7, E16-10, E16-11, E16-12,** and **DO IT!** **16-3.**

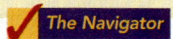

Balance Sheet Presentation

In the balance sheet, companies classify investments as either short-term or long-term.

SHORT-TERM INVESTMENTS

STUDY OBJECTIVE 6
Distinguish between short-term and long-term investments.

Short-term investments (also called **marketable securities**) are securities held by a company that are (1) **readily marketable** and (2) **intended to be converted into cash** within the next year or operating cycle, whichever is longer. Investments that do not meet **both criteria** are classified as **long-term investments**.

HELPFUL HINT
Trading securities are always classified as short-term. Available-for-sale securities can be either short-term or long-term.

Readily Marketable. An investment is readily marketable when it can be sold easily whenever the need for cash arises. Short-term paper[4] meets this criterion. It can be readily sold to other investors. Stocks and bonds traded on organized securities exchanges, such as the New York Stock Exchange, are readily marketable. They can be bought and sold daily. In contrast, there may be only a limited market for the securities issued by small corporations, and no market for the securities of a privately held company.

Intent to Convert. Intent to convert means that management intends to sell the investment within the next year or operating cycle, whichever is longer. Generally, this criterion is satisfied when the investment is considered a resource that the investor will use whenever the need for cash arises. For example, a ski resort may invest idle cash during the summer months with the intent to sell the securities to buy supplies and equipment shortly before the winter season. This investment is

---

[4]**Short-term paper** includes (1) certificates of deposit (CDs) issued by banks, (2) money market certificates issued by banks and savings and loan associations, (3) Treasury bills issued by the U.S. government, and (4) commercial paper (notes) issued by corporations with good credit ratings.

considered short-term even if lack of snow cancels the next ski season and eliminates the need to convert the securities into cash as intended.

Because of their high liquidity, short-term investments appear immediately below Cash in the "Current assets" section of the balance sheet. They are reported at fair value. For example, Pace Corporation would report its trading securities as shown in Illustration 16-9.

PACE CORPORATION
Balance Sheet (partial)

Current assets	
Cash	$ 21,000
Short-term investments, at fair value	147,000

Illustration 16-9
Presentation of short-term investments

HELPFUL HINT
In a recent survey of 600 large U.S. companies, 242 reported short-term investments.

LONG-TERM INVESTMENTS

Companies generally report long-term investments in a separate section of the balance sheet immediately below "Current assets," as shown later in Illustration 16-12 (page 711). Long-term investments in available-for-sale securities are reported at fair value. Investments in common stock accounted for under the equity method are reported at their equity value.

Presentation of Realized and Unrealized Gain or Loss

Companies must present in the financial statements gains and losses on investments, whether realized or unrealized. In the income statement, companies report gains and losses in the nonoperating activities section under the categories listed in Illustration 16-10. Interest and dividend revenue are also reported in that section.

Other Revenue and Gains	Other Expenses and Losses
Interest Revenue	Loss on Sale of Investments
Dividend Revenue	Unrealized Loss—Income
Gain on Sale of Investments	
Unrealized Gain—Income	

Illustration 16-10
Nonoperating items related to investments

As indicated earlier, companies report an unrealized gain or loss on available-for-sale securities as a separate component of stockholders' equity. To illustrate, assume that Dawson Inc. has common stock of $3,000,000, retained earnings of $1,500,000, and an unrealized loss on available-for-sale securities of $100,000. Illustration 16-11 shows the balance sheet presentation of the unrealized loss.

DAWSON INC.
Balance Sheet (partial)

Stockholders' equity	
Common stock	$3,000,000
Retained earnings	1,500,000
Total paid-in capital and retained earnings	4,500,000
Less: Unrealized loss on available-for-sale securities	(100,000)
Total stockholders' equity	$4,400,000

Illustration 16-11
Unrealized loss in stockholders' equity section

Note that the loss decreases stockholders' equity. An unrealized gain is added to stockholders' equity. Reporting the unrealized gain or loss in the stockholders' equity section serves two purposes: (1) It reduces the volatility of net income due to fluctuations in fair value. (2) It informs the financial statement user of the gain or loss that would occur if the securities were sold at fair value.

Companies must report items such as this, which affect stockholders' equity but are not included in the calculation of net income, as part of a more inclusive measure called *comprehensive income*. We discuss comprehensive income briefly in Chapter 18.

Classified Balance Sheet

We have presented many sections of classified balance sheets in this and preceding chapters. The classified balance sheet in Illustration 16-12 includes, in one place, key topics from previous chapters: the issuance of par value common stock, restrictions of retained earnings, and issuance of long-term bonds. From this chapter, the statement includes (highlighted in red) short-term and long-term investments. The investments in short-term securities are considered trading securities. The long-term investments in stock of less than 20% owned companies are considered available-for-sale securities. Illustration 16-12 also includes a long-term investment reported at equity and descriptive notations within the statement, such as the basis for valuing merchandise inventory and one note to the statement.

DO IT!

FINANCIAL STATEMENT PRESENTATION OF INVESTMENTS

Identify where each of the following items would be reported in the financial statements.

1. Interest earned on investments in bonds.
2. Market adjustment—available-for-sale.
3. Unrealized loss on available-for-sale securities.
4. Gain on sale of investments in stock.
5. Unrealized gain on trading securities.

Use the following possible categories:

Balance sheet:

Current assets	Current liabilities
Investments	Long-term liabilities
Property, plant, and equipment	Stockholders' equity
Intangible assets	

Income statement:

| Other revenues and gains | Other expenses and losses |

action plan

✔ Classify investments as current assets if they will be held for less than one year.
✔ Report unrealized gains or losses on trading securities in income.
✔ Report unrealized gains or losses on available-for-sale securities in equity.
✔ Report realized earnings on investments in the income statement as "Other revenues and gains" or as "Other expenses and losses."

Solution

Item	Financial Statement	Category
1. Interest earned on investments in bonds.	Income statement	Other revenues and gains
2. Market adjustment—available-for-sale	Balance sheet	Investments
3. Unrealized loss on available-for-sale securities	Balance sheet	Stockholders' equity
4. Gain on sale of investments in stock	Income statement	Other revenues and gains
5. Unrealized gain on trading securities	Income statement	Other revenues and gains

Related exercise material: **BE16-6, BE16-7, BE16-8, E16-10, E16-11, E16-12,** and **DO IT!** **16-4.**

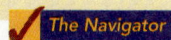

Illustration 16-12
Classified balance sheet

PACE CORPORATION
Balance Sheet
December 31, 2010

Assets

Current assets			
Cash			$ 21,000
Short-term investments, at fair value			**147,000**
Accounts receivable		$ 84,000	
Less: Allowance for doubtful accounts		4,000	80,000
Merchandise inventory, at FIFO cost			43,000
Prepaid insurance			23,000
Total current assets			314,000
Investments			
Investments in stock of less than 20%			
owned companies, at fair value		**50,000**	
Investment in stock of 20–50% owned			
company, at equity		**150,000**	
Total investments			200,000
Property, plant, and equipment			
Land		200,000	
Buildings	$800,000		
Less: Accumulated depreciation	200,000	600,000	
Equipment	180,000		
Less: Accumulated depreciation	54,000	126,000	
Total property, plant, and equipment			926,000
Intangible assets			
Goodwill			270,000
Total assets			$1,710,000

Liabilities and Stockholders' Equity

Current liabilities			
Accounts payable			$ 185,000
Federal income taxes payable			60,000
Bond interest payable			10,000
Total current liabilities			255,000
Long-term liabilities			
Bonds payable, 10%, due 2021		$ 300,000	
Less: Discount on bonds		10,000	
Total long-term liabilities			290,000
Total liabilities			545,000
Stockholders' equity			
Paid-in capital			
Common stock, $10 par value, 200,000 shares			
authorized, 80,000 shares issued and outstanding		800,000	
Paid-in capital in excess of par value		100,000	
Total paid-in capital		900,000	
Retained earnings (Note 1)		255,000	
Total paid-in capital and retained earnings		1,155,000	
Add: Unrealized gain on available-for-sale			
securities		**10,000**	
Total stockholders' equity			1,165,000
Total liabilities and stockholders' equity			$1,710,000

Note 1. Retained earnings of $100,000 is restricted for plant expansion.

Chapter 16 Investments

Comprehensive DO IT!

In its first year of operations, DeMarco Company had the following selected transactions in stock investments that are considered trading securities.

June	1	Purchased for cash 600 shares of Sanburg common stock at $24 per share, plus $300 brokerage fees.
July	1	Purchased for cash 800 shares of Cey common stock at $33 per share, plus $600 brokerage fees.
Sept.	1	Received a $1 per share cash dividend from Cey Corporation.
Nov.	1	Sold 200 shares of Sanburg common stock for cash at $27 per share, less $150 brokerage fees.
Dec.	15	Received a $0.50 per share cash dividend on Sanburg common stock.

At December 31, the fair values per share were: Sanburg $25 and Cey $30.

Instructions
(a) Journalize the transactions.
(b) Prepare the adjusting entry at December 31 to report the securities at fair value.

action plan
✔ Include the price paid plus brokerage fees in the cost of the investment.
✔ Compute the gain or loss on sales as the difference between net selling price and the cost of the securities.
✔ Base the adjustment to fair value on the total difference between the cost and the fair value of the securities.

Solution to Comprehensive DO IT!

(a) June 1 Stock Investments 14,700
    Cash (600 × $24) + $300 14,700
    (To record purchase of 600 shares of Sanburg common stock)

July 1 Stock Investments 27,000
    Cash (800 × $33) + $600 27,000
    (To record purchase of 800 shares of Cey common stock)

Sept. 1 Cash (800 × $1.00) 800
    Dividend Revenue 800
    (To record receipt of $1 per share cash dividend from Cey Corporation)

Nov. 1 Cash (200 × $27) − $150 5,250
    Stock Investments ($14,700 × 200/600) 4,900
    Gain on Sale of Stock Investments 350
    (To record sale of 200 shares of Sanburg common stock)

Dec. 15 Cash (600 − 200) × $0.50 200
    Dividend Revenue 200
    (To record receipt of $0.50 per share dividend from Sanburg Corporation)

(b) Dec. 31 Unrealized Loss—Income 2,800
    Market Adjustment—Trading 2,800
    (To record unrealized loss on trading securities)

Investment	Cost	Fair Value	Unrealized Gain (Loss)
Sanburg common stock	$ 9,800	$10,000	$ 200
Cey common stock	27,000	24,000	(3,000)
Totals	$36,800	$34,000	$(2,800)

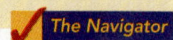

SUMMARY OF STUDY OBJECTIVES

1. **Discuss why corporations invest in debt and stock securities.** Corporations invest for three primary reasons: (a) They have excess cash. (b) They view investments as a significant revenue source. (c) They have strategic goals such as gaining control of a competitor or moving into a new line of business.

2. **Explain the accounting for debt investments.** Companies record investments in debt securities when they purchase bonds, receive or accrue interest, and sell the bonds. They report gains or losses on the sale of bonds in the "Other revenues and gains" or "Other expenses and losses" sections of the income statement.

3. **Explain the accounting for stock investments.** Companies record investments in common stock when they purchase the stock, receive dividends, and sell the stock. When ownership is less than 20%, the cost method is used. When ownership is between 20% and 50%, the equity method should be used. When ownership is more than 50%, companies prepare consolidated financial statements.

4. **Describe the use of consolidated financial statements.** When a company owns more than 50% of the common stock of another company, it usually prepares consolidated financial statements. These statements indicate the magnitude and scope of operations of the companies under common control.

5. **Indicate how debt and stock investments are reported in financial statements.** Investments in debt and stock securities are classified as trading, available-for-sale, or held-to-maturity securities for valuation and reporting purposes. Trading securities are reported as current assets at fair value, with changes from cost reported in net income. Available-for-sale securities are also reported at fair value, with the changes from cost reported in stockholders' equity. Available-for-sale securities are classified as short-term or long-term depending on their expected future sale date.

6. **Distinguish between short-term and long-term investments.** Short-term investments are securities that are (a) readily marketable and (b) intended to be converted to cash within the next year or operating cycle, whichever is longer. Investments that do not meet both criteria are classified as long-term investments.

GLOSSARY

Available-for-sale securities Securities that are held with the intent of selling them sometime in the future. (p. 705).

Consolidated financial statements Financial statements that present the assets and liabilities controlled by the parent company and the total revenues and expenses of the subsidiary companies. (p. 702).

Controlling interest Ownership of more than 50% of the common stock of another entity. (p. 702).

Cost method An accounting method in which the investment in common stock is recorded at cost, and revenue is recognized only when cash dividends are received. (p. 700).

Debt investments Investments in government and corporation bonds. (p. 698).

Equity method An accounting method in which the investment in common stock is initially recorded at cost, and the investment account is then adjusted annually to show the investor's equity in the investee. (p. 701).

Fair value Amount for which a security could be sold in a normal market. (p. 704).

Held-to-maturity securities Debt securities that the investor has the intent and ability to hold to their maturity date. (p. 705).

Investment portfolio A group of stocks and/or debt securities in different corporations held for investment purposes. (p. 699).

Long-term investments Investments that are not readily marketable or that management does not intend to convert into cash within the next year or operating cycle, whichever is longer. (p. 708).

Parent company A company that owns more than 50% of the common stock of another entity. (p. 702).

Short-term investments Investments that are readily marketable and intended to be converted into cash within the next year or operating cycle, whichever is longer. (p. 708).

Stock investments Investments in the capital stock of other corporations. (p. 699).

Subsidiary (affiliated) company A company in which more than 50% of its stock is owned by another company. (p. 702).

Trading securities Securities bought and held primarily for sale in the near term to generate income on short-term price differences. (p. 705).

SELF-STUDY QUESTIONS

Answers are at the end of the chapter.

(SO 1) 1. Which of the following is *not* a primary reason why corporations invest in debt and equity securities?
   a. They wish to gain control of a competitor.
   b. They have excess cash.
   c. They wish to move into a new line of business.
   d. They are required to by law.

(SO 2) 2. Debt investments are initially recorded at:
   a. cost.
   b. cost plus accrued interest.
   c. fair value.
   d. None of the above.

(SO 2) 3. Hanes Company sells debt investments costing $26,000 for $28,000, plus accrued interest that has been recorded. In journalizing the sale, credits are to:
   a. Debt Investments and Loss on Sale of Debt Investments.
   b. Debt Investments, Gain on Sale of Debt Investments, and Bond Interest Receivable.
   c. Stock Investments and Bond Interest Receivable.
   d. No correct answer given.

(SO 3) 4. Pryor Company receives net proceeds of $42,000 on the sale of stock investments that cost $39,500. This transaction will result in reporting in the income statement a:
   a. loss of $2,500 under "Other expenses and losses."
   b. loss of $2,500 under "Operating expenses."
   c. gain of $2,500 under "Other revenues and gains."
   d. gain of $2,500 under "Operating revenues."

(SO 3) 5. The equity method of accounting for long-term investments in stock should be used when the investor has significant influence over an investee and owns:
   a. between 20% and 50% of the investee's common stock.
   b. 20% or more of the investee's common stock.
   c. more than 50% of the investee's common stock.
   d. less than 20% of the investee's common stock.

(SO 3) 6. Assume that Horicon Corp acquired 25% of the common stock of Sheboygan Corp. on January 1, 2010, for $300,000. During 2008 Sheboygan Corp. reported net income of $160,000 and paid total dividends of $60,000. If Horicon uses the equity method to account for its investment, the balance in the investment account on December 31, 2010, will be:
   a. $300,000.
   b. $325,000.
   c. $400,000.
   d. $340,000.

(SO 3) 7. Using the information in question 6, what entry would Horicon make to record the receipt of the dividend from Sheboygan?
   a. Debit Cash and credit Revenue from Investment in Sheboygan Corp.
   b. Debit Dividends and credit Revenue from Investment in Sheboygan Corp.
   c. Debit Cash and credit Stock Investments.
   d. Debit Cash and credit Dividend Revenue.

(SO 3) 8. You have a controlling interest if:
   a. you own more than 20% of a company's stock.
   b. you are the president of the company.
   c. you use the equity method.
   d. you own more than 50% of a company's stock.

(SO 4) 9. Which of the following statements is *not true*? Consolidated financial statements are useful to:
   a. determine the profitability of specific subsidiaries.
   b. determine the total profitability of enterprises under common control.
   c. determine the breadth of a parent company's operations.
   d. determine the full extent of total obligations of enterprises under common control.

(SO 5) 10. At the end of the first year of operations, the total cost of the trading securities portfolio is $120,000. Total fair value is $115,000. The financial statements should show:
   a. a reduction of an asset of $5,000 and a realized loss of $5,000.
   b. a reduction of an asset of $5,000 and an unrealized loss of $5,000 in the stockholders' equity section.
   c. a reduction of an asset of $5,000 in the current assets section and an unrealized loss of $5,000 in "Other expenses and losses."
   d. a reduction of an asset of $5,000 in the current assets section and a realized loss of $5,000 in "Other expenses and losses."

(SO 5) 11. At December 31, 2010, the fair value of available-for-sale securities is $41,300 and the cost is $39,800. At January 1, 2010, there was a credit balance of $900 in the Market Adjustment—Available-for-Sale account. The required adjusting entry would be:
   a. Debit Market Adjustment—Available-for-Sale for $1,500 and credit Unrealized Gain or Loss—Equity for $1,500.
   b. Debit Market Adjustment—Available-for-Sale for $600 and credit Unrealized Gain or Loss—Equity for $600.
   c. Debit Market Adjustment—Available-for-Sale for $2,400 and credit Unrealized Gain or Loss—Equity for $2,400.
   d. Debit Unrealized Gain or Loss—Equity for $2,400 and credit Market Adjustment—Available-for-Sale for $2,400.

(SO 5) 12. In the balance sheet, a debit balance in Unrealized Gain or Loss—Equity is reported as a(n):
   a. increase to stockholders' equity.
   b. decrease to stockholders' equity.
   c. loss in the income statement.
   d. loss in the retained earnings statement.

(SO 6) 13. Short-term debt investments must be readily marketable and expected to be sold within:
   a. 3 months from the date of purchase.
   b. the next year or operating cycle, whichever is shorter.
   c. the next year or operating cycle, whichever is longer.
   d. the operating cycle.

Go to the book's companion website, **www.wiley.com/college/weygandt**, for Additional Self-Study questions.

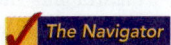

QUESTIONS

1. What are the reasons that corporations invest in securities?
2. (a) What is the cost of an investment in bonds?
   (b) When is interest on bonds recorded?
3. Tino Martinez is confused about losses and gains on the sale of debt investments. Explain to Tino (a) how the gain or loss is computed, and (b) the statement presentation of the gains and losses.
4. Olindo Company sells Gish's bonds costing $40,000 for $45,000, including $500 of accrued interest. In recording the sale, Olindo books a $5,000 gain. Is this correct? Explain.
5. What is the cost of an investment in stock?
6. To acquire Kinston Corporation stock, R. Neal pays $62,000 in cash, plus $1,200 broker's fees. What entry should be made for this investment?
7. (a) When should a long-term investment in common stock be accounted for by the equity method? (b) When is revenue recognized under this method?
8. Rijo Corporation uses the equity method to account for its ownership of 30% of the common stock of Pippen Packing. During 2010 Pippen reported a net income of $80,000 and declares and pays cash dividends of $10,000. What recognition should Rijo Corporation give to these events?
9. What constitutes "significant influence" when an investor's financial interest is below the 50% level?
10. Distinguish between the cost and equity methods of accounting for investments in stocks.
11. What are consolidated financial statements?
12. What are the valuation guidelines for investments at a balance sheet date?
13. Tina Eddings is the controller of Mendez Inc. At December 31, the company's investments in trading securities cost $74,000. They have a fair value of $70,000. Indicate how Tina would report these data in the financial statements prepared on December 31.
14. Using the data in question 13, how would Tina report the data if the investment were long-term and the securities were classified as available-for-sale?
15. Hashmi Company's investments in available-for-sale securities at December 31 show total cost of $195,000 and total fair value of $205,000. Prepare the adjusting entry.
16. Using the data in question 15, prepare the adjusting entry assuming the securities are classified as trading securities.
17. What is the proper statement presentation of the account Unrealized Loss—Equity?
18. What purposes are served by reporting Unrealized Gains (Losses)—Equity in the stockholders' equity section?
19. Altoona Wholesale Supply owns stock in Key Corporation. Altoona intends to hold the stock indefinitely because of some negative tax consequences if sold. Should the investment in Key be classified as a short-term investment? Why or why not?
20.  What does PepsiCo's state regarding its accounting policy involving consolidated financial statements?

BRIEF EXERCISES

BE16-1 Coffey Corporation purchased debt investments for $52,000 on January 1, 2010. On July 1, 2010, Coffey received cash interest of $2,340. Journalize the purchase and the receipt of interest. Assume that no interest has been accrued.

Journalize entries for debt investments.
(SO 2)

BE16-2 On August 1, Wade Company buys 1,000 shares of Morgan common stock for $35,000 cash, plus brokerage fees of $700. On December 1, Wade sells the stock investments for $40,000 in cash. Journalize the purchase and sale of the common stock.

Journalize entries for stock investments.
(SO 3)

BE16-3 Kayser Company owns 25% of Fort Company. For the current year Fort reports net income of $180,000 and declares and pays a $50,000 cash dividend. Record Kayser's equity in Fort's net income and the receipt of dividends from Fort.

Record transactions under the equity method of accounting.
(SO 3)

BE16-4 The cost of the trading securities of Cepeda Company at December 31, 2010, is $62,000. At December 31, 2010, the fair value of the securities is $59,000. Prepare the adjusting entry to record the securities at fair value.

Prepare adjusting entry using fair value.
(SO 5)

BE16-5 For the data presented in BE16-4, show the financial statement presentation of the trading securities and related accounts.

Indicate statement presentation using fair value.
(SO 5, 6)

BE16-6 Garrett Corporation holds as a long-term investment available-for-sale stock securities costing $72,000. At December 31, 2010, the fair value of the securities is $66,000. Prepare the adjusting entry to record the securities at fair value.

Prepare adjusting entry using fair value.
(SO 5)

Chapter 16 Investments

Indicate statements presentation using fair value.
(SO 5, 6)

BE16-7 For the data presented in BE16-6, show the financial statement presentation of the available-for-sale securities and related accounts. Assume the available-for-sale securities are noncurrent.

Prepare investments section of balance sheet.
(SO 5, 6)

BE16-8 Gowdy Corporation has the following long-term investments: (1) Common stock of Dixen Co. (10% ownership) held as available-for-sale securities, cost $108,000, fair value $115,000. (2) Common stock of Ely Inc. (30% ownership), cost $210,000, equity $270,000. Prepare the investments section of the balance sheet.

DO IT! REVIEW

Make journal entry for bond purchase and adjusting entry for interest accrual.
(SO 2)

DO IT! 16-1 Odlaw Corporation had the following transactions relating to debt investments:

Jan. 1   Purchased 50, $1,000, 12% Clinton Company bonds for $50,000 plus broker's fees of $1,500. Interest is payable semiannually on January 1 and July 1.
July 1   Received semiannual interest from Clinton Company bonds.
July 1   Sold 30 Clinton Company bonds for $30,000, less $800 broker's fees.

(a) Journalize the transactions, and (b) prepare the adjusting entry for the accrual of interest on December 31.

Make journal entries for stock investments.
(SO 3)

DO IT! 16-2 Presented below are two independent situations:

1. Potomac Inc. acquired 10% of the 500,000 shares of common stock of Maryland Corporation at a total cost of $11 per share on June 17, 2010. On September 3, Maryland declared and paid a $160,000 dividend. On December 31, Maryland reported net income of $550,000 for the year.

2. Andy Fisher Corporation obtained significant influence over Bandit Company by buying 30% of Bandit's 100,000 outstanding shares of common stock at a cost of $18 per share on January 1, 2010. On May 15, Bandit declared and paid a cash dividend of $150,000. On December 31, Bandit reported net income of $270,000 for the year.

Prepare all necessary journal entries for 2010 for (1) Potomac and (2) Andy Fisher.

Make journal entries for trading and available-for-sale securities.
(SO 5)

DO IT! 16-3 Some of Grand Junction Corporation's investment securities are classified as trading securities and some are classified as available-for-sale. The cost and market value of each category at December 31, 2010, was as follows.

	Cost	Fair Value	Unrealized Gain (Loss)
Trading securities	$96,300	$84,900	$(11,400)
Available-for-sale securities	$59,000	$63,200	$ 4,200

At December 31, 2009, the Market Adjustment—Trading account had a debit balance of $2,200, and the Market Adjustment—Available-for-Sale account had a credit balance of $7,750. Prepare the required journal entries for each group of securities for December 31, 2010.

Indicate financial statement presentation of investments.
(SO 6)

DO IT! 16-4 Identify where each of the following items would be reported in the financial statements.

1. Loss on sale of investments in stock.
2. Unrealized gain on available-for-sale securities.
3. Market adjustment—trading.
4. Interest earned on investments in bonds.
5. Unrealized loss on trading securities.

Use the following possible categories:
Balance sheet:
    Current assets   Current liabilities
    Investments   Long-term liabilities
    Property, plant, and equipment   Stockholders' equity
    Intangible assets
Income statement:
    Other revenues and gains   Other expenses and losses

EXERCISES

E16-1 Max Weinberg is studying for an accounting test and has developed the following questions about investments.
1. What are three reasons why companies purchase investments in debt or stock securities?
2. Why would a corporation have excess cash that it does not need for operations?
3. What is the typical investment when investing cash for short periods of time?
4. What are the typical investments when investing cash to generate earnings?
5. Why would a company invest in securities that provide no current cash flows?
6. What is the typical stock investment when investing cash for strategic reasons?

Understand debt and stock investments.
(SO 1)

Instructions
Provide answers for Max.

E16-2 Foren Corporation had the following transactions pertaining to debt investments.
Jan. 1 Purchased 50 8%, $1,000 Choate Co. bonds for $50,000 cash plus brokerage fees of $900. Interest is payable semiannually on July 1 and January 1.
July 1 Received semiannual interest on Choate Co. bonds.
July 1 Sold 30 Choate Co. bonds for $34,000 less $500 brokerage fees.

Journalize debt investment transactions and accrue interest.
(SO 2)

Instructions
(a) Journalize the transactions.
(b) Prepare the adjusting entry for the accrual of interest at December 31.

E16-3 EmmyLou Company purchased 70 Harris Company 12%, 10-year, $1,000 bonds on January 1, 2010, for $73,000. EmmyLou Company also had to pay $500 of broker's fees. The bonds pay interest semiannually on July 1 and January 1. On January 1, 2011, after receipt of interest, EmmyLou Company sold 40 of the bonds for $40,100.

Journalize debt investment transactions, accrue interest, and record sale.
(SO 2)

Instructions
Prepare the journal entries to record the transactions described above.

E16-4 Dossett Company had the following transactions pertaining to stock investments.
Feb. 1 Purchased 600 shares of Goetz common stock (2%) for $6,000 cash, plus brokerage fees of $200.
July 1 Received cash dividends of $1 per share on Goetz common stock.
Sept. 1 Sold 300 shares of Goetz common stock for $4,400, less brokerage fees of $100.
Dec. 1 Received cash dividends of $1 per share on Goetz common stock.

Journalize stock investment transactions.
(SO 3)

Instructions
(a) Journalize the transactions.
(b) Explain how dividend revenue and the gain (loss) on sale should be reported in the income statement.

E16-5 Wyrick Inc. had the following transactions pertaining to investments in common stock.
Jan. 1 Purchased 2,500 shares of Murphy Corporation common stock (5%) for $140,000 cash plus $2,100 broker's commission.
July 1 Received a cash dividend of $3 per share.
Dec. 1 Sold 500 shares of Murphy Corporation common stock for $32,000 cash, less $800 broker's commission.
Dec. 31 Received a cash dividend of $3 per share.

Journalize transactions for investments in stocks.
(SO 3)

Instructions
Journalize the transactions.

E16-6 On February 1, Neil Company purchased 500 shares (2% ownership) of Young Company common stock for $30 per share plus brokerage fees of $400. On March 20, Neil Company sold 100 shares of Young stock for $2,900, less a $50 brokerage fee. Neil received a dividend of $1.00 per share on April 25. On June 15, Neil sold 200 shares of Young stock for $7,400, less a $90 brokerage fee. On July 28, Neil received a dividend of $1.25 per share.

Journalize transactions for investments in stocks.
(SO 3)

Instructions
Prepare the journal entries to record the transactions described above.

718 Chapter 16 Investments

Journalize and post transactions, and contrast cost and equity method results.
(SO 3)

E16-7 On January 1 Kwun Corporation purchased a 25% equity in Connors Corporation for $180,000. At December 31 Connors declared and paid a $60,000 cash dividend and reported net income of $200,000.

Instructions
(a) Journalize the transactions.
(b) Determine the amount to be reported as an investment in Connors stock at December 31.

Journalize entries under cost and equity methods.
(SO 3, 5)

E16-8 Presented below are two independent situations.

1. Heath Cosmetics acquired 15% of the 200,000 shares of common stock of Van Fashion at a total cost of $13 per share on March 18, 2010. On June 30, Van declared and paid a $60,000 dividend. On December 31, Van reported net income of $122,000 for the year. At December 31, the market price of Van Fashion was $15 per share. The stock is classified as available-for-sale.
2. Yoder, Inc., obtained significant influence over Parks Corporation by buying 30% of Parks 30,000 outstanding shares of common stock at a total cost of $9 per share on January 1, 2010. On June 15, Parks declared and paid a cash dividend of $30,000. On December 31, Parks reported a net income of $80,000 for the year.

Instructions
Prepare all the necessary journal entries for 2010 for (1) Heath Cosmetics and (2) Yoder, Inc.

Understand the usefulness of consolidated statements.
(SO 4)

E16-9 Ryan Company purchased 70% of the outstanding common stock of Wayne Corporation.

Instructions
(a) Explain the relationship between Ryan Company and Wayne Corporation.
(b) How should Ryan account for its investment in Wayne?
(c) Why is the accounting treatment described in (b) useful?

Prepare adjusting entry to record fair value, and indicate statement presentation.
(SO 5, 6)

E16-10 At December 31, 2010, the trading securities for Natoli, Inc. are as follows.

Security	Cost	Fair Value
A	$17,500	$16,000
B	12,500	14,000
C	23,000	19,000
	$53,000	$49,000

Instructions
(a) Prepare the adjusting entry at December 31, 2010, to report the securities at fair value.
(b) Show the balance sheet and income statement presentation at December 31, 2010, after adjustment to fair value.

Prepare adjusting entry to record fair value, and indicate statement presentation.
(SO 5, 6)

E16-11 Data for investments in stock classified as trading securities are presented in E16-10. Assume instead that the investments are classified as available-for-sale securities. They have the same cost and fair value. The securities are considered to be a long-term investment.

Instructions
(a) Prepare the adjusting entry at December 31, 2010, to report the securities at fair value.
(b) Show the statement presentation at December 31, 2010, after adjustment to fair value.
(c) M. Linquist, a member of the board of directors, does not understand the reporting of the unrealized gains or losses. Write a letter to Mr. Linquist explaining the reporting and the purposes that it serves.

Prepare adjusting entries for fair value, and indicate statement presentation for two classes of securities.
(SO 5, 6)

E16-12 McGee Company has the following data at December 31, 2010.

Securities	Cost	Fair Value
Trading	$120,000	$124,000
Available-for-sale	100,000	94,000

The available-for-sale securities are held as a long-term investment.

Instructions
(a) Prepare the adjusting entries to report each class of securities at fair value.
(b) Indicate the statement presentation of each class of securities and the related unrealized gain (loss) accounts.

EXERCISES: SET B

Visit the book's companion website at **www.wiley.com/college/weygandt**, and choose the Student Companion site, to access Exercise Set B.

PROBLEMS: SET A

P16-1A Davison Carecenters Inc. provides financing and capital to the health-care industry, with a particular focus on nursing homes for the elderly. The following selected transactions relate to bonds acquired as an investment by Davison, whose fiscal year ends on December 31.

Journalize debt investment transactions and show financial statement presentation.
(SO 2, 5, 6)

2010

Jan. 1   Purchased at face value $2,000,000 of Hannon Nursing Centers, Inc., 10-year, 8% bonds dated January 1, 2010, directly from Hannon.
July 1   Received the semiannual interest on the Hannon bonds.
Dec. 31 Accrual of interest at year-end on the Hannon bonds.

(Assume that all intervening transactions and adjustments have been properly recorded and that the number of bonds owned has not changed from December 31, 2010, to December 31, 2012.)

2013

Jan. 1   Received the semiannual interest on the Hannon bonds.
Jan. 1   Sold $1,000,000 Hannon bonds at 106. The broker deducted $6,000 for commissions and fees on the sale.
July 1   Received the semiannual interest on the Hannon bonds.
Dec. 31 Accrual of interest at year-end on the Hannon bonds.

Instructions

(a) Journalize the listed transactions for the years 2010 and 2013.
(b) Assume that the fair value of the bonds at December 31, 2010, was $2,200,000. These bonds are classified as available-for-sale securities. Prepare the adjusting entry to record these bonds at fair value.
(c) Based on your analysis in part (b), show the balance sheet presentation of the bonds and interest receivable at December 31, 2010. Assume the investments are considered long-term. Indicate where any unrealized gain or loss is reported in the financial statements.

(a) Gain on sale of debt investment $54,000

P16-2A In January 2010, the management of Noble Company concludes that it has sufficient cash to permit some short-term investments in debt and stock securities. During the year, the following transactions occurred.

Journalize investment transactions, prepare adjusting entry, and show statement presentation.
(SO 2, 3, 5, 6)

Feb. 1   Purchased 600 shares of Hiens common stock for $31,800, plus brokerage fees of $600.
Mar. 1   Purchased 800 shares of Pryce common stock for $20,000, plus brokerage fees of $400.
Apr. 1   Purchased 50 $1,000, 7% Roy bonds for $50,000, plus $1,000 brokerage fees. Interest is payable semiannually on April 1 and October 1.
July 1   Received a cash dividend of $0.60 per share on the Hiens common stock.
Aug. 1   Sold 200 shares of Hiens common stock at $58 per share less brokerage fees of $200.
Sept. 1 Received a $1 per share cash dividend on the Pryce common stock.
Oct. 1   Received the semiannual interest on the Roy bonds.
Oct. 1   Sold the Roy bonds for $50,000 less $1,000 brokerage fees.

At December 31, the fair value of the Hiens common stock was $55 per share. The fair value of the Pryce common stock was $24 per share.

Instructions

(a) Journalize the transactions and post to the accounts Debt Investments and Stock Investments. (Use the T-account form.)
(b) Prepare the adjusting entry at December 31, 2010, to report the investment securities at fair value. All securities are considered to be trading securities.
(c) Show the balance sheet presentation of investment securities at December 31, 2010.
(d) Identify the income statement accounts and give the statement classification of each account.

(a) Gain on stock sale $600

720 Chapter 16 Investments

Journalize transactions and adjusting entry for stock investments.

(SO 3, 5, 6)

P16-3A On December 31, 2010, Ramey Associates owned the following securities, held as a long-term investment. The securities are not held for influence or control of the investee.

Common Stock	Shares	Cost
Hurst Co.	2,000	$60,000
Pine Co.	5,000	45,000
Scott Co.	1,500	30,000

On December 31, 2010, the total fair value of the securities was equal to its cost. In 2011, the following transactions occurred.

July 1	Received $1 per share semiannual cash dividend on Pine Co. common stock.
Aug. 1	Received $0.50 per share cash dividend on Hurst Co. common stock.
Sept. 1	Sold 1,500 shares of Pine Co. common stock for cash at $8 per share, less brokerage fees of $300.
Oct. 1	Sold 800 shares of Hurst Co. common stock for cash at $33 per share, less brokerage fees of $500.
Nov. 1	Received $1 per share cash dividend on Scott Co. common stock.
Dec. 15	Received $0.50 per share cash dividend on Hurst Co. common stock.
31	Received $1 per share semiannual cash dividend on Pine Co. common stock.

At December 31, the fair values per share of the common stocks were: Hurst Co. $32, Pine Co. $8, and Scott Co. $18.

Instructions

(a) Journalize the 2011 transactions and post to the account Stock Investments. (Use the T-account form.)

(b) Unrealized loss $4,100

(b) Prepare the adjusting entry at December 31, 2011, to show the securities at fair value. The stock should be classified as available-for-sale securities.

(c) Show the balance sheet presentation of the investments at December 31, 2011. At this date, Ramey Associates has common stock $1,500,000 and retained earnings $1,000,000.

Prepare entries under the cost and equity methods, and tabulate differences.

(SO 3)

P16-4A Glaser Services acquired 30% of the outstanding common stock of Nickels Company on January 1, 2010, by paying $800,000 for the 45,000 shares. Nickels declared and paid $0.30 per share cash dividends on March 15, June 15, September 15, and December 15, 2010. Nickels reported net income of $320,000 for the year. At December 31, 2010, the market price of Nickels common stock was $24 per share.

Instructions

(a) Total dividend revenue $54,000

(a) Prepare the journal entries for Glaser Services for 2010 assuming Glaser cannot exercise significant influence over Nickels. (Use the cost method and assume that Nickels common stock should be classified as a trading security.)

(b) Revenue from investments $96,000

(b) Prepare the journal entries for Glaser Services for 2010, assuming Glaser can exercise significant influence over Nickels. Use the equity method.

(c) Indicate the balance sheet and income statement account balances at December 31, 2010, under each method of accounting.

Journalize stock investment transactions and show statement presentation.

(SO 3, 5, 6)

P16-5A The following securities are in Pascual Company's portfolio of long-term available-for-sale securities at December 31, 2010.

	Cost
1,000 shares of Abel Corporation common stock	$52,000
1,400 shares of Frey Corporation common stock	84,000
1,200 shares of Weiss Corporation preferred stock	33,600

On December 31, 2010, the total cost of the portfolio equaled total fair value. Pascual had the following transactions related to the securities during 2011.

Jan. 20	Sold 1,000 shares of Abel Corporation common stock at $55 per share less brokerage fees of $600.
28	Purchased 400 shares of $70 par value common stock of Rosen Corporation at $78 per share, plus brokerage fees of $480.
30	Received a cash dividend of $1.15 per share on Frey Corp. common stock.
Feb. 8	Received cash dividends of $0.40 per share on Weiss Corp. preferred stock.
18	Sold all 1,200 shares of Weiss Corp. preferred stock at $27 per share less brokerage fees of $360.

July 30 Received a cash dividend of $1.00 per share on Frey Corp. common stock.
Sept. 6 Purchased an additional 900 shares of $10 par value common stock of Rosen Corporation at $82 per share, plus brokerage fees of $1,200.
Dec. 1 Received a cash dividend of $1.50 per share on Rosen Corporation common stock.

At December 31, 2011, the fair values of the securities were:

Frey Corporation common stock	$64 per share
Rosen Corporation common stock	$72 per share

Pascual Company uses separate account titles for each investment, such as "Investment in Frey Corporation Common Stock."

Instructions
(a) Prepare journal entries to record the transactions.
(b) Post to the investment accounts. (Use T accounts.)
(c) Prepare the adjusting entry at December 31, 2011 to report the portfolio at fair value.
(d) Show the balance sheet presentation at December 31, 2011, for the investment-related accounts.

(a) Loss on sale of preferred stock $1,560
(c) Unrealized loss $7,480

P16-6A The following data, presented in alphabetical order, are taken from the records of Urbina Corporation.

Prepare a balance sheet.
(SO, 5, 6)

Accounts payable	$ 240,000
Accounts receivable	140,000
Accumulated depreciation—building	180,000
Accumulated depreciation—equipment	52,000
Allowance for doubtful accounts	6,000
Bonds payable (10%, due 2018)	500,000
Buildings	950,000
Cash	42,000
Common stock ($10 par value; 500,000 shares authorized, 150,000 shares issued)	1,500,000
Dividends payable	80,000
Equipment	275,000
Goodwill	200,000
Income taxes payable	120,000
Investment in Flott common stock (10% ownership), at cost	278,000
Investment in Portico common stock (30% ownership), at equity	380,000
Land	390,000
Market adjustment—available-for-sale securities (Dr)	8,000
Merchandise inventory	170,000
Notes payable (due 2011)	70,000
Paid-in capital in excess of par value	130,000
Premium on bonds payable	40,000
Prepaid insurance	16,000
Retained earnings	103,000
Short-term stock investment, at fair value (and cost)	180,000
Unrealized gain—available-for-sale securities	8,000

The investment in Flott common stock is considered to be a long-term available-for-sale security.

Instructions
Prepare a classified balance sheet at December 31, 2010.

Total assets $2,791,000

PROBLEMS: SET B

P16-1B Groneman Farms is a grower of hybrid seed corn for Ogleby Genetics Corporation. It has had two exceptionally good years and has elected to invest its excess funds in bonds. The following selected transactions relate to bonds acquired as an investment by Groneman Farms, whose fiscal year ends on December 31.

Journalize debt investment transactions and show financial statement presentation.
(SO 2, 5, 6)

2010

Jan. 1 Purchased at face value $400,000 of Ziemer Corporation 10-year, 9% bonds dated January 1, 2010, directly from the issuing corporation.

722 Chapter 16 Investments

July 1 Received the semiannual interest on the Ziemer bonds.
Dec. 31 Accrual of interest at year-end on the Ziemer bonds.

(Assume that all intervening transactions and adjustments have been properly recorded and the number of bonds owned has not changed from December 31, 2010, to December 31, 2012.)

2013

Jan. 1 Received the semiannual interest on the Ziemer bonds.
Jan. 1 Sold $200,000 of Ziemer bonds at 114. The broker deducted $7,000 for commissions and fees on the sale.
July 1 Received the semiannual interest on the Ziemer bonds.
Dec. 31 Accrual of interest at year-end on the Ziemer bonds.

Instructions

(a) Gain on sale of debt investments $21,000

(a) Journalize the listed transactions for the years 2010 and 2013.
(b) Assume that the fair value of the bonds at December 31, 2010, was $385,000. These bonds are classified as available-for-sale securities. Prepare the adjusting entry to record these bonds at fair value.
(c) Based on your analysis in part (b) show the balance sheet presentation of the bonds and interest receivable at December 31, 2010. Assume the investments are considered long-term. Indicate where any unrealized gain or loss is reported in the financial statements.

Journalize investment transactions, prepare adjusting entry, and show statement presentation.

(SO 2, 3, 5, 6)

P16-2B In January 2010, the management of Prasad Company concludes that it has sufficient cash to purchase some short-term investments in debt and stock securities. During the year, the following transactions occurred.

Feb. 1 Purchased 500 shares of DET common stock for $30,000, plus brokerage fees of $800.
Mar. 1 Purchased 600 shares of STL common stock for $20,000, plus brokerage fees of $300.
Apr. 1 Purchased 40 $1,000, 9% CIN bonds for $40,000, plus $1,200 brokerage fees. Interest is payable semiannually on April 1 and October 1.
July 1 Received a cash dividend of $0.60 per share on the DET common stock.
Aug. 1 Sold 300 shares of DET common stock at $69 per share, less brokerage fees of $350.
Sept. 1 Received a $1 per share cash dividend on the STL common stock.
Oct. 1 Received the semiannual interest on the CIN bonds.
Oct. 1 Sold the CIN bonds for $45,000, less $1,000 brokerage fees.

At December 31, the fair value of the DET common stock was $66 per share. The fair value of the STL common stock was $29 per share.

Instructions

(a) Journalize the transactions and post to the accounts Debt Investments and Stock Investments. (Use the T-account form.)

(b) Unrealized loss $2,020

(b) Prepare the adjusting entry at December 31, 2010, to report the investments at fair value. All securities are considered to be trading securities.
(c) Show the balance sheet presentation of investment securities at December 31, 2010.
(d) Identify the income statement accounts and give the statement classification of each account.

Journalize transactions and adjusting entry for stock investments.

(SO 3, 5, 6)

P16-3B On December 31, 2010, Sauder Associates owned the following securities, held as long-term investments.

Common Stock	Shares	Cost
Adel Co.	4,000	$100,000
Beran Co.	5,000	30,000
Caren Co.	3,000	60,000

On this date, the total fair value of the securities was equal to its cost. The securities are not held for influence or control over the investees. In 2011, the following transactions occurred.

July 1 Received $1 per share semiannual cash dividend on Beran Co. common stock.
Aug. 1 Received $0.50 per share cash dividend on Adel Co. common stock.
Sept. 1 Sold 1,500 shares of Beran Co. common stock for cash at $8 per share, less brokerage fees of $300.
Oct. 1 Sold 600 shares of Adel Co. common stock for cash at $30 per share, less brokerage fees of $600.
Nov. 1 Received $1 per share cash dividend on Caren Co. common stock.

Dec. 15 Received $0.50 per share cash dividend on Adel Co. common stock.
  31 Received $1 per share semiannual cash dividend on Beran Co. common stock.

At December 31, the fair values per share of the common stocks were: Adel Co. $23, Beran Co. $7, and Caren Co. $19.

Instructions
(a) Journalize the 2011 transactions and post to the account Stock Investments. (Use the T-account form.)
(b) Prepare the adjusting entry at December 31, 2011, to show the securities at fair value. The stock should be classified as available-for-sale securities.
(c) Show the balance sheet presentation of the investment-related accounts at December 31, 2011. At this date, Sauder Associates has common stock $2,000,000 and retained earnings $1,200,000.

(a) Gain on sale, $2,700 and $2,400

P16-4B Terry's Concrete acquired 20% of the outstanding common stock of Blakeley, Inc. on January 1, 2010, by paying $1,100,000 for 40,000 shares. Blakeley declared and paid a $0.50 per share cash dividend on June 30 and again on December 31, 2010. Blakeley reported net income of $600,000 for the year. At December 31, 2010, the market price of Blakeley's common stock was $30 per share.

Prepare entries under the cost and equity methods, and tabulate differences.
(SO 3)

Instructions
(a) Prepare the journal entries for Terry's Concrete for 2010 assuming Terry's cannot exercise significant influence over Blakeley. (Use the cost method and assume Blakeley common stock should be classified as available-for-sale.)
(b) Prepare the journal entries for Terry's Concrete for 2010, assuming Terry's can exercise significant influence over Blakeley. (Use the equity method.)
(c) Indicate the balance sheet and income statement account balances at December 31, 2010, under each method of accounting.

(a) Total dividend revenue $40,000

(b) Revenue from investment $120,000

P16-5B The following are in Jamison Company's portfolio of long-term available-for-sale securities at December 31, 2010.

Journalize stock investment transactions and show statement presentation.
(SO 3, 5, 6)

	Cost
700 shares of Adler Corporation common stock	$35,000
900 shares of Lynn Corporation common stock	42,000
800 shares of Swanson Corporation preferred stock	22,400

On December 31, the total cost of the portfolio equaled total fair value. Jamison Company had the following transactions related to the securities during 2011.

Jan. 7 Sold 700 shares of Adler Corporation common stock at $56 per share, less brokerage fees of $700.
  10 Purchased 300 shares, $70 par value common stock of Pesavento Corporation at $78 per share, plus brokerage fees of $240.
  26 Received a cash dividend of $1.15 per share on Lynn Corporation common stock.
Feb. 2 Received cash dividends of $0.40 per share on Swanson Corporation preferred stock.
  10 Sold all 800 shares of Swanson Corporation preferred stock at $26 per share less brokerage fees of $180.
July 1 Received a cash dividend of $1.00 per share on Lynn Corporation common stock.
Sept. 1 Purchased an additional 800 shares of the $70 par value common stock of Pesavento Corporation at $75 per share, plus brokerage fees of $900.
Dec. 15 Received a cash dividend of $1.50 per share on Pesavento Corporation common stock.

At December 31, 2011, the fair values of the securities were:

| Lynn Corporation common stock | $48 per share |
| Pesavento Corporation common stock | $72 per share |

Jamison uses separate account titles for each investment, such as Investment in Lynn Corporation Common Stock.

Instructions
(a) Prepare journal entries to record the transactions.
(b) Post to the investment accounts. (Use T accounts.)
(c) Prepare the adjusting entry at December 31, 2011, to report the portfolio at fair value.
(d) Show the balance sheet presentation at December 31, 2011, for the investment-related accounts.

(a) Loss on sale $1,780

(c) Unrealized loss $4,140

Chapter 16 Investments

Prepare a balance sheet.
(SO 5, 6)

P16-6B The following data, presented in alphabetical order, are taken from the records of Nichols Corporation.

Accounts payable	$ 375,000
Accounts receivable	135,000
Accumulated depreciation—building	270,000
Accumulated depreciation—equipment	80,000
Allowance for doubtful accounts	10,000
Bonds payable (10%, due 2020)	600,000
Buildings	1,350,000
Cash	210,000
Common stock ($5 par value; 500,000 shares authorized, 440,000 shares issued)	2,200,000
Discount on bonds payable	30,000
Dividends payable	75,000
Equipment	415,000
Goodwill	300,000
Income taxes payable	180,000
Investment in Givens Inc. stock (30% ownership), at equity	900,000
Land	780,000
Merchandise inventory	255,000
Notes payable (due 2011)	110,000
Paid-in capital in excess of par value	300,000
Prepaid insurance	25,000
Retained earnings	480,000
Short-term stock investment, at fair value (and cost)	280,000

Total assets $4,290,000

Instructions
Prepare a classified balance sheet at December 31, 2010.

PROBLEMS: SET C

Visit the book's companion website at **www.wiley.com/college/weygandt**, and choose the Student Companion site, to access Problem Set C.

COMPREHENSIVE PROBLEM: CHAPTERS 12 TO 16

Part I Mindy Feldkamp and her two colleagues, Oscar Lopez and Lori Melton, are personal trainers at an upscale health spa/resort in Tampa, Florida. They want to start a health club that specializes in health plans for people in the 50+ age range. The growing population in this age range and strong consumer interest in the health benefits of physical activity have convinced them they can profitably operate their own club. In addition to many other decisions, they need to determine what type of business organization they want. Oscar believes there are more advantages to the corporate form than a partnership, but he hasn't yet convinced Mindy and Lori. They have come to you, a small business consulting specialist, seeking information and advice regarding the choice of starting a partnership versus a corporation.

Instructions

(a) Prepare a memo (dated May 26, 2009) that describes the advantages and disadvantages of both partnerships and corporations. Advise Mindy, Oscar, and Lori regarding which organizational form you believe would better serve their purposes. Make sure to include reasons supporting your advice.

Part II After deciding to incorporate, each of the three investors receives 20,000 shares of $2 par common stock on June 12, 2009, in exchange for their co-owned building ($200,000 market value) and $100,000 total cash they contributed to the business. The next decision that Mindy, Oscar, and Lori need to make is how to obtain financing for renovation and equipment. They understand the difference between equity securities and debt securities, but do not understand the tax, net income, and earnings per share consequences of equity versus debt financing on the future of their business.

Instructions

(b) Prepare notes for a discussion with the three entrepreneurs in which you will compare the consequences of using equity versus debt financing. As part of your notes, show the differences in interest and tax expense assuming $1,400,000 is financed with common stock, and then alternatively with debt. Assume that when common stock is used, 140,000 shares will be issued. When debt is used, assume the interest rate on debt is 9%, the tax rate is 32%, and income before interest and taxes is $300,000. (You may want to use an electronic spreadsheet.)

Part III During the discussion about financing, Lori mentions that one of her clients, Roberto Marino, has approached her about buying a significant interest in the new club. Having an interested investor sways the three to issue equity securities to provide the financing they need. On July 21, 2009, Mr. Marino buys 90,000 shares at a price of $10 per share.

The club, LifePath Fitness, opens on January 12, 2010, and after a slow start, begins to produce the revenue desired by the owners. The owners decide to pay themselves a stock dividend, since cash has been less than abundant since they opened their doors. The 10% stock dividend is declared by the owners on July 27, 2010. The market value of the stock is $3 on the declaration date. The date of record is July 31, 2010 (there have been no changes in stock ownership since the initial issuance), and the issue date is August 15, 2010. By the middle of the fourth quarter of 2010, the cash flow of LifePath Fitness has improved to the point that the owners feel ready to pay themselves a cash dividend. They declare a $0.05 cash dividend on December 4, 2010. The record date is December 14, 2010, and the payment date is December 24, 2010.

Instructions

(c) (1) Record all of the transactions related to the common stock of LifePath Fitness during the years 2009 and 2010. **(2)** Indicate how many shares are issued and outstanding after the stock dividend is issued.

Part IV Since the club opened, a major concern has been the pool facilities. Although the existing pool is adequate, Mindy, Oscar, and Lori all desire to make LifePath a cutting-edge facility. Until the end of 2010, financing concerns prevented this improvement. However, because there has been steady growth in clientele, revenue, and income since the fourth quarter of 2010, the owners have explored possible financing options. They are hesitant to issue stock and change the ownership mix because they have been able to work together as a team with great effectiveness. They have formulated a plan to issue secured term bonds to raise the needed $600,000 for the pool facilities. By the end of April 2011 everything was in place for the bond issue to go ahead. On June 1, 2011, the bonds were issued for $548,000. The bonds pay semiannual interest of 3% (6% annual) on December 1 and June 1 of each year. The bonds mature in 10 years, and amortization is computed using the straight-line method.

Instructions

(d) Record **(1)** the issuance of the secured bonds, **(2)** the interest payment made on December 1, 2011, **(3)** the adjusting entry required at December 31, 2011, and **(4)** the interest payment made on June 1, 2012.

Part V Mr. Marino's purchase of LifePath Fitness was done through his business. The investment has always been accounted for using the cost method on his firm's books. However, early in 2012 he decided to take his company public. He is preparing an IPO (initial public offering), and he needs to have the firm's financial statements audited. One of the issues to be resolved is to restate the investment in LifePath Fitness using the equity method, since Mr. Marino's ownership percentage is greater than 20%.

Instructions

(e) (1) Give the entries that would have been made on Marino's books if the equity method of accounting for investments had been used since the initial investment. Assume the following data for LifePath.

	2009	2010	2011
Net income	$30,000	$70,000	$105,000
Total cash dividends	$ 2,100	$20,000	$ 50,000

(2) Compute the balance in the LifePath Investment account at the end of 2011.

CONTINUING COOKIE CHRONICLE

(*Note:* This is a continuation of the Cookie Chronicle from Chapters 1 through 15.)

CCC 16 Natalie has been approached by Ken Thornton, a shareholder of The Beanery Coffee Inc. Ken wants to retire and would like to sell his 1,000 shares in The Beanery Coffee, which represents 20% of all shares issued. The Beanery is currently operated by Ken's twin daughters, who each own 40% of the common shares. The Beanery not only operates a coffee shop but also roasts and sells beans to retailers, under the name "Rocky Mountain Beanery."

Ken has met with Curtis and Natalie to discuss the business operation. All have concluded that there would be many advantages for Cookie & Coffee Creations Inc. to acquire an interest in The Beanery Coffee. Despite the apparent advantages, Natalie and Curtis are still not convinced that they should participate in this business venture.

Go to the book's companion website,
www.wiley.com/college/weygandt,
to see the completion of this problem.

BROADENING YOUR PERSPECTIVE

FINANCIAL REPORTING AND ANALYSIS

Financial Reporting Problem: Pepsico, Inc.

BYP16-1 The annual report of PepsiCo. is presented in Appendix A.

Instructions
(a) See Note 1 to the financial statements and indicate what the consolidated financial statements include.
(b) Using PepsiCo's consolidated statement of cash flows, determine how much was spent for capital acquisitions during the current year.

Comparative Analysis Problem: PepsiCo, Inc. vs. The Coca-Cola Company

BYP16-2 PepsiCo's financial statements are presented in Appendix A. Financial statements of The Coca-Cola Company are presented in Appendix B.

Instructions
(a) Based on the information contained in these financial statements, determine each of the following for each company.
  (1) Net cash used for investing (investment) activities for the current year (from the statement of cash flows).
  (2) Cash used for capital expenditures during the current year.
(b) Each of PepsiCo's financial statements is labeled "consolidated." What has been consolidated? That is, from the contents of PepsiCo's annual report, identify by name the corporations that have been consolidated (parent and subsidiaries).

Exploring the Web

BYP16-3 Most publicly traded companies are analyzed by numerous analysts. These analysts often don't agree about a company's future prospects. In this exercise you will find analysts' ratings about companies and make comparisons over time and across companies in the same industry. You will also see to what extent the analysts experienced "earnings surprises." Earnings surprises can cause changes in stock prices.

Address: biz.yahoo.com/i, or go to www.wiley.com/college/weygandt

Steps
1. Choose a company.
2. Use the index to find the company's name.
3. Choose **Research**.

Instructions
(a) How many analysts rated the company?
(b) What percentage rated it a strong buy?
(c) What was the average rating for the week?
(d) Did the average rating improve or decline relative to the previous week?
(e) How do the analysts rank this company among all the companies in its industry?
(f) What was the amount of the earnings surprise percentage during the last quarter?

CRITICAL THINKING

Decision Making Across the Organization

BYP16-4 At the beginning of the question and answer portion of the annual stockholders' meeting of Kemper Corporation, stockholder Mike Kerwin asks, "Why did management sell the holdings in UMW Company at a loss when this company has been very profitable during the period its stock was held by Kemper?"

Since president Tony Chavez has just concluded his speech on the recent success and bright future of Kemper, he is taken aback by this question and responds, "I remember we paid $1,300,000 for that stock some years ago, and I am sure we sold that stock at a much higher price. You must be mistaken."

Kerwin retorts, "Well, right here in footnote number 7 to the annual report it shows that 240,000 shares, a 30% interest in UMW, were sold on the last day of the year. Also, it states that UMW earned $520,000 this year and paid out $160,000 in cash dividends. Further, a summary statement indicates that in past years, while Kemper held UMW stock, UMW earned $1,240,000 and paid out $440,000 in dividends. Finally, the income statement for this year shows a loss on the sale of UMW stock of $180,000. So, I doubt that I am mistaken."

Red-faced, president Chavez turns to you.

Instructions
With the class divided into groups, answer the following.
(a) What dollar amount did Kemper receive upon the sale of the UMW stock?
(b) Explain why both stockholder Kerwin and president Chavez are correct.

Communication Activity

BYP16-5 Bunge Corporation has purchased two securities for its portfolio. The first is a stock investment in Longley Corporation, one of its suppliers. Bunge purchased 10% of Longley with the intention of holding it for a number of years, but has no intention of purchasing more shares. The second investment was a purchase of debt securities. Bunge purchased the debt securities because its analysts believe that changes in market interest rates will cause these securities to increase in value in a short period of time. Bunge intends to sell the securities as soon as they have increased in value.

Instructions
Write a memo to Max Scholes, the chief financial officer, explaining how to account for each of these investments. Explain what the implications for reported income are from this accounting treatment.

Ethics Case

BYP16-6 Bartlet Financial Services Company holds a large portfolio of debt and stock securities as an investment. The total fair value of the portfolio at December 31, 2010, is greater than total cost. Some securities have increased in value and others have decreased. Deb Faust, the financial vice president, and Jan McCabe, the controller, are in the process of classifying for the first time the securities in the portfolio.

Faust suggests classifying the securities that have increased in value as trading securities in order to increase net income for the year. She wants to classify the securities that have decreased in value as long-term available-for-sale securities, so that the decreases in value will not affect 2010 net income.

McCabe disagrees. She recommends classifying the securities that have decreased in value as trading securities and those that have increased in value as long-term available-for-sale securities. McCabe argues that the company is having a good earnings year and that recognizing the losses now will help to smooth income for this year. Moreover, for future years, when the company may not be as profitable, the company will have built-in gains.

Instructions
(a) Will classifying the securities as Faust and McCabe suggest actually affect earnings as each says it will?
(b) Is there anything unethical in what Faust and McCabe propose? Who are the stakeholders affected by their proposals?
(c) Assume that Faust and McCabe properly classify the portfolio. Assume, at year-end, that Faust proposes to sell the securities that will increase 2010 net income, and that McCabe proposes to sell the securities that will decrease 2010 net income. Is this unethical?

"All About You" Activity

BYP16-7 The Securities and Exchange Commission (SEC) is the primary regulatory agency of U.S. financial markets. Its job is to ensure that the markets remain fair for all investors. The following SEC sites provide useful information for investors.

Address: www.sec.gov/answers.shtml and **http://www.sec.gov/investor/tools/quiz.htm**, or go to **www.wiley.com/college/weygandt**.

Instructions
(a) Go to the first SEC site and find the definition of the following terms.
   (i) Ask price.
   (ii) Margin account.
   (iii) Prospectus.
   (iv) Index fund.
(b) Go to the second SEC site and take the short quiz.

Answers to Insight and Accounting Across the Organization Questions

p. 703 How Procter & Gamble Accounts for Gillette
Q: Where on Procter & Gamble's balance sheet will you find its investment in Gillette Company?
A: *Because Procter & Gamble owns 9% of Gillette, Procter & Gamble does not report Gillette in the investment section of its balance sheet. Instead, Gillette's assets and liabilities are included and commingled with the assets and liabilities of Procter & Gamble.*

p. 706 And the Correct Way to Report Investments Is . . . ?
Q: Why might the use of the equity method not lead to full disclosure in the financial statements?
A: *Under the equity method, the investment in common stock of another company is initially recorded at cost. After that, the investment account is adjusted at each reporting date to show the investor's equity in the investee. However, on the investor's balance sheet, only the investment account is shown. The pro-rata share of the investee's assets and liabilities are not reported. Because the pro-rata share of the investee's assets and liabilities are not shown, some argue that the full disclosure principle is violated.*

Answers to Self-Study Questions
1. d **2.** a **3.** b **4.** c **5.** a **6.** b **7.** c **8.** d **9.** a **10.** c **11.** c **12.** b **13.** c

Remember to go back to the Navigator box on the chapter-opening page and check off your completed work.

Chapter 17

Statement of Cash Flows

STUDY OBJECTIVES

After studying this chapter, you should be able to:

1. Indicate the usefulness of the statement of cash flows.
2. Distinguish among operating, investing, and financing activities.
3. Prepare a statement of cash flows using the indirect method.
4. Analyze the statement of cash flows.

✓ **The Navigator**

Scan **Study Objectives**	■
Read **Feature Story**	■
Read **Preview**	■
Read text and answer **DO IT!** p. 736 ■ p. 743 ■ p. 746 ■ p. 749 ■	
Work **Comprehensive DO IT!** 1 p. 750	■
Review **Summary of Study Objectives**	■
Work **Comprehensive DO IT!** 2 p. 765	■
Answer **Self-Study Questions**	■
Complete **Assignments**	■

Feature Story

GOT CASH?

In today's environment, companies must be ready to respond to changes quickly in order to survive and thrive. They need to produce new products and expand into new markets continually. To do this takes cash—lots and lots of cash. Keeping lots of cash available is a real challenge for a young company. It requires careful cash management and attention to cash flow.

One company that managed cash successfully in its early years was Microsoft (www.microsoft.com). During those years the company paid much of its payroll with stock options (rights to purchase company stock in the future at a given price) instead of cash. This strategy conserved cash, and turned more than a thousand of its employees into millionaires during the company's first 20 years of business.

In recent years Microsoft has had a different kind of cash problem. Now that it has reached a more "mature" stage in life, it generates so much cash—roughly $1 billion per month—that it cannot always figure out what to do with it. By 2004 Microsoft had accumulated $60 billion.

The company said it was accumulating cash to invest in new opportunities, buy other companies, and pay off pending lawsuits. But for years, the federal government has blocked attempts by Microsoft to buy anything other than small firms because it feared that purchase of a large firm would only increase Microsoft's monopolistic position. In addition, even the largest estimates of Microsoft's legal obligations related to pending lawsuits would use up only about $6 billion in cash.

Microsoft's stockholders have complained for years that holding all this cash was putting a drag on the company's profitability. Why? Because Microsoft had the cash invested in very low-yielding government securities. Stockholders felt that the company either should find new investment projects that would bring higher returns, or return some of the cash to stockholders.

Finally, in July 2004 Microsoft announced a plan to return cash to stockholders, by paying a special one-time $32 billion dividend in December 2004. This special dividend was so large that, according to the U.S. Commerce Department, it caused total personal income in the United States to rise by 3.7% in one month—the largest monthly increase ever recorded by the agency. (It also made the holiday season brighter, especially for retailers in the Seattle area.) Microsoft also doubled its regular annual dividend to $3.50 per share. Further, it announced that it would spend another $30 billion over the next four years buying treasury stock. In addition, in 2008 Microsoft offered to buy Yahoo! for $44.6 billion. These actions will help to deplete some of its massive cash horde, but as you will see in this chapter, for a cash-generating machine like Microsoft, the company will be anything but cash-starved.

Source: "Business: An End to Growth? Microsoft's Cash Bonanza," *The Economist,* July 23, 2005, p. 61.

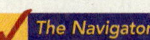

Inside Chapter 17...

- **Net What?** (p. 735)
- **GM Must Sell More Cars** (p. 744)

Preview of Chapter 17

The balance sheet, income statement, and retained earnings statement do not always show the whole picture of the financial condition of a company or institution. In fact, looking at the financial statements of some well-known companies, a thoughtful investor might ask questions like these: How did Eastman Kodak finance cash dividends of $649 million in a year in which it earned only $17 million? How could United Airlines purchase new planes that cost $1.9 billion in a year in which it reported a net loss of over $2 billion? How did the companies that spent a combined fantastic $3.4 trillion on mergers and acquisitions in a recent year finance those deals? Answers to these and similar questions can be found in this chapter, which presents the statement of cash flows.

The content and organization of this chapter are as follows.

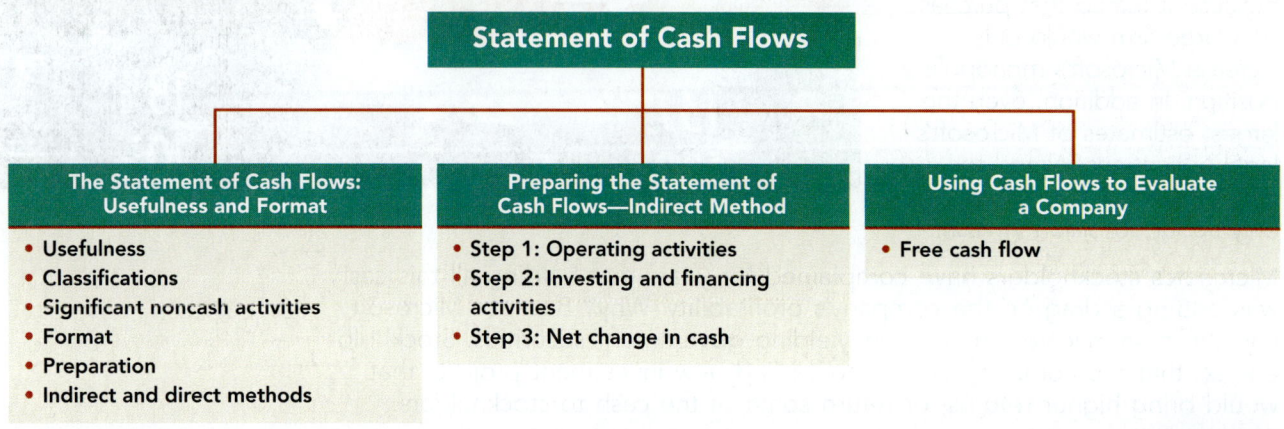

THE STATEMENT OF CASH FLOWS: USEFULNESS AND FORMAT

The balance sheet, income statement, and retained earnings statement provide only limited information about a company's cash flows (cash receipts and cash payments). For example, comparative balance sheets show the increase in property, plant, and equipment during the year. But they do not show how the additions were financed or paid for. The income statement shows net income. But it does not indicate the amount of cash generated by operating activities. The retained earnings statement shows cash dividends declared but not the cash dividends paid during the year. None of these statements presents a detailed summary of where cash came from and how it was used.

Usefulness of the Statement of Cash Flows

STUDY OBJECTIVE 1

Indicate the usefulness of the statement of cash flows.

The **statement of cash flows** reports the cash receipts, cash payments, and net change in cash resulting from operating, investing, and financing activities during a period. The information in a statement of cash flows should help investors, creditors, and others assess:

1. **The entity's ability to generate future cash flows.** By examining relationships between items in the statement of cash flows, investors can make predictions of the amounts, timing, and uncertainty of future cash flows better than they can from accrual basis data.

2. **The entity's ability to pay dividends and meet obligations.** If a company does not have adequate cash, it cannot pay employees, settle debts, or pay dividends. Employees, creditors, and stockholders should be particularly interested in this statement, because it alone shows the flows of cash in a business.
3. **The reasons for the difference between net income and net cash provided (used) by operating activities.** Net income provides information on the success or failure of a business enterprise. However, some financial statement users are critical of accrual-basis net income because it requires many estimates. As a result, users often challenge the reliability of the number. Such is not the case with cash. Many readers of the statement of cash flows want to know the reasons for the difference between net income and net cash provided by operating activities. Then they can assess for themselves the reliability of the income number.
4. **The cash investing and financing transactions during the period.** By examining a company's investing and financing transactions, a financial statement reader can better understand why assets and liabilities changed during the period.

> **ETHICS NOTE**
> Though we would discourage reliance on cash flows to the exclusion of accrual accounting, comparing cash from operations to net income can reveal important information about the "quality" of reported net income. Such a comparison can reveal the extent to which net income provides a good measure of actual performance.

Classification of Cash Flows

The statement of cash flows classifies cash receipts and cash payments as operating, investing, and financing activities. Transactions and other events characteristic of each kind of activity are as follows.

> **STUDY OBJECTIVE 2**
> Distinguish among operating, investing, and financing activities.

1. **Operating activities** include the cash effects of transactions that create revenues and expenses. They thus enter into the determination of net income.
2. **Investing activities** include (a) acquiring and disposing of investments and property, plant, and equipment, and (b) lending money and collecting the loans.
3. **Financing activities** include (a) obtaining cash from issuing debt and repaying the amounts borrowed, and (b) obtaining cash from stockholders, repurchasing shares, and paying dividends.

The operating activities category is the most important. It shows the cash provided by company operations. This source of cash is generally considered to be the best measure of a company's ability to generate sufficient cash to continue as a going concern.

Illustration 17-1 (page 734) lists typical cash receipts and cash payments within each of the three classifications. **Study the list carefully.** It will prove very useful in solving homework exercises and problems.

Note the following general guidelines:

1. Operating activities involve income statement items.
2. Investing activities involve cash flows resulting from changes in investments and long-term asset items.
3. Financing activities involve cash flows resulting from changes in long-term liability and stockholders' equity items.

Companies classify as operating activities some cash flows related to investing or financing activities. For example, receipts of investment revenue (interest and dividends) are classified as operating activities. So are payments of interest to lenders. Why are these considered operating activities? **Because companies report these items in the income statement, where results of operations are shown.**

Illustration 17-1
Typical receipt and payment classifications

Operating activities

Investing activities

Financing activities

TYPES OF CASH INFLOWS AND OUTFLOWS

Operating activities—Income statement items
  Cash inflows:
    From sale of goods or services.
    From interest received and dividends received.
  Cash outflows:
    To suppliers for inventory.
    To employees for services.
    To government for taxes.
    To lenders for interest.
    To others for expenses.

Investing activities—Changes in investments and long-term assets
  Cash inflows:
    From sale of property, plant, and equipment.
    From sale of investments in debt or equity securities of other entities.
    From collection of principal on loans to other entities.
  Cash outflows:
    To purchase property, plant, and equipment.
    To purchase investments in debt or equity securities of other entities.
    To make loans to other entities.

Financing activities—Changes in long-term liabilities and stockholders' equity
  Cash inflows:
    From sale of common stock.
    From issuance of long-term debt (bonds and notes).
  Cash outflows:
    To stockholders as dividends.
    To redeem long-term debt or reacquire capital stock (treasury stock).

Significant Noncash Activities

Not all of a company's significant activities involve cash. Examples of significant noncash activities are:

1. Direct issuance of common stock to purchase assets.
2. Conversion of bonds into common stock.
3. Direct issuance of debt to purchase assets.
4. Exchanges of plant assets.

Companies do not report in the body of the statement of cash flows significant financing and investing activities that do not affect cash. Instead, they report these activities in either a **separate schedule** at the bottom of the statement of cash flows or in a **separate note or supplementary schedule** to the financial statements. The reporting of these noncash activities in a separate schedule satisfies the **full disclosure principle**.

In solving homework assignments you should present significant noncash investing and financing activities in a separate schedule at the bottom of the statement of cash flows. (See the last entry in Illustration 17-2, at the bottom of page 735, for an example.)

> **HELPFUL HINT**
> Do not include noncash investing and financing activities in the body of the statement of cash flows. Report this information in a separate schedule.

ACCOUNTING ACROSS THE ORGANIZATION

Net What?

Net income is not the same as net cash provided by operating activities. Below are some results from recent annual reports (dollars in millions). Note the wide disparity among these companies, all of which engaged in retail merchandising.

Company	Net Income	Net Cash Provided by Operating Activities
Kohl's Corporation	$ 1,083	$ 1,234
Wal-Mart Stores, Inc.	11,284	20,164
J. C. Penney Company, Inc.	1,153	1,255
Costco Wholesale Corp.	1,082	2,076
Target Corporation	2,849	4,125

 In general, why do differences exist between net income and net cash provided by operating activities?

Format of the Statement of Cash Flows

The general format of the statement of cash flows presents the results of the three activities discussed previously—operating, investing, and financing—plus the significant noncash investing and financing activities. Illustration 17-2 shows a widely used form of the statement of cash flows.

Illustration 17-2
Format of statement of cash flows

COMPANY NAME
Statement of Cash Flows
Period Covered

Cash flows from operating activities	
(List of individual items)	XX
Net cash provided (used) by operating activities	XXX
Cash flows from investing activities	
(List of individual inflows and outflows)	XX
Net cash provided (used) by investing activities	XXX
Cash flows from financing activities	
(List of individual inflows and outflows)	XX
Net cash provided (used) by financing activities	XXX
Net increase (decrease) in cash	XXX
Cash at beginning of period	XXX
Cash at end of period	XXX
Noncash investing and financing activities	
(List of individual noncash transactions)	XXX

The cash flows from operating activities section always appears first, followed by the investing activities section and then the financing activities section.

DO IT!

CLASSIFICATION OF CASH FLOWS

action plan

✔ Identify the three types of activities used to report all cash inflows and outflows.

✔ Report as operating activities the cash effects of transactions that create revenues and expenses and enter into the determination of net income.

✔ Report as investing activities transactions that (a) acquire and dispose of investments and long-term assets and (b) lend money and collect loans.

✔ Report as financing activities transactions that (a) obtain cash from issuing debt and repay the amounts borrowed and (b) obtain cash from stockholders and pay them dividends.

During its first week, Duffy & Stevenson Company had these transactions.

1. Issued 100,000 shares of $5 par value common stock for $800,000 cash.
2. Borrowed $200,000 from Castle Bank, signing a 5-year note bearing 8% interest.
3. Purchased two semi-trailer trucks for $170,000 cash.
4. Paid employees $12,000 for salaries and wages.
5. Collected $20,000 cash for services provided.

Classify each of these transactions by type of cash flow activity.

Solution
1. Financing activity
2. Financing activity
3. Investing activity
4. Operating activity
5. Operating activity

Related exercise material: **BE17-1, BE17-2, BE17-3, E17-1, E17-2, E17-3,** and **DO IT!** **17-1.**

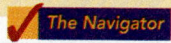

Preparing the Statement of Cash Flows

Companies prepare the statement of cash flows differently from the three other basic financial statements. First, it is not prepared from an adjusted trial balance. It requires detailed information concerning the changes in account balances that occurred between two points in time. An adjusted trial balance will not provide the necessary data. Second, the statement of cash flows deals with cash receipts and payments. As a result, the company **must adjust** the effects of the use of accrual accounting **to determine cash flows**.

The information to prepare this statement usually comes from three sources:

- **Comparative balance sheets.** Information in the comparative balance sheets indicates the amount of the changes in assets, liabilities, and stockholders' equities from the beginning to the end of the period.

- **Current income statement.** Information in this statement helps determine the amount of cash provided or used by operations during the period.

- **Additional information.** Such information includes transaction data that are needed to determine how cash was provided or used during the period.

Preparing the statement of cash flows from these data sources involves three major steps, explained in Illustration 17-3 on the next page.

Illustration 17-3
Three major steps in preparing the statement of cash flows

Step 1: Determine net cash provided/used by operating activities by converting net income from an accrual basis to a cash basis.

This step involves analyzing not only the current year's income statement but also comparative balance sheets and selected additional data.

Step 2: Analyze changes in noncurrent asset and liability accounts and record as investing and financing activities, or disclose as noncash transactions.

This step involves analyzing comparative balance sheet data and selected additional information for their effects on cash.

Step 3: Compare the net change in cash on the statement of cash flows with the change in the cash account reported on the balance sheet to make sure the amounts agree.

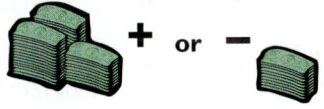

The difference between the beginning and ending cash balances can be easily computed from comparative balance sheets.

Indirect and Direct Methods

In order to perform step 1, a company **must convert net income from an accrual basis to a cash basis**. This conversion may be done by either of two methods: (1) the indirect method or (2) the direct method. **Both methods arrive at the same total amount** for "Net cash provided by operating activities." They differ in **how** they arrive at the amount.

The **indirect method** adjusts net income for items that do not affect cash. A great majority of companies (98.8%) use this method, as shown in the nearby chart.[1] Companies favor the indirect method for two reasons: (1) It is easier and less costly to prepare, and (2) it focuses on the differences between net income and net cash flow from operating activities.

The **direct method** shows operating cash receipts and payments, making it more consistent with the objective of a statement of cash flows. The FASB has expressed a preference for the direct method, but allows the use of either method.

The next section illustrates the more popular indirect method. Appendix 17B illustrates the direct method.

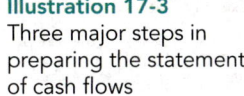

Usage of Methods

99% Indirect Method

1% Direct Method

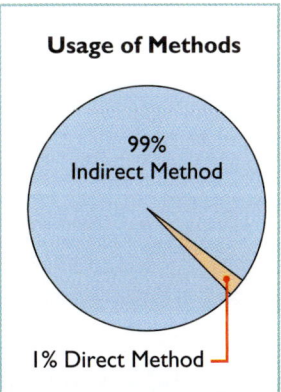

ETHICS NOTE
Some managers have taken actions that artificially increase cash flow from operating activities. They do this by moving negative amounts out of the operating section and into the investing or financing section. One example is **WorldCom, Inc.**, which improperly capitalized expenses and showed them in the investing section.

---

[1] *Accounting Trends and Techniques—2007* (New York: American Institute of Certified Public Accountants, 2007).

PREPARING THE STATEMENT OF CASH FLOWS—INDIRECT METHOD

STUDY OBJECTIVE 3
Prepare a statement of cash flows using the indirect method.

To explain how to prepare a statement of cash flows using the indirect method, we use financial information from Computer Services Company. Illustration 17-4 presents Computer Services' current and previous-year balance sheets, its current-year income statement, and related financial information for the current year.

Illustration 17-4
Comparative balance sheets, income statement, and additional information for Computer Services Company

COMPUTER SERVICES COMPANY
Comparative Balance Sheets
December 31

Assets	2010	2009	Change in Account Balance Increase/Decrease
Current assets			
Cash	$ 55,000	$ 33,000	$ 22,000 Increase
Accounts receivable	20,000	30,000	10,000 Decrease
Merchandise inventory	15,000	10,000	5,000 Increase
Prepaid expenses	5,000	1,000	4,000 Increase
Property, plant, and equipment			
Land	130,000	20,000	110,000 Increase
Building	160,000	40,000	120,000 Increase
Accumulated depreciation—building	(11,000)	(5,000)	6,000 Increase
Equipment	27,000	10,000	17,000 Increase
Accumulated depreciation—equipment	(3,000)	(1,000)	2,000 Increase
Total assets	$398,000	$138,000	
Liabilities and Stockholders' Equity			
Current liabilities			
Accounts payable	$ 28,000	$ 12,000	$ 16,000 Increase
Income tax payable	6,000	8,000	2,000 Decrease
Long-term liabilities			
Bonds payable	130,000	20,000	110,000 Increase
Stockholders' equity			
Common stock	70,000	50,000	20,000 Increase
Retained earnings	164,000	48,000	116,000 Increase
Total liabilities and stockholders' equity	$398,000	$138,000	

COMPUTER SERVICES COMPANY
Income Statement
For the Year Ended December 31, 2010

Revenues		$507,000
Cost of goods sold	$150,000	
Operating expenses (excluding depreciation)	111,000	
Depreciation expense	9,000	
Loss on sale of equipment	3,000	
Interest expense	42,000	315,000
Income before income tax		192,000
Income tax expense		47,000
Net income		$145,000

Additional information for 2010:
1. The company declared and paid a $29,000 cash dividend.
2. Issued $110,000 of long-term bonds in direct exchange for land.
3. A building costing $120,000 was purchased for cash. Equipment costing $25,000 was also purchased for cash.
4. The company sold equipment with a book value of $7,000 (cost $8,000, less accumulated depreciation $1,000) for $4,000 cash.
5. Issued common stock for $20,000 cash.
6. Depreciation expense was comprised of $6,000 for building and $3,000 for equipment.

Illustration 17-4 (continued)

We will now apply the three steps to the information provided for Computer Services Company.

Step 1: Operating Activities

DETERMINE NET CASH PROVIDED/USED BY OPERATING ACTIVITIES BY CONVERTING NET INCOME FROM AN ACCRUAL BASIS TO A CASH BASIS

To determine net cash provided by operating activities under the indirect method, companies **adjust net income in numerous ways**. A useful starting point is to understand **why** net income must be converted to net cash provided by operating activities.

Under generally accepted accounting principles, most companies use the accrual basis of accounting. This basis requires that companies record revenue when earned and record expenses when incurred. Earned revenues may include credit sales for which the company has not yet collected cash. Expenses incurred may include some items that it has not yet paid in cash. Thus, under the accrual basis, net income is not the same as net cash provided by operating activities.

Therefore, under the **indirect method**, companies must adjust net income to convert certain items to the cash basis. The indirect method (or reconciliation method) starts with net income and converts it to net cash provided by operating activities. Illustration 17-5 lists the three types of adjustments.

Net Income	+/−	Adjustments	=	Net Cash Provided/ Used by Operating Activities
		• **Add back noncash expenses**, such as depreciation expense, amortization, or depletion.		
		• **Deduct gains and add losses** that resulted from investing and financing activities.		
		• **Analyze changes** to noncash current asset and current liability accounts.		

Illustration 17-5
Three types of adjustments to convert net income to net cash provided by operating activities

DEPRECIATION EXPENSE

Computer Services' income statement reports depreciation expense of $9,000. Although depreciation expense reduces net income, it does not reduce cash. In other words, depreciation expense is a noncash charge. The company must add it back to net income to arrive at net cash provided by operating activities. Computer Services reports depreciation expense in the statement of cash flows as shown on page 740.

HELPFUL HINT
Depreciation is similar to any other expense in that it reduces net income. It differs in that it does not involve a current cash outflow; that is why it must be *added back* to net income to arrive at cash provided by operating activities.

Illustration 17-6
Adjustment for depreciation

Cash flows from operating activities		
Net income		$145,000
Adjustments to reconcile net income to net cash provided by operating activities:		
Depreciation expense		9,000
Net cash provided by operating activities		$154,000

As the first adjustment to net income in the statement of cash flows, companies frequently list depreciation and similar noncash charges such as amortization of intangible assets, depletion expense, and bad debt expense.

LOSS ON SALE OF EQUIPMENT

Illustration 17-1 states that the investing activities section should report cash received from the sale of plant assets. Because of this, **companies must eliminate from net income all gains and losses related to the disposal of plant assets, to arrive at cash provided by operating activities**.

In our example, Computer Services' income statement reports a $3,000 loss on the sale of equipment (book value $7,000, less $4,000 cash received from sale of equipment). The company's loss of $3,000 should not be included in the operating activities section of the statement of cash flows. Illustration 17-7 shows that the $3,000 loss is eliminated by adding $3,000 back to net income to arrive at net cash provided by operating activities.

Illustration 17-7
Adjustment for loss on sale of equipment

Cash flows from operating activities			
Net income			$145,000
Adjustments to reconcile net income to net cash provided by operating activities:			
Depreciation expense		$9,000	
Loss on sale of equipment		3,000	12,000
Net cash provided by operating activities			$157,000

If a gain on sale occurs, the company deducts the gain from its net income in order to determine net cash provided by operating activities. **In the case of either a gain or a loss, companies report as a source of cash in the investing activities section of the statement of cash flows the actual amount of cash received from the sale.**

CHANGES TO NONCASH CURRENT ASSET AND CURRENT LIABILITY ACCOUNTS

A final adjustment in reconciling net income to net cash provided by operating activities involves examining all changes in current asset and current liability accounts. The accrual accounting process records revenues in the period earned and expenses in the period incurred. For example, companies use Accounts Receivable to record amounts owed to the company for sales that have been made but for which cash collections have not yet been received. They use the Prepaid Insurance account to reflect insurance that has been paid for, but which has not yet expired, and therefore has not been expensed. Similarly, the Salaries Payable account reflects salaries expense that has been incurred by the company but has not been paid.

As a result, we need to adjust net income for these accruals and prepayments to determine net cash provided by operating activities. Thus we must analyze the change in each current asset and current liability account to determine its impact on net income and cash.

CHANGES IN NONCASH CURRENT ASSETS. The adjustments required for changes in noncash current asset accounts are as follows: **Deduct from net income increases in current asset accounts, and add to net income decreases in current asset accounts, to arrive at net cash provided by operating activities.** We can observe these relationships by analyzing the accounts of Computer Services Company.

Decrease in Accounts Receivable. Computer Services Company's accounts receivable decreased by $10,000 (from $30,000 to $20,000) during the period. For Computer Services this means that cash receipts were $10,000 higher than revenues. The Accounts Receivable account in Illustration 17-8 shows that Computer Services Company had $507,000 in revenues (as reported on the income statement), but it collected $517,000 in cash.

	Accounts Receivable			
1/1/10	Balance	30,000	Receipts from customers	517,000
	Revenues	507,000		
12/31/10	Balance	20,000		

Illustration 17-8
Analysis of accounts receivable

To adjust net income to net cash provided by operating activities, the company adds to net income the decrease of $10,000 in accounts receivable (see Illustration 17-9, page 742). When the Accounts Receivable balance increases, cash receipts are lower than revenue earned under the accrual basis. Therefore, the company deducts from net income the amount of the increase in accounts receivable, to arrive at net cash provided by operating activities.

Increase in Merchandise Inventory. Computer Services Company's Merchandise Inventory balance increased $5,000 (from $10,000 to $15,000) during the period. The change in the Merchandise Inventory account reflects the difference between the amount of inventory purchased and the amount sold. For Computer Services this means that the cost of merchandise purchased exceeded the cost of goods sold by $5,000. As a result, cost of goods sold does not reflect $5,000 of cash payments made for merchandise. The company deducts from net income this inventory increase of $5,000 during the period, to arrive at net cash provided by operating activities (see Illustration 17-9, page 742). If inventory decreases, the company adds to net income the amount of the change, to arrive at net cash provided by operating activities.

Increase in Prepaid Expenses. Computer Services' prepaid expenses increased during the period by $4,000. This means that cash paid for expenses is higher than expenses reported on an accrual basis. In other words, the company has made cash payments in the current period, but will not charge expenses to income until future periods (as charges to the income statement). To adjust net income to net cash provided by operating activities, the company deducts from net income the $4,000 increase in prepaid expenses (see Illustration 17-9, page 742).

Illustration 17-9
Adjustments for changes in current asset accounts

Cash flows from operating activities		
Net income		$145,000
Adjustments to reconcile net income to net cash provided by operating activities:		
Depreciation expense	$ 9,000	
Loss on sale of equipment	3,000	
Decrease in accounts receivable	**10,000**	
Increase in merchandise inventory	**(5,000)**	
Increase in prepaid expenses	**(4,000)**	13,000
Net cash provided by operating activities		$158,000

If prepaid expenses decrease, reported expenses are higher than the expenses paid. Therefore, the company adds to net income the decrease in prepaid expenses, to arrive at net cash provided by operating activities.

CHANGES IN CURRENT LIABILITIES. The adjustments required for changes in current liability accounts are as follows: **Add to net income increases in current liability accounts, and deduct from net income decreases in current liability accounts, to arrive at net cash provided by operating activities.**

Increase in Accounts Payable. For Computer Services Company, Accounts Payable increased by $16,000 (from $12,000 to $28,000) during the period. That means the company received $16,000 more in goods than it actually paid for. As shown in Illustration 17-10 (below), to adjust net income to determine net cash provided by operating activities, the company adds to net income the $16,000 increase in Accounts Payable.

Decrease in Income Taxes Payable. When a company incurs income tax expense but has not yet paid its taxes, it records income tax payable. A change in the Income Tax Payable account reflects the difference between income tax expense incurred and income tax actually paid. Computer Services' Income Tax Payable account decreased by $2,000. That means the $47,000 of income tax expense reported on the income statement was $2,000 less than the amount of taxes paid during the period of $49,000. As shown in Illustration 17-10, to adjust net income to a cash basis, the company must reduce net income by $2,000.

Illustration 17-10
Adjustments for changes in current liability accounts

Cash flows from operating activities		
Net income		$145,000
Adjustments to reconcile net income to net cash provided by operating activities:		
Depreciation expense	$ 9,000	
Loss on sale of equipment	3,000	
Decrease in accounts receivable	10,000	
Increase in merchandise inventory	(5,000)	
Increase in prepaid expenses	(4,000)	
Increase in accounts payable	**16,000**	
Decrease in income tax payable	**(2,000)**	27,000
Net cash provided by operating activities		$172,000

Illustration 17-10 shows that, after starting with net income of $145,000, the sum of all of the adjustments to net income was $27,000. This resulted in net cash provided by operating activities of $172,000.

Summary of Conversion to Net Cash Provided by Operating Activities—Indirect Method

As shown in the previous illustrations, the statement of cash flows prepared by the indirect method starts with net income. It then adds or deducts items to arrive at net cash provided by operating activities. The required adjustments are of three types:

1. Noncash charges such as depreciation, amortization, and depletion.
2. Gains and losses on the sale of plant assets.
3. Changes in noncash current asset and current liability accounts.

Illustration 17-11 provides a summary of these changes.

Illustration 17-11
Adjustments required to convert net income to net cash provided by operating activities

		Adjustment Required to Convert Net Income to Net Cash Provided by Operating Activities
Noncash Charges	Depreciation expense	Add
	Patent amortization expense	Add
	Depletion expense	Add
Gains and Losses	Loss on sale of plant asset	Add
	Gain on sale of plant asset	Deduct
Changes in Current Assets and Current Liabilities	Increase in current asset account	Deduct
	Decrease in current asset account	Add
	Increase in current liability account	Add
	Decrease in current liability account	Deduct

DO IT!

CASH FROM OPERATING ACTIVITIES

Josh's PhotoPlus reported net income of $73,000 for 2010. Included in the income statement were depreciation expense of $7,000 and a gain on sale of equipment of $2,500. Josh's comparative balance sheets show the following balances.

	12/31/09	12/31/10
Accounts receivable	$17,000	$21,000
Accounts payable	6,000	2,200

Calculate net cash provided by operating activities for Josh's PhotoPlus.

Solution

Cash flows from operating activities
Net income		$73,000
Adjustments to reconcile net income to net cash provided by operating activities:		
Depreciation expense	$7,000	
Gain on sale of equipment	(2,500)	
Increase in accounts receivable	(4,000)	
Decrease in accounts payable	(3,800)	(3,300)
Net cash provided by operating activities		$69,700

action plan

✔ Add noncash charges such as depreciation back to net income to compute net cash provided by operating activities.

✔ Deduct from net income gains on the sale of plant assets, or add losses back to net income, to compute net cash provided by operating activities.

✔ Use changes in noncash current asset and current liability accounts to compute net cash provided by operating activities.

Related exercise material: **BE17-4, BE17-5, BE17-6, BE17-7, E17-4, E17-5, E17-6, E17-7, E17-8,** and **DO IT! 17-2.**

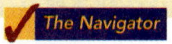

ACCOUNTING ACROSS THE ORGANIZATION

GM Must Sell More Cars

Market share matters—and it shows up in the accounting numbers. Just ask General Motors. In recent years GM has seen its market share erode until, at 25.6% of the market, the company reached the point where it actually consumed more cash than it generated. It isn't time to panic yet—GM has about $20 billion in cash on hand—but it is time to come up with a plan.

To address immediate cash needs, GM management may have to quit paying its $1.1 billion annual dividend, and it may have to sell off some assets and businesses. But in the long term, GM must either increase its market share, or shrink its operations to fit its sales figures. The following table shows net income and cash provided by operating activities at various market-share levels.

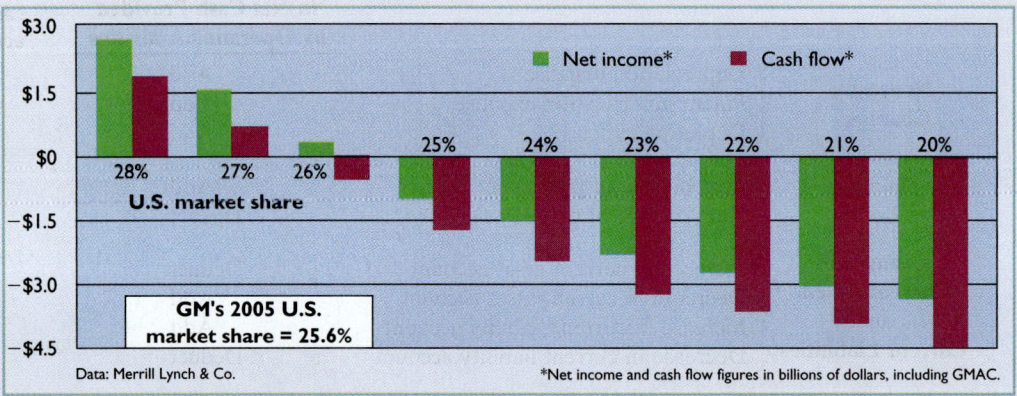

Data: Merrill Lynch & Co.   *Net income and cash flow figures in billions of dollars, including GMAC.

Source: David Welch and Dan Beucke, "Why GM's Plan Won't Work," *Business Week*, May 9, 2005, pp. 85–93.

 Why does GM's cash provided by operating activities drop so precipitously when the company's sales figures decline?

Step 2: Investing and Financing Activities

ANALYZE CHANGES IN NONCURRENT ASSET AND LIABILITY ACCOUNTS AND RECORD AS INVESTING AND FINANCING ACTIVITIES, OR AS NONCASH INVESTING AND FINANCING ACTIVITIES

Increase in Land. As indicated from the change in the Land account and the additional information, the company purchased land of $110,000 through the issuance of long-term bonds. The issuance of bonds payable for land has no effect on cash. But it is a significant noncash investing and financing activity that merits disclosure in a separate schedule. (See Illustration 17-13 on page 746.)

Increase in Building. As the additional data indicate, Computer Services Company acquired an office building for $120,000 cash. This is a cash outflow reported in the investing section. (See Illustration 17-13 on page 746.)

Increase in Equipment. The Equipment account increased $17,000. The additional information explains that this was a net increase that resulted from two transactions: (1) a purchase of equipment of $25,000, and (2) the sale for $4,000 of equipment costing $8,000. These transactions are investing activities. The company should report each transaction separately. Thus it reports the purchase of equipment as an outflow of cash for $25,000. It reports the sale as an inflow of cash for $4,000. The T account below shows the reasons for the change in this account during the year.

Illustration 17-12
Analysis of equipment

Equipment			
1/1/10 Balance	10,000	Cost of equipment sold	8,000
Purchase of equipment	25,000		
12/31/10 Balance	27,000		

The following entry shows the details of the equipment sale transaction.

Cash	4,000	
Accumulated Depreciation	1,000	
Loss on Sale of Equipment	3,000	
Equipment		8,000

A = L + SE
+4,000
+1,000
                  −3,000 Exp
−8,000

Cash Flows
+4,000

Increase in Bonds Payable. The Bonds Payable account increased $110,000. As indicated in the additional information, the company acquired land from the issuance of these bonds. It reports this noncash transaction in a separate schedule at the bottom of the statement.

Increase in Common Stock. The balance sheet reports an increase in Common Stock of $20,000. The additional information section notes that this increase resulted from the issuance of new shares of stock. This is a cash inflow reported in the financing section.

> **HELPFUL HINT**
> When companies issue stocks or bonds for cash, the actual proceeds will appear in the statement of cash flows as a financing inflow (rather than the par value of the stocks or face value of bonds).

Increase in Retained Earnings. Retained earnings increased $116,000 during the year. This increase can be explained by two factors: (1) Net income of $145,000 increased retained earnings. (2) Dividends of $29,000 decreased retained earnings. The company adjusts net income to net cash provided by operating activities in the operating activities section. Payment of the dividends (not the declaration) is a **cash outflow that the company reports as a financing activity**.

STATEMENT OF CASH FLOWS—2010

Using the previous information, we can now prepare a statement of cash flows for 2010 for Computer Services Company as shown in Illustration 17-13 (page 746).

Step 3: Net Change in Cash

COMPARE THE NET CHANGE IN CASH ON THE STATEMENT OF CASH FLOWS WITH THE CHANGE IN THE CASH ACCOUNT REPORTED ON THE BALANCE SHEET TO MAKE SURE THE AMOUNTS AGREE

Illustration 17-13 indicates that the net change in cash during the period was an increase of $22,000. This agrees with the change in Cash account reported on the balance sheet in Illustration 17-4 (page 738).

Illustration 17-13
Statement of cash flows, 2010—indirect method

COMPUTER SERVICES COMPANY
Statement of Cash Flows—Indirect Method
For the Year Ended December 31, 2010

Cash flows from operating activities		
Net income		$145,000
Adjustments to reconcile net income to net cash provided by operating activities:		
Depreciation expense	$ 9,000	
Loss on sale of equipment	3,000	
Decrease in accounts receivable	10,000	
Increase in merchandise inventory	(5,000)	
Increase in prepaid expenses	(4,000)	
Increase in accounts payable	16,000	
Decrease in income tax payable	(2,000)	27,000
Net cash provided by operating activities		172,000
Cash flows from investing activities		
Purchase of building	(120,000)	
Purchase of equipment	(25,000)	
Sale of equipment	4,000	
Net cash used by investing activities		(141,000)
Cash flows from financing activities		
Issuance of common stock	20,000	
Payment of cash dividends	(29,000)	
Net cash used by financing activities		(9,000)
Net increase in cash		22,000
Cash at beginning of period		33,000
Cash at end of period		$ 55,000
Noncash investing and financing activities		
Issuance of bonds payable to purchase land		$110,000

HELPFUL HINT
Note that in the investing and financing activities sections, positive numbers indicate cash inflows (receipts), and negative numbers indicate cash outflows (payments).

DO IT!

INDIRECT METHOD

Use the information below and on page 747 to prepare a statement of cash flows using the indirect method.

action plan
- ✔ Determine net cash provided/used by operating activities by adjusting net income for items that did not affect cash.
- ✔ Determine net cash provided/used by investing activities and financing activities.
- ✔ Determine the net increase/decrease in cash.

REYNOLDS COMPANY
Comparative Balance Sheets
December 31

Assets	2010	2009	Change Increase/Decrease
Cash	$ 54,000	$ 37,000	$ 17,000 Increase
Accounts receivable	68,000	26,000	42,000 Increase
Inventories	54,000	–0–	54,000 Increase
Prepaid expenses	4,000	6,000	2,000 Decrease
Land	45,000	70,000	25,000 Decrease
Buildings	200,000	200,000	–0–
Accumulated depreciation—buildings	(21,000)	(11,000)	10,000 Increase
Equipment	193,000	68,000	125,000 Increase
Accumulated depreciation—equipment	(28,000)	(10,000)	18,000 Increase
Totals	$569,000	$386,000	

Liabilities and Stockholders' Equity			
Accounts payable	$ 23,000	$ 40,000	$ 17,000 Decrease
Accrued expenses payable	10,000	–0–	10,000 Increase
Bonds payable	110,000	150,000	40,000 Decrease
Common stock ($1 par)	220,000	60,000	160,000 Increase
Retained earnings	206,000	136,000	70,000 Increase
Totals	$569,000	$386,000	

REYNOLDS COMPANY
Income Statement
For the Year Ended December 31, 2010

Revenues		$890,000
Cost of goods sold	$465,000	
Operating expenses	221,000	
Interest expense	12,000	
Loss on sale of equipment	2,000	700,000
Income before income taxes		190,000
Income tax expense		65,000
Net income		$125,000

Additional information:
1. Operating expenses include depreciation expense of $33,000 and charges from prepaid expenses of $2,000.
2. Land was sold at its book value for cash.
3. Cash dividends of $55,000 were declared and paid in 2010.
4. Interest expense of $12,000 was paid in cash.
5. Equipment with a cost of $166,000 was purchased for cash. Equipment with a cost of $41,000 and a book value of $36,000 was sold for $34,000 cash.
6. Bonds of $10,000 were redeemed at their face value for cash. Bonds of $30,000 were converted into common stock.
7. Common stock ($1 par) of $130,000 was issued for cash.
8. Accounts payable pertain to merchandise suppliers.

Solution

REYNOLDS COMPANY
Statement of Cash Flows—Indirect Method
For the Year Ended December 31, 2010

Cash flows from operating activities			
Net income			$125,000
Adjustments to reconcile net income to net cash provided by operating activities:			
Depreciation expense		$ 33,000	
Loss on sale of equipment		2,000	
Increase in accounts receivable		(42,000)	
Increase in inventories		(54,000)	
Decrease in prepaid expenses		2,000	
Decrease in accounts payable		(17,000)	
Increase in accrued expenses payable		10,000	(66,000)
Net cash provided by operating activities			59,000

HELPFUL HINT
1. Determine net cash provided/used by operating activities, recognizing that operating activities generally relate to changes in current assets and current liabilities.
2. Determine net cash provided/used by investing activities, recognizing that investing activities generally relate to changes in noncurrent assets.
3. Determine net cash provided/used by financing activities, recognizing that financing activities generally relate to changes in long-term liabilities and stockholders' equity accounts.

Cash flows from investing activities			
Sale of land		25,000	
Sale of equipment		34,000	
Purchase of equipment		(166,000)	
Net cash used by investing activities			(107,000)
Cash flows from financing activities			
Redemption of bonds		(10,000)	
Sale of common stock		130,000	
Payment of dividends		(55,000)	
Net cash provided by financing activities			65,000
Net increase in cash			17,000
Cash at beginning of period			37,000
Cash at end of period			$ 54,000
Noncash investing and financing activities			
Conversion of bonds into common stock			$ 30,000

Related exercise material: **BE17-4, BE17-5, BE17-6, BE17-7, E17-4, E17-5, E17-6, E17-7, E17-8, and E17-9.**

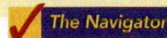

USING CASH FLOWS TO EVALUATE A COMPANY

STUDY OBJECTIVE 4
Analyze the statement of cash flows.

Traditionally, investors and creditors have most commonly used ratios based on accrual accounting. These days, cash-based ratios are gaining increased acceptance among analysts.

Free Cash Flow

In the statement of cash flows, cash provided by operating activities is intended to indicate the cash-generating capability of the company. Analysts have noted, however, that **cash provided by operating activities fails to take into account that a company must invest in new fixed assets** just to maintain its current level of operations. Companies also must at least **maintain dividends at current levels** to satisfy investors. The measurement of free cash flow provides additional insight regarding a company's cash-generating ability. **Free cash flow** describes the cash remaining from operations after adjustment for capital expenditures and dividends.

Consider the following example: Suppose that MPC produced and sold 10,000 personal computers this year. It reported $100,000 cash provided by operating activities. In order to maintain production at 10,000 computers, MPC invested $15,000 in equipment. It chose to pay $5,000 in dividends. Its free cash flow was $80,000 ($100,000 − $15,000 − $5,000). The company could use this $80,000 either to purchase new assets to expand the business or to pay an $80,000 dividend and continue to produce 10,000 computers. In practice, free cash flow is often calculated with the formula in Illustration 17-14. (Alternative definitions also exist.)

Illustration 17-14
Free cash flow

$$\text{Free Cash Flow} = \text{Cash Provided by Operating Activities} - \text{Capital Expenditures} - \text{Cash Dividends}$$

Illustration 17-15 provides basic information (in billions) excerpted from the 2007 statement of cash flows of Microsoft Corporation.

Illustration 17-15
Microsoft cash flow information ($ in millions)

MICROSOFT CORPORATION
Statement of Cash Flows (partial)
2007

Cash provided by operating activities	$17,796
Cash flows from investing activities	
Additions to property and equipment	$ (2,264)
Purchases of investments	(36,308)
Sales of investments	41,451
Acquisitions of companies	(1,150)
Maturities of investments	4,736
Other	(376)
Cash provided by investing activities	6,089
Cash paid for dividends	(3,805)

Microsoft's free cash flow is calculated as shown in Illustration 17-16.

Illustration 17-16
Calculation of Microsoft's free cash flow ($ in millions)

Cash provided by operating activities	$17,796
Less: Expenditures on property, plant, and equipment	2,264
Dividends paid	3,805
Free cash flow	$11,727

This is a tremendous amount of cash generated in a single year. It is available for the acquisition of new assets, the retirement of stock or debt, or the payment of dividends. As indicated in the Feature Story, for example, Microsoft is attempting to buy Yahoo! for over $44 billion as part of its acquisition strategy.

Oracle Corporation is one of the world's largest sellers of database software and information management services. Like Microsoft, its success depends on continuing to improve its existing products while developing new products to keep pace with rapid changes in technology. Oracle's free cash flow for 2007 was $3,955 million. This is impressive, but significantly less than Microsoft's amazing ability to generate cash.

DO IT!

FREE CASH FLOW

Chicago Corporation issued the following statement of cash flows for 2010.

CHICAGO CORPORATION
Statement of Cash Flows—Indirect Method
For the Year Ended December 31, 2010

Cash flows from operating activities		
Net income		$19,000
Adjustments to reconcile net income to net cash		
provided by operating activities:		
Depreciation expense	$ 8,100	
Loss on sale of equipment	1,300	
Decrease in accounts receivable	6,900	
Increase in inventory	(4,000)	

750 Chapter 17 Statement of Cash Flows

Decrease in accounts payable	(2,000)	10,300
Net cash provided by operating activities		29,300
Cash flows from investing activities		
Sale of investments	1,100	
Purchase of equipment	(19,000)	
Net cash used by investing activities		(17,900)
Cash flows from financing activities		
Issuance of stock	10,000	
Payment on long-term note payable	(5,000)	
Payment for dividends	(9,000)	
Net cash used by financing activities		(4,000)
Net increase in cash		7,400
Cash at beginning of year		10,000
Cash at end of year		$17,400

(a) Compute free cash flow for Chicago Corporation. (b) Explain why free cash flow often provides better information than "Net cash provided by operating activities."

action plan

✔ Compute free cash flow as: Cash provided by operating activities − Capital expenditures − Cash dividends.

Solution

(a) Free cash flow = $29,300 − $19,000 − $9,000 = $1,300
(b) Cash provided by operating activities fails to take into account that a company must invest in new plant assets just to maintain the current level of operations. Companies must also maintain dividends at current levels to satisfy investors. The measurement of free cash flow provides additional insight regarding a company's cash-generating ability.

Related exercise material: **BE17-8, BE17-9, BE17-10, BE17-11, E17-7, E17-9,** and **DO IT! 17-3**.

✓ The Navigator

Comprehensive DO IT! 1

The income statement for the year ended December 31, 2010, for Kosinski Manufacturing Company contains the following condensed information.

KOSINSKI MANUFACTURING COMPANY
Income Statement
For the Year Ended December 31, 2010

Revenues		$6,583,000
Operating expenses (excluding depreciation)	$4,920,000	
Depreciation expense	880,000	5,800,000
Income before income taxes		783,000
Income tax expense		353,000
Net income		$ 430,000

Included in operating expenses is a $24,000 loss resulting from the sale of machinery for $270,000 cash. Machinery was purchased at a cost of $750,000.

The following balances are reported on Kosinski's comparative balance sheets at December 31.

KOSINSKI MANUFACTURING COMPANY
Comparative Balance Sheets (partial)

	2010	2009
Cash	$672,000	$130,000
Accounts receivable	775,000	610,000
Inventories	834,000	867,000
Accounts payable	521,000	501,000

Income tax expense of $353,000 represents the amount paid in 2010. Dividends declared and paid in 2010 totaled $200,000.

Instructions
Prepare the statement of cash flows using the indirect method.

Solution to Comprehensive DO IT! 1

KOSINSKI MANUFACTURING COMPANY
Statement of Cash Flows—Indirect Method
For the Year Ended December 31, 2010

Cash flows from operating activities		
Net income		$ 430,000
Adjustments to reconcile net income to net cash provided by operating activities:		
Depreciation expense	$ 880,000	
Loss on sale of machinery	24,000	
Increase in accounts receivable	(165,000)	
Decrease in inventories	33,000	
Increase in accounts payable	20,000	792,000
Net cash provided by operating activities		1,222,000
Cash flows from investing activities		
Sale of machinery	270,000	
Purchase of machinery	(750,000)	
Net cash used by investing activities		(480,000)
Cash flows from financing activities		
Payment of cash dividends		(200,000)
Net increase in cash		542,000
Cash at beginning of period		130,000
Cash at end of period		$ 672,000

action plan
✔ Determine net cash from operating activities. Operating activities generally relate to changes in current assets and current liabilities.

✔ Determine net cash from investing activities. Investing activities generally relate to changes in noncurrent assets.

✔ Determine net cash from financing activities. Financing activities generally relate to changes in long-term liabilities and stockholders' equity accounts.

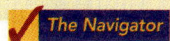

SUMMARY OF STUDY OBJECTIVES

1 Indicate the usefulness of the statement of cash flows. The statement of cash flows provides information about the cash receipts, cash payments, and net change in cash resulting from the operating, investing, and financing activities of a company during the period.

2 Distinguish among operating, investing, and financing activities. Operating activities include the cash effects of transactions that enter into the determination of net income. Investing activities involve cash flows resulting from changes in investments and long-term asset items. Financing activities involve cash flows resulting from changes in long-term liability and stockholders' equity items.

3 Prepare a statement of cash flows using the indirect method. The preparation of a statement of cash flows

752 Chapter 17 Statement of Cash Flows

involves three major steps: (1) Determine net cash provided/used by operating activities by converting net income from an accrual basis to a cash basis. (2) Analyze changes in noncurrent asset and liability accounts and record as investing and financing activities, or disclose as noncash transactions. (3) Compare the net change in cash on the statement of cash flows with the change in the cash account reported on the balance sheet to make sure the amounts agree.

4 Analyze the statement of cash flows. Free cash flow indicates the amount of cash a company generated during the current year that is available for the payment of additional dividends or for expansion.

GLOSSARY

Direct method A method of determining net cash provided by operating activities by adjusting each item in the income statement from the accrual basis to the cash basis and which shows operating cash recipts and payments. (p. 737)

Financing activities Cash flow activities that include (a) obtaining cash from issuing debt and repaying the amounts borrowed and (b) obtaining cash from stockholders, repurchasing shares, and paying dividends. (p. 733).

Free cash flow Cash provided by operating activities adjusted for capital expenditures and dividends paid. (p. 748).

Indirect method A method of preparing a statement of cash flows in which net income is adjusted for items that do not affect cash, to determine net cash provided by operating activities. (pp. 737, 739).

Investing activities Cash flow activities that include (a) purchasing and disposing of investments and property, plant, and equipment using cash and (b) lending money and collecting the loans. (p. 733).

Operating activities Cash flow activities that include the cash effects of transactions that create revenues and expenses and thus enter into the determination of net income. (p. 733).

Statement of cash flows A basic financial statement that provides information about the cash receipts, cash payments, and net change in cash during a period, resulting from operating, investing, and financing activities. (p. 732).

APPENDIX 17A Using a Worksheet to Prepare the Statement of Cash Flows— Indirect Method

STUDY OBJECTIVE 5
Explain how to use a worksheet to prepare the statement of cash flows using the indirect method.

When preparing a statement of cash flows, companies may need to make numerous adjustments of net income. In such cases, they often use **a worksheet to assemble and classify the data that will appear on the statement**. The worksheet is merely an aid in preparing the statement. Its use is optional. Illustration 17A-1 (page 753) shows the skeleton format of the worksheet for preparation of the statement of cash flows.

The following guidelines are important in preparing a worksheet.

1. In the balance sheet accounts section, **list accounts with debit balances separately from those with credit balances**. This means, for example, that Accumulated Depreciation appears under credit balances and not as a contra account under debit balances. Enter the beginning and ending balances of each account in the appropriate columns. Enter as reconciling items in the two middle columns the transactions that caused the change in the account balance during the year.

   After all reconciling items have been entered, each line pertaining to a balance sheet account should "foot across." That is, the beginning balance plus or minus the reconciling item(s) must equal the ending balance. When this agreement exists for all balance sheet accounts, all changes in account balances have been reconciled.

2. The bottom portion of the worksheet consists of the operating, investing, and financing activities sections. It provides the information necessary to prepare the formal statement of cash flows. **Enter inflows of cash as debits in the**

Appendix 17A Using a Worksheet to Prepare the Statement of Cash Flows—Indirect Method

Illustration 17A-1
Format of worksheet

XYZ COMPANY
Worksheet
Statement of Cash Flows For the Year Ended . . .

Balance Sheet Accounts	End of Last Year Balances	Reconciling Items		End of Current Year Balances
		Debit	Credit	
Debit balance accounts	XX	XX	XX	XX
	XX	XX	XX	XX
Totals	XXX			XXX
Credit balance accounts	XX	XX	XX	XX
	XX	XX	XX	XX
Totals	XXX			XXX
Statement of Cash Flows Effects				
Operating activities				
Net income		XX		
Adjustments to net income		XX	XX	
Investing activities				
Receipts and payments		XX	XX	
Financing activities				
Receipts and payments		XX	XX	
Totals		XXX	XXX	
Increase (decrease) in cash		(XX)	XX	
Totals		XXX	XXX	

reconciling columns. **Enter outflows of cash as credits in the reconciling columns.** Thus, in this section, the sale of equipment for cash at book value appears as a debit under investing activities. Similarly, the purchase of land for cash appears as a credit under investing activities.

3. **The reconciling items shown in the worksheet are not entered in any journal or posted to any account.** They do not represent either adjustments or corrections of the balance sheet accounts. They are used only to facilitate the preparation of the statement of cash flows.

Preparing the Worksheet

As in the case of worksheets illustrated in earlier chapters, preparing a worksheet involves a series of prescribed steps. The steps in this case are:

1. Enter in the balance sheet accounts section the balance sheet accounts and their beginning and ending balances.
2. Enter in the reconciling columns of the worksheet the data that explain the changes in the balance sheet accounts other than cash and their effects on the statement of cash flows.
3. Enter on the cash line and at the bottom of the worksheet the increase or decrease in cash. This entry should enable the totals of the reconciling columns to be in agreement.

To illustrate the preparation of a worksheet, we will use the 2010 data for Computer Services Company. Your familiarity with these data (from the chapter) should help you understand the use of a worksheet. For ease of reference, the comparative balance sheets, income statement, and selected data for 2010 are presented in Illustration 17A-2 (on page 754).

Illustration 17A-2
Comparative balance sheets, income statement, and additional information for Computer Services Company

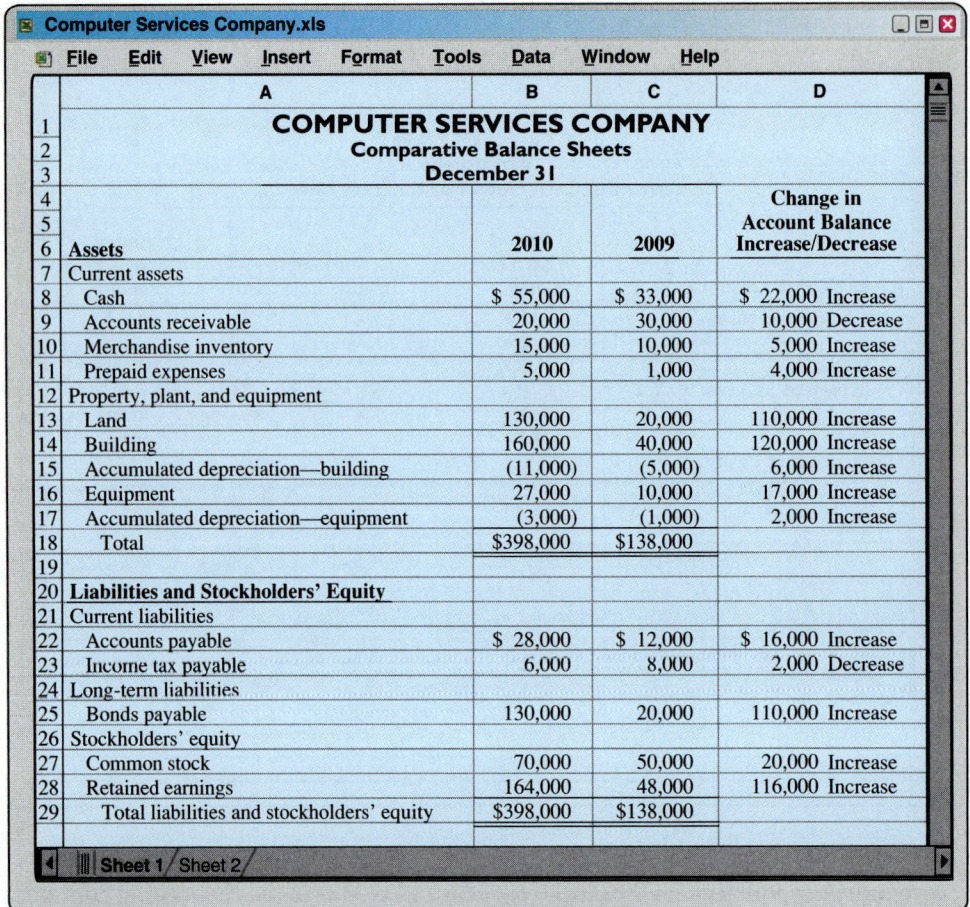

COMPUTER SERVICES COMPANY
Comparative Balance Sheets
December 31

Assets	2010	2009	Change in Account Balance Increase/Decrease
Current assets			
Cash	$ 55,000	$ 33,000	$ 22,000 Increase
Accounts receivable	20,000	30,000	10,000 Decrease
Merchandise inventory	15,000	10,000	5,000 Increase
Prepaid expenses	5,000	1,000	4,000 Increase
Property, plant, and equipment			
Land	130,000	20,000	110,000 Increase
Building	160,000	40,000	120,000 Increase
Accumulated depreciation—building	(11,000)	(5,000)	6,000 Increase
Equipment	27,000	10,000	17,000 Increase
Accumulated depreciation—equipment	(3,000)	(1,000)	2,000 Increase
Total	$398,000	$138,000	
Liabilities and Stockholders' Equity			
Current liabilities			
Accounts payable	$ 28,000	$ 12,000	$ 16,000 Increase
Income tax payable	6,000	8,000	2,000 Decrease
Long-term liabilities			
Bonds payable	130,000	20,000	110,000 Increase
Stockholders' equity			
Common stock	70,000	50,000	20,000 Increase
Retained earnings	164,000	48,000	116,000 Increase
Total liabilities and stockholders' equity	$398,000	$138,000	

COMPUTER SERVICES COMPANY
Income Statement
For the Year Ended December 31, 2010

Revenues		$507,000
Cost of goods sold	$150,000	
Operating expenses (excluding depreciation)	111,000	
Depreciation expense	9,000	
Loss on sale of equipment	3,000	
Interest expense	42,000	315,000
Income before income tax		192,000
Income tax expense		47,000
Net income		$145,000

Additional information for 2010:
1. The company declared and paid a $29,000 cash dividend.
2. Issued $110,000 of long-term bonds in direct exchange for land.
3. A building costing $120,000 was purchased for cash. Equipment costing $25,000 was also purchased for cash.
4. The company sold equipment with a book value of $7,000 (cost $8,000, less accumulated depreciation $1,000) for $4,000 cash.
5. Issued common stock for $20,000 cash.
6. Depreciation expense was comprised of $6,000 for building and $3,000 for equipment.

Appendix 17A Using a Worksheet to Prepare the Statement of Cash Flows—Indirect Method

DETERMINING THE RECONCILING ITEMS

Companies can use one of several approaches to determine the reconciling items. For example, they can first complete the changes affecting net cash provided by operating activities, and then can determine the effects of financing and investing transactions. Or, they can analyze the balance sheet accounts in the order in which they are listed on the worksheet. We will follow this latter approach for Computer Services, except for cash. As indicated in step 3, **cash is handled last**.

Accounts Receivable. The decrease of $10,000 in accounts receivable means that cash collections from revenues are higher than the revenues reported in the income statement. To convert net income to net cash provided by operating activities, we add the decrease of $10,000 to net income. The entry in the reconciling columns of the worksheet is:

(a)   Operating—Decrease in Accounts Receivable   10,000
              Accounts Receivable   10,000

Merchandise Inventory. Computer Services Company's Merchandise Inventory balance increases $5,000 during the period. The Merchandise Inventory account reflects the difference between the amount of inventory that the company purchased and the amount that it sold. For Computer Services this means that the cost of merchandise purchased exceeds the cost of goods sold by $5,000. As a result, cost of goods sold does not reflect $5,000 of cash payments made for merchandise. We deduct this inventory increase of $5,000 during the period from net income to arrive at net cash provided by operating activities. The worksheet entry is:

(b)   Merchandise Inventory   5,000
              Operating—Increase in Merchandise
                 Inventory   5,000

Prepaid Expenses. An increase of $4,000 in prepaid expenses means that expenses deducted in determining net income are less than expenses that were paid in cash. We deduct the increase of $4,000 from net income in determining net cash provided by operating activities. The worksheet entry is:

(c)   Prepaid Expenses   4,000
              Operating—Increase in Prepaid Expenses   4,000

Land. The increase in land of $110,000 resulted from a purchase through the issuance of long-term bonds. The company should report this transaction as a significant noncash investing and financing activity. The worksheet entry is:

(d)   Land   110,000
              Bonds Payable   110,000

> **HELPFUL HINT**
> These amounts are asterisked in the worksheet to indicate that they result from a significant noncash transaction.

Building. The cash purchase of a building for $120,000 is an investing activity cash outflow. The entry in the reconciling columns of the worksheet is:

(e)   Building   120,000
              Investing—Purchase of Building   120,000

Equipment. The increase in equipment of $17,000 resulted from a cash purchase of $25,000 and the sale of equipment costing $8,000. The book value of the equipment was $7,000, the cash proceeds were $4,000, and a loss of $3,000 was recorded. The worksheet entries are:

(f)   Equipment   25,000
              Investing—Purchase of Equipment   25,000

(g)	Investing—Sale of Equipment	4,000	
	Operating—Loss on Sale of Equipment	3,000	
	Accumulated Depreciation—Equipment	1,000	
	Equipment		8,000

Accounts Payable. We must add the increase of $16,000 in accounts payable to net income to determine net cash provided by operating activities. The worksheet entry is:

| (h) | Operating—Increase in Accounts Payable | 16,000 | |
| | Accounts Payable | | 16,000 |

Income Taxes Payable. When a company incurs income tax expense but has not yet paid its taxes, it records income tax payable. A change in the Income Tax Payable account reflects the difference between income tax expense incurred and income tax actually paid. Computer Services' Income Tax Payable account decreases by $2,000. That means the $47,000 of income tax expense reported on the income statement was $2,000 less than the amount of taxes paid during the period of $49,000. To adjust net income to a cash basis, we must reduce net income by $2,000. The worksheet entry is:

| (i) | Income Taxes Payable | 2,000 | |
| | Operating—Decrease in Income Taxes Payable | | 2,000 |

Bonds Payable. The increase of $110,000 in this account resulted from the issuance of bonds for land. This is a significant noncash investing and financing activity. Worksheet entry (d) above is the only entry necessary.

Common Stock. The balance sheet reports an increase in Common Stock of $20,000. The additional information section notes that this increase resulted from the issuance of new shares of stock. This is a cash inflow reported in the financing section. The worksheet entry is:

| (j) | Financing—Issuance of Common Stock | 20,000 | |
| | Common Stock | | 20,000 |

Accumulated Depreciation—Building, and Accumulated Depreciation—Equipment. Increases in these accounts of $6,000 and $3,000, respectively, resulted from depreciation expense. Depreciation expense is a **noncash charge that we must add to net income** to determine net cash provided by operating activities. The worksheet entries are:

(k)	Operating—Depreciation Expense—Building	6,000	
	Accumulated Depreciation—Building		6,000
(l)	Operating—Depreciation Expense—Equipment	3,000	
	Accumulated Depreciation—Equipment		3,000

Retained Earnings. The $116,000 increase in retained earnings resulted from net income of $145,000 and the declaration and payment of a $29,000 cash dividend. Net income is included in net cash provided by operating activities, and the dividends are a financing activity cash outflow. The entries in the reconciling columns of the worksheet are:

(m)	Operating—Net Income	145,000	
	Retained Earnings		145,000
(n)	Retained Earnings	29,000	
	Financing—Payment of Dividends		29,000

Appendix 17A Using a Worksheet to Prepare the Statement of Cash Flows—Indirect Method

Disposition of Change in Cash. The firm's cash increased $22,000 in 2010. The final entry on the worksheet, therefore, is:

(o)	Cash	22,000	
	Increase in Cash		22,000

As shown in the worksheet, we enter the increase in cash in the reconciling credit column as a **balancing** amount. This entry should complete the reconciliation of the changes in the balance sheet accounts. Also, it should permit the totals of the reconciling columns to be in agreement. When all changes have been explained and the reconciling columns are in agreement, the reconciling columns are ruled to complete the worksheet. The completed worksheet for Computer Services Company is shown in Illustration 17A-3.

Illustration 17A-3
Completed worksheet—indirect method

COMPUTER SERVICES COMPANY
Worksheet
Statement of Cash Flows For the Year Ended December 31, 2010

Balance Sheet Accounts	Balance 12/31/09	Reconciling Items Debit	Reconciling Items Credit	Balance 12/31/10
Debits				
Cash	33,000	(o) 22,000		55,000
Accounts Receivable	30,000		(a) 10,000	20,000
Merchandise Inventory	10,000	(b) 5,000		15,000
Prepaid Expenses	1,000	(c) 4,000		5,000
Land	20,000	(d) 110,000*		130,000
Building	40,000	(e) 120,000		160,000
Equipment	10,000	(f) 25,000	(g) 8,000	27,000
Total	144,000			412,000
Credits				
Accounts Payable	12,000		(h) 16,000	28,000
Income Taxes Payable	8,000	(i) 2,000		6,000
Bonds Payable	20,000		(d) 110,000*	130,000
Accumulated Depreciation—Building	5,000		(k) 6,000	11,000
Accumulated Depreciation—Equipment	1,000	(g) 1,000	(l) 3,000	3,000
Common Stock	50,000		(j) 20,000	70,000
Retained Earnings	48,000	(n) 29,000	(m) 145,000	164,000
Total	144,000			412,000
Statement of Cash Flows Effects				
Operating activities				
Net income		(m) 145,000		
Decrease in accounts receivable		(a) 10,000		
Increase in merchandise inventory			(b) 5,000	
Increase in prepaid expenses			(c) 4,000	
Increase in accounts payable		(h) 16,000		
Decrease in income taxes payable			(i) 2,000	
Depreciation expense—building		(k) 6,000		
Depreciation expense—equipment		(l) 3,000		
Loss on sale of equipment		(g) 3,000		
Investing activities				
Purchase of building			(e) 120,000	
Purchase of equipment			(f) 25,000	
Sale of equipment		(g) 4,000		
Financing activities				
Issuance of common stock		(j) 20,000		
Payment of dividends			(n) 29,000	
Totals		525,000	503,000	
Increase in cash			(o) 22,000	
Totals		525,000	525,000	

*Significant noncash investing and financing activity.

758 Chapter 17 Statement of Cash Flows

SUMMARY OF STUDY OBJECTIVE FOR APPENDIX 17A

5 **Explain how to use a worksheet to prepare the statement of cash flows using the indirect method.** When there are numerous adjustments, a worksheet can be a helpful tool in preparing the statement of cash flows. Key guidelines for using a worksheet are: (1) List accounts with debit balances separately from those with credit balances. (2) In the reconciling columns in the bottom portion of the worksheet, show cash inflows as debits and cash outflows as credits. (3) Do not enter reconciling items in any journal or account, but use them only to help prepare the statement of cash flows.

The steps in preparing the worksheet are: (1) Enter beginning and ending balances of balance sheet accounts. (2) Enter debits and credits in reconciling columns. (3) Enter the increase or decrease in cash in two places as a balancing amount.

APPENDIX 17B Statement of Cash Flows—Direct Method

STUDY OBJECTIVE 6
Prepare a statement of cash flows using the direct method.

To explain and illustrate the direct method, we will use the transactions of Juarez Company for 2010, to prepare a statement of cash flows. Illustration 17B-1 presents information related to 2010 for Juarez Company.

Illustration 17B-1
Comparative balance sheets, income statement, and additional information for Juarez Company

JUAREZ COMPANY
Comparative Balance Sheets
December 31

Assets	2010	2009	Change Increase/Decrease
Cash	$191,000	$159,000	$ 32,000 Increase
Accounts receivable	12,000	15,000	3,000 Decrease
Inventory	170,000	160,000	10,000 Increase
Prepaid expenses	6,000	8,000	2,000 Decrease
Land	140,000	80,000	60,000 Increase
Equipment	160,000	-0-	160,000 Increase
Accumulated depreciation—equipment	(16,000)	-0-	16,000 Increase
Total	$663,000	$422,000	

Liabilities and Stockholders' Equity			
Accounts payable	$ 52,000	$ 60,000	$ 8,000 Decrease
Accrued expenses payable	15,000	20,000	5,000 Decrease
Income taxes payable	12,000	-0-	12,000 Increase
Bonds payable	130,000	-0-	130,000 Increase
Common stock	360,000	300,000	60,000 Increase
Retained earnings	94,000	42,000	52,000 Increase
Total	$663,000	$422,000	

JUAREZ COMPANY
Income Statement
For the Year Ended December 31, 2010

Revenues		$975,000
Cost of goods sold	$660,000	
Operating expenses (excluding depreciation)	176,000	
Depreciation expense	18,000	
Loss on sale of store equipment	1,000	855,000
Income before income taxes		120,000
Income tax expense		36,000
Net income		$ 84,000

Appendix 17B Statement of Cash Flows—Direct Method

Illustration 17B-1 (continued)

Additional information:
1. In 2010, the company declared and paid a $32,000 cash dividend.
2. Bonds were issued at face value for $130,000 in cash.
3. Equipment costing $180,000 was purchased for cash.
4. Equipment costing $20,000 was sold for $17,000 cash when the book value of the equipment was $18,000.
5. Common stock of $60,000 was issued to acquire land.

To prepare a statement of cash flows under the direct approach, we will apply the three steps outlined in Illustration 17-3 (page 737).

Step 1: Operating Activities

DETERMINE NET CASH PROVIDED/USED BY OPERATING ACTIVITIES BY CONVERTING NET INCOME FROM AN ACCRUAL BASIS TO A CASH BASIS

Under the **direct method**, companies compute net cash provided by operating activities by **adjusting each item in the income statement** from the accrual basis to the cash basis. To simplify and condense the operating activities section, companies **report only major classes of operating cash receipts and cash payments**. For these major classes, the difference between cash receipts and cash payments is the net cash provided by operating activities. These relationships are as shown in Illustration 17B-2.

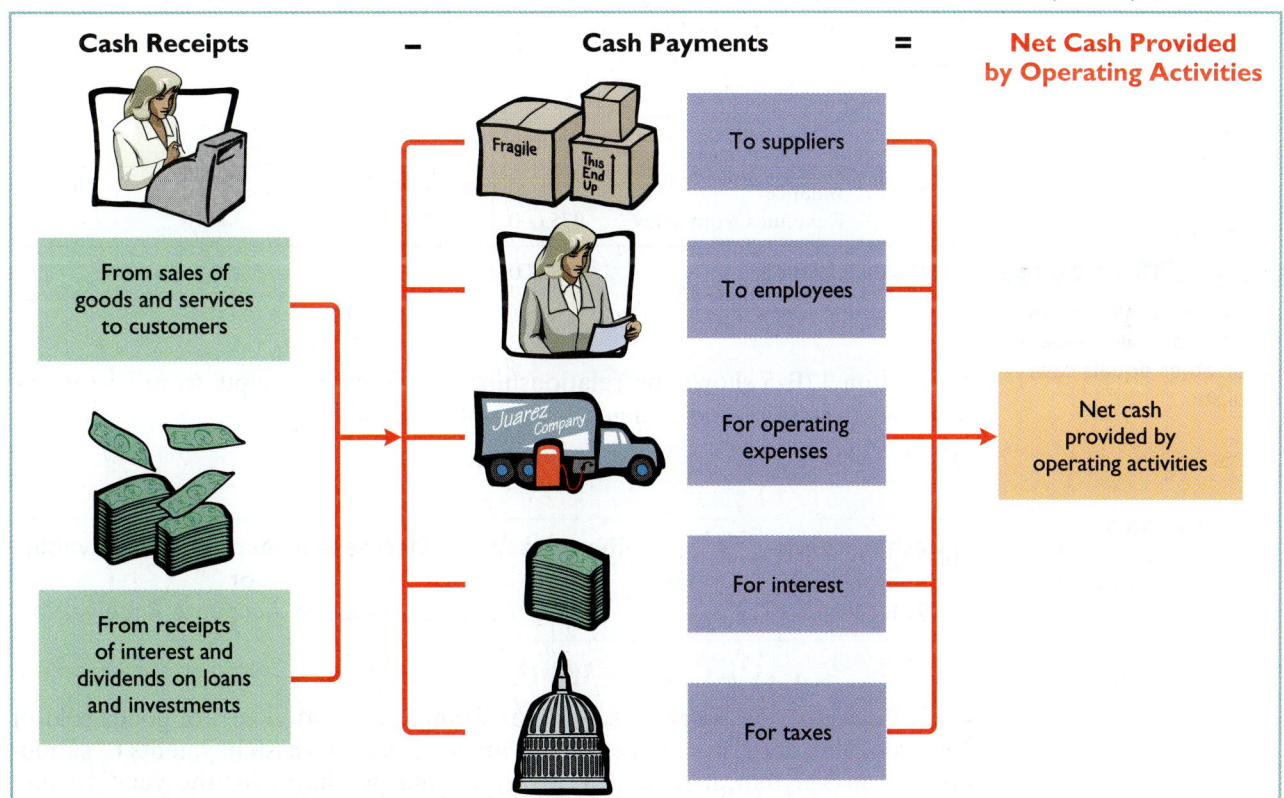

Illustration 17B-2
Major classes of cash receipts and payments

An efficient way to apply the direct method is to analyze the items reported in the income statement in the order in which they are listed. We then determine cash receipts and cash payments related to these revenues and expenses. The following pages present the adjustments required to prepare a statement of cash flows for Juarez Company using the direct approach.

Cash Receipts from Customers. The income statement for Juarez Company reported revenues from customers of $975,000. How much of that was cash receipts? To answer that, companies need to consider the change in accounts receivable during the year. When accounts receivable increase during the year, revenues on an accrual basis are higher than cash receipts from customers. Operations led to revenues, but not all of these revenues resulted in cash receipts.

To determine the amount of cash receipts, the company deducts from sales revenues the increase in accounts receivable. On the other hand, there may be a decrease in accounts receivable. That would occur if cash receipts from customers exceeded sales revenues. In that case, the company adds to sales revenues the decrease in accounts receivable.

For Juarez Company, accounts receivable decreased $3,000. Thus, cash receipts from customers were $978,000, computed as shown in Illustration 17B-3.

Illustration 17B-3
Computation of cash receipts from customers

Revenues from sales	$ 975,000
Add: Decrease in accounts receivable	3,000
Cash receipts from customers	**$ 978,000**

Juarez can also determine cash receipts from customers from an analysis of the Accounts Receivable account, as shown in Illustration 17B-4.

Illustration 17B-4
Analysis of accounts receivable

Accounts Receivable				
1/1/10	Balance	15,000	Receipts from customers	978,000
	Revenues from sales	975,000		
12/31/10	Balance	12,000		

HELPFUL HINT
The T account shows that revenue plus decrease in receivables equals cash receipts.

Illustration 17B-5 shows the relationships among cash receipts from customers, revenues from sales, and changes in accounts receivable.

Illustration 17B-5
Formula to compute cash receipts from customers—direct method

$$\text{Cash Receipts from Customers} = \text{Revenues from Sales} \begin{cases} + \text{Decrease in Accounts Receivable} \\ \text{or} \\ - \text{Increase in Accounts Receivable} \end{cases}$$

Cash Payments to Suppliers. Juarez Company reported cost of goods sold of $660,000 on its income statement. How much of that was cash payments to suppliers? To answer that, it is first necessary to find purchases for the year. To find purchases, companies adjust cost of goods sold for the change in inventory. When inventory increases during the year, purchases for the year have exceeded cost of goods sold. As a result, to determine the amount of purchases, the company adds to cost of goods sold the increase in inventory.

In 2010, Juarez Company's inventory increased $10,000. It computes purchases as follows.

Cost of goods sold	$660,000
Add: Increase in inventory	10,000
Purchases	**$670,000**

Illustration 17B-6
Computation of purchases

After computing purchases, a company can determine cash payments to suppliers. This is done by adjusting purchases for the change in accounts payable. When accounts payable increase during the year, purchases on an accrual basis are higher than they are on a cash basis. As a result, to determine cash payments to suppliers, a company deducts from purchases the increase in accounts payable. On the other hand, if cash payments to suppliers exceed purchases, there will be a decrease in accounts payable. In that case, a company adds to purchases the decrease in accounts payable.

For Juarez Company, cash payments to suppliers were $678,000, computed as follows.

Purchases	$670,000
Add: Decrease in accounts payable	8,000
Cash payments to suppliers	**$678,000**

Illustration 17B-7
Computation of cash payments to suppliers

Juarez also can determine cash payments to suppliers from an analysis of the Accounts Payable account, as shown in Illustration 17B-8.

Accounts Payable

Payments to suppliers	**678,000**	1/1/10 Balance		60,000
		Purchases		670,000
		12/31/10 Balance		52,000

Illustration 17B-8
Analysis of accounts payable

HELPFUL HINT
The T account shows that purchases plus decrease in accounts payable equals payments to suppliers.

Illustration 17B-9 shows the relationships among cash payments to suppliers, cost of goods sold, changes in inventory, and changes in accounts payable.

$$\text{Cash Payments to Suppliers} = \text{Cost of Goods Sold} \begin{Bmatrix} + \text{ Increase in Inventory} \\ \text{or} \\ - \text{ Decrease in Inventory} \end{Bmatrix} \begin{Bmatrix} + \text{ Decrease in Accounts Payable} \\ \text{or} \\ - \text{ Increase in Accounts Payable} \end{Bmatrix}$$

Illustration 17B-9
Formula to compute cash payments to suppliers—direct method

Cash Payments for Operating Expenses. Juarez reported on its income statement operating expenses of $176,000. How much of that amount was cash paid for operating expenses? To answer that, we need to adjust this amount for any changes in prepaid expenses and accrued expenses payable. For example, if prepaid expenses increased during the year, cash paid for operating expenses is higher than operating expenses reported on the income statement. To convert operating expenses to cash payments for operating expenses, a company adds the increase to operating expenses. On the other hand, if prepaid expenses decrease during the year, it deducts the decrease from operating expenses.

Companies must also adjust operating expenses for changes in accrued expenses payable. When accrued expenses payable increase during the year, operating expenses on an accrual basis are higher than they are in a cash basis. As a result, to determine cash payments for operating expenses, a company deducts from operating expenses an increase in accrued expenses payable. On the other hand, a company adds to operating expenses a decrease in accrued expenses payable because cash payments exceed operating expenses.

Juarez Company's cash payments for operating expenses were $179,000, computed as follows.

Illustration 17B-10
Computation of cash payments for operating expenses

Operating expenses	$176,000
Deduct: Decrease in prepaid expenses	(2,000)
Add: Decrease in accrued expenses payable	5,000
Cash payments for operating expenses	**$179,000**

Illustration 17B-11 shows the relationships among cash payments for operating expenses, changes in prepaid expenses, and changes in accrued expenses payable.

Illustration 17B-11
Formula to compute cash payments for operating expenses—direct method

$$\text{Cash Payments for Operating Expenses} = \text{Operating Expenses} \begin{cases} + \text{Increase in Prepaid Expense} \\ \text{or} \\ - \text{Decrease in Prepaid Expense} \end{cases} \begin{cases} + \text{Decrease in Accrued Expenses Payable} \\ \text{or} \\ - \text{Increase in Accrued Expenses Payable} \end{cases}$$

Depreciation Expense and Loss on Sale of Equipment. Companies show operating expenses exclusive of depreciation. Juarez's depreciation expense in 2010 was $18,000. Depreciation expense is not shown on a statement of cash flows because it is a noncash charge. If the amount for operating expenses includes depreciation expense, the company must reduce operating expenses by the amount of depreciation to determine cash payments for operating expenses.

The loss on sale of equipment of $1,000 is also a noncash charge. The loss on sale of equipment reduces net income, but it does not reduce cash. Thus, companies do not report on a statement of cash flows the loss on sale of equipment.

Other charges to expense that do not require the use of cash, such as the amortization of intangible assets, depletion expense, and bad debt expense, are treated in the same manner as depreciation.

Cash Payments for Income Taxes. Juarez reported income tax expense of $36,000 on the income statement. Income taxes payable, however, increased $12,000. This increase means that the company has not yet paid $12,000 of the income taxes. As a result, income taxes paid were less than income taxes reported in the income statement. Cash payments for income taxes were, therefore, $24,000 as shown below.

Illustration 17B-12
Computation of cash payments for income taxes

Income tax expense	$36,000
Deduct: Increase in income taxes payable	12,000
Cash payments for income taxes	**$24,000**

Illustration 17B-13 shows the relationships among cash payments for income taxes, income tax expense, and changes in income taxes payable.

Illustration 17B-13
Formula to compute cash payments for income taxes—direct method

$$\text{Cash Payments for Income Taxes} = \text{Income Tax Expense} \begin{cases} + \text{Decrease in Income Taxes Payable} \\ \text{or} \\ - \text{Increase in Income Taxes Payable} \end{cases}$$

The operating activities section of the statement of cash flows of Juarez Company is shown in Illustration 17B-14.

Illustration 17B-14
Operating activities section of the statement of cash flows

Cash flows from operating activities		
Cash receipts from customers		$978,000
Less: Cash payments:		
To suppliers	$678,000	
For operating expenses	179,000	
For income taxes	24,000	881,000
Net cash provided by operating activities		$ 97,000

When a company uses the direct method, it must also provide in a **separate schedule** (not shown here) the net cash flows from operating activities as computed under the indirect method.

Step 2: Investing and Financing Activities

ANALYZE CHANGES IN NONCURRENT ASSET AND LIABILITY ACCOUNTS AND RECORD AS INVESTING AND FINANCING ACTIVITIES, OR AS SIGNIFICANT NONCASH TRANSACTIONS

Increase in Land. Juarez's land increased $60,000. The additional information section indicates that the company issued common stock to purchase the land. The issuance of common stock for land has no effect on cash. But it is a **significant noncash investing and financing transaction**. This transaction requires disclosure in a separate schedule at the bottom of the statement of cash flows.

Increase in Equipment. The comparative balance sheets show that equipment increased $160,000 in 2010. The additional information in Illustration 17B-1 indicated that the increase resulted from two investing transactions: (1) Juarez purchased for cash equipment costing $180,000. And (2) it sold for $17,000 cash equipment costing $20,000, whose book value was $18,000. The relevant data for the statement of cash flows is the cash paid for the purchase and the cash proceeds from the sale. For Juarez Company, the investing activities section will show the following: The $180,000 purchase of equipment as an outflow of cash, and the $17,000 sale of equipment as an inflow of cash. The company **should not net** the two amounts. **Both individual outflows and inflows of cash should be shown.**

The analysis of the changes in equipment should include the related Accumulated Depreciation account. These two accounts for Juarez Company are shown in Illustration 17B-15.

Illustration 17B-15
Analysis of equipment and related accumulated depreciation

Equipment				
1/1/10	Balance	-0-	Cost of equipment sold	20,000
	Cash purchase	**180,000**		
12/31/10	Balance	160,000		

Accumulated Depreciation—Equipment				
Sale of equipment	2,000	1/1/10	Balance	-0-
			Depreciation expense	18,000
		12/31/10	Balance	16,000

Increase in Bonds Payable. Bonds Payable increased $130,000. The additional information in Illustration 17B-1 indicated that Juarez issued, for $130,000 cash, bonds with a face value of $130,000. The issuance of bonds is a financing activity. For Juarez Company, there is an inflow of cash of $130,000 from the issuance of bonds.

Increase in Common Stock. The Common Stock account increased $60,000. The additional information indicated that Juarez acquired land from the issuance of common stock. This transaction is a **significant noncash investing and financing transaction** which the company should report separately at the bottom of the statement.

Increase in Retained Earnings. The $52,000 net increase in Retained Earnings resulted from net income of $84,000 and the declaration and payment of a cash dividend of $32,000. Companies **do not report net income in the statement of cash flows under the direct method**. Cash dividends paid of $32,000 are reported in the financing activities section as an outflow of cash.

STATEMENT OF CASH FLOWS—2010

Illustration 17B-16 shows the statement of cash flows for Juarez.

Illustration 17B-16
Statement of cash flows, 2010—direct method

JUAREZ COMPANY
Statement of Cash Flows—Direct Method
For the Year Ended December 31, 2010

Cash flows from operating activities		
Cash receipts from customers		$978,000
Less: Cash payments:		
To suppliers	$678,000	
For operating expenses	179,000	
For income taxes	24,000	881,000
Net cash provided by operating activities		97,000
Cash flows from investing activities		
Purchase of equipment	(180,000)	
Sale of equipment	17,000	
Net cash used by investing activities		(163,000)
Cash flows from financing activities		
Issuance of bonds payable	130,000	
Payment of cash dividends	(32,000)	
Net cash provided by financing activities		98,000
Net increase in cash		32,000
Cash at beginning of period		159,000
Cash at end of period		$191,000
Noncash investing and financing activities		
Issuance of common stock to purchase land		$60,000

Step 3: Net Change in Cash

COMPARE THE NET CHANGE IN CASH ON THE STATEMENT OF CASH FLOWS WITH THE CHANGE IN THE CASH ACCOUNT REPORTED ON THE BALANCE SHEET TO MAKE SURE THE AMOUNTS AGREE

Illustration 17B-16 indicates that the net change in cash during the period was an increase of $32,000. This agrees with the change in balances in the cash account reported on the balance sheets in Illustration 17B-1 (page 758).

SUMMARY OF STUDY OBJECTIVE FOR APPENDIX 17B

6 **Prepare a statement of cash flows using the direct method.** The preparation of the statement of cash flows involves three major steps: (1) Determine net cash provided/used by operating activities by converting net income from an accrual basis to a cash basis. (2) Analyze changes in noncurrent asset and liability accounts and record as investing and financing activities, or disclose as noncash transactions. (3) Compare the net change in cash on the statement of cash flows with the change in the cash account reported on the balance sheet to make sure the amounts agree. The direct method reports cash receipts less cash payments to arrive at net cash provided by operating activities.

GLOSSARY FOR APPENDIX 17B

Direct method A method of determining net cash provided by operating activities by adjusting each item in the income statement from the accrual basis to the cash basis. (pp. 737, 759)

Comprehensive DO IT! 2

The income statement for Kosinski Manufacturing Company contains the following condensed information.

KOSINSKI MANUFACTURING COMPANY
Income Statement
For the Year Ended December 31, 2010

Revenues		$6,583,000
Operating expenses, excluding depreciation	$4,920,000	
Depreciation expense	880,000	5,800,000
Income before income taxes		783,000
Income tax expense		353,000
Net income		$ 430,000

Included in operating expenses is a $24,000 loss resulting from the sale of machinery for $270,000 cash. Machinery was purchased at a cost of $750,000. The following balances are reported on Kosinski's comparative balance sheet at December 31.

KOSINSKI MANUFACTURING COMPANY
Comparative Balance Sheets (partial)

	2010	2009
Cash	$672,000	$130,000
Accounts receivable	775,000	610,000
Inventories	834,000	867,000
Accounts payable	521,000	501,000

Income tax expense of $353,000 represents the amount paid in 2010. Dividends declared and paid in 2010 totaled $200,000.

Instructions
Prepare the statement of cash flows using the direct method.

Chapter 17 Statement of Cash Flows

action plan

✔ Determine net cash from operating activities. Each item in the income statement must be adjusted to the cash basis.

✔ Determine net cash from investing activities. Investing activities generally relate to changes in noncurrent assets.

✔ Determine net cash from financing activities. Financing activities generally relate to changes in long-term liabilities and stockholders' equity accounts.

Solution to Comprehensive DO IT! 2

KOSINSKI MANUFACTURING COMPANY
Statement of Cash Flows—Direct Method
For the Year Ended December 31, 2010

Cash flows from operating activities			
Cash collections from customers			$6,418,000*
Cash payments:			
For operating expenses		$4,843,000**	
For income taxes		353,000	5,196,000
Net cash provided by operating activities			1,222,000
Cash flows from investing activities			
Sale of machinery		270,000	
Purchase of machinery		(750,000)	
Net cash used by investing activities			(480,000)
Cash flows from financing activities			
Payment of cash dividends		(200,000)	
Net cash used by financing activities			(200,000)
Net increase in cash			542,000
Cash at beginning of period			130,000
Cash at end of period			$ 672,000

Direct-Method Computations:

*Computation of cash collections from customers:

Revenues per the income statement	$6,583,000
Deduct: Increase in accounts receivable	(165,000)
Cash collections from customers	$6,418,000

**Computation of cash payments for operating expenses:

Operating expenses per the income statement	$4,920,000
Deduct: Loss from sale of machinery	(24,000)
Deduct: Decrease in inventories	(33,000)
Deduct: Increase in accounts payable	(20,000)
Cash payments for operating expenses	$4,843,000

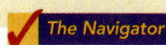

Note: All Questions, Exercises, and Problems marked with an asterisk relate to material in the appendices to the chapter.

SELF-STUDY QUESTIONS

Answers are at the end of the chapter.

(SO 1) **1.** Which of the following is *incorrect* about the statement of cash flows?
  a. It is a fourth basic financial statement.
  b. It provides information about cash receipts and cash payments of an entity during a period.
  c. It reconciles the ending cash account balance to the balance per the bank statement.
  d. It provides information about the operating, investing, and financing activities of the business.

2. Which of the following will *not* be reported in the statement of cash flows? (SO 1)
  a. The net change in plant assets during the year.
  b. Cash payments for plant assets during the year.
  c. Cash receipts from sales of plant assets during the year.
  d. How acquisitions of plant assets during the year were financed.

3. The statement of cash flows classifies cash receipts and cash payments by these activities: (SO 2)

a. operating and nonoperating.
b. investing, financing, and operating.
c. financing, operating, and nonoperating.
d. investing, financing, and nonoperating.

(SO 2) **4.** Which is an example of a cash flow from an operating activity?
a. Payment of cash to lenders for interest.
b. Receipt of cash from the sale of capital stock.
c. Payment of cash dividends to the company's stockholders.
d. None of the above.

(SO 2) **5.** Which is an example of a cash flow from an investing activity?
a. Receipt of cash from the issuance of bonds payable.
b. Payment of cash to repurchase outstanding capital stock.
c. Receipt of cash from the sale of equipment.
d. Payment of cash to suppliers for inventory.

(SO 2) **6.** Cash dividends paid to stockholders are classified on the statement of cash flows as:
a. operating activities.
b. investing activities.
c. a combination of (a) and (b).
d. financing activities.

(SO 2) **7.** Which is an example of a cash flow from a financing activity?
a. Receipt of cash from sale of land.
b. Issuance of debt for cash.
c. Purchase of equipment for cash.
d. None of the above

(SO 2) **8.** Which of the following is *incorrect* about the statement of cash flows?
a. The direct method may be used to report cash provided by operations.
b. The statement shows the cash provided (used) for three categories of activity.
c. The operating section is the last section of the statement.
d. The indirect method may be used to report cash provided by operations.

Questions 9 through 11 apply only to the indirect method.

(SO 3) **9.** Net income is $132,000, accounts payable increased $10,000 during the year, inventory decreased $6,000 during the year, and accounts receivable increased $12,000 during the year. Under the indirect method, what is net cash provided by operating activities?
a. $102,000.   c. $124,000.
b. $112,000.   d. $136,000.

(SO 3) **10.** Items that are added back to net income in determining cash provided by operating activities under the indirect method do *not* include:
a. depreciation expense.   b. an increase in inventory.
c. amortization expense.   d. loss on sale of equipment.

(SO 3) **11.** The following data are available for Allen Clapp Corporation.

Net income	$200,000
Depreciation expense	40,000
Dividends paid	60,000
Gain on sale of land	10,000
Decrease in accounts receivable	20,000
Decrease in accounts payable	30,000

Net cash provided by operating activities is:
a. $160,000.   b. $220,000.
c. $240,000.   d. $280,000.

12. The following data are available for Orange Peels (SO 3) Corporation.

Sale of land	$100,000
Sale of equipment	50,000
Issuance of common stock	70,000
Purchase of equipment	30,000
Payment of cash dividends	60,000

Net cash provided by investing activities is:
a. $120,000.   b. $130,000.
c. $150,000.   d. $190,000.

13. The following data are available for Something Strange! (SO 3)

Increase in accounts payable	$40,000
Increase in bonds payable	100,000
Sale of investment	50,000
Issuance of common stock	60,000
Payment of cash dividends	30,000

Net cash provided by financing activities is:
a. $90,000.
b. $130,000.
c. $160,000.
d. $170,000.

14. The statement of cash flows should *not* be used to evalu- (SO 4) ate an entity's ability to:
a. earn net income.
b. generate future cash flows.
c. pay dividends.
d. meet obligations.

15. Free cash flow provides an indication of a company's abil- (SO4) ity to:
a. generate net income.
b. generate cash to pay dividends.
c. generate cash to invest in new capital expenditures.
d. both (b) and (c).

*__16.__ In a worksheet for the statement of cash flows, a decrease in (SO 5) accounts receivable is entered in the reconciling columns as a credit to Accounts Receivable and a debit in the:
a. investing activities section.
b. operating activities section.
c. financing activities section.
d. None of the above.

*__17.__ In a worksheet for the statement of cash flows, a work- (SO 5) sheet entry that includes a credit to accumulated depreciation will also include a:
a. credit in the operating section and a debit in another section.
b. debit in the operating section.
c. debit in the investing section.
d. debit in the financing section.

Questions 18 and 19 apply only to the direct method.

*__18.__ The beginning balance in accounts receivable is $44,000, (SO 6) the ending balance is $42,000, and sales during the period are $129,000. What are cash receipts from customers?
a. $127,000.   c. $131,000.
b. $129,000.   d. $141,000.

768 Chapter 17 Statement of Cash Flows

(SO 6) *19. Which of the following items is reported on a cash flow statement prepared by the direct method?
   a. Loss on sale of building.
   b. Increase in accounts receivable.
   c. Depreciation expense.
   d. Cash payments to suppliers.

Go to the book's companion website, **www.wiley.com/college/weygandt**, for Additional Self-Study questions.

QUESTIONS

1. (a) What is a statement of cash flows?
   (b) John Norris maintains that the statement of cash flows is an optional financial statement. Do you agree? Explain.
2. What questions about cash are answered by the statement of cash flows?
3. Distinguish among the three types of activities reported in the statement of cash flows.
4. (a) What are the major sources (inflows) of cash in a statement of cash flows?
   (b) What are the major uses (outflows) of cash?
5. Why is it important to disclose certain noncash transactions? How should they be disclosed?
6. Wilma Flintstone and Barny Rublestone were discussing the format of the statement of cash flows of Hart Candy Co. At the bottom of Hart Candy's statement of cash flows was a separate section entitled "Noncash investing and financing activities." Give three examples of significant noncash transactions that would be reported in this section.
7. Why is it necessary to use comparative balance sheets, a current income statement, and certain transaction data in preparing a statement of cash flows?
8. Contrast the advantages and disadvantages of the direct and indirect methods of preparing the statement of cash flows. Are both methods acceptable? Which method is preferred by the FASB? Which method is more popular?
9. When the total cash inflows exceed the total cash outflows in the statement of cash flows, how and where is this excess identified?
10. Describe the indirect method for determining net cash provided (used) by operating activities.
11. Why is it necessary to convert accrual-based net income to cash-basis income when preparing a statement of cash flows?
12. The president of Ferneti Company is puzzled. During the last year, the company experienced a net loss of $800,000, yet its cash increased $300,000 during the same period of time. Explain to the president how this could occur.
13. Identify five items that are adjustments to convert net income to net cash provided by operating activities under the indirect method.
14. Why and how is depreciation expense reported in a statement prepared using the indirect method?
15. Why is the statement of cash flows useful?
16. During 2010 Doubleday Company converted $1,700,000 of its total $2,000,000 of bonds payable into common stock. Indicate how the transaction would be reported on a statement of cash flows, if at all.
*17. Why is it advantageous to use a worksheet when preparing a statement of cash flows? Is a worksheet required to prepare a statement of cash flows?
*18. Describe the direct method for determining net cash provided by operating activities.
*19. Give the formulas under the direct method for computing (a) cash receipts from customers and (b) cash payments to suppliers.
*20. Garcia Inc. reported sales of $2 million for 2010. Accounts receivable decreased $200,000 and accounts payable increased $300,000. Compute cash receipts from customers, assuming that the receivable and payable transactions related to operations.
*21. In the direct method, why is depreciation expense not reported in the cash flows from operating activities section?
22. **PEPSICO** In its 2007 statement of cash flows, what amount did PepsiCo report for net cash (a) provided by operating activities, (b) used for investing activities, and (c) used for financing activities?

BRIEF EXERCISES

Indicate statement presentation of selected transactions.
(SO 2)

BE17-1 Each of these items must be considered in preparing a statement of cash flows for Kiner Co. for the year ended December 31, 2010. For each item, state how it should be shown in the statement of cash flows for 2010.
(a) Issued bonds for $200,000 cash.
(b) Purchased equipment for $150,000 cash.
(c) Sold land costing $20,000 for $20,000 cash.
(d) Declared and paid a $50,000 cash dividend.

BE17-2 Classify each item as an operating, investing, or financing activity. Assume all items involve cash unless there is information to the contrary.

(a) Purchase of equipment.
(b) Sale of building.
(c) Redemption of bonds.
(d) Depreciation.
(e) Payment of dividends.
(f) Issuance of capital stock.

Classify items by activities.
(SO 2)

BE17-3 The following T account is a summary of the cash account of Edmonds Company.

Identify financing activity transactions.
(SO 2)

Cash (Summary Form)

Balance, Jan. 1	8,000		
Receipts from customers	364,000	Payments for goods	200,000
Dividends on stock investments	6,000	Payments for operating expenses	140,000
Proceeds from sale of equipment	36,000	Interest paid	10,000
Proceeds from issuance of		Taxes paid	8,000
bonds payable	300,000	Dividends paid	50,000
Balance, Dec. 31	306,000		

What amount of net cash provided (used) by financing activities should be reported in the statement of cash flows?

Compute cash provided by operating activities—indirect method.
(SO 3)

BE17-4 Martinez, Inc. reported net income of $2.5 million in 2010. Depreciation for the year was $160,000, accounts receivable decreased $350,000, and accounts payable decreased $280,000. Compute net cash provided by operating activities using the indirect method.

BE17-5 The net income for Adcock Co. for 2010 was $280,000. For 2010 depreciation on plant assets was $70,000, and the company incurred a loss on sale of plant assets of $12,000. Compute net cash provided by operating activities under the indirect method.

Compute cash provided by operating activities—indirect method.
(SO 3)

BE17-6 The comparative balance sheets for Goltra Company show these changes in noncash current asset accounts: accounts receivable decrease $80,000, prepaid expenses increase $28,000, and inventories increase $30,000. Compute net cash provided by operating activities using the indirect method assuming that net income is $200,000.

Compute net cash provided by operating activities—indirect method.
(SO 3)

BE17-7 The T accounts for Equipment and the related Accumulated Depreciation for Pettengill Company at the end of 2010 are shown here.

Determine cash received from sale of equipment.
(SO 3)

Equipment					Accumulated Depreciation			
Beg. bal.	80,000	Disposals	22,000		Disposals	5,500	Beg. bal.	44,500
Acquisitions	41,600						Depr. exp.	12,000
End. bal.	99,600						End. bal.	51,000

In addition, Pettengill Company's income statement reported a loss on the sale of equipment of $5,500. What amount was reported on the statement of cash flows as "cash flow from sale of equipment"?

BE17-8 In a recent year, Cypress Semiconductor Corporation reported cash provided by operating activities of $155,793,000, cash used in investing of $207,826,000, and cash used in financing of $33,372,000. In addition, cash spent for fixed assets during the period was $132,280,000. No dividends were paid. Calculate free cash flow.

Calculate free cash flow.
(SO 4)

BE17-9 Lott Corporation reported cash provided by operating activities of $360,000, cash used by investing activities of $250,000, and cash provided by financing activities of $70,000. In addition, cash spent for capital assets during the period was $200,000. No dividends were paid. Calculate free cash flow.

Calculate free cash flow.
(SO 4)

BE17-10 In a recent quarter, Alliance Atlantis Communications Inc. reported cash provided by operating activities of $45,600,000 and revenues of $264,800,000. Cash spent on plant asset additions during the quarter was $1,600,000. Calculate free cash flow.

Calculate free cash flow.
(SO 4)

BE17-11 The management of Radar Inc. is trying to decide whether it can increase its dividend. During the current year it reported net income of $875,000. It had cash provided by operating activities of $734,000, paid cash dividends of $70,000, and had capital expenditures of $280,000.

Calculate and analyze free cash flow.
(SO 4)

770 Chapter 17 Statement of Cash Flows

Compute the company's free cash flow, and discuss whether an increase in the dividend appears warranted. What other factors should be considered?

Indicate entries in worksheet.
(SO 5)

*BE17-12 During the year, prepaid expenses decreased $6,600, and accrued expenses increased $2,400. Indicate how the changes in prepaid expenses and accrued expenses payable should be entered in the reconciling columns of a worksheet. Assume that beginning balances were: Prepaid expenses $18,600 and Accrued expenses payable $8,200.

Compute receipts from customers—direct method.
(SO 6)

*BE17-13 Columbia Sportswear Company had accounts receivable of $206,024,000 at the beginning of a recent year, and $267,653,000 at year-end. Sales revenues were $1,095,307,000 for the year. What is the amount of cash receipts from customers?

Compute cash payments for income taxes—direct method.
(SO 6)

*BE17-14 Young Corporation reported income taxes of $340,000,000 on its 2010 income statement and income taxes payable of $277,000,000 at December 31, 2009, and $522,000,000 at December 31, 2010. What amount of cash payments were made for income taxes during 2010?

Compute cash payments for operating expenses—direct method.
(SO 6)

*BE17-15 Flynn Corporation reports operating expenses of $80,000 excluding depreciation expense of $15,000 for 2010. During the year prepaid expenses decreased $6,600 and accrued expenses payable increased $4,400. Compute the cash payments for operating expenses in 2010.

DO IT! REVIEW

Classify transactions by type of cash flow activity.
(SO 2)

DO IT! 17-1 Rapture Corporation had the following transactions.

1. Issued $200,000 of bonds payable.
2. Paid utilities expense.
3. Issued 500 shares of preferred stock for $45,000.
4. Sold land and a building for $250,000.
5. Lent $30,000 to Dead End Corporation, receiving Dead End's 1-year, 12% note.

Classify each of these transactions by type of cash flow activity (operating, investing, or financing).

Calculate net cash from operating activities.
(SO 3)

DO IT! 17-2 JMB Photography reported net income of $100,000 for 2010. Included in the income statement were depreciation expense of $6,000, patent amortization expense of $2,000, and a gain on sale of equipment of $3,600. JMB's comparative balance sheets show the following balances.

	12/31/09	12/31/10
Accounts receivable	$27,000	$21,000
Accounts payable	6,000	9,200

Calculate net cash provided by operating activities for JMB Photography

Compute and discuss free cash flow.
(SO 4)

DO IT! 17-3 Grinders Corporation issued the following statement of cash flows for 2010.

GRINDERS CORPORATION
Statement of Cash Flows—Indirect Method
For the Year Ended December 31, 2010

Cash flows from operating activities		
Net income		$59,000
Adjustments to reconcile net income to net cash provided by operating activities:		
Depreciation expense	$9,100	
Decrease in accounts receivable	9,500	
Loss on sale of equipment	3,300	
Increase in inventory	(5,000)	
Decrease in accounts payable	(2,200)	14,700
Net cash provided by operating activities		73,700

Cash flows from investing activities
  Sale of investments   3,100
  Purchase of equipment   (27,000)
    Net cash used by investing activities   (23,900)
Cash flows from financing activities
  Issuance of stock   20,000
  Payment on long-term note payable   (10,000)
  Payment for dividends   (15,000)
    Net cash used by financing activities   (5,000)
Net increase in cash   44,800
Cash at beginning of year   13,000
Cash at end of year $57,800

(a) Compute free cash flow for Grinders Corporation. (b) Explain why free cash flow often provides better information than "Net cash provided by operating activities."

EXERCISES

E17-1 Pioneer Corporation had these transactions during 2010.

(a) Issued $50,000 par value common stock for cash.
(b) Purchased a machine for $30,000, giving a long-term note in exchange.
(c) Issued $200,000 par value common stock upon conversion of bonds having a face value of $200,000.
(d) Declared and paid a cash dividend of $18,000.
(e) Sold a long-term investment with a cost of $15,000 for $15,000 cash.
(f) Collected $16,000 of accounts receivable.
(g) Paid $18,000 on accounts payable.

Classify transactions by type of activity.
(SO 2)

Instructions
Analyze the transactions and indicate whether each transaction resulted in a cash flow from operating activities, investing activities, financing activities, or noncash investing and financing activities.

E17-2 An analysis of comparative balance sheets, the current year's income statement, and the general ledger accounts of Gagliano Corp. uncovered the following items. Assume all items involve cash unless there is information to the contrary.

Classify transactions by type of activity.
(SO 2)

(a) Payment of interest on notes payable.
(b) Exchange of land for patent.
(c) Sale of building at book value.
(d) Payment of dividends.
(e) Depreciation.
(f) Receipt of dividends on investment in stock.
(g) Receipt of interest on notes receivable.
(h) Issuance of capital stock.
(i) Amortization of patent.
(j) Issuance of bonds for land.
(k) Purchase of land.
(l) Conversion of bonds into common stock.
(m) Loss on sale of land.
(n) Retirement of bonds.

Instructions
Indicate how each item should be classified in the statement of cash flows using these four major classifications: operating activity (indirect method), investing activity, financing activity, and significant noncash investing and financing activity.

E17-3 Rachael Ray Corporation had the following transactions.

1. Sold land (cost $12,000) for $15,000.
2. Issued common stock for $20,000.
3. Recorded depreciation of $17,000.
4. Paid salaries of $9,000.
5. Issued 1,000 shares of $1 par value common stock for equipment worth $8,000.
6. Sold equipment (cost $10,000, accumulated depreciation $7,000) for $1,200.

Prepare journal entry and determine effect on cash flows.
(SO 2)

Chapter 17 Statement of Cash Flows

Instructions

For each transaction above, **(a)** prepare the journal entry, and **(b)** indicate how it would affect the statement of cash flows.

Prepare the operating activities section—indirect method.
(SO 3)

E17-4 Villa Company reported net income of $195,000 for 2010. Villa also reported depreciation expense of $45,000 and a loss of $5,000 on the sale of equipment. The comparative balance sheet shows a decrease in accounts receivable of $15,000 for the year, a $17,000 increase in accounts payable, and a $4,000 decrease in prepaid expenses.

Instructions

Prepare the operating activities section of the statement of cash flows for 2010. Use the indirect method.

Prepare the operating activities section—indirect method.
(SO 3)

E17-5 The current sections of Bellinham Inc.'s balance sheets at December 31, 2009 and 2010, are presented here.

Bellinham's net income for 2010 was $153,000. Depreciation expense was $24,000.

	2010	2009
Current assets		
Cash	$105,000	$ 99,000
Accounts receivable	110,000	89,000
Inventory	158,000	172,000
Prepaid expenses	27,000	22,000
Total current assets	$400,000	$382,000
Current liabilities		
Accrued expenses payable	$ 15,000	$ 5,000
Accounts payable	85,000	92,000
Total current liabilities	$100,000	$ 97,000

Instructions

Prepare the net cash provided by operating activities section of the company's statement of cash flows for the year ended December 31, 2010, using the indirect method.

Prepare partial statement of cash flows—indirect method.
(SO 3)

E17-6 The three accounts shown below appear in the general ledger of Cesar Corp. during 2010.

Equipment

Date		Debit	Credit	Balance
Jan. 1	Balance			160,000
July 31	Purchase of equipment	70,000		230,000
Sept. 2	Cost of equipment constructed	53,000		283,000
Nov. 10	Cost of equipment sold		49,000	234,000

Accumulated Depreciation—Equipment

Date		Debit	Credit	Balance
Jan. 1	Balance			71,000
Nov. 10	Accumulated depreciation on equipment sold	30,000		41,000
Dec. 31	Depreciation for year		28,000	69,000

Retained Earnings

Date		Debit	Credit	Balance
Jan. 1	Balance			105,000
Aug. 23	Dividends (cash)	14,000		91,000
Dec. 31	Net income		67,000	158,000

Instructions

From the postings in the accounts, indicate how the information is reported on a statement of cash flows using the indirect method. The loss on sale of equipment was $5,000. (*Hint:* Cost of equipment constructed is reported in the investing activities section as a decrease in cash of $53,000.)

E17-7 Scully Corporation's comparative balance sheets are presented below.

Prepare statement of cash flows and compute free cash flow.
(SO 3, 4)

SCULLY CORPORATION
Comparative Balance Sheets
December 31

	2010	2009
Cash	$ 14,300	$ 10,700
Accounts receivable	21,200	23,400
Land	20,000	26,000
Building	70,000	70,000
Accumulated depreciation	(15,000)	(10,000)
Total	$110,500	$120,100
Accounts payable	$12,370	$31,100
Common stock	75,000	69,000
Retained earnings	23,130	20,000
Total	$110,500	$120,100

Additional information:

1. Net income was $22,630. Dividends declared and paid were $19,500.
2. All other changes in noncurrent account balances had a direct effect on cash flows, except the change in accumulated depreciation. The land was sold for $4,900.

Instructions
(a) Prepare a statement of cash flows for 2010 using the indirect method.
(b) Compute free cash flow.

E17-8 Here are comparative balance sheets for Taguchi Company.

Prepare a statement of cash flows—indirect method.
(SO 3)

TAGUCHI COMPANY
Comparative Balance Sheets
December 31

Assets	2010	2009
Cash	$ 73,000	$ 22,000
Accounts receivable	85,000	76,000
Inventories	170,000	189,000
Land	75,000	100,000
Equipment	260,000	200,000
Accumulated depreciation	(66,000)	(32,000)
Total	$597,000	$555,000
Liabilities and Stockholders' Equity		
Accounts payable	$ 39,000	$ 47,000
Bonds payable	150,000	200,000
Common stock ($1 par)	216,000	174,000
Retained earnings	192,000	134,000
Total	$597,000	$555,000

Additional information:

1. Net income for 2010 was $103,000.
2. Cash dividends of $45,000 were declared and paid.
3. Bonds payable amounting to $50,000 were redeemed for cash $50,000.
4. Common stock was issued for $42,000 cash.
5. No equipment was sold during 2010, but land was sold at cost.

774 Chapter 17 Statement of Cash Flows

Instructions
Prepare a statement of cash flows for 2010 using the indirect method.

Prepare statement of cash flows and compute free cash flow.
(SO 3, 4)

E17-9 Muldur Corporation's comparative balance sheets are presented below.

MULDUR CORPORATION
Comparative Balance Sheets
December 31

	2010	2009
Cash	$ 15,200	$ 17,700
Accounts receivable	25,200	22,300
Investments	20,000	16,000
Equipment	60,000	70,000
Accumulated depreciation	(14,000)	(10,000)
Total	$106,400	$116,000
Accounts payable	$ 14,600	$ 11,100
Bonds payable	10,000	30,000
Common stock	50,000	45,000
Retained earnings	31,800	29,900
Total	$106,400	$116,000

Additional information:

1. Net income was $18,300. Dividends declared and paid were $16,400.
2. Equipment which cost $10,000 and had accumulated depreciation of $1,200 was sold for $3,300.
3. All other changes in noncurrent account balances had a direct effect on cash flows, except the change in accumulated depreciation.

Instructions
(a) Prepare a statement of cash flows for 2010 using the indirect method.
(b) Compute free cash flow.

Prepare a worksheet.
(SO 5)

*****E17-10** Comparative balance sheets for Eddie Murphy Company are presented below.

EDDIE MURPHY COMPANY
Comparative Balance Sheets
December 31

Assets	2010	2009
Cash	$ 63,000	$ 22,000
Accounts receivable	85,000	76,000
Inventories	180,000	189,000
Land	75,000	100,000
Equipment	260,000	200,000
Accumulated depreciation	(66,000)	(42,000)
Total	$597,000	$545,000

Liabilities and Stockholders' Equity		
Accounts payable	$ 34,000	$ 47,000
Bonds payable	150,000	200,000
Common stock ($1 par)	214,000	164,000
Retained earnings	199,000	134,000
Total	$597,000	$545,000

Additional information:

1. Net income for 2010 was $125,000.
2. Cash dividends of $60,000 were declared and paid.

3. Bonds payable amounting to $50,000 were redeemed for cash $50,000.
4. Common stock was issued for $50,000 cash.
5. Depreciation expense was $24,000.
6. Sales for the year were $978,000.

Instructions
Prepare a worksheet for a statement of cash flows for 2010 using the indirect method. Enter the reconciling items directly on the worksheet, using letters to cross-reference each entry.

*E17-11 Hairston Company completed its first year of operations on December 31, 2010. Its initial income statement showed that Hairston had revenues of $192,000 and operating expenses of $78,000. Accounts receivable and accounts payable at year-end were $60,000 and $23,000, respectively. Assume that accounts payable related to operating expenses. Ignore income taxes.

Compute cash provided by operating activities—direct method.
(SO 6)

Instructions
Compute net cash provided by operating activities using the direct method.

*E17-12 A recent income statement for McDonald's Corporation shows cost of goods sold $4,852.7 million and operating expenses (including depreciation expense of $1,201 million) $10,671.5 million. The comparative balance sheet for the year shows that inventory increased $18.1 million, prepaid expenses increased $56.3 million, accounts payable (merchandise suppliers) increased $136.9 million, and accrued expenses payable increased $160.9 million.

Compute cash payments—direct method.
(SO 6)

Instructions
Using the direct method, compute (a) cash payments to suppliers and (b) cash payments for operating expenses.

*E17-13 The 2010 accounting records of Verlander Transport reveal these transactions and events.

Compute cash flow from operating activities—direct method.
(SO 6)

Payment of interest	$ 10,000	Collection of accounts receivable	$182,000
Cash sales	48,000	Payment of salaries and wages	53,000
Receipt of dividend revenue	18,000	Depreciation expense	16,000
Payment of income taxes	12,000	Proceeds from sale of vehicles	12,000
Net income	38,000	Purchase of equipment for cash	22,000
Payment of accounts payable		Loss on sale of vehicles	3,000
for merchandise	115,000	Payment of dividends	14,000
Payment for land	74,000	Payment of operating expenses	28,000

Instructions
Prepare the cash flows from operating activities section using the direct method. (Not all of the items will be used.)

*E17-14 The following information is taken from the 2010 general ledger of Pierzynski Company.

Calculate cash flows—direct method.
(SO 6)

Rent	Rent expense	$ 40,000
	Prepaid rent, January 1	5,900
	Prepaid rent, December 31	9,000
Salaries	Salaries expense	$ 54,000
	Salaries payable, January 1	10,000
	Salaries payable, December 31	8,000
Sales	Revenue from sales	$170,000
	Accounts receivable, January 1	16,000
	Accounts receivable, December 31	7,000

Instructions
In each case, compute the amount that should be reported in the operating activities section of the statement of cash flows under the direct method.

EXERCISES: SET B

Visit the book's companion website at **www.wiley.com/college/weygandt**, and choose the Student Companion site, to access Exercise Set B.

776 Chapter 17 Statement of Cash Flows

PROBLEMS: SET A

Distinguish among operating, investing, and financing activities.
(SO 2)

P17-1A You are provided with the following transactions that took place during a recent fiscal year.

Transaction	Where Reported on Statement	Cash Inflow, Outflow, or No Effect?
(a) Recorded depreciation expense on the plant assets.		
(b) Recorded and paid interest expense.		
(c) Recorded cash proceeds from a sale of plant assets.		
(d) Acquired land by issuing common stock.		
(e) Paid a cash dividend to preferred stockholders.		
(f) Distributed a stock dividend to common stockholders.		
(g) Recorded cash sales.		
(h) Recorded sales on account.		
(i) Purchased inventory for cash.		
(j) Purchased inventory on account.		

Instructions
Complete the table indicating whether each item (1) should be reported as an operating (O) activity, investing (I) activity, financing (F) activity, or as a noncash (NC) transaction reported in a separate schedule, and (2) represents a cash inflow or cash outflow or has no cash flow effect. Assume use of the indirect approach.

Determine cash flow effects of changes in equity accounts.
(SO 3)

P17-2A The following account balances relate to the stockholders' equity accounts of Gore Corp. at year-end.

	2010	2009
Common stock, 10,500 and 10,000 shares, respectively, for 2010 and 2009	$160,000	$140,000
Preferred stock, 5,000 shares	125,000	125,000
Retained earnings	300,000	260,000

A small stock dividend was declared and issued in 2010. The market value of the shares was $10,500. Cash dividends were $15,000 in both 2010 and 2009. The common stock has no par or stated value.

Instructions

(a) Net income $65,500

(a) What was the amount of net income reported by Gore Corp. in 2010?
(b) Determine the amounts of any cash inflows or outflows related to the common stock and dividend accounts in 2010.
(c) Indicate where each of the cash inflows or outflows identified in (b) would be classified on the statement of cash flows.

Prepare the operating activities section—indirect method.
(SO 3)

P17-3A The income statement of Elbert Company is presented here.

ELBERT COMPANY
Income Statement
For the Year Ended November 30, 2010

Sales		$7,700,000
Cost of goods sold		
Beginning inventory	$1,900,000	
Purchases	4,400,000	
Goods available for sale	6,300,000	
Ending inventory	1,400,000	

Total cost of goods sold	4,900,000
Gross profit	2,800,000
Operating expenses	1,150,000
Net income	$1,650,000

Additional information:

1. Accounts receivable increased $250,000 during the year, and inventory decreased $500,000.
2. Prepaid expenses increased $150,000 during the year.
3. Accounts payable to suppliers of merchandise decreased $340,000 during the year.
4. Accrued expenses payable decreased $100,000 during the year.
5. Operating expenses include depreciation expense of $90,000.

Instructions

Prepare the operating activities section of the statement of cash flows for the year ended November 30, 2010, for Elbert Company, using the indirect method.

Cash from operations $1,400,000

*P17-4A Data for Elbert Company are presented in P17-3A.

Prepare the operating activities section—direct method.
(SO 6)

Instructions

Prepare the operating activities section of the statement of cash flows using the direct method.

Cash from operations $1,400,000

P17-5A Grania Company's income statement contained the condensed information below.

Prepare the operating activities section—indirect method.
(SO 3)

GRANIA COMPANY
Income Statement
For the Year Ended December 31, 2010

Revenues		$970,000
Operating expenses, excluding depreciation	$624,000	
Depreciation expense	60,000	
Loss on sale of equipment	16,000	700,000
Income before income taxes		270,000
Income tax expense		40,000
Net income		$230,000

Grania's balance sheet contained the comparative data at December 31, shown below.

	2010	2009
Accounts receivable	$75,000	$60,000
Accounts payable	41,000	28,000
Income taxes payable	11,000	7,000

Accounts payable pertain to operating expenses.

Instructions

Prepare the operating activities section of the statement of cash flows using the indirect method.

Cash from operations $308,000

*P17-6A Data for Grania Company are presented in P17-5A.

Prepare the operating activities section—direct method.
(SO 6)

Instructions

Prepare the operating activities section of the statement of cash flows using the direct method.

Cash from operations $308,000

P17-7A Presented on the next page are the financial statements of Weller Company.

Prepare a statement of cash flows—indirect method, and compute free cash flow.

(SO 3, 4)

WELLER COMPANY
Comparative Balance Sheets
December 31

Assets	2010	2009
Cash	$ 35,000	$ 20,000
Accounts receivable	33,000	14,000
Merchandise inventory	27,000	20,000
Property, plant, and equipment	60,000	78,000
Accumulated depreciation	(29,000)	(24,000)
Total	$126,000	$108,000

Liabilities and Stockholders' Equity		
Accounts payable	$ 29,000	$ 15,000
Income taxes payable	7,000	8,000
Bonds payable	27,000	33,000
Common stock	18,000	14,000
Retained earnings	45,000	38,000
Total	$126,000	$108,000

WELLER COMPANY
Income Statement
For the Year Ended December 31, 2010

Sales	$242,000
Cost of goods sold	175,000
Gross profit	67,000
Operating expenses	24,000
Income from operations	43,000
Interest expense	3,000
Income before income taxes	40,000
Income tax expense	8,000
Net income	$ 32,000

Additional data:

1. Dividends declared and paid were $25,000.
2. During the year equipment was sold for $8,500 cash. This equipment cost $18,000 originally and had a book value of $8,500 at the time of sale.
3. All depreciation expense, $14,500, is in the operating expenses.
4. All sales and purchases are on account.

(a) Cash from operations $33,500

Instructions
(a) Prepare a statement of cash flows using the indirect method.
(b) Compute free cash flow.

Prepare a statement of cash flows—direct method, and compute free cash flow.

(SO 4, 6)

(a) Cash from operations $33,500

*P17-8A Data for Weller Company are presented in P17-7A. Further analysis reveals the following.

1. Accounts payable pertain to merchandise suppliers.
2. All operating expenses except for depreciation were paid in cash.

Instructions
(a) Prepare a statement of cash flows for Weller Company using the direct method.
(b) Compute free cash flow.

P17-9A Condensed financial data of Arma Inc. follow.

Prepare a statement of cash flows—indirect method.
(SO 3)

ARMA INC.
Comparative Balance Sheets
December 31

Assets	2010	2009
Cash	$ 90,800	$ 48,400
Accounts receivable	92,800	33,000
Inventories	112,500	102,850
Prepaid expenses	28,400	26,000
Investments	138,000	114,000
Plant assets	270,000	242,500
Accumulated depreciation	(50,000)	(52,000)
Total	$682,500	$514,750

Liabilities and Stockholders' Equity		
Accounts payable	$112,000	$ 67,300
Accrued expenses payable	16,500	17,000
Bonds payable	110,000	150,000
Common stock	220,000	175,000
Retained earnings	224,000	105,450
Total	$682,500	$514,750

ARMA INC.
Income Statement
For the Year Ended December 31, 2010

Sales		$392,780
Less:		
Cost of goods sold	$135,460	
Operating expenses, excluding depreciation	12,410	
Depreciation expense	46,500	
Income taxes	27,280	
Interest expense	4,730	
Loss on sale of plant assets	7,500	233,880
Net income		$158,900

Additional information:

1. New plant assets costing $85,000 were purchased for cash during the year.
2. Old plant assets having an original cost of $57,500 were sold for $1,500 cash.
3. Bonds matured and were paid off at face value for cash.
4. A cash dividend of $40,350 was declared and paid during the year.

Instructions
Prepare a statement of cash flows using the indirect method.

Cash from operations $185,250

*P17-10A Data for Arma Inc. are presented in P17-9A. Further analysis reveals that accounts payable pertain to merchandise creditors.

Prepare a statement of cash flows—direct method.
(SO 6)
Cash from operations $185,250

Instructions
Prepare a statement of cash flows for Arma Inc. using the direct method.

P17-11A The comparative balance sheets for Ramirez Company as of December 31 are presented on the next page.

Prepare a statement of cash flows—indirect method.
(SO 3)

RAMIREZ COMPANY
Comparative Balance Sheets
December 31

Assets	2010	2009
Cash	$ 71,000	$ 45,000
Accounts receivable	44,000	62,000
Inventory	151,450	142,000
Prepaid expenses	15,280	21,000
Land	105,000	130,000
Equipment	228,000	155,000
Accumulated depreciation—equipment	(45,000)	(35,000)
Building	200,000	200,000
Accumulated depreciation—building	(60,000)	(40,000)
Total	$709,730	$680,000

Liabilities and Stockholders' Equity		
Accounts payable	$ 47,730	$ 40,000
Bonds payable	260,000	300,000
Common stock, $1 par	200,000	160,000
Retained earnings	202,000	180,000
Total	$709,730	$680,000

Additional information:

1. Operating expenses include depreciation expense of $42,000 and charges from prepaid expenses of $5,720.
2. Land was sold for cash at book value.
3. Cash dividends of $15,000 were paid.
4. Net income for 2010 was $37,000.
5. Equipment was purchased for $95,000 cash. In addition, equipment costing $22,000 with a book value of $10,000 was sold for $6,000 cash.
6. Bonds were converted at face value by issuing 40,000 shares of $1 par value common stock.

Cash from operations $105,000

Instructions
Prepare a statement of cash flows for the year ended December 31, 2010, using the indirect method.

Prepare a worksheet—indirect method.
(SO 5)

*P17-12A Condensed financial data of Oprah Company appear below.

OPRAH COMPANY
Comparative Balance Sheets
December 31

Assets	2010	2009
Cash	$ 92,700	$ 47,250
Accounts receivable	90,800	57,000
Inventories	121,900	102,650
Investments	84,500	87,000
Plant assets	250,000	205,000
Accumulated depreciation	(49,500)	(40,000)
	$590,400	$458,900

Liabilities and Stockholders' Equity		
Accounts payable	$ 57,700	$ 48,280
Accrued expenses payable	12,100	18,830
Bonds payable	100,000	70,000
Common stock	250,000	200,000
Retained earnings	170,600	121,790
	$590,400	$458,900

OPRAH COMPANY
Income Statement
For the Year Ended December 31, 2010

Sales		$297,500
Gain on sale of plant assets		8,750
		306,250
Less:		
Cost of goods sold	$99,460	
Operating expenses (excluding depreciation expense)	14,670	
Depreciation expense	49,700	
Income taxes	7,270	
Interest expense	2,940	174,040
Net income		$132,210

Additional information:

1. New plant assets costing $92,000 were purchased for cash during the year.
2. Investments were sold at cost.
3. Plant assets costing $47,000 were sold for $15,550, resulting in gain of $8,750.
4. A cash dividend of $83,400 was declared and paid during the year.

Instructions

Prepare a worksheet for the statement of cash flows using the indirect method. Enter the reconciling items directly in the worksheet columns, using letters to cross-reference each entry.

Reconciling items total $610,210

PROBLEMS: SET B

P17-1B You are provided with the following transactions that took place during a recent fiscal year.

Distinguish among operating, investing, and financing activities.

(SO 2)

Transaction	Where Reported on Statement	Cash Inflow, Outflow, or No Effect?
(a) Recorded depreciation expense on the plant assets.		
(b) Incurred a loss on disposal of plant assets.		
(c) Acquired a building by paying cash.		
(d) Made principal repayments on a mortgage.		
(e) Issued common stock.		
(f) Purchased shares of another company to be held as a long-term equity investment.		
(g) Paid dividends to common stockholders.		
(h) Sold inventory on credit. The company uses a perpetual inventory system.		
(i) Purchased inventory on credit.		
(j) Paid wages to employees.		

Instructions

Complete the table indicating whether each item (1) should be reported as an operating (O) activity, investing (I) activity, financing (F) activity, or as a noncash (NC) transaction reported in a separate schedule, and (2) represents a cash inflow or cash outflow or has no cash flow effect. Assume use of the indirect approach.

Determine cash flow effects of changes in plant asset accounts.
(SO 3)

P17-2B The following selected account balances relate to the plant asset accounts of Wegent Inc. at year-end.

	2010	2009
Accumulated depreciation—buildings	$337,500	$300,000
Accumulated depreciation—equipment	144,000	96,000
Buildings	750,000	750,000
Depreciation expense	101,500	85,500
Equipment	300,000	240,000
Land	100,000	70,000
Loss on sale of equipment	8,000	0

Additional information:

1. Wegent purchased $95,000 of equipment and $30,000 of land for cash in 2010.
2. Wegent also sold equipment in 2010.
3. Depreciation expense in 2010 was $37,500 on building and $64,000 on equipment.

Instructions

(a) Cash proceeds $11,000

(a) Determine the amounts of any cash inflows or outflows related to the plant asset accounts in 2010.
(b) Indicate where each of the cash inflows or outflows identified in (a) would be classified on the statement of cash flows.

Prepare the operating activities section—indirect method.
(SO 3)

P17-3B The income statement of Rosenthal Company is presented below.

Additional information:

1. Accounts receivable decreased $320,000 during the year, and inventory increased $120,000.
2. Prepaid expenses increased $175,000 during the year.
3. Accounts payable to merchandise suppliers increased $50,000 during the year.
4. Accrued expenses payable increased $155,000 during the year.

ROSENTHAL COMPANY
Income Statement
For the Year Ended December 31, 2010

Sales		$5,400,000
Cost of goods sold		
Beginning inventory	$1,780,000	
Purchases	3,430,000	
Goods available for sale	5,210,000	
Ending inventory	1,900,000	
Total cost of goods sold		3,310,000
Gross profit		2,090,000
Operating expenses		
Depreciation expense	105,000	
Amortization expense	20,000	
Other expenses	945,000	1,070,000
Net income		$1,020,000

Instructions

Cash from operations $1,375,000

Prepare the operating activities section of the statement of cash flows for the year ended December 31, 2010, for Rosenthal Company, using the indirect method.

Prepare the operating activities section—direct method.
(SO 6)

Cash from operations $1,375,000

***P17-4B** Data for Rosenthal Company are presented in P17-3B.

Instructions

Prepare the operating activities section of the statement of cash flows using the direct method.

P17-5B The income statement of Brislin Inc. reported the following condensed information.

Prepare the operating activities section—indirect method.

(SO 3)

BRISLIN INC.
Income Statement
For the Year Ended December 31, 2010

Revenues	$545,000
Operating expenses	400,000
Income from operations	145,000
Income tax expense	36,000
Net income	$109,000

Brislin's balance sheet contained these comparative data at December 31.

	2010	2009
Accounts receivable	$50,000	$70,000
Accounts payable	30,000	51,000
Income taxes payable	10,000	4,000

Brislin has no depreciable assets. Accounts payable pertain to operating expenses.

Instructions
Prepare the operating activities section of the statement of cash flows using the indirect method.

Cash from operations $114,000

*P17-6B Data for Brislin Inc. are presented in P17-5B.

Prepare the operating activities section—direct method.

(SO 6)

Instructions
Prepare the operating activities section of the statement of cash flows using the direct method.

Cash from operations $114,000

P17-7B Presented below are the financial statements of Ortega Company.

ORTEGA COMPANY
Comparative Balance Sheets
December 31

Assets	2010		2009	
Cash		$ 24,000		$ 33,000
Accounts receivable		25,000		14,000
Merchandise inventory		41,000		25,000
Property, plant, and equipment	$ 70,000		$ 78,000	
Less: Accumulated depreciation	(27,000)	43,000	(24,000)	54,000
Total		$133,000		$126,000

Prepare a statement of cash flows—indirect method, and compute free cash flow.

(SO 3, 4)

Liabilities and Stockholders' Equity		
Accounts payable	$ 31,000	$ 43,000
Income taxes payable	24,000	20,000
Bonds payable	20,000	10,000
Common stock	25,000	25,000
Retained earnings	33,000	28,000
Total	$133,000	$126,000

ORTEGA COMPANY
Income Statement
For the Year Ended December 31, 2010

Sales	$286,000
Cost of goods sold	204,000
Gross profit	82,000

Operating expenses	37,000
Income from operations	45,000
Interest expense	7,000
Income before income taxes	38,000
Income tax expense	10,000
Net income	$ 28,000

Additional data:

1. Dividends of $23,000 were declared and paid.
2. During the year equipment was sold for $10,000 cash. This equipment cost $15,000 originally and had a book value of $10,000 at the time of sale.
3. All depreciation expense, $8,000, is in the operating expenses.
4. All sales and purchases are on account.
5. Additional equipment was purchased for $7,000 cash.

Instructions
(a) Prepare a statement of cash flows using the indirect method.
(b) Compute free cash flow.

P17-8B Data for Ortega Company are presented in P17-7B. Further analysis reveals the following.

1. Accounts payable pertains to merchandise creditors.
2. All operating expenses except for depreciation are paid in cash.

Instructions
(a) Prepare a statement of cash flows using the direct method.
(b) Compute free cash flow.

P17-9B Condensed financial data of Ziebert Company are shown below.

ZIEBERT COMPANY
Comparative Balance Sheets
December 31

Assets	2010	2009
Cash	$102,700	$ 33,400
Accounts receivable	60,800	37,000
Inventories	126,900	102,650
Investments	79,500	107,000
Plant assets	315,000	205,000
Accumulated depreciation	(44,500)	(40,000)
Total	$640,400	$445,050
Liabilities and Stockholders' Equity		
Accounts payable	$ 57,700	$ 48,280
Accrued expenses payable	15,100	18,830
Bonds payable	145,000	70,000
Common stock	250,000	200,000
Retained earnings	172,600	107,940
Total	$640,400	$445,050

ZIEBERT COMPANY
Income Statement
For the Year Ended December 31, 2010

Sales	$297,500
Gain on sale of plant assets	5,000
	302,500

Less:
Cost of goods sold	$99,460	
Operating expenses, excluding depreciation expense	19,670	
Depreciation expense	30,500	
Income taxes	37,270	
Interest expense	2,940	189,840
Net income		$112,660

Additional information:

1. New plant assets costing $146,000 were purchased for cash during the year.
2. Investments were sold at cost.
3. Plant assets costing $36,000 were sold for $15,000, resulting in a gain of $5,000.
4. A cash dividend of $48,000 was declared and paid during the year.

Instructions
Prepare a statement of cash flows using the indirect method.

Cash from operations $95,800

*P17-10B Data for Ziebert Company are presented in P17-9B. Further analysis reveals that accounts payable pertain to merchandise creditors.

Prepare a statement of cash flows—direct method.
(SO 6)

Instructions
Prepare a statement of cash flows for Ziebert Company using the direct method.

Cash from operations $95,800

P17-11B Presented below are the comparative balance sheets for Marin Company at December 31.

Prepare a statement of cash flows—indirect method.
(SO 3)

MARIN COMPANY
Comparative Balance Sheets
December 31

Assets	2010	2009
Cash	$ 41,000	$ 57,000
Accounts receivable	77,000	64,000
Inventory	172,000	140,000
Prepaid expenses	12,140	16,540
Land	110,000	150,000
Equipment	215,000	175,000
Accumulated depreciation—equipment	(70,000)	(42,000)
Building	250,000	250,000
Accumulated depreciation—building	(70,000)	(50,000)
Total	$737,140	$760,540
Liabilities and Stockholders' Equity		
Accounts payable	$ 58,000	$ 45,000
Bonds payable	235,000	265,000
Common stock, $1 par	280,000	250,000
Retained earnings	164,140	200,540
Total	$737,140	$760,540

Additional information:

1. Operating expenses include depreciation expense $55,000 and charges from prepaid expenses of $4,400.
2. Land was sold for cash at cost.
3. Cash dividends of $84,290 were paid.
4. Net income for 2010 was $47,890.
5. Equipment was purchased for $80,000 cash. In addition, equipment costing $40,000 with a book value of $33,000 was sold for $37,000 cash.
6. Bonds were converted at face value by issuing 30,000 shares of $1 par value common stock.

Instructions
Prepare a statement of cash flows for 2010 using the indirect method.

Cash from operations $71,290

786 Chapter 17 Statement of Cash Flows

PROBLEMS: SET C

Visit the book's companion website at **www.wiley.com/college/weygandt** and choose the Student Companion site to access Problem Set C.

CONTINUING COOKIE CHRONICLE

(*Note:* This is a continuation of the Cookie Chronicle from Chapters 1 through 16.)

CCC17 Natalie has prepared the balance sheet and income statement of Cookie & Coffee Creations Inc. and would like you to prepare the cash flow statement.

Go to the book's companion website,
www.wiley.com/college/weygandt,
to see the completion of this problem.

BROADENING YOUR PERSPECTIVE

FINANCIAL REPORTING AND ANALYSIS

Financial Reporting Problem: PepsiCo, Inc.

BYP17-1 Refer to the financial statements of **PepsiCo**'s, presented in Appendix A, and answer the following questions.

(a) What was the amount of net cash provided by operating activities for the year ended December 29, 2007? For the year ended December 30, 2006?
(b) What was the amount of increase or decrease in cash and cash equivalents for the year ended December 29, 2007? For the year ended December 30, 2006?
(c) Which method of computing net cash provided by operating activities does PepsiCo use?
(d) From your analysis of the 2007 statement of cash flows, did the change in accounts and notes receivable require or provide cash? Did the change in inventories require or provide cash? Did the change in accounts payable and other current liabilities require or provide cash?
(e) What was the net outflow or inflow of cash from investing activities for the year ended December 29, 2007?
(f) What was the amount of interest paid in the year ended December 29, 2007? What was the amount of income taxes paid in the year ended December 29, 2007? (See Note 14.)

Comparative Analysis Problem: PepsiCo, Inc. vs. The Coca-Cola Company

BYP17-2 PepsiCo's financial statements are presented in Appendix A. Financial statements of **The Coca-Cola Company** are presented in Appendix B.

Instructions
(a) Based on the information contained in these financial statements, compute free cash flow for each company.
(b) What conclusions concerning the management of cash can be drawn from these data?

Exploring the Web

BYP17-3 Purpose: Learn about the SEC.

Address: www.sec.gov/index.html, or go to **www.wiley.com/college/weygandt**

From the SEC homepage, choose **About the SEC**.

Broadening Your Perspective

Instructions
Answer the following questions.

(a) How many enforcement actions does the SEC take each year against securities law violators? What are typical infractions?

(b) After the Depression, Congress passed the Securities Acts of 1933 and 1934 to improve investor confidence in the markets. What two "common sense" notions are these laws based on?

(c) Who was the President of the United States at the time of the creation of the SEC? Who was the first SEC Chairperson?

BYP17-4 Purpose: Use the Internet to view SEC filings.

Address: biz.yahoo.com/i, or go to **www.wiley.com/college/weygandt**

Steps

1. Type in a company name.
2. Choose **Profile**.
3. Choose **SEC Filings**. (This will take you to Yahoo-Edgar Online.)

Instructions
Answer the following questions.

(a) What company did you select?
(b) Which filing is the most recent? What is the date?
(c) What other recent SEC filings are available for your viewing?

CRITICAL THINKING

Decision Making Across the Organization

BYP17-5 Ron Nord and Lisa Smith are examining the following statement of cash flows for Carpino Company for the year ended January 31, 2010.

CARPINO COMPANY
Statement of Cash Flows
For the Year Ended January 31, 2010

Sources of cash	
From sales of merchandise	$380,000
From sale of capital stock	420,000
From sale of investment (purchased below)	80,000
From depreciation	55,000
From issuance of note for truck	20,000
From interest on investments	6,000
Total sources of cash	961,000
Uses of cash	
For purchase of fixtures and equipment	330,000
For merchandise purchased for resale	258,000
For operating expenses (including depreciation)	160,000
For purchase of investment	75,000
For purchase of truck by issuance of note	20,000
For purchase of treasury stock	10,000
For interest on note payable	3,000
Total uses of cash	856,000
Net increase in cash	$105,000

Ron claims that Carpino's statement of cash flows is an excellent portrayal of a superb first year with cash increasing $105,000. Lisa replies that it was not a superb first year. Rather, she says, the year was an operating failure, that the statement is presented incorrectly, and that $105,000 is not the actual increase in cash. The cash balance at the beginning of the year was $140,000.

Instructions

With the class divided into groups, answer the following.

(a) Using the data provided, prepare a statement of cash flows in proper form using the indirect method. The only noncash items in the income statement are depreciation and the gain from the sale of the investment.

(b) With whom do you agree, Ron or Lisa? Explain your position.

Communication Activity

BYP17-6 Kyle Benson, the owner-president of Computer Services Company, is unfamiliar with the statement of cash flows that you, as his accountant, prepared. He asks for further explanation.

Instructions

Write him a brief memo explaining the form and content of the statement of cash flows as shown in Illustration 17-13 (page 746).

Ethics Case

BYP17-7 Tappit Corp. is a medium-sized wholesaler of automotive parts. It has 10 stockholders who have been paid a total of $1 million in cash dividends for 8 consecutive years. The board's policy requires that, for this dividend to be declared, net cash provided by operating activities as reported in Tappit's current year's statement of cash flows must exceed $1 million. President and CEO Willie Morton's job is secure so long as he produces annual operating cash flows to support the usual dividend.

At the end of the current year, controller Robert Jennings presents president Willie Morton with some disappointing news: The net cash provided by operating activities is calculated by the indirect method to be only $970,000. The president says to Robert, "We must get that amount above $1 million. Isn't there some way to increase operating cash flow by another $30,000?" Robert answers, "These figures were prepared by my assistant. I'll go back to my office and see what I can do." The president replies, "I know you won't let me down, Robert."

Upon close scrutiny of the statement of cash flows, Robert concludes that he can get the operating cash flows above $1 million by reclassifying a $60,000, 2-year note payable listed in the financing activities section as "Proceeds from bank loan—$60,000." He will report the note instead as "Increase in payables—$60,000" and treat it as an adjustment of net income in the operating activities section. He returns to the president, saying, "You can tell the board to declare their usual dividend. Our net cash flow provided by operating activities is $1,030,000." "Good man, Robert! I knew I could count on you," exults the president.

Instructions

(a) Who are the stakeholders in this situation?

(b) Was there anything unethical about the president's actions? Was there anything unethical about the controller's actions?

(c) Are the board members or anyone else likely to discover the misclassification?

"All About You" Activity

BYP17-8 In this chapter you learned that companies prepare a statement of cash flows in order to keep track of their sources and uses of cash and to help them plan for their future cash needs. Planning for your own short- and long-term cash needs is every bit as important as it is for a company.

Instructions

Read the article ("Financial Uh-Oh? No Problem") provided at **www.fool.com/personal-finance/saving/index.aspx**, and answer the following questions.

(a) Describe the three factors that determine how much money you should set aside for short-term needs.

(b) How many months of living expenses does the article suggest to set aside?

(c) Estimate how much you should set aside based upon your current situation. Are you closer to Cliff's scenario or to Prudence's?

Answers to Insight and Accounting Across the Organization Questions

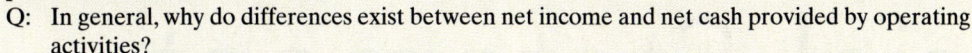

p. 735 Net *What*?

Q: In general, why do differences exist between net income and net cash provided by operating activities?

A: *The differences are explained by differences in the timing of the reporting of revenues and expenses under accrual accounting versus cash. Under accrual accounting, companies report revenues when earned, even if cash hasn't been received, and they report expenses when incurred, even if cash hasn't been paid.*

p. 744 GM Must Sell More Cars

Q: Why does GM's cash provided by operating activities drop so precipitously when the company's sales figures decline?

A: *GM's cash inflow is directly related to how many cars it sells. But many of its cash outflows are not tied to sales—they are "fixed." For example, many of its employee payroll costs are very rigid due to labor contracts. Therefore, even though sales (and therefore cash inflows) fall, these cash outflows don't decline.*

Answers to Self-Study Questions

1. c 2. a 3. b 4. a 5. c 6. d 7. b 8. c 9. d 10. b 11. b 12. a 13. b
14. a 15. d *16. b *17. b *18. c *19. d

Remember to go back to the Navigator box on the chapter-opening page and check off your completed work.

Chapter 18

Financial Statement Analysis

STUDY OBJECTIVES

After studying this chapter, you should be able to:

1 Discuss the need for comparative analysis.
2 Identify the tools of financial statement analysis.
3 Explain and apply horizontal analysis.
4 Describe and apply vertical analysis.
5 Identify and compute ratios used in analyzing a firm's liquidity, profitability, and solvency.
6 Understand the concept of earning power, and how irregular items are presented.
7 Understand the concept of quality of earnings.

✓ The Navigator

Scan **Study Objectives**	■
Read **Feature Story**	■
Read **Preview**	■
Read text and answer **DO IT!** p. 797 ■ p. 810 ■ p. 815 ■ p. 817 ■	
Work **Comprehensive** **DO IT!** p. 818	■
Review **Summary of Study Objectives**	■
Answer **Self-Study Questions**	■
Complete **Assignments**	■

Feature Story

IT PAYS TO BE PATIENT

In 2008 *Forbes* magazine listed Warren Buffett as the richest person in the world. His estimated wealth was $62 billion, give or take a few million. How much is $62 billion? If you invested $62 billion in an investment earning just 4%, you could spend $6.8 million per day—every day—forever. How did Mr. Buffett amass this wealth? Through careful investing.

You think you might want to follow Buffett's example and transform your humble nest-egg into a mountain of cash. His techniques have been widely circulated and emulated, but never practiced with the same degree of success. Buffett epitomizes a "value investor." To this day he applies the same basic techniques he learned in the 1950s from the great value investor

790

Benjamin Graham. That means he spends his time looking for companies that have good long-term potential but are currently underpriced. He invests in companies that have low exposure to debt and that reinvest their earnings for future growth. He does not get caught up in fads or the latest trend. Instead, he looks for companies in industries with sound economics and ones that have high returns on stockholders' equity. He looks for steady earnings trends and high margins.

Buffett sat out on the dot-com mania in the 1990s, when investors put lots of money into fledgling high-tech firms, because he did not find dot-com companies that met his criteria. He didn't get to enjoy the stock price boom on the way up, but on the other hand, he didn't have to ride the price back down to earth. Instead, when the dot-com bubble burst, and nearly everyone else was suffering from investment shock, he swooped in and scooped up deals on companies that he had been following for years.

So, how does Mr. Buffett spend his money? Basically, he doesn't! He still lives in the same house that he purchased in Omaha, Nebraska, in 1958 for $31,500. He still drives his own car (a Cadillac DTS). And in case you were thinking that his kids are riding the road to easy street, think again. Buffett has committed to giving virtually all of his money to charity before he dies.

So, given that neither you nor anyone else will be inheriting Mr. Buffett's riches, you should start honing your financial analysis skills as soon as possible. A good way for you to begin your career as a successful investor is to master the fundamentals of financial analysis discussed in this chapter.

Inside Chapter 18...

- **Keeping Up to Date as an Investor**   (p. 808)
- **What Does "Non-Recurring" Really Mean?** (p. 814)

Preview of Chapter 18

We can learn an important lesson from Warren Buffett. The lesson: Study companies carefully if you wish to invest. Do not get caught up in fads, but instead find companies that are financially healthy. Using some of the basic decision tools presented in this book, you can perform a rudimentary analysis on any U.S. company and draw basic conclusions about its financial health. Although it would not be wise for you to bet your life savings on a company's stock relying solely on your current level of knowledge, we strongly encourage you to practice your new skills wherever possible. Only with practice will you improve your ability to interpret financial numbers.

Before unleashing you on the world of high finance, we will present a few more important concepts and techniques, as well as provide you with one more comprehensive review of corporate financial statements. We use all of the decision tools presented in this text to analyze a single company—J.C. Penney Company, one of the country's oldest and largest retail store chains.

The content and organization of Chapter 18 are as follows.

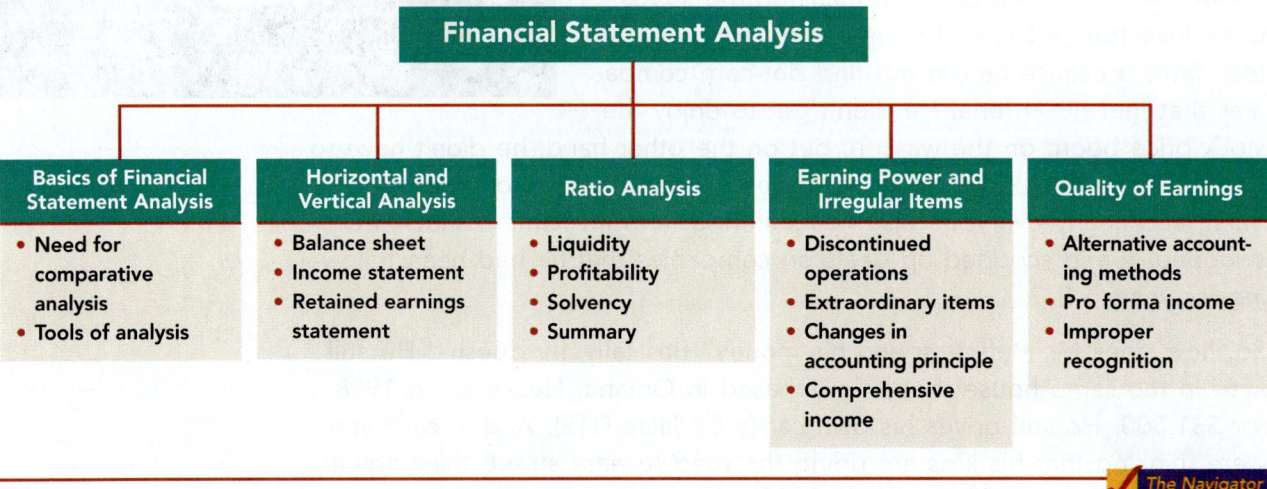

BASICS OF FINANCIAL STATEMENT ANALYSIS

Analyzing financial statements involves evaluating three characteristics: a company's liquidity, profitability, and solvency. A **short-term creditor**, such as a bank, is primarily interested in liquidity—the ability of the borrower to pay obligations when they come due. The liquidity of the borrower is extremely important in evaluating the safety of a loan. A **long-term creditor**, such as a bondholder, looks to profitability and solvency measures that indicate the company's ability to survive over a long period of time. Long-term creditors consider such measures as the amount of debt in the company's capital structure and its ability to meet interest payments. Similarly, **stockholders** look at the profitability and solvency of the company. They want to assess the likelihood of dividends and the growth potential of the stock.

Need for Comparative Analysis

STUDY OBJECTIVE 1
Discuss the need for comparative analysis.

Every item reported in a financial statement has significance. When J.C. Penney Company, Inc. reports cash of $2,471 million on its balance sheet, we know the company had that amount of cash on the balance sheet date. But, we do not know whether the amount represents an increase over prior years, or whether it is adequate in relation to the company's need for cash. To obtain such information, we need to compare the amount of cash with other financial statement data.

Comparisons can be made on a number of different bases. Three are illustrated in this chapter:

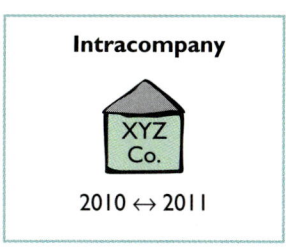

1. **Intracompany basis.** This basis compares an item or financial relationship **within a company** in the current year with the same item or relationship in one or more prior years. For example, J.C. Penney can compare its cash balance at the end of the current year with last year's balance to find the amount of the increase or decrease. Likewise, J.C. Penney can compare the percentage of cash to current assets at the end of the current year with the percentage in one or more prior years. Intracompany comparisons are useful in detecting changes in financial relationships and significant trends.

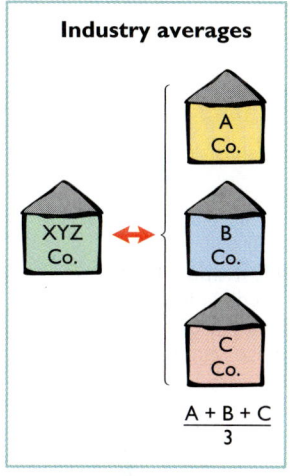

2. **Industry averages.** This basis compares an item or financial relationship of a company with **industry averages** (or **norms**) published by financial ratings organizations such as Dun & Bradstreet, Moody's, and Standard & Poor's. For example, J.C. Penney's net income can be compared with the average net income of all companies in the retail chain-store industry. Comparisons with industry averages provide information as to a company's relative performance within the industry.

3. **Intercompany basis.** This basis compares an item or financial relationship of one company with the same item or relationship in **one or more competing companies.** Analysts make these comparisons on the basis of the published financial statements of the individual companies. For example, we can compare J.C. Penney's total sales for the year with the total sales of a major competitor such as Kmart. Intercompany comparisons are useful in determining a company's competitive position.

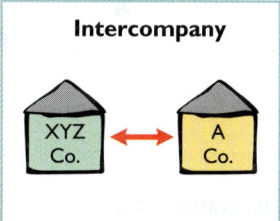

Tools of Analysis

We use various tools to evaluate the significance of financial statement data. Three commonly used tools are these:

> **STUDY OBJECTIVE 2**
> Identify the tools of financial statement analysis.

- **Horizontal analysis** evaluates a series of financial statement data over a period of time.
- **Vertical analysis** evaluates financial statement data by expressing each item in a financial statement as a percent of a base amount.
- **Ratio analysis** expresses the relationship among selected items of financial statement data.

Horizontal analysis is used primarily in intracompany comparisons. Two features in published financial statements facilitate this type of comparison: First, each of the basic financial statements presents comparative financial data for a minimum of two years. Second, a summary of selected financial data is presented for a series of five to ten years or more. *Vertical analysis* is used in both intra- and intercompany comparisons. *Ratio analysis* is used in all three types of comparisons. In the following sections, we explain and illustrate each of the three types of analysis.

HORIZONTAL ANALYSIS

Horizontal analysis, also called **trend analysis**, is a technique for evaluating a series of financial statement data over a period of time. Its purpose is to determine the increase or decrease that has taken place. This change

> **STUDY OBJECTIVE 3**
> Explain and apply horizontal analysis.

794 Chapter 18 Financial Statement Analysis

may be expressed as either an amount or a percentage. For example, the recent net sales figures of J.C. Penney Company are as follows.

Illustration 18-1
J.C. Penney Company's net sales

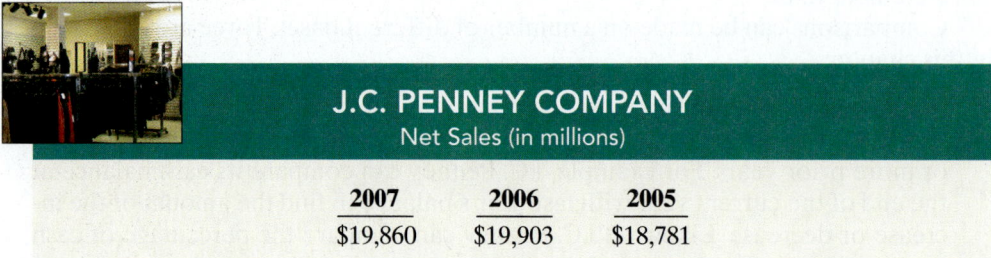

J.C. PENNEY COMPANY
Net Sales (in millions)

2007	2006	2005
$19,860	$19,903	$18,781

If we assume that 2005 is the base year, we can measure all percentage increases or decreases from this base period amount as follows.

Illustration 18-2
Formula for horizontal analysis of changes since base period

$$\text{Change Since Base Period} = \frac{\text{Current Year Amount} - \text{Base Year Amount}}{\text{Base Year Amount}}$$

For example, we can determine that net sales for J.C. Penney increased from 2005 to 2006 approximately 6% [($19,903 − $18,781) ÷ $18,781]. Similarly, we can determine that net sales increased from 2005 to 2007 approximately 5.7% [($19,860 − $18,781) ÷ $18,781].

Alternatively, we can express current year sales as a percentage of the base period. We do this by dividing the current year amount by the base year amount, as shown below.

Illustration 18-3
Formula for horizontal analysis of current year in relation to base year

$$\text{Current Results in Relation to Base Period} = \frac{\text{Current Year Amount}}{\text{Base Year Amount}}$$

Illustration 18-4 presents this analysis for J.C. Penney for a three-year period using 2005 as the base period.

Illustration 18-4
Horizontal analysis of J.C. Penney Company's net sales in relation to base period

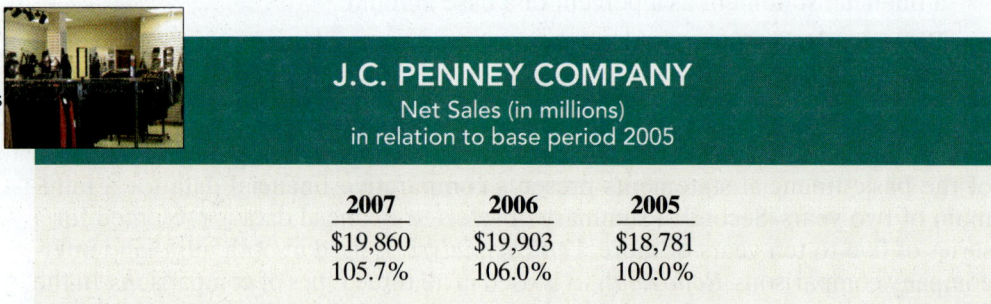

J.C. PENNEY COMPANY
Net Sales (in millions)
in relation to base period 2005

2007	2006	2005
$19,860	$19,903	$18,781
105.7%	106.0%	100.0%

Balance Sheet

To further illustrate horizontal analysis, we will use the financial statements of Quality Department Store Inc., a fictional retailer. Illustration 18-5 presents a horizontal analysis of its two-year condensed balance sheets, showing dollar and percentage changes.

Illustration 18-5
Horizontal analysis of balance sheets

QUALITY DEPARTMENT STORE INC.
Condensed Balance Sheets
December 31

	2007	2006	Increase or (Decrease) during 2007 Amount	Percent
Assets				
Current assets	$1,020,000	$ 945,000	$ 75,000	7.9%
Plant assets (net)	800,000	632,500	167,500	26.5%
Intangible assets	15,000	17,500	(2,500)	(14.3%)
Total assets	$1,835,000	$1,595,000	$240,000	15.0%
Liabilities				
Current liabilities	$ 344,500	$ 303,000	$ 41,500	13.7%
Long-term liabilities	487,500	497,000	(9,500)	(1.9%)
Total liabilities	832,000	800,000	32,000	4.0%
Stockholders' Equity				
Common stock, $1 par	275,400	270,000	5,400	2.0%
Retained earnings	727,600	525,000	202,600	38.6%
Total stockholders' equity	1,003,000	795,000	208,000	26.2%
Total liabilities and stockholders' equity	$1,835,000	$1,595,000	$240,000	15.0%

The comparative balance sheets in Illustration 18-5 show that a number of significant changes have occurred in Quality Department Store's financial structure from 2006 to 2007:

- In the assets section, plant assets (net) increased $167,500, or 26.5%.
- In the liabilities section, current liabilities increased $41,500, or 13.7%.
- In the stockholders' equity section, retained earnings increased $202,600, or 38.6%.

These changes suggest that the company expanded its asset base during 2007 and **financed this expansion primarily by retaining income** rather than assuming additional long-term debt.

Income Statement

Illustration 18-6 (page 796) presents a horizontal analysis of the two-year condensed income statements of Quality Department Store Inc. for the years 2007 and 2006. Horizontal analysis of the income statements shows the following changes:

- Net sales increased $260,000, or 14.2% ($260,000 ÷ $1,837,000).
- Cost of goods sold increased $141,000, or 12.4% ($141,000 ÷ $1,140,000).
- Total operating expenses increased $37,000, or 11.6% ($37,000 ÷ $320,000).

Overall, gross profit and net income were up substantially. Gross profit increased 17.1%, and net income, 26.5%. Quality's profit trend appears favorable.

Illustration 18-6
Horizontal analysis of income statements

QUALITY DEPARTMENT STORE INC.
Condensed Income Statements
For the Years Ended December 31

	2007	2006	Increase or (Decrease) during 2007 Amount	Percent
Sales	$2,195,000	$1,960,000	$235,000	12.0%
Sales returns and allowances	98,000	123,000	(25,000)	(20.3%)
Net sales	2,097,000	1,837,000	260,000	14.2%
Cost of goods sold	1,281,000	1,140,000	141,000	12.4%
Gross profit	816,000	697,000	119,000	17.1%
Selling expenses	253,000	211,500	41,500	19.6%
Administrative expenses	104,000	108,500	(4,500)	(4.1%)
Total operating expenses	357,000	320,000	37,000	11.6%
Income from operations	459,000	377,000	82,000	21.8%
Other revenues and gains				
Interest and dividends	9,000	11,000	(2,000)	(18.2%)
Other expenses and losses				
Interest expense	36,000	40,500	(4,500)	(11.1%)
Income before income taxes	432,000	347,500	84,500	24.3%
Income tax expense	168,200	139,000	29,200	21.0%
Net income	$ 263,800	$ 208,500	$ 55,300	26.5%

HELPFUL HINT
Note that though the amount column is additive (the total is $55,300), the percentage column is not additive (26.5% is not the total). A separate percentage has been calculated for each item.

Retained Earnings Statement

Illustration 18-7 presents a horizontal analysis of Quality Department Store's comparative retained earnings statements. Analyzed horizontally, net income increased $55,300, or 26.5%, whereas dividends on the common stock increased only $1,200, or 2%. We saw in the horizontal analysis of the balance sheet that ending retained earnings increased 38.6%. As indicated earlier, the company retained a significant portion of net income to finance additional plant facilities.

Illustration 18-7
Horizontal analysis of retained earnings statements

QUALITY DEPARTMENT STORE INC.
Retained Earnings Statements
For the Years Ended December 31

	2007	2006	Increase or (Decrease) during 2007 Amount	Percent
Retained earnings, Jan. 1	$525,000	$376,500	$148,500	39.4%
Add: Net income	263,800	208,500	55,300	26.5%
	788,800	585,000	203,800	
Deduct: Dividends	61,200	60,000	1,200	2.0%
Retained earnings, Dec. 31	$727,600	$525,000	$202,600	38.6%

Horizontal analysis of changes from period to period is relatively straightforward and is quite useful. But complications can occur in making the computations. If an item has no value in a base year or preceding year but does have a value in the next year, we cannot compute a percentage change. Similarly, if a negative amount appears in the base or preceding period and a positive amount exists the following year (or vice versa), no percentage change can be computed.

DO IT!

Summary financial information for Rosepatch Company is as follows.

	December 31, 2010	December 31, 2009
Current assets	$234,000	$180,000
Plant assets (net)	756,000	420,000
Total assets	$990,000	$600,000

Compute the amount and percentage changes in 2010 using horizontal analysis, assuming 2009 is the base year.

HORIZONTAL ANALYSIS

action plan
✔ Find the percentage change by dividing the amount of the increase by the 2009 amount (base year).

Solution

	Increase in 2010	
	Amount	Percent
Current assets	$ 54,000	30% [($234,000 − $180,000) ÷ $180,000]
Plant assets (net)	336,000	80% [($756,000 − $420,000) ÷ $420,000]
Total assets	$390,000	65% [($990,000 − $600,000) ÷ $600,000]

Related exercise material: **BE18-2, BE18-3, BE18-5, BE18-6, BE18-7, E18-1, E18-3, E18-4,** and **DO IT!** 18-1.

VERTICAL ANALYSIS

Vertical analysis, also called **common-size analysis**, is a technique that expresses each financial statement item as a percent of a base amount. On a balance sheet we might say that current assets are 22% of total assets—*total assets* being the base amount. Or on an income statement, we might say that selling expenses are 16% of net sales—*net sales* being the base amount.

STUDY OBJECTIVE 4
Describe and apply vertical analysis.

Balance Sheet

Illustration 18-8 (page 798) presents the vertical analysis of Quality Department Store Inc.'s comparative balance sheets. The base for the asset items is **total assets**. The base for the liability and stockholders' equity items is **total liabilities and stockholders' equity**.

Vertical analysis shows the relative size of each category in the balance sheet. It also can show the **percentage change** in the individual asset, liability, and stockholders' equity items. For example, we can see that current assets decreased from 59.2% of total assets in 2006 to 55.6% in 2007 (even though the absolute dollar amount increased $75,000 in that time). Plant assets (net) have increased from 39.7% to 43.6% of total assets. Retained earnings have increased from 32.9% to 39.7% of total liabilities and stockholders' equity. These results reinforce the earlier observations that **Quality is choosing to finance its growth through retention of earnings rather than through issuing additional debt**.

Income Statement

Illustration 18-9 (page 798) shows vertical analysis of Quality's income statements. Cost of goods sold as a percentage of net sales declined 1% (62.1% vs. 61.1%), and total operating expenses declined 0.4% (17.4% vs. 17.0%). As a result, it is not surprising

Illustration 18-8
Vertical analysis of balance sheets

QUALITY DEPARTMENT STORE INC.
Condensed Balance Sheets
December 31

	2007 Amount	2007 Percent	2006 Amount	2006 Percent
Assets				
Current assets	$1,020,000	55.6%	$ 945,000	59.2%
Plant assets (net)	800,000	43.6%	632,500	39.7%
Intangible assets	15,000	0.8%	17,500	1.1%
Total assets	$1,835,000	100.0%	$1,595,000	100.0%
Liabilities				
Current liabilities	$ 344,500	18.8%	$ 303,000	19.0%
Long-term liabilities	487,500	26.5%	497,000	31.2%
Total liabilities	832,000	45.3%	800,000	50.2%
Stockholders' Equity				
Common stock, $1 par	275,400	15.0%	270,000	16.9%
Retained earnings	727,600	39.7%	525,000	32.9%
Total stockholders' equity	1,003,000	54.7%	795,000	49.8%
Total liabilities and stockholders' equity	$1,835,000	100.0%	$1,595,000	100.0%

HELPFUL HINT

The formula for calculating these balance sheet percentages is:

$$\frac{\text{Each item on B/S}}{\text{Total assets}} = \%$$

Illustration 18-9
Vertical analysis of income statements

QUALITY DEPARTMENT STORE INC.
Condensed Income Statements
For the Years Ended December 31

	2007 Amount	2007 Percent	2006 Amount	2006 Percent
Sales	$2,195,000	104.7%	$1,960,000	106.7%
Sales returns and allowances	98,000	4.7%	123,000	6.7%
Net sales	2,097,000	100.0%	1,837,000	100.0%
Cost of goods sold	1,281,000	61.1%	1,140,000	62.1%
Gross profit	816,000	38.9%	697,000	37.9%
Selling expenses	253,000	12.0%	211,500	11.5%
Administrative expenses	104,000	5.0%	108,500	5.9%
Total operating expenses	357,000	17.0%	320,000	17.4%
Income from operations	459,000	21.9%	377,000	20.5%
Other revenues and gains				
Interest and dividends	9,000	0.4%	11,000	0.6%
Other expenses and losses				
Interest expense	36,000	1.7%	40,500	2.2%
Income before income taxes	432,000	20.6%	347,500	18.9%
Income tax expense	168,200	8.0%	139,000	7.5%
Net income	$ 263,800	12.6%	$ 208,500	11.4%

HELPFUL HINT

The formula for calculating these income statement percentages is:

$$\frac{\text{Each item on I/S}}{\text{Net sales}} = \%$$

to see net income as a percent of net sales increase from 11.4% to 12.6%. Quality appears to be a profitable enterprise that is becoming even more successful.

An associated benefit of vertical analysis is that it enables you to compare companies of different sizes. For example, Quality's main competitor is a JC Penney store in a nearby town. Using vertical analysis, we can compare the condensed income statements of Quality Department Store Inc. (a small retail company) with J.C. Penney Company, Inc. (a giant international retailer), as shown in Illustration 18-10.

Illustration 18-10
Intercompany income statement comparison

CONDENSED INCOME STATEMENTS
(in thousands)

	Quality Department Store Inc.		J. C. Penney Company[1]	
	Dollars	Percent	Dollars	Percent
Net sales	$2,097	100.0%	$19,860,000	100.0%
Cost of goods sold	1,281	61.1%	12,189,000	61.4%
Gross profit	816	38.9%	7,671,000	38.6%
Selling and administrative expenses	357	17.0%	5,357,000	27.0%
Income from operations	459	21.9%	2,314,000	11.6%
Other expenses and revenues (including income taxes)	195	9.3%	1,203,000	6.0%
Net income	$ 264	12.6%	$ 1,111,000	5.6%

J.C. Penney's net sales are 9,471 times greater than the net sales of relatively tiny Quality Department Store. But vertical analysis eliminates this difference in size. The percentages show that Quality's and J.C. Penney's gross profit rates were comparable at 38.9% and 38.6%. However, the percentages related to income from operations were significantly different at 21.9% and 11.6%. This disparity can be attributed to Quality's selling and administrative expense percentage (17%) which is much lower than J.C. Penney's (27.0%). Although J.C. Penney earned net income more than 4,208 times larger than Quality's, J.C. Penney's net income as a **percent of each sales dollar** (5.6%) is only 44% of Quality's (12.6%).

RATIO ANALYSIS

Ratio analysis expresses the relationship among selected items of financial statement data. A ratio expresses the mathematical relationship between one quantity and another. The relationship is expressed in terms of either a percentage, a rate, or a simple proportion. To illustrate, in 2007 Nike, Inc., had current assets of $8,076.5 million and current liabilities of $2,584.0 million. We can find the relationship between these two measures by dividing current assets by current liabilities. The alternative means of expression are:

STUDY OBJECTIVE 5
Identify and compute ratios used in analyzing a firm's liquidity, profitability, and solvency.

    Percentage: Current assets are 313% of current liabilities.
    Rate: Current assets are 3.13 times current liabilities.
    Proportion: The relationship of current assets to liabilities is 3.13:1.

To analyze the primary financial statements, we can use ratios to evaluate liquidity, profitability, and solvency. Illustration 18-11 describes these classifications.

---

[1] 2007 Annual Report J.C. Penney Company, Inc. (Dallas, Texas).

Illustration 18-11
Financial ratio classifications

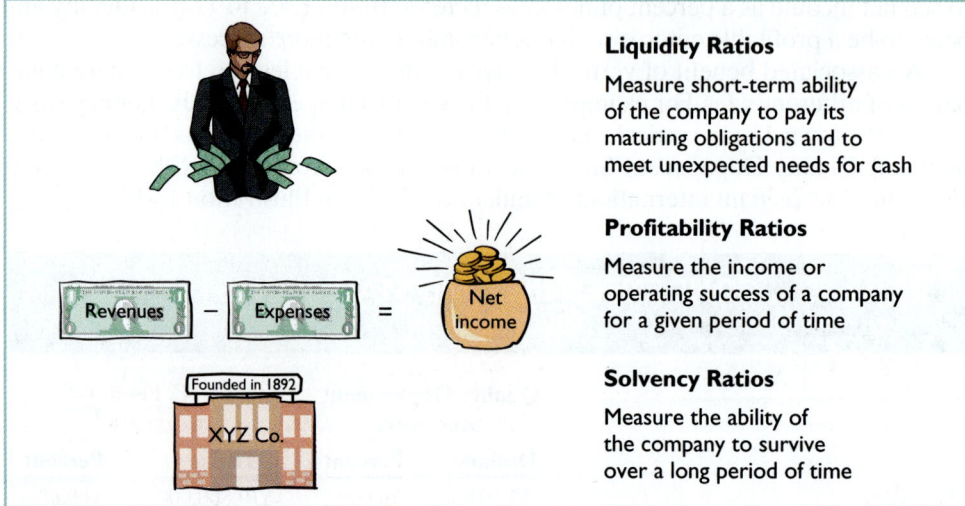

Liquidity Ratios
Measure short-term ability of the company to pay its maturing obligations and to meet unexpected needs for cash

Profitability Ratios
Measure the income or operating success of a company for a given period of time

Solvency Ratios
Measure the ability of the company to survive over a long period of time

INTERNATIONAL NOTE
As more countries adopt international accounting standards, the ability of analysts to compare companies from different countries should improve. However, international standards are open to widely varying interpretations. In addition, some countries adopt international standards "with modifications." As a consequence, most cross-country comparisons are still not as transparent as within-country comparisons.

ETHICS NOTE
Companies can affect the current ratio by speeding up or withholding payments on accounts payable just before the balance sheet date. Management can alter the cash balance by increasing or decreasing long-term assets or long-term debt, or by issuing or purchasing equity shares.

Ratios can provide clues to underlying conditions that may not be apparent from individual financial statement components. However, a single ratio by itself is not very meaningful. Thus, in the discussion of ratios we will use the following types of comparisons.

1. **Intracompany comparisons** for two years for Quality Department Store.
2. **Industry average comparisons** based on median ratios for department stores.
3. **Intercompany comparisons** based on J.C. Penney Company as Quality Department Store's principal competitor.

Liquidity Ratios

Liquidity ratios measure the short-term ability of the company to pay its maturing obligations and to meet unexpected needs for cash. Short-term creditors such as bankers and suppliers are particularly interested in assessing liquidity. The ratios we can use to determine the enterprise's short-term debt-paying ability are the current ratio, the acid-test ratio, receivables turnover, and inventory turnover.

1. CURRENT RATIO
The **current ratio** is a widely used measure for evaluating a company's liquidity and short-term debt-paying ability. The ratio is computed by dividing current assets by current liabilities. Illustration 18-12 shows the 2007 and 2006 current ratios for Quality Department Store and comparative data.

Illustration 18-12
Current ratio

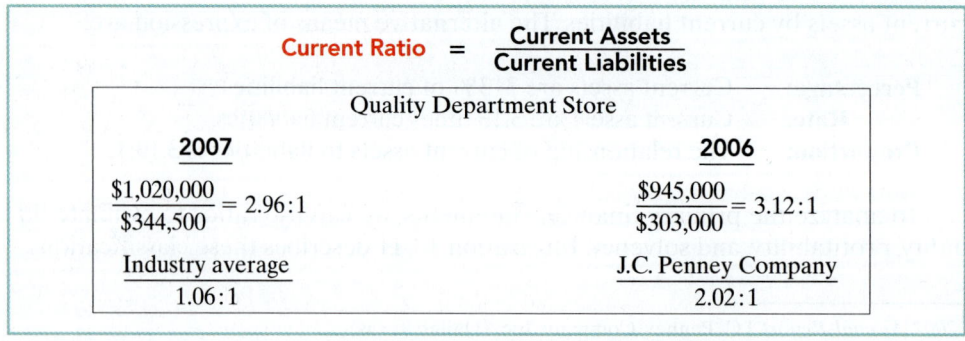

$$\text{Current Ratio} = \frac{\text{Current Assets}}{\text{Current Liabilities}}$$

Quality Department Store

2007	2006
$\dfrac{\$1{,}020{,}000}{\$344{,}500} = 2.96:1$	$\dfrac{\$945{,}000}{\$303{,}000} = 3.12:1$
Industry average	J.C. Penney Company
1.06:1	2.02:1

What does the ratio actually mean? The 2007 ratio of 2.96:1 means that for every dollar of current liabilities, Quality has $2.96 of current assets. Quality's current ratio has decreased in the current year. But, compared to the industry average of 1.06:1, Quality appears to be reasonably liquid. J.C. Penney has a current ratio of 2.02 which indicates it has adequate current assets relative to its current liabilities.

The current ratio is sometimes referred to as the **working capital ratio**; **working capital** is current assets minus current liabilities. The current ratio is a more dependable indicator of liquidity than working capital. Two companies with the same amount of working capital may have significantly different current ratios.

The current ratio is only one measure of liquidity. It does not take into account the **composition** of the current assets. For example, a satisfactory current ratio does not disclose the fact that a portion of the current assets may be tied up in slow-moving inventory. A dollar of cash would be more readily available to pay the bills than a dollar of slow-moving inventory.

2. ACID-TEST RATIO

The **acid-test (quick) ratio** is a measure of a company's immediate short-term liquidity. We compute this ratio by dividing the sum of cash, short-term investments, and net receivables by current liabilities. Thus, it is an important complement to the current ratio. For example, assume that the current assets of Quality Department Store for 2007 and 2006 consist of the items shown in Illustration 18-13.

> **HELPFUL HINT**
> Can any company operate successfully without working capital? Yes, if it has very predictable cash flows and solid earnings. A number of companies (e.g., Whirlpool, American Standard, and Campbell's Soup) are pursuing this goal. The rationale: Less money tied up in working capital means more money to invest in the business.

QUALITY DEPARTMENT STORE INC.
Balance Sheet (partial)

	2007	2006
Current assets		
Cash	$ 100,000	$155,000
Short-term investments	20,000	70,000
Receivables (net*)	230,000	180,000
Inventory	620,000	500,000
Prepaid expenses	50,000	40,000
Total current assets	$1,020,000	$945,000

*Allowance for doubtful accounts is $10,000 at the end of each year.

Illustration 18-13
Current assets of Quality Department Store

Cash, short-term investments, and receivables (net) are highly liquid compared to inventory and prepaid expenses. The inventory may not be readily saleable, and the prepaid expenses may not be transferable to others. Thus, the acid-test ratio measures **immediate** liquidity. The 2007 and 2006 acid-test ratios for Quality Department Store and comparative data are as follows.

$$\text{Acid-Test Ratio} = \frac{\text{Cash + Short-Term Investments + Receivables (Net)}}{\text{Current Liabilities}}$$

Quality Department Store

2007	2006
$\dfrac{\$100{,}000 + \$20{,}000 + \$230{,}000}{\$344{,}500} = 1.02:1$	$\dfrac{\$155{,}000 + \$70{,}000 + \$180{,}000}{\$303{,}000} = 1.34:1$
Industry average	J.C. Penney Company
0.29:1	0.87:1

Illustration 18-14
Acid-test ratio

The ratio has declined in 2007. Is an acid-test ratio of 1.02:1 adequate? This depends on the industry and the economy. When compared with the industry average of 0.29:1 and Penney's of 0.87:1, Quality's acid-test ratio seems adequate.

3. RECEIVABLES TURNOVER

We can measure liquidity by how quickly a company can convert certain assets to cash. How liquid, for example, are the receivables? The ratio used to assess the liquidity of the receivables is **receivables turnover**. It measures the number of times, on average, the company collects receivables during the period. We compute receivables turnover by dividing net credit sales (net sales less cash sales) by the average net receivables. Unless seasonal factors are significant, average net receivables can be computed from the beginning and ending balances of the net receivables.[2]

Assume that all sales are credit sales. The balance of net receivables at the beginning of 2006 is $200,000. Illustration 18-15 shows the receivables turnover for Quality Department Store and comparative data. Quality's receivables turnover improved in 2007. The turnover of 10.2 times is substantially lower than J.C. Penney's 57 times, and is also lower than the department store industry's average of 28.23 times.

Illustration 18-15
Receivables turnover

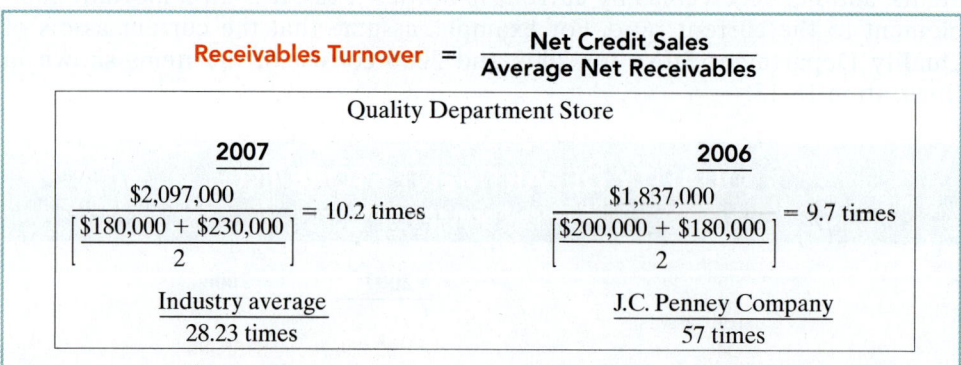

Average Collection Period. A popular variant of the receivables turnover ratio is to convert it to an **average collection period** in terms of days. To do so, we divide the receivables turnover ratio into 365 days. For example, the receivables turnover of 10.2 times divided into 365 days gives an average collection period of approximately 36 days. This means that receivables are collected on average every 36 days, or about every 5 weeks. Analysts frequently use the average collection period to assess the effectiveness of a company's credit and collection policies. The general rule is that the collection period should not greatly exceed the credit term period (the time allowed for payment).

4. INVENTORY TURNOVER

Inventory turnover measures the number of times, on average, the inventory is sold during the period. Its purpose is to measure the liquidity of the inventory. We compute the inventory turnover by dividing cost of goods sold by the average inventory. Unless seasonal factors are significant, we can use the beginning and ending inventory balances to compute average inventory.

Assuming that the inventory balance for Quality Department Store at the beginning of 2006 was $450,000, its inventory turnover and comparative data are as shown in Illustration 18-16. Quality's inventory turnover declined slightly in 2007.

---

[2]If seasonal factors are significant, the average receivables balance might be determined by using monthly amounts.

The turnover of 2.3 times is relatively low compared with the industry average of 7.0 and J.C. Penney's 3.5. Generally, the faster the inventory turnover, the less cash a company has tied up in inventory and the less the chance of inventory obsolescence.

Illustration 18-16
Inventory turnover

$$\text{Inventory Turnover} = \frac{\text{Cost of Goods Sold}}{\text{Average Inventory}}$$

Quality Department Store

2007	2006
$\dfrac{\$1{,}281{,}000}{\left[\dfrac{\$500{,}000 + \$620{,}000}{2}\right]} = 2.3 \text{ times}$	$\dfrac{\$1{,}140{,}000}{\left[\dfrac{\$450{,}000 + \$500{,}000}{2}\right]} = 2.4 \text{ times}$
Industry average 7.0 times	J.C. Penney Company 3.5 times

Days in Inventory. A variant of inventory turnover is the **days in inventory**. We calculate it by dividing the inventory turnover into 365. For example, Quality's 2007 inventory turnover of 2.3 times divided into 365 is approximately 159 days. An average selling time of 159 days is also relatively high compared with the industry average of 52.1 days (365 ÷ 7.0) and J.C. Penney's 104.3 days (365 ÷ 3.5).

Inventory turnover ratios vary considerably among industries. For example, grocery store chains have a turnover of 10 times and an average selling period of 37 days. In contrast, jewelry stores have an average turnover of 1.3 times and an average selling period of 281 days.

Profitability Ratios

Profitability ratios measure the income or operating success of a company for a given period of time. Income, or the lack of it, affects the company's ability to obtain debt and equity financing. It also affects the company's liquidity position and the company's ability to grow. As a consequence, both creditors and investors are interested in evaluating earning power—profitability. Analysts frequently use profitability as the ultimate test of management's operating effectiveness.

5. PROFIT MARGIN

Profit margin is a measure of the percentage of each dollar of sales that results in net income. We can compute it by dividing net income by net sales. Illustration 18-17 shows Quality Department Store's profit margin and comparative data.

ALTERNATIVE TERMINOLOGY
Profit margin is also called the *rate of return on sales*.

Illustration 18-17
Profit margin

$$\text{Profit Margin} = \frac{\text{Net Income}}{\text{Net Sales}}$$

Quality Department Store

2007	2006
$\dfrac{\$263{,}800}{\$2{,}097{,}000} = 12.6\%$	$\dfrac{\$208{,}500}{\$1{,}837{,}000} = 11.4\%$
Industry average 3.7%	J.C. Penney Company 5.6%

Quality experienced an increase in its profit margin from 2006 to 2007. Its profit margin is unusually high in comparison with the industry average of 3.7% and J.C. Penney's 5.6%.

High-volume (high inventory turnover) enterprises such as grocery stores (Safeway or Kroger) and discount stores (Kmart or Wal-Mart) generally experience low profit margins. In contrast, low-volume enterprises such as jewelry stores (Tiffany & Co.) or airplane manufacturers (Boeing Co.) have high profit margins.

6. ASSET TURNOVER

Asset turnover measures how efficiently a company uses its assets to generate sales. It is determined by dividing net sales by average assets. The resulting number shows the dollars of sales produced by each dollar invested in assets. Unless seasonal factors are significant, we can use the beginning and ending balance of total assets to determine average total assets. Assuming that total assets at the beginning of 2006 were $1,446,000, the 2007 and 2006 asset turnover for Quality Department Store and comparative data are shown in Illustration 18-18.

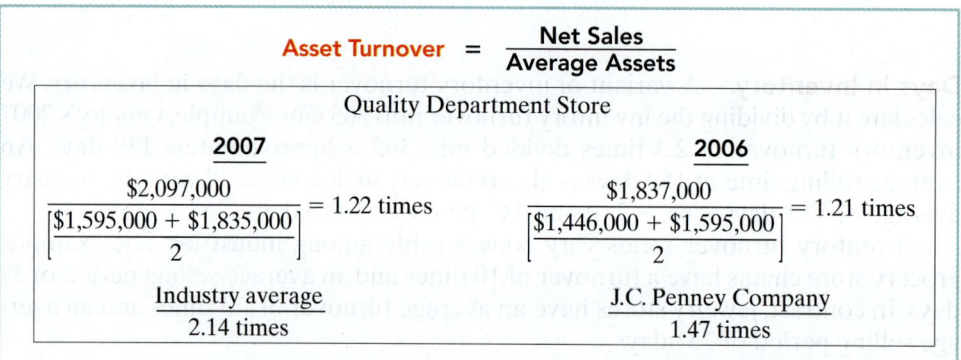

Illustration 18-18
Asset turnover

Asset turnover shows that in 2007 Quality generated sales of $1.22 for each dollar it had invested in assets. The ratio changed little from 2006 to 2007. Quality's asset turnover is below the industry average of 2.14 times and J.C. Penney's ratio of 1.47 times.

Asset turnover ratios vary considerably among industries. For example, a large utility company like Consolidated Edison (New York) has a ratio of 0.49 times, and the large grocery chain Kroger Stores has a ratio of 4.34 times.

7. RETURN ON ASSETS

An overall measure of profitability is **return on assets**. We compute this ratio by dividing net income by average assets. The 2007 and 2006 return on assets for Quality Department Store and comparative data are shown below.

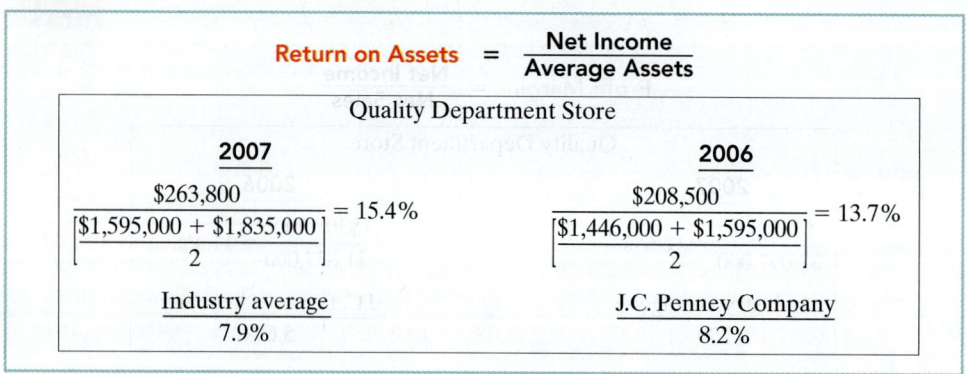

Illustration 18-19
Return on assets

Quality's return on assets improved from 2006 to 2007. Its return of 15.4% is very high compared with the department store industry average of 7.9% and J.C. Penney's 8.2%.

8. RETURN ON COMMON STOCKHOLDERS' EQUITY

Another widely used profitability ratio is **return on common stockholders' equity**. It measures profitability from the common stockholders' viewpoint. This ratio shows how many dollars of net income the company earned for each dollar invested by the owners. We compute it by dividing net income by average common stockholders' equity. Assuming that common stockholders' equity at the beginning of 2006 was $667,000, Illustration 18-20 shows the 2007 and 2006 ratios for Quality Department Store and comparative data.

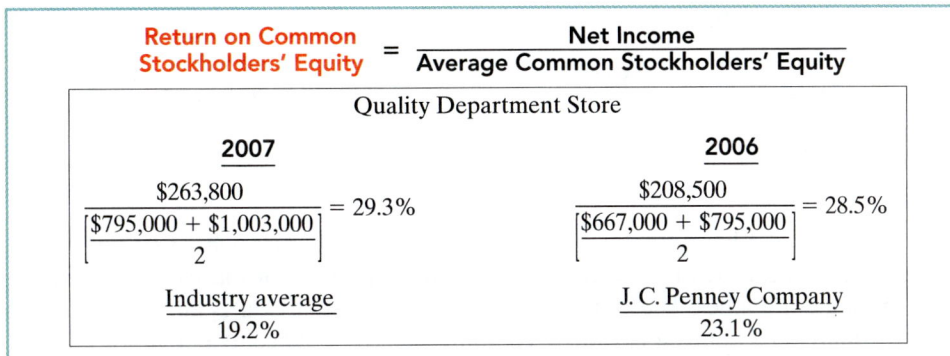

Illustration 18-20
Return on common stockholders' equity

Quality's rate of return on common stockholders' equity is high at 29.3%, considering an industry average of 19.2% and a rate of 23.1% for J.C. Penney.

With Preferred Stock. When a company has preferred stock, we must deduct **preferred dividend** requirements from net income to compute income available to common stockholders. Similarly, we deduct the par value of preferred stock (or call price, if applicable) from total stockholders' equity to determine the amount of common stockholders' equity used in this ratio. The ratio then appears as follows.

$$\text{Return on Common Stockholders' Equity} = \frac{\text{Net Income} - \text{Preferred Dividends}}{\text{Average Common Stockholders' Equity}}$$

Illustration 18-21
Return on common stockholders' equity with preferred stock

Note that Quality's rate of return on stockholders' equity (29.3%) is substantially higher than its rate of return on assets (15.4%). The reason is that Quality has made effective use of **leverage**. **Leveraging** or **trading on the equity** at a gain means that the company has borrowed money at a lower rate of interest than it is able to earn by using the borrowed money. Leverage enables Quality Department Store to use money supplied by nonowners to increase the return to the owners. A comparison of the rate of return on total assets with the rate of interest paid for borrowed money indicates the profitability of trading on the equity. Quality Department Store earns more on its borrowed funds than it has to pay in the form of interest. Thus the return to stockholders exceeds the return on the assets, due to benefits from the positive leveraging.

9. EARNINGS PER SHARE (EPS)

Earnings per share (EPS) is a measure of the net income earned on each share of common stock. It is computed by dividing net income by the number of weighted average common shares outstanding during the year. A measure of net income earned on a per share basis provides a useful perspective for determining profitability. Assuming that there is no change in the number of outstanding shares during 2006 and that the 2007 increase occurred midyear, Illustration 18-22 shows the net income per share for Quality Department Store for 2007 and 2006.

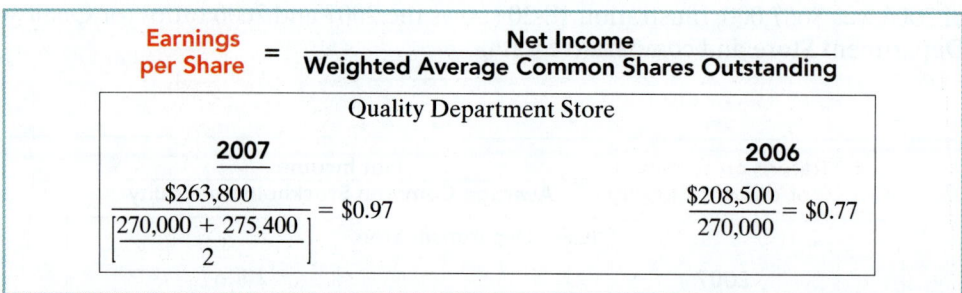

Illustration 18-22
Earnings per share

Note that no industry or J.C. Penney data are presented. Such comparisons are not meaningful because of the wide variations in the number of shares of outstanding stock among companies. The only meaningful EPS comparison is an intracompany trend comparison: Quality's earnings per share increased 20 cents per share in 2007. This represents a 26% increase over the 2006 earnings per share of 77 cents.

The terms "earnings per share" and "net income per share" refer to the amount of net income applicable to each share of **common stock**. Therefore, in computing EPS, if there are preferred dividends declared for the period, we must deduct them from net income to determine income available to the common stockholders.

10. PRICE-EARNINGS RATIO

The **price-earnings (P-E) ratio** is an oft-quoted measure of the ratio of the market price of each share of common stock to the earnings per share. The price-earnings (P-E) ratio reflects investors' assessments of a company's future earnings. We compute it by dividing the market price per share of the stock by earnings per share. Assuming that the market price of Quality Department Store Inc. stock is $8 in 2006 and $12 in 2007, the price-earnings ratio computation is as follows.

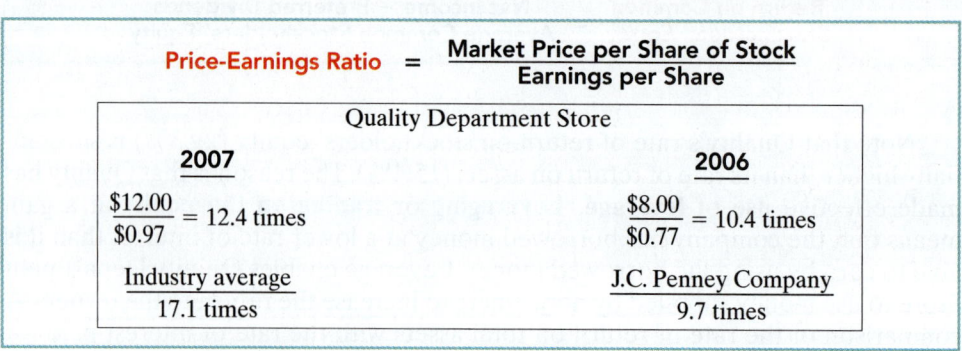

Illustration 18-23
Price-earnings ratio

In 2007 each share of Quality's stock sold for 12.4 times the amount that the company earned on each share. Quality's price-earnings ratio is lower than the industry average of 17.1 times, but 28% higher than the ratio of 9.7 times for J.C. Penney. The average price-earnings ratio for the stocks that constitute the Standard and Poor's 500 Index (500 largest U.S. firms) in early 2007 was approximately 19.1 times.

11. PAYOUT RATIO

The **payout ratio** measures the percentage of earnings distributed in the form of cash dividends. We compute it by dividing cash dividends by net income. Companies that have high growth rates generally have low payout ratios because they reinvest most of their net income into the business. The 2007 and 2006 payout ratios for Quality Department Store are computed as shown in Illustration 18-24.

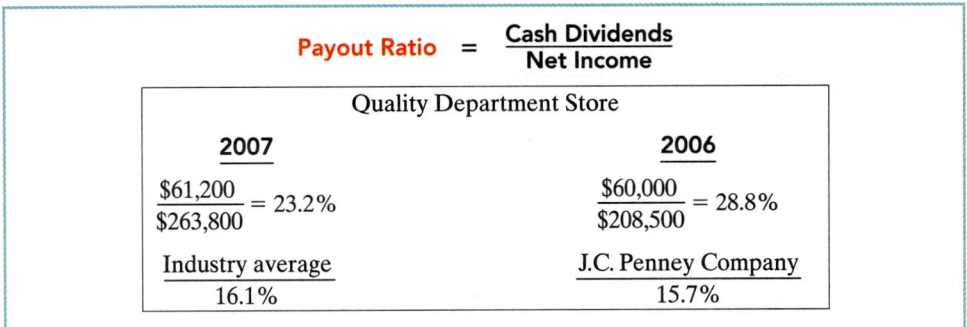

Illustration 18-24
Payout ratio

Quality's payout ratio is higher than J.C. Penney's payout ratio of 15.7%. As indicated earlier (page 797), Quality funded its purchase of plant assets through retention of earnings but still is able to pay dividends.

Solvency Ratios

Solvency ratios measure the ability of a company to survive over a long period of time. Long-term creditors and stockholders are particularly interested in a company's ability to pay interest as it comes due and to repay the face value of debt at maturity. Debt to total assets and times interest earned are two ratios that provide information about debt-paying ability.

12. DEBT TO TOTAL ASSETS RATIO

The **debt to total assets ratio** measures the percentage of the total assets that creditors provide. We compute it by dividing total debt (both current and long-term liabilities) by total assets. This ratio indicates the company's degree of leverage. It also provides some indication of the company's ability to withstand losses without impairing the interests of creditors. The higher the percentage of debt to total assets, the greater the risk that the company may be unable to meet its maturing obligations. The 2007 and 2006 ratios for Quality Department Store and comparative data are as follows.

$$\text{Debt to Total Assets Ratio} = \frac{\text{Total Debt}}{\text{Total Assets}}$$

Quality Department Store

2007	2006
$\frac{\$832,000}{\$1,835,000} = 45.3\%$	$\frac{\$800,000}{\$1,595,000} = 50.2\%$
Industry average	J.C. Penney Company
40.1%	62.9%

Illustration 18-25
Debt to total assets ratio

A ratio of 45.3% means that creditors have provided 45.3% of Quality Department Store's total assets. Quality's 45.3% is above the industry average of 40.1%. It is considerably below the high 62.9% ratio of J.C. Penney. The lower the ratio, the more equity "buffer" there is available to the creditors. Thus, from the creditors' point of view, a low ratio of debt to total assets is usually desirable.

The adequacy of this ratio is often judged in the light of the company's earnings. Generally, companies with relatively stable earnings (such as public utilities) have higher debt to total assets ratios than cyclical companies with widely fluctuating earnings (such as many high-tech companies).

13. TIMES INTEREST EARNED

Times interest earned provides an indication of the company's ability to meet interest payments as they come due. We compute it by dividing income before interest expense and income taxes by interest expense. Illustration 18-26 shows the 2007 and 2006 ratios for Quality Department Store and comparative data. Note that times interest earned uses income before income taxes and interest expense. This represents the amount available to cover interest. For Quality Department Store the 2007 amount of $468,000 is computed by taking the income before income taxes of $432,000 and adding back the $36,000 of interest expense.

> **ALTERNATIVE TERMINOLOGY**
> Times interest earned is also called *interest coverage*.

Illustration 18-26
Times interest earned

$$\text{Times Interest Earned} = \frac{\text{Income before Income Taxes and Interest Expense}}{\text{Interest Expense}}$$

Quality Department Store

2007	2006
$\dfrac{\$468{,}000}{\$36{,}000} = 13$ times	$\dfrac{\$388{,}000}{\$40{,}500} = 9.6$ times
Industry average	J.C. Penney Company
10.7 times	12.3 times

Quality's interest expense is well covered at 13 times, compared with the industry average of 10.7 times and J.C. Penney's 12.3 times.

INVESTOR INSIGHT

Keeping Up to Date as an Investor

Today, investors have access to information provided by corporate managers that used to be available only to professional analysts. Corporate managers have always made themselves available to security analysts for questions at the end of every quarter. Now, because of a combination of new corporate disclosure requirements by the Securities and Exchange Commission and technologies that make communication to large numbers of people possible at a very low price, the average investor can listen in on these discussions. For example, one individual investor, Matthew Johnson, a *Nortel Networks* local area network engineer in Belfast, Northern Ireland, "stayed up past midnight to listen to *Apple Computer*'s Internet conference call. Hearing the company's news 'from the dog's mouth,' he says 'gave me better information' than hunting through chat-rooms."

Source: Jeff D. Opdyke, "Individuals Pick Up on Conference Calls," *Wall Street Journal*, November 20, 2000.

? If you want to keep current with the financial and operating developments of a company in which you own shares, what are some ways you can do so?

Summary of Ratios

Illustration 18-27 summarizes the ratios discussed in this chapter. The summary includes the formula and purpose or use of each ratio.

Illustration 18-27
Summary of liquidity, profitability, and solvency ratios

Ratio	Formula	Purpose or Use
Liquidity Ratios		
1. Current ratio	$\dfrac{\text{Current assets}}{\text{Current liabilities}}$	Measures short-term debt-paying ability.
2. Acid-test (quick) ratio	$\dfrac{\text{Cash + Short-term investments + Receivables (net)}}{\text{Current liabilities}}$	Measures immediate short-term liquidity.
3. Receivables turnover	$\dfrac{\text{Net credit sales}}{\text{Average net receivables}}$	Measures liquidity of receivables.
4. Inventory turnover	$\dfrac{\text{Cost of goods sold}}{\text{Average inventory}}$	Measures liquidity of inventory.
Profitability Ratios		
5. Profit margin	$\dfrac{\text{Net income}}{\text{Net sales}}$	Measures net income generated by each dollar of sales.
6. Asset turnover	$\dfrac{\text{Net sales}}{\text{Average assets}}$	Measures how efficiently assets are used to generate sales.
7. Return on assets	$\dfrac{\text{Net income}}{\text{Average assets}}$	Measures overall profitability of assets.
8. Return on common stockholders' equity	$\dfrac{\text{Net income − Preferred dividends}}{\text{Average common stockholders' equity}}$	Measures profitability of owners' investment.
9. Earnings per share (EPS)	$\dfrac{\text{Net income − Preferred dividends}}{\text{Weighted average common shares outstanding}}$	Measures net income earned on each share of common stock.
10. Price-earnings (P-E) ratio	$\dfrac{\text{Market price per share of stock}}{\text{Earnings per share}}$	Measures the ratio of the market price per share to earnings per share.
11. Payout ratio	$\dfrac{\text{Cash dividends}}{\text{Net income}}$	Measures percentage of earnings distributed in the form of cash dividends.
Solvency Ratios		
12. Debt to total assets ratio	$\dfrac{\text{Total debt}}{\text{Total assets}}$	Measures the percentage of total assets provided by creditors.
13. Times interest earned	$\dfrac{\text{Income before income taxes and interest expense}}{\text{Interest expense}}$	Measures ability to meet interest payments as they come due.

DO IT!

RATIO ANALYSIS

The condensed financial statements of John Cully Company, for the years ended June 30, 2010 and 2009, are presented below.

JOHN CULLY COMPANY
Balance Sheets
June 30

	(in thousands)	
Assets	**2010**	**2009**
Current assets		
Cash and cash equivalents	$ 553.3	$ 611.6
Accounts receivable (net)	776.6	664.9
Inventories	768.3	653.5
Prepaid expenses and other current assets	204.4	269.2
Total current assets	2,302.6	2,199.2
Property, plant, and equipment (net)	694.2	647.0
Investments	12.3	12.6
Intangibles and other assets	876.7	849.3
Total assets	$3,885.8	$3,708.1
Liabilities and Stockholders' Equity		
Current liabilities	$1,497.7	$1,322.0
Long-term liabilities	679.5	637.1
Stockholders' equity—common	1,708.6	1,749.0
Total liabilities and stockholders' equity	$3,885.8	$3,708.1

JOHN CULLY COMPANY
Income Statements
For the Year Ended June 30

	(in thousands)	
	2010	**2009**
Revenues	$6,336.3	$5,790.4
Costs and expenses		
Cost of goods sold	1,617.4	1,476.3
Selling and administrative expenses	4,007.6	3,679.0
Interest expense	13.9	27.1
Total costs and expenses	5,638.9	5,182.4
Income before income taxes	697.4	608.0
Income tax expense	291.3	232.6
Net income	$ 406.1	$ 375.4

Compute the following ratios for 2010 and 2009.

(a) Current ratio.
(b) Inventory turnover. (Inventory on 6/30/08 was $599.0.)
(c) Profit margin ratio.
(d) Return on assets. (Assets on 6/30/08 were $3,349.9.)
(e) Return on common stockholders' equity. (Stockholders' equity on 6/30/08 was $1,795.9.)
(f) Debt to total assets ratio.
(g) Times interest earned.

Solution

	2010	2009
(a) Current ratio:		
$2,302.6 ÷ $1,497.7 =	1.5:1	
$2,199.2 ÷ $1,322.0 =		1.7:1
(b) Inventory turnover:		
$1,617.4 ÷ [($768.3 + $653.5) ÷ 2] =	2.3 times	
$1,476.3 ÷ [($653.5 + $599.0) ÷ 2] =		2.4 times
(c) Profit margin:		
$406.1 ÷ $6,336.3	6.4%	
$375.4 ÷ $5,790.4		6.5%
(d) Return on assets:		
$406.1 ÷ [($3,885.8 + $3,708.1) ÷ 2] =	10.7%	
$375.4 ÷ [($3,708.1 + $3,349.9) ÷ 2] =		10.6%
(e) Return on common stockholders' equity:		
$406.1 ÷ [($1,708.6 + $1,749.0) ÷ 2] =	23.5%	
$375.4 ÷ [($1,749.0 + $1,795.9) ÷ 2] =		21.2%
(f) Debt to total assets ratio:		
($1,497.7 + $679.5) ÷ $3,885.8 =	56.0%	
($1,322.0 + $637.1) ÷ $3,708.1 =		52.8%
(g) Times interest earned:		
($406.1 + $291.3 + $13.9) ÷ $13.9 =	51.2 times	
($375.4 + $232.6 + $27.1) ÷ $27.1 =		23.4 times

action plan
✔ Remember that the current ratio includes all current assets. The acid-test ratio uses only cash, short-term investments, and net receivables.

✔ Use average balances for turnover ratios like inventory, receivables, and assets.

Related exercise material: **BE18-9, BE18-10, BE18-12, BE18-13, E18-5, E18-7, E18-8, E18-9, E18-11,** and **DO IT! 18-2.**

EARNING POWER AND IRREGULAR ITEMS

STUDY OBJECTIVE 6
Understand the concept of earning power, and how irregular items are presented.

Users of financial statements are interested in the concept of earning power. **Earning power** means the normal level of income to be obtained in the future. Earning power differs from actual net income by the amount of irregular revenues, expenses, gains, and losses. Users are interested in earning power because it helps them derive an estimate of future earnings without the "noise" of irregular items.

For users of financial statements to determine earning power or regular income, the "irregular" items are separately identified on the income statement. Companies report two types of "irregular" items.

1. Discontinued operations.
2. Extraordinary items.

These "irregular" items are reported net of income taxes. That is, the income statement first reports income tax on the income before "irregular" items. Then the amount of tax for each of the listed "irregular" items is computed. The general concept is "let the tax follow income or loss."

Discontinued Operations

Discontinued operations refers to the disposal of a **significant component** of a business. Examples involve stopping an entire activity or eliminating a major class of customers. For example, Kmart reported as discontinued operations its decision to terminate its interest in four business activities, including PACE Membership Warehouse and PayLess Drug Stores Northwest.

Following the disposal of a significant component, the company should report on its income statement both income from continuing operations and income (or loss) from discontinued operations. **The income (loss) from discontinued operations consists of two parts: the income (loss) from operations** and **the gain (loss) on disposal of the segment**.

To illustrate, assume that during 2010 Acro Energy Inc. has income before income taxes of $800,000. During 2010 Acro discontinued and sold its unprofitable chemical division. The loss in 2010 from chemical operations (net of $60,000 taxes) was $140,000. The loss on disposal of the chemical division (net of $30,000 taxes) was $70,000. Assuming a 30% tax rate on income, Illustration 18-28 shows Acro's income statement presentation.

Illustration 18-28
Statement presentation of discontinued operations

HELPFUL HINT
Observe the dual disclosures: (1) The results of operations of the discontinued division must be eliminated from the results of continuing operations. (2) The company must also report the disposal of the operation.

ACRO ENERGY INC.
Income Statement (partial)
For the Year Ended December 31, 2010

Income before income taxes		$800,000
Income tax expense		240,000
Income from continuing operations		560,000
Discontinued operations		
Loss from operations of chemical division, net of $60,000 income tax saving	$140,000	
Loss from disposal of chemical division, net of $30,000 income tax saving	70,000	210,000
Net income		$350,000

Note that the statement uses the caption "Income from continuing operations," and adds a new section "Discontinued operations". **The new section reports both the operating loss and the loss on disposal net of applicable income taxes.** This presentation clearly indicates the separate effects of continuing operations and discontinued operations on net income.

Extraordinary Items

Extraordinary items are events and transactions that meet two conditions: They are (1) **unusual in nature**, and (2) **infrequent in occurrence**. To be *unusual*, the item should be abnormal and only incidentally related to the company's customary activities. To be *infrequent*, the item should not be reasonably expected to recur in the foreseeable future.

A company must evaluate both criteria in terms of its operating environment. Thus, Weyerhaeuser Co. reported the $36 million in damages to its timberland caused by the volcanic eruption of Mount St. Helens as an extraordinary item. The eruption was both unusual and infrequent. In contrast, Florida Citrus Company does not report frost damage to its citrus crop as an extraordinary item, because frost damage is not infrequent. Illustration 18-29 (next page) shows the classification of extraordinary and ordinary items.

Companies report extraordinary items net of taxes in a separate section of the income statement, immediately below discontinued operations. To illustrate, assume that in 2010 a foreign government expropriated property held as an investment by Acro Energy Inc. If the loss is $70,000 before applicable income taxes of $21,000, the income statement will report a deduction of $49,000, as shown in

Extraordinary items

1. Effects of major natural casualties, if rare in the area.

2. Expropriation (takeover) of property by a foreign government.

3. Effects of a newly enacted law or regulation, such as a property condemnation action.

Ordinary items

1. Effects of major natural casualties, not uncommon in the area.

2. Write-down of inventories or write-off of receivables.

3. Losses attributable to labor strikes.

4. Gains or losses from sales of property, plant, or equipment.

Illustration 18-29
Examples of extraordinary and ordinary items

Illustration 18-30. When there is an extraordinary item to report, the company adds the caption "Income before extraordinary item" immediately before the section for the extraordinary item. This presentation clearly indicates the effect of the extraordinary item on net income.

Illustration 18-30
Statement presentation of extraordinary items

ACRO ENERGY INC.
Income Statement (partial)
For the Year Ended December 31, 2010

Income before income taxes		$800,000
Income tax expense		240,000
Income from continuing operations		560,000
Discontinued operations		
Loss from operations of chemical division, net of $60,000 income tax saving	$140,000	
Loss from disposal of chemical division, net of $30,000 income tax saving	70,000	210,000
Income before extraordinary item		350,000
Extraordinary item		
Expropriation of investment, net of $21,000 income tax saving		49,000
Net income		$301,000

HELPFUL HINT

If there are no discontinued operations, the third line of the income statement would be labeled "Income before extraordinary item."

What if a transaction or event meets one (but not both) of the criteria for an extraordinary item? In that case the company reports it under either "Other revenues and gains" or "Other expenses and losses" at its gross amount (not net of tax). This is true, for example, of gains (losses) resulting from the sale of property, plant, and equipment, as explained in Chapter 10. It is quite common for companies to use the label "Non-recurring charges" for losses that do not meet the extraordinary item criteria.

INVESTOR INSIGHT

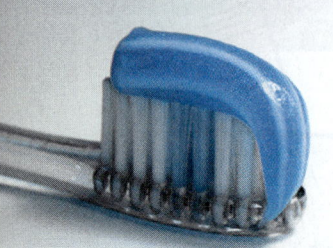

What Does "Non-Recurring" Really Mean?

Many companies incur restructuring charges as they attempt to reduce costs. They often label these items in the income statement as "non-recurring" charges to suggest that they are isolated events which are unlikely to occur in future periods. The question for analysts is, are these costs really one-time, "non-recurring" events, or do they reflect problems that the company will be facing for many periods in the future? If they are one-time events, they can be largely ignored when trying to predict future earnings.

But some companies report "one-time" restructuring charges over and over again. For example, toothpaste and other consumer-goods giant Procter & Gamble Co. reported a restructuring charge in 12 consecutive quarters. Motorola had "special" charges in 14-consecutive quarters. On the other hand, other companies have a restructuring charge only once in a five- or ten-year period. There appears to be no substitute for careful analysis of the numbers that comprise net income.

 If a company takes a large restructuring charge, what is the effect on the company's current income statement versus future ones?

Changes in Accounting Principle

ETHICS NOTE
Changes in accounting principle should result in financial statements that are more informative for statement users. They should *not* be used to artificially improve the reported performance or financial position of the corporation.

For ease of comparison, users of financial statements expect companies to prepare such statements on a basis **consistent** with the preceding period. A **change in accounting principle** occurs when the principle used in the current year is different from the one used in the preceding year. Accounting rules permit a change when management can show that the new principle is preferable to the old principle. An example is a change in inventory costing methods (such as FIFO to average cost).

Companies report most changes in accounting principle retroactively. That is, they report both the current period and previous periods using the new principle. As a result the same principle applies in all periods. This treatment improves the ability to compare results across years.

Comprehensive Income

The income statement reports most revenues, expenses, gains, and losses recognized during the period. However, over time, specific exceptions to this general practice have developed. Certain items now bypass income and are reported directly in stockholders' equity.

For example, in Chapter 16 you learned that companies do not include in income any unrealized gains and losses on available-for-sale securities. Instead, they report such gains and losses in the balance sheet as adjustments to stockholders' equity. Why are these gains and losses on available-for-sale securities excluded from net income? Because disclosing them separately (1) reduces the volatility of net income due to fluctuations in fair value, yet (2) informs the financial statement user of the gain or loss that would be incurred if the securities were sold at fair value.

Many analysts have expressed concern over the significant increase in the number of items that bypass the income statement. They feel that such reporting has reduced the usefulness of the income statement. To address this concern, in addition to reporting net income, a company must also report comprehensive income. **Comprehensive income** includes all changes in stockholders' equity during a period except those resulting from investments by stockholders and distributions to stockholders. A number of alternative formats for reporting comprehensive income are allowed. These formats are discussed in advanced accounting courses.

DO IT!

IRREGULAR ITEMS

In its proposed 2010 income statement, AIR Corporation reports income before income taxes $400,000, extraordinary loss due to earthquake $100,000, income taxes $120,000 (not including irregular items), loss on operation of discontinued flower division $50,000, and loss on disposal of discontinued flower division $90,000. The income tax rate is 30%. Prepare a correct income statement, beginning with "Income before income taxes."

Solution

AIR CORPORATION
Income Statement (partial)
For the Year Ended December 31, 2010

Income before income taxes		$400,000
Income tax expense		120,000
Income from continuing operations		280,000
Discontinued operations		
Loss from operation of flower		
division, net of $15,000 tax saving	$35,000	
Loss on disposal of flower		
division, net of $27,000 tax saving	63,000	98,000
Income before extraordinary item		182,000
Extraordinary earthquake loss, net of		
$30,000 tax saving		70,000
Net income		$112,000

action plan

✔ Recall that a loss is extraordinary if it is both unusual and infrequent.

✔ Disclose the income tax effect of each component of income, beginning with income before any irregular items.

✔ Show discontinued operations before extraordinary items.

Related exercise material: **BE18-14, BE18-15, E18-12, E18-13,** and  **18-3.**

QUALITY OF EARNINGS

In evaluating the financial performance of a company, the quality of a company's earnings is of extreme importance to analysts. A company that has a high **quality of earnings** provides full and transparent information that will not confuse or mislead users of the financial statements.

STUDY OBJECTIVE 7
Understand the concept of quality of earnings.

The issue of quality of earnings has taken on increasing importance because recent accounting scandals suggest that some companies are spending too much time managing their income and not enough time managing their business. Here are some of the factors affecting quality of earnings.

Alternative Accounting Methods

Variations among companies in the application of generally accepted accounting principles may hamper comparability and reduce quality of earnings. For example, one company may use the FIFO method of inventory costing, while another company in the same industry may use LIFO. If inventory is a significant asset to both companies, it is unlikely that their current ratios are comparable. For example, if General Motors Corporation had used FIFO instead of LIFO for inventory valuation, its inventories in a recent year would have been 26% higher, which significantly affects the current ratio (and other ratios as well).

In addition to differences in inventory costing methods, differences also exist in reporting such items as depreciation, depletion, and amortization. Although these differences in accounting methods might be detectable from reading the notes to the financial statements, adjusting the financial data to compensate for the different methods is often difficult, if not impossible.

Pro Forma Income

Companies whose stock is publicly traded are required to present their income statement following generally accepted accounting principles (GAAP). In recent years, many companies have also reported a second measure of income, called pro forma income. Pro forma income usually excludes items that the company thinks are unusual or nonrecurring. For example, at one time, Cisco Systems (a high-tech company) reported a quarterly net loss under GAAP of $2.7 billion. Cisco reported pro forma income for the same quarter as a profit of $230 million. This large difference in profits between GAAP income numbers and pro forma income is not unusual these days. For example, during one 9-month period the 100 largest firms on the Nasdaq stock exchange reported a total pro forma income of $19.1 billion, but a total loss as measured by GAAP of $82.3 billion—a difference of about $100 billion!

To compute pro forma income, companies generally can exclude any items they deem inappropriate for measuring their performance. Many analysts and investors are critical of the practice of using pro forma income because these numbers often make companies look better than they really are. As the financial press noted, pro forma numbers might be called EBS, which stands for "earnings before bad stuff." Companies, on the other hand, argue that pro forma numbers more clearly indicate sustainable income because they exclude unusual and nonrecurring expenses. "Cisco's technique gives readers of financial statements a clear picture of Cisco's normal business activities," the company said in a statement issued in response to questions about its pro forma income accounting.

The SEC has provided some guidance on how companies should present pro forma information. Stay tuned: Everyone seems to agree that pro forma numbers can be useful if they provide insights into determining a company's sustainable income. However, many companies have abused the flexibility that pro forma numbers allow and have used the measure as a way to put their companies in a good light.

Improper Recognition

Because some managers have felt pressure from Wall Street to continually increase earnings, they have manipulated the earnings numbers to meet these expectations. The most common abuse is the improper recognition of revenue. One practice that companies are using is *channel stuffing*: Offering deep discounts on their products to customers, companies encourage their customers to buy early (stuff the channel) rather than later. This lets the company report good earnings in the current period, but it often leads to a disaster in subsequent periods because customers have no need for additional goods. To illustrate, Bristol-Myers Squibb at one time indicated that it used sales incentives to encourage wholesalers to buy more drugs than needed to meet patients' demands. As a result, the company had to issue revised financial statements showing corrected revenues and income.

Another practice is the improper capitalization of operating expenses. The classic case is WorldCom. It capitalized over $7 billion dollars of operating expenses so that it would report positive net income. In other situations, companies fail to report all their liabilities. Enron had promised to make payments on certain contracts if financial difficulty developed, but these guarantees were not reported as liabilities. In addition, disclosure was so lacking in transparency that it was impossible to understand what was happening at the company.

DO IT!

QUALITY OF EARNINGS, FINANCIAL STATEMENT ANALYSIS

Match each of the following terms with the phrase that it best matches.

- Comprehensive income
- Quality of earnings
- Solvency ratio
- Vertical analysis
- Pro forma income
- Extraordinary item

1. _____ Measures the ability of the company to survive over a long period of time.
2. _____ Usually excludes items that a company thinks are unusual or non-recurring.
3. _____ Includes all changes in stockholders' equity during a period except those resulting from investments by stockholders and distributions to stockholders.
4. _____ Indicates the level of full and transparent information provided to users of the financial statements.
5. _____ Describes events and transactions that are unusual in nature and infrequent in occurrence.
6. _____ Expresses each item within a financial statement as a percent of a base amount.

action plan
✔ Develop a sound understanding of basic methods used for financial reporting.
✔ Understand the use of fundamental analysis techniques.

Solution

1. **Solvency ratio:** Measures the ability of the company to survive over a long period of time.
2. **Pro forma income:** Usually excludes items that a company thinks are unusual or non-recurring.
3. **Comprehensive income:** Includes all changes in stockholders' equity during a period except those resulting from investments by stockholders and distributions to stockholders.
4. **Quality of earnings:** Indicates the level of full and transparent information provided to users of the financial statements.
5. **Extraordinary item:** Describes events and transactions that are unusual in nature and infrequent in occurrence.
6. **Vertical analysis:** Expresses each item within a financial statement as a percent of a base amount.

Related exercise material: **DO IT!** 18-4.

Chapter 18 Financial Statement Analysis

Comprehensive DO IT!

The events and transactions of Dever Corporation for the year ending December 31, 2010, resulted in the following data.

Cost of goods sold	$2,600,000
Net sales	4,400,000
Other expenses and losses	9,600
Other revenues and gains	5,600
Selling and administrative expenses	1,100,000
Income from operations of plastics division	70,000
Gain from disposal of plastics division	500,000
Loss from tornado disaster (extraordinary loss)	600,000

Analysis reveals that:

1. All items are before the applicable income tax rate of 30%.
2. The plastics division was sold on July 1.
3. All operating data for the plastics division have been segregated.

Instructions

Prepare an income statement for the year.

action plan

✔ Report material items not typical of continuing operations in separate sections, net of taxes.

✔ Associate income taxes with the item that affects the taxes.

✔ Apply the corporate tax rate to income before income taxes to determine tax expense.

✔ Recall that all data presented in determining income before income taxes are the same as for unincorporated companies.

Solution to Comprehensive DO IT!

DEVER CORPORATION
Income Statement
For the Year Ended December 31, 2010

Net sales			$4,400,000
Cost of goods sold			2,600,000
Gross profit			1,800,000
Selling and administrative expenses			1,100,000
Income from operations			700,000
Other revenues and gains		$5,600	
Other expenses and losses		9,600	4,000
Income before income taxes			696,000
Income tax expense ($696,000 × 30%)			208,800
Income from continuing operations			487,200
Discontinued operations			
Income from operations of plastics division, net of $21,000 income taxes ($70,000 × 30%)		49,000	
Gain from disposal of plastics division, net of $150,000 income taxes ($500,000 × 30%)		350,000	399,000
Income before extraordinary item			886,200
Extraordinary item			
Tornado loss, net of $180,000 income tax saving ($600,000 × 30%)			420,000
Net income			$ 466,200

SUMMARY OF STUDY OBJECTIVES

1 Discuss the need for comparative analysis. There are three bases of comparison: (1) Intracompany, which compares an item or financial relationship with other data within a company. (2) Industry, which compares company data with industry averages. (3) Intercompany, which compares an item or financial relationship of a company with data of one or more competing companies.

2 Identify the tools of financial statement analysis. Financial statements can be analyzed horizontally, vertically, and with ratios.

3 Explain and apply horizontal analysis. Horizontal analysis is a technique for evaluating a series of data over a period of time to determine the increase or decrease that has taken place, expressed as either an amount or a percentage.

4 Describe and apply vertical analysis. Vertical analysis is a technique that expresses each item within a financial statement in terms of a percentage of a relevant total or a base amount.

5 Identify and compute ratios used in analyzing a firm's liquidity, profitability, and solvency. The formula and purpose of each ratio was presented in Illustration 18-27 (page 809).

6 Understand the concept of earning power, and how irregular items are presented. Earning power refers to a company's ability to sustain its profits from operations. "Irregular items"—discontinued operations and extraordinary items—are presented net of tax below income from continuing operations to highlight their unusual nature.

7 Understand the concept of quality of earnings. A high quality of earnings provides full and transparent information that will not confuse or mislead users of the financial statements. Issues related to quality of earnings are (1) alternative accounting methods, (2) pro forma income, and (3) improper recognition.

GLOSSARY

Acid-test (quick) ratio A measure of a company's immediate short-term liquidity; computed by dividing the sum of cash, short-term investments, and net receivables by current liabilities. (p. 801).

Asset turnover A measure of how efficiently a company uses its assets to generate sales; computed by dividing net sales by average assets. (p. 804).

Change in accounting principle The use of a principle in the current year that is different from the one used in the preceding year. (p. 814).

Comprehensive income Includes all changes in stockholders' equity during a period except those resulting from investments by stockholders and distributions to stockholders. (p. 815).

Current ratio A measure used to evaluate a company's liquidity and short-term debt-paying ability; computed by dividing current assets by current liabilities. (p. 800).

Debt to total assets ratio Measures the percentage of total assets provided by creditors; computed by dividing total debt by total assets. (p. 807).

Discontinued operations The disposal of a significant segment of a business. (p. 811).

Earnings per share (EPS) The net income earned on each share of common stock; computed by dividing net income minus preferred dividends (if any) by the number of weighted average common shares outstanding. (p. 806).

Extraordinary items Events and transactions that are unusual in nature and infrequent in occurrence. (p. 812).

Horizontal analysis A technique for evaluating a series of financial statement data over a period of time, to determine the increase (decrease) that has taken place, expressed as either an amount or a percentage. (p. 793).

Inventory turnover A measure of the liquidity of inventory; computed by dividing cost of goods sold by average inventory. (p. 802).

Leveraging See Trading on the equity. (p. 805).

Liquidity ratios Measures of the short-term ability of the enterprise to pay its maturing obligations and to meet unexpected needs for cash. (p. 800).

Payout ratio Measures the percentage of earnings distributed in the form of cash dividends; computed by dividing cash dividends by net income. (p. 807).

Price-earnings (P-E) ratio Measures the ratio of the market price of each share of common stock to the earnings per share; computed by dividing the market price of the stock by earnings per share. (p. 806).

Profit margin Measures the percentage of each dollar of sales that results in net income; computed by dividing net income by net sales. (p. 803).

Profitability ratios Measures of the income or operating success of an enterprise for a given period of time. (p. 803).

Pro forma income A measure of income that usually excludes items that a company thinks are unusual or nonrecurring. (p. 816).

Quality of earnings Indicates the level of full and transparent information provided to users of the financial statements. (p. 815).

Ratio An expression of the mathematical relationship between one quantity and another. The relationship may be expressed either as a percentage, a rate, or a simple proportion. (p. 799).

Ratio analysis A technique for evaluating financial statements that expresses the relationship between selected financial statement data. (p. 799).

Receivables turnover A measure of the liquidity of receivables; computed by dividing net credit sales by average net receivables. (p. 802).

Return on assets An overall measure of profitability; computed by dividing net income by average assets. (p. 804).

Return on common stockholders' equity Measures the dollars of net income earned for each dollar invested by the owners; computed by dividing net income minus preferred dividends (if any) by average common stockholders' equity. (p. 805).

820 Chapter 18 Financial Statement Analysis

Solvency ratios Measures of the ability of the enterprise to survive over a long period of time. (p. 807).

Times interest earned Measures a company's ability to meet interest payments as they come due; computed by dividing income before interest expense and income taxes by interest expense. (p. 808).

Trading on the equity Borrowing money at a lower rate of interest than can be earned by using the borrowed money. (p. 805).

Vertical analysis A technique for evaluating financial statement data that expresses each item within a financial statement as a percent of a base amount. (p. 797).

SELF-STUDY QUESTIONS

Answers are at the end of the chapter.

(SO 1) **1.** Comparisons of data within a company are an example of the following comparative basis:
  a. Industry averages.
  b. Intracompany.
  c. Intercompany.
  d. Both (b) and (c).

(SO 3) **2.** In horizontal analysis, each item is expressed as a percentage of the:
  a. net income amount.
  b. stockholders' equity amount.
  c. total assets amount.
  d. base year amount.

(SO 4) **3.** In vertical analysis, the base amount for depreciation expense is generally:
  a. net sales.
  b. depreciation expense in a previous year.
  c. gross profit.
  d. fixed assets.

(SO 4) **4.** The following schedule is a display of what type of analysis?

	Amount	Percent
Current assets	$200,000	25%
Property, plant, and equipment	600,000	75%
Total assets	$800,000	

  a. Horizontal analysis.
  b. Differential analysis.
  c. Vertical analysis.
  d. Ratio analysis.

(SO 3) **5.** Sammy Corporation reported net sales of $300,000, $330,000, and $360,000 in the years, 2008, 2009, and 2010, respectively. If 2008 is the base year, what is the trend percentage for 2010?
  a. 77%.
  b. 108%.
  c. 120%.
  d. 130%.

(SO 5) **6.** Which of the following measures is an evaluation of a firm's ability to pay current liabilities?
  a. Acid-test ratio.
  b. Current ratio.
  c. Both (a) and (b).
  d. None of the above.

(SO 5) **7.** A measure useful in evaluating the efficiency in managing inventories is:
  a. inventory turnover.
  b. average days to sell inventory.
  c. Both (a) and (b).
  d. None of the above.

Use the following financial statement information as of the end of each year to answer Self-Study Questions 8–12.

	2010	2009
Inventory	$ 54,000	$ 48,000
Current assets	81,000	106,000
Total assets	382,000	326,000
Current liabilities	27,000	36,000
Total liabilities	102,000	88,000
Stockholders' equity	280,000	238,000
Net sales	784,000	697,000
Cost of goods sold	306,000	277,000
Net income	134,000	90,000
Tax expense	22,000	18,000
Interest expense	12,000	12,000
Dividends paid to preferred stockholders	20,000	20,000
Dividends paid to common stockholders	15,000	10,000

(SO 5) **8.** Compute the days in inventory for 2010.
  a. 64.4 days.
  b. 60.8 days.
  c. 6 days.
  d. 24 days.

(SO 5) **9.** Compute the current ratio for 2010.
  a. 1.26:1.
  b. 3.0:1.
  c. .80:1.
  d. 3.75:1.

(SO 5) **10.** Compute the profit margin ratio for 2010.
  a. 17.1%.
  b. 18.1%.
  c. 37.9%.
  d. 5.9%.

(SO 5) **11.** Compute the return on common stockholders' equity for 2010.
  a. 47.9%.
  b. 51.7%.

c. 40.7%.
d. 44.0%.

(SO 5) **12.** Compute the times interest earned for 2010.
a. 11.2 times.
b. 65.3 times.
c. 14.0 times.
d. 13.0 times.

(SO 6) **13.** In reporting discontinued operations, the income statement should show in a special section:
a. gains and losses on the disposal of the discontinued segment.
b. gains and losses from operations of the discontinued segment.
c. Both (a) and (b).
d. Neither (a) nor (b).

(SO 6) **14.** Scout Corporation has income before taxes of $400,000 and an extraordinary loss of $100,000. If the income tax rate is 25% on all items, the income statement should show income before extraordinary items and extraordinary items, respectively, of:
a. $325,000 and $100,000.
b. $325,000 and $75,000.
c. $300,000 and $100,000
d. $300,000 and $75,000.

15. Which situation below might indicate a company has a (SO 7) low quality of earnings?
a. The same accounting principles are used each year.
b. Revenue is recognized when earned.
c. Maintenance costs are expensed as incurred.
d. The company is continually reporting pro forma income numbers.

Go to the book's companion website, **www.wiley.com/college/weygandt**, for Additional Self-Study questions.

QUESTIONS

1. (a) Juan Marichal believes that the analysis of financial statements is directed at two characteristics of a company: liquidity and profitability. Is Juan correct? Explain.
(b) Are short-term creditors, long-term creditors, and stockholders interested primarily in the same characteristics of a company? Explain.

2. (a) Distinguish among the following bases of comparison: (1) intracompany, (2) industry averages, and (3) intercompany.
(b) Give the principal value of using each of the three bases of comparison.

3. Two popular methods of financial statement analysis are horizontal analysis and vertical analysis. Explain the difference between these two methods.

4. (a) If Leonard Company had net income of $360,000 in 2010 and it experienced a 24.5% increase in net income for 2011, what is its net income for 2011?
(b) If six cents of every dollar of Leonard revenue is net income in 2010, what is the dollar amount of 2010 revenue?

5. What is a ratio? What are the different ways of expressing the relationship of two amounts? What information does a ratio provide?

6. Name the major ratios useful in assessing (a) liquidity and (b) solvency.

7. Raphael Ochoa is puzzled. His company had a profit margin of 10% in 2010. He feels that this is an indication that the company is doing well. Cindy Lore, his accountant, says that more information is needed to determine the firm's financial well-being. Who is correct? Why?

8. What do the following classes of ratios measure? (a) Liquidity ratios. (b) Profitability ratios. (c) Solvency ratios.

9. What is the difference between the current ratio and the acid-test ratio?

10. Donte Company, a retail store, has a receivables turnover of 4.5 times. The industry average is 12.5 times. Does Donte have a collection problem with its receivables?

11. Which ratios should be used to help answer the following questions?
(a) How efficient is a company in using its assets to produce sales?
(b) How near to sale is the inventory on hand?
(c) How many dollars of net income were earned for each dollar invested by the owners?
(d) How able is a company to meet interest charges as they fall due?

12. The price-earnings ratio of General Motors (automobile builder) was 8, and the price-earnings ratio of Microsoft (computer software) was 38. Which company did the stock market favor? Explain.

13. What is the formula for computing the payout ratio? Would you expect this ratio to be high or low for a growth company?

14. Holding all other factors constant, indicate whether each of the following changes generally signals good or bad news about a company.
(a) Increase in profit margin.
(b) Decrease in inventory turnover.
(c) Increase in the current ratio.
(d) Decrease in earnings per share.
(e) Increase in price-earnings ratio.
(f) Increase in debt to total assets ratio.
(g) Decrease in times interest earned.

15. The return on assets for Tresh Corporation is 7.6%. During the same year Tresh's return on common stockholders' equity is 12.8%. What is the explanation for the difference in the two rates?

16. Which two ratios do you think should be of greatest interest to:
    (a) A pension fund considering the purchase of 20-year bonds?
    (b) A bank contemplating a short-term loan?
    (c) A common stockholder?
17. Why must preferred stock dividends be subtracted from net income in computing earnings per share?
18. (a) What is meant by trading on the equity?
    (b) How would you determine the profitability of trading on the equity?
19. Hillman Inc. has net income of $160,000, weighted average shares of common stock outstanding of 50,000, and preferred dividends for the period of $40,000. What is Hillman's earnings per share of common stock? Kate Hillman, the president of Hillman Inc., believes the computed EPS of the company is high. Comment.
20. Why is it important to report discontinued operations separately from income from continuing operations?
21. You are considering investing in Shawnee Transportation. The company reports 2010 earnings per share of $6.50 on income before extraordinary items and $4.75 on net income. Which EPS figure would you consider more relevant to your investment decision? Why?
22. STL Inc. reported 2009 earnings per share of $3.20 and had no extraordinary items. In 2010, EPS on income before extraordinary items was $2.99, and EPS on net income was $3.49. Is this a favorable trend?
23. Indicate which of the following items would be reported as an extraordinary item in Mordica Corporation's income statement.
    (a) Loss from damages caused by volcano eruption.
    (b) Loss from sale of temporary investments.
    (c) Loss attributable to a labor strike.
    (d) Loss caused when manufacture of a product was prohibited by the Food and Drug Administration.
    (e) Loss from flood damage. (The nearby Black River floods every 2 to 3 years.)
    (f) Write-down of obsolete inventory.
    (g) Expropriation of a factory by a foreign government.
24. Identify and explain factors that affect quality of earnings.
25.  Identify the specific sections in PepsiCo's 2007 annual report where horizontal and vertical analyses of financial data are presented.

BRIEF EXERCISES

Follow the rounding procedures used in the chapter.

Discuss need for comparative analysis.
(SO 1)

BE18-1 You recently received a letter from your Uncle Frank. A portion of the letter is presented below.

You know that I have a significant amount of money I saved over the years. I am thinking about starting an investment program. I want to do the investing myself, based on my own research and analysis of financial statements. I know that you are studying accounting, so I have a couple of questions for you. I have heard that different users of financial statements are interested in different characteristics of companies. Is this true, and if so, why? Also, some of my friends, who are already investing, have told me that comparisons involving a company's financial data can be made on a number of different bases. Can you explain these bases to me?

Instructions

Write a letter to your Uncle Frank which answers his questions.

Identify and use tools of financial statement analysis.
(SO 2, 3, 4, 5)

BE18-2 Drew Carey Corporation reported the following amounts in 2009, 2010, and 2011.

	2009	2010	2011
Current assets	$200,000	$230,000	$240,000
Current liabilities	$160,000	$168,000	$184,000
Total assets	$500,000	$600,000	$620,000

Instructions
(a) Identify and describe the three tools of financial statement analysis. (b) Perform each of the three types of analysis on Drew Carey's current assets.

Prepare horizontal analysis.
(SO 3)

BE18-3 Using the following data from the comparative balance sheet of Rodenbeck Company, illustrate horizontal analysis.

	December 31, 2011	December 31, 2010
Accounts receivable	$ 520,000	$ 400,000
Inventory	$ 840,000	$ 600,000
Total assets	$ 3,000,000	$2,500,000

BE18-4 Using the same data presented above in BE18-3 for Rodenbeck Company, illustrate vertical analysis.

Prepare vertical analysis.
(SO 4)

BE18-5 Net income was $500,000 in 2009, $450,000 in 2010, and $522,000 in 2011. What is the percentage of change from **(a)** 2009 to 2010 and **(b)** 2010 to 2011? Is the change an increase or a decrease?

Calculate percentage of change.
(SO 3)

BE18-6 If Soule Company had net income of $585,000 in 2011 and it experienced a 30% increase in net income over 2010, what was its 2010 net income?

Calculate net income.
(SO 3)

BE18-7 Horizontal analysis (trend analysis) percentages for Epstein Company's sales, cost of goods sold, and expenses are shown below.

Calculate change in net income.
(SO 3)

Horizontal Analysis	2011	2010	2009
Sales	96.2	106.8	100.0
Cost of goods sold	102.0	97.0	100.0
Expenses	109.6	98.4	100.0

Did Epstein's net income increase, decrease, or remain unchanged over the 3-year period?

BE18-8 Vertical analysis (common size) percentages for Charles Company's sales, cost of goods sold, and expenses are shown below.

Calculate change in net income.
(SO 4)

Vertical Analysis	2011	2010	2009
Sales	100.0	100.0	100.0
Cost of goods sold	59.2	62.4	64.5
Expenses	25.0	25.6	27.5

Did Charles's net income as a percent of sales increase, decrease, or remain unchanged over the 3-year period? Provide numerical support for your answer.

BE18-9 Selected condensed data taken from a recent balance sheet of Perkins Inc. are as follows.

Calculate liquidity ratios.
(SO 5)

PERKINS INC.
Balance Sheet (partial)

Cash	$ 8,041,000
Short-term investments	4,947,000
Accounts receivable	12,545,000
Inventories	14,814,000
Other current assets	5,571,000
Total current assets	$45,918,000
Total current liabilities	$40,644,000

What are the **(a)** working capital, **(b)** current ratio, and **(c)** acid-test ratio?

BE18-10 McLaren Corporation has net income of $11.44 million and net revenue of $80 million in 2010. Its assets are $14 million at the beginning of the year and $18 million at the end of the year. What are McLaren's **(a)** asset turnover and **(b)** profit margin?

Calculate profitability ratios.
(SO 5)

BE18-11 The following data are taken from the financial statements of Morino Company.

Evaluate collection of accounts receivable.
(SO 5)

	2011	2010
Accounts receivable (net), end of year	$ 550,000	$ 520,000
Net sales on account	3,960,000	3,100,000
Terms for all sales are 1/10, n/60.		

(a) Compute for each year (1) the receivables turnover and (2) the average collection period. At the end of 2009, accounts receivable (net) was $480,000.

(b) What conclusions about the management of accounts receivable can be drawn from these data?

824 Chapter 18 Financial Statement Analysis

Evaluate management of inventory.
(SO 5)

BE18-12 The following data are from the income statements of Huntsinger Company.

	2011	2010
Sales	$6,420,000	$6,240,000
Beginning inventory	980,000	860,000
Purchases	4,340,000	4,661,000
Ending inventory	1,020,000	980,000

(a) Compute for each year (1) the inventory turnover and (2) the average days to sell the inventory. (b) What conclusions concerning the management of the inventory can be drawn from these data?

Calculate profitability ratios.
(SO 5)

BE18-13 Gladow Company has owners' equity of $400,000 and net income of $66,000. It has a payout ratio of 20% and a rate of return on assets of 15%. How much did Gladow pay in cash dividends, and what were its average assets?

Prepare income statement including extraordinary items.
(SO 6)

BE18-14 An inexperienced accountant for Ming Corporation showed the following in the income statement: income before income taxes and extraordinary item $400,000, and extraordinary loss from flood (before taxes) $70,000. The extraordinary loss and taxable income are both subject to a 30% tax rate. Prepare a correct income statement.

Prepare discontinued operations section of income statement.
(SO 6)

BE18-15 On June 30, Reeves Corporation discontinued its operations in Mexico. During the year, the operating loss was $300,000 before taxes. On September 1, Reeves disposed of the Mexico facility at a pretax loss of $120,000. The applicable tax rate is 30%. Show the discontinued operations section of the income statement.

DO IT! REVIEW

Prepare horizontal analysis.
(SO 3)

DO IT! 18-1 Summary financial information for Holland Company is as follows.

	December 31, 2011	December 31, 2010
Current assets	$ 199,000	$ 220,000
Plant assets	821,000	780,000
Total assets	$1,020,000	$1,000,000

Compute the amount and percentage changes in 2011 using horizontal analysis, assuming 2010 is the base year.

Compute ratios.
(SO 5)

DO IT! 18-2 The condensed financial statements of Eau Fraîche Company for the years 2009 and 2010 are presented below.

EAU FRAÎCHE COMPANY
Balance Sheets
December 31

	2010	2009
Current assets		
Cash and cash equivalents	$ 330	$ 360
Accounts receivable (net)	470	400
Inventories	460	390
Prepaid expenses	120	160
Total current assets	1,380	1,310
Property, plant, and equipment	420	380
Investments	10	10
Intangibles and other assets	530	510
Total assets	$2,340	$2,210
Current liabilities	$ 900	$ 790
Long-term liabilities	410	380
Stockholders' equity—common	1,030	1,040
Total liabilities and stockholders' equity	$2,340	$2,210

EAU FRAÎCHE COMPANY
Income Statements
For the Year Ended December 31

	2010	2009
Revenues	$3,800	$3,460
Costs and expenses		
Cost of goods sold	970	890
Selling & administrative expenses	2,400	2,330
Interest expense	10	20
Total costs and expenses	3,380	3,240
Income before income taxes	420	220
Income tax expense	168	132
Net income	$ 252	$ 88

Compute the following ratios for 2010 and 2009.
(a) Current ratio.
(b) Inventory turnover. (Inventory on 12/31/08 was $340.)
(c) Profit margin ratio.
(d) Return on assets. (Assets on 12/31/08 were $1,900.)
(e) Return on common stockholders' equity. (Equity on 12/31/08 was $900.)
(f) Debt to total assets ratio.
(g) Times interest earned.

DO IT! 18-3 In its proposed 2010 income statement, Supply Corporation reports income before income taxes $500,000, extraordinary loss due to earthquake $150,000, income taxes $200,000 (not including irregular items), loss on operation of discontinued music division $60,000, and gain on disposal of discontinued music division $40,000. The income tax rate is 40%. Prepare a correct income statement, beginning with income before income taxes.

Prepare income statement, including irregular items.
(SO 6)

DO IT! 18-4 Match each of the following terms with the phrase that it best matches.

Quality of earnings   Pro forma income
Current ratio   Discontinued operations
Horizontal analysis   Comprehensive income

Match terms relating to quality of earnings and financial statement analysis.
(SO 3, 4, 5, 6, 7)

1. _____ A measure used to evaluate a company's liquidity.
2. _____ Usually excludes items that a company thinks are unusual or nonrecurring.
3. _____ Indicates the level of full and transparent information provided to users of the financial statements.
4. _____ The disposal of a significant segment of a business.
5. _____ Determines increases or decreases in a series of financial statement data.
6. _____ Includes all changes in stockholders' equity during a period except those resulting from investments by stockholders and distributions to stockholders.

EXERCISES

Follow the rounding procedures used in the chapter.

E18-1 Financial information for Blevins Inc. is presented below.

Prepare horizontal analysis.
(SO 3)

	December 31, 2011	December 31, 2010
Current assets	$125,000	$100,000
Plant assets (net)	396,000	330,000
Current liabilities	91,000	70,000
Long-term liabilities	133,000	95,000
Common stock, $1 par	161,000	115,000
Retained earnings	136,000	150,000

Instructions
Prepare a schedule showing a horizontal analysis for 2011 using 2010 as the base year.

Chapter 18 Financial Statement Analysis

Prepare vertical analysis.
(SO 4)

E18-2 Operating data for Gallup Corporation are presented below.

	2011	2010
Sales	$750,000	$600,000
Cost of goods sold	465,000	390,000
Selling expenses	120,000	72,000
Administrative expenses	60,000	54,000
Income tax expense	33,000	24,000
Net income	72,000	60,000

Instructions
Prepare a schedule showing a vertical analysis for 2011 and 2010.

Prepare horizontal and vertical analyses.
(SO 3, 4)

E18-3 The comparative condensed balance sheets of Conard Corporation are presented below.

CONARD CORPORATION
Comparative Condensed Balance Sheets
December 31

	2011	2010
Assets		
Current assets	$ 74,000	$ 80,000
Property, plant, and equipment (net)	99,000	90,000
Intangibles	27,000	40,000
Total assets	$200,000	$210,000
Liabilities and stockholders' equity		
Current liabilities	$ 42,000	$ 48,000
Long-term liabilities	143,000	150,000
Stockholders' equity	15,000	12,000
Total liabilities and stockholders' equity	$200,000	$210,000

Instructions
(a) Prepare a horizontal analysis of the balance sheet data for Conard Corporation using 2010 as a base.
(b) Prepare a vertical analysis of the balance sheet data for Conard Corporation in columnar form for 2011.

Prepare horizontal and vertical analyses.
(SO 3, 4)

E18-4 The comparative condensed income statements of Hendi Corporation are shown below.

HENDI CORPORATION
Comparative Condensed Income Statements
For the Years Ended December 31

	2011	2010
Net sales	$600,000	$500,000
Cost of goods sold	483,000	420,000
Gross profit	117,000	80,000
Operating expenses	57,200	44,000
Net income	$ 59,800	$ 36,000

Instructions
(a) Prepare a horizontal analysis of the income statement data for Hendi Corporation using 2010 as a base. (Show the amounts of increase or decrease.)
(b) Prepare a vertical analysis of the income statement data for Hendi Corporation in columnar form for both years.

Compute liquidity ratios and compare results.
(SO 5)

E18-5 Nordstrom, Inc. operates department stores in numerous states. Selected financial statement data for the year ending February 2, 2008, are shown on the next page.

NORDSTROM, INC.
Balance Sheet (partial)

(in millions)	End-of-Year	Beginning-of-Year
Cash and cash equivalents	$ 358	$ 403
Accounts receivable (net)	1,788	684
Merchandise inventory	956	997
Prepaid expenses	78	61
Other current assets	181	597
Total current assets	$3,361	$2,742
Total current liabilities	$1,635	$1,433

For the year, net sales were $8,828, and cost of goods sold was $5,526 (in millions).

Instructions
(a) Compute the four liquidity ratios at the end of the year.
(b) Using the data in the chapter, compare Nordstrom's liquidity with (1) that of J.C. Penney Company, and (2) the industry averages for department stores.

E18-6 Leach Incorporated had the following transactions occur involving current assets and current liabilities during February 2010.

Perform current and acid-test ratio analysis.
(SO 5)

Feb. 3 Accounts receivable of $15,000 are collected.
     7 Equipment is purchased for $28,000 cash.
    11 Paid $3,000 for a 3-year insurance policy.
    14 Accounts payable of $12,000 are paid.
    18 Cash dividends of $5,000 are declared.

Additional information:

1. As of February 1, 2010, current assets were $130,000, and current liabilities were $50,000.
2. As of February 1, 2010, current assets included $15,000 of inventory and $2,000 of prepaid expenses.

Instructions
(a) Compute the current ratio as of the beginning of the month and after each transaction.
(b) Compute the acid-test ratio as of the beginning of the month and after each transaction.

E18-7 Bennis Company has the following comparative balance sheet data.

Compute selected ratios.
(SO 5)

BENNIS COMPANY
Balance Sheets
December 31

	2011	2010
Cash	$ 15,000	$ 30,000
Receivables (net)	70,000	60,000
Inventories	60,000	50,000
Plant assets (net)	200,000	180,000
	$345,000	$320,000
Accounts payable	$50,000	$60,000
Mortgage payable (15%)	100,000	100,000
Common stock, $10 par	140,000	120,000
Retained earnings	55,000	40,000
	$345,000	$320,000

Additional information for 2011:

1. Net income was $25,000.
2. Sales on account were $410,000. Sales returns and allowances were $20,000.
3. Cost of goods sold was $198,000.
4. The allowance for doubtful accounts was $2,500 on December 31, 2011, and $2,000 on December 31, 2010.

Instructions

Compute the following ratios at December 31, 2011.

(a) Current.
(b) Acid-test.
(c) Receivables turnover.
(d) Inventory turnover.

Compute selected ratios.
(SO 5)

E18-8 Selected comparative statement data for Willingham Products Company are presented below. All balance sheet data are as of December 31.

	2011	2010
Net sales	$760,000	$720,000
Cost of goods sold	480,000	440,000
Interest expense	7,000	5,000
Net income	50,000	42,000
Accounts receivable	120,000	100,000
Inventory	85,000	75,000
Total assets	580,000	500,000
Total common stockholders' equity	430,000	325,000

Instructions

Compute the following ratios for 2011.

(a) Profit margin.
(b) Asset turnover.
(c) Return on assets.
(d) Return on common stockholders' equity.

Compute selected ratios.
(SO 5)

E18-9 The income statement for Christensen, Inc., appears below.

CHRISTENSEN, INC.
Income Statement
For the Year Ended December 31, 2010

Sales	$400,000
Cost of goods sold	230,000
Gross profit	170,000
Expenses (including $16,000 interest and $24,000 income taxes)	105,000
Net income	$ 65,000

Additional information:

1. The weighted average common shares outstanding in 2010 were 30,000 shares.
2. The market price of Christensen, Inc. stock was $13 in 2010.
3. Cash dividends of $26,000 were paid, $5,000 of which were to preferred stockholders.

Instructions

Compute the following ratios for 2010.

(a) Earnings per share.
(b) Price-earnings.
(c) Payout.
(d) Times interest earned.

Compute amounts from ratios.
(SO 5)

E18-10 Rees Corporation experienced a fire on December 31, 2011, in which its financial records were partially destroyed. It has been able to salvage some of the records and has ascertained the following balances.

	December 31, 2011	December 31, 2010
Cash	$ 30,000	$ 10,000
Receivables (net)	72,500	126,000
Inventory	200,000	180,000
Accounts payable	50,000	90,000
Notes payable	30,000	60,000
Common stock, $100 par	400,000	400,000
Retained earnings	113,500	101,000

Additional information:

1. The inventory turnover is 3.5 times.
2. The return on common stockholders' equity is 24%. The company had no additional paid-in capital.
3. The receivables turnover is 8.8 times.
4. The return on assets is 20%.
5. Total assets at December 31, 2010, were $605,000.

Instructions
Compute the following for Rees Corporation.

(a) Cost of goods sold for 2011.
(b) Net sales (credit) for 2011.
(c) Net income for 2011.
(d) Total assets at December 31, 2011.

E18-11 Scully Corporation's comparative balance sheets are presented below.

Compute ratios.
(SO 5)

SCULLY CORPORATION
Balance Sheets
December 31

	2010	2009
Cash	$ 4,300	$ 3,700
Accounts receivable	21,200	23,400
Inventory	10,000	7,000
Land	20,000	26,000
Building	70,000	70,000
Accumulated depreciation	(15,000)	(10,000)
Total	$110,500	$120,100
Accounts payable	$ 12,370	$ 31,100
Common stock	75,000	69,000
Retained earnings	23,130	20,000
Total	$110,500	$120,100

Scully's 2010 income statement included net sales of $100,000, cost of goods sold of $60,000, and net income of $15,000.

Instructions
Compute the following ratios for 2010.

(a) Current ratio.
(b) Acid-test ratio.
(c) Receivables turnover.
(d) Inventory turnover.
(e) Profit margin.
(f) Asset turnover.
(g) Return on assets.
(h) Return on common stockholders' equity.
(i) Debt to total assets ratio.

E18-12 For its fiscal year ending October 31, 2010, Molini Corporation reports the following partial data shown on the next page.

Prepare a correct income statement.
(SO 6)

Income before income taxes	$540,000
Income tax expense (30% × $390,000)	117,000
Income before extraordinary items	423,000
Extraordinary loss from flood	150,000
Net income	$273,000

The flood loss is considered an extraordinary item. The income tax rate is 30% on all items.

Instructions

(a) Prepare a correct income statement, beginning with income before income taxes.
(b)  Explain in memo form why the income statement data are misleading.

Prepare income statement.
(SO 6)

E18-13 Yadier Corporation has income from continuing operations of $290,000 for the year ended December 31, 2010. It also has the following items (before considering income taxes).

1. An extraordinary loss of $80,000.
2. A gain of $30,000 on the discontinuance of a division.
3. A correction of an error in last year's financial statements that resulted in a $20,000 understatement of 2009 net income.

Assume all items are subject to income taxes at a 30% tax rate.

Instructions

(a) Prepare an income statement, beginning with income from continuing operations.
(b) Indicate the statement presentation of any item not included in (a) above.

EXERCISES: SET B

Visit the book's companion website at **www.wiley.com/college/weygandt**, and choose the Student Companion site, to access Exercise Set B.

PROBLEMS

Follow the rounding procedures used in the chapter.

Prepare vertical analysis and comment on profitability.
(SO 4, 5)

P18-1 Comparative statement data for Douglas Company and Maulder Company, two competitors, appear below. All balance sheet data are as of December 31, 2011, and December 31, 2010.

	Douglas Company		Maulder Company	
	2011	2010	2011	2010
Net sales	$1,549,035		$339,038	
Cost of goods sold	1,080,490		241,000	
Operating expenses	302,275		79,000	
Interest expense	8,980		2,252	
Income tax expense	54,500		6,650	
Current assets	325,975	$312,410	83,336	$ 79,467
Plant assets (net)	521,310	500,000	139,728	125,812
Current liabilities	65,325	75,815	35,348	30,281
Long-term liabilities	108,500	90,000	29,620	25,000
Common stock, $10 par	500,000	500,000	120,000	120,000
Retained earnings	173,460	146,595	38,096	29,998

Instructions

(a) Prepare a vertical analysis of the 2011 income statement data for Douglas Company and Maulder Company in columnar form.
(b)  Comment on the relative profitability of the companies by computing the return on assets and the return on common stockholders' equity ratios for both companies.

P18-2 The comparative statements of Villa Tool Company are presented below.

Compute ratios from balance sheet and income statement.
(SO 5)

VILLA TOOL COMPANY
Income Statement
For the Year Ended December 31

	2011	2010
Net sales	$1,818,500	$1,750,500
Cost of goods sold	1,011,500	996,000
Gross profit	807,000	754,500
Selling and administrative expense	516,000	479,000
Income from operations	291,000	275,500
Other expenses and losses		
Interest expense	18,000	14,000
Income before income taxes	273,000	261,500
Income tax expense	81,000	77,000
Net income	$ 192,000	$ 184,500

VILLA TOOL COMPANY
Balance Sheets
December 31

Assets	2011	2010
Current assets		
Cash	$ 60,100	$ 64,200
Short-term investments	69,000	50,000
Accounts receivable (net)	117,800	102,800
Inventory	123,000	115,500
Total current assets	369,900	332,500
Plant assets (net)	600,300	520,300
Total assets	$970,200	$852,800

Liabilities and Stockholders' Equity		
Current liabilities		
Accounts payable	$160,000	$145,400
Income taxes payable	43,500	42,000
Total current liabilities	203,500	187,400
Bonds payable	200,000	200,000
Total liabilities	403,500	387,400
Stockholders' equity		
Common stock ($5 par)	280,000	300,000
Retained earnings	286,700	165,400
Total stockholders' equity	566,700	465,400
Total liabilities and stockholders' equity	$970,200	$852,800

All sales were on account. The allowance for doubtful accounts was $3,200 on December 31, 2011, and $3,000 on December 31, 2010.

Instructions
Compute the following ratios for 2011. (Weighted average common shares in 2011 were 57,000.)

(a) Earnings per share.
(b) Return on common stockholders' equity.
(c) Return on assets.
(d) Current.
(e) Acid-test.
(f) Receivables turnover.
(g) Inventory turnover.
(h) Times interest earned.
(i) Asset turnover.
(j) Debt to total assets.

832 Chapter 18 Financial Statement Analysis

Perform ratio analysis, and evaluate financial position and operating results.

(SO 5)

P18-3 Condensed balance sheet and income statement data for Kersenbrock Corporation appear below.

KERSENBROCK CORPORATION
Balance Sheets
December 31

	2011	2010	2009
Cash	$ 25,000	$ 20,000	$ 18,000
Receivables (net)	50,000	45,000	48,000
Other current assets	90,000	95,000	64,000
Investments	75,000	70,000	45,000
Plant and equipment (net)	400,000	370,000	358,000
	$640,000	$600,000	$533,000
Current liabilities	$ 75,000	$ 80,000	$ 70,000
Long-term debt	80,000	85,000	50,000
Common stock, $10 par	340,000	310,000	300,000
Retained earnings	145,000	125,000	113,000
	$640,000	$600,000	$533,000

KERSENBROCK CORPORATION
Income Statement
For the Year Ended December 31

	2011	2010
Sales	$740,000	$700,000
Less: Sales returns and allowances	40,000	50,000
Net sales	700,000	650,000
Cost of goods sold	420,000	400,000
Gross profit	280,000	250,000
Operating expenses (including income taxes)	235,000	220,000
Net income	$ 45,000	$ 30,000

Additional information:
1. The market price of Kersenbrock's common stock was $4.00, $5.00, and $8.00 for 2009, 2010, and 2011, respectively.
2. All dividends were paid in cash.

Instructions
(a) Compute the following ratios for 2010 and 2011.
   (1) Profit margin.
   (2) Asset turnover.
   (3) Earnings per share. (Weighted average common shares in 2011 were 32,000 and in 2010 were 31,000.)
   (4) Price-earnings.
   (5) Payout.
   (6) Debt to total assets.
(b) Based on the ratios calculated, discuss briefly the improvement or lack thereof in financial position and operating results from 2010 to 2011 of Kersenbrock Corporation.

P18-4 Financial information for Hanshew Company is presented below.

Compute ratios, and comment on overall liquidity and profitability.

(SO 5)

HANSHEW COMPANY
Balance Sheets
December 31

Assets	2011	2010
Cash	$ 70,000	$ 65,000
Short-term investments	52,000	40,000
Receivables (net)	98,000	80,000
Inventories	125,000	135,000
Prepaid expenses	29,000	23,000
Land	130,000	130,000
Building and equipment (net)	180,000	175,000
	$684,000	$648,000

Liabilities and Stockholders' Equity		
Notes payable	$100,000	$100,000
Accounts payable	48,000	42,000
Accrued liabilities	50,000	40,000
Bonds payable, due 2012	150,000	150,000
Common stock, $10 par	200,000	200,000
Retained earnings	136,000	116,000
	$684,000	$648,000

HANSHEW COMPANY
Income Statement
For the Years Ended December 31

	2011	2010
Sales	$850,000	$790,000
Cost of goods sold	620,000	575,000
Gross profit	230,000	215,000
Operating expenses	187,000	173,000
Net income	$ 43,000	$ 42,000

Additional information:
1. Inventory at the beginning of 2010 was $118,000.
2. Receivables (net) at the beginning of 2010 were $88,000. The allowance for doubtful accounts was $4,000 at the end of 2011, $3,800 at the end of 2010, and $3,700 at the beginning of 2010.
3. Total assets at the beginning of 2010 were $630,000.
4. No common stock transactions occurred during 2010 or 2011.
5. All sales were on account.

Instructions

(a) Indicate, by using ratios, the change in liquidity and profitability of Hanshew Company from 2010 to 2011. (*Note:* Not all profitability ratios can be computed.)
(b) Given below are three independent situations and a ratio that may be affected. For each situation, compute the affected ratio (1) as of December 31, 2011, and (2) as of December 31, 2012, after giving effect to the situation. Net income for 2012 was $50,000. Total assets on December 31, 2012, were $700,000.

Situation	Ratio
(1) 18,000 shares of common stock were sold at par on July 1, 2012.	Return on common stockholders' equity
(2) All of the notes payable were paid in 2012. The only change in liabilities was that the notes payable were paid.	Debt to total assets
(3) Market price of common stock was $9 on December 31, 2011, and $12.80 on December 31, 2012.	Price-earnings ratio

834 Chapter 18 Financial Statement Analysis

Compute selected ratios, and compare liquidity, profitability, and solvency for two companies.

(SO 5)

P18-5 Selected financial data of Target and Wal-Mart for a recent year are presented here (in millions).

	Target Corporation	Wal-Mart Stores, Inc.
Income Statement Data for Year		
Net sales	$61,471	$374,526
Cost of goods sold	41,895	286,515
Selling and administrative expenses	16,200	70,847
Interest expense	647	1,798
Other income (expense)	1,896	4,273
Income tax expense	1,776	6,908
Net income	$ 2,849	$ 12,731
Balance Sheet Data (End of Year)		
Current assets	$18,906	$ 47,585
Noncurrent assets	25,654	115,929
Total assets	$44,560	$163,514
Current liabilities	$11,782	$ 58,454
Long-term debt	17,471	40,452
Total stockholders' equity	15,307	64,608
Total liabilities and stockholders' equity	$44,560	$163,514
Beginning-of-Year Balances		
Total assets	$37,349	$151,587
Total stockholders' equity	15,633	61,573
Current liabilities	11,117	52,148
Total liabilities	21,716	90,014
Other Data		
Average net receivables	$ 7,124	$ 3,247
Average inventory	6,517	34,433
Net cash provided by operating activities	4,125	20,354

Instructions

(a) For each company, compute the following ratios.
  (1) Current.
  (2) Receivables turnover.
  (3) Average collection period.
  (4) Inventory turnover.
  (5) Days in inventory.
  (6) Profit margin.
  (7) Asset turnover.
  (8) Return on assets.
  (9) Return on common stockholders' equity.
  (10) Debt to total assets.
  (11) Times interest earned.

(b) Compare the liquidity, profitability, and solvency of the two companies.

Compute numerous ratios.

(SO 5)

P18-6 The comparative statements of Dillon Company are presented below.

DILLON COMPANY
Income Statement
For Year Ended December 31

	2011	2010
Net sales (all on account)	$600,000	$520,000
Expenses		
Cost of goods sold	415,000	354,000
Selling and administrative	120,800	114,800
Interest expense	7,800	6,000
Income tax expense	18,000	14,000
Total expenses	561,600	488,800
Net income	$ 38,400	$ 31,200

DILLON COMPANY
Balance Sheets
December 31

Assets	2011	2010
Current assets		
Cash	$ 21,000	$ 18,000
Short-term investments	18,000	15,000
Accounts receivable (net)	86,000	74,000
Inventory	90,000	70,000
Total current assets	215,000	177,000
Plant assets (net)	423,000	383,000
Total assets	$638,000	$560,000
Liabilities and Stockholders' Equity		
Current liabilities		
Accounts payable	$122,000	$110,000
Income taxes payable	23,000	20,000
Total current liabilities	145,000	130,000
Long-term liabilities		
Bonds payable	120,000	80,000
Total liabilities	265,000	210,000
Stockholders' equity		
Common stock ($5 par)	150,000	150,000
Retained earnings	223,000	200,000
Total stockholders' equity	373,000	350,000
Total liabilities and stockholders' equity	$638,000	$560,000

Additional data:

The common stock recently sold at $19.50 per share.
The year-end balance in the allowance for doubtful accounts was $3,000 for 2011 and $2,400 for 2010.

Instructions

Compute the following ratios for 2011.
- (a) Current.
- (b) Acid-test.
- (c) Receivables turnover.
- (d) Inventory turnover.
- (e) Profit margin.
- (f) Asset turnover.
- (g) Return on assets.
- (h) Return on common stockholders' equity.
- (i) Earnings per share.
- (j) Price-earnings.
- (k) Payout.
- (l) Debt to total assets.
- (m) Times interest earned.

P18-7 Presented below is an incomplete income statement and an incomplete comparative balance sheet of Cotte Corporation.

Compute missing information given a set of ratios.

(SO 5)

COTTE CORPORATION
Income Statement
For the Year Ended December 31, 2011

Sales	$11,000,000
Cost of goods sold	?
Gross profit	?
Operating expenses	1,665,000
Income from operations	?
Other expenses and losses	
Interest expense	?
Income before income taxes	?
Income tax expense	560,000
Net income	$?

COTTE CORPORATION
Balance Sheets
December 31

Assets	2011	2010
Current assets		
Cash	$ 450,000	$ 375,000
Accounts receivable (net)	?	950,000
Inventory	?	1,720,000
Total current assets	?	3,045,000
Plant assets (net)	4,620,000	3,955,000
Total assets	$?	$7,000,000
Liabilities and Stockholders' Equity		
Current liabilities	$?	$ 825,000
Long-term notes payable	?	2,800,000
Total liabilities	?	3,625,000
Common stock, $1 par	3,000,000	3,000,000
Retained earnings	400,000	375,000
Total stockholders' equity	3,400,000	3,375,000
Total liabilities and stockholders' equity	$?	$7,000,000

Additional information:

1. The receivables turnover for 2011 is 10 times.
2. All sales are on account.
3. The profit margin for 2011 is 14.5%.
4. Return on assets is 22% for 2011.
5. The current ratio on December 31, 2011, is 3.0.
6. The inventory turnover for 2011 is 4.8 times.

Instructions

Compute the missing information given the ratios above. Show computations. (*Note*: Start with one ratio and derive as much information as possible from it before trying another ratio. List all missing amounts under the ratio used to find the information.)

Prepare income statement with discontinued operations and extraordinary loss.

(SO 6)

P18-8 Cheaney Corporation owns a number of cruise ships and a chain of hotels. The hotels, which have not been profitable, were discontinued on September 1, 2010. The 2010 operating results for the company were as follows.

Operating revenues	$12,850,000
Operating expenses	8,700,000
Operating income	$ 4,150,000

Analysis discloses that these data include the operating results of the hotel chain, which were: operating revenues $2,000,000 and operating expenses $2,400,000. The hotels were sold at a gain of $200,000 before taxes. This gain is not included in the operating results. During the year, Cheaney suffered an extraordinary loss of $800,000 before taxes, which is not included in the operating results. In 2010, the company had other revenues and gains of $100,000, which are not included in the operating results. The corporation is in the 30% income tax bracket.

Instructions

Prepare a condensed income statement.

Prepare income statement with nontypical items.

(SO 6)

P18-9 The ledger of LaRussa Corporation at December 31, 2010, contains the following summary data.

Net sales	$1,700,000	Cost of goods sold	$1,100,000
Selling expenses	120,000	Administrative expenses	150,000
Other revenues and gains	20,000	Other expenses and losses	28,000

Your analysis reveals the following additional information that is not included in the above data.

1. The entire puzzles division was discontinued on August 31. The income from operations for this division before income taxes was $20,000. The puzzles division was sold at a loss of $90,000 before income taxes.
2. On May 15, company property was expropriated for an interstate highway. The settlement resulted in an extraordinary gain of $120,000 before income taxes.
3. The income tax rate on all items is 30%.

Instructions
Prepare an income statement for the year ended December 31, 2010. Use the format illustrated in the Comprehensive **DO IT!** (p. 818).

PROBLEMS: SET B

Visit the book's companion website at **www.wiley.com/college/weygandt**, and choose the Student Companion site, to access Problem Set B.

CONTINUING COOKIE CHRONICLE

(Note: This is a continuation of the Cookie Chronicle from Chapters 1-17.)

CCC18 Natalie and Curtis have comparative balance sheets and income statements for Cookie & Coffee Creations Inc. They have been told that they can use these financial statements to prepare horizontal and vertical analyses, and to calculate financial ratios, to analyze how their business is doing and to make some decisions they have been considering.

Go to the book's companion website,
www.wiley.com/college/weygandt,
to see the completion of this problem.

BROADENING YOUR PERSPECTIVE

FINANCIAL REPORTING AND ANALYSIS

Financial Reporting Problem
PepsiCo, Inc.

BYP18-1 Your parents are considering investing in PepsiCo, common stock. They ask you, as an accounting expert, to make an analysis of the company for them. Fortunately, excerpts from a current annual report of PepsiCo are presented in Appendix A of this textbook. Note that all dollar amounts are in millions.

Instructions
(Follow the approach in the chapter for rounding numbers.)

(a) Make a 5-year trend analysis, using 2003 as the base year, of (1) net sales and (2) net income. Comment on the significance of the trend results.
(b) Compute for 2007 and 2006 the (1) profit margin, (2) asset turnover, (3) return on assets, and (4) return on common stockholders' equity. How would you evaluate PepsiCo's profitability? Total assets at December 31, 2005, were $31,727, and total stockholders' equity at December 31, 2005, was $14,320.
(c) Compute for 2007 and 2006 the (1) debt to total assets and (2) times interest earned ratio. How would you evaluate PepsiCo's long-term solvency?
(d) What information outside the annual report may also be useful to your parents in making a decision about PepsiCo, Inc.?

Comparative Analysis Problem
PepsiCo, Inc. vs. The Coca-Cola Company

BYP18-2 PepsiCo's financial statements are presented in Appendix A. Financial statements of The Coca-Cola Company are presented in Appendix B.

Instructions
(a) Based on the information contained in these financial statements, determine each of the following for each company.
  (1) The percentage increase (decrease) in (i) net sales and (ii) net income from 2006 to 2007.
  (2) The percentage increase in (i) total assets and (ii) total common stockholders' (shareholders') equity from 2006 to 2007.
  (3) The basic earnings per share and price-earnings ratio for 2007. (For both PepsiCo and Coca-Cola, use the basic earnings per share.) Coca-Cola's common stock had a market price of $61.37 at the end of fiscal-year 2007.
(b) What conclusions concerning the two companies can be drawn from these data?

Exploring the Web

BYP18-3 The Management Discussion and Analysis section of an annual report addresses corporate performance for the year, and sometimes uses financial ratios to support its claims.

Address: www.ibm.com/investor/tools/index.phtml or go to **www.wiley.com/college/weygandt**

Steps
1. From IBM's Investor Tools, choose **Investment Guides**.
2. Choose **Guide to Annual Reports**.
3. Choose **Anatomy of an Annual Report**.

Instructions
Using the information from the above site, answer the following questions.

(a) What are the optional elements that are often included in an annual report?
(b) What are the elements of an annual report that are required by the SEC?
(c) Describe the contents of the Management Discussion.
(d) Describe the contents of the Auditors' Report.
(e) Describe the contents of the Selected Financial Data.

CRITICAL THINKING

Decision Making Across the Organization

BYP18-4 As the CPA for Carismo Manufacturing Inc., you have been asked to develop some key ratios from the comparative financial statements. This information is to be used to convince creditors that the company is solvent and will continue as a going concern. The data requested and the computations developed from the financial statements follow.

	2010	2009
Current ratio	3.1 times	2.1 times
Acid-test ratio	.8 times	1.4 times
Asset turnover	2.8 times	2.2 times
Net income	Up 32%	Down 8%
Earnings per share	$3.30	$2.50

Instructions
With the class divided into groups, answer the following.

Carismo Manufacturing Inc. asks you to prepare a list of brief comments stating how each of these items supports the solvency and going-concern potential of the business. The company wishes to use these comments to support its presentation of data to its creditors. You are to prepare the comments as requested, giving the implications and the limitations of each item separately. Then prepare a collective inference that may be drawn from the individual items about Carismo's solvency and going-concern potential.

BYP18-5 **General Dynamics** develops, produces, and supports innovative, reliable, and highly sophisticated military and commercial products. In July of a recent year, the corporation announced that its Quincy Shipbuilding Division (Quincy) will be closed following the completion of the Maritime Prepositioning Ship construction program.

Prior to discontinuance, the operating results of Quincy were net sales $246.8 million, income from operations before income taxes $28.3 million, and income taxes $12.5 million. The corporation's loss on disposition of Quincy was $5.0 million, net of $4.3 million income tax benefits.

From its other operating activities, General Dynamics' financial results were net sales $8,163.8 million, cost of goods sold $6,958.8 million, and selling and administrative expenses $537.0 million. In addition, the corporation had interest expense of $17.2 million and interest revenue of $3.6 million. Income taxes were $282.9 million.

General Dynamics had an average of 42.3 million shares of common stock outstanding during the year.

Instructions
With the class divided into groups, answer the following.

(a) Prepare the income statement for the year, assuming that the year ended on December 31, 2010. Show earnings per share data on the income statement. All dollars should be stated in millions, except for per share amounts. (For example, $8 million would be shown as $8.0)
(b) In the preceding year, Quincy's earnings were $51.6 million before income taxes of $22.8 million. For comparative purposes, General Dynamics reported earnings per share of $0.61 from discontinued operations for Quincy in the preceding year.
  (1) What was the average number of common shares outstanding during the preceding year?
  (2) If earnings per share from continuing operations was $7.47, what was income from continuing operations during the preceding year? (Round to two decimals.)

Communication Activity

BYP18-6 Beth Harlan is the CEO of Lafferty's Electronics. Harlan is an expert engineer but a novice in accounting. She asks you to explain (1) the bases for comparison in analyzing Lafferty's financial statements, and (2) the factors affecting quality of earnings.

Instructions
Write a letter to Beth Harlan that explains the bases for comparison and factors affecting quality of earnings.

Ethics Case

BYP18-7 Jack McClintock, president of McClintock Industries, wishes to issue a press release to bolster his company's image and maybe even its stock price, which has been gradually falling. As controller, you have been asked to provide a list of twenty financial ratios along with some other operating statistics relative to McClintock Industries' first quarter financials and operations.

Two days after you provide the ratios and data requested, Jeremy Phelps, the public relations director of McClintock, asks you to prove the accuracy of the financial and operating data contained in the press release written by the president and edited by Jeremy. In the press release, the president highlights the sales increase of 25% over last year's first quarter and the positive change in the current ratio from 1.5:1 last year to 3:1 this year. He also emphasizes that production was up 50% over the prior year's first quarter.

You note that the press release contains only positive or improved ratios and none of the negative or deteriorated ratios. For instance, no mention is made that the debt to total assets ratio has increased from 35% to 55%, that inventories are up 89%, and that while the current ratio improved, the acid-test ratio fell from 1:1 to .5:1. Nor is there any mention that the reported profit for the quarter would have been a loss had not the estimated lives of McClintock's plant and machinery been increased by 30%. Jeremy emphasized, "The prez wants this release by early this afternoon."

Instructions

(a) Who are the stakeholders in this situation?
(b) Is there anything unethical in president McClintock's actions?
(c) Should you as controller remain silent? Does Jeremy have any responsibility?

"All About You" Activity

BYP18-8 In this chapter you learned how to use many tools for performing a financial analysis of a company. When making personal investments, however, it is most likely that you won't be buying stocks and bonds in individual companies. Instead, when most people want to invest in stock, they buy mutual funds. By investing in a mutual fund, you reduce your risk because the fund diversifies by buying the stock of a variety of different companies, bonds, and other investments, depending on the stated goals of the fund.

Before you invest in a fund, you will need to decide what type of fund you want. For example, do you want a fund that has the potential of high growth (but also high risk), or are you looking for lower risk and a steady stream of income? Do you want a fund that invests only in U.S. companies, or do you want one that invests globally? Many resources are available to help you with these types of decisions.

Instructions

Go to **http://web.archive.org/web/20050210200843/http://www.cnb1.com/invallocmdl.htm** and complete the investment allocation questionnaire. Add up your total points to determine the type of investment fund that would be appropriate for you.

Answers to Insight and Accounting Across the Organization Questions

p. 808 Keeping Up to Date as an Investor

Q: If you want to keep current with the financial and operating developments of a company in which you own shares, what are some ways you can do so?

A: *You can obtain current information on your investments through a company's Web site, financial magazines and newspapers, CNBC television programs, investment letters, and a stockbroker.*

p. 814 What Does "Non-Recurring" Really Mean?

Q: If a company takes a large restructuring charge, what is the effect on the company's current income statement versus future ones?

A: *The current period's net income can be greatly diminished by a large restructuring charge, while the net income in future periods can be enhanced because they are relieved of costs (i.e., depreciation and labor expenses) that would have been charged to them.*

Answers to Self-Study Questions

1. b   2. d   3. a   4. c   5. c   6. c   7. c   8. b   9. b   10. a   11. d   12. c   13. c
14. d   15. d

Remember to go back to the Navigator box on the chapter-opening page and check off your completed work.

Chapter 19

Managerial Accounting

STUDY OBJECTIVES

After studying this chapter, you should be able to:

1. Explain the distinguishing features of managerial accounting.
2. Identify the three broad functions of management.
3. Define the three classes of manufacturing costs.
4. Distinguish between product and period costs.
5. Explain the difference between a merchandising and a manufacturing income statement.
6. Indicate how cost of goods manufactured is determined.
7. Explain the difference between a merchandising and a manufacturing balance sheet.
8. Identify trends in managerial accounting.

✓ The Navigator

Scan **Study Objectives** ☐
Read **Feature Story** ☐
Read **Preview** ☐
Read text and answer **DO IT!**
  p. 848 ☐   p. 851 ☐   p. 854 ☐   p. 861 ☐
Work **Comprehensive** **DO IT!** p. 861 ☐
  p. 863 ☐
Review **Summary of Study Objectives** ☐
Answer **Self-Study Questions** ☐
Complete **Assignments** ☐

✓ The Navigator

Feature Story

WHAT A DIFFERENCE A DAY MAKES

In January 1998 Compaq Computer (www.compaq.com) had just become the largest seller of personal computers, and it was *Forbes* magazine's "company of the year." Its chief executive, Eckhard Pfeiffer, was riding high. But during the next two years Compaq lost $2 billion. The company was in chaos, and Mr. Pfeiffer was out of a job. What happened?

First, Dell happened. Dell Computer (www.dell.com) pioneered a new way of making and selling personal computers. Its customers "custom design" their computer over the Internet or phone. Dell reengineered its "supply chain": It coordinated its efforts with its suppliers and streamlined its order-taking and production process. It can ship a computer within two days of taking an order. Personal computers lose 1 percent of their value every week they sit on a shelf. Thus, having virtually no inventory is a great advantage to Dell. Compaq tried to adopt Dell's approach, but with limited success.

The second shock to Compaq came when it acquired a company even larger than itself—Digital Equipment. Mr. Pfeiffer believed that the purchase of Digital, with its huge and respected technical sales force, opened new opportunities for Compaq as a global service company. But combining the two companies proved to be hugely expensive and extremely complicated. Ultimately Compaq decided to merge with Hewlett-Packard (www.hp.com) in order to survive.

After this merger, HP lost significant market share to Dell because its higher cost structure made it hard to compete with Dell on price. Dell created a buzz in the financial press when it decided to enter the computer printing business—a segment that HP had long dominated. Many predicated that Dell would soon take over printers as well. But just when it appeared that Dell could not be beat, HP regained its footing and Dell stumbled. HP reduced its costs by adopting many of Dell's "lean" practices. Thus Dell lost much of its competitive advantage. In addition, computer purchasing habits changed, and Dell wasn't able to adjust fast enough.

Inside Chapter 19...

- **Even the Best Have to Get Better** (p. 846)
- **Bananas Receive Special Treatment** (p. 860)

Preview of Chapter 19

This chapter focuses on issues illustrated in the Feature Story about **Compaq Computer**, **Hewlett-Packard**, and **Dell**. These include determining and controlling the costs of material, labor, and overhead and the relationship between costs and profits. In previous chapters, you learned about the form and content of **financial statements for external users** of financial information, such as stockholders and creditors. These financial statements represent the principal product of financial accounting. Managerial accounting focuses primarily on the preparation of **reports for internal users** of financial information, such as the managers and officers of a company. In today's rapidly changing global environment, managers often make decisions that determine their company's fate—and their own. Managers are evaluated on the results of their decisions. Managerial accounting provides tools for assisting management in making decisions and for evaluating the effectiveness of those decisions.

The content and organization of this chapter are as follows.

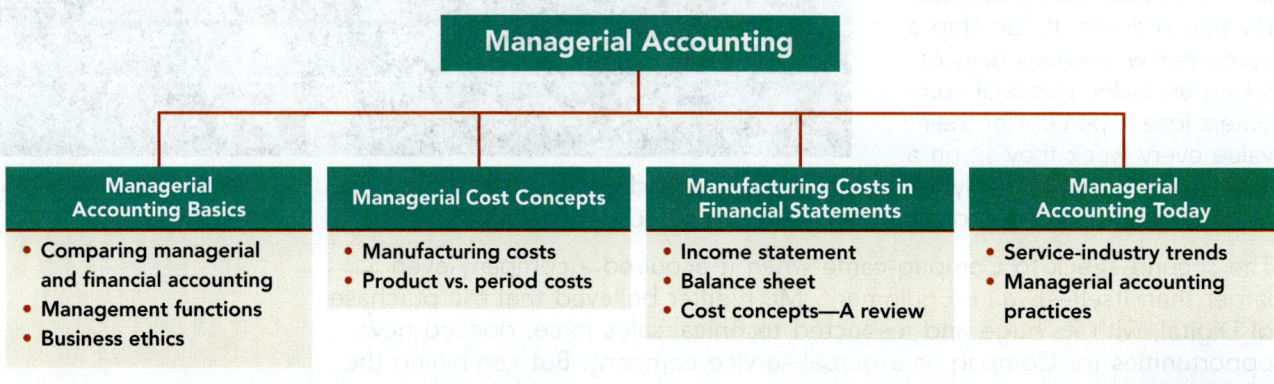

MANAGERIAL ACCOUNTING BASICS

Managerial accounting, also called **management accounting**, is a field of accounting that provides economic and financial information for managers and other internal users. The activities that are part of managerial accounting (and the chapters in which they are discussed in this textbook) are as follows.

1. Explaining manufacturing and nonmanufacturing costs and how they are reported in the financial statements (Chapter 19).
2. Computing the cost of providing a service or manufacturing a product (Chapters 20 and 21).
3. Determining the behavior of costs and expenses as activity levels change and analyzing cost–volume–profit relationships within a company (Chapter 22).
4. Assisting management in profit planning and formalizing these plans in the form of budgets (Chapter 23).
5. Providing a basis for controlling costs and expenses by comparing actual results with planned objectives and standard costs (Chapters 24 and 25).
6. Accumulating and presenting data for management decision making (Chapter 26).

Managerial accounting applies to all types of businesses—service, merchandising, and manufacturing. It also applies to all forms of business organizations—proprietorships, partnerships, and corporations. Not-for-profit entities as well as profit-oriented enterprises need managerial accounting.

In the past, managerial accountants were primarily engaged in cost accounting—collecting and reporting costs to management. Recently that role has changed significantly. First as the business environment has become more automated, methods to determine the amount and type of cost in a product have changed. Second, managerial accountants are now held responsible for strategic cost management; that is, they assist in evaluating how well the company is employing its resources. As a result, managerial accountants now serve as team members alongside personnel from production, marketing, and engineering when the company makes critical strategic decisions.

Opportunities for managerial accountants to advance within the company are considerable. Financial executives must have a background that includes an understanding of managerial accounting concepts. Whatever your position in the company—marketing, sales, or production, knowledge of managerial accounting greatly improves your opportunities for advancement. As the CEO of Microsoft noted: "If you're supposed to be making money in business and supposed to be satisfying customers and building market share, there are numbers that characterize those things. And if somebody can't sort of speak to me quantitatively about it, then I'm nervous."

Comparing Managerial and Financial Accounting

There are both similarities and differences between managerial and financial accounting. First, each field of accounting deals with the economic events of a business. Thus, their interests overlap. For example, *determining* the unit cost of manufacturing a product is part of managerial accounting. *Reporting* the total cost of goods manufactured and sold is part of financial accounting. In addition, both managerial and financial accounting require that a company's economic events be quantified and communicated to interested parties.

Illustration 19-1 illustrates the principal differences between financial accounting and managerial accounting. The need for various types of economic data is responsible for many of the differences.

STUDY OBJECTIVE 1
Explain the distinguishing features of managerial accounting.

Illustration 19-1
Differences between financial and managerial accounting

Financial Accounting		Managerial Accounting
• External users: stockholders, creditors, and regulators.	**Primary Users of Reports**	• Internal users: officers and managers.
• Financial statements. • Quarterly and annually.	**Types and Frequency of Reports**	• Internal reports. • As frequently as needed.
• General-purpose.	**Purpose of Reports**	• Special-purpose for specific decisions.
• Pertains to business as a whole. • Highly aggregated (condensed). • Limited to double-entry accounting and cost data. • Generally accepted accounting principles.	**Content of Reports**	• Pertains to subunits of the business. • Very detailed. • Extends beyond double-entry accounting to any relevant data. • Standard is relevance to decisions.
• Audit by CPA.	**Verification Process**	• No independent audits.

Management Functions

STUDY OBJECTIVE 2
Identify the three broad functions of management.

Managers' activities and responsibilities can be classified into three broad functions:

1. Planning.
2. Directing.
3. Controlling.

In performing these functions, managers make decisions that have a significant impact on the organization.

Planning requires managers to look ahead and to establish objectives. These objectives are often diverse: maximizing short-term profits and market share, maintaining a commitment to environmental protection, and contributing to social programs. For example, Hewlett-Packard, in an attempt to gain a stronger foothold in the computer industry, has greatly reduced its prices to compete with Dell. A key objective of management is to add **value** to the business under its control. Value is usually measured by the trading price of the company's stock and by the potential selling price of the company.

Directing involves coordinating a company's diverse activities and human resources to produce a smooth-running operation. This function relates to implementing planned objectives and providing necessary incentives to motivate employees. For example, manufacturers such as Campbell Soup Company, General Motors, and Dell must coordinate purchasing, manufacturing, warehousing, and selling. Service corporations such as American Airlines, FedEx, and AT&T must coordinate scheduling, sales, service, and acquisitions of equipment and supplies. Directing also involves selecting executives, appointing managers and supervisors, and hiring and training employees.

MANAGEMENT INSIGHT

Even the Best Have to Get Better

Louis Vuitton is a French manufacturer of high-end handbags, wallets, and suitcases. Its reputation for quality and style allows it to charge extremely high prices—for example, $700 for a tote bag. But often in the past, when demand was hot, supply was nonexistent—shelves were empty, and would-be buyers left empty-handed.

Luxury-goods manufacturers used to consider stock-outs to be a good thing, but recently Louis Vuitton changed its attitude. The company adopted "lean" processes used by car manufacturers and electronics companies to speed up production of "hot" products. Work is done by flexible teams, with jobs organized based on how long a task takes. By reducing wasted time and eliminating bottlenecks, what used to take 20 to 30 workers eight days to do now takes 6 to 12 workers one day. Also, production employees who used to specialize on a single task on a single product are now multiskilled. This allows them to quickly switch products to meet demand.

To make sure that the factory is making the right products, within a week of a product launch, Louis Vuitton stores around the world feed sales information to the headquarters in France, and production is adjusted accordingly. Finally, the new production processes have also improved quality. Returns of some products are down by two-thirds, which makes quite a difference to the bottom line when the products are pricey.

Source: Christina Passariello, "Louis Vuitton Tries Modern Methods on Factory Lines," *Wall Street Journal,* October 9, 2006.

 What are some of the steps that this company has taken in order to ensure that production meets demand?

The third management function, **controlling**, is the process of keeping the company's activities on track. In controlling operations, managers determine whether planned goals are being met. When there are deviations from targeted objectives, managers must decide what changes are needed to get back on track. Recent scandals at companies like Enron, Lucent, and Xerox attest to the fact that companies must have adequate controls to ensure that the company develops and distributes accurate information.

How do managers achieve control? A smart manager in a small operation can make personal observations, ask good questions, and know how to evaluate the answers. But using this approach in a large organization would result in chaos. Unless there is some record of what has happened and what is expected to occur, imagine the president of Dell attempting to determine whether the company is meeting its planned objectives. Thus, large businesses typically use a formal system of evaluation. These systems include such features as budgets, responsibility centers, and performance evaluation reports—all of which are features of managerial accounting.

Decision making is not a separate management function. Rather, it is the outcome of the exercise of good judgment in planning, directing, and controlling.

Business Ethics

As indicated in Chapter 1, all employees within an organization are expected to act ethically in their business activities. Given the importance of ethical behavior to corporations and their owners (stockholders), an increasing number of organizations provide codes of business ethics for their employees.

Despite these efforts, recent business scandals resulted in massive investment losses and numerous employee layoffs. A recent survey of fraud by international accounting firm KPMG reported a 13% increase in instances of corporate fraud compared to five years earlier. It noted that while employee fraud (such things as expense-account abuse, payroll fraud, and theft of assets) represented 60% of all instances of fraud, financial reporting fraud (the intentional misstatement of financial reports) was the most costly to companies. That should not be surprising given the long list of companies such as Enron, Global Crossing, WorldCom, and others that engaged in massive financial frauds which led to huge financial losses and thousands of lost jobs.

CREATING PROPER INCENTIVES
Companies like Motorola, IBM, and Nike use complex systems to control and evaluate the actions of managers. They dedicate substantial resources to monitor and effectively evaluate the actions of employees. Unfortunately, these systems and controls sometimes unwittingly create incentives for managers to take unethical actions. For example, companies prepare budgets to provide direction. Because the budget is also used as an evaluation tool, some managers try to "game" the budgeting process by underestimating their division's predicted performance so that it will be easier to meet their performance targets. On the other hand, if the budget is set at unattainable levels, managers sometimes take unethical actions to meet the targets in order to receive higher compensation or, in some cases, to keep their jobs.

For example, in recent years, airline manufacturer Boeing was plagued by a series of scandals including charges of over-billing, corporate espionage, and illegal conflicts of interest. Some long-time employees of Boeing blame the decline in ethics on a change in the corporate culture that took place after Boeing merged with McDonnell Douglas. They suggest that evaluation systems implemented after the merger to monitor results and evaluate employee performance made employees believe they needed to succeed no matter what.

As another example, manufacturing companies need to establish production goals for their processes. Again, if controls are not effective and realistic, problems develop. To illustrate, Schering-Plough, a pharmaceutical manufacturer, found that employees were so concerned with meeting production standards that they failed to monitor the quality of the product, and as a result the dosages were often wrong.

CODE OF ETHICAL STANDARDS

In response to ethical scandals in 2000 and 2001, the U.S. Congress enacted legislation to help prevent lapses in internal control. This legislation, referred to as the **Sarbanes-Oxley Act of 2002 (SOX)** has important implications for the financial community. One result of SOX was to clarify top management's responsibility for the company's financial statements. CEOs and CFOs must now certify that financial statements give a fair presentation of the company's operating results and its financial condition. In addition, top managers must certify that the company maintains an adequate system of internal controls to safeguard the company's assets and ensure accurate financial reports.

Another result of Sarbanes-Oxley is that companies now pay more attention to the composition of the board of directors. In particular, the audit committee of the board of directors must be comprised entirely of independent members (that is, nonemployees) and must contain at least one financial expert.

Finally, to increase the likelihood of compliance with the rules that are part of the new legislation, the law substantially increases the penalties for misconduct.

To provide guidance for managerial accountants, the Institute of Management Accountants (IMA) has developed a code of ethical standards, entitled *IMA Statement of Ethical Professional Practice*. Management accountants should not commit acts in violation of these standards. Nor should they condone such acts by others within their organizations. We include the IMA code of ethical standards in Appendix E at the end of the book. Throughout the chapters on managerial accounting, we will address various ethical issues faced by managers.

DO IT!

MANAGERIAL ACCOUNTING CONCEPTS

Indicate whether the following statements are true or false.

1. Managerial accountants have a single role within an organization, collecting and reporting costs to management.
2. Financial accounting reports are general-purpose and intended for external users.
3. Managerial accounting reports are special-purpose and issued as frequently as needed.
4. Managers' activities and responsibilities can be classified into three broad functions: cost accounting, budgeting, and internal control.
5. As a result of the Sarbanes-Oxley Act of 2002, managerial accounting reports must now comply with generally accepted accounting principles (GAAP).
6. Top managers must certify that a company maintains an adequate system of internal controls.

action plan

✔ Understand that managerial accounting is a field of accounting that provides economic and financial information for managers and other internal users.

✔ Understand that financial accounting provides information for external users.

✔ Analyze which users require which different types of information.

Solution

1. False. Managerial accounts today must help determine the amount and type of a cost in product. In addition, managerial accountants are now held responsible for evaluating how well the company is employing its resources. As a result, when the company makes critical strategic decisions, managerial accountants now serve as team members alongside personnel from production, marketing, and engineering.

2. True.
3. True.
4. False. Managers' activities are classified into three broad functions: planning, directing, and controlling. Planning requires managers to look ahead to establish objectives. Directing involves coordinating a company's diverse activities and human resources to produce a smooth-running operation. Controlling is keeping the company's activities on track.
5. False. SOX clarifies top management's responsibility for the company's financial statements. In addition, top managers must certify that the company maintains an adequate system of internal control to safeguard the company's assets and ensure accurate financial reports.
6. True.

Related exercise material: **BE19-1, BE19-2, BE19-3, E19-1,** and **DO IT! 19-1.**

✓ The Navigator

MANAGERIAL COST CONCEPTS

In order for managers at companies like Dell or Hewlett-Packard to plan, direct, and control operations effectively, they need good information. One very important type of information is related to costs. Managers should ask questions such as the following.

1. What costs are involved in making a product or providing a service?
2. If we decrease production volume, will costs decrease?
3. What impact will automation have on total costs?
4. How can we best control costs?

To answer these questions, managers need reliable and relevant cost information. We now explain and illustrate the various cost categories that companies use.

Manufacturing Costs

Manufacturing consists of activities and processes that convert raw materials into finished goods. Contrast this type of operation with merchandising, which sells merchandise in the form in which it is purchased. Manufacturing costs are typically classified as shown in Illustration 19-2.

STUDY OBJECTIVE 3
Define the three classes of manufacturing costs.

Illustration 19-2
Classifications of manufacturing costs

Manufacturing Costs

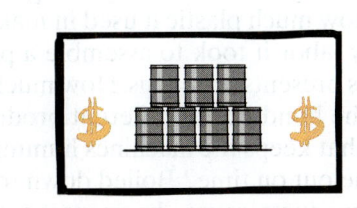
Direct Materials

Direct Labor

Manufacturing Overhead

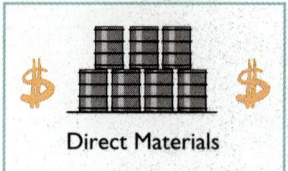
Direct Materials

DIRECT MATERIALS

To obtain the materials that will be converted into the finished product, the manufacturer purchases raw materials. **Raw materials** are the basic materials and parts used in the manufacturing process. For example, auto manufacturers such as General Motors, Ford, and Toyota use steel, plastics, and tires as raw materials in making cars.

Raw materials that can be physically and directly associated with the finished product during the manufacturing process are direct materials. Examples include flour in the baking of bread, syrup in the bottling of soft drinks, and steel in the making of automobiles. Direct materials for Hewlett-Packard and Dell Computer include plastic, glass, hard drives, and processing chips.

But some raw materials cannot be easily associated with the finished product. These are called indirect materials. Indirect materials have one of two characteristics: (1) They do not physically become part of the finished product (such as lubricants and polishing compounds). Or (2) they cannot be traced because their physical association with the finished product is too small in terms of cost (such as cotter pins and lock washers). Companies account for indirect materials as part of **manufacturing overhead**.

Direct Labor

DIRECT LABOR

The work of factory employees that can be physically and directly associated with converting raw materials into finished goods is direct labor. Bottlers at Coca-Cola, bakers at Sara Lee, and typesetters at Aptara Corp. are employees whose activities are usually classified as direct labor. Indirect labor refers to the work of employees that has no physical association with the finished product, or for which it is impractical to trace costs to the goods produced. Examples include wages of maintenance people, time-keepers, and supervisors. Like indirect materials, companies classify indirect labor as **manufacturing overhead**.

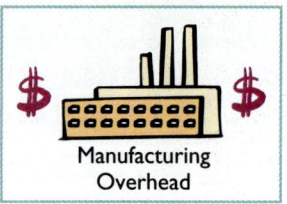
Manufacturing Overhead

MANUFACTURING OVERHEAD

Manufacturing overhead consists of costs that are indirectly associated with the manufacture of the finished product. These costs may also be manufacturing costs that cannot be classified as direct materials or direct labor. Manufacturing overhead includes indirect materials, indirect labor, depreciation on factory buildings and machines, and insurance, taxes, and maintenance on factory facilities.

One study found the following magnitudes of the three different product costs as a percentage of the total product cost: direct materials 54%, direct labor 13%, and manufacturing overhead 33%. Note that the direct labor component is the smallest. This component of product cost is dropping substantially because of automation. Companies are working hard to increase productivity by decreasing labor. A Nissan Motor plant in Tennessee produces Altima automobiles using only 15.74 labor hours per vehicle compared to 26 to 28 hours per vehicle at Ford and Daimler plants, for example. In some companies, direct labor has become as little as 5% of the total cost.

Allocating materials and labor costs to specific products is fairly straightforward. Good record keeping can tell a company how much plastic it used in making each type of gear, or how many hours of factory labor it took to assemble a part. But allocating overhead costs to specific products presents problems. How much of the purchasing agent's salary is attributable to the hundreds of different products made in the same plant? What about the grease that keeps the machines humming, or the computers that make sure paychecks come out on time? Boiled down to its simplest form, the question becomes: Which products cause the incurrence of which costs? In subsequent chapters we show various methods of allocating overhead to products.

ALTERNATIVE TERMINOLOGY

Some companies use terms such as *factory overhead*, *indirect manufacturing costs*, and *burden* instead of manufacturing overhead.

Product versus Period Costs

Each of the manufacturing cost components—direct materials, direct labor, and manufacturing overhead—are product costs. As the term suggests, **product costs** are costs that are a necessary and integral part of producing the finished product. Companies record product costs, when incurred, as inventory. Under the matching principle, these costs do not become expenses until the company sells the finished goods inventory. At that point, the company records the expense as cost of goods sold.

Period costs are costs that are matched with the revenue of a specific time period rather than included as part of the cost of a salable product. These are nonmanufacturing costs. Period costs include selling and administrative expenses. In order to determine net income, companies deduct these costs from revenues in the period in which they are incurred.

Illustration 19-3 summarizes these relationships and cost terms. Our main concern in this chapter is with product costs.

STUDY OBJECTIVE 4
Distinguish between product and period costs.

ALTERNATIVE TERMINOLOGY
Product costs are also called *inventoriable costs*.

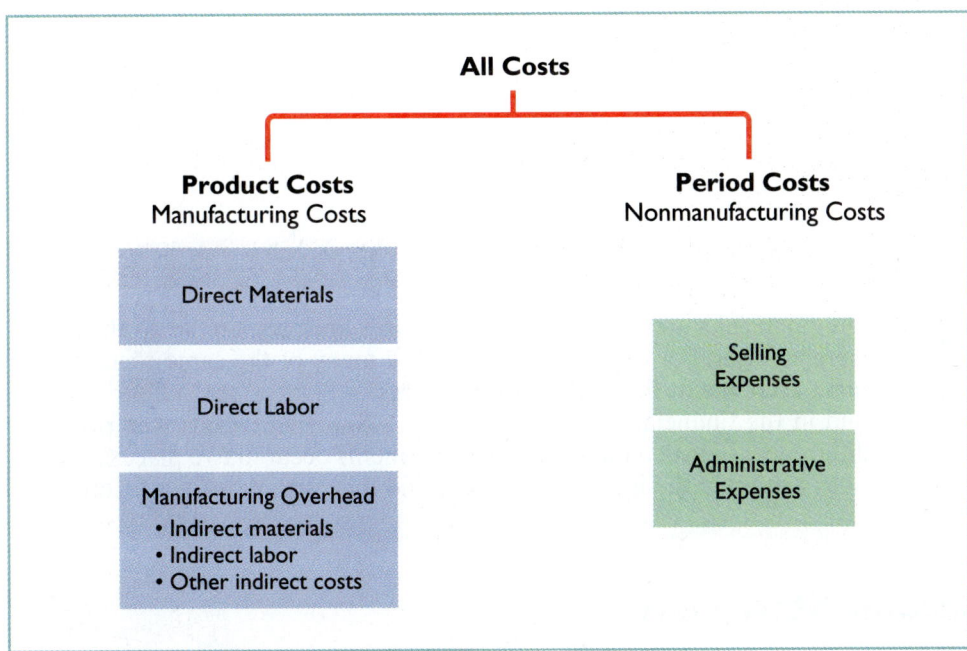

Illustration 19-3
Product versus period costs

DO IT!

A bicycle company has these costs:

Tires
Advertising
Factory building depreciation
Wheel lubricant
Salary of factory manager

Office utilities expense
Salaries of employees who put tires on wheels
Spokes
Salaries of factory maintenance employees
Handlebars

Classify each cost as a period or a product cost. Within the product cost category, indicate if the cost is part of direct materials (DM), direct labor (DL), or manufacturing overhead (MO).

MANAGERIAL COST CONCEPTS

852 Chapter 19 Managerial Accounting

action plan

✔ Product costs are costs that are a necessary and integral part of producing the finished product.

✔ Direct materials can be physically and directly associated with the finished product.

✔ Direct labor is the work of factory employees that can be physically and directly associated with the finished product.

✔ Manufacturing overhead includes any costs that are indirectly associated with the finished product.

✔ Period costs are costs that are matched with the revenue of a specific time period. They are nonmanufacturing costs.

Solution

Period costs:

Office utilities expense
Advertising

Product costs:

Tires (DM)	Salaries of employees who put tires on wheels (DL)
Factory building depreciation (MO)	Spokes (DM)
Wheel lubricant (MO)	Salaries of factory maintenance employees (MO)
Salary of factory manager (MO)	Handlebars (DM)

Related exercise material: **BE19-4, BE19-5, BE19-6, BE19-7, E19-2, E19-3, E19-4, E19-5, E19-6, E19-7,** and **DO IT! 19-2.**

MANUFACTURING COSTS IN FINANCIAL STATEMENTS

STUDY OBJECTIVE 5

Explain the difference between a merchandising and a manufacturing income statement.

The financial statements of a manufacturer are very similar to those of a merchandiser. For example, you will find many of the same sections and same accounts in the financial statements of Procter & Gamble that you find in the financial statements of Dick's Sporting Goods. The principal differences between their financial statements occur in two places: the cost of goods sold section in the income statement and the current assets section in the balance sheet.

Income Statement

Under a periodic inventory system, the income statements of a merchandiser and a manufacturer differ in the cost of goods sold section. Merchandisers compute cost of goods sold by adding the beginning merchandise inventory to the **cost of goods purchased** and subtracting the ending merchandise inventory. Manufacturers compute cost of goods sold by adding the beginning finished goods inventory to the **cost of goods manufactured** and subtracting the ending finished goods inventory. Illustration 19-4 (next page) shows these different methods.

Illustration 19-5 (next page) shows the different presentations of the cost of goods sold sections for merchandising and manufacturing companies. The other sections of an income statement are similar for merchandisers and manufacturers.

A number of accounts are involved in determining the cost of goods manufactured. To eliminate excessive detail, income statements typically show only the total cost of goods manufactured. A separate statement, called a Cost of Goods Manufactured Schedule, presents the details. (For more information, see the discussion on page 854 and Illustration 19-7.)

Manufacturing Costs in Financial Statements

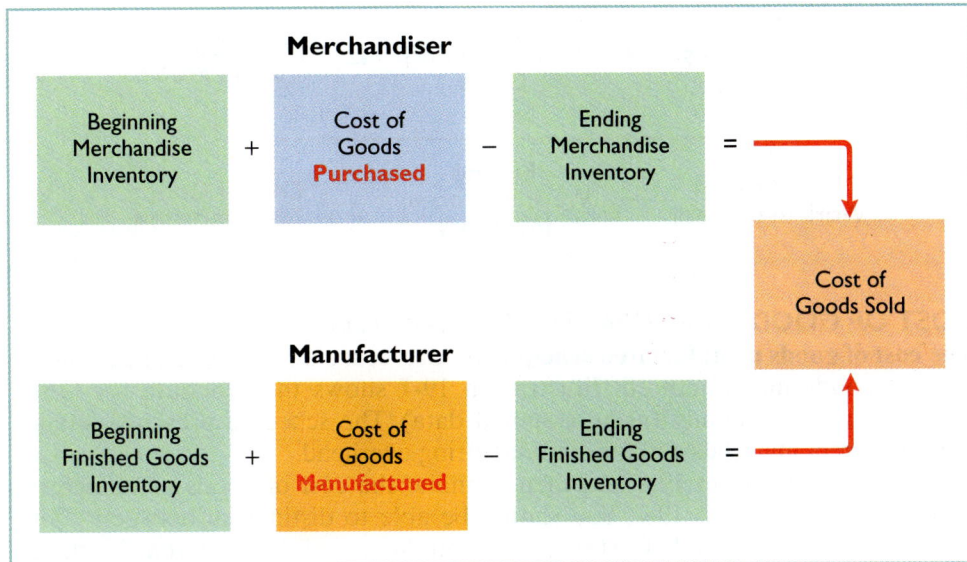

Illustration 19-4
Cost of goods sold components

HELPFUL HINT
We assume a periodic inventory system in this illustration.

Illustration 19-5
Cost of goods sold sections of merchandising and manufacturing income statements

MERCHANDISING COMPANY Income Statement (partial) For the Year Ended December 31, 2010		MANUFACTURING COMPANY Income Statement (partial) For the Year Ended December 31, 2010	
Cost of goods sold		Cost of goods sold	
Merchandise inventory, January 1	$ 70,000	Finished goods inventory, January 1	$ 90,000
Cost of goods purchased	650,000	Cost of goods manufactured	
		(see Illustration 19-7)	370,000
Cost of goods available for sale	720,000	Cost of goods available for sale	460,000
Merchandise inventory, December 31	400,000	Finished goods inventory, December 31	80,000
Cost of goods sold	$320,000	Cost of goods sold	$380,000

DETERMINING THE COST OF GOODS MANUFACTURED

An example may help show how companies determine the cost of goods manufactured. Assume that Dell has a number of computers in various stages of production on January 1. In total, these partially completed units are called **beginning work in process inventory**. The costs the company assigns to beginning work in process inventory are based on the **manufacturing costs incurred in the prior period**.

STUDY OBJECTIVE 6
Indicate how cost of goods manufactured is determined.

Dell first uses the manufacturing costs incurred in the current year to complete the work that was in process on January 1. It then incurs manufacturing costs for production of new orders. The sum of the direct materials costs, direct labor costs, and manufacturing overhead incurred in the current year is the **total manufacturing costs** for the current period.

We now have two cost amounts: (1) the cost of the beginning work in process and (2) the total manufacturing costs for the current period. The sum of these costs is the **total cost of work in process** for the year.

At the end of the year, Dell may have some computers that are only partially completed. The costs of these units become the cost of the **ending work in process inventory**. To find the **cost of goods manufactured**, we subtract this cost from the total cost of work in process. Illustration 19-6 (next page) shows the formula for determining the cost of goods manufactured.

854 Chapter 19 Managerial Accounting

Illustration 19-6
Cost of goods manufactured formula

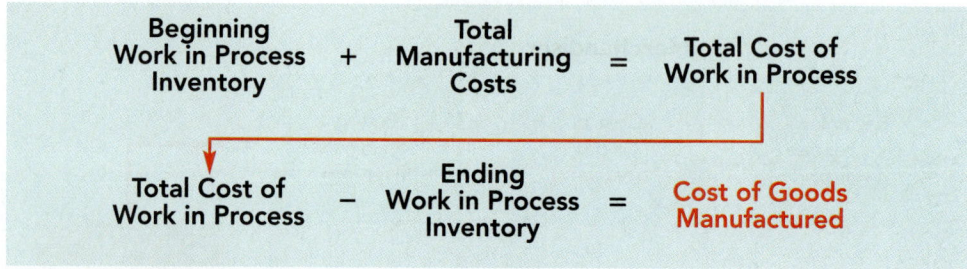

COST OF GOODS MANUFACTURED SCHEDULE

The **cost of goods manufactured schedule** reports cost elements used in calculating cost of goods manufactured. Illustration 19-7 shows the schedule for Olsen Manufacturing Company (using assumed data). The schedule presents detailed data for direct materials and for manufacturing overhead.

Review Illustration 19-6 and then examine the cost of goods manufactured schedule in Illustration 19-7. You should be able to distinguish between "Total manufacturing costs" and "Cost of goods manufactured." The difference is the effect of the change in work in process during the period.

Illustration 19-7
Cost of goods manufactured schedule

OLSEN MANUFACTURING COMPANY
Cost of Goods Manufactured Schedule
For the Year Ended December 31, 2010

Work in process, January 1			$ 18,400
Direct materials			
Raw materials inventory, January 1	$ 16,700		
Raw materials purchases	152,500		
Total raw materials available for use	169,200		
Less: Raw materials inventory, December 31	22,800		
Direct materials used		$146,400	
Direct labor		175,600	
Manufacturing overhead			
Indirect labor	14,300		
Factory repairs	12,600		
Factory utilities	10,100		
Factory depreciation	9,440		
Factory insurance	8,360		
Total manufacturing overhead		54,800	
Total manufacturing costs			376,800
Total cost of work in process			395,200
Less: Work in process, December 31			25,200
Cost of goods manufactured			$370,000

DO IT!

COST OF GOODS MANUFACTURED

The following information is available for Keystone Manufacturing Company.

	March 1	March 31
Raw material inventory	$12,000	$10,000
Work in process inventory	2,500	4,000

Materials purchased in March $90,000
Direct labor in March 75,000
Manufacturing overhead in March 220,000

Prepare the cost of goods manufactured schedule for the month of March.

Solution

KEYSTONE MANUFACTURING COMPANY
Cost of Goods Manufactured Schedule
For the Month Ended March 31

Work in process, March 1		$ 2,500
Direct materials		
Raw materials, March 1	$ 12,000	
Raw material purchases	90,000	
Total raw materials available for use	102,000	
Less: Raw materials, March 31	10,000	
Direct materials used		$ 92,000
Direct labor		75,000
Manufacturing overhead		220,000
Total manufacturing costs		387,000
Total cost of work in process		389,500
Less: Work in process, March 31		4,000
Cost of goods manufactured		$385,500

action plan

✔ Start with beginning work in process as the first item in the cost of goods manufactured schedule.

✔ Sum direct materials used, direct labor, and total manufacturing overhead to determine total manufacturing costs.

✔ Sum beginning work in process and total manufacturing costs to determine total cost of work in process.

✔ Cost of goods manufactured is the total cost of work in process less ending work in process.

Related exercise material: **BE19-8, BE19-10, BE19-11, E19-8, E19-9, E19-10, E19-11, E19-12, E19-13, E19-14, E19-15, E19-16, E19-17,** and **DO IT! 19-3**.

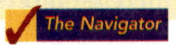

Balance Sheet

The balance sheet for a merchandising company shows just one category of inventory. In contrast, the balance sheet for a manufacturer may have three inventory accounts, as shown in Illustration 19-8.

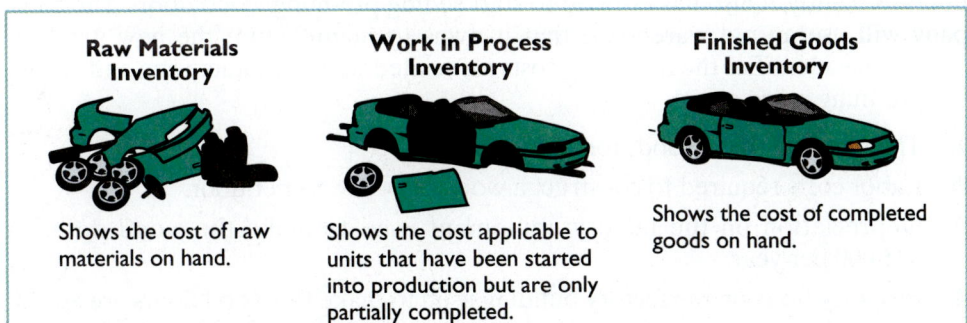

Illustration 19-8
Inventory accounts for a manufacturer

Finished Goods Inventory is to a manufacturer what Merchandise Inventory is to a merchandiser. Each of these classifications represents the goods that are available for sale.

The current assets sections presented in Illustration 19-9 (page 856) contrast the presentations of inventories for merchandising and manufacturing companies. Manufacturing companies generally list their inventories in the order of their liquidity—the order in which they are expected to be realized in cash. Thus, finished goods inventory comes first. The remainder of the balance sheet is similar for the two types of companies.

STUDY OBJECTIVE 7
Explain the difference between a merchandising and a manufacturing balance sheet.

MERCHANDISING COMPANY		MANUFACTURING COMPANY		
Balance Sheet December 31, 2010		Balance Sheet December 31, 2010		
Current assets		Current assets		
Cash	$100,000	Cash		$180,000
Receivables (net)	210,000	Receivables (net)		210,000
Merchandise inventory	400,000	Inventories		
Prepaid expenses	22,000	Finished goods	$80,000	
Total current assets	$732,000	Work in process	25,200	
		Raw materials	22,800	128,000
		Prepaid expenses		18,000
		Total current assets		$536,000

Illustration 19-9
Current assets sections of merchandising and manufacturing balance sheets

For expanded coverage, go to the Student Companion site and select Chapter 19, Accounting Cycle (Worksheet) for a Manufacturing Company.

Each step in the accounting cycle for a merchandiser applies to a manufacturer. For example, prior to preparing financial statements, manufacturers make adjusting entries. The adjusting entries are essentially the same as those of a merchandiser. The closing entries are also similar for manufacturers and merchandisers.

Cost Concepts—A Review

You have learned a number of cost concepts in this chapter. Because many of these concepts are new, here we provide an extended example for review.

Assume that Northridge Company manufactures and sells pre-hung metal doors. Recently, it also has decided to start selling pre-hung wood doors. The company will use an old warehouse that it owns to manufacture the new product. Northridge identifies the following costs associated with manufacturing and selling the pre-hung wood doors.

1. The material cost (wood) for each door is $10.
2. Labor costs required to construct a wood door are $8 per door.
3. Depreciation on the factory equipment used to make the wood doors is $25,000 per year.
4. Property taxes on the factory building used to make the wood doors are $6,000 per year.
5. Advertising costs for the pre-hung wood doors total $2,500 per month or $30,000 per year.
6. Sales commissions related to pre-hung wood doors sold are $4 per door.
7. Salaries for employees who maintain the factory facilities are $28,000.
8. The salary of the plant manager in charge of pre-hung wood doors is $70,000.
9. The cost of shipping pre-hung wood doors is $12 per door sold.

Illustration 19-10 shows how Northridge would assign these manufacturing and selling costs to the various categories.

Illustration 19-10
Assignment of costs to cost categories

Cost Item	Direct Materials	Direct Labor	Manufacturing Overhead	Period Costs
1. Material cost ($10) per door	X			
2. Labor costs ($8) per door		X		
3. Depreciation on factory equipment ($25,000 per year)			X	
4. Property taxes on factory building ($6,000 per year)			X	
5. Advertising costs ($30,000 per year)				X
6. Sales commissions ($4 per door)				X
7. Maintenance salaries (factory facilities) ($28,000 per year)			X	
8. Salary of plant manager ($70,000)			X	
9. Cost of shipping pre-hung doors ($12 per door)				X

Remember that total manufacturing costs are the sum of the **product costs**—direct materials, direct labor, and manufacturing overhead. If Northridge Company produces 10,000 pre-hung wood doors the first year, the total manufacturing costs would be $309,000 as shown in Illustration 19-11.

Illustration 19-11
Computation of total manufacturing costs

Cost Number and Item	Manufacturing Cost
1. Material cost ($10 × 10,000)	$100,000
2. Labor cost ($8 × 10,000)	80,000
3. Depreciation on factory equipment	25,000
4. Property taxes on factory building	6,000
7. Maintenance salaries (factory facilities)	28,000
8. Salary of plant manager	70,000
Total manufacturing costs	**$309,000**

Knowing the total manufacturing costs, Northridge can compute the manufacturing cost per unit. Assuming 10,000 units, the cost to produce one pre-hung wood door is $30.90 ($309,000 ÷ 10,000 units).

In subsequent chapters we will use extensively the cost concepts discussed in this chapter. Study Illustration 19-10 carefully. If you do not understand any of these classifications, go back and reread the appropriate section in this chapter.

MANAGERIAL ACCOUNTING TODAY

STUDY OBJECTIVE 8
Identify trends in managerial accounting.

In recent years, the competitive environment for U.S. business has changed significantly. For example, the airline, financial services, and telecommunications industries have been deregulated. Global competition has intensified. The world economy now has the European Union, NAFTA, and ASEAN. Countries like China and India are becoming economic powerhouses. As indicated earlier, managerial accountants must be forward-looking, acting as advisors and information providers to different parts of the organization. Some of the issues they face are discussed below.

Service-Industry Trends

The Feature Story notes that at the peak of its success as a personal computer manufacturer, Compaq purchased Digital Equipment. Its management believed that the future of computing was in providing computer services, rather than in manufacturing computer hardware. In fact, the U.S. economy in general has shifted toward an emphasis on providing services, rather than goods. Today over 50% of U.S. workers work in service companies, and that percentage is projected to increase in coming years. Much of this chapter focused on manufacturers, but most of the techniques that you will learn in this course apply equally to service companies.

ETHICS NOTE
Do telecommunications companies have an obligation to provide service to remote or low-user areas for a fee that may be less than the cost of the service?

Managers of service companies look to managerial accounting to answer many questions. In some instances the managerial accountant may need to develop new systems for measuring the cost of serving individual customers. In others, companies may need new operating controls to improve the quality and efficiency of specific services. Many of the examples we present in subsequent chapters will be based on service companies.

Managerial Accounting Practices

As discussed earlier, the practice of managerial accounting has changed significantly in recent years to better address the needs of managers. The following sections explain some recent managerial accounting practices.

THE VALUE CHAIN

The **value chain** refers to all activities associated with providing a product or service. For a manufacturer these include research and development, product design, acquisition of raw materials, production, sales and marketing, delivery, customer relations, and subsequent service. Illustration 19-12 depicts the value chain for a manufacturer. In recent years, companies have made huge strides in analyzing all stages of the value chain in an effort to improve productivity and eliminate waste. Japanese automobile manufacturer Toyota pioneered many of these innovations.

Illustration 19-12
A manufacturer's value chain

In the 1980s many companies purchased giant machines to replace humans in the manufacturing process. These machines were designed to produce large batches of products. In recent years these large-batch manufacturing processes have been recognized as wasteful. They require vast amounts of inventory storage capacity and considerable movement of materials. Consequently, many companies have reengineered their manufacturing processes. As one example, the manufacturing company Pratt and Whitney has replaced many large machines with smaller, more flexible ones and has begun reorganizing its plants for more efficient flow of goods. Pratt and Whitney was able to reduce the time that its turbine engine blades spend in the grinding section of its factory from 10 days down to 2 hours. It cut the total amount of time spent making a blade from 22 days to 7 days. Analysis of the value chain has made companies far more responsive to customer needs and has improved profitability.

JUST-IN-TIME INVENTORY METHODS

Many companies have significantly lowered inventory levels and costs using **just-in-time (JIT) inventory** methods. Under a just-in-time method, goods are manufactured or purchased just in time for use. As noted in the Feature Story, Dell is famous for having developed a system for making computers in response to individual customer requests. Even though each computer is custom-made to meet each customer's specifications, it takes Dell less than 48 hours to assemble the computer and put it on a truck. By integrating its information systems with those of its suppliers, Dell reduced its inventories to nearly zero. This is a huge advantage in an industry where products become obsolete nearly overnight.

> **ETHICS NOTE**
> Does just-in-time inventory justify "just-in-time" employees obtained through temporary employment services?

QUALITY

JIT inventory systems require an increased emphasis on product quality. If products are produced only as they are needed, it is very costly for the company to have to stop production because of defects or machine breakdowns. Many companies have installed **total quality management (TQM)** systems to reduce defects in finished products. The goal is to achieve zero defects. These systems require timely data on defective products, rework costs, and the cost of honoring warranty contracts. Often, companies use this information to help redesign the product in a way that makes it less prone to defect. Or they may use the information to reengineer the production process to reduce setup time and decrease the potential for error. TQM systems also provide information on nonfinancial measures such as customer satisfaction, number of service calls, and time to generate reports. Attention to these measures, which employees can control, leads to increased profitability.

ACTIVITY-BASED COSTING

As discussed earlier, overhead costs have become an increasingly large component of product and service costs. By definition, overhead costs cannot be directly traced to individual products. But to determine each product's cost, overhead must be **allocated** to the various products. In order to obtain more accurate product costs, many companies now allocate overhead using **activity-based costing (ABC)**. Under ABC, companies allocate overhead based on each product's use of activities in making the product. For example, companies can keep track of their cost of setting up machines for each batch of a production process. Then companies can allocate part of the total set-up cost to a particular product based on the number of set-ups that product required.

Activity-based costing is beneficial because it results in more accurate product costing and in more careful scrutiny of all activities in the value chain. For example, if a product's cost is high because it requires a high number of set-ups, management will be motivated to determine how to produce the product using the optimal number of machine set-ups. Both manufacturing and service companies now widely use ABC. Allied Signal and Coca-Cola have both enjoyed improved results from ABC. Fidelity Investments uses ABC to identify which customers cost the most to serve.

MANAGEMENT INSIGHT

Bananas Receive Special Treatment

When it comes to total quality management, few companies can compare with Chiquita Brands International. Grocery store customers are very picky about bananas—bad bananas are consistently the number one grocery store complaint. Because bananas often account for up to 3% of a grocery store's sales, Chiquita goes to great lengths to protect the popular fruit. While bananas are in transit from Central America, "black box" recording devices attached to shipping crates ensure that they are kept in an environment of 90% humidity and an unvarying 55-degree temperature. Upon arrival in the U.S., bananas are ripened in airtight warehouses that use carefully monitored levels of ethylene gas. Regular checks are made of each warehouse using ultrasonic detectors that can detect leaks the size of a pinhole. Says one grocery store executive, "No other item in the store has this type of attention and resources devoted to it."

Source: Devon Spurgeon, "When Grocers in U.S. Go Bananas Over Bad Fruit, They Call Laubenthal," *Wall Street Journal,* August 14, 2000, p. A1.

 Why is it important to keep track of costs that are incurred to improve product quality?

BALANCED SCORECARD

As companies implement various business practice innovations, managers sometimes focus too enthusiastically on the latest innovation, to the detriment of other areas of the business. For example, in focusing on improving quality, companies sometimes have lost sight of cost/benefit considerations. Similarly, in focusing on reducing inventory levels through just-in-time, companies sometimes have lost sales due to inventory shortages. The **balanced scorecard** is a performance-measurement approach that uses both financial and nonfinancial measures to evaluate all aspects of a company's operations in an **integrated** fashion. The performance measures are linked in a cause-and-effect fashion to ensure that they all tie to the company's overall objectives.

For example, the company may desire to increase its return on assets, a common financial performance measure (calculated as net income divided by average total assets). It will then identify a series of linked goals. If the company accomplishes each goal, the ultimate result will be an increase in return on assets. For example, in order to increase return on assets, sales must increase. In order to increase sales, customer satisfaction must be increased. In order to increase customer satisfaction, product defects must be reduced. In order to reduce product defects, employee training must be increased. Note the linkage, which starts with employee training and ends with return on assets. Each objective will have associated performance measures.

The use of the balanced scorecard is widespread among well-known and respected companies. For example, Hilton Hotels Corporation uses the balanced scorecard to evaluate the performance of employees at all of its hotel chains. Wal-Mart employs the balanced scorecard, and actually extends its use to evaluation of its suppliers. For example, Wal-Mart recently awarded Welch Company the "Dry Grocery Division Supplier of the Year Award" for its balanced scorecard results. We discuss the balanced scorecard further in Chapter 25.

DO IT!

Match the descriptions that follow with the corresponding terms.

TRENDS IN MANAGERIAL ACCOUNTING

Descriptions:

1. _____ All activities associated with providing a product or service.
2. _____ A method of allocating overhead based on each product's use of activities in making the product.
3. _____ Systems implemented to reduce defects in finished products with the goal of achieving zero defects.
4. _____ A performance-measurement approach that uses both financial and nonfinancial measures, tied to company objectives, to evaluate a company's operations in an integrated fashion.
5. _____ Inventory system in which goods are manufactured or purchased just as they are needed for use.

Terms:

a. Activity-based costing
b. Balanced scorecard
c. Just-in-time (JIT) inventory
d. Total quality management (TQM)
e. Value chain

Solution

1. e   2. a   3. d   4. b   5. c

Related exercise material: **E19-18** and  **19-4**.

action plan

✔ Develop a forward-looking view, in order to advise and provide information to various members of the organization.
✔ Understand current business trends and issues.

Comprehensive DO IT! 1

Giant Manufacturing Co. specializes in manufacturing different models of bicycles. Assume that the market has responded enthusiastically to a new model, the Jaguar. As a result, the company has established a separate manufacturing facility to produce these bicycles. The company produces 1,000 of these bicycles per month. Giant's monthly manufacturing cost and other expenses data related to these bicycles are as follows.

1. Rent on manufacturing equipment (lease cost) — $2,000/month
2. Insurance on manufacturing building — $750/month
3. Raw materials (frames, tires, etc.) — $80/bicycle
4. Utility costs for manufacturing facility — $1,000/month
5. Supplies for administrative office — $800/month
6. Wages for assembly line workers in manufacturing facility — $30/bicycle
7. Depreciation on office equipment — $650/month
8. Miscellaneous materials (lubricants, solders, etc.) — $1.20/bicycle
9. Property taxes on manufacturing building — $2,400/year
10. Manufacturing supervisor's salary — $3,000/month
11. Advertising for bicycles — $30,000/year
12. Sales commissions — $10/bicycle
13. Depreciation on manufacturing building — $1,500/month

Instructions

(a) Prepare an answer sheet with the following column headings.

Cost Item	Product Costs			Period Costs
	Direct Materials	Direct Labor	Manufacturing Overhead	

Enter each cost item on your answer sheet, placing an "X" mark under the appropriate headings.

(b) Compute total manufacturing costs for the month.

Solution to Comprehensive DO IT! 1

(a)

Cost Item	Product Costs			Period Costs
	Direct Materials	Direct Labor	Manufacturing Overhead	
1. Rent on manufacturing equipment ($2,000/month)			X	
2. Insurance on manufacturing building ($750/month)			X	
3. Raw materials ($80/bicycle)	X			
4. Manufacturing utilities ($1,000/month)			X	
5. Office supplies ($800/month)				X
6. Wages for workers ($30/bicycle)		X		
7. Depreciation on office equipment ($650/month)				X
8. Miscellaneous materials ($1.20/bicycle)			X	
9. Property taxes on manufacturing building ($2,400/year)			X	
10. Manufacturing supervisor's salary ($3,000/month)			X	
11. Advertising cost ($30,000/year)				X
12. Sales commissions ($10/bicycle)				X
13. Depreciation on manufacturing building ($1,500/month)			X	

(b)

Cost Item	Manufacturing Cost
Rent on manufacturing equipment	$ 2,000
Insurance on manufacturing building	750
Raw materials ($80 × 1,000)	80,000
Manufacturing utilities	1,000
Labor ($30 × 1,000)	30,000
Miscellaneous materials ($1.20 × 1,000)	1,200
Property taxes on manufacturing building ($2,400 ÷ 12)	200
Manufacturing supervisor's salary	3,000
Depreciation on manufacturing building	1,500
Total manufacturing costs	$119,650

Comprehensive DO IT! 2

Superior Manufacturing Company has the following cost and expense data for the year ending December 31, 2010.

Raw materials, 1/1/10	$ 30,000	Insurance, factory	$ 14,000
Raw materials, 12/31/10	20,000	Property taxes, factory building	6,000
Raw materials purchases	205,000	Sales (net)	1,500,000
Indirect materials	15,000	Delivery expenses	100,000
Work in process, 1/1/10	80,000	Sales commissions	150,000
Work in process, 12/31/10	50,000	Indirect labor	90,000
Finished goods, 1/1/10	110,000	Factory machinery rent	40,000
Finished goods, 12/31/10	120,000	Factory utilities	65,000
Direct labor	350,000	Depreciation, factory building	24,000
Factory manager's salary	35,000	Administrative expenses	300,000

Instructions

(a) Prepare a cost of goods manufactured schedule for Superior Company for 2010.
(b) Prepare an income statement for Superior Company for 2010.
(c) Assume that Superior Company's ledgers show the balances of the following current asset accounts: Cash $17,000, Accounts Receivable (net) $120,000, Prepaid Expenses $13,000, and Short-term Investments $26,000. Prepare the current assets section of the balance sheet for Superior Company as of December 31, 2010.

Solution to Comprehensive DO IT! 2

(a)
SUPERIOR MANUFACTURING COMPANY
Cost of Goods Manufactured Schedule
For the Year Ended December 31, 2010

Work in process, 1/1			$ 80,000
Direct materials			
Raw materials inventory, 1/1	$ 30,000		
Raw materials purchases	205,000		
Total raw materials available for use	235,000		
Less: Raw materials inventory, 12/31	20,000		
Direct materials used		$215,000	
Direct labor		350,000	
Manufacturing overhead			
Indirect labor	90,000		
Factory utilities	65,000		
Factory machinery rent	40,000		
Factory manager's salary	35,000		
Depreciation on building	24,000		
Indirect materials	15,000		
Factory insurance	14,000		
Property taxes	6,000		
Total manufacturing overhead		289,000	
Total manufacturing costs			854,000
Total cost of work in process			934,000
Less: Work in process, 12/31			50,000
Cost of goods manufactured			$884,000

action plan

✔ Start with beginning work in process as the first item in the cost of goods manufactured schedule.
✔ Sum direct materials used, direct labor, and total manufacturing overhead to determine total manufacturing costs.
✔ Sum beginning work in process and total manufacturing costs to determine total cost of work in process.
✔ Cost of goods manufactured is the total cost of work in process less ending work in process.
✔ In the cost of goods sold section of the income statement, show beginning and ending finished goods inventory and cost of goods manufactured.
✔ In the balance sheet, list manufacturing inventories in the order of their expected realization in cash, with finished goods first.

(b)

SUPERIOR MANUFACTURING COMPANY
Income Statement
For the Year Ended December 31, 2010

Sales (net)		$1,500,000
Cost of goods sold		
Finished goods inventory, January 1	$110,000	
Cost of goods manufactured	884,000	
Cost of goods available for sale	994,000	
Less: Finished goods inventory, December 31	120,000	
Cost of goods sold		874,000
Gross profit		626,000
Operating expenses		
Administrative expenses	300,000	
Sales commissions	150,000	
Delivery expenses	100,000	
Total operating expenses		550,000
Net income		$ 76,000

(c)

SUPERIOR MANUFACTURING COMPANY
Balance Sheet (partial)
December 31, 2010

Current assets		
Cash		$ 17,000
Short-term investments		26,000
Accounts receivable (net)		120,000
Inventories		
Finished goods	$120,000	
Work in process	50,000	
Raw materials	20,000	190,000
Prepaid expenses		13,000
Total current assets		$366,000

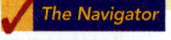

SUMMARY OF STUDY OBJECTIVES

1 Explain the distinguishing features of managerial accounting. The *primary users* of managerial accounting reports are internal users, who are officers, department heads, managers, and supervisors in the company. Managerial accounting issues internal reports as frequently as the need arises. The purpose of these reports is to provide special-purpose information for a particular user for a specific decision. The content of managerial accounting reports pertains to subunits of the business, may be very detailed, and may extend beyond the double-entry accounting system. The reporting standard is relevance to the decision being made. No independent audits are required in managerial accounting.

2 Identify the three broad functions of management. The three functions are planning, directing, and controlling. Planning requires management to look ahead and to establish objectives. Directing involves coordinating the diverse activities and human resources of a company to produce a smooth-running operation. Controlling is the process of keeping the activities on track.

3 Define the three classes of manufacturing costs. Manufacturing costs are typically classified as either (1) direct materials, (2) direct labor, or (3) manufacturing overhead. Raw materials that can be physically and directly associated with the finished product during the manufacturing process are called direct materials. The work of factory employees that can be physically and directly associated with converting raw materials into finished goods is considered direct labor. Manufacturing overhead consists of costs that are indirectly associated with the manufacture of the finished product.

4 **Distinguish between product and period costs.** Product costs are costs that are a necessary and integral part of producing the finished product. Product costs are also called inventoriable costs. Under the matching principle, these costs do not become expenses until the company sells the finished goods inventory. Period costs are costs that are identified with a specific time period rather than with a salable product. These costs relate to nonmanufacturing costs and therefore are not inventoriable costs.

5 **Explain the difference between a merchandising and a manufacturing income statement.** The difference between a merchandising and a manufacturing income statement is in the cost of goods sold section. A manufacturing cost of goods sold section shows beginning and ending finished goods inventories and the cost of goods manufactured.

6 **Indicate how cost of goods manufactured is determined.** Companies add the cost of the beginning work in process to the total manufacturing costs for the current year to arrive at the total cost of work in process for the year. They then subtract the ending work in process from the total cost of work in process to arrive at the cost of goods manufactured.

7 **Explain the difference between a merchandising and a manufacturing balance sheet.** The difference between a merchandising and a manufacturing balance sheet is in the current assets section. The current assets section of a manufacturing company's balance sheet presents three inventory accounts: finished goods inventory, work in process inventory, and raw materials inventory.

8 **Identify trends in managerial accounting.** Managerial accounting has experienced many changes in recent years. Among these are a shift toward addressing the needs of service companies and improving practices to better meet the needs of managers. Improved practices include a focus on managing the value chain through techniques such as just-in-time inventory and total quality management. In addition, techniques such as activity-based costing (ABC) have been developed to improve decision making. Finally, the balanced scorecard is now used by many companies in order to attain a more comprehensive view of the company's operations.

GLOSSARY

Activity-based costing (ABC) A method of allocating overhead based on each product's use of activities in making the product. (p. 859).

Balanced scorecard A performance-measurement approach that uses both financial and nonfinancial measures, tied to company objectives, to evaluate a company's operations in an integrated fashion. (p. 860).

Cost of goods manufactured Total cost of work in process less the cost of the ending work in process inventory. (p. 853).

Direct labor The work of factory employees that can be physically and directly associated with converting raw materials into finished goods. (p. 850).

Direct materials Raw materials that can be physically and directly associated with manufacturing the finished product. (p. 850).

Indirect labor Work of factory employees that has no physical association with the finished product, or for which it is impractical to trace the costs to the goods produced. (p. 850).

Indirect materials Raw materials that do not physically become part of the finished product or cannot be traced because their physical association with the finished product is too small. (p. 850).

Just-in-time (JIT) inventory Inventory system in which goods are manufactured or purchased just in time for use. (p. 859).

Managerial accounting A field of accounting that provides economic and financial information for managers and other internal users. (p. 844).

Manufacturing overhead Manufacturing costs that are indirectly associated with the manufacture of the finished product. (p. 850).

Period costs Costs that are matched with the revenue of a specific time period and charged to expense as incurred. (p. 851).

Product costs Costs that are a necessary and integral part of producing the finished product. (p. 851).

Sarbanes-Oxley Act of 2002 (SOX) Law passed by Congress in 2002, intended to reduce unethical corporate behavior. (p. 848).

Total cost of work in process Cost of the beginning work in process plus total manufacturing costs for the current period. (p. 853).

Total manufacturing costs The sum of direct materials, direct labor, and manufacturing overhead incurred in the current period. (p. 853).

Total quality management (TQM) Systems implemented to reduce defects in finished products with the goal of achieving zero defects. (p. 859).

Value chain All activities associated with providing a product or service. (p. 858).

SELF-STUDY QUESTIONS

Answers are at the end of the chapter.

(SO 1) **1.** Managerial accounting:
  a. is governed by generally accepted accounting principles.
  b. places emphasis on special-purpose information.
  c. pertains to the entity as a whole and is highly aggregated.
  d. is limited to cost data.

(SO 2) **2.** The management of an organization performs several broad functions. They are:
  a. planning, directing, and selling.
  b. planning, directing, and controlling.
  c. planning, manufacturing, and controlling.
  d. directing, manufacturing, and controlling.

(SO 2) **3.** After passage of the Sarbanes-Oxley Act of 2002:
  a. reports prepared by managerial accountants must by audited by CPAs.
  b. CEOs and CFOs must certify that financial statements give a fair presentation of the company's operating results.
  c. the audit committee, rather than top management, is responsible for the company's financial statements.
  d. reports prepared by managerial accountants must comply with generally accepted accounting principles (GAAP).

(SO 3) **4.** Direct materials are a:

	Product Cost	Manufacturing Overhead	Period Cost
a.	Yes	Yes	No
b.	Yes	No	No
c.	Yes	Yes	Yes
d.	No	No	No

(SO 3) **5.** Which of the following costs would a computer manufacturer include in manufacturing overhead?
  a. The cost of the disk drives.
  b. The wages earned by computer assemblers.
  c. The cost of the memory chips.
  d. Depreciation on testing equipment.

(SO 3) **6.** Which of the following is *not* an element of manufacturing overhead?
  a. Sales manager's salary.
  b. Plant manager's salary.
  c. Factory repairman's wages.
  d. Product inspector's salary.

(SO 4) **7.** Indirect labor is a:
  a. nonmanufacturing cost.
  b. raw material cost.
  c. product cost.
  d. period cost.

(SO 4) **8.** Which of the following costs are classified as a period cost?
  a. Wages paid to a factory custodian.
  b. Wages paid to a production department supervisor.
  c. Wages paid to a cost accounting department supervisor.
  d. Wages paid to an assembly worker.

(SO 5) **9.** For the year, Redder Company has cost of goods manufactured of $600,000, beginning finished goods inventory of $200,000, and ending finished goods inventory of $250,000. The cost of goods sold is:
  a. $450,000.
  b. $500,000.
  c. $550,000.
  d. $600,000.

(SO 5) **10.** Cost of goods available for sale is reported on the income statement of:
  a. a merchandising company but not a manufacturing company.
  b. a manufacturing company but not a merchandising company.
  c. a merchandising company and a manufacturing company.
  d. neither a manufacturing company nor a merchandising company.

(SO 6) **11.** A cost of goods manufactured schedule shows beginning and ending inventories for:
  a. raw materials and work in process only.
  b. work in process only.
  c. raw materials only.
  d. raw materials, work in process, and finished goods.

(SO 6) **12.** The formula to determine the cost of goods manufactured is:
  a. Beginning raw materials inventory + Total manufacturing costs − Ending work in process inventory.
  b. Beginning work in process inventory + Total manufacturing costs − Ending finished goods inventory.
  c. Beginning finished good inventory + Total manufacturing costs − Ending finished goods inventory.
  d. Beginning work in process inventory + Total manufacturing costs − Ending work in process inventory.

(SO 7) **13.** A manufacturer may report three inventories in its balance sheet: (1) raw materials, (2) work in process, and (3) finished goods. Indicate in what sequence these inventories generally appear on a balance sheet.
  a. (1), (2), (3)   c. (3), (1), (2)
  b. (2), (3), (1)   d. (3), (2), (1)

(SO 8) **14.** Which of the following managerial accounting techniques attempts to allocate manufacturing overhead in a more meaningful fashion?
  a. Just-in-time inventory.
  b. Total-quality management.
  c. Balanced scorecard.
  d. Activity-based costing.

(SO 8) **15.** Examples of recent trends in the economic environment of U.S. businesses are:
  a. increasing deregulation, decreasing global competition, and a shift toward providing services rather than goods.
  b. increasing deregulation, increasing global competition, and a shift toward providing goods rather than services.

c. decreasing deregulation, decreasing global competition, and a shift toward providing services rather than goods.
d. increasing deregulation, increasing global competition, and a shift toward providing services rather than goods.

Go to the book's companion website, **www.wiley.com/college/weygandt**, for Additional Self-Study questions.

QUESTIONS

1. (a) "Managerial accounting is a field of accounting that provides economic information for all interested parties." Do you agree? Explain.
   (b) Mary Barett believes that managerial accounting serves only manufacturing firms. Is Mary correct? Explain.
2. Distinguish between managerial and financial accounting as to (a) primary users of reports, (b) types and frequency of reports, and (c) purpose of reports.
3. How does the content of reports and the verification of reports differ between managerial and financial accounting?
4. In what ways can the budgeting process create incentives for unethical behavior?
5. Karen Fritz is studying for the next accounting mid-term examination. Summarize for Karen what she should know about management functions.
6. "Decision making is management's most important function." Do you agree? Why or why not?
7. What new rules were enacted under the Sarbanes-Oxley Act to address unethical accounting practices?
8. Stan Kaiser is studying for his next accounting examination. Explain to Stan what he should know about the differences between the income statements for a manufacturing and for a merchandising company.
9. Terry Lemay is unclear as to the difference between the balance sheets of a merchandising company and a manufacturing company. Explain the difference to Terry.
10. How are manufacturing costs classified?
11. Matt Litkee claims that the distinction between direct and indirect materials is based entirely on physical association with the product. Is Matt correct? Why?
12. Megan Neill is confused about the differences between a product cost and a period cost. Explain the differences to Megan.
13. Identify the differences in the cost of goods sold section of an income statement between a merchandising company and a manufacturing company.
14. The determination of the cost of goods manufactured involves the following factors: (A) beginning work in process inventory, (B) total manufacturing costs, and (C) ending work in process inventory. Identify the meaning of x in the following formulas:
    (a) $A + B = x$
    (b) $A + B - C = x$
15. Ohmie Manufacturing has beginning raw materials inventory $12,000, ending raw materials inventory $15,000, and raw materials purchases $170,000. What is the cost of direct materials used?
16. Neff Manufacturing Inc. has beginning work in process $26,000, direct materials used $240,000, direct labor $200,000, total manufacturing overhead $180,000, and ending work in process $32,000. What are total manufacturing costs?
17. Using the data in Q16, what are (a) the total cost of work in process and (b) the cost of goods manufactured?
18. In what order should manufacturing inventories be listed in a balance sheet?
19. What is the value chain? Describe, in sequence, the main components of a manufacturer's value chain.
20. Why is product quality important for companies that implement a just-in-time inventory system?
21. Explain what is meant by "balanced" in the balanced scorecard approach.
22. What is activity-based costing, and what are its potential benefits?

BRIEF EXERCISES

BE19-1 Complete the following comparison table between managerial and financial accounting.

Distinguish between managerial and financial accounting.
(SO 1)

	Financial Accounting	Managerial Accounting
Primary users		
Types of reports		
Frequency of reports		
Purpose of reports		
Content of reports		
Verification		

868 Chapter 19 Managerial Accounting

Identify important regulatory changes.
(SO 2)

BE19-2 The Sarbanes Oxley Act of 2002 (SOX) has important implications for the financial community. Explain two implications of SOX.

BE19-3 Listed below are the three functions of the management of an organization.

Identify the three management functions.
(SO 2)

1. Planning   2. Directing   3. Controlling

Identify which of the following statements best describes each of the above functions.

(a) ____ require(s) management to look ahead and to establish objectives. A key objective of management is to add value to the business.

(b) ____ involves coordinating the diverse activities and human resources of a company to produce a smooth-running operation. This function relates to the implementation of planned objectives.

(c) ____ is the process of keeping the activities on track. Management must determine whether goals are being met and what changes are necessary when there are deviations.

Classify manufacturing costs.
(SO 3)

BE19-4 Determine whether each of the following costs should be classified as direct materials (DM), direct labor (DL), or manufacturing overhead (MO).

(a) ____Frames and tires used in manufacturing bicycles.
(b) ____Wages paid to production workers.
(c) ____Insurance on factory equipment and machinery.
(d) ____Depreciation on factory equipment.

Classify manufacturing costs.
(SO 3)

BE19-5 Indicate whether each of the following costs of an automobile manufacturer would be classified as direct materials, direct labor, or manufacturing overhead.

(a) ____Windshield.
(b) ____Engine.
(c) ____Wages of assembly line worker.
(d) ____Depreciation of factory machinery.
(e) ____Factory machinery lubricants.
(f) ____Tires.
(g) ____Steering wheel.
(h) ____Salary of painting supervisor.

Identify product and period costs.
(SO 4)

BE19-6 Identify whether each of the following costs should be classified as product costs or period costs.

(a) ____Manufacturing overhead.
(b) ____Selling expenses.
(c) ____Administrative expenses.
(d) ____Advertising expenses.
(e) ____Direct labor.
(f) ____Direct material.

Classify manufacturing costs.
(SO 3)

BE19-7 Presented below are Lang Company's monthly manufacturing cost data related to its personal computer products.

(a) Utilities for manufacturing equipment $116,000
(b) Raw material (CPU, chips, etc.) $ 85,000
(c) Depreciation on manufacturing building $880,000
(d) Wages for production workers $191,000

Enter each cost item in the following table, placing an "X" under the appropriate headings.

	Product Costs		
	Direct Materials	Direct Labor	Factory Overhead
(a)			
(b)			
(c)			
(d)			

Compute total manufacturing costs and total cost of work in process.
(SO 6)

BE19-8 Francum Manufacturing Company has the following data: direct labor $229,000, direct materials used $180,000, total manufacturing overhead $208,000, and beginning work in process $25,000. Compute (a) total manufacturing costs and (b) total cost of work in process.

Prepare current assets section.
(SO 7)

BE19-9 In alphabetical order below are current asset items for Dieker Company's balance sheet at December 31, 2010. Prepare the current assets section (including a complete heading).

Accounts receivable	$200,000
Cash	62,000
Finished goods	71,000
Prepaid expenses	38,000
Raw materials	73,000
Work in process	87,000

BE19-10 Presented below are incomplete manufacturing cost data. Determine the missing amounts for three different situations.

Determine missing amounts in computing total manufacturing costs.
(SO 6)

	Direct Materials Used	Direct Labor Used	Factory Overhead	Total Manufacturing Costs
(1)	$25,000	$61,000	$ 50,000	?
(2)	?	$75,000	$140,000	$296,000
(3)	$55,000	?	$111,000	$310,000

BE19-11 Use the same data from BE19–10 above and the data below. Determine the missing amounts.

Determine missing amounts in computing cost of goods manufactured.
(SO 6)

	Total Manufacturing Costs	Work in Process (1/1)	Work in Process (12/31)	Cost of Goods Manufactured
(1)	?	$120,000	$82,000	?
(2)	$296,000	?	$98,000	$321,000
(3)	$310,000	$463,000	?	$715,000

DO IT! REVIEW

DO IT! 19-1 Indicate whether the following statements are true or false.

Identify managerial accounting concepts.
(SO 1, 2)

1. Managerial accountants explain and report manufacturing and nonmanufacturing costs, determine cost behaviors, and perform C-V-P analysis, but are not involved in the budget process.
2. Financial accounting reports pertain to subunits of the business and are very detailed.
3. Managerial accounting reports must follow GAAP and are audited by CPAs.
4. Managers' activities and responsibilities can be classified into three broad functions: planning, directing, and controlling.
5. As a result of the Sarbanes-Oxley Act of 2002 (SOX), top managers must certify that the company maintains an adequate system of internal control.
6. Management accountants follow a code of ethics developed by the Institute of Management Accountants.

DO IT! 19-2 A music company has these costs:

Advertising
Blank CDs
Depreciation of CD image burner
Salary of factory manager
Factory supplies used
Paper inserts for CD cases
CD plastic cases
Salaries of sales representatives
Salaries of factory maintenance employees
Salaries of employees who burn music onto CDs

Identify managerial cost concepts.
(SO 3, 4)

Classify each cost as a period or a product cost. Within the product cost category, indicate if the cost is part of direct materials (DM), direct labor (DL), or manufacturing overhead (MO).

DO IT! 19-3 The following information is available for Kopps Manufacturing Company.

Prepare cost of goods manufactured schedule.
(SO 6)

	April 1	April 31
Raw material inventory	$10,000	$14,000
Work in process inventory	5,000	3,500
Materials purchased in April		$ 98,000
Direct labor in April		60,000
Manufacturing overhead in April		180,000

Prepare the cost of goods manufactured schedule for the month of April.

DO IT! 19-4 Match the descriptions that follow with the corresponding terms.

Identify trends in managerial accounting.
(SO 8)

Descriptions:
1. _____ Inventory system in which goods are manufactured or purchased just as they are needed for use.
2. _____ A method of allocating overhead based on each product's use of activities in making the product.

3. _____ Systems that are especially important to firms adopting just-in-time inventory methods.
4. _____ One part of the value chain for a manufacturing company.
5. _____ The U.S. economy is trending towards this.
6. _____ A performance-measurement approach that uses both financial and nonfinancial measures, tied to company objectives, to evaluate a company's operations in an integrated fashion.

Terms:
(a) Activity-based costing
(b) Balanced scorecard
(c) Total quality management (TQM)
(d) Research and development, and product design
(e) Service industries
(f) Just-in-time (JIT) inventory

EXERCISES

Identify distinguishing features of managerial accounting.
(SO 1)

E19-1 Chris Martin has prepared the following list of statements about managerial accounting and financial accounting.

1. Financial accounting focuses on providing information to internal users.
2. Analyzing cost-volume-profit relationships is part of managerial accounting.
3. Preparation of budgets is part of financial accounting.
4. Managerial accounting applies only to merchandising and manufacturing companies.
5. Both managerial accounting and financial accounting deal with many of the same economic events.
6. Managerial accounting reports are prepared only quarterly and annually.
7. Financial accounting reports are general-purpose reports.
8. Managerial accounting reports pertain to subunits of the business.
9. Managerial accounting reports must comply with generally accepted accounting principles.
10. Although managerial accountants are expected to behave ethically, there is no code of ethical standards for managerial accountants.

Instructions
Identify each statement as true or false. If false, indicate how to correct the statement.

Classify costs into three classes of manufacturing costs.
(SO 3)

E19-2 Presented below is a list of costs and expenses usually incurred by Burrand Corporation, a manufacturer of furniture, in its factory.

1. Salaries for assembly line inspectors.
2. Insurance on factory machines.
3. Property taxes on the factory building.
4. Factory repairs.
5. Upholstery used in manufacturing furniture.
6. Wages paid to assembly line workers.
7. Factory machinery depreciation.
8. Glue, nails, paint, and other small parts used in production.
9. Factory supervisors' salaries.
10. Wood used in manufacturing furniture.

Instructions
Classify the above items into the following categories: (a) direct materials, (b) direct labor, and (c) manufacturing overhead.

Identify types of cost and explain their accounting.
(SO 3, 4)

E19-3 Coldplay Corporation incurred the following costs while manufacturing its product.

Materials used in product	$100,000	Advertising expense	$45,000
Depreciation on plant	60,000	Property taxes on plant	14,000
Property taxes on store	7,500	Delivery expense	21,000
Labor costs of assembly-line workers	110,000	Sales commissions	35,000
Factory supplies used	13,000	Salaries paid to sales clerks	50,000

Instructions
(a) Identify each of the costs as direct materials, direct labor, manufacturing overhead, or period costs.
(b) Explain the basic difference in accounting for product costs and period costs.

E19-4 Caroline Company reports the following costs and expenses in May.

Determine the total amount of various types of costs.
(SO 3, 4)

Factory utilities	$ 11,500	Direct labor	$69,100
Depreciation on factory equipment	12,650	Sales salaries	46,400
		Property taxes on factory building	2,500
Depreciation on delivery trucks	3,800	Repairs to office equipment	1,300
Indirect factory labor	48,900	Factory repairs	2,000
Indirect materials	80,800	Advertising	18,000
Direct materials used	137,600	Office supplies used	2,640
Factory manager's salary	8,000		

Instructions
From the information, determine the total amount of:
(a) Manufacturing overhead.
(b) Product costs.
(c) Period costs.

E19-5 Sota Company is a manufacturer of personal computers. Various costs and expenses associated with its operations are as follows.

Classify various costs into different cost categories.
(SO 3, 4)

1. Property taxes on the factory building.
2. Production superintendents' salaries.
3. Memory boards and chips used in assembling computers.
4. Depreciation on the factory equipment.
5. Salaries for assembly line quality control inspectors.
6. Sales commissions paid to sell personal computers.
7. Electrical components used in assembling computers.
8. Wages of workers assembling personal computers.
9. Soldering materials used on factory assembly lines.
10. Salaries for the night security guards for the factory building.

The company intends to classify these costs and expenses into the following categories: (a) direct materials, (b) direct labor, (c) manufacturing overhead, and (d) period costs.

Instructions
List the items (1) through (10). For each item, indicate the cost category to which it belongs.

E19-6 The administrators of San Diego County's Memorial Hospital are interested in identifying the various costs and expenses that are incurred in producing a patient's X-ray. A list of such costs and expenses in presented below.

Classify various costs into different cost categories.
(SO 3)

1. Salaries for the X-ray machine technicians.
2. Wages for the hospital janitorial personnel.
3. Film costs for the X-ray machines.
4. Property taxes on the hospital building.
5. Salary of the X-ray technicians' supervisor.
6. Electricity costs for the X-ray department.
7. Maintenance and repairs on the X-ray machines.
8. X-ray department supplies.
9. Depreciation on the X-ray department equipment.
10. Depreciation on the hospital building.

The administrators want these costs and expenses classified as: (a) direct materials, (b) direct labor, or (c) service overhead.

Instructions
List the items (1) through (10). For each item, indicate the cost category to which the item belongs.

872 Chapter 19 Managerial Accounting

Classify various costs into different cost categories.
(SO 4)

E19-7 Rapid Delivery Service reports the following costs and expenses in June 2010.

Indirect materials	$ 5,400	Drivers' salaries	$11,000
Depreciation on delivery equipment	11,200	Advertising	1,600
Dispatcher's salary	5,000	Delivery equipment repairs	300
Property taxes on office building	870	Office supplies	650
CEO's salary	12,000	Office utilities	990
Gas and oil for delivery trucks	2,200	Repairs on office equipment	180

Instructions
Determine the total amount of (a) delivery service (product) costs and (b) period costs.

Compute cost of goods manufactured and sold.
(SO 5, 6)

E19-8 Coldplay Corporation incurred the following costs while manufacturing its product.

Materials used in product	$100,000	Advertising expense	$45,000
Depreciation on plant	60,000	Property taxes on plant	14,000
Property taxes on store	7,500	Delivery expense	21,000
Labor costs of assembly-line workers	110,000	Sales commissions	35,000
Factory supplies used	23,000	Salaries paid to sales clerks	50,000

Work-in-process inventory was $12,000 at January 1 and $15,500 at December 31. Finished goods inventory was $60,000 at January 1 and $55,600 at December 31.

Instructions
(a) Compute cost of goods manufactured.
(b) Compute cost of goods sold.

Determine missing amounts in cost of goods manufactured schedule.
(SO 6)

E19-9 An incomplete cost of goods manufactured schedule is presented below.

CEPEDA MANUFACTURING COMPANY
Cost of Goods Manufactured Schedule
For the Year Ended December 31, 2010

Work in process (1/1)			$210,000
Direct materials			
Raw materials inventory (1/1)	$?		
Add: Raw materials purchases	158,000		
Total raw materials available for use	?		
Less: Raw materials inventory (12/31)	12,500		
Direct materials used		$190,000	
Direct labor		?	
Manufacturing overhead			
Indirect labor	$ 18,000		
Factory depreciation	36,000		
Factory utilities	68,000		
Total overhead		122,000	
Total manufacturing costs			?
Total cost of work in process			?
Less: Work in process (12/31)			81,000
Cost of goods manufactured			$510,000

Instructions
Complete the cost of goods manufactured schedule for Cepeda Manufacturing Company.

Determine the missing amount of different cost items.
(SO 6)

E19-10 Manufacturing cost data for Criqui Company are presented below.

	Case A	Case B	Case C
Direct materials used	(a)	$58,400	$130,000
Direct labor	$ 57,000	86,000	(g)
Manufacturing overhead	46,500	81,600	102,000

Total manufacturing costs	185,650	(d)	253,700
Work in process 1/1/10	(b)	16,500	(h)
Total cost of work in process	221,500	(e)	337,000
Work in process 12/31/10	(c)	11,000	70,000
Cost of goods manufactured	185,275	(f)	(i)

Instructions
Indicate the missing amount for each letter (a) through (i).

E19-11 Incomplete manufacturing cost data for Ikerd Company for 2010 are presented as follows for four different situations.

Determine the missing amount of different cost items, and prepare a condensed cost of goods manufactured schedule.
(SO 6)

	Direct Materials Used	Direct Labor Used	Manufacturing Overhead	Total Manufacturing Costs	Work in Process 1/1	Work in Process 12/31	Cost of Goods Manufactured
(1)	$127,000	$140,000	$ 77,000	(a)	$33,000	(b)	$360,000
(2)	(c)	200,000	132,000	$450,000	(d)	$40,000	470,000
(3)	80,000	100,000	(e)	245,000	60,000	80,000	(f)
(4)	70,000	(g)	75,000	288,000	45,000	(h)	270,000

Instructions
(a) Indicate the missing amount for each letter.
(b) Prepare a condensed cost of goods manufactured schedule for situation (1) for the year ended December 31, 2010.

E19-12 Aikman Corporation has the following cost records for June 2010.

Prepare a cost of goods manufactured schedule and a partial income statement.
(SO 5, 6)

Indirect factory labor	$ 4,500	Factory utilities	$ 400
Direct materials used	20,000	Depreciation, factory equipment	1,400
Work in process, 6/1/10	3,000	Direct labor	30,000
Work in process, 6/30/10	3,800	Maintenance, factory equipment	1,800
Finished goods, 6/1/10	5,000	Indirect materials	2,200
Finished goods, 6/30/10	7,500	Factory manager's salary	3,000

Instructions
(a) Prepare a cost of goods manufactured schedule for June 2010.
(b) Prepare an income statement through gross profit for June 2010 assuming net sales are $87,100.

E19-13 Sara Collier, the bookkeeper for Danner, Cheney, and Howe, a political consulting firm, has recently completed an accounting course at her local college. One of the topics covered in the course was the cost of goods manufactured schedule. Sara wondered if such a schedule could be prepared for her firm. She realized that, as a service-oriented company, it would have no Work in Process inventory to consider.

Classify various costs into different categories and prepare cost of services provided schedule.
(SO 4, 5, 6)

Listed below are the costs her firm incurred for the month ended August 31, 2010.

Supplies used on consulting contracts	$ 1,200
Supplies used in the administrative offices	1,500
Depreciation on equipment used for contract work	900
Depreciation used on administrative office equipment	1,050
Salaries of professionals working on contracts	12,600
Salaries of administrative office personnel	7,700
Janitorial services for professional offices	400
Janitorial services for administrative offices	500
Insurance on contract operations	800
Insurance on administrative operations	900
Utilities for contract operations	1,400
Utilities for administrative offices	1,300

Instructions
(a) Prepare a schedule of cost of contract services provided (similar to a cost of goods manufactured schedule) for the month.
(b) For those costs not included in (a), explain how they would be classified and reported in the financial statements.

874 Chapter 19 Managerial Accounting

Prepare a cost of goods manufactured schedule and a partial income statement.

(SO 5, 6, 7)

E19-14 The following information is available for Sassafras Company.

	January 1, 2010	2010	December 31, 2010
Raw materials inventory	$ 21,000		$30,000
Work in process inventory	13,500		17,200
Finished goods inventory	27,000		21,000
Materials purchased		$150,000	
Direct labor		200,000	
Manufacturing overhead		180,000	
Sales		900,000	

Instructions
(a) Compute cost of goods manufactured.
(b) Prepare an income statement through gross profit.
(c) Show the presentation of the ending inventories on the December 31, 2010, balance sheet.
(d) How would the income statement and balance sheet of a merchandising company be different from Sassafras's financial statements?

Indicate in which schedule or financial statement(s) different cost items will appear.

(SO 5, 6, 7)

E19-15 Corbin Manufacturing Company produces blankets. From its accounting records it prepares the following schedule and financial statements on a yearly basis.
(a) Cost of goods manufactured schedule.
(b) Income statement.
(c) Balance sheet.

The following items are found in its ledger and accompanying data.

1. Direct labor
2. Raw materials inventory, 1/1
3. Work in process inventory, 12/31
4. Finished goods inventory, 1/1
5. Indirect labor
6. Depreciation on factory machinery
7. Work in process, 1/1
8. Finished goods inventory, 12/31
9. Factory maintenance salaries
10. Cost of goods manufactured
11. Depreciation on delivery equipment
12. Cost of goods available for sale
13. Direct materials used
14. Heat and electricity for factory
15. Repairs to roof of factory building
16. Cost of raw materials purchases

Instructions
List the items (1)–(16). For each item, indicate by using the appropriate letter or letters, the schedule and/or financial statement(s) in which the item will appear.

Prepare a cost of goods manufactured schedule, and present the ending inventories of the balance sheet.

(SO 6, 7)

E19-16 An analysis of the accounts of Chamberlin Manufacturing reveals the following manufacturing cost data for the month ended June 30, 2010.

Inventories	Beginning	Ending
Raw materials	$9,000	$13,100
Work in process	5,000	7,000
Finished goods	9,000	6,000

Costs incurred: Raw materials purchases $54,000, direct labor $57,000, manufacturing overhead $19,900. The specific overhead costs were: indirect labor $5,500, factory insurance $4,000, machinery depreciation $4,000, machinery repairs $1,800, factory utilities $3,100, miscellaneous factory costs $1,500. Assume that all raw materials used were direct materials.

Instructions
(a) Prepare the cost of goods manufactured schedule for the month ended June 30, 2010.
(b) Show the presentation of the ending inventories on the June 30, 2010, balance sheet.

Determine the amount of cost to appear in various accounts, and indicate in which financial statements these accounts would appear.

(SO 5, 6, 7)

E19-17 Todd Motor Company manufactures automobiles. During September 2010 the company purchased 5,000 head lamps at a cost of $9 per lamp. Todd withdrew 4,650 lamps from the warehouse during the month. Fifty of these lamps were used to replace the head lamps in autos used by traveling sales staff. The remaining 4,600 lamps were put in autos manufactured during the month.

Of the autos put into production during September 2010, 90% were completed and transferred to the company's storage lot. Of the cars completed during the month, 75% were sold by September 30.

Instructions

(a) Determine the cost of head lamps that would appear in each of the following accounts at September 30, 2010: Raw Materials, Work in Process, Finished Goods, Cost of Goods Sold, and Selling Expenses.

(b) Write a short memo to the chief accountant, indicating whether and where each of the accounts in (a) would appear on the income statement or on the balance sheet at September 30, 2010.

E19-18 The following is a list of terms related to managerial accounting practices.

Identify various managerial accounting practices.
(SO 8)

1. Activity-based costing.
2. Just-in-time inventory.
3. Balanced scorecard.
4. Value chain.

Instructions
Match each of the terms with the statement below that best describes the term.

(a) _____ A performance-measurement technique that attempts to consider and evaluate all aspects of performance using financial and nonfinancial measures in an integrated fashion.
(b) _____ The group of activities associated with providing a product or service.
(c) _____ An approach used to reduce the cost associated with handling and holding inventory by reducing the amount of inventory on hand.
(d) _____ A method used to allocate overhead to products based on each product's use of the activities that cause the incurrence of the overhead cost.

EXERCISES: SET B

Visit the book's companion website at **www.wiley.com/college/weygandt**, and choose the Student Companion site, to access Exercise Set B.

PROBLEMS: SET A

P19-1A Bjerg Company specializes in manufacturing a unique model of bicycle helmet. The model is well accepted by consumers, and the company has enough orders to keep the factory production at 10,000 helmets per month (80% of its full capacity). Bjerg's monthly manufacturing cost and other expense data are as follows.

Classify manufacturing costs into different categories and compute the unit cost.
(SO 3, 4)

Rent on factory equipment	$ 7,000
Insurance on factory building	1,500
Raw materials (plastics, polystyrene, etc.)	75,000
Utility costs for factory	900
Supplies for general office	300
Wages for assembly line workers	43,000
Depreciation on office equipment	800
Miscellaneous materials (glue, thread, etc.)	1,100
Factory manager's salary	5,700
Property taxes on factory building	400
Advertising for helmets	14,000
Sales commissions	7,000
Depreciation on factory building	1,500

Instructions
(a) Prepare an answer sheet with the following column headings.

	Product Costs			
Cost Item	Direct Materials	Direct Labor	Manufacturing Overhead	Period Costs

(a) DM $75,000
DL $43,000
MO $18,100
PC $22,100

Chapter 19 Managerial Accounting

Enter each cost item on your answer sheet, placing the dollar amount under the appropriate headings. Total the dollar amounts in each of the columns.

(b) Compute the cost to produce one helmet.

Classify manufacturing costs into different categories and compute the unit cost.

(SO 3, 4)

P19-2A Copa Company, a manufacturer of stereo systems, started its production in October 2010. For the preceding 3 years Copa had been a retailer of stereo systems. After a thorough survey of stereo system markets, Copa decided to turn its retail store into a stereo equipment factory.

Raw materials cost for a stereo system will total $74 per unit. Workers on the production lines are on average paid $12 per hour. A stereo system usually takes 5 hours to complete. In addition, the rent on the equipment used to assemble stereo systems amounts to $4,900 per month. Indirect materials cost $5 per system. A supervisor was hired to oversee production; her monthly salary is $3,000.

Factory janitorial costs are $1,300 monthly. Advertising costs for the stereo system will be $8,500 per month. The factory building depreciation expense is $7,200 per year. Property taxes on the factory building will be $9,000 per year.

Instructions

(a) Prepare an answer sheet with the following column headings.

(a) DM $96,200
DL $78,000
MO $17,050
PC $ 8,500

	Product Costs			
Cost Item	Direct Materials	Direct Labor	Manufacturing Overhead	Period Costs

Assuming that Copa manufactures, on average, 1,300 stereo systems per month, enter each cost item on your answer sheet, placing the dollar amount per month under the appropriate headings. Total the dollar amounts in each of the columns.

(b) Compute the cost to produce one stereo system.

Indicate the missing amount of different cost items, and prepare a condensed cost of goods manufactured schedule, an income statement, and a partial balance sheet.

(SO 5, 6, 7)

P19-3A Incomplete manufacturing costs, expenses, and selling data for two different cases are as follows.

	Case 1	Case 2
Direct Materials Used	$ 7,600	$ (g)
Direct Labor	5,000	8,000
Manufacturing Overhead	8,000	4,000
Total Manufacturing Costs	(a)	18,000
Beginning Work in Process Inventory	1,000	(h)
Ending Work in Process Inventory	(b)	3,000
Sales	24,500	(i)
Sales Discounts	2,500	1,400
Cost of Goods Manufactured	17,000	22,000
Beginning Finished Goods Inventory	(c)	3,300
Goods Available for Sale	18,000	(j)
Cost of Goods Sold	(d)	(k)
Ending Finished Goods Inventory	3,400	2,500
Gross Profit	(e)	7,000
Operating Expenses	2,500	(l)
Net Income	(f)	5,000

Instructions

(a) Indicate the missing amount for each letter.

(b) Ending WIP $4,600
(c) Current assets $28,000

(b) Prepare a condensed cost of goods manufactured schedule for Case 1.

(c) Prepare an income statement and the current assets section of the balance sheet for Case 1. Assume that in Case 1 the other items in the current assets section are as follows: Cash $4,000, Receivables (net) $15,000, Raw Materials $600, and Prepaid Expenses $400.

P19-4A The following data were taken from the records of Stellar Manufacturing Company for the fiscal year ended June 30, 2010.

Raw Materials Inventory 7/1/09	$ 48,000	Factory Insurance	$ 4,600
Raw Materials Inventory 6/30/10	39,600	Factory Machinery Depreciation	16,000
Finished Goods Inventory 7/1/09	96,000	Factory Utilities	27,600
Finished Goods Inventory 6/30/10	95,900	Office Utilities Expense	8,650
Work in Process Inventory 7/1/09	19,800	Sales	554,000
Work in Process Inventory 6/30/10	18,600	Sales Discounts	4,200
Direct Labor	149,250	Plant Manager's Salary	29,000
Indirect Labor	24,460	Factory Property Taxes	9,600
Accounts Receivable	27,000	Factory Repairs	1,400
		Raw Materials Purchases	96,400
		Cash	32,000

Prepare a cost of goods manufactured schedule, a partial income statement, and a partial balance sheet.
(SO 5, 6, 7)

Instructions
(a) Prepare a cost of goods manufactured schedule. (Assume all raw materials used were direct materials.)
(b) Prepare an income statement through gross profit.
(c) Prepare the current assets section of the balance sheet at June 30, 2010.

(a) CGM $367,910
(b) Gross profit $181,790
(c) Current assets $213,100

P19-5A Tombert Company is a manufacturer of computers. Its controller resigned in October 2010. An inexperienced assistant accountant has prepared the following income statement for the month of October 2010.

Prepare a cost of goods manufactured schedule and a correct income statement.
(SO 5, 6)

TOMBERT COMPANY
Income Statement
For the Month Ended October 31, 2010

Sales (net)		$780,000
Less: Operating expenses		
Raw materials purchases	$264,000	
Direct labor cost	190,000	
Advertising expense	90,000	
Selling and administrative salaries	75,000	
Rent on factory facilities	60,000	
Depreciation on sales equipment	45,000	
Depreciation on factory equipment	31,000	
Indirect labor cost	28,000	
Utilities expense	12,000	
Insurance expense	8,000	803,000
Net loss		$(23,000)

Prior to October 2010 the company had been profitable every month. The company's president is concerned about the accuracy of the income statement. As her friend, you have been asked to review the income statement and make necessary corrections. After examining other manufacturing cost data, you have acquired additional information as follows.

1. Inventory balances at the beginning and end of October were:

	October 1	October 31
Raw materials	$18,000	$34,000
Work in process	16,000	14,000
Finished goods	30,000	48,000

2. Only 70% of the utilities expense and 60% of the insurance expense apply to factory operations. The remaining amounts should be charged to selling and administrative activities.

878 Chapter 19 Managerial Accounting

(a) CGM $572,200
(b) NI $ 9,000

Instructions

(a) Prepare a schedule of cost of goods manufactured for October 2010.
(b) Prepare a correct income statement for October 2010.

PROBLEMS: SET B

Classify manufacturing costs into different categories and compute the unit cost.

(SO 3, 4)

P19-1B Petra Company specializes in manufacturing motorcycle helmets. The company has enough orders to keep the factory production at 1,000 motorcycle helmets per month. Petra's monthly manufacturing cost and other expense data are as follows.

Maintenance costs on factory building	$ 1,500
Factory manager's salary	4,000
Advertising for helmets	8,000
Sales commissions	5,000
Depreciation on factory building	700
Rent on factory equipment	6,000
Insurance on factory building	3,000
Raw materials (plastic, polystyrene, etc.)	20,000
Utility costs for factory	800
Supplies for general office	200
Wages for assembly line workers	54,000
Depreciation on office equipment	500
Miscellaneous materials (glue, thread, etc.)	2,000

Instructions

(a) Prepare an answer sheet with the following column headings.

(a) DM $20,000
    DL $54,000
    MO $18,000
    PC $13,700

	Product Costs			
Cost Item	Direct Materials	Direct Labor	Manufacturing Overhead	Period Costs

Enter each cost item on your answer sheet, placing the dollar amount under the appropriate headings. Total the dollar amounts in each of the columns.

(b) Compute the cost to produce one motorcycle helmet.

Classify manufacturing costs into different categories and compute the unit cost.

(SO 3, 4)

P19-2B Net Play Company, a manufacturer of tennis rackets, started production in November 2010. For the preceding 5 years Net Play had been a retailer of sports equipment. After a thorough survey of tennis racket markets, Net Play decided to turn its retail store into a tennis racket factory.

Raw materials cost for a tennis racket will total $23 per racket. Workers on the production lines are paid on average $13 per hour. A racket usually takes 2 hours to complete. In addition, the rent on the equipment used to produce rackets amounts to $1,300 per month. Indirect materials cost $3 per racket. A supervisor was hired to oversee production; her monthly salary is $3,500.

Janitorial costs are $1,400 monthly. Advertising costs for the rackets will be $6,000 per month. The factory building depreciation expense is $8,400 per year. Property taxes on the factory building will be $7,200 per year.

Instructions

(a) Prepare an answer sheet with the following column headings.

(a) DM $57,500
    DL $65,000
    MO $15,000
    PC $ 6,000

	Product Costs			
Cost Item	Direct Materials	Direct Labor	Manufacturing Overhead	Period Costs

Assuming that Net Play manufactures, on average, 2,500 tennis rackets per month, enter each cost item on your answer sheet, placing the dollar amount per month under the appropriate headings. Total the dollar amounts in each of the columns.

(b) Compute the cost to produce one racket.

P19-3B Incomplete manufacturing costs, expenses, and selling data for two different cases are as follows.

Indicate the missing amount of different cost items, and prepare a condensed cost of goods manufactured schedule, an income statement, and a partial balance sheet.

(SO 5, 6, 7)

	Case A	Case B
Direct Materials Used	$ 6,300	$ (g)
Direct Labor	3,000	4,000
Manufacturing Overhead	6,000	5,000
Total Manufacturing Costs	(a)	16,000
Beginning Work in Process Inventory	1,000	(h)
Ending Work in Process Inventory	(b)	2,000
Sales	22,500	(i)
Sales Discounts	1,500	1,200
Cost of Goods Manufactured	15,800	20,000
Beginning Finished Goods Inventory	(c)	5,000
Goods Available for Sale	18,300	(j)
Cost of Goods Sold	(d)	(k)
Ending Finished Goods Inventory	1,200	2,500
Gross Profit	(e)	6,000
Operating Expenses	2,700	(l)
Net Income	(f)	2,200

Instructions
(a) Indicate the missing amount for each letter.
(b) Prepare a condensed cost of goods manufactured schedule for Case A.
(c) Prepare an income statement and the current assets section of the balance sheet for Case A. Assume that in Case A the other items in the current assets section are as follows: Cash $3,000, Receivables (net) $10,000, Raw Materials $700, and Prepaid Expenses $200.

(c) Current assets $15,600

P19-4B The following data were taken from the records of Dosey Manufacturing Company for the year ended December 31, 2010.

Prepare a cost of goods manufactured schedule, a partial income statement, and a partial balance sheet.

(SO 5, 6, 7)

Raw Materials Inventory 1/1/10	$ 47,000	Factory Insurance	$ 7,400
Raw Materials Inventory 12/31/10	44,200	Factory Machinery Depreciation	7,700
Finished Goods Inventory 1/1/10	85,000	Factory Utilities	12,900
Finished Goods Inventory 12/31/10	67,800	Office Utilities Expense	8,600
Work in Process Inventory 1/1/10	9,500	Sales	465,000
Work in Process Inventory 12/31/10	8,000	Sales Discounts	2,500
Direct Labor	145,100	Plant Manager's Salary	40,000
Indirect Labor	18,100	Factory Property Taxes	6,100
Accounts Receivable	27,000	Factory Repairs	800
		Raw Materials Purchases	62,500
		Cash	28,000

Instructions
(a) Prepare a cost of goods manufactured schedule. (Assume all raw materials used were direct materials.)
(b) Prepare an income statement through gross profit.
(c) Prepare the current assets section of the balance sheet at December 31.

(a) CGM $304,900

(b) Gross profit $140,400

(c) Current assets $175,000

P19-5B Cinta Company is a manufacturer of toys. Its controller resigned in August 2010. An inexperienced assistant accountant has prepared the following income statement for the month of August 2010.

Prepare a cost of goods manufactured schedule and a correct income statement.

(SO 5, 6)

880 Chapter 19 Managerial Accounting

CINTA COMPANY
Income Statement
For the Month Ended August 31, 2010

Sales (net)		$675,000
Less: Operating expenses		
Raw materials purchases	$220,000	
Direct labor cost	160,000	
Advertising expense	75,000	
Selling and administrative salaries	70,000	
Rent on factory facilities	60,000	
Depreciation on sales equipment	50,000	
Depreciation on factory equipment	35,000	
Indirect labor cost	20,000	
Utilities expense	10,000	
Insurance expense	5,000	705,000
Net loss		$ (30,000)

Prior to August 2010 the company had been profitable every month. The company's president is concerned about the accuracy of the income statement. As her friend, you have been asked to review the income statement and make necessary corrections. After examining other manufacturing cost data, you have acquired additional information as follows.

1. Inventory balances at the beginning and end of August were:

	August 1	August 31
Raw materials	$19,500	$30,000
Work in process	25,000	21,000
Finished goods	40,000	59,000

2. Only 50% of the utilities expense and 70% of the insurance expense apply to factory operations; the remaining amounts should be charged to selling and administrative activities.

Instructions

(a) CGM $497,000
(b) NL $ (4,500)

(a) Prepare a cost of goods manufactured schedule for August 2010.
(b) Prepare a correct income statement for August 2010.

PROBLEMS: SET C

Visit the book's companion website at **www.wiley.com/college/weygandt**, and choose the Student Companion site, to access Problem Set C.

WATERWAYS CONTINUING PROBLEM

The Waterways Problem starts in this chapter and continues in every chapter. Here, we provide some details about the company introduced in this new continuing problem. You will find the complete problem for each chapter at the book's companion website

(*Note:* The Waterways problem begins in Chapter 19 and continues in every managerial-accounting chapter. You can also find this problem at the book's Student Companion site.)

WCP19 Waterways Corporation is a private corporation formed for the purpose of providing the products and the services needed to irrigate farms, parks, commercial projects, and private lawns. It has a centrally located factory in a U.S. city that manufactures the products it markets to retail outlets across the nation. It also maintains a division that provides installation and warranty servicing in six metropolitan areas.

The mission of Waterways is to manufacture quality parts that can be used for effective irrigation projects that also conserve water. By that effort, the company hopes to satisfy its customers, provide rapid and responsible service, and serve the community and the employees who represent them in each community.

The company has been growing rapidly, so management is considering new ideas to help the company continue its growth and maintain the high quality of its products.

Waterways was founded by Will Winkman, who is the company president and chief executive officer(CEO). Working with him from the company's inception was Will's brother, Ben, whose sprinkler designs and ideas about the installation of proper systems have been a major basis of the company's success. Ben is the vice president who oversees all aspects of design and production in the company.

The factory itself is managed by Todd Senter who hires his line managers to supervise the factory employees. The factory makes all of the parts for the irrigation systems. The purchasing department is managed by Hector Hines.

The installation and training division is overseen by vice president Henry Writer, who supervises the managers of the six local installation operations. Each of these local managers hires his or her own local service people. These service employees are trained by the home office under Henry Writer's direction because of the uniqueness of the company's products.

There is a small human resources department under the direction of Sally Fenton, a vice president who handles the employee paperwork, though hiring is actually performed by the separate departments. Sam Totter is the vice president who heads the sales and marketing area; he oversees 10 well-trained salespeople.

The accounting and finance division of the company is headed by Abe Headman, who is the chief financial officer (CFO) and a company vice president; he is a member of the Institute of Management Accountants and holds a certificate in management accounting. He has a small staff of Certified Public Accountants, including a controller and a treasurer, and a staff of accounting input operators who maintain the financial records.

Go to the book's companion website, www.wiley.com/college/weygandt, to see the completion of this problem.

BROADENING YOUR PERSPECTIVE

Decision Making Across the Organization

BYP19-1 Mismatch Manufacturing Company specializes in producing fashion outfits. On July 31, 2010, a tornado touched down at its factory and general office. The inventories in the warehouse and the factory were completely destroyed as was the general office nearby. Next morning, through a careful search of the disaster site, however, Ross Clarkson, the company's controller, and Catherine Harper, the cost accountant, were able to recover a small part of manufacturing cost data for the current month.

"What a horrible experience," sighed Ross. "And the worst part is that we may not have enough records to use in filing an insurance claim."

"It was terrible," replied Catherine. "However, I managed to recover some of the manufacturing cost data that I was working on yesterday afternoon. The data indicate that our direct labor cost in July totaled $240,000 and that we had purchased $345,000 of raw materials. Also, I recall that the amount of raw materials used for July was $350,000. But I'm not sure this information will help. The rest of our records are blown away."

"Well, not exactly," said Ross. "I was working on the year-to-date income statement when the tornado warning was announced. My recollection is that our sales in July were $1,260,000 and our gross profit ratio has been 40% of sales. Also, I can remember that our cost of goods available for sale was $770,000 for July."

"Maybe we can work something out from this information!" exclaimed Catherine. "My experience tells me that our manufacturing overhead is usually 60% of direct labor."

"Hey, look what I just found," cried Catherine. "It's a copy of this June's balance sheet, and it shows that our inventories as of June 30 are Finished goods $38,000, Work in process $25,000, and Raw materials $19,000."

"Super," yelled Ross. "Let's go work something out."

In order to file an insurance claim, Mismatch Company must determine the amount of its inventories as of July 31, 2010, the date of the tornado touchdown.

Instructions

With the class divided into groups, determine the amount of cost in the Raw Materials, Work in Process, and Finished Goods inventory accounts as of the date of the tornado touchdown.

MANAGERIAL ANALYSIS

BYP19-2 Love All is a fairly large manufacturing company located in the southern United States. The company manufactures tennis rackets, tennis balls, tennis clothing, and tennis shoes, all bearing the company's distinctive logo, a large green question mark on a white flocked tennis ball. The company's sales have been increasing over the past 10 years.

The tennis racket division has recently implemented several advanced manufacturing techniques. Robot arms hold the tennis rackets in place while glue dries, and machine vision systems check for defects. The engineering and design team uses computerized drafting and testing of new products. The following managers work in the tennis racket division.

> Andre Agassi, Sales Manager (supervises all sales representatives).
> Serena Williams, technical specialist (supervises computer programmers).
> Pete Sampras, cost accounting manager (supervises cost accountants).
> Andy Roddick, production supervisor (supervises all manufacturing employees).
> Venus Williams, engineer (supervises all new-product design teams).

Instructions

(a) What are the primary information needs of each manager?
(b) Which, if any, financial accounting report(s) is each likely to use?
(c) Name one special-purpose management accounting report that could be designed for each manager. Include the name of the report, the information it would contain, and how frequently it should be issued.

REAL-WORLD FOCUS

BYP19-3 **Anchor Glass Container Corporation**, the third largest manufacturer of glass containers in the U.S., supplies beverage and food producers and consumer products manufacturers nationwide. Parent company **Consumers Packaging Inc.** *(Toronto Stock Exchange:* CGC) is a leading international designer and manufacturer of glass containers.

The following management discussion appeared in a recent annual report of Anchor Glass.

ANCHOR GLASS CONTAINER CORPORATION
Management Discussion

Cost of Products Sold Cost of products sold as a percentage of net sales was 89.3% in the current year compared to 87.6% in the prior year. The increase in cost of products sold as a percentage of net sales principally reflected the impact of operational problems during the second quarter of the current year at a major furnace at one of the Company's plants, higher downtime, and costs and expenses associated with an increased number of scheduled capital improvement projects, increases in labor, and certain other manufacturing costs (with no corresponding selling price increases in the current year). Reduced fixed costs from the closing of the Streator, Illinois, plant in June of the current year and productivity and efficiency gains partially offset these cost increases.

Instructions

What factors affect the costs of products sold at Anchor Glass Container Corporation?

EXPLORING THE WEB

BYP19-4 The Institute of Management Accountants (IMA) is an organization dedicated to excellence in the practice of management accounting and financial management.

Address: www.imanet.org, or go to www.wiley.com/college/weygandt

Instructions
At the IMA's home page, locate the answers to the following questions.

(a) How many members does the IMA have, and what are their job titles?
(b) What are some of the benefits of joining the IMA as a student?
(c) Use the chapter locator function to locate the IMA chapter nearest you, and find the name of the chapter president.

COMMUNICATION ACTIVITY

BYP19-5 Refer to Problem 19-5A and add the following requirement.

Prepare a letter to the president of the company, Sue Tombert, describing the changes you made. Explain clearly why net income is different after the changes. Keep the following points in mind as you compose your letter.

1. This is a letter to the president of a company, who is your friend. The style should be generally formal, but you may relax some requirements. For example, you may call the president by her first name.
2. Executives are very busy. Your letter should tell the president your main results first (for example, the amount of net income).
3. You should include brief explanations so that the president can understand the changes you made in the calculations.

ETHICS CASE

BYP19-6 Wayne Terrago, controller for Robbin Industries, was reviewing production cost reports for the year. One amount in these reports continued to bother him—advertising. During the year, the company had instituted an expensive advertising campaign to sell some of its slower-moving products. It was still too early to tell whether the advertising campaign was successful.

There had been much internal debate as how to report advertising cost. The vice president of finance argued that advertising costs should be reported as a cost of production, just like direct materials and direct labor. He therefore recommended that this cost be identified as manufacturing overhead and reported as part of inventory costs until sold. Others disagreed. Terrago believed that this cost should be reported as an expense of the current period, based on the conservatism principle. Others argued that it should be reported as Prepaid Advertising and reported as a current asset.

The president finally had to decide the issue. He argued that these costs should be reported as inventory. His arguments were practical ones. He noted that the company was experiencing financial difficulty and expensing this amount in the current period might jeopardize a planned bond offering. Also, by reporting the advertising costs as inventory rather than as prepaid advertising, less attention would be directed to it by the financial community.

Instructions
(a) Who are the stakeholders in this situation?
(b) What are the ethical issues involved in this situation?
(c) What would you do if you were Wayne Terrago?

"All About You" Activity

BYP19-7 The primary purpose of managerial accounting is to provide information useful for management decisions. Many of the managerial accounting techniques that you learn in this course will be useful for decisions you make in your everyday life.

Instructions

For each of the following managerial accounting techniques, read the definition provided and then provide an example of a personal situation that would benefit from use of this technique.

(a) Break-even analysis (page 986).   **(c)** Balanced scorecard (page 860).
(b) Budgeting (page 1018).   **(d)** Capital budgeting (page 1166).

Answers to Insight and Accounting Across the Organization Questions

p. 846 Even the Best Have to Get Better

Q: What are some of the steps that this company has taken in order to ensure that production meets demand?

A: *The company has organized flexible teams, with jobs arranged by the amount of time a task takes. Employees now are multiskilled, so they can switch between tasks and products. Also, the stores now provide sales data more quickly to the manufacturing facility, so that production levels can be changed more quickly to respond to demand.*

p. 860 Bananas Receive Special Treatment

Q: Why is it important to keep track of costs that are incurred to improve product quality?

A: *Most companies are concerned about product quality, but managers need to consider the cost/benefit tradeoff. If you spend too much on improving product quality, your customers might not be willing to pay the price needed to recover costs. Therefore it is very important that Chiquita closely track all of the costs that it incurs to protect the bananas, to ensure that these costs are factored into the price that it ultimately charges for the bananas.*

Answers to Self-Study Questions

1. b **2.** b **3.** b **4.** b **5.** d **6.** a **7.** c **8.** c **9.** c **10.** c **11.** a **12.** d **13.** d **14.** d **15.** d

Remember to go back to the Navigator box on the chapter-opening page and check off your completed work.

Chapter 20

Job Order Costing

STUDY OBJECTIVES

After studying this chapter, you should be able to:

1. Explain the characteristics and purposes of cost accounting.
2. Describe the flow of costs in a job order costing system.
3. Explain the nature and importance of a job cost sheet.
4. Indicate how the predetermined overhead rate is determined and used.
5. Prepare entries for jobs completed and sold.
6. Distinguish between under- and overapplied manufacturing overhead.

✓ The Navigator

Scan **Study Objectives**	■
Read **Feature Story**	■
Read **Preview**	■
Read text and answer **DO IT!** p. 893 p. 899 p. 903 p. 905	■
Work **Comprehensive** **DO IT!** p. 907	■
Review **Summary of Study Objectives**	■
Answer **Self-Study Questions**	■
Complete **Assignments**	■

✓ The Navigator

Feature Story

"... AND WE'D LIKE IT IN RED"

Western States Fire Apparatus, Inc., of Cornelius, Oregon, is one of the few U.S. companies that makes fire trucks. The company builds about 25 trucks per year. Founded in 1941, the company is run by the children and grandchildren of the original founder.

"We buy the chassis, which is the cab and the frame," says Susan Scott, the company's bookkeeper. "In our computer, we set up an account into which all of the direct material that is purchased for that particular job is charged." Other direct materials include the water pump—which can cost $10,000—the lights, the siren, ladders, and hoses.

As for direct labor, the production workers fill out time tickets that tell what jobs they worked on. Usually, the company is building four trucks at any one

time. On payday, the controller allocates the payroll to the appropriate job record.

The company allocates indirect materials, such as nuts and bolts, wiring, lubricants, and abrasives, to each job in proportion to direct material dollars. It allocates other costs, such as insurance and supervisors' salaries, based on direct labor hours. "We need to allocate overhead in order to know what kind of price we have to charge when we submit our bids," she says.

Western gets orders through a "blind-bidding" process. That is, Western submits its bid without knowing the bid prices made by its competitors. "If we bid too low, we won't make a profit. If we bid too high, we don't get the job."

Regardless of the final price for the truck, the quality had better be first-rate. "The fire departments let you know if they don't like what you did, and you usually end up fixing it."

✓ The Navigator

Inside Chapter 20

- **Jobs Won, Money Lost** (p. 890)
- **Working a 25-Hour Day** (p. 905)
- ***All About You:* Minding Your Own Business** (p. 906)

887

Preview of Chapter 20

The Feature Story about Western States Fire Apparatus describes the manufacturing costs used in making a fire truck. It demonstrates that accurate costing is critical to the company's success. For example, in order to submit accurate bids on new jobs and to know whether it profited from past jobs, the company needs a good costing system. This chapter illustrates how these manufacturing costs are assigned to specific jobs, such as the manufacture of individual fire trucks. We begin the discussion in this chapter with an overview of the flow of costs in a job order cost accounting system. We then use a case study to explain and illustrate the documents, entries, and accounts in this type of cost accounting system.

The content and organization of Chapter 20 are as follows.

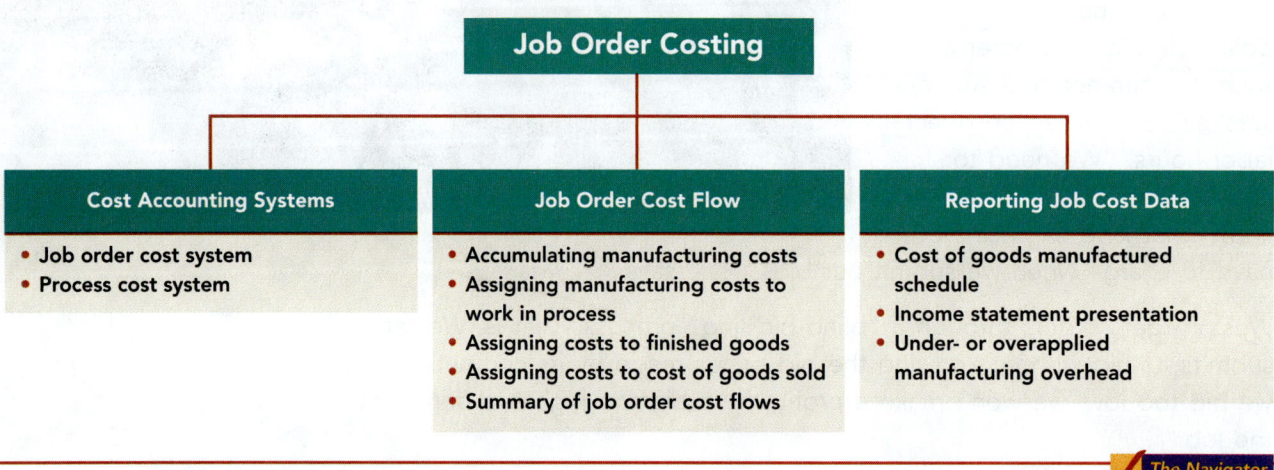

COST ACCOUNTING SYSTEMS

STUDY OBJECTIVE 1
Explain the characteristics and purposes of cost accounting.

Cost accounting involves the measuring, recording, and reporting of product costs. From the data accumulated, companies determine both the total cost and the unit cost of each product. The accuracy of the product cost information produced by the cost accounting system is critical to the success of the company. Companies use this information to determine which products to produce, what price to charge, and the amounts to produce. Accurate product cost information is also vital for effective evaluation of employee performance.

A cost accounting system consists of accounts for the various manufacturing costs. These accounts are fully integrated into the general ledger of a company. An important feature of a cost accounting system is the use of **a perpetual inventory system**. Such a system **provides immediate, up-to-date information on the cost of a product**.

There are two basic types of cost accounting systems: (1) a job order cost system and (2) a process cost system. Although cost accounting systems differ widely from company to company, most involve one of these two traditional product costing systems.

Job Order Cost System

Under a job order cost system, the company assigns costs to each **job** or to each **batch** of goods. An example of a job is the manufacture of a mainframe computer by IBM, the production of a movie by Disney, or the making of a fire truck by Western States. An example of a batch is the printing of 225 wedding invitations by a local print shop, or the printing of a weekly issue of *Fortune* magazine by a hi-tech printer such as Quad Graphics. Companies may complete jobs or batches to fill a specific customer order or to replenish inventory.

An important feature of job order costing is that each job or batch has its own distinguishing characteristics. For example, each house is custom built, each consulting engagement by a CPA firm is unique, and each printing job is different. **The objective is to compute the cost per job.** At each point in manufacturing a product or providing a service, the company can identify the job and its associated costs. A job order cost system measures costs for each completed job, rather than for set time periods. Illustration 20-1 shows the recording of costs in a job order cost system.

Illustration 20-1
Job order cost system

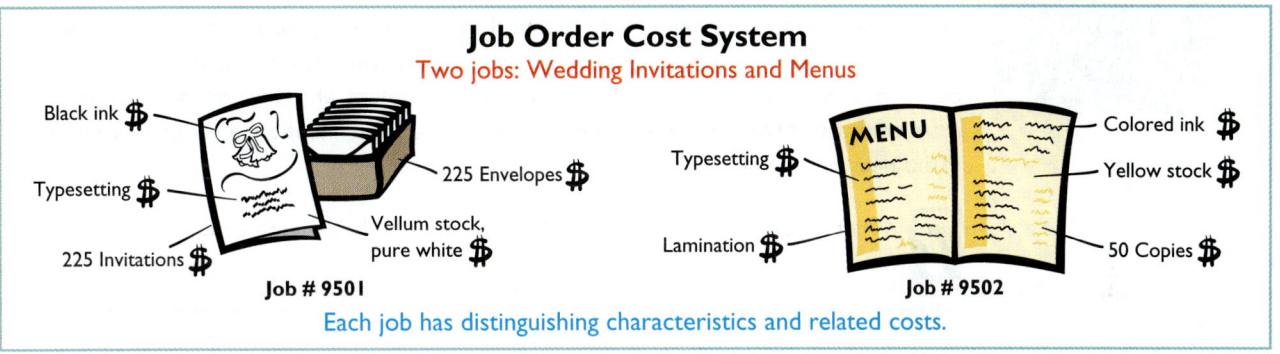

Process Cost System

A company uses a **process cost system** when it manufactures a large volume of similar products. Production is continuous. Examples of a process cost system are the manufacture of cereal by Kellogg, the refining of petroleum by ExxonMobil, and the production of automobiles by General Motors. Process costing accumulates product-related costs **for a period of time** (such as a week or a month) instead of assigning costs to specific products or job orders. In process costing, companies assign the costs to departments or processes for the specified period of time. Illustration 20-2 shows examples of the use of a process cost system. We will discuss the process cost system further in Chapter 21.

Illustration 20-2
Process cost system

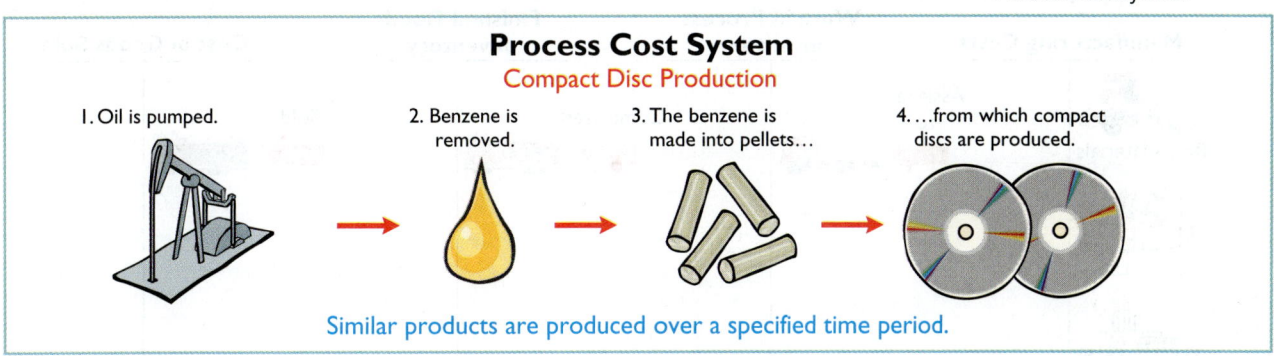

Can a company use both types of cost systems? Yes. For example, General Motors uses process cost accounting for its standard model cars, such as Saturns

MANAGEMENT INSIGHT

Jobs Won, Money Lost

Many companies suffer from poor cost accounting. As a result, they sometimes make products they should not be selling at all, or they buy other products that they could more profitably make themselves. Also, inaccurate cost data lead companies to misallocate capital and frustrate efforts by plant managers to improve efficiency.

For example, consider the case of a diversified company in the business of rebuilding diesel locomotives. The managers thought they were making money, but a consulting firm found that the company had seriously underestimated costs. The company bailed out of the business, and not a moment too soon. Says the consultant who advised the company, "The more contracts it won, the more money it lost." Given that situation, a company cannot stay in business very long!

 What type of costs do you think the company had been underestimating?

JOB ORDER COST FLOW

STUDY OBJECTIVE 2
Describe the flow of costs in a job order costing system.

The flow of costs (direct materials, direct labor, and manufacturing overhead) in job order cost accounting parallels the physical flow of the materials as they are converted into finished goods. As shown in Illustration 20-3, companies assign manufacturing costs to the Work in Process Inventory account. When a job is completed, the company transfers the cost of the job to Finished Goods Inventory. Later when the goods are sold, the company transfers their cost to Cost of Goods Sold.

Illustration 20-3
Flow of costs in job order costing

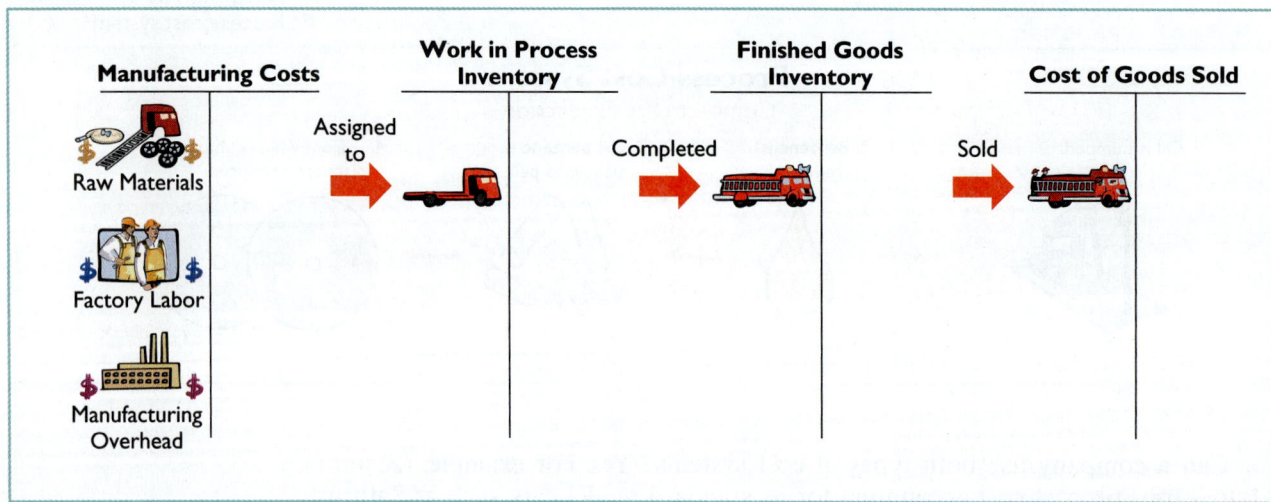

Illustration 20-3 provides a basic overview of the flow of costs in a manufacturing setting. A more detailed presentation of the flow of costs is shown in Illustration 20-4. The box in the lower corner of Illustration 20-4 indicates two

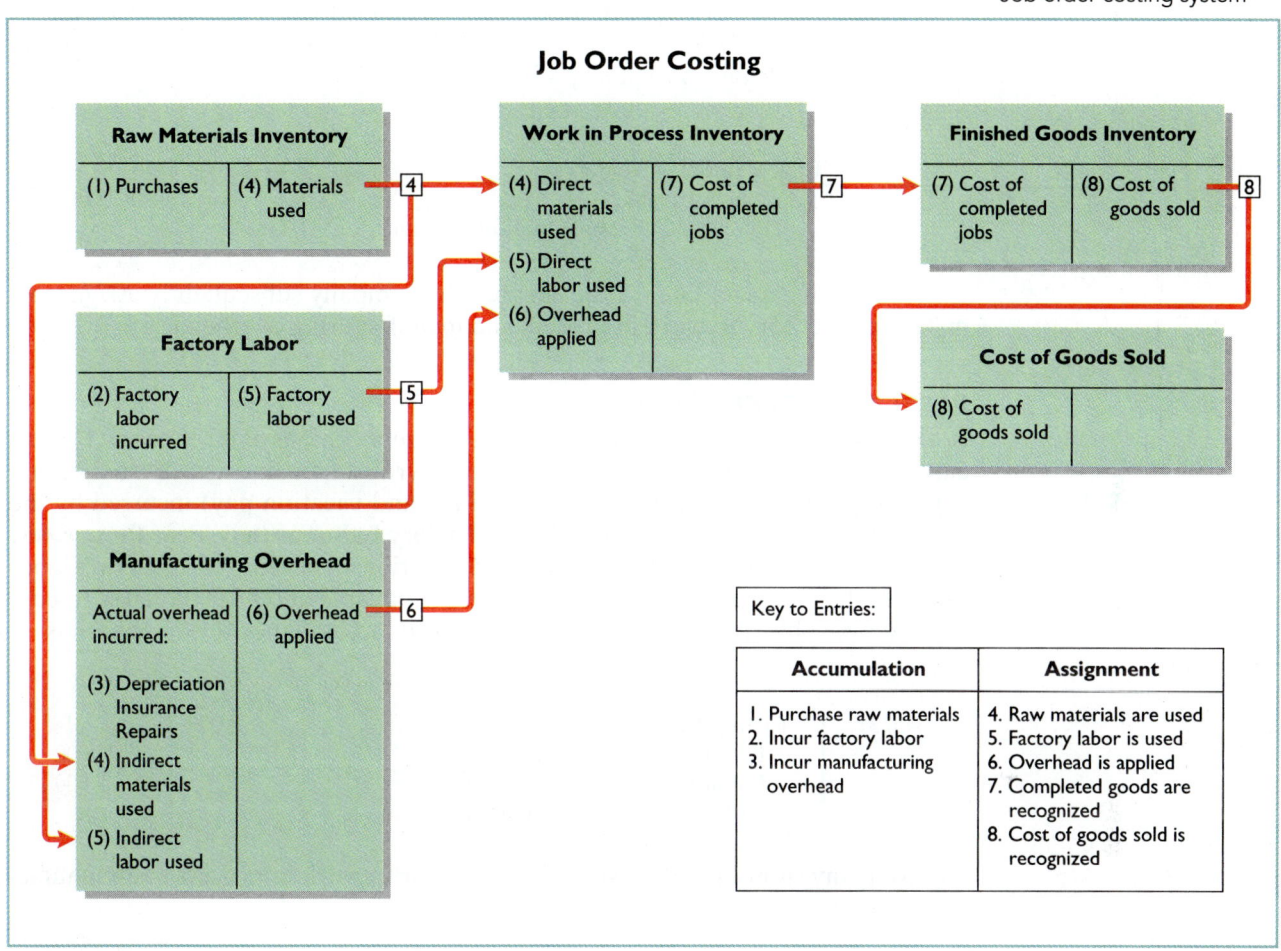

Illustration 20-4
Job order costing system

major steps in the flow of costs: (1) *accumulating* the manufacturing costs incurred, and (2) *assigning* the accumulated costs to the work done. As shown, the company accumulates manufacturing costs incurred in entries 1–3 by debits to Raw Materials Inventory, Factory Labor, and Manufacturing Overhead. When the company incurs these costs, it does not attempt to associate the costs with specific jobs. The remaining entries (entries 4–8) assign manufacturing costs incurred. In the remainder of this chapter, we will use a case study to explain how a job order system operates.

Accumulating Manufacturing Costs

To illustrate a job order cost system, we will use the January transactions of Wallace Manufacturing Company, which makes machine tools.

RAW MATERIALS COSTS

When Wallace receives the raw materials it has purchased, **it debits the costs of the materials to Raw Materials Inventory**. The company would debit this account for the invoice cost of the raw materials and freight costs chargeable to the purchaser. It would credit the account for purchase discounts taken and purchase returns and allowances. Wallace makes **no effort at this point to associate the cost of materials with specific jobs or orders**.

To illustrate, assume that Wallace Manufacturing purchases 2,000 handles (Stock No. AA2746) at $5 per unit ($10,000) and 800 modules (Stock No. AA2850) at $40 per unit ($32,000) for a total cost of $42,000 ($10,000 + $32,000). The entry to record this purchase on January 4 is:

(1)
Jan. 4	Raw Materials Inventory	42,000	
	Accounts Payable		42,000
	(Purchase of raw materials on account)		

As we will explain later in the chapter, the company subsequently assigns raw materials inventory to work in process and manufacturing overhead.

FACTORY LABOR COSTS

In a manufacturing company, the cost of factory labor consists of three costs: (1) gross earnings of factory workers, (2) employer payroll taxes on these earnings, and (3) fringe benefits (such as sick pay, pensions, and vacation pay) incurred by the employer. **Companies debit labor costs to Factory Labor as they incur those costs.**

To illustrate, assume that Wallace Manufacturing incurs $32,000 of factory labor costs. Of that amount, $27,000 relates to wages payable and $5,000 relates to payroll taxes payable in January. The entry to record factory labor for the month is:

(2)
Jan. 31	Factory Labor	32,000	
	Factory Wages Payable		27,000
	Employer Payroll Taxes Payable		5,000
	(To record factory labor costs)		

The company subsequently assigns factory labor to work in process and manufacturing overhead.

MANUFACTURING OVERHEAD COSTS

A company has many types of overhead costs. It may recognize these costs **daily**, as in the case of machinery repairs and the use of indirect materials and indirect labor. Or, it may record overhead costs **periodically** through adjusting entries. Companies record property taxes, depreciation, and insurance periodically, for example. This is done using a **summary entry**, which summarizes the totals from multiple transactions.

Using assumed data, the summary entry for manufacturing overhead in Wallace Manufacturing Company is:

(3)
Jan. 31	Manufacturing Overhead	13,800	
	Utilities Payable		4,800
	Prepaid Insurance		2,000
	Accounts Payable (for repairs)		2,600
	Accumulated Depreciation		3,000
	Property Taxes Payable		1,400
	(To record overhead costs)		

DO IT!

During the current month, Ringling Company incurs the following manufacturing costs:

(a) Raw material purchases of $4,200 on account.

(b) Incurs factory labor of $18,000. Of that amount, $15,000 relates to wages payable and $3,000 relates to payroll taxes payable.

(c) Factory utilities of $2,200 are payable, prepaid factory insurance of $1,800 has expired, and depreciation on the factory building is $3,500.

Prepare journal entries for each type of manufacturing cost.

MANUFACTURING COSTS

Solution

(a)	Raw Materials Inventory	4,2000	
	Accounts Payable		4,200
	(Purchases of raw materials on account)		
(b)	Factory Labor	18,000	
	Factory Wages Payable		15,000
	Employer Payroll Taxes Payable		3,000
	(To record factory labor costs)		
(c)	Manufacturing Overhead	7,500	
	Utilities Payable		2,200
	Prepaid Insurance		1,800
	Accumulated Depreciation		3,500
	(To record overhead costs)		

action plan

✔ In accumulating manufacturing costs, debit at least one of three accounts: Raw Materials Inventory, Factory Labor, and Manufacturing Overhead.

✔ Manufacturing overhead costs may be recognized daily. Or manufacturing overhead may be recorded periodically through a summary entry.

Related exercise material: **BE20-1, BE20-2; E20-1, E20-7, E20-8, E20-11,** and  **20-1.**

Assigning Manufacturing Costs to Work in Process

As Illustration 20-4 (page 891) shows, assigning manufacturing costs to work in process results in the following entries:

STUDY OBJECTIVE 3
Explain the nature and importance of a job cost sheet.

1. **Debits** made to Work in Process Inventory.
2. **Credits** made to Raw Materials Inventory, Factory Labor, and Manufacturing Overhead.

An essential accounting record in assigning costs to jobs is a **job cost sheet**, shown in Illustration 20-5 (page 894). A **job cost sheet** is a form used to record the costs chargeable to a specific job and to determine the total and unit costs of the completed job.

Companies keep a separate job cost sheet for each job. The job cost sheets constitute the subsidiary ledger for the Work in Process Inventory account. A **subsidiary ledger** consists of individual records for each individual item—in this case, each job. The Work in Process account is referred to as a **control account** because it summarizes the detailed data regarding specific jobs contained in the job cost sheets. **Each entry to Work in Process Inventory must be accompanied by a corresponding posting to one or more job cost sheets.**

894 Chapter 20 Job Order Costing

Illustration 20-5
Job cost sheet

Job Cost Sheet

Job No. _____ Quantity _____
Item _____ Date Requested _____
For _____ Date Completed _____

Date	Direct Materials	Direct Labor	Manufacturing Overhead

Cost of completed job
   Direct materials $ _____
   Direct labor _____
   Manufacturing overhead _____
  Total cost $ _____
  Unit cost (total dollars ÷ quantity) $ _____

> **HELPFUL HINT**
> In today's electronic environment, companies typically maintain job cost sheets as computer files.

RAW MATERIALS COSTS

Companies assign raw materials costs when their materials storeroom issues the materials. Requests for issuing raw materials are made on a prenumbered **materials requisition slip**. The materials issued may be used directly on a job, or they may be considered indirect materials. As Illustration 20-6 shows, the requisition should indicate the quantity and type of materials withdrawn and the account to be charged. The company will charge direct materials to Work in Process Inventory, and indirect materials to Manufacturing Overhead.

Illustration 20-6
Materials requisition slip

Wallace Manufacturing Company
Materials Requisition Slip

Deliver to: Assembly Department   Req. No. R247
Charge to: Work in Process–Job No. 101   Date: 1/6/10

Quantity	Description	Stock No.	Cost per Unit	Total
200	Handles	AA2746	$5.00	$1,000

Requested by *Bruce Howart*   Received by *Herb Crowley*
Approved by *Kap Shin*   Costed by *Heather Remmers*

The company may use any of the inventory costing methods (FIFO, LIFO, or average-cost) in costing the requisitions **to the individual job cost sheets**.

Periodically, the company journalizes the requisitions. For example, if Wallace Manufacturing uses $24,000 of direct materials and $6,000 of indirect materials in January, the entry is:

> **ETHICS NOTE**
> The internal control principle of documentation includes prenumbering to enhance accountability.

	(4)		
Jan. 31	Work in Process Inventory	24,000	
	Manufacturing Overhead	6,000	
	Raw Materials Inventory		30,000
	(To assign materials to jobs and overhead)		

The requisition slips show total direct materials costs of $12,000 for Job No. 101, $7,000 for Job No. 102, and $5,000 for Job No. 103. Illustration 20-7 shows the posting of requisition slip R247 and other assumed postings to the job cost sheets for materials. After the company has completed all postings, the sum of the direct materials columns of the job cost sheets (the subsidiary accounts) should equal the direct materials debited to Work in Process Inventory (the control account).

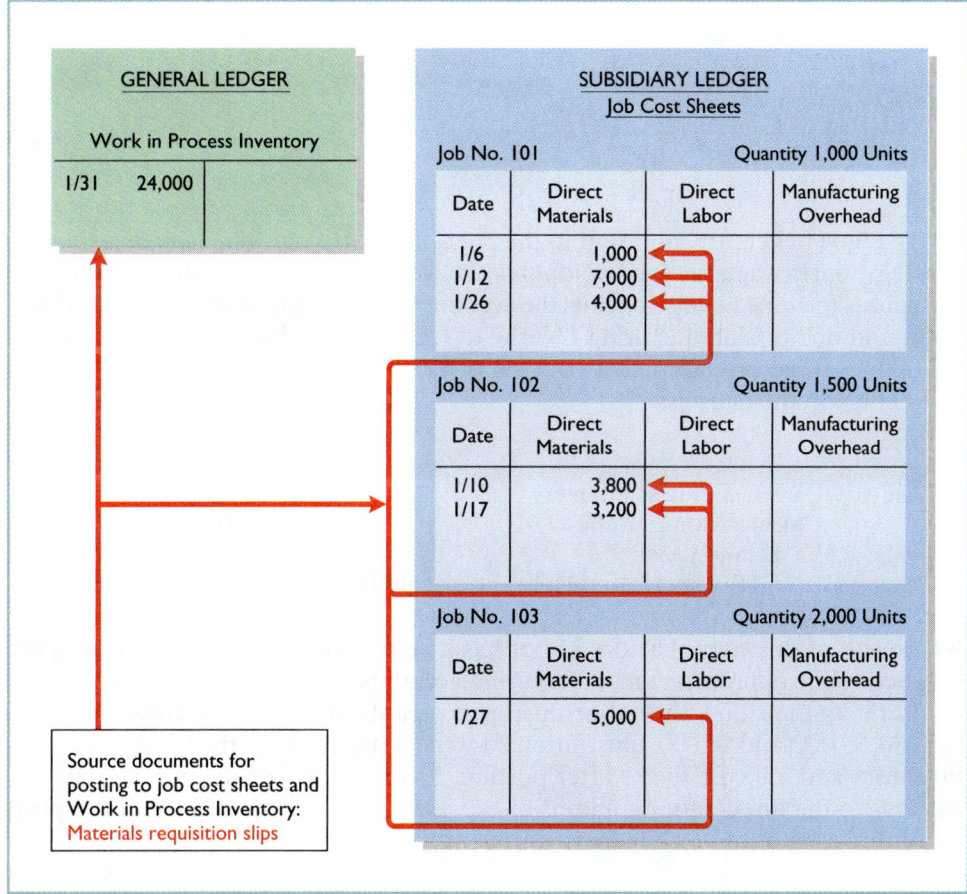

Illustration 20-7
Job cost sheets—direct materials

> **HELPFUL HINT**
> Companies post to control accounts monthly and post to job cost sheets daily.

FACTORY LABOR COSTS
Companies assign factory labor costs to jobs on the basis of time tickets prepared when the work is performed. The **time ticket** indicates the employee, the hours worked, the account and job to be charged, and the total labor cost. Many companies

accumulate these data through the use of bar coding and scanning devices. When they start and end work, employees scan bar codes on their identification badges and bar codes associated with each job they work on. When direct labor is involved, the time ticket must indicate the job number, as shown in Illustration 20-8. The employee's supervisor should approve all time tickets.

Illustration 20-8
Time ticket

HELPFUL HINT
Some companies use different colored time tickets for direct and for indirect labor.

Wallace Manufacturing Company
Time Ticket

Date: 1/6/10
Employee: John Nash
Employee No.: 124
Charge to: Work in Process
Job No.: 101

Time			Hourly Rate	Total Cost
Start	Stop	Total Hours		
0800	1200	4	10.00	40.00

Approved by: Bob Kadler
Costed by: M Cher

The time tickets are later sent to the payroll department, which applies the employee's hourly wage rate and computes the total labor cost. Finally, the company journalizes the time tickets. It debits the account Work in Process Inventory for direct labor, and debits Manufacturing Overhead for indirect labor. For example, if the $32,000 total factory labor cost consists of $28,000 of direct labor and $4,000 of indirect labor, the entry is:

		(5)		
Jan. 31	Work in Process Inventory		28,000	
	Manufacturing Overhead		4,000	
	Factory Labor			32,000
	(To assign labor to jobs and overhead)			

As a result of this entry, Factory Labor has a zero balance, and gross earnings are assigned to the appropriate manufacturing accounts.

Let's assume that the labor costs chargeable to Wallace's three jobs are $15,000, $9,000, and $4,000. Illustration 20-9 (next page) shows the Work in Process Inventory and job cost sheets after posting. As in the case of direct materials, the postings to the direct labor columns of the job cost sheets should equal the posting of direct labor to Work in Process Inventory.

MANUFACTURING OVERHEAD COSTS

STUDY OBJECTIVE 4
Indicate how the predetermined overhead rate is determined and used.

Companies charge the actual costs of direct materials and direct labor to specific jobs. In contrast, manufacturing **overhead** relates to production operations **as a whole**. As a result, overhead costs cannot be assigned to specific jobs on the basis of actual costs incurred. Instead, companies

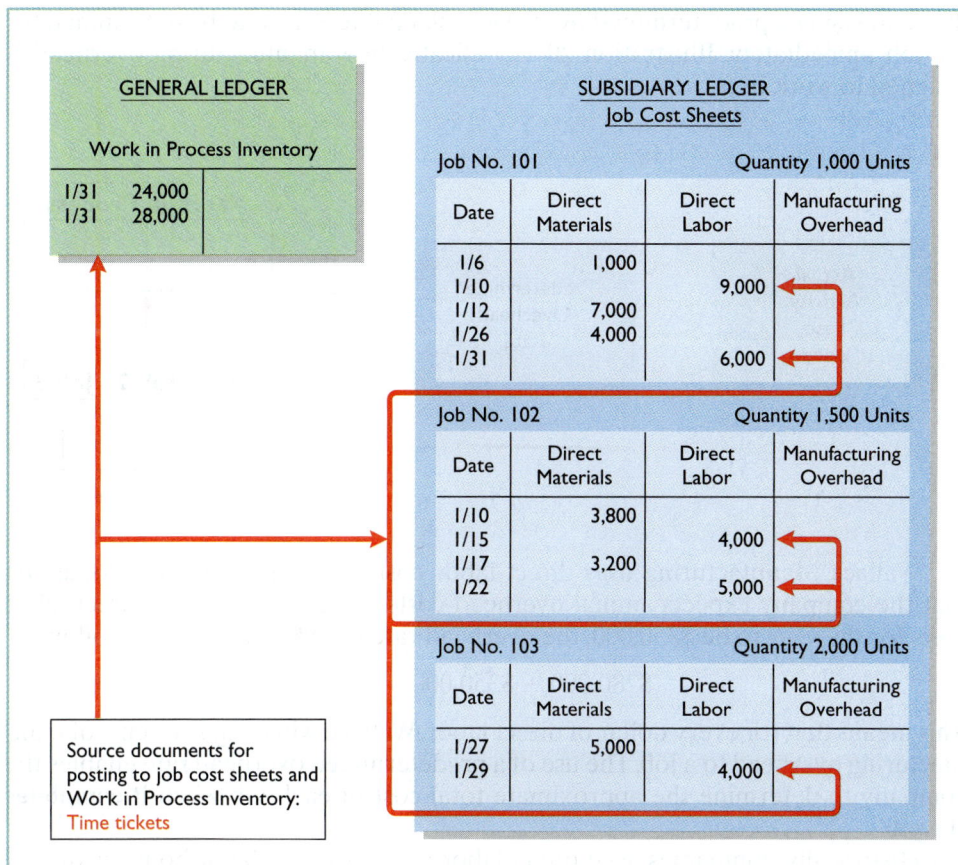

Illustration 20-9
Job cost sheets—direct labor

HELPFUL HINT
Prove the $28,000 by totaling the charges by jobs:
101   $15,000
102   9,000
103   4,000
       $28,000

assign manufacturing overhead to work in process and to specific jobs **on an estimated basis through the use of a predetermined overhead rate**.

The **predetermined overhead rate** is based on the relationship between estimated annual overhead costs and expected annual operating activity, expressed in terms of a common **activity base**. The company may state the activity in terms of direct labor costs, direct labor hours, machine hours, or any other measure that will provide an equitable basis for applying overhead costs to jobs. Companies establish the predetermined overhead rate at the beginning of the year. Small companies often use a single, company-wide predetermined overhead rate. Large companies often use rates that vary from department to department. The formula for a predetermined overhead rate is as follows.

$$\text{Estimated Annual Overhead Costs} \div \text{Expected Annual Operating Activity} = \text{Predetermined Overhead Rate}$$

Illustration 20-10
Formula for predetermined overhead rate

Overhead relates to production operations as a whole. To know what "the whole" is, the logical thing is to wait until the end of the year's operations. At that time the company knows all of its costs for the period. As a practical matter, though, managers cannot wait until the end of the year. To price products accurately, they need information about product costs of specific jobs completed during the year. Using a predetermined overhead rate enables a cost to be determined for the job immediately. Illustration 20-11 indicates how manufacturing overhead is assigned to work in process.

Illustration 20-11
Using predetermined overhead rates

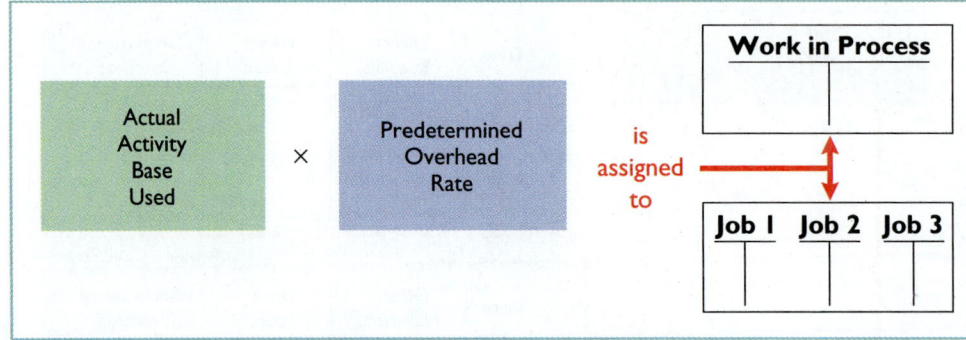

Wallace Manufacturing uses direct labor cost as the activity base. Assuming that the company expects annual overhead costs to be $280,000 and direct labor costs for the year to be $350,000, the overhead rate is 80%, computed as follows:

$$\$280,000 \div \$350,000 = 80\%$$

This means that for every dollar of direct labor, Wallace will assign 80 cents of manufacturing overhead to a job. The use of a predetermined overhead rate enables the company to determine the approximate total cost of each job **when it completes the job**.

Historically, companies used direct labor costs or direct labor hours as the activity base. The reason was the relatively high correlation between direct labor and manufacturing overhead. Today more companies are using **machine hours as the activity base, due to increased reliance on automation in manufacturing operations**. Or, as mentioned in Chapter 19, many companies now use activity-based costing in an attempt to more accurately allocate overhead costs based on the activities that give rise to the costs.

A company may use more than one activity base. For example, if a job is manufactured in more than one factory department, each department may have its own overhead rate. In the Feature Story about fire trucks, Western States Fire Apparatus uses two bases in assigning overhead to jobs: direct materials dollars for indirect materials, and direct labor hours for such costs as insurance and supervisors' salaries.

Companies apply manufacturing overhead to work in process when they assign direct labor costs. They also apply manufacturing overhead to specific jobs at the same time. For Wallace Manufacturing, overhead applied for January is $22,400 (direct labor cost of $28,000 × 80%). The following entry records this application.

		(6)		
Jan. 31	Work in Process Inventory		22,400	
	Manufacturing Overhead			22,400
	(To assign overhead to jobs)			

The overhead that Wallace applies to each job will be 80% of the direct labor cost of the job for the month. Illustration 20-12 shows the Work in Process Inventory account and the job cost sheets after posting. Note that the debit of $22,400 to Work in Process Inventory equals the sum of the overhead applied to jobs: Job 101 $12,000 + Job 102 $7,200 + Job 103 $3,200.

> **HELPFUL HINT**
> Service industries also use job order costing systems extensively. A service company will report actual direct labor and apply overhead using a predetermined rate. Although service companies do not produce inventory, many incur significant materials costs that are charged to each job.

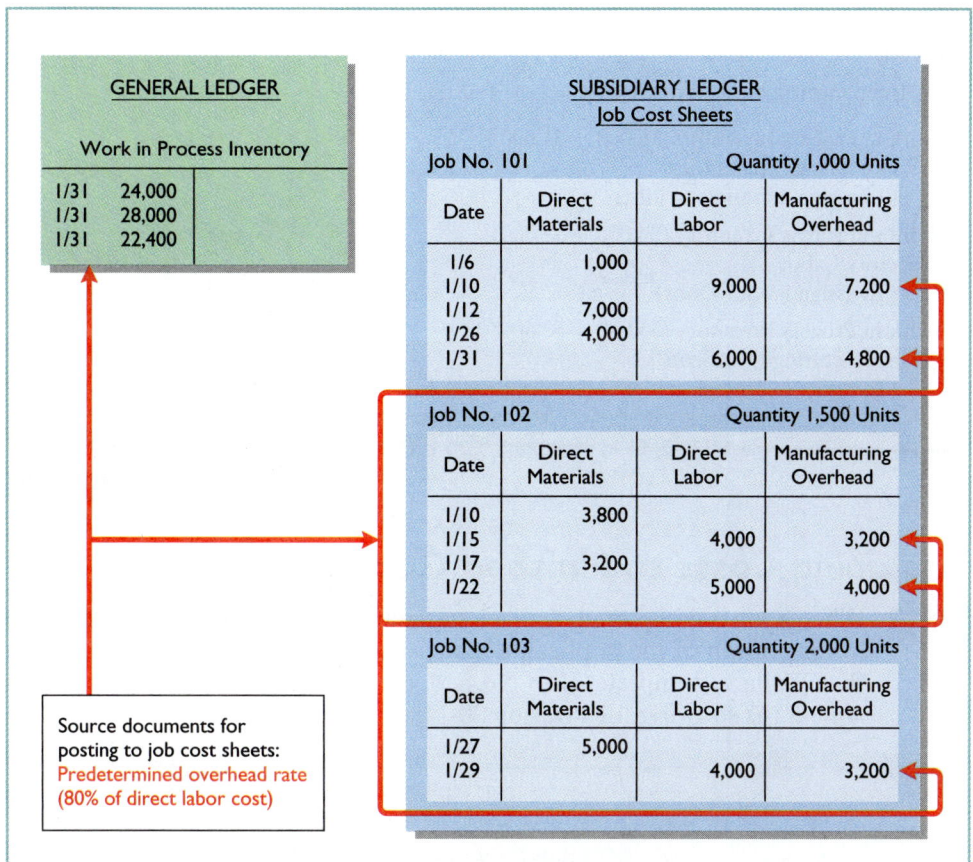

Illustration 20-12
Job cost sheets—manufacturing overhead applied

At the end of each month, **the balance in Work in Process Inventory should equal the sum of the costs shown on the job cost sheets of unfinished jobs.** Illustration 20-13 presents proof of the agreement of the control and subsidiary accounts in Wallace Manufacturing. (It assumes that all jobs are still in process.)

Work in Process Inventory		Job Cost Sheets	
Jan. 31	24,000	No. 101	$39,000
31	28,000	102	23,200
31	22,400	103	12,200
	74,400		$74,400

Illustration 20-13
Proof of job cost sheets to work in process inventory

DO IT!

WORK IN PROCESS

Danielle Company is working on two job orders. The job cost sheets show the following:

    Direct materials—Job 120 $6,000, Job 121 $3,600
    Direct labor—Job 120 $4,000, Job 121 $2,000
    Manufacturing overhead—Job 120 $5,000, Job 121 $2,500

Prepare the three summary entries to record the assignment of costs to Work in Process from the data on the job cost sheets.

900 Chapter 20 Job Order Costing

action plan

✔ Recognize that Work in Process Inventory is the control account for all unfinished job cost sheets.

✔ Debit Work in Process Inventory for the materials, labor, and overhead charged to the job cost sheets.

✔ Credit the accounts that were debited when the manufacturing costs were accumulated.

Solution

The three summary entries are:

Work in Process Inventory ($6,000 + $3,600)	9,600	
Raw Materials Inventory		9,600
(To assign materials to jobs)		
Work in Process Inventory ($4,000 + $2,000)	6,000	
Factory Labor		6,000
(To assign labor to jobs)		
Work in Process Inventory ($5,000 + $2,500)	7,500	
Manufacturing Overhead		7,500
(To assign overhead to jobs)		

Related exercise material: **BE20-3, BE20-4, BE20-5, E20-1, E20-2, E20-7, E20-8,** and **DO IT!** **20-2.**

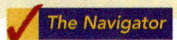

Assigning Costs to Finished Goods

STUDY OBJECTIVE 5

Prepare entries for jobs completed and sold.

When a job is completed, Wallace summarizes the costs and completes the lower portion of the applicable job cost sheet. For example, if we assume that Wallace completes Job No. 101 on January 31, the job cost sheet appears as shown in Illustration 20-14.

Illustration 20-14
Completed job cost sheet

Job Cost Sheet

Job No. __101__   Quantity __1,000__
Item __Magnetic Sensors__   Date Requested __February 5__
For __Tanner Company__   Date Completed __January 31__

Date	Direct Materials	Direct Labor	Manufacturing Overhead
1/6	$ 1,000		
1/10		$ 9,000	$ 7,200
1/12	7,000		
1/26	4,000		
1/31		6,000	4,800
	$12,000	$15,000	$12,000

Cost of completed job
  Direct materials $ 12,000
  Direct labor   15,000
  Manufacturing overhead   12,000
Total cost $ 39,000
Unit cost ($39,000 ÷ 1,000) $ 39.00

When a job is finished, Wallace makes an entry to transfer its total cost to finished goods inventory. The entry is as follows:

(7)
Jan. 31	Finished Goods Inventory		39,000	
	Work in Process Inventory			39,000
	(To record completion of Job No. 101)			

Finished Goods Inventory is a control account. It controls individual finished goods records in a finished goods subsidiary ledger. The company posts directly from completed job cost sheets to the receipts columns. Illustration 20-15 shows the finished goods inventory record for Job No. 101.

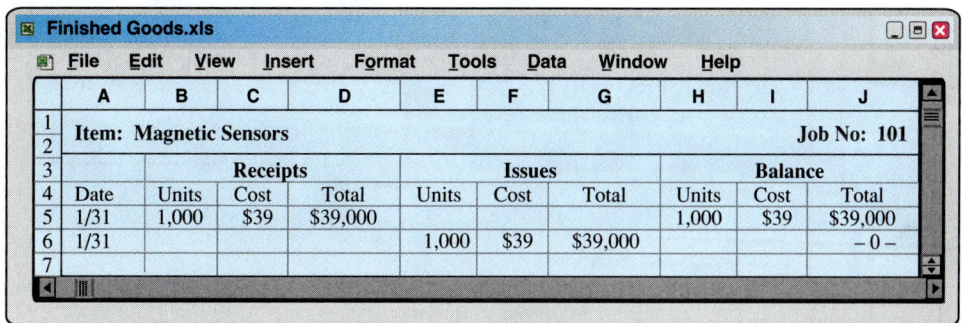

Illustration 20-15
Finished goods record

Assigning Costs to Cost of Goods Sold

Companies recognize cost of goods sold when each sale occurs. To illustrate the entries a company makes when it sells a completed job, assume that on January 31 Wallace Manufacturing sells on account Job 101. The job cost $39,000, and it sold for $50,000. The entries to record the sale and recognize cost of goods sold are:

		(8)		
Jan. 31	Accounts Receivable		50,000	
	Sales			50,000
	(To record sale of Job No. 101)			
31	Cost of Goods Sold		39,000	
	Finished Goods Inventory			39,000
	(To record cost of Job No. 101)			

As Illustration 20-15 above shows, Wallace records, in the issues section of the finished goods record, the units sold, the cost per unit, and the total cost of goods sold for each job sold.

Summary of Job Order Cost Flows

Illustration 20-16 (page 902) shows a completed flow chart for a job order cost accounting system. All postings are keyed to entries 1–8 in Wallace Manufacturing's accounts presented in the cost flow graphic in Illustration 20-4 (page 891).

The cost flows in the diagram can be categorized as one of four types:

- **Accumulation:** The company first accumulates costs by (1) purchasing raw materials, (2) incurring labor costs, and (3) incurring manufacturing overhead costs.
- **Assignment to Jobs:** Once the company has incurred manufacturing costs, it must assign them to specific jobs. For example, as it uses raw materials on specific jobs (4), it assigns them to work in process, or treats them as manufacturing overhead if the raw materials cannot be associated with a specific job. Similarly, it either assigns factory labor (5) to work in process, or treats it as manufacturing overhead if the factory labor cannot be associated with a specific job. Finally it assigns manufacturing overhead (6) to work in process using a *predetermined overhead rate*. This deserves emphasis: **Do not assign overhead using actual overhead costs, but instead use a predetermined rate**.

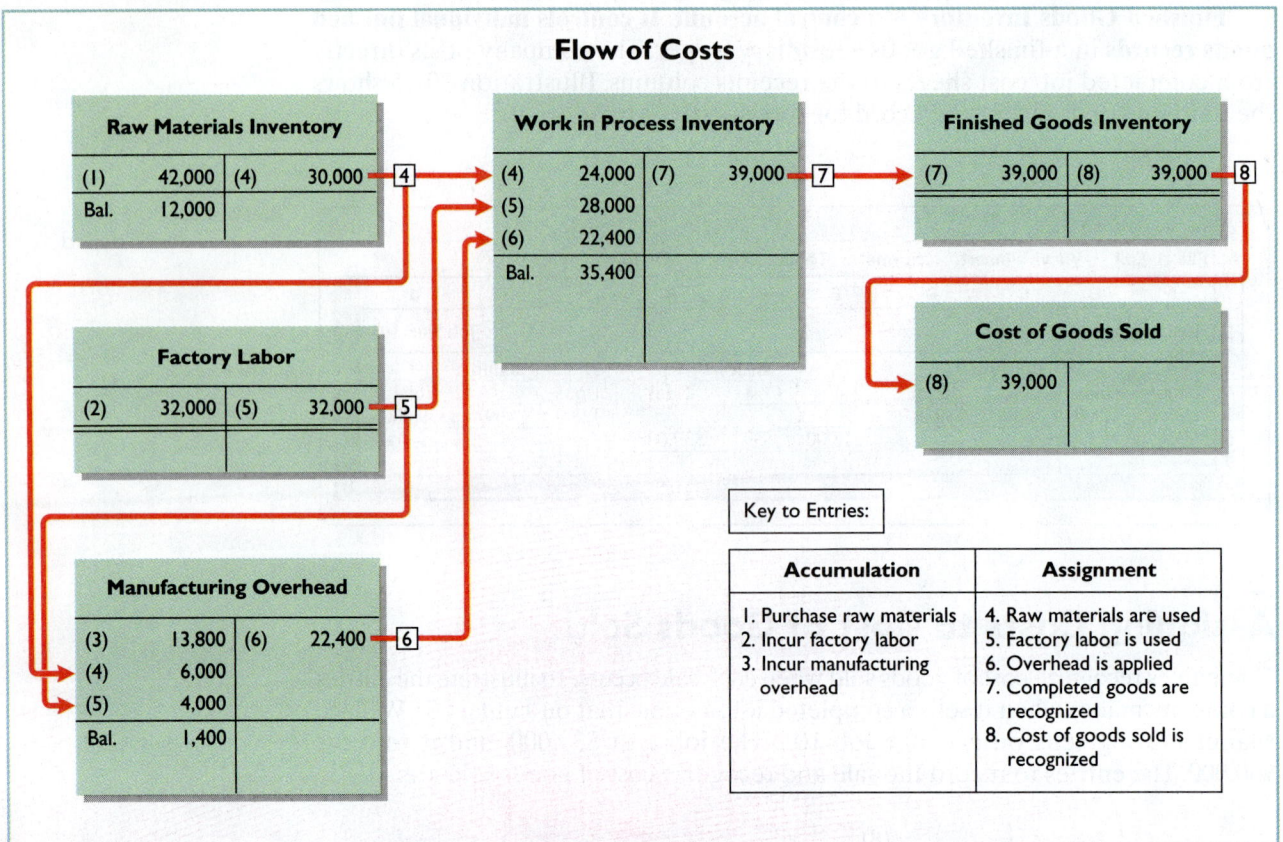

Illustration 20-16
Flow of costs in a job order cost system

- **Completed Jobs:** As jobs are completed (7), the company transfers the cost of the completed job out of work in process inventory into finished goods inventory.
- **When Goods Are Sold:** As specific items are sold (8), the company transfers their cost out of finished goods inventory into cost of goods sold.

Illustration 20-17 summarizes the flow of documents in a job order cost system.

Illustration 20-17
Flow of documents in a job order cost system

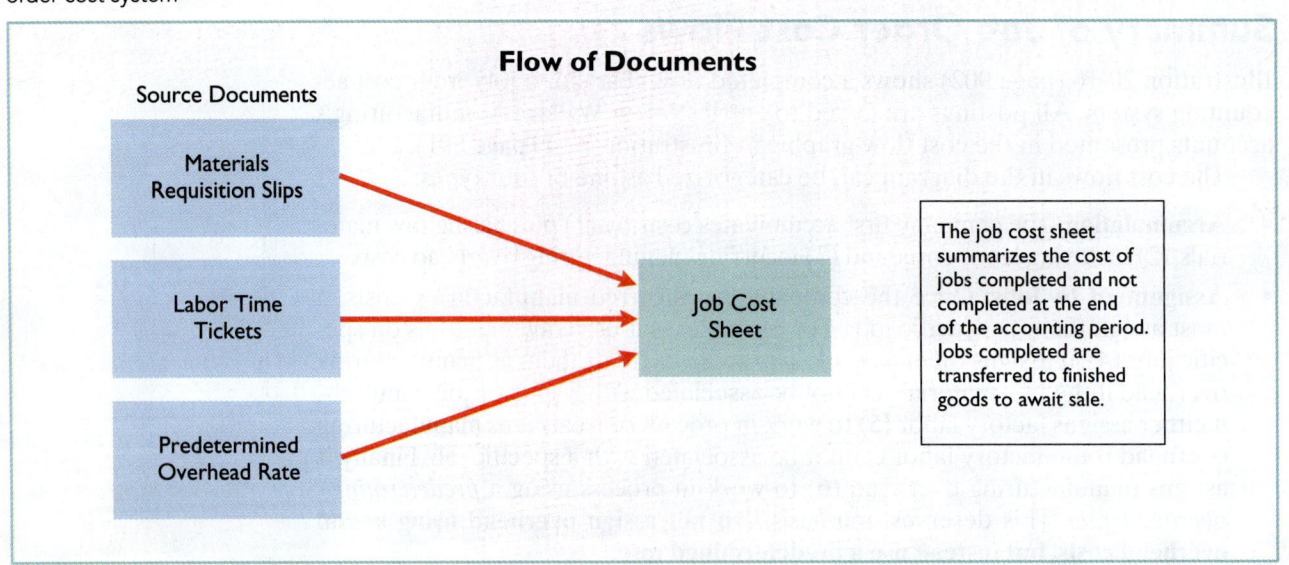

DO IT!

COMPLETION AND SALE OF JOBS

During the current month, Onyx Corporation completed Job 109 and Job 112. Job 109 cost $19,000 and Job 112 costs $27,000. Job 112 was sold on account for $42,000. Journalize the entries for the completion of the two jobs and the sale of Job 112.

Solution

Finished Goods Inventory	46,000	
Work in Process Inventory		46,000
(To record completion of Job 109, costing $19,000 and Job 112, costing $27,000)		
Accounts Receivable	42,000	
Sales		42,000
(To record sale of Job 112)		
Cost of Goods Sold	27,000	
Finished Goods Inventory		27,000
(To record cost of goods sold for Job 112)		

action plan
✔ Debit Finished Goods for the cost of completed jobs.
✔ Debit Cost of Goods Sold for the cost of jobs sold.

Related exercise material: **BE20-8, E20-2, E20-3, E20-4, E20-6, E20-7, E20-10,** and **DO IT! 20-3.**

REPORTING JOB COST DATA

At the end of a period, companies prepare financial statements that present aggregate data on all jobs manufactured and sold. The cost of goods manufactured schedule in job order costing is the same as in Chapter 19 with one exception: **The schedule shows manufacturing overhead applied, rather than actual overhead costs. The company adds manufacturing overhead applied to direct materials and direct labor to determine total manufacturing costs.**

Companies prepare the cost of goods manufactured schedule directly from the Work in Process Inventory account. Illustration 20-18 shows a condensed schedule for Wallace Manufacturing Company for January.

> **HELPFUL HINT**
> Monthly financial statements are usually prepared for management use only.

Illustration 20-18
Cost of goods manufactured schedule

WALLACE MANUFACTURING COMPANY
Cost of Goods Manufactured Schedule
For the Month Ended January 31, 2010

Work in process, January 1		$ –0–
Direct materials used	$24,000	
Direct labor	28,000	
Manufacturing overhead applied	**22,400**	
Total manufacturing costs		74,400
Total cost of work in process		74,400
Less: Work in process, January 31		35,400
Cost of goods manufactured		$39,000

Note that the cost of goods manufactured ($39,000) agrees with the amount transferred from Work in Process Inventory to Finished Goods Inventory in journal entry no. 7 in Illustration 20-16 (page 902).

The income statement and balance sheet are the same as those illustrated in Chapter 19. For example, Illustration 20-19 shows the partial income statement for Wallace Manufacturing for the month of January.

Illustration 20-19
Partial income statement

WALLACE MANUFACTURING COMPANY
Income Statement (partial)
For the Month Ending January 31, 2010

Sales		$50,000
Cost of goods sold		
Finished goods inventory, January 1	$ –0–	
Cost of goods manufactured (See Illustration 20-18)	**39,000**	
Cost of goods available for sale	39,000	
Less: Finished goods inventory, January 31	–0–	
Cost of goods sold		39,000
Gross profit		$11,000

Under- or Overapplied Manufacturing Overhead

STUDY OBJECTIVE 6
Distinguish between under- and overapplied manufacturing overhead.

When Manufacturing Overhead has a **debit balance**, overhead is said to be underapplied. **Underapplied overhead** means that the overhead assigned to work in process is less than the overhead incurred. Conversely, when manufacturing overhead has a **credit balance**, overhead is overapplied. **Overapplied overhead** means that the overhead assigned to work in process is greater than the overhead incurred. Illustration 20-20 shows these concepts.

Illustration 20-20
Under- and overapplied overhead

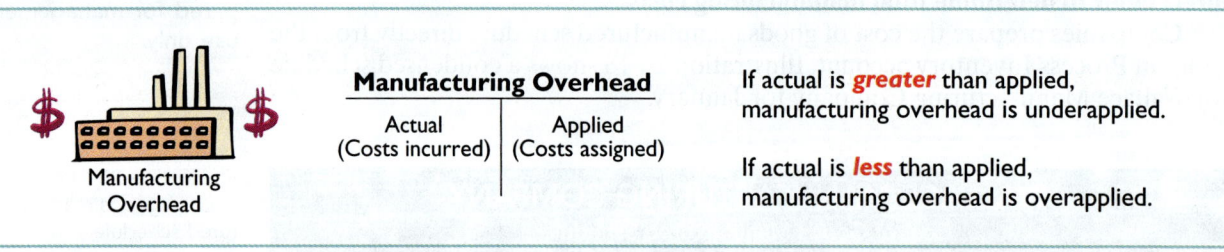

YEAR-END BALANCE

At the end of the year, all manufacturing overhead transactions are complete. There is no further opportunity for offsetting events to occur. At this point, Wallace eliminates any balance in Manufacturing Overhead by an adjusting entry. It considers under- or overapplied overhead to be an **adjustment to cost of goods sold**. Thus, Wallace **debits underapplied overhead to Cost of Goods Sold**. It **credits overapplied overhead to Cost of Goods Sold**.

To illustrate, assume that Wallace Manufacturing has a $2,500 credit balance in Manufacturing Overhead at December 31. The adjusting entry for the overapplied overhead is:

Dec. 31	Manufacturing Overhead	2,500	
	Cost of Goods Sold		2,500
	(To transfer overapplied overhead to		
	cost of goods sold)		

After Wallace posts this entry, Manufacturing Overhead has a zero balance. In preparing an income statement for the year, Wallace reports cost of goods sold **after adjusting it** for either under- or overapplied overhead.

Conceptually, some argue, under- or overapplied overhead at the end of the year should be allocated among ending work in process, finished goods, and cost of goods sold. The discussion of this possible allocation approach is left to more advanced courses.

ETHICS INSIGHT

Working a 25-Hour Day

In some industries, companies bill jobs on a "cost plus profit" basis. For example, law offices bill their customers based upon the "billable hours" incurred by their legal staff. This creates an incentive for law offices to pad their bills—that is, to overstate the costs incurred on particular jobs so as to inflate their bills. In one survey, two-thirds of attorneys reported knowledge of bill padding.

Similarly, suppliers to the government have often been accused of overbilling by misstating their cost accounting records. For example, the government recently filed a lawsuit against Northrop Grumman. This suit accused the company of intentionally concealing cost-accounting and material-tracking problems related to radar-jamming devices that the company made for the U.S. government more than 20 years before. These problems, the suit alleged, resulted in the government overpaying by $27 million. Company memos discussed strategies for training cost-accounting managers on how to conceal the problem from the government. One memo stated, "We can't tell the truth."

Sources: Nathan Koppel, "Lawyer's Charge Opens Window on Bill Padding," *Wall Street Journal*, August 30, 2006; and Andy Pasztor and Jonathan Karp, "Northrup Papers Indicate Coverup," *Wall Street Journal*, April 19, 2004.

 What feature of these businesses creates an incentive to misstate cost accounting data on particular jobs? What can customers do to protect themselves from overbilling?

DO IT!

For Karr Company, the predetermined overhead rate is 140% of direct labor cost. During the month, Karr incurred $90,000 of factory labor costs, of which $80,000 is direct labor and $10,000 is indirect labor. Actual overhead incurred was $119,000.

Compute the amount of manufacturing overhead applied during the month. Determine the amount of under- or overapplied manufacturing overhead.

APPLIED MANUFACTURING OVERHEAD

action plan
✔ Calculate the amount of overhead applied by multiplying the predetermined overhead rate by actual activity.
✔ If actual manufacturing overhead is greater than applied, manufacturing overhead is underapplied.
✔ If actual manufacturing overhead is less than applied, manufacturing overhead is overapplied.

Solution
Manufacturing overhead applied = (140% × $80,000) = $112,000
Underapplied manufacturing overhead = ($119,000 − $112,000) = $7,000

Related exercise material: **BE20-9, E20-5, E20-12, E20-13,** and **DO IT!** **20-4.**

 Be sure to read **ALL ABOUT YOU: *Minding Your Own Business*** on page 906 for information on how topics in this chapter apply to your personal life.

all about YOU

Minding Your Own Business

After graduating you might decide to start a small business. As discussed in this chapter, owners of any business need to know how to calculate the cost of their products. In fact, many small businesses fail because they do not accurately calculate their product costs, so they don't know if they are making money or losing money—until it is too late.

Some Facts

* There are about 17.6 million sole proprietorships in the U.S. The most common type of sole proprietorship is construction contractor.

* During a recent year, 25% of all sole proprietorships reported losses. The safest business is surveying and mapping, with only 6% of firms reporting losses. The riskiest business is hunting and trapping, with 76% of firms reporting losses.

* *Inc.* Magazine ranked the following as the top ten best places to start a business in 2006: Yuma, AZ; St. George, UT; Cape Coral–Fort Myers, FL; Fort Walton Beach–Crestview–Destin, FL; Coeur d'Alene, ID; Bellingham, WA; Port St. Lucie–Fort Pierce, FL; Naples–Marco Island, FL; Las Vegas–Paradise, NV; Idaho Fall, ID.

* About.com ranked the top ten business opportunities for 2005: business coach (motivates managers); business broker (brings together buyers and sellers of businesses); garage-organizing service; designing and producing smart (customized) clothes; medical transcription; trash removal; anti-aging spas; college admissions consulting; translation services; gaming-related businesses.

About the Numbers

Instead of starting your own business from scratch, perhaps you think it makes more sense to purchase a franchise. Initial investment varies, and annual franchise fees range from about $20,000 up to $80,000. The nearby chart of some well-known franchises shows the investment you typically need to make for these franchises. As you can see, you have to generate considerable revenue to cover the investment and related franchise fees. That's a lot of overhead.

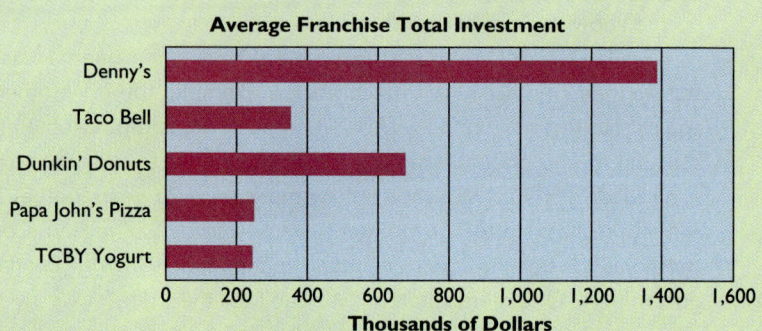

Source: AllBusiness.com, www.allbusiness.com/franchise/listings.asp?cat=4933&sub=4970 (accessed June 2006).

What Do You Think?

Suppose that you decide to start a landscape business. You use an old pickup truck that you've fully paid for. You store the truck and other equipment in your parents' barn, and you store trees and shrubs on their land. Your parents will not charge you for the use of these facilities for the first two years, but beginning in the third year they will charge a reasonable rent. Your mother helps you by answering phone calls and providing customers with information. She doesn't charge you for this service, but she plans on doing it for only your first two years in business.

In pricing your services, should you include charges for the truck, the barn, the land, and your mother's services when calculating your product cost?

YES: If you don't include charges for these costs, your costs are understated and your profitability is overstated.

NO: At this point you are not actually incurring costs related to these activities, therefore you shouldn't record charges.

Sources: www.bizstats.com; Darrel Zahorsky, "10 Best Small Business Opportunities for 2005," sbinformation.about.com (accessed June 2006); Joel Kotkin, "Boomtowns '06," *Inc.* Magazine, May 2006, p. 97.

Comprehensive DO IT!

During February, Cardella Manufacturing works on two jobs: A16 and B17. Summary data concerning these jobs are as follows.

Manufacturing Overhead
Cardella Manufacturing uses a predetermined overhead rate with direct labor costs as the activity base. It expects annual overhead costs to be $760,000 and direct labor costs for the year to be $950,000.

Manufacturing Costs Incurred
Purchased $54,000 of raw materials on account.
Factory labor $76,000, plus $4,000 employer payroll taxes.
Manufacturing overhead exclusive of indirect materials and indirect labor $59,800.

Assignment of Costs

Direct materials:	Job A16 $27,000, Job B17 $21,000
Indirect materials:	$3,000
Direct labor:	Job A16 $52,000, Job B17 $26,000
Indirect labor:	$2,000

Job A16 was completed and sold on account for $150,000. Job B17 was only partially completed.

Instructions

(a) Compute the predetermined overhead rate.
(b) Journalize the February transactions in the sequence followed in the chapter.
(c) What was the amount of under- or overapplied manufacturing overhead?

Solution to Comprehensive DO IT!

(a)

Estimated annual overhead costs	÷	Expected annual operating activity	=	Predetermined overhead rate
$760,000	÷	$950,000	=	80%

(b)

1.

Feb. 28	Raw Materials Inventory	54,000	
	Accounts Payable		54,000
	(Purchase of raw materials on account)		

2.

28	Factory Labor	80,000	
	Factory Wages Payable		76,000
	Employer Payroll Taxes Payable		4,000
	(To record factory labor costs)		

3.

28	Manufacturing Overhead	59,800	
	Accounts Payable, Accumulated Depreciation, and Prepaid Insurance		59,800
	(To record overhead costs)		

4.

28	Work in Process Inventory	48,000	
	Manufacturing Overhead	3,000	
	Raw Materials Inventory		51,000
	(To assign raw materials to production)		

action plan

✔ Predetermined overhead rate = Estimated annual overhead costs ÷ Expected annual operating activity.

✔ In accumulating costs, debit three accounts: Raw Materials Inventory, Factory Labor, and Manufacturing Overhead.

✔ When Work in Process Inventory is debited, credit one of the three accounts listed above.

✔ Debit Finished Goods Inventory for the cost of completed jobs. Debit Cost of Goods Sold for the cost of jobs sold.

✔ Overhead is underapplied when Manufacturing Overhead has a debit balance.

			5.		
Feb. 28		Work in Process Inventory		78,000	
		Manufacturing Overhead		2,000	
		Factory Labor			80,000
		(To assign factory labor to production)			
			6.		
28		Work in Process Inventory		62,400	
		Manufacturing Overhead			62,400
		(To assign overhead to jobs—			
		80% × $78,000)			
			7.		
28		Finished Goods Inventory		120,600	
		Work in Process Inventory			120,600
		(To record completion of Job A16: direct			
		materials $27,000, direct labor $52,000,			
		and manufacturing overhead $41,600)			
			8.		
28		Accounts Receivable		150,000	
		Sales			150,000
		(To record sale of Job A16)			
28		Cost of Goods Sold		120,600	
		Finished Goods Inventory			120,600
		(To record cost of sale for Job A16)			

(c) Manufacturing Overhead has a debit balance of $2,400 as shown below.

Manufacturing Overhead

(3)	59,800	(6)	62,400
(4)	3,000		
(5)	2,000		
Bal.	2,400		

Thus, manufacturing overhead is underapplied for the month.

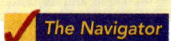

SUMMARY OF STUDY OBJECTIVES

1. **Explain the characteristics and purposes of cost accounting.** Cost accounting involves the procedures for measuring, recording, and reporting product costs. From the data accumulated, companies determine the total cost and the unit cost of each product. The two basic types of cost accounting systems are job order cost and process cost.

2. **Describe the flow of costs in a job order costing system.** In job order costing, manufacturing costs are first accumulated in three accounts: Raw Materials Inventory, Factory Labor, and Manufacturing Overhead. The accumulated costs are then assigned to Work in Process Inventory and eventually to Finished Goods Inventory and Cost of Goods Sold.

3. **Explain the nature and importance of a job cost sheet.** A job cost sheet is a form used to record the costs chargeable to a specific job and to determine the total and unit costs of the completed job. Job cost sheets constitute the subsidiary ledger for the Work in Process Inventory control account.

4. **Indicate how the predetermined overhead rate is determined and used.** The predetermined overhead rate is based on the relationship between estimated annual overhead costs and expected annual operating activity. This is expressed in terms of a common activity base, such as direct labor cost. The rate is used in assigning overhead costs to work in process and to specific jobs.

5 Prepare entries for jobs completed and sold. When jobs are completed, the cost is debited to Finished Goods Inventory and credited to Work in Process Inventory. When a job is sold the entries are: (a) Debit Cash or Accounts Receivable and credit Sales for the selling price. And (b) debit Cost of Goods Sold and credit Finished Goods Inventory for the cost of the goods.

6 Distinguish between under- and overapplied manufacturing overhead. Underapplied manufacturing overhead means that the overhead assigned to work in process is less than the overhead incurred. Overapplied overhead means that the overhead assigned to work in process is greater than the overhead incurred.

GLOSSARY

Cost accounting An area of accounting that involves measuring, recording, and reporting product costs. (p. 888)

Cost accounting system Manufacturing cost accounts that are fully integrated into the general ledger of a company. (p. 888)

Job cost sheet A form used to record the costs chargeable to a specific job and to determine the total and unit costs of the completed job. (p. 893)

Job order cost system A cost accounting system in which costs are assigned to each job or batch. (p. 888)

Materials requisition slip A document authorizing the issuance of raw materials from the storeroom to production. (p. 894)

Overapplied overhead A situation in which overhead assigned to work in process is greater than the overhead incurred. (p. 904)

Predetermined overhead rate A rate based on the relationship between estimated annual overhead costs and expected annual operating activity, expressed in terms of a common activity base. (p. 897)

Process cost system A system of accounting used when a large quantity of similar products are manufactured. (p. 889)

Summary entry A journal entry that summarizes the totals from multiple transactions. (p. 892)

Time ticket A document that indicates the employee, the hours worked, the account and job to be charged, and the total labor cost. (p. 895)

Underapplied overhead A situation in which overhead assigned to work in process is less than the overhead incurred. (p. 904)

SELF-STUDY QUESTIONS

Answers are at the end of the chapter.

(SO 1) **1.** Cost accounting involves the measuring, recording, and reporting of:
  a. product costs.
  b. future costs.
  c. manufacturing processes.
  d. managerial accounting decisions.

(SO 1) **2.** A company is more likely to use a job costing system if:
  a. it manufactures a large volume of similar products.
  b. its production is continuous.
  c. it manufactures products with unique characteristics.
  d. it uses a periodic inventory system.

(SO 2) **3.** In accumulating raw materials costs, the cost of raw materials purchased in a perpetual system is debited to:
  a. Raw Materials Purchases.
  b. Raw Materials Inventory.
  c. Purchases.
  d. Work in Process.

(SO 2) **4.** When incurred, factory labor costs are debited to:
  a. Work in Process.
  b. Factory Wages Expense.
  c. Factory Labor.
  d. Factory Wages Payable.

5. The flow of costs in job order costing: (SO 2)
  a. begins with work in process inventory and ends with finished goods inventory.
  b. begins as soon as a sale occurs.
  c. parallels the physical flow of materials as they are converted into finished goods.
  d. is necessary to prepare the cost of goods manufactured schedule.

6. Raw materials are assigned to a job when: (SO 3)
  a. the job is sold.
  b. the materials are purchased.
  c. the materials are received from the vendor.
  d. the materials are issued by the materials storeroom.

7. The source documents for assigning costs to job cost (SO 3) sheets are:
  a. invoices, time tickets, and the predetermined overhead rate.
  b. materials requisition slips, time tickets, and the actual overhead costs.
  c. materials requisition slips, payroll register, and the predetermined overhead rate.
  d. materials requisition slips, time tickets, and the predetermined overhead rate.

910 Chapter 20 Job Order Costing

(SO 3) 8. In recording the issuance of raw materials in a job order cost system, it would be *incorrect* to:
a. debit Work in Process Inventory.
b. debit Finished Goods Inventory.
c. debit Manufacturing Overhead.
d. credit Raw Materials Inventory.

(SO 3) 9. The entry when direct factory labor is assigned to jobs is a debit to:
a. Work in Process Inventory and a credit to Factory Labor.
b. Manufacturing Overhead and a credit to Factory Labor.
c. Factory Labor and a credit to Manufacturing Overhead.
d. Factory Labor and a credit to Work in Process Inventory.

(SO 4) 10. The formula for computing the predetermined manufacturing overhead rate is estimated annual overhead costs divided by an expected annual operating activity, expressed as:
a. direct labor cost.
b. direct labor hours.
c. machine hours.
d. any of the above.

(SO 4) 11. In Crawford Company, the predetermined overhead rate is 80% of direct labor cost. During the month, $210,000 of factory labor costs are incurred, of which $180,000 is direct labor and $30,000 is indirect labor. Actual overhead incurred was $200,000. The amount of overhead debited to Work in Process Inventory should be:
a. $120,000.
b. $144,000.
c. $168,000.
d. $160,000.

(SO 5) 12. In Mynex Company, Job No. 26 is completed at a cost of $4,500 and later sold for $7,000 cash. A correct entry is:
a. Debit Finished Goods Inventory $7,000 and credit Work in Process Inventory $7,000.
b. Debit Cost of Goods Sold $7,000 and credit Finished Goods Inventory $7,000.
c. Debit Finished Goods Inventory $4,500 and credit Work in Process Inventory $4,500.
d. Debit Accounts Receivable $7,000 and credit Sales $7,000.

(SO 5) 13. At the end of an accounting period, a company using a job costing system prepares the cost of goods manufactured:
a. from the job cost sheet.
b. from the Work in Process Inventory account.
c. by adding direct materials used, direct labor incurred, and manufacturing overhead incurred.
d. from the Cost of Goods Sold account.

(SO 6) 14. At end of the year a company has a $1,200 debit balance in Manufacturing Overhead. The company:
a. makes an adjusting entry by debiting Manufacturing Overhead Applied for $1,200 and crediting Manufacturing Overhead for $1,200.
b. makes an adjusting entry by debiting Manufacturing Overhead Expense for $1,200 and crediting Manufacturing Overhead for $1,200.
c. makes an adjusting entry by debiting Cost of Goods Sold for $1,200 and crediting Manufacturing Overhead for $1,200.
d. makes no adjusting entry because differences between actual overhead and the amount applied are a normal part of job costing and will average out over the next year.

(SO 6) 15. Manufacturing overhead is underapplied if:
a. actual overhead is less than applied.
b. actual overhead is greater than applied.
c. the predetermined rate equals the actual rate.
d. actual overhead equals applied overhead.

Go to the book's companion website,
www.wiley.com/college/weygandt,
for Additional Self-Study questions.

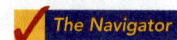

QUESTIONS

1. (a) Joe Delong is not sure about the difference between cost accounting and a cost accounting system. Explain the difference to Joe. (b) What is an important feature of a cost accounting system?
2. (a) Distinguish between the two types of cost accounting systems. (b) May a company use both types of cost accounting systems?
3. What type of industry is likely to use a job order cost system? Give some examples.
4. What type of industry is likely to use a process cost system? Give some examples.
5. Your roommate asks your help in understanding the major steps in the flow of costs in a job order cost system. Identify the steps for your roommate.
6. There are two inventory control accounts in a job order system. Identify the control accounts and their subsidiary ledgers.
7. What source documents are used in accumulating direct labor costs?
8. "Entries to Manufacturing Overhead normally are only made daily." Do you agree? Explain.
9. Tony Andres is confused about the source documents used in assigning materials and labor costs. Identify the documents and give the entry for each document.
10. What is the purpose of a job cost sheet?
11. Indicate the source documents that are used in charging costs to specific jobs.
12. Explain how a "materials requisition slip" is used in a job order cost system.
13. Mel Finney believes actual manufacturing overhead should be charged to jobs. Do you agree? Why or why not?
14. What relationships are involved in computing a predetermined overhead rate?
15. How can the agreement of Work in Process Inventory and job cost sheets be verified?

16. Tina Birk believes that the cost of goods manufactured schedule in job order cost accounting is the same as shown in Chapter 19. Is Tina correct? Explain.

17. Jeff Gillum is confused about under- and overapplied manufacturing overhead. Define the terms for Jeff, and indicate the balance in the manufacturing overhead account applicable to each term.

18. "At the end of the year, under- or overapplied overhead is closed to Income Summary." Is this correct? If not, indicate the customary treatment of this amount.

BRIEF EXERCISES

BE20-1 Reyes Tool & Die begins operations on January 1. Because all work is done to customer specifications, the company decides to use a job order cost accounting system. Prepare a flow chart of a typical job order system with arrows showing the flow of costs. Identify the eight transactions.

Prepare a flowchart of a job order cost accounting system, and identify transactions.
(SO 2)

BE20-2 During January, its first month of operations, Reyes Tool & Die accumulated the following manufacturing costs: raw materials $4,000 on account, factory labor $5,000 of which $4,200 relates to factory wages payable and $800 relates to payroll taxes payable, and utilities payable $2,000. Prepare separate journal entries for each type of manufacturing cost.

Prepare entries in accumulating manufacturing costs.
(SO 2)

BE20-3 In January, Reyes Tool & Die requisitions raw materials for production as follows: Job 1 $900, Job 2 $1,200, Job 3 $700, and general factory use $600. Prepare a summary journal entry to record raw materials used.

Prepare entry for the assignment of raw materials costs.
(SO 3)

BE20-4 Factory labor data for Reyes Tool & Die is given in BE20-2. During January, time tickets show that the factory labor of $5,000 was used as follows: Job 1 $1,200, Job 2 $1,600 Job 3 $1,400, and general factory use $800. Prepare a summary journal entry to record factory labor used.

Prepare entry for the assignment of factory labor costs.
(SO 3)

BE20-5 Data pertaining to job cost sheets for Reyes Tool & Die are given in BE20-3 and BE20-4. Prepare the job cost sheets for each of the three jobs. (*Note*: You may omit the column for Manufacturing Overhead.)

Prepare job cost sheets.
(SO 3)

BE20-6 Marquis Company estimates that annual manufacturing overhead costs will be $800,000. Estimated annual operating activity bases are: direct labor cost $500,000, direct labor hours 50,000, and machine hours 100,000. Compute the predetermined overhead rate for each activity base.

Compute predetermined overhead rates.
(SO 4)

BE20-7 During the first quarter, Diaz Company incurs the following direct labor costs: January $40,000, February $30,000, and March $50,000. For each month, prepare the entry to assign overhead to production using a predetermined rate of 90% of direct labor cost.

Assign manufacturing overhead to production.
(SO 4)

BE20-8 In March, Hollaway Company completes Jobs 10 and 11. Job 10 cost $25,000 and Job 11 $30,000. On March 31, Job 10 is sold to the customer for $35,000 in cash. Journalize the entries for the completion of the two jobs and the sale of Job 10.

Prepare entries for completion and sale of completed jobs.
(SO 5)

BE20-9 At December 31, balances in Manufacturing Overhead are: Lott Company—debit $1,500, Perez Company—credit $900. Prepare the adjusting entry for each company at December 31, assuming the adjustment is made to cost of goods sold.

Prepare adjusting entries for under- and overapplied overhead.
(SO 6)

DO IT! REVIEW

DO IT! 20-1 During the current month, Barnum Company incurs the following manufacturing costs:

a. Purchased raw materials of $13,000 on account.
b. Incurred factory labor of $40,000. Of that amount, $31,000 relates to wages payable and $9,000 relates to payroll taxes payable.

Prepare journal entries for manufacturing costs.
(SO 2)

912 Chapter 20 Job Order Costing

c. Factory utilities of $3,100 are payable, prepaid factory property taxes of $2,400 have expired, and depreciation on the factory building is $9,500.

Prepare journal entries for each type of manufacturing cost. (Use a summary entry to record manufacturing overhead.)

Assign costs to work in process.
(SO 3, 4)

DO IT! 20-2 Fishel Company is working on two job orders. The job cost sheets show the following:

	Job 201	Job 202
Direct materials	$7,200	$9,000
Direct labor	4,000	6,000
Manufacturing overhead	5,200	7,800

Prepare the three summary entries to record the assignment of costs to Work in Process from the data on the job cost sheets.

Prepare entries for completion and sale of jobs.
(SO 5)

DO IT! 20-3 During the current month, Seeza Corporation completed Job 310 and Job 312. Job 310 cost $60,000 and Job 312 cost $40,000. Job 312 was sold on account for $90,000. Journalize the entries for the completion of the two jobs and the sale of Job 312.

Apply manufacturing overhead and determine under- or overapplication.
(SO 6)

DO IT! 20-4 For KnightRider Company, the predetermined overhead rate is 150% of direct labor cost. During the month, KnightRider incurred $100,000 of factory labor costs, of which $85,000 is direct labor and $15,000 is indirect labor. Actual overhead incurred was $120,000.

Compute the amount of manufacturing overhead applied during the month. Determine the amount of under- or overapplied manufacturing overhead.

EXERCISES

Prepare entries for factory labor.
(SO 2, 3)

E20-1 The gross earnings of the factory workers for Brantley Company during the month of January are $60,000. The employer's payroll taxes for the factory payroll are $8,000. The fringe benefits to be paid by the employer on this payroll are $4,000. Of the total accumulated cost of factory labor, 85% is related to direct labor and 15% is attributable to indirect labor.

Instructions
(a) Prepare the entry to record the factory labor costs for the month of January.
(b) Prepare the entry to assign factory labor to production.

Prepare journal entries for manufacturing costs.
(SO 3, 4, 5)

E20-2 Milner Manufacturing uses a job order cost accounting system. On May 1, the company has a balance in Work in Process Inventory of $3,200 and two jobs in process: Job No. 429 $2,000, and Job No. 430 $1,200. During May, a summary of source documents reveals the following.

Job Number	Materials Requisition Slips		Labor Time Tickets	
429	$2,500		$1,900	
430	3,500		3,000	
431	4,400	$10,400	7,600	$12,500
General use	800		1,200	
		$11,200		$13,700

Milner Manufacturing applies manufacturing overhead to jobs at an overhead rate of 80% of direct labor cost. Job No. 429 is completed during the month.

Instructions
(a) Prepare summary journal entries on May 31 to record: (i) the requisition slips, (ii) the time tickets, (iii) the assignment of manufacturing overhead to jobs, and (iv) the completion of Job No. 429.
(b) Post the entries to Work in Process Inventory, and prove the agreement of the control account with the job cost sheets of the unfinished jobs.

E20-3 A job order cost sheet for Rolen Company is shown below.

Analyze a job cost sheet and prepare entries for manufacturing costs.
(SO 3, 4, 5)

Job No. 92			For 2,000 Units
Date	Direct Materials	Direct Labor	Manufacturing Overhead
Beg. bal. Jan. 1	5,000	6,000	4,500
8	6,000		
12		8,000	6,400
25	2,000		
27		4,000	3,200
	13,000	18,000	14,100

Cost of completed job:	
Direct materials	$13,000
Direct labor	18,000
Manufacturing overhead	14,100
Total cost	$45,100
Unit cost ($45,100 ÷ 2,000)	$22.55

Instructions
(a) On the basis of the foregoing data answer the following questions.
 (1) What was the balance in Work in Process Inventory on January 1 if this was the only unfinished job?
 (2) If manufacturing overhead is applied on the basis of direct labor cost, what overhead rate was used in each year?
(b) Prepare summary entries at January 31 to record the current year's transactions pertaining to Job No. 92.

E20-4 Manufacturing cost data for Pena Company, which uses a job order cost system, are presented below.

Analyze costs of manufacturing and determine missing amounts.
(SO 5)

	Case A	Case B	Case C
Direct materials used	$ (a)	$ 83,000	$ 63,150
Direct labor	50,000	120,000	(h)
Manufacturing overhead applied	42,500	(d)	(i)
Total manufacturing costs	155,650	(e)	213,000
Work in process 1/1/10	(b)	15,500	18,000
Total cost of work in process	201,500	(f)	(j)
Work in process 12/31/10	(c)	11,800	(k)
Cost of goods manufactured	192,300	(g)	222,000

Instructions
Indicate the missing amount for each letter. Assume that in all cases manufacturing overhead is applied on the basis of direct labor cost and the rate is the same.

E20-5 Renteria Company applies manufacturing overhead to jobs on the basis of machine hours used. Overhead costs are expected to total $305,000 for the year, and machine usage is estimated at 125,000 hours.
 For the year, $322,000 of overhead costs are incurred and 130,000 hours are used.

Compute the manufacturing overhead rate and under- or overapplied overhead.
(SO 4, 6)

Instructions
(a) Compute the manufacturing overhead rate for the year.
(b) What is the amount of under- or overapplied overhead at December 31?
(c) Assuming the under- or overapplied overhead for the year is not allocated to inventory accounts, prepare the adjusting entry to assign the amount to cost of goods sold.

Chapter 20 Job Order Costing

Analyze job cost sheet and prepare entry for completed job.

(SO 2, 3, 4, 5)

E20-6 A job cost sheet of Nilson Company is given below.

Job Cost Sheet

JOB NO. 469   Quantity 2,000
ITEM White Lion Cages   Date Requested 7/2
FOR Tesla Company   Date Completed 7/31

Date	Direct Materials	Direct Labor	Manufacturing Overhead
7/10	825		
12	900		
15		440	550
22		380	475
24	1,600		
27	1,500		
31		540	675

Cost of completed job:
- Direct materials _____
- Direct labor _____
- Manufacturing overhead _____
- Total cost _____
- Unit cost _____

Instructions

(a) Answer the following questions.
   (1) What are the source documents for direct materials, direct labor, and manufacturing overhead costs assigned to this job?
   (2) What is the predetermined manufacturing overhead rate?
   (3) What are the total cost and the unit cost of the completed job?

(b) Prepare the entry to record the completion of the job.

Prepare entries for manufacturing costs.

(SO 2, 3, 4, 5)

E20-7 Elder Corporation incurred the following transactions.

1. Purchased raw materials on account $46,300.
2. Raw Materials of $36,000 were requisitioned to the factory. An analysis of the materials requisition slips indicated that $6,800 was classified as indirect materials.
3. Factory labor costs incurred were $53,900, of which $49,000 pertained to factory wages payable and $4,900 pertained to employer payroll taxes payable.
4. Time tickets indicated that $48,000 was direct labor and $5,900 was indirect labor.
5. Overhead costs incurred on account were $80,500.
6. Manufacturing overhead was applied at the rate of 150% of direct labor cost.
7. Goods costing $88,000 were completed and transferred to finished goods.
8. Finished goods costing $75,000 to manufacture were sold on account for $103,000.

Instructions

Journalize the transactions. (Omit explanations.)

Prepare entries for manufacturing costs.

(SO 2, 3, 4, 5)

E20-8 Garnett Printing Corp. uses a job order cost system. The following data summarize the operations related to the first quarter's production.

1. Materials purchased on account $192,000, and factory wages incurred $87,300.
2. Materials requisitioned and factory labor used by job:

Job Number	Materials	Factory Labor
A20	$ 35,240	$18,000
A21	42,920	22,000
A22	36,100	15,000
A23	39,270	25,000
General factory use	4,470	7,300
	$158,000	$87,300

3. Manufacturing overhead costs incurred on account $39,500.
4. Depreciation on machinery and equipment $14,550.
5. Manufacturing overhead rate is 80% of direct labor cost.
6. Jobs completed during the quarter: A20, A21, and A23.

Instructions
Prepare entries to record the operations summarized above. (Prepare a schedule showing the individual cost elements and total cost for each job in item 6.)

E20-9 At May 31, 2010, the accounts of Hannifan Manufacturing Company show the following.

Prepare a cost of goods manufactured schedule and partial financial statements.
(SO 2, 5)

1. May 1 inventories—finished goods $12,600, work in process $14,700, and raw materials $8,200.
2. May 31 inventories—finished goods $9,500, work in process $17,900, and raw materials $7,100.
3. Debit postings to work in process were: direct materials $62,400, direct labor $32,000, and manufacturing overhead applied $40,000.
4. Sales totaled $200,000.

Instructions
(a) Prepare a condensed cost of goods manufactured schedule.
(b) Prepare an income statement for May through gross profit.
(c) Indicate the balance sheet presentation of the manufacturing inventories at May 31, 2010.

E20-10 Tomlin Company begins operations on April 1. Information from job cost sheets shows the following.

Compute work in process and finished goods from job cost sheets.
(SO 3, 5)

Job Number	Manufacturing Costs Assigned			Month Completed
	April	May	June	
10	$5,200	$4,400		May
11	4,100	3,900	$3,000	June
12	1,200			April
13		4,700	4,500	June
14		4,900	3,600	Not complete

Job 12 was completed in April. Job 10 was completed in May. Jobs 11 and 13 were completed in June. Each job was sold for 25% above its cost in the month following completion.

Instructions
(a) What is the balance in Work in Process Inventory at the end of each month?
(b) What is the balance in Finished Goods Inventory at the end of each month?
(c) What is the gross profit for May, June, and July?

E20-11 Shown below are the job cost related accounts for the law firm of Barnes, King, and Morton and their manufacturing-company equivalents:

Prepare entries for costs of services provided.
(SO 2, 4, 5)

Law Firm Accounts	Manufacturing-Company Accounts
Supplies	Raw Materials
Salaries Payable	Factory Wages Payable
Operating Overhead	Manufacturing Overhead
Work in Process	Work in Process
Cost of Completed Work	Cost of Goods Sold

Cost data for the month of March follow.

1. Purchased supplies on account $1,500.
2. Issued supplies $1,200 (60% direct and 40% indirect).
3. Time cards for the month indicated labor costs of $50,000 (80% direct and 20% indirect).
4. Operating overhead costs incurred for cash totaled $40,000.
5. Operating overhead is applied at a rate of 90% of direct attorney cost.
6. Work completed totaled $70,000.

Instructions
(a) Journalize the transactions for March. Omit explanations.
(b) Determine the balance of the Work in Process account. Use a T account.

Chapter 20 Job Order Costing

Determine cost of jobs and ending balance in work in process and overhead accounts.
(SO 3, 4, 6)

E20-12 Pedro Morales and Associates, a C.P.A. firm, uses job order costing to capture the costs of its audit jobs. There were no audit jobs in process at the beginning of November. Listed below are data concerning the three audit jobs conducted during November.

	Gonzalez	Navarro	Rojas
Direct materials	$600	$400	$200
Auditor labor costs	$5,400	$6,600	$3,375
Auditor hours	72	88	45

Overhead costs are applied to jobs on the basis of auditor hours, and the predetermined overhead rate is $55 per auditor hour. The Gonzalez job is the only incomplete job at the end of November. Actual overhead for the month was $12,000.

Instructions
(a) Determine the cost of each job.
(b) Indicate the balance of the Work in Process account at the end of November.
(c) Calculate the ending balance of the Manufacturing Overhead account for November.

Determine predetermined overhead rate, apply overhead and determine whether balance under- or overapplied.
(SO 4, 6)

E20-13 Easy Decorating uses a job order costing system to collect the costs of its interior decorating business. Each client's consultation is treated as a separate job. Overhead is applied to each job based on the number of decorator hours incurred. Listed below are data for the current year.

Budgeted overhead	$960,000
Actual overhead	$982,800
Budgeted decorator hours	40,000
Actual decorator hours	40,500

The company uses Operating Overhead in place of Manufacturing Overhead.

Instructions
(a) Compute the predetermined overhead rate.
(b) Prepare the entry to apply the overhead for the year.
(c) Determine whether the overhead was under- or overapplied and by how much.

EXERCISES: SET B

Visit the book's companion website at **www.wiley.com/college/weygandt**, and choose the Student Companion site, to access Exercise Set B.

PROBLEMS: SET A

Prepare entries in a job cost system and job cost sheets.
(SO 2, 3, 4, 5, 6)

P20-1A Garcia Manufacturing uses a job order cost system and applies overhead to production on the basis of direct labor costs. On January 1, 2010, Job No. 50 was the only job in process. The costs incurred prior to January 1 on this job were as follows: direct materials $20,000, direct labor $12,000, and manufacturing overhead $16,000. As of January 1, Job No. 49 had been completed at a cost of $90,000 and was part of finished goods inventory. There was a $15,000 balance in the Raw Materials Inventory account.

During the month of January, Garcia Manufacturing began production on Jobs 51 and 52, and completed Jobs 50 and 51. Jobs 49 and 50 were also sold on account during the month for $122,000 and $158,000, respectively. The following additional events occurred during the month.

1. Purchased additional raw materials of $90,000 on account.
2. Incurred factory labor costs of $65,000. Of this amount $16,000 related to employer payroll taxes.
3. Incurred manufacturing overhead costs as follows: indirect materials $17,000; indirect labor $15,000; depreciation expense $19,000, and various other manufacturing overhead costs on account $20,000.

4. Assigned direct materials and direct labor to jobs as follows.

Job No.	Direct Materials	Direct Labor
50	$10,000	$ 5,000
51	39,000	25,000
52	30,000	20,000

Instructions
(a) Calculate the predetermined overhead rate for 2010, assuming Garcia Manufacturing estimates total manufacturing overhead costs of $1,050,000, direct labor costs of $700,000, and direct labor hours of 20,000 for the year.
(b) Open job cost sheets for Jobs 50, 51, and 52. Enter the January 1 balances on the job cost sheet for Job No. 50.
(c) Prepare the journal entries to record the purchase of raw materials, the factory labor costs incurred, and the manufacturing overhead costs incurred during the month of January.
(d) Prepare the journal entries to record the assignment of direct materials, direct labor, and manufacturing overhead costs to production. In assigning manufacturing overhead costs, use the overhead rate calculated in (a). Post all costs to the job cost sheets as necessary.
(e) Total the job cost sheets for any job(s) completed during the month. Prepare the journal entry (or entries) to record the completion of any job(s) during the month.
(f) Prepare the journal entry (or entries) to record the sale of any job(s) during the month.
(g) What is the balance in the Finished Goods Inventory account at the end of the month? What does this balance consist of?
(h) What is the amount of over- or underapplied overhead?

(e) Job 50, $70,500
Job 51, $101,500

P20-2A For the year ended December 31, 2010, the job cost sheets of DeVoe Company contained the following data.

Prepare entries in a job cost system and partial income statement.
(SO 2, 3, 4, 5, 6)

Job Number	Explanation	Direct Materials	Direct Labor	Manufacturing Overhead	Total Costs
7640	Balance 1/1	$25,000	$24,000	$28,800	$ 77,800
	Current year's costs	30,000	36,000	43,200	109,200
7641	Balance 1/1	11,000	18,000	21,600	50,600
	Current year's costs	43,000	48,000	57,600	148,600
7642	Current year's costs	48,000	55,000	66,000	169,000

Other data:

1. Raw materials inventory totaled $15,000 on January 1. During the year, $140,000 of raw materials were purchased on account.
2. Finished goods on January 1 consisted of Job No. 7638 for $87,000 and Job No. 7639 for $92,000.
3. Job No. 7640 and Job No. 7641 were completed during the year.
4. Job Nos. 7638, 7639, and 7641 were sold on account for $530,000.
5. Manufacturing overhead incurred on account totaled $120,000.
6. Other manufacturing overhead consisted of indirect materials $14,000, indirect labor $20,000, and depreciation on factory machinery $8,000.

Instructions
(a) Prove the agreement of Work in Process Inventory with job cost sheets pertaining to unfinished work. *Hint:* Use a single T account for Work in Process Inventory. Calculate each of the following, then post each to the T account: (1) beginning balance, (2) direct materials, (3) direct labor, (4) manufacturing overhead, and (5) completed jobs.
(b) Prepare the adjusting entry for manufacturing overhead, assuming the balance is allocated entirely to Cost of Goods Sold.
(c) Determine the gross profit to be reported for 2010.

(a) $169,000; Job 7642: $169,000

(b) Amount = $4,800

(c) $156,600

P20-3A Enos Inc. is a construction company specializing in custom patios. The patios are constructed of concrete, brick, fiberglass, and lumber, depending upon customer preference. On June 1, 2010, the general ledger for Enos Inc. contains the following data.

Prepare entries in a job cost system and cost of goods manufactured schedule.
(SO 2, 3, 4, 5)

| Raw Materials Inventory | $4,200 | Manufacturing Overhead Applied | $32,640 |
| Work in Process Inventory | $5,540 | Manufacturing Overhead Incurred | $31,650 |

Subsidiary data for Work in Process Inventory on June 1 are as follows.

Job Cost Sheets

Cost Element	Customer Job		
	Fowler	Haines	Krantz
Direct materials	$ 600	$ 800	$ 900
Direct labor	320	540	580
Manufacturing overhead	400	675	725
	$1,320	$2,015	$2,205

During June, raw materials purchased on account were $3,900, and all wages were paid. Additional overhead costs consisted of depreciation on equipment $700 and miscellaneous costs of $400 incurred on account.

A summary of materials requisition slips and time tickets for June shows the following.

Customer Job	Materials Requisition Slips	Time Tickets
Fowler	$ 800	$ 450
Elgin	2,000	800
Haines	500	360
Krantz	1,300	1,600
Fowler	300	390
	4,900	3,600
General use	1,500	1,200
	$6,400	$4,800

Overhead was charged to jobs at the same rate of $1.25 per dollar of direct labor cost. The patios for customers Fowler, Haines, and Krantz were completed during June and sold for a total of $18,900. Each customer paid in full.

Instructions
(a) Journalize the June transactions: (i) for purchase of raw materials, factory labor costs incurred, and manufacturing overhead costs incurred; (ii) assignment of raw materials, labor, and overhead to production; and (iii) completion of jobs and sale of goods.
(b) Post the entries to Work in Process Inventory.
(c) Reconcile the balance in Work in Process Inventory with the costs of unfinished jobs.
(d) Prepare a cost of goods manufactured schedule for June.

(d) Cost of goods manufactured $14,740

Compute predetermined overhead rates, apply overhead and calculate under- or overapplied overhead.
(SO 4, 6)

P20-4A Mabry Manufacturing Company uses a job order cost system in each of its three manufacturing departments. Manufacturing overhead is applied to jobs on the basis of direct labor cost in Department D, direct labor hours in Department E, and machine hours in Department K.

In establishing the predetermined overhead rates for 2010 the following estimates were made for the year.

	Department		
	D	E	K
Manufacturing overhead	$1,050,000	$1,500,000	$840,000
Direct labor costs	$1,500,000	$1,250,000	$450,000
Direct labor hours	100,000	125,000	40,000
Machine hours	400,000	500,000	120,000

During January, the job cost sheets showed the following costs and production data.

	Department		
	D	E	K
Direct materials used	$140,000	$126,000	$78,000
Direct labor costs	$120,000	$110,000	$37,500
Manufacturing overhead incurred	$ 89,000	$124,000	$74,000
Direct labor hours	8,000	11,000	3,500
Machine hours	34,000	45,000	10,400

Instructions
(a) Compute the predetermined overhead rate for each department.
(b) Compute the total manufacturing costs assigned to jobs in January in each department.
(c) Compute the under- or overapplied overhead for each department at January 31.

(a) 70%, $12, $7.00
(b) $344,000, $368,000
  $188,300
(c) $5,000, $(8,000), $1,200

P20-5A Vargas Corporation's fiscal year ends on November 30. The following accounts are found in its job order cost accounting system for the first month of the new fiscal year.

Analyze manufacturing accounts and determine missing amounts.
(SO 2, 3, 4, 5, 6)

Raw Materials Inventory

Dec. 1	Beginning balance	(a)	Dec. 31	Requisitions	18,850
31	Purchases	19,225			
Dec. 31	Ending balance	7,975			

Work in Process Inventory

Dec. 1	Beginning balance	(b)	Dec. 31	Jobs completed	(f)
31	Direct materials	(c)			
31	Direct labor	8,800			
31	Overhead	(d)			
Dec. 31	Ending balance	(e)			

Finished Goods Inventory

Dec. 1	Beginning balance	(g)	Dec. 31	Cost of goods sold	(i)
31	Completed jobs	(h)			
Dec. 31	Ending balance	(j)			

Factory Labor

Dec. 31	Factory wages	12,465	Dec. 31	Wages assigned	(k)

Manufacturing Overhead

Dec. 31	Indirect materials	1,900	Dec. 31	Overhead applied	(m)
31	Indirect labor	(l)			
31	Other overhead	1,245			

Other data:
1. On December 1, two jobs were in process: Job No. 154 and Job No. 155. These jobs had combined direct materials costs of $9,750 and direct labor costs of $15,000. Overhead was applied at a rate that was 80% of direct labor cost.
2. During December, Job Nos. 156, 157, and 158 were started. On December 31, Job No. 158 was unfinished. This job had charges for direct materials $3,800 and direct labor $4,800, plus manufacturing overhead. All jobs, except for Job No. 158, were completed in December.
3. On December 1, Job No. 153 was in the finished goods warehouse. It had a total cost of $5,000. On December 31, Job No. 157 was the only job finished that was not sold. It had a cost of $4,000.
4. Manufacturing overhead was $230 overapplied in December.

Instructions
List the letters (a) through (m) and indicate the amount pertaining to each letter.

(c) $16,950
(f) $57,100
(i) $58,100

PROBLEMS: SET B

P20-1B Weinrich Manufacturing uses a job order cost system and applies overhead to production on the basis of direct labor hours. On January 1, 2010, Job No. 25 was the only job in process. The costs incurred prior to January 1 on this job were as follows: direct materials $10,000; direct labor $6,000; and manufacturing overhead $9,000. Job No. 23 had been completed at a cost of $42,000 and was part of finished goods inventory. There was a $5,000 balance in the Raw Materials Inventory account.

During the month of January, the company began production on Jobs 26 and 27, and completed Jobs 25 and 26. Jobs 23 and 25 were sold on account during the month for $63,000 and $74,000, respectively. The following additional events occurred during the month.

Prepare entries in a job cost system and job cost sheets.
(SO 2, 3, 4, 5, 6)

1. Purchased additional raw materials of $40,000 on account.
2. Incurred factory labor costs of $31,500. Of this amount $7,500 related to employer payroll taxes.
3. Incurred manufacturing overhead costs as follows: indirect materials $10,000; indirect labor $7,500; depreciation expense $12,000; and various other manufacturing overhead costs on account $11,000.
4. Assigned direct materials and direct labor to jobs as follows.

Job No.	Direct Materials	Direct Labor
25	$ 5,000	$ 3,000
26	17,000	12,000
27	13,000	9,000

5. The company uses direct labor hours as the activity base to assign overhead. Direct labor hours incurred on each job were as follows: Job No. 25, 200; Job No. 26, 800; and Job No. 27, 600.

Instructions
(a) Calculate the predetermined overhead rate for the year 2010, assuming Weinrich Manufacturing estimates total manufacturing overhead costs of $480,000, direct labor costs of $300,000, and direct labor hours of 20,000 for the year.
(b) Open job cost sheets for Jobs 25, 26, and 27. Enter the January 1 balances on the job cost sheet for Job No. 25.
(c) Prepare the journal entries to record the purchase of raw materials, the factory labor costs incurred, and the manufacturing overhead costs incurred during the month of January.
(d) Prepare the journal entries to record the assignment of direct materials, direct labor, and manufacturing overhead costs to production. In assigning manufacturing overhead costs, use the overhead rate calculated in (a). Post all costs to the job cost sheets as necessary.
(e) Total the job cost sheets for any job(s) completed during the month. Prepare the journal entry (or entries) to record the completion of any job(s) during the month.
(f) Prepare the journal entry (or entries) to record the sale of any job(s) during the month.
(g) What is the balance in the Work in Process Inventory account at the end of the month? What does this balance consist of?
(h) What is the amount of over- or underapplied overhead?

(e) Job 25, $37,800
Job 26, $48,200

Prepare entries in a job cost system and partial income statement.

(SO 2, 3, 4, 5, 6)

P20-2B For the year ended December 31, 2010, the job cost sheets of Moxie Company contained the following data.

Job Number	Explanation	Direct Materials	Direct Labor	Manufacturing Overhead	Total Costs
7650	Balance 1/1	$18,000	$20,000	$25,000	$ 63,000
	Current year's costs	32,000	36,000	45,000	113,000
7651	Balance 1/1	12,000	16,000	20,000	48,000
	Current year's costs	30,000	40,000	50,000	120,000
7652	Current year's costs	45,000	68,000	85,000	198,000

Other data:
1. Raw materials inventory totaled $20,000 on January 1. During the year, $100,000 of raw materials were purchased on account.
2. Finished goods on January 1 consisted of Job No. 7648 for $93,000 and Job No. 7649 for $62,000.
3. Job No. 7650 and Job No. 7651 were completed during the year.
4. Job Nos. 7648, 7649, and 7650 were sold on account for $490,000.
5. Manufacturing overhead incurred on account totaled $135,000.
6. Other manufacturing overhead consisted of indirect materials $12,000, indirect labor $18,000 and depreciation on factory machinery $19,500.

Instructions
(a) Prove the agreement of Work in Process Inventory with job cost sheets pertaining to unfinished work. (*Hint*: Use a single T account for Work in Process Inventory.) Calculate each of the following, then post each to the T account: (1) beginning balance, (2) direct materials, (3) direct labor, (4) manufacturing overhead, and (5) completed jobs.

(a) (1) $111,000
(4) $180,000
Unfinished job 7652, $198,000

(b) Prepare the adjusting entry for manufacturing overhead, assuming the balance is allocated entirely to cost of goods sold.

(c) Determine the gross profit to be reported for 2010.

(b) Amount = $4,500

(c) $154,500

P20-3B Michael Ortiz is a contractor specializing in custom-built jacuzzis. On May 1, 2010, his ledger contains the following data.

Raw Materials Inventory	$30,000
Work in Process Inventory	12,200
Manufacturing Overhead	2,500 (dr.)

Prepare entries in a job cost system and cost of goods manufactured schedule.

(SO 2, 3, 4, 5)

The Manufacturing Overhead account has debit totals of $12,500 and credit totals of $10,000. Subsidiary data for Work in Process Inventory on May 1 include:

Job Cost Sheets

Job by Customer	Direct Materials	Direct Labor	Manufacturing Overhead
Taylor	$2,500	$2,000	$1,400
Baker	2,000	1,200	840
Joiner	900	800	560
	$5,400	$4,000	$2,800

During May, the following costs were incurred: (a) raw materials purchased on account $4,000, (b) labor paid $7,600, (c) manufacturing overhead paid $1,400.

A summary of materials requisition slips and time tickets for the month of May reveals the following.

Job by Customer	Materials Requisition Slips	Time Tickets
Taylor	$ 500	$ 400
Baker	600	1,000
Joiner	2,300	1,300
Smith	1,900	2,900
	5,300	5,600
General use	1,500	2,000
	$6,800	$7,600

Overhead was charged to jobs on the basis of $0.70 per dollar of direct labor cost.

The jacuzzis for customers Taylor, Baker, and Joiner were completed during May. Each jacuzzi was sold for $12,000 cash.

Instructions

(a) Prepare journal entries for the May transactions: (i) for purchase of raw materials, factory labor costs incurred, and manufacturing overhead costs incurred; (ii) assignment of raw materials, labor, and overhead to production; and (iii) completion of jobs and sale of goods.

(b) Post the entries to Work in Process Inventory.

(c) Reconcile the balance in Work in Process Inventory with the costs of unfinished jobs.

(d) Prepare a cost of goods manufactured schedule for May.

(d) Cost of goods manufactured $20,190.

P20-4B Elliott Manufacturing uses a job order cost system in each of its three manufacturing departments. Manufacturing overhead is applied to jobs on the basis of direct labor cost in Department A, direct labor hours in Department B, and machine hours in Department C.

In establishing the predetermined overhead rates for 2010 the following estimates were made for the year.

Compute predetermined overhead rates, apply overhead, and calculate under- or overapplied overhead.

(SO 4, 6)

	Department		
	A	B	C
Manufacturing overhead	$780,000	$640,000	$750,000
Direct labor cost	$600,000	$100,000	$600,000
Direct labor hours	50,000	40,000	40,000
Machine hours	100,000	120,000	150,000

922 Chapter 20 Job Order Costing

During January, the job cost sheets showed the following costs and production data.

	Department		
	A	B	C
Direct materials used	$92,000	$86,000	$64,000
Direct labor cost	$48,000	$35,000	$50,400
Manufacturing overhead incurred	$66,000	$60,000	$62,100
Direct labor hours	4,000	3,500	4,200
Machine hours	8,000	10,500	12,600

(a) 130%, $16, $5
(b) $202,400, $177,000 $177,400
(c) $3,600 $4,000 $(900)

Instructions
(a) Compute the predetermined overhead rate for each department.
(b) Compute the total manufacturing costs assigned to jobs in January in each department.
(c) Compute the under- or overapplied overhead for each department at January 31.

Analyze manufacturing accounts and determine missing amounts.

(SO 2, 3, 4, 5, 6)

P20-5B Bell Company's fiscal year ends on June 30. The following accounts are found in its job order cost accounting system for the first month of the new fiscal year.

Raw Materials Inventory

July 1	Beginning balance	19,000	July 31	Requisitions	(a)
31	Purchases	90,400			
July 31	Ending balance	(b)			

Work in Process Inventory

July 1	Beginning balance	(c)	July 31	Jobs completed	(f)
31	Direct materials	75,000			
31	Direct labor	(d)			
31	Overhead	(e)			
July 31	Ending balance	(g)			

Finished Goods Inventory

July 1	Beginning balance	(h)	July 31	Cost of goods sold	(j)
31	Completed jobs	(i)			
July 31	Ending balance	(k)			

Factory Labor

July 31	Factory wages	(l)	July 31	Wages assigned	(m)

Manufacturing Overhead

July 31	Indirect materials	8,900	July 31	Overhead applied	114,000
31	Indirect labor	16,000			
31	Other overhead	(n)			

Other data:
1. On July 1, two jobs were in process: Job No. 4085 and Job No. 4086, with costs of $19,000 and $13,200, respectively.
2. During July, Job Nos. 4087, 4088, and 4089 were started. On July 31, only Job No. 4089 was unfinished. This job had charges for direct materials $2,000 and direct labor $1,500, plus manufacturing overhead. Manufacturing overhead was applied at the rate of 120% of direct labor cost.
3. On July 1, Job No. 4084, costing $145,000, was in the finished goods warehouse. On July 31, Job No. 4088, costing $138,000, was in finished goods.
4. Overhead was $3,000 underapplied in July.

(d) $ 95,000
(f) $310,900
(l) $111,000

Instructions
List the letters (a) through (n) and indicate the amount pertaining to each letter. Show computations.

PROBLEMS: SET C

Visit the book's companion website at www.wiley.com/college/weygandt, and choose the Student Companion site, to access Problem Set C.

WATERWAYS CONTINUING PROBLEM

(*Note:* This is a continuation of the Waterways Problem from Chapter 19.)

WCP20 Waterways has two major public-park projects to provide with comprehensive irrigation in one of its service locations this month. Job J57 and Job K52 involve 15 acres of landscaped terrain which will require special-order sprinkler heads to meet the specifications of the project. This problem asks you to help Waterways use a job cost system to account for production of these parts.

Go to the book's companion website,
www.wiley.com/college/weygandt,
to see the completion of this problem.

BROADENING YOUR PERSPECTIVE

Decision Making Across the Organization

BYP20-1 Pine Products Company uses a job order cost system. For a number of months there has been an ongoing rift between the sales department and the production department concerning a special-order product, TC-1. TC-1 is a seasonal product that is manufactured in batches of 1,000 units. TC-1 is sold at cost plus a markup of 40% of cost.

The sales department is unhappy because fluctuating unit production costs significantly affect selling prices. Sales personnel complain that this has caused excessive customer complaints and the loss of considerable orders for TC-1.

The production department maintains that each job order must be fully costed on the basis of the costs incurred during the period in which the goods are produced. Production personnel maintain that the only real solution to the problem is for the sales department to increase sales in the slack periods.

Regina Newell, president of the company, asks you as the company accountant to collect quarterly data for the past year on TC-1. From the cost accounting system, you accumulate the following production quantity and cost data.

Costs	Quarter 1	Quarter 2	Quarter 3	Quarter 4
Direct materials	$100,000	$220,000	$ 80,000	$200,000
Direct labor	60,000	132,000	48,000	120,000
Manufacturing overhead	105,000	123,000	97,000	125,000
Total	$265,000	$475,000	$225,000	$445,000
Production in batches	5	11	4	10
Unit cost (per batch)	$ 53,000	$ 43,182	$ 56,250	$ 44,500

Instructions
With the class divided into groups, answer the following questions.

(a) What manufacturing cost element is responsible for the fluctuating unit costs? Why?
(b) What is your recommended solution to the problem of fluctuating unit cost?
(c) Restate the quarterly data on the basis of your recommended solution.

Managerial Analysis

BYP20-2 In the course of routine checking of all journal entries prior to preparing year-end reports, Diane Riser discovered several strange entries. She recalled that the president's son Ron had come in to help out during an especially busy time and that he had recorded some journal entries. She was relieved that there were only a few of his entries, and even more relieved that he had included rather lengthy explanations. The entries Ron made were:

(1)

Work in Process Inventory	25,000	
Cash		25,000

(This is for materials put into process. I don't find the record that we paid for these, so I'm crediting Cash, because I know we'll have to pay for them sooner or later.)

(2)

Manufacturing Overhead	12,000	
Cash		12,000

(This is for bonuses paid to salespeople. I know they're part of overhead, and I can't find an account called "Non-factory Overhead" or "Other Overhead" so I'm putting it in Manufacturing Overhead. I have the check stubs, so I know we paid these.)

(3)

Wages Expense	120,000	
Cash		120,000

(This is for the factory workers' wages. I have a note that payroll taxes are $15,000. I still think that's part of wages expense, and that we'll have to pay it all in cash sooner or later, so I credited Cash for the wages and the taxes.)

(4)

Work in Process Inventory	3,000	
Raw Materials Inventory		3,000

(This is for the glue used in the factory. I know we used this to make the products, even though we didn't use very much on any one of the products. I got it out of inventory, so I credited an inventory account.)

Instructions
(a) How should Ron have recorded each of the four events?
(b) If the entry was not corrected, which financial statements (income statement or balance sheet) would be affected? What balances would be overstated or understated?

Real-World Focus

BYP20-3 Founded in 1970, **Parlex Corporation** is a world leader in the design and manufacture of flexible interconnect products. Utilizing proprietary and patented technologies, Parlex produces custom flexible interconnects including flexible circuits, polymer thick film, laminated cables, and value-added assemblies for sophisticated electronics used in automotive, telecommunications, computer, diversified electronics, and aerospace applications. In addition to manufacturing sites in Methuen, Massachusetts; Salem, New Hampshire; Cranston, Rhode Island; San Jose, California; Shanghai, China; Isle of Wight, UK; and Empalme, Mexico, Parlex has logistic support centers and strategic alliances throughout North America, Asia, and Europe.

The following information was provided in the company's annual report.

> **PARLEX COMPANY**
> Notes to the Financial Statements
>
> The Company's products are manufactured on a job order basis to customers' specifications. Customers submit requests for quotations on each job, and the Company prepares bids based on its own cost estimates. The Company attempts to reflect the impact of changing costs when establishing prices. However, during the past several years, the market conditions for flexible circuits and the resulting price sensitivity haven't always allowed this to transpire. Although still not satisfactory, the Company was able to reduce the cost of products sold as a percentage of sales to 85% this year versus 87% that was experienced in the two immediately preceding years. Management continues to focus on improving operational efficiency and further reducing costs.

Instructions
(a) Parlex management discusses the job order cost system employed by their company. What are several advantages of using the job order approach to costing?
(b) Contrast the products produced in a job order environment, like Parlex, to those produced when process cost systems are used.

Exploring the Web

BYP20-4 The Institute of Management Accountants sponsors a certification for management accountants, allowing them to obtain the title of Certified Management Accountant.

Address: www.imanet.org, or go to www.wiley.com/college/weygandt

Steps
1. Go to the site shown above.
2. Choose **Certification**, and then, **Getting Started**.

Instructions
(a) What is the experience qualification requirement?
(b) How many hours of continuing education are required, and what types of activities qualify?

Communication Activity

BYP20-5 You are the management accountant for Newberry Manufacturing. Your company does custom carpentry work and uses a job order cost accounting system. Newberry sends detailed job cost sheets to its customers, along with an invoice. The job cost sheets show the date materials were used, the dollar cost of materials, and the hours and cost of labor. A predetermined overhead application rate is used, and the total overhead applied is also listed.

Donna Werly is a customer who recently had custom cabinets installed. Along with her check in payment for the work done, she included a letter. She thanked the company for including the detailed cost information but questioned why overhead was estimated. She stated that she would be interested in knowing exactly what costs were included in overhead, and she thought that other customers would, too.

Instructions
Prepare a letter to Ms. Werly (address: 123 Cedar Lane, Altoona, Kansas 66651) and tell her why you did not send her information on exact costs of overhead included in her job. Respond to her suggestion that you provide this information.

Ethics Case

BYP20-6 SEK Printing provides printing services to many different corporate clients. Although SEK bids most jobs, some jobs, particularly new ones, are negotiated on a "cost-plus" basis. Cost-plus means that the buyer is willing to pay the actual cost plus a return (profit) on these costs to SEK.

Betty Keiser, controller for SEK, has recently returned from a meeting where SEK's president stated that he wanted her to find a way to charge most costs to any project that was on a cost-plus basis. The president noted that the company needed more profits to meet its stated goals this period. By charging more costs to the cost-plus projects and therefore fewer costs to the jobs that were bid, the company should be able to increase its profit for the current year.

Betty knew why the president wanted to take this action. Rumors were that he was looking for a new position and if the company reported strong profit, the president's opportunities would be enhanced. Betty also recognized that she could probably increase the cost of certain jobs by changing the basis used to allocate manufacturing overhead.

Instructions
(a) Who are the stakeholders in this situation?
(b) What are the ethical issues in this situation?
(c) What would you do if you were Betty Keiser?

"All About You" Activity

BYP20-7 Many of you will work for a small business. As noted in the **All About You** feature in this chapter, some of you will even own your own business. In order to operate a small business you will need a good understanding of managerial accounting, as well as many other skills. Much information is available to assist people who are interested in starting a new business. A great place to start is the website provided by the Small Business Administration which is an agency of the federal government whose purpose is to support small business.

Instructions
Go to **www.sba.gov** and in the "Starting Your Business" link, review the material under the "Are You Ready?" Answer the following questions.

(a) What are some of the characteristics required of a small business owner?
(b) What are the top 10 reasons given for business failure?

Answers to Insight and Accounting Across the Organization Questions

p. 890 Jobs Won, Money Lost
Q: What type of costs do you think the company had been underestimating?
A: *It is most likely that the company failed to estimate and track overhead. In a highly diversified company, overhead associated with the diesel locomotive jobs may have been "lost" in the total overhead pool for the entire company.*

p. 905 Working a 25-Hour Day
Q: What feature of these businesses creates an incentive to misstate cost accounting data on particular jobs? What can customers do to protect themselves from overbilling?
A: *In these business situations, the compensation to the supplier depends on the costs incurred by the supplier. This so-called "cost-plus" arrangement creates an incentive for the supplier to overstate costs. Customers should stipulate that they have the right to have the suppliers' records audited.*

Authors' Comments on *All About You:* Minding Your Own Business (p. 906)

The situation presented is a difficult one because you are presently receiving some help for free. It would seem that the best strategy is to price your services based on what it would cost you to do the landscape business without any free help. In the long run, it is going to be impossible to continue unless you can cover these costs. In addition, if you under-price your services today, it may lead to an expectation by your customers that your prices will remain low in the future. That probably cannot happen, given that your costs will increase substantially after the first two years. However, we should note that it is not unusual to start a small business with some assets available to you. Then, as your business grows, you acquire additional assets to meet your needs. After all, you may need a low price to get started and as you gain experience you will be able to charge more or become more efficient.

So what to do? Let's address your old truck first. You should treat the truck as an asset owned by your business. Put it on your books at its fair value, and depreciate it over a reasonable life. This will result in an overhead charge. You need to cover the cost of that truck, as you will have to buy another one some day.

The land, barn, and your mother's services are a little more difficult. If you rented the land and barn and if you paid an assistant, all of these costs would be charged to overhead. (The assistant would be indirect labor.) You are currently getting all these services for free. This is a good situation now, and you may need this situation early in your business to help you get started. But you should recognize that even if you run your business profitably for the first two years, you may have problems starting in the third year. Thus, it would seem prudent to establish a budget based on both scenarios for the first two years. If you can charge based on your expected costs in the future, do so. If that is not realistic, because you need to establish yourself and get more experience, then charge less. But be sure from the start to cover a reasonable amount of your costs, or the business does not make sense for you financially.

Answers to Self-Study Questions

1. a   2. c   3. b   4. c   5. c   6. d   7. d   8. b   9. a   10. d   11. b   12. c   13. b   14. c   15. b

✓ *Remember to go back to the Navigator box on the chapter-opening page and check off your completed work.*

Chapter 21

Process Costing

STUDY OBJECTIVES

After studying this chapter, you should be able to:

1. Understand who uses process cost systems.
2. Explain the similarities and differences between job order cost and process cost systems.
3. Explain the flow of costs in a process cost system.
4. Make the journal entries to assign manufacturing costs in a process cost system.
5. Compute equivalent units.
6. Explain the four steps necessary to prepare a production cost report.
7. Prepare a production cost report.
8. Explain just-in-time (JIT) processing.
9. Explain activity-based costing (ABC).

✓ The Navigator

✓ The Navigator

Scan **Study Objectives** ■
Read **Feature Story** ■
Read **Preview** ■
Read text and answer **DO IT!**
  p. 935 ■ p. 938 ■ p. 944 ■ p. 949 ■
Work **Comprehensive** **DO IT!** p. 949 ■
Review **Summary of Study Objectives** ■
Answer **Self-Study Questions** ■
Complete **Assignments** ■

Feature Story

BEN & JERRY'S TRACKS ITS MIX-UPS

Ben & Jerry's Homemade, Inc. (*www.benjerry.com*) is one of the "hottest" and "coolest" U.S. companies. Based in Waterbury, Vermont, the ice cream company that started out of a garage in 1978 is now a public company.

Making ice cream is a process—a movement of product from a mixing department to a prepping department to a pint department. The mixing department is where the ice cream is created. In the prep area the production process adds extras such as cherries and walnuts to make plain ice cream into "Cherry Garcia," Ben & Jerry's most popular flavor, or fudge-covered waffle cone pieces and a swirl of caramel for "Stephen Colbert's

Americone Dream," one of B & J's newest flavors. The pint department is where the ice cream is actually put into containers. As the product is processed from one department to the next, the appropriate materials, labor, and overhead are added to it.

"The incoming ingredients from the shipping and receiving departments are stored in certain locations, either in a freezer or dry warehouse," says Beecher Eurich, staff accountant. "As ingredients get added, so do the costs associated with them." How much ice cream is produced? Running plants around the clock, the company produces 18 million gallons a year.

With the company's process costing system, Eurich can tell you how much a certain batch of ice cream costs to make—its materials, labor, and overhead in each of the production departments. She generates reports for the production department heads, but makes sure not to overdo it. "You can get bogged down in numbers," says Eurich. "If you're generating a report that no one can use, then that's a waste of time."

It's more likely, though, Ben & Jerry's production people want to know how efficient they are. Why? Many own stock in the company.

The Navigator

Inside Chapter 21...

- **Choosing a Cost Driver** (p. 935)
- **Keeping Score for the Xbox** (p. 940)

Preview of Chapter 21

The cost accounting system used by companies such as Ben & Jerry's is **process cost accounting**. In contrast to job order cost accounting, which focuses on the individual job, process cost accounting focuses on the *processes* involved in mass-producing products that are identical or very similar in nature. The primary objective of the chapter is to explain and illustrate process costing.

The content and organization of this chapter are as follows.

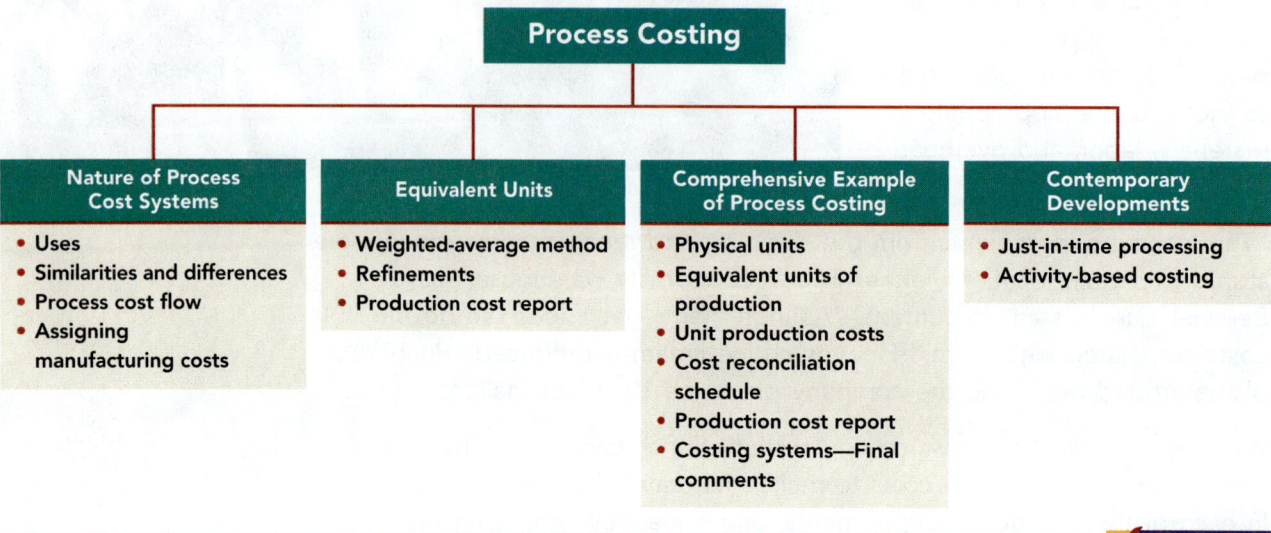

THE NATURE OF PROCESS COST SYSTEMS

STUDY OBJECTIVE 1
Understand who uses process cost systems.

Uses of Process Cost Systems

Companies use **process cost systems** to apply costs to similar products that are mass-produced in a continuous fashion. Ben & Jerry's uses a process cost system: Production of the ice cream, once it begins, continues until the ice cream emerges, and the processing is the same for the entire run—with precisely the same amount of materials, labor, and overhead. Each finished pint of ice cream is indistinguishable from another.

A company such as USX uses process costing in the manufacturing of steel. Kellogg and General Mills use process costing for cereal production; ExxonMobil uses process costing for its oil refining; Sherwin Williams uses process costing for its paint products. At a bottling company like Coca-Cola, the manufacturing process begins with the blending of ingredients. Next, automated machinery moves the bottles into position and fills them. The production process then caps, packages, and forwards the bottles to the finished goods warehouse. Illustration 21-1 shows this process.

Illustration 21-1
Manufacturing processes

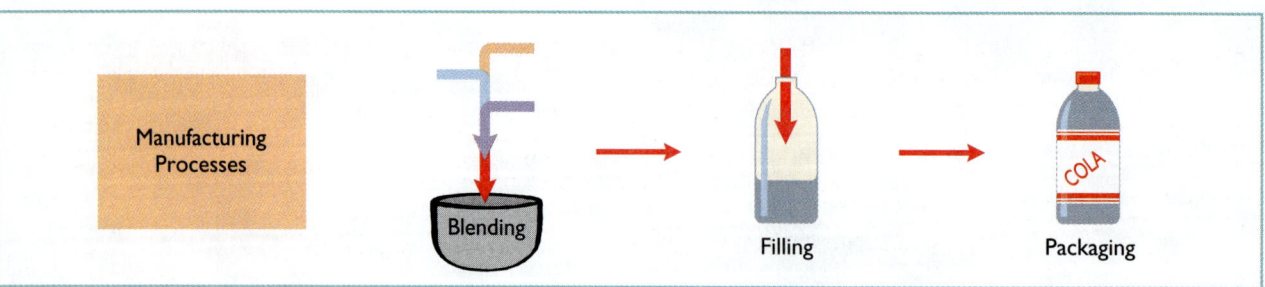

For Coca-Cola, as well as the other companies just mentioned, once the production begins, it continues until the finished product emerges, and each unit of finished product is like every other unit.

In comparison, in a job order cost system companies assign costs to a *specific job*. Examples are the construction of a customized home, the making of a motion picture, or the manufacturing of a specialized machine. Illustration 21-2 provides examples of companies that primarily use either a process cost system or a job order cost system.

Illustration 21-2
Process cost and job order cost companies and products

Process Cost System Company	Product	Job Order Cost System Company	Product
Coca-Cola, PepsiCo	Soft drinks	Young & Rubicam, Omnicom	Advertising
ExxonMobil, Royal Dutch Shell	Oil	Walt Disney, Warner Brothers	Motion pictures
Intel, Advanced Micro Devices	Computer chips	Center Ice Consultants, Ice Rink Events	Ice rinks
Dow Chemical, DuPont	Chemicals	Kaiser Permanente, Mayo Clinic	Patient health care

Frequently, when we think of service companies, we think of specific, nonroutine tasks, such as rebuilding an automobile engine, providing consulting services on a business acquisition, or working on a major lawsuit. However, many service companies specialize in performing repetitive, routine aspects of a particular business. For example, auto-care vendors such as Jiffy Lube focus on the routine aspects of car care. H&R Block focuses on the routine aspects of basic tax practice, and many large law firms focus on routine legal services, such as uncomplicated divorces. Service companies that provide specific, nonroutine services will probably benefit from using a job order cost system. Those that perform routine, repetitive services will probably be better off with a process cost system.

Similarities and Differences Between Job Order Cost and Process Cost Systems

In a job order cost system, companies assign costs to each job. In a process cost system, companies track costs through a series of connected manufacturing processes or departments, rather than by individual jobs. Thus, companies use process cost systems when they produce a large volume of uniform or relatively homogeneous products. Illustration 21-3 shows the basic flow of costs in these two systems.

Illustration 21-3 (next page) highlights the basic similarities and differences between these two systems.

STUDY OBJECTIVE 2
Explain the similarities and differences between job order cost and process cost systems.

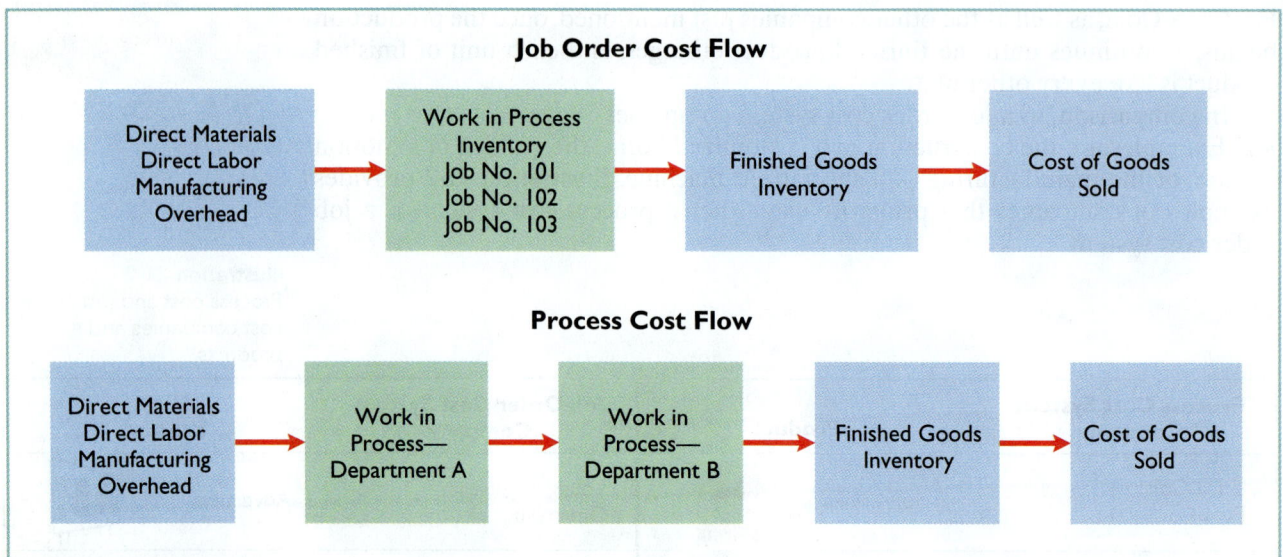

Illustration 21-3
Job order cost and process cost flow

SIMILARITIES
Job order cost and process cost systems are similar in three ways:

1. **The manufacturing cost elements.** Both costing systems track three manufacturing cost elements—direct materials, direct labor, and manufacturing overhead.
2. **The accumulation of the costs of materials, labor, and overhead.** Both costing systems debit raw materials to Raw Materials Inventory; factory labor to Factory Labor; and manufacturing overhead costs to Manufacturing Overhead.
3. **The flow of costs.** As noted above, both systems accumulate all manufacturing costs by debits to Raw Materials Inventory, Factory Labor, and Manufacturing Overhead. Both systems then assign these costs to the same accounts—Work in Process, Finished Goods Inventory, and Cost of Goods Sold. **The methods of assigning costs, however, differ significantly.** These differences are explained and illustrated later in the chapter.

DIFFERENCES
The differences between a job order cost and a process cost system are as follows.

1. **The number of work in process accounts used.** A job order cost system uses only one Work in Process account. A process cost system uses multiple work in process accounts.
2. **Documents used to track costs.** A job order cost system charges costs to individual jobs and summarizes them in a job cost sheet. A process cost system summarizes costs in a production cost report for each department.
3. **The point at which costs are totaled.** A job order cost system totals costs when the job is completed. A process cost system totals costs at the end of a period of time.
4. **Unit cost computations.** In a job order cost system, the unit cost is the total cost per job divided by the units produced. In a process cost system, the unit cost is total manufacturing costs for the period divided by the units produced during the period.

Illustration 21-4 summarizes the major differences between a job order cost and a process cost system.

The Nature of Process Cost Systems

Features	Job Order Cost System	Process Cost System
Work in process accounts	• One work in process account	• Multiple work in process accounts
Documents used	• Job cost sheets	• Production cost reports
Determination of total manufacturing costs	• Each job	• Each period
Unit-cost computations	• Cost of each job ÷ Units produced for the job	• Total manufacturing costs ÷ Units produced during the period

Illustration 21-4
Job order versus process cost systems

Process Cost Flow

Illustration 21-5 shows the flow of costs in the process cost system for Tyler Company. Tyler Company manufactures automatic can openers that it sells to retail outlets. Manufacturing consists of two processes: machining and assembly. The Machining Department shapes, hones, and drills the raw materials. The Assembly Department assembles and packages the parts.

STUDY OBJECTIVE 3
Explain the flow of costs in a process cost system.

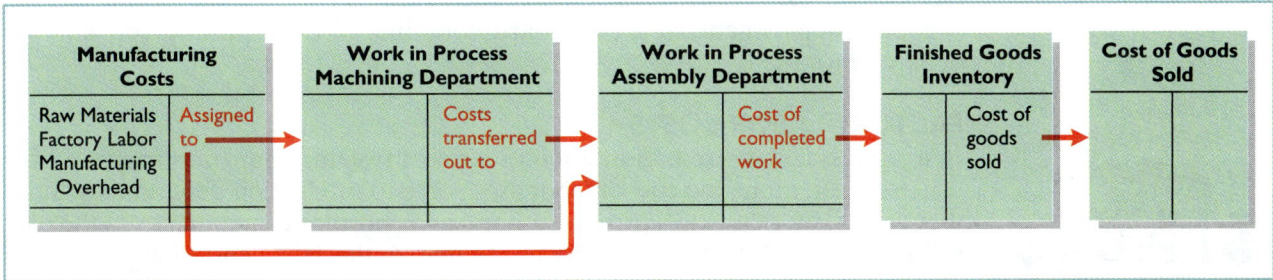

Illustration 21-5
Flow of costs in process cost system

As the flow of costs indicates, the company can add materials, labor, and manufacturing overhead in both the Machining and Assembly departments. When it finishes its work, the Machining Department transfers the partially completed units to the Assembly Department. The Assembly Department finishes the goods and then transfers them to the finished goods inventory. Upon sale, Tyler removes the goods from the finished goods inventory. Within each department, a similar set of activities is performed on each unit processed.

Assigning Manufacturing Costs—Journal Entries

As indicated, the accumulation of the costs of materials, labor, and manufacturing overhead is the same in a process cost system as in a job order cost system. That is, both systems follow these procedures:

STUDY OBJECTIVE 4
Make the journal entries to assign manufacturing costs in a process cost system.

- Companies debit all raw materials to Raw Materials Inventory at the time of purchase.
- They debit all factory labor to Factory Labor as the labor costs are incurred.
- They debit overhead costs to Manufacturing Overhead as these costs are incurred.

However, the assignment of the three manufacturing cost elements to Work in Process in a process cost system is different from a job order cost system. Here we'll look at how companies assign these manufacturing cost elements in a process cost system.

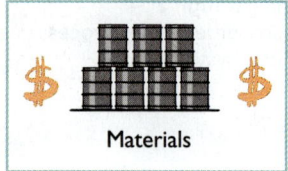

MATERIALS COSTS

All raw materials issued for production are a materials cost to the producing department. A process cost system may use materials requisition slips, but **it generally requires fewer requisitions than in a job order cost system, because the materials are used for processes rather than for specific jobs** and therefore typically are for larger quantities.

At the beginning of the first process, a company usually adds most of the materials needed for production. However, other materials may be added at various points. For example, in the manufacture of Hershey candy bars, the chocolate and other ingredients are added at the beginning of the first process, and the wrappers and cartons are added at the end of the packaging process. Tyler Company adds materials at the beginning of each process. Tyler makes the following entry to record the materials used:

Work in Process—Machining	XXXX	
Work in Process—Assembly	XXXX	
Raw Materials Inventory		XXXX
(To record materials used)		

Ice cream maker Ben & Jerry's adds materials in three departments: milk and flavoring in the mixing department; extras such as cherries and walnuts in the prepping department; and cardboard containers in the pinting (packaging) department.

FACTORY LABOR COSTS

In a process cost system, as in a job order cost system, companies may use time tickets to determine the cost of labor assignable to production departments. Since they assign labor costs to a process rather than a job, they can obtain from the payroll register or departmental payroll summaries the labor cost chargeable to a process.

Labor costs for the Machining Department will include the wages of employees who shape, hone, and drill the raw materials. The entry to assign these costs for Tyler Company is:

Work in Process—Machining	XXXX	
Work in Process—Assembly	XXXX	
Factory Labor		XXXX
(To assign factory labor to production)		

MANUFACTURING OVERHEAD COSTS

The objective in assigning overhead in a process cost system is to allocate the overhead costs to the production departments on an objective and equitable basis. That basis is the activity that "drives" or causes the costs. A primary driver of overhead costs in continuous manufacturing operations is **machine time used**, not direct labor. Thus, companies **widely use machine hours** in allocating manufacturing overhead costs. Tyler's entry to allocate overhead to the two processes is:

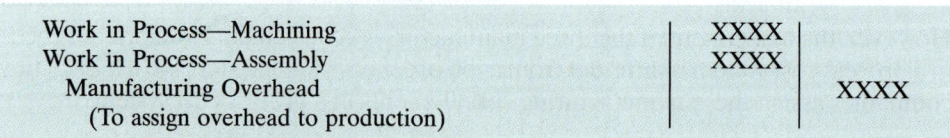

Work in Process—Machining	XXXX	
Work in Process—Assembly	XXXX	
Manufacturing Overhead		XXXX
(To assign overhead to production)		

MANAGEMENT INSIGHT

Choosing a Cost Driver

In one of its automated cost centers, Caterpillar feeds work into the cost center, where robotic machines process it and transfer the finished job to the next cost center without human intervention. One person tends all of the machines and spends more time maintaining machines than operating them. In such cases, overhead rates based on direct labor hours may be misleading. Surprisingly, some companies continue to assign manufacturing overhead on the basis of direct labor despite the fact that there is no cause-and-effect relationship between labor and overhead.

 What is the result if a company uses the wrong "cost driver" to assign manufacturing overhead?

TRANSFER TO NEXT DEPARTMENT

At the end of the month, Tyler needs an entry to record the cost of the goods transferred out of the department. In this case, the transfer is to the Assembly Department, and Tyler makes the following entry.

Work in Process—Assembly	XXXXX	
Work in Process—Machining		XXXXX
(To record transfer of units to the Assembly Department)		

TRANSFER TO FINISHED GOODS

When the Assembly Department completes the units, it transfers them to the finished goods warehouse. The entry for this transfer is as follows.

Finished Goods Inventory	XXXXX	
Work in Process—Assembly		XXXXX
(To record transfer of units to finished goods)		

TRANSFER TO COST OF GOODS SOLD

When Tyler sells the finished goods, it records the cost of goods sold as follows.

Cost of Goods Sold	XXXXX	
Finished Goods Inventory		XXXXX
(To record cost of units sold)		

DO IT!

MANUFACTURING COSTS IN PROCESS COSTING

Ruth Company manufactures ZEBO through two processes: blending and bottling. In June, raw materials used were Blending $18,000 and Bottling $4,000. Factory labor costs were Blending $12,000 and Bottling $5,000. Manufacturing overhead costs were Blending $6,000 and Bottling $2,500. The company transfers units completed at a cost of $19,000 in the Blending Department to the Bottling Department. The Bottling Department transfers units completed at a cost of $11,000 to Finished Goods. Journalize the assignment of these costs to the two processes and the transfer of units as appropriate.

936 Chapter 21 Process Costing

action plan

✔ In process cost accounting, keep separate work in process accounts for each process.

✔ When the costs are assigned to production, debit the separate work in process accounts.

✔ Transfer cost of completed units to the next process or to Finished Goods.

Solution

The entries are:

Work in Process—Blending	18,000	
Work in Process—Bottling	4,000	
Raw Materials Inventory		22,000
(To record materials used)		
Work in Process—Blending	12,000	
Work in Process—Bottling	5,000	
Factory Labor		17,000
(To assign factory labor to production)		
Work in Process—Blending	6,000	
Work in Process—Bottling	2,500	
Manufacturing Overhead		8,500
(To assign overhead to production)		
Work in Process—Bottling	19,000	
Work in Process—Blending		19,000
(To record transfer of units to the Bottling Department)		
Finished Goods Inventory	11,000	
Work in Process—Bottling		11,000
(To record transfer of units to finished goods)		

Related exercise material: **BE21-1, BE21-2, BE21-3, E21-2, E21-4,** and **DO IT!** **21-1.**

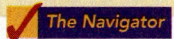

EQUIVALENT UNITS

STUDY OBJECTIVE 5
Compute equivalent units.

Suppose you have a work-study job in the office of your college's president, and she asks you to compute the cost of instruction per full-time equivalent student at your college. The college's vice president for finance provides the following information.

Illustration 21-6
Information for full-time student example

Costs:	
Total cost of instruction	$9,000,000
Student population:	
Full-time students	900
Part-time students	1,000

Part-time students take 60% of the classes of a full-time student during the year. To compute the number of full-time equivalent students per year, you would make the following computation.

Illustration 21-7
Full-time equivalent unit computation

Full-time Students	+	Equivalent Units of Part-time Students	=	Full-time Equivalent Students
900	+	(60% × 1,000)	=	**1,500**

The cost of instruction per full-time equivalent student is therefore the total cost of instruction ($9,000,000) divided by the number of full-time equivalent students (1,500), which is $6,000 ($9,000,000 ÷ 1,500).

A process cost system uses the same idea, called equivalent units of production. **Equivalent units of production** measure the work done during the period, expressed in fully completed units. Companies use this measure to determine the cost per unit of completed product.

Weighted-Average Method

The formula to compute equivalent units of production is as follows.

| Units Completed and Transferred Out | + | Equivalent Units of Ending Work in Process | = | Equivalent Units of Production |

Illustration 21-8
Equivalent units of production formula

To better understand this concept of equivalent units, consider the following two separate examples.

Example 1: In a specific period the entire output of Sullivan Company's Blending Department consists of ending work in process of 4,000 units which are 60% complete as to materials, labor, and overhead. The equivalent units of production for the Blending Department are therefore 2,400 units (4,000 × 60%).

Example 2: The output of Kori Company's Packaging Department during the period consists of 10,000 units completed and transferred out, and 5,000 units in ending work in process which are 70% completed. The equivalent units of production are therefore 13,500 [10,000 + (5,000 × 70%)].

This method of computing equivalent units is referred to as the **weighted-average method**. It considers the degree of completion (weighting) of the units completed and transferred out and the ending work in process. *Use the weighted-average method to compute equivalent units in the homework.*

Refinements on the Weighted-Average Method

Kellogg Company has produced Eggo® Waffles since 1970. Three departments produce these waffles: Mixing, Baking, and Freezing/Packaging. The Mixing Department combines dry ingredients, including flour, salt, and baking powder, with liquid ingredients, including eggs and vegetable oil, to make waffle batter. Illustration 21-9 provides information related to the Mixing Department at the end of June.

MIXING DEPARTMENT

		Percentage Complete	
	Physical Units	Materials	Conversion Costs
Work in process, June 1	100,000	100%	70%
Started into production	800,000		
Total units	900,000		
Units transferred out	700,000		
Work in process, June 30	200,000	100%	60%
Total units	900,000		

Illustration 21-9
Information for Mixing Department

Illustration 21-9 indicates that the beginning work in process is 100% complete as to materials cost and 70% complete as to conversion costs. **Conversion costs are the sum of labor costs and overhead costs.** In other words, Kellogg adds both the dry and liquid ingredients (materials) at the beginning of the waffle-making process. The conversion costs (labor and overhead) related to the mixing of these ingredients are incurred uniformly and are 70% complete. The ending work in process is 100% complete as to materials cost and 60% complete as to conversion costs.

We then use the Mixing Department information to determine equivalent units. **In computing equivalent units, the beginning work in process is not part of the equivalent-units-of-production formula.** The units transferred out to the Baking Department are fully complete as to both materials and conversion costs. The ending work in process is fully complete as to materials, but only 60% complete as to conversion costs. We therefore need to make **two equivalent unit computations**: one for materials, and the other for conversion costs. Illustration 21-10 shows these computations.

Illustration 21-10
Computation of equivalent units—Mixing Department

MIXING DEPARTMENT

	Equivalent Units	
	Materials	Conversion Costs
Units transferred out	700,000	700,000
Work in process, June 30		
200,000 × 100%	200,000	
200,000 × 60%		120,000
Total equivalent units	900,000	820,000

We can refine the earlier formula used to compute equivalent units of production (Illustration 21-8) (page 937) to show the computations for materials and for conversion costs, as follows.

Illustration 21-11
Refined equivalent units of production formula

Units Completed and Transferred Out—Materials	+	Equivalent Units of Ending Work in Process—Materials	=	Equivalent Units of Production—Materials
Units Completed and Transferred Out—Conversion Costs	+	Equivalent Units of Ending Work in Process—Conversion Costs	=	Equivalent Units of Production—Conversion Costs

DO IT!

EQUIVALENT UNITS

The fabricating department has the following production and cost data for the current month.

Beginning Work in Process	Units Transferred Out	Ending Work in Process
–0–	15,000	10,000

Materials are entered at the beginning of the process. The ending work in process units are 30% complete as to conversion costs. Compute the equivalent units of production for (a) materials and (b) conversion costs.

Solution

(a) Since materials are entered at the beginning of the process, the equivalent units of ending work in process are 10,000. Thus, 15,000 units + 10,000 units = 25,000 equivalent units of production for materials.

(b) Since ending work in process is only 30% complete as to conversion costs, the equivalent units of ending work in process are 3,000 (30% × 10,000 units). Thus, 15,000 units + 3,000 units = 18,000 equivalent units of production for conversion costs.

Related exercise material: **BE21-5, BE21-10, E21-5, E21-6, E21-7, E21-8, E21-9, E21-10, E21-11, E21-13,** and **DO IT! 21-2.**

action plan

✔ To measure the work done during the period, expressed in fully completed units, compute equivalent units of production.

✔ Use the appropriate formula: Units completed and transferred out + Equivalent units of ending work in process = Equivalent units of production.

✓ The Navigator

Production Cost Report

As mentioned earlier, companies prepare a production cost report for each department. A **production cost report** is the key document that management uses to understand the activities in a department; it shows the production quantity and cost data related to that department. For example, in producing Eggo® Waffles, **Kellogg Company** uses three production cost reports: Mixing, Baking, and Freezing/Packaging. Illustration 21-12 shows the flow of costs to make an Eggo® Waffle and the related production cost reports for each department.

Illustration 21-12
Flow of costs in making Eggo® Waffles

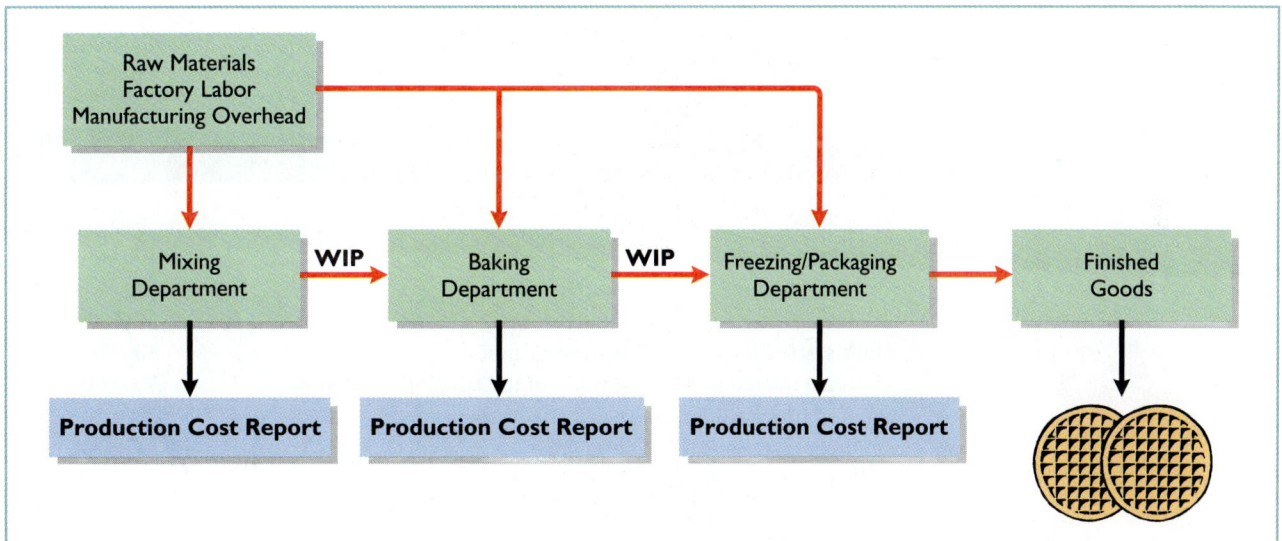

In order to complete a production cost report, the company must perform four steps, which as a whole, make up the process costing system.

1. Compute the physical unit flow.
2. Compute the equivalent units of production.
3. Compute unit production costs.
4. Prepare a cost reconciliation schedule.

The next section explores these steps in an extended example.

STUDY OBJECTIVE 6
Explain the four steps necessary to prepare a production cost report.

MANAGEMENT INSIGHT

Keeping Score for the Xbox

When you are as big and as profitable as Microsoft, you get to a point where continued rapid growth is very difficult. For example, many believe it is unlikely that Microsoft will see much growth in software sales. As a result, the company is looking for new markets, such as the video game market with its Xbox player.

Profitability in the video-game hardware market has been elusive. Microsoft has struggled to control the costs of both manufacturing and distribution. One analyst predicted that Microsoft's "snowballing" costs in the next period could exceed budget by $2.4 billion. Microsoft's Chief Financial Officer blamed the high costs on unexpectedly high volumes, saying, "We pushed market volumes very high in the Xbox business. As a result of that we incurred some costs in the supply chain." Given these issues and, despite its incredible success as a software company, some observers question whether Microsoft will be able to make the changes that are required to become a successful hardware manufacturer.

Source: Rober A. Guth, "Microsoft Net Rises 16%, but Costs Damp Results," *Wall Street Journal Online*, April 28, 2006.

 In what ways has cost accounting probably become more critical for Microsoft in recent years?

COMPREHENSIVE EXAMPLE OF PROCESS COSTING

Illustration 21-13 shows assumed data for the Mixing Department at Kellogg Company for the month of June. We will use this information to complete a production cost report for the Mixing Department.

Illustration 21-13
Unit and cost data—Mixing Department

MIXING DEPARTMENT

Units

Work in process, June 1	100,000
Direct materials: 100% complete	
Conversion costs: 70% complete	
Units started into production during June	800,000
Units completed and transferred out to Baking Department	700,000
Work in process, June 30	200,000
Direct materials: 100% complete	
Conversion costs: 60% complete	

Costs

Work in process, June 1	
Direct materials: 100% complete	$ 50,000
Conversion costs: 70% complete	35,000
Cost of work in process, June 1	$ 85,000
Costs incurred during production in June	
Direct materials	$400,000
Conversion costs	170,000
Costs incurred in June	$570,000

Compute the Physical Unit Flow (Step 1)

Physical units are the actual units to be accounted for during a period, irrespective of any work performed. To keep track of these units, add the units started (or transferred) into production during the period to the units in process at the beginning of the period. This amount is referred to as the **total units to be accounted for**.

The total units then are accounted for by the output of the period. The output consists of units transferred out during the period and any units in process at the end of the period. This amount is referred to as the **total units accounted for**. Illustration 21-14 shows the flow of physical units for Kellogg's Mixing Department for the month of June.

MIXING DEPARTMENT

	Physical Units
Units to be accounted for	
Work in process, June 1	100,000
Started (transferred) into production	800,000
Total units	**900,000**
Units accounted for	
Completed and transferred out	700,000
Work in process, June 30	200,000
Total units	**900,000**

Illustration 21-14
Physical unit flow—Mixing Department

The records indicate that the Mixing Department must account for 900,000 units. Of this sum, 700,000 units were transferred to the Baking Department and 200,000 units were still in process.

Compute Equivalent Units of Production (Step 2)

Once the physical flow of the units is established, Kellogg must measure the Mixing Department's productivity in terms of equivalent units of production. The Mixing Department adds materials at the beginning of the process, and incurs conversion costs uniformly during the process. Thus, we need two computations of equivalent units: one for materials and one for conversion costs. The equivalent unit computation is as follows.

HELPFUL HINT
Materials are not always added at the beginning of the process. For example, materials are sometimes added uniformly during the process.

	Equivalent Units	
	Materials	Conversion Costs
Units transferred out	700,000	700,000
Work in process, June 30		
200,000 × 100%	200,000	
200,000 × 60%		120,000
Total equivalent units	**900,000**	**820,000**

Illustration 21-15
Computation of equivalent units—Mixing Department

HELPFUL HINT
Remember that we ignore the beginning work in process in this computation.

Compute Unit Production Costs (Step 3)

Armed with the knowledge of the equivalent units of production, we can now compute the unit production costs. **Unit production costs** are costs expressed in terms of equivalent units of production. When equivalent units of production are different for materials and conversion costs, we compute three unit costs: (1) materials, (2) conversion, and (3) total manufacturing.

The computation of total materials cost related to Eggo® Waffles is as follows.

Illustration 21-16
Total materials cost computation

Work in process, June 1	
Direct materials cost	$ 50,000
Costs added to production during June	
Direct materials cost	400,000
Total materials cost	**$450,000**

The computation of unit materials cost is as follows.

Illustration 21-17
Unit materials cost computation

Total Materials Cost	÷	Equivalent Units of Materials	=	Unit Materials Cost
$450,000	÷	900,000	=	**$0.50**

Illustration 21-18 shows the computation of total conversion costs.

Illustration 21-18
Total conversion costs computation

Work in process, June 1	
Conversion costs	$ 35,000
Costs added to production during June	
Conversion costs	170,000
Total conversion costs	**$205,000**

The computation of unit conversion cost is as follows.

Illustration 21-19
Unit conversion cost computation

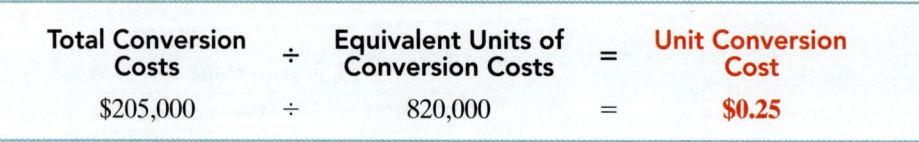

Total Conversion Costs	÷	Equivalent Units of Conversion Costs	=	Unit Conversion Cost
$205,000	÷	820,000	=	**$0.25**

Total manufacturing cost per unit is therefore computed as shown in Illustration 21-20 on the next page.

Unit Materials Cost	+	Unit Conversion Cost	=	Total Manufacturing Cost per Unit
$0.50	+	$0.25	=	**$0.75**

Illustration 21-20
Total manufacturing cost per unit

Prepare a Cost Reconciliation Schedule (Step 4)

We are now ready to determine the cost of goods transferred out of the Mixing Department to the Baking Department and the costs in ending work in process. Kellogg charged total costs of $655,000 to the Mixing Department in June, calculated as follows.

Costs to be accounted for	
Work in process, June 1	$ 85,000
Started into production	570,000
Total costs	**$655,000**

Illustration 21-21
Costs charged to Mixing Department

The company then prepares a cost reconciliation schedule to assign these costs to (a) units transferred out to the Baking Department and (b) ending work in process.

MIXING DEPARTMENT
Cost Reconciliation Schedule

Costs accounted for		
Transferred out (700,000 × $0.75)		$ 525,000
Work in process, June 30		
Materials (200,000 × $0.50)	$100,000	
Conversion costs (120,000 × $0.25)	30,000	130,000
Total costs		**$655,000**

Illustration 21-22
Cost reconciliation schedule—Mixing Department

Kellogg uses the total manufacturing cost per unit, $0.75, in costing the **units completed** and transferred to the Baking Department. In contrast, the unit cost of materials and the unit cost of conversion are needed in costing **units in process**. The **cost reconciliation schedule** shows that the **total costs accounted for** (Illustration 21-22) equal the **total costs to be accounted for** (see Illustration 21-21).

Preparing the Production Cost Report

At this point, Kellogg is ready to prepare the production cost report for the Mixing Department. As indicated earlier, this report is an internal document for management that shows production quantity and cost data for a production department.

STUDY OBJECTIVE 7
Prepare a production cost report.

There are four steps in preparing a production cost report. They are:

(1) Prepare a physical unit schedule.
(2) Compute equivalent units.
(3) Compute unit costs.
(4) Prepare a cost reconciliation schedule.

944 Chapter 21 Process Costing

Illustration 21-23 shows the production cost report for the Mixing Department. The report identifies the four steps.

Illustration 21-23
Production cost report

Mixing Department
Production Cost Report
For the Month Ended June 30, 2010

		Physical Units	Equivalent Units		
			Materials	Conversion Costs	
QUANTITIES		Step 1	Step 2		
Units to be accounted for					
Work in process, June 1		100,000			
Started into production		800,000			
Total units		900,000			
Units accounted for					
Transferred out		700,000	700,000	700,000	
Work in process, June 30		200,000	200,000	120,000	(200,000 × 60%)
Total units		900,000	900,000	820,000	

COSTS			Materials	Conversion Costs	Total
Unit costs		Step 3			
Costs in June		(a)	$450,000	$205,000	$655,000
Equivalent units		(b)	900,000	820,000	
Unit costs [(a) ÷ (b)]			$0.50	$0.25	$0.75
Costs to be accounted for					
Work in process, June 1					$85,000
Started into production					570,000
Total costs					$655,000
Cost Reconciliation Schedule		Step 4			
Costs accounted for					
Transferred out (700,000 × $0.75)					$525,000
Work in process, June 30					
Materials (200,000 × $0.50)				$100,000	
Conversion costs (120,000 × $0.25)				30,000	130,000
Total costs					$655,000

Production cost reports provide a basis for evaluating the productivity of a department. In addition, managers can use the cost data to assess whether unit costs and total costs are reasonable. By comparing the quantity and cost data with predetermined goals, top management can also judge whether current performance is meeting planned objectives.

DO IT!

COST RECONCILIATION SCHEDULE

In March, Rodayo Manufacturing had the following unit production costs: materials $6 and conversion costs $9. On March 1, it had zero work in process. During March, Rodayo transferred out 12,000 units. As of March 31, 800 units that were 25% complete as to conversion costs and 100% complete as to materials were in ending work in process. Total costs to be accounted for are $186,600.

(a) Compute the total units to be accounted for.
(b) Compute the equivalent units of production.
(c) Prepare a cost reconciliation schedule, including the costs of materials transferred out and the costs of materials in process.

Solution

(a) 0 (work in process, March 1) + 12,800 (started into production) = 12,800 units

(b) Equivalent units of production:

	Materials	Conversion
Units transferred out	12,000	12,000
Work in process, March 31	800	200 (800 × 25%)
Total	12,800	12,200

(c) Cost reconciliation schedule:

Costs accounted for		
Transferred out (12,000 × $15)		$180,000
Work in process, March 31		
Materials (800 × $6)	$4,800	
Conversion costs (200 × $9)	1,800	6,600
Total costs		$186,600

Related exercise material: **BE21-4, BE21-5, BE21-6, BE21-7, BE21-8, BE21-9, BE21-10, E21-5, E21-6, E21-8, E21-9, E21-10, E21-11, E21-12, E21-14,** and **DO IT! 21-3.**

action plan

✔ To find units to be accounted for, add the units started into production during the month to the units in process at the beginning of the month.

✔ Realize that equivalent units of production for materials will differ from equivalent units of production for conversion costs. The units in ending work in process are 100% complete as to materials but only 25% complete as to conversion costs.

✔ Assign the total manufacturing cost of $15 per unit to the 12,000 units transferred out.

✔ Assign the materials cost and conversion costs based on equivalent units of production to units in process.

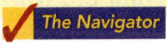

Costing Systems—Final Comments

Companies often use a combination of a process cost and a job order cost system. Called **operations costing**, this hybrid system is similar to process costing in its assumption that standardized methods are used to manufacture the product. At the same time, the product may have some customized, individual features that require the use of a job order cost system.

Consider, for example, the automobile manufacturer Ford Motor Company. Each vehicle at a given plant goes through the same assembly line, but Ford uses different materials (such as seat coverings, paint, and tinted glass) for different vehicles. Similarly, Kellogg's Pop-Tarts Toaster Pastries® go through numerous standardized processes—mixing, filling, baking, frosting, and packaging. The pastry dough, though, comes in different flavors—plain, chocolate, and graham—and fillings include Smucker's® real fruit, chocolate fudge, vanilla creme, brown sugar cinnamon, and S'mores.

A cost-benefit tradeoff occurs as a company decides which costing system to use. A job order system, for example, provides detailed information related to the cost of the product. Because each job has its own distinguishing characteristics, the system can provide an accurate cost per job. This information is useful in controlling costs and pricing products. However, the cost of implementing a job order cost system is often expensive because of the accounting costs involved.

On the other hand, for a company like Intel, which makes computer chips, is there a benefit in knowing whether the cost of the one hundredth chip produced is different from the one thousandth chip produced? Probably not. An average cost of the product will suffice for control and pricing purposes.

In summary, when deciding to use one of these systems, or a combination system, a company must weigh the costs of implementing the system against the benefits from the additional information provided.

CONTEMPORARY DEVELOPMENTS

As indicated in Chapter 19, two contemporary developments in managerial accounting are just-in-time processing and activity-based costing. We explain these innovations in the following sections.

Just-In-Time Processing

STUDY OBJECTIVE 8
Explain just-in-time (JIT) processing.

Traditionally, continuous process manufacturing has been based on a **just-in-case** philosophy: Companies hold inventories of raw materials *just in case* some items are of poor quality or a key supplier is shut down by a strike. They manufacture and store subassembly parts *just in case* these parts are needed later in the manufacturing process. Companies complete and store finished goods *just in case* they receive unexpected and rush customer orders. This philosophy often results in a **"push approach"**: Raw materials and subassembly parts are pushed through each process. Traditional processing often results in the buildup of extensive manufacturing inventories.

Primarily in response to foreign competition, many U.S. firms have switched to **just-in-time (JIT) processing**. JIT manufacturing is dedicated to having the right amount of materials, parts, or products just as they are needed. JIT first hit the United States in the early 1980s when automobile companies adopted it to compete with foreign automakers. Many companies, including Dell, Caterpillar, and Harley-Davidson now successfully use JIT. Under JIT processing, companies receive raw materials *just in time* for use in production, they complete subassembly parts *just in time* for use in finished goods, and they complete finished goods *just in time* to be sold. Illustration 21-24 shows the sequence of activities in just-in-time processing.

Illustration 21-24
Just-in-time processing

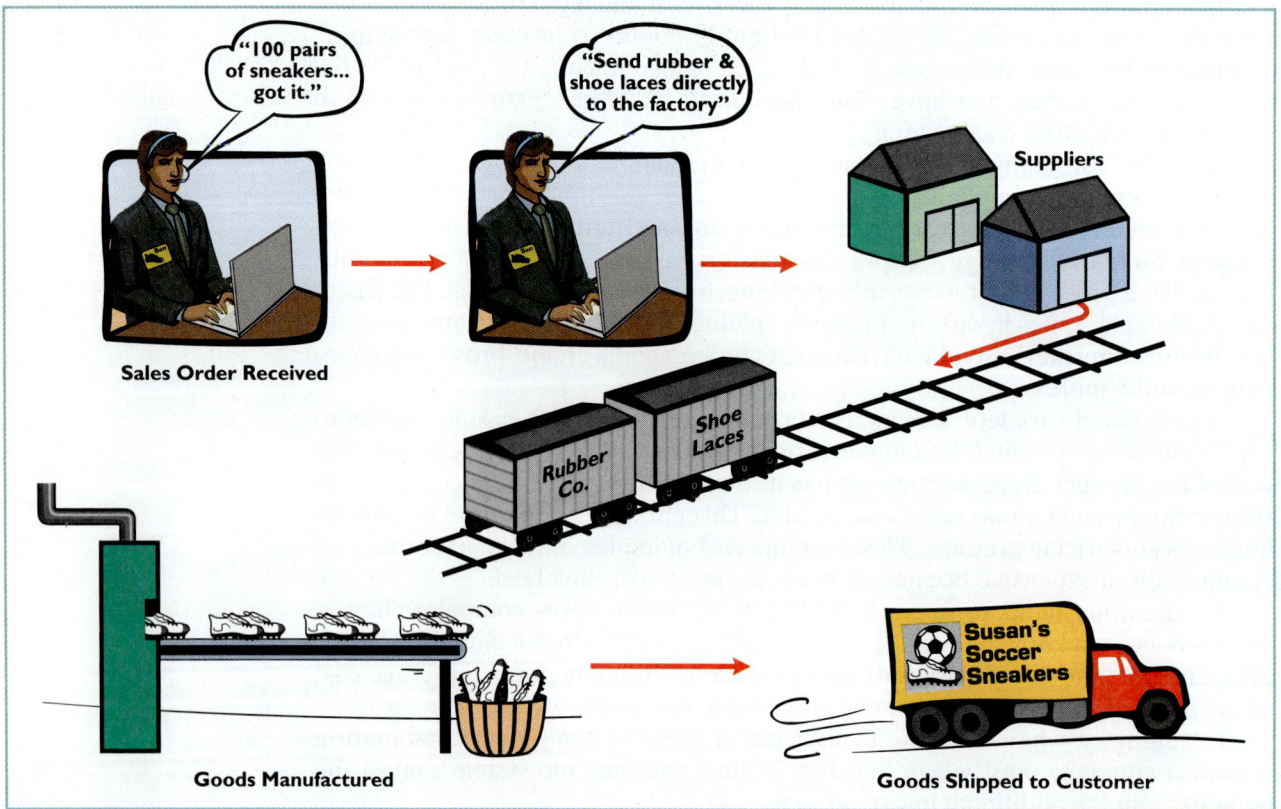

OBJECTIVE OF JIT PROCESSING

A primary objective of JIT is to eliminate all manufacturing inventories. Inventories have an adverse effect on net income because they tie up funds and storage space that could be put to more productive uses. JIT strives to eliminate inventories by using a **"pull approach"** in manufacturing. This approach begins with the customer placing an order with the company, which starts the process of pulling the product through the manufacturing process. A computer at the final work station sends a signal to the preceding work station. This signal indicates the exact materials (parts and subassemblies) needed to complete the production of a specified product for a specified time period, such as an eight-hour shift. The next preceding process, in turn, sends its signal to other processes back up the line. The goal is a smooth continuous flow in the manufacturing process and no buildup of inventories at any point.

ELEMENTS OF JIT PROCESSING

There are three important elements in JIT processing:

1. **Dependable suppliers.** Suppliers must be willing to deliver on short notice exact quantities of raw materials according to precise quality specifications (even including multiple deliveries within the same day). Suppliers must also be willing to deliver the raw materials at specified work stations rather than at a central receiving department. This type of purchasing requires constant and direct communication. Such communication is facilitated by an online computer linkage between the company and its suppliers.

2. A **multiskilled workforce.** Under JIT, machines are often strategically grouped around work cells or work stations. Much of the work is automated. As a result, one worker may have the responsibility to operate and maintain several different types of machines.

3. A **total quality control system.** The company must establish total quality control throughout the manufacturing operations. Total quality control means **no defects**. Since the **pull approach** signals only required quantities, any defects at any work station will shut down operations at subsequent work stations. Total quality control requires continuous monitoring by both employees and supervisors at each work station.

BENEFITS OF JIT PROCESSING

The major benefits of JIT processing are:

1. Significant reduction or elimination of manufacturing inventories.
2. Enhanced product quality.
3. Reduction or elimination of rework costs and inventory storage costs.
4. Production cost savings from the improved flow of goods through the processes.

The effects in many cases have been dramatic. For example, after using JIT for two years, a major division of Hewlett-Packard found that work in process inventories (in dollars) were down 82%, scrap/rework costs were down 30%, space utilization improved by 40%, and labor efficiency improved 50%. As indicated, JIT not only reduces inventory but also enables a manufacturer to produce a better product faster and with less waste.

One of the major accounting benefits of JIT is the elimination of raw materials and work in process inventory accounts. In place of these accounts is **one account**, Raw and In-Process Inventory. All materials and conversion costs are charged to this account. The reduction (or elimination) of in-process inventories results in a simplified computation of equivalent units of production.

Activity-Based Costing

STUDY OBJECTIVE 9
Explain activity-based costing (ABC).

Activity-based costing focuses on the activities performed in producing a product. An ABC system is similar to conventional costing systems in accounting for direct materials and direct labor, but it differs in regard to manufacturing overhead.

A conventional cost system uses a **single unit-level** basis to allocate overhead costs to products. The basis may be direct labor or machine hours used to manufacture the product. The assumption in this approach is that as volume of units produced increases, so does the cost of overhead. However, in recent years the amount of direct labor used in many industries has greatly *decreased*, and total overhead costs resulting from depreciation on expensive equipment and machinery, utilities, repairs, and maintenance have significantly *increased*.

In ABC costing, the cost of a product is equal to the sum of the costs of all activities performed to manufacture it. ABC recognizes that to have accurate and meaningful cost data, **more than one basis** of allocating activity costs to products is needed.

In selecting the allocation basis, ABC seeks to identify the **cost drivers** that measure the activities performed on the product. A **cost driver** may be any factor or activity that has a direct cause–effect relationship with the resources consumed. Examples of activities and possible cost drivers are as follows.

Illustration 21-25
Activities and cost drivers in ABC

Activity	Cost Driver
Ordering raw materials	Ordering hours; number of orders
Receiving raw materials	Receiving hours; number of shipments
Materials handling	Number of requisitions; weight of materials; handling hours
Production scheduling	Number of orders
Machine setups	Setup hours; number of setups
Machining (fabricating, assembling, etc.)	Machine hours
Quality control inspections	Number of inspections
Factory supervision	Number of employees

Two important assumptions must be met in order to obtain accurate product costs under ABC:

1. All overhead costs related to the activity must be driven by the cost driver used to assign costs to products.
2. All overhead costs related to the activity should respond proportionally to changes in the activity level of the cost driver.

For example, if there is little or no correlation between changes in the cost driver and consumption of the overhead cost, inaccurate product costs are inevitable. An example of the use of ABC is illustrated in the appendix at the end of this chapter.

Activity-based costing may be used with either a job order or a process cost accounting system. The primary benefit of ABC is more accurate and meaningful product costing. Also, improved cost data about an activity can lead to reduced costs for the activity. In sum, ABC makes managers realize that it is *activities*, and not products, that determine the profitability of a company—a realization that should lead to better management decisions.

DO IT!

Indicate whether each of the following statements is true or false.

JIT AND ABC

1. Continuous process manufacturing often results in a reduction of inventory.
2. Companies that use just-in-time processing complete and store finished goods all the time to meet rush orders from customers.
3. A major benefit of just-in-time processing is production cost savings from the improved flow of goods through the processes.
4. An ABC system is similar to traditional costing systems in accounting for manufacturing costs but differs in regard to period costs.
5. The primary benefit of ABC is more accurate and meaningful costs.
6. In recent years, the amount of direct labor used in many industries has greatly increased and total overhead costs have significantly decreased.

action plan

✔ JIT manufacturing is dedicated to having the right amounts of materials, parts, or products just as they are needed.

✔ ABC focuses on the activities performed in producing a product. It recognizes that to have accurate and meaningful cost data, more than one basis of allocating costs to products is needed.

Solution
1. False. 2. False. 3. True. 4. False. 5. True. 6. False.

Related exercise material: **BE21-11** and **DO IT! 21-4**.

Comprehensive DO IT!

Essence Company manufactures a high-end after-shave lotion, called Eternity, in 10-ounce plastic bottles. Because the market for after-shave lotion is highly competitive, the company is very concerned about keeping its costs under control. Eternity is manufactured through three processes: mixing, filling, and corking. Materials are added at the beginning of each of the processes, and labor and overhead are incurred uniformly throughout each process. The company uses a weighted-average method to cost its product. A partially completed production cost report for the month of May for the Mixing Department is shown below.

ESSENCE COMPANY
Mixing Department
Production Cost Report
For the Month Ended May 31, 2010

QUANTITIES	Physical Units	Equivalent Units — Materials	Equivalent Units — Conversion Costs
Units to be accounted for	Step 1	Step 2	
Work in process, May 1	1,000		
Started into production	2,000		
Total units	3,000		
Units accounted for			
Transferred out	2,200	?	?
Work in process, May 31	800	?	?
Total units	3,000	?	?

950 Chapter 21 Process Costing

COSTS		Materials	Conversion Costs	Total
Unit costs Step 3				
Costs in May	(a)	?	?	?
Equivalent units	(b)	?	?	
Unit costs [(a) ÷ (b)]		?	?	?
Costs to be accounted for				
Work in process, May 1				$ 56,300
Started into production				119,320
Total costs				$175,620

COST RECONCILIATION SCHEDULE Step 4

	Materials	Conversion Costs	Total
Costs accounted for			
Transferred out			?
Work in process, May 31			
Materials	?		
Conversion costs		?	?
Total costs			?

Additional information:
  Work in process, May 1, 1000 units
    Materials cost, 1,000 units (100% complete) $49,100
    Conversion costs, 1,000 units (70% complete)   7,200 $56,300
  Materials cost for May, 2,000 units $100,000
  Conversion costs for May $19,320
  Work in process, May 31, 800 units, 100% complete as to materials and 50% complete as to conversion costs.

Instructions

(a) Prepare a production cost report for the Mixing Department for the month of May.
(b) Prepare the journal entry to record the transfer of goods from the Mixing Department to the Filling Department.
(c) Explain why Essence Company is using a process cost system to account for its costs.

action plan

✔ Compute the physical unit flow—that is, the total units to be accounted for.
✔ Compute the equivalent units of production.
✔ Compute the unit production costs, expressed in terms of equivalent units of production.
✔ Prepare a cost reconciliation schedule, which shows that the total costs accounted for equal the total costs to be accounted for.

Solution to Comprehensive DO IT!

(a) A completed production cost report for the Mixing Department is shown below. Computations to support the amounts reported follow the report.

ESSENCE COMPANY
Mixing Department
Production Cost Report
For the Month Ended May 31, 2010

QUANTITIES	Physical Units	Equivalent Units	
		Materials	Conversion Costs
Units to be accounted for	Step 1	Step 2	
Work in process, May 1	1,000		
Started into production	2,000		
Total units	3,000		

QUANTITIES	Physical Units	Equivalent Units	
		Materials	Conversion Costs
Units accounted for			
Transferred out	2,200	2,200	2,200
Work in process, May 31	800	800	400 (800 × 50%)
Total units	3,000	3,000	2,600

COSTS		Materials	Conversion Costs	Total
Unit costs Step 3				
Costs in May	(a)	$149,100	$26,520	$175,620
Equivalent units	(b)	3,000	2,600	
Unit costs [(a) ÷ (b)]		$49.70	$10.20	$59.90
Costs to be accounted for				
Work in process, May 1				$ 56,300
Started into production				119,320
Total costs				$175,620

COST RECONCILIATION SCHEDULE Step 4

Costs accounted for			
Transferred out (2,200 × $59.90)			$131,780
Work in process, May 31			
Materials (800 × $49.70)		$39,760	
Conversion costs (400 × $10.20)		4,080	43,840
Total costs			$175,620

Additional computations to support production cost report data:
  Materials cost—$49,100 + $100,000
  Conversion costs—$7,200 + $19,320 ($119,320 − $100,000)

(b) Work in Process—Filling   131,780
      Work in Process—Mixing   131,780

(c) Companies use process cost systems to apply costs to similar products that are mass-produced in a continuous fashion. Essence Company uses a process cost system because production of the after-shave lotion, once it begins, continues until the after-shave lotion emerges. The processing is the same for the entire run—with precisely the same amount of materials, labor, and overhead. Each bottle of Eternity after-shave lotion is indistinguishable from another.

SUMMARY OF STUDY OBJECTIVES

1 Understand who uses process cost systems. Companies that mass-produce similar products in a continuous fashion use process cost systems. Once production begins, it continues until the finished product emerges. Each unit of finished product is indistinguishable from every other unit.

2 Explain the similarities and differences between job order cost and process cost systems. Job order cost systems are similar to process cost systems in three ways: (1) Both systems track the same cost elements—direct materials, direct labor, and manufacturing overhead. (2) Both accumulate costs in the same accounts—Raw Materials Inventory, Factory Labor, and Manufacturing Overhead. (3) Both assign accumulated costs to the same accounts—Work in Process, Finished Goods Inventory, and Cost of Goods Sold. However, the method of assigning costs differs significantly.

There are four main differences between the two cost systems: (1) A process cost system uses separate accounts for each department or manufacturing process, rather than only one work in process account used in a job order cost system.

(2) A process cost system summarizes costs in a production cost report for each department. A job cost system charges costs to individual jobs and summarizes them in a job cost sheet. (3) Costs are totaled at the end of a time period in a process cost system, but at the completion of a job in a job cost system. (4) A process cost system calculates unit cost as: Total manufacturing costs for the period ÷ Units produced during the period. A job cost system calculates unit cost as: Total cost per job ÷ Units produced.

3 Explain the flow of costs in a process cost system. A process cost system assigns manufacturing costs for raw materials, labor, and overhead to work in process accounts for various departments or manufacturing processes. It transfers the costs of units completed from one department to another as those units move through the manufacturing process. The system transfers the costs of completed work to Finished Goods Inventory. Finally, when inventory is sold, the system transfers costs to Cost of Goods Sold.

4 Make the journal entries to assign manufacturing costs in a process cost system. Entries to assign the costs of raw materials, labor, and overhead consist of a credit to Raw Materials Inventory, Factory Labor, and Manufacturing Overhead, and a debit to Work in Process for each department. Entries to record the cost of goods transferred to another department are a credit to Work in Process for the department whose work is finished and a debit to the department to which the goods are transferred. The entry to record units completed and transferred to the warehouse is a credit for the department whose work is finished and a debit to Finished Goods Inventory. The entry to record the sale of goods is a credit to Finished Goods Inventory and a debit to Cost of Goods Sold.

5 Compute equivalent units. Equivalent units of production measure work done during a period, expressed in fully completed units. Companies use this measure to determine the cost per unit of completed product. Equivalent units are the sum of units completed and transferred out plus equivalent units of ending work in process.

6 Explain the four steps necessary to prepare a production cost report. The four steps to complete a production cost report are: (1) Compute the physical unit flow—that is, the total units to be accounted for. (2) Compute the equivalent units of production. (3) Compute the unit production costs, expressed in terms of equivalent units of production. (4) Prepare a cost reconciliation schedule, which shows that the total costs accounted for equal the total costs to be accounted for.

7 Prepare a production cost report. The production cost report contains both quantity and cost data for a production department. There are four sections in the report: (1) number of physical units, (2) equivalent units determination, (3) unit costs, and (4) cost reconciliation schedule.

8 Explain just-in-time (JIT) processing. JIT is a manufacturing technique dedicated to producing the right products at the right time as needed. One of the principal accounting effects is that a Raw and In-Process Inventory account replaces both the raw materials and work in process inventory accounts.

9 Explain activity-based costing (ABC). ABC is a method of product costing that focuses on the activities performed to produce products. It assigns the cost of the activities to products by using cost drivers that measure the activities performed. The primary objective of ABC is accurate and meaningful product costs.

GLOSSARY

Activity-based costing A cost accounting system that focuses on the activities performed in manufacturing a specific product. (p. 948).

Conversion costs The sum of labor costs and overhead costs. (p. 937).

Cost driver Any factor or activity that has a direct cause–effect relationship with the resources consumed. (p. 948).

Cost reconciliation schedule A schedule that shows that the total costs accounted for equal the total costs to be accounted for. (p. 943).

Equivalent units of production A measure of the work done during the period, expressed in fully completed units. (p. 937).

Just-in-time processing A processing system dedicated to producing the right products (or parts) as they are needed. (p. 946).

Operations costing A combination of a process cost and a job order cost system, in which products are manufactured primarily by standardized methods, with some customization. (p. 945).

Physical units Actual units to be accounted for during a period, irrespective of any work performed. (p. 941).

Process cost systems An accounting system used to apply costs to similar products that are mass-produced in a continuous fashion. (p. 930).

Production cost report An internal report for management that shows both production quantity and cost data for a production department. (p. 939).

Total units (costs) accounted for The sum of the units (costs) transferred out during the period plus the units (costs) in process at the end of the period. (pp. 941, 943).

Total units (costs) to be accounted for The sum of the units (costs) started (or transferred) into production during the period plus the units (costs) in process at the beginning of the period. (pp. 941, 943).

Unit production costs Costs expressed in terms of equivalent units of production. (p. 942).

Weighted-average method Method used to compute equivalent units of production which considers the degree of completion (weighting) of the units completed and transferred out and the ending work in process. (p. 937).

APPENDIX Example of Traditional Costing versus Activity-Based Costing

Production and Cost Data

In this appendix we present an example that compares activity-based costing to traditional costing. Assume that Atlas Company produces two products, The Boot and The Club. The Boot is a high-volume item totaling 25,000 units annually. The Club is a low-volume item totaling only 5,000 units per year. Each product requires one hour of direct labor for completion. Therefore, total annual direct labor hours are 30,000 (25,000 + 5,000). Expected annual manufacturing overhead costs are $900,000. The predetermined overhead rate is $30 ($900,000 ÷ 30,000) per direct labor hour.

The direct materials cost per unit is $40 for The Boot and $30 for The Club. The direct labor cost is $12 per unit for each product.

STUDY OBJECTIVE 10
Apply activity-based costing to specific company data.

Unit Costs Under Traditional Costing

Illustration 21A-1 shows the unit cost for each product under traditional costing.

	Product	
Manufacturing Costs	**The Boot**	**The Club**
Direct materials	$40	$30
Direct labor	12	12
Overhead	30*	30*
Total unit cost	**$82**	**$72**

*Predetermined overhead rate × Direct labor hours ($30 × 1 hr = $30)

Illustration 21A-1
Units costs—traditional costing

Unit Costs Under ABC

Let's now calculate unit costs under ABC, in order to compare activity-based costing with a traditional costing system. The first step is to determine overhead rates under ABC.

DETERMINING OVERHEAD RATES UNDER ABC

Analysis reveals that Atlas Company's expected annual overhead costs of $900,000 relate to three activities—machine setups, machining, and inspections. Illustration 21A-2 shows the cost driver and overhead rate for each activity.

Activity	Cost Driver	Total Expected Overhead Cost	Total Expected Use of Driver	Activity Based Overhead Rate
Machine setups	Number of setups	$300,000	1,500	**$200** per setup
Machining	Machine hours	500,000	50,000	**$10** per machine hour
Inspections	Number of inspections	100,000	2,000	**$50** per inspection

Illustration 21A-2
Computing overhead rates—ABC

ASSIGNING OVERHEAD COSTS TO PRODUCTS UNDER ABC

In assigning costs, it is necessary to know the expected number of cost drivers for each product. Because of its low volume, The Club requires more setups and inspections than The Boot. The expected number of cost drivers for each product is as follows.

Illustration 21A-3
Expected number of cost drivers

Cost Driver	Product		Total Usage
	The Boot	The Club	
Number of machine setups	500	1,000	1,500
Machine hours	30,000	20,000	50,000
Number of inspections	500	1,500	2,000

Using these data, Atlas can assign the expected annual overhead cost to each product as follows.

Illustration 21A-4
Assignment of overhead costs to products

Activity	The Boot		The Club		Total Cost
	Number	Cost	Number	Cost	
Machine setups ($200)	500	$100,000	1,000	$200,000	$300,000
Machining ($10)	30,000	300,000	20,000	200,000	500,000
Inspections ($50)	500	25,000	1,500	75,000	100,000
Total assigned costs (a)		$425,000		$475,000	$900,000
Units produced (b)		25,000		5,000	
Overhead cost per unit [(a) ÷ (b)]		**$17**		**$95**	

These data show that under ABC, overhead costs are shifted from the high-volume product (The Boot) to the low-volume product (The Club). This shift results in more accurate costing for two reasons:

1. Low-volume products often require more special handling, such as more machine setups and inspections, than high-volume products. This is true for Atlas Company. Thus, the low-volume product frequently is responsible for more overhead costs per unit than a high-volume product.

2. Assigning overhead using ABC will usually increase the cost per unit for low-volume products as compared to a traditional overhead allocation. Therefore, traditional cost drivers such as direct labor hours are usually not appropriate for assigning overhead costs to low-volume products.

Comparing Unit Costs

A comparison of unit manufacturing costs under traditional costing and ABC shows the following significant differences.

Illustration 21A-5
Comparison of unit product costs

Manufacturing Costs	The Boot		The Club	
	Traditional Costing	ABC	Traditional Costing	ABC
Direct materials	$40	$40	$30	$ 30
Direct labor	12	12	12	12
Overhead	30	17	30	95
Total cost per unit	**$82**	**$69**	**$72**	**$137**
	Overstated $13		Understated $65	

The comparison shows that unit costs under traditional costing have been significantly distorted. The cost of The Boot has been overstated $13 per unit ($82−$69). The cost of The Club has been understated $65 per unit ($137−$72). The differences are attributable to how Atlas Company assigns manufacturing overhead. A likely consequence of the differences is that Atlas has been overpricing The Boot and possibly losing market share to competitors. It also has been sacrificing profitability by underpricing The Club.

As illustrated in the above case, ABC involves the following steps.

1. Identify the major activities that pertain to the manufacture of specific products.
2. Accumulate manufacturing overhead costs by activities.
3. Identify the cost driver(s) that accurately measure(s) each activity's contribution to the finished product.
4. Assign manufacturing overhead costs for each activity to products, using the cost driver(s).

Benefits and Limitations of Activity-Based Costing

We have already seen that a primary benefit of ABC is more accurate product costing. In addition, ABC offers the following other benefits:

1. **Enhanced control over overhead costs.** Under ABC, companies can trace many overhead costs directly to activities—allowing some indirect costs to be identified as direct costs. Thus, managers have become more aware of their responsibility to control the activities that generate the costs.
2. **Better management decisions.** More accurate product costing should contribute to setting selling prices that can help achieve desired product profitability levels. In addition, more accurate cost data could be helpful in deciding whether to make or buy a component, and sometimes even whether to discontinue or expand a product.

The principal disadvantages of ABC generally focus on two factors. First, **the expense of obtaining the cost data** required by the system is relatively high. ABC requires data that are not normally generated within a company. Examples of such data are the number of setups, inspections, orders placed, and orders received. In addition, many computations are involved in assigning overhead costs to individual products.

Second, **ABC does not eliminate arbitrary assignments** of overhead. For example, plant-wide overhead costs such as depreciation, insurance, and property taxes on the factory building should be allocated to the activity centers in determining the cost of a product. With ABC, these allocations may be more difficult to do accurately because of the increased number of activity centers. As a result, accuracy of product costs could be adversely affected.

SUMMARY OF STUDY OBJECTIVE FOR APPENDIX

10. **Apply activity-based costing to specific company data.** In applying ABC, it is necessary to compute the overhead rate for each activity by dividing total expected overhead by the total expected usage of the cost driver. The overhead cost for each activity is then assigned to products on the basis of each product's use of the cost driver.

*Note: All **asterisked** Questions, Exercises, and Problems relate to material contained in the appendix to the chapter.

SELF-STUDY QUESTIONS

Answers are at the end of the chapter.

(SO 1) 1. Which of the following items is *not* characteristic of a process cost system?
   a. Once production begins, it continues until the finished product emerges.
   b. The products produced are heterogeneous in nature.
   c. The focus is on continually producing homogeneous products.
   d. When the finished product emerges, all units have precisely the same amount of materials, labor, and overhead.

(SO 2) 2. Indicate which of the following statements is *not* correct.
   a. Both a job order and a process cost system track the same three manufacturing cost elements—direct materials, direct labor, and manufacturing overhead.
   b. A job order cost system uses only one work in process account, whereas a process cost system uses multiple work in process accounts.
   c. Manufacturing costs are accumulated the same way in a job order and in a process cost system.
   d. Manufacturing costs are assigned the same way in a job order and in a process cost system.

(SO 3) 3. In a process cost system, costs are assigned only:
   a. to one work in process account.
   b. to work in process and finished goods inventory.
   c. to work in process, finished goods, and cost of goods sold.
   d. to work in process accounts.

(SO 4) 4. In making the journal entry to assign raw materials costs, a company:
   a. debits Finished Goods Inventory.
   b. often debits two or more work in process accounts.
   c. generally credits two or more work in process accounts.
   d. credits Finished Goods Inventory.

(SO 4) 5. In a process cost system, manufacturing overhead:
   a. is assigned to finished goods at the end of each accounting period.
   b. is assigned to a work in process account for each job as the job is completed.
   c. is assigned to a work in process account for each production department on the basis of a predetermined overhead rate.
   d. is assigned to a work in process account for each production department as overhead costs are incurred.

(SO 5) 6. Conversion costs are the sum of:
   a. fixed and variable overhead costs.
   b. labor costs and overhead costs.
   c. direct material costs and overhead costs.
   d. direct labor and indirect labor costs.

(SO 5) 7. The Mixing Department's output during the period consists of 20,000 units completed and transferred out, and 5,000 units in ending work in process 60% complete as to materials and conversion costs. Beginning inventory is 1,000 units, 40% complete as to materials and conversion costs. The equivalent units of production are:
   a. 22,600.   c. 24,000.
   b. 23,000.   d. 25,000.

8. In RYZ Company, there are zero units in beginning work **(SO 6)** in process, 7,000 units started into production, and 500 units in ending work in process 20% completed. The physical units to be accounted for are:
   a. 7,000.   c. 7,600.
   b. 7,360.   d. 7,340.

9. Stock Company has 2,000 units in beginning work in **(SO 6)** process, 20% complete as to conversion costs, 23,000 units transferred out to finished goods, and 3,000 units in ending work in process 33⅓% complete as to conversion costs. The beginning and ending inventory is fully complete as to materials costs. Equivalent units for materials and conversion costs are, respectively:
   a. 22,000, 24,000.
   b. 24,000, 26,000.
   c. 26,000, 24,000.
   d. 26,000, 26,000.

10. Fortner Company has no beginning work in process; 9,000 **(SO 6)** units are transferred out and 3,000 units in ending work in process are one-third finished as to conversion costs and fully complete as to materials cost. If total materials cost is $60,000, the unit materials cost is:
    a. $5.00.
    b. $5.45 rounded.
    c. $6.00.
    d. No correct answer is given.

11. Largo Company has unit costs of $10 for materials and **(SO 6)** $30 for conversion costs. If there are 2,500 units in ending work in process, 40% complete as to conversion costs, and fully complete as to materials cost, the total cost assignable to the ending work in process inventory is:
    a. $45,000.   c. $75,000.
    b. $55,000.   d. $100,000.

12. A production cost report **(SO 7)**
    a. is an external report.
    b. shows costs charged to a department and costs accounted for.
    c. shows equivalent units of production but not physical units.
    d. contains six sections.

13. In a production cost report, units to be accounted for are **(SO 7)** calculated as:
    a. Units started into production + Units in ending work in process.
    b. Units started into production − Units in beginning work in process.
    c. Units transferred out + Units in beginning work in process.
    d. Units started into production + Units in beginning work in process.

14. Just-in-time processing (JIT): **(SO 8)**
    a. strives to eliminate inventories.
    b. uses a pull approach in manufacturing.
    c. Neither of the above.
    d. Both (a) and (b).

(SO 8) **15.** The sequence of activities in just-in-time processing begins when the manufacturer:
   a. orders raw materials from a supplier.
   b. issues raw materials to work in process inventory.
   c. receives a sales order from a customer.
   d. calculates its predetermined overhead rates.

(SO 9) **16.** Activity-based costing:
   a. assumes that the cost of a product is equal to the sum of the costs of all activities performed to manufacture it.
   b. has become more widespread as overhead costs have been decreasing relative to materials and labor costs.
   c. is similar to a conventional cost accounting system in accounting for direct labor and manufacturing overhead but differs in regard to direct materials.
   d. uses a single unit-level basis to allocate overhead costs to products.

17. Activity-based costing (ABC): (SO 9)
   a. can be used only in a process cost system.
   b. focuses on units of production.
   c. focuses on activities performed to produce a product.
   d. uses only a single basis of allocation.

*18. The overhead rate for Machine Setups is $100 per setup. (SO 10) Products A and B have 80 and 60 setups, respectively. The overhead assigned to each product is:
   a. Product A $8,000, Product B $8,000.
   b. Product A $8,000, Product B $6,000.
   c. Product A $6,000, Product B $6,000.
   d. Product A $6,000, Product B $8,000.

Go to the book's companion website, **www.wiley.com/college/weygandt**, for additional Self-Study Questions.

QUESTIONS

1. Identify which costing system—job order or process cost—the following companies would primarily use: (a) Quaker Oats, (b) Ford Motor Company, (c) Kinko's Print Shop, and (d) Warner Bros. Motion Pictures.
2. Contrast the primary focus of job order cost accounting and of process cost accounting.
3. What are the similarities between a job order and a process cost system?
4. Your roommate is confused about the features of process cost accounting. Identify and explain the distinctive features for your roommate.
5. Mel Storrer believes there are no significant differences in the flow of costs between job order cost accounting and process cost accounting. Is Storrer correct? Explain.
6. (a) What source documents are used in assigning (1) materials and (2) labor to production in a process cost system?
   (b) What criterion and basis are commonly used in allocating overhead to processes?
7. At Ace Company, overhead is assigned to production departments at the rate of $5 per machine hour. In July, machine hours were 3,000 in the Machining Department and 2,400 in the Assembly Department. Prepare the entry to assign overhead to production.
8. Gary Weiss is uncertain about the steps used to prepare a production cost report. State the procedures that are required in the sequence in which they are performed.
9. Rich Mordica is confused about computing physical units. Explain to Rich how physical units to be accounted for and physical units accounted for are determined.
10. What is meant by the term "equivalent units of production"?
11. How are equivalent units of production computed?
12. Mason Company had zero units of beginning work in process. During the period, 9,000 units were completed, and there were 600 units of ending work in process. What were the units started into production?
13. Mendle Co. had zero units of beginning work in process. During the period 12,000 units were completed, and there were 800 units of ending work in process one-fifth complete as to conversion cost and 100% complete as to materials cost. What were the equivalent units of production for (a) materials and (b) conversion costs?
14. Reyes Co. started 3,000 units in the period. Its beginning inventory is 500 units one-fourth complete as to conversion costs and 100% complete as to materials cost. Its ending inventory is 200 units one-fifth complete as to conversion cost and 100% complete as to materials costs. How many units were transferred out this period?
15. Kiner Company transfers out 14,000 units and has 2,000 units of ending work in process that are 25% complete. Materials are entered at the beginning of the process and there is no beginning work in process. Assuming unit materials costs of $3 and unit conversion costs of $6, what are the costs to be assigned to units (a) transferred out and (b) in ending work in process?
16. (a) Eve Adams believes the production cost report is an external report for stockholders. Is Eve correct? Explain.
   (b) Identify the sections in a production cost report.
17. What purposes are served by a production cost report?
18. At Frank Company, there are 800 units of ending work in process that are 100% complete as to materials and 40% complete as to conversion costs. If the unit cost of materials is $4 and the costs assigned to the 800 units is $6,000, what is the per-unit conversion cost?
19. What is the difference between operations costing and a process costing system?
20. How does a company decide whether to use a job order or a process cost system?
21. (a) Describe the philosophy and approach of just-in-time processing.
    (b) Identify the major elements of JIT processing.
22. (a) What are the principal differences between activity-based costing (ABC) and traditional product costing?
    (b) What assumptions must be met for ABC costing to be useful?

958 Chapter 21 Process Costing

23. Dipak Co. identifies the following activities that pertain to manufacturing overhead: Materials Handling, Machine Setups, Factory Machine Maintenance, Factory Supervision, and Quality Control. For each activity identify an appropriate cost driver.

*24. (a) Identify the steps that pertain to activity-based costing.
(b) What are the advantages of ABC costing?

BRIEF EXERCISES

Journalize entries for accumulating costs.
(SO 4)

BE21-1 Sanchez Manufacturing purchases $45,000 of raw materials on account, and it incurs $50,000 of factory labor costs. Journalize the two transactions on March 31 assuming the labor costs are not paid until April.

Journalize the assignment of materials and labor costs.
(SO 4)

BE21-2 Data for Sanchez Manufacturing are given in BE21-1. Supporting records show that (a) the Assembly Department used $24,000 of raw materials and $30,000 of the factory labor, and (b) the Finishing Department used the remainder. Journalize the assignment of the costs to the processing departments on March 31.

Journalize the assignment of overhead costs.
(SO 4)

BE21-3 Factory labor data for Sanchez Manufacturing are given in BE21-2. Manufacturing overhead is assigned to departments on the basis of 200% of labor costs. Journalize the assignment of overhead to the Assembly and Finishing Departments.

Compute physical units of production.
(SO 6)

BE21-4 Bowyer Manufacturing Company has the following production data for selected months.

			Ending Work in Process	
Month	Beginning Work in Process	Units Transferred Out	Units	% Complete as to Conversion Cost
January	–0–	30,000	10,000	40%
March	–0–	40,000	8,000	75
July	–0–	40,000	16,000	25

Compute the physical units for each month.

Compute equivalent units of production.
(SO 5)

BE21-5 Using the data in BE21-4, compute equivalent units of production for materials and conversion costs, assuming materials are entered at the beginning of the process.

Compute unit costs of production.
(SO 6)

BE21-6 In Montego Company, total material costs are $32,000, and total conversion costs are $54,000. Equivalent units of production are materials 10,000 and conversion costs 12,000. Compute the unit costs for materials, conversion costs, and total manufacturing costs.

Assign costs to units transferred out and in process.
(SO 6)

BE21-7 Hindi Company has the following production data for April: units transferred out 40,000, and ending work in process 5,000 units that are 100% complete for materials and 40% complete for conversion costs. If unit materials cost is $4 and unit conversion cost is $9, determine the costs to be assigned to the units transferred out and the units in ending work in process.

Compute unit costs.
(SO 6)

BE21-8 Production costs chargeable to the Finishing Department in June in Castilla Company are materials $15,000, labor $29,500, overhead $18,000. Equivalent units of production are materials 20,000 and conversion costs 19,000. Compute the unit costs for materials and conversion costs.

Prepare cost reconciliation schedule.
(SO 6)

BE21-9 Data for Castilla Company are given in BE21-8. Production records indicate that 18,000 units were transferred out, and 2,000 units in ending work in process were 50% complete as to conversion cost and 100% complete as to materials. Prepare a cost reconciliation schedule.

Compute equivalent units of production.
(SO 5)

BE21-10 The Smelting Department of Massaro Manufacturing Company has the following production and cost data for November.

Production: Beginning work in process 2,000 units that are 100% complete as to materials and 20% complete as to conversion costs; units transferred out 8,000 units; and ending work in process 5,000 units that are 100% complete as to materials and 40% complete as to conversion costs.

Compute the equivalent units of production for (a) materials and (b) conversion costs for the month of November.

BE21-11 Ernie Els has formulated the following list of statements about contemporary developments in managerial accounting.

Understand contemporary developments.
(SO 8, 9)

1. Just-in-time processing results in a push approach; that is, raw materials are pushed through each process.
2. A primary objective of just-in-time processing is to eliminate all manufacturing inventories.
3. A major disadvantage of just-in-time processing is lower product quality.
4. A primary benefit of activity-based costing is more accurate and meaningful product costing.
5. A major advantage of activity-based costing is that it uses a single unit-level basis, such as direct labor or machine hours, to allocate overhead.

Identify each statement as true or false. If false, indicate how to correct the statement to make it true.

*BE21-12 Bristol Company identifies three activities in its manufacturing process: machine setups, machining, and inspections. Estimated annual overhead cost for each activity is $120,000, $300,000, and $70,000, respectively. The cost driver for each activity and the expected annual usage are: number of setups 1,000, machine hours 25,000, and number of inspections 2,000. Compute the overhead rate for each activity.

Compute overhead rates for activities.
(SO 10)

DO IT! REVIEW

DO IT! 21-1 Boaz Company manufactures CH-21 through two processes: Mixing and Packaging. In July, the following costs were incurred.

Assign and journalize manufacturing costs.
(SO 4)

	Mixing	Packaging
Raw Materials used	$10,000	$24,000
Factory Labor costs	8,000	36,000
Manufacturing Overhead costs	12,000	54,000

Units completed at a cost of $21,000 in the Mixing Department are transferred to the Packaging Department. Units completed at a cost of $102,000 in the Packaging Department are transferred to Finished Goods. Journalize the assignment of these costs to the two processes and the transfer of units as appropriate.

DO IT! 21-2 The assembly department has the following production and cost data for the current month.

Compute equivalent units.
(SO 5)

Beginning Work in Process	Units Transferred Out	Ending Work in Process
–0–	20,000	16,000

Materials are entered at the beginning of the process. The ending work in process units are 70% complete as to conversion costs. Compute the equivalent units of production for (a) materials and (b) conversion costs.

DO IT! 21-3 In March, Lasso Manufacturing had the following unit production costs: materials $10 and conversion costs $8. On March 1, it had zero work in process. During March, Lasso transferred out 22,000 units. As of March 31, 2,000 units that were 40% complete as to conversion costs and 100% complete as to materials were in ending work in process.

Prepare cost reconciliation schedule.
(SO 6, 7)

(a) Compute the total units to be accounted for.
(b) Compute the equivalent units of production.
(c) Prepare a cost reconciliation schedule, including the costs of materials transferred out and the costs of materials in process.

DO IT! 21-4 Indicate whether each of the following statements is true or false.

Answer questions about JIT and ABC.
(SO 8, 9)

1. Just-in-time processing is also known as just-in-case processing.
2. Companies that use just-in-time processing complete finished goods just in time to be sold.
3. A major benefit of just-in-time processing is enhanced product quality.
4. An ABC system is similar to conventional costing systems in accounting for period costs but differs in regard to manufacturing costs.

5. The primary benefit of ABC is significant reduction or elimination of manufacturing inventories.
6. In recent years, the amount of direct labor used in many industries has greatly decreased and total overhead costs have significantly increased.

EXERCISES

Understand process cost accounting.
(SO 1, 2)

E21-1 Doc Gibbs has prepared the following list of statements about process cost accounting.

1. Process cost systems are used to apply costs to similar products that are mass-produced in a continuous fashion.
2. A process cost system is used when each finished unit is indistinguishable from another.
3. Companies that produce soft drinks, motion pictures, and computer chips would all use process cost accounting.
4. In a process cost system, costs are tracked by individual jobs.
5. Job order costing and process costing track different manufacturing cost elements.
6. Both job order costing and process costing account for direct materials, direct labor, and manufacturing overhead.
7. Costs flow through the accounts in the same basic way for both job order costing and process costing.
8. In a process cost system, only one work in process account is used.
9. In a process cost system, costs are summarized in a job cost sheet.
10. In a process cost system, the unit cost is total manufacturing costs for the period divided by the units produced during the period.

Instructions
Identify each statement as true or false. If false, indicate how to correct the statement.

Journalize transactions.
(SO 4)

E21-2 Fernando Company manufactures pizza sauce through two production departments: Cooking and Canning. In each process, materials and conversion costs are incurred evenly throughout the process. For the month of April, the work in process accounts show the following debits.

	Cooking	Canning
Beginning work in process	$ –0–	$ 4,000
Materials	21,000	6,000
Labor	8,500	7,000
Overhead	29,500	25,800
Costs transferred in		53,000

Instructions
Journalize the April transactions.

Answer questions on costs and production.
(SO 3, 5, 6)

E21-3 The ledger of Molindo Company has the following work in process account.

	Work in Process—Painting				
5/1	Balance	3,590	5/31	Transferred out	?
5/31	Materials	5,160			
5/31	Labor	2,740			
5/31	Overhead	1,650			
5/31	Balance	?			

Production records show that there were 400 units in the beginning inventory, 30% complete, 1,100 units started, and 1,200 units transferred out. The beginning work in process had materials cost of $2,040 and conversion costs of $1,550. The units in ending inventory were 40% complete. Materials are entered at the beginning of the painting process.

Instructions
(a) How many units are in process at May 31?
(b) What is the unit materials cost for May?
(c) What is the unit conversion cost for May?
(d) What is the total cost of units transferred out in May?
(e) What is the cost of the May 31 inventory?

E21-4 Douglas Manufacturing Company has two production departments: Cutting and Assembly. July 1 inventories are Raw Materials $4,200, Work in Process—Cutting $2,900, Work in Process—Assembly $10,600, and Finished Goods $31,000. During July, the following transactions occurred.

Journalize transactions for two processes.
(SO 4)

1. Purchased $62,500 of raw materials on account.
2. Incurred $56,000 of factory labor. (Credit Wages Payable.)
3. Incurred $70,000 of manufacturing overhead; $40,000 was paid and the remainder is unpaid.
4. Requisitioned materials for Cutting $15,700 and Assembly $8,900.
5. Used factory labor for Cutting $29,000 and Assembly $27,000.
6. Applied overhead at the rate of $15 per machine hour. Machine hours were Cutting 1,680 and Assembly 1,720.
7. Transferred goods costing $67,600 from the Cutting Department to the Assembly Department.
8. Transferred goods costing $134,900 from Assembly to Finished Goods.
9. Sold goods costing $150,000 for $200,000 on account.

Instructions
Journalize the transactions. (Omit explanations.)

E21-5 In Ramirez Company, materials are entered at the beginning of each process. Work in process inventories, with the percentage of work done on conversion costs, and production data for its Sterilizing Department in selected months during 2010 are as follows.

Compute physical units and equivalent units of production.
(SO 5, 6)

Month	Beginning Work in Process		Units Transferred Out	Ending Work in Process	
	Units	Conversion Cost%		Units	Conversion Cost%
January	–0–	—	7,000	2,000	60
March	–0–	—	12,000	3,000	30
May	–0–	—	16,000	5,000	80
July	–0–	—	10,000	1,500	40

Instructions
(a) Compute the physical units for January and May.
(b) Compute the equivalent units of production for (1) materials and (2) conversion costs for each month.

E21-6 The Cutting Department of Groneman Manufacturing has the following production and cost data for July.

Determine equivalent units, unit costs, and assignment of costs.
(SO 5, 6)

Production	Costs	
1. Transferred out 9,000 units.	Beginning work in process	$ –0–
2. Started 3,000 units that are 60% complete as to conversion costs and 100% complete as to materials at July 31.	Materials	45,000
	Labor	16,200
	Manufacturing overhead	18,900

Materials are entered at the beginning of the process. Conversion costs are incurred uniformly during the process.

Instructions
(a) Determine the equivalent units of production for (1) materials and (2) conversion costs.
(b) Compute unit costs and prepare a cost reconciliation schedule.

E21-7 The Sanding Department of Ortiz Furniture Company has the following production and manufacturing cost data for March 2010, the first month of operation.

Prepare a production cost report.
(SO 5, 6, 7)

Production: 12,000 units finished and transferred out; 3,000 units started that are 100% complete as to materials and 20% complete as to conversion costs.
Manufacturing costs: Materials $33,000; labor $27,000; overhead $36,000.

Instructions
Prepare a production cost report.

Determine equivalent units, unit costs, and assignment of costs.
(SO 5, 6)

E21-8 The Blending Department of Hancock Company has the following cost and production data for the month of April.

Costs:		
Work in process, April 1		
Direct materials: 100% complete		$100,000
Conversion costs: 20% complete		70,000
Cost of work in process, April 1		$170,000
Costs incurred during production in April		
Direct materials		$ 800,000
Conversion costs		362,000
Costs incurred in April		$1,162,000

Units transferred out totaled 14,000. Ending work in process was 1,000 units that are 100% complete as to materials and 40% complete as to conversion costs.

Instructions
(a) Compute the equivalent units of production for (1) materials and (2) conversion costs for the month of April.
(b) Compute the unit costs for the month.
(c) Determine the costs to be assigned to the units transferred out and in ending work in process.

Determine equivalent units, unit costs, and assignment of costs.
(SO 5, 6)

E21-9 Podsednik Company has gathered the following information.

Units in beginning work in process	–0–
Units started into production	36,000
Units in ending work in process	6,000
Percent complete for conversion costs in ending work in process	40%
Costs incurred:	
Direct materials	$72,000
Direct labor	$81,000
Overhead	$97,200

Instructions
(a) Compute equivalent units of production for materials and for conversion costs.
(b) Determine the unit costs of production.
(c) Show the assignment of costs to units transferred out and in process.

Determine equivalent units, unit costs, and assignment of costs.
(SO 5, 6)

E21-10 Pink Martini Company has gathered the following information.

Units in beginning work in process	20,000
Units started into production	72,000
Units in ending work in process	24,000
Percent complete for conversion costs in ending work in process	60%
Costs incurred (includes beginning work in process):	
Direct materials	$101,200
Direct labor	$164,800
Overhead	$123,600

Instructions
(a) Compute equivalent units of production for materials and for conversion costs.
(b) Determine the unit costs of production.
(c) Show the assignment of costs to units transferred out and in process.

E21-11 The Polishing Department of Estaban Manufacturing Company has the following production and manufacturing cost data for September. Materials are entered at the beginning of the process.

Compute equivalent units, unit costs, and costs assigned.
(SO 5, 6)

Production: Beginning inventory 1,600 units that are 100% complete as to materials and 30% complete as to conversion costs; units started during the period are 18,400; ending inventory of 5,000 units 10% complete as to conversion costs.

Manufacturing costs: Beginning inventory costs, comprised of $20,000 of materials and $43,180 of conversion costs; materials costs added in Polishing during the month, $177,200; labor and overhead applied in Polishing during the month, $102,680 and $257,140, respectively.

Instructions
(a) Compute the equivalent units of production for materials and conversion costs for the month of September.
(b) Compute the unit costs for materials and conversion costs for the month.
(c) Determine the costs to be assigned to the units transferred out and in process.

E21-12 Stan Maley has recently been promoted to production manager, and so he has just started to receive various managerial reports. One of the reports he has received is the production cost report that you prepared. It showed that his department had 2,000 equivalent units in ending inventory. His department has had a history of not keeping enough inventory on hand to meet demand. He has come to you, very angry, and wants to know why you credited him with only 2,000 units when he knows he had at least twice that many on hand.

Explain the production cost report.
(SO 7)

Instructions
Explain to him why his production cost report showed only 2,000 equivalent units in ending inventory. Write an informal memo. Be kind and explain very clearly why he is mistaken.

E21-13 The Welding Department of Batista Manufacturing Company has the following production and manufacturing cost data for February 2010. All materials are added at the beginning of the process.

Prepare a production cost report.
(SO 5, 6, 7)

Manufacturing Costs			Production Data	
Beginning work in process			Beginning work in process	15,000 units
Materials	$18,000			1/10 complete
Conversion costs	14,175	$32,175	Units transferred out	49,000
Materials		180,000	Units started	60,000
Labor		32,780	Ending work in process	26,000 units
Overhead		61,445		1/5 complete

Instructions
Prepare a production cost report for the Welding Department for the month of February.

*E21-14 Carmeli Instrument Inc. manufactures two products: missile range instruments and space pressure gauges. During January, 50 range instruments and 300 pressure gauges were produced, and overhead costs of $81,000 were incurred. An analysis of overhead costs reveals the following activities.

Compute overhead rates and assign overhead using ABC.
(SO 10)

Activity	Cost Driver	Total Cost
1. Materials handling	Number of requisitions	$30,000
2. Machine setups	Number of setups	27,000
3. Quality inspections	Number of inspections	24,000

The cost driver volume for each product was as follows.

Cost Driver	Instruments	Gauges	Total
Number of requisitions	400	600	1,000
Number of setups	150	300	450
Number of inspections	200	400	600

Chapter 21 Process Costing

Instructions

(a) Determine the overhead rate for each activity.

(b) Assign the manufacturing overhead costs for January to the two products using activity-based costing.

(c)  Write a memo to the president of Carmeli Instrument, explaining the benefits of activity-based costing.

Compute product cost using traditional costing and ABC.
(SO 10)

*E21-15 Oakenfeld Company manufactures a number of specialized machine parts. Part Bunkka-22 uses $35 of direct materials and $15 of direct labor per unit.

Oakenfeld's estimated manufacturing overhead is as follows:

Materials handling	$100,000
Machining	200,000
Factory supervision	150,000
Total	$450,000

Overhead is applied based on direct labor costs, which were estimated at $200,000.

Oakenfeld is considering adopting activity-based costing. The cost drivers are estimated at:

Activity	Cost driver	Expected use
Materials handling	Weight of materials	50,000 pounds
Machining	Machine hours	20,000 hours
Factory supervision	Direct labor hours	12,000 hours

Instructions

(a) Compute the cost of 1,000 units of Bunkka-22 using the current traditional costing system.

(b) Compute the cost of 1,000 units of Bunkka-22 using the proposed activity-based costing system. Assume the 1,000 units use 2,500 pounds of materials, 500 machine hours, and 1,000 direct labor hours.

EXERCISES: SET B

Visit the book's companion website at **www.wiley.com/college/weygandt**, and choose the Student Companion site, to access Exercise Set B.

PROBLEMS: SET A

Complete four steps necessary to prepare a production cost report.
(SO 5, 6, 7)

P21-1A Kasten Company manufactures bowling balls through two processes: Molding and Packaging. In the Molding Department, the urethane, rubber, plastics, and other materials are molded into bowling balls. In the Packaging Department, the balls are placed in cartons and sent to the finished goods warehouse. All materials are entered at the beginning of each process. Labor and manufacturing overhead are incurred uniformly throughout each process. Production and cost data for the Molding Department during June 2010 are presented below.

Production Data	June
Beginning work in process units	–0–
Units started into production	20,000
Ending work in process units	2,000
Percent complete—ending inventory	60%
Cost Data	
Materials	$198,000
Labor	50,400
Overhead	112,800
Total	$361,200

Instructions

(a) Prepare a schedule showing physical units of production.
(b) Determine the equivalent units of production for materials and conversion costs.
(c) Compute the unit costs of production.
(d) Determine the costs to be assigned to the units transferred and in process for June.
(e) Prepare a production cost report for the Molding Department for the month of June.

P21-2A Ortega Industries Inc. manufactures in separate processes furniture for homes. In each process, materials are entered at the beginning, and conversion costs are incurred uniformly. Production and cost data for the first process in making two products in two different manufacturing plants are as follows.

Complete four steps necessary to prepare a production cost report.

(SO 5, 6, 7)

	Cutting Department	
Production Data—July	Plant 1 T12-Tables	Plant 2 C10-Chairs
Work in process units, July 1	–0–	–0–
Units started into production	20,000	16,000
Work in process units, July 31	3,000	500
Work in process percent complete	60	80
Cost Data—July		
Work in process, July 1	$ –0–	$ –0–
Materials	380,000	288,000
Labor	234,400	125,900
Overhead	104,000	96,700
Total	$718,400	$510,600

Instructions

(a) For each plant:
  (1) Compute the physical units of production.
  (2) Compute equivalent units of production for materials and for conversion costs.
  (3) Determine the unit costs of production.
  (4) Show the assignment of costs to units transferred out and in process.
(b) Prepare the production cost report for Plant 1 for July 2010.

P21-3A Fiedel Company manufactures its product, Vitadrink, through two manufacturing processes: Mixing and Packaging. All materials are entered at the beginning of each process. On October 1, 2010, inventories consisted of Raw Materials $26,000, Work in Process—Mixing $0, Work in Process—Packaging $250,000, and Finished Goods $289,000. The beginning inventory for Packaging consisted of 10,000 units that were 50% complete as to conversion costs and fully complete as to materials. During October, 50,000 units were started into production in the Mixing Department and the following transactions were completed.

Journalize transactions.

(SO 3, 4)

1. Purchased $300,000 of raw materials on account.
2. Issued raw materials for production: Mixing $210,000 and Packaging $45,000.
3. Incurred labor costs of $248,900.
4. Used factory labor: Mixing $182,500 and Packaging $66,400.
5. Incurred $790,000 of manufacturing overhead on account.
6. Applied manufacturing overhead on the basis of $22 per machine hour. Machine hours were 28,000 in Mixing and 6,000 in Packaging.
7. Transferred 45,000 units from Mixing to Packaging at a cost of $979,000.
8. Transferred 53,000 units from Packaging to Finished Goods at a cost of $1,315,000.
9. Sold goods costing $1,604,000 for $2,500,000 on account.

Instructions
Journalize the October transactions.

Chapter 21 Process Costing

Assign costs and prepare production cost report.
(SO 5, 6, 7)

P21-4A Cavalier Company has several processing departments. Costs charged to the Assembly Department for November 2010 totaled $2,229,000 as follows.

Work in process, November 1		
Materials	$69,000	
Conversion costs	48,150	$117,150
Materials added		1,548,000
Labor		225,920
Overhead		337,930

Production records show that 35,000 units were in beginning work in process 30% complete as to conversion costs, 700,000 units were started into production, and 25,000 units were in ending work in process 40% complete as to conversion costs. Materials are entered at the beginning of each process.

Instructions
(a) Determine the equivalent units of production and the unit production costs for the Assembly Department.
(b) Determine the assignment of costs to goods transferred out and in process.
(c) Prepare a production cost report for the Assembly Department.

Determine equivalent units and unit costs and assign costs.
(SO 5, 6, 7)

P21-5A Chen Company manufactures basketballs. Materials are added at the beginning of the production process and conversion costs are incurred uniformly. Production and cost data for the month of July 2010 are as follows.

Production Data—Basketballs	Units	Percent Complete
Work in process units, July 1	500	60%
Units started into production	1,000	
Work in process units, July 31	600	30%

Cost Data—Basketballs		
Work in process, July 1		
Materials	$750	
Conversion costs	600	$1,350
Direct materials		2,400
Direct labor		1,580
Manufacturing overhead		1,060

Instructions
(a) Calculate the following.
   (1) The equivalent units of production for materials and conversion.
   (2) The unit costs of production for materials and conversion costs.
   (3) The assignment of costs to units transferred out and in process at the end of the accounting period.
(b) Prepare a production cost report for the month of July for the basketballs.

Compute equivalent units and complete production cost report.
(SO 5, 7)

P21-6A Luther Processing Company uses a weighted-average process costing system and manufactures a single product—a premium rug shampoo and cleaner. The manufacturing activity for the month of October has just been completed. A partially completed production cost report for the month of October for the mixing and cooking department is shown on page 967.

Instructions
(a) Prepare a schedule that shows how the equivalent units were computed so that you can complete the "Quantities: Units accounted for" equivalent units section shown in the production cost report, and compute October unit costs.
(b) Complete the "Cost Reconciliation Schedule" part of the production cost report on page 967.

LUTHER PROCESSING COMPANY
Mixing and Cooking Department
Production Cost Report
For the Month Ended October 31

QUANTITIES	Physical Units	Equivalent Units Materials	Equivalent Units Conversion Costs
Units to be accounted for			
Work in process, October 1	20,000		
Started into production	160,000		
Total units	180,000		
Units accounted for			
Transferred out	130,000	?	?
Work in process, October 31 (60% materials, 40% conversion costs)	50,000	?	?
Total units	180,000	?	?

COSTS	Materials	Conversion Costs	Total
Unit costs			
Costs in October	$240,000	$105,000	$345,000
Equivalent units	?	?	
Unit costs	$? +	$? =	$?
Costs to be accounted for			
Work in process, October 1			$ 30,000
Started into production			315,000
Total costs			$345,000

COST RECONCILIATION SCHEDULE

Costs accounted for			
Transferred out			$?
Work in process, October 31			
Materials		?	
Conversion costs		?	?
Total costs			?

*P21-7A Darby Electronics manufactures two large-screen television models: the Royale which sells for $1,500, and a new model, the Majestic, which sells for $1,200. The production cost per unit for each model in 2010 was as follows.

Assign overhead to products using ABC.

(SO 10)

	Royale	Majestic
Direct materials	$ 700	$420
Direct labor ($20 per hour)	100	80
Manufacturing overhead ($40 per DLH)	200	160
Total per unit cost	$1,000	$660

In 2010, Darby manufactured 30,000 units of the Royale and 10,000 units of the Majestic. The overhead rate of $40 per direct labor hour was determined by dividing total expected manufacturing overhead of $7,600,000 by the total direct labor hours (190,000) for the two models.

The gross profit on the model was: Royale $500 ($1,500 − $1,000) and Majestic $540 ($1,200 − $660). Because of this difference, management is considering phasing out the Royale model and increasing the production of the Majestic model.

Before finalizing its decision, management asks the controller, Marie Stumfall, to prepare an analysis using activity-based costing. Marie accumulates the following information about overhead for the year ended December 31, 2010.

Activity	Cost Driver	Total Cost	Cost Driver Volume	Overhead Rate
Purchase orders	Number of orders	$1,200,000	30,000	$40
Machine setups	Number of setups	900,000	15,000	60
Machining	Machine hours	4,800,000	160,000	30
Quality control	Number of inspections	700,000	35,000	20

The cost driver volume for each product was:

Cost Driver	Royale	Majestic	Total
Purchase orders	16,000	14,000	30,000
Machine setups	5,000	10,000	15,000
Machine hours	100,000	60,000	160,000
Inspections	10,000	25,000	35,000

Instructions
(a) Assign the total 2010 manufacturing overhead costs to the two products using activity-based costing (ABC).
(b) What was the cost per unit and gross profit of each model using ABC costing?
(c) Are management's future plans for the two models sound?

PROBLEMS: SET B

Complete four steps necessary to prepare a production cost report.
(SO 5, 6, 7)

P21-1B Walters Corporation manufactures water skis through two processes: Molding and Packaging. In the Molding Department fiberglass is heated and shaped into the form of a ski. In the Packaging Department, the skis are placed in cartons and sent to the finished goods warehouse. Materials are entered at the beginning of both processes. Labor and manufacturing overhead are incurred uniformly throughout each process. Production and cost data for the Molding Department for January 2010 are presented below.

Production Data	January
Beginning work in process units	–0–
Units started into production	42,500
Ending work in process units	2,500
Percent complete—ending inventory	40%

Cost Data	
Materials	$510,000
Labor	96,000
Overhead	150,000
Total	$756,000

Instructions
(a) Compute the physical units of production.
(b) Determine the equivalent units of production for materials and conversion costs.
(c) Compute the unit costs of production.
(d) Determine the costs to be assigned to the units transferred out and in process.
(e) Prepare a production cost report for the Molding Department for the month of January.

Complete four steps necessary to prepare a production cost report.
(SO 5, 6, 7)

P21-2B Slocum Corporation manufactures in separate processes refrigerators and freezers for homes. In each process, materials are entered at the beginning and conversion costs are incurred uniformly. Production and cost data for the first process in making two products in two different manufacturing plants are as follows.

	Stamping Department	
Production Data—June	Plant A R12 Refrigerators	Plant B F24 Freezers
Work in process units, June 1	–0–	–0–
Units started into production	21,000	20,000
Work in process units, June 30	4,000	2,500
Work in process percent complete	75	60
Cost Data—June		
Work in process, June 1	$ –0–	$ –0–
Materials	840,000	720,000
Labor	220,000	221,000
Overhead	420,000	292,000
Total	$1,480,000	$1,233,000

Instructions
(a) For each plant:
  (1) Compute the physical units of production.
  (2) Compute equivalent units of production for materials and for conversion costs.
  (3) Determine the unit costs of production.
  (4) Show the assignment of costs to units transferred out and in process.
(b) Prepare the production cost report for Plant A for June 2010.

P21-3B Buehler Company manufactures a nutrient, Everlife, through two manufacturing processes: Blending and Packaging. All materials are entered at the beginning of each process. On August 1, 2010, inventories consisted of Raw Materials $5,000, Work in Process—Blending $0, Work in Process—Packaging $3,945, and Finished Goods $7,500. The beginning inventory for Packaging consisted of 500 units, two-fifths complete as to conversion costs and fully complete as to materials. During August, 9,000 units were started into production in Blending, and the following transactions were completed.

Journalize transactions.
(SO 3, 4)

1. Purchased $25,000 of raw materials on account.
2. Issued raw materials for production: Blending $18,930 and Packaging $9,140.
3. Incurred labor costs of $23,770.
4. Used factory labor: Blending $13,320 and Packaging $10,450.
5. Incurred $41,500 of manufacturing overhead on account.
6. Applied manufacturing overhead at the rate of $25 per machine hour. Machine hours were Blending 900 and Packaging 300.
7. Transferred 8,200 units from Blending to Packaging at a cost of $44,940.
8. Transferred 8,600 units from Packaging to Finished Goods at a cost of $67,490.
9. Sold goods costing $62,000 for $90,000 on account.

Instructions
Journalize the August transactions.

P21-4B McNair Company has several processing departments. Costs charged to the Assembly Department for October 2010 totaled $1,249,500 as follows.

Assign costs and prepare production cost report.
(SO 5, 6, 7)

Work in process, October 1		
Materials	$29,000	
Conversion costs	16,500	$ 45,500
Materials added		1,006,000
Labor		90,000
Overhead		108,000

Production records show that 25,000 units were in beginning work in process 40% complete as to conversion cost, 425,000 units were started into production, and 35,000 units were in ending work in process 40% complete as to conversion costs. Materials are entered at the beginning of each process.

Instructions
(a) Determine the equivalent units of production and the unit production costs for the Assembly Department.
(b) Determine the assignment of costs to goods transferred out and in process.
(c) Prepare a production cost report for the Assembly Department.

Determine equivalent units and unit costs and assign costs.
(SO 5, 7)

P21-5B Marte Company manufactures bicycles and tricycles. For both products, materials are added at the beginning of the production process, and conversion costs are incurred uniformly. Production and cost data for the month of May are as follows.

Production Data—Bicycles	Units	Percent Complete
Work in process units, May 1	500	80%
Units started in production	1,500	
Work in process units, May 31	800	25%

Cost Data—Bicycles		
Work in process, May 1		
Materials	$15,000	
Conversion costs	18,000	$ 33,000
Direct materials		50,000
Direct labor		18,320
Manufacturing overhead		33,680

Instructions
(a) Calculate the following.
  (1) The equivalent units of production for materials and conversion.
  (2) The unit costs of production for materials and conversion costs.
  (3) The assignment of costs to units transferred out and in process at the end of the accounting period.
(b) Prepare a production cost report for the month of May for the bicycles.

Compute equivalent units and complete production cost report.
(SO 5, 6, 7)

P21-6B Guthrie Cleaner Company uses a weighted-average process costing system and manufactures a single product—an all-purpose liquid cleaner. The manufacturing activity for the month of March has just been completed. A partially completed production cost report for the month of March for the mixing and blending department is shown below.

GUTHRIE CLEANER COMPANY
Mixing and Blending Department
Production Cost Report
For the Month Ended March 31

		Equivalent Units	
QUANTITIES	Physical Units	Materials	Conversion Costs
Units to be accounted for			
Work in process, March 1	10,000		
Started into production	100,000		
Total units	110,000		
Units accounted for			
Transferred out	95,000	?	?
Work in process, March 31 (60% materials, 20% conversion costs)	15,000	?	?
Total units	110,000	?	?

COSTS	Materials	Conversion Costs	Total
Unit costs			
Costs in March	$156,000	$98,000	$254,000
Equivalent units	?	?	
Unit costs	$?	+ $?	= $?

Costs to be accounted for
Work in process, March 1 $ 8,700
Started into production   245,300
Total costs $254,000

COST RECONCILIATION SCHEDULE

Costs accounted for
Transferred out $?
Work in process, March 31
  Materials   ?
  Conversion costs   ?   ?
    Total costs   ?

Instructions

(a) Prepare a schedule that shows how the equivalent units were computed so that you can complete the "Quantities: Units accounted for" equivalent units section shown in the production cost report above, and compute March unit costs.

(b) Complete the "Cost Reconciliation Schedule" part of the production cost report above.

PROBLEMS: SET C

Visit the book's companion website at **www.wiley.com/college/weygandt**, and choose the Student Companion site, to access Problem Set C.

WATERWAYS CONTINUING PROBLEM

(Note: This is a continuation of the Waterways Problem from Chapters 19 and 20.)

WCP21 Because most of the parts for its irrigation systems are standard, Waterways handles the majority of its manufacturing as a process cost system. There are multiple process departments. Three of these departments are the Molding, Cutting, and Welding departments. All items eventually end up in the Packaging department which prepares items for sale in kits or individually. This problem asks you to help Waterways calculate equivalent units and prepare a production cost report.

Go to the book's companion website,
www.wiley.com/college/weygandt,
to find the remainder of this problem.

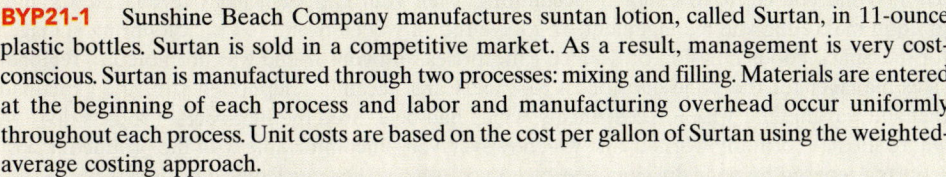

Decision Making Across the Organization

BYP21-1 Sunshine Beach Company manufactures suntan lotion, called Surtan, in 11-ounce plastic bottles. Surtan is sold in a competitive market. As a result, management is very cost-conscious. Surtan is manufactured through two processes: mixing and filling. Materials are entered at the beginning of each process and labor and manufacturing overhead occur uniformly throughout each process. Unit costs are based on the cost per gallon of Surtan using the weighted-average costing approach.

On June 30, 2010, Jill Ritzman, the chief accountant for the past 20 years, opted to take early retirement. Her replacement, Sid Benili, had extensive accounting experience with motels in the area but only limited contact with manufacturing accounting. During July, Sid correctly accumulated the following production quantity and cost data for the Mixing Department.

Production quantities: Work in process, July 1, 8,000 gallons 75% complete; started into production 91,000 gallons; work in process, July 31, 5,000 gallons 20% complete. Materials are added at the beginning of the process.

Production costs: Beginning work in process $88,000, comprised of $21,000 of materials costs and $67,000 of conversion costs; incurred in July: materials $573,000, conversion costs $769,000.

Sid then prepared a production cost report on the basis of physical units started into production. His report showed a production cost of $15.71 per gallon of Surtan. The management of Sunshine Beach was surprised at the high unit cost. The president comes to you, as Jill's top assistant, to review Sid's report and prepare a correct report if necessary.

Instructions
With the class divided into groups, answer the following questions.

(a) Show how Sid arrived at the unit cost of $15.71 per gallon of Surtan.
(b) What error(s) did Sid make in preparing his production cost report?
(c) Prepare a correct production cost report for July.

Managerial Analysis

BYP21-2 Guion Furniture Company manufactures living room furniture through two departments: Framing and Upholstering. Materials are entered at the beginning of each process. For May, the following cost data are obtained from the two work in process accounts.

	Framing	Upholstering
Work in process, May 1	$ –0–	$?
Materials	420,000	?
Conversion costs	280,000	330,000
Costs transferred in	–0–	600,000
Costs transferred out	600,000	?
Work in process, May 31	100,000	?

Instructions
Answer the following questions.

(a) If 3,000 sofas were started into production on May 1 and 2,500 sofas were transferred to Upholstering, what was the unit cost of materials for May in the Framing Department?
(b) Using the data in (a) above, what was the per unit conversion cost of the sofas transferred to Upholstering?
(c) Continuing the assumptions in (a) above, what is the percentage of completion of the units in process at May 31 in the Framing Department?

Exploring the Web

BYP21-3 Search the Internet and find the websites of two manufacturers that you think are likely to use process costing. Are there any specifics included in their websites that confirm the use of process costing for each of these companies?

Communication Activity

BYP21-4 Carol Gorden was a good friend of yours in high school and is from your home town. While you chose to major in accounting when you both went away to college, she majored in marketing and management. You have recently been promoted to accounting manager for the Snack Foods Division of Koonce Enterprises, and your friend was promoted to regional sales manager for the same division of Koonce. Carol recently telephoned you. She explained that she was familiar with job cost sheets, which had been used by the Special Projects division where she had formerly worked. She was, however, very uncomfortable with the production cost reports prepared by your division. She faxed you a list of her particular questions:

1. Since Koonce occasionally prepares snack foods for special orders in the Snack Foods Division, why don't we track costs of the orders separately?
2. What is an equivalent unit?
3. Why am I getting four production cost reports? Isn't there one Work in Process account?

Instructions
Prepare a memo to Carol. Answer her questions, and include any additional information you think would be helpful. You may write informally, but do use proper grammar and punctuation.

Ethics Case

BYP21-5 R. B. Patrick Company manufactures a high-tech component that passes through two production processing departments, Molding and Assembly. Department managers are partially compensated on the basis of units of products completed and transferred out relative to units of product put into production. This was intended as encouragement to be efficient and to minimize waste.

Sue Wooten is the department head in the Molding Department, and Fred Barando is her quality control inspector. During the month of June, Sue had three new employees who were not yet technically skilled. As a result, many of the units produced in June had minor molding defects. In order to maintain the department's normal high rate of completion, Sue told Fred to pass through inspection and on to the Assembly Department all units that had defects nondetectable to the human eye. "Company and industry tolerances on this product are too high anyway," says Sue. "Less than 2% of the units we produce are subjected in the market to the stress tolerance we've designed into them. The odds of those 2% being any of this month's units are even less. Anyway, we're saving the company money."

Instructions
(a) Who are the potential stakeholders involved in this situation?
(b) What alternatives does Fred have in this situation? What might the company do to prevent this situation from occurring?

"All About You" Activity

BYP21-6 Many of you ultimately will work in service environments, such as medical facilities. Many service organizations have adopted activity-based management systems, which incorporate activity-based costing concepts throughout the organization.

East Valley Hospital is a primary medical health-care facility and trauma center that serves 11 small, rural Midwestern communities within a 40-mile radius. The hospital offers all the medical/surgical services of a typical small hospital. It has a staff of 18 full-time doctors and 20 part-time visiting specialists. East Valley has a payroll of 150 employees, consisting of nurses, technicians, therapists, dieticians, managers, directors, administrators, secretaries, data processors, and janitors.

Instructions
(a) Using your existing knowledge (however limited, moderate, or in-depth) of a hospital's operations, identify as many *activities* as you can that would serve as the basis for implementing an activity-based costing system.
(b) For each of the activities listed in (a), identify a *cost driver* that would serve as a valid measure of the resources consumed in the activity.

Answers to Insight and Accounting Across the Organization Questions

p. 935 Choosing a Cost Driver
Q: What is the result if a company uses the wrong "cost driver" to assign manufacturing overhead?
A: *Incorrect application of manufacturing overhead will result in some products receiving too much overhead and others receiving too little.*

p. 940 Keeping Score for the Xbox
Q: In what ways has cost accounting probably become more critical for Microsoft in recent years?
A: *In the past Microsoft enjoyed very high profit margins on its software sales. As a consequence, it could afford to be less cost-conscious than most companies. In addition, in producing software, manufacturing costs represented a very small part of its total product cost. But the video-game hardware market is very competitive. In order to achieve its profitability goals, Microsoft will have to manufacture its product efficiently in order to meet its cost targets to ensure adequate margins. The information provided by process cost accounting will be critical to its efforts.*

Answers to Self-Study Questions
1. b 2. d 3. c 4. b 5. c 6. b 7. b 8. a 9. c 10. a 11. b 12. b 13. d
14. d 15. c 16. a 17. c 18. b

Remember to go back to the Navigator box on the chapter-opening page and check off your completed work.

Chapter 22

Cost-Volume-Profit

STUDY OBJECTIVES

After studying this chapter, you should be able to:

1. Distinguish between variable and fixed costs.
2. Explain the significance of the relevant range.
3. Explain the concept of mixed costs.
4. List the five components of cost-volume-profit analysis.
5. Indicate what contribution margin is and how it can be expressed.
6. Identify the three ways to determine the break-even point.
7. Give the formulas for determining sales required to earn target net income.
8. Define margin of safety, and give the formulas for computing it.
9. Describe the essential features of a cost-volume-profit income statement.

✓ The Navigator

Scan **Study Objectives**	■
Read **Feature Story**	■
Read **Preview**	■
Read text and answer **DO IT!** p. 981 ■ p. 983 ■ p. 989 ■ p. 994 ■	
Work **Comprehensive** 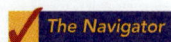 p. 996	
Review **Summary of Study Objectives**	■
Answer **Self-Study Questions**	■
Complete **Assignments**	■

✓ The Navigator

Feature Story

GROWING BY LEAPS AND LEOTARDS

When the last of her three children went off to school, Amy began looking for a job. At this same time, her daughter asked to take dance classes. The nearest dance studio was over 20 miles away, and Amy didn't know how she would balance a new job and drive her daughter to dance class. Suddenly it hit her—why not start her own dance studio?

Amy sketched out a business plan: A local church would rent its basement to her for $6 per hour. The size of the basement limited the number of students she could teach, but the rent was low. Insurance for a small studio was $50 per month. Initially she would teach only classes for young kids since that was all she felt qualified to do. She thought she could charge $2.50 for a one-hour class. There was room for eight students per class. She wouldn't get rich—but at least it would be fun, and she didn't have much at risk.

Amy soon realized that the demand for dance classes far exceeded her capacity. She considered renting a bigger space that could serve 15 students per class. But her rent would also increase significantly. Also, rather than paying rent by the hour, she would have to pay $600 per month, even during the summer months when demand for dance classes was low. She also would have to pay utilities—roughly $70 per month.

However, with a bigger space Amy could offer classes for teens and adults. Teens and adults would pay a higher fee—$5 per hour—though the number of students per class would have to be smaller, probably only eight per class. She could hire a part-time instructor at about $18 per hour to teach advanced classes. Insurance costs could increase to $100 per month. In addition, she would need a part-time administrator at $100 per month to keep records. Amy also realized she could increase her income by selling dance supplies such as shoes, towels, and leotards.

Amy laid out a new business plan based on these estimates. If she failed, she stood to lose real money. Convinced she could make a go of it, she made the big plunge.

Her planning paid off: Within 10 years of starting her business in a church basement Amy had over 800 students, seven instructors, two administrators, and a facility with three separate studios.

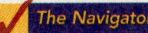

Inside Chapter 22...

- **Charter Flights Offer a Good Deal** (p. 988)
- **How a Rolling Stones' Tour Makes Money** (p. 991)
- ***All About You:* A Hybrid Dilemma** (p. 995)

Preview of Chapter 22

As the Feature Story indicates, to manage any size business you must understand how costs respond to changes in sales volume and the effect of costs and revenues on profits. A prerequisite to understanding cost-volume-profit (CVP) relationships is knowledge of how costs behave. In this chapter, we first explain the considerations involved in cost behavior analysis. Then we discuss and illustrate CVP analysis.

The content and organization of Chapter 22 are as follows.

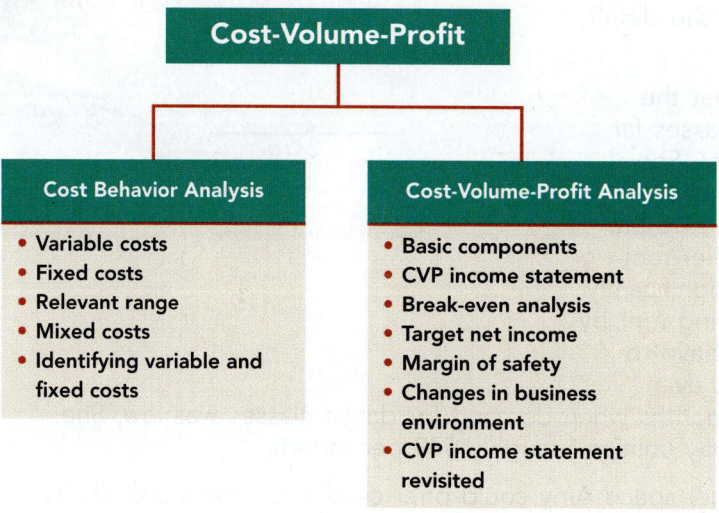

COST BEHAVIOR ANALYSIS

Cost behavior analysis is the study of how specific costs respond to changes in the level of business activity. As you might expect, some costs change, and others remain the same. For example, for an airline company such as Southwest or United, the longer the flight the higher the fuel costs. On the other hand, Massachusetts General Hospital's costs to staff the emergency room on any given night are relatively constant regardless of the number of patients treated. A knowledge of cost behavior helps management plan operations and decide between alternative courses of action. Cost behavior analysis applies to all types of entities, as the Feature Story about Amy's dance studio indicates.

The starting point in cost behavior analysis is measuring the key business activities. Activity levels may be expressed in terms of sales dollars (in a retail company), miles driven (in a trucking company), room occupancy (in a hotel), or dance classes taught (by a dance studio). Many companies use more than one measurement base. A manufacturer, for example, may use direct labor hours or units of output for manufacturing costs and sales revenue or units sold for selling expenses.

For an activity level to be useful in cost behavior analysis, changes in the level or volume of activity should be correlated with changes in costs. The activity level selected is referred to as the activity (or volume) index. The **activity index** identifies the activity that causes changes in the behavior of costs. With an appropriate activity index, companies can classify the behavior of costs in response to changes in activity levels into three categories: variable, fixed, or mixed.

Variable Costs

Variable costs are costs that vary **in total** directly and proportionately with changes in the activity level. If the level increases 10%, total variable costs will increase 10%. If the level of activity decreases by 25%, variable costs will decrease 25%. Examples of variable costs include direct materials and direct labor for a manufacturer; cost of goods sold, sales commissions, and freight-out for a merchandiser; and gasoline in airline and trucking companies. A variable cost may also be defined as a cost that **remains the same *per unit* at every level of activity**.

> **STUDY OBJECTIVE 1**
> Distinguish between variable and fixed costs.

To illustrate the behavior of a variable cost, assume that Damon Company manufactures radios that contain a $10 digital clock. The activity index is the number of radios produced. As Damon manufactures each radio, the total cost of the clocks increases by $10. As part (a) of Illustration 22-1 shows, total cost of the clocks will be $20,000 if Damon produces 2,000 radios, and $100,000 when it produces 10,000 radios. We also can see that a variable cost remains the same per unit as the level of activity changes. As part (b) of Illustration 22-1 shows, the unit cost of $10 for the clocks is the same whether Damon produces 2,000 or 10,000 radios.

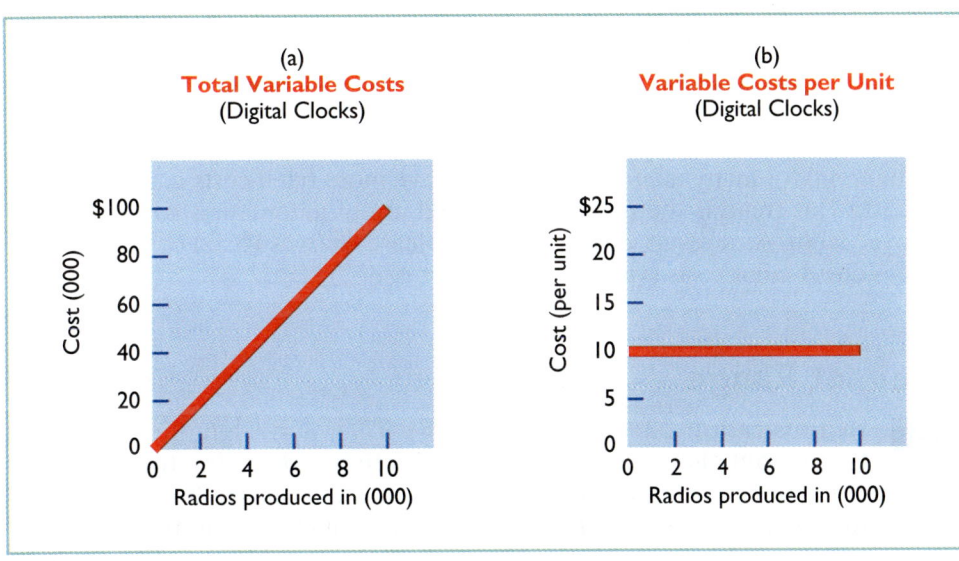

Illustration 22-1
Behavior of total and unit variable costs

> **HELPFUL HINT**
> True or false: Variable cost per unit changes directly and proportionately with changes in activity.
> Answer: False. Per unit cost remains constant at all levels of activity.

Companies that rely heavily on labor to manufacture a product, such as Nike or Reebok, or to provide a service, such as Hilton or Marriott, are likely to have many variable costs. In contrast, companies that use a high proportion of machinery and equipment in producing revenue, such as AT&T or Duke Energy Co., may have few variable costs.

Fixed Costs

Fixed costs are costs that **remain the same in total** regardless of changes in the activity level. Examples include property taxes, insurance, rent, supervisory salaries, and depreciation on buildings and equipment. Because total fixed costs remain constant as activity changes, it follows that **fixed costs *per unit* vary inversely with activity: As volume increases, unit cost declines, and vice versa**.

To illustrate the behavior of fixed costs, assume that Damon Company leases its productive facilities at a cost of $10,000 per month. Total fixed costs of the facilities will remain constant at every level of activity, as part (a) of Illustration 22-2 (page 978) shows. But, on a per unit basis, the cost of rent will

978 Chapter 22 Cost-Volume-Profit

decline as activity increases, as part (b) of Illustration 22-2 shows. At 2,000 units, the unit cost is $5 ($10,000 ÷ 2,000). When Damon produces 10,000 radios, the unit cost is only $1 ($10,000 ÷ 10,000).

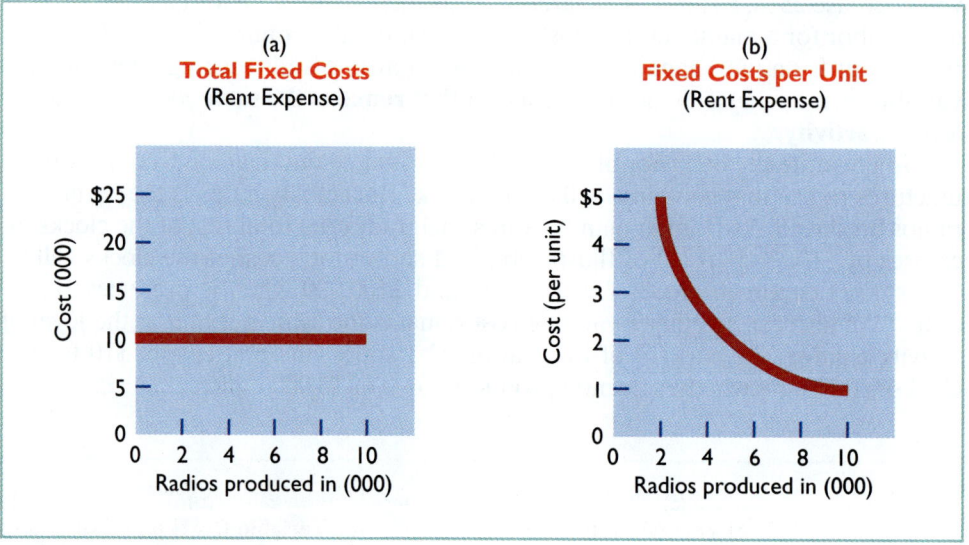

Illustration 22-2
Behavior of total and unit fixed costs

The trend for many manufacturers is to have more fixed costs and fewer variable costs. This trend is the result of increased use of automation and less use of employee labor. As a result, depreciation and lease charges (fixed costs) increase, whereas direct labor costs (variable costs) decrease.

Relevant Range

> **STUDY OBJECTIVE 2**
> Explain the significance of the relevant range.

In Illustration 22-1, part (a), (page 977), a straight line is drawn throughout the entire range of the activity index for total variable costs. In essence, the assumption is that the costs are **linear**. If a relationship is linear (that is, straight-line), then changes in the activity index will result in a direct, proportional change in the variable cost. For example, if the activity level doubles, the cost doubles.

It is now necessary to ask: Is the straight-line relationship realistic? Does the linear assumption produce useful data for CVP analysis?

In most business situations, a straight-line relationship **does not exist** for variable costs throughout the entire range of possible activity. At abnormally low levels of activity, it may be impossible to be cost-efficient. Small-scale operations may not allow the company to obtain quantity discounts for raw materials or to use specialized labor. In contrast, at abnormally high levels of activity, labor costs may increase sharply because of overtime pay. Also at high activity levels, materials costs may jump significantly because of excess spoilage caused by worker fatigue.

As a result, in the real world, the relationship between the behavior of a variable cost and changes in the activity level is often **curvilinear**, as shown in part (a) of Illustration 22-3 (next page). In the curved sections of the line, a change in the activity index will not result in a direct, proportional change in the variable cost. That is, a doubling of the activity index will not result in an exact doubling of the variable cost. The variable cost may more than double, or it may be less than double.

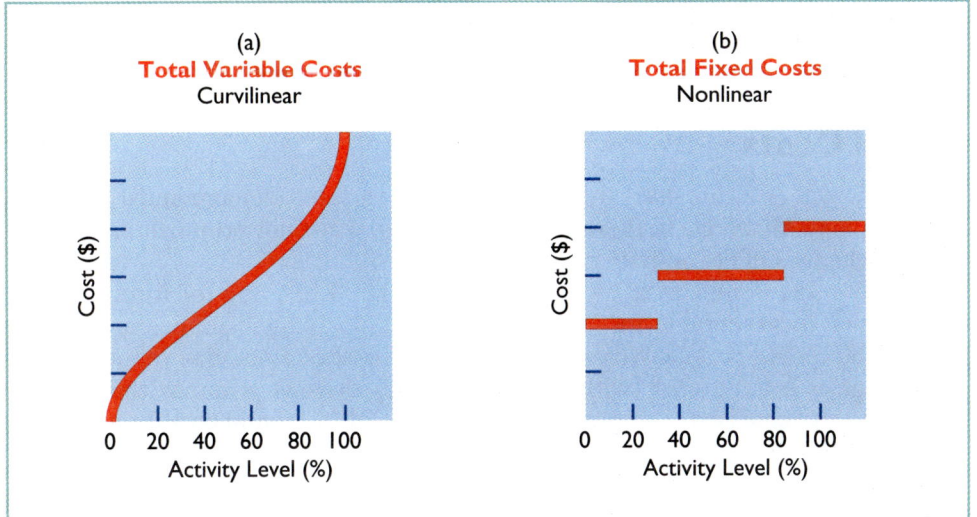

Illustration 22-3
Nonlinear behavior of variable and fixed costs

Total fixed costs also do not have a straight-line relationship over the entire range of activity. Some fixed costs will not change. But it is possible for management to change other fixed costs. For example, in the Feature Story the dance studio's rent was originally variable and then became fixed at a certain amount. It then increased to a new fixed amount when the size of the studio increased beyond a certain point. Illustration 23-3, part (b), shows an example of the behavior of total fixed costs through all potential levels of activity.

For most companies, operating at almost zero or at 100% capacity is the exception rather than the rule. Instead, companies often operate over a somewhat narrower range, such as 40–80% of capacity. The range over which a company expects to operate during a year is called the **relevant range** of the activity index. Within the relevant range, as both diagrams in Illustration 22-4 show, a straight-line relationship generally exists for both variable and fixed costs.

> **HELPFUL HINT**
> Fixed costs that may be changeable include research, such as new product development, and management training programs.

> **ALTERNATIVE TERMINOLOGY**
> The relevant range is also called the *normal* or *practical range*.

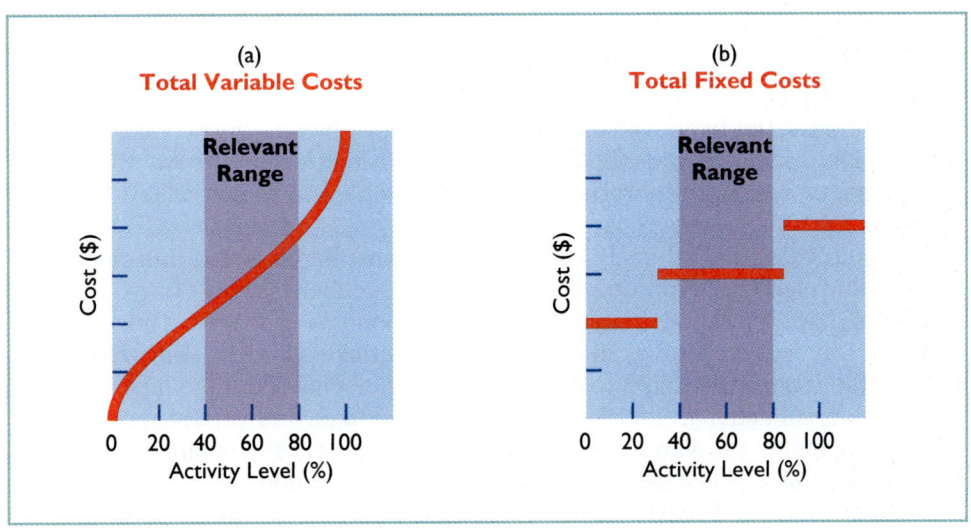

Illustration 22-4
Linear behavior within relevant range

980 Chapter 22 Cost-Volume-Profit

As you can see, although the linear (straight-line) relationship may not be completely realistic, **the linear assumption produces useful data for CVP analysis as long as the level of activity remains within the relevant range**.

Mixed Costs

STUDY OBJECTIVE 3
Explain the concept of mixed costs.

Mixed costs are costs that contain both a variable element and a fixed element. **Mixed costs, therefore, change in total but not proportionately with changes in the activity level**.

The rental of a U-Haul truck is a good example of a mixed cost. Assume that local rental terms for a 17-foot truck, including insurance, are $50 per day plus 50 cents per mile. When determining the cost of a one-day rental, the per day charge is a fixed cost (with respect to miles driven), whereas the mileage charge is a variable cost. The graphic presentation of the rental cost for a one-day rental is as follows.

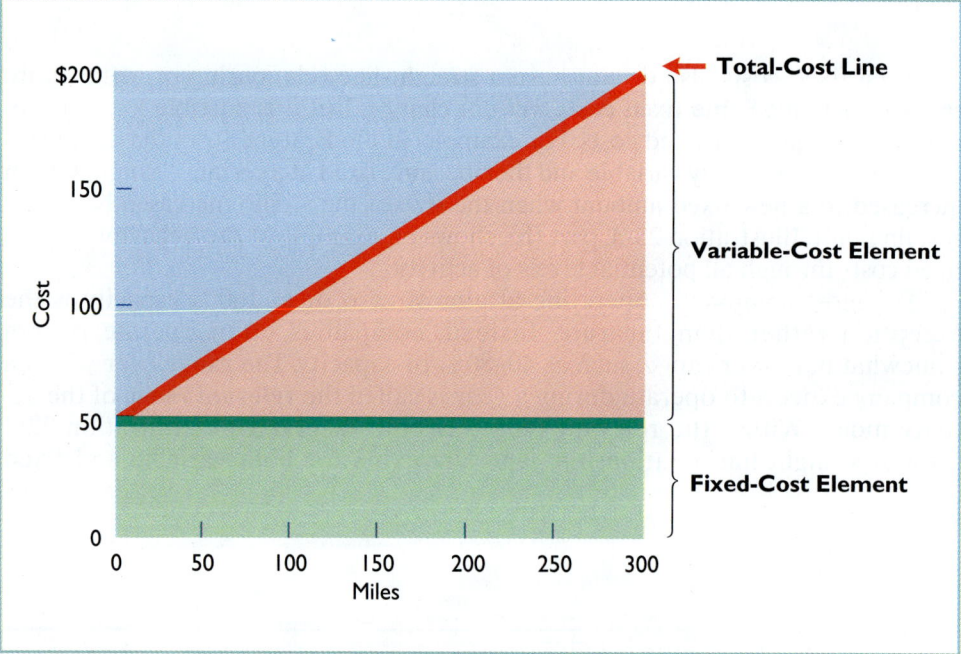

Illustration 22-5
Behavior of a mixed cost

In this case, the fixed-cost element is the cost of having the service available. The variable-cost element is the cost of actually using the service. Another example of a mixed cost is utility costs (electric, telephone, and so on), where there is a flat service fee plus a usage charge.

For purposes of CVP analysis, **mixed costs must be classified into their fixed and variable elements**. How does management make the classification? One possibility is to determine the variable and fixed components each time a mixed cost is incurred. But because of time and cost constraints, this approach is rarely followed. Instead, the usual approach is to collect data on the behavior of the mixed costs at various levels of activity. Analysts then identify the fixed and variable cost components. Companies use various types of analysis. One type of analysis, called the **high-low method**, is discussed on page 981. Other methods, such as the scatter diagram method and least squares regression analysis, are more appropriately explained in cost accounting courses.

DO IT!

TYPES OF COSTS

Helena Company reports the following total costs at two levels of production.

	10,000 Units	20,000 Units
Direct materials	$20,000	$40,000
Maintenance	8,000	10,000
Direct labor	17,000	34,000
Indirect materials	1,000	2,000
Depreciation	4,000	4,000
Utilities	3,000	5,000
Rent	6,000	6,000

Classify each cost as variable, fixed, or mixed.

Solution

Variable costs: Direct materials, direct labor, and indirect materials are variable costs.

Fixed costs: Depreciation and rent are fixed costs.

Mixed costs: Maintenance and utilities are mixed costs.

Related exercise material: **BE22-1, BE22-2, E22-1, E22-2, E22-3,** and **DO IT!** 22-1.

action plan

✔ Recall that a variable cost varies in total directly and proportionately with each change in activity.

✔ Recall that a fixed cost remains the same in total with each change in activity.

✔ Recall that a mixed cost changes in total but not proportionately with each change in activity.

HIGH-LOW METHOD

The **high-low method** uses the total costs incurred at the high and low levels of activity to classify mixed costs into fixed and variable components. The difference in costs between the high and low levels represents variable costs, since only the variable cost element can change as activity levels change.

The steps in computing fixed and variable costs under this method are as follows.

1. Determine variable cost per unit from the following formula.

| Change in Total Costs | ÷ | High minus Low Activity Level | = | Variable Cost per Unit |

Illustration 22-6
Formula for variable cost per unit using high-low method

To illustrate, assume that Metro Transit Company has the following maintenance costs and mileage data for its fleet of buses over a 4-month period.

Month	Miles Driven	Total Cost	Month	Miles Driven	Total Cost
January	20,000	$30,000	March	35,000	$49,000
February	40,000	48,000	April	50,000	63,000

Illustration 22-7
Assumed maintenance costs and mileage data

The high and low levels of activity are 50,000 miles in April and 20,000 miles in January. The maintenance costs at these two levels are $63,000 and $30,000, respectively. The difference in maintenance costs is $33,000 ($63,000 − $30,000), and the difference in miles is 30,000 (50,000 − 20,000). Therefore, for Metro Transit, variable cost per unit is $1.10, computed as follows.

$$\$33,000 \div 30,000 = \$1.10$$

2. **Determine the fixed cost by subtracting the total variable cost at either the high or the low activity level from the total cost at that activity level.**

For Metro Transit, the computations are shown in Illustration 22-8.

Illustration 22-8
High-low method computation of fixed costs

	A	B	C	D
1			METRO TRANSIT	
2			Activity Level	
3			High	Low
4	Total cost		$63,000	$30,000
5	Less:	Variable costs		
6		50,000 × $1.10	55,000	
7		20,000 × $1.10		22,000
8	Total fixed costs		$ 8,000	$ 8,000

Maintenance costs are therefore $8,000 per month plus $1.10 per mile. This is represented by the following formula:

$$\text{Maintenance costs} = \text{Fixed costs} + (\$1.10 \times \text{miles driven})$$

For example, at 45,000 miles, estimated maintenance costs would be $8,000 fixed and $49,500 variable ($1.10 × 45,000) for a total of $57,500.

The high-low method generally produces a reasonable estimate for analysis. However, it does not produce a precise measurement of the fixed and variable elements in a mixed cost because it ignores other activity levels in the computation.

Importance of Identifying Variable and Fixed Costs

Why is it important to segregate costs into variable and fixed elements? The answer may become apparent if we look at the following four business decisions.

1. If American Airlines is to make a profit when it reduces all domestic fares by 30%, what reduction in costs or increase in passengers will be required?
   Answer: To make a profit when it cuts domestic fares by 30%, American Airlines will have to increase the number of passengers or cut its variable costs for those flights. Its fixed costs will not change.

2. If Ford Motor Company meets workers' demands for higher wages, what increase in sales revenue will be needed to maintain current profit levels?
   Answer: Higher wages at Ford Motor Company will increase the variable costs of manufacturing automobiles. To maintain present profit levels, Ford will have to cut other variable costs or increase the price of its automobiles.

3. If United States Steel Corp.'s program to modernize plant facilities through significant equipment purchases reduces the work force by 50%, what will be the effect on the cost of producing one ton of steel?
   Answer: The modernizing of plant facilities at United States Steel Corp. changes the proportion of fixed and variable costs of producing one ton of steel. Fixed costs increase because of higher depreciation charges, whereas variable costs decrease due to the reduction in the number of steelworkers.

4. What happens if Kellogg Company increases its advertising expenses but cannot increase prices because of competitive pressure?
   Answer: Sales volume must be increased to cover the increase in fixed advertising costs.

Cost-Volume-Profit Analysis 983

DO IT!

Byrnes Company accumulates the following data concerning a mixed cost, using units produced as the activity level.

HIGH-LOW METHOD

	Units Produced	Total Cost
March	9,800	$14,740
April	8,500	13,250
May	7,000	11,100
June	7,600	12,000
July	8,100	12,460

(a) Compute the variable and fixed cost elements using the high-low method.
(b) Estimate the total cost if the company produces 6,000 units.

action plan

✔ Determine the highest and lowest levels of activity.

✔ Compute variable cost per unit as: Change in total costs ÷ High − Low activity level = Variable cost per unit.

✔ Compute fixed cost as: Total cost − (Variable cost per unit × Units produced) = Fixed cost.

Solution

(a) Variable cost: ($14,740 − $11,100) ÷ (9,800 − 7,000) = $1.30 per unit
Fixed cost: $14,740 − $12,740 ($1.30 × 9,800 units) = $2,000
or $11,100 − $9,100 ($1.30 × 7,000) = $2,000

(b) Total cost to produce 6,000 units: $2,000 + $7,800 ($1.30 × 6,000) = $9,800

Related exercise material: **BE22-3, BE22-4, E22-1, E22-2, E22-3,** and **DO IT! 22-2.**

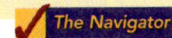

COST-VOLUME-PROFIT ANALYSIS

Cost-volume-profit (CVP) analysis is the study of the effects of changes in costs and volume on a company's profits. CVP analysis is important in profit planning. It also is a critical factor in such management decisions as setting selling prices, determining product mix, and maximizing use of production facilities.

STUDY OBJECTIVE 4
List the five components of cost-volume-profit analysis.

Basic Components

CVP analysis considers the interrelationships among the components shown in Illustration 22-9.

Illustration 22-9
Components of CVP analysis

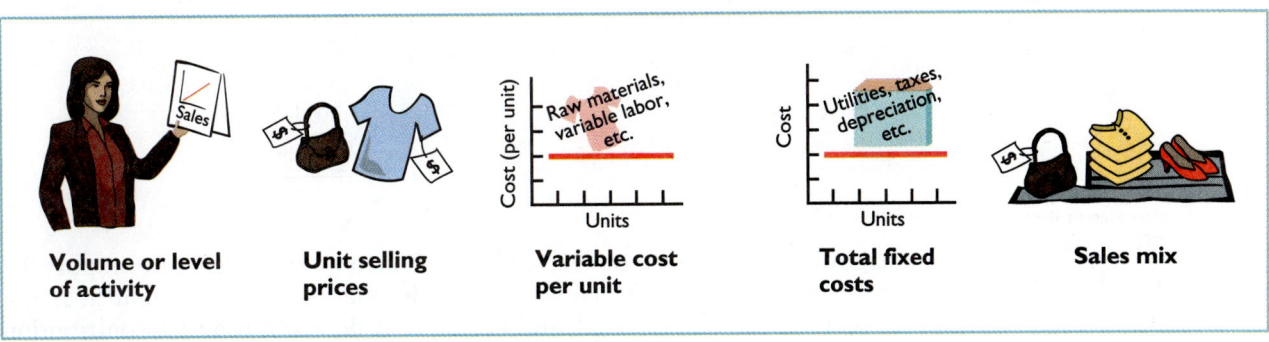

Volume or level of activity | Unit selling prices | Variable cost per unit | Total fixed costs | Sales mix

The following assumptions underlie each CVP analysis.

1. The behavior of both costs and revenues is linear throughout the relevant range of the activity index.
2. Costs can be classified accurately as either variable or fixed.

3. Changes in activity are the only factors that affect costs.
4. All units produced are sold.
5. When more than one type of product is sold, the sales mix will remain constant. That is, the percentage that each product represents of total sales will stay the same. Sales mix complicates CVP analysis because different products will have different cost relationships. In this chapter we assume a single product.

When these assumptions are not valid, the CVP analysis may be inaccurate.

CVP Income Statement

STUDY OBJECTIVE 5
Indicate what contribution margin is and how it can be expressed.

Because CVP is so important for decision making, management often wants this information reported in a **CVP income statement** format for internal use. The CVP income statement classifies costs as variable or fixed and computes a contribution margin. **Contribution margin** is the amount of revenue remaining after deducting variable costs. It is often stated both as a total amount and on a per unit basis.

We will use Vargo Video Company to illustrate a CVP income statement. Vargo Video produces a high-end, progressive-scan DVD player/recorder with up to 160-hour recording capacity and MP3 playback capability. Relevant data for the DVD players sold by this company in June 2010 are as follows.

Illustration 22-10
Assumed selling and cost data for Vargo Video

Unit selling price of DVD player	$500
Unit variable costs	$300
Total monthly fixed costs	$200,000
Units sold	1,600

The CVP income statement for Vargo Video therefore would be reported as follows.

Illustration 22-11
CVP income statement, with net income

VARGO VIDEO COMPANY
CVP Income Statement
For the Month Ended June 30, 2010

	Total	Per Unit
Sales (1,600 DVD players)	$800,000	$500
Variable costs	480,000	300
Contribution margin	**320,000**	**$200**
Fixed costs	200,000	
Net income	**$120,000**	

A traditional income statement and a CVP income statement both report the same net income of $120,000. However a traditional income statement does not classify costs as variable or fixed, and therefore it does not report a contribution margin. In addition, both a total and a per unit amount are often shown on a CVP income statement to facilitate CVP analysis.

In the applications of CVP analysis that follow, we assume that the term "cost" includes all costs and expenses related to production and sale of the product. That is, cost includes manufacturing costs plus selling and administrative expenses.

CONTRIBUTION MARGIN PER UNIT

Vargo Video's CVP income statement shows a contribution margin of $320,000, and a contribution margin per unit of $200 ($500 − $300). The formula for **contribution margin per unit** and the computation for Vargo Video are:

Unit Selling Price	−	Unit Variable Costs	=	Contribution Margin per Unit
$500	−	$300	=	$200

Illustration 22-12
Formula for contribution margin per unit

Contribution margin per unit indicates that for every DVD player sold, Vargo has $200 to cover fixed costs and contribute to net income. Because Vargo Video has fixed costs of $200,000, it must sell 1,000 DVD players ($200,000 ÷ $200) before it earns any net income. Vargo's CVP income statement, assuming a zero net income, is as follows.

VARGO VIDEO COMPANY
CVP Income Statement
For the Month Ended June 30, 2010

	Total	Per Unit
Sales (1,000 DVD players)	$500,000	$500
Variable costs	300,000	300
Contribution margin	200,000	$200
Fixed costs	200,000	
Net income	$ –0–	

Illustration 22-13
CVP income statement, with zero net income

It follows that for every DVD player sold above 1,000 units, net income increases $200. For example, assume that Vargo sold one more DVD player, for a total of 1,001 DVD players sold. In this case Vargo reports net income of $200 as shown in Illustration 22-14.

VARGO VIDEO COMPANY
CVP Income Statement
For the Month Ended June 30, 2010

	Total	Per Unit
Sales (1,001 DVD players)	$500,500	$500
Variable costs	300,300	300
Contribution margin	200,200	$200
Fixed costs	200,000	
Net income	$ 200	

Illustration 22-14
CVP income statement, with net income

CONTRIBUTION MARGIN RATIO

Some managers prefer to use a contribution margin ratio in CVP analysis. The **contribution margin ratio** is the contribution margin per unit divided by the unit selling price. For Vargo Video, the ratio is shown in illustration 22-15 on the next page.

Illustration 22-15
Formula for contribution margin ratio

Contribution Margin per Unit	÷	Unit Selling Price	=	Contribution Margin Ratio
$200	÷	$500	=	40%

The contribution margin ratio of 40% means that $0.40 of each sales dollar ($1 × 40%) is available to apply to fixed costs and to contribute to net income.

This expression of contribution margin is very helpful in determining the effect of changes in sales dollars on net income. For example, if sales increase $100,000, net income will increase $40,000 (40% × $100,000). Thus, by using the contribution margin ratio, managers can quickly determine increases in net income from any change in sales dollars.

We can also see this effect through a CVP income statement. Assume that Vargo Video's current sales are $500,000 and it wants to know the effect of a $100,000 increase in sales. Vargo prepares a comparative CVP income statement analysis as follows.

Illustration 22-16
Comparative CVP income statements

VARGO VIDEO COMPANY
CVP Income Statements
For the Month Ended June 30, 2010

	No Change Total	No Change Per Unit	With Change Total	With Change Per Unit
Sales	$500,000	$500	$600,000	$500
Variable costs	300,000	300	360,000	300
Contribution margin	200,000	$200	240,000	$200
Fixed costs	200,000		200,000	
Net income	$ –0–		$ 40,000	

Study these CVP income statements carefully. The concepts presented in these statements are used extensively in this and later chapters.

Break-even Analysis

STUDY OBJECTIVE 6
Identify the three ways to determine the break-even point.

A key relationship in CVP analysis is the level of activity at which total revenues equal total costs (both fixed and variable). This level of activity is called the **break-even point**. At this volume of sales, the company will realize no income but will suffer no loss. The process of finding the break-even point is called **break-even analysis**. Knowledge of the break-even point is useful to management when it decides whether to introduce new product lines, change sales prices on established products, or enter new market areas.

The break-even point can be:

1. Computed from a mathematical equation.
2. Computed by using contribution margin.
3. Derived from a cost-volume-profit (CVP) graph.

The break-even point can be expressed either in **sales units** or **sales dollars**.

MATHEMATICAL EQUATION
Illustration 22-17 shows a common equation used for CVP analysis.

Illustration 22-17
Basic CVP equation

Sales	=	Variable Costs	+	Fixed Costs	+	Net Income

Identifying the break-even point is a special case of CVP analysis. Because at the break-even point net income is zero, **break-even occurs where total sales equal variable costs plus fixed costs**.

We can compute the break-even point **in units** directly from the equation by using **unit selling prices** and **unit variable costs**. The computation for Vargo Video is:

Sales	=	Variable Costs	+	Fixed Costs	+	Net Income
$500Q	=	$300Q	+	$200,000	+	$0

$$200Q = \$200,000$$
$$Q = \textbf{1,000 units}$$

where

$$Q = \text{sales volume in units}$$
$$\$500 = \text{selling price}$$
$$\$300 = \text{variable cost per unit}$$
$$\$200,000 = \text{total fixed costs}$$

Illustration 22-18
Computation of break-even point

Thus, Vargo Video must sell 1,000 units to break even.

To find **sales dollars** required to break even, we multiply the units sold at the break-even point times the selling price per unit, as shown below.

$$1,000 \times \$500 = \$500,000 \text{ (break-even sales dollars)}$$

CONTRIBUTION MARGIN TECHNIQUE

We know that contribution margin equals total revenues less variable costs. It follows that at the break-even point, **contribution margin must equal total fixed costs**. On the basis of this relationship, we can compute the break-even point using either the contribution margin per unit or the contribution margin ratio.

When a company uses the contribution margin per unit, the formula to compute break-even point in units is fixed costs divided by contribution margin per unit. For Vargo Video the computation is as follows.

Fixed Costs	÷	Contribution Margin per Unit	=	Break-even Point in Units
$200,000	÷	$200	=	**1,000 units**

Illustration 22-19
Formula for break-even point in units using contribution margin

One way to interpret this formula is that Vargo Video generates $200 of contribution margin with each unit that it sells. This $200 goes to pay off fixed costs. Therefore, the company must sell 1,000 units to pay off $200,000 in fixed costs.

When a company uses the contribution margin ratio, the formula to compute break-even point in dollars is fixed costs divided by the contribution margin ratio. We know that the contribution margin ratio for Vargo Video is 40% ($200 ÷ $500), which means that every dollar of sales generates 40 cents to pay off fixed costs. Thus, the break-even point in dollars is:

Fixed Costs	÷	Contribution Margin Ratio	=	Break-even Point in Dollars
$200,000	÷	40%	=	**$500,000**

Illustration 22-20
Formula for break-even point in dollars using contribution margin ratio

ACCOUNTING ACROSS THE ORGANIZATION

Charter Flights Offer a Good Deal

The Internet is wringing inefficiencies out of nearly every industry. While commercial aircraft spend roughly 4,000 hours a year in the air, chartered aircraft spend only 500 hours flying. That means that they are sitting on the ground—not making any money—about 90% of the time. One company, FlightServe, saw a business opportunity in that fact. For about the same cost as a first-class ticket, FlightServe decided to match up executives with charter flights in small "private jets." The executive would get a more comfortable ride and could avoid the hassle of big airports. FlightServe noted that the average charter jet has eight seats. When all eight seats were full, the company would have an 80% profit margin. It would break even at an average of 3.3 full seats per flight.

Source: "Jet Set Go," *The Economist,* March 18, 2000, p. 68.

 How did FlightServe determine that it would break even with 3.3 seats full per flight?

GRAPHIC PRESENTATION

An effective way to find the break-even point is to prepare a break-even graph. Because this graph also shows costs, volume, and profits, it is referred to as a **cost-volume-profit (CVP) graph**.

As the CVP graph in Illustration 22-21 shows, sales volume is recorded along the horizontal axis. This axis should extend to the maximum level of expected sales. Both total revenues (sales) and total costs (fixed plus variable) are recorded on the vertical axis.

Illustration 22-21
CVP graph

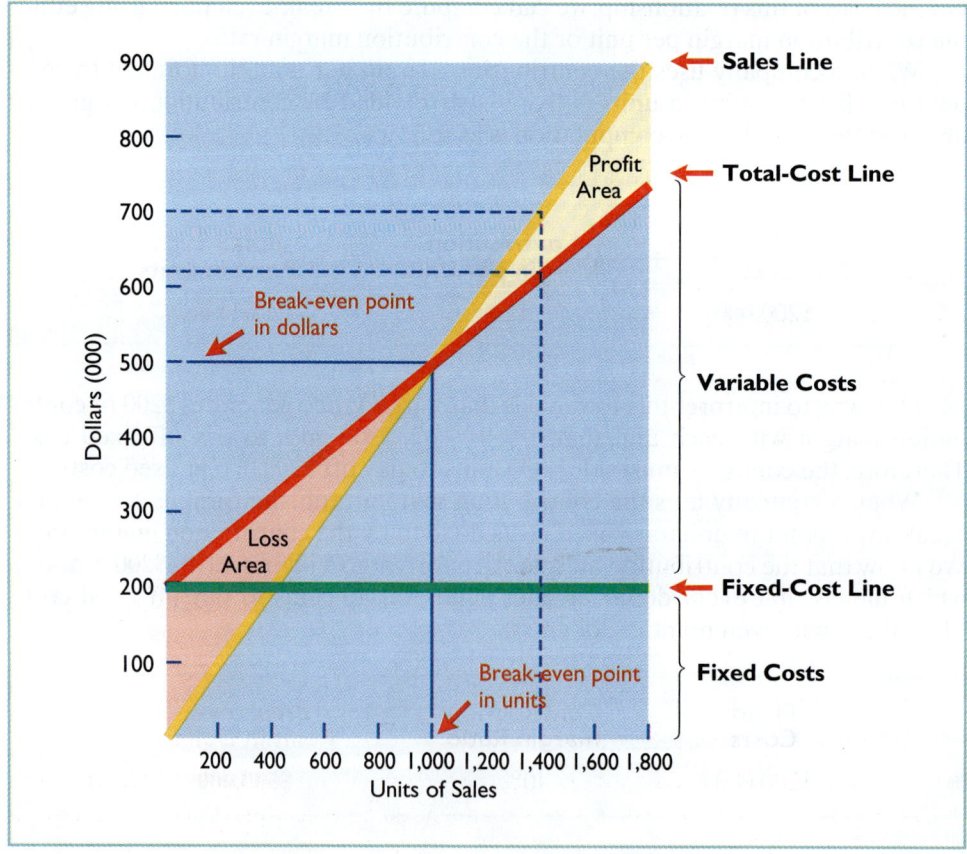

The construction of the graph, using the data for Vargo Video, is as follows.

1. Plot the total-sales line, starting at the zero activity level. For every DVD player sold, total revenue increases by $500. For example, at 200 units, sales are $100,000. At the upper level of activity (1,800 units), sales are $900,000. The revenue line is assumed to be linear through the full range of activity.
2. Plot the total fixed cost using a horizontal line. For the DVD players, this line is plotted at $200,000. The fixed cost is the same at every level of activity.
3. Plot the total-cost line. This starts at the fixed-cost line at zero activity. It increases by the variable cost at each level of activity. For each DVD player, variable costs are $300. Thus, at 200 units, total variable cost is $60,000, and the total cost is $260,000. At 1,800 units total variable cost is $540,000, and total cost is $740,000. On the graph, the amount of the variable cost can be derived from the difference between the total cost and fixed cost lines at each level of activity.
4. Determine the break-even point from the intersection of the total-cost line and the total-revenue line. The break-even point in dollars is found by drawing a horizontal line from the break-even point to the vertical axis. The break-even point in units is found by drawing a vertical line from the break-even point to the horizontal axis. For the DVD players, the break-even point is $500,000 of sales, or 1,000 units. At this sales level, Vargo Video will cover costs but make no profit.

The CVP graph also shows both the net income and net loss areas. Thus, the amount of income or loss at each level of sales can be derived from the total sales and total cost lines.

A CVP graph is useful because the effects of a change in any element in the CVP analysis can be quickly seen. For example, a 10% increase in selling price will change the location of the total revenue line. Likewise, the effects on total costs of wage increases can be quickly observed.

DO IT!

Lombardi Company has a unit selling price of $400, variable costs per unit of $240, and fixed costs of $180,000. Compute the break-even point in units using **(a)** a mathematical equation and **(b)** contribution margin per unit.

BREAK-EVEN ANALYSIS

action plan

✔ Apply the formula: Sales = Variable costs + Fixed costs + Net income.
✔ Apply the formula: Fixed costs ÷ Contribution margin per unit = Break-even point in units.

Solution
(a) The formula is $400Q = $240Q + $180,000. The break-even point in units is 1,125 ($180,000 ÷ $160).
(b) The contribution margin per unit is $160 ($400 − $240). The formula therefore is $180,000 ÷ $160, and the break-even point in units is 1,125.

Related exercise material: **BE22-5, BE22-6, E22-4, E22-5, E22-6, E22-7, E22-8,** and **DO IT! 22-3.**

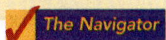

Target Net Income

Rather than simply "breaking even," management usually sets an income objective often called **target net income**. It indicates the sales necessary to achieve a specified level of income. Companies determine the sales necessary to achieve target net income by using one of the three approaches discussed earlier.

STUDY OBJECTIVE 7
Give the formulas for determining sales required to earn target net income.

MATHEMATICAL EQUATION
We know that at the break-even point no profit or loss results for the company. By adding an amount for target net income to the same basic equation, we obtain the following formula for determining required sales.

Illustration 22-22
Formula for required sales to meet target net income

| Required Sales | = | Variable Costs | + | Fixed Costs | + | Target Net Income |

Required sales may be expressed in either **sales units** or **sales dollars**. Assuming that target net income is $120,000 for Vargo Video, the computation of required sales in units is as follows.

Illustration 22-23
Computation of required unit sales

| Required Sales | = | Variable Costs | + | Fixed Costs | + | Target Net Income |
| $500Q | = | $300Q | + | $200,000 | + | $120,000 |

$$200Q = \$320,000$$
$$Q = \mathbf{1{,}600}$$

where

Q = sales volume
$500 = selling price
$300 = variable costs per unit
$200,000 = total fixed costs
$120,000 = target net income

The sales dollars required to achieve the target net income is found by multiplying the units sold by the unit selling price [(1,600 × $500) = $800,000].

CONTRIBUTION MARGIN TECHNIQUE

As in the case of break-even sales, we can compute in either units or dollars the sales required to meet a target net income. The formula to compute required sales in units for Vargo Video using the contribution margin per unit is as follows.

Illustration 22-24
Formula for required sales in units using contribution margin per unit

| Fixed Costs + Target Net Income | ÷ | Contribution Margin Per Unit | = | Required Sales in Units |
| ($200,000 + $120,000) | ÷ | $200 | = | **1,600 units** |

This computation tells Vargo that to achieve its desired target net income of $120,000, it must sell 1,600 DVD players.

The formula to compute the required sales in dollars for Vargo Video using the contribution margin ratio is as follows.

Illustration 22-25
Formula for required sales in dollars using contribution margin ratio

| Fixed Costs + Target Net Income | ÷ | Contribution Margin Ratio | = | Required Sales in Dollars |
| ($200,000 + $120,000) | ÷ | 40% | = | **$800,000** |

This computation tells Vargo that to achieve its desired target net income of $120,000, it must generate sales of $800,000.

GRAPHIC PRESENTATION

We also can use the CVP graph in Illustration 22-21 (on page 988) to find the sales required to meet target net income. In the profit area of the graph, the distance between the sales line and the total cost line at any point equals net income. We can find required sales by analyzing the differences between the two lines until the desired net income is found.

For example, suppose Vargo Video sells 1,400 DVD players. Illustration 22-21 shows that a vertical line drawn at 1,400 units intersects the sales line at $700,000 and the total cost line at $620,000. The difference between the two amounts represents the net income (profit) of $80,000.

Margin of Safety

The margin of safety is another relationship used in CVP analysis. **Margin of safety** is the difference between actual or expected sales and sales at the break-even point. This relationship measures the "cushion" that management has, allowing it to still break even if expected sales fail to materialize. The margin of safety is expressed in dollars or as a ratio.

STUDY OBJECTIVE 8
Define margin of safety, and give the formulas for computing it.

The formula for stating the **margin of safety in dollars** is actual (or expected) sales minus break-even sales. Assuming that actual (expected) sales for Vargo Video are $750,000, the computation is:

Actual (Expected) Sales	−	Break-even Sales	=	Margin of Safety in Dollars
$750,000	−	$500,000	=	**$250,000**

Illustration 22-26
Formula for margin of safety in dollars

Vargo's margin of safety is $250,000. Its sales must fall $250,000 before it operates at a loss.

The **margin of safety ratio** is the margin of safety in dollars divided by actual (or expected) sales. The formula and computation for determining the margin of safety ratio are:

Margin of Safety in Dollars	÷	Actual (Expected) Sales	=	Margin of Safety Ratio
$250,000	÷	$750,000	=	**33%**

Illustration 22-27
Formula for margin of safety ratio

This means that the company's sales could fall by 33% before it would be operating at a loss.

The higher the dollars or the percentage, the greater the margin of safety. Management continuously evaluates the adequacy of the margin of safety in terms of such factors as the vulnerability of the product to competitive pressures and to downturns in the economy.

MANAGEMENT INSIGHT

How a Rolling Stones' Tour Makes Money

Computation of break-even and margin of safety is important for service companies as well. Consider how the promoter for the Rolling Stones' tour used the break-even point and margin of safety. For example, one outdoor show should bring 70,000 individuals for a gross of $2.45 million. The promoter guarantees $1.2 million to the Rolling Stones. In addition, 20% of gross goes to the stadium in which the performance is staged. Add another $400,000 for other expenses such as ticket takers, parking attendants, advertising, and so on. The promoter also shares in sales of T-shirts and memorabilia for which the promoter will net over $7 million during the tour. From a successful Rolling Stones' tour, the promoter could make $35 million!

 What amount of sales dollars are required for the promoter to break even?

CVP and Changes in the Business Environment

When the personal computer was introduced, it sold for $2,500; today similar computers sell for much less. Recently, when oil prices rose, the break-even point for airline companies such as American and Northwest rose dramatically. Because of lower prices for imported steel, the demand for domestic steel dropped significantly. The point should be clear: Business conditions change rapidly, and management must respond intelligently to these changes. CVP analysis can help.

To better understand how CVP analysis works, let's look at three independent situations that might occur at Vargo Video. Each case uses the original DVD player sales and cost data, which were:

Illustration 22-28
Original DVD player sales and cost data

Unit selling price	$500
Unit variable cost	$300
Total fixed costs	$200,000
Break-even sales	$500,000 or 1,000 units

Case 1. A competitor is offering a 10% discount on the selling price of its DVD players. Management must decide whether to offer a similar discount.

Question: What effect will a 10% discount on selling price have on the break-even point for DVD players?

Answer: A 10% discount on selling price reduces the selling price per unit to $450 [$500 − ($500 × 10%)]. Variable costs per unit remain unchanged at $300. Thus, the contribution margin per unit is $150. Assuming no change in fixed costs, break-even point is 1,333 units, computed as follows.

Illustration 22-29
Computation of break-even sales in units

Fixed Costs	÷	Contribution Margin per Unit	=	Break-even Point in Units
$200,000	÷	$150	=	1,333 units (rounded)

For Vargo Video, this change requires monthly sales to increase by 333 units, or 33⅓%, in order to break even. In reaching a conclusion about offering a 10% discount to customers, management must determine how likely it is to achieve the increased sales. Also, management should estimate the possible loss of sales if the competitor's discount price is not matched.

Case 2. To meet the threat of foreign competition, management invests in new robotic equipment that will lower the amount of direct labor required to make DVD players. The company estimates that total fixed costs will increase 30% and that variable cost per unit will decrease 30%.

Question: What effect will the new equipment have on the sales volume required to break even?

Answer: Total fixed costs become $260,000 [$200,000 + (30% × $200,000)]. The variable cost per unit becomes $210 [$300 − (30% × $300)]. The new break-even point is approximately 897 units, computed as follows.

Cost-Volume-Profit Analysis

Fixed Costs	÷	Contribution Margin per Unit	=	**Break-even Point in Units**
$260,000	÷	($500 − $210)	=	**897 units (rounded)**

Illustration 22-30
Computation of break-even sales in units

These changes appear to be advantageous for Vargo Video. The break-even point is reduced by 10%, or 100 units.

Case 3. Vargo's principal supplier of raw materials has just announced a price increase. The higher cost is expected to increase the variable cost of DVD players by $25 per unit. Management decides to hold the line on the selling price of the DVD players. It plans a cost-cutting program that will save $17,500 in fixed costs per month. Vargo is currently realizing monthly net income of $80,000 on sales of 1,400 DVD players.

Question: What increase in units sold will be needed to maintain the same level of net income?

Answer: The variable cost per unit increases to $325 ($300 + $25). Fixed costs are reduced to $182,500 ($200,000 − $17,500). Because of the change in variable cost, the contribution margin per unit becomes $175 ($500 − $325). The required number of units sold to achieve the target net income is computed as follows.

Fixed Costs + Target Net Income	÷	Contribution Margin per Unit	=	**Required Sales in Units**
($182,500 + $80,000)	÷	$175	=	**1,500**

Illustration 22-31
Computation of required sales

To achieve the required sales, Vargo will have to sell 1,500 DVD players, an increase of 100 units. If this does not seem to be a reasonable expectation, management will either have to make further cost reductions or accept less net income if the selling price remains unchanged.

CVP Income Statement Revisited

Earlier in the chapter we presented a simple CVP income statement. When companies prepare a CVP income statement, they provide more detail about specific variable and fixed-cost items.

STUDY OBJECTIVE 9
Describe the essential features of a cost-volume-profit income statement.

To illustrate a more detailed CVP income statement, we will assume that Vargo Video reaches its target net income of $120,000 (see Illustration 22-23 on page 990). The following information is obtained on the $680,000 of costs that were incurred in June to produce and sell 1,600 units.

	Variable	Fixed	Total
Cost of goods sold	$400,000	$120,000	$520,000
Selling expenses	60,000	40,000	100,000
Administrative expenses	20,000	40,000	60,000
	$480,000	$200,000	$680,000

Illustration 22-32
Assumed cost and expense data

The detailed CVP income statement for Vargo is shown on page 994.

Illustration 22-33
Detailed CVP income statement

VARGO VIDEO COMPANY
CVP Income Statement
For the Month Ended June 30, 2010

	Total	Per Unit
Sales	$800,000	$500
Variable expenses		
Cost of goods sold $400,000		
Selling expenses 60,000		
Administrative expenses 20,000		
Total variable expenses	480,000	300
Contribution margin	**320,000**	**$200**
Fixed expenses		
Cost of goods sold 120,000		
Selling expenses 40,000		
Administrative expenses 40,000		
Total fixed expenses	200,000	
Net income	**$120,000**	

DO IT!

MARGIN OF SAFETY; REQUIRED SALES

Mabo Company makes calculators that sell for $20 each. For the coming year, management expects fixed costs to total $220,000 and variable costs to be $9 per unit.

(a) Compute break-even point in dollars using the contribution margin (CM) ratio.
(b) Compute the margin of safety percentage assuming actual sales are $500,000.
(c) Compute the sales required in dollars to earn net income of $165,000.

action plan

✔ Know the formulas.
✔ Recognize that variable costs change with sales volume; fixed costs do not.
✔ Avoid computational errors.

Solution

(a) Contribution margin per unit = Unit selling price − Unit variable costs
$11 = $20 − $9
Contribution margin ratio = Contribution margin per unit ÷ Unit selling price
55% = $11 ÷ $20
Break-even point in dollars = Fixed cost ÷ Contribution margin ratio
= $220,000 ÷ 55%
= $400,000

(b) Margin of safety = $\dfrac{\text{Actual sales} - \text{Break-even sales}}{\text{Actual sales}}$

= $\dfrac{\$500{,}000 - \$400{,}000}{\$500{,}000}$

= 20%

(c) Required sales = Variable costs + Fixed costs + Net income
$20Q = $9Q + $220,000 + $165,000
$11Q = $385,000
Q = 35,000 units
35,000 units × $20 = $700,000 required sales

Related exercise material: BE22-6, BE22-7, BE22-8, E22-5, E22-6, E22-7, E22-8, E22-9, E22-10, and **DO IT!** 22-4.

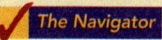

Be sure to read **ALL ABOUT YOU: *A Hybrid Dilemma*** on the next page for information on how topics in this chapter apply to your personal life.

all about Y*U

A Hybrid Dilemma

Have high gas prices got you down? Maybe you should consider a hybrid. These half-gas and half-electric vehicles are generating a lot of interest. They burn less fuel and therefore are easier on the environment. But are they easier on your pocketbook? Is a hybrid car at least a break-even investment, or is it more likely a losing proposition?

*Some Facts

* Ford plans to sell at least seven different models of hybrid cars, about 250,000 vehicles annually, by the end of the decade.
* Hybrid vehicles typically cost $3,000 to $5,000 more than their conventional counterpart, although for some models the premium is higher.
* Bank of America and Timberland offer $3,000 to employees who purchase hybrids. Google offers $5,000 to employees who purchase cars that get at least 45 miles per gallon.
* The most fuel-efficient hybrids—the Toyota Prius and the Honda Civic—can save about $630 per year in fuel costs relative to a similar conventional car. However some other hybrids provide only slight fuel savings.
* Each gallon of gasoline that is not consumed reduces carbon dioxide emissions by 19 pounds. Many believe carbon dioxide contributes to global warming.
* The federal government initially provided tax credits of up to $3,400 to buyers of hybrids. These credits are to be phased out as automakers reach sales caps determined by the Internal Revenue Service (IRS).

*About the Numbers

Sales of hybrid cars started very strong in 2005, but then tapered off. The following graph shows that sales of the Toyota Prius far exceed other brands.

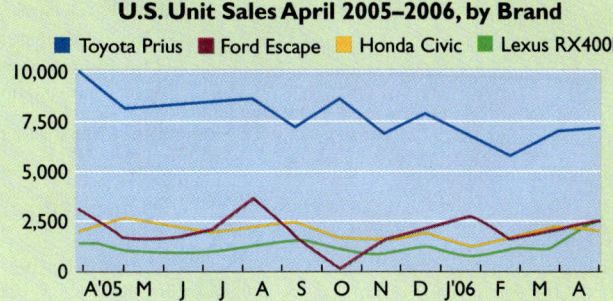

Source: J.D. Power and Associates, 2006, "Happening Hybrids," as reported in the *Wall Street Journal*, May 23, 2006.

*What Do You Think?

Gas prices are depleting your wallet so fast that you might even have to give up your old car and resort to walking or riding your bike on occasion. Will making the investment in a hybrid slow the outflow from your wallet and spare your feet?

YES: At 44 miles per gallon, I can drive forever without ever having to fill up.

NO: Because of the premium price charged for hybrids, I will never drive enough miles to break even on my investment.

Sources: "The Dollars and Sense of Hybrids," *Consumer Reports*, April, 2006, pp. 18-22.; John D. Stoll and Gina Chon, "Consumer Drive for Hybrid Autos Is Slowing Down," *Wall Street Journal*, April 7, 2006, p. A2. Associated Press, "Bank Workers Get Hybrid Reward," *Wall Street Journal*, June 8, 2006, p. D2.

The authors' comments on this situation appear on page 1014.

Comprehensive DO IT!

B.T. Hernandez Company, maker of high-quality flashlights, has experienced steady growth over the last 6 years. However, increased competition has led Mr. Hernandez, the president, to believe that an aggressive campaign is needed next year to maintain the company's present growth. The company's accountant has presented Mr. Hernandez with the following data for the current year, 2010, for use in preparing next year's advertising campaign.

Cost Schedules

Variable costs		
Direct labor per flashlight		$ 8.00
Direct materials		4.00
Variable overhead		3.00
Variable cost per flashlight		$15.00
Fixed costs		
Manufacturing		$ 25,000
Selling		40,000
Administrative		70,000
Total fixed costs		$135,000
Selling price per flashlight		$25.00
Expected sales, 2010 (20,000 flashlights)		$500,000

Mr. Hernandez has set the sales target for the year 2011 at a level of $550,000 (22,000 flashlights).

Instructions

(Ignore any income tax considerations.)

(a) What is the projected operating income for 2010?
(b) What is the contribution margin per unit for 2010?
(c) What is the break-even point in units for 2010?
(d) Mr. Hernandez believes that to attain the sales target in the year 2011, the company must incur an additional selling expense of $10,000 for advertising in 2011, with all other costs remaining constant. What will be the break-even point in dollar sales for 2011 if the company spends the additional $10,000?
(e) If the company spends the additional $10,000 for advertising in 2011, what is the sales level in dollars required to equal 2010 operating income?

action plan

✔ Know the formulas.
✔ Recognize that variable costs change with sales volume; fixed costs do not.
✔ Avoid computational errors.

Solution to Comprehensive DO IT!

(a)

Expected sales		$500,000
Less:		
Variable cost (20,000 flashlights × $15)	$300,000	
Fixed costs	135,000	435,000
Projected operating income		$ 65,000

(b)

Selling price per flashlight	$25
Variable cost per flashlight	15
Contribution margin per unit	$10

(c) Fixed costs ÷ Contribution margin per unit = Break-even point in units
$135,000 ÷ $10 = 13,500 units

(d) Fixed costs ÷ Contribution margin ratio = Break-even point in dollars
$145,000 ÷ 40% = $362,500

Fixed costs (from 2010)	$135,000
Additional advertising expense	10,000
Fixed costs (2011)	$145,000

Contribution margin per unit (b) $10
Contribution margin ratio = Contribution margin per unit ÷ Unit selling price
40% = $10 ÷ $25

(e) Required sales = (Fixed costs + Target net income) ÷ Contribution margin ratio
$525,000 = ($145,000 + $65,000) ÷ 40%

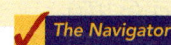

SUMMARY OF STUDY OBJECTIVES

1 **Distinguish between variable and fixed costs.** Variable costs are costs that vary in total directly and proportionately with changes in the activity index. Fixed costs are costs that remain the same in total regardless of changes in the activity index.

2 **Explain the significance of the relevant range.** The relevant range is the range of activity in which a company expects to operate during a year. It is important in CVP analysis because the behavior of costs is assumed to be linear throughout the relevant range.

3 **Explain the concept of mixed costs.** Mixed costs increase in total but not proportionately with changes in the activity level. For purposes of CVP analysis, mixed costs must be classified into their fixed and variable elements. One method that management may use to classify these costs is the high-low method.

4 **List the five components of cost-volume-profit analysis.** The five components of CVP analysis are (a) volume or level of activity, (b) unit selling prices, (c) variable cost per unit, (d) total fixed costs, and (e) sales mix.

5 **Indicate what contribution margin is and how it can be expressed.** Contribution margin is the amount of revenue remaining after deducting variable costs. It is identified in a CVP income statement, which classifies costs as variable or fixed. It can be expressed as a per unit amount or as a ratio.

6 **Identify the three ways to determine the break-even point.** The break-even point can be (a) computed from a mathematical equation, (b) computed by using a contribution margin technique, and (c) derived from a CVP graph.

7 **Give the formulas for determining sales required to earn target net income.** The general formula is: Required sales = Variable costs + Fixed costs + Target net income. Two other formulas are: Required sales in units = (Fixed costs + Target net income) ÷ Contribution margin per unit, and Required sales in dollars = (Fixed costs + Target net income) ÷ Contribution margin ratio.

8 **Define margin of safety, and give the formulas for computing it.** Margin of safety is the difference between actual or expected sales and sales at the break-even point. The formulas for margin of safety are: Actual (expected) sales − Break-even sales = Margin of safety in dollars; Margin of safety in dollars ÷ Actual (expected) sales = Margin of safety ratio.

9 **Describe the essential features of a cost-volume-profit income statement.** The CVP income statement classifies costs and expenses as variable or fixed and reports contribution margin in the body of the statement.

GLOSSARY

Activity index The activity that causes changes in the behavior of costs. (p. 976).

Break-even point The level of activity at which total revenues equal total costs. (p. 986).

Contribution margin (CM) The amount of revenue remaining after deducting variable costs. (p. 984).

Contribution margin per unit The amount of revenue remaining per unit after deducting variable costs; calculated as unit selling price minus unit variable cost. (p. 985).

Contribution margin ratio The percentage of each dollar of sales that is available to apply to fixed costs and contribute to net income; calculated as contribution margin per unit divided by unit selling price. (p. 985).

Chapter 22 Cost-Volume-Profit

...avior analysis The study of how specific costs re-...d to changes in the level of business activity. (p. 976).

...volume-profit (CVP) analysis The study of the effects ...f changes in costs and volume on a company's profits. (p. 983).

Cost-volume-profit (CVP) graph A graph showing the relationship between costs, volume, and profits. (p. 988).

Cost-volume-profit (CVP) income statement A statement for internal use that classifies costs as fixed or variable and reports contribution margin in the body of the statement. (p. 984).

Fixed costs Costs that remain the same in total regardless of changes in the activity level. (p. 977).

High-low method A mathematical method that uses the total costs incurred at the high and low levels of activity to classify mixed costs into fixed and variable components. (p. 981).

Margin of safety The difference between actual or expected sales and sales at the break-even point. (p. 991).

Mixed costs Costs that contain both a variable and a fixed cost element and change in total but not proportionately with changes in the activity level. (p. 980).

Relevant range The range of the activity index over which the company expects to operate during the year. (p. 979).

Target net income The income objective set by management. (p. 989).

Variable costs Costs that vary in total directly and proportionately with changes in the activity level. (p. 977).

APPENDIX Variable Costing

STUDY OBJECTIVE 10
Explain the difference between absorption costing and variable costing.

In earlier chapters, we classified both variable and fixed manufacturing costs as product costs. In job order costing, for example, a job is assigned the costs of direct materials, direct labor, and both variable and fixed manufacturing overhead. This costing approach is called **absorption costing** (or **full costing**). It is so named because all manufacturing costs are charged to, or absorbed by, the product.

An alternative approach is to use variable costing. Under **variable costing** only direct materials, direct labor, and variable manufacturing overhead costs are considered product costs. Companies recognize fixed manufacturing overhead costs as period costs (expenses) when incurred. Illustration 22A-1 shows the difference between absorption costing and variable costing.

Illustration 22A-1
Difference between absorption costing and variable costing

Under both absorption and variable costing selling and administrative expenses are period costs.

To illustrate the computation of unit production cost under absorption and variable costing, assume that Premium Products Corporation manufactures a polyurethane sealant, called Fix-It, for car windshields. Relevant data for Fix-It in January 2010, the first month of production, are as follows.

Illustration 22A-2
Sealant sales and cost data for Premium Products Corporation

Selling price	$20 per unit.
Units	Produced 30,000; sold 20,000; beginning inventory zero.
Variable unit costs	Manufacturing $9 (direct materials $5, direct labor $3, and variable overhead $1). Selling and administrative expenses $2.
Fixed costs	Manufacturing overhead $120,000. Selling and administrative expenses $15,000.

The per unit production cost of Fix-It under each costing approach is:

Type of Cost	Absorption Costing	Variable Costing
Direct materials	$ 5	$5
Direct labor	3	3
Variable manufacturing overhead	1	1
Fixed manufacturing overhead ($120,000 ÷ 30,000 units produced)	4	0
Total unit cost	**$13**	**$9**

Illustration 22A-3
Computation of per unit production cost

The total unit cost is $4 higher ($13 − $9) for absorption costing. This occurs because fixed manufacturing costs are a product cost under absorption costing. Under variable costing, they are, instead, a period cost, and so are expensed. Based on these data, each unit sold and each unit remaining in inventory is costed at $13 under absorption costing and at $9 under variable costing.

Effects of Variable Costing on Income

Illustrations 22A-4 below and 22A-5 (page 1000) show the income statements under the two costing approaches. Absorption costing uses the traditional income statement format. Variable costing uses the cost-volume-profit format. We have inserted computations parenthetically in the statements to facilitate your understanding of the amounts.

PREMIUM PRODUCTS CORPORATION
Income Statement
For the Month Ended January 31, 2010
(Absorption Costing)

Sales (20,000 units × $20)		$400,000
Cost of goods sold		
Inventory, January 1	$ -0-	
Cost of goods manufactured (30,000 units × $13)	390,000	
Cost of goods available for sale	390,000	
Inventory, January 31 (10,000 units × $13)	**130,000**	
Cost of goods sold (20,000 units × $13)		260,000
Gross profit		140,000
Selling and administrative expenses		
(Variable 20,000 units × $2 + fixed $15,000)		55,000
Income from operations		**$ 85,000**

Illustration 22A-4
Absorption costing income statement

HELPFUL HINT
This is the traditional statement that would result from job order and processing costing explained in Chapters 20 and 21.

Income from operations under absorption costing (Illustration 22A-4) is $40,000 ($85,000 − $45,000) higher than under variable costing (Illustration 22A-5). The reason: There is a $40,000 difference in the ending inventories ($130,000 under absorption costing versus $90,000 under variable costing). Under absorption costing, the company defers $40,000 of the fixed overhead costs (10,000 units × $4) to a future period as a product cost. In contrast, under variable costing the company expenses the entire fixed manufacturing costs when incurred.

Chapter 22 Cost-Volume-Profit

Illustration 22A-5
Variable costing income statement

PREMIUM PRODUCTS CORPORATION
Income Statement
For the Month Ended January 31, 2010
(Variable Costing)

Sales (20,000 units × $20)		$400,000
Variable expenses		
Variable cost of goods sold		
Inventory, January 1	$ –0–	
Variable manufacturing costs (30,000 units × $9)	270,000	
Cost of goods available for sale	270,000	
Inventory, January 31 (10,000 units × $9)	**90,000**	
Variable cost of goods sold	180,000	
Variable selling and administrative expenses		
(20,000 units × $2)	40,000	
Total variable expenses		220,000
Contribution margin		180,000
Fixed expenses		
Manufacturing overhead	120,000	
Selling and administrative expenses	15,000	
Total fixed expenses		135,000
Income from operations		**$ 45,000**

HELPFUL HINT
Note the difference in the computation of the ending inventory: $9 per unit here, $13 per unit in Illustration 22A-4.

The following relationships apply:

- When units produced exceed units sold (as shown), income from operations under absorption costing is higher.
- When units produced are less than units sold, income from operations under absorption costing is lower.
- When units produced and sold are the same, income from operations will be equal under the two costing approaches. In this case, there is no increase in ending inventory. So fixed overhead costs of the current period are not deferred to future periods through the ending inventory.

Illustration 22A-6 summarizes the foregoing effects of the two costing approaches on income from operations.

Illustration 22A-6
Summary of income effects

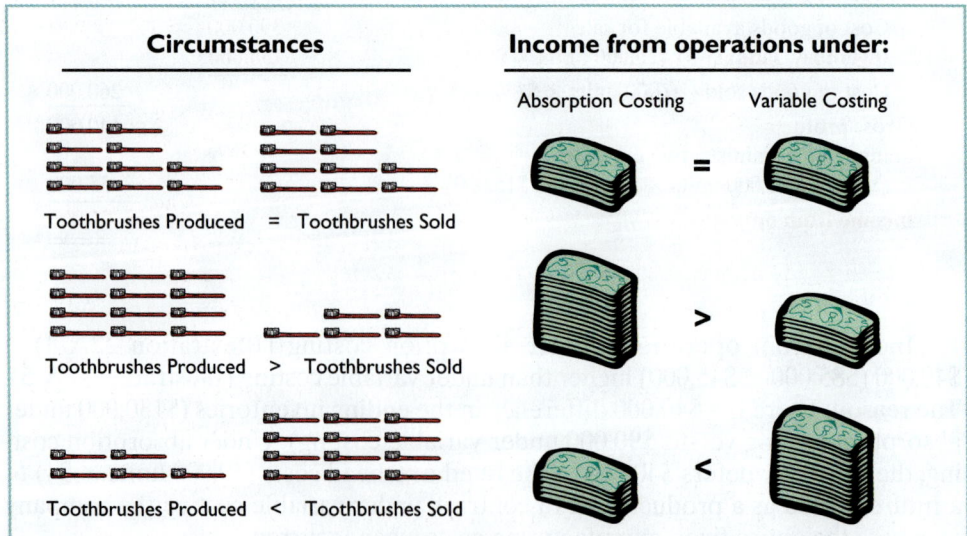

Rationale for Variable Costing

The purpose of fixed manufacturing costs is **to have productive facilities available for use**. A company incurs these costs whether it operates at zero or at 100% of capacity. Thus, proponents of variable costing argue that these costs are period costs and therefore should be expensed when incurred.

Supporters of absorption costing defend the assignment of fixed manufacturing overhead costs to inventory. They say that these costs are as much a cost of getting a product ready for sale as direct materials or direct labor. Accordingly, they contend, these costs should not be matched with revenues until the product is sold.

The use of variable costing is acceptable **only for internal use by management**. It cannot be used in determining product costs in financial statements prepared in accordance with generally accepted accounting principles because it understates inventory costs. To comply with the matching principle, a company must use absorption costing for its work in process and finished goods inventories. Similarly, companies must use absorption costing for income tax purposes.

SUMMARY OF STUDY OBJECTIVE FOR APPENDIX

10 Explain the difference between absorption costing and variable costing. Under absorption costing, fixed manufacturing costs are product costs. Under variable costing, fixed manufacturing costs are period costs.

GLOSSARY FOR APPENDIX

Absorption costing A costing approach in which all manufacturing costs are charged to the product. (p. 998).

Variable costing A costing approach in which only variable manufacturing costs are product costs, and fixed manufacturing costs are period costs (expenses). (p. 998).

*Note: All asterisked Questions, Exercises, and Problems relate to material in the appendix to the chapter.

SELF-STUDY QUESTIONS

Answers are at the end of the chapter.

(SO 1) **1.** Variable costs are costs that:
  a. vary in total directly and proportionately with changes in the activity level.
  b. remain the same per unit at every activity level.
  c. Neither of the above.
  d. Both (a) and (b) above.

(SO 2) **2.** The relevant range is:
  a. the range of activity in which variable costs will be curvilinear.
  b. the range of activity in which fixed costs will be curvilinear.
  c. the range over which the company expects to operate during a year.
  d. usually from zero to 100% of operating capacity.

(SO 3) **3.** Mixed costs consist of a:
  a. variable cost element and a fixed cost element.
  b. fixed cost element and a controllable cost element.
  c. relevant cost element and a controllable cost element.
  d. variable cost element and a relevant cost element.

4. Your phone service provider offers a plan that is classified (SO 3) as a mixed cost. The cost per month for 1,000 minutes is $50. If you use 2,000 minutes this month, your cost will be:
  a. $50.   c. more than $100.
  b. $100.   d. between $50 and $100.

5. One of the following is *not* involved in CVP analysis. That (SO 4) factor is:
  a. sales mix.   c. fixed costs per unit.
  b. unit selling prices.   d. volume or level of activity.

6. Contribution margin: (SO 5)
  a. is revenue remaining after deducting variable costs.
  b. may be expressed as contribution margin per unit.
  c. is selling price less cost of goods sold.
  d. Both (a) and (b) above.

7. When comparing a traditional income statement to a CVP (SO 5) income statement:
  a. net income will always be greater on the traditional statement.
  b. net income will always be less on the traditional statement.

1002 Chapter 22 Cost-Volume-Profit

c. net income will always be identical on both.
d. net income will be greater or less depending on the sales volume.

(SO 6) 8. Brownstone Company's contribution margin ratio is 30%. If Brownstone's sales revenue is $100 greater than its break-even sales in dollars, its net income:
a. will be $100.
b. will be $70.
c. will be $30.
d. cannot be determined without knowing fixed costs.

(SO 6) 9. Gossen Company is planning to sell 200,000 pliers for $4 per unit. The contribution margin ratio is 25%. If Gossen will break even at this level of sales, what are the fixed costs?
a. $100,000.
b. $160,000.
c. $200,000.
d. $300,000.

(SO 7) 10. The mathematical equation for computing required sales to obtain target net income is: Required sales =
a. Variable costs + Target net income.
b. Variable costs + Fixed costs + Target net income.
c. Fixed costs + Target net income.
d. No correct answer is given.

(SO 8) 11. Marshall Company had actual sales of $600,000 when break-even sales were $420,000. What is the margin of safety ratio?
a. 25%.
b. 30%.
c. 33⅓%.
d. 45%.

12. Margin of safety is computed as: (SO 8)
a. Actual sales − Break-even sales.
b. Contribution margin − Fixed costs.
c. Break-even sales − Variable costs.
d. Actual sales − Contribution margin.

13. On a CVP income statement: (SO 9)
a. Sales − Cost of goods sold = Contribution margin.
b. Sales − Variable costs − Fixed costs = Contribution margin.
c. Sales − Variable costs = Contribution margin.
d. Sales − Fixed costs = Contribution margin.

14. Cournot Company sells 100,000 wrenches for $12 a unit. (SO 9) Fixed costs are $300,000, and net income is $200,000. What should be reported as variable expenses in the CVP income statement?
a. $700,000.
b. $900,000.
c. $500,000.
d. $1,000,000.

*15. Under variable costing, fixed manufacturing costs are (SO 10) classified as:
a. period costs.
b. product costs.
c. both (a) and (b).
d. neither (a) nor (b).

Go to the book's companion website,
www.wiley.com/college/weygandt,
for Additional Self-Study questions.

QUESTIONS

1. (a) What is cost behavior analysis?
   (b) Why is cost behavior analysis important to management?

2. (a) Jenny Kent asks your help in understanding the term "activity index." Explain the meaning and importance of this term for Jenny.
   (b) State the two ways that variable costs may be defined.

3. Contrast the effects of changes in the activity level on total fixed costs and on unit fixed costs.

4. A. J. Hernandez claims that the relevant range concept is important only for variable costs.
   (a) Explain the relevant range concept.
   (b) Do you agree with A. J.'s claim? Explain.

5. "The relevant range is indispensable in cost behavior analysis." Is this true? Why or why not?

6. Ryan Ricketts is confused. He does not understand why rent on his apartment is a fixed cost and rent on a Hertz rental truck is a mixed cost. Explain the difference to Ryan.

7. How should mixed costs be classified in CVP analysis? What approach is used to effect the appropriate classification?

8. At the high and low levels of activity during the month, direct labor hours are 90,000 and 40,000, respectively. The related costs are $160,000 and $100,000. What are the fixed and variable costs at any level of activity?

9. "Cost-volume-profit (CVP) analysis is based entirely on unit costs." Do you agree? Explain.

10. Jill Nott defines contribution margin as the amount of profit available to cover operating expenses. Is there any truth in this definition? Discuss.

11. Kosko Company's Speedo calculator sells for $40. Variable costs per unit are estimated to be $28. What are the contribution margin per unit and the contribution margin ratio?

12. "Break-even analysis is of limited use to management because a company cannot survive by just breaking even." Do you agree? Explain.

13. Total fixed costs are $25,000 for Haag Inc. It has a contribution margin per unit of $15, and a contribution margin ratio of 25%. Compute the break-even sales in dollars.

14. Nancy Tobias asks your help in constructing a CVP graph. Explain to Nancy (a) how the break-even point is plotted, and (b) how the level of activity and dollar sales at the break-even point are determined.

15. Define the term "margin of safety." If Peine Company expects to sell 1,250 units of its product at $12 per unit, and break-even sales for the product are $12,000, what is the margin of safety ratio?

16. Ortega Company's break-even sales are $600,000. Assuming fixed costs are $180,000, what sales volume is needed to achieve a target net income of $60,000?

17. The traditional income statement for Mallon Company shows sales $900,000, cost of goods sold $500,000, and operating expenses $200,000. Assuming all costs and

expenses are 70% variable and 30% fixed, prepare a CVP income statement through contribution margin.

*18. Distinguish between absorption costing and variable costing.

*19. (a) What is the major rationale for the use of variable costing? (b) Discuss why variable costing may not be used for financial reporting purposes.

BRIEF EXERCISES

BE22-1 Monthly production costs in Pesavento Company for two levels of production are as follows.

Cost	3,000 units	6,000 units
Indirect labor	$10,000	$20,000
Supervisory salaries	5,000	5,000
Maintenance	4,000	7,000

Indicate which costs are variable, fixed, and mixed, and give the reason for each answer.

Classify costs as variable, fixed, or mixed.
(SO 1, 3)

BE22-2 For Loder Company, the relevant range of production is 40–80% of capacity. At 40% of capacity, a variable cost is $4,000 and a fixed cost is $6,000. Diagram the behavior of each cost within the relevant range assuming the behavior is linear.

Diagram the behavior of costs within the relevant range.
(SO 2)

BE22-3 For Hunt Company, a mixed cost is $20,000 plus $16 per direct labor hour. Diagram the behavior of the cost using increments of 500 hours up to 2,500 hours on the horizontal axis and increments of $20,000 up to $80,000 on the vertical axis.

Diagram the behavior of a mixed cost.
(SO 3)

BE22-4 Deines Company accumulates the following data concerning a mixed cost, using miles as the activity level.

	Miles Driven	Total Cost		Miles Driven	Total Cost
January	8,000	$14,150	March	8,500	$15,000
February	7,500	13,600	April	8,200	14,490

Compute the variable and fixed cost elements using the high-low method.

Determine variable and fixed cost elements using the high-low method.
(SO 3)

BE22-5 Determine the missing amounts.

	Unit Selling Price	Unit Variable Costs	Contribution Margin per Unit	Contribution Margin Ratio
1.	$250	$170	(a)	(b)
2.	$500	(c)	$200	(d)
3.	(e)	(f)	$300	30%

Determine missing amounts for contribution margin.
(SO 5)

BE22-6 Hamby Company has a unit selling price of $400, variable costs per unit of $260, and fixed costs of $210,000. Compute the break-even point in units using (a) the mathematical equation and (b) contribution margin per unit.

Compute the break-even point.
(SO 6)

BE22-7 For Markowis Company, variable costs are 70% of sales, and fixed costs are $210,000. Management's net income goal is $60,000. Compute the required sales needed to achieve management's target net income of $60,000. (Use the mathematical equation approach.)

Compute sales for target net income.
(SO 7)

BE22-8 For Briggs Company actual sales are $1,200,000 and break-even sales are $900,000. Compute (a) the margin of safety in dollars and (b) the margin of safety ratio.

Compute the margin of safety and the margin of safety ratio.
(SO 8)

BE22-9 Dilts Manufacturing Inc. had sales of $1,800,000 for the first quarter of 2010. In making the sales, the company incurred the following costs and expenses.

	Variable	Fixed
Cost of goods sold	$760,000	$540,000
Selling expenses	95,000	60,000
Administrative expenses	79,000	66,000

Prepare a CVP income statement for the quarter ended March 31, 2010.

Prepare CVP income statement.
(SO 9)

1004 Chapter 22 Cost-Volume-Profit

Compute net income under absorption and variable costing.
(SO 10)

*BE22-10 Gore Company's fixed overhead costs are $3 per unit, and its variable overhead costs are $8 per unit. In the first month of operations, 50,000 units are produced, and 47,000 units are sold. Write a short memo to the chief financial officer explaining which costing approach will produce the higher income and what the difference will be.

DO IT! REVIEW

Classify types of costs.
(SO 1, 3)

DO IT! 22-1 Montana Company reports the following total costs at two levels of production.

	5,000 Units	10,000 Units
Indirect labor	$ 3,000	$ 6,000
Property taxes	7,000	7,000
Direct labor	27,000	54,000
Direct materials	22,000	44,000
Depreciation	4,000	4,000
Utilities	3,000	5,000
Maintenance	9,000	11,000

Classify each cost as variable, fixed, or mixed.

Compute costs using high-low method and estimate total cost.
(SO 3)

DO IT! 22-2 Amanda Company accumulates the following data concerning a mixed cost, using units produced as the activity level.

	Units Produced	Total Cost
March	10,000	$18,000
April	9,000	16,650
May	10,500	18,750
June	8,800	16,200
July	9,500	17,100

(a) Compute the variable and fixed cost elements using the high-low method.
(b) Estimate the total cost if the company produces 8,500 units.

Compute break-even point in units.
(SO 6)

DO IT! 22-3 Vince Company has a unit selling price of $250, variable cost per unit of $160, and fixed costs of $135,000. Compute the breakeven point in units using (a) a mathematical equation and (b) contribution margin per unit.

Compute margin of safety percentage and required sales.
(SO 8, 9)

DO IT! 22-4 Queensland Company makes radios that sell for $30 each. For the coming year, management expects fixed costs to total $200,000 and variable costs to be $20 per unit.

(a) Compute the break-even point in dollars using the contribution margin (CM) ratio.
(b) Compute the margin of safety percentage assuming actual sales are $750,000.
(c) Compute the sales required in dollars to earn net income of $120,000.

EXERCISES

Define and classify variable, fixed, and mixed costs.
(SO 1, 3)

E22-1 Dye Company manufactures a single product. Annual production costs incurred in the manufacturing process are shown below for two levels of production.

	Costs Incurred			
Production in Units	5,000		10,000	
Production Costs	Total Cost	Cost/Unit	Total Cost	Cost/Unit
Direct materials	$8,250	$1.65	$16,500	$1.65
Direct labor	9,500	1.90	19,000	1.90
Utilities	1,500	0.30	2,500	0.25
Rent	4,000	0.80	4,000	0.40
Maintenance	800	0.16	1,100	0.11
Supervisory salaries	1,000	0.20	1,000	0.10

Instructions
(a) Define the terms variable costs, fixed costs, and mixed costs.
(b) Classify each cost above as either variable, fixed, or mixed.

E22-2 The controller of Dugan Industries has collected the following monthly expense data for use in analyzing the cost behavior of maintenance costs.

Determine fixed and variable costs using the high-low method and prepare graph.

(SO 1, 3)

Month	Total Maintenance Costs	Total Machine Hours
January	$2,400	300
February	3,000	400
March	3,600	600
April	4,500	790
May	3,200	500
June	4,900	800

Instructions
(a) Determine the fixed and variable cost components using the high-low method.
(b) Prepare a graph showing the behavior of maintenance costs, and identify the fixed and variable cost elements. Use 200 unit increments and $1,000 cost increments.

E22-3 Black Brothers Furniture Corporation incurred the following costs.

Classify variable, fixed, and mixed costs.

(SO 1, 3)

1. Wood used in the production of furniture.
2. Fuel used in delivery trucks.
3. Straight-line depreciation on factory building.
4. Screws used in the production of furniture.
5. Sales staff salaries.
6. Sales commissions.
7. Property taxes.
8. Insurance on buildings.
9. Hourly wages of furniture craftsmen.
10. Salaries of factory supervisors.
11. Utilities expense.
12. Telephone bill.

Instructions
Identify the costs above as variable, fixed, or mixed.

E22-4 Jim Thome wants Thome Company to use CVP analysis to study the effects of changes in costs and volume on the company. Thome has heard that certain assumptions must be valid in order for CVP analysis to be useful.

Explain assumptions underlying CVP analysis.

(SO 4)

Instructions
Prepare a memo to Jim Thome concerning the assumptions that underlie CVP analysis.

E22-5 In the month of June, Barbara's Beauty Salon gave 2,700 haircuts, shampoos, and permanents at an average price of $30. During the month, fixed costs were $18,000 and variable costs were 70% of sales.

Compute contribution margin, break-even point, and margin of safety.

(SO 5, 6, 8)

Instructions
(a) Determine the contribution margin in dollars, per unit, and as a ratio.
(b) Using the contribution margin technique, compute the break-even point in dollars and in units.
(c) Compute the margin of safety in dollars and as a ratio.

E22-6 Grissom Company estimates that variable costs will be 60% of sales, and fixed costs will total $800,000. The selling price of the product is $4.

Prepare a CVP graph and compute break-even point and margin of safety.

(SO 6, 8)

Instructions
(a) Prepare a CVP graph, assuming maximum sales of $3,200,000. (*Note*: Use $400,000 increments for sales and costs and 100,000 increments for units.)
(b) Compute the break-even point in (1) units and (2) dollars.
(c) Compute the margin of safety in (1) dollars and (2) as a ratio, assuming actual sales are $2.5 million.

Chapter 22 Cost-Volume-Profit

Compute variable cost per unit, contribution margin ratio, and increase in fixed costs.
(SO 5, 6)

E22-7 In 2010, Hadicke Company had a break-even point of $350,000 based on a selling price of $7 per unit and fixed costs of $105,000. In 2011, the selling price and the variable cost per unit did not change, but the break-even point increased to $420,000.

Instructions
(a) Compute the variable cost per unit and the contribution margin ratio for 2010.
(b) Compute the increase in fixed costs for 2011.

Prepare CVP income statements.
(SO 5, 6)

E22-8 NIU Company has the following information available for September 2010.

Unit selling price of video game consoles	$ 400
Unit variable costs	$ 270
Total fixed costs	$52,000
Units sold	620

Instructions
(a) Prepare a CVP income statement that shows both total and per unit amounts.
(b) Compute NIU's breakeven point in units.
(c) Prepare a CVP income statement for the breakeven point that shows both total and per unit amounts.

Compute various components to derive target net income under different assumptions.
(SO 6, 7)

E22-9 Lynn Company had $150,000 of net income in 2010 when the selling price per unit was $150, the variable costs per unit were $90, and the fixed costs were $570,000. Management expects per unit data and total fixed costs to remain the same in 2011. The president of Lynn Company is under pressure from stockholders to increase net income by $60,000 in 2011.

Instructions
(a) Compute the number of units sold in 2010.
(b) Compute the number of units that would have to be sold in 2011 to reach the stockholders' desired profit level.
(c) Assume that Lynn Company sells the same number of units in 2011 as it did in 2010. What would the selling price have to be in order to reach the stockholders' desired profit level?

Compute net income under different alternatives.
(SO 7)

E22-10 Moran Company reports the following operating results for the month of August: Sales $350,000 (units 5,000); variable costs $210,000; and fixed costs $90,000. Management is considering the following independent courses of action to increase net income.

1. Increase selling price by 10% with no change in total variable costs.
2. Reduce variable costs to 55% of sales.
3. Reduce fixed costs by $10,000.

Instructions
Compute the net income to be earned under each alternative. Which course of action will produce the highest net income?

Prepare a CVP income statement before and after changes in business environment.
(SO 9)

E22-11 Polzin Company had sales in 2010 of $1,500,000 on 60,000 units. Variable costs totaled $840,000, and fixed costs totaled $500,000.

A new raw material is available that will decrease the variable costs per unit by 20% (or $2.80). However, to process the new raw material, fixed operating costs will increase by $60,000. Management feels that one-half of the decline in the variable costs per unit should be passed on to customers in the form of a sales price reduction. The marketing department expects that this sales price reduction will result in a 7% increase in the number of units sold.

Instructions
Prepare a CVP income statement for 2010, assuming the changes are made as described.

Compute total product cost and prepare an income statement using variable costing.
(SO 10)

*E22-12 Titus Equipment Company manufactures and distributes industrial air compressors. The following costs are available for the year ended December 31, 2010. The company has no beginning inventory. In 2010, 1,500 units were produced, but only 1,300 units were sold. The unit selling price was $4,500. Costs and expenses were:

Variable costs per unit	
Direct materials	$ 1,000
Direct labor	1,500
Variable manufacturing overhead	300
Variable selling and administrative expenses	70
Annual fixed costs and expenses	
Manufacturing overhead	$1,400,000
Selling and administrative expenses	100,000

Instructions

(a) Compute the manufacturing cost of one unit of product using variable costing.
(b) Prepare a 2010 income statement for Titus Company using variable costing.

E22-13 Cowell Corporation produces one product. Its cost includes direct materials ($10 per unit), direct labor ($8 per unit), variable overhead ($6 per unit), fixed manufacturing ($250,000), and fixed selling and administrative ($30,000). In October 2010, Cowell produced 25,000 units and sold 20,000 at $50 each.

Prepare absorption cost and variable cost income statements.
(SO 10)

Instructions

(a) Prepare an absorption costing income statement.
(b) Prepare a variable costing income statement.
(c) Explain the difference in net income in the two income statements.

EXERCISES: SET B

Visit the book's compaion website at **www.wiley.com/college/weygandt**, and choose the Student Companion site, to access Exercise Set B.

PROBLEMS: SET A

P22-1A Matt Reiss owns the Fredonia Barber Shop. He employs five barbers and pays each a base rate of $1,000 per month. One of the barbers serves as the manager and receives an extra $500 per month. In addition to the base rate, each barber also receives a commission of $5.50 per haircut.

Other costs are as follows.

Advertising	$200 per month
Rent	$900 per month
Barber supplies	$0.30 per haircut
Utilities	$175 per month plus $0.20 per haircut
Magazines	$25 per month

Determine variable and fixed costs, compute break-even point, prepare a CVP graph, and determine net income.
(SO 1, 3, 5, 6)

Matt currently charges $10 per haircut.

Instructions

(a) Determine the variable cost per haircut and the total monthly fixed costs.
(b) Compute the break-even point in units and dollars.
(c) Prepare a CVP graph, assuming a maximum of 1,800 haircuts in a month. Use increments of 300 haircuts on the horizontal axis and $3,000 on the vertical axis.
(d) Determine net income, assuming 1,900 haircuts are given in a month.

P22-2A Utech Company bottles and distributes Livit, a diet soft drink. The beverage is sold for 50 cents per 16-ounce bottle to retailers, who charge customers 75 cents per bottle. For the year 2010, management estimates the following revenues and costs.

Prepare a CVP income statement, compute break-even point, contribution margin ratio, margin of safety ratio, and sales for target net income.
(SO 5, 6, 7, 8, 9)

Net sales	$1,800,000	Selling expenses—variable	$70,000
Direct materials	430,000	Selling expenses—fixed	65,000
Direct labor	352,000	Administrative expenses—	
Manufacturing overhead—		variable	20,000
variable	316,000	Administrative expenses—	
Manufacturing overhead—		fixed	60,000
fixed	283,000		

Instructions

(a) Prepare a CVP income statement for 2010 based on management's estimates.
(b) Compute the break-even point in (1) units and (2) dollars.
(c) Compute the contribution margin ratio and the margin of safety ratio. (Round to full percents.)
(d) Determine the sales dollars required to earn net income of $238,000.

Chapter 22 Cost-Volume-Profit

Compute break-even point under alternative courses of action.

(SO 5, 6)

P22-3A Gorham Manufacturing's sales slumped badly in 2010. For the first time in its history, it operated at a loss. The company's income statement showed the following results from selling 600,000 units of product: Net sales $2,400,000; total costs and expenses $2,540,000; and net loss $140,000. Costs and expenses consisted of the amounts shown below.

	Total	Variable	Fixed
Cost of goods sold	$2,100,000	$1,440,000	$660,000
Selling expenses	240,000	72,000	168,000
Administrative expenses	200,000	48,000	152,000
	$2,540,000	$1,560,000	$980,000

Management is considering the following independent alternatives for 2011.

1. Increase unit selling price 20% with no change in costs, expenses, and sales volume.
2. Change the compensation of salespersons from fixed annual salaries totaling $150,000 to total salaries of $60,000 plus a 3% commission on net sales.
3. Purchase new automated equipment that will change the proportion between variable and fixed cost of goods sold to 54% variable and 46% fixed.

Instructions

(a) Compute the break-even point in dollars for 2010.
(b) Compute the break-even point in dollars under each of the alternative courses of action. (Round all ratios to nearest full percent.) Which course of action do you recommend?

Compute break-even point and margin of safety ratio, and prepare a CVP income statement before and after changes in business environment.

(SO 6, 8, 9)

P22-4A Alice Shoemaker is the advertising manager for Value Shoe Store. She is currently working on a major promotional campaign. Her ideas include the installation of a new lighting system and increased display space that will add $34,000 in fixed costs to the $270,000 currently spent. In addition, Alice is proposing that a 5% price decrease ($40 to $38) will produce a 20% increase in sales volume (20,000 to 24,000). Variable costs will remain at $22 per pair of shoes. Management is impressed with Alice's ideas but concerned about the effects that these changes will have on the break-even point and the margin of safety.

Instructions

(a) Compute the current break-even point in units, and compare it to the break-even point in units if Alice's ideas are used.
(b) Compute the margin of safety ratio for current operations and after Alice's changes are introduced. (Round to nearest full percent.)
(c) Prepare a CVP income statement for current operations and after Alice's changes are introduced. Would you make the changes suggested?

Compute break-even point and margin of safety ratio, and prepare a CVP income statement before and after changes in business environment.

(SO 5, 6, 7, 8)

P22-5A Poole Corporation has collected the following information after its first year of sales. Net sales were $1,600,000 on 100,000 units; selling expenses $240,000 (40% variable and 60% fixed); direct materials $511,000; direct labor $285,000; administrative expenses $280,000 (20% variable and 80% fixed); manufacturing overhead $360,000 (70% variable and 30% fixed). Top management has asked you to do a CVP analysis so that it can make plans for the coming year. It has projected that unit sales will increase by 10% next year.

Instructions

(a) Compute (1) the contribution margin for the current year and the projected year, and (2) the fixed costs for the current year. (Assume that fixed costs will remain the same in the projected year.)
(b) Compute the break-even point in units and sales dollars for the current year.
(c) The company has a target net income of $310,000. What is the required sales in dollars for the company to meet its target?
(d) If the company meets its target net income number, by what percentage could its sales fall before it is operating at a loss? That is, what is its margin of safety ratio?
(e) The company is considering a purchase of equipment that would reduce its direct labor costs by $104,000 and would change its manufacturing overhead costs to 30% variable and 70% fixed (assume total manufacturing overhead cost is $360,000, as above). It is also

considering switching to a pure commission basis for its sales staff. This would change selling expenses to 90% variable and 10% fixed (assume total selling expense is $240,000, as above). Assuming that net sales remain at first-year levels, compute (1) the contribution margin and (2) the contribution margin ratio, and recompute (3) the break-even point in sales dollars. Comment on the effect each of management's proposed changes has on the break-even point.

P22-6A TLR produces plastic that is used for injection molding applications such as gears for small motors. In 2010, the first year of operations, TLR produced 6,000 tons of plastic and sold 5,000 tons. In 2011, the production and sales results were exactly reversed. In each year, selling price per ton was $1,000, variable manufacturing costs were 15% of the sales price of units produced, variable selling expenses were 10% of the selling price of units sold, fixed manufacturing costs were $2,100,000, and fixed administrative expenses were $500,000.

Prepare income statements under absorption and variable costing.
(SO 10)

Instructions
(a) Prepare comparative income statements for each year using variable costing.
(b) Prepare comparative income statements for each year using absorption costing.
(c) Reconcile the differences each year in income from operations under the two costing approaches.
(d) Comment on the effects of production and sales on net income under the two costing approaches.

PROBLEMS: SET B

P22-1B The McCune Barber Shop employs four barbers. One barber, who also serves as the manager, is paid a salary of $3,900 per month. The other barbers are paid $1,900 per month. In addition, each barber is paid a commission of $2 per haircut. Other monthly costs are: store rent $700 plus 60 cents per haircut, depreciation on equipment $500, barber supplies 40 cents per haircut, utilities $300, and advertising $100. The price of a haircut is $10.

Determine variable and fixed costs, compute break-even point, prepare a CVP graph, and determine net income.
(SO 1, 3, 5, 6)

Instructions
(a) Determine the variable cost per haircut and the total monthly fixed costs.
(b) Compute the break-even point in units and dollars.
(c) Prepare a CVP graph, assuming a maximum of 1,800 haircuts in a month. Use increments of 300 haircuts on the horizontal axis and $3,000 increments on the vertical axis.
(d) Determine the net income, assuming 1,700 haircuts are given in a month.

P22-2B Huber Company bottles and distributes No-FIZZ, a fruit drink. The beverage is sold for 50 cents per 16-ounce bottle to retailers, who charge customers 70 cents per bottle. For the year 2010, management estimates the following revenues and costs.

Prepare a CVP income statement, compute break-even point, contribution margin ratio, margin of safety ratio, and sales for target net income.
(SO 5, 6, 7, 8, 9)

Net sales	$2,000,000	Selling expenses—variable	$ 80,000
Direct materials	360,000	Selling expenses—fixed	150,000
Direct labor	450,000	Administrative expenses— variable	40,000
Manufacturing overhead— variable	270,000	Administrative expenses— fixed	70,000
Manufacturing overhead— fixed	280,000		

Instructions
(a) Prepare a CVP income statement for 2010 based on management's estimates.
(b) Compute the break-even point in (1) units and (2) dollars.
(c) Compute the contribution margin ratio and the margin of safety ratio.
(d) Determine the sales dollars required to earn net income of $390,000.

P22-3B Keppel Manufacturing had a bad year in 2010. For the first time in its history it operated at a loss. The company's income statement showed the following results from selling 60,000 units of product: Net sales $1,500,000; total costs and expenses $1,890,000; and net loss $390,000. Costs and expenses consisted of the amounts shown on the next page.

Compute break-even point under alternative courses of action.
(SO 5, 6)

	Total	Variable	Fixed
Cost of goods sold	$1,350,000	$930,000	$420,000
Selling expenses	420,000	65,000	355,000
Administrative expenses	120,000	55,000	65,000
	$1,890,000	$1,050,000	$840,000

Management is considering the following independent alternatives for 2011.
1. Increase unit selling price 40% with no change in costs, expenses, and sales volume.
2. Change the compensation of salespersons from fixed annual salaries totaling $200,000 to total salaries of $30,000 plus a 4% commission on net sales.
3. Purchase new high-tech factory machinery that will change the proportion between variable and fixed cost of goods sold to 50:50.

Instructions
(a) Compute the break-even point in dollars for 2010.
(b) Compute the break-even point in dollars under each of the alternative courses of action. Which course of action do you recommend?

Compute break-even point and margin of safety ratio, and prepare a CVP income statement before and after changes in business environment.

(SO 6, 8, 9)

P22-4B Jane Greinke is the advertising manager for Payless Shoe Store. She is currently working on a major promotional campaign. Her ideas include the installation of a new lighting system and increased display space that will add $24,000 in fixed costs to the $210,000 currently spent. In addition, Jane is proposing that a 6⅔% price decrease (from $30 to $28) will produce an increase in sales volume from 16,000 to 20,000 units. Variable costs will remain at $15 per pair of shoes. Management is impressed with Jane's ideas but concerned about the effects that these changes will have on the break-even point and the margin of safety.

Instructions
(a) Compute the current break-even point in units, and compare it to the break-even point in units if Jane's ideas are used.
(b) Compute the margin of safety ratio for current operations and after Jane's changes are introduced. (Round to nearest full percent.)
(c) Prepare a CVP income statement for current operations and after Jane's changes are introduced. Would you make the changes suggested?

Compute break-even point and margin of safety ratio, and prepare a CVP income statement before and after changes in business environment.

(SO 5, 6, 7, 8)

P22-5B Mortonsen Corporation has collected the following information after its first year of sales. Net sales were $2,000,000 on 100,000 units; selling expenses $400,000 (30% variable and 70% fixed); direct materials $600,000; direct labor $340,000; administrative expenses $500,000 (30% variable and 70% fixed); manufacturing overhead $480,000 (20% variable and 80% fixed). Top management has asked you to do a CVP analysis so that it can make plans for the coming year. It has projected that unit sales will increase by 20% next year.

Instructions
(a) Compute (1) the contribution margin for the current year and the projected year, and (2) the fixed costs for the current year. (Assume that fixed costs will remain the same in the projected year.)
(b) Compute the break-even point in units and sales dollars.
(c) The company has a target net income of $374,000. What is the required sales in dollars for the company to meet its target?
(d) If the company meets its target net income number, by what percentage could its sales fall before it is operating at a loss? That is, what is its margin of safety ratio?
(e) The company is considering a purchase of equipment that would reduce its direct labor costs by $140,000 and would change its manufacturing overhead costs to 10% variable and 90% fixed (assume total manufacturing overhead cost is $480,000, as above). It is also considering switching to a pure commission basis for its sales staff. This would change selling expenses to 80% variable and 20% fixed (assume total selling expense is $400,000, as above). Compute (1) the contribution margin and (2) the contribution margin ratio, and recompute (3) the break-even point in sales dollars. Comment on the effect each of management's proposed changes has on the break-even point.

Prepare income statements under absorption and variable costing.

(SO 10)

*P22-6B Blanco Metal Company produces the steel wire that goes into the production of paper clips. In 2010, the first year of operations, Blanco produced 50,000 miles of wire and sold 45,000 miles. In 2011, the production and sales results were exactly reversed. In each year, selling price per mile was $60, variable manufacturing costs were 20% of the sales price, variable selling expenses were $8.00 per mile sold, fixed manufacturing costs were $1,200,000, and fixed administrative expenses were $230,000.

Instructions

(a) Prepare comparative income statements for each year using variable costing.
(b) Prepare comparative income statements for each year using absorption costing.
(c) Reconcile the differences each year in income from operations under the two costing approaches.
(d) Comment on the effects of production and sales on net income under the two costing approaches.

PROBLEMS: SET C

Visit the book's companion website at **www.wiley.com/college/weygandt**, and choose the Student Companion site, to access Problem Set C.

WATERWAYS CONTINUING PROBLEM

(*Note:* This is a continuation of the Waterways Problem from Chapters 19 through 21.)

WCP22 The Vice President for Sales and Marketing at Waterways Corporation is planning for production needs to meet sales demand in the coming year. He is also trying to determine how the company's profits might be increased in the coming year. This problem asks you to use cost-volume-profit concepts to help Waterways understand contribution margins of some of its products and to decide whether to mass-produce certain products.

Go to the book's companion website,
www.wiley.com/college/weygandt,
to find the remainder of this problem.

BROADENING YOUR PERSPECTIVE

Decision Making Across the Organization

BYP22-1 Gagliano Company has decided to introduce a new product. The new product can be manufactured by either a capital-intensive method or a labor-intensive method. The manufacturing method will not affect the quality of the product. The estimated manufacturing costs by the two methods are as follows.

	Capital-Intensive	Labor-Intensive
Direct materials	$5 per unit	$5.50 per unit
Direct labor	$6 per unit	$8.00 per unit
Variable overhead	$3 per unit	$4.50 per unit
Fixed manufacturing costs	$2,508,000	$1,538,000

Gagliano's market research department has recommended an introductory unit sales price of $30. The incremental selling expenses are estimated to be $502,000 annually plus $2 for each unit sold, regardless of manufacturing method.

Instructions

With the class divided into groups, answer the following.

(a) Calculate the estimated break-even point in annual unit sales of the new product if Gagliano Company uses the:
   (1) capital-intensive manufacturing method.
   (2) labor-intensive manufacturing method.
(b) Determine the annual unit sales volume at which Gagliano Company would be indifferent between the two manufacturing methods.
(c) Explain the circumstance under which Gagliano should employ each of the two manufacturing methods.

(CMA adapted)

Managerial Analysis

BYP22-2 The condensed income statement for the Terri and Jerri partnership for 2010 is as follows.

TERRI AND JERRI COMPANY
Income Statement
For the Year Ended December 31, 2010

Sales (200,000 units)		$1,200,000
Cost of goods sold		800,000
Gross profit		400,000
Operating expenses		
Selling	$280,000	
Administrative	160,000	440,000
Net loss		($40,000)

A cost behavior analysis indicates that 75% of the cost of goods sold are variable, 50% of the selling expenses are variable, and 25% of the administrative expenses are variable.

Instructions

(Round to nearest unit, dollar, and percentage, where necessary. Use the CVP income statement format in computing profits.)

(a) Compute the break-even point in total sales dollars and in units for 2010.
(b) Terri has proposed a plan to get the partnership "out of the red" and improve its profitability. She feels that the quality of the product could be substantially improved by spending $0.25 more per unit on better raw materials. The selling price per unit could be increased to only $6.25 because of competitive pressures. Terri estimates that sales volume will increase by 30%. What effect would Terri's plan have on the profits and the break-even point in dollars of the partnership? (Round the contribution margin ratio to two decimal places.)
(c) Jerri was a marketing major in college. She believes that sales volume can be increased only by intensive advertising and promotional campaigns. She therefore proposed the following plan as an alternative to Terri's. (1) Increase variable selling expenses to $0.79 per unit, (2) lower the selling price per unit by $0.30, and (3) increase fixed selling expenses by $35,000. Jerri quoted an old marketing research report that said that sales volume would increase by 60% if these changes were made. What effect would Jerri's plan have on the profits and the break-even point in dollars of the partnership?
(d) Which plan should be accepted? Explain your answer.

Real-World Focus

BYP22-3 **The Coca-Cola Company** hardly needs an introduction. A line taken from the cover of a recent annual report says it all: If you measured time in servings of Coca-Cola, "a billion Coca-Cola's ago was yesterday morning." On average, every U.S. citizen drinks 363 8-ounce servings of Coca-Cola products each year. Coca-Cola's primary line of business is the making and selling of syrup to bottlers. These bottlers then sell the finished bottles and cans of Coca-Cola to the consumer.

The annual report of Coca-Cola provided the following information.

> **THE COCA-COLA COMPANY**
> **Management Discussion**
>
> Our gross margin declined to 61 percent this year from 62 percent in the prior year, primarily due to costs for materials such as sweeteners and packaging.
>
> The increases [in selling expenses] in the last two years were primarily due to higher marketing expenditures in support of our Company's volume growth.
>
> We measure our sales volume in two ways: (1) gallon shipments of concentrates and syrups and (2) unit cases of finished product (bottles and cans of Coke sold by bottlers).

Instructions
Answer the following questions.

(a) Are sweeteners and packaging a variable cost or a fixed cost? What is the impact on the contribution margin of an increase in the per unit cost of sweeteners or packaging? What are the implications for profitability?

(b) In your opinion, are marketing expenditures a fixed cost, variable cost, or mixed cost to The Coca-Cola Company? Give justification for your answer.

(c) Which of the two measures cited for measuring volume represents the activity index as defined in this chapter? Why might Coca-Cola use two different measures?

Exploring the Web

BYP22-4 **Ganong Bros. Ltd.**, located in St. Stephen, New Brunswick, is Canada's oldest independent candy company. Its products are distributed worldwide. In 1885, Ganong invented the popular "chicken bone," a cinnamon flavored, pink, hard candy jacket over a chocolate center. The home page of Ganong, listed below, includes information about the company and its products.

Address: www.ganong.com/retail/chicken_bones.html, or go to **www.wiley.com/college/weygandt**

Instructions
Read the description of "chicken bones," and answer the following.

(a) Describe the steps in making "chicken bones."

(b) Identify at least two variable and two fixed costs that are likely to affect the production of "chicken bones."

Communication Activity

BYP22-5 Your roommate asks your help on the following questions about CVP analysis formulas.

(a) How can the mathematical equation for break-even sales show both sales units and sales dollars?

(b) How do the formulas differ for contribution margin per unit and contribution margin ratio?

(c) How can contribution margin be used to determine break-even sales in units and in dollars?

Instructions
Write a memo to your roommate stating the relevant formulas and answering each question.

Ethics Case

BYP22-6 Kenny Hampton is an accountant for Bartley Company. Early this year Kenny made a highly favorable projection of sales and profits over the next 3 years for Bartley's hot-selling computer PLEX. As a result of the projections Kenny presented to senior management, they decided to expand production in this area. This decision led to dislocations of some plant personnel who were reassigned to one of the company's newer plants in another state. However, no one was fired, and in fact the company expanded its work force slightly.

Unfortunately Kenny rechecked his computations on the projections a few months later and found that he had made an error that would have reduced his projections substantially. Luckily, sales of PLEX have exceeded projections so far, and management is satisfied with its decision. Kenny, however, is not sure what to do. Should he confess his honest mistake and jeopardize his possible promotion? He suspects that no one will catch the error because sales of PLEX have exceeded his projections, and it appears that profits will materialize close to his projections.

Instructions
(a) Who are the stakeholders in this situation?
(b) Identify the ethical issues involved in this situation.
(c) What are the possible alternative actions for Kenny? What would you do in Kenny's position?

"All About You" Activity

BYP22-7 In the **All About You** feature in this chapter, you learned that cost-volume-profit analysis can be used in making personal financial decisions. The purchase of a new car is one of your biggest personal expenditures. It is important that you carefully analyze your options.

Suppose that you are considering the purchase of a hybrid vehicle. Let's assume the following facts: The hybrid will initially cost an additional $3,000 above the cost of a traditional vehicle. The hybrid will get 40 miles per gallon of gas, and the traditional car will get 25 miles per gallon. Also, assume that the cost of gas is $4 per gallon.

Instructions
Using the facts above, answer the following questions.
(a) What is the variable gasoline cost of going one mile in the hybrid car? What is the variable cost of going one mile in the traditional car?
(b) Using the information in part (a), if "miles" is your unit of measure, what is the "contribution margin" of the hybrid vehicle relative to the traditional vehicle? That is, express the variable cost savings on a per-mile basis.
(c) How many miles would you have to drive in order to break even on your investment in the hybrid car?
(d) What other factors might you want to consider?

Answers to Insight and Accounting Across the Organization Questions

p. 988 Charter Flights Offer a Good Deal
Q: How did FlightServe determine that it would break even with 3.3 seats full per flight?
A: *FlightServe determined its break-even point with the following formula:*
Fixed costs ÷ Contribution margin per seat occupied = Break-even point in seats.

p. 991 How a Rolling Stones' Tour Makes Money
Q: What amount of sales dollars are required for the promoter to break even?
A: Fixed costs = $1,200,000 + $400,000 = $1,600,000
Contribution margin ratio = 80%
Break-even sales = $1,600,000 ÷ .80 = $2,000,000

Authors' Comments on All About You: A Hybrid Dilemma (p. 995)

Just like the break-even analysis that a company would perform on an investment in a new piece of equipment, the break-even analysis of a hybrid car requires a lot of assumptions. After deciding on a car, you need to estimate how many miles you would drive each year and how many years you would own the car. If you trade cars every two or three years, it is unlikely, with the hybrids available today, that you will recoup your initial investment. Your chances of recouping the investment increase the longer you keep the car and the more miles you drive. You need to determine whether you will get a federal tax credit or a rebate from your employer. You also need to estimate what the car would be worth when you sell it. Based on assumed values for the average driver, *Consumer Reports* determined that only the most fuel-efficient hybrids save enough on fuel to cover their additional costs, but individual results will vary depending on the factors mentioned above.

Answers to Self-Study Questions
1. d **2.** c **3.** a **4.** d **5.** c **6.** d **7.** c **8.** c **9.** c **10.** b **11.** b **12.** a **13.** c **14.** a **15.** a

Remember to go back to the Navigator box on the chapter-opening page and check off your completed work.

Chapter 23

Budgetary Planning

STUDY OBJECTIVES

After studying this chapter, you should be able to:

1. Indicate the benefits of budgeting.
2. State the essentials of effective budgeting.
3. Identify the budgets that comprise the master budget.
4. Describe the sources for preparing the budgeted income statement.
5. Explain the principal sections of a cash budget.
6. Indicate the applicability of budgeting in non-manufacturing companies.

✓ The Navigator

Scan **Study Objectives**	■
Read **Feature Story**	■
Read **Preview**	■
Read text and answer **DO IT!** p. 1023 p. 1026 p. 1030 p. 1035	■
Work **Comprehensive** **DO IT!** p. 1039	■
Review **Summary of Study Objectives**	■
Answer **Self-Study Questions**	■
Complete **Assignments**	■

✓ The Navigator

Feature Story

THE NEXT AMAZON.COM? NOT QUITE

The bursting of the dot-com bubble resulted in countless stories of dot-com failures. Many of these ventures were half-baked, get-rich-quick schemes, rarely based on sound business practices. Initially they saw money flowing in faster than they knew what to do with—which was precisely the problem. Without proper planning and budgeting, much of the money went to waste. In some cases, failure was actually brought on by rapid, uncontrolled growth.

One such example was online discount bookseller, www.Positively-You.com. One of the website's co-founders, Lyle Bowline, had never run a business. However, his experience as an assistant director of an entrepreneurial center had provided him with knowledge about the do's and don'ts of small business. To minimize costs, he started the company small and simple. He invested $5,000 in computer equipment and ran the business out of his basement. In the early months, even though sales were only about $2,000 a month, the

1016

company actually made a profit because it kept its costs low (a feat few other dot-coms could boast of).

Things changed dramatically when the company received national publicity in the financial press. Suddenly the company's sales increased to $50,000 a month—fully 25 times the previous level. The "simple" little business suddenly needed a business plan, a strategic plan, and a budget. It needed to rent office space and to hire employees.

Initially, members of a local book club donated time to help meet the sudden demand. Some put in so much time that eventually the company hired them. Quickly the number of paid employees ballooned. The sudden growth necessitated detailed planning and budgeting. The need for a proper budget was accentuated by the fact that the company's gross profit was only 16 cents on each dollar of goods sold. This meant that after paying for its inventory, the company had only 16 cents of every dollar to cover its remaining operating costs.

Unfortunately, the company never got things under control. Within a few months, sales had plummeted to $12,000 per month. At this level of sales the company could not meet the mountain of monthly expenses that it had accumulated in trying to grow. Ironically, the company's sudden success, and the turmoil it created, appears to have been what eventually caused the company to fail.

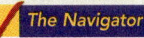

Inside Chapter 23...

- **Businesses Often Feel Too Busy to Plan for the Future** (p. 1020)
- **Without a Budget, Can the Games Begin?** (p. 1034)
- *All About You:* **Avoiding Personal Financial Disaster** (p. 1038)

Preview of Chapter 23

As the Feature Story about Positively-You.com indicates, budgeting is critical to financial well-being. As a student, you budget your study time and your money. Families budget income and expenses. Governmental agencies budget revenues and expenditures. Business enterprises use budgets in planning and controlling their operations.

Our primary focus in this chapter is budgeting—specifically, how budgeting is used as a *planning tool* by management. Through budgeting, it should be possible for management to maintain enough cash to pay creditors, to have sufficient raw materials to meet production requirements, and to have adequate finished goods to meet expected sales.

The content and organization of Chapter 23 are as follows.

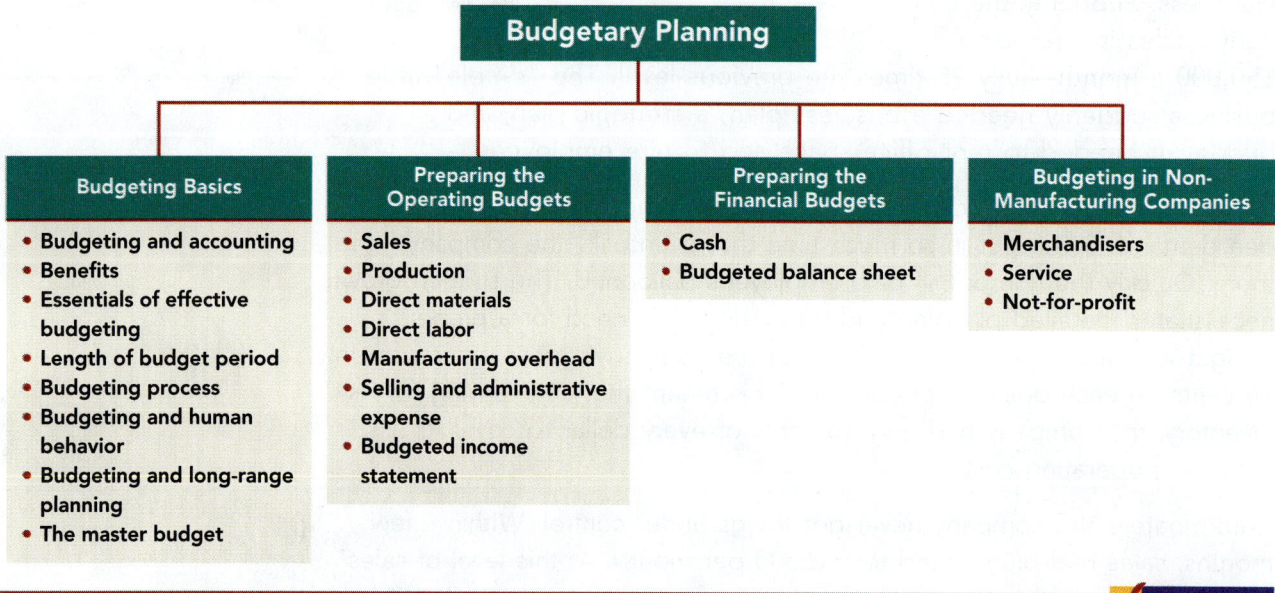

BUDGETING BASICS

One of management's major responsibilities is planning. As explained in Chapter 19, **planning** is the process of establishing enterprise-wide objectives. A successful organization makes both long-term and short-term plans. These plans set forth the objectives of the company and the proposed way of accomplishing them.

A **budget** is a formal written statement of management's plans for a specified future time period, expressed in financial terms. It normally represents the primary method of communicating agreed-upon objectives throughout the organization. Once adopted, a budget becomes an important basis for evaluating performance. It promotes efficiency and serves as a deterrent to waste and inefficiency. We consider the role of budgeting as a **control device** in Chapter 24.

Budgeting and Accounting

Accounting information makes major contributions to the budgeting process. From the accounting records, companies can obtain historical data on revenues, costs, and expenses. These data are helpful in formulating future budget goals.

Normally, accountants have the responsibility for presenting management's budgeting goals in financial terms. In this role, they translate management's plans

1018

and communicate the budget to employees throughout the company. They prepare periodic budget reports that provide the basis for measuring performance and comparing actual results with planned objectives. The budget itself, and the administration of the budget, however, are entirely management responsibilities.

The Benefits of Budgeting

The primary benefits of budgeting are:

1. It requires all levels of management to **plan ahead** and to formalize goals on a recurring basis.
2. It provides **definite objectives** for evaluating performance at each level of responsibility.
3. It creates an **early warning system** for potential problems so that management can make changes before things get out of hand.
4. It facilitates the **coordination of activities** within the business. It does this by correlating the goals of each segment with overall company objectives. Thus, the company can integrate production and sales promotion with expected sales.
5. It results in greater **management awareness** of the entity's overall operations and the impact on operations of external factors, such as economic trends.
6. It **motivates personnel** throughout the organization to meet planned objectives.

> **STUDY OBJECTIVE 1**
> Indicate the benefits of budgeting.

A budget is an aid to management; it is not a *substitute* for management. A budget cannot operate or enforce itself. Companies can realize the benefits of budgeting only when managers carefully administer budgets.

Essentials of Effective Budgeting

Effective budgeting depends on a **sound organizational structure**. In such a structure, authority and responsibility for all phases of operations are clearly defined. Budgets based on **research and analysis** should result in realistic goals that will contribute to the growth and profitability of a company. And, the effectiveness of a budget program is directly related to its **acceptance by all levels of management**.

> **STUDY OBJECTIVE 2**
> State the essentials of effective budgeting.

Once adopted, the budget should be an important tool for evaluating performance. Managers should systematically and periodically review variations between actual and expected results to determine their cause(s). However, individuals should not be held responsible for variations that are beyond their control.

Length of the Budget Period

The budget period is not necessarily one year in length. **A budget may be prepared for any period of time.** Various factors influence the length of the budget period. These factors include the type of budget, the nature of the organization, the need for periodic appraisal, and prevailing business conditions. For example, cash may be budgeted monthly, whereas a plant expansion budget may cover a 10-year period.

The budget period should be long enough to provide an attainable goal under normal business conditions. Ideally, the time period should minimize the impact of seasonal or cyclical fluctuations. On the other hand, the budget period should not be so long that reliable estimates are impossible.

The **most common budget period is one year**. The annual budget, in turn, is often supplemented by monthly and quarterly budgets. Many companies use **continuous 12-month budgets**. These budgets drop the month just ended and add a future month. One advantage of continuous budgeting is that it keeps management planning a full year ahead.

The Budgeting Process

The development of the budget for the coming year generally starts several months before the end of the current year. The budgeting process usually begins with the collection of data from each organizational unit of the company. Past performance is often the starting point from which future budget goals are formulated.

The budget is developed within the framework of a **sales forecast**. This forecast shows potential sales for the industry and the company's expected share of such sales. Sales forecasting involves a consideration of various factors: (1) general economic conditions, (2) industry trends, (3) market research studies, (4) anticipated advertising and promotion, (5) previous market share, (6) changes in prices, and (7) technological developments. The input of sales personnel and top management is essential to the sales forecast.

In small companies like Positively-You.com, the budgeting process is often informal. In larger companies, a **budget committee** has responsibility for coordinating the preparation of the budget. The committee ordinarily includes the president, treasurer, chief accountant (controller), and management personnel from each of the major areas of the company, such as sales, production, and research. The budget committee serves as a review board where managers can defend their budget goals and requests. Differences are reviewed, modified if necessary, and reconciled. The budget is then put in its final form by the budget committee, approved, and distributed.

ACCOUNTING ACROSS THE ORGANIZATION

Businesses Often Feel Too Busy to Plan for the Future

A recent study by Willard & Shullman Group Ltd. found that fewer than 14% of businesses with fewer than 500 employees prepare an annual budget or have a written business plan. In all, nearly 60% of these businesses have no plans on paper at all. For many small businesses the basic assumption is that, "As long as I sell as much as I can, and keep my employees paid, I'm doing OK." A few small business owners even say that they see no need for budgeting and planning. Most small business owners, though, say that they understand that budgeting and planning are critical for survival and growth. But given the long hours that they already work addressing day-to-day challenges, they also say that they are "just too busy to plan for the future."

? Describe a situation in which a business "sells as much as it can" but cannot "keep its employees paid."

Budgeting and Human Behavior

A budget can have a significant impact on human behavior. It may inspire a manager to higher levels of performance. Or, it may discourage additional effort and pull down the morale of a manager. Why do these diverse effects occur? The answer is found in how the budget is developed and administered.

In developing the budget, each level of management should be invited to participate. This "bottom-to-top" approach is referred to as **participative budgeting**. The advantages of participative budgeting are, first, that lower-level managers have more detailed knowledge of their specific area and thus are able to provide more accurate budgetary estimates. Second, when lower-level managers participate in the budgeting process, they are more likely to perceive the resulting budget as fair. The overall goal is to reach agreement on a budget that the managers consider fair and achievable, but which also meets the corporate goals set by top management.

When this goal is met, the budget will provide positive motivation for the managers. In contrast, if the managers view the budget as being unfair and unrealistic, they may feel discouraged and uncommitted to budget goals. The risk of having unrealistic budgets is generally greater when the budget is developed from top management down to lower management than vice versa.

Participative budgeting does, however, have potential disadvantages. First, it is more time-consuming (and thus more costly) than a "top-down" approach, in which the budget is simply dictated to lower-level managers. A second disadvantage is that participative budgeting can foster budgetary "gaming" through budgetary slack. **Budgetary slack** occurs when managers intentionally underestimate budgeted revenues or overestimate budgeted expenses in order to make it easier to achieve budgetary goals. To minimize budgetary slack, higher-level managers must carefully review and thoroughly question the budget projections provided to them by employees whom they supervise. Illustration 23-1 graphically displays the appropriate flow of budget data from bottom to top in an organization.

> **ETHICS NOTE**
> Unrealistic budgets can lead to unethical employee behavior such as cutting corners on the job or distorting internal financial reports.

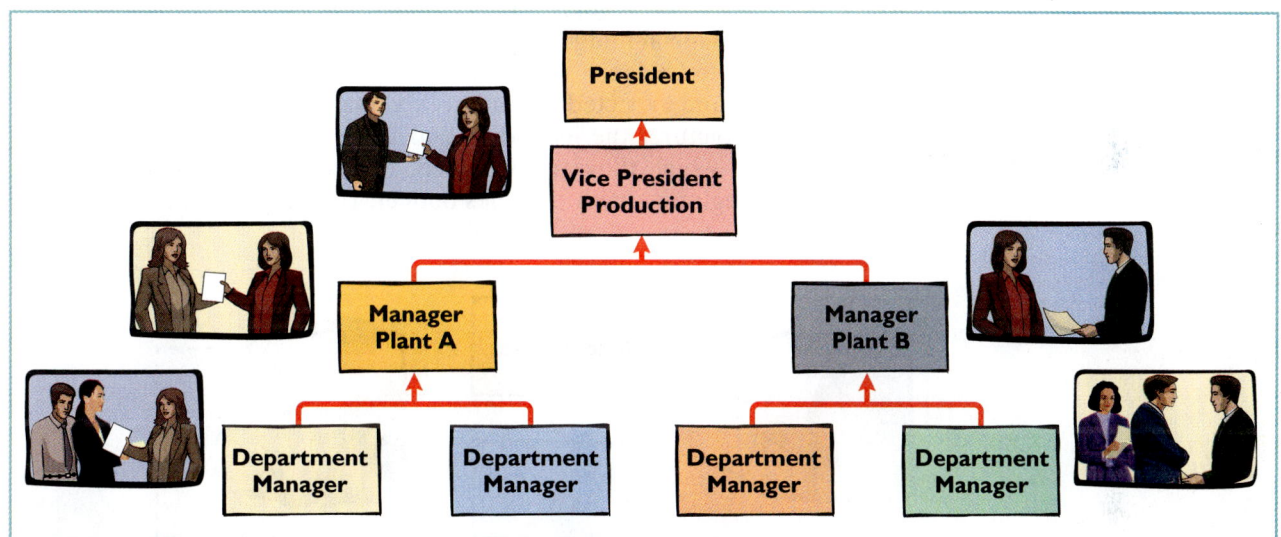

Illustration 23-1
Flow of budget data from lower levels of management to top levels

For the budget to be effective, top management must completely support the budget. The budget is an important basis for evaluating performance. It also can be used as a positive aid in achieving projected goals. The effect of an evaluation is positive when top management tempers criticism with advice and assistance. In contrast, a manager is likely to respond negatively if top management uses the budget exclusively to assess blame. A budget should not be used as a pressure device to force improved performance. In sum, a budget can be a manager's friend or a foe.

Budgeting and Long-Range Planning

Budgeting and long-range planning are not the same. One important difference is the **time period involved**. The maximum length of a budget is usually one year, and budgets are often prepared for shorter periods of time, such as a month or a quarter. In contrast, long-range planning usually encompasses a period of at least five years.

A second significant difference is in **emphasis**. Budgeting focuses on achieving specific short-term goals, such as meeting annual profit objectives. **Long-range planning**, on the other hand, identifies long-term goals, selects strategies to achieve those goals, and develops policies and plans to implement the strategies.

> **HELPFUL HINT**
> In comparing a budget with a long-range plan: (1) Which has more detail? (2) Which is done for a longer period of time? (3) Which is more concerned with short-term goals?
> Answers: (1) Budget. (2) Long-range plan. (3) Budget.

In long-range planning, management also considers anticipated trends in the economic and political environment and how the company should cope with them.

The final difference between budgeting and long-range planning relates to the **amount of detail presented**. Budgets, as you will see in this chapter, can be very detailed. Long-range plans contain considerably less detail. The data in long-range plans are intended more for a review of progress toward long-term goals than as a basis of control for achieving specific results. The primary objective of long-range planning is to develop the best strategy to maximize the company's performance over an extended future period.

The Master Budget

> **STUDY OBJECTIVE 3**
> Identify the budgets that comprise the master budget.

The term "budget" is actually a shorthand term to describe a variety of budget documents. All of these documents are combined into a master budget. The **master budget** is a set of interrelated budgets that constitutes a plan of action for a specified time period.

The master budget contains two classes of budgets. **Operating budgets** are the individual budgets that result in the preparation of the budgeted income statement. These budgets establish goals for the company's sales and production personnel. In contrast, **financial budgets** are the capital expenditure budget, the cash budget, and the budgeted balance sheet. These budgets focus primarily on the cash resources needed to fund expected operations and planned capital expenditures.

Illustration 23-2 pictures the individual budgets included in a master budget, and the sequence in which they are prepared. The company first develops the operating budgets, beginning with the sales budget. Then it prepares the financial

Illustration 23-2
Components of the master budget

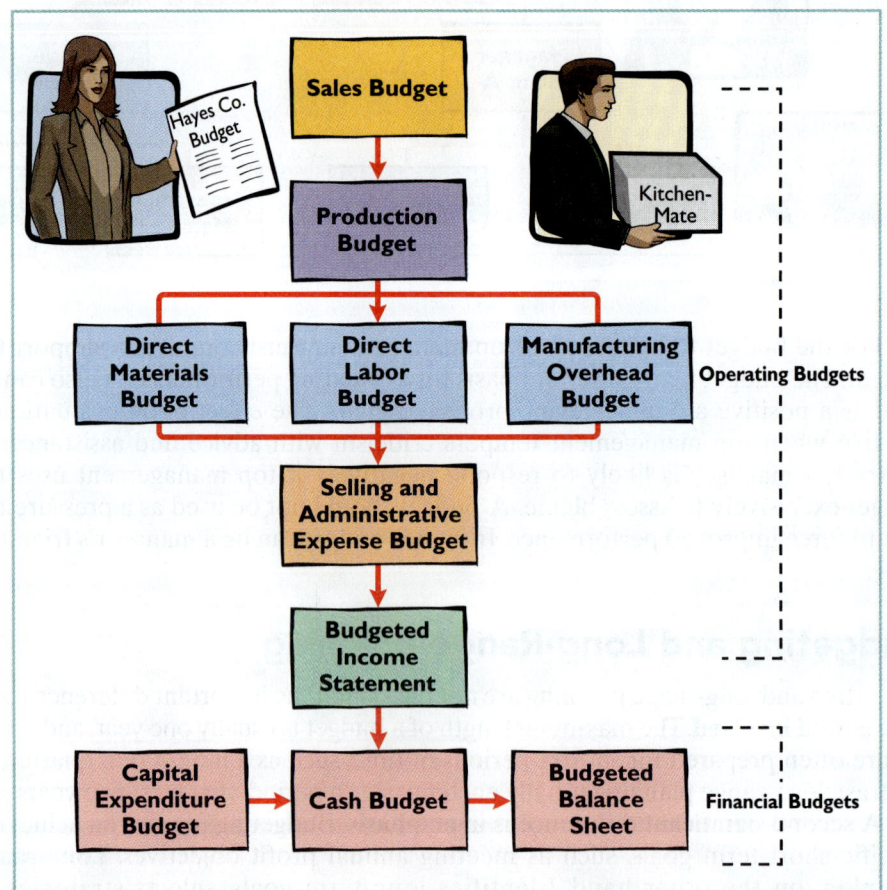

budgets. We will explain and illustrate each budget shown in Illustration 23-2 except the capital expenditure budget. That budget is discussed under the topic of capital budgeting in Chapter 26.

DO IT!

BUDGET TERMINOLOGY

Use this list of terms to complete the sentences that follow.

Long-range planning   Participative budgeting
Sales forecast   Operating budgets
Master budget   Financial budgets

1. A _____ shows potential sales for the industry and a company's expected share of such sales.
2. _____ are used as the basis for the preparation of the budgeted income statement.
3. The _____ is a set of interrelated budgets that constitutes a plan of action for a specified time period.
4. _____ identifies long-term goals, selects strategies to achieve these goals, and develops policies and plans to implement the strategies.
5. Lower-level managers are more likely to perceive results as fair and achievable under a _____ approach.
6. _____ focus primarily on the cash resources needed to fund expected operations and planned capital expenditures.

Solution
1. Sales forecast.
2. Operating budgets.
3. Master budget.
4. Long-range planning.
5. Participative budgeting.
6. Financial budgets.

Related exercise material: **BE23-1, E23-1,** and **DO IT! 23-1.**

action plan
✔ Understand the budgeting process, including the importance of the sales forecast.
✔ Understand the difference between an operating and a financial budget.
✔ Differentiate budgeting from long-range planning.
✔ Realize that the master budget is a set of interrelated budgets.

PREPARING THE OPERATING BUDGETS

We use a case study of Hayes Company in preparing the operating budgets. Hayes manufactures and sells a single product, Kitchen-Mate. The budgets are prepared by quarters for the year ending December 31, 2010. Hayes Company begins its annual budgeting process on September 1, 2009, and it completes the budget for 2010 by December 1, 2009.

Sales Budget

As shown in the master budget in Illustration 23-2, **the sales budget is the first budget prepared**. Each of the other budgets depends on the sales budget. The **sales budget** is derived from the sales forecast. It represents management's best estimate of sales revenue for the budget period. An inaccurate sales budget may adversely affect net income. For example, an overly optimistic sales budget may result in excessive inventories that may have to be sold at reduced prices. In contrast, an unduly conservative budget may result in loss of sales revenue due to inventory shortages.

HELPFUL HINT

For a retail or manufacturing company, what is the starting point in preparing the master budget, and why? Answer: The sales budget is the starting point for the master budget. It sets the level of activity for other functions such as production and purchasing.

Forecasting sales is challenging. For example, consider the forecasting challenges faced by major sports arenas, whose revenues depend on the success of the home team. Madison Square Garden's revenues from April to June were $193 million when the Knicks made the NBA playoffs. But revenues were only $133.2 million a couple of years later when the team did not make the playoffs. Or consider the challenges faced by Hollywood movie producers in predicting the complicated revenue stream produced by a new movie. Movie theater ticket sales represent only 20% of total revenue. The bulk of revenue comes from global sales, DVDs, video-on-demand, merchandising products, and videogames, all of which are difficult to forecast.

The sales budget is prepared by multiplying the expected unit sales volume for each product by its anticipated unit selling price. Hayes Company expects sales volume to be 3,000 units in the first quarter, with 500-unit increases in each succeeding quarter. Illustration 23-3 shows the sales budget for the year, by quarters, based on a sales price of $60 per unit.

Illustration 23-3
Sales budget

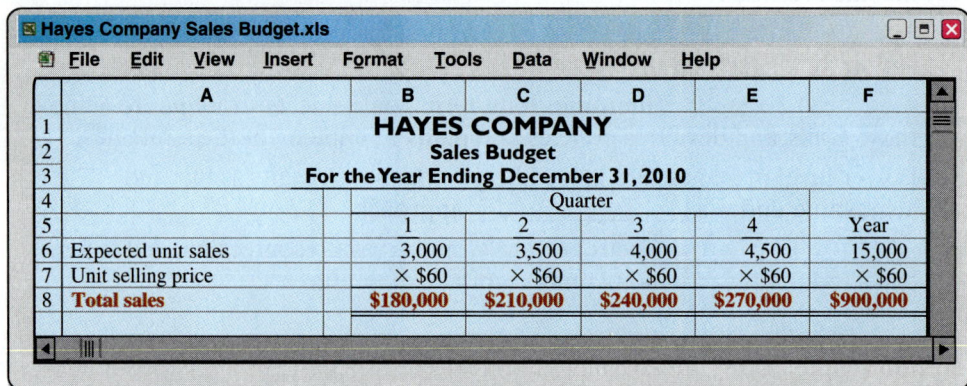

Some companies classify the anticipated sales revenue as cash or credit sales and by geographical regions, territories, or salespersons.

Production Budget

The **production budget** shows the units to produce to meet anticipated sales. Production requirements are determined from the following formula.[1]

Illustration 23-4
Production requirements formula

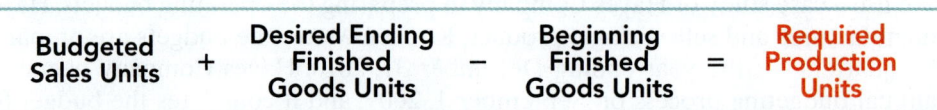

A realistic estimate of ending inventory is essential in scheduling production requirements. Excessive inventories in one quarter may lead to cutbacks in production and employee layoffs in a subsequent quarter. On the other hand, inadequate inventories may result either in added costs for overtime work or in lost sales. Hayes Company believes it can meet future sales requirements by maintaining

---

[1] This formula ignores any work in process inventories, which are assumed to be nonexistent in Hayes Company.

an ending inventory equal to 20% of the next quarter's budgeted sales volume. For example, the ending finished goods inventory for the first quarter is 700 units (20% × anticipated second-quarter sales of 3,500 units). Illustration 23-5 shows the production budget.

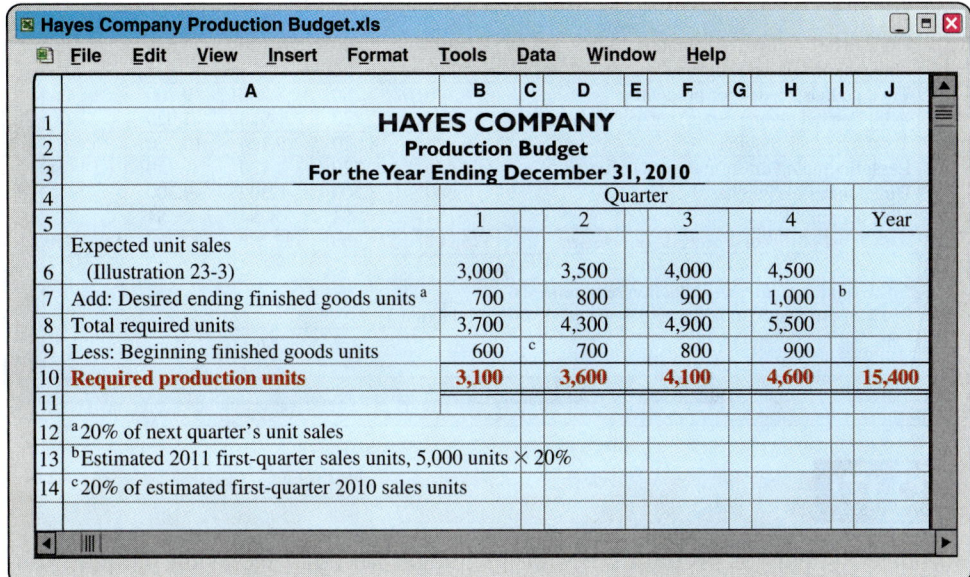

Illustration 23-5
Production budget

The production budget, in turn, provides the basis for the budgeted costs for each manufacturing cost element, as explained in the following pages.

Direct Materials Budget

The **direct materials budget** shows both the quantity and cost of direct materials to be purchased. The quantities of direct materials are derived from the following formula.

Illustration 23-6
Formula for direct materials quantities

The company then computes the budgeted cost of direct materials to be purchased by multiplying the required units of direct materials by the anticipated cost per unit.

The desired ending inventory is again a key component in the budgeting process. For example, inadequate inventories could result in temporary shutdowns of production. Because of its close proximity to suppliers, Hayes Company maintains an ending inventory of raw materials equal to 10% of the next quarter's production requirements. The manufacture of each Kitchen-Mate requires 2 pounds of raw materials, and the expected cost per pound is $4. Illustration 23-7 (page 1026) shows the direct materials budget. Assume that the desired ending direct materials amount is 1,020 pounds for the fourth quarter of 2010.

Illustration 23-7
Direct materials budget

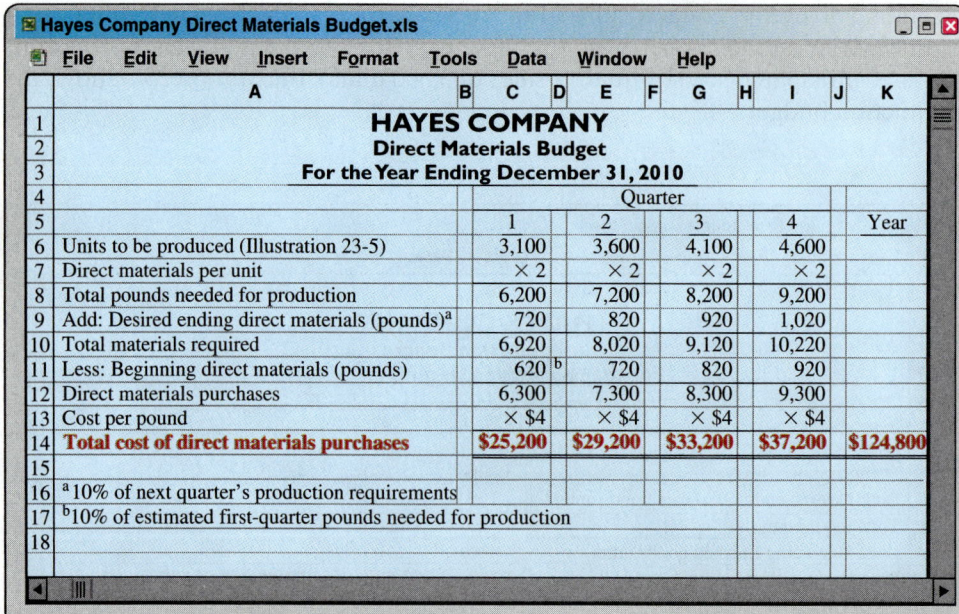

DO IT!

MASTER BUDGET

Soriano Company is preparing its master budget for 2010. Relevant data pertaining to its sales, production, and direct materials budgets are as follows:

Sales: Sales for the year are expected to total 1,200,000 units. Quarterly sales are 20%, 25%, 30%, and 25% respectively. The sales price is expected to be $50 per unit for the first three quarters and $55 per unit beginning in the fourth quarter. Sales in the first quarter of 2011 are expected to be 10% higher than the budgeted sales for the first quarter of 2010.

Production: Management desires to maintain the ending finished goods inventories at 25% of the next quarter's budgeted sales volume.

Direct materials: Each unit requires 3 pounds of raw materials at a cost of $5 per pound. Management desires to maintain raw materials inventories at 5% of the next quarter's production requirements. Assume the production requirements for the first quarter of 2011 are 810,000 pounds.

Prepare the sales, production, and direct materials budgets by quarters for 2010.

action plan

✔ Know the form and content of the sales budget.

✔ Prepare the sales budget first, as the basis for the other budgets.

✔ Determine the units that must be produced to meet anticipated sales.

✔ Know how to compute the beginning and ending finished goods units.

✔ Determine the materials required to meet production needs.

✔ Know how to compute the beginning and ending direct materials units.

Solution

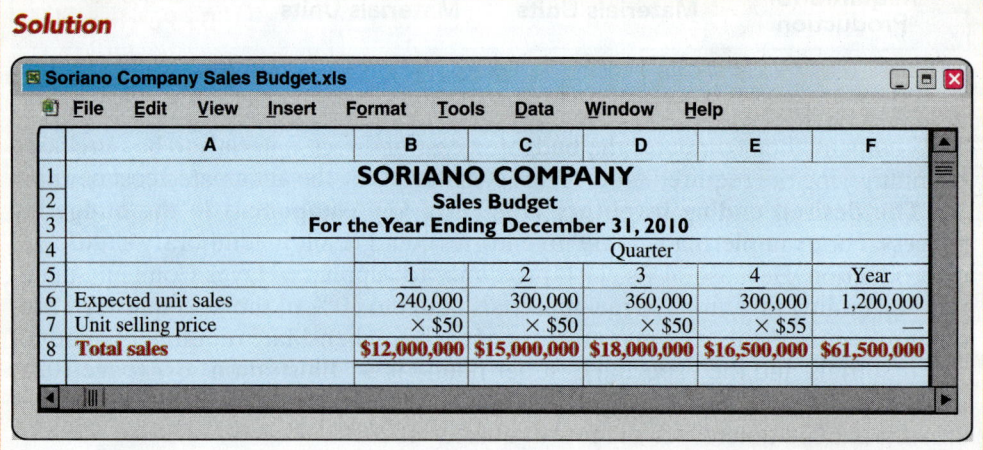

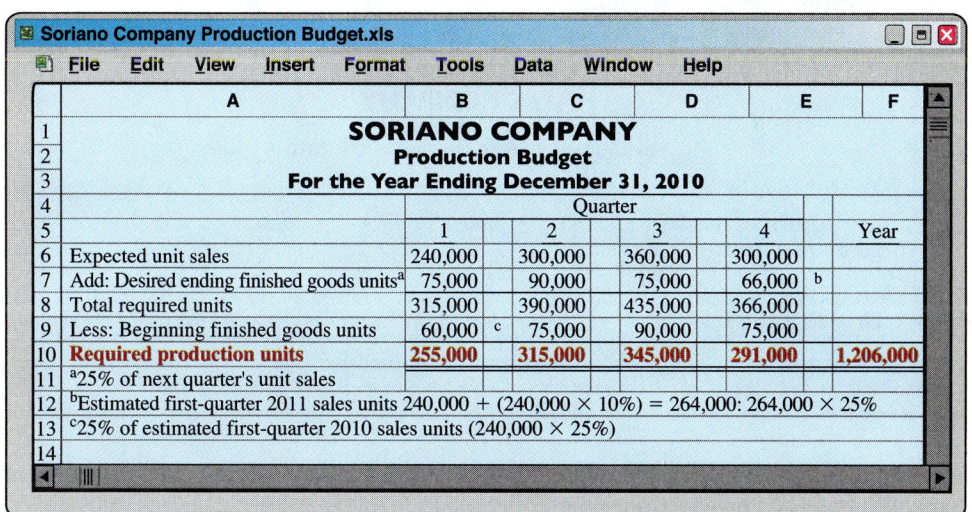

Related exercise material: **BE23-2, BE23-3, BE23-4, E23-2, E23-3, E23-4, E23-5, E23-6,** and **DO IT! 23-2**.

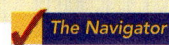

Direct Labor Budget

Like the direct materials budget, the **direct labor budget** contains the quantity (hours) and cost of direct labor necessary to meet production requirements. The total direct labor cost is derived from the following formula.

| Units to Be Produced | × | Direct Labor Time per Unit | × | Direct Labor Cost per Hour | = | **Total Direct Labor Cost** |

Illustration 23-8
Formula for direct labor cost

Direct labor hours are determined from the production budget. At Hayes Company, two hours of direct labor are required to produce each unit of finished goods. The anticipated hourly wage rate is $10. Illustration 23-9 shows these data.

Illustration 23-9
Direct labor budget

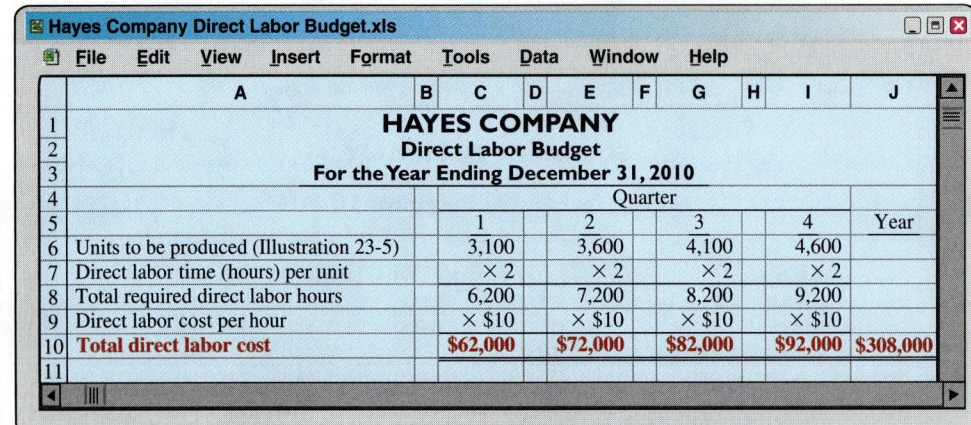

HELPFUL HINT

An important assumption in Illustration 23-9 is that the company can add to and subtract from its work force as needed so that the $10 per hour labor cost applies to a wide range of possible production activity.

The direct labor budget is critical in maintaining a labor force that can meet the expected levels of production.

Manufacturing Overhead Budget

The **manufacturing overhead budget** shows the expected manufacturing overhead costs for the budget period. As Illustration 23-10 shows, **this budget distinguishes between variable and fixed overhead costs.** Hayes Company expects variable costs to fluctuate with production volume on the basis of the following rates per direct labor hour: indirect materials $1.00, indirect labor $1.40, utilities $0.40, and maintenance $0.20. Thus, for the 6,200 direct labor hours to produce 3,100 units, budgeted indirect materials are $6,200 (6,200 × $1), and budgeted indirect labor is $8,680 (6,200 × $1.40). Hayes also recognizes that some maintenance is fixed. The amounts reported for fixed costs are assumed for our example. The accuracy of budgeted fixed overhead cost estimates can be greatly improved by employing activity-based costing.

Illustration 23-10
Manufacturing overhead budget

HAYES COMPANY
Manufacturing Overhead Budget
For the Year Ending December 31, 2010

	Quarter 1	Quarter 2	Quarter 3	Quarter 4	Year
Variable costs					
Indirect materials ($1.00/hour)	$ 6,200	$ 7,200	$ 8,200	$ 9,200	$ 30,800
Indirect labor ($1.40/hour)	8,680	10,080	11,480	12,880	43,120
Utilities ($0.40/hour)	2,480	2,880	3,280	3,680	12,320
Maintenance ($0.20/hour)	1,240	1,440	1,640	1,840	6,160
Total variable costs	18,600	21,600	24,600	27,600	92,400
Fixed costs					
Supervisory salaries	20,000	20,000	20,000	20,000	80,000
Depreciation	3,800	3,800	3,800	3,800	15,200
Property taxes and insurance	9,000	9,000	9,000	9,000	36,000
Maintenance	5,700	5,700	5,700	5,700	22,800
Total fixed costs	38,500	38,500	38,500	38,500	154,000
Total manufacturing overhead	**$57,100**	**$60,100**	**$63,100**	**$66,100**	**$246,400**
Direct labor hours (Illustration 23-9)	6,200	7,200	8,200	9,200	30,800
Manufacturing overhead rate per direct labor hour ($246,400 ÷ 30,800)					**$ 8**

At Hayes Company, overhead is applied to production on the basis of direct labor hours. Thus, as Illustration 23-10 shows, the annual rate is $8 per hour ($246,400 ÷ 30,800).

Selling and Administrative Expense Budget

Hayes Company combines its operating expenses into one budget, the **selling and administrative expense budget**. This budget projects anticipated selling and administrative expenses for the budget period. This budget (Illustration 23-11) also classifies expenses as either variable or fixed. In this case, the variable expense rates per unit of sales are sales commissions $3 and freight-out $1. Variable expenses per quarter are based on the unit sales from the sales budget (Illustration 23-3). For example, Hayes expects sales in the first quarter to be 3,000 units. Thus, Sales Commissions Expense is $9,000 (3,000 × $3), and Freight-out is $3,000 (3,000 × $1). Fixed expenses are based on assumed data. Illustration 23-11 shows the selling and administrative expense budget.

Illustration 23-11
Selling and administrative expense budget

HAYES COMPANY
Selling and Administrative Expense Budget
For the Year Ending December 31, 2010

	Quarter 1	Quarter 2	Quarter 3	Quarter 4	Year
Budgeted sales in units (Illustration 23-3)	3,000	3,500	4,000	4,500	15,000
Variable expenses					
Sales commissions ($3 per unit)	$ 9,000	$10,500	$12,000	$13,500	$ 45,000
Freight-out ($1 per unit)	3,000	3,500	4,000	4,500	15,000
Total variable expenses	12,000	14,000	16,000	18,000	60,000
Fixed expenses					
Advertising	5,000	5,000	5,000	5,000	20,000
Sales salaries	15,000	15,000	15,000	15,000	60,000
Office salaries	7,500	7,500	7,500	7,500	30,000
Depreciation	1,000	1,000	1,000	1,000	4,000
Property taxes and insurance	1,500	1,500	1,500	1,500	6,000
Total fixed expenses	30,000	30,000	30,000	30,000	120,000
Total selling and administrative expenses	**$42,000**	**$44,000**	**$46,000**	**$48,000**	**$180,000**

Budgeted Income Statement

The **budgeted income statement** is the important end-product of the operating budgets. This budget indicates the expected profitability of operations for the budget period. The budgeted income statement provides the basis for evaluating company performance. Budgeted income statements often act as a call to action. For example, a board member at XM Satellite Radio Holdings felt that budgeted costs were too high relative to budgeted revenues. When management refused to cut its marketing and programming costs, the board member resigned; he felt that without the cuts, the company risked financial crisis.

STUDY OBJECTIVE 4
Describe the sources for preparing the budgeted income statement.

As you would expect, the budgeted income statement is prepared from the various operating budgets. For example, to find the cost of goods sold, it is first necessary to determine the total unit cost of producing one Kitchen-Mate, as follows.

Chapter 23 Budgetary Planning

Illustration 23-12
Computation of total unit cost

Cost of One Kitchen-Mate

Cost Element	Illustration	Quantity	Unit Cost	Total
Direct materials	23-7	2 pounds	$ 4.00	$ 8.00
Direct labor	23-9	2 hours	$10.00	20.00
Manufacturing overhead	23-10	2 hours	$ 8.00	16.00
Total unit cost				**$44.00**

Hayes Company then determines cost of goods sold by multiplying the units sold by the unit cost. Its budgeted cost of goods sold is $660,000 (15,000 × $44). All data for the statement come from the individual operating budgets except the following: (1) interest expense is expected to be $100, and (2) income taxes are estimated to be $12,000. Illustration 23-13 shows the budgeted income statement.

Illustration 23-13
Budgeted income statement

HAYES COMPANY
Budgeted Income Statement
For the Year Ending December 31, 2010

Sales (Illustration 23-3)	$900,000
Cost of goods sold (15,000 × $44)	660,000
Gross profit	240,000
Selling and administrative expenses (Illustration 23-11)	180,000
Income from operations	60,000
Interest expense	100
Income before income taxes	59,900
Income tax expense	12,000
Net income	$ 47,900

DO IT!

BUDGETED INCOME STATEMENT

Soriano Company is preparing its budgeted income statement for 2010. Relevant data pertaining to its sales, production, and direct materials budgets can be found in the Do It! exercise on page 1026.

In addition, Soriano budgets 0.5 hours of direct labor per unit, labor costs at $15 per hour, and manufacturing overhead at $25 per direct labor hour. Its budgeted selling and administrative expenses for 2010 are $12,000,000.

(a) Calculate the budgeted total unit cost. (b) Prepare the budgeted income statement for 2010.

action plan

✔ Recall that total unit cost consists of direct materials, direct labor, and manufacturing overhead.
✔ Recall that direct materials costs are included in the direct materials budget.
✔ Know the form and content of the income statement.
✔ Use the total unit sales information from the sales budget to compute annual sales and cost of goods sold.

Solution
(a)

Cost Element	Quantity	Unit Cost	Total
Direct materials	3.0 pounds	$ 5	$15.00
Direct labor	0.5 hours	$15	7.50
Manufacturing overhead	0.5 hours	$25	12.50
Total unit cost			**$35.00**

(b)

SORIANO COMPANY
Budgeted Income Statement
For the Year Ending December 31, 2010

Sales (1,200,000 units from sales budget, page 1026)	$61,500,000
Cost of goods sold (1,200,000 × $35.00/unit)	42,000,000
Gross profit	19,500,000
Selling and administrative expenses	12,000,000
Net income	$ 7,500,000

Related exercise material: **BE23-8, E23-11**, and **DO IT!** **23-3**.

PREPARING THE FINANCIAL BUDGETS

As shown in Illustration 23-2 (page 1022), the financial budgets consist of the capital expenditure budget, the cash budget, and the budgeted balance sheet. We will discuss the capital expenditure budget in Chapter 26; the other budgets are explained in the following sections.

Cash Budget

The **cash budget** shows anticipated cash flows. Because cash is so vital, this budget is often considered to be the most important financial budget.

STUDY OBJECTIVE 5
Explain the principal sections of a cash budget.

The cash budget contains three sections (cash receipts, cash disbursements, and financing) and the beginning and ending cash balances, as shown in Illustration 23-14.

ANY COMPANY
Cash Budget

Beginning cash balance	$X,XXX
Add: Cash receipts (Itemized)	X,XXX
Total available cash	X,XXX
Less: Cash disbursements (Itemized)	X,XXX
Excess (deficiency) of available cash over cash disbursements	X,XXX
Financing	X,XXX
Ending cash balance	$X,XXX

Illustration 23-14
Basic form of a cash budget

The **cash receipts section** includes expected receipts from the company's principal source(s) of revenue. These are usually cash sales and collections from customers on credit sales. This section also shows anticipated receipts of interest and dividends, and proceeds from planned sales of investments, plant assets, and the company's capital stock.

HELPFUL HINT
Why is the cash budget prepared after the other budgets are prepared? Answer: Because the information generated by the other budgets dictates the expected inflows and outflows of cash.

The **cash disbursements section** shows expected cash payments. Such payments include direct materials, direct labor, manufacturing overhead, and selling and administrative expenses. This section also includes projected payments for income taxes, dividends, investments, and plant assets.

The **financing section** shows expected borrowings and the repayment of the borrowed funds plus interest. Companies need this section when there is a cash deficiency or when the cash balance is below management's minimum required balance.

Data in the cash budget are prepared in sequence. The ending cash balance of one period becomes the beginning cash balance for the next period. Companies obtain data for preparing the cash budget from other budgets and from information provided by management. In practice, cash budgets are often prepared for the year on a monthly basis.

To minimize detail, we will assume that Hayes Company prepares an annual cash budget by quarters. Hayes Company's cash budget is based on the following assumptions.

1. The January 1, 2010, cash balance is expected to be $38,000.
2. Sales (Illustration 23-3, page 1024): 60% are collected in the quarter sold and 40% are collected in the following quarter. Accounts receivable of $60,000 at December 31, 2009, are expected to be collected in full in the first quarter of 2010.
3. Short-term investments are expected to be sold for $2,000 cash in the first quarter.
4. Direct materials (Illustration 23-7, page 1026): 50% are paid in the quarter purchased and 50% are paid in the following quarter. Accounts payable of $10,600 at December 31, 2009, are expected to be paid in full in the first quarter of 2010.
5. Direct labor (Illustration 23-9, page 1028): 100% is paid in the quarter incurred.
6. Manufacturing overhead (Illustration 23-10, page 1028) and selling and administrative expenses (Illustration 23-11, page 1029): All items except depreciation are paid in the quarter incurred.
7. Management plans to purchase a truck in the second quarter for $10,000 cash.
8. Hayes makes equal quarterly payments of its estimated annual income taxes.
9. Loans are repaid in the earliest quarter in which there is sufficient cash (that is, when the cash on hand exceeds the $15,000 minimum required balance).

In preparing the cash budget, it is useful to prepare schedules for collections from customers (assumption No. 2, above) and cash payments for direct materials (assumption No. 4, above). These schedules are shown in Illustrations 23-15 and 23-16.

Illustration 23-15
Collections from customers

HAYES COMPANY
Schedule of Expected Collections from Customers

	Quarter			
	1	2	3	4
Accounts receivable, 12/31/09	$ 60,000			
First quarter ($180,000)	108,000	$ 72,000		
Second quarter ($210,000)		126,000	$ 84,000	
Third quarter ($240,000)			144,000	$ 96,000
Fourth quarter ($270,000)				162,000
Total collections	$168,000	$198,000	$228,000	$258,000

Illustration 23-16
Payments for direct materials

HAYES COMPANY
Schedule of Expected Payments for Direct Materials

	Quarter			
	1	2	3	4
Accounts payable, 12/31/09	$10,600			
First quarter ($25,200)	12,600	$12,600		
Second quarter ($29,200)		14,600	$14,600	
Third quarter ($33,200)			16,600	$16,600
Fourth quarter ($37,200)				18,600
Total payments	$23,200	$27,200	$31,200	$35,200

Illustration 23-17 shows the cash budget for Hayes Company. The budget indicates that Hayes will need $3,000 of financing in the second quarter to maintain a minimum cash balance of $15,000. Since there is an excess of available cash over disbursements of $22,500 at the end of the third quarter, the borrowing, plus $100 interest, is repaid in this quarter.

Illustration 23-17
Cash budget

HAYES COMPANY
Cash Budget
For the Year Ending December 31, 2010

	Assumption	Quarter 1	Quarter 2	Quarter 3	Quarter 4
Beginning cash balance	1	$ 38,000	$ 25,500	$ 15,000	$ 19,400
Add: Receipts					
Collections from customers	2	168,000	198,000	228,000	258,000
Sale of securities	3	2,000	0	0	0
Total receipts		170,000	198,000	228,000	258,000
Total available cash		208,000	223,500	243,000	277,400
Less: Disbursements					
Direct materials	4	23,200	27,200	31,200	35,200
Direct labor	5	62,000	72,000	82,000	92,000
Manufacturing overhead	6	53,300 [a]	56,300	59,300	62,300
Selling and administrative expenses	6	41,000 [b]	43,000	45,000	47,000
Purchase of truck	7	0	10,000	0	0
Income tax expense	8	3,000	3,000	3,000	3,000
Total disbursements		182,500	211,500	220,500	239,500
Excess (deficiency) of available cash over cash disbursements		25,500	12,000	22,500	37,900
Financing					
Borrowings		0	3,000	0	0
Repayments-plus $100 interest	9	0	0	3,100	0
Ending cash balance		$ 25,500	$ 15,000	$ 19,400	$ 37,900

[a] $57,100-$3,800 depreciation
[b] $42,000-$1,000 depreciation

A cash budget contributes to more effective cash management. It shows managers when additional financing is necessary well before the actual need arises. And, it indicates when excess cash is available for investments or other purposes.

MANAGEMENT INSIGHT

Without a Budget, Can the Games Begin?

Behind the grandeur of the Olympic Games lies a huge financial challenge—how to keep budgeted costs in line with revenues. For example, the 2006 Winter Olympics in Turin, Italy, narrowly avoided going into bankruptcy before the Games even started. In order for the event to remain solvent, organizers cancelled glitzy celebrations and shifted promotional responsibilities to an Italian state-run agency. Despite these efforts, after the Games were over, the Italian government created a lottery game to cover its financial losses.

As another example, organizers of the 2002 Winter Olympics in Salt Lake City cut budgeted costs by $200 million shortly before the events began. According to the chief operating and financial officer, the organizers went through every line item in the budget, sorting each one into "must have" versus "nice to have." As a result, the Salt Lake City Games produced a surplus of $100 million.

Source: Gabriel Kahn and Roger Thurow, "In Turin, Paying for Games Went Down to the Wire," *Wall Street Journal*, February 10, 2006.

 Why does it matter whether the Olympic Games exceed their budget?

Budgeted Balance Sheet

The **budgeted balance sheet** is a projection of financial position at the end of the budget period. This budget is developed from the budgeted balance sheet for the preceding year and the budgets for the current year. Pertinent data from the budgeted balance sheet at December 31, 2009, are as follows.

| Buildings and equipment | $182,000 | Common stock | $225,000 |
| Accumulated depreciation | $ 28,800 | Retained earnings | $ 46,480 |

Illustration 23-18 on page 1035 shows Hayes Company's budgeted balance sheet at December 31, 2010.

The computations and sources of the amounts are explained below.

Cash: Ending cash balance $37,900, shown in the cash budget (Illustration 23-17, page 1033).

Accounts receivable: 40% of fourth-quarter sales $270,000, shown in the schedule of expected collections from customers (Illustration 23-15, page 1032).

Finished goods inventory: Desired ending inventory 1,000 units, shown in the production budget (Illustration 23-5, page 1025) times the total unit cost $44 (shown in Illustration 23-12, page 1030).

Raw materials inventory: Desired ending inventory 1,020 pounds, times the cost per pound $4, shown in the direct materials budget (Illustration 23-7, page 1026).

Buildings and equipment: December 31, 2009, balance $182,000, plus purchase of truck for $10,000.

HAYES COMPANY
Budgeted Balance Sheet
December 31, 2010

Assets

Cash		$ 37,900
Accounts receivable		108,000
Finished goods inventory		44,000
Raw materials inventory		4,080
Buildings and equipment	$192,000	
Less: Accumulated depreciation	48,000	144,000
Total assets		$337,980

Liabilities and Stockholders' Equity

Accounts payable	$ 18,600
Common stock	225,000
Retained earnings	94,380
Total liabilities and stockholders' equity	$337,980

Illustration 23-18
Budgeted balance sheet

Accumulated depreciation: December 31, 2009, balance $28,800, plus $15,200 depreciation shown in manufacturing overhead budget (Illustration 23-10, page 1028) and $4,000 depreciation shown in selling and administrative expense budget (Illustration 23-11, page 1029).

Accounts payable: 50% of fourth-quarter purchases $37,200, shown in schedule of expected payments for direct materials (Illustration 23-16, page 1033).

Common stock: Unchanged from the beginning of the year.

Retained earnings: December 31, 2009, balance $46,480, plus net income $47,900, shown in budgeted income statement (Illustration 23-13, page 1030).

After budget data are entered into the computer, Hayes prepares the various budgets (sales, cash, etc.), as well as the budgeted financial statements. Using spreadsheets, management can also perform "what if" (sensitivity) analyses based on different hypothetical assumptions. For example, suppose that sales managers project that sales will be 10% higher in the coming quarter. What impact does this change have on the rest of the budgeting process and the financing needs of the business? The impact of the various assumptions on the budget is quickly determined by the spreadsheet. Armed with these analyses, managers make more informed decisions about the impact of various projects. They also anticipate future problems and business opportunities. As seen in this chapter, budgeting is an excellent use of electronic spreadsheets.

DO IT!

CASH BUDGET

Martian Company management wants to maintain a minimum monthly cash balance of $15,000. At the beginning of March, the cash balance is $16,500, expected cash receipts for March are $210,000, and cash disbursements are expected to be $220,000. How much cash, if any, must be borrowed to maintain the desired minimum monthly balance?

Action Plan

- ✔ Write down the basic form of the cash budget, starting with the beginning cash balance, adding cash receipts for the period, deducting cash disbursements, and identifying the needed financing to achieve the desired minimum ending cash balance.
- ✔ Insert the data given into the outlined form of the cash budget.

Solution

MARTIAN COMPANY
Cash Budget
For the Month Ending March 31, 2010

Beginning cash balance	$ 16,500
Add: Cash receipts for March	210,000
Total available cash	226,500
Less: Cash disbursements for March	220,000
Excess of available cash over cash disbursements	6,500
Financing	8,500
Ending cash balance	$ 15,000

To maintain the desired minimum cash balance of $15,000, Martian Company must borrow $8,500 cash.

Related exercise material: **BE23-9, E23-12, E23-13, E23-16,** and **DO IT! 23-4**.

BUDGETING IN NON-MANUFACTURING COMPANIES

STUDY OBJECTIVE 6
Indicate the applicability of budgeting in non-manufacturing companies.

Budgeting is not limited to manufacturers. Budgets are also used by merchandisers, service enterprises, and not-for-profit organizations.

Merchandisers

As in manufacturing operations, the sales budget for a merchandiser is both the starting point and the key factor in the development of the master budget. The major differences between the master budgets of a merchandiser and a manufacturer are these:

1. A merchandiser **uses a merchandise purchases budget instead of a production budget**.
2. A merchandiser **does not use the manufacturing budgets (direct materials, direct labor, and manufacturing overhead)**.

The **merchandise purchases budget** shows the estimated cost of goods to be purchased to meet expected sales. The formula for determining budgeted merchandise purchases is:

Illustration 23-19
Merchandise purchases formula

Budgeted Cost of Goods Sold	+	Desired Ending Merchandise Inventory	−	Beginning Merchandise Inventory	=	Required Merchandise Purchases

To illustrate, assume that the budget committee of Lima Company is preparing the merchandise purchases budget for July 2010. It estimates that budgeted sales will be $300,000 in July and $320,000 in August. Cost of goods sold is expected to be 70% of sales—that is, $210,000 in July (.70 × $300,000) and $224,000 in August (.70 × $320,000). Lima's desired ending inventory is 30% of the following month's cost of goods sold. Required merchandise purchases for July are $214,200, as shown in Illustration 23-20.

When a merchandiser is departmentalized, it prepares separate budgets for each department. For example, a grocery store prepares sales budgets and purchases budgets for each of its major departments, such as meats, dairy, and produce. The store then combines these budgets into a master budget for the store. When a retailer has

Illustration 23-20
Merchandise purchases budget

LIMA COMPANY
Merchandise Purchases Budget
For the Month Ending July 31, 2010

Budgeted cost of goods sold ($300,000 × 70%)	$ 210,000
Add: Desired ending merchandise inventory ($224,000 × 30%)	67,200
Total	277,200
Less: Beginning merchandise inventory ($210,000 × 30%)	63,000
Required merchandise purchases for July	**$214,200**

branch stores, it prepares separate master budgets for each store. Then it incorporates these budgets into master budgets for the company as a whole.

Service Enterprises

In a service enterprise, such as a public accounting firm, a law office, or a medical practice, the critical factor in budgeting is **coordinating professional staff needs with anticipated services**. If a firm is overstaffed, several problems may result: Labor costs are disproportionately high. Profits are lower because of the additional salaries. Staff turnover sometimes increases because of lack of challenging work. In contrast, if a service enterprise is understaffed, it may lose revenue because existing and prospective client needs for service cannot be met. Also, professional staff may seek other jobs because of excessive work loads.

Service enterprises can obtain budget data for service revenue from **expected output** or **expected input**. When output is used, it is necessary to determine the expected billings of clients for services provided. In a public accounting firm, for example, output is the sum of its billings in auditing, tax, and consulting services. When input data are used, each professional staff member projects his or her billable time. The firm then applies billing rates to billable time to produce expected service revenue.

Not-for-Profit Organizations

Budgeting is just as important for not-for-profit organizations as for profit-oriented enterprises. The budget process, however, is different. In most cases, not-for-profit entities budget **on the basis of cash flows (expenditures and receipts), rather than on a revenue and expense basis**. Further, the starting point in the process is usually expenditures, not receipts. For the not-for-profit entity, management's task generally is to find the receipts needed to support the planned expenditures. The activity index is also likely to be significantly different. For example, in a not-for-profit entity, such as a university, budgeted faculty positions may be based on full-time equivalent students or credit hours expected to be taught in a department.

For some governmental units, voters approve the budget. In other cases, such as state governments and the federal government, legislative approval is required. After the budget is adopted, it must be followed. Overspending is often illegal. In governmental budgets, authorizations tend to be on a line-by-line basis. That is, the budget for a municipality may have a specified authorization for police and fire protection, garbage collection, street paving, and so on. The line-item authorization of governmental budgets significantly limits the amount of discretion management can exercise. The city manager often cannot use savings from one line item, such as street paving, to cover increased spending in another line item, such as snow removal.

 Be sure to read **ALL ABOUT YOU:** *Avoiding Personal Financial Disaster* on page 1038 for information on how topics in this chapter apply to your personal life.

all about Y✹U

Avoiding Personal Financial Disaster

You might hear people say that they "need to learn to live within a budget." The funny thing is that most people who say this haven't actually prepared a personal budget, nor do they intend to. Instead, what they are referring to is a vaguely defined, poorly specified, collection of rough ideas of how much they should spend on various aspects of their life. You can't live within or even outside of something that doesn't exist. With that in mind, let's take a look at personal budgets.

✹ Some Facts

* The average American household income is $58,712, before taxes.

* The average family spends $5,931 on food each year. Of this, $3,297 is for food consumed at home, and $2,635 is for food consumed away from home.

* The average family spends $15,167 annually on housing costs. Of this amount, $8,805 is the actual cost of shelter, $3,183 is for utilities, and $1,767 is for furnishings and equipment.

* The average family spends $8,344 per year on transportation. Of this, $3,544 goes to vehicle purchase payments, and $2,013 is spent on fuel. The average family spends only $448 per year on public transportation.

✹ About the Numbers

Obviously people spend their income in different ways. For example, the percentage of your income spent on necessities declines as your income increases. Nonetheless, it is interesting to see how the average family spends its money.

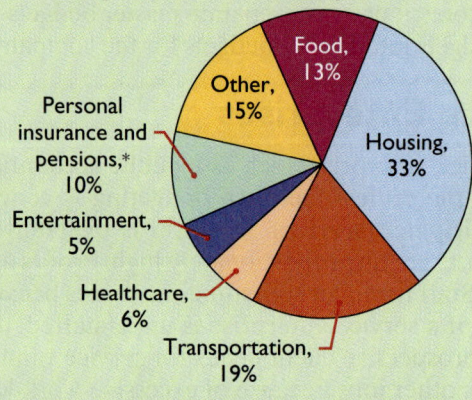

Average U.S. Household Expenditures

- Food, 13%
- Other, 15%
- Personal insurance and pensions,* 10%
- Entertainment, 5%
- Healthcare, 6%
- Transportation, 19%
- Housing, 33%

* This includes Social Security tax.

Source: "Consumer Expenditures in 2004," U.S. Department of Labor and U.S. Bureau of Labor Statistics, Report 992, April 2006.

✹ What Do You Think?

Many worksheet templates that are provided for personal budgets for college students treat student loans as an income source. See, for example, the template provided at **http://financialplan.about.com/cs/budgeting/l/blmocolbud.htm**. Based on your knowledge of accounting, is this correct?

YES: Student loans provide a source of cash which can be used to pay costs. As the saying goes, "It all spends the same." Therefore student loans are income.

NO: Student loans must eventually be repaid; therefore they are not income. As the name suggests, they are loans.

Source: U.S. Department of Labor and U.S. Bureau of Labor Statistics, "Consumer Expenditures in 2004," April 2006, Report 992.

Comprehensive DO IT!

Barrett Company has completed all operating budgets other than the income statement for 2010. Selected data from these budgets follow.

Sales: $300,000
Purchases of raw materials: $145,000
Ending inventory of raw materials: $15,000
Direct labor: $40,000
Manufacturing overhead: $73,000, including $3,000 of depreciation expense
Selling and administrative expenses: $36,000 including depreciation expense of $1,000
Interest expense: $1,000
Principal payment on note: $2,000
Dividends declared: $2,000
Income tax rate: 30%

Other information:
Year-end accounts receivable: 4% of 2010 sales
Year-end accounts payable: 50% of ending inventory of raw materials
Interest, direct labor, manufacturing overhead, and selling and administrative expenses other than depreciation are paid as incurred.
Dividends declared and income taxes for 2010 will not be paid until 2011.

BARRETT COMPANY
Balance Sheet
December 31, 2009

Assets

Cash		$20,000
Raw materials inventory		10,000
Equipment	$40,000	
Less: Accumulated depreciation	4,000	36,000
Total assets		$66,000

Liabilities and Stockholders' Equity

Accounts payable	$ 5,000	
Notes payable	22,000	
Total liabilities		$27,000
Common stock	25,000	
Retained earnings	14,000	39,000
Total liabilities and stockholders' equity		$66,000

Instructions

(a) Calculate budgeted cost of goods sold.
(b) Prepare a budgeted income statement for the year ending December 31, 2010.
(c) Prepare a budgeted balance sheet as of December 31, 2010.

Solution to Comprehensive DO IT!

(a) Beginning raw materials + Purchases − Ending raw materials = Cost of direct materials used ($10,000 + $145,000 − $15,000 = $140,000)
Direct materials used + Direct labor + Manufacturing overhead = ($140,000 + $40,000 + $73,000 = $253,000)

action plan

✔ Recall that beginning raw materials inventory plus purchases less ending raw materials inventory equals direct materials used.

✔ Prepare the budgeted income statement before the budgeted balance sheet.

✔ Use the standard form of a cash budget to determine cash on the budgeted balance sheet.

✔ Add budgeted depreciation expense to accumulated depreciation at the beginning of the year to determine accumulated depreciation on the budgeted balance sheet.

✔ Add budgeted net income to retained earnings from the beginning of the year and subtract dividends declared to determine retained earnings on the budgeted balance sheet.

✔ Verify that total assets equal total liabilities and stockholders' equity on the budgeted balance sheet.

(b)

BARRETT COMPANY
Budgeted Income Statement
For the Year Ending December 31, 2010

Sales		$300,000
Cost of goods sold		253,000
Gross profit		47,000
Selling and administrative expenses	$36,000	
Interest expense	1,000	37,000
Income before income tax expense		10,000
Income tax expense (30%)		3,000
Net income		$ 7,000

(c)

BARRETT COMPANY
Budgeted Balance Sheet
December 31, 2010

Assets

Cash[(1)]		$17,500
Accounts receivable (4% × $300,000)		12,000
Raw materials inventory		15,000
Equipment	$40,000	
Less: Accumulated depreciation	8,000	32,000
Total assets		$76,500

Liabilities and Stockholders' Equity

Accounts payable (50% × $15,000)	$ 7,500	
Income taxes payable	3,000	
Dividends payable	2,000	
Note payable	20,000	
Total liabilities		$32,500
Common stock	25,000	
Retained earnings[(2)]	19,000	44,000
Total liabilities and stockholders' equity		$76,500

[(1)]Beginning cash balance		$ 20,000
Add: Collections from customers (96% × $300,000 sales)		288,000
Total available cash		308,000
Less: Disbursements		
Direct materials ($5,000 + $145,000 − $7,500)	$142,500	
Direct labor	40,000	
Manufacturing overhead	70,000	
Selling and administrative expenses	35,000	
Total disbursements		287,500
Excess of available cash over cash disbursements		20,500
Financing		
Repayments of principal	2,000	
Interest payments	1,000	3,000
Ending cash balance		$ 17,500

[(2)]Beginning retained earnings + Net income − Dividends declared = Ending retained earnings
($14,000 + 7,000 − 2,000 = $19,000)

SUMMARY OF STUDY OBJECTIVES

1. **Indicate the benefits of budgeting.** The primary advantages of budgeting are that it (a) requires management to plan ahead, (b) provides definite objectives for evaluating performance, (c) creates an early warning system for potential problems, (d) facilitates coordination of activities, (e) results in greater management awareness, and (f) motivates personnel to meet planned objectives.

2. **State the essentials of effective budgeting.** The essentials of effective budgeting are (a) sound organizational structure, (b) research and analysis, and (c) acceptance by all levels of management.

3. **Identify the budgets that comprise the master budget.** The master budget consists of the following budgets: (a) sales, (b) production, (c) direct materials, (d) direct labor, (e) manufacturing overhead, (f) selling and administrative expense, (g) budgeted income statement, (h) capital expenditure budget, (i) cash budget, and (j) budgeted balance sheet.

4. **Describe the sources for preparing the budgeted income statement.** The budgeted income statement is prepared from (a) the sales budget, (b) the budgets for direct materials, direct labor, and manufacturing overhead, and (c) the selling and administrative expense budget.

5. **Explain the principal sections of a cash budget.** The cash budget has three sections (receipts, disbursements, and financing) and the beginning and ending cash balances.

6. **Indicate the applicability of budgeting in nonmanufacturing companies.** Budgeting may be used by merchandisers for development of a master budget. In service enterprises budgeting is a critical factor in coordinating staff needs with anticipated services. In not-for-profit organizations, the starting point in budgeting is usually expenditures, not receipts.

GLOSSARY

Budget A formal written statement of management's plans for a specified future time period, expressed in financial terms. (p. 1018).

Budget committee A group responsible for coordinating the preparation of the budget. (p. 1020).

Budgetary slack The amount by which a manager intentionally underestimates budgeted revenues or overestimates budgeted expenses in order to make it easier to achieve budgetary goals. (p. 1021).

Budgeted balance sheet A projection of financial position at the end of the budget period. (p. 1034).

Budgeted income statement An estimate of the expected profitability of operations for the budget period. (p. 1029).

Cash budget A projection of anticipated cash flows. (p. 1031).

Direct labor budget A projection of the quantity and cost of direct labor necessary to meet production requirements. (p. 1027).

Direct materials budget An estimate of the quantity and cost of direct materials to be purchased. (p. 1025).

Financial budgets Individual budgets that focus primarily on the cash resources needed to fund expected operations and planned capital expenditures. (p. 1022).

Long-range planning A formalized process of selecting strategies to achieve long-term goals and developing policies and plans to implement the strategies. (p. 1021).

Manufacturing overhead budget An estimate of expected manufacturing overhead costs for the budget period. (p. 1028).

Master budget A set of interrelated budgets that constitutes a plan of action for a specific time period. (p. 1022).

Merchandise purchases budget The estimated cost of goods to be purchased by a merchandiser to meet expected sales. (p. 1036).

Operating budgets Individual budgets that result in a budgeted income statement. (p. 1022).

Participative budgeting A budgetary approach that starts with input from lower-level managers and works upward so that managers at all levels participate. (p. 1020).

Production budget A projection of the units that must be produced to meet anticipated sales. (p. 1024).

Sales budget An estimate of expected sales revenue for the budget period. (p. 1023).

Sales forecast The projection of potential sales for the industry and the company's expected share of such sales. (p. 1020).

Selling and administrative expense budget A projection of anticipated selling and administrative expenses for the budget period. (p. 1029).

1042 Chapter 23 Budgetary Planning

SELF-STUDY QUESTIONS

Answers are at the end of the chapter.

(SO 1) **1.** Which of the following is not a benefit of budgeting?
   a. Management can plan ahead.
   b. An early warning system is provided for potential problems.
   c. It enables disciplinary action to be taken at every level of responsibility.
   d. The coordination of activities is facilitated.

(SO 1) **2.** A budget:
   a. is the responsibility of management accountants.
   b. is the primary method of communicating agreed-upon objectives throughout an organization.
   c. ignores past performance because it represents management's plans for a future time period.
   d. may promote efficiency but has no role in evaluating performance.

(SO 2) **3.** The essentials of effective budgeting do *not* include:
   a. top-down budgeting.
   b. management acceptance.
   c. research and analysis.
   d. sound organizational structure.

(SO 2) **4.** Compared to budgeting, long-range planning generally has the:
   a. same amount of detail.
   b. longer time period.
   c. same emphasis.
   d. same time period.

(SO 3) **5.** A sales budget is:
   a. derived from the production budget.
   b. management's best estimate of sales revenue for the year.
   c. not the starting point for the master budget.
   d. prepared only for credit sales.

(SO 3) **6.** The formula for the production budget is budgeted sales in units plus:
   a. desired ending merchandise inventory less beginning merchandise inventory.
   b. beginning finished goods units less desired ending finished goods units.
   c. desired ending direct materials units less beginning direct materials units.
   d. desired ending finished goods units less beginning finished goods units.

(SO 3) **7.** Direct materials inventories are kept in pounds in Byrd Company, and the total pounds of direct materials needed for production is 9,500. If the beginning inventory is 1,000 pounds and the desired ending inventory is 2,200 pounds, the total pounds to be purchased is:
   a. 9,400.
   b. 9,500.
   c. 9,700.
   d. 10,700.

(SO 4) **8.** The formula for computing the direct labor budget is to multiply the direct labor cost per hour by the:
   a. total required direct labor hours.
   b. physical units to be produced.
   c. equivalent units to be produced.
   d. No correct answer is given.

(SO 4) **9.** Each of the following budgets is used in preparing the budgeted income statement *except* the:
   a. sales budget.
   b. selling and administrative budget.
   c. capital expenditure budget.
   d. direct labor budget.

(SO 4) **10.** The budgeted income statement is:
   a. the end-product of the operating budgets.
   b. the end-product of the financial budgets.
   c. the starting point of the master budget.
   d. dependent on cash receipts and cash disbursements.

(SO 5) **11.** The budgeted balance sheet is:
   a. developed from the budgeted balance sheet for the preceding year and the budgets for the current year.
   b. the last operating budget prepared.
   c. used to prepare the cash budget.
   d. All of the above.

(SO 5) **12.** The format of a cash budget is:
   a. Beginning cash balance + Cash receipts + Cash from financing − Cash disbursements = Ending cash balance.
   b. Beginning cash balance + Cash receipts − Cash disbursements +/− Financing = Ending cash balance.
   c. Beginning cash balance + Net income − Cash dividends = Ending cash balance.
   d. Beginning cash balance + Cash revenues − Cash expenses = Ending cash balance.

(SO 5) **13.** Expected direct materials purchases in Read Company are $70,000 in the first quarter and $90,000 in the second quarter. Forty percent of the purchases are paid in cash as incurred, and the balance is paid in the following quarter. The budgeted cash payments for purchases in the second quarter are:
   a. $96,000.
   b. $90,000.
   c. $78,000.
   d. $72,000.

(SO 6) **14.** The budget for a merchandiser differs from a budget for a manufacturer because:
   a. a merchandise purchases budget replaces the production budget.
   b. the manufacturing budgets are not applicable.
   c. None of the above.
   d. Both (a) and (b) above.

(SO 6) **15.** In most cases, not-for-profit entities:
   a. prepare budgets using the same steps as those used by profit-oriented enterprises.
   b. know budgeted cash receipts at the beginning of a time period, so they budget only for expenditures.
   c. begin the budgeting process by budgeting expenditures rather than receipts.
   d. can ignore budgets because they are not expected to generate net income.

Go to the book's companion website, **www.wiley.com/college/weygandt**, for Additional Self-Study questions.

QUESTIONS

1. (a) What is a budget?
   (b) How does a budget contribute to good management?
2. Karen Bay and Frank Barone are discussing the benefits of budgeting. They ask you to identify the primary advantages of budgeting. Comply with their request.
3. Tina Haworth asks your help in understanding the essentials of effective budgeting. Identify the essentials for Tina.
4. (a) "Accounting plays a relatively unimportant role in budgeting." Do you agree? Explain.
   (b) What responsibilities does management have in budgeting?
5. What criteria are helpful in determining the length of the budget period? What is the most common budget period?
6. Megan Pedigo maintains that the only difference between budgeting and long-range planning is time. Do you agree? Why or why not?
7. What is participative budgeting? What are its potential benefits? What are its potential shortcomings?
8. What is budgetary slack? What incentive do managers have to create budgetary slack?
9. Distinguish between a master budget and a sales forecast.
10. What budget is the starting point in preparing the master budget? What may result if this budget is inaccurate?
11. "The production budget shows both unit production data and unit cost data." Is this true? Explain.
12. Cali Company has 15,000 beginning finished goods units. Budgeted sales units are 160,000. If management desires 20,000 ending finished goods units, what are the required units of production?
13. In preparing the direct materials budget for Mast Company, management concludes that required purchases are 64,000 units. If 52,000 direct materials units are required in production and there are 7,000 units of beginning direct materials, what is the desired units of ending direct materials?
14. The production budget of Rooney Company calls for 80,000 units to be produced. If it takes 30 minutes to make one unit and the direct labor rate is $16 per hour, what is the total budgeted direct labor cost?
15. Morales Company's manufacturing overhead budget shows total variable costs of $198,000 and total fixed costs of $162,000. Total production in units is expected to be 160,000. It takes 15 minutes to make one unit, and the direct labor rate is $15 per hour. Express the manufacturing overhead rate as (a) a percentage of direct labor cost, and (b) an amount per direct labor hour.
16. Elbert Company's variable selling and administrative expenses are 10% of net sales. Fixed expenses are $50,000 per quarter. The sales budget shows expected sales of $200,000 and $250,000 in the first and second quarters, respectively. What are the total budgeted selling and administrative expenses for each quarter?
17. For Nolte Company, the budgeted cost for one unit of product is direct materials $10, direct labor $20, and manufacturing overhead 90% of direct labor cost. If 25,000 units are expected to be sold at $69 each, what is the budgeted gross profit?
18. Indicate the supporting schedules used in preparing a budgeted income statement through gross profit for a manufacturer.
19. Identify the three sections of a cash budget. What balances are also shown in this budget?
20. Van Gundy Company has credit sales of $500,000 in January. Past experience suggests that 45% is collected in the month of sale, 50% in the month following the sale, and 5% in the second month following the sale. Compute the cash collections from January sales in January, February, and March.
21. What is the formula for determining required merchandise purchases for a merchandiser?
22. How may expected revenues in a service enterprise be computed?

BRIEF EXERCISES

BE23-1 Noble Manufacturing Company uses the following budgets: Balance Sheet, Capital Expenditure, Cash, Direct Labor, Direct Materials, Income Statement, Manufacturing Overhead, Production, Sales, and Selling and Administrative. Prepare a diagram of the interrelationships of the budgets in the master budget. Indicate whether each budget is an operating or a financial budget.

Prepare a diagram of a master budget.
(SO 3)

BE23-2 Goody Company estimates that unit sales will be 10,000 in quarter 1; 12,000 in quarter 2; 14,000 in quarter 3; and 18,000 in quarter 4. Using a sales price of $80 per unit, prepare the sales budget by quarters for the year ending December 31, 2010.

Prepare a sales budget.
(SO 3)

BE23-3 Sales budget data for Goody Company are given in BE23-2. Management desires to have an ending finished goods inventory equal to 20% of the next quarter's expected unit sales. Prepare a production budget by quarters for the first 6 months of 2010.

Prepare a production budget for 2 quarters.
(SO 3)

BE23-4 Ortiz Company has 1,600 pounds of raw materials in its December 31, 2010, ending inventory. Required production for January and February of 2011 are 4,000 and 5,500 units, respectively. Two pounds of raw materials are needed for each unit, and the estimated cost per pound

Prepare a direct materials budget for 1 month.
(SO 3)

Chapter 23 Budgetary Planning

is $6. Management desires an ending inventory equal to 20% of next month's materials requirements. Prepare the direct materials budget for January.

Prepare a direct labor budget for 2 quarters.
(SO 3)

BE23-5 For Everly Company, units to be produced are 5,000 in quarter 1 and 6,000 in quarter 2. It takes 1.5 hours to make a finished unit, and the expected hourly wage rate is $14 per hour. Prepare a direct labor budget by quarters for the 6 months ending June 30, 2010.

Prepare a manufacturing overhead budget.
(SO 3)

BE23-6 For Justus Inc. variable manufacturing overhead costs are expected to be $20,000 in the first quarter of 2010 with $4,000 increments in each of the remaining three quarters. Fixed overhead costs are estimated to be $35,000 in each quarter. Prepare the manufacturing overhead budget by quarters and in total for the year.

Prepare a selling and administrative expense budget.
(SO 3)

BE23-7 Mize Company classifies its selling and administrative expense budget into variable and fixed components. Variable expenses are expected to be $25,000 in the first quarter, and $5,000 increments are expected in the remaining quarters of 2010. Fixed expenses are expected to be $40,000 in each quarter. Prepare the selling and administrative expense budget by quarters and in total for 2010.

Prepare a budgeted income statement for the year.
(SO 4)

BE23-8 Perine Company has completed all of its operating budgets. The sales budget for the year shows 50,000 units and total sales of $2,000,000. The total unit cost of making one unit of sales is $22. Selling and administrative expenses are expected to be $300,000. Income taxes are estimated to be $150,000. Prepare a budgeted income statement for the year ending December 31, 2010.

Prepare data for a cash budget.
(SO 5)

BE23-9 Agee Industries expects credit sales for January, February, and March to be $200,000, $260,000, and $310,000, respectively. It is expected that 70% of the sales will be collected in the month of sale, and 30% will be collected in the following month. Compute cash collections from customers for each month.

Determine required merchandise purchases for 1 month.
(SO 6)

BE23-10 Palermo Wholesalers is preparing its merchandise purchases budget. Budgeted sales are $400,000 for April and $475,000 for May. Cost of goods sold is expected to be 60% of sales. The company's desired ending inventory is 20% of the following month's cost of goods sold. Compute the required purchases for April.

DO IT! REVIEW

Identify budget terminology.
(SO 2, 3)

DO IT! 23-1 Use this list of terms to complete the sentences that follow.

Long-range plans   Participative budgeting
Sales forecast   Operating budgets
Master budget   Financial budgets

1. _____ establish goals for the company's sales and production personnel.
2. The _____ is a set of interrelated budgets that constitutes a plan of action for a specified time period.
3. _____ reduces the risk of having unrealistic budgets.
4. _____ include the cash budget and the budgeted balance sheet.
5. The budget is formed within the framework of a _____.
6. _____ contain considerably less detail than budgets.

Prepare sales, production, and direct materials budgets.
(SO 3)

DO IT! 23-2 Oak Creek Company is preparing its master budget for 2010. Relevant data pertaining to its sales, production, and direct materials budgets are as follows.

Sales: Sales for the year are expected to total 1,000,000 units. Quarterly sales are 20%, 25%, 25%, and 30% respectively. The sales price is expected to be $40 per unit for the first three quarters and $45 per unit beginning in the fourth quarter. Sales in the first quarter of 2011 are expected to be 10% higher than the budgeted sales for the first quarter of 2010.

Production: Management desires to maintain the ending finished goods inventories at 20% of the next quarter's budgeted sales volume.

Direct materials: Each unit requires 2 pounds of raw materials at a cost of $10 per pound. Management desires to maintain raw materials inventories at 10% of the next quarter's production requirements. Assume the production requirements for first quarter of 2011 are 500,000 pounds.

Prepare the sales, production, and direct materials budgets by quarters for 2010.

DO IT! 23-3 Oak Creek Company is preparing its budgeted income statement for 2010. Relevant data pertaining to its sales, production, and direct materials budgets can be found in Do It! exercise 23-2 on page 1044.

Calculate budgeted total unit cost and prepare budgeted income statement.
(SO 4)

In addition, Oak Creek budgets 0.3 hours of direct labor per unit, labor costs at $14 per hour, and manufacturing overhead at $20 per direct labor hour. Its budgeted selling and administrative expenses for 2010 are $7,000,000.

(a) Calculate the budgeted total unit cost.
(b) Prepare the budgeted income statement for 2010.

DO IT! 23-4 Venetian Company management wants to maintain a minimum monthly cash balance of $20,000. At the beginning of April, the cash balance is $22,000, expected cash receipts for March are $245,000, and cash disbursements are expected to be $256,000. How much cash, if any, must be borrowed to maintain the desired minimum monthly balance?

Determine amount of financing needed.
(SO 5)

EXERCISES

E23-1 Black Rose Company has always done some planning for the future, but the company has never prepared a formal budget. Now that the company is growing larger, it is considering preparing a budget.

Explain the concept of budgeting.
(SO 1, 2, 3)

Instructions
Write a memo to Jack Bruno, the president of Black Rose Company, in which you define budgeting, identify the budgets that comprise the master budget, identify the primary benefits of budgeting, and discuss the essentials of effective budgeting.

E23-2 Zeller Electronics Inc. produces and sells two models of pocket calculators, XQ-103 and XQ-104. The calculators sell for $12 and $25, respectively. Because of the intense competition Zeller faces, management budgets sales semiannually. Its projections for the first 2 quarters of 2010 are as follows.

Prepare a sales budget for 2 quarters.
(SO 3)

	Unit Sales	
Product	**Quarter 1**	**Quarter 2**
XQ-103	20,000	25,000
XQ-104	12,000	15,000

No changes in selling prices are anticipated.

Instructions
Prepare a sales budget for the 2 quarters ending June 30, 2010. List the products and show for each quarter and for the 6 months, units, selling price, and total sales by product and in total.

E23-3 Roche and Young, CPAs, are preparing their service revenue (sales) budget for the coming year (2010). The practice is divided into three departments: auditing, tax, and consulting. Billable hours for each department, by quarter, are provided below.

Prepare a sales budget for four quarters.
(SO 3, 6)

Department	Quarter 1	Quarter 2	Quarter 3	Quarter 4
Auditing	2,200	1,600	2,000	2,400
Tax	3,000	2,400	2,000	2,500
Consulting	1,500	1,500	1,500	1,500

Average hourly billing rates are: auditing $80, tax $90, and consulting $100.

Instructions
Prepare the service revenue (sales) budget for 2010 by listing the departments and showing for each quarter and the year in total, billable hours, billable rate, and total revenue.

Prepare quarterly production budgets.
(SO 3)

E23-4 Turney Company produces and sells automobile batteries, the heavy-duty HD-240. The 2010 sales budget is as follows.

Quarter	HD-240
1	5,000
2	7,000
3	8,000
4	10,000

The January 1, 2010, inventory of HD-240 is 2,500 units. Management desires an ending inventory each quarter equal to 50% of the next quarter's sales. Sales in the first quarter of 2011 are expected to be 30% higher than sales in the same quarter in 2010.

Instructions
Prepare quarterly production budgets for each quarter and in total for 2010.

Prepare a direct materials purchases budget.
(SO 3)

E23-5 Moreno Industries has adopted the following production budget for the first 4 months of 2011.

Month	Units	Month	Units
January	10,000	March	5,000
February	8,000	April	4,000

Each unit requires 3 pounds of raw materials costing $2 per pound. On December 31, 2010, the ending raw materials inventory was 9,000 pounds. Management wants to have a raw materials inventory at the end of the month equal to 30% of next month's production requirements.

Instructions
Prepare a direct materials purchases budget by month for the first quarter.

Prepare production and direct materials budgets by quarters for 6 months.
(SO 3)

E23-6 On January 1, 2011 the Batista Company budget committee has reached agreement on the following data for the 6 months ending June 30, 2011.

Sales units: First quarter 5,000; second quarter 6,000; third quarter 7,000
Ending raw materials inventory: 50% of the next quarter's production requirements
Ending finished goods inventory: 30% of the next quarter's expected sales units
Third-quarter production: 7,250 units

The ending raw materials and finished goods inventories at December 31, 2010, follow the same percentage relationships to production and sales that occur in 2011. Three pounds of raw materials are required to make each unit of finished goods. Raw materials purchased are expected to cost $4 per pound.

Instructions
(a) Prepare a production budget by quarters for the 6-month period ended June 30, 2011.
(b) Prepare a direct materials budget by quarters for the 6-month period ended June 30, 2011.

Prepare a direct labor budget.
(SO 3)

E23-7 Neely, Inc., is preparing its direct labor budget for 2010 from the following production budget based on a calendar year.

Quarter	Units	Quarter	Units
1	20,000	3	35,000
2	25,000	4	30,000

Each unit requires 1.6 hours of direct labor.

Instructions
Prepare a direct labor budget for 2010. Wage rates are expected to be $15 for the first 2 quarters and $16 for quarters 3 and 4.

Prepare a manufacturing overhead budget for the year.
(SO 3)

E23-8 Hardin Company is preparing its manufacturing overhead budget for 2010. Relevant data consist of the following.

Units to be produced (by quarters): 10,000, 12,000, 14,000, 16,000.

Direct labor: Time is 1.5 hours per unit.

Variable overhead costs per direct labor hour: Indirect materials $0.70; indirect labor $1.20; and maintenance $0.50.

Fixed overhead costs per quarter: Supervisory salaries $35,000; depreciation $16,000; and maintenance $12,000.

Instructions
Prepare the manufacturing overhead budget for the year, showing quarterly data.

E23-9 Edington Company combines its operating expenses for budget purposes in a selling and administrative expense budget. For the first 6 months of 2010, the following data are available.

1. Sales: 20,000 units quarter 1; 22,000 units quarter 2.
2. Variable costs per dollar of sales: Sales commissions 5%, delivery expense 2%, and advertising 3%.
3. Fixed costs per quarter: Sales salaries $10,000, office salaries $6,000, depreciation $4,200, insurance $1,500, utilities $800, and repairs expense $600.
4. Unit selling price: $20.

Prepare a selling and administrative expense budget for 2 quarters.
(SO 3)

Instructions
Prepare a selling and administrative expense budget by quarters for the first 6 months of 2010.

E23-10 Tyson Chandler Company's sales budget projects unit sales of part 198Z of 10,000 units in January, 12,000 units in February, and 13,000 units in March. Each unit of part 198Z requires 2 pounds of materials, which cost $3 per pound. Tyson Chandler Company desires its ending raw materials inventory to equal 40% of the next month's production requirements, and its ending finished goods inventory to equal 25% of the next month's expected unit sales. These goals were met at December 31, 2009.

Prepare a production and a direct materials budget.
(SO 3)

Instructions
(a) Prepare a production budget for January and February 2010.
(b) Prepare a direct materials budget for January 2010.

E23-11 Fuqua Company has accumulated the following budget data for the year 2010.

1. Sales: 30,000 units, unit selling price $80.
2. Cost of one unit of finished goods: Direct materials 2 pounds at $5 per pound, direct labor 3 hours at $12 per hour, and manufacturing overhead $6 per direct labor hour.
3. Inventories (raw materials only): Beginning, 10,000 pounds; ending, 15,000 pounds.
4. Raw materials cost: $5 per pound.
5. Selling and administrative expenses: $200,000.
6. Income taxes: 30% of income before income taxes.

Prepare a budgeted income statement for the year.
(SO 3, 4)

Instructions
(a) Prepare a schedule showing the computation of cost of goods sold for 2010.
(b) Prepare a budgeted income statement for 2010.

E23-12 Garza Company expects to have a cash balance of $46,000 on January 1, 2010. Relevant monthly budget data for the first 2 months of 2010 are as follows.

Collections from customers: January $85,000, February $150,000.

Payments for direct materials: January $50,000, February $70,000.

Direct labor: January $30,000, February $45,000. Wages are paid in the month they are incurred.

Manufacturing overhead: January $21,000, February $25,000. These costs include depreciation of $1,000 per month. All other overhead costs are paid as incurred.

Selling and administrative expenses: January $15,000, February $20,000. These costs are exclusive of depreciation. They are paid as incurred.

Sales of marketable securities in January are expected to realize $10,000 in cash. Garza Company has a line of credit at a local bank that enables it to borrow up to $25,000. The company wants to maintain a minimum monthly cash balance of $20,000.

Prepare a cash budget for 2 months.
(SO 5)

Instructions
Prepare a cash budget for January and February.

E23-13 Pink Martini Corporation is projecting a cash balance of $31,000 in its December 31, 2009, balance sheet. Pink Martini's schedule of expected collections from customers for the

Prepare a cash budget.
(SO 5)

first quarter of 2010 shows total collections of $180,000. The schedule of expected payments for direct materials for the first quarter of 2010 shows total payments of $41,000. Other information gathered for the first quarter of 2010 is: sale of equipment $3,500; direct labor $70,000, manufacturing overhead $35,000, selling and administrative expenses $45,000; and purchase of securities $12,000. Pink Martini wants to maintain a balance of at least $25,000 cash at the end of each quarter.

Instructions
Prepare a cash budget for the first quarter.

Prepare schedules of expected collections and payments.
(SO 5)

E23-14 NIU Company's budgeted sales and direct materials purchases are as follows.

	Budgeted Sales	Budgeted D.M. Purchases
January	$200,000	$30,000
February	220,000	35,000
March	270,000	41,000

NIU's sales are 40% cash and 60% credit. Credit sales are collected 10% in the month of sale, 50% in the month following sale, and 36% in the second month following sale; 4% are uncollectible. NIU's purchases are 50% cash and 50% on account. Purchases on account are paid 40% in the month of purchase, and 60% in the month following purchase.

Instructions
(a) Prepare a schedule of expected collections from customers for March.
(b) Prepare a schedule of expected payments for direct materials for March.

Prepare schedules for cash receipts and cash payments, and determine ending balances for balance sheet.
(SO 5, 6)

E23-15 Environmental Landscaping Inc. is preparing its budget for the first quarter of 2010. The next step in the budgeting process is to prepare a cash receipts schedule and a cash payments schedule. To that end the following information has been collected.

Clients usually pay 60% of their fee in the month that service is provided, 30% the month after, and 10% the second month after receiving service.

Actual service revenue for 2009 and expected service revenues for 2010 are: November 2009, $90,000; December 2009, $80,000; January 2010, $100,000; February 2010, $120,000; March 2010, $130,000.

Purchases on landscaping supplies (direct materials) are paid 40% in the month of purchase and 60% the following month. Actual purchases for 2009 and expected purchases for 2010 are: December 2009, $14,000; January 2010, $12,000; February 2010, $15,000; March 2010, $18,000.

Instructions
(a) Prepare the following schedules for each month in the first quarter of 2010 and for the quarter in total:
  (1) Expected collections from clients.
  (2) Expected payments for landscaping supplies.
(b) Determine the following balances at March 31, 2010:
  (1) Accounts receivable.
  (2) Accounts payable.

Prepare a cash budget for two quarters.
(SO 5, 6)

E23-16 Donnegal Dental Clinic is a medium-sized dental service specializing in family dental care. The clinic is currently preparing the master budget for the first 2 quarters of 2010. All that remains in this process is the cash budget. The following information has been collected from other portions of the master budget and elsewhere.

Beginning cash balance	$ 30,000
Required minimum cash balance	25,000
Payment of income taxes (2nd quarter)	4,000
Professional salaries:	
1st quarter	140,000
2nd quarter	140,000
Interest from investments (2nd quarter)	5,000
Overhead costs:	
1st quarter	75,000
2nd quarter	100,000

Selling and administrative costs, including $3,000 depreciation:	
1st quarter	50,000
2nd quarter	70,000
Purchase of equipment (2nd quarter)	50,000
Sale of equipment (1st quarter)	15,000
Collections from clients:	
1st quarter	230,000
2nd quarter	380,000
Interest payments (2nd quarter)	300

Instructions
Prepare a cash budget for each of the first two quarters of 2010.

E23-17 In May 2010, the budget committee of Dalby Stores assembles the following data in preparation of budgeted merchandise purchases for the month of June.

Prepare a purchases budget and budgeted income statement for a merchandiser.
(SO 6)

1. Expected sales: June $500,000, July $600,000.
2. Cost of goods sold is expected to be 70% of sales.
3. Desired ending merchandise inventory is 40% of the following (next) month's cost of goods sold.
4. The beginning inventory at June 1 will be the desired amount.

Instructions
(a) Compute the budgeted merchandise purchases for June.
(b) Prepare the budgeted income statement for June through gross profit.

EXERCISES: SET B

Visit the book's companion website at **www.wiley.com/college/weygandt**, and choose the Student Companion site, to access Exercise Set B.

PROBLEMS: SET A

P23-1A Danner Farm Supply Company manufactures and sells a pesticide called Snare. The following data are available for preparing budgets for Snare for the first 2 quarters of 2011.

Prepare budgeted income statement and supporting budgets.
(SO 3, 4)

1. Sales: Quarter 1, 28,000 bags; quarter 2, 42,000 bags. Selling price is $60 per bag.
2. Direct materials: Each bag of Snare requires 4 pounds of Gumm at a cost of $4 per pound and 6 pounds of Tarr at $1.50 per pound.
3. Desired inventory levels:

Type of Inventory	January 1	April 1	July 1
Snare (bags)	8,000	12,000	18,000
Gumm (pounds)	9,000	10,000	13,000
Tarr (pounds)	14,000	20,000	25,000

4. Direct labor: Direct labor time is 15 minutes per bag at an hourly rate of $14 per hour.
5. Selling and administrative expenses are expected to be 15% of sales plus $175,000 per quarter.
6. Income taxes are expected to be 30% of income from operations.

Your assistant has prepared two budgets: (1) The manufacturing overhead budget shows expected costs to be 150% of direct labor cost. (2) The direct materials budget for Tarr shows the cost of Tarr purchases to be $297,000 in quarter 1 and $421,500 in quarter 2.

Instructions
Prepare the budgeted income statement for the first 6 months and all required supporting budgets by quarters. (*Note*: Use variable and fixed in the selling and administrative expense budget). Do not prepare the manufacturing overhead budget or the direct materials budget for Tarr.

Net income $600,250
Cost per bag $33.75

1050 Chapter 23 Budgetary Planning

Prepare sales, production, direct materials, direct labor, and income statement budgets.

(SO 3, 4)

P23-2A Larussa Inc. is preparing its annual budgets for the year ending December 31, 2011. Accounting assistants furnish the data shown below.

	Product JB 50	Product JB 60
Sales budget:		
Anticipated volume in units	400,000	200,000
Unit selling price	$20	$25
Production budget:		
Desired ending finished goods units	25,000	15,000
Beginning finished goods units	30,000	10,000
Direct materials budget:		
Direct materials per unit (pounds)	2	3
Desired ending direct materials pounds	30,000	15,000
Beginning direct materials pounds	40,000	10,000
Cost per pound	$3	$4
Direct labor budget:		
Direct labor time per unit	0.4	0.6
Direct labor rate per hour	$12	$12
Budgeted income statement:		
Total unit cost	$12	$21

An accounting assistant has prepared the detailed manufacturing overhead budget and the selling and administrative expense budget. The latter shows selling expenses of $660,000 for product JB 50 and $360,000 for product JB 60, and administrative expenses of $540,000 for product JB 50 and $340,000 for product JB 60. Income taxes are expected to be 30%.

(a) Total sales $13,000,000
(b) Required production units: JB 50, 395,000 JB 60, 205,000
(c) Total cost of direct materials purchases $4,820,000
(d) Total direct labor cost $3,372,000
(e) Net income $1,470,000

Instructions
Prepare the following budgets for the year. Show data for each product. You do not need to prepare quarterly budgets.

(a) Sales
(b) Production
(c) Direct materials
(d) Direct labor
(e) Income statement (*Note*: Income taxes are not allocated to the products.)

Prepare sales and production budgets and compute cost per unit under two plans.

(SO 3, 4)

P23-3A Colt Industries had sales in 2010 of $6,400,000 and gross profit of $1,100,000. Management is considering two alternative budget plans to increase its gross profit in 2011.

Plan A would increase the selling price per unit from $8.00 to $8.40. Sales volume would decrease by 5% from its 2010 level. Plan B would decrease the selling price per unit by $0.50. The marketing department expects that the sales volume would increase by 150,000 units.

At the end of 2010, Colt has 40,000 units of inventory on hand. If Plan A is accepted, the 2011 ending inventory should be equal to 5% of the 2011 sales. If Plan B is accepted, the ending inventory should be equal to 50,000 units. Each unit produced will cost $1.80 in direct labor, $2.00 in direct materials, and $1.20 in variable overhead. The fixed overhead for 2011 should be $1,895,000.

(c) Unit cost: Plan A $7.50, Plan B $6.97
(d) Gross profit:
 Plan A $684,000
 Plan B $503,500

Instructions
(a) Prepare a sales budget for 2011 under each plan.
(b) Prepare a production budget for 2011 under each plan.
(c) Compute the production cost per unit under each plan. Why is the cost per unit different for each of the two plans? (Round to two decimals.)
(d) Which plan should be accepted? (*Hint*: Compute the gross profit under each plan.)

Prepare cash budget for 2 months.

(SO 5)

P23-4A Haas Company prepares monthly cash budgets. Relevant data from operating budgets for 2011 are:

	January	February
Sales	$350,000	$400,000
Direct materials purchases	110,000	130,000
Direct labor	90,000	100,000
Manufacturing overhead	70,000	75,000
Selling and administrative expenses	79,000	86,000

All sales are on account. Collections are expected to be 50% in the month of sale, 30% in the first month following the sale, and 20% in the second month following the sale. Sixty percent (60%) of direct materials purchases are paid in cash in the month of purchase, and the balance due is paid in the month following the purchase. All other items above are paid in the month incurred except for selling and administrative expenses that include $1,000 of depreciation per month.

Other data:

1. Credit sales: November 2010, $260,000; December 2010, $320,000.
2. Purchases of direct materials: December 2010, $100,000.
3. Other receipts: January—Collection of December 31, 2010, notes receivable $15,000; February—Proceeds from sale of securities $6,000.
4. Other disbursements: February—Withdrawal of $5,000 cash for personal use of owner, Dewey Yaeger.

The company's cash balance on January 1, 2011, is expected to be $60,000. The company wants to maintain a minimum cash balance of $50,000.

Instructions

(a) Prepare schedules for (1) expected collections from customers and (2) expected payments for direct materials purchases.

(b) Prepare a cash budget for January and February in columnar form.

(a) January: collections $323,000 payments $106,000
(b) Ending cash balance: January $54,000 February $50,000

P23-5A The budget committee of Deleon Company collects the following data for its San Miguel Store in preparing budgeted income statements for May and June 2011.

1. Sales for May are expected to be $800,000. Sales in June and July are expected to be 10% higher than the preceding month.
2. Cost of goods sold is expected to be 75% of sales.
3. Company policy is to maintain ending merchandise inventory at 20% of the following month's cost of goods sold.
4. Operating expenses are estimated to be:

Sales salaries	$30,000 per month
Advertising	5% of monthly sales
Delivery expense	3% of monthly sales
Sales commissions	4% of monthly sales
Rent expense	$5,000 per month
Depreciation	$800 per month
Utilities	$600 per month
Insurance	$500 per month

5. Income taxes are estimated to be 30% of income from operations.

Prepare purchases and income statement budgets for a merchandiser.
(SO 6)

Instructions

(a) Prepare the merchandise purchases budget for each month in columnar form.
(b) Prepare budgeted income statements for each month in columnar form. Show in the statements the details of cost of goods sold.

(a) Purchases:
May $612,000
June $673,200
(b) Net income:
May $46,970
June $54,250

P23-6A Glendo Industries' balance sheet at December 31, 2010, is presented below and on the next page.

Prepare budgeted income statement and balance sheet.
(SO 4, 5)

GLENDO INDUSTRIES
Balance Sheet
December 31, 2010

Assets

Current assets		
Cash		$ 7,500
Accounts receivable		82,500
Finished goods inventory (2,000 units)		30,000
Total current assets		120,000
Property, plant, and equipment		
Equipment	$40,000	
Less: Accumulated depreciation	10,000	30,000
Total assets		$150,000

Liabilities and Stockholders' Equity

Liabilities		
Notes payable		$ 25,000
Accounts payable		45,000
Total liabilities		70,000
Stockholders' equity		
Common stock	$50,000	
Retained earnings	30,000	
Total stockholders' equity		80,000
Total liabilities and stockholders' equity		$150,000

Additional information accumulated for the budgeting process is as follows.
Budgeted data for the year 2011 include the following.

	4th Qtr. of 2011	Year 2011 Total
Sales budget (8,000 units at $35)	$84,000	$280,000
Direct materials used	17,000	69,400
Direct labor	12,500	56,600
Manufacturing overhead applied	10,000	54,000
Selling and administrative expenses	18,000	76,000

To meet sales requirements and to have 3,000 units of finished goods on hand at December 31, 2011, the production budget shows 9,000 required units of output. The total unit cost of production is expected to be $20. Glendo Industries uses the first-in, first-out (FIFO) inventory costing method. Selling and administrative expenses include $4,000 for depreciation on equipment. Interest expense is expected to be $3,500 for the year. Income taxes are expected to be 30% of income before income taxes.

All sales and purchases are on account. It is expected that 60% of quarterly sales are collected in cash within the quarter and the remainder is collected in the following quarter. Direct materials purchased from suppliers are paid 50% in the quarter incurred and the remainder in the following quarter. Purchases in the fourth quarter were the same as the materials used. In 2011, the company expects to purchase additional equipment costing $19,000. It expects to pay $8,000 on notes payable plus all interest due and payable to December 31 (included in interest expense $3,500, above). Accounts payable at December 31, 2011, includes amounts due suppliers (see above) plus other accounts payable of $5,700. In 2011, the company expects to declare and pay a $5,000 cash dividend. Unpaid income taxes at December 31 will be $5,000. The company's cash budget shows an expected cash balance of $7,950 at December 31, 2011.

Instructions

Net income $35,350
Total assets $146,550

Prepare a budgeted income statement for 2011 and a budgeted balance sheet at December 31, 2011. In preparing the income statement, you will need to compute cost of goods manufactured (direct materials + direct labor + manufacturing overhead) and finished goods inventory (December 31, 2011).

PROBLEMS: SET B

Prepare budgeted income statement and supporting budgets.
(SO 3, 4)

P23-1B Suppan Farm Supply Company manufactures and sells a fertilizer called Basic II. The following data are available for preparing budgets for Basic II for the first 2 quarters of 2010.

1. Sales: Quarter 1, 40,000 bags; quarter 2, 50,000 bags. Selling price is $65 per bag.
2. Direct materials: Each bag of Basic II requires 6 pounds of Crup at a cost of $4 per pound and 10 pounds of Dert at $1.50 per pound.

3. Desired inventory levels:

Type of Inventory	January 1	April 1	July 1
Basic II (bags)	10,000	15,000	20,000
Crup (pounds)	9,000	12,000	15,000
Dert (pounds)	15,000	20,000	25,000

4. Direct labor: Direct labor time is 15 minutes per bag at an hourly rate of $10 per hour.
5. Selling and administrative expenses are expected to be 10% of sales plus $160,000 per quarter.
6. Income taxes are expected to be 30% of income from operations.

Your assistant has prepared two budgets: (1) The manufacturing overhead budget shows expected costs to be 100% of direct labor cost. (2) The direct materials budget for Dert which shows the cost of Dert to be $682,500 in quarter 1 and $825,00 in quarter 2.

Instructions
Prepare the budgeted income statement for the first 6 months of 2010 and all required supporting budgets by quarters. (*Note*: Use variable and fixed in the selling and administrative expense budget.) Do not prepare the manufacturing overhead budget or the direct materials budget for Dert.

Net income $689,500
Cost per bag $44.00

P23-2B Durham Inc. is preparing its annual budgets for the year ending December 31, 2010. Accounting assistants furnish the following data.

Prepare sales, production, direct materials, direct labor, and income statement budgets.
(SO 3, 4)

	Product LN 35	Product LN 40
Sales budget:		
Anticipated volume in units	400,000	240,000
Unit selling price	$25	$35
Production budget:		
Desired ending finished goods units	30,000	25,000
Beginning finished goods units	20,000	15,000
Direct materials budget:		
Direct materials per unit (pounds)	2	3
Desired ending direct materials pounds	50,000	20,000
Beginning direct materials pounds	40,000	10,000
Cost per pound	$2	$3
Direct labor budget:		
Direct labor time per unit	0.5	0.75
Direct labor rate per hour	$12	$12
Budgeted income statement:		
Total unit cost	$11	$20

An accounting assistant has prepared the detailed manufacturing overhead budget and the selling and administrative expense budget. The latter shows selling expenses of $750,000 for product LN 35 and $590,000 for product LN 40, and administrative expenses of $420,000 for product LN 35 and $380,000 for product LN 40. Income taxes are expected to be 30%.

Instructions
Prepare the following budgets for the year. Show data for each product. You do not need to prepare quarterly budgets.

(a) Sales
(b) Production
(c) Direct materials
(d) Direct labor
(e) Income statement (*Note*: Income taxes are not allocated to the products.)

(a) Total sales $18,400,000
(b) Required production units:
LN 35, 410,000
(c) Total cost of direct materials purchases $3,940,000
(d) Total direct labor cost $4,710,000
(e) Net income $4,942,000

P23-3B Speier Industries has sales in 2010 of $5,600,000 (800,000 units) and gross profit of $1,344,000. Management is considering two alternative budget plans to increase its gross profit in 2011.

Plan A would increase the selling price per unit from $7.00 to $7.60. Sales volume would decrease by 10% from its 2010 level. Plan B would decrease the selling price per unit by 5%. The marketing department expects that the sales volume would increase by 100,000 units.

At the end of 2010, Speier has 70,000 units on hand. If Plan A is accepted, the 2011 ending inventory should be equal to 90,000 units. If Plan B is accepted, the ending inventory should be

Prepare sales and production budgets and compute cost per unit under two plans.
(SO 3, 4)

1054 Chapter 23 Budgetary Planning

equal to 100,000 units. Each unit produced will cost $2.00 in direct materials, $1.50 in direct labor, and $0.50 in variable overhead. The fixed overhead for 2011 should be $925,000.

Instructions
(a) Prepare a sales budget for 2011 under (1) Plan A and (2) Plan B.
(b) Prepare a production budget for 2011 under (1) Plan A and (2) Plan B.
(c) Compute the cost per unit under (1) Plan A and (2) Plan B. Explain why the cost per unit is different for each of the two plans. (Round to two decimals.)
(d) Which plan should be accepted? (*Hint:* Compute the gross profit under each plan.)

(c) Unit cost: Plan A $5.25
Plan B $4.99
(d) Gross profit:
Plan A $1,692,000
Plan B $1,494,000

Prepare cash budget for 2 months.
(SO 5)

P23-4B Vidro Company prepares monthly cash budgets. Relevant data from operating budgets for 2011 are:

	January	February
Sales	$350,000	$400,000
Direct materials purchases	120,000	110,000
Direct labor	85,000	115,000
Manufacturing overhead	60,000	75,000
Selling and administrative expenses	75,000	80,000

All sales are on account. Collections are expected to be 60% in the month of sale, 30% in the first month following the sale, and 10% in the second month following the sale. Thirty percent (30%) of direct materials purchases are paid in cash in the month of purchase, and the balance due is paid in the month following the purchase. All other items above are paid in the month incurred. Depreciation has been excluded from manufacturing overhead and selling and administrative expenses.

Other data:

1. Credit sales: November 2010, $200,000; December 2010, $280,000.
2. Purchases of direct materials: December 2010, $90,000.
3. Other receipts: January—Collection of December 31, 2010, interest receivable $3,000; February—Proceeds from sale of securities $5,000.
4. Other disbursements: February—payment of $20,000 for land.

The company's cash balance on January 1, 2011, is expected to be $50,000. The company wants to maintain a minimum cash balance of $40,000.

(a) January: collections $314,000
payments $99,000
(b) Ending cash balance:
January $48,000
February $40,000

Instructions
(a) Prepare schedules for (1) expected collections from customers and (2) expected payments for direct materials purchases.
(b) Prepare a cash budget for January and February in columnar form.

Prepare purchases and income statement budgets for a merchandiser.
(SO 6)

P23-5B The budget committee of Guzman Company collects the following data for its Westwood Store in preparing budgeted income statements for July and August 2010.

1. Expected sales: July $400,000, August $450,000, September $500,000.
2. Cost of goods sold is expected to be 60% of sales.
3. Company policy is to maintain ending merchandise inventory at 20% of the following month's cost of goods sold.
4. Operating expenses are estimated to be:

Sales salaries	$50,000 per month
Advertising	4% of monthly sales
Delivery expense	2% of monthly sales
Sales commissions	3% of monthly sales
Rent expense	$3,000 per month
Depreciation	$700 per month
Utilities	$500 per month
Insurance	$300 per month

5. Income taxes are estimated to be 30% of income from operations.

(a) Purchases: July $246,000
August $276,000
(b) Net income: July $48,650
August $59,500

Instructions
(a) Prepare the merchandise purchases budget for each month in columnar form.
(b) Prepare budgeted income statements for each month in columnar form. Show the details of cost of goods sold in the statements.

PROBLEMS: SET C

Visit the book's companion website at **www.wiley.com/college/weygandt**, and choose the Student Companion site, to access Problem Set C.

WATERWAYS CONTINUING PROBLEM

(This is a continuation of the Waterways Problem from Chapters 19 through 22.)

WCP23 Waterways Corporation is preparing its budget for the coming year, 2011. The first step is to plan for the first quarter of that coming year. The company has gathered information from its managers in preparation of the budgeting process. This problem asks you to prepare the various budgets that comprise the master budget for 2011.

Go to the book's companion website,
www.wiley.com/college/weygandt,
to find the remainder of this problem.

BROADENING YOUR PERSPECTIVE

Decision Making Across the Organization

BYP23-1 Lanier Corporation operates on a calendar-year basis. It begins the annual budgeting process in late August when the president establishes targets for the total dollar sales and net income before taxes for the next year.

The sales target is given first to the marketing department. The marketing manager formulates a sales budget by product line in both units and dollars. From this budget, sales quotas by product line in units and dollars are established for each of the corporation's sales districts. The marketing manager also estimates the cost of the marketing activities required to support the target sales volume and prepares a tentative marketing expense budget.

The executive vice president uses the sales and profit targets, the sales budget by product line, and the tentative marketing expense budget to determine the dollar amounts that can be devoted to manufacturing and corporate office expense. The executive vice president prepares the budget for corporate expenses. She then forwards to the production department the product-line sales budget in units and the total dollar amount that can be devoted to manufacturing.

The production manager meets with the factory managers to develop a manufacturing plan that will produce the required units when needed within the cost constraints set by the executive vice president. The budgeting process usually comes to a halt at this point because the production department does not consider the financial resources allocated to be adequate.

When this standstill occurs, the vice president of finance, the executive vice president, the marketing manager, and the production manager meet together to determine the final budgets for each of the areas. This normally results in a modest increase in the total amount available for manufacturing costs and cuts in the marketing expense and corporate office expense budgets. The total sales and net income figures proposed by the president are seldom changed. Although the participants are seldom pleased with the compromise, these budgets are final. Each executive then develops a new detailed budget for the operations in his or her area.

None of the areas has achieved its budget in recent years. Sales often run below the target. When budgeted sales are not achieved, each area is expected to cut costs so that the president's profit target can be met. However, the profit target is seldom met because costs are not cut enough. In fact, costs often run above the original budget in all functional areas (marketing, production, and corporate office).

The president is disturbed that Lanier has not been able to meet the sales and profit targets. He hired a consultant with considerable experience with companies in Lanier's industry. The consultant reviewed the budgets for the past 4 years. He concluded that the product line sales budgets were reasonable and that the cost and expense budgets were adequate for the budgeted sales and production levels.

Instructions

With the class divided into groups, answer the following.

(a) Discuss how the budgeting process employed by Lanier Corporation contributes to the failure to achieve the president's sales and profit targets.

(b) Suggest how Lanier Corporation's budgeting process could be revised to correct the problems.

(c) Should the functional areas be expected to cut their costs when sales volume falls below budget? Explain your answer. (CMA adapted.)

Managerial Analysis

BYP23-2 Bedner & Flott Inc. manufactures ergonomic devices for computer users. Some of their more popular products include glare screens (for computer monitors), keyboard stands with wrist rests, and carousels that allow easy access to magnetic disks. Over the past 5 years, they experienced rapid growth, with sales of all products increasing 20% to 50% each year.

Last year, some of the primary manufacturers of computers began introducing new products with some of the ergonomic designs, such as glare screens and wrist rests, already built in. As a result, sales of Bedner & Flott's accessory devices have declined somewhat. The company believes that the disk carousels will probably continue to show growth, but that the other products will probably continue to decline. When the next year's budget was prepared, increases were built in to research and development so that replacement products could be developed or the company could expand into some other product line. Some product lines being considered are general-purpose ergonomic devices including back supports, foot rests, and sloped writing pads.

The most recent results have shown that sales decreased more than was expected for the glare screens. As a result, the company may have a shortage of funds. Top management has therefore asked that all expenses be reduced 10% to compensate for these reduced sales. Summary budget information is as follows.

Direct materials	$240,000
Direct labor	110,000
Insurance	50,000
Depreciation	90,000
Machine repairs	30,000
Sales salaries	50,000
Office salaries	80,000
Factory salaries (indirect labor)	50,000
Total	$700,000

Instructions

Using the information above, answer the following questions.

(a) What are the implications of reducing each of the costs? For example, if the company reduces direct materials costs, it may have to do so by purchasing lower-quality materials. This may affect sales in the long run.

(b) Based on your analysis in (a), what do you think is the best way to obtain the $70,000 in cost savings requested? Be specific. Are there any costs that cannot or should not be reduced? Why?

Real-World Focus

BYP23-3 Network Computing Devices Inc. was founded in 1988 in Mountain View, California. The company develops software products such as X-terminals, Z-mail, PC X-ware, and related hardware products. Presented below is a discussion by management in its annual report.

> # NETWORK COMPUTING DEVICES, INC.
> ### Management Discussion
>
> The Company's operating results have varied significantly, particularly on a quarterly basis, as a result of a number of factors, including general economic conditions affecting industry demand for computer products, the timing and market acceptance of new product introductions by the Company and its competitors, the timing of significant orders from large customers, periodic changes in product pricing and discounting due to competitive factors, and the availability of key components, such as video monitors and electronic subassemblies, some of which require substantial order lead times. The Company's operating results may fluctuate in the future as a result of these and other factors, including the Company's success in developing and introducing new products, its product and customer mix, and the level of competition which it experiences. The Company operates with a small backlog. Sales and operating results, therefore, generally depend on the volume and timing of orders received, which are difficult to forecast. The Company has experienced slowness in orders from some customers during the first quarter of each calendar year due to budgeting cycles common in the computer industry. In addition, sales in Europe typically are adversely affected in the third calendar quarter as many European customers reduce their business activities during the month of August.
>
> Due to the Company's rapid growth rate and the effect of new product introductions on quarterly revenues, these seasonal trends have not materially impacted the Company's results of operations to date. However, as the Company's product lines mature and its rate of revenue growth declines, these seasonal factors may become more evident. Additionally, the Company's international sales are denominated in U.S. dollars, and an increase or decrease in the value of the U.S. dollar relative to foreign currencies could make the Company's products less or more competitive in those markets.

Instructions
(a) Identify the factors that affect the budgeting process at Network Computing Devices, Inc.
(b) Explain the additional budgeting concerns created by the international operations of the company.

Communication Activity

BYP23-4 In order to better serve their rural patients, Drs. Dan and Jack Fleming (brothers) began giving safety seminars. Especially popular were their "emergency-preparedness" talks given to farmers. Many people asked whether the "kit" of materials the doctors recommended for common farm emergencies was commercially available.

After checking with several suppliers, the doctors realized that no other company offered the supplies they recommended in their seminars, packaged in the way they described. Their wives, Julie and Amy, agreed to make a test package by ordering supplies from various medical supply companies and assembling them into a "kit" that could be sold at the seminars. When these kits proved a runaway success, the sisters-in-law decided to market them. At the advice of their accountant, they organized this venture as a separate company, called Life Protection Products (LPP), with Julie Fleming as CEO and Amy Fleming as Secretary-Treasurer.

LPP soon started receiving requests for the kits from all over the country, as word spread about their availability. Even without advertising, LPP was able to sell its full inventory every month. However, the company was becoming financially strained. Julie and Amy had about $100,000 in savings, and they invested about half that amount initially. They believed that this venture would allow them to make money. However, at the present time, only about $30,000 of the cash remains, and the company is constantly short of cash.

Julie has come to you for advice. She does not understand why the company is having cash flow problems. She and Amy have not even been withdrawing salaries. However, they have rented a local building and have hired two more full-time workers to help them cope with the increasing demand. They do not think they could handle the demand without this additional help.

Julie is also worried that the cash problems mean that the company may not be able to support itself. She has prepared the cash budget shown below. All seminar customers pay for their products in full at the time of purchase. In addition, several large companies have ordered the kits for use by employees who work in remote sites. They have requested credit terms and have been allowed to pay in the month following the sale. These large purchasers amount to about 25% of the sales at the present time. LPP purchases the materials for the kits about 2 months ahead of time. Julie and Amy are considering slowing the growth of the company by simply purchasing less materials, which will mean selling fewer kits.

The workers are paid in cash weekly. Julie and Amy need about $15,000 cash on hand at the beginning of the month to pay for purchases of raw materials. Right now they have been using cash from their savings, but as noted, only $30,000 is left.

Instructions

Write a response to Julie Fleming. Explain why LPP is short of cash. Will this company be able to support itself? Explain your answer. Make any recommendations you deem appropriate.

LIFE PROTECTION PRODUCTS
Cash Budget
For the Quarter Ending June 30, 2011

	April	May	June
Cash balance, beginning	$15,000	$15,000	$15,000
Cash received			
From prior month sales	5,000	7,500	12,500
From current sales	15,000	22,500	37,500
Total cash on hand	35,000	45,000	65,000
Cash payments			
To employees	3,000	3,000	3,000
For products	25,000	35,000	45,000
Miscellaneous expenses	5,000	6,000	7,000
Postage	1,000	1,000	1,000
Total cash payments	34,000	45,000	56,000
Cash balance	$ 1,000	$ 0	$ 9,000
Borrow from savings	$14,000	$15,000	$ 1,000
Borrow from bank?	$ 0	$ 0	$ 5,000

Ethics Case

BYP23-5 You are an accountant in the budgetary, projections, and special projects department of American Conductor, Inc., a large manufacturing company. The president, William Brown, asks you on very short notice to prepare some sales and income projections covering the next 2 years of the company's much heralded new product lines. He wants these projections for a series of speeches he is making while on a 2-week trip to eight East Coast brokerage firms. The president hopes to bolster American's stock sales and price.

You work 23 hours in 2 days to compile the projections, hand deliver them to the president, and are swiftly but graciously thanked as he departs. A week later you find time to go over some of your computations and discover a miscalculation that makes the projections grossly overstated. You quickly inquire about the president's itinerary and learn that he has made half of his speeches and has half yet to make. You are in a quandary as to what to do.

Instructions
(a) What are the consequences of telling the president of your gross miscalculations?
(b) What are the consequences of *not* telling the president of your gross miscalculations?
(c) What are the ethical considerations to you and the president in this situation?

"All About You" Activity

BYP23-6 The **All About You** feature in this chapter emphasizes that in order to get your personal finances under control, you need to prepare a personal budget. Assume that you have compiled the following information regarding your expected cash flows for a typical month.

Rent payment	$ 400	Miscellaneous costs	$110
Interest income	50	Savings	50
Income tax withheld	300	Eating out	150
Electricity bill	22	Telephone and Internet costs	90
Groceries	80	Student loan payments	275
Wages earned	2,000	Entertainment costs	250
Insurance	100	Transportation costs	150

Instructions

Using the information above, prepare a personal budget. In preparing this budget, use the format found at **http://financialplan.about.com/cs/budgeting/l/blbudget.htm**. Just skip any unused line items.

Answers to Insight and Accounting Across the Organization Questions

p. 1020 Business Often Feel Too Busy to Plan for the Future

Q: Describe a situation in which a business "sells as much as it can" but cannot "keep its employees paid."

A: *If sales are made to customers on credit and collection is slow, the company may find that it does not have enough cash to pay employees or suppliers. Without these resources, the company will fail to survive.*

p. 1034 Without a Budget, Can the Games Begin?

Q: Why does it matter whether the Olympic Games exceed their budget?

A: *If the Olympic Games exceed their budget, taxpayers of the sponsoring community and country will end up footing the bill. Depending on the size of the losses, and the resources of the community, this could produce a substantial burden. As a result, other communities might be reluctant to host the Olympics in the future.*

Authors' Comments on All About You: Avoiding Personal Financial Disaster (p. 1038)

We are concerned that the personal budgets presented on websites and in financial planning textbooks often list student loans among the sources of income. This type of thinking can lead to an over-reliance on debt during college, and will result in accumulation of large amounts of debt that must be repaid. We would prefer a format that lists non-debt sources of income, then subtracts expenses, then shows debt borrowed. This format emphasizes an important point: Just like a business, in the short run you can borrow money when your cash inflows are not sufficient to meet your outflows, but in the long run you need to learn to live within your income, and your budget.

Answers to Self-Study Questions

1. c 2. b 3. a 4. b 5. b 6. d 7. d 8. a 9. c 10. a 11. a 12. b 13. c
14. d 15. c

Chapter 24

Budgetary Control and Responsibility Accounting

STUDY OBJECTIVES

After studying this chapter, you should be able to:

1. Describe the concept of budgetary control.
2. Evaluate the usefulness of static budget reports.
3. Explain the development of flexible budgets and the usefulness of flexible budget reports.
4. Describe the concept of responsibility accounting.
5. Indicate the features of responsibility reports for cost centers.
6. Identify the content of responsibility reports for profit centers.
7. Explain the basis and formula used in evaluating performance in investment centers.

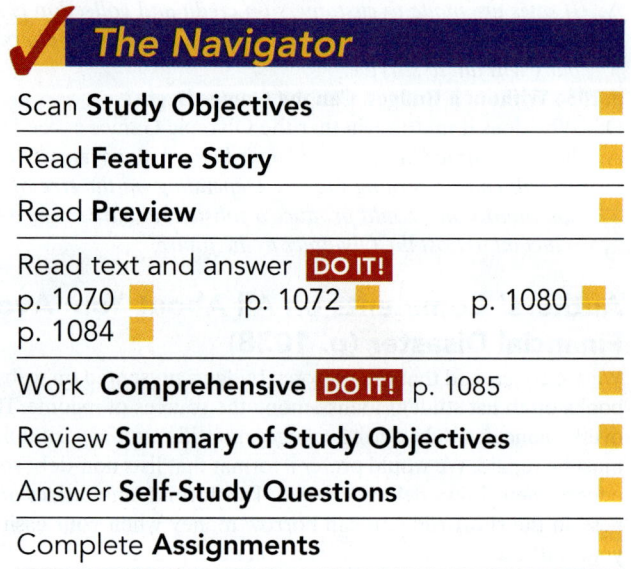

✓ The Navigator

- Scan **Study Objectives**
- Read **Feature Story**
- Read **Preview**
- Read text and answer **DO IT!** p. 1070 p. 1072 p. 1080 p. 1084
- Work **Comprehensive DO IT!** p. 1085
- Review **Summary of Study Objectives**
- Answer **Self-Study Questions**
- Complete **Assignments**

Feature Story

TRYING TO AVOID AN ELECTRIC SHOCK

Budgets are critical to evaluating an organization's success. They are based on management's expectations of what is most likely to happen in the future. In order to be useful, they must be accurate. But what if management's expectations are wrong? Estimates are never exactly correct, and

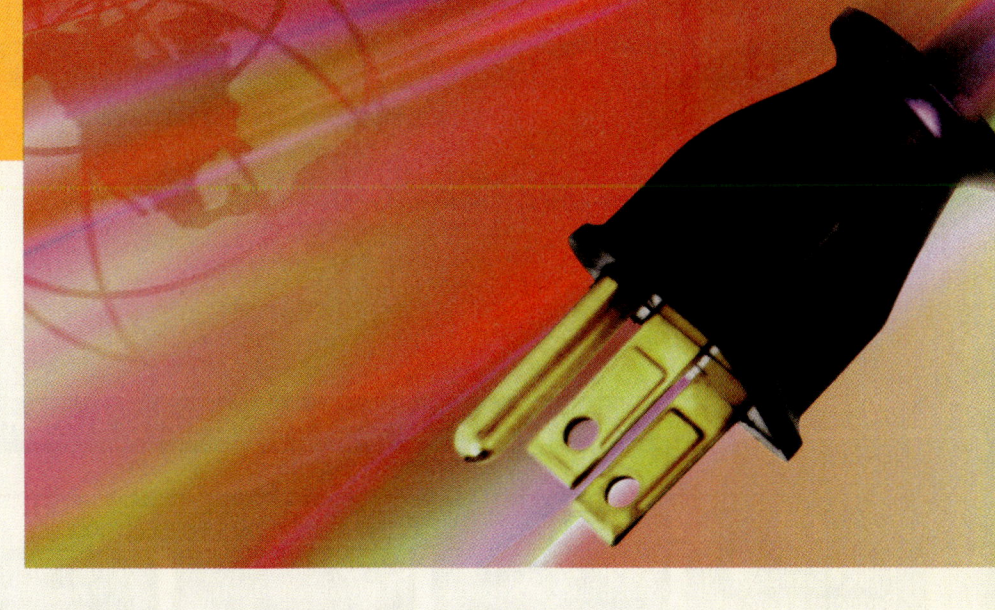

sometimes, especially in volatile industries, estimates can be "off by a mile."

In recent years the electric utility industry has become very volatile. Deregulation, volatile prices for natural gas, coal, and oil, changes in environmental regulations, and economic swings have all contributed to large changes in the profitability of electric utility companies. This means that for planning and budgeting purposes, utilities must plan and budget based on multiple "what if" scenarios that take into account factors beyond management's control. For example, in recent years, Duke Energy Corporation (www.duke-energy.com), headquartered in Charlotte, North Carolina, built budgeting and planning models based on three different scenarios of what the future might hold. One scenario assumes that the U.S. economy will slow considerably. A second scenario assumes that the company will experience "pricing pressure" as the market for energy becomes more efficient as a result of more energy being traded in Internet auctions. A third scenario assumes a continuation of the current environment of rapid growth, changing regulation, and large swings in the prices for the fuels the company uses to create energy.

Compounding this budgeting challenge is the fact that changes in many indirect costs can also significantly affect the company. For example, even a tiny change in market interest rates has a huge effect on the company because it has massive amounts of outstanding debt. And finally, as a result of the California energy crisis, there is mounting pressure for government intervention and regulation. This pressure has resulted in setting "rate caps" that limit the amount that utilities and energy companies can charge, thus lowering profits. The bottom line is that for budgeting and planning purposes, utility companies must remain alert and flexible.

✓ The Navigator

Inside Chapter 24...

- **Competition versus Collaboration** (p. 1074)
- **Does Hollywood Look at ROI?** (p. 1083)

Preview of Chapter 24

In contrast to Chapter 23, we now consider how budgets are used by management to control operations. In the Feature Story on **Duke Energy**, we saw that budgeting must take into account factors beyond management's control. This chapter focuses on two aspects of management control: (1) budgetary control and (2) responsibility accounting.

The content and organization of Chapter 24 are as follows.

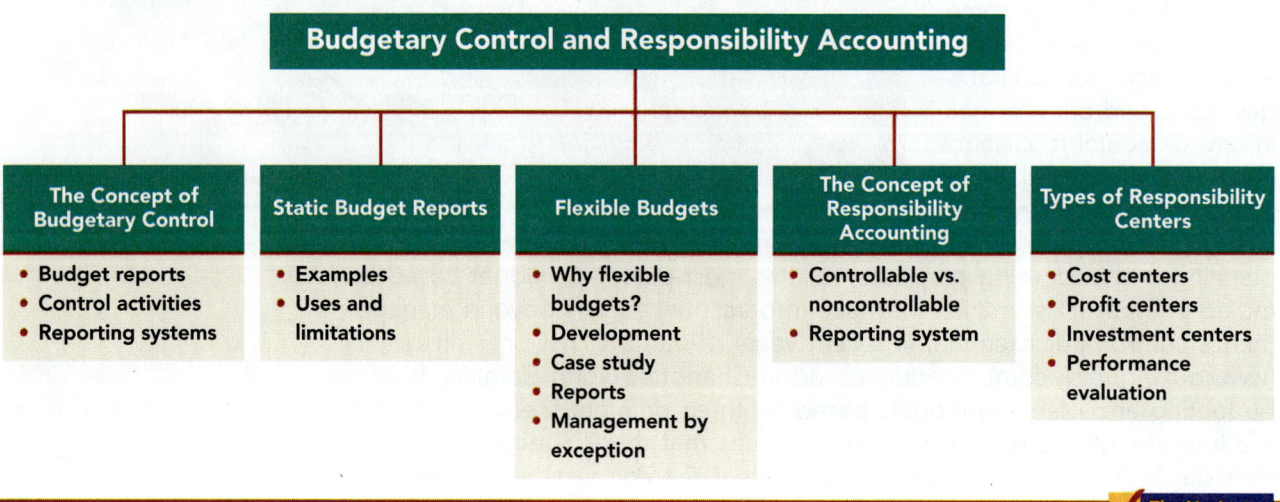

THE CONCEPT OF BUDGETARY CONTROL

STUDY OBJECTIVE 1
Describe the concept of budgetary control.

One of management's major functions is to control company operations. Control consists of the steps taken by management to see that planned objectives are met. We now ask: How do budgets contribute to control of operations?

The use of budgets in controlling operations is known as **budgetary control**. Such control takes place by means of **budget reports** that compare actual results with planned objectives. The use of budget reports is based on the belief that planned objectives lose much of their potential value without some monitoring of progress along the way. Just as your professors give midterm exams to evaluate your progress, so top management requires periodic reports on the progress of department managers toward their planned objectives.

Budget reports provide management with feedback on operations. The feedback for a crucial objective, such as having enough cash on hand to pay bills, may be made daily. For other objectives, such as meeting budgeted annual sales and operating expenses, monthly budget reports may suffice. Budget reports are prepared as frequently as needed. From these reports, management analyzes any differences between actual and planned results and determines their causes. Management then takes corrective action, or it decides to modify future plans.

Budgetary control involves activities shown in Illustration 24-1.

Illustration 24-1
Budgetary control activities

Budgetary control works best when a company has a formalized reporting system. The system does the following:

1. Identifies the name of the budget report, such as the sales budget or the manufacturing overhead budget.
2. States the frequency of the report, such as weekly or monthly.
3. Specifies the purpose of the report.
4. Indicates the primary recipient(s) of the report.

Illustration 24-2 provides a partial budgetary control system for a manufacturing company. Note the frequency of the reports and their emphasis on control. For example, there is a daily report on scrap and a weekly report on labor.

Illustration 24-2
Budgetary control reporting system

Name of Report	Frequency	Purpose	Primary Recipient(s)
Sales	Weekly	Determine whether sales goals are being met	Top management and sales manager
Labor	Weekly	Control direct and indirect labor costs	Vice president of production and production department managers
Scrap	Daily	Determine efficient use of materials	Production manager
Departmental overhead costs	Monthly	Control overhead costs	Department manager
Selling expenses	Monthly	Control selling expenses	Sales manager
Income statement	Monthly and quarterly	Determine whether income objectives are being met	Top management

STATIC BUDGET REPORTS

You learned in Chapter 23 that the master budget formalizes management's planned objectives for the coming year. When used in budgetary control, each budget included in the master budget is considered to be static. A **static budget** is a projection of budget data **at one level of activity**. These budgets do not consider data for different levels of activity. As a result, companies always compare actual results with budget data at the activity level that was used in developing the master budget.

STUDY OBJECTIVE 2
Evaluate the usefulness of static budget reports.

Examples

To illustrate the role of a static budget in budgetary control, we will use selected data prepared for Hayes Company in Chapter 23. Budget and actual sales data for the Kitchen-Mate product in the first and second quarters of 2010 are as follows.

Illustration 24-3
Budget and actual sales data

Sales	First Quarter	Second Quarter	Total
Budgeted	$180,000	$210,000	$390,000
Actual	179,000	199,500	378,500
Difference	$ 1,000	$ 10,500	$ 11,500

The sales budget report for Hayes Company's first quarter is shown below. The right-most column reports the difference between the budgeted and actual amounts.

Illustration 24-4
Sales budget report—first quarter

ALTERNATIVE TERMINOLOGY

The difference between budget and actual is sometimes called a *budget variance*.

HAYES COMPANY
Sales Budget Report
For the Quarter Ended March 31, 2010

Product Line	Budget	Actual	Difference Favorable F Unfavorable U
Kitchen-Mate[a]	$180,000	$179,000	**$1,000 U**

[a] In practice, each product line would be included in the report.

The report shows that sales are $1,000 under budget—an unfavorable result. This difference is less than 1% of budgeted sales ($1,000 ÷ $180,000 = .0056). Top management's reaction to unfavorable differences is often influenced by the materiality (significance) of the difference. Since the difference of $1,000 is immaterial in this case, we assume that Hayes Company management takes no specific corrective action.

Illustration 24-5 shows the budget report for the second quarter. It contains one new feature: cumulative year-to-date information. This report indicates that sales for the second quarter are $10,500 below budget. This is 5% of budgeted sales ($10,500 ÷ $210,000). Top management may now conclude that the difference between budgeted and actual sales requires investigation.

Illustration 24-5
Sales budget report—second quarter

HAYES COMPANY
Sales Budget Report
For the Quarter Ended June 30, 2010

	Second Quarter			Year-to-Date		
Product Line	Budget	Actual	Difference Favorable F Unfavorable U	Budget	Actual	Difference Favorable F Unfavorable U
Kitchen-Mate	$210,000	$199,500	**$10,500 U**	$390,000	$378,500	**$11,500 U**

Management's analysis should start by asking the sales manager the cause(s) of the shortfall. Managers should consider the need for corrective action. For example, management may decide to spur sales by offering sales incentives to customers or by increasing the advertising of Kitchen-Mates. Or, if management concludes that a downturn in the economy is responsible for the lower sales, it may modify planned sales and profit goals for the remainder of the year.

Uses and Limitations

From these examples, you can see that a master sales budget is useful in evaluating the performance of a sales manager. It is now necessary to ask: Is the master budget appropriate for evaluating a manager's performance in controlling costs? Recall that in a static budget, data are not modified or adjusted, regardless of changes in activity. It follows, then, that a static budget is appropriate in evaluating a manager's effectiveness in controlling costs when:

1. The actual level of activity closely approximates the master budget activity level, and/or
2. The behavior of the costs in response to changes in activity is fixed.

A static budget report is, therefore, appropriate for **fixed manufacturing costs** and for **fixed selling and administrative expenses**. But, as you will see shortly, static budget reports may not be a proper basis for evaluating a manager's performance in controlling variable costs.

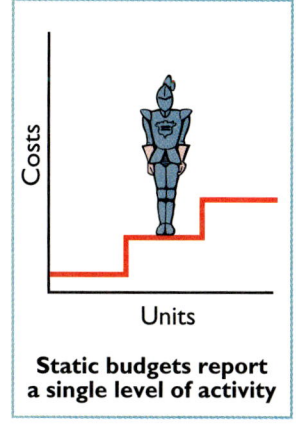

Static budgets report a single level of activity

FLEXIBLE BUDGETS

In contrast to a static budget, which is based on one level of activity, a **flexible budget** projects budget data for various levels of activity. In essence, **the flexible budget is a series of static budgets at different levels of activity**. The flexible budget recognizes that the budgetary process is more useful if it is adaptable to changed operating conditions.

Flexible budgets can be prepared for each of the types of budgets included in the master budget. For example, Marriott Hotels can budget revenues and net income on the basis of 60%, 80%, and 100% of room occupancy. Similarly, American Van Lines can budget its operating expenses on the basis of various levels of truck miles driven. Likewise, in the Feature Story, Duke Energy can budget revenue and net income on the basis of estimated billions of kwh (kilowatt hours) of residential, commercial, and industrial electricity generated. In the following pages, we will illustrate a flexible budget for manufacturing overhead.

STUDY OBJECTIVE 3

Explain the development of flexible budgets and the usefulness of flexible budget reports.

Why Flexible Budgets?

Assume that you are the manager in charge of manufacturing overhead in the Forging Department of Barton Steel. In preparing the manufacturing overhead budget for 2010, you prepare the following static budget based on a production volume of 10,000 units of steel ingots.

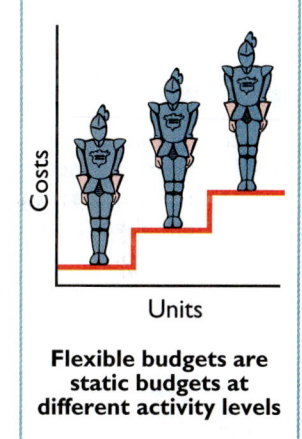

Flexible budgets are static budgets at different activity levels

Illustration 24-6
Static overhead budget

BARTON STEEL
Manufacturing Overhead Static Budget
Forging Department
For the Year Ended December 31, 2010

Budgeted production in units (steel ingots)	10,000
Budgeted costs	
Indirect materials	$ 250,000
Indirect labor	260,000
Utilities	190,000
Depreciation	280,000
Property taxes	70,000
Supervision	50,000
	$1,100,000

HELPFUL HINT

The static budget is the master budget described in Chapter 23.

Fortunately for the company, the demand for steel ingots has increased, and Barton produces and sells 12,000 units during the year, rather than 10,000. You are elated: Increased sales means increased profitability, which should mean a bonus or a raise for you and the employees in your department. Unfortunately, a comparison of Forging Department actual and budgeted costs has put you on the spot. The budget report is shown below.

Illustration 24-7
Static overhead budget report

BARTON STEEL
Manufacturing Overhead Static Budget Report
For the Year Ended December 31, 2010

	Budget	Actual	Difference Favorable - F Unfavorable - U	
Production in units	10,000	12,000		
Costs				
Indirect materials	$ 250,000	$ 295,000	$ 45,000	U
Indirect labor	260,000	312,000	52,000	U
Utilities	190,000	225,000	35,000	U
Depreciation	280,000	280,000	0	
Property taxes	70,000	70,000	0	
Supervision	50,000	50,000	0	
	$1,100,000	$1,232,000	$132,000	U

HELPFUL HINT
A static budget is not useful for performance evaluation if a company has substantial variable costs.

This comparison uses budget data based on the original activity level (10,000 steel ingots). It indicates that the Forging Department is significantly **over budget** for three of the six overhead costs. And, there is a total unfavorable difference of $132,000, which is 12% over budget ($132,000 ÷ $1,100,000). Your supervisor is very unhappy! Instead of sharing in the company's success, you may find yourself looking for another job. What went wrong?

When you calm down and carefully examine the manufacturing overhead budget, you identify the problem: The budget data are not relevant! At the time the budget was developed, the company anticipated that only 10,000 units of steel ingots would be produced, **not** 12,000. Comparing actual with budgeted variable costs is meaningless. As production increases, the budget allowances for variable costs should increase proportionately. The variable costs in this example are indirect materials, indirect labor, and utilities.

Analyzing the budget data for these costs at 10,000 units, you arrive at the following per unit results.

Illustration 24-8
Variable costs per unit

Item	Total Cost	Per Unit
Indirect materials	$250,000	$25
Indirect labor	260,000	26
Utilities	190,000	19
	$700,000	$70

Illustration 24-9 calculates the budgeted variable costs at 12,000 units.

Item	Computation	Total
Indirect materials	$25 × 12,000	$300,000
Indirect labor	26 × 12,000	312,000
Utilities	19 × 12,000	228,000
		$840,000

Illustration 24-9
Budgeted variable costs, 12,000 units

Because fixed costs do not change in total as activity changes, the budgeted amounts for these costs remain the same. Illustration 24-10 shows the budget report based on the flexible budget for **12,000 units** of production. (Compare this with Illustration 24-7, on page 1066.)

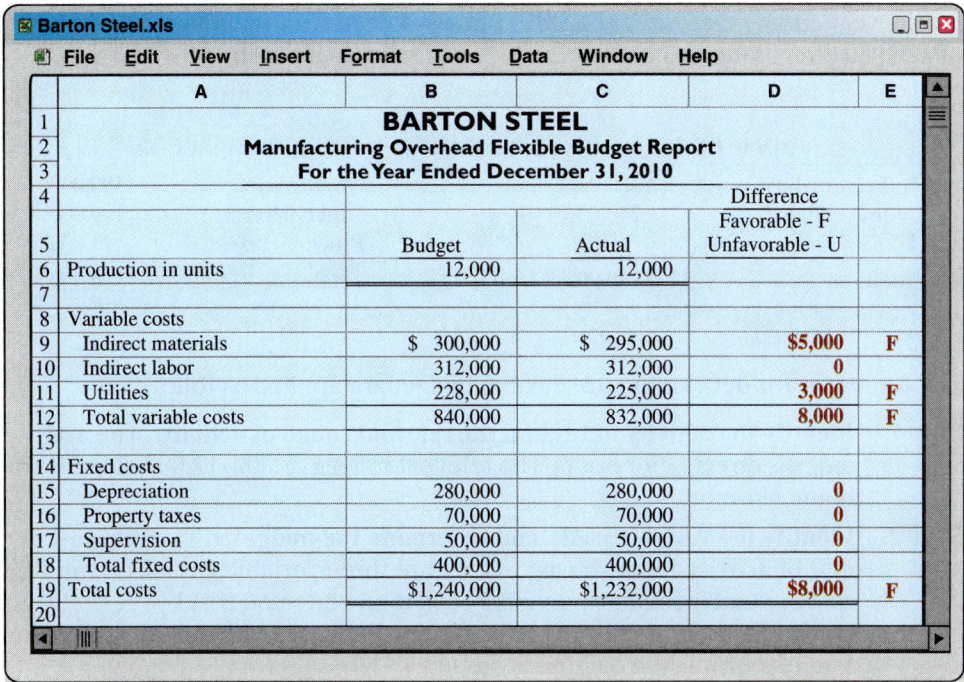

Illustration 24-10
Flexible overhead budget report

BARTON STEEL
Manufacturing Overhead Flexible Budget Report
For the Year Ended December 31, 2010

	Budget	Actual	Difference Favorable - F Unfavorable - U	
Production in units	12,000	12,000		
Variable costs				
Indirect materials	$ 300,000	$ 295,000	$5,000	F
Indirect labor	312,000	312,000	0	
Utilities	228,000	225,000	3,000	F
Total variable costs	840,000	832,000	8,000	F
Fixed costs				
Depreciation	280,000	280,000	0	
Property taxes	70,000	70,000	0	
Supervision	50,000	50,000	0	
Total fixed costs	400,000	400,000	0	
Total costs	$1,240,000	$1,232,000	$8,000	F

This report indicates that the Forging Department is *below budget*—a favorable difference. Instead of worrying about being fired, you may be in line for a bonus or a raise after all! As this analysis shows, the only appropriate comparison is between actual costs at 12,000 units of production and budgeted costs at 12,000 units. Flexible budget reports provide this comparison.

Developing the Flexible Budget

The flexible budget uses the master budget as its basis. To develop the flexible budget, management uses the following steps.

1. Identify the activity index and the relevant range of activity.
2. Identify the variable costs, and determine the budgeted variable cost per unit of activity for each cost.
3. Identify the fixed costs, and determine the budgeted amount for each cost.
4. Prepare the budget for selected increments of activity within the relevant range.

The activity index chosen should significantly influence the costs being budgeted. For manufacturing overhead costs, for example, the activity index is usually the same as the index used in developing the predetermined overhead rate—that is, direct labor hours or machine hours. For selling and administrative expenses, the activity index usually is sales or net sales.

The choice of the increment of activity is largely a matter of judgment. For example, if the relevant range is 8,000 to 12,000 direct labor hours, increments of 1,000 hours may be selected. The flexible budget is then prepared for each increment within the relevant range.

Flexible Budget—A Case Study

To illustrate the flexible budget, we use Fox Manufacturing Company. Fox's management uses a **flexible budget for monthly comparisons** of actual and budgeted manufacturing overhead costs of the Finishing Department. The master budget for the year ending December 31, 2010, shows expected annual operating capacity of 120,000 direct labor hours and the following overhead costs.

Illustration 24-11
Master budget data

Variable Costs		Fixed Costs	
Indirect materials	$180,000	Depreciation	$180,000
Indirect labor	240,000	Supervision	120,000
Utilities	60,000	Property taxes	60,000
Total	$480,000	Total	$360,000

The four steps for developing the flexible budget are applied as follows.

STEP 1. **Identify the activity index and the relevant range of activity.** The activity index is direct labor hours. The relevant range is 8,000–12,000 direct labor hours per month.

STEP 2. **Identify the variable costs, and determine the budgeted variable cost per unit of activity for each cost.** There are three variable costs. The variable cost per unit is found by dividing each total budgeted cost by the direct labor hours used in preparing the master budget (120,000 hours). For Fox Manufacturing, the computations are:

Illustration 24-12
Computation of variable costs per direct labor hour

Variable Cost	Computation	Variable Cost per Direct Labor Hour
Indirect materials	$180,000 ÷ 120,000	$1.50
Indirect labor	$240,000 ÷ 120,000	2.00
Utilities	$ 60,000 ÷ 120,000	0.50
Total		$4.00

STEP 3. **Identify the fixed costs, and determine the budgeted amount for each cost.** There are three fixed costs. Since Fox desires **monthly budget data**, it divides each annual budgeted cost by 12 to find the monthly amounts. For Fox Manufacturing, the monthly budgeted fixed costs are: depreciation $15,000, supervision $10,000, and property taxes $5,000.

STEP 4. **Prepare the budget for selected increments of activity within the relevant range.** Management prepares the budget in increments of 1,000 direct labor hours.

Illustration 24-13 shows Fox's flexible budget.

Illustration 24-13
Monthly overhead flexible budget

FOX MANUFACTURING COMPANY
Monthly Manufacturing Overhead Flexible Budget
Finishing Department
For the Year 2010

Activity level					
Direct labor hours	8,000	9,000	10,000	11,000	12,000
Variable costs					
Indirect materials	$12,000	$13,500	$15,000	$16,500	$18,000
Indirect labor	16,000	18,000	20,000	22,000	24,000
Utilities	4,000	4,500	5,000	5,500	6,000
Total variable costs	32,000	36,000	40,000	44,000	48,000
Fixed costs					
Depreciation	15,000	15,000	15,000	15,000	15,000
Supervision	10,000	10,000	10,000	10,000	10,000
Property taxes	5,000	5,000	5,000	5,000	5,000
Total fixed costs	30,000	30,000	30,000	30,000	30,000
Total costs	$62,000	$66,000	$70,000	$74,000	$78,000

Fox uses the formula below to determine total budgeted costs at any level of activity.

Illustration 24-14
Formula for total budgeted costs

Fixed Costs + Variable Costs* = Total Budgeted Costs

*Total variable cost per unit of activity × Activity level.

HELPFUL HINT
Using the data given for Fox, what amount of total costs would be budgeted for 10,600 direct labor hours? Answer: $30,000 fixed + $42,400 variable (i.e, 10,600 × $4) = $72,400 total.

For Fox, fixed costs are $30,000, and total variable cost per direct labor hour is $4. At 9,000 direct labor hours, total budgeted costs are $66,000 [$30,000 + ($4 × 9,000)]. At 8,622 direct labor hours, total budgeted costs are $64,488 [$30,000 + ($4 × 8,622)].

Total budgeted costs can also be shown graphically, as in Illustration 24-15.

Illustration 24-15
Flexible budget graph highlighting 10,000 and 12,000 hours of activity levels

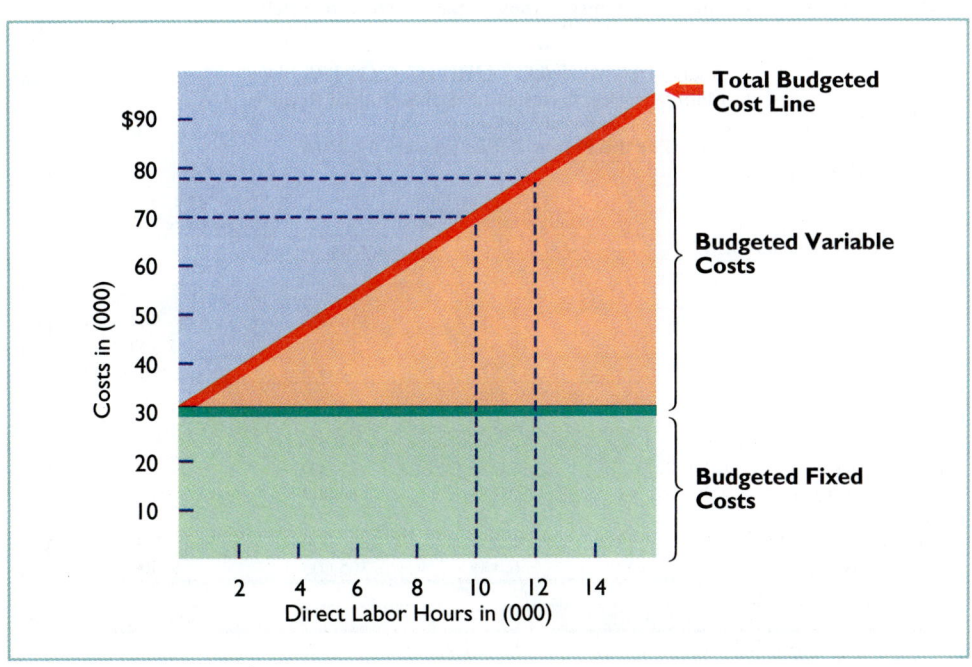

1070 Chapter 24 Budgetary Control and Responsibility Accounting

In the graph, the horizontal axis represents the activity index, and costs are indicated on the vertical axis. The graph highlights two activity levels (10,000 and 12,000). As shown, total budgeted costs at these activity levels are $70,000 [$30,000 + ($4 × 10,000)] and $78,000 [$30,000 + ($4 × 12,000)], respectively.

DO IT!

FLEXIBLE BUDGETS

In Strassel Company's flexible budget graph, the fixed cost line and the total budgeted cost line intersect the vertical axis at $36,000. The total budgeted cost line is $186,000 at an activity level of 50,000 direct labor hours. Compute total budgeted costs at 30,000 direct labor hours.

action plan

✔ Apply the formula: Fixed costs + Variable costs (Total variable costs per unit × Activity level) = Total budgeted costs.

Solution

Using the graph, fixed costs are $36,000, and variable costs are $3 per direct labor hour [($186,000 − $36,000) ÷ 50,000]. Thus, at 30,000 direct labor hours, total budgeted costs are $126,000 [$36,000 + ($3 × 30,000)].

Related exercise material: **BE24-4, E24-3, E24-5, E24-10** and **DO IT! 24-1**.

Flexible Budget Reports

As shown in Illustration 24-10 (page 1067), the flexible budget report consists of two sections: (1) production data for a selected activity index, such as direct labor hours, and (2) cost data for variable and fixed costs. The report provides a basis for evaluating a manager's performance in two areas: production control and cost control. Flexible budget reports are widely used in production and service departments.

Illustration 24-16 shows a budget report for the Finishing Department of Fox Company for the month of January. In this month, 9,000 hours are worked. The

Illustration 24-16
Overhead flexible budget report

FOX MANUFACTURING COMPANY
Manufacturing Overhead Flexible Budget Report
Finishing Department
For the Month Ended January 31, 2010

	Budget at 9,000 DLH	Actual costs at 9,000 DLH	Difference Favorable - F Unfavorable - U	
Direct labor hours (DLH)				
Variable costs				
Indirect materials	$13,500	$14,000	$ 500	U
Indirect labor	18,000	17,000	1,000	F
Utilities	4,500	4,600	100	U
Total variable costs	36,000	35,600	400	F
Fixed costs				
Depreciation	15,000	15,000	0	
Supervision	10,000	10,000	0	
Property taxes	5,000	5,000	0	
Total fixed costs	30,000	30,000	0	
Total costs	$66,000	$65,600	$ 400	F

budget data are therefore based on the flexible budget for 9,000 hours in Illustration 24-13 (page 1069). The actual cost data are assumed.

How appropriate is this report in evaluating the Finishing Department manager's performance in controlling overhead costs? The report clearly provides a reliable basis. Both actual and budget costs are based on the activity level worked during January. Since variable costs generally are incurred directly by the department, the difference between the budget allowance for those hours and the actual costs is the responsibility of the department manager.

In subsequent months, Fox Manufacturing will prepare other flexible budget reports. For each month, the budget data are based on the actual activity level attained. In February that level may be 11,000 direct labor hours, in July 10,000, and so on.

Note that this flexible budget is based on a single cost driver. A more accurate budget often can be developed using the activity-based costing concepts explained in Chapter 21.

Management by Exception

Management by exception means that top management's review of a budget report is focused either entirely or primarily on differences between actual results and planned objectives. This approach enables top management to focus on problem areas. For example, many companies now use online reporting systems for employees to file their travel and entertainment expense reports. In addition to cutting reporting time in half, the online system enables managers to quickly analyze variances from travel budgets. This enables companies to cut down on expense account "padding" such as spending too much on meals or falsifying documents for costs that were never actually incurred.

Management by exception does not mean that top management will investigate every difference. For this approach to be effective, there must be guidelines for identifying an exception. The usual criteria are materiality and controllability.

MATERIALITY

Without quantitative guidelines, management would have to investigate every budget difference regardless of the amount. Materiality is usually expressed as a percentage difference from budget. For example, management may set the percentage difference at 5% for important items and 10% for other items. Managers will investigate all differences either over or under budget by the specified percentage. Costs over budget warrant investigation to determine why they were not controlled. Likewise, costs under budget merit investigation to determine whether costs critical to profitability are being curtailed. For example, if maintenance costs are budgeted at $80,000 but only $40,000 is spent, major unexpected breakdowns in productive facilities may occur in the future.

Alternatively, a company may specify a single percentage difference from budget for all items and supplement this guideline with a minimum dollar limit. For example, the exception criteria may be stated at 5% of budget or more than $10,000.

CONTROLLABILITY OF THE ITEM

Exception guidelines are more restrictive for controllable items than for items the manager cannot control. In fact, there may be no guidelines for noncontrollable items. For example, a large unfavorable difference between actual and budgeted property tax expense may not be flagged for investigation because the only possible causes are an unexpected increase in the tax rate or in the assessed value of the property. An investigation into the difference would be useless: the manager cannot control either cause.

Chapter 24 Budgetary Control and Responsibility Accounting

DO IT!

FLEXIBLE BUDGET REPORTS

Lawler Company expects to produce 40,000 units of product CV93 during the current year. Budgeted variable manufacturing costs per unit are direct materials $6, direct labor $15, and overhead $24. Annual budgeted fixed manufacturing overhead costs are $120,000 for depreciation and $60,000 for supervision.

In the current month, Lawler produced 5,000 units and incurred the following costs: direct materials $33,900, direct labor $74,200, variable overhead $120,500, depreciation $10,000, and supervision $5,000.

Prepare a flexible budget report. (Note: You do not have to prepare the heading.) Were costs controlled?

action plan

✔ Use budget for actual units produced.
✔ Classify each cost as variable or fixed.
✔ Determine monthly fixed costs by dividing annual amounts by 12.
✔ Determine the difference as favorable or unfavorable.
✔ Determine the difference in total variable costs, total fixed costs, and total costs.

Solution

	Budget at 5,000 units	Actual costs at 5,000 units	Difference Favorable - F Unfavorable - U	
Units produced				
Variable costs				
Direct materials	$ 30,000	$ 33,900	$3,900	U
Direct labor	75,000	74,200	800	F
Overhead	120,000	120,500	500	U
Total variable costs	225,000	228,600	3,600	U
Fixed costs				
Depreciation	10,000	10,000	0	
Supervision	5,000	5,000	0	
Total fixed costs	15,000	15,000	0	
Total costs	$240,000	$243,600	$3,600	U

The responsibility report indicates that actual direct labor was only about 1% different from the budget, and overhead was less than half a percent different. Both appear to have been well controlled.

This was not the case for direct materials. Its 13% unfavorable difference should probably be investigated.

Actual fixed costs had no difference from budget and were well controlled.

Related exercise material: **BE24-5, E24-4, E24-6, E24-7, E24-8,** and **DO IT! 24-2.**

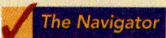

THE CONCEPT OF RESPONSIBILITY ACCOUNTING

STUDY OBJECTIVE 4
Describe the concept of responsibility accounting.

Like budgeting, responsibility accounting is an important part of management accounting. **Responsibility accounting** involves accumulating and reporting costs (and revenues, where relevant) on the basis of the manager who has the authority to make the day-to-day decisions about the items.

Under responsibility accounting, a manager's performance is evaluated on matters directly under that manager's control. Responsibility accounting can be used at every level of management in which the following conditions exist.

1. Costs and revenues can be directly associated with the specific level of management responsibility.
2. The costs and revenues can be controlled by employees at the level of responsibility with which they are associated.
3. Budget data can be developed for evaluating the manager's effectiveness in controlling the costs and revenues.

Illustration 24-17 depicts levels of responsibility for controlling costs.

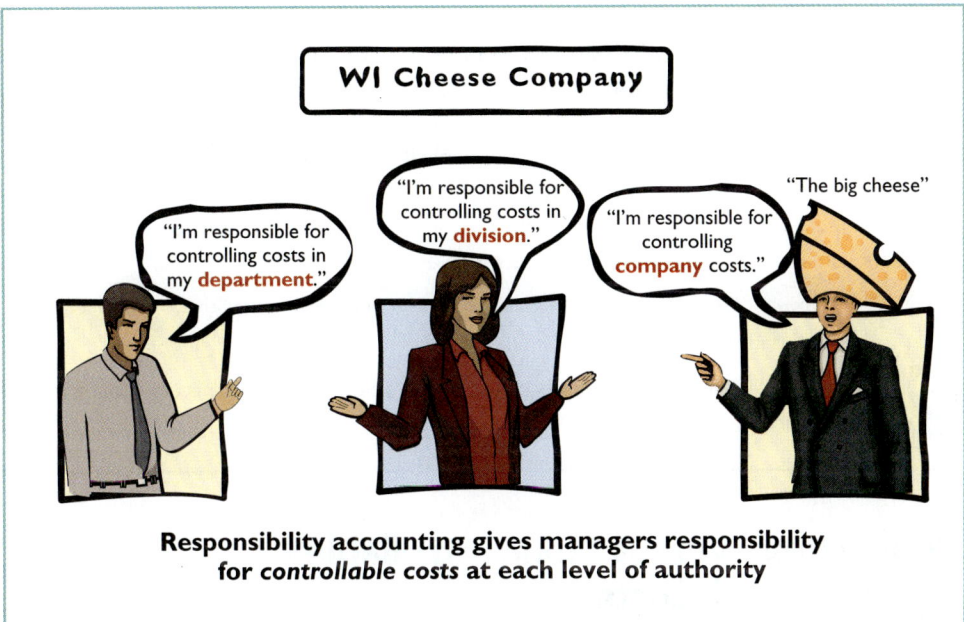

Illustration 24-17
Responsibility for controllable costs at varying levels of management

Under responsibility accounting, any individual who controls a specified set of activities can be a responsibility center. Thus, responsibility accounting may extend from the lowest level of control to the top strata of management. Once responsibility is established, the company first measures and reports the effectiveness of the individual's performance for the specified activity. It then reports that measure upward throughout the organization.

Responsibility accounting is especially valuable in a decentralized company. **Decentralization** means that the control of operations is delegated to many managers throughout the organization. The term **segment** is sometimes used to identify an area of responsibility in decentralized operations. Under responsibility accounting, companies prepare segment reports periodically, such as monthly, quarterly, and annually, to evaluate managers' performance.

Responsibility accounting is an essential part of any effective system of budgetary control. The reporting of costs and revenues under responsibility accounting differs from budgeting in two respects:

1. A distinction is made between controllable and noncontrollable items.
2. Performance reports either emphasize or include only items controllable by the individual manager.

HELPFUL HINT
All companies use responsibility accounting. Without some form of responsibility accounting, there would be chaos in discharging management's control function.

Responsibility accounting applies to both profit and not-for-profit entities. For-profit entities seek to maximize net income. Not-for-profit entities wish to provide services as efficiently as possible.

MANAGEMENT INSIGHT

Competition versus Collaboration

Many compensation and promotion programs encourage competition among employees for pay raises. To get ahead you have to perform better than your fellow employees. While this may encourage hard work, it does not foster collaboration, and it can lead to distrust and disloyalty. Such results have led some companies to believe that cooperation and collaboration are essential in order to succeed in today's environment. For example, division managers might increase collaboration (and reduce costs) by sharing design and marketing resources or by jointly negotiating with suppliers. In addition, companies can reduce the need to hire and lay off employees by sharing employees across divisions as human resource needs increase and decrease.

As a consequence, many companies now explicitly include measures of collaboration in their performance measures. For example, Procter & Gamble measures collaboration in employees' annual performance reviews. At Cisco Systems the assessment of an employee's teamwork can affect the annual bonus by as much as 20%.

Source: Carol Hymowitz, "Rewarding Competitors Over Collaboration No Longer Makes Sense," *Wall Street Journal*, February 13, 2006.

 How might managers of separate divisions be able to reduce division costs through collaboration?

Controllable versus Noncontrollable Revenues and Costs

All costs and revenues are controllable at some level of responsibility within a company. This truth underscores the adage by the CEO of any organization that "the buck stops here." Under responsibility accounting, the critical issue is **whether the cost or revenue is controllable at the level of responsibility with which it is associated**. A cost over which a manager has control is called a **controllable cost**. From this definition, it follows that:

1. All costs are controllable by top management because of the broad range of its authority.
2. Fewer costs are controllable as one moves down to each lower level of managerial responsibility because of the manager's decreasing authority.

> **HELPFUL HINT**
> Are there more or fewer controllable costs as you move to higher levels of management?
> Answer: More.

In general, **costs incurred directly by a level of responsibility are controllable at that level**. In contrast, costs incurred indirectly and allocated to a responsibility level are **noncontrollable costs** at that level.

> **HELPFUL HINT**
> The longer the time span, the more likely that the cost becomes controllable.

Responsibility Reporting System

A **responsibility reporting system** involves the preparation of a report for each level of responsibility in the company's organization chart. To illustrate such a system, we use the partial organization chart and production departments of Francis Chair Company in Illustration 24-18.

The Concept of Responsibility Accounting 1075

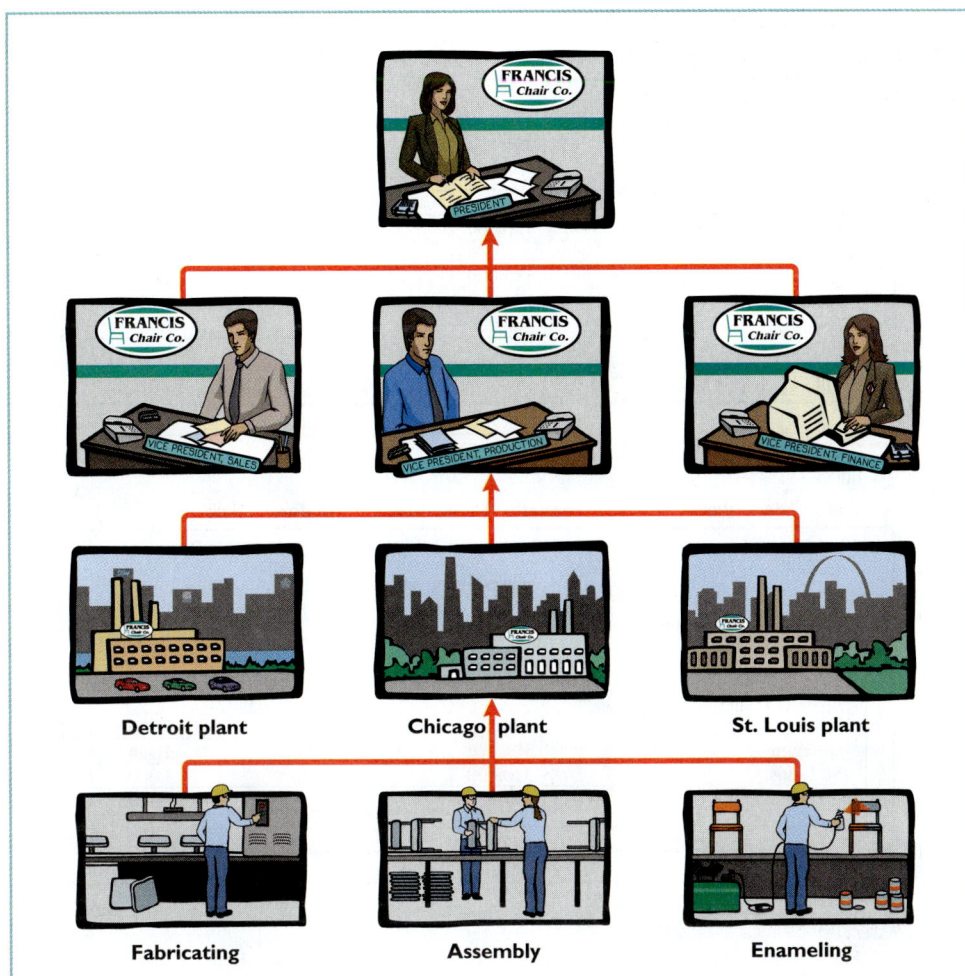

Illustration 24-18
Partial organization chart

Report A
President sees summary data of vice presidents.

Report B
Vice president sees summary of controllable costs in his/her functional area.

Report C
Plant manager sees summary of controllable costs for each department in the plant.

Report D
Department manager sees controllable costs of his/her department.

The responsibility reporting system begins with the lowest level of responsibility for controlling costs and moves upward to each higher level. Illustration 24-19 (page 1076) details the connections between levels. A brief description of the four reports for Francis Chair Company is as follows.

1. **Report D** is typical of reports that go to managers at the lowest level of responsibility shown in the organization chart—department managers. Similar reports are prepared for the managers of the Fabricating, Assembly, and Enameling Departments.

2. **Report C** is an example of reports that are sent to plant managers. It shows the costs of the Chicago plant that are controllable at the second level of responsibility. In addition, Report C shows summary data for each department that is controlled by the plant manager. Similar reports are prepared for the Detroit and St. Louis plant managers.

3. **Report B** illustrates the reports at the third level of responsibility. It shows the controllable costs of the vice president of production and summary data on the three assembly plants for which this officer is responsible. Similar reports are prepared for the vice presidents of sales and finance.

4. **Report A** is typical of reports that go to the top level of responsibility—the president. It shows the controllable costs and expenses of this office and summary data on the vice presidents that are accountable to the president.

Illustration 24-19
Responsibility reporting system

Report A
President sees summary data of vice presidents.

Report B
Vice president sees summary of controllable costs in his/her functional area.

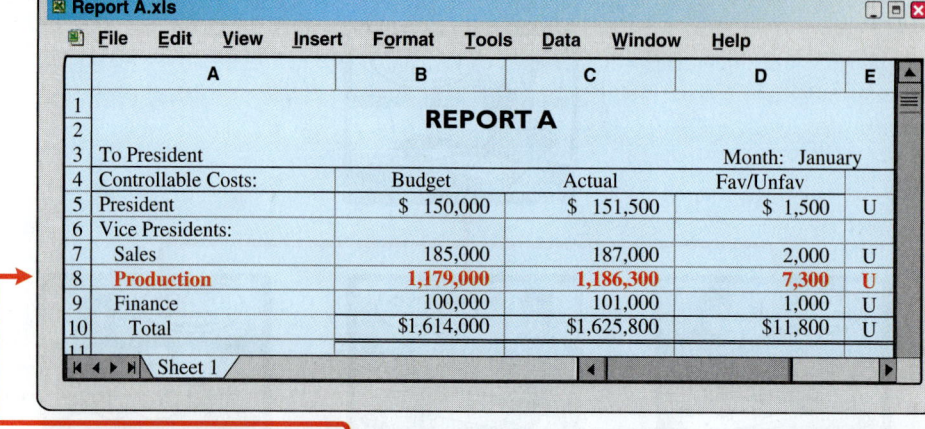

Report C
Plant manager sees summary of controllable costs for each department in the plant.

Report D
Department manager sees controllable costs of his/her department.

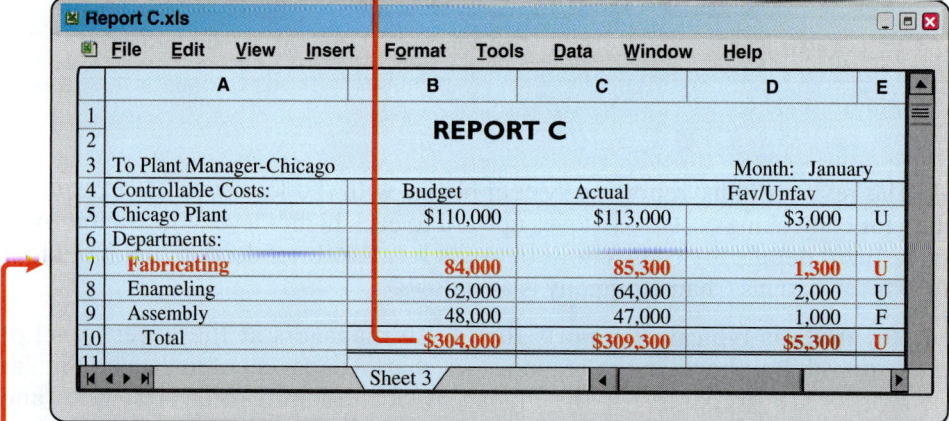

A responsibility reporting system permits management by exception at each level of responsibility. And, each higher level of responsibility can obtain the detailed report for each lower level of responsibility. For example, the vice president of production in the Francis Chair Company may request the Chicago plant manager's report because this plant is $5,300 over budget.

This type of reporting system also permits comparative evaluations. In Illustration 24-19, the Chicago plant manager can easily rank the department managers' effectiveness in controlling manufacturing costs. Comparative rankings provide further incentive for a manager to control costs.

TYPES OF RESPONSIBILITY CENTERS

There are three basic types of responsibility centers: cost centers, profit centers, and investment centers. These classifications indicate the degree of responsibility the manager has for the performance of the center.

A **cost center** incurs costs (and expenses) but does not directly generate revenues. Managers of cost centers have the authority to incur costs. They are evaluated on their ability to control costs. **Cost centers are usually either production departments or service departments.** Production departments participate directly in making the product. Service departments provide only support services. In a Ford Motor Company automobile plant, the welding, painting, and assembling departments are production departments. Ford's maintenance, cafeteria, and human resources departments are service departments. All of them are cost centers.

A **profit center** incurs costs (and expenses) and also generates revenues. Managers of profit centers are judged on the profitability of their centers. Examples of profit centers include the individual departments of a retail store, such as clothing, furniture, and automotive products, and branch offices of banks.

Like a profit center, an **investment center** incurs costs (and expenses) and generates revenues. In addition, an investment center has control over decisions regarding the assets available for use. Investment center managers are evaluated on both the profitability of the center and the rate of return earned on the funds invested. Investment centers are often associated with subsidiary companies. Utility Duke Energy has operating divisions such as electric utility, energy trading, and natural gas. Investment center managers control or significantly influence investment decisions related to such matters as plant expansion and entry into new market areas. Illustration 24-20 depicts these three types of responsibility centers.

> **HELPFUL HINT**
> (1) Is the jewelry department of Macy's department store a profit center or a cost center? (2) Is the props department of a movie studio a profit center or a cost center? Answers: (1) Profit center. (2) Cost center.

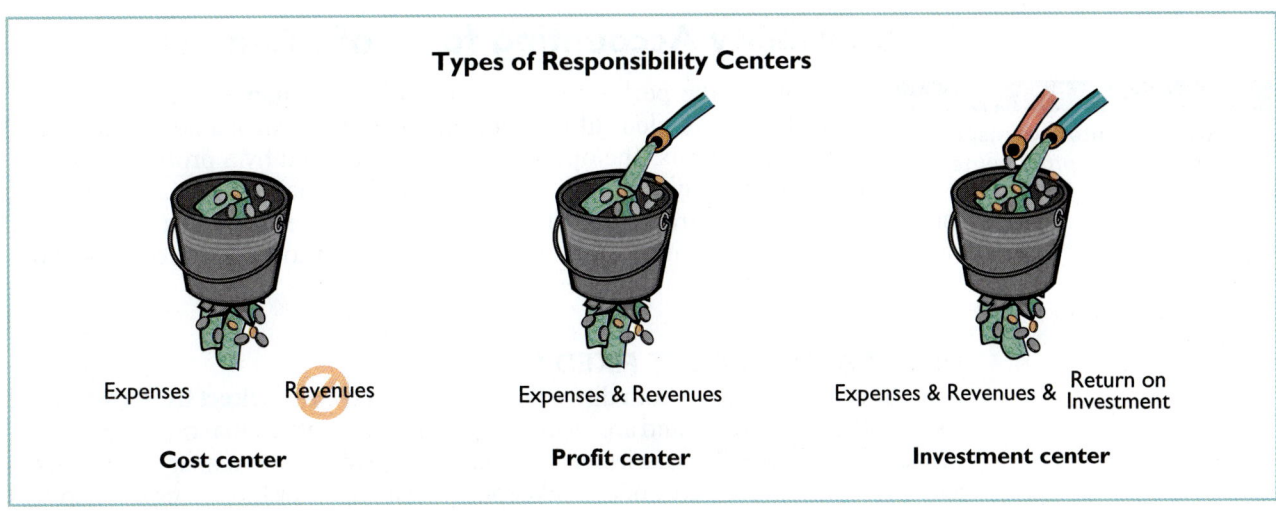

Illustration 24-20
Types of responsibility centers

Responsibility Accounting for Cost Centers

STUDY OBJECTIVE 5
Indicate the features of responsibility reports for cost centers.

The evaluation of a manager's performance for cost centers is based on his or her ability to meet budgeted goals for controllable costs. **Responsibility reports for cost centers compare actual controllable costs with flexible budget data.**

Illustration 24-21 shows a responsibility report. The report is adapted from the flexible budget report for Fox Manufacturing Company in Illustration 24-16 on page 1070. It assumes that the Finishing Department manager is able to control all manufacturing overhead costs except depreciation, property taxes, and his own monthly salary of $6,000. The remaining $4,000 ($10,000 − $6,000) of supervision costs are assumed to apply to other supervisory personnel within the Finishing Department, whose salaries are controllable by the manager.

Illustration 24-21
Responsibility report for a cost center

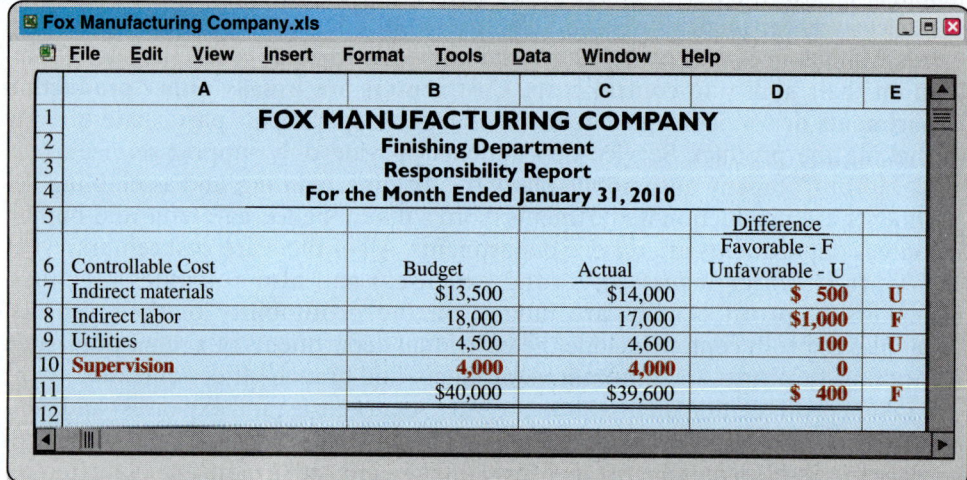

The report in Illustration 24-21 includes **only controllable costs**, and no distinction is made between variable and fixed costs. The responsibility report continues the concept of management by exception. In this case, top management may request an explanation of the $1,000 favorable difference in indirect labor and/or the $500 unfavorable difference in indirect materials.

Responsibility Accounting for Profit Centers

STUDY OBJECTIVE 6
Identify the content of responsibility reports for profit centers.

To evaluate the performance of a profit center manager, upper management needs detailed information about both controllable revenues and controllable costs. The operating revenues earned by a profit center, such as sales, are controllable by the manager. All variable costs (and expenses) incurred by the center are also controllable by the manager because they vary with sales. However, to determine the controllability of fixed costs, it is necessary to distinguish between direct and indirect fixed costs.

DIRECT AND INDIRECT FIXED COSTS

A profit center may have both direct and indirect fixed costs. **Direct fixed costs** relate specifically to one center and are incurred for the sole benefit of that center. Examples of such costs include the salaries established by the profit center manager for supervisory personnel and the cost of a timekeeping department for the center's employees.

Since these fixed costs can be traced directly to a center, they are also called **traceable costs**. **Most direct fixed costs are controllable by the profit center manager.**

In contrast, **indirect fixed costs** pertain to a company's overall operating activities and are incurred for the benefit of more than one profit center. Management allocates indirect fixed costs to profit centers on some type of equitable basis. For example, property taxes on a building occupied by more than one center may be allocated on the basis of square feet of floor space used by each center. Or, the costs of a company's human resources department may be allocated to profit centers on the basis of the number of employees in each center. Because these fixed costs apply to more than one center, they are also called **common costs**. **Most indirect fixed costs are not controllable by the profit center manager.**

RESPONSIBILITY REPORT

The responsibility report for a profit center shows budgeted and actual **controllable revenues and costs**. The report is prepared using the cost-volume-profit income statement explained in Chapter 22. In the report:

1. Controllable fixed costs are deducted from contribution margin.
2. The excess of contribution margin over controllable fixed costs is identified as **controllable margin**.
3. Noncontrollable fixed costs are not reported.

Illustration 24-22 shows the responsibility report for the manager of the Marine Division, a profit center of Mantle Manufacturing Company. For the year, the Marine Division also had $60,000 of indirect fixed costs that were not controllable by the profit center manager.

Controllable margin is considered to be the best measure of the manager's performance **in controlling revenues and costs**. The report in Illustration 24-22 shows that the manager's performance was below budgeted expectations by 10% ($36,000 ÷ $360,000). Top management would likely investigate the causes of this unfavorable result. Note that the report does not show the Marine Division's noncontrollable fixed costs of $60,000. These costs would be included in a report on the profitability of the profit center.

Illustration 24-22
Responsibility report for profit center

MANTLE MANUFACTURING COMPANY
Marine Division
Responsibility Report
For the Year Ended December 31, 2010

	Budget	Actual	Difference Favorable - F Unfavorable - U	
Sales	$1,200,000	$1,150,000	$50,000	U
Variable costs				
Cost of goods sold	500,000	490,000	10,000	F
Selling and administrative	160,000	156,000	4,000	F
Total	660,000	646,000	14,000	F
Contribution margin	540,000	504,000	36,000	U
Controllable fixed costs				
Cost of goods sold	100,000	100,000	0	
Selling and administrative	80,000	80,000	0	
Total	180,000	180,000	0	
Controllable margin	$ 360,000	$ 324,000	$36,000	U

Chapter 24 Budgetary Control and Responsibility Accounting

Management also may choose to see monthly responsibility reports for profit centers. In addition, responsibility reports may include cumulative year-to-date results.

DO IT!

RESPONSIBILITY REPORTS FOR PROFIT CENTERS

Midwest Division operates as a profit center. It reports the following for the year.

	Budgeted	Actual
Sales	$1,500,000	$1,700,000
Variable costs	700,000	800,000
Controllable fixed costs	400,000	400,000
Noncontrollable fixed costs	200,000	200,000

Prepare a responsibility report for the Midwest Division for December 31, 2010.

action plan

✔ Deduct variable costs from sales to show contribution margin.
✔ Deduct controllable fixed costs from the contribution margin to show controllable margin.
✔ Do not report noncontrollable fixed costs.

Solution

MIDWEST DIVISION
Responsibility Report
For the Year Ended December 31, 2010

	Budget	Actual	Difference Favorable F Unfavorable U
Sales	$1,500,000	$1,700,000	$200,000 F
Variable costs	700,000	800,000	100,000 U
Contribution margin	800,000	900,000	100,000 F
Controllable fixed costs	400,000	400,000	–0–
Controllable margin	$ 400,000	$ 500,000	$100,000 F

Related exercise material: **BE24-7, E24-9, E24-13,** and **DO IT! 24-3.**

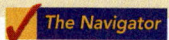

Responsibility Accounting for Investment Centers

STUDY OBJECTIVE 7
Explain the basis and formula used in evaluating performance in investment centers.

As explained earlier, an investment center manager can control or significantly influence the investment funds available for use. Thus, the primary basis for evaluating the performance of a manager of an investment center is **return on investment (ROI)**. The return on investment is considered to be a useful performance measurement because it shows the **effectiveness of the manager in utilizing the assets at his or her disposal**.

RETURN ON INVESTMENT (ROI)

The formula for computing ROI for an investment center, together with assumed illustrative data, is shown in Illustration 24-23.

Illustration 24-23
ROI formula

Controllable Margin	÷	Average Operating Assets	=	Return on Investment (ROI)
$1,000,000	÷	$5,000,000	=	20%

Both factors in the formula are controllable by the investment center manager. Operating assets consist of current assets and plant assets used in operations by the center and controlled by the manager. Nonoperating assets such as idle plant assets and land held for future use are excluded. Average operating assets are usually based on the cost or book value of the assets at the beginning and end of the year.

RESPONSIBILITY REPORT

The scope of the investment center manager's responsibility significantly affects the content of the performance report. Since an investment center is an independent entity for operating purposes, **all fixed costs are controllable by its manager**. For example, the manager is responsible for depreciation on investment center assets. Therefore, more fixed costs are identified as controllable in the performance report for an investment center manager than in a performance report for a profit center manager. The report also shows budgeted and actual ROI below controllable margin.

To illustrate this responsibility report, we will now assume that the Marine Division of Mantle Manufacturing Company is an investment center. It has budgeted and actual average operating assets of $2,000,000. The manager can control $60,000 of fixed costs that were not controllable when the division was a profit center. Illustration 24-24 shows the division's responsibility report.

Illustration 24-24
Responsibility report for investment center

MANTLE MANUFACTURING COMPANY
Marine Division
Responsibility Report
For the Year Ended December 31, 2010

	Budget	Actual	Difference Favorable - F Unfavorable - U	
Sales	$1,200,000	$1,150,000	$ 50,000	U
Variable costs				
Cost of goods sold	500,000	490,000	10,000	F
Selling and administrative	160,000	156,000	4,000	F
Total	660,000	646,000	14,000	F
Contribution margin	540,000	504,000	36,000	U
Controllable fixed costs				
Cost of goods sold	100,000	100,000	0	
Selling and administrative	80,000	80,000	0	
Other fixed costs	**60,000**	**60,000**	**0**	
Total	240,000	240,000	0	
Controllable margin	**$ 300,000**	**$ 264,000**	**$ 36,000**	**U**
Return on investment	**15.0%**	**13.2%**	**1.8%**	**U**
	(a)	(b)	(c)	
	(a) $ 300,000 / $2,000,000	(b) $ 264,000 / $2,000,000	(c) $ 36,000 / $2,000,000	

The report shows that the manager's performance based on ROI was below budget expectations by 1.8% (15.0% versus 13.2%). Top management would likely want an explanation of the reasons for this unfavorable result.

JUDGMENTAL FACTORS IN ROI

The return on investment approach includes two judgmental factors:

1. **Valuation of operating assets.** Operating assets may be valued at acquisition cost, book value, appraised value, or market value. The first two bases are readily available from the accounting records.
2. **Margin (income) measure.** This measure may be controllable margin, income from operations, or net income.

Each of the alternative values for operating assets can provide a reliable basis for evaluating a manager's performance as long as it is consistently applied between reporting periods. However, the use of income measures other than controllable margin will not result in a valid basis for evaluating the performance of an investment center manager.

IMPROVING ROI

The manager of an investment center can improve ROI in two ways: (1) increase controllable margin, and/or (2) reduce average operating assets. To illustrate, we will use the following assumed data for the Laser Division of Berra Manufacturing.

Illustration 24-25
Assumed data for Laser Division

Sales	$2,000,000
Variable costs	1,100,000
Contribution margin (45%)	900,000
Controllable fixed costs	300,000
Controllable margin (a)	$ 600,000
Average operating assets (b)	$5,000,000
Return on investment (a) ÷ (b)	**12%**

Increasing Controllable Margin. Controllable margin can be increased by increasing sales or by reducing variable and controllable fixed costs as follows.

1. **Increase sales 10%.** Sales will increase $200,000 ($2,000,000 × .10). Assuming no change in the contribution margin percentage of 45%, contribution margin will increase $90,000 ($200,000 × .45). Controllable margin will increase by the same amount because controllable fixed costs will not change. Thus, controllable margin becomes $690,000 ($600,000 + $90,000). The new ROI is 13.8%, computed as follows.

Illustration 24-26
ROI computation—increase in sales

$$\text{ROI} = \frac{\text{Controllable margin}}{\text{Average operating assets}} = \frac{\$690,000}{\$5,000,000} = \mathbf{13.8\%}$$

An increase in sales benefits both the investment center and the company if it results in new business. It would not benefit the company if the increase was achieved at the expense of other investment centers.

2. **Decrease variable and fixed costs 10%.** Total costs decrease $140,000 [($1,100,000 + $300,000) × .10]. This reduction results in a corresponding increase in controllable margin. Thus, controllable margin becomes $740,000 ($600,000 + $140,000). The new ROI is 14.8%, computed as follows.

Illustration 24-27
ROI computation—decrease in costs

$$\text{ROI} = \frac{\text{Controllable margin}}{\text{Average operating assets}} = \frac{\$740,000}{\$5,000,000} = \mathbf{14.8\%}$$

This course of action is clearly beneficial when waste and inefficiencies are eliminated. But, a reduction in vital costs such as required maintenance and inspections is not likely to be acceptable to top management.

Reducing Average Operating Assets. Assume that average operating assets are reduced 10% or $500,000 ($5,000,000 × .10). Average operating assets become $4,500,000 ($5,000,000 − $500,000). Since controllable margin remains unchanged at $600,000, the new ROI is 13.3%, computed as follows.

$$\text{ROI} = \frac{\text{Controllable margin}}{\text{Average operating assets}} = \frac{\$600,000}{\$4,500,000} = \mathbf{13.3\%}$$

Illustration 24-28
ROI computation—decrease in operating assets

Reductions in operating assets may or may not be prudent. It is beneficial to eliminate overinvestment in inventories and to dispose of excessive plant assets. However, it is unwise to reduce inventories below expected needs or to dispose of essential plant assets.

ACCOUNTING ACROSS THE ORGANIZATION

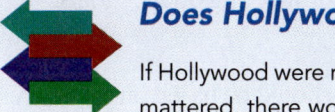

Does Hollywood Look at ROI?

If Hollywood were run like a real business, where things like return on investment mattered, there would be one unchallenged, sacred principle that studio chieftains would never violate: Make lots of G-rated movies.

No matter how you slice the movie business—by star vehicles, by budget levels, by sequels or franchises—by far the best return on investment comes from the not-so-glamorous world of G-rated films. The problem is, these movies represent only 3% of the total films made in a typical year.

Take 2003: According to Motion Picture Association of America statistics, of the 940 movies released that year, only 29 were G-rated. Yet the highest-grossing movie of the year, *Finding Nemo*, was G-rated. . . . On the flip side are the R-rated films, which dominate the total releases and yet yield the worst return on investment. A whopping 646 R-rated films were released in 2003—69% of the total output—but only four of the top-20 grossing movies of the year were R-rated films.

This trend—G-rated movies are good for business but underproduced; R-rated movies are bad for business, and yet overdone—is something that has been driving economists batty for the past several years.

Source: Grainger, David, "The Dysfunctional Family-Film Business," *Fortune*, January 10, 2005, pp. 20–21.

 What might be the reason that movie studios do not produce G-rated movies as often as R-rated ones?

Principles of Performance Evaluation

Performance evaluation is at the center of responsibility accounting. **Performance evaluation** is a management function that compares actual results with budget goals. It involves both behavioral and reporting principles.

BEHAVIORAL PRINCIPLES
The human factor is critical in evaluating performance. Behavioral principles include the following.

1. **Managers of responsibility centers should have direct input into the process of establishing budget goals of their area of responsibility.** Without such input, managers may view the goals as unrealistic or arbitrarily set by top management. Such views adversely affect the managers' motivation to meet the targeted objectives.

2. **The evaluation of performance should be based entirely on matters that are controllable by the manager being evaluated.** Criticism of a manager on matters outside his or her control reduces the effectiveness of the evaluation process. It leads to negative reactions by a manager and to doubts about the fairness of the company's evaluation policies.

3. **Top management should support the evaluation process.** As explained earlier, the evaluation process begins at the lowest level of responsibility and extends upward to the highest level of management. Managers quickly lose faith in the process when top management ignores, overrules, or bypasses established procedures for evaluating a manager's performance.

4. **The evaluation process must allow managers to respond to their evaluations.** Evaluation is not a one-way street. Managers should have the opportunity to defend their performance. Evaluation without feedback is both impersonal and ineffective.

5. **The evaluation should identify both good and poor performance.** Praise for good performance is a powerful motivating factor for a manager. This is especially true when a manager's compensation includes rewards for meeting budget goals.

REPORTING PRNCIPLES

Performance evaluation under responsibility accounting should be based on certain reporting principles. These principles pertain primarily to the internal reports that provide the basis for evaluating performance. Performance reports should:

1. Contain only data that are controllable by the manager of the responsibility center.
2. Provide accurate and reliable budget data to measure performance.
3. Highlight significant differences between actual results and budget goals.
4. Be tailor-made for the intended evaluation.
5. Be prepared at reasonable intervals.

In recent years companies have come under increasing pressure from influential shareholder groups to do a better job of linking executive pay to corporate performance. For example, software maker **Siebel Systems** unveiled a new incentive plan after lengthy discussions with the California Public Employees' Retirement System. One unique feature of the plan is that managers' targets will be publicly disclosed at the beginning of each year for investors to evaluate.

DO IT!

PERFORMANCE EVALUATION

action plan

✔ Recall key formulas: Sales − Variable cost = Contribution margin.

✔ Contribution margin ÷ Sales = Contribution margin percentage.

✔ Contribution margin − Controllable fixed costs = Controllable margin.

✔ Return on investment = Controllable margin ÷ Average operating assets.

The service division of Metro Industries reported the following results for 2010.

Sales	$400,000
Variable costs	320,000
Controllable fixed costs	40,800
Average operating assets	280,000

Management is considering the following independent courses of action in 2011 in order to maximize the return on investment for this division.

1. Reduce average operating assets by $80,000, with no change in controllable margin.
2. Increase sales $80,000, with no change in the contribution margin percentage.

(a) Compute the controllable margin and the return on investment for 2010.
(b) Compute the controllable margin and the expected return on investment for each proposed alternative.

Solution

(a) Return on investment for 2010

Sales		$400,000
Variable costs		320,000
Contribution margin		80,000
Controllable fixed costs		40,800
Controllable margin		$ 39,200
Return on investment	$\dfrac{\$39,200}{\$280,000}$ =	14%

(b) Expected return on investment for alternative 1:

$$\dfrac{\$39,200}{\$200,000} = 19.6\%$$

Expected return on investment for alternative 2:

Sales ($400,000 + 80,000)	$480,000
Variable costs ($320,000/400,000 × $480,000)	384,000
Contribution margin	96,000
Controllable fixed costs	40,800
Controllable margin	$ 55,200
Return on investment $\dfrac{\$55,200}{\$280,000}$ =	19.7%

Related exercise material: **BE24-8, BE24-9, BE24-10, E24-14, E24-15, E24-16, E24-17,** and **DO IT! 24-4.**

Comprehensive DO IT!

Glenda Company uses a flexible budget for manufacturing overhead based on direct labor hours. For 2010 the master overhead budget for the Packaging Department based on 300,000 direct labor hours was as follows.

Variable Costs		Fixed Costs	
Indirect labor	$360,000	Supervision	$ 60,000
Supplies and lubricants	150,000	Depreciation	24,000
Maintenance	210,000	Property taxes	18,000
Utilities	120,000	Insurance	12,000
	$840,000		$114,000

During July, 24,000 direct labor hours were worked. The company incurred the following variable costs in July: indirect labor $30,200, supplies and lubricants $11,600, maintenance $17,500, and utilities $9,200. Actual fixed overhead costs were the same as monthly budgeted fixed costs.

Instructions

Prepare a flexible budget report for the Packaging Department for July.

action plan

✔ Compute the cost per direct labor hour for all variable costs.
✔ Use budget data for actual direct labor hours worked.
✔ Classify each cost as variable or fixed.
✔ Determine the difference between budgeted and actual costs.
✔ Identify the difference as favorable or unfavorable.
✔ Determine the difference in total variable costs, total fixed costs, and total costs.

Solution to Comprehensive DO IT!

GLENDA COMPANY
Manufacturing Overhead Flexible Budget Report
Packaging Department
For the Month Ended July 31, 2010

Direct labor hours (DLH)	Budget 24,000 DLH	Actual Costs 24,000 DLH	Difference Favorable F Unfavorable U
Variable costs			
Indirect labor ($1.20)	$28,800	$30,200	$1,400 U
Supplies and lubricants ($0.50)	12,000	11,600	400 F
Maintenance ($0.70)	16,800	17,500	700 U
Utilities ($0.40)	9,600	9,200	400 F
Total variable	67,200	68,500	1,300 U
Fixed costs			
Supervision	$ 5,000	$ 5,000	–0–
Depreciation	2,000	2,000	–0–
Property taxes	1,500	1,500	–0–
Insurance	1,000	1,000	–0–
Total fixed	9,500	9,500	–0–
Total costs	$76,700	$78,000	$1,300 U

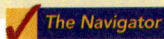

SUMMARY OF STUDY OBJECTIVES

1. **Describe the concept of budgetary control.** Budgetary control consists of (a) preparing periodic budget reports that compare actual results with planned objectives, (b) analyzing the differences to determine their causes, (c) taking appropriate corrective action, and (d) modifying future plans, if necessary.

2. **Evaluate the usefulness of static budget reports.** Static budget reports are useful in evaluating the progress toward planned sales and profit goals. They are also appropriate in assessing a manager's effectiveness in controlling costs when (a) actual activity closely approximates the master budget activity level, and/or (b) the behavior of the costs in response to changes in activity is fixed.

3. **Explain the development of flexible budgets and the usefulness of flexible budget reports.** To develop the flexible budget it is necessary to: (a) Identify the activity index and the relevant range of activity. (b) Identify the variable costs, and determine the budgeted variable cost per unit of activity for each cost. (c) Identify the fixed costs, and determine the budgeted amount for each cost. (d) Prepare the budget for selected increments of activity within the relevant range. Flexible budget reports permit an evaluation of a manager's performance in controlling production and costs.

4. **Describe the concept of responsibility accounting.** Responsibility accounting involves accumulating and reporting revenues and costs on the basis of the individual manager who has the authority to make the day-to-day decisions about the items. The evaluation of a manager's performance is based on the matters directly under the manager's control. In responsibility accounting, it is necessary to distinguish between controllable and noncontrollable fixed costs and to identify three types of responsibility centers: cost, profit, and investment.

5. **Indicate the features of responsibility reports for cost centers.** Responsibility reports for cost centers compare actual costs with flexible budget data. The reports show only controllable costs, and no distinction is made between variable and fixed costs.

6. **Identify the content of responsibility reports for profit centers.** Responsibility reports show contribution margin, controllable fixed costs, and controllable margin for each profit center.

7. **Explain the basis and formula used in evaluating performance in investment centers.** The primary basis for evaluating performance in investment centers is return on investment (ROI). The formula for computing ROI for investment centers is: Controllable margin ÷ Average operating assets.

GLOSSARY

Budgetary control The use of budgets to control operations. (p. 1062).

Controllable cost A cost over which a manager has control. (p. 1074).

Controllable margin Contribution margin less controllable fixed costs. (p. 1079).

Cost center A responsibility center that incurs costs but does not directly generate revenues. (p. 1077).

Decentralization Control of operations is delegated to many managers throughout the organization. (p. 1073).

Direct fixed costs Costs that relate specifically to a responsibility center and are incurred for the sole benefit of the center. (p. 1078).

Flexible budget A projection of budget data for various levels of activity. (p. 1065).

Indirect fixed costs Costs that are incurred for the benefit of more than one profit center. (p. 1079).

Investment center A responsibility center that incurs costs, generates revenues, and has control over decisions regarding the assets available for use. (p. 1077).

Management by exception The review of budget reports by top management focused entirely or primarily on differences between actual results and planned objectives. (p. 1071).

Noncontrollable costs Costs incurred indirectly and allocated to a responsibility center that are not controllable at that level. (p. 1074).

Profit center A responsibility center that incurs costs and also generates revenues. (p. 1077).

Responsibility accounting A part of management accounting that involves accumulating and reporting revenues and costs on the basis of the manager who has the authority to make the day-to-day decisions about the items. (p. 1072).

Responsibility reporting system The preparation of reports for each level of responsibility in the company's organization chart. (p. 1074).

Return on investment (ROI) A measure of management's effectiveness in utilizing assets at its disposal in an investment center. (p.1080).

Segment An area of responsibility in decentralized operations. (p. 1073).

Static budget A projection of budget data at one level of activity. (p. 1063).

SELF-STUDY QUESTIONS

Answers are at the end of the chapter.

(SO 1) **1.** Budgetary control involves all but one of the following:
  a. modifying future plans.
  b. analyzing differences.
  c. using static budgets.
  d. determining differences between actual and planned results.

(SO 1) **2.** Budget reports are prepared:
  a. daily.   c. monthly.
  b. weekly.   d. All of the above.

(SO 1) **3.** A production manager in a manufacturing company would most likely receive a:
  a. sales report.
  b. income statement.
  c. scrap report.
  d. shipping department overhead report.

(SO 2) **4.** A static budget is:
  a. a projection of budget data at several levels of activity within the relevant range of activity.
  b. a projection of budget data at a single level of activity.
  c. compared to a flexible budget in a budget report.
  d. never appropriate in evaluating a manager's effectiveness in controlling costs.

(SO 2) **5.** A static budget is useful in controlling costs when cost behavior is:
  a. mixed.   c. variable.
  b. fixed.   d. linear.

(SO 3) **6.** At zero direct labor hours in a flexible budget graph, the total budgeted cost line intersects the vertical axis at $30,000. At 10,000 direct labor hours, a horizontal line drawn from the total budgeted cost line intersects the vertical axis at $90,000. Fixed and variable costs may be expressed as:
  a. $30,000 fixed plus $6 per direct labor hour variable.
  b. $30,000 fixed plus $9 per direct labor hour variable.
  c. $60,000 fixed plus $3 per direct labor hour variable.
  d. $60,000 fixed plus $6 per direct labor hour variable.

(SO 3) **7.** At 9,000 direct labor hours, the flexible budget for indirect materials is $27,000. If $28,000 of indirect materials costs are incurred at 9,200 direct labor hours, the flexible budget report should show the following difference for indirect materials:
  a. $1,000 unfavorable.
  b. $1,000 favorable.
  c. $400 favorable.
  d. $400 unfavorable.

(SO 4) **8.** Under responsibility accounting, the evaluation of a manager's performance is based on matters that the manager:
  a. directly controls.
  b. directly and indirectly controls.
  c. indirectly controls.
  d. has shared responsibility for with another manager.

(SO 4) **9.** Responsibility centers include:
  a. cost centers.   c. investment centers.
  b. profit centers. d All of the above.

1088 Chapter 24 Budgetary Control and Responsibility Accounting

(SO 5) 10. Responsibility reports for cost centers:
  a. distinguish between fixed and variable costs.
  b. use static budget data.
  c. include both controllable and noncontrollable costs.
  d. include only controllable costs.

(SO 5) 11. The accounting department of a manufacturing company is an example of:
  a. a cost center.
  b. a profit center.
  c. an investment center.
  d. a contribution center.

(SO 6) 12. To evaluate the performance of a profit center manager, upper management needs detailed information about:
  a. controllable costs.
  b. controllable revenues.
  c. controllable costs and revenues.
  d. controllable costs and revenues and average operating assets.

(SO 6) 13. In a responsibility report for a profit center, controllable fixed costs are deducted from contribution margin to show:
  a. profit center margin.
  b. controllable margin.
  c. net income.
  d. income from operations.

(SO 7) 14. In the formula for return on investment (ROI), the factors for controllable margin and operating assets are, respectively:
  a. controllable margin percentage and total operating assets.
  b. controllable margin dollars and average operating assets.
  c. controllable margin dollars and total assets.
  d. controllable margin percentage and average operating assets.

(SO 7) 15. A manager of an investment center can improve ROI by:
  a. increasing average operating assets.
  b. reducing sales.
  c. increasing variable costs.
  d. reducing variable and/or controllable fixed costs.

Go to the book's companion website, **www.wiley.com/college/weygandt**, for Additional Self-Study questions.

QUESTIONS

1. (a) What is budgetary control?
   (b) Greg Gilligan is describing budgetary control. What steps should be included in Greg's description?

2. The following purposes are part of a budgetary reporting system: (a) Determine efficient use of materials. (b) Control overhead costs. (c) Determine whether income objectives are being met. For each purpose, indicate the name of the report, the frequency of the report, and the primary recipient(s) of the report.

3. How may a budget report for the second quarter differ from a budget report for the first quarter?

4. Joe Cey questions the usefulness of a master sales budget in evaluating sales performance. Is there justification for Joe's concern? Explain.

5. Under what circumstances may a static budget be an appropriate basis for evaluating a manager's effectiveness in controlling costs?

6. "A flexible budget is really a series of static budgets." Is this true? Why?

7. The static manufacturing overhead budget based on 40,000 direct labor hours shows budgeted indirect labor costs of $54,000. During March, the department incurs $65,000 of indirect labor while working 45,000 direct labor hours. Is this a favorable or unfavorable performance? Why?

8. A static overhead budget based on 40,000 direct labor hours shows Factory Insurance $6,500 as a fixed cost. At the 50,000 direct labor hours worked in March, factory insurance costs were $6,200. Is this a favorable or unfavorable performance? Why?

9. Kate Coulter is confused about how a flexible budget is prepared. Identify the steps for Kate.

10. Alou Company has prepared a graph of flexible budget data. At zero direct labor hours, the total budgeted cost line intersects the vertical axis at $25,000. At 10,000 direct labor hours, the line drawn from the total budgeted cost line intersects the vertical axis at $85,000. How may the fixed and variable costs be expressed?

11. The flexible budget formula is fixed costs $40,000 plus variable costs of $4 per direct labor hour. What is the total budgeted cost at (a) 9,000 hours and (b) 12,345 hours?

12. What is management by exception? What criteria may be used in identifying exceptions?

13. What is responsibility accounting? Explain the purpose of responsibility accounting.

14. Ann Wilkins is studying for an accounting examination. Describe for Ann what conditions are necessary for responsibility accounting to be used effectively.

15. Distinguish between controllable and noncontrollable costs.

16. How do responsibility reports differ from budget reports?

17. What is the relationship, if any, between a responsibility reporting system and a company's organization chart?

18. Distinguish among the three types of responsibility centers.

19. (a) What costs are included in a performance report for a cost center? (b) In the report, are variable and fixed costs identified?

20. How do direct fixed costs differ from indirect fixed costs? Are both types of fixed costs controllable?

21. Lori Quan is confused about controllable margin reported in an income statement for a profit center. How is this margin computed, and what is its primary purpose?

22. What is the primary basis for evaluating the performance of the manager of an investment center? Indicate the formula for this basis.

23. Explain the ways that ROI can be improved.

24. Indicate two behavioral principles that pertain to (a) the manager being evaluated and (b) top management.

BRIEF EXERCISES

BE24-1 For the quarter ended March 31, 2010, Voorhees Company accumulates the following sales data for its product, Garden-Tools: $310,000 budget; $304,000 actual. Prepare a static budget report for the quarter.

Prepare static budget report.
(SO 2)

BE24-2 Data for Voorhees Company are given in BE24-1. In the second quarter, budgeted sales were $380,000, and actual sales were $383,000. Prepare a static budget report for the second quarter and for the year to date.

Prepare static budget report for 2 quarters.
(SO 2)

BE24-3 In Mussatto Company, direct labor is $20 per hour. The company expects to operate at 10,000 direct labor hours each month. In January 2008, direct labor totaling $203,000 is incurred in working 10,400 hours. Prepare (a) a static budget report and (b) a flexible budget report. Evaluate the usefulness of each report.

Show usefulness of flexible budgets in evaluating performance.
(SO 3)

BE24-4 Hannon Company expects to produce 1,200,000 units of Product XX in 2010. Monthly production is expected to range from 80,000 to 120,000 units. Budgeted variable manufacturing costs per unit are: direct materials $4, direct labor $6, and overhead $8. Budgeted fixed manufacturing costs per unit for depreciation are $2 and for supervision are $1. Prepare a flexible manufacturing budget for the relevant range value using 20,000 unit increments.

Prepare a flexible budget for variable costs.
(SO 3)

BE24-5 Data for Hannon Company are given in BE24-4. In March 2010, the company incurs the following costs in producing 100,000 units: direct materials $425,000, direct labor $590,000, and variable overhead $805,000. Prepare a flexible budget report for March. Were costs controlled?

Prepare flexible budget report.
(SO 3)

BE24-6 In the Assembly Department of Cobb Company, budgeted and actual manufacturing overhead costs for the month of April 2010 were as follows.

Prepare a responsibility report for a cost center.
(SO 5)

	Budget	Actual
Indirect materials	$15,000	$14,300
Indirect labor	20,000	20,600
Utilities	10,000	10,750
Supervision	5,000	5,000

All costs are controllable by the department manager. Prepare a responsibility report for April for the cost center.

BE24-7 Eckert Manufacturing Company accumulates the following summary data for the year ending December 31, 2010, for its Water Division which it operates as a profit center: sales—$2,000,000 budget, $2,080,000 actual; variable costs—$1,000,000 budget, $1,050,000 actual; and controllable fixed costs—$300,000 budget, $310,000 actual. Prepare a responsibility report for the Water Division.

Prepare a responsibility report for a profit center.
(SO 6)

BE24-8 For the year ending December 31, 2010, Kaspar Company accumulates the following data for the Plastics Division which it operates as an investment center: contribution margin—$700,000 budget, $715,000 actual; controllable fixed costs—$300,000 budget, $309,000 actual. Average operating assets for the year were $2,000,000. Prepare a responsibility report for the Plastics Division beginning with contribution margin.

Prepare a responsibility report for an investment center.
(SO 7)

BE24-9 For its three investment centers, Paige Company accumulates the following data:

Compute return on investment using the ROI formula.
(SO 7)

	I	II	III
Sales	$2,000,000	$3,000,000	$ 4,000,000
Controllable margin	1,200,000	2,000,000	3,200,000
Average operating assets	5,000,000	8,000,000	10,000,000

Compute the return on investment (ROI) for each center.

Chapter 24 Budgetary Control and Responsibility Accounting

Compute return on investment under changed conditions.
(SO 7)

BE24-10 Data for the investment centers for Paige Company are given in BE24-9. The centers expect the following changes in the next year: (I) increase sales 15%; (II) decrease costs $200,000; (III) decrease average operating assets $400,000. Compute the expected return on investment (ROI) for each center. Assume center I has a contribution margin percentage of 75%.

DO IT! REVIEW

Compute total budgeted costs in flexible budget.
(SO 3)

DO IT! 24-1 In Moore Company's flexible budget graph, the fixed cost line and the total budgeted cost line intersect the vertical axis at $90,000. The total budgeted cost line is $330,000 at an activity level of 60,000 direct labor hours. Compute total budgeted costs at 70,000 direct labor hours.

Prepare and evaluate a flexible budget report.
(SO 3)

DO IT! 24-2 Chickasaw Company expects to produce 50,000 units of product IOA during the current year. Budgeted variable manufacturing costs per unit are direct materials $7, direct labor $12, and overhead $18. Annual budgeted fixed manufacturing overhead costs are $96,000 for depreciation and $45,000 for supervision.

In the current month, Chickasaw produced 6,000 units and incurred the following costs: direct materials $38,900, direct labor $70,200, variable overhead $116,500, depreciation $8,000, and supervision $4,000.

Prepare a flexible budget report. (*Note*: You do not need to prepare the heading.) Were costs controlled?

Prepare a responsibility report.
(SO 6)

DO IT! 24-3 The Deep South Division operates as a profit center. It reports the following for the year.

	Budgeted	Actual
Sales	$2,000,000	$1,800,000
Variable costs	800,000	750,000
Controllable fixed costs	550,000	550,000
Noncontrollable fixed costs	250,000	250,000

Prepare a responsibility report for the Deep South Division at December 31, 2010.

Compute ROI and expected return on investments.
(SO 7)

DO IT! 24-4 The service division of Retro Industries reported the following results for 2010.

Sales	$500,000
Variable costs	300,000
Controllable fixed costs	75,000
Average operating assets	450,000

Management is considering the following independent courses of action in 2011 in order to maximize the return on investment for this division.

1. Reduce average operating assets by $50,000, with no change in controllable margin.
2. Increase sales $100,000, with no change in the contribution margin percentage.

(a) Compute the controllable margin and the return on investment for 2010. (b) Compute the controllable margin and the expected return on investment for each proposed alternative.

EXERCISES

Understand the concept of budgetary control.
(SO 1, 2, 3)

E24-1 Jim Thome has prepared the following list of statements about budgetary control.
1. Budget reports compare actual results with planned objectives.
2. All budget reports are prepared on a weekly basis.
3. Management uses budget reports to analyze differences between actual and planned results and determine their causes.
4. As a result of analyzing budget reports, management may either take corrective action or modify future plans.

5. Budgetary control works best when a company has an informal reporting system.
6. The primary recipients of the sales report are the sales manager and the vice-president of production.
7. The primary recipient of the scrap report is the production manager.
8. A static budget is a projection of budget data at one level of activity.
9. Top management's reaction to unfavorable differences is not influenced by the materiality of the difference.
10. A static budget is not appropriate in evaluating a manager's effectiveness in controlling costs unless the actual activity level approximates the static budget activity level or the behavior of the costs is fixed.

Instructions
Identify each statement as true or false. If false, indicate how to correct the statement.

E24-2 Pargo Company budgeted selling expenses of $30,000 in January, $35,000 in February, and $40,000 in March. Actual selling expenses were $31,000 in January, $34,500 in February, and $47,000 in March.

Prepare and evaluate static budget report.
(SO 2)

Instructions
(a) Prepare a selling expense report that compares budgeted and actual amounts by month and for the year to date.
(b) What is the purpose of the report prepared in (a), and who would be the primary recipient?
(c) What would be the likely result of management's analysis of the report?

E24-3 Raney Company uses a flexible budget for manufacturing overhead based on direct labor hours. Variable manufacturing overhead costs per direct labor hour are as follows.

Prepare manufacturing flexible overhead budget.
(SO 3)

Indirect labor	$1.00
Indirect materials	0.50
Utilities	0.40

Fixed overhead costs per month are: Supervision $4,000, Depreciation $1,500, and Property Taxes $800. The company believes it will normally operate in a range of 7,000–10,000 direct labor hours per month.

Instructions
Prepare a monthly manufacturing overhead flexible budget for 2010 for the expected range of activity, using increments of 1,000 direct labor hours.

E24-4 Using the information in E24-3, assume that in July 2010, Raney Company incurs the following manufacturing overhead costs.

Prepare flexible budget reports for manufacturing overhead costs, and comment on findings.
(SO 3)

Variable Costs		Fixed Costs	
Indirect labor	$8,700	Supervision	$4,000
Indirect materials	4,300	Depreciation	1,500
Utilities	3,200	Property taxes	800

Instructions
(a) Prepare a flexible budget performance report, assuming that the company worked 9,000 direct labor hours during the month.
(b) Prepare a flexible budget performance report, assuming that the company worked 8,500 direct labor hours during the month.
(c) Comment on your findings.

E24-5 Trusler Company uses flexible budgets to control its selling expenses. Monthly sales are expected to range from $170,000 to $200,000. Variable costs and their percentage relationship to sales are: Sales Commissions 5%, Advertising 4%, Traveling 3%, and Delivery 2%. Fixed selling expenses will consist of Sales Salaries $34,000, Depreciation on Delivery Equipment $7,000, and Insurance on Delivery Equipment $1,000.

Prepare flexible selling expense budget.
(SO 3)

Instructions
Prepare a monthly flexible budget for each $10,000 increment of sales within the relevant range for the year ending December 31, 2010.

Chapter 24 Budgetary Control and Responsibility Accounting

Prepare flexible budget reports for selling expenses.
(SO 3)

E24-6 The actual selling expenses incurred in March 2010 by Trusler Company are as follows.

Variable Expenses		Fixed Expenses	
Sales commissions	$9,200	Sales salaries	$34,000
Advertising	7,000	Depreciation	7,000
Travel	5,100	Insurance	1,000
Delivery	3,500		

Instructions
(a) Prepare a flexible budget performance report for March using the budget data in E24-5, assuming that March sales were $170,000. Expected and actual sales are the same.
(b) Prepare a flexible budget performance report, assuming that March sales were $180,000. Expected sales and actual sales are the same.
(c) Comment on the importance of using flexible budgets in evaluating the performance of the sales manager.

Prepare flexible budget and responsibility report for manufacturing overhead.
(SO 3, 5)

E24-7 Pletcher Company's manufacturing overhead budget for the first quarter of 2010 contained the following data.

Variable Costs		Fixed Costs	
Indirect materials	$12,000	Supervisory salaries	$36,000
Indirect labor	10,000	Depreciation	7,000
Utilities	8,000	Property taxes and insurance	8,000
Maintenance	6,000	Maintenance	5,000

Actual variable costs were: indirect materials $13,800, indirect labor $9,600, utilities $8,700, and maintenance $4,900. Actual fixed costs equaled budgeted costs except for property taxes and insurance, which were $8,200.

All costs are considered controllable by the production department manager except for depreciation, and property taxes and insurance.

Instructions
(a) Prepare a manufacturing overhead flexible budget report for the first quarter.
(b) Prepare a responsibility report for the first quarter.

Prepare flexible budget report, and answer question.
(SO 2, 3)

E24-8 As sales manager, Terry Dewitt was given the following static budget report for selling expenses in the Clothing Department of Garber Company for the month of October.

GARBER COMPANY
Clothing Department
Selling Expense Budget Report
For the Month Ended October 31, 2010

	Budget	Actual	Difference Favorable F Unfavorable U
Sales in units	8,000	10,000	2,000 F
Variable expenses			
Sales commissions	$ 2,000	$ 2,600	$ 600 U
Advertising expense	800	850	50 U
Travel expense	3,600	4,000	400 U
Free samples given out	1,600	1,300	300 F
Total variable	8,000	8,750	750 U
Fixed expenses			
Rent	1,500	1,500	–0–
Sales salaries	1,200	1,200	–0–
Office salaries	800	800	–0–
Depreciation—autos (sales staff)	500	500	–0–
Total fixed	4,000	4,000	–0–
Total expenses	$12,000	$12,750	$ 750 U

As a result of this budget report, Terry was called into the president's office and congratulated on his fine sales performance. He was reprimanded, however, for allowing his costs to get out of control. Terry knew something was wrong with the performance report that he had been given. However, he was not sure what to do, and comes to you for advice.

Instructions
(a) Prepare a budget report based on flexible budget data to help Terry.
(b) Should Terry have been reprimanded? Explain.

E24-9 Pronto Plumbing Company is a newly formed company specializing in plumbing services for home and business. The owner, Paul Pronto, had divided the company into two segments: Home Plumbing Services and Business Plumbing Services. Each segment is run by its own supervisor, while basic selling and administrative services are shared by both segments.

Prepare and discuss a responsibility report.
(SO 3, 5)

Paul has asked you to help him create a performance reporting system that will allow him to measure each segment's performance in terms of its profitability. To that end, the following information has been collected on the Home Plumbing Services segment for the first quarter of 2010.

	Budgeted	Actual
Service revenue	$25,000	$26,000
Allocated portion of:		
Building depreciation	11,000	11,000
Advertising	5,000	4,200
Billing	3,500	3,000
Property taxes	1,200	1,000
Material and supplies	1,500	1,200
Supervisory salaries	9,000	9,400
Insurance	4,000	3,500
Wages	3,000	3,300
Gas and oil	2,700	3,400
Equipment depreciation	1,600	1,300

Instructions
(a) Prepare a responsibility report for the first quarter of 2010 for the Home Plumbing Services segment.
(b) Write a memo to Paul Pronto discussing the principles that should be used when preparing performance reports.

E24-10 Rensing Company has two production departments, Fabricating and Assembling. At a department managers' meeting, the controller uses flexible budget graphs to explain total budgeted costs. Separate graphs based on direct labor hours are used for each department. The graphs show the following.

State total budgeted cost formulas, and prepare flexible budget graph.
(SO 3)

1. At zero direct labor hours, the total budgeted cost line and the fixed cost line intersect the vertical axis at $40,000 in the Fabricating Department and $30,000 in the Assembling Department.
2. At normal capacity of 50,000 direct labor hours, the line drawn from the total budgeted cost line intersects the vertical axis at $150,000 in the Fabricating Department, and $110,000 in the Assembling Department.

Instructions
(a) State the total budgeted cost formula for each department.
(b) Compute the total budgeted cost for each department, assuming actual direct labor hours worked were 53,000 and 47,000, in the Fabricating and Assembling Departments, respectively.
(c) Prepare the flexible budget graph for the Fabricating Department, assuming the maximum direct labor hours in the relevant range is 100,000. Use increments of 10,000 direct labor hours on the horizontal axis and increments of $50,000 on the vertical axis.

E24-11 Lovell Company's organization chart includes the president; the vice president of production; three assembly plants—Dallas, Atlanta, and Tucson; and two departments within each plant—Machining and Finishing. Budget and actual manufacturing cost data for July 2010 are as follows:

Prepare reports in a responsibility reporting system.
(SO 4)

Finishing Department—Dallas: Direct materials $41,500 actual, $45,000 budget; direct labor $83,000 actual, $82,000 budget; manufacturing overhead $51,000 actual, $49,200 budget.

Machining Department—Dallas: Total manufacturing costs $220,000 actual, $216,000 budget.

Atlanta Plant: Total manufacturing costs $424,000 actual, $421,000 budget.

Tucson Plant: Total manufacturing costs $494,000 actual, $496,500 budget.

The Dallas plant manager's office costs were $95,000 actual and $92,000 budget. The vice president of production's office costs were $132,000 actual and $130,000 budget. Office costs are not allocated to departments and plants.

Instructions

Using the format on page 1076, prepare the reports in a responsibility system for:

(a) The Finishing Department—Dallas.
(b) The plant manager—Dallas.
(c) The vice president of production.

Prepare a responsibility report for a cost center.

(SO 5)

E24-12 The Mixing Department manager of Crede Company is able to control all overhead costs except rent, property taxes, and salaries. Budgeted monthly overhead costs for the Mixing Department, in alphabetical order, are:

Indirect labor	$12,000	Property taxes	$ 1,000
Indirect materials	7,500	Rent	1,800
Lubricants	1,700	Salaries	10,000
Maintenance	3,500	Utilities	5,000

Actual costs incurred for January 2010 are indirect labor $12,200; indirect materials $10,200; lubricants $1,650; maintenance $3,500; property taxes $1,100; rent $1,800; salaries $10,000; and utilities $6,500.

Instructions

(a) Prepare a responsibility report for January 2010.
(b) What would be the likely result of management's analysis of the report?

Compute missing amounts in responsibility reports for three profit centers, and prepare a report.

(SO 6)

E24-13 Gonzales Manufacturing Inc. has three divisions which are operated as profit centers. Actual operating data for the divisions listed alphabetically are as follows.

Operating Data	Women's Shoes	Men's Shoes	Children's Shoes
Contribution margin	$240,000	(3)	$180,000
Controllable fixed costs	100,000	(4)	(5)
Controllable margin	(1)	$ 90,000	96,000
Sales	600,000	450,000	(6)
Variable costs	(2)	330,000	250,000

Instructions

(a) Compute the missing amounts. Show computations.
(b) Prepare a responsibility report for the Women's Shoe Division assuming (1) the data are for the month ended June 30, 2010, and (2) all data equal budget except variable costs which are $10,000 over budget.

Prepare a responsibility report for a profit center, and compute ROI.

(SO 6, 7)

E24-14 The Sports Equipment Division of Brandon McCarthy Company is operated as a profit center. Sales for the division were budgeted for 2010 at $900,000. The only variable costs budgeted for the division were cost of goods sold ($440,000) and selling and administrative ($60,000). Fixed costs were budgeted at $100,000 for cost of goods sold, $90,000 for selling and administrative and $70,000 for noncontrollable fixed costs. Actual results for these items were:

Sales	$880,000
Cost of goods sold	
Variable	409,000
Fixed	105,000
Selling and administrative	
Variable	61,000
Fixed	67,000
Noncontrollable fixed	80,000

Instructions

(a) Prepare a responsibility report for the Sports Equipment Division for 2010.
(b) Assume, instead, the division is an investment center, and average operating assets were $1,000,000. Compute ROI.

E24-15 The Green Division of Frizell Company reported the following data for the current year.

Sales	$3,000,000
Variable costs	1,950,000
Controllable fixed costs	600,000
Average operating assets	5,000,000

Compute ROI for current year and for possible future changes.
(SO 7)

Top management is unhappy with the investment center's return on investment (ROI). It asks the manager of the Green Division to submit plans to improve ROI in the next year. The manager believes it is feasible to consider the following independent courses of action.

1. Increase sales by $320,000 with no change in the contribution margin percentage.
2. Reduce variable costs by $100,000.
3. Reduce average operating assets by 4%.

Instructions
(a) Compute the return on investment (ROI) for the current year.
(b) Using the ROI formula, compute the ROI under each of the proposed courses of action. (Round to one decimal.)

E24-16 The Medina and Ortiz Dental Clinic provides both preventive and orthodontic dental services. The two owners, Martin Medina and Olga Ortiz, operate the clinic as two separate investment centers: Preventive Services and Orthodontic Services. Each of them is in charge of one of the centers: Martin for Preventive Services and Olga for Orthodontic Services. Each month they prepare an income statement on the two centers to evaluate performance and make decisions about how to improve the operational efficiency and profitability of the clinic.

Prepare a responsibility report for an investment center.
(SO 7)

Recently they have been concerned about the profitability of the Preventive Services operations. For several months it has been reporting a loss. Shown below is the responsibility report for the month of May 2010.

	Actual	Difference from Budget
Service revenue	$ 40,000	$1,000 F
Variable costs:		
Filling materials	5,000	100 U
Novocain	4,000	200 U
Supplies	2,000	250 F
Dental assistant wages	2,500	–0–
Utilities	500	50 U
Total variable costs	14,000	100 U
Fixed costs:		
Allocated portion of receptionist's salary	3,000	200 U
Dentist salary	10,000	500 U
Equipment depreciation	6,000	–0–
Allocated portion of building depreciation	15,000	1,000 U
Total fixed costs	34,000	1,700 U
Operating income (loss)	$ (8,000)	$ 800 U

In addition, the owners know that the investment in operating assets at the beginning of the month was $82,400, and it was $77,600 at the end of the month. They have asked for your assistance in evaluating their current performance reporting system.

Instructions
(a) Prepare a responsibility report for an investment center as illustrated in the chapter.
(b) Write a memo to the owners discussing the deficiencies of their current reporting system.

E24-17 The Transamerica Transportation Company uses a responsibility reporting system to measure the performance of its three investment centers: Planes, Taxis, and Limos. Segment performance is measured using a system of responsibility reports and return on investment

Prepare missing amounts in responsibility reports for three investment centers.
(SO 7)

1096 Chapter 24 Budgetary Control and Responsibility Accounting

calculations. The allocation of resources within the company and the segment managers' bonuses are based in part on the results shown in these reports.

Recently, the company was the victim of a computer virus that deleted portions of the company's accounting records. This was discovered when the current period's responsibility reports were being prepared. The printout of the actual operating results appeared as follows.

	Planes	Taxis	Limos
Service revenue	$?	$500,000	$?
Variable costs	5,500,000	?	320,000
Contribution margin	?	200,000	480,000
Controllable fixed costs	1,500,000	?	?
Controllable margin	?	80,000	240,000
Average operating assets	25,000,000	?	1,600,000
Return on investment	12%	10%	?

Instructions
Determine the missing pieces of information above.

EXERCISES: SET B

Visit the book's companion website at **www.wiley.com/college/weygandt**, and choose the Student Companion site, to access Exercise Set B.

PROBLEMS: SET A

Prepare flexible budget and budget report for manufacturing overhead.
(SO 3)

P24-1A Malone Company estimates that 360,000 direct labor hours will be worked during the coming year, 2010, in the Packaging Department. On this basis, the following budgeted manufacturing overhead cost data are computed for the year.

Fixed Overhead Costs		Variable Overhead Costs	
Supervision	$ 90,000	Indirect labor	$126,000
Depreciation	60,000	Indirect materials	90,000
Insurance	30,000	Repairs	54,000
Rent	24,000	Utilities	72,000
Property taxes	18,000	Lubricants	18,000
	$222,000		$360,000

It is estimated that direct labor hours worked each month will range from 27,000 to 36,000 hours.
During October, 27,000 direct labor hours were worked and the following overhead costs were incurred.

Fixed overhead costs: Supervision $7,500, Depreciation $5,000, Insurance $2,470, Rent $2,000, and Property taxes $1,500.
Variable overhead costs: Indirect labor $10,360, Indirect materials, $6,400, Repairs $4,000, Utilities $5,700, and Lubricants $1,640.

Instructions

(a) Total costs: DLH 27,000, $45,500; DLH 36,000, $54,500
(b) Total $1,070 U

(a) Prepare a monthly manufacturing overhead flexible budget for each increment of 3,000 direct labor hours over the relevant range for the year ending December 31, 2010.
(b) Prepare a flexible budget report for October.
(c)  Comment on management's efficiency in controlling manufacturing overhead costs in October.

Prepare flexible budget, budget report, and graph for manufacturing overhead.
(SO 3)

P24-2A Fultz Company manufactures tablecloths. Sales have grown rapidly over the past 2 years. As a result, the president has installed a budgetary control system for 2010. The following data were used in developing the master manufacturing overhead budget for the Ironing Department, which is based on an activity index of direct labor hours.

Variable Costs	Rate per Direct Labor Hour	Annual Fixed Costs	
Indirect labor	$0.40	Supervision	$42,000
Indirect materials	0.50	Depreciation	18,000
Factory utilities	0.30	Insurance	12,000
Factory repairs	0.20	Rent	24,000

The master overhead budget was prepared on the expectation that 480,000 direct labor hours will be worked during the year. In June, 42,000 direct labor hours were worked. At that level of activity, actual costs were as shown below.

Variable—per direct labor hour: Indirect labor $0.43, Indirect materials $0.49, Factory utilities $0.32, and Factory repairs $0.24.

Fixed: same as budgeted.

Instructions

(a) Prepare a monthly manufacturing overhead flexible budget for the year ending December 31, 2010, assuming production levels range from 35,000 to 50,000 direct labor hours. Use increments of 5,000 direct labor hours.

(b) Prepare a budget report for June comparing actual results with budget data based on the flexible budget.

(c) Were costs effectively controlled? Explain.

(d) State the formula for computing the total budgeted costs for Fultz Company.

(e) Prepare the flexible budget graph, showing total budgeted costs at 35,000 and 45,000 direct labor hours. Use increments of 5,000 direct labor hours on the horizontal axis and increments of $10,000 on the vertical axis.

(a) Total costs: 35,000 DLH, $57,000; 50,000 DLH, $78,000

(b) Budget $66,800 Actual $70,160

P24-3A Zelmer Company uses budgets in controlling costs. The August 2010 budget report for the company's Assembling Department is as follows.

State total budgeted cost formula, and prepare flexible budget reports for 2 time periods.

(SO 2, 3)

ZELMER COMPANY
Budget Report
Assembling Department
For the Month Ended August 31, 2010

Manufacturing Costs	Budget	Actual	Difference Favorable F Unfavorable U
Variable costs			
Direct materials	$ 48,000	$ 47,000	$1,000 F
Direct labor	54,000	51,300	2,700 F
Indirect materials	24,000	24,200	200 U
Indirect labor	18,000	17,500	500 F
Utilities	15,000	14,900	100 F
Maintenance	9,000	9,200	200 U
Total variable	168,000	164,100	3,900 F
Fixed costs			
Rent	12,000	12,000	–0–
Supervision	17,000	17,000	–0–
Depreciation	7,000	7,000	–0–
Total fixed	36,000	36,000	–0–
Total costs	$204,000	$200,100	$3,900 F

The monthly budget amounts in the report were based on an expected production of 60,000 units per month or 720,000 units per year. The Assembling Department manager is pleased with the report and expects a raise, or at least praise for a job well done. The company president, however, is unhappy with the results for August, because only 58,000 units were produced.

Instructions

(a) State the total monthly budgeted cost formula.

(b) Prepare a budget report for August using flexible budget data. Why does this report provide a better basis for evaluating performance than the report based on static budget data?

(c) In September, 64,000 units were produced. Prepare the budget report using flexible budget data, assuming (1) each variable cost was 10% higher than its actual cost in August, and (2) fixed costs were the same in September as in August.

Prepare responsibility report for a profit center.
(SO 6)

P24-4A Jantzen Manufacturing Inc. operates the Patio Furniture Division as a profit center. Operating data for this division for the year ended December 31, 2010, are as shown below.

	Budget	Difference from Budget
Sales	$2,500,000	$60,000 F
Cost of goods sold		
Variable	1,300,000	41,000 F
Controllable fixed	200,000	6,000 U
Selling and administrative		
Variable	220,000	7,000 U
Controllable fixed	50,000	2,000 U
Noncontrollable fixed costs	70,000	4,000 U

In addition, Jantzen Manufacturing incurs $180,000 of indirect fixed costs that were budgeted at $175,000. Twenty percent (20%) of these costs are allocated to the Patio Furniture Division.

Instructions

(a) Prepare a responsibility report for the Patio Furniture Division for the year.

(b) ✏️ Comment on the manager's performance in controlling revenues and costs.

(c) Identify any costs excluded from the responsibility report and explain why they were excluded.

Prepare responsibility report for an investment center, and compute ROI.
(SO 7)

P24-5A Dinkle Manufacturing Company manufactures a variety of tools and industrial equipment. The company operates through three divisions. Each division is an investment center. Operating data for the Home Division for the year ended December 31, 2010, and relevant budget data are as follows.

	Actual	Comparison with Budget
Sales	$1,500,000	$100,000 favorable
Variable cost of goods sold	700,000	60,000 unfavorable
Variable selling and administrative expenses	125,000	25,000 unfavorable
Controllable fixed cost of goods sold	170,000	On target
Controllable fixed selling and administrative expenses	80,000	On target

Average operating assets for the year for the Home Division were $2,500,000 which was also the budgeted amount.

Instructions

(a) Prepare a responsibility report (in thousands of dollars) for the Home Division.

(b) Evaluate the manager's performance. Which items will likely be investigated by top management?

(c) Compute the expected ROI in 2011 for the Home Division, assuming the following independent changes to actual data.
  (1) Variable cost of goods sold is decreased by 6%.
  (2) Average operating assets are decreased by 10%.

(3) Sales are increased by $200,000, and this increase is expected to increase contribution margin by $90,000.

P24-6A Nieto Company uses a responsibility reporting system. It has divisions in Denver, Seattle, and San Diego. Each division has three production departments: Cutting, Shaping, and Finishing. The responsibility for each department rests with a manager who reports to the division production manager. Each division manager reports to the vice president of production. There are also vice presidents for marketing and finance. All vice presidents report to the president.

Prepare reports for cost centers under responsibility accounting, and comment on performance of managers.
(SO 4)

In January 2010, controllable actual and budget manufacturing overhead cost data for the departments and divisions were as shown below.

Manufacturing Overhead	Actual	Budget
Individual costs—Cutting Department—Seattle		
Indirect labor	$ 73,000	$ 70,000
Indirect materials	47,700	46,000
Maintenance	20,500	18,000
Utilities	20,100	17,000
Supervision	22,000	20,000
	$183,300	$171,000
Total costs		
Shaping Department—Seattle	$158,000	$148,000
Finishing Department—Seattle	210,000	206,000
Denver division	676,000	673,000
San Diego division	722,000	715,000

Additional overhead costs were incurred as follows: Seattle division production manager—actual costs $52,500, budget $51,000; vice president of production—actual costs $65,000, budget $64,000; president—actual costs $76,400, budget $74,200. These expenses are not allocated.

The vice presidents who report to the president, other than the vice president of production, had the following expenses.

Vice president	Actual	Budget
Marketing	$133,600	$130,000
Finance	109,000	105,000

Instructions

(a) Using the format on page 1076, prepare the following responsibility reports.
   (1) Manufacturing overhead—Cutting Department manager—Seattle division.
   (2) Manufacturing overhead—Seattle division manager.
   (3) Manufacturing overhead—vice president of production.
   (4) Manufacturing overhead and expenses—president.
(b) Comment on the comparative performances of:
   (1) Department managers in the Seattle division.
   (2) Division managers.
   (3) Vice presidents.

(a) (1) $12,300 U
(2) $27,800 U
(3) $38,800 U
(4) $48,600 U

PROBLEMS: SET B

P24-1B Ogleby Company estimates that 240,000 direct labor hours will be worked during 2010 in the Assembly Department. On this basis, the following budgeted manufacturing overhead data are computed.

Prepare flexible budget and budget report for manufacturing overhead.
(SO 3)

Variable Overhead Costs		Fixed Overhead Costs	
Indirect labor	$ 72,000	Supervision	$ 75,000
Indirect materials	48,000	Depreciation	30,000
Repairs	36,000	Insurance	12,000
Utilities	26,400	Rent	9,000
Lubricants	9,600	Property taxes	6,000
	$192,000		$132,000

It is estimated that direct labor hours worked each month will range from 18,000 to 24,000 hours. During January, 20,000 direct labor hours were worked and the following overhead costs were incurred.

Variable Overhead Costs		Fixed Overhead Costs	
Indirect labor	$ 6,200	Supervision	$ 6,250
Indirect materials	3,600	Depreciation	2,500
Repairs	2,400	Insurance	1,000
Utilities	1,700	Rent	850
Lubricants	830	Property taxes	500
	$14,730		$11,100

Instructions

(a) Prepare a monthly manufacturing overhead flexible budget for each increment of 2,000 direct labor hours over the relevant range for the year ending December 31, 2010.

(b) Prepare a manufacturing overhead budget report for January.

(c) Comment on management's efficiency in controlling manufacturing overhead costs in January.

(a) Total costs: 18,000 DLH, $25,400; 24,000 DLH, $30,200

(b) Budget $27,000 Actual, $25,830

Prepare flexible budget, budget report, and graph for manufacturing overhead.

(SO 3)

P24-2B Parcells Manufacturing Company produces one product, Olpe. Because of wide fluctuations in demand for Olpe, the Assembly Department experiences significant variations in monthly production levels.

The annual master manufacturing overhead budget is based on 300,000 direct labor hours. In July 27,500 labor hours were worked. The master manufacturing overhead budget for the year and the actual overhead costs incurred in July are as follows.

Overhead Costs	Master Budget (annual)	Actual in July
Variable		
Indirect labor	$330,000	$29,000
Indirect materials	180,000	14,000
Utilities	90,000	8,100
Maintenance	60,000	5,400
Fixed		
Supervision	150,000	12,500
Depreciation	96,000	8,000
Insurance and taxes	60,000	5,000
Total	$966,000	$82,000

Instructions

(a) Prepare a monthly overhead flexible budget for the year ending December 31, 2010, assuming monthly production levels range from 22,500 to 30,000 direct labor hours. Use increments of 2,500 direct labor hours.

(b) Prepare a budget report for the month of July 2010 comparing actual results with budget data based on the flexible budget.

(c) Were costs effectively controlled? Explain.

(d) State the formula for computing the total monthly budgeted costs in the Parcells Manufacturing Company.

(e) Prepare the flexible budget graph showing total budgeted costs at 25,000 and 27,500 direct labor hours. Use increments of 5,000 on the horizontal axis and increments of $10,000 on the vertical axis.

(a) Total costs: 22,500 DLH, $75,000; 30,000 DLH, $91,500

(b) Budget $86,000 Actual $82,000

P24-3B Fernetti Company uses budgets in controlling costs. The May 2010 budget report for the company's Packaging Department is as follows.

State total budgeted cost formula, and prepare flexible budget reports for 2 time periods.
(SO 2, 3)

FERNETTI COMPANY
Budget Report
Packaging Department
For the Month Ended May 31, 2010

Manufacturing Costs	Budget	Actual	Difference Favorable F Unfavorable U
Variable costs			
Direct materials	$ 40,000	$ 41,000	$1,000 U
Direct labor	45,000	47,000	2,000 U
Indirect materials	15,000	15,200	200 U
Indirect labor	12,500	13,000	500 U
Utilities	10,000	9,600	400 F
Maintenance	5,000	5,200	200 U
Total variable	127,500	131,000	3,500 U
Fixed costs			
Rent	10,000	10,000	–0–
Supervision	7,000	7,000	–0–
Depreciation	5,000	5,000	–0–
Total fixed	22,000	22,000	–0–
Total costs	$149,500	$153,000	$3,500 U

The monthly budget amounts in the report were based on an expected production of 50,000 units per month or 600,000 units per year.

The company president was displeased with the department manager's performance. The department manager, who thought he had done a good job, could not understand the unfavorable results. In May, 55,000 units were produced.

Instructions
(a) State the total budgeted cost formula.
(b) Prepare a budget report for May using flexible budget data. Why does this report provide a better basis for evaluating performance than the report based on static budget data?
(c) In June, 40,000 units were produced. Prepare the budget report using flexible budget data, assuming (1) each variable cost was 20% less in June than its actual cost in May, and (2) fixed costs were the same in the month of June as in May.

(b) Budget $162,250

(c) Budget $124,000
Actual $126,800

P24-4B Widnet Manufacturing Inc. operates the Home Appliance Division as a profit center. Operating data for this division for the year ended December 31, 2010, are shown below.

Prepare responsibility report for a profit center.
(SO 6)

	Budget	Difference from Budget
Sales	$2,400,000	$100,000 U
Cost of goods sold		
Variable	1,200,000	60,000 U
Controllable fixed	200,000	8,000 F
Selling and administrative		
Variable	240,000	8,000 F
Controllable fixed	60,000	4,000 U
Noncontrollable fixed costs	50,000	2,000 U

In addition, Widnet Manufacturing incurs $150,000 of indirect fixed costs that were budgeted at $155,000. Twenty percent (20%) of these costs are allocated to the Home Appliance Division. None of these costs are controllable by the division manager.

1102 Chapter 24 Budgetary Control and Responsibility Accounting

(a) Contribution margin
$152,000 U
Controllable margin
$148,000 U

Instructions

(a) Prepare a responsibility report for the Home Appliance Division (a profit center) for the year.
(b)  Comment on the manager's performance in controlling revenues and costs.
(c) Identify any costs excluded from the responsibility report and explain why they were excluded.

Prepare responsibility report for an investment center, and compute ROI.
(SO 7)

P24-5B Schwinn Manufacturing Company manufactures a variety of garden and lawn equipment. The company operates through three divisions. Each division is an investment center. Operating data for the Lawnmower Division for the year ended December 31, 2010, and relevant budget data are as follows.

	Actual	Comparison with Budget
Sales	$2,900,000	$120,000 unfavorable
Variable cost of goods sold	1,400,000	90,000 unfavorable
Variable selling and administrative expenses	300,000	50,000 favorable
Controllable fixed cost of goods sold	270,000	On target
Controllable fixed selling and administrative expenses	140,000	On target

Average operating assets for the year for the Lawnmower Division were $5,000,000 which was also the budgeted amount.

Instructions

(a) Controllable margin:
Budget $950
Actual $790

(a) Prepare a responsibility report (in thousands of dollars) for the Lawnmower Division.
(b) Evaluate the manager's performance. Which items will likely be investigated by top management?
(c) Compute the expected ROI in 2011 for the Lawnmower Division, assuming the following independent changes.
  (1) Variable cost of goods sold is decreased by 15%.
  (2) Average operating assets are decreased by 20%.
  (3) Sales are increased by $500,000 and this increase is expected to increase contribution margin by $210,000.

PROBLEMS: SET C

Visit the book's companion website at **www.wiley.com/college/weygandt**, and choose the Student Companion site, to access Problem Set C.

WATERWAYS CONTINUING PROBLEM

(*Note:* This is a continuation of the Waterways Problem from Chapters 19 through 23.)

WCP24 Waterways Corporation is continuing its budget preparations. This problem gives you static budget information as well as actual overhead costs and asks you to calculate amounts related to budgetary control and responsibility accounting.

Go to the book's companion website,
www.wiley.com/college/weygandt,
to find the completion of this problem.

BROADENING YOUR PERSPECTIVE

Decision Making Across the Organization

BYP24-1 G-Bar Pastures is a 400-acre farm on the outskirts of the Kentucky Bluegrass, specializing in the boarding of broodmares and their foals. A recent economic downturn in the thoroughbred industry has led to a decline in breeding activities, and it has made the boarding business extremely competitive. To meet the competition, G-Bar Pastures planned in 2010 to entertain clients, advertise more extensively, and absorb expenses formerly paid by clients such as veterinary and blacksmith fees.

The budget report for 2010 is presented below. As shown, the static income statement budget for the year is based on an expected 21,900 boarding days at $25 per mare. The variable expenses per mare per day were budgeted: Feed $5, Veterinary fees $3, Blacksmith fees $0.30, and Supplies $0.55. All other budgeted expenses were either semifixed or fixed.

During the year, management decided not to replace a worker who quit in March, but it did issue a new advertising brochure and did more entertaining of clients.[1]

G-BAR PASTURES
Static Budget Income Statement
Year Ended December 31, 2010

	Actual	Master Budget	Difference
Number of mares per day	52	60	8*
Number of boarding days	18,980	21,900	2,920*
Sales	$379,600	$547,500	$167,900*
Less variable expenses:			
Feed	104,390	109,500	5,110
Veterinary fees	58,838	65,700	6,862
Blacksmith fees	6,074	6,570	496
Supplies	10,178	12,045	1,867
Total variable expenses	179,480	193,815	14,335
Contribution margin	200,120	353,685	153,565*
Less fixed expenses:			
Depreciation	40,000	40,000	–0–
Insurance	11,000	11,000	–0–
Utilities	12,000	14,000	2,000
Repairs and maintenance	10,000	11,000	1,000
Labor	88,000	96,000	8,000
Advertisement	12,000	8,000	4,000*
Entertainment	7,000	5,000	2,000*
Total fixed expenses	180,000	185,000	5,000
Net income	$ 20,120	$168,685	$148,565*

*Unfavorable.

Instructions
With the class divided into groups, answer the following.

(a) Based on the static budget report:
  (1) What was the primary cause(s) of the loss in net income?
  (2) Did management do a good, average, or poor job of controlling expenses?
  (3) Were management's decisions to stay competitive sound?

---

[1]Data for this case are based on Hans Sprohge and John Talbott, "New Applications for Variance Analysis," *Journal of Accountancy* (AICPA, New York), April 1989, pp. 137–141.

(b) Prepare a flexible budget report for the year based on boarding days.
(c) Based on the flexible budget report, answer the three questions in part (a) above.
(d) What course of action do you recommend for the management of G-Bar Pastures?

Managerial Analysis

BYP24-2 Fugate Company manufactures expensive watch cases sold as souvenirs. Three of its sales departments are: Retail Sales, Wholesale Sales, and Outlet Sales. The Retail Sales Department is a profit center. The Wholesale Sales Department is a cost center. Its managers merely take orders from customers who purchase through the company's wholesale catalog. The Outlet Sales Department is an investment center, because each manager is given full responsibility for an outlet store location. The manager can hire and discharge employees, purchase, maintain, and sell equipment, and in general is fairly independent of company control.

Jane Duncan is a manager in the Retail Sales Department. Richard Wayne manages the Wholesale Sales Department. Jose Lopez manages the Golden Gate Club outlet store in San Francisco. The following are the budget responsibility reports for each of the three departments.

	Budget		
	Retail Sales	Wholesale Sales	Outlet Sales
Sales	$ 750,000	$ 400,000	$200,000
Variable costs			
Cost of goods sold	150,000	100,000	25,000
Advertising	100,000	30,000	5,000
Sales salaries	75,000	15,000	3,000
Printing	10,000	20,000	5,000
Travel	20,000	30,000	2,000
Fixed costs			
Rent	50,000	30,000	10,000
Insurance	5,000	2,000	1,000
Depreciation	75,000	100,000	40,000
Investment in assets	$1,000,000	$1,200,000	$800,000

	Actual Results		
	Retail Sales	Wholesale Sales	Outlet Sales
Sales	$ 750,000	$ 400,000	$200,000
Variable costs			
Cost of goods sold	195,000	120,000	26,250
Advertising	100,000	30,000	5,000
Sales salaries	75,000	15,000	3,000
Printing	10,000	20,000	5,000
Travel	15,000	20,000	1,500
Fixed costs			
Rent	40,000	50,000	12,000
Insurance	5,000	2,000	1,000
Depreciation	80,000	90,000	60,000
Investment in assets	$1,000,000	$1,200,000	$800,000

Instructions
(a) Determine which of the items should be included in the responsibility report for each of the three managers.
(b) Compare the actual results with the budget. Decide which results should be called to the attention of each manager.

Real-World Focus

BYP24-3 Computer Associates International, Inc., the world's leading business software company, delivers the end-to-end infrastructure to enable e-business through innovative technology, services, and education. CA has 19,000 employees worldwide and recently had revenue of over $6 billion.

Presented below is information from the company's annual report.

COMPUTER ASSOCIATES INTERNATIONAL
Management Discussion

The Company has experienced a pattern of business whereby revenue for its third and fourth fiscal quarters reflects an increase over first- and second-quarter revenue. The Company attributes this increase to clients' increased spending at the end of their calendar year budgetary periods and the culmination of its annual sales plan. Since the Company's costs do not increase proportionately with the third- and fourth-quarters' increase in revenue, the higher revenue in these quarters results in greater profit margins and income. Fourth-quarter profitability is traditionally affected by significant new hirings, training, and education expenditures for the succeeding year.

Instructions
(a) Why don't the company's costs increase proportionately as the revenues increase in the third and fourth quarters?
(b) What type of budgeting seems appropriate for the Computer Associates situation?

Exploring the Web

BYP24-4 There are many useful online resources regarding budgeting. The following activity investigates the results of a comprehensive budgeting study performed by a very large international accounting firm.

Address:
www.pwc.com/extweb/pwcpublications.nsf/docid/C2D9FB96F792CFA3852572B10049C87D, or go to **www.wiley.com/college/weygandt**

Steps
Go to the address above, click on the link to download the full report, and then register to receive the report. (Remove the checkmark to receive future reports.)

Instructions
Scan the report to answer the following questions.
(a) What percentage of respondents report that they are "very satisfied" with their financial planning process?
(b) What are the top six key elements that companies forecast?
(c) What is the percentage of total budget time spent on each of the following budgeting activities?
  (1) Data collection/consolidation
  (2) Analysis
  (3) Strategy/target setting
  (4) Review/approval
  (5) Report preparation
(d) What percentage of firms spend more than four months to complete a budget?
(e) What percentage of surveyed firms update their forecasts on a monthly basis?

Communication Activity

BYP24-5 The manufacturing overhead budget for Edmonds Company contains the following items.

Variable costs		Fixed costs	
Indirect materials	$24,000	Supervision	$18,000
Indirect labor	12,000	Inspection costs	1,000
Maintenance expense	10,000	Insurance expense	2,000
Manufacturing supplies	6,000	Depreciation	15,000
Total variable	$52,000	Total fixed	$36,000

The budget was based on an estimated 2,000 units being produced. During the past month, 1,500 units were produced, and the following costs incurred.

Variable costs		Fixed costs	
Indirect materials	$24,200	Supervision	$19,300
Indirect labor	13,500	Inspection costs	1,200
Maintenance expense	8,200	Insurance expense	2,200
Manufacturing supplies	5,100	Depreciation	14,700
Total variable	$51,000	Total fixed	$37,400

Instructions
(a) Determine which items would be controllable by Mark Farris, the production manager.
(b) How much should have been spent during the month for the manufacture of the 1,500 units?
(c) Prepare a manufacturing overhead flexible budget report for Mr. Farris.
(d) Prepare a responsibility report. Include only the costs that would have been controllable by Mr. Farris. Assume that the supervision cost above includes Mr. Farris's salary of $10,000, both at budget and actual. In an attached memo, describe clearly for Mr. Farris the areas in which his performance needs to be improved.

Ethics Case

BYP24-6 National Products Corporation participates in a highly competitive industry. In order to meet this competition and achieve profit goals, the company has chosen the decentralized form of organization. Each manager of a decentralized investment center is measured on the basis of profit contribution, market penetration, and return on investment. Failure to meet the objectives established by corporate management for these measures has not been acceptable and usually has resulted in demotion or dismissal of an investment center manager.

An anonymous survey of managers in the company revealed that the managers feel the pressure to compromise their personal ethical standards to achieve the corporate objectives. For example, at certain plant locations there was pressure to reduce quality control to a level which could not assure that all unsafe products would be rejected. Also, sales personnel were encouraged to use questionable sales tactics to obtain orders, including gifts and other incentives to purchasing agents.

The chief executive officer is disturbed by the survey findings. In his opinion such behavior cannot be condoned by the company. He concludes that the company should do something about this problem.

Instructions
(a) Who are the stakeholders (the affected parties) in this situation?
(b) Identify the ethical implications, conflicts, or dilemmas in the above described situation.
(c) What might the company do to reduce the pressures on managers and decrease the ethical conflicts?

(CMA adapted)

 ## "All About You" Activity

BYP24-7 It is one thing to prepare a personal budget; it is another thing to stick to it. Financial planners have suggested various mechanisms to provide support for enforcing personal budgets. One approach is called "envelope budgeting."

Instructions
Read the article provided at **http://en.wikipedia.org/wiki/Envelope_budgeting**, and answer the following questions.

(a) Summarize the process of envelope budgeting.
(b) Evaluate whether you think you would benefit from envelope budgeting. What do you think are its strengths and weaknesses relative to your situation?

Answers to Insight and Accounting Across the Organization Questions

p. 1074 Competition versus Collaboration
Q: How might managers of separate divisions be able to reduce division costs through collaboration?
A: *Division managers might reduce costs by sharing design and marketing resources or by jointly negotiating with suppliers. In addition, they can reduce the need to hire and lay off employees by sharing staff across divisions as human resource needs change.*

p. 1083 Does Hollywood Look at ROI?
Q: What might be the reason that movie studios do not produce G-rated movies as often as R-rated movies?
A: *Perhaps Hollywood believes that big-name stars or large budgets, both of which are typical of R-rated movies, sell movies. However, one study recently concluded, "We can't find evidence that stars help movies, and we can't find evidence that bigger budgets increase return on investment." Some film companies are going out of their way to achieve at least a PG rating.*

Answers to Self-Study Questions
1. c 2. d 3. c 4. b 5. b 6. a 7. d 8. a 9. d 10. d 11. a 12. c 13. b
14. b 15. d

Remember to go back to the Navigator box on the chapter-opening page and check off your completed work.

Chapter 25

Standard Costs and Balanced Scorecard

STUDY OBJECTIVES

After studying this chapter, you should be able to:

1. Distinguish between a standard and a budget.
2. Identify the advantages of standard costs.
3. Describe how companies set standards.
4. State the formulas for determining direct materials and direct labor variances.
5. State the formula for determining the total manufacturing overhead variance.
6. Discuss the reporting of variances.
7. Prepare an income statement for management under a standard costing system.
8. Describe the balanced scorecard approach to performance evaluation.

✓ The Navigator

Scan **Study Objectives**

Read **Feature Story**

Read **Preview**

Read text and answer **DO IT!**
p. 1115   p. 1118   p. 1122
p. 1127

Work **Comprehensive** **DO IT!** p. 1127

Review **Summary of Study Objectives**

Answer **Self-Study Questions**

Complete **Assignments**

✓ The Navigator

Feature Story

HIGHLIGHTING PERFORMANCE EFFICIENCY

There's a very good chance that the highlighter you're holding in your hand was made by Sanford (www.sanfordcorp.com), a maker of permanent markers and other writing instruments. Sanford, headquartered in Illinois, annually sells hundreds of millions of dollars' worth of Accent® highlighters, fine-point pens, Sharpie permanent markers, Expo dry-erase markers for overhead projectors, and other writing instruments.

Since Sanford makes literally billions of writing utensils per year, the company must keep tight control over manufacturing costs. A very important part of Sanford's manufacturing process is determining how much direct materials, labor, and overhead should cost. The company then compares these costs to actual costs to assess performance efficiency. Raw materials for Sanford's markers include a barrel, plug, cap, ink reservoir, and a nib (tip). Machines assemble these parts to produce thousands of units per hour. A major component of manufacturing overhead is machine maintenance—some fixed, some variable.

"Labor costs are associated with material handling and equipment maintenance functions. Although the assembly process is highly automated, labor is still required to move raw materials to the machine and to package the finished product. In addition, highly skilled technicians are required to service and maintain each piece of equipment," says Mike Orr, vice president, operations.

Labor rates are predictable because the hourly workers are covered by a union contract. The story is the same with the fringe benefits and some supervisory salaries. Even volume levels are fairly predictable—demand for the product is high—so fixed overhead is efficiently absorbed. Raw material standard costs are based on the previous year's actual prices plus any anticipated inflation. For the past several years, though, inflation had been so low that the company was considering any price increase in raw material to be unfavorable because its standards remained unchanged.

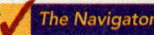

Inside Chapter 25...

- **How Can We Make Susan's Chili Profitable?** (p. 1115)
- **It May Be Time to Fly United Again** (p. 1126)

Preview of Chapter 25

Standards are a fact of life. You met the admission standards for the school you are attending. The vehicle that you drive had to meet certain governmental emissions standards. The hamburgers and salads you eat in a restaurant have to meet certain health and nutritional standards before they can be sold. As described in our Feature Story, Sanford Corp. has standards for the costs of its materials, labor, and overhead. The reason for standards in these cases is very simple: They help to ensure that overall product quality is high while keeping costs under control.

In this chapter we continue the study of controlling costs. You will learn how to evaluate performance using standard costs and a balanced scorecard.

The content and organization of Chapter 25 are as follows.

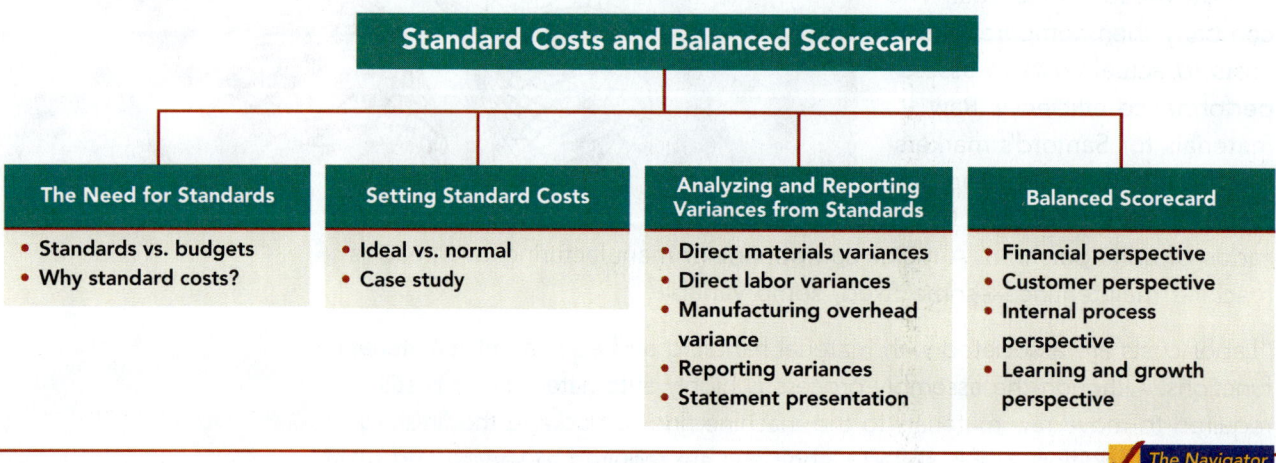

THE NEED FOR STANDARDS

Standards are common in business. Those imposed by government agencies are often called **regulations**. They include the Fair Labor Standards Act, the Equal Employment Opportunity Act, and a multitude of environmental standards. Standards established internally by a company may extend to personnel matters, such as employee absenteeism and ethical codes of conduct, quality control standards for products, and standard costs for goods and services. In managerial accounting, standard costs are predetermined unit costs, which companies use as measures of performance.

We will focus on manufacturing operations in this chapter. But you should also recognize that standard costs also apply to many types of service businesses as well. For example, a fast-food restaurant such as McDonald's knows the price it should pay for pickles, beef, buns, and other ingredients. It also knows how much time it should take an employee to flip hamburgers. If the company pays too much for pickles or if employees take too much time to prepare Big Macs, McDonald's notices the deviations and takes corrective action. Not-for-profit enterprises such as universities, charitable organizations, and governmental agencies also may use standard costs.

Distinguishing between Standards and Budgets

Both **standards** and **budgets** are predetermined costs, and both contribute to management planning and control. There is a difference, however, in the way the terms are expressed. A standard is a **unit** amount. A budget is a **total** amount. Thus, it is customary to state that the **standard cost** of direct labor for a unit of product is, say, $10. If the company produces 5,000 units of the product, the $50,000 of direct labor is the **budgeted** labor cost. A standard is the budgeted **cost per unit** of product. A standard is therefore concerned with each individual cost component that makes up the entire budget.

There are important accounting differences between budgets and standards. Except in the application of manufacturing overhead to jobs and processes, budget data are not journalized in cost accounting systems. In contrast, as we illustrate in the appendix to this chapter, standard costs may be incorporated into cost accounting systems. Also, a company may report its inventories at standard cost in its financial statements, but it would not report inventories at budgeted costs.

> **STUDY OBJECTIVE 1**
> Distinguish between a standard and a budget.

Why Standard Costs?

Standard costs offer a number of advantages to an organization, as shown in Illustration 25-1.

Illustration 25-1
Advantages of standard costs

Advantages of standard costs

Facilitate management planning

Promote greater economy by making employees more "cost-conscious"

Useful in setting selling prices

Contribute to management control by providing basis for evaluation of cost control

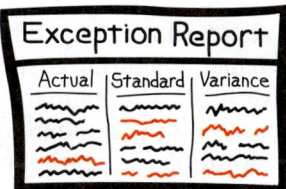
Useful in highlighting variances in management by exception

Simplify costing of inventories and reduce clerical costs

The organization will realize these advantages only when standard costs are carefully established and prudently used. Using standards solely as a way to place blame can have a negative effect on managers and employees. To minimize this effect, many companies offer wage incentives to those who meet the standards.

> **STUDY OBJECTIVE 2**
> Identify the advantages of standard costs.

SETTING STANDARD COSTS—A DIFFICULT TASK

STUDY OBJECTIVE 3
Describe how companies set standards.

The setting of standard costs to produce a unit of product is a difficult task. It requires input from all persons who have responsibility for costs and quantities. To determine the standard cost of direct materials, management consults purchasing agents, product managers, quality control engineers, and production supervisors. In setting the cost standard for direct labor, managers obtain pay rate data from the payroll department. Industrial engineers generally determine the labor time requirements. The managerial accountant provides important input for the standard-setting process by accumulating historical cost data and by knowing how costs respond to changes in activity levels.

To be effective in controlling costs, standard costs need to be current at all times. Thus, standards are under continuous review. They should change whenever managers determine that the existing standard is not a good measure of performance. Circumstances that warrant revision of a standard include changed wage rates resulting from a new union contract, a change in product specifications, or the implementation of a new manufacturing method.

Ideal versus Normal Standards

Companies set standards at one of two levels: ideal or normal. **Ideal standards** represent optimum levels of performance under perfect operating conditions. **Normal standards** represent efficient levels of performance that are attainable under expected operating conditions.

Some managers believe ideal standards will stimulate workers to ever-increasing improvement. However, most managers believe that ideal standards lower the morale of the entire workforce because they are difficult, if not impossible, to meet. Very few companies use ideal standards.

ETHICS NOTE
When standards are set too high, employees sometimes feel pressure to consider unethical practices to meet these standards.

Most companies that use standards set them at a normal level. Properly set, normal standards should be **rigorous but attainable**. Normal standards allow for rest periods, machine breakdowns, and other "normal" contingencies in the production process. In the remainder of this chapter we will assume that standard costs are set at a normal level.

A Case Study

To establish the standard cost of producing a product, it is necessary to establish standards for each manufacturing cost element—direct materials, direct labor, and manufacturing overhead. The standard for each element is derived from the standard price to be paid and the standard quantity to be used.

To illustrate, we look at a case study of how standard costs are set. In this extended example, we assume that Xonic, Inc. wishes to use standard costs to measure performance in filling an order for 1,000 gallons of Weed-O, a liquid weed killer.

DIRECT MATERIALS

The **direct materials price standard** is the cost per unit of direct materials that should be incurred. This standard should be based on the purchasing department's best estimate of the **cost of raw materials**. This cost is frequently based on current purchase prices. The price standard also includes an amount for related costs such as receiving, storing, and handling. The materials price standard per pound of material for Xonic's weed killer is:

Item	Price
Purchase price, net of discounts	$2.70
Freight	0.20
Receiving and handling	0.10
Standard direct materials price per pound	**$3.00**

Illustration 25-2
Setting direct materials price standard

The **direct materials quantity standard** is the quantity of direct materials that should be used per unit of finished goods. This standard is expressed as a physical measure, such as pounds, barrels, or board feet. In setting the standard, management considers both the quality and quantity of materials required to manufacture the product. The standard includes allowances for unavoidable waste and normal spoilage. The standard quantity per unit for Xonic, Inc. is as follows.

Item	Quantity (Pounds)
Required materials	3.5
Allowance for waste	0.4
Allowance for spoilage	0.1
Standard direct materials quantity per unit	**4.0**

Illustration 25-3
Setting direct materials quantity standard

The standard direct materials cost per unit is the standard direct materials price times the standard direct materials quantity. For Xonic, Inc., the standard direct materials cost per gallon of Weed-O is $12.00 ($3.00 × 4.0 pounds).

DIRECT LABOR

The **direct labor price standard** is the rate per hour that should be incurred for direct labor. This standard is based on current wage rates, adjusted for anticipated changes such as cost of living adjustments (COLAs). The price standard also generally includes employer payroll taxes and fringe benefits, such as paid holidays and vacations. For Xonic, Inc., the direct labor price standard is as follows.

ALTERNATIVE TERMINOLOGY

The direct labor price standard is also called the *direct labor rate standard*.

Item	Price
Hourly wage rate	$ 7.50
COLA	0.25
Payroll taxes	0.75
Fringe benefits	1.50
Standard direct labor rate per hour	**$10.00**

Illustration 25-4
Setting direct labor price standard

The **direct labor quantity standard** is the time that should be required to make one unit of the product. This standard is especially critical in labor-intensive companies. Allowances should be made in this standard for rest periods, cleanup, machine setup, and machine downtime. For Xonic, Inc., the direct labor quantity standard is as follows.

ALTERNATIVE TERMINOLOGY

The direct labor quantity standard is also called the *direct labor efficiency standard*.

Item	Quantity (Hours)
Actual production time	1.5
Rest periods and cleanup	0.2
Setup and downtime	0.3
Standard direct labor hours per unit	**2.0**

Illustration 25-5
Setting direct labor quantity standard

The standard direct labor cost per unit is the standard direct labor rate times the standard direct labor hours. For Xonic, Inc., the standard direct labor cost per gallon of Weed-O is $20 ($10.00 × 2.0 hours).

MANUFACTURING OVERHEAD

For manufacturing overhead, companies use a **standard predetermined overhead rate** in setting the standard. This overhead rate is determined by dividing budgeted overhead costs by an expected standard activity index. For example, the index may be standard direct labor hours or standard machine hours.

As discussed in Chapter 21, many companies employ activity-based costing (ABC) to allocate overhead costs. Because ABC uses multiple activity indices to allocate overhead costs, it results in a better correlation between activities and costs incurred than do other methods. As a result, the use of ABC can significantly improve the usefulness of standard costing for management decision making.

Xonic, Inc. uses standard direct labor hours as the activity index. The company expects to produce 13,200 gallons of Weed-O during the year at normal capacity. **Normal capacity** is the average activity output that a company should experience in the long run. Since it takes 2 direct labor hours for each gallon, total standard direct labor hours are 26,400 (13,200 gallons × 2 hours).

At normal capacity of 26,400 direct labor hours, overhead costs are expected to be $132,000. Of that amount, $79,200 are variable and $52,800 are fixed. Illustration 25-6 shows computation of the standard predetermined overhead rates for Xonic, Inc.

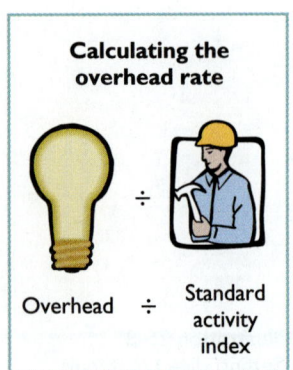

Calculating the overhead rate

Overhead ÷ Standard activity index

Illustration 25-6
Computing predetermined overhead rates

Budgeted Overhead Costs	Amount	÷	Standard Direct Labor Hours	=	Overhead Rate per Direct Labor Hour
Variable	$ 79,200		26,400		$3.00
Fixed	52,800		26,400		2.00
Total	$132,000		26,400		**$5.00**

The standard manufacturing overhead rate per unit is the predetermined overhead rate times the activity index quantity standard. For Xonic, Inc., which uses direct labor hours as its activity index, the standard manufacturing overhead rate per gallon of Weed-O is $10 ($5 × 2 hours).

TOTAL STANDARD COST PER UNIT

After a company has established the standard quantity and price per unit of product, it can determine the total standard cost. The total standard cost per unit is the sum of the standard costs of direct materials, direct labor, and manufacturing overhead. For Xonic, Inc., the total standard cost per gallon of Weed-O is $42, as shown on the following standard cost card.

Illustration 25-7
Standard cost per gallon of Weed-O

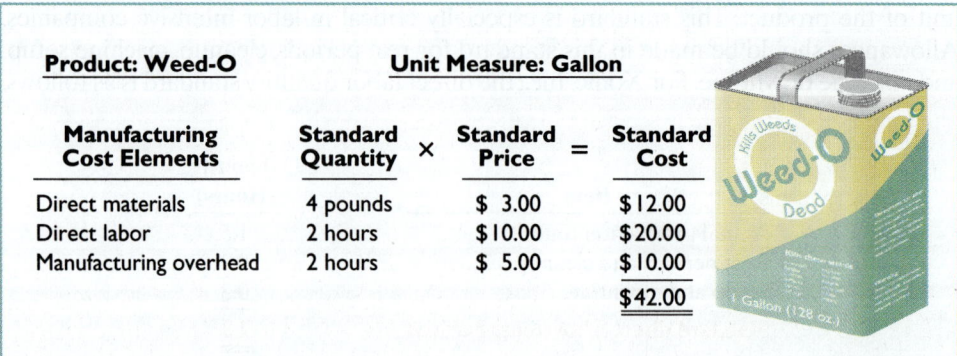

Product: Weed-O   **Unit Measure: Gallon**

Manufacturing Cost Elements	Standard Quantity	×	Standard Price	=	Standard Cost
Direct materials	4 pounds		$ 3.00		$12.00
Direct labor	2 hours		$10.00		$20.00
Manufacturing overhead	2 hours		$ 5.00		$10.00
					$42.00

The company prepares a standard cost card for each product. This card provides the basis for determining variances from standards.

MANAGEMENT INSIGHT

How Can We Make Susan's Chili Profitable?

Setting standards can be difficult. Consider Susan's Chili Factory, which manufactures and sells chili. The cost of manufacturing Susan's chili consists of the costs of raw materials, labor to convert the basic ingredients to chili, and overhead. We will use materials cost as an example. Managers need to develop three standards: (1) What should be the formula (mix) of ingredients for one gallon of chili? (2) What should be the normal wastage (or shrinkage) for the individual ingredients? (3) What should be the standard cost for the individual ingredients that go into the chili?

Susan's Chili Factory also illustrates how managers can use standard costs in controlling costs. Suppose that summer droughts have reduced crop yields. As a result, prices have doubled for beans, onions, and peppers. In this case, actual costs will be significantly higher than standard costs, which will cause management to evaluate the situation. Similarly, assume that poor maintenance caused the onion-dicing blades to become dull. As a result, usage of onions to make a gallon of chili tripled. Because this deviation is quickly highlighted through standard costs, managers can take corrective action promptly.

Source: Adapted from David R. Beran, "Cost Reduction Through Control Reporting," *Management Accounting*, April 1982, pp. 29–33.

 How might management use this raw material cost information?

DO IT!

STANDARD COSTS

Ridette Inc. accumulated the following standard cost data concerning product Cty31.

   Materials per unit: 1.5 pounds at $4 per pound
   Labor per unit: 0.25 hours at $13 per hour.
   Manufacturing overhead: Predetermined rate is 120% of direct labor cost.

Compute the standard cost of one unit of product Cty31.

Solution

Manufacturing Cost Element	Standard Quantity	×	Standard Price	=	Standard Cost
Direct materials	1.5 pounds		$4.00		$6.00
Direct labor	0.25 hours		$13.00		3.25
Manufacturing overhead	120%		$3.25		3.90
Total					$13.15

Related exercise material: **BE25-2, E25-1, E25-2, E25-3,** and **DO IT! 25-1.**

action plan

✔ Know that standard costs are predetermined unit costs.

✔ To establish the standard cost of producing a product, establish the standard for each manufacturing cost element—direct materials, direct labor, and manufacturing overhead.

✔ Compute the standard cost for each element from the standard price to be paid and the standard quantity to be used.

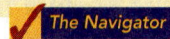

ANALYZING AND REPORTING VARIANCES FROM STANDARDS

ALTERNATIVE TERMINOLOGY

In business, the term *variance* is also used to indicate differences between total budgeted and total actual costs.

One of the major management uses of standard costs is to identify variances from standards. **Variances** are the differences between total actual costs and total standard costs.

To illustrate, we will assume that in producing 1,000 gallons of Weed-O in the month of June, Xonic, Inc. incurred the following costs.

Illustration 25-8
Actual production costs

Direct materials	$13,020
Direct labor	20,580
Variable overhead	6,500
Fixed overhead	4,400
Total actual costs	$44,500

Companies determine total standard costs by multiplying the units produced by the standard cost per unit. The total standard cost of Weed-O is $42,000 (1,000 gallons × $42). Thus, the total variance is $2,500, as shown below.

Illustration 25-9
Computation of total variance

Actual costs	$44,500
Less: Standard costs	42,000
Total variance	**$ 2,500**

Note that the variance is expressed in total dollars, and not on a per unit basis.

When actual costs exceed standard costs, the variance is **unfavorable**. The $2,500 variance in June for Weed-O is unfavorable. An unfavorable variance has a negative connotation. It suggests that the company paid too much for one or more of the manufacturing cost elements or that it used the elements inefficiently.

If actual costs are less than standard costs, the variance is **favorable**. A favorable variance has a positive connotation. It suggests efficiencies in incurring manufacturing costs and in using direct materials, direct labor, and manufacturing overhead.

However, be careful: A favorable variance could be obtained by using inferior materials. In printing wedding invitations, for example, a favorable variance could result from using an inferior grade of paper. Or, a favorable variance might be achieved in installing tires on an automobile assembly line by tightening only half of the lug bolts. A variance is not favorable if the company has sacrificed quality control standards.

Direct Materials Variances

STUDY OBJECTIVE 4
State the formulas for determining direct materials and direct labor variances.

In completing the order for 1,000 gallons of Weed-O, Xonic used 4,200 pounds of direct materials. These were purchased at a cost of $3.10 per unit. The **total materials variance** is computed from the following formula.

Illustration 25-10
Formula for total materials variance

Actual Quantity × Actual Price (AQ) × (AP)	−	Standard Quantity × Standard Price (SQ) × (SP)	=	Total Materials Variance (TMV)

For Xonic, Inc., the total materials variance is $1,020 ($13,020 − $12,000) unfavorable, as shown below.

$$(4{,}200 \times \$3.10) - (4{,}000 \times \$3.00) = \$1{,}020 \text{ U}$$

Next, the company analyzes the total variance to determine the amount attributable to price (costs) and to quantity (use). The **materials price variance** is computed from the following formula.[1]

Actual Quantity × Actual Price (AQ) × (AP)	−	Actual Quantity × Standard Price (AQ) × (SP)	=	Materials Price Variance (MPV)

Illustration 25-11
Formula for materials price variance

For Xonic, Inc., the materials price variance is $420 ($13,020 − $12,600) unfavorable, as shown below.

$$(4{,}200 \times \$3.10) - (4{,}200 \times \$3.00) = \$420 \text{ U}$$

The price variance can also be computed by multiplying the actual quantity purchased by the difference between the actual and standard price per unit. The computation in this case is 4,200 × ($3.10 − $3.00) = $420 U.

The **materials quantity variance** is determined from the following formula.

HELPFUL HINT
The alternative formula is:
$$\boxed{AQ} \times \boxed{AP - SP} = \boxed{MPV}$$

Actual Quantity × Standard Price (AQ) × (SP)	−	Standard Quantity × Standard Price (SQ) × (SP)	=	Materials Quantity Variance (MQV)

Illustration 25-12
Formula for materials quantity variance

For Xonic, Inc., the materials quantity variance is $600 ($12,600 − $12,000) unfavorable, as shown below.

$$(4{,}200 \times \$3.00) - (4{,}000 \times \$3.00) = \$600 \text{ U}$$

The price variance can also be computed by applying the standard price to the difference between actual and standard quantities used. The computation in this example is $3.00 × (4,200 − 4,000) = $600 U.

The total materials variance of $1,020 U, therefore, consists of the following.

HELPFUL HINT
The alternative formula is:
$$\boxed{SP} \times \boxed{AQ - SQ} = \boxed{MQV}$$

Materials price variance	$ 420 U
Materials quantity variance	600 U
Total materials variance	**$1,020 U**

Illustration 25-13
Summary of materials variances

Companies sometimes use a matrix to analyze a variance. **When the matrix is used, a company computes the formulas for each cost element first and then computes the variances.** Illustration 25-14 (page 1118) shows the completed matrix for the direct materials variance for Xonic, Inc. The matrix provides a convenient structure for determining each variance.

---

[1] We will assume that all materials purchased during the period are used in production and that no units remain in inventory at the end of the period.

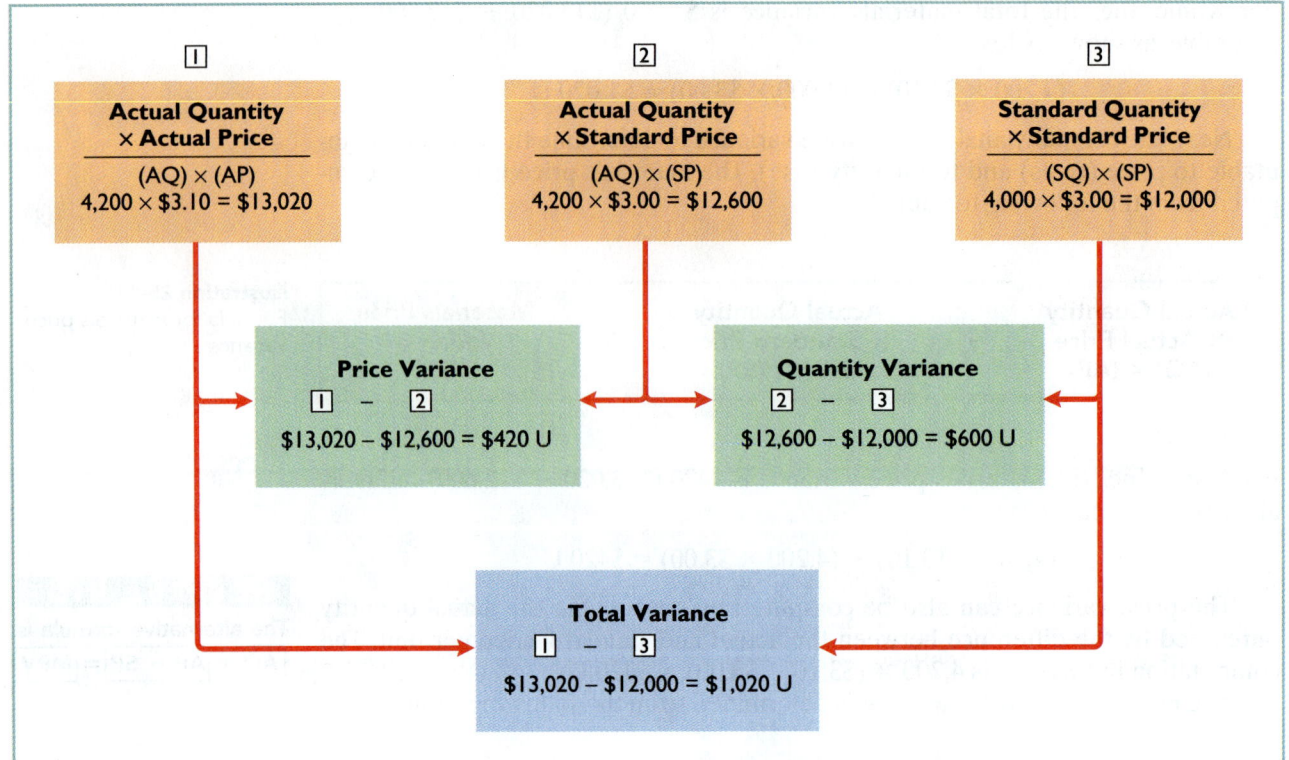

Illustration 25-14
Matrix for direct materials variances

CAUSES OF MATERIALS VARIANCES

What are the causes of a variance? The causes may relate to both internal and external factors. The investigation of a **materials price variance usually begins in the purchasing department**. Many factors affect the price paid for raw materials. These include availability of quantity and cash discounts, the quality of the materials requested, and the delivery method used. To the extent that these factors are considered in setting the price standard, the purchasing department is responsible for any variances.

However, a variance may be beyond the control of the purchasing department. Sometimes, for example, prices may rise faster than expected. Moreover, actions by groups over which the company has no control, such as the OPEC nations' oil price increases, may cause an unfavorable variance. There are also times when a production department may be responsible for the price variance. This may occur when a rush order forces the company to pay a higher price for the materials.

The starting point for determining the cause(s) of an unfavorable **materials quantity variance is in the production department**. If the variances are due to inexperienced workers, faulty machinery, or carelessness, the production department is responsible. However, if the materials obtained by the purchasing department were of inferior quality, then the purchasing department is responsible.

DO IT!

MATERIALS VARIANCES

The standard cost of Product XX includes two units of direct materials at $8.00 per unit. During July, the company buys 22,000 units of direct materials at $7.50 and uses those materials to produce 10,000 units. Compute the total, price, and quantity variances for materials.

Solution
Substituting amounts into the formulas, the variances are:

Total materials variance = (22,000 × $7.50) − (20,000 × $8.00) = $5,000 unfavorable.

Materials price variance = (22,000 × $7.50) − (22,000 × $8.00) = $11,000 favorable.

Materials quantity variance = (22,000 × $8.00) − (20,000 × $8.00) = $16,000 unfavorable.

Related exercise material: **BE25-4, E25-5,** and **DO IT! E25-2.**

action plan
✔ Use the formulas for computing each of the materials variances:

Total materials variance = (AQ × AP) − (SQ × SP)

Materials price variance = (AQ × AP) − (AQ × SP)

Materials quantity variance = (AQ × SP) − (SQ × SP)

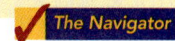

Direct Labor Variances

The process of determining direct labor variances is the same as for determining the direct materials variances. In completing the Weed-O order, Xonic, Inc. incurred 2,100 direct labor hours at an average hourly rate of $9.80. The standard hours allowed for the units produced were 2,000 hours (1,000 gallons × 2 hours). The standard labor rate was $10 per hour. The **total labor variance** is computed from the following formula.

| Actual Hours × Actual Rate (AH) × (AR) | − | Standard Hours × Standard Rate (SH) × (SR) | = | Total Labor Variance (TLV) |

Illustration 25-15 Formula for total labor variance

The total labor variance is $580 ($20,580 − $20,000) unfavorable, as shown below.

(2,100 × $9.80) − (2,000 × $10.00) = $580 U

The formula for the **labor price variance** is as follows.

| Actual Hours × Actual Rate (AH) × (AR) | − | Actual Hours × Standard Rate (AH) × (SR) | = | Labor Price Variance (LPV) |

Illustration 25-16 Formula for labor price variance

For Xonic, Inc., the labor price variance is $420 ($20,580 − $21,000) favorable, as shown below.

(2,100 × $9.80) − (2,100 × $10.00) = $420 F

The labor price variance can also be computed by multiplying actual hours worked by the difference between the actual pay rate and the standard pay rate. The computation in this example is 2,100 × ($10.00 − $9.80) = $420 F.

The **labor quantity variance** is derived from the following formula.

HELPFUL HINT
The alternative formula is:
AH × |AR − SR| = LPV

| Actual Hours × Standard Rate (AH) × (SR) | − | Standard Hours × Standard Rate (SH) × (SR) | = | Labor Quantity Variance (LQV) |

Illustration 25-17 Formula for labor quantity variance

For Xonic, Inc., the labor quantity variance is $1,000 ($21,000 − $20,000) unfavorable:

$$(2,100 \times \$10.00) - (2,000 \times \$10.00) = \$1,000 \ U$$

HELPFUL HINT
The alternative formula is:
$$SR \times |AH - SH| = LQV$$

The same result can be obtained by multiplying the standard rate by the difference between actual hours worked and standard hours allowed. In this case the computation is $10.00 × (2,100 − 2,000) = $1,000 U.

The total direct labor variance of $580 U, therefore, consists of:

Illustration 25-18
Summary of labor variances

Labor price variance	$ 420 F
Labor quantity variance	1,000 U
Total direct labor variance	**$ 580 U**

These results can also be obtained from the matrix in Illustration 25-19.

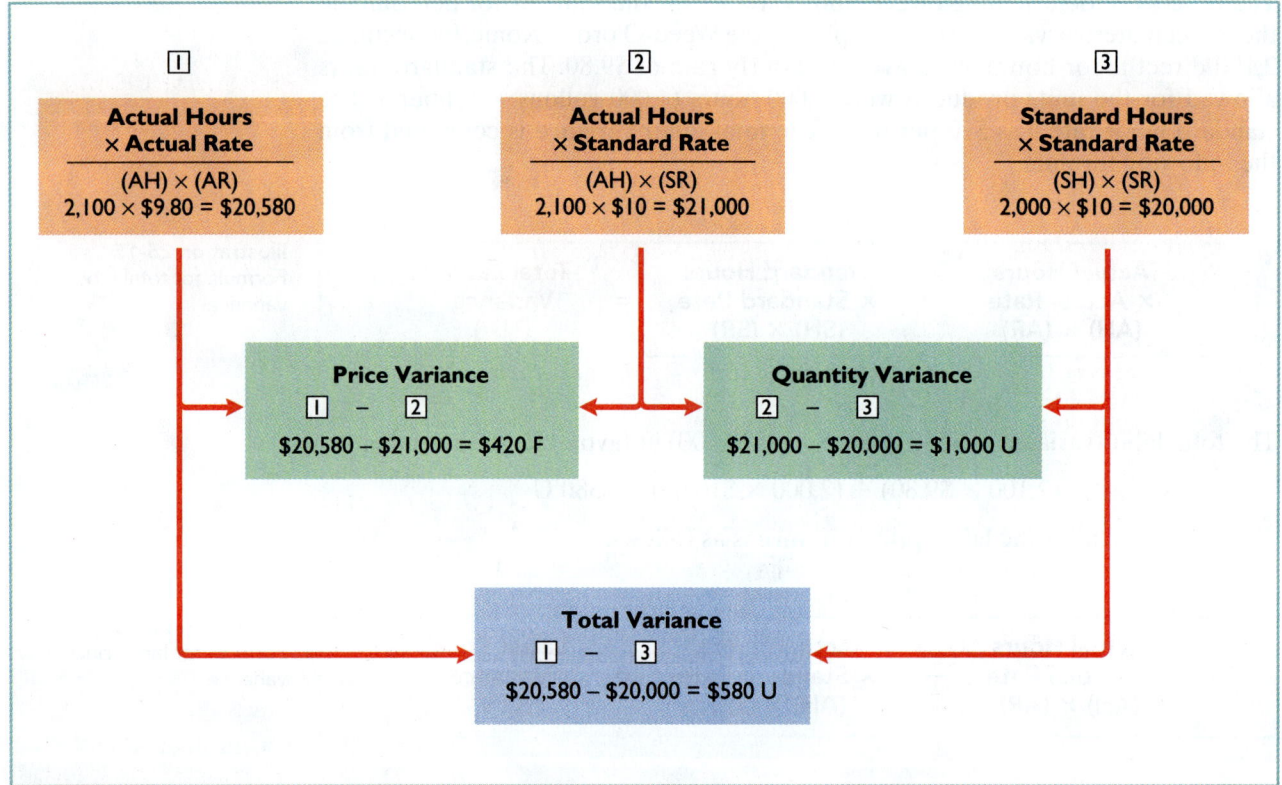

Illustration 25-19
Matrix for direct labor variances

CAUSES OF LABOR VARIANCES

Labor price variances usually result from two factors: (1) paying workers **higher wages than expected**, and (2) **misallocation of workers**. In companies where pay rates are determined by union contracts, labor price variances should be infrequent. When workers are not unionized, there is a much higher likelihood of such variances. The responsibility for these variances rests with the manager who authorized the wage increase.

Misallocation of the workforce refers to using skilled workers in place of unskilled workers and vice versa. The use of an inexperienced worker instead of an experienced one will result in a favorable price variance because of the lower pay rate of the unskilled worker. An unfavorable price variance would result if a skilled worker were substituted for an inexperienced one. The production department generally is responsible for labor price variances resulting from misallocation of the workforce.

Labor quantity variances relate to the **efficiency of workers**. The cause of a quantity variance generally can be traced to the production department. The causes of an unfavorable variance may be poor training, worker fatigue, faulty machinery, or carelessness. These causes are the responsibility of the **production department**. However, if the excess time is due to inferior materials, the responsibility falls outside the production department.

Manufacturing Overhead Variance

The **total overhead variance** is the difference between the actual overhead costs and overhead costs applied based on standard hours allowed. As indicated in Illustration 25-8, Xonic incurred overhead costs of $10,900 ($6,500 + $4,400) to produce 1,000 gallons of Weed-O in June. The computation of the actual overhead is comprised of a variable and a fixed component. Illustration 25-20 shows this computation.

> **STUDY OBJECTIVE 5**
> State the formula for determining the total manufacturing overhead variance.

Variable overhead	$ 6,500
Fixed overhead	4,400
Total actual overhead	**$10,900**

Illustration 25-20
Actual overhead costs

We then determine the overhead costs applied based on standard hours allowed times the predetermined overhead rate. **Standard hours allowed** are the hours that *should* have been worked for the units produced. Because it takes two hours of direct labor to produce one gallon of Weed-O, for the 1,000-gallon Weed-O order, the standard hours allowed are 2,000 hours (1,000 gallons × 2 hours). We then apply the predetermined overhead rate to the 2,000 standard hours allowed.

The predetermined rate for Weed-O is $5, comprised of a variable overhead rate of $3 and a fixed rate of $2. Recall from Illustration 25-6 that the amount of budgeted overhead costs at normal capacity of $132,000 was divided by normal capacity of 26,400 direct labor hours, to arrive at a predetermined overhead rate of $5 ($132,000 ÷ 26,400). The predetermined rate of $5 is then multiplied by the 2,000 standard hours allowed, to determine the overhead costs applied.

Illustration 25-21 shows the formula for the total overhead variance and the calculation for Xonic, Inc. for the month of June.

Actual Overhead	−	Overhead Applied*	=	Total Overhead Variance
$10,900 ($6,500 + $4,400)	−	$10,000 ($5 × 2,000 hours)	=	$900 U

*Based on standard hours allowed.

Illustration 25-21
Formula for total overhead variance

Thus, for Xonic, Inc. the total overhead variance is $900 unfavorable.

The overhead variance is generally analyzed through a price and quantity variance. The name usually given to the price variance is the **overhead controllable variance**; the quantity variance is referred to as the **overhead volume variance**. Appendix 25B discusses how the total overhead volume variance can be broken down into these two variances.

CAUSES OF MANUFACTURING OVERHEAD VARIANCES

One reason for an overhead variance relates to over- or under-spending on overhead items. For example, overhead may include indirect labor for which a company paid wages higher than the standard labor price allowed. Or the price of electricity to run the company's machines increased, and the company did not anticipate this additional cost. Companies should investigate any spending variances, to determine whether they will continue in the future. Generally, the responsibility for these variances rests with the production department.

The overhead variance can also result from the inefficient use of overhead. For example, because of poor maintenance, a number of the manufacturing machines are experiencing breakdowns on a consistent basis, leading to reduced production. Or the flow of materials through the production process is impeded because of a lack of skilled labor to perform the necessary production tasks, due to a lack of planning. In both of these cases, the production department is responsible for the cause of these variances. On the other hand, overhead can also be underutilized because of a lack of sales orders. When the cause is a lack of sales orders, the responsibility rests outside the production department.

DO IT!

LABOR AND MANUFACTURING OVERHEAD VARIANCES

The standard cost of Product YY includes 3 hours of direct labor at $12.00 per hour. The predetermind overhead rate is $20.00 per direct labor hour. During July, the company incurred 3,500 hours of direct labor at an average rate of $12.40 per hour and $71,300 of manufacturing overhead costs. It produced 1,200 units.

(a) Compute the total, price, and quantity variances for labor. **(b)** Compute the total overhead variance.

action plan

✔ Use the formulas for computing each of the variances:

Total labor variance = (AH × AR) − (SH × SR)

Labor price variance = (AH × AR) − (AH × SR)

Labor quantity variance = (AH × SR) − (SH × SR)

Total overhead variance = Actual overhead − Overhead applied*

*Based on standard hours allowed.

Solution

Substituting amounts into the formulas, the variances are:

Total labor variance = (3,500 × $12.40) − (3,600 × $12.00) = $200 Unfavorable
Labor price variance = (3,500 × $12.40) − (3,500 × $12.00) = $1,400 Unfavorable
Labor quantity variance = (3,500 × $12.00) − (3,600 × $12.00) = $1,200 Favorable
Total overhead variance = $71,300 − $72,000* = $700 Favorable

*3,600 hours × $20.00

Related exercise material: **BE25-5, BE25-6, E25-4, E25-6, E25-7, E25-8, E25-10, E25-11,** and **DO IT! 25-3.**

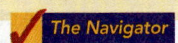

Reporting Variances

STUDY OBJECTIVE 6
Discuss the reporting of variances.

All variances should be reported to appropriate levels of management as soon as possible. The sooner managers are informed, the sooner they can evaluate problems and take corrective action.

The form, content, and frequency of variance reports vary considerably among companies. One approach is to prepare a weekly report for each department that has primary responsibility for cost control. Under this approach, materials price variances are reported to the purchasing department, and all other variances are reported to the production department that did the work. Illustration 25-22 is a materials price variance report for Xonic, Inc., with the materials for the Weed-O order listed first.

XONIC, INC.
Variance Report — Purchasing Department
For Week Ended June 8, 2010

Type of Materials	Quantity Purchased	Actual Price	Standard Price	Price Variance	Explanation
X100	4,200 lbs.	$3.10	$3.00	$420 U	Rush order
X142	1,200 units	2.75	2.80	60 F	Quantity discount
A85	600 doz.	5.20	5.10	60 U	Regular supplier on strike
Total price variance				**$420 U**	

Illustration 25-22
Materials price variance report

The explanation column is completed after consultation with the purchasing department manager.

Variance reports facilitate the principle of "management by exception" explained in Chapter 24. For example, the vice president of purchasing can use the report shown above to evaluate the effectiveness of the purchasing department manager. Or, the vice president of production can use production department variance reports to determine how well each production manager is controlling costs. In using variance reports, top management normally looks for **significant variances**. These may be judged on the basis of some quantitative measure, such as more than 10% of the standard or more than $1,000.

Statement Presentation of Variances

In income statements **prepared for management** under a standard cost accounting system, **cost of goods sold is stated at standard cost and the variances are disclosed separately**. Illustration 25-23 shows this format. Based entirely on the production and sale of Weed-O, it assumes selling and administrative costs of $3,000. Observe that each variance is shown, as well as the total net variance. In this example, variations from standard costs reduced net income by $2,500.

STUDY OBJECTIVE 7
Prepare an income statement for management under a standard costing system.

XONIC, INC.
Income Statement
For the Month Ended June 30, 2010

Sales		$60,000
Cost of goods sold (at standard)		42,000
Gross profit (at standard)		18,000
Variances		
Materials price	$ 420	
Materials quantity	600	
Labor price	(420)	
Labor quantity	1,000	
Overhead variance	900	
Total variance unfavorable		2,500
Gross profit (actual)		15,500
Selling and administrative expenses		3,000
Net income		$12,500

Illustration 25-23
Variances in income statement for management

1124 Chapter 25 Standard Costs and Balanced Scorecard

Standard costs may be used in financial statements prepared for stockholders and other external users. The costing of inventories at standard costs is in accordance with generally accepted accounting principles when there are no significant differences between actual costs and standard costs. Hewlett-Packard and Jostens, Inc., for example, report their inventories at standard costs. However, if there are significant differences between actual and standard costs, the financial statements must report inventories and cost of goods sold at actual costs.

It is also possible to show the variances in an income statement prepared in the variable costing (CVP) format. To do so, it is necessary to analyze the overhead variances into variable and fixed components. This type of analysis is explained in cost accounting textbooks.

BALANCED SCORECARD

STUDY OBJECTIVE 8
Describe the balanced scorecard approach to performance evaluation.

Financial measures (measurement of dollars), such as variance analysis and return on investment (ROI), are useful tools for evaluating performance. However, many companies now supplement these financial measures with nonfinancial measures to better assess performance and anticipate future results. For example, airlines, like Delta, American, and United, use capacity utilization as an important measure to understand and predict future performance. Newspaper publishers, such as the *New York Times* and the *Chicago Tribune*, use circulation figures as another measure by which to assess performance. Illustration 25-24 lists some key nonfinancial measures used in various industries.

Illustration 25-24
Nonfinancial measures used in various industries

Industry	Measure
Automobiles	Capacity utilization of plants. Average age of key assets. Impact of strikes. Brand-loyalty statistics.
Computer Systems	Market profile of customer end-products. Number of new products. Employee stock ownership percentages. Number of scientists and technicians used in R&D.
Chemicals	Customer satisfaction data. Factors affecting customer product selection. Number of patents and trademarks held. Customer brand awareness.
Regional Banks	Number of ATMs by state. Number of products used by average customer. Percentage of customer service calls handled by interactive voice response units. Personnel cost per employee. Credit card retention rates.

Source: Financial Accounting Standards Board, *Business Reporting: Insights into Enhancing Voluntary Disclosures* (Norwalk, Conn.: FASB, 2001).

Most companies recognize that both financial and nonfinancial measures can provide useful insights into what is happening in the company. As a result, many companies now use a broad-based measurement approach, called the **balanced scorecard**, to evaluate performance. The balanced scorecard incorporates financial and nonfinancial measures in an integrated system that links performance measurement and a company's strategic goals. Nearly 50% of the largest companies in the United States including Unilever, Chase, and Wal-Mart, are using the balanced scorecard approach.

The balanced scorecard evaluates company performance from a series of "perspectives." The four most commonly employed perspectives are as follows.

1. The financial perspective is the most traditional view of the company. It employs financial measures of performance used by most firms.

2. The customer perspective evaluates how well the company is performing from the viewpoint of those people who buy and use its products or services. This view measures how well the company compares to competitors in terms of price, quality, product innovation, customer service, and other dimensions.

3. The internal process perspective evaluates the internal operating processes critical to success. All critical aspects of the value chain—including product development, production, delivery and after-sale service—are evaluated to ensure that the company is operating effectively and efficiently.

4. The learning and growth perspective evaluates how well the company develops and retains its employees. This would include evaluation of such things as employee skills, employee satisfaction, training programs, and information dissemination.

Within each perspective, the balanced scorecard identifies objectives that will contribute to attainment of strategic goals. Illustration 25-25 shows examples of objectives within each perspective.

Financial perspective
Return on assets
Net income
Credit rating
Share price
Profit per employee

Customer perspective
Percentage of customers who would recommend product
Customer retention
Response time per customer request
Brand recognition
Customer service expense per customer

Internal process perspective
Percentage of defect-free products
Stockouts
Labor utilization rates
Waste reduction
Planning accuracy

Learning and growth perspective
Percentage of employees leaving in less than one year
Number of cross-trained employees
Ethics violations
Training hours
Reportable accidents

Illustration 25-25
Examples of objectives within the four perspectives of balanced scorecard

The objectives are linked across perspectives in order to tie performance measurement to company goals. The financial objectives are normally set first, and then objectives are set in the other perspectives in order to accomplish the financial objectives.

For example, within the financial perspective, a common goal is to increase profit per dollars invested as measured by ROI. In order to increase ROI, a customer-perspective objective might be to increase customer satisfaction as measured by the percentage of customers who would recommend the product to a friend. In order to increase customer satisfaction, an internal business process perspective objective might be to increase product quality as measured by the percentage of defect-free units. Finally, in order to increase the percentage of defect-free units, the learning and growth perspective objective might be to reduce factory employee turnover as measured by the percentage of employees leaving in under one year. Illustration 25-26 illustrates this linkage across perspectives.

Illustration 25-26
Linked process across balanced scorecard perspectives

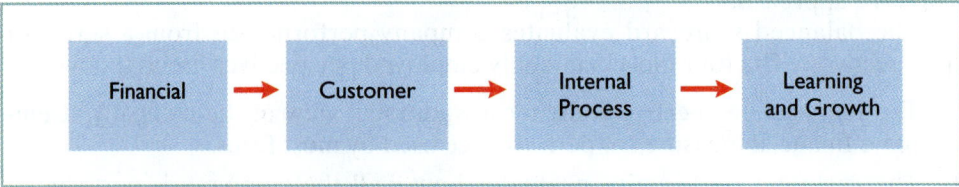

Through this linked process, the company can better understand how to achieve its goals and what measures to use to evaluate performance. In summary, the balanced scorecard does the following:

1. Employs both financial and nonfinancial measures. (For example, ROI is a financial measure; employee turnover is a nonfinancial measure.)
2. Creates linkages so that high-level corporate goals can be communicated all the way down to the shop floor.
3. Provides measurable objectives for such nonfinancial measures as product quality, rather than vague statements such as "We would like to improve quality."
4. Integrates all of the company's goals into a single performance measurement system, so that an inappropriate amount of weight will not be placed on any single goal.

ACCOUNTING ACROSS THE ORGANIZATION

It May Be Time to Fly United Again

Many of the benefits of a balanced scorecard approach are evident in the improved operations at United Airlines. At the time it filed for bankruptcy in 2002, United had a reputation for some of the worst service in the airline business. But when Glenn Tilton took over as United's Chief Executive Officer in September 2002, he recognized that things had to change.

One thing he did was to implement an incentive program that allows all of United's 63,000 employees to earn a bonus of 2.5% or more of their wages if the company "exceeds its goals for on-time flight departures and for customer intent to fly United again." Since instituting this program the company's on-time departures are among the best, its customer complaints have been reduced considerably, and its number of customers who say that they would fly United again is at its highest level ever. While none of these things guarantees that United will survive (given the substantial increase in oil prices), these improvements certainly increase its chances.

Source: Susan Carey, "Friendlier Skies: In Bankruptcy, United Airlines Forges a Path to Better Service," *Wall Street Journal*, June 15, 2004.

 Which of the perspectives of a balanced scorecard were the focus of United's CEO?

DO IT!

Indicate which of the four perspectives in the balanced scorecard is most likely associated with the objectives that follow.

BALANCED SCORECARD

1. Percentage of repeat customers.
2. Number of suggestions for improvement from employees.
3. Contribution margin.
4. Market share.
5. Number of cross-trained employees.
6. Amount of setup time.

action plan

✔ The financial perspective employs traditional financial measures of performance.
✔ The customer perspective evaluates company performance as seen by the people who buy its products or services.
✔ The internal process perspective evaluates the internal operating processes critical to success.
✔ The learning and growth perspective evaluates how well the company develops and retains its employees.

Solution

1. Customer perspective.
2. Learning and growth perspective.
3. Financial perspective.
4. Customer perspective.
5. Learning and growth perspective.
6. Internal process perspective.

Related exercise material: **BE25-7**, **E25-16**, and **DO IT!** **25-4**.

Comprehensive DO IT!

Manlow Company makes a cologne called Allure. The standard cost for one bottle of Allure is as follows.

Manufacturing Cost Elements	Quantity	×	Standard Price	=	Cost
Direct materials	6 oz.	×	$ 0.90	=	$ 5.40
Direct labor	0.5 hrs.	×	$12.00	=	6.00
Manufacturing overhead	0.5 hrs.	×	$ 4.80	=	2.40
					$13.80

During the month, the following transactions occurred in manufacturing 10,000 bottles of Allure.

1. 58,000 ounces of materials were purchased at $1.00 per ounce.
2. All the materials purchased were used to produce the 10,000 bottles of Allure.
3. 4,900 direct labor hours were worked at a total labor cost of $56,350.
4. Variable manufacturing overhead incurred was $15,000 and fixed overhead incurred was $10,400.

The manufacturing overhead rate of $4.80 is based on a normal capacity of 5,200 direct labor hours. The total budget at this capacity is $10,400 fixed and $14,560 variable.

Instructions

(a) Compute the total variance and the price and quantity variances for direct material and direct labor elements.
(b) Compute the total variance for manufacturing overhead.

1128 Chapter 25 Standard Costs and Balanced Scorecard

action plan

✔ Check to make sure the total variance and the sum of the individual variances are equal.

✔ Find the price variance first, then the quantity variance.

✔ Base overhead applied on standard hours allowed.

✔ Ignore actual hours worked in computing overhead variance.

Solution to Comprehensive DO IT!

(a)

Total Variance

Actual costs incurred	
Direct materials	$ 58,000
Direct labor	56,350
Manufacturing overhead	25,400
	139,750
Standard cost (10,000 × $13.80)	138,000
Total variance	$ 1,750 U

Direct Materials Variances

Total	=	$58,000 (58,000 × $1.00)	−	$54,000 (60,000 × $0.90)	= $4,000 U
Price	=	$58,000 (58,000 × $1.00)	−	$52,200 (58,000 × $0.90)	= $5,800 U
Quantity	=	$52,200 (58,000 × $0.90)	−	$54,000 (60,000 × $0.90)	= $1,800 F

Direct Labor Variances

Total	=	$56,350 (4,900 × $11.50)	−	$60,000 (5,000 × $12.00)	= $3,650 F
Price	=	$56,350 (4,900 × $11.50)	−	$58,800 (4,900 × $12.00)	= $2,450 F
Quantity	=	$58,800 (4,900 × $12.00)	−	$60,000 (5,000 × $12.00)	= $1,200 F

(b)

Overhead Variance

Total	=	$25,400 ($15,000 + $10,400)	−	$24,000 (5,000 × $4.80)	= $ 1,400 U

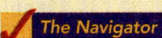

SUMMARY OF STUDY OBJECTIVES

1 Distinguish between a standard and a budget. Both standards and budgets are predetermined costs. The primary difference is that a standard is a unit amount, whereas a budget is a total amount. A standard may be regarded as the budgeted cost per unit of product.

2 Identify the advantages of standard costs. Standard costs offer a number of advantages. They (a) facilitate management planning, (b) promote greater economy, (c) are useful in setting selling prices, (d) contribute to management control, (e) permit "management by exception," and (f) simplify the costing of inventories and reduce clerical costs.

3 Describe how companies set standards. The direct materials price standard should be based on the delivered cost of raw materials plus an allowance for receiving and handling. The direct materials quantity standard should establish the required quantity plus an allowance for waste and spoilage.

The direct labor price standard should be based on current wage rates and anticipated adjustments such as COLAs. It also generally includes payroll taxes and fringe benefits. Direct labor quantity standards should be based on required production time plus an allowance for rest periods, cleanup, machine setup, and machine downtime.

For manufacturing overhead, a standard predetermined overhead rate is used. It is based on an expected standard activity index such as standard direct labor hours or standard machine hours.

4 **State the formulas for determining direct materials and direct labor variances.** The formulas for the direct materials variances are:

$$\begin{pmatrix} \text{Actual quantity} \\ \times \text{ Actual price} \end{pmatrix} - \begin{pmatrix} \text{Standard quantity} \\ \times \text{ Standard price} \end{pmatrix} = \begin{matrix} \text{Total} \\ \text{materials} \\ \text{variance} \end{matrix}$$

$$\begin{pmatrix} \text{Actual quantity} \\ \times \text{ Actual price} \end{pmatrix} - \begin{pmatrix} \text{Actual quantity} \\ \times \text{ Standard price} \end{pmatrix} = \begin{matrix} \text{Materials} \\ \text{price} \\ \text{variance} \end{matrix}$$

$$\begin{pmatrix} \text{Actual quantity} \\ \times \text{ Standard price} \end{pmatrix} - \begin{pmatrix} \text{Standard quantity} \\ \times \text{ Standard price} \end{pmatrix} = \begin{matrix} \text{Materials} \\ \text{quantity} \\ \text{variance} \end{matrix}$$

The formulas for the direct labor variances are:

$$\begin{pmatrix} \text{Actual hours} \\ \times \text{ Actual rate} \end{pmatrix} - \begin{pmatrix} \text{Standard hours} \\ \times \text{ Standard rate} \end{pmatrix} = \begin{matrix} \text{Total} \\ \text{labor} \\ \text{variance} \end{matrix}$$

$$\begin{pmatrix} \text{Actual hours} \\ \times \text{ Actual rate} \end{pmatrix} - \begin{pmatrix} \text{Actual hours} \\ \times \text{ Standard rate} \end{pmatrix} = \begin{matrix} \text{Labor} \\ \text{price} \\ \text{variance} \end{matrix}$$

$$\begin{pmatrix} \text{Actual hours} \\ \times \text{ Standard rate} \end{pmatrix} - \begin{pmatrix} \text{Standard hours} \\ \times \text{ Standard rate} \end{pmatrix} = \begin{matrix} \text{Labor} \\ \text{quantity} \\ \text{variance} \end{matrix}$$

5 **State the formula for determining the total manufacturing overhead variance.** The formula for the total manufacturing overhead variance is:

$$\begin{pmatrix} \text{Actual} \\ \text{overhead} \end{pmatrix} - \begin{pmatrix} \text{Overhead} \\ \text{applied at} \\ \text{standard} \\ \text{hours} \\ \text{allowed} \end{pmatrix} = \begin{matrix} \text{Total overhead} \\ \text{variance} \end{matrix}$$

6 **Discuss the reporting of variances.** Variances are reported to management in variance reports. The reports facilitate management by exception by highlighting significant differences.

7 **Prepare an income statement for management under a standard costing system.** Under a standard costing system, an income statement prepared for management will report cost of goods sold at standard cost and then disclose each variance separately.

8 **Describe the balanced scorecard approach to performance evaluation.** The balanced scorecard incorporates financial and nonfinancial measures in an integrated system that links performance measurement and a company's strategic goals. It employs four perspectives: financial, customer, internal processes, and learning and growth. Objectives are set within each of these perspectives that link to objectives within the other perspectives.

GLOSSARY

Balanced scorecard An approach that incorporates financial and nonfinancial measures in an integrated system that links performance measurement and a company's strategic goals. (p. 1125)

Customer perspective A viewpoint employed in the balanced scorecard to evaluate the company from the perspective of those people who buy and use its products or services. (p. 1125)

Direct labor price standard The rate per hour that should be incurred for direct labor. (p. 1113)

Direct labor quantity standard The time that should be required to make one unit of product. (p. 1113)

Direct materials price standard The cost per unit of direct materials that should be incurred. (p. 1112)

Direct materials quantity standard The quantity of direct materials that should be used per unit of finished goods. (p. 1113)

Financial perspective A viewpoint employed in the balanced scorecard to evaluate a company's performance using financial measures. (p. 1125)

Ideal standards Standards based on the optimum level of performance under perfect operating conditions. (p. 1112)

Internal process perspective A viewpoint employed in the balanced scorecard to evaluate the effectiveness and efficiency of a company's value chain, including product development, production, delivery, and after-sale service. (p. 1125)

Labor price variance The difference between the actual hours times the actual rate and the actual hours times the standard rate for labor. (p. 1119)

Labor quantity variance The difference between actual hours times the standard rate and standard hours times the standard rate for labor. (p. 1119)

Learning and growth perspective A viewpoint employed in the balanced scorecard to evaluate how well a company develops and retains its employees. (p. 1125)

Materials price variance The difference between the actual quantity times the actual price and the actual quantity times the standard price for materials. (p. 1117)

Materials quantity variance The difference between the actual quantity times the standard price and the standard quantity times the standard price for materials. (p. 1117)

Normal capacity The average activity output that a company should experience over the long run. (p. 1114)

Normal standards Standards based on an efficient level of performance that are attainable under expected operating conditions. (p. 1112)

Standard costs Predetermined unit costs which companies use as measures of performance. (p. 1110)

1130 Chapter 25 Standard Costs and Balanced Scorecard

Standard hours allowed The hours that should have been worked for the units produced. (p. 1121)

Standard predetermined overhead rate An overhead rate determined by dividing budgeted overhead costs by an expected standard activity index. (p. 1114)

Total labor variance The difference between actual hours times the actual rate and standard hours times the standard rate for labor. (p. 1119)

Total materials variance The difference between the actual quantity times the actual price and the standard quantity times the standard price of materials. (p. 1116)

Total overhead variance The difference between actual overhead costs and overhead costs applied to work done. (p.1121)

Variances The difference between total actual costs and total standard costs. (p. 1116)

APPENDIX 25A Standard Cost Accounting System

STUDY OBJECTIVE 9
Identify the features of a standard cost accounting system.

A **standard cost accounting system** is a double-entry system of accounting. In this system, companies use standard costs in making entries, and they formally recognize variances in the accounts. Companies may use a standard cost system with either job order or process costing.

In this appendix, we will explain and illustrate a **standard cost, job order cost accounting system**. The system is based on two important assumptions:

(1) Variances from standards are recognized at the earliest opportunity.
(2) The Work in Process account is maintained exclusively on the basis of standard costs.

In practice, there are many variations among standard cost systems. The system described here should prepare you for systems you see in the "real world."

Journal Entries

We will use the transactions of Xonic, Inc. to illustrate the journal entries. Note as you study the entries that the major difference between the entries here and those for the job order cost accounting system in Chapter 20 is the **variance accounts**.

1. Purchase raw materials on account for $13,020 when the standard cost is $12,600.

Raw Materials Inventory	12,600	
Materials Price Variance	420	
Accounts Payable		13,020
(To record purchase of materials)		

   Xonic debits the inventory account for actual quantities at standard cost. This enables the perpetual materials records to show actual quantities. Xonic debits the price variance, which is unfavorable, to Materials Price Variance.

2. Incur direct labor costs of $20,580 when the standard labor cost is $21,000.

Factory Labor	21,000	
Labor Price Variance		420
Wages Payable		20,580
(To record direct labor costs)		

   Like the raw materials inventory account, Xonic debits Factory Labor for actual hours worked at the standard hourly rate of pay. In this case, the labor variance is favorable. Thus, Xonic credits Labor Price Variance.

3. Incur actual manufacturing overhead costs of $10,900.

Manufacturing Overhead	10,900	
Accounts Payable/Cash/Acc. Depreciation		10,900
(To record overhead incurred)		

The controllable overhead variance is not recorded at this time. It depends on standard hours applied to work in process. This amount is not known at the time overhead is incurred.

4. Issue raw materials for production at a cost of $12,600 when the standard cost is $12,000.

Work in Process Inventory	12,000	
Materials Quantity Variance	600	
Raw Materials Inventory		12,600
(To record issuance of raw materials)		

Xonic debits Work in Process Inventory for standard materials quantities used at standard prices. It debits the variance account because the variance is unfavorable. The company credits Raw Materials Inventory for actual quantities at standard prices.

5. Assign factory labor to production at a cost of $21,000 when standard cost is $20,000.

Work in Process Inventory	20,000	
Labor Quantity Variance	1,000	
Factory Labor		21,000
(To assign factory labor to jobs)		

Xonic debits Work in Process Inventory for standard labor hours at standard rates. It debits the unfavorable variance to Labor Quantity Variance. The credit to Factory Labor produces a zero balance in this account.

6. Applying manufacturing overhead to production $10,000.

Work in Process Inventory	10,000	
Manufacturing Overhead		10,000
(To assign overhead to jobs)		

Xonic debits Work in Process Inventory for standard hours allowed multiplied by the standard overhead rate.

7. Transfer completed work to finished goods $42,000.

Finished Goods Inventory	42,000	
Work in Process Inventory		42,000
(To record transfer of completed work to finished goods)		

In this example, both inventory accounts are at standard cost.

8. The 1,000 gallons of Weed-O are sold for $60,000.

Accounts Receivable	60,000	
Cost of Goods Sold	42,000	
Sales		60,000
Finished Goods Inventory		42,000
(To record sale of finished goods and the cost of goods sold)		

The company debits Cost of Goods Sold at standard cost. Gross profit, in turn, is the difference between sales and the standard cost of goods sold.

9. Recognize unfavorable total overhead variance:

Overhead Variance	900	
Manufacturing Overhead		900
(To recognize total overhead variance)		

Prior to this entry, a debit balance of $900 existed in Manufacturing Overhead. This entry therefore produces a zero balance in the Manufacturing Overhead account. The information needed for this entry is often not available until the end of the accounting period.

Ledger Accounts

Illustration 25A-1 shows the cost accounts for Xonic, Inc., after posting the entries. Note that six variance accounts are included in the ledger. The remaining accounts are the same as those illustrated for a job order cost system in Chapter 20, in which only actual costs were used.

Illustration 25A-1
Cost accounts with variances

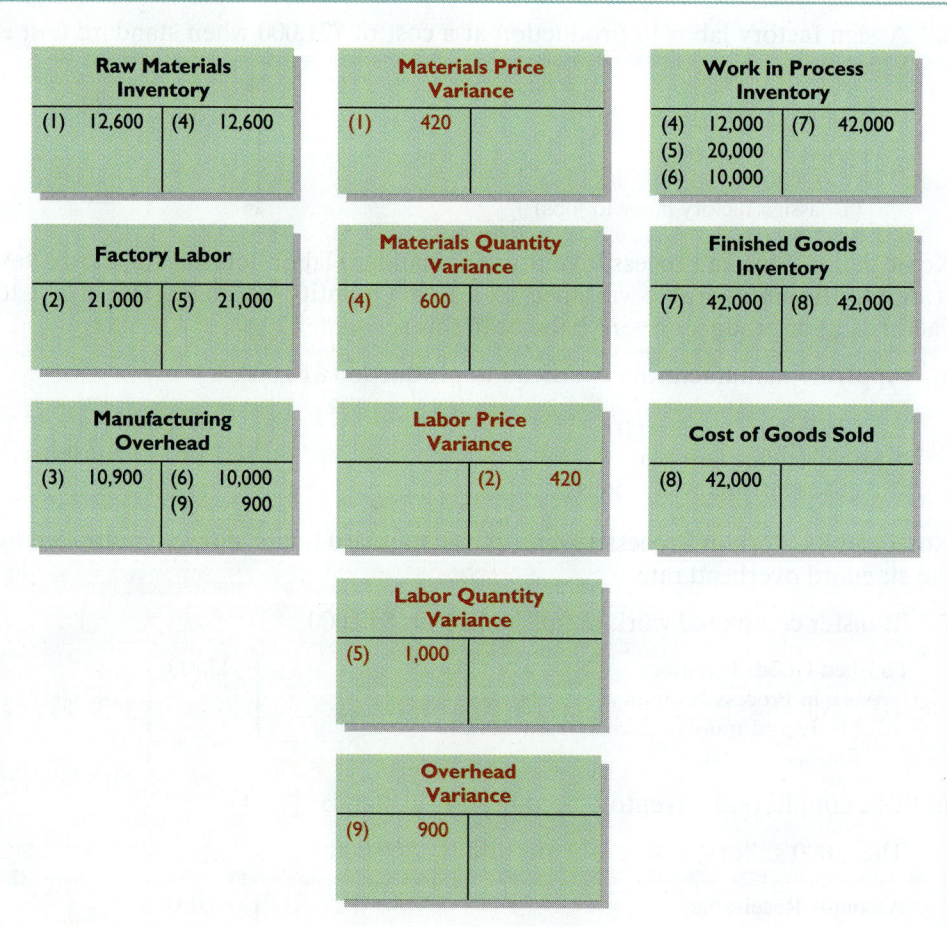

HELPFUL HINT
All debit balances in variance accounts indicate unfavorable variances; all credit balances indicate favorable variances.

SUMMARY OF STUDY OBJECTIVE FOR APPENDIX

9 Identify the features of a standard cost accounting system. In a standard cost accounting system, companies journalize and post standard costs, and they maintain separate variance accounts in the ledger.

GLOSSARY FOR APPENDIX 25A

Standard cost accounting system A double-entry system of accounting in which standard costs are used in making entries and variances are recognized in the accounts. (p. 1130)

APPENDIX 25B A Closer Look at Overhead Variances

As indicated in the chapter, the total overhead variance is generally analyzed through a price variance and a quantity variance. The name usually given to the price variance is the **overhead controllable variance**; the quantity variance is referred to as the **overhead volume variance**.

> **STUDY OBJECTIVE 10**
> Compute overhead controllable and volume variance.

OVERHEAD CONTROLLABLE VARIANCE

The **overhead controllable variance** shows whether overhead costs are effectively controlled. To compute this variance, the company compares actual overhead costs incurred with budgeted costs for the **standard hours allowed**. The budgeted costs are determined from a manufacturing overhead flexible budget. The concepts related to a flexible budget were discussed in Chapter 24.

For Xonic the budget formula for manufacturing overhead is variable manufacturing overhead cost of $3 per hour of labor plus fixed manufacturing overhead costs of $4,400. Illustration 25B-1 shows the flexible budget for Xonic, Inc.

Illustration 25B-1
Flexible budget using standard direct labor hours

XONIC, INC
Manufacturing Overhead Flexible Budget

Activity Index				
Standard direct labor hours	1,800	2,000	2,200	2,400
Costs				
Variable costs				
Indirect materials	$1,800	$ 2,000	$ 2,200	$ 2,400
Indirect labor	2,700	3,000	3,300	3,600
Utilities	900	1,000	1,100	1,200
Total variable costs	5,400	6,000	6,600	7,200
Fixed costs				
Supervision	3,000	3,000	3,000	3,000
Depreciation	1,400	1,400	1,400	1,400
Total fixed costs	4,400	4,400	4,400	4,400
Total costs	$9,800	$10,400	$11,000	$11,600

As shown, the budgeted costs for 2,000 standard hours are $10,400 ($6,000 variable and $4,400 fixed).

Illustration 25B-2 shows the formula for the overhead controllable variance and the calculation for Xonic, Inc.

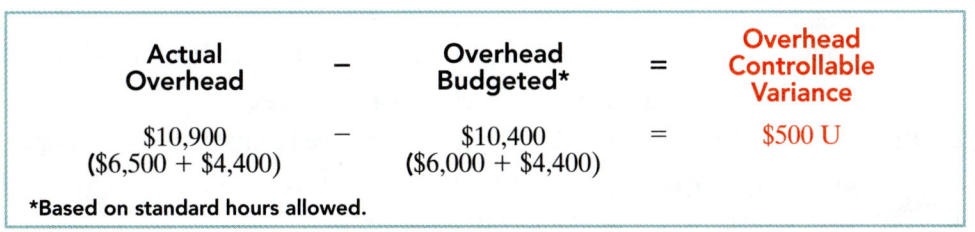

Illustration 25B-2
Formula for overhead controllable variance

Actual Overhead − Overhead Budgeted* = Overhead Controllable Variance

$10,900 − $10,400 = $500 U
($6,500 + $4,400) ($6,000 + $4,400)

*Based on standard hours allowed.

The overhead controllable variance for Xonic, Inc. is $500 unfavorable.

Most controllable variances are associated with variable costs, which are controllable costs. Fixed costs are often known at the time the budget is prepared and are therefore not as likely to deviate from the budgeted amount. In Xonic's case, all of the overhead controllable variance is due to the difference between the actual variable overhead costs ($6,500) and the budgeted variable costs ($6,000).

Management can compare actual and budgeted overhead for each manufacturing overhead cost that contributes to the controllable variance. In addition, management can develop cost and quantity variances for each overhead cost, such as indirect materials and indirect labor.

OVERHEAD VOLUME VARIANCE

The **overhead volume variance** is the difference between normal capacity hours and standard hours allowed times the fixed overhead rate. The overhead volume variance relates to whether fixed costs were under- or over-applied during the year. For example, the overhead volume variance answers the question of whether Xonic effectively used its fixed costs. If Xonic produces less Weed-O than normal capacity would allow, an unfavorable variance results. Conversely, if Xonic produces more Weed-O than what is considered normal capacity, a favorable variance results.

The formula for computing the overhead volume variance is as follows.

Illustration 25B-3
Formula for overhead volume variance

| Fixed Overhead Rate | × | (Normal Capacity Hours − Standard Hours Allowed) | = | Overhead Volume Variance |

To illustrate the fixed overhead rate computation, recall that Xonic Inc. budgeted fixed overhead cost for the year of $52,800 (Illustration 25-6 on page 1114). At normal capacity, 26,400 standard direct labor hours are required. The fixed overhead rate is therefore $2 ($52,800 ÷ 26,400 hours).

Xonic produced 1,000 units of Weed-O in June. The standard hours allowed for the 1,000 gallons produced in June is 2,000 (1,000 gallons × 2 hours). For Xonic, standard direct labor hours for June at normal capacity is 2,200 (26,400 annual hours ÷ 12 months). The computation of the overhead volume variance in this case is as follows.

Illustration 25B-4
Computation of overhead volume variance for Xonic Co.

Fixed Overhead Rate	×	(Normal Capacity Hours − Standard Hours Allowed)	=	Overhead Volume Variance
$2	×	(2,200 − 2,000)	=	$400 U

In Xonic's case, a $400 unfavorable volume variance results. The volume variance is unfavorable because Xonic produced only 1,000 gallons rather than the normal capacity of 1,100 gallons in the month of June. As a result, it underapplied fixed overhead for that period.

In computing the overhead variances, it is important to remember the following.

1. Standard hours allowed are used in each of the variances.
2. Budgeted costs for the controllable variance are derived from the flexible budget.
3. The controllable variance generally pertains to variable costs.
4. The volume variance pertains solely to fixed costs.

SUMMARY OF STUDY OBJECTIVE FOR APPENDIX 25B

10 Compute overhead controllable and volume variance. The total overhead variance is generally analyzed through a price variance and a quantity variance. The name usually given to the price variance is the overhead controllable variance. The quantity variance is referred to as the overhead volume variance.

GLOSSARY FOR APPENDIX 25B

Overhead controllable variance The difference between actual overhead incurred and overhead budgeted for the standard hours allowed. (p. 1133)

Overhead volume variance The difference between normal capacity hours and standard hours allowed times the fixed overhead rate. (p. 1134)

Note: All asterisked Questions, Exercises, and Problems relate to material in the appendices to the chapter.

SELF-STUDY QUESTIONS

Answers are at the end of the chapter.

(SO 1) **1.** Standards differ from budgets in that:
   a. budgets but not standards may be used in valuing inventories.
   b. budgets but not standards may be journalized and posted.
   c. budgets are a total amount and standards are a unit amount.
   d. only budgets contribute to management planning and control.

(SO 1) **2.** Standard costs:
   a. are imposed by governmental agencies.
   b. are predetermined unit costs which companies use as measures of performance.
   c. can be used by manufacturing companies but not by service or not-for-profit companies.
   d. All of the above.

(SO 2) **3.** The advantages of standard costs include all of the following *except*:
   a. management by exception may be used.
   b. management planning is facilitated.
   c. they may simplify the costing of inventories.
   d. management must use a static budget.

(SO 3) **4.** Normal standards:
   a. allow for rest periods, machine breakdowns, and setup time.
   b. represent levels of performance under perfect operating conditions.
   c. are rarely used because managers believe they lower workforce morale.
   d. are more likely than ideal standards to result in unethical practices.

(SO 3) **5.** The setting of standards is:
   a. a managerial accounting decision.
   b. a management decision.
   c. a worker decision.
   d. preferably set at the ideal level of performance.

(SO 4) **6.** Each of the following formulas is correct except:
   a. Labor price variance = (Actual hours × Actual rate) − (Actual hours × Standard rate).
   b. Overhead controllable variance = Actual overhead − Overhead budgeted.
   c. Materials price variance = (Actual quantity × Actual price) − (Standard quantity × Standard price).
   d. Overhead volume variance = Fixed overhead rate × (Normal capacity hours − Standard hours allowed).

(SO 4) **7.** In producing product AA, 6,300 pounds of direct materials were used at a cost of $1.10 per pound. The standard was 6,000 pounds at $1.00 per pound. The direct materials quantity variance is:
   a. $330 unfavorable.   c. $600 unfavorable.
   b. $300 unfavorable.   d. $630 unfavorable.

(SO 4) **8.** In producing product ZZ, 14,800 direct labor hours were used at a rate of $8.20 per hour. The standard was 15,000 hours at $8.00 per hour. Based on these data, the direct labor:
   a. quantity variance is $1,600 favorable.
   b. quantity variance is $1,600 unfavorable.
   c. price variance is $2,960 favorable.
   d. price variance is $3,000 unfavorable.

(SO 5) **9.** Which of the following is *correct* about the total overhead variance?
   a. Budgeted overhead and overhead applied are the same.
   b. Total actual overhead is composed of variable overhead, fixed overhead, and period costs.
   c. Standard hours actually worked are used in computing the variance.
   d. Standard hours allowed for the work done is the measure used in computing the variance.

(SO 5) **10.** The formula for computing the total overhead variance is:
   a. actual overhead less overhead applied.
   b. overhead budgeted less overhead applied.
   c. actual overhead less overhead budgeted.
   d. No correct answer given.

1136 Chapter 25 Standard Costs and Balanced Scorecard

(SO 6) **11.** Which of the following is *incorrect* about variance reports?
   a. They facilitate "management by exception."
   b. They should only be sent to the top level of management.
   c. They should be prepared as soon as possible.
   d. They may vary in form, content, and frequency among companies.

(SO 6) **12.** In using variance reports to evaluate cost control, management normally looks into:
   a. all variances.
   b. favorable variances only.
   c. unfavorable variances only.
   d. both favorable and unfavorable variances that exceed a predetermined quantitative measure such as a percentage or dollar amount.

(SO 7) **13.** Generally accepted accounting principles allow a company to:
   a. report inventory at standard cost but cost of goods sold must be reported at actual cost.
   b. report cost of goods sold at standard cost but inventory must be reported at actual cost.
   c. report inventory and cost of goods sold at standard cost as long as there are no significant differences between actual and standard cost.
   d. report inventory and cost of goods sold only at actual costs; standard costing is never permitted.

(SO 8) **14.** Which of the following would *not* be an objective used in the customer perspective of the balanced scorecard approach?
   a. Percentage of customers who would recommend product to a friend.
   b. Customer retention.
   c. Brand recognition.
   d. Earnings per share.

(SO 9) ***15.** Which of the following is *incorrect* about a standard cost accounting system?
   a. It is applicable to job order costing.
   b. It is applicable to process costing.
   c. It reports only favorable variances.
   d. It keeps separate accounts for each variance.

(SO 10) ***16.** The formula to compute the overhead volume variance is:
   a. Fixed overhead rate × (Standard hours − Actual hours).
   b. Fixed overhead rate × (Normal capacity hours − Actual hours).
   c. Fixed overhead rate × (Normal capacity hours − Standard hours allowed).
   d. (Variable overhead rate + Fixed overhead rate) × (Normal capacity hours − Standard hours allowed).

Go to the book's companion website, **www.wiley.com/college/weygandt**, for Additional Self-Study questions.

QUESTIONS

1. **(a)** "Standard costs are the expected total cost of completing a job." Is this correct? Explain.
   (b) "A standard imposed by a governmental agency is known as a regulation." Do you agree? Explain.

2. **(a)** Explain the similarities and differences between standards and budgets.
   (b) Contrast the accounting for standards and budgets.

3. Standard costs facilitate management planning. What are the other advantages of standard costs?

4. Contrast the roles of the management accountant and management in setting standard costs.

5. Distinguish between an ideal standard and a normal standard.

6. What factors should be considered in setting (a) the direct materials price standard and (b) the direct materials quantity standard?

7. "The objective in setting the direct labor quantity standard is to determine the aggregate time required to make one unit of product." Do you agree? What allowances should be made in setting this standard?

8. How is the predetermined overhead rate determined when standard costs are used?

9. What is the difference between a favorable cost variance and an unfavorable cost variance?

10. In each of the following formulas, supply the words that should be inserted for each number in parentheses.
    (a) (Actual quantity × (1)) − (Standard quantity × (2)) = Total materials variance
    (b) ((3) × Actual price) − (Actual quantity × (4)) = Materials price variance
    (c) (Actual quantity × (5)) − ((6) × Standard price) = Materials quantity variance

11. In the direct labor variance matrix, there are three factors: (1) Actual hours × Actual rate, (2) Actual hours × Standard rate, and (3) Standard hours × Standard rate. Using the numbers, indicate the formulas for each of the direct labor variances.

12. Greer Company's standard predetermined overhead rate is $8 per direct labor hour. For the month of June, 26,000 actual hours were worked, and 27,000 standard hours were allowed. Normal capacity hours were 28,000. How much overhead was applied?

13. How often should variances be reported to management? What principle may be used with variance reports?

14. What circumstances may cause the purchasing department to be responsible for both an unfavorable materials price variance and an unfavorable materials quantity variance?

15. What are the four perspectives used in the balanced scorecard? Discuss the nature of each, and how the perspectives are linked.

16. Tom Jones says that the balanced scorecard was created to replace financial measures as the primary mechanism for performance evaluation. He says that it uses only nonfinancial measures. Is this true?

17. What are some examples of nonfinancial measures used by companies to evaluate performance?

18. **(a)** How are variances reported in income statements prepared for management? **(b)** May standard costs be used in preparing financial statements for stockholders? Explain.

*19. (a) Explain the basic features of a standard cost accounting system. (b) What type of balance will exist in the variance account when (1) the materials price variance is unfavorable and (2) the labor quantity variance is favorable?

*20. If the $8 per hour overhead rate in question 12 includes $5 variable, and actual overhead costs were $218,000, what is the overhead controllable variance for June? The normal capacity hours were 28,000. Is the variance favorable or unfavorable?

*21. What is the purpose of computing the overhead volume variance? What is the basic formula for this variance?

*22. Janet Finney does not understand why the overhead volume variance indicates that fixed overhead costs are under- or overapplied. Clarify this matter for Janet.

*23. Nick Menke is attempting to outline the important points about overhead variances on a class examination. List four points that Nick should include in his outline.

BRIEF EXERCISES

BE25-1 Orasco Company uses both standards and budgets. For the year, estimated production of Product X is 500,000 units. Total estimated cost for materials and labor are $1,200,000 and $1,600,000. Compute the estimates for (a) a standard cost and (b) a budgeted cost.

Distinguish between a standard and a budget.
(SO 1)

BE25-2 Asaki Company accumulates the following data concerning raw materials in making one gallon of finished product: (1) Price—net purchase price $2.20, freight-in $0.20 and receiving and handling $0.10. (2) Quantity—required materials 2.6 pounds, allowance for waste and spoilage 0.4 pounds. Compute the following.

(a) Standard direct materials price per gallon.
(b) Standard direct materials quantity per gallon.
(c) Total standard materials cost per gallon.

Set direct materials standard.
(SO 3)

BE25-3 Labor data for making one gallon of finished product in Asaki Company are as follows: (1) Price—hourly wage rate $12.00, payroll taxes $0.80, and fringe benefits $1.20. (2) Quantity—actual production time 1.2 hours, rest periods and clean up 0.25 hours, and setup and downtime 0.15 hours. Compute the following.

(a) Standard direct labor rate per hour.
(b) Standard direct labor hours per gallon.
(c) Standard labor cost per gallon.

Set direct labor standard.
(SO 3)

BE25-4 Neville Company's standard materials cost per unit of output is $10 (2 pounds × $5). During July, the company purchases and uses 3,200 pounds of materials costing $16,160 in making 1,500 units of finished product. Compute the total, price, and quantity materials variances.

Compute direct materials variances.
(SO 4)

BE25-5 Wamser Company's standard labor cost per unit of output is $20 (2 hours × $10 per hour). During August, the company incurs 2,100 hours of direct labor at an hourly cost of $10.50 per hour in making 1,000 units of finished product. Compute the total, price, and quantity labor variances.

Compute direct labor variances.
(SO 4)

BE25-6 In October, Keane Company reports 21,000 actual direct labor hours, and it incurs $115,000 of manufacturing overhead costs. Standard hours allowed for the work done is 20,000 hours. The predetermined overhead rate is $6 per direct labor hour. Compute the total overhead variance.

Compute total overhead variance.
(SO 5)

BE25-7 The four perspectives in the balanced scorecard are (1) financial, (2) customer, (3) internal process, and (4) learning and growth. Match each of the following objectives with the perspective it is most likely associated with: (a) Plant capacity utilization. (b) Employee work days missed due to injury. (c) Return on assets. (d) Brand recognition.

Match balanced scorecard perspectives.
(SO 8)

***BE25-8** Journalize the following transactions for Orkin Manufacturing.
(a) Purchased 6,000 units of raw materials on account for $11,100. The standard cost was $12,000.
(b) Issued 5,500 units of raw materials for production. The standard units were 5,800.

Journalize materials variances.
(SO 9)

***BE25-9** Journalize the following transactions for Rogler Manufacturing.
(a) Incurred direct labor costs of $24,000 for 3,000 hours. The standard labor cost was $25,200.
(b) Assigned 3,000 direct labor hours costing $24,000 to production. Standard hours were 3,100.

Journalize labor variances.
(SO 9)

***BE25-10** Some overhead data for Keane Company are given in BE25-6. In addition, the flexible manufacturing overhead budget shows that budgeted costs are $4 variable per direct labor hour and $50,000 fixed. Compute the overhead controllable variance.

Compute the overhead controllable variance.
(SO 10)

***BE25-11** Using the data in BE25-6 and BE25-10, compute the overhead volume variance. Normal capacity was 25,000 direct labor hours.

Compute overhead volume variance.
(SO 10)

Chapter 25 Standard Costs and Balanced Scorecard

DO IT! REVIEW

Compute standard cost.
(SO 3)

DO IT! 25-1 Riuto Company accumulated the following standard cost data concerning product I-Tal.

Materials per unit: 2 pounds at $5 per pound
Labor per unit: 0.2 hours at $14 per hour
Manufacturing overhead: Predetermined rate is 125% of direct labor cost

Compute the standard cost of one unit of product I-Tal.

Compute materials variance.
(SO 4)

DO IT! 25-2 The standard cost of product 999 includes 2 units of direct materials at $6.00 per unit. During August, the company bought 29,000 units of materials at $6.20 and used those materials to produce 15,000 units. Compute the total, price, and quantity variances for materials.

Compute labor and manufacturing overhead variances.
(SO 4, 5)

DO IT! 25-3 The standard cost of product 2525 includes 2 hours of direct labor at $14.00 per hour. The predetermined overhead rate is $21.00 per direct labor hour. During July, the company incurred 4,100 hours of direct labor at an average rate of $14.40 per hour and $81,300 of manufacturing overhead costs. It produced 2,000 units.

(a) Compute the total, price, and quantity variances for labor. (b) Compute the total overhead variance.

Match balance scorecard perspectives and their objectives.
(SO 8)

DO IT! 25-4 Indicate which of the four perspectives in the balanced scorecard is most likely associated with the objectives that follow.

1. Ethics violations.
2. Credit rating.
3. Customer retention.
4. Stockouts.
5. Reportable accidents.
6. Brand recognition.

EXERCISES

Compute budget and standard.
(SO 1, 2, 3)

E25-1 Lovitz Company is planning to produce 2,000 units of product in 2010. Each unit requires 3 pounds of materials at $6 per pound and a half hour of labor at $14 per hour. The overhead rate is 70% of direct labor.

Instructions
(a) Compute the budgeted amounts for 2010 for direct materials to be used, direct labor, and applied overhead.
(b) Compute the standard cost of one unit of product.
(c) What are the potential advantages to a corporation of using standard costs?

Compute standard materials costs.
(SO 3)

E25-2 Tony Rondeli manufactures and sells homemade wine, and he wants to develop a standard cost per gallon. The following are required for production of a 50-gallon batch.

  3,000 ounces of grape concentrate at $0.04 per ounce
  54 pounds of granulated sugar at $0.35 per pound
  60 lemons at $0.60 each
  50 yeast tablets at $0.25 each
  50 nutrient tablets at $0.20 each
  2,500 ounces of water at $0.004 per ounce

Tony estimates that 4% of the grape concentrate is wasted, 10% of the sugar is lost, and 20% of the lemons cannot be used.

Instructions
Compute the standard cost of the ingredients for one gallon of wine. (Carry computations to two decimal places.)

Compute standard cost per unit.
(SO 3)

E25-3 Muhsin Company has gathered the information shown on the next page about its product.

Direct materials: Each unit of product contains 4.5 pounds of materials. The average waste and spoilage per unit produced under normal conditions is 0.5 pounds. Materials cost $4 per pound, but Muhsin always takes the 2% cash discount all of its suppliers offer. Freight costs average $0.25 per pound.

Direct labor: Each unit requires 2 hours of labor. Setup, cleanup, and downtime average 0.2 hours per unit. The average hourly pay rate of Muhsin's employees is $12. Payroll taxes and fringe benfits are an additional $3 per hour.

Manufacturing overhead: Overhead is applied at a rate of $6 per direct labor hour.

Instructions
Compute Muhsin's total standard cost per unit.

E25-4 Rapid Repair Services, Inc. is trying to establish the standard labor cost of a typical oil change. The following data have been collected from time and motion studies conducted over the past month.

Compute labor quantity variance.
(SO 3, 4)

Actual time spent on the oil change	1.0 hour
Hourly wage rate	$10
Payroll taxes	10% of wage rate
Setup and downtime	10% of actual labor time
Cleanup and rest periods	30% of actual labor time
Fringe benefits	25% of wage rate

Instructions
(a) Determine the standard direct labor hours per oil change.
(b) Determine the standard direct labor hourly rate.
(c) Determine the standard direct labor cost per oil change.
(d) If an oil change took 1.5 hours at the standard hourly rate, what was the direct labor quantity variance?

E25-5 The standard cost of Product B manufactured by Mateo Company includes three units of direct materials at $5.00 per unit. During June, 28,000 units of direct materials are purchased at a cost of $4.70 per unit, and 28,000 units of direct materials are used to produce 9,000 units of Product B.

Compute materials price and quantity variances.
(SO 4)

Instructions
(a) Compute the total materials variance and the price and quantity variances.
(b) Repeat (a), assuming the purchase price is $5.20 and the quantity purchased and used is 26,200 units.

E25-6 Scheer Company's standard labor cost of producing one unit of Product DD is 4 hours at the rate of $12.00 per hour. During August, 40,800 hours of labor are incurred at a cost of $12.10 per hour to produce 10,000 units of Product DD.

Compute labor price and quantity variances.
(SO 4)

Instructions
(a) Compute the total labor variance.
(b) Compute the labor price and quantity variances.
(c) Repeat (b), assuming the standard is 4.2 hours of direct labor at $12.25 per hour.

E25-7 Haslett Inc., which produces a single product, has prepared the following standard cost sheet for one unit of the product.

Compute materials and labor variances.
(SO 4)

Direct materials (8 pounds at $2.50 per pound)	$20
Direct labor (3 hours at $12.00 per hour)	$36

During the month of April, the company manufactures 230 units and incurs the following actual costs.

Direct materials purchased and used (1,900 pounds)	$4,940
Direct labor (700 hours)	$8,120

Instructions
Compute the total, price, and quantity variances for materials and labor.

E25-8 The direct materials and direct labor data shown on the next page pertain to the operations of Solario Manufacturing Company for the month of August.

Compute the materials and labor variances and list reasons for unfavorable variances.
(SO 4)

	Costs		Quantities	
Actual labor rate	$13 per hour	Actual hours incurred and used	4,200 hours
Actual materials price	$128 per ton	Actual quantity of materials purchased and used	1,225 tons
Standard labor rate	$12 per hour	Standard hours used	4,300 hours
Standard materials price	$130 per ton	Standard quantity of materials used	1,200 tons

Instructions

(a) Compute the total, price, and quantity variances for materials and labor.

(b) ✎ Provide two possible explanations for each of the unfavorable variances calculated above, and suggest where responsibility for the unfavorable result might be placed.

Prepare a variance report for direct labor.
(SO 4, 6)

E25-9 During March 2010, Hinton Tool & Die Company worked on four jobs. A review of direct labor costs reveals the following summary data.

Job Number	Actual Hours	Actual Costs	Standard Hours	Standard Costs	Total Variance
A257	220	$ 4,400	225	$4,500	$ 100 F
A258	450	9,900	430	8,600	1,300 U
A259	300	6,150	300	6,000	150 U
A260	115	2,070	110	2,200	130 F
Total variance					$1,220 U

Analysis reveals that Job A257 was a repeat job. Job A258 was a rush order that required overtime work at premium rates of pay. Job A259 required a more experienced replacement worker on one shift. Work on Job A260 was done for one day by a new trainee when a regular worker was absent.

Instructions

Prepare a report for the plant supervisor on direct labor cost variances for March. The report should have columns for (1) Job No., (2) Actual Hours, (3) Standard Hours, (4) Quantity Variance, (5) Actual Rate, (6) Standard Rate, (7) Price Variance, and (8) Explanation.

Compute overhead variance.
(SO 5)

E25-10 Manufacturing overhead data for the production of Product H by Norland Company are as follows.

Overhead incurred for 52,000 actual direct labor hours worked	$213,000
Overhead rate (variable $3; fixed $1) at normal capacity of 54,000 direct labor hours	$4
Standard hours allowed for work done	51,000

Instructions

Compute the total overhead variance.

Compute overhead variance.
(SO 5)

E25-11 Jay Levitt Company produces one product, a putter called GO-Putter. Levitt uses a standard cost system and determines that it should take one hour of direct labor to produce one GO-Putter. The normal production capacity for this putter is 100,000 units per year. The total budgeted overhead at normal capacity is $800,000 comprised of $200,000 of variable costs and $600,000 of fixed costs. Levitt applies overhead on the basis of direct labor hours.

During the current year, Levitt produced 90,000 putters, worked 94,000 direct labor hours, and incurred variable overhead costs of $186,000 and fixed overhead costs of $600,000.

Instructions

(a) Compute the predetermined variable overhead rate and the predetermined fixed overhead rate.

(b) Compute the applied overhead for Levitt for the year.

(c) Compute the total overhead variance.

Compute variances for materials.
(SO 4)

E25-12 Buerhle Company purchased (at a cost of $10,900) and used 2,300 pounds of materials during May. Buerhle's standard cost of materials per unit produced is based on 2 pounds per unit at a cost $5 per pound. Production in May was 1,070 units.

Instructions

(a) Compute the total, price, and quantity variances for materials.
(b) Assume Buerhle also had an unfavorable labor quantity variance. What is a possible scenario that would provide one cause for the variances computed in (a) and the unfavorable labor quantity variance?

E25-13 Imperial Landscaping plants grass seed as the basic landscaping for business campuses. During a recent month the company worked on three projects (Ames, Korman, and Stilles). The company is interested in controlling the material costs, namely the grass seed, for these plantings projects.

Prepare a variance report.
(SO 4, 6)

In order to provide management with useful cost control information, the company uses standard costs and prepares monthly variance reports. Analysis reveals that the purchasing agent mistakenly purchased poor-quality seed for the Ames project. The Korman project, however, received higher-than-standard-quality seed that was on sale. The Stilles project received standard-quality seed; however, the price had increased and a new employee was used to spread the seed.

Shown below are quantity and cost data for each project.

Project	Actual Quantity	Actual Costs	Standard Quantity	Standard Costs	Total Variance
Ames	500 lbs.	$1,175	460 lbs.	$1,150	$ 25 U
Korman	400	960	410	1,025	65 F
Stilles	500	1,300	480	1,200	100 U
Total variance					$ 60 U

Instructions

(a) Prepare a variance report for the purchasing department with the following columns: (1) Project, (2) Actual pounds purchased, (3) Actual price, (4) Standard price, (5) Price variance, and (6) Explanation.
(b) Prepare a variance report for the production department with the following columns: (1) Project, (2) Actual pounds, (3) Standard pounds, (4) Standard price, (5) Quantity variance, and (6) Explanation.

E25-14 Archangel Corporation prepared the following variance report.

Complete variance report.
(SO 6)

ARCHANGEL CORPORATION
Variance Report—Purchasing Department
for Week Ended January 9, 2011

Type of Materials	Quantity Purchased	Actual Price	Standard Price	Price Variance	Explanation
Rogue11	? lbs.	$5.20	$5.00	$5,200 ?	Price increase
Storm17	7,000 oz.	?	3.25	1,050 U	Rush order
Beast29	22,000 units	0.45	?	440 F	Bought larger quantity

Instructions
Fill in the appropriate amounts or letters for the question marks in the report.

E25-15 Cepeda Company uses a standard cost accounting system. During January, the company reported the following manufacturing variances.

Prepare income statement for management.
(SO 7)

Materials price variance	$1,250 U	Labor quantity variance	$ 725 U
Materials quantity variance	700 F	Overhead variance	800 U
Labor price variance	525 U		

In addition, 8,000 units of product were sold at $8.00 per unit. Each unit sold had a standard cost of $6.00. Selling and administrative expenses were $6,000 for the month.

Instructions
Prepare an income statement for management for the month ended January 31, 2010.

Chapter 25 Standard Costs and Balanced Scorecard

Identify performance evaluation terminology.

(SO 3, 8)

E25-16 The following is a list of terms related to performance evaluation.

(1) Balanced scorecard
(2) Variance
(3) Learning and growth perspective
(4) Nonfinancial measures
(5) Customer perspective
(6) Internal process perspective
(7) Ideal standards
(8) Normal standards

Instructions

Match each of the following descriptions with one of the terms above.

(a) The difference between total actual costs and total standard costs.
(b) An efficient level of performance that is attainable under expected operating conditions.
(c) An approach that incorporates financial and nonfinancial measures in an integrated system that links performance measurement and a company's strategic goals.
(d) A viewpoint employed in the balanced scorecard to evaluate how well a company develops and retains its employees.
(e) An evaluation tool that is not based on dollars.
(f) A viewpoint employed in the balanced scorecard to evaluate the company from the perspective of those people who buy and use its products or services.
(g) An optimum level of performance under perfect operating conditions.
(h) A viewpoint employed in the balanced scorecard to evaluate the efficiency and effectiveness of the company's value chain.

Journalize entries in a standard cost accounting system.

(SO 9)

*E25-17 Peyton Company installed a standard cost system on January 1. Selected transactions for the month of January are as follows.

1. Purchased 18,000 units of raw materials on account at a cost of $4.50 per unit. Standard cost was $4.30 per unit.
2. Issued 18,000 units of raw materials for jobs that required 17,600 standard units of raw materials.
3. Incurred 15,200 actual hours of direct labor at an actual rate of $4.80 per hour. The standard rate is $5.50 per hour. (Credit Wages Payable)
4. Performed 15,200 hours of direct labor on jobs when standard hours were 15,400.
5. Applied overhead to jobs at the rate of 100% of direct labor cost for standard hours allowed.

Instructions

Journalize the January transactions.

Answer questions concerning missing entries and balances.

(SO 4, 5, 9)

*E25-18 Cesar Company uses a standard cost accounting system. Some of the ledger accounts have been destroyed in a fire. The controller asks your help in reconstructing some missing entries and balances.

Instructions

Answer the following questions.

(a) Materials Price Variance shows a $2,000 favorable balance. Accounts Payable shows $128,000 of raw materials purchases. What was the amount debited to Raw Materials Inventory for raw materials purchased?
(b) Materials Quantity Variance shows a $3,000 unfavorable balance. Raw Materials Inventory shows a zero balance. What was the amount debited to Work in Process Inventory for direct materials used?
(c) Labor Price Variance shows a $1,500 unfavorable balance. Factory Labor shows a debit of $140,000 for wages incurred. What was the amount credited to Wages Payable?
(d) Factory Labor shows a credit of $140,000 for direct labor used. Labor Quantity Variance shows a $900 unfavorable balance. What was the amount debited to Work in Process for direct labor used?
(e) Overhead applied to Work in Process totaled $165,000. If the total overhead variance was $1,200 unfavorable, what was the amount of overhead costs debited to Manufacturing Overhead?

Journalize entries for materials and labor variances.

(SO 9)

*E25-19 Data for Haslett Inc. are given in E25-7.

Instructions

Journalize the entries to record the materials and labor variances.

*E25-20 The following information was taken from the annual manufacturing overhead cost budget of Granada Company.

Variable manufacturing overhead costs	$33,000
Fixed manufacturing overhead costs	$19,800
Normal production level in labor hours	16,500
Normal production level in units	4,125
Standard labor hours per unit	4

During the year, 4,000 units were produced, 16,100 hours were worked, and the actual manufacturing overhead was $54,000. Actual fixed manufacturing overhead costs equaled budgeted fixed manufacturing overhead costs. Overhead is applied on the basis of direct labor hours.

Compute manufacturing overhead variances and interpret findings.
(SO 10)

Instructions
(a) Compute the total, fixed, and variable predetermined manufacturing overhead rates.
(b) Compute the total, controllable, and volume overhead variances.
(c) Briefly interpret the overhead controllable and volume variances computed in (b).

*E25-21 The loan department of Local Bank uses standard costs to determine the overhead cost of processing loan applications. During the current month a fire occurred, and the accounting records for the department were mostly destroyed. The following data were salvaged from the ashes.

Compute overhead variances.
(SO 10)

Standard variable overhead rate per hour	$9
Standard hours per application	2
Standard hours allowed	2,000
Standard fixed overhead rate per hour	$6
Actual fixed overhead cost	$13,200
Variable overhead budget based on standard hours allowed	$18,000
Fixed overhead budget	$13,200
Overhead controllable variance	$ 1,500 U

Instructions
(a) Determine the following.
 (1) Total actual overhead cost.
 (2) Actual variable overhead cost.
 (3) Variable overhead cost applied.
 (4) Fixed overhead cost applied.
 (5) Overhead volume variance.
(b) Determine how many loans were processed.

*E25-22 Jackson Company's annual overhead rate was based on estimates of $200,000 for overhead costs and 20,000 direct labor hours. Jackson's standards allow 2 hours of direct labor per unit produced. Production in May was 900 units, and actual overhead incurred in May was $18,800. The overhead budgeted for 1,800 standard direct labor hours is $17,600 ($5,000 fixed and $12,600 variable).

Compute variances.
(SO 10)

Instructions
(a) Compute the total, controllable, and volume variances for overhead.
(b) What are possible causes of the variances computed in part (a)?

EXERCISES: SET B

Visit the book's companion website at **www.wiley.com/college/weygandt**, and choose the Student Companion site, to access Exercise Set B.

PROBLEMS: SET A

P25-1A Putnam Corporation manufactures a single product. The standard cost per unit of product is shown below.

Compute variances.
(SO 4, 5)

Direct materials—1 pound plastic at $7.00 per pound	$ 7.00
Direct labor—1.5 hours at $12.00 per hour	18.00
Variable manufacturing overhead	11.25
Fixed manufacturing overhead	3.75
Total standard cost per unit	$40.00

The predetermined manufacturing overhead rate is $10 per direct labor hour ($15.00 ÷ 1.5). It was computed from a master manufacturing overhead budget based on normal production of 7,500 direct labor hours (5,000 units) for the month. The master budget showed total variable costs of $56,250 ($7.50 per hour) and total fixed overhead costs of $18,750 ($2.50 per hour). Actual costs for October in producing 4,900 units were as follows.

Direct materials (5,100 pounds)	$ 37,230
Direct labor (7,000 hours)	87,500
Variable overhead	56,170
Fixed overhead	19,680
Total manufacturing costs	$200,580

The purchasing department buys the quantities of raw materials that are expected to be used in production each month. Raw materials inventories, therefore, can be ignored.

Instructions
(a) Compute all of the materials and labor variances.
(b) Compute the total overhead variance.

Compute variances, and prepare income statement.
(SO 4, 5, 7)

P25-2A Dinkel Manufacturing Corporation accumulates the following data relative to jobs started and finished during the month of June 2010.

Costs and Production Data	Actual	Standard
Raw materials unit cost	$2.25	$2.00
Raw materials units used	10,600	10,000
Direct labor payroll	$122,400	$120,000
Direct labor hours worked	14,400	15,000
Manufacturing overhead incurred	$184,500	
Manufacturing overhead applied		$189,000
Machine hours expected to be used at normal capacity		42,500
Budgeted fixed overhead for June		$51,000
Variable overhead rate per hour		$3.00
Fixed overhead rate per hour		$1.20

Overhead is applied on the basis of standard machine hours. Three hours of machine time are required for each direct labor hour. The jobs were sold for $400,000. Selling and administrative expenses were $40,000. Assume that the amount of raw materials purchased equaled the amount used.

Instructions
(a) Compute all of the variances for (1) direct materials and (2) direct labor.
(b) Compute the total overhead variance.
(c) Prepare an income statement for management. Ignore income taxes.

Compute and identify significant variances.
(SO 4, 5, 6)

P25-3A Rapache Clothiers is a small company that manufactures tall-men's suits. The company has used a standard cost accounting system. In May 2010, 11,200 suits were produced. The following standard and actual cost data applied to the month of May when normal capacity was 14,000 direct labor hours. All materials purchased were used.

Cost Element	Standard (per unit)	Actual
Direct materials	8 yards at $4.30 per yard	$371,050 for 90,500 yards ($4.10 per yard)
Direct labor	1.2 hours at $13.50 per hour	$201,630 for 14,300 hours ($14.10 per hour)
Overhead	1.2 hours at $6.00 per hour (fixed $3.50; variable $2.50)	$49,000 fixed overhead $37,000 variable overhead

Overhead is applied on the basis of direct labor hours. At normal capacity, budgeted fixed overhead costs were $49,000, and budgeted variable overhead was $35,000.

Instructions
(a) Compute the total, price, and quantity variances for (1) materials and (2) labor.
(b) Compute the total overhead variance.
(c) Which of the materials and labor variances should be investigated if management considers a variance of more than 4% from standard to be significant?

P25-4A Dorantes Manufacturing Company uses a standard cost accounting system. In 2010, the company produced 28,000 units. Each unit took several pounds of direct materials and 1½ standard hours of direct labor at a standard hourly rate of $12.00. Normal capacity was 50,000 direct labor hours. During the year, 131,000 pounds of raw materials were purchased at $0.92 per pound. All materials purchased were used during the year.

Answer questions about variances.
(SO 4, 5)

Instructions
(a) If the materials price variance was $2,620 favorable, what was the standard materials price per pound?
(b) If the materials quantity variance was $4,700 unfavorable, what was the standard materials quantity per unit?
(c) What were the standard hours allowed for the units produced?
(d) If the labor quantity variance was $7,200 unfavorable, what were the actual direct labor hours worked?
(e) If the labor price variance was $10,650 favorable, what was the actual rate per hour?
(f) If total budgeted manufacturing overhead was $350,000 at normal capacity, what was the predetermined overhead rate?
(g) What was the standard cost per unit of product?
(h) How much overhead was applied to production during the year?
(i) Using one or more answers above, what were the total costs assigned to work in process?

P25-5A Farm Labs, Inc. provides mad cow disease testing for both state and federal governmental agricultural agencies. Because the company's customers are governmental agencies, prices are strictly regulated. Therefore, Farm Labs must constantly monitor and control its testing costs. Shown below are the standard costs for a typical test.

Compute variances, prepare an income statement, and explain unfavorable variances.
(SO 4, 5, 7)

Direct materials (2 test tubes @ $1.50 per tube)	$ 3
Direct labor (1 hour @ $25 per hour)	25
Variable overhead (1 hour @ $5 per hour)	5
Fixed overhead (1 hour @ $10 per hour)	10
Total standard cost per test	$43

The lab does not maintain an inventory of test tubes. Therefore, the tubes purchased each month are used that month. Actual activity for the month of November 2010, when 1,500 tests were conducted, resulted in the following:

Direct materials (3,050 test tubes)	$ 4,270
Direct labor (1,600 hours)	36,800
Variable overhead	7,400
Fixed overhead	14,000

Monthly budgeted fixed overhead is $14,000. Revenues for the month were $75,000, and selling and administrative expenses were $4,000.

Instructions
(a) Compute the price and quantity variances for direct materials and direct labor.
(b) Compute the total overhead variance.
(c) Prepare an income statement for management.
(d) Provide possible explanations for each unfavorable variance.

*P25-6A Adcock Corporation uses standard costs with its job order cost accounting system. In January, an order (Job No. 12) for 1,900 units of Product B was received. The standard cost of one unit of Product B is as follows:

Journalize and post standard cost entries, and prepare income statement.
(SO 4, 5, 7, 9)

Direct materials	3 pounds at $1.00 per pound	$ 3.00
Direct labor	1 hour at $8.00 per hour	8.00
Overhead	2 hours (variable $4.00 per machine hour; fixed $2.25 per machine hour)	12.50
Standard cost per unit		$23.50

1146 Chapter 25 Standard Costs and Balanced Scorecard

Normal capacity for the month was 4,200 machine hours. During January, the following transactions applicable to Job No. 12 occurred.

1. Purchased 6,250 pounds of raw materials on account at $1.06 per pound.
2. Requisitioned 6,250 pounds of raw materials for Job No. 12.
3. Incurred 2,100 hours of direct labor at a rate of $7.75 per hour.
4. Worked 2,100 hours of direct labor on Job No. 12.
5. Incurred manufacturing overhead on account $25,800.
6. Applied overhead to Job No. 12 on basis of standard machine hours allowed.
7. Completed Job No. 12.
8. Billed customer for Job No. 12 at a selling price of $70,000.
9. Incurred selling and administrative expenses on account $2,000.

Instructions
(a) Journalize the transactions.
(b) Post to the job order cost accounts.
(c) Prepare the entry to recognize the total overhead variance.
(d) Prepare the January 2010 income statement for management.

Compute overhead controllable and volume variances.
(SO 10)

*P25-7A Using the information in P25-1A, compute the overhead controllable variance and the overhead volume variance.

Compute overhead controllable and volume variances.
(SO 10)

*P25-8A Using the information in P25-2A, compute the overhead controllable variance and the overhead volume variance.

Compute overhead controllable and volume variances.
(SO 10)

*P25-9A Using the information in P25-3A, compute the overhead controllable variance and the overhead volume variance.

Compute overhead controllable and volume variances.
(SO 10)

*P25-10A Using the information in P25-5A, compute the overhead controllable variance and the overhead volume variance.

PROBLEMS: SET B

Compute variances.
(SO 4, 5)

P25-1B Maris Corporation manufactures a single product. The standard cost per unit of product is as follows.

Direct materials—2 pounds of plastic at $5 per pound	$10
Direct labor—2 hours at $12 per hour	24
Variable manufacturing overhead	8
Fixed manufacturing overhead	6
Total standard cost per unit	$48

The master manufacturing overhead budget for the month based on normal productive capacity of 20,000 direct labor hours (10,000 units) shows total variable costs of $80,000 ($4 per labor hour) and total fixed costs of $60,000 ($3 per labor hour). Normal productive capacity is 20,000 direct labor hours. Overhead is applied on the basis of direct labor hours. Actual costs for November in producing 9,700 units were as follows.

Direct materials (20,000 pounds)	$ 98,000
Direct labor (19,600 hours)	239,120
Variable overhead	79,100
Fixed overhead	59,000
Total manufacturing costs	$475,220

The purchasing department normally buys the quantities of raw materials that are expected to be used in production each month. Raw materials inventories, therefore, can be ignored.

Instructions
(a) Compute all of the materials and labor variances.
(b) Compute the total overhead variance.

Compute variances, and prepare income statement.
(SO 4, 5, 7)

P25-2B Sanchez Manufacturing Company uses a standard cost accounting system to account for the manufacture of exhaust fans. In July 2010, it accumulates the following data relative to 1,800 units started and finished.

Cost and Production Data	Actual	Standard
Raw materials		
Units purchased	21,000	
Units used	21,000	22,000
Unit cost	$3.40	$3.00
Direct labor		
Hours worked	3,450	3,600
Hourly rate	$11.80	$12.50
Manufacturing overhead		
Incurred	$101,500	
Applied		$108,000

Manufacturing overhead was applied on the basis of direct labor hours. Normal capacity for the month was 3,400 direct labor hours. At normal capacity, budgeted overhead costs were $20 per labor hour variable and $10 per labor hour fixed. Total budgeted fixed overhead costs were $34,000.

Jobs finished during the month were sold for $280,000. Selling and administrative expenses were $25,000.

Instructions
(a) Compute all of the variances for (1) direct materials and (2) direct labor.
(b) Compute the total overhead variance.
(c) Prepare an income statement for management. Ignore income taxes.

P25-3B Sadler Clothiers manufactures women's business suits. The company uses a standard cost accounting system. In March 2010, 15,700 suits were made. The following standard and actual cost data applied to the month of March when normal capacity was 20,000 direct labor hours. All materials purchased were used in production.

Compute and identify significant variances.
(SO 4, 5, 6)

Cost Element	Standard (per unit)	Actual
Direct materials	5 yards at $6.80 per yard	$547,200 for 76,000 yards ($7.20 per yard)
Direct labor	1.0 hours at $11.50 per hour	$166,880 for 14,900 hours ($11.20 per hour)
Overhead	1.0 hours at $9.30 per hour (fixed $6.30; variable $3.00)	$120,000 fixed overhead $49,000 variable overhead

Overhead is applied on the basis of direct labor hours. At normal capacity, budgeted fixed overhead costs were $126,000, and budgeted variable overhead costs were $60,000.

Instructions
(a) Compute the total, price, and quantity variances for (1) materials and (2) labor.
(b) Compute the total overhead variance.
(c) Which of the materials and labor variances should be investigated if management considers a variance of more than 5% from standard to be significant?

P25-4B Dobbs Manufacturing Company uses a standard cost accounting system. In 2010, 50,000 units were produced. Each unit took several pounds of direct materials and 2 standard hours of direct labor at a standard hourly rate of $12.00. Normal capacity was 96,000 direct labor hours. During the year, 200,000 pounds of raw materials were purchased at $1.00 per pound. All materials purchased were used during the year.

Answer questions about variances.
(SO 4, 5)

Instructions
(a) If the materials price variance was $8,000 unfavorable, what was the standard materials price per pound?
(b) If the materials quantity variance was $24,000 favorable, what was the standard materials quantity per unit?
(c) What were the standard hours allowed for the units produced?
(d) If the labor quantity variance was $10,800 unfavorable, what were the actual direct labor hours worked?
(e) If the labor price variance was $25,225 favorable, what was the actual rate per hour?

(f) If total budgeted manufacturing overhead was $792,000 at normal capacity, what was the predetermined overhead rate per direct labor hour?
(g) What was the standard cost per unit of product?
(h) How much overhead was applied to production during the year?
(i) Using selected answers above, what were the total costs assigned to work in process?

Compute variances, prepare an income statement, and explain unfavorable variances.
(SO 4, 5, 7)

P25-5B Moran Labs performs steroid testing services to high schools, colleges, and universities. Because the company deals solely with educational institutions, the price of each test is strictly regulated. Therefore, the costs incurred must be carefully monitored and controlled. Shown below are the standard costs for a typical test.

Direct materials (1 petrie dish @ $2 per dish)	$ 2.00
Direct labor (0.5 hours @ $20 per hour)	10.00
Variable overhead (0.5 hours @ $8 per hour)	4.00
Fixed overhead (0.5 hours @ $4 per hour)	2.00
Total standard cost per test	$18.00

The lab does not maintain an inventory of petrie dishes. Therefore, the dishes purchased each month are used that month. Actual activity for the month of May 2010, when 2,500 tests were conducted, resulted in the following.

Direct materials (2,530 dishes)	$ 5,313
Direct labor (1,240 hours)	26,040
Variable overhead	10,100
Fixed overhead	5,700

Monthly budgeted fixed overhead is $6,000. Revenues for the month were $58,000, and selling and administrative expenses were $2,000.

Instructions
(a) Compute the price and quantity variances for direct materials and direct labor.
(b) Compute the total overhead variance.
(c) Prepare an income statement for management.
(d) Provide possible explanations for each unfavorable variance.

Journalize and post standard cost entries, and prepare income statement.
(SO 4, 5, 7, 9)

*P25-6B Harter Manufacturing Company uses standard costs with its job order cost accounting system. In January, an order (Job No. 84) was received for 5,500 units of Product D. The standard cost of 1 unit of Product D is as follows.

Direct materials—1.4 pounds at $4.00 per pound	$ 5.60
Direct labor—1 hour at $9.00 per hour	9.00
Overhead—1 hour (variable $7.40; fixed $8.00)	15.40
Standard cost per unit	$30.00

Overhead is applied on the basis of direct labor hours. Normal capacity for the month of January was 6,000 direct labor hours. During January, the following transactions applicable to Job No. 84 occurred.

1. Purchased 8,100 pounds of raw materials on account at $3.60 per pound.
2. Requisitioned 8,100 pounds of raw materials for production.
3. Incurred 5,100 hours of direct labor at $9.25 per hour.
4. Worked 5,100 hours of direct labor on Job No. 84.
5. Incurred $87,650 of manufacturing overhead on account.
6. Applied overhead to Job No. 84 on the basis of direct labor hours.
7. Transferred Job No. 84 to finished goods.
8. Billed customer for Job No. 84 at a selling price of $280,000.
9. Incurred selling and administrative expenses on account $61,000.

Instructions
(a) Journalize the transactions.
(b) Post to the job order cost accounts.
(c) Prepare the entry to recognize the total overhead variance.
(d) Prepare the January 2010 income statement for management.

Compute overhead controllable and volume variances.
(SO 10)

*P25-7B Using the information in P25-1B, compute the overhead controllable variance and the overhead volume variance.

*P25-8B Using the information in P25-2B, compute the overhead controllable variance and the overhead volume variance.

Compute overhead controllable and volume variances.
(SO 10)

*P25-9B Using the information in P25-3B, compute the overhead controllable variance and the overhead volume variance.

Compute overhead controllable and volume variances.
(SO 10)

*P25-10B Using the information in P25-5B, compute the overhead controllable variance and the overhead volume variance.

Compute overhead controllable and volume variances.
(SO 10)

PROBLEMS: SET C

Visit the book's companion website at **www.wiley.com/college/weygandt**, and choose the Student Companion site, to access Problem Set C.

WATERWAYS CONTINUING PROBLEM

(This is a continuation of the Waterways Problem from Chapters 19 through 24.)

WCP25 Waterways Corporation uses very stringent standard costs in evaluating its manufacturing efficiency. These standards are not "ideal" at this point, but the management is working toward that as a goal. This problem asks you to calculate and evaluate the company's variances.

Go to the book's companion website, www.wiley.com/college/weygandt, to find the remainder of this problem.

BROADENING YOUR PERSPECTIVE

Decision Making Across the Organization

BYP25-1 Colaw Professionals, a management consulting firm, specializes in strategic planning for financial institutions. Ken Comer and Mary Linden, partners in the firm, are assembling a new strategic planning model for use by clients. The model is designed for use on most personal computers and replaces a rather lengthy manual model currently marketed by the firm. To market the new model Ken and Mary will need to provide clients with an estimate of the number of labor hours and computer time needed to operate the model. The model is currently being test marketed at five small financial institutions. These financial institutions are listed below, along with the number of combined computer/labor hours used by each institution to run the model one time.

Financial Institutions	Computer/Labor Hours Required
Midland National	25
First State	45
Financial Federal	40
Pacific America	30
Lakeview National	30
Total	170
Average	34

Any company that purchases the new model will need to purchase user manuals for the system. User manuals will be sold to clients in cases of 20, at a cost of $300 per case. One manual must be used each time the model is run because each manual includes a nonreusable computer-accessed password for operating the system. Also required are specialized computer forms that are sold only by Colaw. The specialized forms are sold in packages of 250, at a cost of $50 per package. One application of the model requires the use of 50 forms. This amount includes two forms that are generally wasted in each application due to printer alignment errors. The overall cost of the strategic planning model to clients is $12,000. Most clients will use the model four times annually.

Colaw must provide its clients with estimates of ongoing costs incurred in operating the new planning model, and would like to do so in the form of standard costs.

Instructions

With the class divided into groups, answer the following.
(a) What factors should be considered in setting a standard for computer/labor hours?
(b) What alternatives for setting a standard for computer/labor hours might be used?
(c) What standard for computer/labor hours would you select? Justify your answer.
(d) Determine the standard materials cost associated with the user manuals and computer forms for each application of the strategic planning model.

Managerial Analysis

*BYP25-2 Ed Widner and Associates is a medium-sized company located near a large metropolitan area in the Midwest. The company manufactures cabinets of mahogany, oak, and other fine woods for use in expensive homes, restaurants, and hotels. Although some of the work is custom, many of the cabinets are a standard size.

One such non-custom model is called Luxury Base Frame. Normal production is 1,000 units. Each unit has a direct labor hour standard of 5 hours. Overhead is applied to production based on standard direct labor hours. During the most recent month, only 900 units were produced; 4,500 direct labor hours were allowed for standard production, but only 4,000 hours were used. Standard and actual overhead costs were as follows.

	Standard (1,000 units)	Actual (900 units)
Indirect materials	$ 12,000	$ 12,300
Indirect labor	43,000	51,000
(Fixed) Manufacturing supervisors salaries	22,000	22,000
(Fixed) Manufacturing office employees salaries	13,000	11,500
(Fixed) Engineering costs	27,000	25,000
Computer costs	10,000	10,000
Electricity	2,500	2,500
(Fixed) Manufacturing building depreciation	8,000	8,000
(Fixed) Machinery depreciation	3,000	3,000
(Fixed) Trucks and forklift depreciation	1,500	1,500
Small tools	700	1,400
(Fixed) Insurance	500	500
(Fixed) Property taxes	300	300
Total	$143,500	$149,000

Instructions
(a) Determine the overhead application rate.
(b) Determine how much overhead was applied to production.
(c) Calculate the controllable overhead variance and the overhead volume variance.
(d) Decide which overhead variances should be investigated.
(e) Discuss causes of the overhead variances. What can management do to improve its performance next month?

Real-World Focus

BYP25-3 Glassmaster Co. is organized as two divisions and one subsidiary. One division focuses on the manufacture of filaments such as fishing line and sewing thread; the other division manufactures antennas and specialty fiberglass products. Its subsidiary manufactures flexible steel wire controls and molded control panels.

The annual report of Glassmaster provides the following information.

> **GLASSMASTER COMPANY**
> **Management Discussion**
>
> Gross profit margins for the year improved to 20.9% of sales compared to last year's 18.5%. All operations reported improved margins due in large part to improved operating efficiencies as a result of cost reduction measures implemented during the second and third quarters of the fiscal year and increased manufacturing throughout due to higher unit volume sales. Contributing to the improved margins was a favorable materials price variance due to competitive pricing by suppliers as a result of soft demand for petrochemical-based products. This favorable variance is temporary and will begin to reverse itself as stronger worldwide demand for commodity products improves in tandem with the economy. Partially offsetting these positive effects on profit margins were competitive pressures on sales prices of certain product lines. The company responded with pricing strategies designed to maintain and/or increase market share.

Instructions
(a) Is it apparent from the information whether Glassmaster utilizes standard costs?
(b) Do you think the price variance experienced should lead to changes in standard costs for the next fiscal year?

Exploring the Web

BYP25-4 The Balanced Scorecard Institute **(www.balancedscorecard.org)** is a great resource for information about implementing the balanced scorecard. One item of interest provided at its website is an example of a balanced scorecard for a regional airline.

Address: http://www.balancedscorecard.org/files/Regional_Airline.pdf, or go to **www.wiley.com/college/weygandt**

Instructions
Go to the address above and answer the following questions.
(a) What are the objectives identified for the airline for each perspective?
(b) What measures are used for the objective in the customer perspective?
(c) What initiatives are planned to achieve the objective in the learning perspective?

Communication Activity

BYP25-5 The setting of standards is critical to the effective use of standards in evaluating performance.

Instructions
Explain the following in a memo to your instructor.
(a) The comparative advantages and disadvantages of ideal versus normal standards.
(b) The factors that should be included in setting the price and quantity standards for direct materials, direct labor, and manufacturing overhead.

Ethics Case

BYP25-6 At Camden Manufacturing Company, production workers in the Painting Department are paid on the basis of productivity. The labor time standard for a unit of production is established through periodic time studies conducted by the Lowery Management Department. In a time study, the actual time required to complete a specific task by a worker is observed. Allowances are then made for preparation time, rest periods, and clean-up time. Ron Orlano is one of several veterans in the Painting Department.

Ron is informed by Lowery Management that he will be used in the time study for the painting of a new product. The findings will be the basis for establishing the labor time standard for the next 6 months. During the test, Ron deliberately slows his normal work pace in an effort to obtain a labor time standard that will be easy to meet. Because it is a new product, the Lowery Management representative who conducted the test is unaware that Ron did not give the test his best effort.

Instructions
(a) Who was benefited and who was harmed by Ron's actions?
(b) Was Ron ethical in the way he performed the time study test?
(c) What measure(s) might the company take to obtain valid data for setting the labor time standard?

"All About You" Activity

BYP25-7 From the time you first entered school many years ago, instructors have been measuring and evaluating you by imposing standards. In addition, many of you will pursue professions that administer professional examinations to attain recognized certification. Recently a federal commission presented proposals suggesting all public colleges and universities should require standardized tests to measure their students' learning.

Instructions
Read the following article at **www.signonsandiego.com/uniontrib/20060811/news_1n11colleges.html**, and answer the following questions.

(a) What areas of concern did the panel's recommendations address?
(b) What are possible advantages of standard testing?
(c) What are possible disadvantages of standard testing?
(d) Would you be in favor of standardized tests?

Answers to Insight and Accounting Across the Organization Questions

p. 1115 How Can We Make Susan's Chili Profitable?
Q: How might management use this raw material cost information?
A: *Management might decide to increase the price of its chili. Or it might revise its recipes to use cheaper ingredients. Or it might eliminate some products until ingredients are available at costs closer to standard.*

p. 1126 It May Be Time to Fly United Again
Q: Which of the perspectives of a balanced scorecard were the focus of United's CEO?
A: *Improving on-time flight departures is an objective within the internal process perspective. Customer intent to fly United again is an objective within the customer perspective.*

Answers to Self-Study Questions
1. c **2.** b **3.** d **4.** a **5.** b **6.** c **7.** b **8.** a **9.** d **10.** a **11.** b **12.** d **13.** c **14.** d ***15.** c ***16.** c

Remember to go back to the Navigator box on the chapter-opening page and check off your completed work.

Chapter 26

Incremental Analysis and Capital Budgeting

STUDY OBJECTIVES

After studying this chapter, you should be able to:

1. Identify the steps in management's decision-making process.
2. Describe the concept of incremental analysis.
3. Identify the relevant costs in accepting an order at a special price.
4. Identify the relevant costs in a make-or-buy decision.
5. Give the decision rule for whether to sell or process materials further.
6. Identify the factors to consider in retaining or replacing equipment.
7. Explain the relevant factors in whether to eliminate an unprofitable segment.
8. Determine which products to make and sell when resources are limited.
9. Contrast annual rate of return and cash payback in capital budgeting.
10. Distinguish between the net present value and internal rate of return methods.

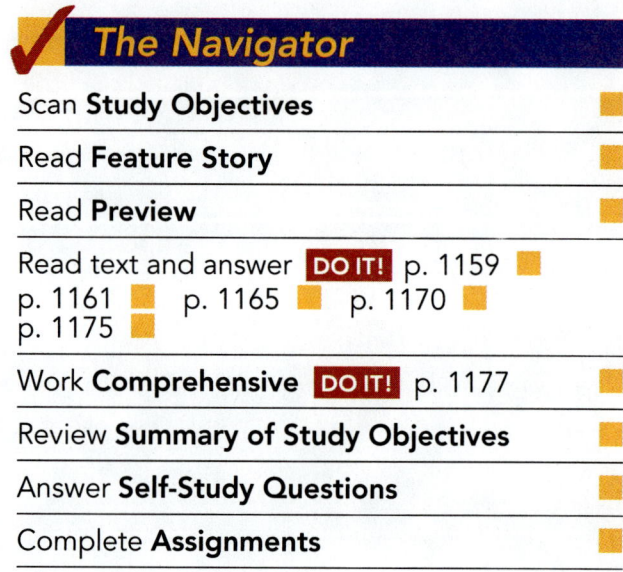

The Navigator

- Scan **Study Objectives**
- Read **Feature Story**
- Read **Preview**
- Read text and answer **DO IT!** p. 1159, p. 1161, p. 1165, p. 1170, p. 1175
- Work **Comprehensive** **DO IT!** p. 1177
- Review **Summary of Study Objectives**
- Answer **Self-Study Questions**
- Complete **Assignments**

Feature Story

SOUP IS GOOD FOOD

When you hear the word *Campbell*, what is the first thing that comes to mind? Soup. Campbell *is* soup. It sells 38 percent of all the soup—including homemade—consumed in the United States.

But can a company survive on soup alone? In an effort to expand its operations and to lessen its reliance on soup, Campbell Soup Company (www.campbellsoup.com) in 1990 began searching for an additional line of business. Campbell's management believed it saw an opportunity in convenient meals that were low in fat, nutritionally rich, and had therapeutic value for heart patients and diabetics. This venture would require a huge investment—but the rewards were potentially tremendous.

The initial investment required building food labs, hiring nutritional scientists, researching prototype products, constructing new production facilities, and marketing the new products. Management predicted that with an initial investment of roughly $55 million, the company might generate sales of $200 million per year.

By 1994 the company had created 24 meals, and an extensive field-study revealed considerable health benefits from the products. Unfortunately, initial sales of the new product line, called Intelligent Quisine, were less than stellar. In 1997 Campbell hired a consulting firm to evaluate whether to continue the project. Product development of the new line was costing $20 million per year—a sum that some managers felt could be better spent developing new products in other divisions, or expanding overseas operations. In 1998 Campbell discontinued the project.

Campbell was not giving up on growth, but simply had decided to refocus its efforts on soup. The company's annual report stated management's philosophy: "Soup will be our growth engine." Campbell has sold off many of its non-soup businesses and in a recent year introduced 20 new soup products.

Source: Vanessa O'Connell, "Food for Thought: How Campbell Saw a Breakthrough Menu Turn into Leftovers," *Wall Street Journal*, October 6, 1998.

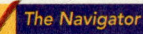

The Navigator

Inside Chapter 26...

- **These Wheels Have Miles Before Installation** (p. 1162)
- **Are You Ready for the 50-Inch Screen?** (p. 1170)
- ***All About You:* What Is a Degree Worth?** (p. 1176)

1155

Preview of Chapter 26

An important purpose of management accounting is to provide relevant information for decision making. Examples of these decisions include the following: (1) Campbell Soup's decision to produce "therapeutic meals" rather than some other food product. (2) Boeing's strategic decisions to spend $5 billion to build a plane for the 21st century—the B-777—and to cancel development of a larger version of the B-747. (3) The Coca-Cola Company's decision to spend $750 million to build twelve plants in Russia.

This chapter begins with an explanation of management's decision-making process. It then considers the topics of incremental analysis and capital budgeting. The content and organization of Chapter 26 are as follows.

Incremental Analysis and Capital Budgeting

Incremental Analysis
- Management's decision-making process
- Accept special-price order
- Make or buy
- Sell or process further
- Retain or replace equipment
- Eliminate unprofitable segment
- Allocate limited resources

Capital Budgeting
- Evaluation process
- Annual rate of return
- Cash payback
- Discounted cash flow: NPV and IRR

✓ The Navigator

SECTION 1 Incremental Analysis

MANAGEMENT'S DECISION-MAKING PROCESS

STUDY OBJECTIVE 1
Identify the steps in management's decision-making process.

Making decisions is an important management function. Management's decision-making process does not always follow a set pattern, because decisions vary significantly in their scope, urgency, and importance. It is possible, though, to identify some steps that are frequently involved in the process. These steps are shown in Illustration 26-1.

Illustration 26-1
Management's decision-making process

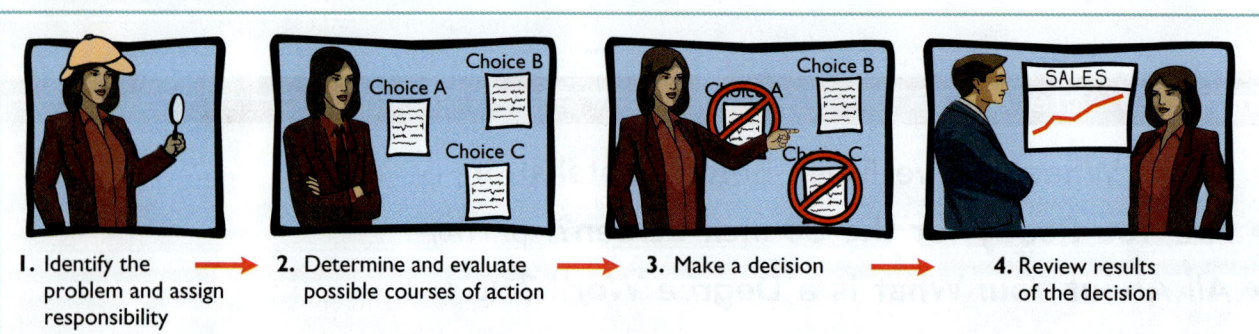

1. Identify the problem and assign responsibility
2. Determine and evaluate possible courses of action
3. Make a decision
4. Review results of the decision

Accounting's contribution to the decision-making process occurs primarily in Steps 2 and 4—evaluating possible courses of action, and reviewing the results. In Step 2, for each possible course of action, accounting provides relevant revenue and cost data. These show the expected overall effect on net income. In Step 4, accounting prepares internal reports that review the actual impact of the decision.

In making business decisions, management ordinarily considers both financial and nonfinancial information. *Financial information* is related to revenues and costs and their effect on the company's overall profitability. *Nonfinancial information* relates to such factors as the effect of the decision on employee turnover, the environment, or the overall image of the company in the community. Although the nonfinancial information can be as important as the financial information, we focus primarily on financial information that is relevant to the decision.

The Incremental Analysis Approach

Decisions involve a choice among alternative courses of action. Suppose that you were deciding whether to purchase or lease a computer for use in doing your accounting homework. The financial data relate to the cost of leasing versus the cost of purchasing. For example, leasing involves periodic lease payments; purchasing requires "up-front" payment of the purchase price. In other words, the financial data relevant to the decision are the data that vary among the possible alternatives. The process used to identify the financial data that change under alternative courses of action is called **incremental analysis**. In some cases, when you use incremental analysis, both costs **and** revenues will change. In other cases, only costs **or** revenues will change.

STUDY OBJECTIVE 2
Describe the concept of incremental analysis.

ALTERNATIVE TERMINOLOGY
Incremental analysis is also called *differential analysis* because the analysis focuses on differences.

Just as your decision to buy or lease a PC affects your future, similar decisions, on a larger scale, affect a company's future. Incremental analysis identifies the probable effects of those decisions on future earnings. Such analysis inevitably involves estimates and uncertainty. Gathering data for incremental analyses may involve market analysts, engineers, and accountants. In quantifying the data, the accountant is expected to produce the most reliable information available at the time the decision must be made.

How Incremental Analysis Works

The following example illustrates the basic approach in incremental analysis.

	Alternative A	Alternative B	Net Income Increase (Decrease)
Revenues	$125,000	$110,000	$ (15,000)
Costs	100,000	80,000	20,000
Net income	$ 25,000	$ 30,000	$ 5,000

Illustration 26-2
Basic approach in incremental analysis

This example compares alternative B with alternative A. The net income column shows the differences between the alternatives. In this case, incremental revenue will be $15,000 less under alternative B than under alternative A, but a $20,000 incremental cost saving will be realized.[1] Thus, alternative B will produce $5,000 more net income than alternative A.

Incremental analysis sometimes involves changes that at first glance might seem contrary to your intuition. For example, sometimes variable costs *do not change* under the alternative courses of action. Also, sometimes fixed costs *do change*. For example, direct labor, normally a variable cost, is not an incremental cost in deciding between two new factory machines if each asset requires the same amount of direct labor. In contrast, rent expense, normally a fixed cost, is an incremental cost in a decision to continue occupancy of a building or to purchase or lease a new building.

TYPES OF INCREMENTAL ANALYSIS

A number of different types of decisions involve incremental analysis. The more common types of decisions are:

1. Accept an order at a special price.
2. Make or buy.
3. Sell or process further.
4. Retain or replace equipment.
5. Eliminate an unprofitable business segment.
6. Allocate limited resources.

We consider each of these types of analysis in the following pages.

Accept an Order at a Special Price

STUDY OBJECTIVE 3
Identify the relevant costs in accepting an order at a special price.

Sometimes, a company has an opportunity to obtain additional business if it is willing to make a major price concession to a specific customer. To illustrate, assume that Sunbelt Company produces 100,000 automatic blenders per month, which is 80% of plant capacity. Variable manufacturing costs are $8 per unit. Fixed manufacturing costs are $400,000, or $4 per unit. The blenders are normally sold directly to retailers at $20 each. Sunbelt has an offer from Mexico Co. (a foreign wholesaler) to purchase an additional 2,000 blenders at $11 per unit. Acceptance of the offer would not affect normal sales of the product, and the additional units can be manufactured without increasing plant capacity. What should management do?

If management makes its decision on the basis of the total cost per unit of $12 ($8 + $4), the order would be rejected, because costs ($12) would exceed revenues ($11) by $1 per unit. However, since the units can be produced within existing plant capacity, the special order **will not increase fixed costs**. The relevant data for the decision, therefore, are the variable manufacturing costs per unit of $8 and the expected revenue of $11 per unit. Thus, as shown in Illustration 26-3, Sunbelt will increase its net income by $6,000 by accepting this special order.

---

[1]Although income taxes are sometimes important in incremental analysis, they are ignored in the chapter for simplicity's sake.

Illustration 26-3
Incremental analysis—accepting an order at a special price

	Reject Order	Accept Order	Net Income Increase (Decrease)
Revenues	$0	$22,000	$ 22,000
Costs	0	16,000	(16,000)
Net income	$0	$ 6,000	$ 6,000

Two points should be emphasized: First, we assume that sales of the product in other markets are not affected by this special order. If other sales are affected, then Sunbelt must consider the lost sales in making the decision. Second, if Sunbelt is operating at full capacity, it is likely that the special order would be rejected. Under such circumstances, the company would have to expand plant capacity. In that case, the special order would have to absorb these additional fixed manufacturing costs, as well as the variable manufacturing costs.

DO IT!

SPECIAL ORDERS

Cobb Company incurs a cost of $28 per unit, of which $18 is variable, to make a product that normally sells for $42. A foreign wholesaler offers to buy 5,000 units at $25 each. Cobb will incur shipping costs of $1 per unit. Compute the increase or decrease in net income Cobb will realize by accepting the special order, assuming Cobb has excess operating capacity. Should Cobb Company accept the special order?

action plan

✔ Identify all revenues that will change as a result of accepting the order.
✔ Identify all costs that will change as a result of accepting the order, and net this amount against the change in revenues.

Solution

	Reject	Accept	Net Income Increase (Decrease)
Revenues	$–0–	$125,000	$125,000
Costs	–0–	95,000*	(95,000)
Net income	$–0–	$ 30,000	$ 30,000

*(5,000 × $18) + (5,000 × $1)

Given the result of the analysis, Cobb Company should accept the special order.

Related exercise material: **BE26-2, BE26-3, E26-2, E26-3**, and **DO IT! 26-1**.

Make or Buy

When a manufacturer assembles component parts in producing a finished product, management must decide whether to make or buy the components. For example, General Motors Corporation may either make or buy the batteries, tires, and radios used in its cars. Similarly, Hewlett-Packard Corporation may make or buy the electronic circuitry, cases, and printer heads for its printers. Boeing recently sold some of its commercial aircraft factories in an effort to cut production costs and focus instead on engineering and final assembly rather than manufacturing. The decision to make or buy components should be made on the basis of incremental analysis.

STUDY OBJECTIVE 4
Identify the relevant costs in a make-or-buy decision.

Chapter 26 Incremental Analysis and Capital Budgeting

To illustrate the analysis, assume that Baron Company incurs the following annual costs in producing 25,000 ignition switches for motor scooters.

Illustration 26-4
Annual product cost data

Direct materials	$ 50,000
Direct labor	75,000
Variable manufacturing overhead	40,000
Fixed manufacturing overhead	60,000
Total manufacturing costs	$225,000
Total cost per unit ($225,000 ÷ 25,000)	**$9.00**

Or, instead of making its own switches, Baron Company might purchase the ignition switches from Ignition Inc. at a price of $8 per unit. The question again is, "What should management do?"

At first glance, it appears that management should purchase the ignition switches for $8, rather than make them at a cost of $9. However, a review of operations indicates that if Baron purchases the ignition switches from Ignition Inc., it will eliminate *all* of its variable costs but only $10,000 of its fixed manufacturing costs. Thus, $50,000 of the fixed manufacturing costs will remain if the ignition switches are purchased. The relevant costs for incremental analysis, therefore, are as follows.

Illustration 26-5
Incremental analysis—make or buy

Incremental Analysis - Make or buy.xls

	Make	Buy	Net Income Increase (Decrease)
Direct materials	$ 50,000	$ 0	$ 50,000
Direct labor	75,000	0	75,000
Variable manufacturing costs	40,000	0	40,000
Fixed manufacturing costs	60,000	50,000	10,000
Purchase price (25,000 × $8)	0	200,000	(200,000)
Total annual cost	$225,000	$250,000	$ (25,000)

> **ETHICS NOTE**
> In the make-or-buy decision it is important for management to take into account the social impact of its choice. For instance, buying may be the most economically feasible solution, but such action could result in the closure of a manufacturing plant that employs many good workers.

This analysis indicates that Baron Company will incur $25,000 of additional costs by buying the ignition switches. Therefore, Baron should continue to make the ignition switches, even though the total manufacturing cost is $1 higher than the purchase price. The reason is that if the company purchases the ignition switches, it will still have fixed costs of $50,000 to absorb.

OPPORTUNITY COST

The foregoing make-or-buy analysis is complete only if the productive capacity used to make the ignition switches cannot be converted to another purpose. If there is an opportunity to use this productive capacity in some other manner, then this opportunity cost must be considered. **Opportunity cost** is the potential benefit that may be obtained by following an alternative course of action.

To illustrate, assume that through buying the switches, Baron Company can use the released productive capacity to generate additional income of $28,000. This lost income is an additional cost of continuing to make the switches in the make-or-buy decision. This opportunity cost therefore is added to the "Make" column, for comparison. Illustration 26-6 shows that it is now advantageous to buy the ignition switches.

Illustration 26-6
Incremental analysis—make or buy, with opportunity cost

	Make	Buy	Net Income Increase (Decrease)
Total annual cost	$225,000	$250,000	$(25,000)
Opportunity cost	**28,000**	**0**	**28,000**
Total cost	$253,000	$250,000	$ 3,000

The qualitative factors in this decision include the possible loss of jobs for employees who produce the ignition switches. In addition, management must assess how long the supplier will be able to satisfy the company's quality control standards at the quoted price per unit.

DO IT!

MAKE OR BUY

Juanita Company must decide whether to make or buy some of its components. The costs of producing 50,000 electrical cords for its floor lamps are as follows.

Direct materials	$60,000	Variable overhead	$12,000
Direct labor	$30,000	Fixed overhead	$8,000

Instead of making the electrical cords at an average cost per unit of $2.20 ($110,000 ÷ 50,000), the company has an opportunity to buy the cords at $2.15 per unit. If the company purchases the cords, all variable costs and one-half of the fixed costs will be eliminated.

(a) Prepare an incremental analysis showing whether the company should make or buy the electrical cords. **(b)** Will your answer be different if the released productive capacity will generate additional income of $25,000?

action plan
✔ Look for the costs that change.
✔ Ignore the costs that do not change.
✔ Use the format in the chapter for your answer.
✔ Recognize that opportunity cost can make a difference.

Solution
(a)

	Make	Buy	Net Income Increase (Decrease)
Direct materials	$ 60,000	$ –0–	$ 60,000
Direct labor	30,000	–0–	30,000
Variable manufacturing costs	12,000	–0–	12,000
Fixed manufacturing costs	8,000	4,000	4,000
Purchase price	–0–	107,500	(107,500)
Total cost	$110,000	$111,500	$ (1,500)

This analysis indicates that Juanita Company will incur $1,500 of additional costs if it buys the electrical cords.

(b)

	Make	Buy	Net Income Increase (Decrease)
Total cost	$110,000	$111,500	$ (1,500)
Opportunity cost	25,000		25,000
Total cost	$135,000	$111,500	$ 23,500

Yes, the answer is different: The analysis shows that net income will be increased by $23,500 if Juanita Company purchases the electrical cords.

Related exercise material: **BE26-4, E26-4,** and **DO IT! 26-2**.

ACCOUNTING ACROSS THE ORGANIZATION

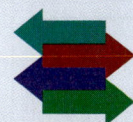

These Wheels Have Miles Before Installation

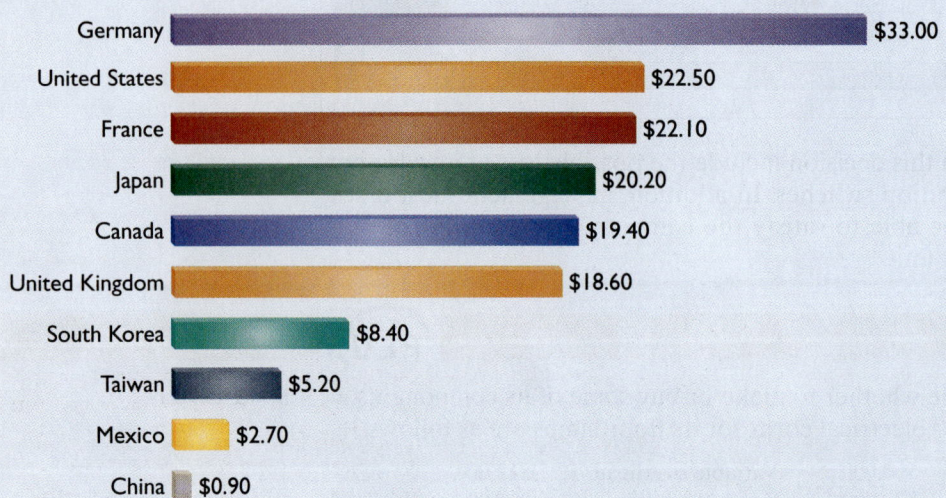

Consider the make-or-buy decision faced by Superior Industries International, Inc., a big aluminum-wheel maker in Van Nuys, California. For years, president Steve Borick had ignored the possibility of Chinese manufacturing. Then Mr. Borick started getting a blunt message from General Motors and Ford, with whom Superior does 85% of its business: Match the prices of Chinese wheel suppliers. Both auto makers said separately that if Superior could not agree to the lower prices, they would go directly to Chinese manufacturers or turn to other North American wheel-makers.

Stories like this, repeated in various industries, illustrate why manufacturers engage in overseas *off-shoring* (outsourcing). For example, compare the relative labor costs in major auto-producing nations, in dollars per hour, to see why incremental analysis often leads to outsourcing production to countries like China.

Source: Norihiko Shirouzu, "Big Three's Outsourcing Plan: Make Parts Suppliers Do It," *Wall Street Journal*, June 10, 2004, p. A1.

 What are the disadvantages of outsourcing to a foreign country?

Sell or Process Further

STUDY OBJECTIVE 5
Give the decision rule for whether to sell or process materials further.

Many manufacturers have the option of selling products at a given point in the production cycle or continuing to process with the expectation of selling them at a higher price. For example, a bicycle manufacturer such as Schwinn could sell its 10-speed bicycles to retailers either unassembled or assembled. A furniture manufacturer such as Ethan Allen could sell its dining room sets to furniture stores either unfinished or finished. The sell-or-process-further decision should be made on the basis of incremental analysis. The basic decision rule is: **Process further as long as the incremental revenue from such processing exceeds the incremental processing costs.**

Assume, for example, that Woodmasters Inc. makes tables. The cost to manufacture an unfinished table is $35, computed as follows.

Illustration 26-7
Per unit cost of unfinished table

Direct material	$15
Direct labor	10
Variable manufacturing overhead	6
Fixed manufacturing overhead	4
Manufacturing cost per unit	**$35**

The selling price per unfinished unit is $50. Woodmasters currently has unused productive capacity that is expected to continue indefinitely. Management concludes that some of this capacity can be used to finish the tables and sell them at $60 per unit. For a finished table, direct materials will increase $2 and direct labor costs will increase $4. Variable manufacturing overhead costs will increase by $2.40 (60% of direct labor). No increase is anticipated in fixed manufacturing overhead. Illustration 26-8 shows the incremental analysis on a per unit basis.

Illustration 26-8
Incremental analysis—sell or process further

	Sell	Process Further	Net Income Increase (Decrease)
Sales per unit	$50.00	$60.00	$10.00
Cost per unit			
Direct materials	15.00	17.00	(2.00)
Direct labor	10.00	14.00	(4.00)
Variable manufacturing overhead	6.00	8.40	(2.40)
Fixed manufacturing overhead	4.00	4.00	0.00
Total	35.00	43.40	(8.40)
Net income per unit	$15.00	$16.60	$ 1.60

HELPFUL HINT
Current net income is known. Net income from processing further is an estimate. In making its decision, management could add a "risk" factor for the estimate.

It is advantageous for Woodmasters to process the tables further. The incremental revenue of $10.00 from the additional processing is $1.60 higher than the incremental processing costs of $8.40.

Retain or Replace Equipment

Management often has to decide whether to continue using an asset or replace it. To illustrate, assume that Jeffcoat Company has a factory machine with a book value of $40,000 and a remaining useful life of four years. A new machine is available that costs $120,000. It is expected to have zero salvage value at the end of its four-year useful life. If Jeffcoat acquires the new machine, variable manufacturing costs are expected to decrease from $160,000 to $125,000 annually, and the old unit will be scrapped. The incremental analysis for the four-year period is as follows.

STUDY OBJECTIVE 6
Identify the factors to consider in retaining or replacing equipment.

Illustration 26-9
Incremental analysis—retain or replace equipment

	Retain Equipment		Replace Equipment		Net Income Increase (Decrease)
Variable manufacturing costs	$640,000	a	$500,000	b	$140,000
New machine cost			120,000		(120,000)
Total	$640,000		$620,000		$ 20,000

a(4 years × $160,000)
b(4 years × $125,000)

1164 Chapter 26 Incremental Analysis and Capital Budgeting

In this case, it is advantageous to replace the equipment. The lower variable manufacturing costs related to the new equipment more than offset its purchase cost.

One other point about Jeffcoat's decision: **The book value of the old machine does not affect the decision.** Book value is a **sunk cost**, which is a cost that cannot be changed by any present or future decision. Sunk costs **are not relevant in incremental analysis**. In this example, if the company retains the asset, book value is depreciated over its remaining useful life. Or, if the company acquires the new unit, book value is recognized as a loss of the current period. Thus, the effect of book value on current and future earnings is the same regardless of the replacement decision. However, **any trade-in allowance or cash disposal value of the existing asset is relevant** to the decision, because the company will not realize this value if the old asset is continued in use.

Eliminate an Unprofitable Segment

STUDY OBJECTIVE 7
Explain the relevant factors in whether to eliminate an unprofitable segment.

Management sometimes must decide whether to eliminate an unprofitable business segment. For example, in recent years many airlines have quit servicing certain cities or have cut back on the number of flights; and Goodyear recently quit producing several brands in the low-end tire market. Again, the key is to **focus on the relevant costs—the data that change under the alternative courses of action**. To illustrate, assume that Martina Company manufactures tennis racquets in three models: Pro, Master, and Champ. Pro and Master are profitable lines. Champ (highlighted in color in Illustration 26-10) operates at a loss. Condensed income statement data for the three segments are:

Illustration 26-10
Segment income data

	Pro	Master	Champ	Total
Sales	$800,000	$300,000	**$100,000**	$1,200,000
Variable expenses	520,000	210,000	**90,000**	820,000
Contribution margin	280,000	90,000	**10,000**	380,000
Fixed expenses	80,000	50,000	**30,000**	160,000
Net income	$200,000	$ 40,000	**$ (20,000)**	$ 220,000

It might be expected that total net income will increase by $20,000 to $240,000 if Martina Company eliminates the unprofitable Champ line of racquets. However, **net income may decrease if that line is discontinued**. The reason is that the other products will have to absorb the fixed expenses allocated to the Champ racquets. To illustrate, assume that the $30,000 of fixed costs applicable to the unprofitable segment are allocated ⅔ and ⅓ to the Pro and Master product lines, respectively. Fixed expenses will increase to $100,000 ($80,000 + $20,000) in the Pro line and to $60,000 ($50,000 + $10,000) in the Master line. Illustration 26-11 shows the revised income statements.

HELPFUL HINT
A decision to discontinue a segment based solely on the bottom line—net loss—is inappropriate.

Illustration 26-11
Income data after eliminating unprofitable product line

	Pro	Master	Total
Sales	$800,000	$300,000	$1,100,000
Variable expenses	520,000	210,000	730,000
Contribution margin	280,000	90,000	370,000
Fixed expenses	**100,000**	**60,000**	160,000
Net income	$180,000	$ 30,000	**$ 210,000**

Total net income has decreased $10,000 ($220,000 − $210,000). This result is also obtained in the following incremental analysis of the Champ racquets.

Illustration 26-12
Incremental analysis—eliminating an unprofitable segment

	Continue	Eliminate	Net Income Increase (Decrease)
Sales	$100,000	$ 0	$(100,000)
Variable costs	90,000	0	90,000
Contribution margin	10,000	0	(10,000)
Fixed costs	30,000	30,000	0
Net income	$ (20,000)	$(30,000)	$ (10,000)

The loss in net income is attributable to the contribution margin ($10,000) that the company will not realize if it discontinues the segment.

In deciding on the future status of an unprofitable segment, management should consider the effect of elimination on related product lines. It may be possible for continuing product lines to obtain some or all of the sales lost by the discontinued product line. In some businesses, services or products may be linked—for example, free checking accounts at a bank, or coffee at a donut shop. In addition, management should consider the effect of eliminating the product line on employees who may have to be discharged or retrained.

DO IT!

UNPROFITABLE SEGMENTS

Lambert, Inc. manufactures several types of accessories. For the year, the knit hats and scarves line had sales of $400,000, variable expenses of $310,000, and fixed expenses of $120,000. Therefore, the knit hats and scarves line had a net loss of $30,000. If Lambert eliminates the knit hats and scarves line, $20,000 of fixed costs will remain. Prepare an analysis showing whether the company should eliminate the knit hats and scarves line.

action plan

✔ Identify the revenues that will change as a result of eliminating a product line.

✔ Identify all costs that will change as a result of eliminating a product line, and net the amount against the revenues.

Solution

	Continue	Eliminate	Net Income Increase (Decrease)
Sales	$400,000	$ 0	$(400,000)
Variable costs	310,000	0	310,000
Contribution margin	90,000	0	(90,000)
Fixed costs	120,000	20,000	100,000
Net income	$ (30,000)	$(20,000)	$ 10,000

The analysis indicates that Lambert should eliminate the knit hats and scarves line because net income will increase $10,000.

Related exercise material: **BE26-7, E26-8, E26-9,** and **DO IT! 26-3.**

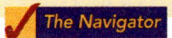

Allocate Limited Resources

Companies, like individuals, face limited resources. For a retail department store, the limited resource may be floor space. For a manufacturing company, the limited resource may be raw materials, direct labor hours, or machine capacity. When a company has limited resources, management must decide which products to make and sell in order to maximize net income.

STUDY OBJECTIVE 8
Determine which products to make and sell when resources are limited.

To illustrate, assume that Collins Company manufactures deluxe and standard pen and pencil sets. The limiting resource is machine capacity, which is 3,600 hours per month. Relevant data consist of the following.

Illustration 26-13
Contribution margin and machine hours

	Deluxe Sets	Standard Sets
Contribution margin per unit	$8	$6
Machine hours required	0.4	0.2

HELPFUL HINT
CM alone is not enough in this decision. The key factor is CM per unit of limited resource.

The deluxe sets may appear to be more profitable: They have a higher contribution margin ($8) than the standard sets ($6). However, the standard sets take fewer machine hours to produce than the deluxe sets. Therefore, Collins needs to find the **contribution margin per unit of limited resource**—in this case, contribution margin per machine hour. This is obtained by dividing the contribution margin per unit of each product by the number of units of the limited resource required for each product, as shown in Illustration 26-14.

Illustration 26-14
Contribution margin per unit of limited resource

	Deluxe Sets	Standard Sets
Contribution margin per unit (a)	$8	$6
Machine hours required (b)	0.4	0.2
Contribution margin per unit of limited resource [(a) ÷ (b)]	**$20**	**$30**

The computation shows that the standard sets have a higher contribution margin per unit of limited resource. This suggests that, given sufficient demand for standard sets, the company should shift the sales mix to standard sets or should increase machine capacity. If Collins Company is able to increase machine capacity from 3,600 hours to 4,200 hours, the additional 600 hours could be used to produce either the standard or deluxe pen and pencil sets. The total contribution margin under each alternative is found by multiplying the machine hours by the contribution margin per unit of limited resource, as shown below.

Illustration 26-15
Incremental analysis—computation of total contribution margin

	Produce Deluxe Sets	Produce Standard Sets
Machine hours (a)	600	600
Contribution margin per unit of limited resource (b)	$20	$30
Contribution margin [(a) × (b)]	**$12,000**	**$18,000**

From this analysis, we see that to maximize net income, Collins should use all of the increased capacity to make and sell the standard sets.

SECTION 2 Capital Budgeting

Individuals make capital expenditures when they buy a new home, car, or television set. Similarly, businesses make capital expenditures when they modernize plant facilities or expand operations. Companies like Campbell Soup must constantly determine how to invest their resources. Other examples: Hollywood studios recently built 25 new sound stage projects to allow for additional filming in future years. Also, Union Pacific Resources Group Inc. announced that it would cut its capital budget by 19% in order to use the funds to reduce its outstanding debt.

In business, as for individuals, the amount of possible capital expenditures usually exceeds the funds available for such expenditures. Thus, the resources available must be allocated (budgeted) among the competing alternatives. The process of making capital expenditure decisions in business is known as **capital budgeting**. Capital budgeting involves choosing among various capital projects to find the one(s) that will maximize a company's return on its financial investment.

EVALUATION PROCESS

Many companies follow a standard process in capital budgeting. At least once a year, top management requests proposals for projects from each department. A capital budgeting committee screens the proposals and submits its findings to the officers of the company. The officers, in turn, select the projects they believe to be most worthy of funding. They submit this list to the board of directors. Ultimately, the directors approve the capital expenditure budget for the year.

The involvement of top management and the board of directors in the process demonstrates the importance of capital budgeting decisions. These decisions often have a significant impact on a company's future profitability. In fact, poor capital budgeting decisions have led to the bankruptcy of some companies.

Accounting data are indispensable in assessing the probable effects of capital expenditures. To provide management with relevant data for capital budgeting decisions, you should be familiar with the quantitative techniques that may be used. The three most common techniques are: (1) annual rate of return, (2) cash payback, and (3) discounted cash flow. We demonstrate each of these techniques in the following sections. To illustrate the three quantitative techniques, assume that Tappan Company is considering an investment of $130,000 in new equipment. The new equipment is expected to last 10 years. It will have zero salvage value at the end of its useful life. Tappan uses the straight-line method of depreciation for accounting purposes. The expected annual revenues and costs of the new product that will be produced from the investment are:

Sales		$200,000
Less: Costs and expenses		
Manufacturing costs (exclusive of depreciation)	$145,000	
Depreciation expenses ($130,000 ÷ 10)	13,000	
Selling and administrative expenses	22,000	180,000
Income before income taxes		20,000
Income tax expense		7,000
Net income		$ 13,000

Illustration 26-16
Estimated annual net income from capital expenditure

ANNUAL RATE OF RETURN

The **annual rate of return technique** is based directly on accounting data. It indicates **the profitability of a capital expenditure** by dividing expected annual net income by the average investment. Illustration 26-17 shows the formula for computing annual rate of return.

STUDY OBJECTIVE 9
Contrast annual rate of return and cash payback in capital budgeting.

$$\text{Expected Annual Net Income} \div \text{Average Investment} = \text{Annual Rate of Return}$$

Illustration 26-17
Annual rate of return formula

Expected annual net income is obtained from the projected income statement. Tappan Company's expected annual net income is $13,000. Average investment is derived from the following formula.

Illustration 26-18
Formula for computing average investment

$$\text{Average Investment} = \frac{\text{Original Investment} + \text{Value at End of Useful Life}}{2}$$

The "value at the end of useful life" is the asset's salvage value, if any.

For Tappan Company, average investment is $65,000 ($130,000 + $0) ÷ 2. The expected annual rate of return for Tappan Company's investment in new equipment is therefore 20%, computed as follows:

$$\$13,000 \div \$65,000 = 20\%$$

Management then compares this annual rate of return with its required **minimum rate of return** for investments of similar risk. The minimum rate of return is generally based on the company's **cost of capital**. The **cost of capital** is the rate of return that management expects to pay on all borrowed and equity funds. The cost of capital is a company-wide (or sometimes a division-wide) rate; it does not relate to the cost of funding a specific project.

> **ALTERNATIVE TERMINOLOGY**
> The minimum rate of return is also called the *hurdle rate* or *cutoff rate*.

> **HELPFUL HINT**
> A capital budgeting decision based on only one technique may be misleading. It is often wise to analyze the investment from a number of different perspectives.

The annual rate of return decision rule is: **A project is acceptable if its rate of return is greater than management's minimum rate of return. It is unacceptable when the reverse is true.** When companies use the rate of return technique in deciding among several acceptable projects, **the higher the rate of return for a given risk, the more attractive the investment.**

The principal advantages of this technique are simplicity of calculation and management's familiarity with the accounting terms used in the computation. A major limitation of the annual rate of return approach is that it does not consider the time value of money. For example, no consideration is given as to whether cash inflows will occur early or late in the life of the investment. As explained in Appendix C at the back of the book, recognition of the time value of money can make a significant difference between the future value and the present value of an investment.

CASH PAYBACK

The **cash payback technique** identifies the time period required to recover the cost of the capital investment from the annual cash inflow produced by the investment. Illustration 26-19 presents the formula for computing the cash payback period.

Illustration 26-19
Cash payback formula

$$\text{Cost of Capital Investment} \div \text{Net Annual Cash Flow} = \text{Cash Payback Period}$$

> **HELPFUL HINT**
> Net annual cash flow can also be approximated by net cash provided by operating activities from the statement of cash flows.

Net annual cash flow is approximated by taking net income and adding back depreciation expense. Depreciation expense is added back because depreciation on the capital expenditure does not involve an annual outflow of cash. Accordingly, the depreciation deducted in determining net income must be added back to determine net annual cash flows.

In the Tappan Company example, net annual cash flow is $26,000, as shown below.

Illustration 26-20
Computation of net annual cash flow

Net income	$13,000
Add: Depreciation expense	13,000
Net annual cash flow	**$26,000**

The cash payback period in this example is therefore five years, computed as follows.

$$\$130{,}000 \div \$26{,}000 = 5 \text{ years}$$

Evaluation of the payback period is often related to the expected useful life of the asset. For example, assume that at Tappan Company a project is unacceptable if the payback period is longer than 60% of the asset's expected useful life. The five-year payback period in this case is 50% of the project's expected useful life. Thus, the project is acceptable.

It follows that when companies use the payback method to decide among acceptable alternative projects, **the shorter the payback period, the more attractive the investment**. This is true for two reasons: First, the earlier the investment is recovered, the sooner the company can use the cash funds for other purposes. Second, the risk of loss from obsolescence and changed economic conditions is less in a shorter payback period.

The preceding computation of the cash payback period assumes **equal** cash flows in each year of the investment's life. In many cases, this assumption is not valid. In the case of **uneven** cash flows, the company determines the cash payback period when the cumulative net cash flows from the investment equal the cost of the investment.

To illustrate, assume that Chen Company proposes an investment in a new website that is estimated to cost $300,000. Illustration 26-21 shows the proposed investment cost, net annual cash flows, cumulative net cash flows, and the cash payback period.

Illustration 26-21
Net annual cash flow schedule

Year	Investment	Net Annual Cash Flow	Cumulative Net Cash Flow
0	$300,000		
1		$ 60,000	$ 60,000
2		90,000	150,000
3		90,000	240,000
4		120,000	360,000
5		100,000	460,000

Cash payback period = **3.5 years**

As Illustration 26-21 shows, at the end of year 3, cumulative cash flow of $240,000 is less than the investment cost of $300,000. However, at the end of year 4 the cumulative net cash flow of $360,000 exceeds the investment cost. The net cash flow needed in year 4 to equal the investment cost is $60,000 ($300,000 − $240,000). Assuming the net cash flow occurs evenly during year 4, we then divide this amount by the annual net cash flow in year 4 ($120,000) to determine the point during the year when the cash payback occurs. Thus, we get 0.50 ($60,000/$120,000), or half of the year, and the cash payback period is 3.5 years.

The cash payback method may be useful as an initial screening tool. It may be the most critical factor in the capital budgeting decision for a company that desires a fast turnaround of its investment because of a weak cash position. Like the annual rate of return, cash payback is relatively easy to compute and understand.

However, cash payback is not ordinarily the only basis for the capital budgeting decision because it ignores the expected profitability of the project. To illustrate, assume that Projects X and Y have the same payback period, but Project X's useful life is double the useful life of Project Y's. Project X's earning power, therefore, is twice as long as Project Y's. A further—and major—disadvantage of this technique is that it ignores the time value of money.

1170 Chapter 26 Incremental Analysis and Capital Budgeting

DO IT!

CAPITAL BUDGETING

action plan

Use appropriate formulas:

✔ Annual rate of return = Expected annual net income ÷ Average investment.

✔ Average investment = (Original investment + Value at end of useful life) ÷ 2.

✔ Cash payback period = Cost of capital investment ÷ Net annual cash flow.

✔ Net annual cash flow = Net income + Depreciation expense.

Rochelle Company is considering purchasing new equipment for $250,000. The equipment has a 5-year useful life, and depreciation would be $50,000 (assuming straight-line depreciation and zero salvage value). The purchase of the equipment should increase net income by $25,000 each year for 5 years. **(a)** Compute the annual rate of return. **(b)** Compute the cash payback period.

Solution

(a) Average investment = ($250,000 + 0) ÷ 2 = $125,000
Annual rate of return = $25,000 ÷ $125,000 = 20%

(b) Net annual cash flow = $25,000 + $50,000 = $75,000
Cash payback period = $250,000 ÷ $75,000 = 3.3 years

Related exercise material: **BE26-9, BE26-10, E26-11, E26-12, E26-13,** and **DO IT! 26-4.**

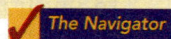

MANAGEMENT INSIGHT

Are You Ready for the 50-Inch Screen?

Building a new factory to produce 50-inch-plus TV screens can cost $4 billion at a time when prices for flat screens are tumbling. Now the makers of those giant liquid-crystal displays are wondering whether such investments are worth the gamble.

If LCD makers decide to hold off on building new factories, price declines for wide-screen TVs could slow in two or three years as production falls behind added consumer demand. Experts also say a slowdown in factory building could also bring welcome relief for the industry by reducing its volatile profit swings.

Since 2000, LCD makers have been on a nonstop construction binge, building new factories to produce the latest generation of screens arriving every 18 months or so. . . . Now, with the eighth generation of screens, the cost to build new factories is higher than ever—running between $3 billion to $4 billion each. And this generation of factories is optimized for screens measuring 50 inches or more diagonally, which so far is a much smaller potential market than that targeted by previous screen generations.

Source: Evan Ramstad, "The 50-Inch Screen Poses a Gamble," *Wall Street Journal*, June 8, 2006, p. B3.

 In building factories to manufacture 50-inch TV screens, how might companies build risk factors into their financial analyses?

DISCOUNTED CASH FLOW

STUDY OBJECTIVE 10
Distinguish between the net present value and internal rate of return methods.

The **discounted cash flow technique** is generally recognized as the best conceptual approach to making capital budgeting decisions. This technique considers both the estimated total net cash flows from the investment and the time value of money. The expected total net cash flow consists of the sum of the annual net cash flows plus the estimated liquidation proceeds when the asset is sold for salvage at the end of its useful life. But because liquidation proceeds are generally immaterial, we ignore them in subsequent discussions.

Two methods are used with the discounted cash flow technique: (1) net present value, and (2) internal rate of return. **Before we discuss the methods, we recommend that you examine Appendix C if you need a review of present value concepts.**

Net Present Value Method

The **net present value (NPV) method** involves discounting net cash flows to their present value and then comparing that present value with the capital outlay required by the investment. The difference between these two amounts is referred to as **net present value (NPV)**. Company management determines what interest rate to use in discounting the future net cash flows. This rate, often referred to as the **discount rate** or **required rate of return** is discussed in a later section.

The NVP decision rule is this: **A proposal is acceptable when net present value is zero or positive.** At either of those values, the rate of return on the investment equals or exceeds the required rate of return. When net present value is negative, the project is unacceptable. Illustration 26-22 shows the net present value decision criteria.

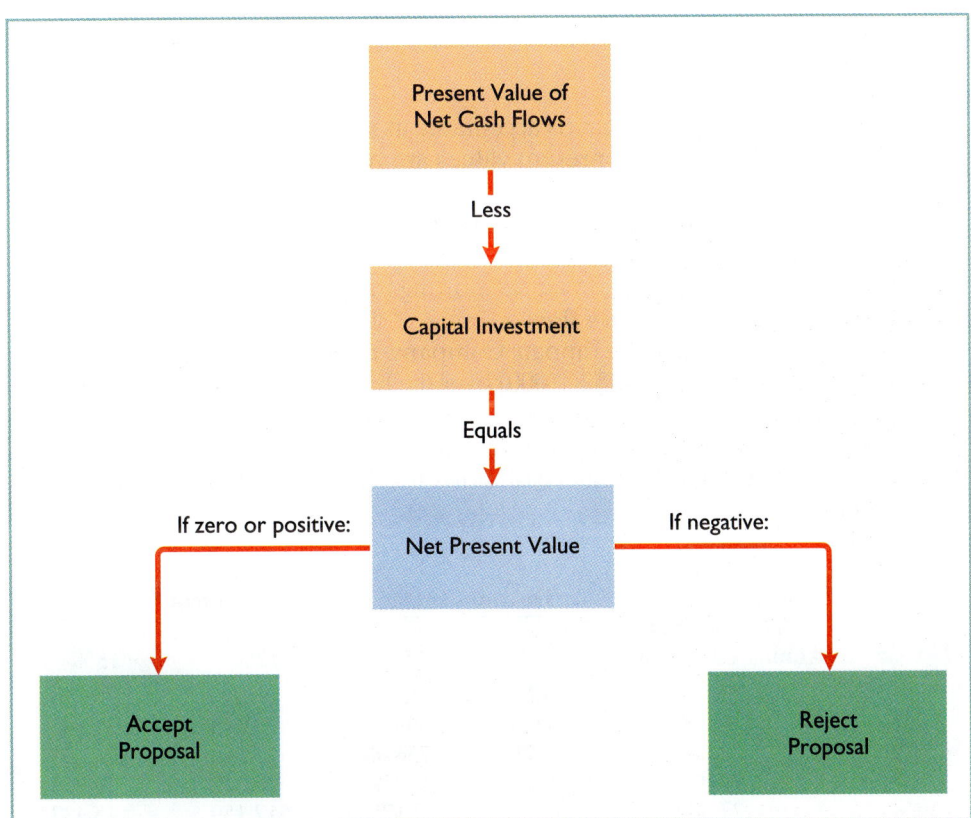

Illustration 26-22
Net present value decision criteria

When making a selection among acceptable proposals, **the higher the positive net present value, the more attractive the investment.** The next two sections demonstrate use of this method. In each case, we assume that the investment has no salvage value.

EQUAL NET ANNUAL CASH FLOWS

Tappan Company's net annual cash flows are $26,000. If we assume this amount **is uniform over the asset's useful life**, we can compute the present value of the net annual cash flows by using the present value of an annuity

> **ETHICS NOTE**
> Discounted future cash flows may not take into account all of the important considerations needed to make an informed capital budgeting decision. Other issues, for example, could include worker safety, product quality, and environmental impact.

of 1 for 10 periods (in Table 2, Appendix C). The computations at rates of return of 12% and 15%, respectively, are:

Illustration 26-23
Present value of net annual cash flows

	Present Values at Different Discount Rates	
	12%	15%
Discount factor for 10 periods	5.65022	5.01877
Present value of net annual cash flows:		
$26,000 × 5.65022	$146,906	
$26,000 × 5.01877		$130,488

The analysis of the proposal by the net present value method is as follows:

Illustration 26-24
Computations of net present value

	12%	15%
Present value of net annual cash flows	$146,906	$130,488
Capital investment	130,000	130,000
Positive (negative) net present value	$ 16,906	$ 488

> **HELPFUL HINT**
> The ABC Co. expects equal cash flows over an asset's 5-year useful life.
> What discount factor should it use in determining present values if management wants (1) a 12% return or (2) a 15% return?
> Answer: Using Table 2, the factors are (1) 3.60478 and (2) 3.35216.

The proposed capital expenditure is acceptable at a required rate of return of both 12% and 15% because the net present values are positive.

UNEQUAL NET ANNUAL CASH FLOWS

When net annual cash flows are unequal, we cannot use annuity tables to calculate their present value. Instead, we use tables showing the **present value of a single future amount for each net annual cash flow**.

To illustrate, assume that Tappan Company management expects the same aggregate net annual cash flow ($260,000) over the life of the investment. But because of a declining market demand for the new product over the life of the equipment, the net annual cash flows are higher in the early years and lower in the later years. The present value of the net annual cash flows is calculated as follows using Table 1 in Appendix C.

Illustration 26-25
Computing present value of unequal annual cash flows

Year	Assumed Net Annual Cash Flows	Discount Factor 12%	Discount Factor 15%	Present Value 12%	Present Value 15%
	(1)	(2)	(3)	(1) × (2)	(1) × (3)
1	$ 36,000	.89286	.86957	$ 32,143	$ 31,305
2	32,000	.79719	.75614	25,510	24,196
3	29,000	.71178	.65752	20,642	19,068
4	27,000	.63552	.57175	17,159	15,437
5	26,000	.56743	.49718	14,753	12,927
6	24,000	.50663	.43233	12,159	10,376
7	23,000	.45235	.37594	10,404	8,647
8	22,000	.40388	.32690	8,885	7,192
9	21,000	.36061	.28426	7,573	5,969
10	20,000	.32197	.24719	6,439	4,944
	$260,000			**$155,667**	**$140,061**

Therefore, the analysis of the proposal by the net present value method is as follows.

	12%	15%
Present value of net annual cash flows	$155,667	$140,061
Capital investment	130,000	130,000
Positive (negative) net present value	**$ 25,667**	**$ 10,061**

Illustration 26-26
Analysis of proposal using net present value method

In this example, the present values of the net annual cash flows are greater than the $130,000 capital investment. Thus, the project is acceptable at both a 12% and 15% required rate of return. The difference between the present values using the 12% rate under equal cash flows ($146,906) and unequal net annual cash flows ($155,667) is due to the pattern of the net cash flows.

Internal Rate of Return Method

The **internal rate of return method** differs from the net present value method in that it finds the **interest yield of the potential investment**. The **internal rate of return** (IRR) is the interest rate that will cause the present value of the proposed capital expenditure to equal the present value of the expected net annual cash flows. The determination of the internal rate of return involves two steps.

Step 1. Compute the internal rate of return factor. The formula for this factor is:

Capital Investment	÷	Net Annual Cash Flows	=	Internal Rate of Return Factor

Illustration 26-27
Formula for internal rate of return factor

The computation for Tappan Company, assuming equal net annual cash flows,[2] is:

$$\$130,000 \div \$26,000 = 5.0$$

Step 2. Use the factor and the present value of an annuity of 1 table to find the internal rate of return. Table 2 of Appendix C is used in this step. The internal rate of return is the discount factor that is closest to the internal rate of return factor for the time period covered by the net annual cash flows.

For Tappan Company, the net annual cash flows are expected to continue for 10 years. Thus, it is necessary to read across the period-10 row in Table 2 to find the discount factor. The row for 10 periods is reproduced below for your convenience.

TABLE 2
PRESENT VALUE OF AN ANNUITY OF 1

(n) Periods	5%	6%	8%	9%	10%	11%	12%	15%
10	7.72173	7.36009	6.71008	6.41766	6.14457	5.88923	5.65022	**5.01877**

In this case, the closest discount factor to 5.0 is 5.01877, which represents an interest rate of approximately 15%. The rate of return can be further determined by interpolation, but since we are using estimated net annual cash flows, such precision is seldom required.

---

[2] When net annual cash flows are equal, the internal rate of return factor is the same as the cash payback period.

Once managers know the internal rate of return, they compare it to the company's required rate of return (the discount rate). The IRR decision rule is as follows: **Accept the project when the internal rate of return is equal to or greater than the required rate of return. Reject the project when the internal rate of return is less than the required rate of return.** Illustration 26-28 below shows these relationships. Assuming the minimum required rate of return is 10% for Tappan Company, the project is acceptable because the 15% internal rate of return is greater than the required rate.

Illustration 26-28
Internal rate of return decision criteria

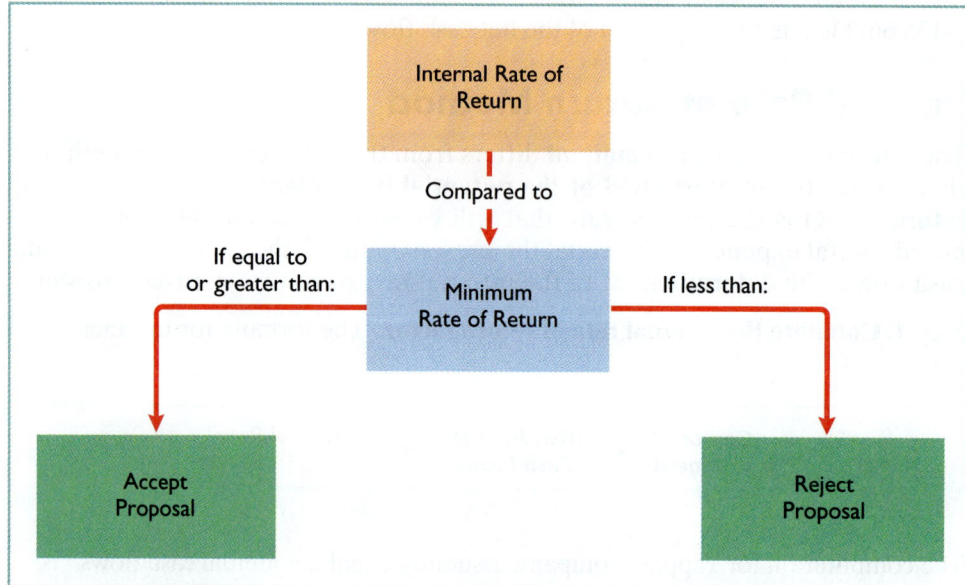

The IRR method is widely used in practice. Most managers find the internal rate of return easy to interpret.

Comparing Discounted Cash Flow Methods

Illustration 26-29 compares the two discounted cash flow methods—net present value and internal rate of return. When properly used, either method provides management with relevant quantitative data for making capital budgeting decisions.

Illustration 26-29
Comparison of discounted cash flow methods

Item	Net Present Value	Internal Rate of Return
1. Objective	Compute net present value (a dollar amount).	Compute internal rate of return (a percentage).
2. Decision rule	If net present value is zero or positive, accept the proposal. If net present value is negative, reject the proposal.	If internal rate of return is equal to or greater than the minimum required rate of return, accept the proposal. If internal rate of return is less than the minimum required rate, reject the proposal.

DO IT!

Watertown Paper Corporation is considering adding another machine for the manufacture of corrugated cardboard. The machine would cost $900,000. It would have an estimated life of 6 years and no salvage value. The company estimates that annual cash inflows would increase by $400,000 and that annual cash outflows would increase by $190,000. Management has a required rate of return of 9%.

(a) Calculate the net present value on this project, and discuss whether it should be accepted.

(b) Calculate the internal rate of return on this project, and discuss whether it should be accepted.

DISCOUNTED CASH FLOW

Solution

(a)
Estimated annual cash inflows	$400,000
Estimated annual cash outflows	190,000
Net annual cash flow	$210,000

	Cash Flow	9% Discount Factor	Present Value
Present value of net annual cash flows	$210,000	4.48592*	$942,043
Capital investment			900,000
Net present value			$ 42,043

*Table 2, Appendix C

Since the net present value is greater than zero, Watertown should accept the project.

(b) $900,000 ÷ 210,000 = 4.285714. Using Table 2 of Appendix C and the factors that correspond with the six-period row, 4.285714 is between the factors for 10% and 11%. Since the project has an internal rate that is greater than 10% and the required rate of return is only 9%, Watertown should accept the project.

action plan

✔ Compute net annual cash flow: Estimated annual cash inflows ÷ Estimated annual cash outflows.

✔ Use the NPV technique to calculate the difference between net cash flows and the initial investment.

✔ Accept the project if the net present value is positive.

✔ Compute the IRR factor: Capital investment ÷ Net annual cash flows.

✔ Look up the factor in the present value of an annuity table to find the internal rate of return.

✔ Accept the project if the internal rate of return is equal to or greater than the required rate of return.

Related exercise material: **BE26-11, BE26-12, BE26-13, E26-12, E26-13, E26-14, E26-15,** and **DO IT! 26-5.**

 Be sure to read **ALL ABOUT YOU: What Is a Degree Worth?** on page 1176 for information on how topics in this chapter apply to your personal life.

all about YOU

What Is a Degree Worth?

It may not have occurred to you at the time, but you already made a huge decision in your life that was ideally suited to both incremental analysis and capital budgeting. No, it's not your choice of whether to have pizza or Chinese food at lunch today. We are referring to your decision to pursue a post–high-school degree. If you weren't going to college, you could be working full-time. School costs money, which is an expenditure that you could have avoided. Also, if you did not go to college, many of you would avoid mountains of school-related debt. While you cannot go back and redo your initial decision, we can look at some facts to evaluate the wisdom of your decision.

❋ About the Numbers

Tuition is very expensive. As a result, many students have high "unmet needs"—the portion of college expenses not provided by family or student aid. The graph below suggests that in the coming decade an increasing number of students with high "unmet" financial needs will decide not to pursue any form of post–high-school education. This has obvious implications for their long-term personal financial well-being. It also has significant implications for the well-being of the United States as a society. Research shows that people with post–high-school degrees pay more in taxes. Also, without adequate educational training of its citizenry, the United States will be less able to compete in a high-tech world.

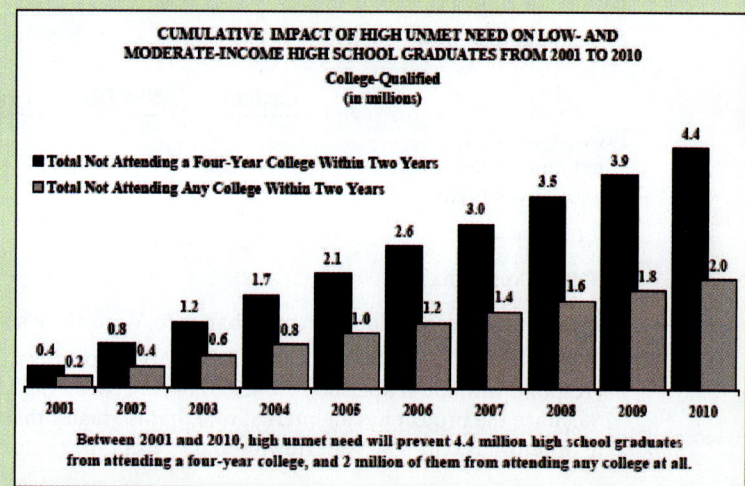

Source: "Empty Promises: The Myth of College Access in America," A Report of the Advisory Committee on Student Financial Assistance, June 2002, www.ed.gov/about/bdscomm/list/acsfa/emptypromises.pdf, p. 28 (accessed August 2006).

❋ Some Facts

* Over a lifetime of work, high-school graduates earn an average of $1.2 million, associate's degree holders earn an average of $1.6 million, and people with bachelor's degrees earn about $2.1 million.
* A year of tuition at a public four-year college costs about $8,655, and a year of tuition at a public two-year college costs about $1,359.
* There has also been considerable research on other, less-tangible benefits of post–high-school education. For example, some have suggested that there is a relationship between higher education and good health. Research also suggests that college-educated people are more optimistic.
* About 600,000 students drop out of four-year colleges each year.

❋ What Do You Think?

Each year many students decide to drop out of school. Many of them never return. Suppose that you are working two jobs and going to college and that you are not making ends meet. Your grades are suffering due to your lack of available study time. You feel depressed. Should you drop out of school?

YES: You can always go back to school. If your grades are bad, and you are depressed, what good is school doing you anyway?

NO: Once you drop out, it is very hard to get enough momentum to go back. Dropping out will dramatically reduce your long-term opportunities. It is better to stay in school, even if you take only one class per semester.

Sources: Kathleen Porter, "The Value of a College Degree," ERIC Clearinghouse on Higher Education, Washington DC, www.ericdigests.org/2003-3/value.htm (accessed August 2006).

The authors' comments on this situation appear on page 1196.

Comprehensive DO IT!

Sierra Company is considering a long-term capital investment project called ZIP. The project will require an investment of $120,000, and it will have a useful life of 4 years. Annual net income for ZIP is expected to be: Year 1 $12,000; Year 2 $10,000; Year 3 $8,000; and Year 4 $6,000. Depreciation is computed by the straight-line method with no salvage value. The company's cost of capital is 12%.

Instructions

(a) Compute the annual rate of return for the project.
(b) Compute the cash payback period for the project. (Round to two decimals.)
(c) Compute the net present value for the project. (Round to nearest dollar.)
(d) Should the project be accepted? Why?

Solution to Comprehensive DO IT!

(a) $9,000 ($36,000 ÷ 4) ÷ $60,000 ($120,000 ÷ 2) = 15%
(b) Depreciation expense is $120,000 ÷ 4 years = $30,000.
   Net annual cash flows are:
   Year 1 $12,000 + $30,000 = $42,000
   Year 2 $10,000 + $30,000 = $40,000
   Year 3 $8,000 + $30,000 = $38,000
   Year 4 $6,000 + $30,000 = $36,000

   Cumulative net cash flows would be $82,000 ($42,000 + $40,000) at the end of year 2 and $120,000 ($42,000 + $40,000 + $38,000) at the end of year 3. Since the cumulative net cash flows at the end of year 3 exactly equal the initial cash investment of $120,000, the cash payback period is 3 years.

(c)

Year	Discount Factor	Net Annual Cash Flow	Present Value
1	.89286	$42,000	$ 37,500
2	.79719	40,000	31,888
3	.71178	38,000	27,048
4	.63552	36,000	22,879
			119,315
		Capital investment	120,000
		Negative net present value	$ (685)

(d) The annual rate of return of 15% is good. However, the cash payback period is 75% of the project's useful life, and net present value is negative. The recommendation is to reject the project.

action plan

✔ To compute annual rate of return, divide expected annual net income by average investment.

✔ To compute cash payback, divide cost of the investment by net annual cash flows.

✔ Recall that net annual cash flow equals annual net income plus annual depreciation expense.

✔ Be careful to use the correct discount factor in using the net present value method.

SUMMARY OF STUDY OBJECTIVES

1 **Identify the steps in management's decision-making process.** Management's decision-making process is: (a) identify the problem and assign responsibility, (b) determine and evaluate possible courses of action, (c) make the decision, and (d) review the results of the decision.

2 **Describe the concept of incremental analysis.** Incremental analysis identifies financial data that change under alternative courses of action. These data are relevant to the decision because they will vary in the future among the possible alternatives.

3 **Identify the relevant costs in accepting an order at a special price.** The relevant information in accepting an order at a special price is the difference between the variable costs to produce the special order and expected revenues.

1178 Chapter 26 Incremental Analysis and Capital Budgeting

4 Identify the relevant costs in a make-or-buy decision. In a make-or-buy decision, the relevant costs are (a) the manufacturing costs that will be saved, (b) the purchase price, and (c) opportunity costs.

5 Give the decision rule for whether to sell or process materials further. The decision rule for whether to sell or process materials further is: Process further as long as the incremental revenue from processing exceeds the incremental processing costs.

6 Identify the factors to consider in retaining or replacing equipment. The factors to consider in determining whether equipment should be retained or replaced are the effects on variable costs and the cost of the new equipment. Also, any trade-in allowance or cash disposal value of the existing asset must be considered.

7 Explain the relevant factors in whether to eliminate an unprofitable segment. In deciding whether to eliminate an unprofitable segment, determine the contribution margin, if any, produced by the segment and the disposition of the segment's fixed expenses.

8 Determine which products to make and sell when resources are limited. When a company has limited resources, find the contribution margin per unit of limited resource. Then multiply this amount by the units of limited resource to determine which product maximizes net income.

9 Contrast annual rate of return and cash payback in capital budgeting. The *annual rate of return* is obtained by dividing expected annual net income by the average investment. The higher the rate of return, the more attractive the investment. The *cash payback* technique identifies the time period to recover the cost of the investment. The formula is: Cost of capital expenditure divided by estimated net annual cash flow equals cash payback period. The shorter the payback period, the more attractive the investment.

10 Distinguish between the net present value and internal rate of return methods. Under the *net present value* method, compare the present value of future net cash flows with the capital investment to determine net present value. The NPV decision rule is: Accept the project if net present value is zero or positive. Reject the investment if net present value is negative.

Under the *internal rate of return* method, find the interest yield of the potential investment. The IRR decision rule is: Accept the project when the internal rate of return is equal to or greater than the required rate of return. Reject the project when the internal rate of return is less than the required rate.

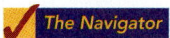

GLOSSARY

Annual rate of return technique Determines the profitability of a capital expenditure by dividing expected annual net income by the average investment. (p. 1167).

Capital budgeting The process of making capital expenditure decisions in business. (p. 1167).

Cash payback technique Identifies the time period required to recover the cost of a capital investment from the net annual cash flow produced by the investment. (p. 1168).

Cost of capital The rate of return that management expects to pay on all borrowed and equity funds. (p. 1168).

Discounted cash flow technique Considers both the estimated total net cash flows from the investment and the time value of money. (p. 1170).

Discount rate Interest rate used in discounting the future net cash flows. (p. 1171).

Incremental analysis The process of identifying the financial data that change under alternative courses of action. (p. 1157).

Internal rate of return (IRR) The rate that will cause the present value of the proposed capital expenditure to equal the present value of the expected net annual cash flows. (p. 1173).

Internal rate of return method Finds the interest yield of the potential investment. (p. 1173).

Net present value (NPV) The difference that results when the original capital outlay is subtracted from the discounted net cash flows. (p. 1171).

Net present value method Discounts net cash flows to their present value and then compares that present value to the capital outlay required by the investment. (p. 1171).

Opportunity cost The potential benefit that may be obtained from following an alternative course of action. (p. 1160).

Sunk cost A cost that cannot be changed by any present or future decision. (p. 1164).

SELF-STUDY QUESTIONS

Answers are at the end of the chapter.

(SO 1) **1.** Three of the steps in management's decision process are: (1) Review results of decision. (2) Identify the problem. (3) Make the decision. The steps are performed in the following order.
  a. (1), (2), (3).
  b. (3), (2), (1).
  c. (2), (1), (3).
  d. (2), (3), (1).

2. Incremental analysis is the process of identifying the financial data that: (SO 2)
  a. do not change under alternative courses of action.
  b. change under alternative courses of action.
  c. are mixed under alternative courses of action.
  d. No correct answer is given.

3. It costs a company $14 of variable costs and $6 of fixed (SO 3) costs to produce product A that sells for $30. A foreign buyer offers to purchase 3,000 units at $18 each. If the

special offer is accepted and produced with unused capacity, net income will:
  a. decrease $6,000.
  b. increase $6,000.
  c. increase $12,000.
  d. increase $9,000.

(SO 3) 4. Jobart Company is currently operating at full capacity. It is considering buying a part from an outside supplier rather than making it in-house. If Jobart purchases the part, it can use the released productive capacity to generate additional income of $30,000 from producing a different product. When conducting incremental analysis in this make-or-buy decision, the company should:
  a. ignore the $30,000.
  b. add $30,000 to other costs in the "Make" column.
  c. add $30,000 to other costs in the "Buy" column.
  d. subtract $30,000 from the other costs in the "Make" column.

(SO 4) 5. In a make-or-buy decision, relevant costs are:
  a. manufacturing costs that will be saved.
  b. the purchase price of the units.
  c. opportunity costs.
  d. all of the above.

(SO 5) 6. The decision rule in a sell-or-process-further decision is: Process further as long as the incremental revenue from processing exceeds:
  a. incremental processing costs.
  b. variable processing costs.
  c. fixed processing costs.
  d. No correct answer is given.

(SO 5) 7. Walton, Inc. makes an unassembled product that it currently sells for $55. Production costs are $20. Walton is considering assembling the product and selling it for $68. The cost to assemble the product is estimated at $12. What decision should Walton make?
  a. Sell before assembly; net income per unit will be $12 greater.
  b. Sell before assembly; net income per unit will be $1 greater.
  c. Process further; net income per unit will be $13 greater.
  d. Process further; net income per unit will be $1 greater.

(SO 6) 8. In a decision to retain or replace equipment, the book value of the old equipment is a(n):
  a. opportunity cost.   c. incremental cost.
  b. sunk cost.   d. marginal cost.

(SO 7) 9. If an unprofitable segment is eliminated:
  a. net income will always increase.
  b. variable expenses of the eliminated segment will have to be absorbed by other segments.
  c. fixed expenses allocated to the eliminated segment will have to be absorbed by other segments.
  d. net income will always decrease.

10. A segment of Hazard Inc. has the following data. (SO 7)
    Sales $200,000
    Variable costs $140,000
    Fixed costs $100,000
    If this segment is eliminated, 50% of the fixed costs will be eliminated, and the rest will be allocated to the remaining segments. What should Hazard do?
    a. Eliminate the segment; net income will be $50,000 greater.
    b. Eliminate the segment; net income will be $10,000 greater.
    c. Keep the segment; net income will be $200,000 greater.
    d. Keep the segment; net income will be $10,000 greater.

11. If the contribution margin per unit is $15 and it takes 3.0 (SO 8) machine hours to produce the unit, the contribution margin per unit of limited resource is:
    a. $25.   c. $45.
    b. $5.   d. No correct answer is given.

12. Which of the following is *incorrect* about the annual rate (SO 9) of return technique?
    a. The calculation is simple.
    b. The accounting terms used are familiar to management.
    c. The timing of the net cash flows is not considered.
    d. The time value of money is considered.

13. What is a weakness of the cash payback approach? (SO 9)
    a. It uses accrual-based accounting numbers.
    b. It ignores the time value of money.
    c. It is complicated to compute.
    d. It cannot be used if a project has uneven net annual cash flows.

14. A project should be accepted if its internal rate of return (SO 10) exceeds:
    a. zero.
    b. the rate of return on a government bond.
    c. the company's required rate of return.
    d. the rate the company pays on borrowed funds.

15. A positive net present value means that the: (SO 10)
    a. project's rate of return is less than the cutoff rate.
    b. project's rate of return exceeds the required rate of return.
    c. project's rate of return equals the required rate of return.
    d. project is unacceptable.

Go to the book's companion website, **www.wiley.com/college/weygandt**, for Additional Self-Study questions.

QUESTIONS

1. What steps are frequently involved in management's decision-making process?
2. Your roommate, Matt Mikan, contends that accounting contributes to most of the steps in management's decision-making process. Is your roommate correct? Explain.
3. "Incremental analysis involves the accumulation of information concerning a single course of action." Do you agree? Why?
4. Jerry Karr asks your help concerning the relevance of variable and fixed costs in incremental analysis. Help Jerry with his problem.

5. What data are relevant in deciding whether to accept an order at a special price?
6. Perney Company has an opportunity to buy parts at $7 each that currently cost $10 to make. What manufacturing costs are relevant to this make-or-buy decision?
7. Define the term "opportunity cost." How may this cost be relevant in a make-or-buy decision?
8. What is the decision rule in deciding whether to sell a product or process it further?
9. Your roommate, Betty Melton, is confused about sunk costs. Explain to your roommate the meaning of sunk costs and their relevance to a decision to retain or replace equipment.
10. Slocum Inc. has one product line that is unprofitable. What circumstances may cause overall company net income to be lower if the unprofitable product line is eliminated?
11. How is the contribution margin per unit of limited resources computed?
12. Describe the process a company may use in screening and approving the capital expenditure budget.
13. Your classmate, Laura Elder, is confused about the factors that are included in the annual rate of return technique. What is the formula for this technique?
14. Hector Ruiz is trying to understand the term "cost of capital." Define the term, and indicate its relevance to the decision rule under the annual rate of return technique.
15. Pete Hetzel claims the formula for the cash payback technique is the same as the formula for the annual rate of return technique. Is Pete correct? What is the formula for the cash payback technique?
16. What are the advantages and disadvantages of the cash payback technique?
17. Two types of present value tables may be used with the discounted cash flow technique. Identify the tables and the circumstance(s) when each table should be used.
18. What is the decision rule under the net present value method?
19. Identify the steps required in using the internal rate of return method.
20. Gillaspie Company uses the internal rate of return method. What is the decision rule for this method?

BRIEF EXERCISES

Identify the steps in management's decision-making process.
(SO 1)

BE26-1 The steps in management's decision-making process are listed in random order below. Indicate the order in which the steps should be executed.
—Make a decision.
—Identify the problem and assign responsibility.
—Review results of the decision.
—Determine and evaluate possible courses of action.

Determine incremental changes.
(SO, 2)

BE26-2 Ming Company is considering two alternatives. Alternative A will have sales of $150,000 and costs of $100,000. Alternative B will have sales of $180,000 and costs of $120,000. Compare Alternative A to Alternative B showing incremental revenues, costs, and net income. Which alternative should you choose?

Determine whether to accept a special order.
(SO 3)

BE26-3 In Karnes Company it costs $30 per unit ($20 variable and $10 fixed) to make a product that normally sells for $45. A foreign wholesaler offers to buy 4,000 units at $23 each. Karnes will incur special shipping costs of $1 per unit. Assuming that Karnes has excess operating capacity, prepare an incremental analysis that indicates the net income (loss) Karnes would realize by accepting the special order. Should the order be accepted?

Determine whether to make or buy a part.
(SO 4)

BE26-4 Bartley Manufacturing incurs unit costs of $8 ($5 variable and $3 fixed) in making a sub-assembly part for its finished product. A supplier offers to make 10,000 of the part at $5.30 per unit. If the offer is accepted, Bartley will save all variable costs but no fixed costs. Prepare an analysis showing the total cost saving, if any, Bartley will realize by buying the part. What should they do?

Determine whether to sell or process further.
(SO 5)

BE26-5 Stanton Inc. makes unfinished bookcases that it sells for $60. Production costs are $30 variable and $10 fixed. Because it has unused capacity, Stanton is considering finishing the bookcases and selling them for $72. Variable finishing costs are expected to be $8 per unit with no increase in fixed costs. Prepare an analysis on a per unit basis showing whether Stanton should sell unfinished or finished bookcases.

Determine whether to retain or replace equipment.
(SO 6)

BE26-6 Felton Company has a factory machine with a book value of $90,000 and a remaining useful life of 4 years. A new machine is available at a cost of $200,000. This machine will have a 4-year useful life with no salvage value. The new machine will lower annual variable manufacturing costs from $600,000 to $440,000. Prepare an analysis showing whether the old machine should be retained or replaced.

BE26-7 Derby, Inc. manufactures golf clubs in three models. For the year, the Eagle line has a net loss of $20,000 from sales $200,000, variable expenses $180,000, and fixed expenses $40,000. If the Eagle line is eliminated, $34,000 of fixed costs will remain. Prepare an analysis showing whether the Eagle line should be eliminated.

Determine whether to eliminate an unprofitable segment.
(SO 7)

BE26-8 In Nevitt Company, data concerning two products are: Contribution margin per unit—Product A $11, Product B $12; machine hours required for one unit—Product A 2, Product B 2.5. Compute the contribution margin per unit of limited resource for each product.

Show allocation of limited resources.
(SO 8)

BE26-9 Adler Company is considering purchasing new equipment for $300,000. It is expected that the equipment will produce annual net income of $10,000 over its 10-year useful life. Annual depreciation will be $30,000. Compute the cash payback period.

Compute the cash payback period for a capital investment.
(SO 9)

BE26-10 Engles Oil Company is considering investing in a new oil well. It is expected that the oil well will increase annual revenues by $130,000 and will increase annual expenses by $80,000 including depreciation. The oil well will cost $490,000 and will have a $10,000 salvage value at the end of its 10-year useful life. Calculate the annual rate of return.

Compute annual rate of return.
(SO 9)

BE26-11 Harry Company is considering two different, mutually exclusive capital expenditure proposals. Project A will cost $395,000, has an expected useful life of 10 years, a salvage value of zero, and is expected to increase net annual cash flows by $70,000. Project B will cost $270,000, has an expected useful life of 10 years, a salvage value of zero, and is expected to increase net annual cash flows by $50,000. A discount rate of 9% is appropriate for both projects. Compute the net present value of each project. Which project should be accepted?

Compute net present value.
(SO 10)

BE26-12 Frost Company is evaluating the purchase of a rebuilt spot-welding machine to be used in the manufacture of a new product. The machine will cost $170,000, has an estimated useful life of 7 years, a salvage value of zero, and will increase net annual cash flows by $33,740. What is its approximate internal rate of return?

Calculate internal rate of return.
(SO 10)

BE26-13 Horak Company accumulates the following data concerning a proposed capital investment: cash cost $225,000, net annual cash flow $34,000, present value factor of cash inflows for 10 years 6.71 (rounded). Determine the net present value, and indicate whether the investment should be made.

Compute net present value of an investment.
(SO 10)

DO IT! REVIEW

DO IT! 26-1 Corn Company incurs a cost of $35 per unit, of which $20 is variable, to make a product that normally sells for $58. A foreign wholesaler offers to buy 6,000 units at $31 each. Corn will incur additional costs of $2 per unit to imprint a logo and to pay for shipping. Compute the increase or decrease in net income Corn will realize by accepting the special order, assuming Corn has sufficient excess operating capacity. Should Corn Company accept the special order?

Evaluate special order.
(SO 3)

DO IT! 26-2 Barney Company must decide whether to make or buy some of its components. The costs of producing 60,000 switches for its generators are as follows.

Evaluate make-or-buy opportunity.
(SO 4)

| Direct materials | $30,000 | Variable overhead | $45,000 |
| Direct labor | $42,000 | Fixed overhead | $60,000 |

Instead of making the switches at an average cost of $2.95 ($177,000 ÷ 60,000), the company has an opportunity to buy the switches at $2.75 per unit. If the company purchases the switches, all the variable costs and one-third of the fixed costs will be eliminated.

(a) Prepare an incremental analysis showing whether the company should make or buy the switches. **(b)** Would your answer be different if the released productive capacity will generate additional income of $30,000?

DO IT! 26-3 Lion Corporation manufactures several types of accessories. For the year, the gloves and mittens line had sales of $500,000, variable expenses of $375,000, and fixed expenses of $150,000. Therefore, the gloves and mittens line had a net loss of $25,000. If Lion eliminates the line, $40,000 of fixed costs will remain.

Prepare an analysis showing whether the company should eliminate the gloves and mittens line.

Analyze whether to eliminate unprofitable segment.
(SO 7)

DO IT! 26-4 Beacon Company is considering purchasing new equipment for $350,000. The equipment has a 5-year useful life, and depreciation would be $70,000 (assuming straight-line depreciation

Compute capital budgeting measures.
(SO 9)

1182 Chapter 26 Incremental Analysis and Capital Budgeting

Compute discounted cash flow measures.
(SO 10)

and zero salvage value). The purchase of the equipment should increase net income by $40,000 each year for 5 years. **(a)** Compute the annual rate of return. **(b)** Compute the cash payback period.

DO IT! 26-5 Maranantha Box Corporation is considering adding another machine for the manufacture of corrugated cardboard. The machine would cost $700,000. It would have an estimated life of 6 years and no salvage value. The company estimates that annual cash inflows would increase by $300,000 and that annual cash outflows would increase by $140,000. Management has a required rate of return of 9%.

(a) Calculate the net present value on this project, and discuss whether it should be accepted. **(b)** Calculate the internal rate of return on this project, and discuss whether it should be accepted.

EXERCISES

Analyze statements about decision making and incremental analysis.
(SO 1, 2)

E26-1 Pender has prepared the following list of statements about decision making and incremental analysis.

1. The first step in management's decision-making process is, "Determine and evaluate possible courses of action."
2. The final step in management's decision-making process is to actually make the decision.
3. Accounting's contribution to management's decision-making process occurs primarily in evaluating possible courses of action and in reviewing the results.
4. In making business decisions, management ordinarily considers only financial information because it is objectively determined.
5. Decisions involve a choice among alternative courses of action.
6. The process used to identify the financial data that change under alternative courses of action is called incremental analysis.
7. Costs that are the same under all alternative courses of action sometimes affect the decision.
8. When using incremental analysis, some costs will always change under alternative courses of action, but revenues will not.
9. Variable costs will change under alternative courses of action, but fixed costs will not.

Instructions
Identify each statement as true or false. If false, indicate how to correct the statement.

Make incremental analysis for special order.
(SO 3)

E26-2 Wyco Company manufactures toasters. For the first 8 months of 2011, the company reported the following operating results while operating at 75% of plant capacity.

Sales (400,000 units)	$4,000,000
Cost of goods sold	2,400,000
Gross profit	1,600,000
Operating expenses	900,000
Net income	$ 700,000

Cost of goods sold was 70% variable and 30% fixed. Operating expenses were 60% variable and 40% fixed.

In September, Wyco Company receives a special order for 40,000 toasters at $6.00 each from Salono Company of Mexico City. Acceptance of the order would result in $8,000 of shipping costs but no increase in fixed operating expenses.

Instructions
(a) Prepare an incremental analysis for the special order.
(b)  Should Wyco Company accept the special order? Why or why not?

Make incremental analysis for special-order decision.
(SO 3)

E26-3 Innova Company produces golf discs which it normally sells to retailers for $7 each. The cost of manufacturing 20,000 golf discs is:

Materials	$ 10,000
Labor	30,000
Variable overhead	20,000
Fixed overhead	40,000
Total	$100,000

Innova also incurs 5% sales commission ($0.35) on each disc sold.

Mudd Corporation offers Innova $4.75 per disc for 5,000 discs. Mudd would sell the discs under its own brand name in foreign markets not yet served by Innova. If Innova accepts the offer, its fixed overhead will increase from $40,000 to $45,000 due to the purchase of a new imprinting machine. No sales commission will result from the special order.

Instructions
(a) Prepare an incremental analysis for the special order.
(b) Should Innova accept the special order? Why or why not?
(c) What assumptions underlie the decision made in part (b)?

E26-4 Shannon Inc. has been manufacturing its own shades for its table lamps. The company is currently operating at 100% of capacity. Variable manufacturing overhead is charged to production at the rate of 50% of direct labor cost. The direct materials and direct labor cost per unit to make the lamp shades are $4.00 and $6.00, respectively. Normal production is 40,000 table lamps per year.

Make incremental analysis for make-or-buy decision.
(SO 4)

A supplier offers to make the lamp shades at a price of $13.50 per unit. If Shannon Inc. accepts the supplier's offer, all variable manufacturing costs will be eliminated, but the $40,000 of fixed manufacturing overhead currently being charged to the lamp shades will have to be absorbed by other products.

Instructions
(a) Prepare the incremental analysis for the decision to make or buy the lamp shades.
(b) Should Shannon Inc. buy the lamp shades?
(c) Would your answer be different in (b) if the productive capacity released by not making the lamp shades could be used to produce income of $35,000?

E26-5 Stacy McGuire recently opened her own basketweaving studio. She sells finished baskets in addition to the raw materials needed by customers to weave baskets of their own. Stacy has put together a variety of raw material kits, each including materials at various stages of completion. Unfortunately, owing to space limitations, Stacy is unable to carry all varieties of kits originally assembled and must choose between two basic packages.

Make incremental analysis for further processing of materials.
(SO 5)

The basic introductory kit includes undyed, uncut reeds (with dye included) for weaving one basket. This basic package costs Stacy $12 and sells for $27. The second kit, called Stage 2, includes cut reeds that have already been dyed. With this kit the customer need only soak the reeds and weave the basket. Stacy is able to produce the second kit by using the basic materials included in the first kit and adding one hour of her own time (to produce two kits), which she values at $18 per hour. Because she is more efficient at cutting and dying reeds than her average customer, Stacy is able to make two kits of the dyed reeds, in one hour, from one kit of undyed reeds. The kit of dyed and cut reeds sells for $33.

Instructions
Determine whether Stacy's basketweaving shop should carry the basic introductory kit with undyed and uncut reeds, or the Stage 2 kit with reeds already dyed and cut. Prepare an incremental analysis to support your answer.

E26-6 Donkey Bikes could sell its bicycles to retailers either assembled or unassembled. The cost of an unassembled bike is as follows.

Make incremental analysis for sell-or-process-further decision.
(SO 5)

Direct materials	$150
Direct labor	70
Variable overhead (70% of direct labor)	49
Fixed overhead (30% of direct labor)	21
Manufacturing cost per unit	$290

The unassembled bikes are sold to retailers at $400 each.

Donkey currently has unused productive capacity that is expected to continue indefinitely; management has concluded that some of this capacity can be used to assemble the bikes and sell them at $450 each. Assembling the bikes will increase direct materials by $5 per bike, and direct labor by $20 per bike. Additional variable overhead will be incurred at the normal rates, but there will be no additional fixed overhead as a result of assembling the bikes.

Instructions
(a) Prepare an incremental analysis for the sell-or-process-further decision.
(b) Should Donkey sell or process further? Why or why not?

1184 Chapter 26 Incremental Analysis and Capital Budgeting

Make incremental analysis for retaining or replacing equipment.
(SO 6)

E26-7 Crone Enterprises uses a word processing computer to handle its sales invoices. Lately, business has been so good that it takes an extra 3 hours per night, plus every third Saturday, to keep up with the volume of sales invoices. Management is considering updating its computer with a faster model that would eliminate all of the overtime processing.

	Current Machine	New Machine
Original purchase cost	$15,000	$21,000
Accumulated depreciation	6,000	—
Estimated operating costs	24,000	20,000
Useful life	5 years	5 years

If sold now, the current machine would have a salvage value of $5,000. If operated for the remainder of its useful life, the current machine would have zero salvage value. The new machine is expected to have zero salvage value after 5 years.

Instructions
Should the current machine be replaced? (Ignore the time value of money.)

Make incremental analysis for elimination of division.
(SO 7)

E26-8 Judy Herzog, a recent graduate of Rolling's accounting program, evaluated the operating performance of Klumpe Company's six divisions. Judy made the following presentation to the Klumpe board of directors and suggested the Ketchum Division be eliminated. "If the Ketchum Division is eliminated," she said, "our total profits would increase by $16,870."

	The Other Five Divisions	Ketchum Division	Total
Sales	$1,664,200	$ 98,200	$1,762,400
Cost of goods sold	978,520	76,470	1,054,990
Gross profit	685,680	21,730	707,410
Operating expenses	527,940	38,600	566,540
Net income	$ 157,740	$(16,870)	$ 140,870

In the Ketchum Division, cost of goods sold is $56,000 variable and $20,470 fixed, and operating expenses are $12,000 variable and $26,600 fixed. None of the Ketchum Division's fixed costs will be eliminated if the division is discontinued.

Instructions
Is Judy right about eliminating the Ketchum Division? Prepare a schedule to support your answer.

Make incremental analysis for elimination of a product line.
(SO 7)

E26-9 Shatner Company makes three models of phasers. Information on the three products is given below.

	Stunner	Double-Set	Mega-Power
Sales	$300,000	$500,000	$200,000
Variable expenses	150,000	200,000	140,000
Contribution margin	150,000	300,000	60,000
Fixed expenses	120,000	225,000	90,000
Net income	$ 30,000	$ 75,000	$(30,000)

Fixed expenses consist of $300,000 of common costs allocated to the three products based on relative sales, and additional fixed expenses of $30,000 (Stunner), $75,000 (Double-Set), and $30,000 (Mega-Power). The common costs will be incurred regardless of how many models are produced. The other fixed expenses would be eliminated if a model is phased out.

Jim Kirk, an executive with the company, feels the Mega-Power line should be discontinued to increase the company's net income.

Instructions
(a) Compute current net income for Shatner Company.
(b) Compute net income by product line and in total for Shatner Company if the company discontinues the Mega-Power product line. (*Hint:* Allocate the $300,000 common costs to the two remaining product lines based on their relative sales.)
(c) Should Shatner eliminate the Mega-Power product line? Why or why not?

E26-10 Freese Company manufactures and sells three products. Relevant per unit data concerning each product are given below.

Compute contribution margin and determine the product to be manufactured.
(SO 8)

	Product		
	A	B	C
Selling price	$11	$12	$15
Variable costs and expenses	$4	$8	$9
Machine hours to produce	2	1	2

Instructions
(a) Compute the contribution margin per unit of the limited resource (machine hour) for each product.
(b) Assuming 3,000 additional machine hours are available, which product should be manufactured?
(c) Prepare an analysis showing the total contribution margin if the additional hours are (1) divided equally among the products, and (2) allocated entirely to the product identified in (b) above.

E26-11 Carleton Service Center just purchased an automobile hoist for $15,000. The hoist has a 5-year life and an estimated salvage value of $1,080. Installation costs were $2,900, and freight charges were $820. Carleton uses straight-line depreciation.

Compute cash payback period and annual rate of return.
(SO 9)

The new hoist will be used to replace mufflers and tires on automobiles. Carleton estimates that the new hoist will enable his mechanics to replace four extra mufflers per week. Each muffler sells for $65 installed. The cost of a muffler is $35, and the labor cost to install a muffler is $10.

Instructions
(a) Compute the payback period for the new hoist.
(b) Compute the annual rate of return for the new hoist. (Round to one decimal.)

E26-12 Suzaki Manufacturing Company is considering three new projects, each requiring an equipment investment of $22,000. Each project will last for 3 years and produce the following cash inflows.

Compute cash payback period and net present value.
(SO 9, 10)

Year	AA	BB	CC
1	$ 7,000	$ 9,500	$13,000
2	9,000	9,500	10,000
3	15,000	9,500	9,000
Total	$31,000	$28,500	$32,000

The equipment's salvage value is zero. Suzaki uses straight-line depreciation. Suzaki will not accept any project with a payback period over 2 years. Suzaki's minimum required rate of return is 12%.

Instructions
(a) Compute each project's payback period, indicating the most desirable project and the least desirable project using this method. (Round to two decimals.)
(b) Compute the net present value of each project. Does your evaluation change? (Round to nearest dollar.)

E26-13 Rondello Company is considering a capital investment of $150,000 in additional productive facilities. The new machinery is expected to have a useful life of 5 years with no salvage value. Depreciation is by the straight-line method. During the life of the investment, annual net income and cash inflows are expected to be $18,000 and $48,000, respectively. Rondello has a 12% cost of capital rate, which is the minimum acceptable rate of return on the investment.

Compute annual rate of return, cash payback period, and net present value.
(SO 9, 10)

Instructions
(Round to two decimals.)
(a) Compute (1) the annual rate of return and (2) the cash payback period on the proposed capital expenditure.
(b) Using the discounted cash flow technique, compute the net present value.

Chapter 26 Incremental Analysis and Capital Budgeting

Determine internal rate of return.
(SO 10)

E26-14 Omega Company is considering three capital expenditure projects. Relevant data for the projects are as follows.

Project	Investment	Annual Income	Life of Project
22A	$240,000	$13,300	6 years
23A	270,000	21,000	9 years
24A	288,000	20,000	8 years

Annual income is constant over the life of the project. Each project is expected to have zero salvage value at the end of the project. Omega Company uses the straight-line method of depreciation.

Instructions
(a) Determine the internal rate of return for each project. Round the internal rate of return factor to three decimals.
(b) If Omega Company's minimum required rate of return is 11%, which projects are acceptable?

Compute net present value and recommend project.
(SO 10)

E26-15 Vasquez Corporation is considering investing in two different projects. It could invest in both, neither, or just one of the projects. The forecasts for the projects are as follows.

	Project A	Project B
Capital investment	$200,000	$300,000
Net annual cash flows	$50,000	$65,000
Length of project	5 years	7 years

The minimum rate of return acceptable to Vasquez is 10%.

Instructions
(a) Compute the net present value of the two projects.
(b) What capital budgeting decision should Vasquez make?
(c) Project A could be modified. By spending $20,000 more initially, the net annual cash flows could be increased by $10,000 per year. Would this change Vasquez's decision?

EXERCISES: SET B

Visit the book's website at **www.wiley.com/college/weygandt**, and choose the Student Companion site, to access Exercise Set B.

PROBLEMS: SET A

Make incremental analysis for special order, and identify non-financial factors in decision.
(SO 3)

P26-1A Korte Company is currently producing 16,000 units per month, which is 80% of its production capacity. Variable manufacturing costs are currently $8.00 per unit. Fixed manufacturing costs are $56,000 per month. Korte pays a 9% sales commission to its sales people, has $30,000 in fixed administrative expenses per month, and is averaging $320,000 in sales per month.

A special order received from a foreign company would enable Korte Company to operate at 100% capacity. The foreign company offered to pay 75% of Korte's current selling price per unit. If the order is accepted, Korte will have to spend an extra $2.00 per unit to package the product for overseas shipping. Also, Korte Company would need to lease a new stamping machine to imprint the foreign company's logo on the product, at a monthly cost of $2,500. The special order would require a sales commission of $3,500.

Instructions
(a) Compute the number of units involved in the special order and the foreign company's offered price per unit.
(b) What is the manufacturing cost of producing one unit of Korte's product for regular customers?
(c) Prepare an incremental analysis of the special order. Should management accept the order?
(d) What is the lowest price that Korte could accept for the special order to earn net income of $1.20 per unit?
(e)  What nonfinancial factors should management consider in making its decision?

P26-2A The management of Martinez Manufacturing Company has asked for your assistance in deciding whether to continue manufacturing a part or to buy it from an outside supplier. The part, called Tropica, is a component of Martinez's finished product.

An analysis of the accounting records and the production data revealed the following information for the year ending December 31, 2010.

1. The Machinery Department produced 36,000 units of Tropica.
2. Each Tropica unit requires 10 minutes to produce. Three people in the Machinery Department work full time (2,000 hours per year) producing Tropica. Each person is paid $11.00 per hour.
3. The cost of materials per Tropica unit is $2.00.
4. Manufacturing overhead costs directly applicable to the production of Tropica are: indirect labor, $5,500; utilities, $1,300; depreciation, $1,600; property taxes and insurance, $1,000. All of the costs will be eliminated if Tropica is purchased.
5. The lowest price for a Tropica from an outside supplier is $3.90 per unit. Freight charges will be $0.30 per unit, and a part-time receiving clerk at $8,500 per year will be required.
6. If Tropica is purchased, the excess space will be used to store Martinez's finished product. Currently, Martinez rents storage space at approximately $0.60 per unit stored per year. Approximately 6,000 units per year are stored in the rented space.

Make incremental analysis related to make or buy; consider opportunity cost, and identify nonfinancial factors.
(SO 4)

Instructions
(a) Prepare an incremental analysis for the make-or-buy decision. Should Martinez make or buy the part? Why?
(b) Prepare an incremental analysis, assuming the released facilities can be used to produce $10,000 of net income in addition to the savings on the rental of storage space. What decision should now be made?
(c) What nonfinancial factors should be considered in the decision?

P26-3A Deskins Manufacturing Company has four operating divisions. During the first quarter of 2010 the company reported total income from operations of $61,000 and the following results for the divisions.

Compute contribution margin, and prepare incremental analysis concerning elimination of divisions.
(SO 7)

	Division			
	Denver	**Miami**	**San Diego**	**Tacoma**
Sales	$455,000	$730,000	$920,000	$515,000
Cost of goods sold	380,000	480,000	576,000	430,000
Selling and administrative expenses	120,000	207,000	246,000	120,000
Income (loss) from operations	$ (45,000)	$ 43,000	$ 98,000	$ (35,000)

Analysis reveals the following percentages of variable costs in each division.

	Denver	**Miami**	**San Diego**	**Tacoma**
Cost of goods sold	95%	80%	90%	90%
Selling and administrative expenses	80	60	70	60

Discontinuance of any division would save 60% of the fixed costs and expenses for that division.

Top management is deeply concerned about the unprofitable divisions (Denver and Tacoma). The consensus is that one or both of the divisions should be eliminated.

Instructions
(a) Compute the contribution margin for the two unprofitable divisions.
(b) Prepare an incremental analysis concerning the possible elimination of (1) the Denver Division and (2) the Tacoma Division. What course of action do you recommend for each division?
(c) Prepare a columnar condensed income statement using the CVP format for Deskins Manufacturing Company, assuming (1) the Denver Division is eliminated, and (2) the unavoidable fixed costs and expenses of the Denver Division are allocated 30% to Miami, 50% to San Diego, and 20% to Tacoma.
(d) Compare the total income from operations with the Denver Division ($61,000) to total income from operations without this division.

Compute annual rate of return, cash payback, and net present value.

(SO 9, 10)

P26-4A Timmons Corporation is considering three long-term capital investment proposals. Relevant data on each project are as follows.

	Project		
	Brown	**Red**	**Yellow**
Capital investment	$190,000	$220,000	$250,000
Annual net income:			
Year 1	25,000	20,000	26,000
2	16,000	20,000	24,000
3	13,000	20,000	23,000
4	10,000	20,000	17,000
5	8,000	20,000	20,000
Total	$ 72,000	$100,000	$110,000

Salvage value is expected to be zero at the end of each project. Depreciation is computed by the straight-line method. The company's minimum rate of return is the company's cost of capital which is 12%.

Instructions

(a) Compute the annual rate of return for each project. (Round to one decimal.)
(b) Compute the cash payback period for each project. (Round to two decimals.)
(c) Compute the net present value for each project. (Round to nearest dollar.)
(d) Rank the projects on each of the foregoing bases. Which project do you recommend?

Compute annual rate of return, cash payback, and net present value.

(SO 9, 10)

P26-5A Wendy Dobson is the managing director of the Wichita Day Care Center. Wichita is currently set up as a full-time child care facility for children between the ages of 12 months and 6 years. Wendy is trying to determine whether the center should expand its facilities to incorporate a newborn care room for infants between the ages of 6 weeks and 12 months. The necessary space already exists. An investment of $25,000 would be needed, however, to purchase cribs, high chairs, etc. The equipment purchased for the room would have a 5-year useful life with zero salvage value.

The newborn nursery would be staffed to handle 12 infants on a full-time basis. The parents of each infant would be charged $200 weekly, and the facility would operate 52 weeks of the year. Staffing the nursery would require two full-time specialists and five part-time assistants at an annual cost of $103,800. Food, diapers, and other miscellaneous supplies are expected to total $14,000 annually.

Instructions

(a) Determine (1) annual net income and (2) net cash flow for the new nursery.
(b) Compute (1) the annual rate of return and (2) the cash payback period for the new nursery. (Round to two decimals.)
(c) Assuming that Wichita can borrow the money needed for expansion at 10%, compute the net present value of the new room. (Round to the nearest dollar.)
(d) ✎ What should Wendy conclude from these computations?

Compute net present value and internal rate of return.

(SO 10)

P26-6A Aqua Tech Testing is considering investing in a new testing device. It has two options: Option A would have an initial lower cost but would require a significant expenditure for rebuilding after 5 years. Option B would require no rebuilding expenditure, but its maintenance costs would be higher. Since the option B machine is of initial higher quality, it is expected to have a salvage value at the end of its useful life. The following estimates were provided. The company's cost of capital is 9%.

	Option A	**Option B**
Initial cost	$90,000	$170,000
Net annual cash flows	$20,000	$32,000
Cost to rebuild (end of year 5)	$26,500	$0
Salvage value	$0	$27,500
Estimated useful life	8 years	8 years

Instructions

(a) Compute the (1) net present value, and (2) internal rate of return for each option. (*Hint:* To solve for internal rate of return, experiment with alternative discount rates to arrive at a net present value of zero.)
(b) Which option should be accepted?

PROBLEMS: SET B

P26-1B Haslett Inc. manufactures basketballs for the National Basketball Association (NBA). For the first 6 months of 2011, the company reported the following operating results while operating at 90% of plant capacity.

	Amount	Per Unit
Sales	$4,500,000	$50.00
Cost of goods sold	3,150,000	35.00
Selling and administrative expenses	360,000	4.00
Net income	$ 990,000	$11.00

Make incremental analysis for special order, and identify nonfinancial factors in decision.
(SO 3)

Fixed costs for the period were: Cost of goods sold $900,000, and selling and administrative expenses $135,000.

In July, normally a slack manufacturing month, Haslett receives a special order for 9,000 basketballs at $32 each from the European Basketball Association (EBA). Acceptance of the order would increase variable selling and administrative expenses $0.50 per unit because of shipping costs but would not increase fixed costs and expenses.

Instructions
(a) Prepare an incremental analysis for the special order.
(b) Should Haslett Inc. accept the special order?
(c) What is the minimum selling price on the special order to produce net income of $5.00 per ball?
(d) What nonfinancial factors should management consider in making its decision?

P26-2B The management of Finnigan Manufacturing Company is trying to decide whether to continue manufacturing a part or to buy it from an outside supplier. The part, called BIZBE, is a component of the company's finished product.

The following information was collected from the accounting records and production data for the year ending December 31, 2010.

Make incremental analysis related to make or buy; consider opportunity cost, and identify nonfinancial factors.
(SO 4)

1. 6,000 units of BIZBE were produced in the Machining Department.
2. Variable manufacturing costs applicable to the production of each BIZBE unit were: direct materials $4.75, direct labor $4.60, indirect labor $0.45, utilities $0.35.
3. Fixed manufacturing costs applicable to the production of BIZBE were:

Cost Item	Direct	Allocated
Depreciation	$1,100	$ 900
Property taxes	500	200
Insurance	900	600
	$2,500	$1,700

All variable manufacturing and direct fixed costs will be eliminated if BIZBE is purchased. Allocated costs will have to be absorbed by other production departments.

4. The lowest quotation for 6,000 BIZBE units from a supplier is $66,000.
5. If BIZBE units are purchased, freight and inspection costs would be $0.30 per unit, and receiving costs totaling $750 per year would be incurred by the Machining Department.

Instructions
(a) Prepare an incremental analysis for BIZBE. Your analysis should have columns for (1) Make BIZBE, (2) Buy BIZBE, and (3) Net Income Increase/Decrease.
(b) Based on your analysis, what decision should management make?
(c) Would the decision be different if Finnegan Company has the opportunity to produce $6,000 of net income with the facilities currently being used to manufacture BIZBE? Show computations.
(d) What nonfinancial factors should management consider in making its decision?

P26-3B Tryon Manufacturing Company has four operating divisions. During the first quarter of 2011, the company reported aggregate income from operations of $135,000 and the divisional results shown on the next page.

Compute contribution margin, and prepare incremental analysis concerning elimination of divisions.
(SO 7)

	Division			
	I	II	III	IV
Sales	$510,000	$390,000	$310,000	$170,000
Cost of goods sold	300,000	250,000	270,000	150,000
Selling and administrative expenses	60,000	80,000	65,000	70,000
Income (loss) from operations	$150,000	$ 60,000	$ (25,000)	$(50,000)

Analysis reveals the following percentages of variable costs in each division.

	I	II	III	IV
Cost of goods sold	70%	80%	75%	90%
Selling and administrative expenses	40	50	60	70

Discontinuance of any division would save 50% of the fixed costs and expenses for that division. Top management is very concerned about the unprofitable divisions (III and IV). Consensus is that one or both of the divisions should be discontinued.

Instructions
(a) Compute the contribution margin for Divisions III and IV.
(b) Prepare an incremental analysis concerning the possible discontinuance of (1) Division III and (2) Division IV. What course of action do you recommend for each division?
(c) Prepare a columnar condensed income statement for Tryon Manufacturing, assuming Division IV is eliminated. Use the CVP format. Division IV's unavoidable fixed costs are allocated equally to the continuing divisions.
(d) Reconcile the total income from operations ($135,000) with the total income from operations without Division IV.

Compute annual rate of return, cash payback, and net present value.
(SO 9, 10)

P26-4B Bensen Corporation is considering three long-term capital investment proposals. Each investment has a useful life of 5 years. Relevant data on each project are as follows.

	Project Ric	Project Rac	Project Roe
Capital investment	$140,000	$150,000	$180,000
Annual net income:			
Year 1	13,000	18,000	27,000
2	13,000	17,000	22,000
3	13,000	13,000	16,000
4	13,000	12,000	13,000
5	13,000	9,000	12,000
Total	$ 65,000	$ 69,000	$ 90,000

Depreciation is computed by the straight-line method with no salvage value. The company's cost of capital is 15%.

Instructions
(a) Compute the annual rate of return for each project. (Round to one decimal.)
(b) Compute the cash payback period for each project. (Round to two decimals.)
(c) Compute the net present value for each project. (Round to nearest dollar.)
(d) Rank the projects on each of the foregoing bases. Which project do you recommend?

Compute annual rate of return, cash payback, and net present value.
(SO, 9, 10)

P26-5B Betty Dillman is an accounting major at a midwestern state university located approximately 60 miles from a major city. Many of the students attending the university are from the metropolitan area and visit their homes regularly on the weekends. Betty, an entrepreneur at heart, realizes that few good commuting alternatives are available for students doing weekend travel. She believes that a weekend commuting service could be organized and run profitably from several suburban and downtown shopping mall locations. Betty has gathered the following investment information.

1. Six used vans would cost a total of $96,000 to purchase and would have a 3-year useful life with negligible salvage value. Betty plans to use straight-line depreciation.
2. Ten drivers would have to be employed at a total payroll expense of $70,000.

3. Other annual out of pocket expenses associated with running the commuter service would include Gasoline $28,000, Maintenance $2,800, Repairs $3,500, Insurance $3,200, Advertising $1,500. (Exclude interest expense.)
4. Betty has visited several financial institutions to discuss funding for her new venture. The best interest rate she has been able to negotiate is 10%. Use this rate for cost of capital.
5. Betty expects each van to make ten round trips weekly and carry an average of five students each trip. The service is expected to operate 30 weeks each years. Each student will be charged $16.00 for a round-trip ticket.

Instructions
(a) Determine the annual (1) net income, and (2) net cash flow for the commuter service.
(b) Compute (1) the annual rate of return, and (2) the cash payback period. (Round to two decimals.)
(c) Compute the net present value of the commuter service. (Round to the nearest dollar.)
(d) What should Betty conclude from these computations?

P26-6B Oklahoma Clinic is considering investing in new heart-monitoring equipment. It has two options: Option A would have an initial lower cost but would require a significant expenditure for rebuilding after 4 years. Option B would require no rebuilding expenditure, but its maintenance costs would be higher. Since the option B machine is of initial higher quality, it is expected to have a salvage value at the end of its useful life. The following estimates were made of the cash flows. The company's cost of capital is 8%.

Compute net present value, and internal rate of return.
(SO 10)

	Option A	Option B
Initial cost	$135,000	$203,000
Net annual cash flows	$31,000	$40,000
Cost to rebuild (end of year 4)	$50,000	$0
Salvage value	$0	$10,000
Estimated useful life	8 years	8 years

Instructions
(a) Compute the (1) net present value and (2) internal rate of return for each option. (*Hint:* To solve for internal rate of return, experiment with alternative discount rates to arrive at a net present value of zero.)
(b) Which option should be accepted?

PROBLEMS: SET C

Visit the book's companion website at **www.wiley.com/college/weygandt**, and choose the Student Companion site, to access Problem Set C.

COMPREHENSIVE PROBLEM: CHAPTERS 19 TO 26

You would like to start a business manufacturing a unique model of bicycle helmet. In preparation for an interview with the bank to discuss your financing needs, you develop answers to the following questions. A number of assumptions are required; clearly note all assumptions that you make.

Instructions
(a) Identify the types of costs that would likely be involved in making this product.
(b) Set up five columns as indicated.

	Product Costs			
Item	Direct Materials	Direct Labor	Manufacturing Overhead	Period Costs

Classify the costs you identified in (a) into the manufacturing cost classifications of product costs (direct materials, direct labor, and manufacturing overhead) and period costs.

(c) Assign hypothetical monthly dollar figures to the costs you identified in (a) and (b).

(d) Assume you have no raw materials or work in process beginning or ending inventories. Prepare a projected cost of goods manufactured schedule for the first month of operations.

(e) Project the number of helmets you expect to produce the first month of operations. Compute the cost to produce one bicycle helmet. Review the result to ensure it is reasonable; if not, return to part (c) and adjust the monthly dollar figures you assigned accordingly.

(f) What type of cost accounting system will you likely use—job order or process costing?

(g) Explain how you would assign costs in either the job order or process costing system you plan to use.

(h) Classify your costs as either variable or fixed costs. For simplicity, assign all costs to either variable or fixed, assuming there are no mixed costs, using the format shown.

Item	Variable Costs	Fixed Costs	Total Costs

(i) Compute the unit variable cost, using the production number you determined in (e).

(j) Project the number of helmets you anticipate selling the first month of operations. Set a unit selling price, and compute both the contribution margin per unit and the contribution margin ratio.

(k) Determine your break-even point in dollars and in units.

(l) Prepare projected operating budgets (sales, production, direct materials, direct labor, manufacturing overhead, selling and administrative expense, and income statement). You will need to make assumptions for each of the following:

Direct materials budget:	Quantity of direct materials required to produce one helmet; cost per unit of quantity; desired ending direct materials (assume none).
Direct labor budget:	Direct labor time required per helmet; direct labor cost per hour.
Budgeted income statement:	Income tax expense is 45% of income from operations.

(m) Prepare a cash budget for the month. Assume the percentage of sales that will be collected from customers is 75%, and the percentage of direct materials that will be paid in the current month is 75%.

(n) Determine a relevant range of activity, using the number of helmets produced as your activity index. Recast your manufacturing overhead budget into a flexible monthly budget for two additional activity levels.

(o) Identify one potential cause of materials, direct labor, and manufacturing overhead variances for your product.

(p) Assume that you wish to purchase production equipment that costs $720,000. Determine the cash payback period, utilizing the monthly cash flow that you computed in part (m) multiplied by 12 months (for simplicity).

(q) Identify any nonfinancial factors that should be considered before commencing your business venture.

WATERWAYS CONTINUING PROBLEM

(This is a continuation of the Waterways Problem from Chapters 19 through 25.)

WCP26 Waterways Corporation puts much emphasis on cash flow when it plans for capital investments. The company chose its discount rate of 8% based on the rate of return it must pay its owners and creditors. Using that rate, Waterways then uses different methods to determine the best decisions for making capital outlays. Waterways is considering buying five new backhoes to replace the backhoes it now has. This problem asks you to evaluate that decision, using various capital budgeting techniques.

Go to the book's companion website, www.wiley.com/college/weygandt, to find the remainder of this problem.

BROADENING YOUR PERSPECTIVE

Decision Making Across the Organization

BYP26-1 Morganstern Company is considering the purchase of a new machine. The invoice price of the machine is $170,000, freight charges are estimated to be $4,000, and installation costs are expected to be $6,000. Salvage value of the new equipment is expected to be zero after a useful life of 4 years. Existing equipment could be retained and used for an additional 4 years if the new machine is not purchased. At that time, the salvage value of the equipment would be zero. If the new machine is purchased now, the existing machine would be scrapped. Morganstern's accountant, Diane Gallup, has accumulated the following data regarding annual sales and expenses with and without the new machine.

1. Without the new machine, Morganstern can sell 10,000 units of product annually at a per unit selling price of $100. If the new unit is purchased, the number of units produced and sold would increase by 20%. The selling price would remain the same.
2. The new machine is faster than the old machine, and it is more efficient in its usage of materials. With the old machine the gross profit rate will be 25% of sales. With the new machine the rate will be 28% of sales.
3. Annual selling expenses are $135,000 with the current equipment. Because the new equipment would produce a greater number of units to be sold, annual selling expenses are expected to increase by 10% if it is purchased.
4. Annual administrative expenses are expected to be $100,000 with the old machine and $113,000 with the new machine.
5. The current book value of the existing machine is $36,000. Morganstern uses straight-line depreciation.
6. Morganstern's management wants a minimum rate of return of 15% on its investment and a payback period of no more than 3 years.

Instructions
With the class divided into groups, answer the following. (Ignore income tax effects.)
(a) Prepare an incremental analysis for the 4 years showing whether Morganstern should keep the existing machine or buy the new machine.
(b) Calculate the annual rate of return for the new machine. (Round to two decimals.)
(c) Compute the payback period for the new machine. (Round to two decimals.)
(d) Compute the net present value of the new machine. (Round to the nearest dollar.)
(e) On the basis of the foregoing data, would you recommend that Morganstern buy the machine? Why?

Managerial Analysis

BYP26-2 Barone Company manufactures private-label small electronic products, such as alarm clocks, calculators, kitchen timers, stopwatches, and automatic pencil sharpeners. Some of the products are sold as sets, and others are sold individually. Products are studied as to their sales potential, and then cost estimates are made. The Engineering Department develops production plans, and then production begins. The company has generally had very successful product introduction. Only two products introduced by the company have been discontinued.

One of the products currently sold is a multi-alarm alarm clock. The clock has four alarms that can be programmed to sound at various times and for varying lengths of time. The company has experienced a great deal of difficulty in making the circuit boards for the clocks. The production process has never operated smoothly. The product is unprofitable at the present time, primarily because of warranty repairs and product recalls. Two models of the clocks were recalled, for example, because they sometimes caused an electric shock when the alarms were being shut off. The Engineering Department is attempting to revise the manufacturing process, but the revision will take another 6 months at least.

The clocks were very popular when they were introduced, and since they are private-label, the company has not suffered much from the recalls. Presently, the company has a very large order for several items from Kmart Stores. The order includes 5,000 of the multi-alarm clocks.

When Barone suggested that Kmart purchase the clocks from another manufacturer, Kmart threatened to rescind the entire order unless the clocks were included.

Barone has therefore investigated the possibility of having another company make the clocks for them. The clocks were bid for the Kmart order, based on an estimated $5.50 cost to manufacture, as follows.

Circuit board, 1 each @ $1.00	$1.00
Plastic case, 1 each @ $0.50	0.50
Alarms, 4 @ $0.15 each	0.60
Labor, 15 minutes @ $12/hour	3.00
Overhead, $1.60 per labor hour	0.40

Barone could purchase clocks to fill the Kmart order for $9 from Silver Star, a Korean manufacturer with a very good quality record. Silver Star has offered to reduce the price to $7.50 after Barone has been a customer for 6 months, placing an order of at least 1,000 units per month. If Barone becomes a "preferred customer" by purchasing 15,000 units per year, the price would be reduced still further to $4.50.

Sigma Products, a local manufacturer, has also offered to make clocks for Barone. They have offered to sell 5,000 clocks for $5 each. However, Sigma Products has been in business for only 6 months. They have experienced significant turnover in their labor force, and the local media have reported that the owners may soon face tax evasion charges. The owner of Sigma Products is an electronic engineer, however, and the quality of the clocks is likely to be good.

If Barone decides to purchase the clocks from either Silver Star or Sigma, all the costs to manufacturer could be avoided, except a total of $5,000 in overhead costs for machine depreciation. The machinery is fairly new, and has no alternate use.

Instructions

(a) What is the difference in profit under each of the alternatives if the clocks are to be sold for $13.00 each to Kmart?

(b) What are the most important nonfinancial factors that Barone should consider when making this decision?

(c) What should Barone do in regard to the Kmart order? What should it do in regard to continuing to manufacture the multi-alarm alarm clocks? Be prepared to defend your answer.

Real-World Focus

BYP26-3 Founded in 1983, the Beverly Hills Fan Company is located in Woodland Hills, California. With 23 employees and sales of less than $10 million, the company is relatively small. Management feels that there is potential for growth in the upscale market for ceiling fans and lighting. They are particularly optimistic about growth in Mexican and Canadian markets.

Presented below is information from the president's letter in the company's annual report.

BEVERLY HILLS FAN COMPANY
President's Letter

An aggressive product development program was initiated during the past year resulting in new ceiling fan models planned for introduction next year. Award winning industrial designer Ron Rezek created several new fan models for the Beverly Hills Fan and L.A. Fan lines, including a new Showroom Collection, designed specifically for the architectural and designer markets. Each of these models has received critical acclaim, and order commitments for next year have been outstanding. Additionally, our Custom Color and special order fans continued to enjoy increasing popularity and sales gains as more and more customers desire fans that match their specific interior decors. Currently, Beverly Hills Fan Company offers a product line of over 100 models of contemporary, traditional, and transitional ceiling fans.

Instructions

(a) What points did the company management need to consider before deciding to offer the special-order fans to customers?

(b) How would incremental analysis be employed to assist in this decision?

Exploring the Web

BYP26-4 **Campbell Soup Company** is an international provider of soup products. Management is very interested in continuing to grow the company in its core business, while "spinning off" those businesses that are not part of its core operation.

Address: www.campbellsoups.com, or go to **www.wiley.com/college/weygandt**

Steps
1. Go to the home page of Campbell Soup Company at the address shown above.
2. Choose **Our Company** and then **Investor Center**.
3. Choose **Financial Reports**.
4. Choose the 2007 annual report, or the current annual report if 2007 is no longer available.

Instructions
Review the financial statements and management's discussion and analysis, and answer the following questions.

(a) What was the total amount reported as "Purchases of Plant Assets" in the 2007 statement of cash flows? How does this amount compare with the previous year?
(b) What range of interest rates does the company report on its long-term liabilities in the notes to its financial statements?
(c) Assume that this year's capital expenditures are expected to increase cash flows by $45 million. What is the expected internal rate of return (IRR) for these capital expenditures? (Assume a 10-year period for the cash flows.)

Communication Activity

BYP26-5 Refer back to E26-11 to address the following.

Instructions
Prepare a memo to Angie Baden, your supervisor. Show your calculations from E26-11, parts (a) and (b). In one or two paragraphs, discuss important nonfinancial considerations. Make any assumptions you believe to be necessary. Make a recommendation, based on your analysis.

Ethics Case

BYP26-6 DeVito Company operates in a state where corporate taxes and workmen's compensation insurance rates have recently doubled. DeVito's president has assigned you the task of preparing an economic analysis and making a recommendation about whether to move the company's entire operation to Missouri. The president is slightly in favor of such a move because Missouri is his boyhood home, and he also owns a fishing lodge there.

You have just completed building your dream house, moved in, and sodded the lawn. Your children are all doing well in school and sports and, along with your spouse, want no part of a move to Missouri. If the company does move, so will you because your town is a one-industry community, and you and your spouse will have to move to have employment. Moving when everyone else does will cause you to take a big loss on the sale of your house. The same hardships will be suffered by your coworkers, and the town will be devastated.

In compiling the costs of moving versus not moving, you have latitude in the assumptions you make, the estimates you compute, and the discount rates and time periods you project. You are in a position to influence the decision singlehandedly.

Instructions
(a) Who are the stakeholders in this situation?
(b) What are the ethical issues in this situation?
(c) What would you do in this situation?

"All About You" Activity

BYP26-7 Managerial accounting techniques can be used in a wide variety of settings. As we have frequently pointed out, you can use them in many personal situations. They also can be useful in trying to find solutions for societal issues that appear to be hard to solve.

Instructions

Read the *Fortune* article "The Toughest Customers: How Hardheaded Business Metrics Can Help the Hard-core Homeless," by Cait Murphy, available at *http://money.cnn.com/magazines/fortune/fortune_archive/2006/04/03/8373067/index.htm*. Answer the following questions.

(a) How does the article define "chronic" homelessness?
(b) In what ways does homelessness cost a city money? What are the estimated costs of a chronic homeless person to various cities?
(c) What are the steps suggested to address the problem?
(d) What is the estimated cost of implementing this program in New York? What results have been seen?
(e) In terms of incremental analysis, frame the relevant costs in this situation.

Answers to Insight and Accounting Across the Organization Questions

p. 1162 These Wheels Have Miles Before Installation

Q: What are the disadvantages of outsourcing to a foreign country?

A: *Possible disadvantages of outsourcing are that the supplier loses control over the quality of the product, as well as the timing of production. Also, the company exposes itself to price changes caused by changes in the value of the foreign currency. In addition, shipping large, heavy products such as tires is costly, and disruptions in shipping (due to strikes, weather, etc.) can cause delays in final assembly of vehicles. As a result of the outsourcing, the company will have to re-assign, or even lay off, many skilled workers. Not only is this very disruptive to the lives of those employees, it also hurts morale of the remaining employees. As more U.S employers begin to use robotic automation in their facilities, they are able to reduce the amount of labor required, and thus are beginning to be able to compete more favorably with foreign suppliers.*

p. 1170 Are You Ready for the 50-Inch Screen?

Q: In building factories to manufacture 50-inch TV screens, how might companies build risk factors into their financial analyses?

A: *One approach is to use sensitivity analysis. Sensitivity analysis uses a number of outcome estimates to get a sense of the variability among potential returns. In addition, more distant cash flows can be discarded or given a low weighting because of their high uncertainty.*

Authors' Comments on *All About You:* What Is a Degree Worth? (p. 1176)

This is a very difficult decision. All of the evidence suggests that your short-term and long-term prospects will be far greater with some form of post–high-school degree. Because of this, we feel strongly that you should make every effort to continue your education. Many of the discussions provided in this text presented ideas on how to get control of your individual financial situation. We would encourage you to use these tools to identify ways to reduce your financial burden in order to continue your education. We also want to repeat that even taking only one course a semester is better than dropping out. Your instructors and advisors frequently provide advice to students who are faced with the decision about whether to continue with their education. If you are in this situation, we would encourage you to seek their advice since the implications of this decision can be long-lasting.

Answers to Self-Study Questions

1. d   2. b   3. c   4. b   5. d   6. a   7. d   8. b   9. c   10. d   11. b   12. d   13. b
14. c   15. b

Appendix A

SPECIMEN FINANCIAL STATEMENTS:
PepsiCo, Inc.

THE ANNUAL REPORT

Once each year a corporation communicates to its stockholders and other interested parties by issuing a complete set of audited financial statements. The **annual report**, as this communication is called, summarizes the financial results of the company's operations for the year and its plans for the future. Many annual reports are attractive, multicolored, glossy public relations pieces, containing pictures of corporate officers and directors as well as photos and descriptions of new products and new buildings. Yet the basic function of every annual report is to report financial information, almost all of which is a product of the corporation's accounting system.

The content and organization of corporate annual reports have become fairly standardized. Excluding the public relations part of the report (pictures, products, etc.), the following are the traditional financial portions of the annual report:

- Financial Highlights
- Letter to the Stockholders
- Management's Discussion and Analysis
- Financial Statements
- Notes to the Financial Statements
- Management's Report on Internal Control
- Management Certification of Financial Statements
- Auditor's Report
- Supplementary Financial Information

In this appendix we illustrate current financial reporting with a comprehensive set of corporate financial statements that are prepared in accordance with generally accepted accounting principles and audited by an international independent certified public accounting firm. We are grateful for permission to use the actual financial statements and other accompanying financial information from the annual report of a large, publicly held company, PepsiCo, Inc.

FINANCIAL HIGHLIGHTS

Companies usually present the financial highlights section inside the front cover of the annual report or on its first two pages. This section generally reports the total or per share amounts for five to ten financial items for the current year and one or more previous years. Financial items from the income statement and the balance sheet that typically are presented are sales, income from continuing operations, net income, net income per share, net cash provided by operating activities, dividends per common share, and the amount of capital expenditures. The financial highlights section from PepsiCo's Annual Report is shown on page A-2.

The financial information herein is reprinted with permission from the PepsiCo, Inc. 2007 Annual Report. The complete financial statements are available through a link at the book's companion website.

A1

Appendix A Specimen Financial Statements: PepsiCo, Inc.

Financial Highlights

PepsiCo, Inc. and Subsidiaries
($ in millions except per share amounts; all per share amounts assume dilution)

	2007	2006	Chg[a]
Summary of Operations			
Total net revenue	$39,474	$35,137	12%
Division operating profit[b]	$8,025	$7,307	10%
Total operating profit[c]	$7,272	$6,569	11%
Net income[d]	$5,599	$5,065	11%
Earnings per share[d]	$3.38	$3.00	13%
Other Data			
Management operating cash flow[e]	$4,551	$4,065	12%
Net cash provided by operating activities	$6,934	$6,084	14%
Capital spending	$2,430	$2,068	17%
Common share repurchases	$4,300	$3,000	43%
Dividends paid	$2,204	$1,854	19%
Long-term debt	$4,203	$2,550	65%

(a) Percentage changes are based on unrounded amounts.
(b) Excludes corporate unallocated expenses and restructuring and impairment charges.
See page 86 for a reconciliation to the most directly comparable financial measure in accordance with GAAP.
(c) Excludes restructuring and impairment charges.
See page 86 for a reconciliation to the most directly comparable financial measure in accordance with GAAP.
(d) Excludes restructuring and impairment charges and certain tax items.
See page 86 for a reconciliation to the most directly comparable financial measure in accordance with GAAP.
(e) Includes the impact of net capital spending. Also, see "Our Liquidity and Capital Resources" in Management's Discussion and Analysis.

PepsiCo Estimated Worldwide Retail Sales: $98 Billion*

*Includes estimated retail sales of all PepsiCo products, including those sold by our partners and franchised bottlers.

Largest PepsiCo Brands

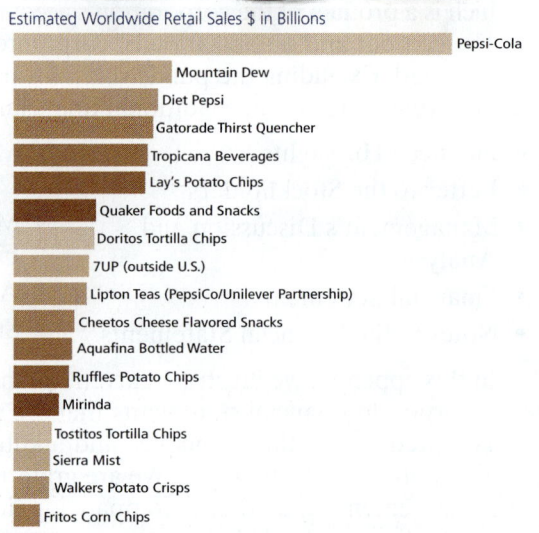

Estimated Worldwide Retail Sales $ in Billions

- Pepsi-Cola
- Mountain Dew
- Diet Pepsi
- Gatorade Thirst Quencher
- Tropicana Beverages
- Lay's Potato Chips
- Quaker Foods and Snacks
- Doritos Tortilla Chips
- 7UP (outside U.S.)
- Lipton Teas (PepsiCo/Unilever Partnership)
- Cheetos Cheese Flavored Snacks
- Aquafina Bottled Water
- Ruffles Potato Chips
- Mirinda
- Tostitos Tortilla Chips
- Sierra Mist
- Walkers Potato Crisps
- Fritos Corn Chips

PepsiCo has 18 mega-brands that generate $1 billion or more each in annual retail sales.

LETTER TO THE STOCKHOLDERS

Nearly every annual report contains a letter to the stockholders from the chairman of the board or the president, or both. This letter typically discusses the company's accomplishments during the past year and highlights significant events such as mergers and acquisitions, new products, operating achievements, business philosophy, changes in officers or directors, financing commitments, expansion plans, and future prospects. The letter to the stockholders is signed by Indra Nooyi, Chairman of the Board and Chief Executive Officer, of PepsiCo.

Only a short summary of the letter is provided below. The full letter can be accessed at the book's companion website at www.wiley.com/college/weygandt.

Delivering Performance with Purpose in 2007

Dear Shareholders:

We have titled this year's annual report "Performance with Purpose: The Journey Continues." That's because in 2007 PepsiCo made great progress toward the long-term corporate objectives we set for ourselves last year: To achieve business and financial success while leaving a positive imprint on society.

Once more, our extraordinary associates around the world delivered terrific performance, and I am delighted to share with you the following 2007 financial results:

- Net revenue grew 12%, roughly three times the rate of global GDP growth.
- Division operating profit grew 10%.
- Earnings per share grew 13%.
- Total return to shareholders was 26%.
- Return on invested capital was 29%.
- Cash flow from operations was $6.9 billion.

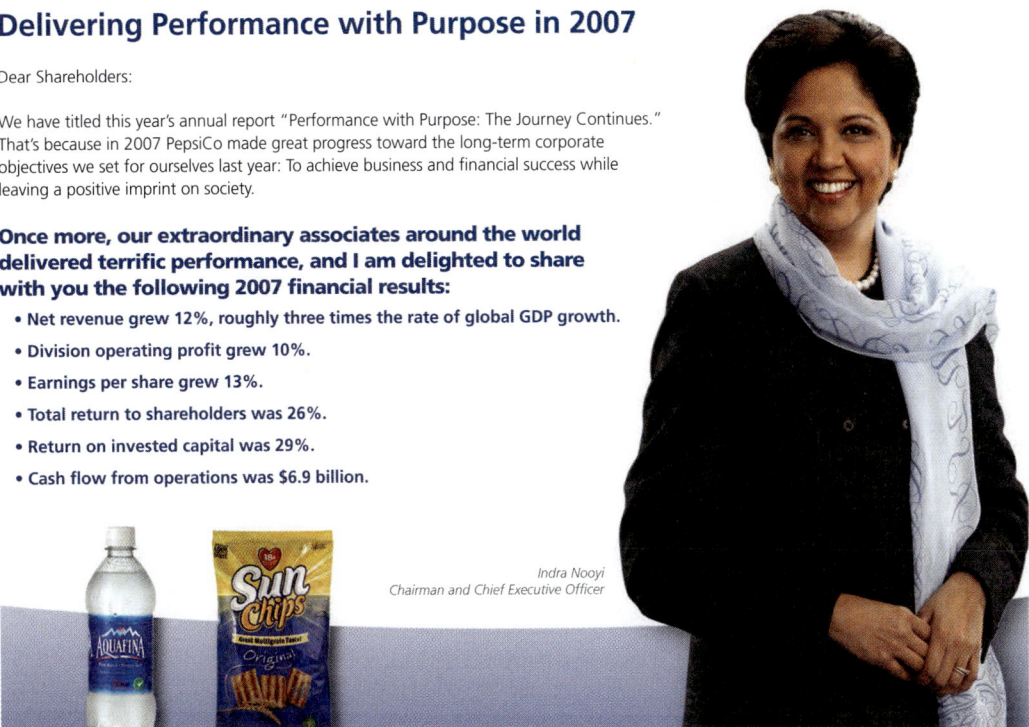

Indra Nooyi
Chairman and Chief Executive Officer

MANAGEMENT'S DISCUSSION AND ANALYSIS

The **management's discussion and analysis (MD&A)** section covers three financial aspects of a company: its results of operations, its ability to pay near-term obligations, and its ability to fund operations and expansion. Management must highlight favorable or unfavorable trends and identity significant events and uncertainties that affect these three factors. This discussion obviously involves a number of subjective estimates and opinions. In its MD&A section, PepsiCo breaks its discussion into four major headings: Our Business, Our Critical Accounting Policies, Our Financial Results, and Our Liquidity and Capital Resources. You can access the full MD&A section at www.wiley.com/college/weygandt.

FINANCIAL STATEMENTS AND ACCOMPANYING NOTES

The standard set of financial statements consists of: (1) a comparative income statement for three years, (2) a comparative statement of cash flows for three years, (3) a comparative balance sheet for two years, (4) a statement of stockholders' equity for three years, and (5) a set of accompanying notes that are considered an integral part of the financial statements. The auditor's report, unless stated otherwise, covers the financial statements and the accompanying notes. PepsiCo's financial statements and accompanying notes plus supplementary data and analyses follow.

Consolidated Statement of Income

PepsiCo, Inc. and Subsidiaries
Fiscal years ended December 29, 2007, December 30, 2006 and December 31, 2005

(in millions except per share amounts)	2007	2006	2005
Net Revenue	**$39,474**	$35,137	$32,562
Cost of sales	18,038	15,762	14,176
Selling, general and administrative expenses	14,208	12,711	12,252
Amortization of intangible assets	58	162	150
Operating Profit	**7,170**	6,502	5,984
Bottling equity income	560	553	495
Interest expense	(224)	(239)	(256)
Interest income	125	173	159
Income before Income Taxes	**7,631**	6,989	6,382
Provision for Income Taxes	**1,973**	1,347	2,304
Net Income	**$ 5,658**	$ 5,642	$ 4,078
Net Income per Common Share			
Basic	$3.48	$3.42	$2.43
Diluted	$3.41	$3.34	$2.39

See accompanying notes to consolidated financial statements.

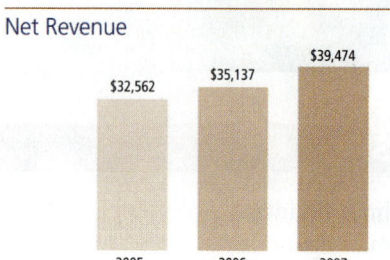

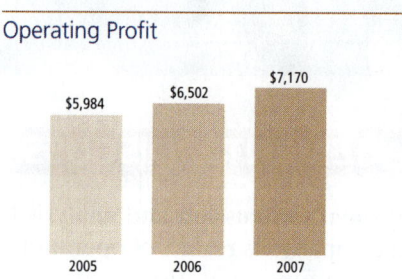

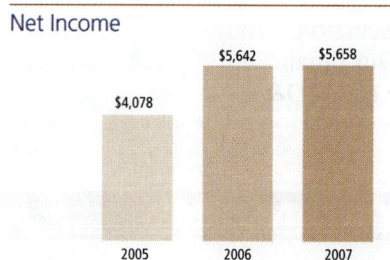

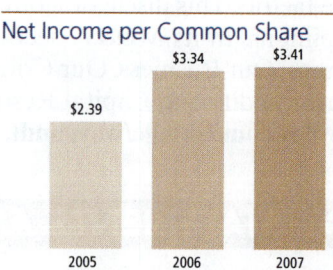

Consolidated Statement of Cash Flows

PepsiCo, Inc. and Subsidiaries
Fiscal years ended December 29, 2007, December 30, 2006 and December 31, 2005

(in millions)	2007	2006	2005
Operating Activities			
Net income	$ 5,658	$ 5,642	$ 4,078
Depreciation and amortization	1,426	1,406	1,308
Stock-based compensation expense	260	270	311
Excess tax benefits from share-based payment arrangements	(208)	(134)	–
Cash payments for merger-related costs and restructuring charges	–	–	(22)
Pension and retiree medical plan contributions	(310)	(131)	(877)
Pension and retiree medical plan expenses	535	544	464
Bottling equity income, net of dividends	(441)	(442)	(414)
Deferred income taxes and other tax charges and credits	118	(510)	440
Change in accounts and notes receivable	(405)	(330)	(272)
Change in inventories	(204)	(186)	(132)
Change in prepaid expenses and other current assets	(16)	(37)	(56)
Change in accounts payable and other current liabilities	500	223	188
Change in income taxes payable	128	(295)	609
Other, net	(107)	64	227
Net Cash Provided by Operating Activities	6,934	6,084	5,852
Investing Activities			
Capital spending	(2,430)	(2,068)	(1,736)
Sales of property, plant and equipment	47	49	88
Proceeds from (Investment in) finance assets	27	(25)	–
Acquisitions and investments in noncontrolled affiliates	(1,320)	(522)	(1,095)
Cash proceeds from sale of PBG stock	315	318	214
Divestitures	–	37	3
Short-term investments, by original maturity			
More than three months — purchases	(83)	(29)	(83)
More than three months — maturities	113	25	84
Three months or less, net	(413)	2,021	(992)
Net Cash Used for Investing Activities	(3,744)	(194)	(3,517)
Financing Activities			
Proceeds from issuances of long-term debt	2,168	51	25
Payments of long-term debt	(579)	(157)	(177)
Short-term borrowings, by original maturity			
More than three months — proceeds	83	185	332
More than three months — payments	(133)	(358)	(85)
Three months or less, net	(345)	(2,168)	1,601
Cash dividends paid	(2,204)	(1,854)	(1,642)
Share repurchases — common	(4,300)	(3,000)	(3,012)
Share repurchases — preferred	(12)	(10)	(19)
Proceeds from exercises of stock options	1,108	1,194	1,099
Excess tax benefits from share-based payment arrangements	208	134	–
Net Cash Used for Financing Activities	(4,006)	(5,983)	(1,878)
Effect of exchange rate changes on cash and cash equivalents	75	28	(21)
Net (Decrease)/Increase in Cash and Cash Equivalents	(741)	(65)	436
Cash and Cash Equivalents, Beginning of Year	1,651	1,716	1,280
Cash and Cash Equivalents, End of Year	$ 910	$ 1,651	$ 1,716

See accompanying notes to consolidated financial statements.

Consolidated Balance Sheet

PepsiCo, Inc. and Subsidiaries
December 29, 2007 and December 30, 2006

(in millions except per share amounts)	2007	2006
ASSETS		
Current Assets		
Cash and cash equivalents	$ 910	$ 1,651
Short-term investments	1,571	1,171
Accounts and notes receivable, net	4,389	3,725
Inventories	2,290	1,926
Prepaid expenses and other current assets	991	657
Total Current Assets	10,151	9,130
Property, Plant and Equipment, net	11,228	9,687
Amortizable Intangible Assets, net	796	637
Goodwill	5,169	4,594
Other nonamortizable intangible assets	1,248	1,212
Nonamortizable Intangible Assets	6,417	5,806
Investments in Noncontrolled Affiliates	4,354	3,690
Other Assets	1,682	980
Total Assets	$34,628	$29,930
LIABILITIES AND SHAREHOLDERS' EQUITY		
Current Liabilities		
Short-term obligations	$ —	$ 274
Accounts payable and other current liabilities	7,602	6,496
Income taxes payable	151	90
Total Current Liabilities	7,753	6,860
Long-Term Debt Obligations	4,203	2,550
Other Liabilities	4,792	4,624
Deferred Income Taxes	646	528
Total Liabilities	17,394	14,562
Commitments and Contingencies		
Preferred Stock, no par value	41	41
Repurchased Preferred Stock	(132)	(120)
Common Shareholders' Equity		
Common stock, par value 1 2/3¢ per share (authorized 3,600 shares, issued 1,782 shares)	30	30
Capital in excess of par value	450	584
Retained earnings	28,184	24,837
Accumulated other comprehensive loss	(952)	(2,246)
	27,712	23,205
Less: repurchased common stock, at cost (177 and 144 shares, respectively)	(10,387)	(7,758)
Total Common Shareholders' Equity	17,325	15,447
Total Liabilities and Shareholders' Equity	$34,628	$29,930

See accompanying notes to consolidated financial statements.

Consolidated Statement of Common Shareholders' Equity

PepsiCo, Inc. and Subsidiaries
Fiscal years ended December 29, 2007, December 30, 2006 and December 31, 2005

(in millions)	2007 Shares	2007 Amount	2006 Shares	2006 Amount	2005 Shares	2005 Amount
Common Stock	1,782	$ 30	1,782	$ 30	1,782	$ 30
Capital in Excess of Par Value						
Balance, beginning of year		584		614		618
Stock-based compensation expense		260		270		311
Stock option exercises/RSUs converted[a]		(347)		(300)		(315)
Withholding tax on RSUs converted		(47)		–		–
Balance, end of year		450		584		614
Retained Earnings						
Balance, beginning of year		24,837		21,116		18,730
Adoption of FIN 48		7		–		–
Adjusted balance, beginning of year		24,844				
Net income		5,658		5,642		4,078
Cash dividends declared — common		(2,306)		(1,912)		(1,684)
Cash dividends declared — preferred		(2)		(1)		(3)
Cash dividends declared — RSUs		(10)		(8)		(5)
Balance, end of year		28,184		24,837		21,116
Accumulated Other Comprehensive Loss						
Balance, beginning of year		(2,246)		(1,053)		(886)
Currency translation adjustment		719		465		(251)
Cash flow hedges, net of tax:						
Net derivative (losses)/gains		(60)		(18)		54
Reclassification of losses/(gains) to net income		21		(5)		(8)
Adoption of SFAS 158		–		(1,782)		–
Pension and retiree medical, net of tax:						
Net pension and retiree medical gains		464		–		–
Reclassification of net losses to net income		135		–		–
Minimum pension liability adjustment, net of tax		–		138		16
Unrealized gain on securities, net of tax		9		9		24
Other		6		–		(2)
Balance, end of year		(952)		(2,246)		(1,053)
Repurchased Common Stock						
Balance, beginning of year	(144)	(7,758)	(126)	(6,387)	(103)	(4,920)
Share repurchases	(64)	(4,300)	(49)	(3,000)	(54)	(2,995)
Stock option exercises	28	1,582	31	1,619	31	1,523
Other, primarily RSUs converted	3	89	–	10	–	5
Balance, end of year	(177)	(10,387)	(144)	(7,758)	(126)	(6,387)
Total Common Shareholders' Equity		$17,325		$15,447		$14,320

	2007	2006	2005
Comprehensive Income			
Net income	$5,658	$5,642	$4,078
Currency translation adjustment	719	465	(251)
Cash flow hedges, net of tax	(39)	(23)	46
Minimum pension liability adjustment, net of tax	–	5	16
Pension and retiree medical, net of tax:			
Net prior service cost	(105)	–	–
Net gains	704	–	–
Unrealized gain on securities, net of tax	9	9	24
Other	6	–	(2)
Total Comprehensive Income	$6,952	$6,098	$3,911

(a) Includes total tax benefits of $216 million in 2007, $130 million in 2006 and $125 million in 2005.
See accompanying notes to consolidated financial statements.

Notes to Consolidated Financial Statements

Note 1 — Basis of Presentation and Our Divisions

Basis of Presentation

Our financial statements include the consolidated accounts of PepsiCo, Inc. and the affiliates that we control. In addition, we include our share of the results of certain other affiliates based on our economic ownership interest. We do not control these other affiliates, as our ownership in these other affiliates is generally less than 50%. Our share of the net income of our anchor bottlers is reported in our income statement as bottling equity income. Bottling equity income also includes any changes in our ownership interests of these affiliates. Bottling equity income includes $174 million, $186 million and $126 million of pre-tax gains on our sales of PBG stock in 2007, 2006 and 2005, respectively. See Note 8 for additional information on our significant noncontrolled bottling affiliates. Intercompany balances and transactions are eliminated. In 2005, we had an additional week of results (53rd week). Our fiscal year ends on the last Saturday of each December, resulting in an additional week of results every five or six years.

Beginning in the first quarter of 2007, income for certain non-consolidated international bottling interests was reclassified from bottling equity income and corporate unallocated results to PI's division operating results, to be consistent with PepsiCo's internal management accountability. Prior period amounts have been adjusted to reflect this reclassification.

Raw materials, direct labor and plant overhead, as well as purchasing and receiving costs, costs directly related to production planning, inspection costs and raw material handling facilities, are included in cost of sales. The costs of moving, storing and delivering finished product are included in selling, general and administrative expenses.

The preparation of our consolidated financial statements in conformity with generally accepted accounting principles requires us to make estimates and assumptions that affect reported amounts of assets, liabilities, revenues, expenses and disclosure of contingent assets and liabilities. Estimates are used in determining, among other items, sales incentives accruals, tax reserves, stock-based compensation, pension and retiree medical accruals, useful lives for intangible assets, and future cash flows associated with impairment testing for perpetual brands, goodwill and other long-lived assets. Actual results could differ from these estimates.

See "Our Divisions" below and for additional unaudited information on items affecting the comparability of our consolidated results, see "Items Affecting Comparability" in Management's Discussion and Analysis.

Tabular dollars are in millions, except per share amounts. All per share amounts reflect common per share amounts, assume dilution unless noted, and are based on unrounded amounts. Certain reclassifications were made to prior years' amounts to conform to the 2007 presentation.

Our Divisions

We manufacture or use contract manufacturers, market and sell a variety of salty, sweet and grain-based snacks, carbonated and non-carbonated beverages, and foods through our North American and international business divisions. Our North American divisions include the U.S. and Canada. Division results are based on how our Chief Executive Officer assesses the performance of and allocates resources to our divisions. For additional unaudited information on our divisions, see "Our Operations" in Management's Discussion and Analysis. The accounting policies for the divisions are the same as those described in Note 2, except for the following certain allocation methodologies:
- stock-based compensation expense,
- pension and retiree medical expense, and
- derivatives.

Stock-Based Compensation Expense

Our divisions are held accountable for stock-based compensation expense and, therefore, this expense is allocated to our divisions as an incremental employee compensation cost. The allocation of stock-based compensation expense in 2007 was approximately 29% to FLNA, 17% to PBNA, 34% to PI, 4% to QFNA and 16% to corporate unallocated expenses. We had similar allocations of stock-based compensation expense to our divisions in 2006 and 2005. The expense allocated to our divisions excludes any impact of changes in our Black-Scholes assumptions during the year which reflect market conditions over which division management has no control. Therefore, any variances between allocated expense and our actual expense are recognized in corporate unallocated expenses.

Pension and Retiree Medical Expense

Pension and retiree medical service costs measured at a fixed discount rate, as well as amortization of gains and losses due to demographics, including salary experience, are reflected in division results for North American employees. Division results also include interest costs, measured at a fixed discount rate, for retiree medical plans. Interest costs for the pension plans, pension asset returns and the impact of pension funding, and gains and losses other than those due to demographics, are all reflected in corporate unallocated expenses. In addition, corporate unallocated expenses include the difference between the service costs measured at a fixed discount rate (included in division results as noted above) and the total service costs determined using the Plans' discount rates as disclosed in Note 7.

Financial Statements and Accompanying Notes

Derivatives

Beginning in the fourth quarter of 2005, we began centrally managing commodity derivatives on behalf of our divisions. Certain of the commodity derivatives, primarily those related to the purchase of energy for use by our divisions, do not qualify for hedge accounting treatment. These derivatives hedge underlying commodity price risk and were not entered into for speculative purposes. Such derivatives are marked to market with the resulting gains and losses recognized in corporate unallocated expenses. These gains and losses are subsequently reflected in division results when the divisions take delivery of the underlying commodity. Therefore, division results reflect the contract purchase price of the energy or other commodities.

In the second quarter of 2007, we expanded our commodity hedging program to include derivative contracts used to mitigate our exposure to price changes associated with our purchases of fruit. Similar to our energy contracts, these contracts do not qualify for hedge accounting treatment and are marked to market with the resulting gains and losses recognized in corporate unallocated expenses. These gains and losses are then subsequently reflected in divisional results.

New Organizational Structure

In the fourth quarter of 2007, we announced a strategic realignment of our organizational structure. For additional unaudited information on our new organizational structure, see "Our Operations" in Management's Discussion and Analysis. In the first quarter of 2008, our historical segment reporting will be restated to reflect the new structure. The segment amounts and discussions reflected in this annual report reflect the management reporting that existed through fiscal year-end 2007.

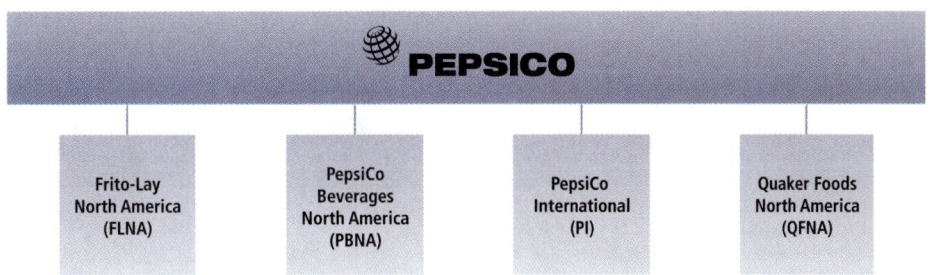

	Net Revenue			Operating Profit		
	2007	2006	2005	**2007**	2006	2005
FLNA	**$11,586**	$10,844	$10,322	**$2,845**	$2,615	$2,529
PBNA	**10,230**	9,565	9,146	**2,188**	2,055	2,037
PI	**15,798**	12,959	11,376	**2,322**	2,016	1,661
QFNA	**1,860**	1,769	1,718	**568**	554	537
Total division	**39,474**	35,137	32,562	**7,923**	7,240	6,764
Corporate	–	–	–	**(753)**	(738)	(780)
	$39,474	$35,137	$32,562	**$7,170**	$6,502	$5,984

Net Revenue

QFNA 5%
FLNA 29%
PI 40%
PBNA 26%

Division Operating Profit

QFNA 7%
FLNA 36%
PI 29%
PBNA 28%

Corporate

Corporate includes costs of our corporate headquarters, centrally managed initiatives, such as our ongoing business transformation initiative in North America, unallocated insurance and benefit programs, foreign exchange transaction gains and losses, and certain commodity derivative gains and losses, as well as profit-in-inventory elimination adjustments for our noncontrolled bottling affiliates and certain other items.

Other Division Information

	Total Assets			Capital Spending		
	2007	2006	2005	**2007**	2006	2005
FLNA	**$ 6,270**	$ 5,969	$ 5,948	**$ 624**	$ 499	$ 512
PBNA	**7,130**	6,567	6,316	**430**	492	320
PI	**14,747**	11,571	10,229	**1,108**	835	667
QFNA	**1,002**	1,003	989	**41**	31	31
Total division	**29,149**	25,110	23,482	**2,203**	1,857	1,530
Corporate(a)	**2,124**	1,739	5,331	**227**	211	206
Investments in bottling affiliates	**3,355**	3,081	2,914	**–**	–	–
	$34,628	$29,930	$31,727	**$2,430**	$2,068	$1,736

(a) Corporate assets consist principally of cash and cash equivalents, short-term investments, and property, plant and equipment.

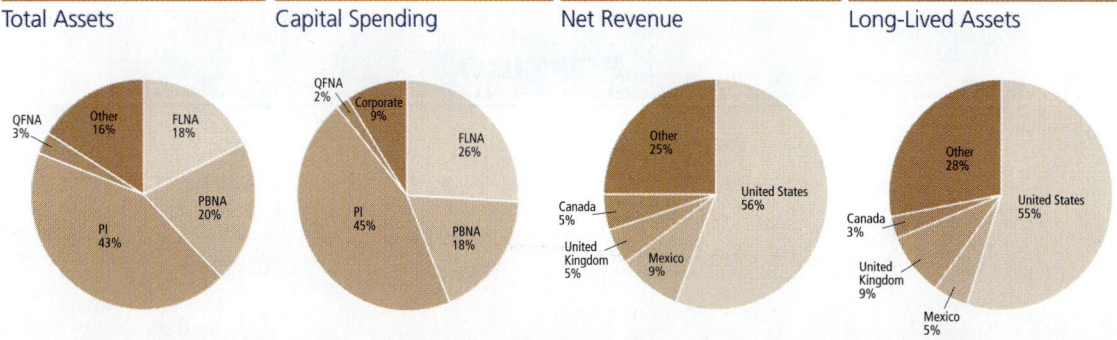

	Amortization of Intangible Assets			Depreciation and Other Amortization		
	2007	2006	2005	**2007**	2006	2005
FLNA	**$ 9**	$ 9	$ 3	**$ 437**	$ 432	$ 419
PBNA	**11**	77	76	**302**	282	264
PI	**38**	76	71	**564**	478	420
QFNA	**–**	–	–	**34**	33	34
Total division	**58**	162	150	**1,337**	1,225	1,137
Corporate	**–**	–	–	**31**	19	21
	$58	$162	$150	**$1,368**	$1,244	$1,158

	Net Revenue(a)			Long-Lived Assets(b)		
	2007	2006	2005	**2007**	2006	2005
U.S.	**$21,978**	$20,788	$19,937	**$12,498**	$11,515	$10,723
Mexico	**3,498**	3,228	3,095	**1,067**	996	902
United Kingdom	**1,987**	1,839	1,821	**2,090**	1,995	1,715
Canada	**1,961**	1,702	1,509	**699**	589	582
All other countries	**10,050**	7,580	6,200	**6,441**	4,725	3,948
	$39,474	$35,137	$32,562	**$22,795**	$19,820	$17,870

(a) Represents net revenue from businesses operating in these countries.
(b) Long-lived assets represent property, plant and equipment, nonamortizable intangible assets, amortizable intangible assets, and investments in noncontrolled affiliates. These assets are reported in the country where they are primarily used.

Note 2 — Our Significant Accounting Policies

Revenue Recognition

We recognize revenue upon shipment or delivery to our customers based on written sales terms that do not allow for a right of return. However, our policy for DSD and chilled products is to remove and replace damaged and out-of-date products from store shelves to ensure that our consumers receive the product quality and freshness that they expect. Similarly, our policy for warehouse-distributed products is to replace damaged and out-of-date products. Based on our historical experience with this practice, we have reserved for anticipated damaged and out-of-date products. For additional unaudited information on our revenue recognition and related policies, including our policy on bad debts, see "Our Critical Accounting Policies" in Management's Discussion and Analysis. We are exposed to concentration of credit risk by our customers, Wal-Mart and PBG. In 2007, Wal-Mart (including Sam's) represented approximately 12% of our total net revenue, including concentrate sales to our bottlers which are used in finished goods sold by them to Wal-Mart; and PBG represented approximately 9%. We have not experienced credit issues with these customers.

Sales Incentives and Other Marketplace Spending

We offer sales incentives and discounts through various programs to our customers and consumers. Sales incentives and discounts are accounted for as a reduction of revenue and totaled $11.3 billion in 2007, $10.1 billion in 2006 and $8.9 billion in 2005. While most of these incentive arrangements have terms of no more than one year, certain arrangements, such as fountain pouring rights, extend beyond one year. Costs incurred to obtain these arrangements are recognized over the shorter of the economic or contractual life, as a reduction of revenue, and the remaining balances of $287 million at December 29, 2007 and $297 million at December 30, 2006 are included in current assets and other assets on our balance sheet. For additional unaudited information on our sales incentives, see "Our Critical Accounting Policies" in Management's Discussion and Analysis.

Other marketplace spending, which includes the costs of advertising and other marketing activities, totaled $2.9 billion in 2007, $2.7 billion in 2006 and $2.8 billion in 2005 and is reported as selling, general and administrative expenses. Included in these amounts were advertising expenses of $1.9 billion in 2007, $1.7 billion in 2006 and $1.8 billion in 2005. Deferred advertising costs are not expensed until the year first used and consist of:
- media and personal service prepayments,
- promotional materials in inventory, and
- production costs of future media advertising.

Deferred advertising costs of $160 million and $171 million at year-end 2007 and 2006, respectively, are classified as prepaid expenses on our balance sheet.

Distribution Costs

Distribution costs, including the costs of shipping and handling activities, are reported as selling, general and administrative expenses. Shipping and handling expenses were $5.1 billion in 2007, $4.6 billion in 2006 and $4.1 billion in 2005.

Cash Equivalents

Cash equivalents are investments with original maturities of three months or less which we do not intend to rollover beyond three months.

Software Costs

We capitalize certain computer software and software development costs incurred in connection with developing or obtaining computer software for internal use when both the preliminary project stage is completed and it is probable that the software will be used as intended. Capitalized software costs include only (i) external direct costs of materials and services utilized in developing or obtaining computer software, (ii) compensation and related benefits for employees who are directly associated with the software project and (iii) interest costs incurred while developing internal-use computer software. Capitalized software costs are included in property, plant and equipment on our balance sheet and amortized on a straight-line basis when placed into service over the estimated useful lives of the software, which approximate five to seven years. Net capitalized software and development costs were $652 million at December 29, 2007 and $537 million at December 30, 2006.

Commitments and Contingencies

We are subject to various claims and contingencies related to lawsuits, taxes and environmental matters, as well as commitments under contractual and other commercial obligations. We recognize liabilities for contingencies and commitments when a loss is probable and estimable. For additional information on our commitments, see Note 9.

Research and Development

We engage in a variety of research and development activities. These activities principally involve the development of new products, improvement in the quality of existing products, improvement and modernization of production processes, and the development and implementation of new technologies to enhance the quality and value of both current and proposed product lines. Consumer research is excluded from research and development costs and included in other marketing costs. Research and development costs were $364 million in 2007, $282 million in 2006 and $280 million in 2005 and are reported as selling, general and administrative expenses.

Other Significant Accounting Policies

Our other significant accounting policies are disclosed as follows:
- Property, Plant and Equipment and Intangible Assets — Note 4, and for additional unaudited information on brands and goodwill, see "Our Critical Accounting Policies" in Management's Discussion and Analysis.
- Income Taxes — Note 5, and for additional unaudited information, see "Our Critical Accounting Policies" in Management's Discussion and Analysis.
- Pension, Retiree Medical and Savings Plans — Note 7, and for additional unaudited information, see "Our Critical Accounting Policies" in Management's Discussion and Analysis.
- Risk Management — Note 10, and for additional unaudited information, see "Our Business Risks" in Management's Discussion and Analysis.

Recent Accounting Pronouncements

In September 2006, the SEC issued SAB 108 to address diversity in practice in quantifying financial statement misstatements. SAB 108 requires that we quantify misstatements based on their impact on each of our financial statements and related disclosures. On December 30, 2006, we adopted SAB 108. Our adoption of SAB 108 did not impact our financial statements.

In September 2006, the FASB issued SFAS 157 which defines fair value, establishes a framework for measuring fair value, and expands disclosures about fair value measurements. The provisions of SFAS 157 are effective as of the beginning of our 2008 fiscal year. However, the FASB has deferred the effective date of SFAS 157, until the beginning of our 2009 fiscal year, as it relates to fair value measurement requirements for nonfinancial assets and liabilities that are not remeasured at fair value on a recurring basis. We are currently evaluating the impact of adopting SFAS 157 on our financial statements. We do not expect our adoption to have a material impact on our financial statements.

In February 2007, the FASB issued SFAS 159 which permits entities to choose to measure many financial instruments and certain other items at fair value. The provisions of SFAS 159 are effective as of the beginning of our 2008 fiscal year. Our adoption of SFAS 159 will not impact our financial statements.

In December 2007, the FASB issued SFAS 141R and SFAS 160 to improve, simplify, and converge internationally the accounting for business combinations and the reporting of noncontrolling interests in consolidated financial statements. The provisions of SFAS 141R and SFAS 160 are effective as of the beginning of our 2009 fiscal year. We are currently evaluating the impact of adopting SFAS 141R and SFAS 160 on our financial statements.

Note 3 — Restructuring and Impairment Charges

2007 Restructuring and Impairment Charge

In 2007, we incurred a charge of $102 million ($70 million after-tax or $0.04 per share) in conjunction with restructuring actions primarily to close certain plants and rationalize other production lines across FLNA, PBNA and PI. The charge was comprised of $57 million of asset impairments, $33 million of severance and other employee-related costs and $12 million of other costs and was recorded in selling, general and administrative expenses in our income statement. Employee-related costs primarily reflect the termination costs for approximately 1,100 employees. Substantially all cash payments related to this charge are expected to be paid by the end of 2008.

A summary of the restructuring and impairment charge by division is as follows:

	Asset Impairments	Severance and Other Employee Costs	Other Costs	Total
FLNA	$19	$ –	$ 9	$ 28
PBNA	–	11	–	11
PI	38	22	3	63
	$57	$33	$12	$102

2006 Restructuring and Impairment Charge

In 2006, we incurred a charge of $67 million ($43 million after-tax or $0.03 per share) in conjunction with consolidating the manufacturing network at FLNA by closing two plants in the U.S., and rationalizing other assets, to increase manufacturing productivity and supply chain efficiencies. The charge was comprised of $43 million of asset impairments, $14 million of severance and other employee-related costs and $10 million of other costs. Employee-related costs primarily reflect the termination costs for approximately 380 employees. All cash payments related to this charge were paid by the end of 2007.

2005 Restructuring Charge

In 2005, we incurred a charge of $83 million ($55 million after-tax or $0.03 per share) in conjunction with actions taken to reduce costs in our operations, principally through headcount reductions. Of this charge, $34 million related to FLNA, $21 million to PBNA, $16 million to PI and $12 million to Corporate. Most of this charge related to the termination of approximately 700 employees. As of December 30, 2006, all terminations had occurred, and as of December 29, 2007, no accrual remains.

Note 4 — Property, Plant and Equipment and Intangible Assets

	Average Useful Life	2007	2006	2005
Property, plant and equipment, net				
Land and improvements	10 – 34 yrs.	$ 864	$ 756	
Buildings and improvements	20 – 44	4,577	4,095	
Machinery and equipment, including fleet and software	5 – 14	14,471	12,768	
Construction in progress		1,984	1,439	
		21,896	19,058	
Accumulated depreciation		(10,668)	(9,371)	
		$ 11,228	$ 9,687	
Depreciation expense		$1,304	$1,182	$1,103
Amortizable intangible assets, net				
Brands	5 – 40	$ 1,476	$1,288	
Other identifiable intangibles	3 – 15	344	290	
		1,820	1,578	
Accumulated amortization		(1,024)	(941)	
		$ 796	$ 637	
Amortization expense		$58	$162	$150

Property, plant and equipment is recorded at historical cost. Depreciation and amortization are recognized on a straight-line basis over an asset's estimated useful life. Land is not depreciated and construction in progress is not depreciated until ready for service. Amortization of intangible assets for each of the next five years, based on average 2007 foreign exchange rates, is expected to be $62 million in 2008, $60 million in 2009, $60 million in 2010, $59 million in 2011 and $59 million in 2012.

Depreciable and amortizable assets are only evaluated for impairment upon a significant change in the operating or macroeconomic environment. In these circumstances, if an evaluation of the undiscounted cash flows indicates impairment, the asset is written down to its estimated fair value, which is based on discounted future cash flows. Useful lives are periodically evaluated to determine whether events or circumstances have occurred which indicate the need for revision. For additional unaudited information on our amortizable brand policies, see "Our Critical Accounting Policies" in Management's Discussion and Analysis.

Nonamortizable Intangible Assets

Perpetual brands and goodwill are assessed for impairment at least annually. If the carrying amount of a perpetual brand exceeds its fair value, as determined by its discounted cash flows, an impairment loss is recognized in an amount equal to that excess. No impairment charges resulted from the required impairment evaluations. The change in the book value of nonamortizable intangible assets is as follows:

	Balance, Beginning 2006	Acquisitions	Translation and Other	Balance, End of 2006	Acquisitions	Translation and Other	Balance, End of 2007
FLNA							
Goodwill	$ 145	$139	$ –	$ 284	$ –	$ 27	$ 311
PBNA							
Goodwill	2,164	39	–	2,203	146	20	2,369
Brands	59	–	–	59	–	–	59
	2,223	39	–	2,262	146	20	2,428
PI							
Goodwill	1,604	183	145	1,932	236	146	2,314
Brands	1,026	–	127	1,153	–	36	1,189
	2,630	183	272	3,085	236	182	3,503
QFNA							
Goodwill	175	–	–	175	–	–	175
Corporate							
Pension intangible	1	–	(1)	–	–	–	–
Total goodwill	4,088	361	145	4,594	382	193	5,169
Total brands	1,085	–	127	1,212	–	36	1,248
Total pension intangible	1	–	(1)	–	–	–	–
	$5,174	$361	$271	$5,806	$382	$229	$6,417

Note 5 — Income Taxes

	2007	2006	2005
Income before income taxes			
U.S.	$4,085	$3,844	$3,175
Foreign	3,546	3,145	3,207
	$7,631	$6,989	$6,382
Provision for income taxes			
Current: U.S. Federal	$1,422	$ 776	$1,638
Foreign	489	569	426
State	104	56	118
	2,015	1,401	2,182
Deferred: U.S. Federal	22	(31)	137
Foreign	(66)	(16)	(26)
State	2	(7)	11
	(42)	(54)	122
	$1,973	$1,347	$2,304
Tax rate reconciliation			
U.S. Federal statutory tax rate	35.0%	35.0%	35.0%
State income tax, net of U.S. Federal tax benefit	0.9	0.5	1.4
Lower taxes on foreign results	(6.5)	(6.5)	(6.5)
Tax settlements	(1.7)	(8.6)	–
Taxes on AJCA repatriation	–	–	7.0
Other, net	(1.8)	(1.1)	(0.8)
Annual tax rate	25.9%	19.3%	36.1%
Deferred tax liabilities			
Investments in noncontrolled affiliates	$1,163	$1,103	
Property, plant and equipment	828	784	
Intangible assets other than nondeductible goodwill	280	169	
Pension benefits	148	–	
Other	136	248	
Gross deferred tax liabilities	2,555	2,304	
Deferred tax assets			
Net carryforwards	722	667	
Stock-based compensation	425	443	
Retiree medical benefits	528	541	
Other employee-related benefits	447	342	
Pension benefits	–	38	
Deductible state tax and interest benefits	189	–	
Other	618	592	
Gross deferred tax assets	2,929	2,623	
Valuation allowances	(695)	(624)	
Deferred tax assets, net	2,234	1,999	
Net deferred tax liabilities	$ 321	$ 305	
Deferred taxes included within:			
Assets:			
Prepaid expenses and other current assets	$325	$223	
Liabilities:			
Deferred income taxes	$646	$528	
Analysis of valuation allowances			
Balance, beginning of year	$624	$532	$564
Provision/(benefit)	39	71	(28)
Other additions/(deductions)	32	21	(4)
Balance, end of year	$695	$624	$532

For additional unaudited information on our income tax policies, including our reserves for income taxes, see "Our Critical Accounting Policies" in Management's Discussion and Analysis.

In 2007, we recognized $129 million of non-cash tax benefits related to the favorable resolution of certain foreign tax matters. In 2006, we recognized non-cash tax benefits of $602 million, substantially all of which related to the IRS's examination of our consolidated income tax returns for the years 1998 through 2002. In 2005, we repatriated approximately $7.5 billion in earnings previously considered indefinitely reinvested outside the U.S. and recorded income tax expense of $460 million related to the AJCA. The AJCA created a one-time incentive for U.S. corporations to repatriate undistributed international earnings by providing an 85% dividends received deduction.

Reserves

A number of years may elapse before a particular matter, for which we have established a reserve, is audited and finally resolved. The number of years with open tax audits varies depending on the tax jurisdiction. Our major taxing jurisdictions and the related open tax audits are as follows:

- the U.S. — in 2006, the IRS issued a Revenue Agent's Report (RAR) related to the years 1998 through 2002. We are in agreement with their conclusion, except for one matter which we continue to dispute. We made the appropriate cash payment during 2006 to settle the agreed-upon issues, and we do not anticipate the resolution of the open matter will significantly impact our financial statements. In 2007, the IRS initiated their audit of our U.S. tax returns for the years 2003 through 2005;
- Mexico — in 2006, we completed and agreed with the conclusions of an audit of our tax returns for the years 2001 through 2005;
- the United Kingdom — audits have been completed for all taxable years prior to 2004; and
- Canada — audits have been completed for all taxable years through 2004. We are disputing some of the adjustments for the years 1999 through 2004. We do not anticipate the resolution of the 1999 through 2004 tax years will significantly impact our financial statements. The Canadian tax return for 2005 is currently under audit and no adjustments are expected to significantly impact our financial statements.

While it is often difficult to predict the final outcome or the timing of resolution of any particular tax matter, we believe that our reserves reflect the probable outcome of known tax contingencies. We adjust these reserves, as well as the related interest, in light of changing facts and circumstances. Settlement of any particular issue would usually require the use of cash. Favorable resolution would be recognized as a reduction to our annual tax rate in the year of resolution.

For further unaudited information on the impact of the resolution of open tax issues, see "Other Consolidated Results."

In 2006, the FASB issued FIN 48, which clarifies the accounting for uncertainty in tax positions. FIN 48 requires that we recognize in our financial statements the impact of a tax position, if that position is more likely than not of being sustained on audit, based on the technical merits of the position. We adopted the provisions of FIN 48 as of the beginning of our 2007 fiscal year. As a result of our adoption of FIN 48, we recognized a $7 million decrease to reserves for income taxes, with a corresponding increase to opening retained earnings.

As of December 29, 2007, the total gross amount of reserves for income taxes, reported in other liabilities, was $1.5 billion. Of that amount, $1.4 billion, if recognized, would affect our effective tax rate. Any prospective adjustments to our reserves for income taxes will be recorded as an increase or decrease to our provision for income taxes and would impact our effective tax rate. In addition, we accrue interest related to reserves for income taxes in our provision for income taxes and any associated penalties are recorded in selling, general and administrative expenses. The gross amount of interest accrued, reported in other liabilities, was $338 million as of December 29, 2007, of which $34 million was recognized in 2007.

A rollforward of our reserves in 2007 for all federal, state and foreign tax jurisdictions, is as follows:

Balance, beginning of year	$1,435
FIN 48 adoption adjustment to retained earnings	(7)
Reclassification of deductible state tax and interest benefits to other balance sheet accounts	(144)
Adjusted balance, beginning of year	1,284
Additions for tax positions related to the current year	264
Additions for tax positions from prior years	151
Reductions for tax positions from prior years	(73)
Settlement payments	(174)
Statute of limitations expiration	(7)
Currency translation adjustment	16
Balance, end of year	$1,461

Carryforwards and Allowances

Operating loss carryforwards totaling $7.1 billion at year-end 2007 are being carried forward in a number of foreign and state jurisdictions where we are permitted to use tax operating losses from prior periods to reduce future taxable income. These operating losses will expire as follows: $0.5 billion in 2008, $5.6 billion between 2009 and 2027 and $1.0 billion may be carried forward indefinitely. We establish valuation allowances for our deferred tax assets if, based on the available evidence, it is more likely than not that some portion or all of the deferred tax assets will not be realized.

Undistributed International Earnings

At December 29, 2007, we had approximately $14.7 billion of undistributed international earnings. We intend to continue to reinvest earnings outside the U.S. for the foreseeable future and, therefore, have not recognized any U.S. tax expense on these earnings.

Mexico Tax Legislation

In October 2007, Mexico enacted new tax legislation effective January 1, 2008. The deferred tax impact was not material and is reflected in our effective tax rate in 2007.

Note 6 — Stock-Based Compensation

Our stock-based compensation program is a broad-based program designed to attract and retain employees while also aligning employees' interests with the interests of our shareholders. A majority of our employees participate in our stock-based compensation program, which includes our broad-based SharePower program established in 1989 to grant an annual award of stock options to all eligible employees, based on job level or classification and, in the case of international employees, tenure as well. In addition, members of our Board of Directors participate in our stock-based compensation program in connection with their service on our Board. Beginning in 2007, members of our Board of Directors no longer receive stock-based compensation grants. Stock options and restricted stock units (RSU) are granted to employees under the shareholder-approved 2007 Long-Term Incentive Plan (LTIP), our only active stock-based plan. Stock-based compensation expense was $260 million in 2007, $270 million in 2006 and $311 million in 2005. Related income tax benefits recognized in earnings were $77 million in 2007, $80 million in 2006 and $87 million in 2005. Stock-based compensation cost capitalized in connection with our ongoing business transformation initiative was $3 million in 2007, $3 million in 2006 and $4 million in 2005. At year-end 2007, 67 million shares were available for future stock-based compensation grants.

Method of Accounting and Our Assumptions

We account for our employee stock options, which include grants under our executive program and broad-based SharePower program, under the fair value method of accounting using a Black-Scholes valuation model to measure stock option expense at the date of grant. All stock option grants have an exercise price equal to the fair market value of our common stock on the date of grant and generally have a 10-year term. The fair value of stock option grants is amortized to expense over the vesting period, generally three years. Executives who are awarded long-term incentives based on their performance are offered the choice of stock options or RSUs. Executives who elect RSUs receive one RSU for every four stock options that would have otherwise been granted. Senior officers do not have a choice and are granted 50% stock options and 50% RSUs. RSU expense is based on the fair value of PepsiCo stock on the date of grant and is amortized over the vesting period, generally three years. Each RSU is settled in a share of our stock after the vesting period. Vesting of RSU awards for senior officers is contingent upon the achievement of pre-established performance targets. There have been no reductions to the exercise price of previously issued awards, and any repricing of awards would require approval of our shareholders.

On January 1, 2006, we adopted SFAS 123R under the modified prospective method. Since we had previously accounted for our stock-based compensation plans under the fair value provisions of SFAS 123, our adoption did not significantly impact our financial position or our results of operations. Under SFAS 123R, actual tax benefits recognized in excess of tax benefits previously established upon grant are reported as a financing cash inflow. Prior to adoption, such excess tax benefits were reported as an operating cash inflow.

Our weighted-average Black-Scholes fair value assumptions are as follows:

	2007	2006	2005
Expected life	6 yrs.	6 yrs.	6 yrs.
Risk free interest rate	4.8%	4.5%	3.8%
Expected volatility	15%	18%	23%
Expected dividend yield	1.9%	1.9%	1.8%

The expected life is the period over which our employee groups are expected to hold their options. It is based on our historical experience with similar grants. The risk free interest rate is based on the expected U.S. Treasury rate over the expected life. Volatility reflects movements in our stock price over the most recent historical period equivalent to the expected life. Dividend yield is estimated over the expected life based on our stated dividend policy and forecasts of net income, share repurchases and stock price.

A summary of our stock-based compensation activity for the year ended December 29, 2007 is presented below:

Our Stock Option Activity	Options[a]	Average Price[b]	Average Life (years)[c]	Aggregate Intrinsic Value[d]
Outstanding at December 30, 2006	127,749	$44.24		
Granted	11,671	65.12		
Exercised	(28,116)	39.34		
Forfeited/expired	(2,496)	56.04		
Outstanding at December 29, 2007	108,808	$47.47	5.26	$3,216,316
Exercisable at December 29, 2007	75,365	$42.65	3.97	$2,590,994

(a) Options are in thousands and include options previously granted under Quaker plans. No additional options or shares may be granted under the Quaker plans.
(b) Weighted-average exercise price.
(c) Weighted-average contractual life remaining.
(d) In thousands.

Our RSU Activity	RSUs[a]	Average Intrinsic Value[b]	Average Life (years)[c]	Aggregate Intrinsic Value[d]
Outstanding at December 30, 2006	7,885	$53.38		
Granted	2,342	65.21		
Converted	(2,361)	47.83		
Forfeited/expired	(496)	$57.73		
Outstanding at December 29, 2007	7,370	$58.63	1.28	$567,706

(a) RSUs are in thousands.
(b) Weighted-average intrinsic value at grant date.
(c) Weighted-average contractual life remaining.
(d) In thousands.

Other Stock-Based Compensation Data	2007	2006	2005
Stock Options			
Weighted-average fair value of options granted	$13.56	$12.81	$13.45
Total intrinsic value of options exercised[a]	$826,913	$686,242	$632,603
RSUs			
Total number of RSUs granted[a]	2,342	2,992	3,097
Weighted-average intrinsic value of RSUs granted	$65.21	$58.22	$53.83
Total intrinsic value of RSUs converted[a]	$125,514	$10,934	$4,974

(a) In thousands.

At December 29, 2007, there was $287 million of total unrecognized compensation cost related to nonvested share-based compensation grants. This unrecognized compensation is expected to be recognized over a weighted-average period of 1.5 years.

Note 7 — Pension, Retiree Medical and Savings Plans

Our pension plans cover full-time employees in the U.S. and certain international employees. Benefits are determined based on either years of service or a combination of years of service and earnings. U.S. and Canada retirees are also eligible for medical and life insurance benefits (retiree medical) if they meet age and service requirements. Generally, our share of retiree medical costs is capped at specified dollar amounts, which vary based upon years of service, with retirees contributing the remainder of the costs.

Other gains and losses resulting from actual experience differing from our assumptions and from changes in our assumptions are also determined at each measurement date. If this net accumulated gain or loss exceeds 10% of the greater of plan assets or liabilities, a portion of the net gain or loss is included in expense for the following year. The cost or benefit of plan changes that increase or decrease benefits for prior employee service (prior service cost/(credit)) is included in earnings on a straight-line basis over the average remaining service period of active plan participants, which is approximately 11 years for pension expense and approximately 13 years for retiree medical expense.

On December 30, 2006, we adopted SFAS 158. In connection with our adoption, we recognized the funded status of our Plans on our balance sheet as of December 30, 2006 with subsequent changes in the funded status recognized in comprehensive income in the years in which they occur. In accordance with SFAS 158, amounts prior to the year of adoption have not been adjusted. SFAS 158 also requires that, no later than 2008, our assumptions used to measure our annual pension and retiree medical expense be determined as of the balance sheet date, and all plan assets and liabilities be reported as of that date. Accordingly, as of the beginning of our 2008 fiscal year, we will change the measurement date for our annual pension and retiree medical expense and all plan assets and liabilities from September 30 to our year-end balance sheet date. As a result of this change in measurement date, we will record an after-tax $7 million reduction to 2008 opening shareholders' equity which will be reflected in our 2008 first quarter Form 10-Q.

Selected financial information for our pension and retiree medical plans is as follows:

	Pension				Retiree Medical	
	2007	2006	2007	2006	2007	2006
	U.S.		International			
Change in projected benefit liability						
Liability at beginning of year	$5,947	$5,771	$1,511	$1,263	$1,370	$1,312
Service cost	244	245	59	52	48	46
Interest cost	338	319	81	68	77	72
Plan amendments	147	11	4	8	–	–
Participant contributions	–	–	14	12	–	–
Experience (gain)/loss	(309)	(163)	(155)	20	(80)	(34)
Benefit payments	(319)	(233)	(46)	(38)	(77)	(75)
Settlement/curtailment loss	–	(7)	–	(6)	–	–
Special termination benefits	–	4	–	–	–	1
Foreign currency adjustment	–	–	96	126	9	–
Other	–	–	31	6	7	48
Liability at end of year	$6,048	$5,947	$1,595	$1,511	$1,354	$1,370
Change in fair value of plan assets						
Fair value at beginning of year	$5,378	$5,086	$1,330	$1,099	$ –	$ –
Actual return on plan assets	654	513	122	112	–	–
Employer contributions/funding	69	19	58	30	77	75
Participant contributions	–	–	14	12	–	–
Benefit payments	(319)	(233)	(46)	(38)	(77)	(75)
Settlement/curtailment loss	–	(7)	–	–	–	–
Foreign currency adjustment	–	–	91	116	–	–
Other	–	–	26	(1)	–	–
Fair value at end of year	$5,782	$5,378	$1,595	$1,330	$ –	$ –
Reconciliation of funded status						
Funded status	$(266)	$(569)	$ –	$(181)	$(1,354)	$(1,370)
Adjustment for fourth quarter contributions	15	6	107	13	19	16
Adjustment for fourth quarter special termination benefits	(5)	–	–	–	–	–
Net amount recognized	$(256)	$(563)	$107	$(168)	$(1,335)	$(1,354)
Amounts recognized						
Other assets	$ 440	$ 185	$187	$ 6	$ –	$ –
Other current liabilities	(24)	(19)	(3)	(2)	(88)	(84)
Other liabilities	(672)	(729)	(77)	(172)	(1,247)	(1,270)
Net amount recognized	$(256)	$(563)	$107	$(168)	$(1,335)	$(1,354)
Amounts included in accumulated other comprehensive loss (pre-tax)						
Net loss	$1,136	$1,836	$287	$475	$276	$ 364
Prior service cost/(credit)	156	13	28	24	(88)	(101)
Total	$1,292	$1,849	$315	$499	$188	$ 263
Components of the (decrease)/increase in net loss						
Change in discount rate	$(292)	$(123)	$(224)	$ 2	$(50)	$(30)
Employee-related assumption changes	–	(45)	61	6	(9)	–
Liability-related experience different from assumptions	(17)	5	7	6	(21)	(4)
Actual asset return different from expected return	(255)	(122)	(25)	(30)	–	–
Amortization of losses	(136)	(164)	(30)	(29)	(18)	(21)
Other, including foreign currency adjustments and 2003 Medicare Act	–	(3)	23	46	10	17
Total	$(700)	$(452)	$(188)	$ 1	$(88)	$(38)
Liability at end of year for service to date	$5,026	$4,998	$1,324	$1,239		

Components of benefit expense are as follows:

	Pension						Retiree Medical		
	2007	2006	2005	2007	2006	2005	2007	2006	2005
	U.S.			International					
Components of benefit expense									
Service cost	$ 244	$ 245	$ 213	$ 59	$ 52	$ 32	$ 48	$ 46	$ 40
Interest cost	338	319	296	81	68	55	77	72	78
Expected return on plan assets	(399)	(391)	(344)	(97)	(81)	(69)	–	–	–
Amortization of prior service cost/(credit)	5	3	3	3	2	1	(13)	(13)	(11)
Amortization of net loss	136	164	106	30	29	15	18	21	26
	324	340	274	76	70	34	130	126	133
Settlement/curtailment loss	–	3	–	–	–	–	–	–	–
Special termination benefits	5	4	21	–	–	–	–	1	2
Total	$ 329	$ 347	$ 295	$ 76	$ 70	$ 34	$130	$127	$135

The estimated amounts to be amortized from accumulated other comprehensive loss into benefit expense in 2008 for our pension and retiree medical plans are as follows:

	Pension		Retiree Medical
	U.S.	International	
Net loss	$56	$20	$ 7
Prior service cost/(credit)	20	3	(12)
Total	$76	$23	$ (5)

The following table provides the weighted-average assumptions used to determine projected benefit liability and benefit expense for our pension and retiree medical plans:

	Pension						Retiree Medical		
	2007	2006	2005	2007	2006	2005	2007	2006	2005
	U.S.			International					
Weighted-average assumptions									
Liability discount rate	6.2%	5.8%	5.7%	5.8%	5.2%	5.1%	6.1%	5.8%	5.7%
Expense discount rate	5.8%	5.7%	6.1%	5.2%	5.1%	6.1%	5.8%	5.7%	6.1%
Expected return on plan assets	7.8%	7.8%	7.8%	7.3%	7.3%	8.0%			
Rate of salary increases	4.7%	4.5%	4.4%	3.9%	3.9%	4.1%			

The following table provides selected information about plans with liability for service to date and total benefit liability in excess of plan assets:

	Pension				Retiree Medical	
	2007	2006	2007	2006	2007	2006
	U.S.		International			
Selected information for plans with liability for service to date in excess of plan assets						
Liability for service to date	$(364)	$(387)	$(72)	$(286)		
Fair value of plan assets	$–	$1	$13	$237		
Selected information for plans with benefit liability in excess of plan assets						
Benefit liability	$(707)	$(754)	$(384)	$(1,387)	$(1,354)	$(1,370)
Fair value of plan assets	$–	$1	$278	$1,200		

Of the total projected pension benefit liability at year-end 2007, $658 million relates to plans that we do not fund because the funding of such plans does not receive favorable tax treatment.

Future Benefit Payments and Funding

Our estimated future benefit payments are as follows:

	2008	2009	2010	2011	2012	2013-17
Pension	$290	$315	$350	$385	$425	$2,755
Retiree medical[a]	$95	$100	$105	$110	$115	$640

(a) Expected future benefit payments for our retiree medical plans do not reflect any estimated subsidies expected to be received under the 2003 Medicare Act. Subsidies are expected to be approximately $10 million for each of the years from 2008 through 2012 and approximately $70 million in total for 2013 through 2017.

These future benefits to beneficiaries include payments from both funded and unfunded pension plans.

In 2008, we expect to make pension contributions of up to $150 million, with up to $75 million expected to be discretionary. Our cash payments for retiree medical are estimated to be approximately $85 million in 2008.

Pension Assets

Our pension plan investment strategy is reviewed annually and is established based upon plan liabilities, an evaluation of market conditions, tolerance for risk, and cash requirements for benefit payments. Our investment objective is to ensure that funds are available to meet the plans' benefit obligations when they are due. Our overall investment strategy is to prudently invest plan assets in high-quality and diversified equity and debt securities to achieve our long-term return expectation. As part of our investment strategy, we employ certain equity strategies which, in addition to investing in U.S. and international common and preferred stock, include investing in certain equity- and debt-based securities used collectively to generate returns in excess of certain equity-based indices. Debt-based securities represent approximately a third of our equity strategy portfolio as of year-end 2007 and 2006. Our investment policy also permits the use of derivative instruments to enhance the overall return of the portfolio. Our expected long-term rate of return on U.S. plan assets is 7.8%, reflecting estimated long-term rates of return of 9.3% from our equity strategies, and 5.8% from our fixed income strategies. Our target investment allocation is 60% for equity strategies and 40% for fixed income strategies. Our actual pension plan asset allocations, consistent with our investment approach and with how we view and manage our overall investment portfolio, for the plan years 2007 and 2006, are as follows:

	Actual Allocation	
Asset Category	2007	2006
Equity strategies	61%	61%
Fixed income strategies	38%	39%
Other, primarily cash	1%	–
Total	100%	100%

The expected return on pension plan assets is based on our historical experience, our pension plan investment strategy and our expectations for long-term rates of return. We use a market-related valuation method for recognizing investment gains or losses. For this purpose, investment gains or losses are the difference between the expected and actual return based on the market-related value of assets. This market-related valuation method recognizes investment gains or losses over a five-year period from the year in which they occur, which has the effect of reducing year-to-year volatility. Pension expense in future periods will be impacted as gains or losses are recognized in the market-related value of assets over the five-year period.

Pension assets include 5.5 million shares of PepsiCo common stock with a market value of $401 million in 2007, and 5.5 million shares with a market value of $358 million in 2006. Our investment policy limits the investment in PepsiCo stock at the time of investment to 10% of the fair value of plan assets.

As of December 29, 2007, approximately 3%, or approximately $165 million, of securities in the investment portfolio of our U.S. pension plans are subprime mortgage holdings. We do not believe that the ultimate realization of such investments will result in a material impact to future pension expense, future contributions or the funded status of our plans.

Retiree Medical Cost Trend Rates

An average increase of 8.5% in the cost of covered retiree medical benefits is assumed for 2008. This average increase is then projected to decline gradually to 5% in 2014 and thereafter. These assumed health care cost trend rates have an impact on the retiree medical plan expense and liability. However, the cap on our share of retiree medical costs limits the impact. A 1-percentage-point change in the assumed health care trend rate would have the following effects:

	1% Increase	1% Decrease
2007 service and interest cost components	$5	$(4)
2007 benefit liability	$55	$(48)

Savings Plan

Our U.S. employees are eligible to participate in 401(k) savings plans, which are voluntary defined contribution plans. The plans are designed to help employees accumulate additional savings for retirement. We make matching contributions on a portion of eligible pay based on years of service. In 2007 and 2006, our matching contributions were $62 million and $56 million, respectively.

For additional unaudited information on our pension and retiree medical plans and related accounting policies and assumptions, see "Our Critical Accounting Policies" in Management's Discussion and Analysis.

Note 8 — Noncontrolled Bottling Affiliates

Our most significant noncontrolled bottling affiliates are PBG and PAS. Sales to PBG reflect approximately 9% of our total net revenue in 2007 and approximately 10% in 2006 and 2005.

The Pepsi Bottling Group

In addition to approximately 35% and 38% of PBG's outstanding common stock that we own at year-end 2007 and 2006, respectively, we own 100% of PBG's class B common stock and approximately 7% of the equity of Bottling Group, LLC, PBG's principal operating subsidiary. Bottling equity income includes $174 million, $186 million and $126 million of pre-tax gains on our sales of PBG stock in 2007, 2006 and 2005, respectively.

PBG's summarized financial information is as follows:

	2007	2006	2005
Current assets	$ 3,086	$ 2,749	
Noncurrent assets	10,029	9,178	
Total assets	$13,115	$11,927	
Current liabilities	$ 2,215	$2,051	
Noncurrent liabilities	7,312	7,252	
Minority interest	973	540	
Total liabilities	$10,500	$9,843	
Our investment	$2,022	$1,842	
Net revenue	$13,591	$12,730	$11,885
Gross profit	$6,221	$5,830	$5,540
Operating profit	$1,071	$1,017	$1,023
Net income	$532	$522	$466

Our investment in PBG, which includes the related goodwill, was $507 million and $500 million higher than our ownership interest in their net assets at year-end 2007 and 2006, respectively. Based upon the quoted closing price of PBG shares at year-end 2007 and 2006, the calculated market value of our shares in PBG exceeded our investment balance, excluding our investment in Bottling Group, LLC, by approximately $1.7 billion and $1.4 billion, respectively.

Additionally, in 2007, we formed a joint venture with PBG, comprising our concentrate and PBG's bottling businesses in Russia. PBG holds a 60% majority interest in the joint venture and consolidates the entity. We account for our interest of 40% under the equity method of accounting.

PepsiAmericas

At year-end 2007 and 2006, we owned approximately 44% of PAS, and their summarized financial information is as follows:

	2007	2006	2005
Current assets	$ 922	$ 675	
Noncurrent assets	4,386	3,532	
Total assets	$5,308	$4,207	
Current liabilities	$ 903	$ 694	
Noncurrent liabilities	2,274	1,909	
Minority interest	273	—	
Total liabilities	$3,450	$2,603	
Our investment	$1,118	$1,028	
Net revenue	$4,480	$3,972	$3,726
Gross profit	$1,823	$1,608	$1,562
Operating profit	$436	$356	$393
Net income	$212	$158	$195

Our investment in PAS, which includes the related goodwill, was $303 million and $316 million higher than our ownership interest in their net assets at year-end 2007 and 2006, respectively. Based upon the quoted closing price of PAS shares at year-end 2007 and 2006, the calculated market value of our shares in PAS exceeded our investment by $855 million and $173 million, respectively.

Additionally, in 2007, we completed the joint purchase of Sandora, LLC with PAS. PAS holds a 60% majority interest in the joint venture and consolidates the entity. We account for our interest of 40% under the equity method of accounting.

Related Party Transactions

Our significant related party transactions include our noncontrolled bottling affiliates. We sell concentrate to these affiliates, which they use in the production of CSDs and non-carbonated beverages. We also sell certain finished goods to these affiliates, and we receive royalties for the use of our trademarks for certain products. Sales of concentrate and finished goods are reported net of bottler funding. For further unaudited information on these bottlers, see "Our Customers" in Management's Discussion and Analysis. These transactions with our bottling affiliates are reflected in our consolidated financial statements as follows:

	2007	2006	2005
Net revenue	$4,874	$4,837	$4,633
Selling, general and administrative expenses	$91	$87	$143
Accounts and notes receivable	$163	$175	
Accounts payable and other current liabilities	$106	$62	

Such amounts are settled on terms consistent with other trade receivables and payables. See Note 9 regarding our guarantee of certain PBG debt.

In addition, we coordinate, on an aggregate basis, the contract negotiations of sweeteners and other raw material requirements for certain of our bottlers. Once we have negotiated the contracts, the bottlers order and take delivery directly from the supplier and pay the suppliers directly. Consequently, these transactions are not reflected in our consolidated financial statements. As the contracting party, we could be liable to these suppliers in the event of any nonpayment by our bottlers, but we consider this exposure to be remote.

Note 9 — Debt Obligations and Commitments

	2007	2006
Short-term debt obligations		
Current maturities of long-term debt	$ 526	$ 605
Commercial paper (4.3% and 5.3%)	361	792
Other borrowings (7.2% and 7.3%)	489	377
Amounts reclassified to long-term debt	(1,376)	(1,500)
	$ —	$ 274
Long-term debt obligations		
Short-term borrowings, reclassified	$1,376	$1,500
Notes due 2008-2026 (5.3% and 6.0%)	2,673	1,148
Zero coupon notes, $375 million due 2008-2012 (13.3%)	285	299
Other, due 2008-2016 (6.1% and 6.1%)	395	208
	4,729	3,155
Less: current maturities of long-term debt obligations	(526)	(605)
	$4,203	$2,550

The interest rates in the above table reflect weighted-average rates at year-end.

In the second quarter of 2007, we issued $1 billion of senior unsecured notes maturing in 2012. We used a portion of the proceeds from the issuance of the notes to repay existing short-term debt of $500 million, bearing interest at 3.2% per year and maturing on May 15, 2007, with the balance of the proceeds used primarily for general corporate purposes. Additionally, in the second quarter of 2007, we extended the maturity of our $1.5 billion unsecured revolving credit agreement by one year to 2012, and, in the third quarter of 2007, we increased the amount of this agreement from $1.5 billion to $2 billion. Funds borrowed under this agreement may be used for general corporate purposes, including supporting our outstanding commercial paper issuances. This line of credit remains unused as of December 29, 2007.

In the third quarter of 2007, we updated our U.S. $2.5 billion euro medium term note program following the expiration of the existing program. Under the program, we may issue unsecured notes under mutually agreed upon terms with the purchasers of the notes. Proceeds from any issuance of notes may be used for general corporate purposes, except as otherwise specified in the related prospectus. As of December 29, 2007, we have no outstanding notes under the program.

In the fourth quarter of 2007, we issued $1 billion of senior unsecured notes maturing in 2013. We used the proceeds from the issuance of the notes for general corporate purposes, including the repayment of outstanding short-term indebtedness.

As of December 29, 2007, we have reclassified $1.4 billion of short-term debt to long-term based on our intent and ability to refinance on a long-term basis.

In addition, as of December 29, 2007, $806 million of our debt related to borrowings from various lines of credit is maintained for our international divisions. These lines of credit are subject to normal banking terms and conditions and are fully committed to the extent of our borrowings.

Interest Rate Swaps

In connection with the issuance of the $1 billion notes in the second quarter of 2007, we entered into an interest rate swap to effectively convert the interest rate from a fixed rate of 5.15% to a variable rate based on LIBOR. We previously entered into an interest rate swap in 2004 to effectively convert the interest rate of a specific debt issuance from a fixed rate to a variable rate. This interest rate swap matured in May 2007. The terms of the swaps match the terms of the debt they modify. The notional amounts of the interest rate swaps outstanding at December 29, 2007 and December 30, 2006 were $1 billion and $500 million, respectively.

At December 29, 2007, approximately 56% of total debt, after the impact of the related interest rate swap, was exposed to variable interest rates, compared to 63% at December 30, 2006. In addition to variable rate long-term debt, all debt with maturities of less than one year is categorized as variable for purposes of this measure.

Cross Currency Interest Rate Swaps

In 2004, we entered into a cross currency interest rate swap to hedge the currency exposure on U.S. dollar denominated debt of $50 million held by a foreign affiliate. The terms of this swap match the terms of the debt it modifies. The swap matures in 2008. The unrealized loss related to this swap was approximately $8 million at December 29, 2007, resulting in a U.S. dollar liability of $58 million. The unrealized gain related to this swap was less than $1 million at December 30, 2006, resulting in a U.S. dollar liability of $50 million.

We also entered into cross currency interest rate swaps to hedge the currency exposure on U.S. dollar denominated intercompany debt of $45 million at December 29, 2007 and $95 million at December 30, 2006. The terms of the swaps match the terms of the debt they modify. The net unrealized losses related to these swaps was less than $1 million at December 29, 2007 and December 30, 2006. The outstanding swap matures in 2008.

Long-Term Contractual Commitments[a]

Payments Due by Period	Total	2008	2009-2010	2011-2012	2013 and beyond
Long-term debt obligations[b]	$ 2,827	$ —	$ 171	$1,340	$1,316
Interest on debt obligations[c]	938	184	300	285	169
Operating leases	1,105	260	340	191	314
Purchasing commitments	3,767	1,182	1,713	509	363
Marketing commitments	1,251	329	551	278	93
Other commitments	248	44	127	75	2
	$10,136	$1,999	$3,202	$2,678	$2,257

(a) Reflects non-cancelable commitments as of December 29, 2007 based on year-end foreign exchange rates and excludes any reserves for income taxes under FIN 48 as we are unable to reasonably predict the ultimate amount or timing of settlement of our reserves for income taxes.
(b) Excludes short-term borrowings reclassified as long-term debt of $1,376 million and includes $273 million of accrued interest related to our zero coupon notes.
(c) Interest payments on floating-rate debt are estimated using interest rates effective as of December 29, 2007.

Most long-term contractual commitments, except for our long-term debt obligations, are not recorded on our balance sheet. Non-cancelable operating leases primarily represent building leases. Non-cancelable purchasing commitments are primarily for oranges and orange juice, packaging materials and cooking oil. Non-cancelable marketing commitments are primarily for sports marketing. Bottler funding is not reflected in our long-term contractual commitments as it is negotiated on an annual basis. See Note 7 regarding our pension and retiree medical obligations and discussion below regarding our commitments to noncontrolled bottling affiliates and former restaurant operations.

Off-Balance-Sheet Arrangements

It is not our business practice to enter into off-balance-sheet arrangements, other than in the normal course of business. However, certain guarantees were necessary to facilitate the separation of our bottling and restaurant operations from us. In connection with these transactions, we have guaranteed $2.3 billion of Bottling Group, LLC's long-term debt through 2012 and $18 million of YUM! Brands, Inc.'s (YUM) outstanding obligations, primarily property leases, through 2020. The terms of our Bottling Group, LLC debt guarantee are intended to preserve the structure of PBG's separation from us and our payment obligation would be triggered if Bottling Group, LLC failed to perform under these debt obligations or the structure significantly changed. Our guarantees of certain obligations ensured YUM's continued use of certain properties. These guarantees would require our cash payment if YUM failed to perform under these lease obligations. See Note 8 regarding contracts related to certain of our bottlers.

See "Our Liquidity and Capital Resources" in Management's Discussion and Analysis for further unaudited information on our borrowings.

Note 10 — Risk Management

We are exposed to market risks arising from adverse changes in:
- commodity prices, affecting the cost of our raw materials and energy,
- foreign exchange risks, and
- interest rates.

In the normal course of business, we manage these risks through a variety of strategies, including the use of derivatives. Certain derivatives are designated as either cash flow or fair value hedges and qualify for hedge accounting treatment, while others do not qualify and are marked to market through earnings. See "Our Business Risks" in Management's Discussion and Analysis for further unaudited information on our business risks.

For cash flow hedges, changes in fair value are deferred in accumulated other comprehensive loss within shareholders' equity until the underlying hedged item is recognized in net income. For fair value hedges, changes in fair value are recognized immediately in earnings, consistent with the underlying hedged item. Hedging transactions are limited to an underlying exposure. As a result, any change in the value of our derivative instruments would be substantially offset by an opposite change in the value of the underlying hedged items. Hedging ineffectiveness and a net earnings impact occur when the change in the value of the hedge does not offset the change in the value of the underlying hedged item. If the derivative instrument is terminated, we continue to defer the related gain or loss and include it as a component of the cost of the underlying hedged item. Upon determination that the underlying hedged item will not be part of an actual transaction, we recognize the related gain or loss in net income in that period.

We also use derivatives that do not qualify for hedge accounting treatment. We account for such derivatives at market value with the resulting gains and losses reflected in our income statement. We do not use derivative instruments for trading or speculative purposes, and we limit our exposure to individual counterparties to manage credit risk.

Commodity Prices

We are subject to commodity price risk because our ability to recover increased costs through higher pricing may be limited in the competitive environment in which we operate. This risk is managed through the use of fixed-price purchase orders, pricing agreements, geographic diversity and derivatives. We use derivatives, with terms of no more than two years, to economically hedge price fluctuations related to a portion of our anticipated commodity purchases, primarily for natural gas, diesel fuel and fruit. For those derivatives that qualify for hedge accounting, any ineffectiveness is recorded immediately. However, such commodity cash flow hedges have not had any significant ineffectiveness for all periods presented. We classify both the earnings and cash flow impact from these derivatives consistent with the underlying hedged item. During the next 12 months, we expect to reclassify net gains of $1 million related to cash flow hedges from accumulated other comprehensive loss into net income. Derivatives used to hedge commodity price risks that do not qualify for hedge accounting are marked to market each period and reflected in our income statement.

Foreign Exchange

Our operations outside of the U.S. generate 44% of our net revenue, with Mexico, the United Kingdom and Canada comprising 19% of our net revenue. As a result, we are exposed to foreign currency risks. On occasion, we enter into hedges, primarily forward contracts with terms of no more than two years, to reduce the effect of foreign exchange rates. Ineffectiveness of these hedges has not been material.

Interest Rates

We centrally manage our debt and investment portfolios considering investment opportunities and risks, tax consequences and overall financing strategies. We may use interest rate and cross currency interest rate swaps to manage our overall interest expense and foreign exchange risk. These instruments effectively change the interest rate and currency of specific debt issuances. These swaps are entered into concurrently with the issuance of the debt that they are intended to modify. The notional amount, interest payment and maturity date of the swaps match the principal, interest payment and maturity date of the related debt. These swaps are entered into only with strong creditworthy counterparties and are settled on a net basis.

Fair Value

All derivative instruments are recognized on our balance sheet at fair value. The fair value of our derivative instruments is generally based on quoted market prices. Book and fair values of our derivative and financial instruments are as follows:

	2007		2006	
	Book Value	Fair Value	Book Value	Fair Value
Assets				
Cash and cash equivalents[a]	$910	$910	$1,651	$1,651
Short-term investments[b]	$1,571	$1,571	$1,171	$1,171
Forward exchange contracts[c]	$32	$32	$8	$8
Commodity contracts[d]	$10	$10	$2	$2
Prepaid forward contracts[e]	$74	$74	$73	$73
Interest rate swaps[f]	$36	$36	$—	$—
Cross currency interest rate swaps[f]	$—	$—	$1	$1
Liabilities				
Forward exchange contracts[c]	$61	$61	$24	$24
Commodity contracts[d]	$7	$7	$29	$29
Debt obligations	$4,203	$4,352	$2,824	$2,955
Interest rate swaps[g]	$—	$—	$4	$4
Cross currency interest rate swaps[g]	$8	$8	$—	$—

The above items are included on our balance sheet under the captions noted or as indicated below. In addition, derivatives qualify for hedge accounting unless otherwise noted below.

(a) Book value approximates fair value due to the short maturity.
(b) Principally short-term time deposits and includes $189 million at December 29, 2007 and $145 million at December 30, 2006 of mutual fund investments used to manage a portion of market risk arising from our deferred compensation liability.
(c) The 2007 asset includes $20 million related to derivatives that do not qualify for hedge accounting and the 2007 liability includes $5 million related to derivatives that do not qualify for hedge accounting. The 2006 liability includes $10 million related to derivatives that do not qualify for hedge accounting. Assets are reported within current assets and other assets, and liabilities are reported within current liabilities and other liabilities.
(d) The 2007 asset includes $10 million related to derivatives that do not qualify for hedge accounting and the 2007 liability includes $7 million related to derivatives that do not qualify for hedge accounting. The 2006 liability includes $28 million related to derivatives that do not qualify for hedge accounting. Assets are reported within current assets and other assets, and liabilities are reported within current liabilities and other liabilities.
(e) Included in current assets and other assets.
(f) Asset included within other assets.
(g) Reported in other liabilities.

This table excludes guarantees, including our guarantee of $2.3 billion of Bottling Group, LLC's long-term debt. The guarantee had a fair value of $35 million at December 29, 2007 and December 30, 2006 based on our estimate of the cost to us of transferring the liability to an independent financial institution. See Note 9 for additional information on our guarantees.

Note 11 — Net Income per Common Share

Basic net income per common share is net income available to common shareholders divided by the weighted average of common shares outstanding during the period. Diluted net income per common share is calculated using the weighted average of common shares outstanding adjusted to include the effect that would occur if in-the-money employee stock options were exercised and RSUs and preferred shares were converted into common shares. Options to purchase 2.7 million shares in 2007, 0.1 million shares in 2006 and 3.0 million shares in 2005 were not included in the calculation of diluted earnings per common share because these options were out-of-the-money. Out-of-the-money options had average exercise prices of $65.18 in 2007, $65.24 in 2006 and $53.77 in 2005.

The computations of basic and diluted net income per common share are as follows:

	2007		2006		2005	
	Income	Shares[a]	Income	Shares[a]	Income	Shares[a]
Net income	$5,658		$5,642		$4,078	
Preferred shares:						
Dividends	(2)		(2)		(2)	
Redemption premium	(10)		(9)		(16)	
Net income available for common shareholders	$5,646	1,621	$5,631	1,649	$4,060	1,669
Basic net income per common share	$3.48		$3.42		$2.43	
Net income available for common shareholders	$5,646	1,621	$5,631	1,649	$4,060	1,669
Dilutive securities:						
Stock options and RSUs	–	35	–	36	–	35
ESOP convertible preferred stock	12	2	11	2	18	2
Diluted	$5,658	1,658	$5,642	1,687	$4,078	1,706
Diluted net income per common share	$3.41		$3.34		$2.39	

(a) Weighted-average common shares outstanding.

Note 12 — Preferred Stock

As of December 29, 2007 and December 30, 2006, there were 3 million shares of convertible preferred stock authorized. The preferred stock was issued only for an ESOP established by Quaker and these shares are redeemable for common stock by the ESOP participants. The preferred stock accrues dividends at an annual rate of $5.46 per share. At year-end 2007 and 2006, there were 803,953 preferred shares issued and 287,553 and 320,853 shares outstanding, respectively. The outstanding preferred shares had a fair value of $108 million as of December 29, 2007 and $100 million as of December 30, 2006. Each share is convertible at the option of the holder into 4.9625 shares of common stock. The preferred shares may be called by us upon written notice at $78 per share plus accrued and unpaid dividends. Quaker made the final award to its ESOP plan in June 2001.

	2007		2006		2005	
	Shares	Amount	Shares	Amount	Shares	Amount
Preferred stock	0.8	$41	0.8	$41	0.8	$41
Repurchased preferred stock						
Balance, beginning of year	0.5	$120	0.5	$110	0.4	$ 90
Redemptions	–	12	–	10	0.1	19
Balance, end of year	0.5	$132	0.5	$120	0.5	$110[a]

(a) Does not sum due to rounding.

Note 13 — Accumulated Other Comprehensive Loss

Comprehensive income is a measure of income which includes both net income and other comprehensive income or loss. Other comprehensive income or loss results from items deferred from recognition into our income statement. Accumulated other comprehensive loss is separately presented on our balance sheet as part of common shareholders' equity. Other comprehensive income/(loss) was $1,294 million in 2007, $456 million in 2006 and $(167) million in 2005. The accumulated balances for each component of other comprehensive loss were as follows:

	2007	2006	2005
Currency translation adjustment	$ 213	$ (506)	$ (971)
Cash flow hedges, net of tax[a]	(35)	4	27
Unamortized pension and retiree medical, net of tax[b]	(1,183)	(1,782)	–
Minimum pension liability adjustment[c]	–	–	(138)
Unrealized gain on securities, net of tax	49	40	31
Other	4	(2)	(2)
Accumulated other comprehensive loss	$ (952)	$(2,246)	$(1,053)

(a) Includes $3 million after-tax gain in 2007 and 2006 and no impact in 2005 for our share of our equity investees' accumulated derivative activity.
(b) Net of taxes of $645 million in 2007 and $919 million in 2006.
(c) Net of taxes of $72 million in 2005. Also includes $120 million for our share of our equity investees' minimum pension liability adjustments, net of tax.

Note 14 — Supplemental Financial Information

	2007	2006	2005
Accounts receivable			
Trade receivables	$3,670	$3,147	
Other receivables	788	642	
	4,458	3,789	
Allowance, beginning of year	64	75	$ 97
Net amounts charged/(credited) to expense	5	10	(1)
Deductions[a]	(7)	(27)	(22)
Other[b]	7	6	1
Allowance, end of year	69	64	$ 75
Net receivables	$4,389	$3,725	
Inventories[c]			
Raw materials	$1,056	$ 860	
Work-in-process	157	140	
Finished goods	1,077	926	
	$2,290	$1,926	

(a) Includes accounts written off.
(b) Includes currency translation effects and other adjustments.
(c) Inventories are valued at the lower of cost or market. Cost is determined using the average, first-in, first-out (FIFO) or last-in, first-out (LIFO) methods. Approximately 14% in 2007 and 19% in 2006 of the inventory cost was computed using the LIFO method. The differences between LIFO and FIFO methods of valuing these inventories were not material.

	2007	2006
Other assets		
Noncurrent notes and accounts receivable	$ 121	$149
Deferred marketplace spending	205	232
Unallocated purchase price for recent acquisitions	451	196
Pension plans	635	197
Other	270	206
	$1,682	$980
Accounts payable and other current liabilities		
Accounts payable	$2,562	$2,102
Accrued marketplace spending	1,607	1,444
Accrued compensation and benefits	1,287	1,143
Dividends payable	602	492
Other current liabilities	1,544	1,315
	$7,602	$6,496

Other supplemental information	2007	2006	2005
Rent expense	$303	$291	$228
Interest paid	$251	$215	$213
Income taxes paid, net of refunds	$1,731	$2,155	$1,258
Acquisitions[a]			
Fair value of assets acquired	$ 1,611	$ 678	$ 1,089
Cash paid and debt issued	(1,320)	(522)	(1,096)
SVE minority interest eliminated	–	–	216
Liabilities assumed	$ 291	$ 156	$ 209

(a) In 2005, these amounts include the impact of our acquisition of General Mills, Inc.'s 40.5% ownership interest in SVE for $750 million. The excess of our purchase price over the fair value of net assets acquired was $250 million and reported in goodwill. We also reacquired rights to distribute global brands for $263 million which is included in other nonamortizable intangible assets.

ADDITIONAL INFORMATION

In addition to the financial statements and accompanying notes, companies are required to provide a report on internal control over financial reporting and to have an auditor's report on the financial statements. In addition, PepsiCo has provided a report indicating that financial reporting is management's responsibility. Finally, PepsiCo also provides selected financial data it believes is useful. The two required reports are further explained below.

Management's Report on Internal Control over Financial Reporting

The Sarbanes-Oxley Act of 2002 requires managers of publicly traded companies to establish and maintain systems of internal control over the company's financial reporting processes. In addition, management must express its responsibility for financial reporting, and it must provide certifications regarding the accuracy of the financial statements.

Auditor's Report

All publicly held corporations, as well as many other enterprises and organizations engage the services of independent certified public accountants for the purpose of obtaining an objective, expert report on their financial statements. Based on a comprehensive examination of the company's accounting system, accounting records, and the financial statements, the outside CPA issues the auditor's report.

The standard auditor's report identifies who and what was audited and indicates the responsibilities of management and the auditor relative to the financial statements. It states that the audit was conducted in accordance with generally accepted auditing standards and discusses the nature and limitations of the audit. It then expresses an informed opinion as to (1) the fairness of the financial statements and (2) their conformity with generally accepted accounting principles. It also expresses an opinion regarding the effectiveness of the company's internal controls. All of this additional information for PepsiCo is provided on the following pages.

Management's Responsibility for Financial Reporting

To Our Shareholders:

At PepsiCo, our actions — the actions of all our associates — are governed by our Worldwide Code of Conduct. This code is clearly aligned with our stated values — a commitment to sustained growth, through empowered people, operating with responsibility and building trust. Both the code and our core values enable us to operate with integrity — both within the letter and the spirit of the law. Our code of conduct is reinforced consistently at all levels and in all countries. We have maintained strong governance policies and practices for many years.

The management of PepsiCo is responsible for the objectivity and integrity of our consolidated financial statements. The Audit Committee of the Board of Directors has engaged independent registered public accounting firm, KPMG LLP, to audit our consolidated financial statements and they have expressed an unqualified opinion.

We are committed to providing timely, accurate and understandable information to investors. Our commitment encompasses the following:

Maintaining strong controls over financial reporting. Our system of internal control is based on the control criteria framework of the Committee of Sponsoring Organizations of the Treadway Commission published in their report titled *Internal Control — Integrated Framework*. The system is designed to provide reasonable assurance that transactions are executed as authorized and accurately recorded; that assets are safeguarded; and that accounting records are sufficiently reliable to permit the preparation of financial statements that conform in all material respects with accounting principles generally accepted in the U.S. We maintain disclosure controls and procedures designed to ensure that information required to be disclosed in reports under the Securities Exchange Act of 1934 is recorded, processed, summarized and reported within the specified time periods. We monitor these internal controls through self-assessments and an ongoing program of internal audits. Our internal controls are reinforced through our Worldwide Code of Conduct, which sets forth our commitment to conduct business with integrity, and within both the letter and the spirit of the law.

Exerting rigorous oversight of the business. We continuously review our business results and strategies. This encompasses financial discipline in our strategic and daily business decisions. Our Executive Committee is actively involved — from understanding strategies and alternatives to reviewing key initiatives and financial performance. The intent is to ensure we remain objective in our assessments, constructively challenge our approach to potential business opportunities and issues, and monitor results and controls.

Engaging strong and effective Corporate Governance from our Board of Directors. We have an active, capable and diligent Board that meets the required standards for independence, and we welcome the Board's oversight as a representative of our shareholders. Our Audit Committee is comprised of independent directors with the financial literacy, knowledge and experience to provide appropriate oversight. We review our critical accounting policies, financial reporting and internal control matters with them and encourage their direct communication with KPMG LLP, with our General Auditor, and with our General Counsel. We also have a senior compliance officer to lead and coordinate our compliance policies and practices.

Providing investors with financial results that are complete, transparent and understandable. The consolidated financial statements and financial information included in this report are the responsibility of management. This includes preparing the financial statements in accordance with accounting principles generally accepted in the U.S., which require estimates based on management's best judgment.

PepsiCo has a strong history of doing what's right. We realize that great companies are built on trust, strong ethical standards and principles. Our financial results are delivered from that culture of accountability, and we take responsibility for the quality and accuracy of our financial reporting.

Management's Report on Internal Control over Financial Reporting

To Our Shareholders:

Our management is responsible for establishing and maintaining adequate internal control over financial reporting, as such term is defined in Rule 13a-15(f) of the Exchange Act. Under the supervision and with the participation of our management, including our Chief Executive Officer and Chief Financial Officer, we conducted an evaluation of the effectiveness of our internal control over financial reporting based upon the framework in *Internal Control — Integrated Framework* issued by the Committee of Sponsoring Organizations of the Treadway Commission. Based on that evaluation, our management concluded that our internal control over financial reporting is effective as of December 29, 2007.

KPMG LLP, an independent registered public accounting firm, has audited the consolidated financial statements included in this Annual Report and, as part of their audit, has issued their report, included herein, on the effectiveness of our internal control over financial reporting.

During our fourth fiscal quarter of 2007, we continued migrating certain of our financial processing systems to SAP software. This software implementation is part of our ongoing global business transformation initiative, and we plan to continue implementing such software throughout other parts of our businesses over the course of the next few years. In connection with the SAP implementation and resulting business process changes, we continue to enhance the design and documentation of our internal control processes to ensure suitable controls over our financial reporting.

Except as described above, there were no changes in our internal control over financial reporting that have materially affected, or are reasonably likely to materially affect, our internal control over financial reporting during our fourth fiscal quarter of 2007.

Peter A. Bridgman
Senior Vice President and Controller

Richard Goodman
Chief Financial Officer

Indra K. Nooyi
Chairman of the Board of Directors and Chief Executive Officer

Report of Independent Registered Public Accounting Firm

The Board of Directors and Shareholders
PepsiCo, Inc.:

We have audited the accompanying Consolidated Balance Sheet of PepsiCo, Inc. and Subsidiaries ("PepsiCo, Inc." or the "Company") as of December 29, 2007 and December 30, 2006, and the related Consolidated Statements of Income, Cash Flows and Common Shareholders' Equity for each of the years in the three-year period ended December 29, 2007. We also have audited PepsiCo, Inc.'s internal control over financial reporting as of December 29, 2007, based on criteria established in Internal Control — Integrated Framework issued by the Committee of Sponsoring Organizations of the Treadway Commission ("COSO"). PepsiCo, Inc.'s management is responsible for these consolidated financial statements, for maintaining effective internal control over financial reporting, and for its assessment of the effectiveness of internal control over financial reporting, included in Management's Report on Internal Control over Financial Reporting. Our responsibility is to express an opinion on these consolidated financial statements and an opinion on the Company's internal control over financial reporting based on our audits.

We conducted our audits in accordance with the standards of the Public Company Accounting Oversight Board (United States). Those standards require that we plan and perform the audits to obtain reasonable assurance about whether the financial statements are free of material misstatement and whether effective internal control over financial reporting was maintained in all material respects. Our audits of the consolidated financial statements included examining, on a test basis, evidence supporting the amounts and disclosures in the financial statements, assessing the accounting principles used and significant estimates made by management, and evaluating the overall financial statement presentation. Our audit of internal control over financial reporting included obtaining an understanding of internal control over financial reporting, assessing the risk that a material weakness exists, and testing and evaluating the design and operating effectiveness of internal control based on the assessed risk. Our audits also included performing such other procedures as we considered necessary in the circumstances. We believe that our audits provide a reasonable basis for our opinions.

A company's internal control over financial reporting is a process designed to provide reasonable assurance regarding the reliability of financial reporting and the preparation of financial statements for external purposes in accordance with generally accepted accounting principles. A company's internal control over financial reporting includes those policies and procedures that (1) pertain to the maintenance of records that, in reasonable detail, accurately and fairly reflect the transactions and dispositions of the assets of the company; (2) provide reasonable assurance that transactions are recorded as necessary to permit preparation of financial statements in accordance with generally accepted accounting principles, and that receipts and expenditures of the company are being made only in accordance with authorizations of management and directors of the company; and (3) provide reasonable assurance regarding prevention or timely detection of unauthorized acquisition, use, or disposition of the company's assets that could have a material effect on the financial statements.

Because of its inherent limitations, internal control over financial reporting may not prevent or detect misstatements. Also, projections of any evaluation of effectiveness to future periods are subject to the risk that controls may become inadequate because of changes in conditions, or that the degree of compliance with the policies or procedures may deteriorate.

In our opinion, the consolidated financial statements referred to above present fairly, in all material respects, the financial position of PepsiCo, Inc. as of December 29, 2007 and December 30, 2006, and the results of its operations and its cash flows for each of the years in the three-year period ended December 29, 2007, in conformity with accounting principles generally accepted in the United States of America. Also in our opinion, PepsiCo, Inc. maintained, in all material respects, effective internal control over financial reporting as of December 29, 2007, based on criteria established in Internal Control — Integrated Framework issued by COSO.

KPMG LLP

New York, New York
February 15, 2008

Appendix A Specimen Financial Statements: PepsiCo, Inc.

Selected Financial Data (in millions except per share amounts, unaudited)

Quarterly	First Quarter	Second Quarter	Third Quarter	Fourth Quarter
Net revenue				
2007	$7,350	$9,607	$10,171	$12,346
2006	$6,719	$8,714	$9,134	$10,570
Gross profit				
2007	$4,065	$5,265	$5,544	$6,562
2006	$3,757	$4,852	$5,026	$5,740
Restructuring and impairment charges[a]				
2007	–	–	–	$102
2006	–	–	–	$67
Tax benefits[b]				
2007	–	–	$(115)	$(14)
2006	–	–	–	$(602)
Net income				
2007	$1,096	$1,557	$1,743	$1,262
2006	$947	$1,375	$1,494	$1,826
Net income per common share — basic				
2007	$0.67	$0.96	$1.08	$0.78
2006	$0.57	$0.83	$0.90	$1.11
Net income per common share — diluted				
2007	$0.65	$0.94	$1.06	$0.77
2006	$0.56	$0.81	$0.89	$1.09
Cash dividends declared per common share				
2007	$0.30	$0.375	$0.375	$0.375
2006	$0.26	$0.30	$0.30	$0.30
2007 stock price per share[c]				
High	$65.54	$69.64	$70.25	$79.00
Low	$61.89	$62.57	$64.25	$68.02
Close	$64.09	$66.68	$67.98	$77.03
2006 stock price per share[c]				
High	$60.55	$61.19	$65.99	$65.99
Low	$56.00	$56.51	$58.65	$61.15
Close	$59.34	$59.70	$64.73	$62.55

2006 results reflect our change in reporting calendars of certain operating units within PI.

(a) The restructuring and impairment charge in 2007 was $102 million ($70 million or $0.04 per share after-tax). The restructuring and impairment charge in 2006 was $67 million ($43 million or $0.03 per share after-tax). See Note 3.
(b) In 2007, represents non-cash tax benefits related to the favorable resolution of certain foreign tax matters. In 2006, represents non-cash tax benefits primarily related to the IRS's examination of our consolidated income tax returns for the years 1998 through 2002. See Note 5.
(c) Represents the composite high and low sales price and quarterly closing prices for one share of PepsiCo common stock.

Five-Year Summary	2007	2006	2005
Net revenue	$39,474	$35,137	$32,562
Net income	$5,658	$5,642	$4,078
Income per common share — basic	$3.48	$3.42	$2.43
Income per common share — diluted	$3.41	$3.34	$2.39
Cash dividends declared per common share	$1.425	$1.16	$1.01
Total assets	$34,628	$29,930	$31,727
Long-term debt	$4,203	$2,550	$2,313
Return on invested capital[a]	28.9%	30.4%	22.7%

Five-Year Summary (cont.)	2004	2003
Net revenue	$29,261	$26,971
Income from continuing operations	$4,174	$3,568
Net income	$4,212	$3,568
Income per common share — basic, continuing operations	$2.45	$2.07
Income per common share — diluted, continuing operations	$2.41	$2.05
Cash dividends declared per common share	$0.85	$0.63
Total assets	$27,987	$25,327
Long-term debt	$2,397	$1,702
Return on invested capital[a]	27.4%	27.5%

(a) Return on invested capital is defined as adjusted net income divided by the sum of average shareholders' equity and average total debt. Adjusted net income is defined as net income plus net interest expense after-tax. Net interest expense after-tax was $63 million in 2007, $72 million in 2006, $62 million in 2005, $60 million in 2004 and $72 million in 2003.

- Includes restructuring and impairment charges of:

	2007	2006	2005	2004	2003
Pre-tax	$102	$67	$83	$150	$147
After-tax	$70	$43	$55	$96	$100
Per share	$0.04	$0.03	$0.03	$0.06	$0.06

- Includes Quaker merger-related costs of:

	2003
Pre-tax	$59
After-tax	$42
Per share	$0.02

- In 2007, we recognized $129 million ($0.08 per share) of non-cash tax benefits related to the favorable resolution of certain foreign tax matters. In 2006, we recognized non-cash tax benefits of $602 million ($0.36 per share) primarily in connection with the IRS's examination of our consolidated income tax returns for the years 1998 through 2002. In 2005, we recorded income tax expense of $460 million ($0.27 per share) related to our repatriation of earnings in connection with the AJCA. In 2004, we reached agreement with the IRS for an open issue related to our discontinued restaurant operations which resulted in a tax benefit of $38 million ($0.02 per share).
- On December 30, 2006, we adopted SFAS 158 which reduced total assets by $2,016 million, total common shareholders' equity by $1,643 million and total liabilities by $373 million.
- The 2005 fiscal year consisted of 53 weeks compared to 52 weeks in our normal fiscal year. The 53rd week increased 2005 net revenue by an estimated $418 million and net income by an estimated $57 million ($0.03 per share).

Appendix B

SPECIMEN FINANCIAL STATEMENTS:
The Coca-Cola Company

THE COCA-COLA COMPANY AND SUBSIDIARIES
CONSOLIDATED STATEMENTS OF INCOME

Year Ended December 31, (In millions except per share data)	2007	2006	2005
NET OPERATING REVENUES	$ 28,857	$ 24,088	$ 23,104
Cost of goods sold	10,406	8,164	8,195
GROSS PROFIT	18,451	15,924	14,909
Selling, general and administrative expenses	10,945	9,431	8,739
Other operating charges	254	185	85
OPERATING INCOME	7,252	6,308	6,085
Interest income	236	193	235
Interest expense	456	220	240
Equity income—net	668	102	680
Other income (loss)—net	173	195	(93)
Gains on issuances of stock by equity method investees	—	—	23
INCOME BEFORE INCOME TAXES	7,873	6,578	6,690
Income taxes	1,892	1,498	1,818
NET INCOME	$ 5,981	$ 5,080	$ 4,872
BASIC NET INCOME PER SHARE	$ 2.59	$ 2.16	$ 2.04
DILUTED NET INCOME PER SHARE	$ 2.57	$ 2.16	$ 2.04
AVERAGE SHARES OUTSTANDING	2,313	2,348	2,392
Effect of dilutive securities	18	2	1
AVERAGE SHARES OUTSTANDING ASSUMING DILUTION	2,331	2,350	2,393

Refer to Notes to Consolidated Financial Statements.

The financial information herein is reprinted with permission from The Coca-Cola Company 2007 Annual Report. The accompanying Notes are an integral part of the consolidated financial statements. The complete financial statements are available through a link at the book's companion website.

THE COCA-COLA COMPANY AND SUBSIDIARIES
CONSOLIDATED BALANCE SHEETS

December 31,	2007	2006
(In millions except par value)		
ASSETS		
CURRENT ASSETS		
Cash and cash equivalents	$ 4,093	$ 2,440
Marketable securities	215	150
Trade accounts receivable, less allowances of $56 and $63, respectively	3,317	2,587
Inventories	2,220	1,641
Prepaid expenses and other assets	2,260	1,623
TOTAL CURRENT ASSETS	12,105	8,441
INVESTMENTS		
Equity method investments:		
Coca-Cola Enterprises Inc.	1,637	1,312
Coca-Cola Hellenic Bottling Company S.A.	1,549	1,251
Coca-Cola FEMSA, S.A.B. de C.V.	996	835
Coca-Cola Amatil Limited	806	817
Other, principally bottling companies and joint ventures	2,301	2,095
Cost method investments, principally bottling companies	488	473
TOTAL INVESTMENTS	7,777	6,783
OTHER ASSETS	2,675	2,701
PROPERTY, PLANT AND EQUIPMENT—net	8,493	6,903
TRADEMARKS WITH INDEFINITE LIVES	5,153	2,045
GOODWILL	4,256	1,403
OTHER INTANGIBLE ASSETS	2,810	1,687
TOTAL ASSETS	$ 43,269	$ 29,963
LIABILITIES AND SHAREOWNERS' EQUITY		
CURRENT LIABILITIES		
Accounts payable and accrued expenses	$ 6,915	$ 5,055
Loans and notes payable	5,919	3,235
Current maturities of long-term debt	133	33
Accrued income taxes	258	567
TOTAL CURRENT LIABILITIES	13,225	8,890
LONG-TERM DEBT	3,277	1,314
OTHER LIABILITIES	3,133	2,231
DEFERRED INCOME TAXES	1,890	608
SHAREOWNERS' EQUITY		
Common stock, $0.25 par value; Authorized—5,600 shares; Issued—3,519 and 3,511 shares, respectively	880	878
Capital surplus	7,378	5,983
Reinvested earnings	36,235	33,468
Accumulated other comprehensive income (loss)	626	(1,291)
Treasury stock, at cost—1,201 and 1,193 shares, respectively	(23,375)	(22,118)
TOTAL SHAREOWNERS' EQUITY	21,744	16,920
TOTAL LIABILITIES AND SHAREOWNERS' EQUITY	$ 43,269	$ 29,963

Refer to Notes to Consolidated Financial Statements.

THE COCA-COLA COMPANY AND SUBSIDIARIES
CONSOLIDATED STATEMENTS OF CASH FLOWS

Year Ended December 31, (In millions)	2007	2006	2005
OPERATING ACTIVITIES			
Net income	$ 5,981	$ 5,080	$ 4,872
Depreciation and amortization	1,163	938	932
Stock-based compensation expense	313	324	324
Deferred income taxes	109	(35)	(88)
Equity income or loss, net of dividends	(452)	124	(446)
Foreign currency adjustments	9	52	47
Gains on issuances of stock by equity investees	—	—	(23)
Gains on sales of assets, including bottling interests	(244)	(303)	(9)
Other operating charges	166	159	85
Other items	99	233	299
Net change in operating assets and liabilities	6	(615)	430
Net cash provided by operating activities	7,150	5,957	6,423
INVESTING ACTIVITIES			
Acquisitions and investments, principally beverage and bottling companies	(5,653)	(901)	(637)
Purchases of other investments	(99)	(82)	(53)
Proceeds from disposals of other investments	448	640	33
Purchases of property, plant and equipment	(1,648)	(1,407)	(899)
Proceeds from disposals of property, plant and equipment	239	112	88
Other investing activities	(6)	(62)	(28)
Net cash used in investing activities	(6,719)	(1,700)	(1,496)
FINANCING ACTIVITIES			
Issuances of debt	9,979	617	178
Payments of debt	(5,638)	(2,021)	(2,460)
Issuances of stock	1,619	148	230
Purchases of stock for treasury	(1,838)	(2,416)	(2,055)
Dividends	(3,149)	(2,911)	(2,678)
Net cash provided by (used in) financing activities	973	(6,583)	(6,785)
EFFECT OF EXCHANGE RATE CHANGES ON CASH AND CASH EQUIVALENTS	249	65	(148)
CASH AND CASH EQUIVALENTS			
Net increase (decrease) during the year	1,653	(2,261)	(2,006)
Balance at beginning of year	2,440	4,701	6,707
Balance at end of year	$ 4,093	$ 2,440	$ 4,701

Refer to Notes to Consolidated Financial Statements.

THE COCA-COLA COMPANY AND SUBSIDIARIES
CONSOLIDATED STATEMENTS OF SHAREOWNERS' EQUITY

Year Ended December 31, (In millions except per share data)	2007	2006	2005
NUMBER OF COMMON SHARES OUTSTANDING			
Balance at beginning of year	2,318	2,369	2,409
Stock issued to employees exercising stock options	8	4	7
Purchases of stock for treasury[1]	(35)	(55)	(47)
Treasury stock issued to employees exercising stock options	23	—	—
Treasury stock issued to former shareholders of glacéau	4	—	—
Balance at end of year	2,318	2,318	2,369
COMMON STOCK			
Balance at beginning of year	$ 878	$ 877	$ 875
Stock issued to employees exercising stock options	2	1	2
Balance at end of year	880	878	877
CAPITAL SURPLUS			
Balance at beginning of year	5,983	5,492	4,928
Stock issued to employees exercising stock options	1,001	164	229
Tax (charge) benefit from employees' stock option and restricted stock plans	(28)	3	11
Stock-based compensation	309	324	324
Stock purchased by former shareholders of glacéau	113	—	—
Balance at end of year	7,378	5,983	5,492
REINVESTED EARNINGS			
Balance at beginning of year	33,468	31,299	29,105
Adjustment for the cumulative effect on prior years of the adoption of Interpretation No. 48	(65)		
Net income	5,981	5,080	4,872
Dividends (per share—$1.36, $1.24 and $1.12 in 2007, 2006 and 2005, respectively)	(3,149)	(2,911)	(2,678)
Balance at end of year	36,235	33,468	31,299
ACCUMULATED OTHER COMPREHENSIVE INCOME (LOSS)			
Balance at beginning of year	(1,291)	(1,669)	(1,348)
Net foreign currency translation adjustment	1,575	603	(396)
Net gain (loss) on derivatives	(64)	(26)	57
Net change in unrealized gain on available-for-sale securities	14	43	13
Net change in pension liability	392	—	—
Net change in pension liability, prior to adoption of SFAS No. 158	—	46	5
Net other comprehensive income adjustments	1,917	666	(321)
Adjustment to initially apply SFAS No. 158	—	(288)	—
Balance at end of year	626	(1,291)	(1,669)
TREASURY STOCK			
Balance at beginning of year	(22,118)	(19,644)	(17,625)
Stock issued to employees exercising stock options	428	—	—
Stock purchased by former shareholders of glacéau	66	—	—
Purchases of treasury stock	(1,751)	(2,474)	(2,019)
Balance at end of year	(23,375)	(22,118)	(19,644)
TOTAL SHAREOWNERS' EQUITY	$ 21,744	$ 16,920	$ 16,355
COMPREHENSIVE INCOME			
Net income	$ 5,981	$ 5,080	$ 4,872
Net other comprehensive income adjustments	1,917	666	(321)
TOTAL COMPREHENSIVE INCOME	$ 7,898	$ 5,746	$ 4,551

[1] Common stock purchased from employees exercising stock options numbered approximately zero shares, zero shares and 0.5 million shares for the years ended December 31, 2007, 2006 and 2005, respectively.

Refer to Notes to Consolidated Financial Statements.

Appendix C

Time Value of Money

STUDY OBJECTIVES

After studying this appendix, you should be able to:

1. Distinguish between simple and compound interest.
2. Identify the variables fundamental to solving present value problems.
3. Solve for present value of a single amount.
4. Solve for present value of an annuity.
5. Compute the present value of notes and bonds.

Would you rather receive $1,000 today or a year from now? You should prefer to receive the $1,000 today because you can invest the $1,000 and earn interest on it. As a result, you will have more than $1,000 a year from now. What this example illustrates is the concept of the **time value of money**. Everyone prefers to receive money today rather than in the future because of the interest factor.

NATURE OF INTEREST

Interest is payment for the use of another person's money. It is the difference between the amount borrowed or invested (called the **principal**) and the amount repaid or collected. The amount of interest to be paid or collected is usually stated as a **rate** over a specific period of time. The rate of interest is generally stated as an **annual rate**.

The amount of interest involved in any financing transaction is based on three elements:

1. **Principal (p):** The original amount borrowed or invested.
2. **Interest Rate (i):** An annual percentage of the principal.
3. **Time (n):** The number of years that the principal is borrowed or invested.

Simple Interest

Simple interest is computed on the principal amount only. It is the return on the principal for one period. Simple interest is usually expressed as shown in Illustration C-1 on the next page.

> **STUDY OBJECTIVE 1**
> Distinguish between simple and compound interest.

C1

Illustration C-1
Interest computation

| Interest | = | Principal
p | × | Rate
i | × | Time
n |

For example, if you borrowed $5,000 for 2 years at a simple interest rate of 12% annually, you would pay $1,200 in total interest computed as follows:

$$\text{Interest} = p \times i \times n$$
$$= \$5,000 \times .12 \times 2$$
$$= \$1,200$$

Compound Interest

Compound interest is computed on principal **and** on any interest earned that has not been paid or withdrawn. It is the return on the principal for two or more time periods. Compounding computes interest not only on the principal but also on the interest earned to date on that principal, assuming the interest is left on deposit.

To illustrate the difference between simple and compound interest, assume that you deposit $1,000 in Bank Two, where it will earn *simple interest* of 9% per year, and you deposit another $1,000 in Citizens Bank, where it will earn compound interest of 9% per year *compounded annually*. Also assume that in both cases you will not withdraw any interest until three years from the date of deposit. Illustration C-2 shows the computation of interest you will receive and the accumulated year-end balances.

Illustration C-2
Simple versus compound interest

Bank Two				Citizens Bank		
Simple Interest Calculation	Simple Interest	Accumulated Year-end Balance		Compound Interest Calculation	Compound Interest	Accumulated Year-end Balance
Year 1 $1,000.00 × 9%	$ 90.00	$1,090.00		Year 1 $1,000.00 × 9%	$ 90.00	$1,090.00
Year 2 $1,000.00 × 9%	90.00	$1,180.00		Year 2 $1,090.00 × 9%	98.10	$1,188.10
Year 3 $1,000.00 × 9%	90.00	$1,270.00		Year 3 $1,188.10 × 9%	106.93	$1,295.03
	$ 270.00		$25.03 Difference		$ 295.03	

Note in Illustration C-2 that simple interest uses the initial principal of $1,000 to compute the interest in all three years. Compound interest uses the accumulated balance (principal plus interest to date) at each year-end to compute interest in the succeeding year—which explains why your compound interest account is larger.

Obviously, if you had a choice between investing your money at simple interest or at compound interest, you would choose compound interest, all other things—especially risk—being equal. In the example, compounding provides $25.03 of additional interest income. For practical purposes, compounding assumes that unpaid interest earned becomes a part of the principal, and the accumulated balance at the end of each year becomes the new principal on which interest is earned during the next year.

Illustration C-2 indicates that you should invest your money at the bank that compounds interest annually. Most business situations use compound interest. Simple interest is generally applicable only to short-term situations of one year or less.

PRESENT VALUE VARIABLES

The **present value** is the value now of a given amount to be paid or received in the future, assuming compound interest. The present value is based on three variables: (1) the dollar amount to be received (future amount), (2) the length of time until the amount is received (number of periods), and (3) the interest rate (the discount rate). The process of determining the present value is referred to as **discounting the future amount**.

> **STUDY OBJECTIVE 2**
> Identify the variables fundamental to solving present value problems.

In this textbook, we use present value computations in measuring several items. For example, Chapter 15 computed the present value of the principal and interest payments to determine the market price of a bond. In addition, determining the amount to be reported for notes payable and lease liabilities involves present value computations.

PRESENT VALUE OF A SINGLE AMOUNT

To illustrate present value, assume that you want to invest a sum of money that will yield $1,000 at the end of one year. What amount would you need to invest today to have $1,000 one year from now? Illustration C-3 shows the formula for calculating present value.

> **STUDY OBJECTIVE 3**
> Solve for present value of a single amount.

$$\text{Present Value} = \text{Future Value} \div (1 + i)^n$$

Illustration C-3
Formula for present value

Thus, if you want a 10% rate of return, you would compute the present value of $1,000 for one year as follows:

$$\begin{aligned} PV &= FV \div (1 + i)^n \\ &= \$1{,}000 \div (1 + .10)^1 \\ &= \$1{,}000 \div 1.10 \\ &= \$909.09 \end{aligned}$$

We know the future amount ($1,000), the discount rate (10%), and the number of periods (1). These variables are depicted in the time diagram in Illustration C-4.

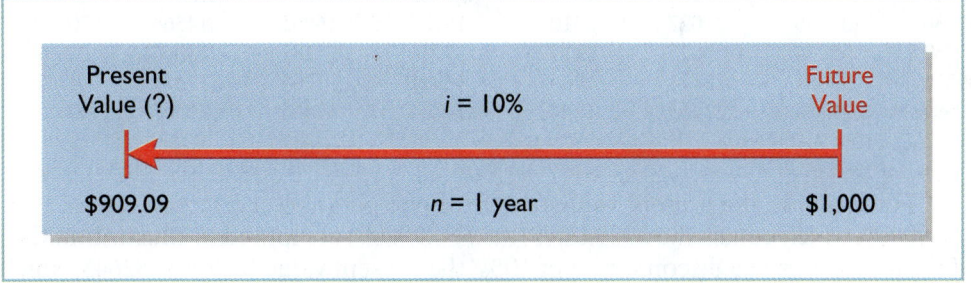

Illustration C-4
Finding present value if discounted for one period

If you receive the single amount of $1,000 **in two years**, discounted at 10% [$PV = \$1{,}000 \div (1 + .10)^2$], the present value of your $1,000 is $826.45 [($1,000 ÷ 1.21), depicted as shown in Illustration C-5 on the next page.

Illustration C-5
Finding present value if discounted for two periods

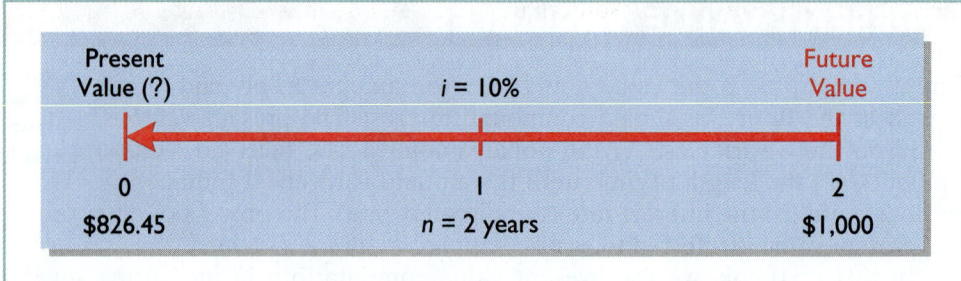

You also could find the present value of your amount through tables that show the present value of 1 for *n* periods. In Table 1, below, *n* (represented in the table's rows) is the number of discounting periods involved. The percentages (represented in the table's columns) are the periodic interest rates or discount rates. The 5-digit decimal numbers in the intersections of the rows and columns are called the **present value of 1 factors**.

When using Table 1 to determine present value, you multiply the future value by the present value factor specified at the intersection of the number of periods and the discount rate.

TABLE 1
Present Value of 1

(*n*) Periods	4%	5%	6%	8%	9%	10%	11%	12%	15%
1	.96154	.95238	.94340	.92593	.91743	.90909	.90090	.89286	.86957
2	.92456	.90703	.89000	.85734	.84168	.82645	.81162	.79719	.75614
3	.88900	.86384	.83962	.79383	.77218	.75132	.73119	.71178	.65752
4	.85480	.82270	.79209	.73503	.70843	.68301	.65873	.63552	.57175
5	.82193	.78353	.74726	.68058	.64993	.62092	.59345	.56743	.49718
6	.79031	.74622	.70496	.63017	.59627	.56447	.53464	.50663	.43233
7	.75992	.71068	.66506	.58349	.54703	.51316	.48166	.45235	.37594
8	.73069	.67684	.62741	.54027	.50187	.46651	.43393	.40388	.32690
9	.70259	.64461	.59190	.50025	.46043	.42410	.39092	.36061	.28426
10	.67556	.61391	.55839	.46319	.42241	.38554	.35218	.32197	.24719
11	.64958	.58468	.52679	.42888	.38753	.35049	.31728	.28748	.21494
12	.62460	.55684	.49697	.39711	.35554	.31863	.28584	.25668	.18691
13	.60057	.53032	.46884	.36770	.32618	.28966	.25751	.22917	.16253
14	.57748	.50507	.44230	.34046	.29925	.26333	.23199	.20462	.14133
15	.55526	.48102	.41727	.31524	.27454	.23939	.20900	.18270	.12289
16	.53391	.45811	.39365	.29189	.25187	.21763	.18829	.16312	.10687
17	.51337	.43630	.37136	.27027	.23107	.19785	.16963	.14564	.09293
18	.49363	.41552	.35034	.25025	.21199	.17986	.15282	.13004	.08081
19	.47464	.39573	.33051	.23171	.19449	.16351	.13768	.11611	.07027
20	.45639	.37689	.31180	.21455	.17843	.14864	.12403	.10367	.06110

For example, the present value factor for one period at a discount rate of 10% is .90909, which equals the $909.09 ($1,000 × .90909) computed in Illustration C-4. For two periods at a discount rate of 10%, the present value factor is .82645, which equals the $826.45 ($1,000 × .82645) computed previously.

Note that a higher discount rate produces a smaller present value. For example, using a 15% discount rate, the present value of $1,000 due one year from now is $869.57, versus $909.09 at 10%. Also note that the further removed from the present the future value is, the smaller the present value. For example, using the same discount rate of 10%, the present value of $1,000 due in **five years** is $620.92, versus the present value of $1,000 due in **one year**, which is $909.09.

The following two demonstration problems (Illustrations C-6, C-7) illustrate how to use Table 1.

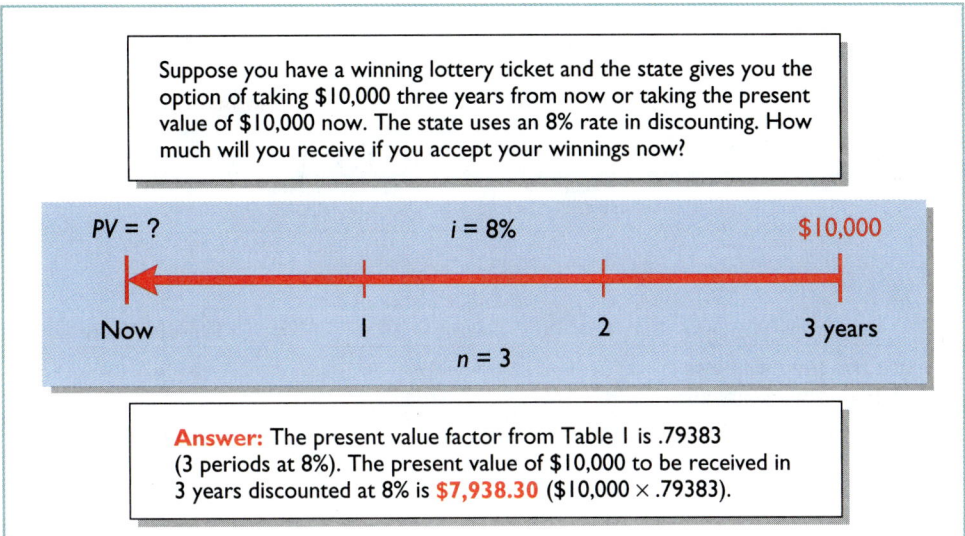

Illustration C-6
Demonstration problem—
Using Table 1 for PV of 1

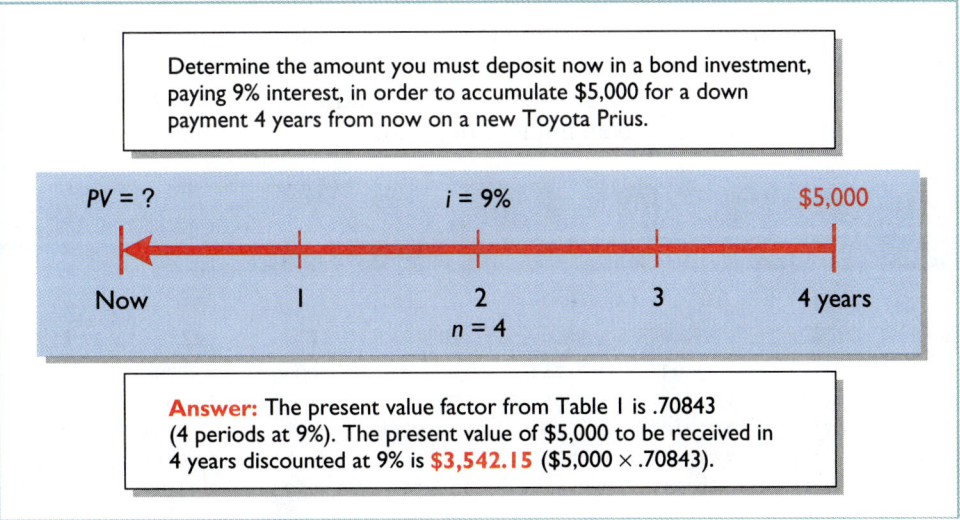

Illustration C-7
Demonstration problem—
Using Table 1 for PV of 1

PRESENT VALUE OF AN ANNUITY

The preceding discussion involved the discounting of only a single future amount. Businesses and individuals frequently engage in transactions in which a *series* of equal dollar amounts are to be received or paid periodically. Examples of a series of periodic receipts or payments are loan agreements, installment sales, mortgage notes, lease (rental) contracts, and pension obligations. As discussed in Chapter 15, these periodic receipts or payments are **annuities**.

The **present value of an annuity** is the value now of a series of future receipts or payments, discounted assuming compound interest. In computing the present value of an annuity, you need to know: (1) the discount rate, (2) the number of discount periods, and (3) the amount of the periodic receipts or payments.

STUDY OBJECTIVE 4
Solve for present value of an annuity.

To illustrate how to compute the present value of an annuity, assume that you will receive $1,000 cash annually for three years at a time when the discount rate is 10%. Illustration C-8 depicts this situation, and Illustration C-9 shows the computation of its present value.

Illustration C-8
Time diagram for a three-year annuity

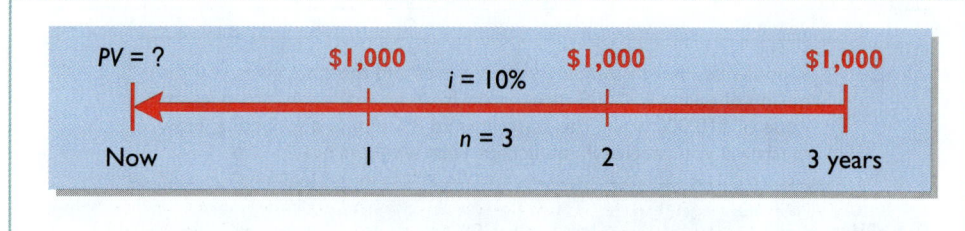

Illustration C-9
Present value of a series of future amounts computation

Future Amount	×	Present Value of 1 Factor at 10%	=	Present Value
$1,000 (one year away)		.90909		$ 909.09
1,000 (two years away)		.82645		826.45
1,000 (three years away)		.75132		751.32
		2.48686		**$2,486.86**

This method of calculation is required when the periodic cash flows are not uniform in each period. However, when the future receipts are the same in each period, there are two other ways to compute present value. First, you can multiply the annual cash flow by the sum of the three present value factors. In the previous example, $1,000 × 2.48686 equals $2,486.86. The second method is to use annuity tables. As illustrated in Table 2 below, these tables show the present value of 1 to be received periodically for a given number of periods.

TABLE 2
Present Value of an Annuity of 1

(n) Periods	4%	5%	6%	8%	9%	10%	11%	12%	15%
1	.96154	.95238	.94340	.92593	.91743	.90909	.90090	.89286	.86957
2	1.88609	1.85941	1.83339	1.78326	1.75911	1.73554	1.71252	1.69005	1.62571
3	2.77509	2.72325	2.67301	2.57710	2.53130	2.48685	2.44371	2.40183	2.28323
4	3.62990	3.54595	3.46511	3.31213	3.23972	3.16986	3.10245	3.03735	2.85498
5	4.45182	4.32948	4.21236	3.99271	3.88965	3.79079	3.69590	3.60478	3.35216
6	5.24214	5.07569	4.91732	4.62288	4.48592	4.35526	4.23054	4.11141	3.78448
7	6.00205	5.78637	5.58238	5.20637	5.03295	4.86842	4.71220	4.56376	4.16042
8	6.73274	6.46321	6.20979	5.74664	5.53482	5.33493	5.14612	4.96764	4.48732
9	7.43533	7.10782	6.80169	6.24689	5.99525	5.75902	5.53705	5.32825	4.77158
10	8.11090	7.72173	7.36009	6.71008	6.41766	6.14457	5.88923	5.65022	5.01877
11	8.76048	8.30641	7.88687	7.13896	6.80519	6.49506	6.20652	5.93770	5.23371
12	9.38507	8.86325	8.38384	7.53608	7.16073	6.81369	6.49236	6.19437	5.42062
13	9.98565	9.39357	8.85268	7.90378	7.48690	7.10336	6.74987	6.42355	5.58315
14	10.56312	9.89864	9.29498	8.24424	7.78615	7.36669	6.98187	6.62817	5.72448
15	11.11839	10.37966	9.71225	8.55948	8.06069	7.60608	7.19087	6.81086	5.84737
16	11.65230	10.83777	10.10590	8.85137	8.31256	7.82371	7.37916	6.97399	5.95424
17	12.16567	11.27407	10.47726	9.12164	8.54363	8.02155	7.54879	7.11963	6.04716
18	12.65930	11.68959	10.82760	9.37189	8.75563	8.20141	7.70162	7.24967	6.12797
19	13.13394	12.08532	11.15812	9.60360	8.95012	8.36492	7.83929	7.36578	6.19823
20	13.59033	12.46221	11.46992	9.81815	9.12855	8.51356	7.96333	7.46944	6.25933

Table 2 shows that the present value of an annuity of 1 factor for three periods at 10% is 2.48685.[1] (This present value factor is the total of the three individual present value factors, as shown in Illustration C-9.) Applying this amount to the annual cash flow of $1,000 produces a present value of $2,486.85.

The following demonstration problem (Illustration C-10) illustrates how to use Table 2.

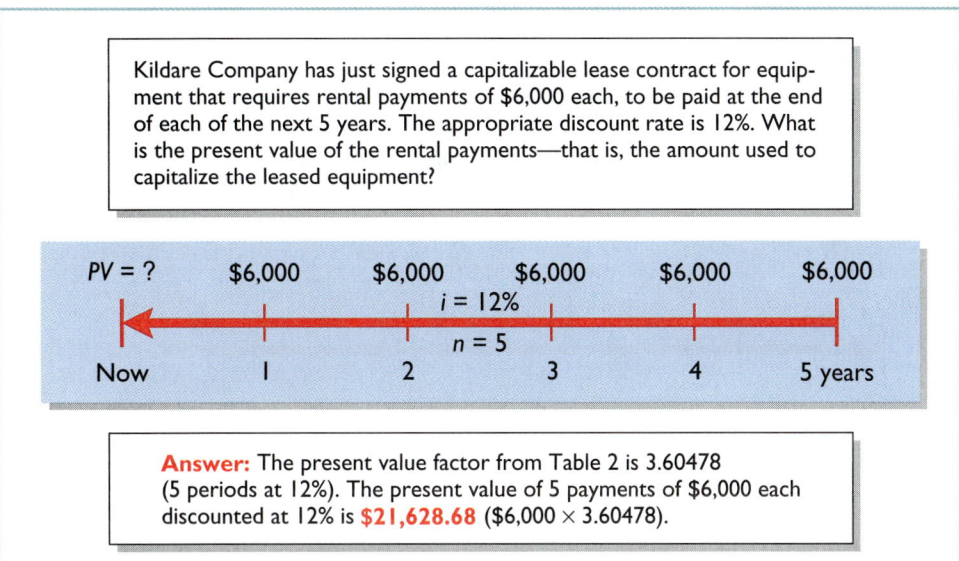

Illustration C-10
Demonstration problem—Using Table 2 for PV of an annuity of 1

TIME PERIODS AND DISCOUNTING

In the preceding calculations, the discounting was done on an *annual* basis using an *annual* interest rate. Discounting may also be done over shorter periods of time such as monthly, quarterly, or semiannually.

When the time frame is less than one year, you need to convert the annual interest rate to the applicable time frame. Assume, for example, that the investor in Illustration C-8 received $500 **semiannually** for three years instead of $1,000 annually. In this case, the number of periods becomes six (3×2), the discount rate is 5% ($10\% \div 2$), the present value factor from Table 2 is 5.07569, and the present value of the future cash flows is $2,537.85 (5.07569 × $500). This amount is slightly higher than the $2,486.86 computed in Illustration C-9 because interest is paid twice during the same year; therefore interest is earned on the first half year's interest.

COMPUTING THE PRESENT VALUE OF A LONG-TERM NOTE OR BOND

The present value (or market price) of a long-term note or bond is a function of three variables: (1) the payment amounts, (2) the length of time until the amounts are paid, and (3) the discount rate. Our illustration uses a five-year bond issue.

STUDY OBJECTIVE 5
Compute the present value of notes and bonds.

---
[1] The difference of .00001 between 2.48686 and 2.48685 is due to rounding.

The first variable—dollars to be paid—is made up of two elements: (1) a series of interest payments (an annuity), and (2) the principal amount (a single sum). To compute the present value of the bond, we must discount both the interest payments and the principal amount—two different computations. The time diagrams for a bond due in five years are shown in Illustration C-11.

Illustration C-11
Present value of a bond time diagram

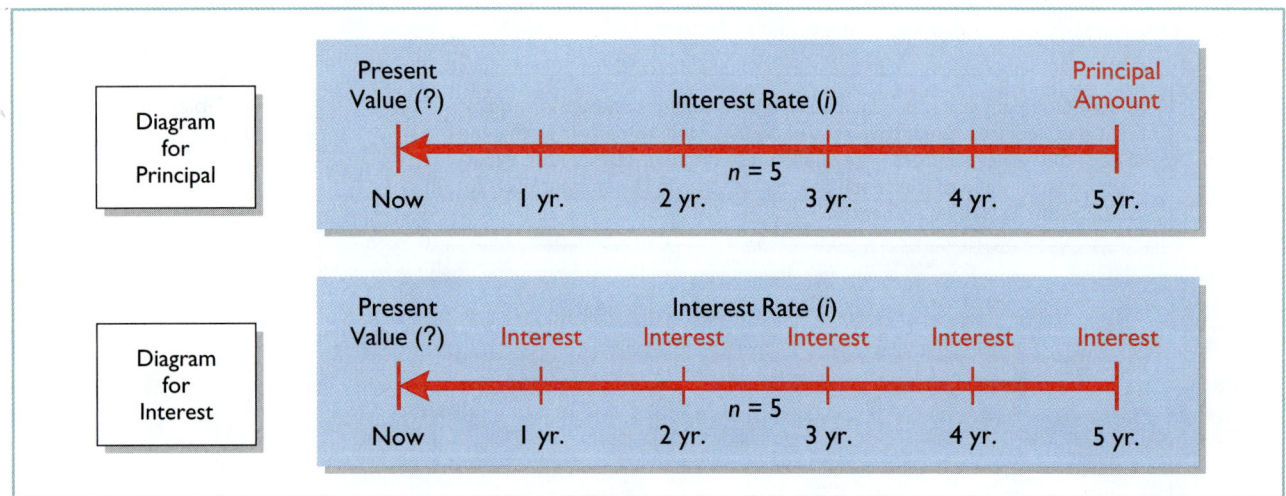

When the investor's market interest rate is equal to the bond's contractual interest rate, the present value of the bonds will *equal* the face value of the bonds. To illustrate, assume a bond issue of 10%, five-year bonds with a face value of $100,000 with interest payable **semiannually** on January 1 and July 1. If the discount rate is the same as the contractual rate, the bonds will sell at face value. In this case, the investor will receive the following: (1) $100,000 at maturity, and (2) a series of ten $5,000 interest payments [($100,000 × 10%) ÷ 2] over the term of the bonds. The length of time is expressed in terms of interest periods—in this case—10, and the discount rate per interest period, 5%. The following time diagram (Illustration C-12) depicts the variables involved in this discounting situation.

Illustration C-12
Time diagram for present value of a 10%, five-year bond paying interest semiannually

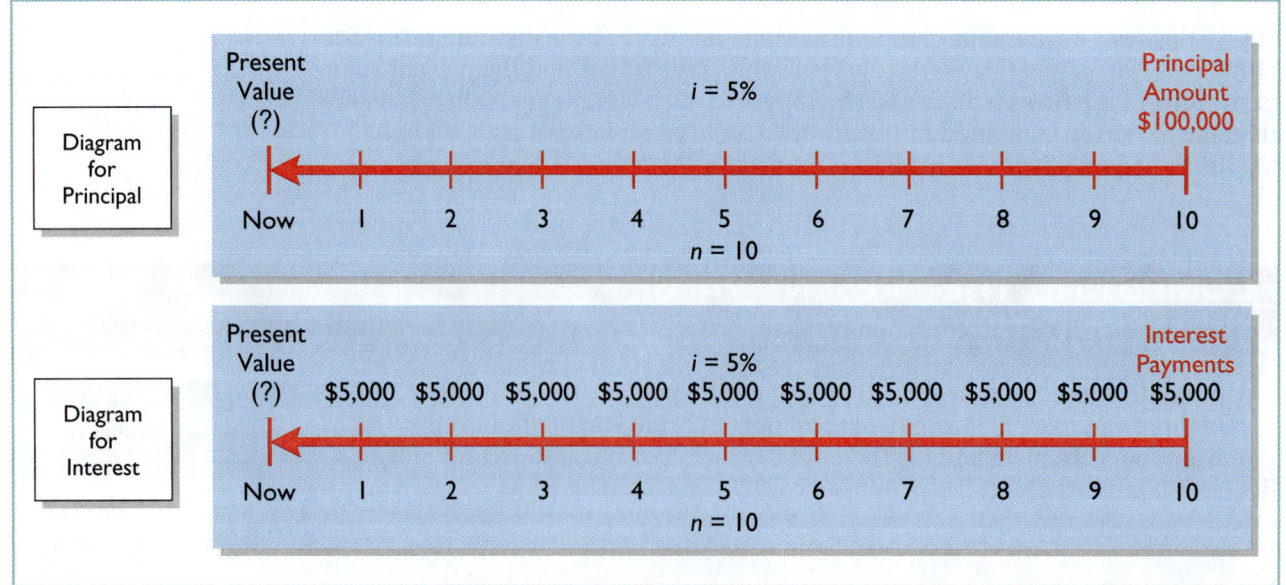

Illustration C-13 shows the computation of the present value of these bonds.

Illustration C-13
Present value of principal and interest—face value

10% Contractual Rate—10% Discount Rate	
Present value of principal to be received at maturity	
$100,000 × PV of 1 due in 10 periods at 5%	
$100,000 × .61391 (Table 1)	$ 61,391
Present value of interest to be received periodically over the term of the bonds	
$5,000 × PV of 1 due periodically for 10 periods at 5%	
$5,000 × 7.72173 (Table 2)	38,609*
Present value of bonds	**$100,000**

*Rounded

Now assume that the investor's required rate of return is 12%, not 10%. The future amounts are again $100,000 and $5,000, respectively, but now a discount rate of 6% (12% ÷ 2) must be used. The present value of the bonds is $92,639, as computed in Illustration C-14.

Illustration C-14
Present value of principal and interest—discount

10% Contractual Rate—12% Discount Rate	
Present value of principal to be received at maturity	
$100,000 × .55839 (Table 1)	$55,839
Present value of interest to be received periodically over the term of the bonds	
$5,000 × 7.36009 (Table 2)	36,800
Present value of bonds	**$92,639**

Conversely, if the discount rate is 8% and the contractual rate is 10%, the present value of the bonds is $108,111, computed as shown in Illustration C-15.

Illustration C-15
Present value of principal and interest—premium

10% Contractual Rate—8% Discount Rate	
Present value of principal to be received at maturity	
$100,000 × .67556 (Table 1)	$ 67,556
Present value of interest to be received periodically over the term of the bonds	
$5,000 × 8.11090 (Table 2)	40,555
Present value of bonds	**$108,111**

The above discussion relies on present value tables in solving present value problems. Many people use spreadsheets such as Excel or Financial calculators (some even on websites) to compute present values, without the use of tables. Many calculators, especially "financial calculators," have present value (*PV*) functions that allow you to calculate present values by merely inputting the proper amount, discount rate, and periods, and pressing the PV key. Appendix D illustrates how to use a financial calculator in various business situations.

Appendix C Time Value of Money

SUMMARY OF STUDY OBJECTIVES

1. **Distinguish between simple and compound interest.** Simple interest is computed on the principal only, while compound interest is computed on the principal and any interest earned that has not been withdrawn.

2. **Identify the variables fundamental to solving present value problems.** The following three variables are fundamental to solving present value problems: (1) the future amount, (2) the number of periods, and (3) the interest rate (the discount rate).

3. **Solve for present value of a single amount.** Prepare a time diagram of the problem. Identify the future amount, the number of discounting periods, and the discount (interest) rate. Using the present value of a single amount table, multiply the future amount by the present value factor specified at the intersection of the number of periods and the discount rate.

4. **Solve for present value of an annuity.** Prepare a time diagram of the problem. Identify the future annuity payments, the number of discounting periods, and the discount (interest) rate. Using the present value of an annuity of 1 table, multiply the amount of the annuity payments by the present value factor specified at the intersection of the number of periods and the interest rate.

5. **Compute the present value of notes and bonds.** To determine the present value of the principal amount: Multiply the principal amount (a single future amount) by the present value factor (from the present value of 1 table) intersecting at the number of periods (number of interest payments) and the discount rate.

   To determine the present value of the series of interest payments: Multiply the amount of the interest payment by the present value factor (from the present value of an annuity of 1 table) intersecting at the number of periods (number of interest payments) and the discount rate. Add the present value of the principal amount to the present value of the interest payments to arrive at the present value of the note or bond.

GLOSSARY

Annuity A series of equal dollar amounts to be paid or received periodically. (p. C5).

Compound interest The interest computed on the principal and any interest earned that has not been paid or withdrawn. (p. C2)

Discounting the future amount(s) The process of determining present value. (p. C3).

Interest Payment for the use of another's money. (p. C1).

Present value The value now of a given amount to be paid or received in the future assuming compound interest. (p. C3).

Present value of an annuity The value now of a series of future receipts or payments, discounted assuming compound interest. (p. C5).

Principal The amount borrowed or invested. (p. C1).

Simple interest The interest computed on the principal only. (p. C1).

BRIEF EXERCISES

Use tables to solve exercises.

Use present value tables.

BEC-1 For each of the following cases, indicate (a) to what interest rate columns, and (b) to what number of periods you would refer in looking up the discount rate.

1. In Table 1 (present value of 1):

	Annual Rate	Number of Years Involved	Compounding Per Year
(a)	12%	6	Annually
(b)	10%	15	Annually
(c)	8%	12	Semiannually

2. In Table 2 (present value of an annuity of 1):

	Annual Rate	Number of Years Involved	Number of Payments Involved	Frequency of Payments
(a)	8%	20	20	Annually
(b)	10%	5	5	Annually
(c)	12%	4	8	Semiannually

Determine present values.

BEC-2 (a) What is the present value of $30,000 due 8 periods from now, discounted at 8%?
(b) What is the present value of $30,000 to be received at the end of each of 6 periods, discounted at 9%?

BEC-3 Ramirez Company is considering an investment that will return a lump sum of $600,000 5 years from now. What amount should Ramirez Company pay for this investment in order to earn a 10% return?

Compute the present value of a single-sum investment.

BEC-4 LaRussa Company earns 9% on an investment that will return $700,000 8 years from now. What is the amount LaRussa should invest now in order to earn this rate of return?

Compute the present value of a single-sum investment.

BEC-5 Polley Company sold a 5-year, zero-interest-bearing $36,000 note receivable to Valley Inc. Valley wishes to earn 10% over the remaining 4 years of the note. How much cash will Polley receive upon sale of the note?

Compute the present value of a single-sum zero-interest-bearing note.

BEC-6 Marichal Company issues a 3-year, zero-interest-bearing $60,000 note. The interest rate used to discount the zero-interest-bearing note is 8%. What are the cash proceeds that Marichal Company should receive?

Compute the present value of a single-sum zero-interest-bearing note.

BEC-7 Colaw Company is considering investing in an annuity contract that will return $40,000 annually at the end of each year for 15 years. What amount should Colaw Company pay for this investment if it earns a 6% return?

Compute the present value of an annuity investment.

BEC-8 Sauder Enterprises earns 11% on an investment that pays back $100,000 at the end of each of the next 4 years. What is the amount Sauder Enterprises invested to earn the 11% rate of return?

Compute the present value of an annuity investment.

BEC-9 Chicago Railroad Co. is about to issue $200,000 of 10-year bonds paying a 10% interest rate, with interest payable semiannually. The discount rate for such securities is 8%. How much can Chicago expect to receive for the sale of these bonds?

Compute the present value of bonds.

BEC-10 Assume the same information as in BEC-9 except that the discount rate is 10% instead of 8%. In this case, how much can Chicago expect to receive from the sale of these bonds?

Compute the present value of bonds.

BEC-11 Berghaus Company receives a $75,000, 6-year note bearing interest of 8% (paid annually) from a customer at a time when the discount rate is 9%. What is the present value of the note received by Berghaus Company?

Compute the present value of a note.

BEC-12 Troutman Enterprises issued 8%, 8-year, $1,000,000 par value bonds that pay interest semiannually on October 1 and April 1. The bonds are dated April 1, 2010, and are issued on that date. The discount rate of interest for such bonds on April 1, 2010, is 10%. What cash proceeds did Troutman receive from issuance of the bonds?

Compute the present value of bonds.

BEC-13 Ricky Cleland owns a garage and is contemplating purchasing a tire retreading machine for $16,280. After estimating costs and revenues, Ricky projects a net cash flow from the retreading machine of $2,800 annually for 8 years. Ricky hopes to earn a return of 11% on such investments. What is the present value of the retreading operation? Should Ricky Cleland purchase the retreading machine?

Compute the value of a machine for purposes of making a purchase decision.

BEC-14 Martinez Company issues a 10%, 6-year mortgage note on January 1, 2010, to obtain financing for new equipment. Land is used as collateral for the note. The terms provide for semiannual installment payments of $78,978. What were the cash proceeds received from the issuance of the note?

Compute the present value of a note.

BEC-15 Durler Company is considering purchasing equipment. The equipment will produce the following cash flows: Year 1, $30,000; Year 2, $40,000; Year 3, $60,000. Durler requires a minimum rate of return of 12%. What is the maximum price Durler should pay for this equipment?

Compute the maximum price to pay for a machine.

BEC-16 If Carla Garcia invests $2,745 now, she will receive $10,000 at the end of 15 years. What annual rate of interest will Carla earn on her investment? (*Hint:* Use Table 1.)

Compute the interest rate on a single sum.

BEC-17 Sara Altom has been offered the opportunity of investing $51,316 now. The investment will earn 10% per year and at the end of that time will return Sara $100,000. How many years must Sara wait to receive $100,000? (*Hint:* Use Table 1.)

Compute the number of periods of a single sum.

BEC-18 Stacy Dains purchased an investment for $11,469.92. From this investment, she will receive $1,000 annually for the next 20 years, starting one year from now. What rate of interest will Stacy's investment be earning for her? (*Hint:* Use Table 2.)

Compute the interest rate on an annuity.

BEC-19 Diana Rossi invests $8,559.48 now for a series of $1,000 annual returns, beginning one year from now. Diana will earn a return of 8% on the initial investment. How many annual payments of $1,000 will Diana receive? (*Hint:* Use Table 2.)

Compute the number of periods of an annuity.

Appendix C Time Value of Money

Compute the amount to be invested.

BEC-20 Minitori Company needs $10,000 on January 1, 2013. It is starting a fund on January 1, 2010.

Instructions
Compute the amount that must be invested in the fund on January 1, 2010, to produce a $10,000 balance on January 1, 2013 if.

(a) The fund earns 8% per year compounded annually.
(b) The fund earns 8% per year compounded semiannually.
(c) The fund earns 12% per year compounded annually.
(d) The fund earns 12% per year compounded semiannually.

Compute the amount to be invested.

BEC-21 Venuchi Company needs $10,000 on January 1, 2015. It is starting a fund to produce that amount.

Instructions
Compute the amount that must be invested in the fund to produce a $10,000 balance on January 1, 2015, if:

(a) The initial investment is made January 1, 2010, and the fund earns 6% per year.
(b) The initial investment is made January 1, 2012, and the fund earns 6% per year.
(c) The initial investment is made January 1, 2010, and the fund earns 10% per year.
(d) The initial investment is made January 1, 2012, and the fund earns 10% per year.

Select the better payment option.

BEC-22 Letterman Corporation is buying new equipment. It can pay $39,500 today (option 1), or $10,000 today and 5 yearly payments of $8,000 each, starting in one year (option 2).

Instructions
Which option should Letterman select? (Assume a discount rate of 10%.)

Compute the cost of an investment, amount received, and rate of return.

BEC-23 Carmen Corporation is considering several investments.

Instructions
(a) One investment returns $10,000 per year for 5 years and provides a return of 10%. What is the cost of this investment?
(b) Another investment costs $50,000 and returns a certain amount per year for 10 years, providing an 8% return. What amount is received each year?
(c) A third investment costs $70,000 and returns $11,971 each year for 15 years. What is the rate of return on this investment?

Select the best payment option.

BEC-24 You are the beneficiary of a trust fund. The fund gives you the option of receiving $5,000 per year for 10 years, $9,000 per year for 5 years, or $30,000 today.

Instructions
If the desired rate of return is 8%, which option should you select?

Compute the semiannual car payment.

BEC-25 You are purchasing a car for $24,000, and you obtain financing as follows: $2,400 down payment, 12% interest, semiannual payments over 5 years.

Instructions
Compute the payment you will make every 6 months

Compute the present value of bonds.

BEC-26 Contreras Corporation is considering purchasing bonds of Jose Company as an investment. The bonds have a face value of $40,000 with a 10% interest rate. The bonds mature in 4 years and pay interest semiannually.

Instructions
(a) What is the most Contreras should pay for the bonds if it desires a 12% return?
(b) What is the most Contreras should pay for the bonds if it desires an 8% return?

Compute the present value of bonds.

BEC-27 Garcia Corporation is considering purchasing bonds of Fred Company as an investment. The bonds have a face value of $90,000 with a 9% interest rate. The bonds mature in 6 years and pay interest semiannually.

Instructions
(a) What is the most Garcia should pay for the bonds if it desires a 10% return?
(b) What is the most Garcia should pay for the bonds if it desires an 8% return?

Appendix D

Using Financial Calculators

STUDY OBJECTIVE

After studying this appendix, you should be able to:

1 Use a financial calculator to solve time value of money problems.

Business professionals, once they have mastered the underlying concepts in Appendix C, often use a financial (business) calculator to solve time value of money problems. In many cases, they must use calculators if interest rates or time periods do not correspond with the information provided in the compound interest tables.

To use financial calculators, you enter the time value of money variables into the calculator. Illustration D-1 shows the five most common keys used to solve time value of money problems.[1]

STUDY OBJECTIVE 1
Use a financial calculator to solve time value of money problems.

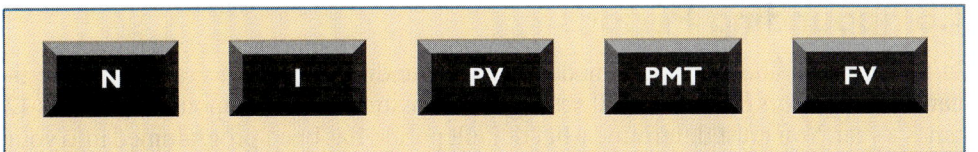

Illustration D-1
Financial calculator keys

where

N = number of periods

I = interest rate per period (some calculators use I/YR or i)

PV = present value (occurs at the beginning of the first period)

PMT = payment (all payments are equal, and none are skipped)

FV = future value (occurs at the end of the last period)

In solving time value of money problems in this appendix, you will generally be given three of four variables and will have to solve for the remaining variable. The fifth key (the key not used) is given a value of zero to ensure that this variable is not used in the computation.

PRESENT VALUE OF A SINGLE SUM

To illustrate how to solve a present value problem using a financial calculator, assume that you want to know the present value of $84,253 to be received in five years, discounted at 11% compounded annually. Illustration D-2 pictures this problem.

---

[1] On many calculators, these keys are actual buttons on the face of the calculator; on others they appear on the display after the user accesses a present value menu.

Illustration D-2
Calculator solution for present value of a single sum

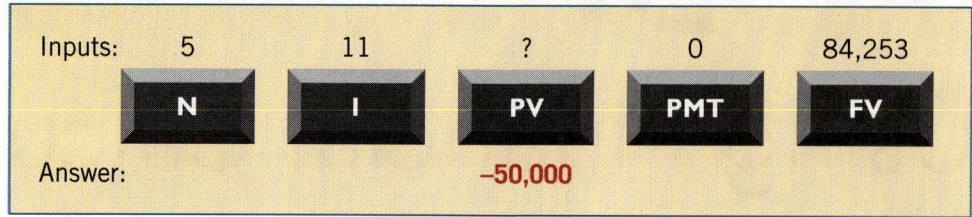

The diagram shows you the information (inputs) to enter into the calculator: N = 5, I = 11, PMT = 0, and FV = 84,253. You then press PV for the answer: −$50,000. As indicated, the PMT key was given a value of zero because a series of payments did not occur in this problem.

Plus and Minus

The use of plus and minus signs in time value of money problems with a financial calculator can be confusing. Most financial calculators are programmed so that the positive and negative cash flows in any problem offset each other. In the present value problem above, we identified the $84,253 future value initial investment as a positive (inflow); the answer −$50,000 was shown as a negative amount, reflecting a cash outflow. If the 84,253 were entered as a negative, then the final answer would have been reported as a positive 50,000.

Hopefully, the sign convention will not cause confusion. If you understand what is required in a problem, you should be able to interpret a positive or negative amount in determining the solution to a problem.

Compounding Periods

In the problem above, we assumed that compounding occurs once a year. Some financial calculators have a default setting, which assumes that compounding occurs 12 times a year. You must determine what default period has been programmed into your calculator and change it as necessary to arrive at the proper compounding period.

Rounding

Most financial calculators store and calculate using 12 decimal places. As a result, because compound interest tables generally have factors only up to 5 decimal places, a slight difference in the final answer can result. In most time value of money problems, the final answer will not include more than two decimal points.

PRESENT VALUE OF AN ANNUITY

To illustrate how to solve a present value of an annuity problem using a financial calculator, assume that you are asked to determine the present value of rental receipts of $6,000 each to be received at the end of each of the next five years, when discounted at 12%, as pictured in Illustration D-3.

Illustration D-3
Calculator solution for present value of an annuity

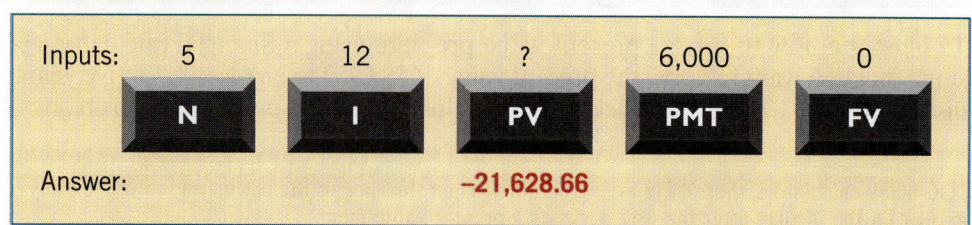

In this case, you enter N = 5, I = 12, PMT = 6,000, FV = 0, and then press PV to arrive at the answer of $21,628.66.

USEFUL APPLICATIONS OF THE FINANCIAL CALCULATOR

With a financial calculator you can solve for any interest rate or for any number of periods in a time value of money problem. Here are some examples of these applications.

Auto Loan

Assume you are financing a car with a three-year loan. The loan has a 9.5% nominal annual interest rate, compounded monthly. The price of the car is $6,000, and you want to determine the monthly payments, assuming that the payments start one month after the purchase. This problem is pictured in Illustration D-4.

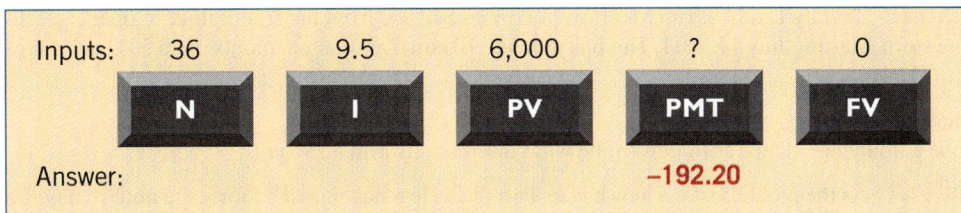

Illustration D-4
Calculator solution for auto loan payments

To solve this problem, you enter N = 36 (12 × 3), I = 9.5, PV = 6,000, FV = 0, and then press PMT. You will find that the monthly payments will be $192.20. Note that the payment key is usually programmed for 12 payments per year. Thus, you must change the default (compounding period) if the payments are other than monthly.

Mortgage Loan Amount

Let's say you are evaluating financing options for a loan on a house. You decide that the maximum mortgage payment you can afford is $700 per month. The annual interest rate is 8.4%. If you get a mortgage that requires you to make monthly payments over a 15-year period, what is the maximum purchase price you can afford? Illustration D-5 depicts this problem.

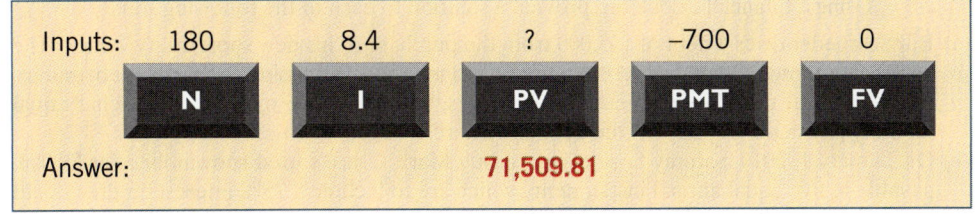

Illustration D-5
Calculator solution for mortgage amount

You enter N = 180 (12 × 15 years), I = 8.4, PMT = −700, FV = 0, and press PV. You find a present value of $71,509.81—the maximum house price you can afford, given that you want to keep your mortgage payments at $700. Note that by changing any of the variables, you can quickly conduct "what-if" analyses for different situations.

Appendix D Using Financial Calculators

SUMMARY OF LEARNING OBJECTIVE

1. **Use a financial calculator to solve time value of money problems.** Financial calculators can be used to solve the same and additional problems as those solved with time value of money tables. One enters into the financial calculator the amounts for all but one of the unknown elements of a time value of money problem (periods, interest rate, payments, future or present value). Particularly useful situations involve interest rates and compounding periods not presented in the tables.

BRIEF EXERCISES

Determine interest rate.

BED-1 Reba McEntire wishes to invest $19,000 on July 1, 2010, and have it accumulate to $49,000 by July 1, 2020.

Instructions
Use a financial calculator to determine at what exact annual rate of interest Reba must invest the $19,000.

Determine interest rate.

BED-2 On July 17, 2010, Tim McGraw borrowed $42,000 from his grandfather to open a clothing store. Starting July 17, 2011, Tim has to make 10 equal annual payments of $6,500 each to repay the loan.

Instructions
Use a financial calculator to determine what interest rate Tim is paying.

Determine interest rate.

BED-3 As the purchaser of a new house, Patty Loveless has signed a mortgage note to pay the Memphis National Bank and Trust Co. $14,000 every 6 months for 20 years, at the end of which time she will own the house. At the date the mortgage is signed the purchase price was $198,000, and Loveless made a down payment of $20,000. The first payment will be made 6 months after the date the mortgage is signed.

Instructions
Using a financial calculator, compute the exact rate of interest earned on the mortgage by the bank.

Various time value of money situations.

BED-4 Using a financial calculator, solve for the unknowns in each of the following situations.

(a) On June 1, 2010, Shelley Long purchases lakefront property from her neighbor, Joey Brenner, and agrees to pay the purchase price in seven payments of $16,000 each, the first payment to be payable June 1, 2011. (Assume that interest compounded at an annual rate of 7.35% is implicit in the payments.) What is the purchase price of the property?

(b) On January 1, 2010, Cooke Corporation purchased 200 of the $1,000 face value, 8% coupon, 10-year bonds of Howe Inc. The bonds mature on January 1, 2020, and pay interest annually beginning January 1, 2011. Cooke purchased the bonds to yield 10.65%. How much did Cooke pay for the bonds?

Various time value of money situations.

BED-5 Using a financial calculator, provide a solution to each of the following situations.

(a) Bill Schroeder owes a debt of $35,000 from the purchase of his new sport utility vehicle. The debt bears annual interest of 9.1% compounded monthly. Bill wishes to pay the debt and interest in equal monthly payments over 8 years, beginning one month hence. What equal monthly payments will pay off the debt and interest?

(b) On January 1, 2010, Sammy Sosa offers to buy Mark Grace's used snowmobile for $8,000, payable in five equal annual installments, which are to include 8.25% interest on the unpaid balance and a portion of the principal. If the first payment is to be made on December 31, 2010, how much will each payment be?

Appendix E

Standards of Ethical Conduct for Management Accountants

Management accountants have an obligation to the organizations they serve, their profession, the public, and themselves to maintain the highest standards of ethical conduct. In recognition of this obligation, the **Institute of Management Accountants (IMA)** has published and promoted the following standards of ethical conduct for management accountants.[1]

IMA STATEMENT OF ETHICAL PROFESSIONAL PRACTICE

Members of IMA shall behave ethically. A commitment to ethical professional practice includes: overarching principles that express our values, and standards that guide our conduct.

Principles

IMA's overarching ethical principles include: Honesty, Fairness, Objectivity, and Responsibility. Members shall act in accordance with these principles and shall encourage others within their organizations to adhere to them.

Standards

A member's failure to comply with the following standards may result in disciplinary action.

I. COMPETENCE

Each member has a responsibility to:

1. Maintain an appropriate level of professional expertise by continually developing knowledge and skills.
2. Perform professional duties in accordance with relevant laws, regulations, and technical standards.
3. Provide decision support information and recommendations that are accurate, clear, concise, and timely.
4. Recognize and communicate professional limitations or other constraints that would preclude responsible judgment or successful performance of an activity.

---

[1] Reprinted by permission of the Institute of Management Accountants, *www.imanet.org/pdf/981.pdf*.

II. CONFIDENTIALITY

Each member has a responsibility to:

1. Keep information confidential except when disclosure is authorized or legally required.
2. Inform all relevant parties regarding appropriate use of confidential information. Monitor subordinates' activities to ensure compliance.
3. Refrain from using confidential information for unethical or illegal advantage.

III. INTEGRITY

Each member has a responsibility to:

1. Mitigate actual conflicts of interest. Regularly communicate with business associates to avoid apparent conflicts of interest. Advise all parties of any potential conflicts.
2. Refrain from engaging in any conduct that would prejudice carrying out duties ethically.
3. Abstain from engaging in or supporting any activity that might discredit the profession.

IV. CREDIBILITY

Each member has a responsibility to:

1. Communicate information fairly and objectively.
2. Disclose all relevant information that could reasonably be expected to influence an intended user's understanding of the reports, analyses, or recommendations.
3. Disclose delays or deficiencies in information, timeliness, processing, or internal controls in conformance with organization policy and/or applicable law.

Resolution of Ethical Conflict

In applying the Standards of Ethical Professional Practice, you may encounter problems identifying unethical behavior or resolving an ethical conflict. When faced with ethical issues, you should follow your organization's established policies on the resolution of such conflict. If these policies do not resolve the ethical conflict, you should consider the following courses of action:

1. Discuss the issue with your immediate supervisor except when it appears that the supervisor is involved. In that case, present the issue to the next level. If you cannot achieve a satisfactory resolution, submit the issue to the next management level. If your immediate superior is the chief executive officer or equivalent, the acceptable reviewing authority may be a group such as the audit committee, executive committee, board of directors, board of trustees, or owners. Contact with levels above the immediate superior should be initiated only with your superior's knowledge, assuming he or she is not involved. Communication of such problems to authorities or individuals not employed or engaged by the organization is not considered appropriate, unless you believe there is a clear violation of the law.
2. Clarify relevant ethical issues by initiating a confidential discussion with an IMA Ethics Counselor or other impartial advisor to obtain a better understanding of possible courses of action.
3. Consult your own attorney as to legal obligations and rights concerning the ethical conflict.

PHOTO CREDITS

Chapter 13   Page 569 David Young-Wolf/PhotoEdit Page 576 Brandon Laufenberg/iStockphoto Page 584 Norm Betts/Bloomberg News/Landov LLC

Chapter 14   Page 607 Tim Boyle/Bloomberg News/Landov LLC Page 611 Tomasz Resiak/iStockphoto Page 615 PhotoDisc, Inc./Getty Images Page 617 Arpad Benedek/iStockphoto

Chapter 15   Page 643 Corporation of London/HIP/The Image Works Page 656 Greg Nicholas/iStockphoto Page 660 Corbis Stock Market

Chapter 16   Page 694 Warner Bros./Legendary Pictures/The Kobal Collection/The Picture Desk

Chapter 17   Page 730 Rudi Von Briel/PhotoEdit Page 735 Darren McCollester/Getty Images News and Sport Services Page 749 PhotoDisc, Inc./Getty Images

Chapter 18   Page 791 AFP PHOTO/Nicholas ROBERTS/NewsCom Page 794 iStockphoto Page 794 iStockphoto Page 808 Royalty-Free/Corbis Images Page 814 Martina Misar/iStockphoto

Chapter 19   Page 843 Alamy Images Page 846 Peter Kramer/Getty Images, Inc. Page 860 Octavio Campos/iStockphoto

Chapter 20   Page 887 PhotoDisc, Inc./Getty Images Page 890 iStockphoto Page 905 Marcin Balcerzak/iStockphoto

Chapter 21   Page 929 Kevin Foy/Alamy Page 935 iStockphoto Page 940 Yoshikazu Tsuno/Getty Images, Inc.

Chapter 22   Page 975 Tad Denson/iStockphoto Page 988 Digital Vision/Getty Images Page 991 Yael/Retna

Chapter 23   Page 1017 ©2000 Artville, Inc Page 1020 iStockphoto Page 1034 Popperfoto/Alamy Images

Chapter 24   Page 1061 ©EyeWire Page 1074 Digital Vision/Getty Images, Inc Page 1083 Sandy Jones/iStockphoto

Chapter 25   Page 1109 Luria Digital Productions/Taxi/Getty Images Page 1115 Hywit Dimyadi/iStockphoto Page 1126 PhotoDisc, Inc./Getty Images

Chapter 26   Page 1155 Royalty-Free/Corbis Images Page 1170 Rebecca Ellis/iStockphoto

COMPANY INDEX

A
About.com, 906
Advanced Micro Devices, 575, 931
Alcoa (Aluminum Company of America), 597
Allied Signal, 860
Aluminum Company of America (Alcoa), 597
American Airlines, 846, 982, 992, 1124
American Cancer Society, 570
American Standard, 801
American Van Lines, 1065
America Online (AOL), 695, 697
Anaheim Angels, 703
Anchor Glass Container Corporation, 882
AOL, *see* America Online
AOL Time Warner, Inc., 697
Apple Computer, 808
Aptara Corp., 850
AT&T, 703, 846, 977
Avis, 703

B
Babies "R" Us, 703
BankAmerica, 624
Bank of America, 995
Ben & Jerry's Homemade, Inc., 928–930, 934
Berkshire Hathaway, 615
Beverly Hills Fan Company, 1194
Bill & Melinda Gates Foundation, 570
Boeing Capital Corporation, 847
Boeing Company, 608, 804, 1159
Bristol-Myers Squibb, 816–817

C
Campbell Soup Company, 801, 846, 1154–1156, 1166, 1195
Capital Cities/ABC, Inc., 703
Cargill Inc., 571
Carlin Corporation, 691
Caterpillar Inc., 570, 935, 946
Cendant Corp., 624, 703
Center Ice Consultants, 931
Century 21, 703
Chase, 1125
Chicago Tribune, 1124
Chiquita Brands International, 860, 884
Cisco Systems, 816, 1074
The Coca-Cola Company, 603, 638–639, 690–691, 726, 786, 838, 850, 860, 930–931, 1012–1013, 1156, B1–B2
Coldwell Banker, 703
Compaq Computer, 842–844, 858
Computer Associates International, Inc., 1105
Consolidated Edison, 804
Consumers Packaging Inc., 883
Costco Wholesale Corp., 735
Crane Company, 586

D
Daimler, 850
DaimlerChrysler Corporation, 653
Davison Carecenters Inc., 719
Dell Computer Corp., 704, 843, 844, 846, 847, 849, 853, 859, 946
Delta Airlines, 1124
Denny's, 906
Dick's Sporting Goods, 852
Digital Equipment, 843, 858
The Disney Company, 703, 889
Disneyland, 703
Disney World, 703
Dow Chemical, 931
Duke Energy Co., 977, 1061, 1062, 1065, 1077
Dunkin' Donuts Inc., 906
DuPont, 646, 647, 931

E
Eastman Kodak Company, 732
Enron Corp., 624, 817, 847
ESPN, 703
Ethan Allen, 1162
ExxonMobil Corporation, 582, 889, 930, 931

F
FedEx, 846
Fidelity Investments, 860
FlightServe, 988, 1014
Florida Citrus Company, 812
Ford Motor Company, 568–572, 582, 850, 945, 957, 982, 995, 1077, 1162

G
Ganong Bros. Ltd., 1013
GE, *see* General Electric
General Dynamics, 839
General Electric (GE), 570, 697, 947
General Mills, 789, 930
General Motors (GM), 574, 744, 789, 816, 821, 846, 889–890, 947, 1159, 1162
Gillette Company, 703, 728
Glassmaster Co., 1150–1151
Global Crossing, 847
GM, *see* General Motors
Google, 570, 576, 995
Gulf Oil, 574

H
Hanes Company, 714
Harley-Davidson, 946
Hershey Foods Corp., 608
Hertz Car Rental, 657, 1002
Hewlett-Packard (HP), 843, 846, 849, 947, 1124, 1159
Hilton Hotels Corporation, 860, 977
Honda, 995
Howard Johnson, 703
HP, *see* Hewlett-Packard
H&R Block, 931

I
IBM, 570, 574*n*.2, 593, 847, 889
Ice Rink Events, 931
Imaginarium, 703
Intel, 570, 931, 945

J
J.C. Penney Company, Inc., 735, 792–794, 799, 800, 802–808
Jiffy Lube, 931
Jostens, Inc., 1124

K
Kaiser Permanente, 931
Kellogg Company, 588, 659, 889, 930, 937, 939–945, 982
Kids "R" Us, 703
Kinko's Print Shop, 957
Kmart Stores, 793, 804, 811, 1193–1194
Kohl's Corporation, 735
KPMG, 847
Kraft Foods, 697
Kroger Co., 804

L
Lockheed Martin Corporation, 617
Louis Vuitton, 846
Lucent Technologies, 624, 847

M
McCabe Co., 801
McDonald's Corporation, 570, 608, 655, 775, 1110
McDonnell Douglas, 847
Macy's, 1077
Madison Square Garden, 1024
Marco Chemical Corp., 604–605
Marriott Hotels, 977, 1065
Massachusetts General Hospital, 976
Mayo Clinic, 931
Microsoft Corporation, 582, 730–731, 749, 821, 845, 940, 973
Mighty Ducks, 703
Moody's Investment Service, 691
Morgan Stanley, 707
Motorola, 814, 847

N
NationsBank, 624
Network Computing Devices Inc., 1056–1057
New York Times, 1124
Nike Inc., 577, 608–609, 614, 799, 847, 977
Nissan Motors, 850
Nordstrom, Inc., 826–827
Nortel Networks, 808
North American Van Lines, 577
Northrop Grumman, 905
Northwest Airlines, 992

O
Omnicom, 931
Oracle Corporation, 749

P
PACE Membership Warehouse, 811
Papa John's Pizza, 906
Parlex Corporation, 924–925
PayLess Drug Stores Northwest, 811
PepsiCo Inc., 570, 576, 586, 593, 603, 605, 628, 638–639, 678, 690–691, 715, 726, 768, 786, 793, 822, 837–838, 931, A1–A34
Phillip Morris, 697
Positively-You.com, 1016–1018, 1020
Pratt and Whitney, 859
The Procter & Gamble Company, 577, 703, 728, 814, 852, 1074

Q
Quad Graphics, 889
Quaker Oats, 957
Qualcomm, 574

R
Ramada Inn, 703
Reebok, 577, 584, 977
Royal Dutch/Shell, 931

S
Safeway, 804
Salvation Army, 570
Sanford, 1108–1110
Sara Lee, 850
Sarbanes-Oxley Act (2002), 848
Schering-Plough, 847–848
Siebel Systems, 1084
Smucker's, 945
Southwest Airlines, 976
Superior Industries International, Inc., 1162

T
Taco Bell, 906
Target Corporation, 735, 834

I-1

Company Index

TCBY Yogurt, 906
Tektronix Inc., 617–618
Tiffany & Co., 804
Timberland, 995
Time Warner, Inc., 582, 694–697, 701–703
Toyota, 995
Toys "R" Us, Inc., 703
Toysrus.com, 703
Turner Broadcasting, 697, 701–703

U
U-Haul, 980
Unilever, 1125
Union Pacific Resources Group Inc., 1167
United Airlines, 976, 1124, 1126, 1152

United States Steel Corp., 982
USAir, 653
USX Corp., 653, 930

V
Van Meter Industrial, Inc., 606–607

W
Wall Street Journal, 576
Wal-Mart Stores, Inc., 570, 647, 735, 804, 834, 860, 1125
Walt Disney Company, 621, 931
Warner Brothers, 931, 957
Welch Company, 860

Western States Fire Apparatus, Inc., 886–889, 898
Weyerhaeuser Co., 812
Whirlpool, 801
Willard & Shullman Group Ltd., 1020
WorldCom, Inc., 624, 737, 817, 847

X
Xerox, 847
XM Satellite Radio Holdings, 1029

Y
Yahoo! Inc., 731, 749
Young & Rubicam, 931

SUBJECT INDEX

A

ABC, *see* Activity-based costing
Absorption costing, 998
Accounts payable, 756
Accounts receivable, 755
Accounting:
  cost, 888–890
  financial, 845
  managerial, *see* Managerial accounting
  responsibility, *see* Responsibility accounting
Accounting information, in budgeting process, 1018–1019
Acid-test ratio, 801–802
Activity base, 897, 898
Activity-based costing (ABC), 859–860, 948–949, 953–955
Activity index (CVP), 976
Adjustable interest rates, 655
Adjusting entries, prior period, 618
Affiliated company, 702
Agents, of corporations, 571
Alternative accounting methods, 816
American Stock Exchange, 577
Amortization:
  effective-interest method, 669–672
  straight-line, 673–675
Annual rate of return, 1167–1168
Annual reports:
  of The Coca-Cola Company, B1–B2
  of PepsiCo, Inc., A1–A34
Annuities, present value of, 665–666, C5–C7, D2–D3
Articles of incorporation, 573
Assets, capital leases as, 657–658
Asset turnover ratio, 804
Authorized stock, 575
Available-for-sale securities, 705, 707
Average collection period, 802

B

Balanced scorecard, 860, 1124–1126
Balanced Scorecard Institute, 1151
Balance sheet:
  budget, 1034–1035
  horizontal analysis of, 794–795
  investments on, 708–710
  merchandising and manufacturing costs on, 855–856
  stockholders' equity section of, 587–589
  unpaid notes payable on, 655
  vertical analysis of, 797, 798
Bankruptcy law, 643
Batch jobs, 888, 889
Bearer bonds, 646
Best-efforts contracts, 576*n*.3
Bonds, 644–654
  converting into common stock, 653–654
  discount/premium on, 649–650
  issued for credit, 745
  issuing, 646–652
  market value of, 648
  present value of, 663–668, C7–C9
  recording transactions with, 698–699
  redeeming, 653
  trading, 646–647
  types of, 645–646
Bonds payable, 756, 764
Bond amortization, 669–672
  effective interest method, 669–672
  straight-line, 673–675
Bond indentures, 646
Bond interest expense, 651
Bond issues, 646–652
  at a discount, 650–651
  at face value, 649
  at a premium, 651–652
  procedures for, 646

Book (carrying) value, 650
Borick, Steve, 1162
Bowline, Lyle, 1016
Break-even analysis, 986–989
Break-even point, 986
Budgets, 1018
  continuous 12-month, 1019
  flexible, 1065–1072
  standards vs., 1111
  static, 1063–1065
Budgetary control, 1062–1072
  flexible budgets, 1065–1072
  static budgets, 1063–1065
Budgetary planning, 1018–1040
  accounting information in, 1018–1019
  budget balance sheet, 1034–1035
  budget income statement, 1029–1031
  cash budget, 1031–1034
  direct labor budget, 1027–1028
  direct materials budget, 1025–1027
  financial budgets, 1031–1036
  foundation for, 1019
  and human behavior, 1020–1021
  length of budget period, 1019
  and long-range planning, 1021–1022
  manufacturing overhead budget, 1028–1029
  master budget, 1022–1023
  for merchandisers, 1036–1037
  in non-manufacturing companies, 1036–1037
  for not-for-profit organizations, 1037
  personal, 1038
  process for, 1020
  production budget, 1024–1025
  sales and administrative expense budget, 1029
  sales budget, 1023–1024
  for service enterprises, 1037
Budgetary slack, 1021
Budget balance sheet, 1034–1035
Budget committee, 1020
Budget income statement, 1029–1031
Budget period, length of, 1019
Budget reports, 1062, 1065, 1070–1072
Buffett, Warren, 615, 790–792
Buildings, 755
Burden, 850
Business opportunities, 906
By-laws of corporations, 573

C

Callable bonds, 646
Capital, corporate acquisition of, 571
Capital budgeting, 1166–1175
  annual rate of return, 1167–1168
  cash payback, 1168–1169
  discounted cash flow, 1170–1175
  evaluation process in, 1167
Capital leases, 657–658
Capital stock, 587
Carrying value, *see* Book value
Carrying (book) value method, 654
Cash:
  net change in, 745–746
  for statement of cash flows, 757
Cash budget, 1031–1034
Cash dividends, 608–612
Cash flows. *See also* Statement of cash flows
  ability to generate, 732
  classification of, 733–734
  free, 748–749
Cash management, 1034
Cash payback, 1168–1169
Cash payments, 760–762
Cash receipts, 760
CEO (chief executive officer), 572
Changes in accounting principle, 814
Channel stuffing, 816–817
Charter, corporate, 573

Chief executive officer (CEO), 572
Classified balance sheet, investments on, 710–711
Closely held corporations, 570. *See also* Privately held corporations
Code of ethics, 624, 848
Collaboration, 1074
Common-size analysis, 797. *See also* Vertical analysis
Common stock, 574, 579–582
  allocating cash dividends to, 610–611
  converting bonds into, 653–654
  earnings per share for, 622
  no-par value, 580
  par value, 579–580
  for services or noncash assets, 580–581
  for statement of cash flows, 756, 764
Competitive environment, 858
Components, make-or-buy decisions for, 1159–1160
Compound interest, C2, D2
Comprehensive income, 710, 814–815
Consolidated financial statements, 702–703
Continuous 12-month budgets, 1019
Contra accounts:
  for bonds at a discount, 650
  for stockholders' equity, 583
Contractual interest rate, 646, 649
Contributed capital, 587. *See also* Paid-in capital
Contribution margin per unit (CVP analysis), 985, 987, 990, 1166
Contribution margin ratio (CVP analysis), 985–987, 990
Control accounts, 893
Controllability of items, 1071
Controllable margin, 1079, 1082
Controllable revenues/costs, 1074
Controllable variance (overhead), 1121, 1133–1134
Controllers, 572
Controlling interest, 702
Convertible bonds, 646, 653–654
Corporate capital, 577–578
Corporations, 570–579
  characteristics of, 571–573
  corporate capital, 577–578
  forming, 573–574
  ownership rights of stockholders, 574–575
  reasons for investing, 696–697
  stock issues, 575–577. *See also* Stock
Cost(s):
  controllable vs. noncontrollable, 1074
  factory labor, 892, 895–896
  fixed, *see* Fixed costs
  in incremental analysis, 1158
  inventoriable, 851
  labor, 850, 892, 895–896, 932–934
  in managerial accounting, 849
  manufacturing, *see* Manufacturing costs
  material, 932–934
  materials, 850, 892, 894–895
  mixed, 980–982
  in noncash transactions, 581
  non-recurring, 814
  opportunity, 1160–1161
  organization, 574
  period, 851–852
  product, 850–852
  standard, *see* Standard costs
  unit production, 942
  variable, 977, 1028, 1068
Cost accounting systems, 888–890
Cost behavior analysis, 976–983
Cost centers, 1077, 1078
Cost drivers, 948
Cost flows, in process vs. job order cost systems, 932
Cost method:
  for stock investments, 700
  for treasury stock, 582–583

I-3

I-4 Subject Index

Cost of goods manufactured, 852–854
Cost of goods manufactured schedule, 854
Cost of goods purchased, 852
Cost of goods sold, 901
Cost reconciliation schedule, 943
Cost-volume-profit (CVP) analysis, 983–997
   break-even analysis, 986–989
   and changes in business environment, 992–993
   CVP income statement, 984–986, 993–994
   margin of safety, 991
   target net income, 989–991
Cost-volume-profit (CVP) graph, 988–991
Cost-volume-profit (CVP) relationships, 976–983
   cost behavior analysis, 976–983
   fixed costs, 977–978
   identifying cost types in, 982–983
   mixed costs, 980–982
   relevant range in, 978–980
   variable costs, 977
Coupon bonds, 646
Covenants, 660
Cumulative dividends, 587
Current assets, 740–742
Current liabilities:
   bond interest payable, 649
   leases, 658
   noncash, 740–743
Current ratio, 800–801
Cutoff rate, 1168
CVP analysis, *see* Cost-volume-profit analysis
CVP graph, *see* Cost-volume-profit graph
CVP income statement, 984–986, 993–994
CVP relationships, *see* Cost-volume-profit relationships

D

Days in inventory, 803
Debenture bonds, 646
Debt covenants, 660
Debt investments, 698–699
Debtors' prison, 642–643
Debt to total assets ratio, 659, 807–808
Decentralized companies, 1073
Decision making, *see* Management decision-making
Declaration date (cash dividends), 609
Depreciation:
   in direct method, 762
   for statement of cash flows, 756
Depreciation expense, 739–740
Differential analysis, 1167. *See also* Incremental analysis
Direct fixed costs, 1078–1079
Direct labor, 850
Direct labor budget, 1027–1028
Direct labor price standard, 1113
Direct labor quantity, 1113
Direct labor variances, 1119–1121
Direct materials, 850
Direct materials budget, 1025–1027
Direct materials price standard, 1112–1113
Direct materials quantity standard, 1113–1114
Direct materials variances, 1116–1119
Direct method (statement of cash flows), 737, 758–764
   investing and financing activities, 763–764
   net change in cash, 764
   operating activities, 759–763
Discontinued operations, 811–812
Discounts, bond, 649–651, 669–671, 673–674
Discounted cash flow method, 1170–1175
Discounting, time value of money and, C7
Discount rate, 1171
Disposal of treasury stock, 584–585
Dividends, 608–614
   ability to pay, 733
   cash, 608–612
   on preferred stock, 586–587
   stock, 612–614
   from stock investments, 700, 702
Dividends in arrears, 587
Double taxation, 573

E

Earnings, quality of, 815–817
Earnings per share (EPS), 622, 806

Earnings statement, *see* Income statement
Earning power, 811
Education, worth of, 1176
Effective-interest amortization, 669–672
Envelope budgeting, 1106
EPS, *see* Earnings per share
Equal Employment Opportunity Act, 1110
Equipment:
   retaining vs. replacing, 1163–1164
   for statement of cash flows, 755–756, 763
Equity method (stock investments), 701
Equivalent units, 936–939, 941
Ethics issues:
   artificial increasing cash flow, 737
   available-for-sale securities, 707
   changes in accounting principle, 814
   comparing cash from operations to net income, 733
   discounted future cash flows, 1171
   documentation control, 895
   expectations for EPS, 622
   lease accounting, 658
   length of workday, 905
   in managerial accounting, 847–849
   manipulating current ratio/cash balance, 800
   meeting standards, 1112
   minimizing debt reported, 646
   non-owner managers, 572
   overstating market value, 707
   standards of conduct for management accountants, E1–E2
   telecommunications to remote areas, 858
   temporary employees, 859
   treasury stock purchase, 583
   unrealistic budgets, 1021
Eurich, Beecher, 929
Evaluation of companies, 748–750. *See also* Financial statement analysis
Extraordinary items, 712–814

F

Face value of bonds, 646, 649, 664–665
Factory labor costs, 892
Factory overhead, 850
Fair Labor Standards Act, 1110
Fair value, 704–705
FIFO (first-in, first-out), 816
Financial accounting, managerial accounting vs., 845
Financial budgets, 1022, 1031–1036
Financial calculators, D1–D3
Financial statement analysis, 792–818
   changes in accounting principle, 814
   comprehensive income, 814–815
   earning power, 811
   horizontal, 793–797
   irregular items, 811–815
   need for, 792–793
   quality of earnings, 815–817
   ratio, 799–809
   vertical, 797–799
Financial statements. *See also individual statements*
   consolidated, 702–703
   investments on, 704–712
   long-term liabilities on, 658–660
   manufacturing costs in, 852–857
   monthly, 893
   stockholders' equity on, 587–589, 620–623
Financing activities, 733–734, 744–745, 763–764
Finished goods inventory, 900–901
First-in, first-out (FIFO), 816
Fixed costs:
   in CVP, 977–978
   in flexible budget, 1068
   in manufacturing overhead budget, 1028
   for profit centers, 1078–1079
   static budget reports for, 1065
Fixed interest rates, 655
Flexible budgets, 1065–1072
   case study of, 1068–1070
   developing, 1067–1068
   and management by exception, 1071–1072
   uses of, 1065–1067
Flexible budget reports, 1070–1072
Ford, Henry, 568–569

For-profit corporations, 570
Franchises, 906
Fraud, 847
Free cash flow, 748–749
Full costing, 998
Full disclosure principle, 734

G

GAAP, *see* Generally accepted accounting principles
Gains, 705, 709–710, 812
Generally accepted accounting principles (GAAP), 815, 816
Governmental budgets, 1037
Graham, Benjamin, 791

H

Held-to-maturity securities, 705
High-low method (CVP), 980–982
Horizontal analysis, 793–797
Human behavior:
   budgetary planning and, 1020–1021
   and performance evaluation, 1083–1084
Hurdle rate, 1168
Hybrid vehicles, 995

I

Ideal standards, 1112
IMA, *see* Institute of Management Accountants
IMA Statement of Ethical Professional Practice, 848
Improper recognition, 816–817
Inc. Magazine, 906
Incentives, creating, 847–848
Income statement:
   budget, 1029–1031
   CVP, 984–986, 993–994
   horizontal analysis of, 795–796
   merchandising and manufacturing costs in, 852–855
   stockholders' equity on, 621–623
   variances on, 1123
   vertical analysis of, 797–790
Income taxes:
   on corporation income statements, 621–622
   for corporations, 573
Income taxes payable, 742, 756
Incremental analysis, 1156–1166
   for accepting an order at a special price, 1158–1159
   for allocating limited resources, 1165–1166
   for eliminating unprofitable segments, 1164–1165
   for making vs. buying, 1159–1162
   management decision-making process in, 1156–1158
   for retaining vs. replacing equipment, 1163–1164
   for selling vs. processing further, 1162–1163
   types of decisions involving, 1158
Indirect fixed costs, 1079
Indirect labor, 850
Indirect manufacturing costs, 850
Indirect materials, 850
Indirect method (statement of cash flows), 737–748
   investing and financing activities, 744–745
   net change in cash, 745–747
   operating activities, 739–744
   worksheet for, 752–757
Industry averages (norms), 793
Institute of Management Accountants (IMA), 848, 883, 925
Intercompany comparisons, 793
Interest, C1–C2
   on bonds, 645, 698
   compound, C2
   simple, C1–C2
Interest coverage, 808
Interest payments (annuities), 665–666
Interest rates:
   for bonds, 646, 649
   for mortgages, 655
   shopping for, 656
Internal rate of return (IRR) method, 1173–1174
Intracompany comparisons, 793
Inventoriable costs, 851
Inventory(-ies):
   for merchandising companies, 855–856
   for statement of cash flows, 755

Subject Index I-5

Inventory turnover, 802–803
Investing activities:
  cash flows from, 733, 734
  direct method for, 763–764
  indirect method for, 744–745
  noncash, 734
Investment centers, 1077, 1080–1083
Investment portfolio, 699
Investments, 696–712
  debt investments, 698–699
  reasons for making, 696–697
  short-term, 708–709
  stock investments, 699–704
  valuing and reporting, 704–712
Irregular items, 811–815
IRR method, *see* Internal rate of return method

J

JIT inventory, *see* Just-in-time inventory
JIT processing, *see* Just-in-time processing
Job cost data, reporting, 903–905
Job cost sheet, 893, 894
Job order cost flow, 890–903
  accumulating manufacturing costs, 890–893
  assigning costs to cost of goods sold, 901
  assigning costs to finished goods, 900–901
  assigning manufacturing costs to work in process, 893–900
Job order costing, 888–908
  cost accounting systems, 888–890
  job order cost flow, 890–903
  reporting job cost data, 903–905
Job order cost systems, 888–889, 931
  process cost systems vs., 931–933
  standard cost accounting system with, 1130–1132
Johnson, Matthew, 808
Journalizing:
  for bonds, 647
  with standard cost accounting system, 1130–1132
Just-in-time (JIT) inventory, 859
Just-in-time (JIT) processing, 946–947

L

Labor costs, 850, 892, 895–896, 932–934
Labor variances:
  direct, 1119–1121
  price, 1120–1121
  quantity, 1119–1121
  total, 1119
Land, 755, 763
Last-in, first-out (LIFO), 816
Leases, 656–658
Ledgers, 1132. *See also* Subsidiary ledgers
Leveraging, 805
Liabilities, long-term, *see* Long-term liabilities
Life of a corporation, 571–572
LIFO (last-in, first-out), 816
Limited liability, 571
Liquidating dividends, 608
Liquidation of preferred stocks, 587
Liquidity, short-term creditor interest in, 792
Liquidity ratios, 800–803
Long-range planning, budgetary planning and, 1021–1022
Long-term debt, C7–C9
Long-term investments, 709
Long-term liabilities, 644–662
  bonds, 644–654
  on financial statements, 658–660
  leases, 656–658
  notes payable, long-term, 654–656
Losses:
  from discontinued operations, 812
  realized, 709–710
  on sale of equipment, 740
  unrealized, 705, 709–710

M

Machine time used, 934
Make-or-buy decisions, 1159–1160
Management accountants, ethical conduct for, E1–E2
Management accounting, *see* Managerial accounting
Management by exception, 1071–1072

Management decision-making:
  for accepting an order at a special price, 1158–1159
  for allocating limited resources, 1165–1166
  for eliminating unprofitable segments, 1164–1165
  financial and nonfinancial information in, 1157
  incremental analysis for, 1156–1158
  for making vs. buying, 1159–1162
  process for, 1156–1158
  for retaining vs. replacing equipment, 1163–1164
  for selling vs. processing further, 1162–1163
Management of corporations, 572
Managers, functions of, 846–847
Managerial accounting, 844–864
  activities in, 844
  business ethics in, 847–849
  cost concepts in, 849
  financial accounting vs., 845
  managers' functions in, 846–847
  manufacturing costs, 849–850, 852–857
  practices of, 858–860
  product vs. period costs, 851–852
  service-industry trends, 858
Mann, Bruce, 643
Manufacturing companies, 849, 930–931
Manufacturing costs, 849–850. *See also* Job order cost flow; Process cost system
  accumulating, 890–893
  assigning, to work in process, 893–900
  in financial statements, 852
  in income statement, 852–855
  in job order cost system, 932
  journal entries for, 933–934
  in process cost system, 932–936
Manufacturing overhead, 850, 892–893, 896–899
  under activity-based costing, 953–954
  journal entries for, 933, 934
  process vs. job order cost systems for, 932
  under- or overapplied, 904–905
Manufacturing overhead budget, 1028–1029
Manufacturing overhead variance, 1121–1122
Margin of safety, 991
Margin of safety ratio (CVP), 991
Marketable securities, 708–709
Market interest rate, 649
Market value:
  of bonds, 648
  of stock, 576
Marshall, John, 570
Master budget, 1022–1023
Materials, sell-vs.-processing further decisions for, 1162–1163
Materials costs, 850, 892, 894–895
  journal entries for, 933, 934
  process vs. job order cost systems for, 932
Materials variances:
  direct, 1116–1119
  price, 1118
  quantity, 1118
Materiality, 1071
Maturity date, for bonds, 653
Merchandise purchases budget, 1036–1037
Merchandising companies, 849
  budgetary planning for, 1036–1037
  cost of goods in, 853, 855, 856
Minimum rate of return, 1168
Mixed costs, in CVP, 980–982
Morris, Robert, 643
Mortgages, 655
Mortgage bonds, 645
Motion Picture Association of America, 1083

N

NASDAQ, 577
Net annual cash flow, 1168–1169, 1171–1173
Net cash from operating activities, net income vs., 735
Net change in cash:
  direct method, 764
  indirect method, 745–746
Net income:
  converting from accrual to cash basis, 737, 739–744, 759–763
  net cash from operating activities vs., 735
Net losses, closing entry for, 616–617
Net present value (NPV) method, 1171–1173

New York Stock Exchange (NYSE), 576, 577
Noncash activities, 734
Noncash current assets, changes to, 740–742
Noncash current liabilities, changes to, 740–743
Noncontrollable revenues/costs, 1074
Non-manufacturing companies, budgetary planning for, 1036–1037
Non-recurring charges, 814
No-par value stocks, 577, 580
Normal capacity, 1114
Normal range, *see* Relevant range
Normal standards, 1112
Notes payable:
  long-term, 654–656
  present value of, C7–C9
Not-for-profit corporations/organizations, 570, 1037, 1110
NYSE, *see* New York Stock Exchange

O

Off-balance-sheet financing, 658
Olympic Games, 1034
Operating activities:
  cash flows from, 733, 734
  direct method, 759–763
  indirect method, 733, 735, 739–744
Operating budgets, 1022
Operating leases, 657
Operations costing, 945
Opportunity cost, 1160–1161
Organization costs, 574
Orr, Mike, 1109
Overbilling, 905
Overhead:
  under activity-based costing, 953–954
  journal entries for, 933, 934
  manufacturing, 850, 892–893, 896–899, 904–905
  process vs. job order cost systems for, 932
  standard predetermined, 1114
Overhead variances, 1133–1134
  controllable, 1121, 1133–1134
  manufacturing, 1121–1122
  total, 1121
  volume, 1121, 1134
Over-the-counter stock trades, 577
Ownership rights:
  in corporations, 570, 571
  preemptive, 574
  of stockholders, 574–575

P

Paid-in capital, 578, 587, 608
Paid-in capital in excess of par value, 580
Parent company, 702
Participative budgeting, 1020–1021
Par value, 577, 579–580
Payment date (cash dividends), 610
Payout ratio, 807
P/E (price/earnings) ratio, 622n.3
Performance evaluation, 1083–1084
Period costs, 851–852
Perpetual inventory systems, 888
Pfeiffer, Eckhard, 842, 843
Physical unit flow, 941
Physical units, 941
Practical range, *see* Relevant range
Preferred stock, 586–587, 610–611, 805
Premium:
  on bonds, 649–652, 671–672, 674–675
  on stock, 580
Prepaid expenses (prepayments), for statement of cash flows, 755
Present value, 648
  of an annuity, 665–666, C5–C7, D2–D3
  and bond pricing, 663–668
  of bonds, 648
  of face value, 664–665
  of interest payments (annuities), 665–666
  of leases, 658
  of long-term notes/bonds, C7–C9
  of a single amount, C3–C5
  time periods in computing, 667
  using financial calculator for, D1–D2
  variables in, C3
Present value of 1 factors, C4
Price/earnings (P/E) ratio, 622n.3, 806–807

Price variances:
  labor, 1120–1121
  materials, 1118
Prior period adjustments, 618
Private accounting, *see* Managerial accounting
Privately held corporations, 570–571
Process cost flow, 933
Process cost system, 889–890, 930–951
  and activity-based costing, 948–949
  assigning manufacturing costs, 933–936
  equivalent units, 936–939
  example of, 940–945
  job order cost systems vs., 931–933
  and just-in-time processing, 946–947
  process cost flow, 933
  uses of, 930–931
Products, sell-vs.-processing further decisions for, 1162–1163
Product costs, 850–852
Production budget, 1024–1025
Production cost report, 939, 943–944
Profitability, creditor interest in, 792
Profitability ratios, 803–807
Profit and loss statement, *see* Income statement
Profit centers, 1077–1080
Profit margin, 803–804
Pro forma income, 816
Publicly held corporations, 570
Pull approach to manufacturing, 947
Push approach to manufacturing, 946

Q
Quality of earnings, 815–817
Quantity variances:
  labor, 1119–1121
  materials, 1118
Quick ratio, 801. *See also* Acid-test ratio

R
Ratio analysis, 793, 799–809
  liquidity ratios, 800–803
  profitability ratios, 803–807
  solvency ratios, 807–808
Raw materials, 850
Raw materials costs, 892, 894–895
Realized gain/loss, 709–710
Receivables turnover, 802
Reconciling items, for statement of cash flows, 755–757
Record date (cash dividends), 609–610
Redeeming bonds, 653
Registered bonds, 646
Regulations, government, 1110
  for corporations, 573
  as standards, 1110. *See also* Standard costs
Relevant range, 978–980, 1068
Republic of Debtors (Bruce Mann), 643
Repurchase of shares, 584
Required rate of return, 1171
Residual claims, 574
Resource allocation decisions, 1165–1166
Responsibility accounting, 1072–1084
  controllable vs. noncontrollable revenues/costs, 1074
  responsibility centers, 1077–1084
  responsibility reporting system, 1074–1077
Responsibility centers, 1077–1084
Responsibility reporting system, 1074–1077
Retained earnings, 578, 616–619
  payment of cash dividends from, 608
  prior period adjustments, 618
  restrictions on, 617–618
  for statement of cash flows, 756, 764
Retained earnings statement, 619, 796–797
Return on assets, 804–805
Return on common stockholders' equity, 621, 805
Return on investment (ROI), 1080–1083, 1125, 1126
Revenues:
  controllable vs. noncontrollable, 1074
  from stock investments, 702
ROI, *see* Return on investment
Rolling Stones, 991

S
Sales:
  of bonds, 698–699
  of equipment, loss on, 740
  of stocks, 701
Sales and administrative expense budget, 1029
Sales budget, 1023–1024
Sales forecasts, 1020, 1024
Sarbanes-Oxley Act (2002), 624
Sarbox, *see* Sarbanes-Oxley Act (2002)
Scott, Susan, 886
SEC, *see* Securities and Exchange Commission
Secured bonds, 645
Securities:
  available-for-sale, 705, 707
  held-to-maturity, 705
  marketable, 708–709
  trading, 705–706, 708–709
Securities Acts (1933, 1934), 767
Securities and Exchange Commission (SEC), 707, 728, 767
Segments, in responsibility accounting, 1073
Serial bonds, 646
Service companies:
  budgetary planning for, 1037
  job order costing in, 898
  process vs. job order cost systems for, 931
Shareholders' equity, 577. *See also* Corporate capital
Short-term investments, 708–709
Short-term paper, 708
Simple interest, C1–C2
Sinking fund bonds, 645
Sole proprietorships, 906
Solvency, creditor interest in, 792
Solvency ratios, 807–808
SOX, *see* Sarbanes-Oxley Act (2002)
Special order-price decisions, 1158–1159
Standards. *See also* Standard costs
  budgets vs., 1111
  government, 1110
  ideal vs. normal, 1112
Standard costs, 1110–1124
  analyzing variances from, 1116–1122
  need for, 1110–1111
  reporting variances from, 1122–1124
  setting, 1112–1115
Standard cost accounting system, 1130–1132
Standard hours, 1121
Standard predetermined overhead, 1114
Statement of cash flows, 732–751
  classification of cash flows, 733–734
  company evaluation based on, 748–750
  direct method for, 737, 758–764
  format of, 735–736
  indirect method for, 737–748
  preparation of, 736–748
  significant noncash activities, 734
  usefulness of, 732–733
  worksheet for, 752–757
Statement of operations, *see* Income statement
Static budgets, 1063–1065
Static budget reports, 1065
Stocks, 575–577
  authorized, 575
  capital, 587
  common, 574, 579–582
  direct issues, 575
  indirect issues, 575–576
  issued for credit, 745
  market value of, 576
  no-par value, 577
  par value of, 577
  preferred, 586–587
  treasury, 582–586
Stock certificates, 575
Stock dividends, 612–614
Stockholders:
  limited liability of, 571
  ownership rights of, 574–575
Stockholders' equity, 577. *See also* Corporate capital
  on balance sheet, 587–589
  contra account for, 583
  effect of dividends on, 614
  on financial statements, 620–623

Stock investments, 699–704
Stock splits, 614–615
Straight-line amortization, 673–675
Subsidiary (affiliated) company, 702
Subsidiary ledgers, job cost sheets as, 893, 894
Summary entries, 892
"Surplus," use of term, 588

T
Target net income, 989–991
Taxes:
  on corporations, 573
  on dividends, 611
  double taxation, 573
  income, *see* Income taxes
Term bonds, 646
Tilton, Glenn, 1126
Time periods, C7
Times interest earned, 808
Times interest earned ratio, 659
Time value of money, 648, C1–C9
  interest, C1–C2
  present value of an annuity, C5–C7
  present value of a single amount, C3–C5
  present value of long-term notes/bonds, C7–C9
  present value variables, C3
  time periods and discounting, C7
Total labor variance, 1119
Total materials variance, 1116–1117
Total overhead variance, 1121
Total quality management (TQM), 859
Total standard cost per unit, 1114–1115
TQM (total quality management), 859
Trading bonds, 646
Trading on the equity, 805
Trading securities, 705–706, 708–709
Treasurers of corporations, 572
Treasury stock, 582–586
Trend analysis, 793. *See also* Horizontal analysis
Trustees (bonds), 646
Turner, Ted, 695

U
Underwriting, 576
Unit production costs, 942
Unprofitable segment elimination decisions, 1164–1165
Unrealized gains/losses, 705, 709–710
Unsecured bonds, 646

V
Valuation of investments, 704–706
Value chain, 858–859
Variable costs:
  in CVP, 977
  in flexible budget, 1068
  in manufacturing overhead budget, 1028
Variable costing, 998–1001
Variances from standards, 1116–1124
  direct labor variances, 1119–1121
  direct materials variances, 1116–1119
  manufacturing overhead variance, 1121–1122
  overhead, 1133–1134
  reporting, 1122–1124
Vertical analysis, 793, 797–799

W
Weighted average method, 937–938
Working capital ratio, 801
Work in process, 893–900
Work in process inventory, 853
Worksheets, for statement of cash flows, 752–757
World economy, 858

Y
Year-end balance, 904

Z
Zero-interest bonds, 648